Contemporary Authors®

NEW REVISION SERIES

Explore your options!
Gale databases offered in
a variety of formats

DISKETTE/MAGNETIC TAPE

Many Gale databases are available on diskette or magnetic tape, allowing systemwide access to your most-used information sources through existing computer systems. Data can be delivered on a variety of mediums (DOS formatted diskette, 9-track tape, 8mm data tape) and in industry-standard formats (comma-delimited, tagged, fixed-field). Retrieval software is also available with many of Gale's databases that allows you to search, display, print and download the data.

ONLINE

For your convenience, many Gale databases are available through popular online services, including DIALOG, NEXIS (Mead Data Central), Data-Star, Orbit, Questel, OCLC, I/Plus and HRIN.

CD-ROM

A variety of Gale titles is available on CD-ROM, offering maximum flexibility and powerful search software.

The information in this Gale publication is also available in some or all of the formats described here. Your Customer Service Representative will be happy to fill you in.

For information, call

GALE

Gale Research Inc.
1 - 8 0 0 - 8 7 7 - G A L E

ISSN 0275-7176

Contemporary Authors®

A Bio-Bibliographical Guide to
Current Writers in Fiction, General Nonfiction,
Poetry, Journalism, Drama, Motion Pictures,
Television, and Other Fields

PAMELA S. DEAR
Editor

NEW REVISION SERIES
volume 47

 Gale Research Inc.

An International Thomson Publishing Company

ITP
Changing the Way the World Learns

NEW YORK • LONDON • BONN • BOSTON • DETROIT • MADRID
MELBOURNE • MEXICO CITY • PARIS • SINGAPORE • TOKYO
TORONTO • WASHINGTON • ALBANY NY • BELMONT CA • CINCINNATI OH

∞ ™ This book is printed on acid-free paper that meets the minimum requirements
of American National Standard for Information Sciences-
Permanence Paper for Printed Library Materials, ANSI Z39.48-1984.

Library of Congress Catalog Card Number 81-640179

ISBN 0-8103-5750-X
ISSN 0275-7176

Printed in the United States of America.

I(T)P™ Gale Research Inc., an International Thomson Publishing Company.
ITP logo is a trademark under license.

10 9 8 7 6 5 4 3 2 1

Contents

Preface vii

CA Numbering System and
Volume Update Charts xi

Authors and Media People
Featured in This Volume xiii

Author Listings 1

Indexing note: All *Contemporary Authors New Revision Series* entries are indexed in the *Contemporary Authors* cumulative index, which is published separately and distributed with even-numbered *Contemporary Authors* original volumes and odd-numbered *Contemporary Authors New Revision Series* volumes.

As always, the most recent *Contemporary Authors* cumulative index continues to be the user's guide to the location of an individual author's listing.

Contemporary Authors
was named an
**"Outstanding
Reference Source"** *by
the American Library
Association Reference
and Adult Services
Division after its 1962
inception.
In 1985 it was listed by
the same organization
as one of the
twenty-five most
distinguished reference
titles published in the
past twenty-five years.*

Preface

The *Contemporary Authors New Revision Series* (*CANR*) provides completely updated information on authors listed in earlier volumes of *Contemporary Authors* (*CA*). Entries for individual authors from *any* volume of *CA* may be included in a volume of the *New Revision Series*. *CANR* updates only those sketches requiring significant change.

Authors are included on the basis of specific criteria that indicate the need for significant revision. These criteria include bibliographical additions, changes in addresses or career, major awards, and personal information such as name changes or death dates. All listings in this volume have been revised or augmented in various ways. Some sketches have been extensively rewritten, and many include informative new sidelights. As always, a *CANR* listing entails no charge or obligation.

How to Get the Most out of *CA*: Use the Index

The key to locating an author's most recent entry is the *CA* cumulative index, which is published separately and distributed with even-numbered original volumes and odd-numbered revision volumes. It provides access to *all* entries in *CA* and *CANR*. Always consult the latest index to find an author's most recent entry.

For the convenience of users, the *CA* cumulative index also includes references to all entries in these Gale literary series: *Authors and Artists for Young Adults, Authors in the News, Bestsellers, Black Literature Criticism, Black Writers, Children's Literature Review, Concise Dictionary of American Literary Biography, Concise Dictionary of British Literary Biography, Contemporary Authors Autobiography Series, Contemporary Authors Bibliographical Series, Contemporary Literary Criticism, Dictionary of Literary Biography, DISCovering Authors, Drama Criticism, Hispanic Literature Criticism, Hispanic Writers, Junior DISCovering Authors, Major Authors and Illustrators for Children and Young Adults, Major 20th-Century Writers, Native North American Literature, Poetry Criticism, Short Story Criticism, Something about the Author, Something about the Author Autobiography Series, Twentieth-Century Literary Criticism, World Literature Criticism,* and *Yesterday's Authors of Books for Children.*

A Sample Index Entry:

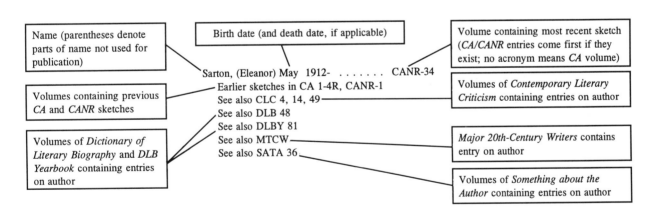

For the most recent *CA* information on Sarton, users should refer to Volume 34 of the *New Revision Series,* as designated by "CANR-34"; if that volume is unavailable, refer to CANR-1. And if CANR-1 is unavailable, refer to CA 1-4R, published in 1967, for Sarton's First Revision entry.

How Are Entries Compiled?

The editors make every effort to secure new information directly from the authors. Copies of all sketches in selected *CA* and *CANR* volumes previously published are routinely sent to listees at their last-known addresses, and returns from these authors are then assessed. For deceased writers, or those who fail to reply to requests for data, we consult other reliable biographical sources, such as those indexed in Gale's *Biography and Genealogy Master Index,* and bibliographical sources, such as *National Union Catalog, LC MARC,* and *British National Bibliography.* Further details come from published interviews, feature stories, and book reviews, and often the authors' publishers supply material.

* Indicates that a listing has been compiled from secondary sources believed to be reliable but has not been personally verified for this edition by the author sketched.

What Kinds of Information Does an Entry Provide?

Sketches in *CANR* contain the following biographical and bibliographical information:

- **Entry heading:** the most complete form of author's name, plus any pseudonyms or name variations used for writing

- **Personal information:** author's date and place of birth, family data, educational background, political and religious affiliations, and hobbies and leisure interests

- **Addresses:** author's home, office, or agent's addresses as available

- **Career summary:** name of employer, position, and dates held for each career post; résumé of other vocational achievements; military service

- **Membership information:** professional, civic, and other association memberships and any official posts held

- **Awards and honors:** military and civic citations, major prizes and nominations, fellowships, grants, and honorary degrees

- **Writings:** a comprehensive, chronological list of titles, publishers, dates of original publication and revised editions, and production information for plays, television scripts, and screenplays

- **Adaptations:** a list of films, plays, and other media which have been adapted from the author's work

- **Work in progress:** current or planned projects, with dates of completion and/or publication, and expected publisher, when known

- **Sidelights:** a biographical portrait of the author's development; information about the critical reception of the author's works; revealing comments, often by the author, on personal interests, aspirations, motivations, and thoughts on writing

- **Biographical and critical sources:** a list of books and periodicals in which additional information on an author's life and/or writings appears

Related Titles in the *CA* Series

Contemporary Authors Autobiography Series complements *CA* original and revised volumes with specially commissioned autobiographical essays by important current authors, illustrated with personal photographs they provide. Common topics include their motivations for writing, the people and experiences that shaped their careers, the rewards they derive from their work, and their impressions of the current literary scene.

Contemporary Authors Bibliographical Series surveys writings by and about important American authors since World War II. Each volume concentrates on a specific genre and features approximately ten writers; entries list works written by and about the author and contain a bibliographical essay discussing the merits and deficiencies of major critical and scholarly studies in detail.

Available in Electronic Formats

CD-ROM. Full-text bio-bibliographic entries from the entire *CA* series, covering approximately 100,000 writers, are available on CD-ROM through lease and purchase plans. The disc combines entries from the *CA, CANR,* and *Contemporary Authors Permanent Series* (*CAP*) print series to provide the most recent author listing. It can be searched by name, title, subject/genre, and personal data, and by using boolean logic. The disc will be updated every six months. For more information, call 1-800-877-GALE.

Magnetic Tape. *CA* is available for licensing on magnetic tape in a fielded format. Either the complete database or a custom selection of entries may be ordered. The database is available for internal data processing and nonpublishing purposes only. For more information, call 1-800-877-GALE.

Online. The *Contemporary Authors* database is made available online to libraries and their patrons through online public access catalog (OPAC) vendors. Currently, *CA* is offered through Ameritech Library Services' Vista Online (formerly Dynix), and is expected to become available through CARL Systems, The Library Corporation, and Winnebago Software. More OPAC vendor offerings will follow soon.

Suggestions Are Welcome

The editors welcome comments and suggestions from users on any aspects of the *CA* series. If readers would like to recommend authors whose entries should appear in future volumes of the series, they are cordially invited to write: The Editors, *Contemporary Authors,* 835 Penobscot Bldg., Detroit, MI 48226-4094; call toll-free at 1-800-347-GALE; or fax to 1-313-961-6599.

CA Numbering System and Volume Update Chart

Occasionally questions arise about the *CA* numbering system and which volumes, if any, can be discarded. Despite numbers like "29-32R," "97-100" and "146," the entire *CA* series consists of only 120 physical volumes with the publication of *CA New Revision Series* Volume 47. The following charts note changes in the numbering system and cover design, and indicate which volumes are essential for the most complete, up-to-date coverage.

CA First Revision	● 1-4R through 41-44R (11 books) *Cover:* Brown with black and gold trim. There will be no further First Revision volumes because revised entries are now being handled exclusively through the more efficient *New Revision Series* mentioned below.
CA Original Volumes	● 45-48 through 97-100 (14 books) *Cover:* Brown with black and gold trim. ● 101 through 146 (46 books) *Cover:* Blue and black with orange bands. The same as previous *CA* original volumes but with a new, simplified numbering system and new cover design.
CA Permanent Series	● *CAP*-1 and *CAP*-2 (2 books) *Cover:* Brown with red and gold trim. There will be no further *Permanent Series* volumes because revised entries are now being handled exclusively through the more efficient *New Revision Series* mentioned below.
CA New Revision Series	● *CANR*-1 through *CANR*-47 (47 books) *Cover:* Blue and black with green bands. Includes only sketches requiring extensive changes; **sketches are taken from any previously published *CA*, *CAP*, or *CANR* volume.**

If You Have:	**You May Discard:**
CA First Revision Volumes 1-4R through 41-44R **and** *CA Permanent Series* Volumes 1 and 2	*CA* Original Volumes 1, 2, 3, 4 Volumes 5-6 through 41-44
CA Original Volumes 45-48 through 97-100 **and** 101 through 146	**NONE:** These volumes will not be superseded by corresponding revised volumes. Individual entries from these and all other volumes appearing in the left column of this chart may be revised and included in the various volumes of the *New Revision Series*.
CA New Revision Series Volumes *CANR*-1 through *CANR*-47	**NONE:** The *New Revision Series* does not replace any single volume of *CA*. Instead, volumes of *CANR* include entries from many previous *CA* series volumes. All *New Revision Series* volumes must be retained for full coverage.

A Sampling of Authors and Media People
Featured in This Volume

Chinua Achebe
A Nigerian-born poet and novelist, Achebe successfully employs European novel-writing conventions in a distinctly African style in such works as *Things Fall Apart* and *Anthills of the Savannah.*

Harriet Doerr
American Book Award winner Doerr is praised for her masterful fictive technique and insightful study of the cultural differences between Mexicans and Americans in the novels *Stones for Ibarra* and *Consider This, Senora.*

Alasdair Gray
Gray's self-illustrated works are noted for their mixture of realistic social commentary and vivid fantasy; many, such as *The Fall of Kelvin Walker* and the widely-acclaimed *Lanark,* are set in his native Scotland.

John Grisham
Grisham's highly successful legal thrillers--*The Firm, The Pelican Brief,* and *The Client,* each of which has been made into a motion picture--have made the former attorney one of America's best-selling authors.

Michael Hamburger
A respected and prolific poet born in Germany and residing in England, Hamburger is praised as a representative of German and English literature "capable of doing equal justice to both."

John Hawkes
Critics remark on the dreamlike, often nightmarish quality of Hawkes' fiction and offer widely varying opinions of its worth. His controversial works include *The Lime Twig, The Cannibal,* and *Whistlejacket.*

William Least Heat-Moon
Heat-Moon's *Blue Highways: A Journey into America* and *PrairyErth (a deep map)* examine the American psyche in a manner reminiscent of Henry David Thoreau and John Steinbeck.

Jack Heifner
American playwright Heifner's *Vanities* became the longest-running nonmusical production in Off-Broadway history. His other successful plays include *Patio/Porch* and *Running on Empty.*

Isabelle Holland
Holland is respected for the realistic topics of her young-adult novels such as *Cecily, The Man without a Face,* and the National Book Award nominee *Of Love and Death and Other Journeys.*

Ernst Juenger
Juenger's depictions of the ravages of war and the danger of tyranny in such works as *Storm of Steel, On the Marble Cliffs* and *The Glass Bees* have placed him among Germany's foremost literary figures.

Jamaica Kincaid
Kincaid was widely praised for her first two works, *At the Bottom of the River* and *Annie John,* both set in her native Antigua. The novel *Lucy* parallels Kincaid's experiences in moving to America at age seventeen.

James Laughlin
Poet Laughlin is best known as the founder of New Directions, an early publisher of experimental and avant-garde authors including Ezra Pound, Gertrude Stein, and E. E. Cummings.

Christobel Mattingley
An Australian author of books for children and young adults, Mattingley examines contemporary problems in stories such as *The Sack, No Gun for Asmir,* and *The Miracle Tree.*

Amos Oz
Oz is internationally recognized for his portrayal of life in his native Israel. Among his works in English translation are the novels *My Michael* and *Elsewhere, Perhaps,* and *In the Land of Israel,* a collection of interviews with Israelis.

Leopold Sedar Senghor
African poet Senghor gained acclaim with the publication of his first volume in 1945 and later served as president of Senegal. He is best known for developing "negritude," a movement that influenced black culture worldwide.

Stephen Sondheim
A composer and lyricist responsible for many of America's best-loved musicals, Sondheim's credits include *West Side Story, A Funny Thing Happened on the Way to the Forum, Sweeney Todd,* and *Sunday in the Park with George.*

Derek Walcott
Poet and playwright Walcott is the first Caribbean writer to receive the Nobel Prize for Literature. With his skillful combination of the varying ethnic elements of his heritage, he is considered West Indian culture's greatest poet.

Robert Penn Warren
Warren was the first U.S. Poet Laureate and the only person to receive the Pulitzer Prize in both fiction and poetry. Among his most acclaimed works are *All the King's Men* and *Promises: Poems, 1954-56.*

Contemporary Authors®

NEW REVISION SERIES

*Indicates that a listing has been compiled from secondary sources believed to be reliable
but has not been personally verified for this edition by the author sketched.*

ABBOTT, Keith 1944-

PERSONAL: Born February 2, 1944, in Tacoma, WA;
son of Lenard (a miller) and Gertrude (Retka) Abbott;
married Lani Kae Hansen (a costumer), 1966; children:
Persephone.

ADDRESSES: Home and office—Naropa Writing Institute, 2130 Arapahoe, Boulder, Colorado 80302.

AWARDS, HONORS: Grants from Poets Foundation,
1973; Djerrassi Foundation, 1984 and 1985.

WRITINGS:

Gush (novel), Blue Wind Press (Berkeley, CA), 1975.
Erase Words (poems), Blue Wind Press, 1977.
Rhino Ritz: An American Mystery (novel), Blue Wind
    Press, 1979.
Enter the Turkish Navy (two-act play), first produced in
    San Francisco, CA, at Eureka Theatre, 1981.
Welcome Nugget (two-act play, adaptation of Nikolay
    Gogol's *Inspector General*,) first produced in Berke-
    ley, CA, at London School of Drama, 1982.
Burnt Arms of a Slow Day Hero (two-act play), first pro-
    duced in San Francisco at People's Theatre, 1984.
Harum Scarum (short stories), Coffee House Press (Min-
    neapolis, MN), 1984.
Mordecai of Monterey (novel), City Miner, 1985.
The First Thing Coming (short stories), Coffee House
    Press, 1987.
Racer (novel), Marovenlag, 1987.
*Downstream from Trout Fishing in America: A Memoir of
    Richard Brautigan,* Capra (Santa Barbara, CA), 1989.
The Last Part of the First Thing (short story), Grayspider,
    1993.
Skin and Bone (short story), Tangram, 1993.

*WORK IN PROGRESS: False Courage, Good Golly Miss
Molly,* and *Boy Scout Cookies,* all novels.

SIDELIGHTS: Keith Abbott told *CA:* "Currently I am at
work on a novel: *Boy Scout Cookies.* This is the second of
a series of crime novels set in California. The first novel,
Good Golly Miss Molly, is with my agent. My work has
been translated into German, French, Italian, Romanian,
Czech, and Russian. I am presently working at Naropa Institute in Boulder, teaching fiction. My painting and calligraphy have been widely exhibited and published; forthcoming is a cover for a University of New Mexico Press
anthology of Naropa lectures, *Dis-Embodied Poetics.*"

BIOGRAPHICAL/CRITICAL SOURCES:

PERIODICALS

Review of Contemporary Fiction, spring, 1981.

*   *   *

ACHEBE, (Albert) Chinua(lumogu) 1930-

PERSONAL: Born November 16, 1930, in Ogidi, Nigeria;
son of Isaiah Okafo (a Christian churchperson) and Janet
N. (Iloegbunam) Achebe; married Christie Chinwe Okoli,
September 10, 1961; children: Chinelo (daughter),
Ikechukwu (son), Chidi (son), Nwando (daughter). *Education:* Attended University College, Ibadan, 1948-53;
London University, B.A., 1953; studied broadcasting at
the British Broadcasting Corporation, London, 1956. *Avocational interests:* Music.

ADDRESSES: Home—P.O. Box 53 Nsukka, Anambra
State, Nigeria. *Office*—Institute of African Studies, Uni-
versity of Nigeria, Nsukka, Anambra State, Nigeria; and
University of Massachusetts, Amherst, MA 01003.

CAREER: Writer. Nigerian Broadcasting Corporation,
Lagos, Nigeria, talks producer, 1954-57, controller of
Eastern Region in Enugu, Nigeria, 1958-61, founder and

director of Voice of Nigeria, 1961-66; University of Nigeria, Nsukka, senior research fellow, 1967-72, professor of English, 1976-81, professor emeritus, 1985—; Anambra State University of Technology, Enugu, pro-chancellor and chair of council, 1986—; University of Massachusetts—Amherst, professor, 1987-88. Served on diplomatic missions for Biafra during the Nigerian Civil War, 1967-69. Visiting professor of English at University of Massachusetts—Amherst, 1972-75, and University of Connecticut, 1975-76. Lecturer at University of California, Los Angeles, and at universities in Nigeria and the United States; speaker at events in numerous countries throughout the world. Chair, Citadel Books Ltd., Enugu, Nigeria, 1967; director, Heinemann Educational Books Ltd., Ibadan, Nigeria, 1970—; director, Nwamife Publishers Ltd., Enugu, Nigeria, 1970—. Founder and publisher, *Uwa Ndi Igbo: A Bilingual Journal of Igbo Life and Arts,* 1984—. Governor, Newsconcern International Foundation, 1983. Member, University of Lagos Council, 1966, East Central State Library Board, 1971-72, Anambra State Arts Council, 1977-79, and National Festival Committee, 1983; director, Okike Arts Centre, Nsukka, 1984—. Deputy national president of People's Redemption Party, 1983; president of town union, Ogidi, Nigeria, 1986—.

MEMBER: International Social Prospects Academy (Geneva), Writers and Scholars International (London), Writers and Scholars Educational Trust (London), Commonwealth Arts Organization (member of executive committee, 1981—), Association of Nigerian Authors (founder; president, 1981-86), Ghana Association of Writers (fellow), Royal Society of Literature (London), Modern Language Association of America (honorary fellow), American Academy and Institute of Arts and Letters (honorary member).

AWARDS, HONORS: Margaret Wrong Memorial Prize, 1959, for *Things Fall Apart;* Rockefeller travel fellowship to East and Central Africa, 1960; Nigerian National Trophy, 1961, for *No Longer at Ease;* UNESCO fellowship for creative artists for travel to United States and Brazil, 1963; Jock Campbell/*New Statesman* Award, 1965, for *Arrow of God;* Commonwealth Poetry Prize, 1972, for *Beware, Soul-Brother, and Other Poems;* Neil Gunn international fellow, Scottish Arts Council, 1975; Lotus Award for Afro-Asian Writers, 1975; Nigerian National Merit Award, 1979; named to the Order of the Federal Republic of Nigeria, 1979; Commonwealth Foundation senior visiting practitioner award, 1984; *A Man of the People* was cited in Anthony Burgess's 1984 book *Ninety-nine Novels: The Best in England since 1939;* Booker Prize nomination, 1987, for *Anthills of the Savannah.* D.Litt., Dartmouth College, 1972, University of Southampton, 1975, University of Ife, 1978, University of Nigeria, Nsukka, 1981,

University of Kent, 1982, Mount Allison University, 1984, University of Guelph, 1984, and Franklin Pierce College, 1985; D.Univ., University of Stirling, 1975; LL.D., University of Prince Edward Island, 1976; D.H.L., University of Massachusetts—Amherst, 1977.

WRITINGS:

NOVELS

Things Fall Apart, Heinemann (London), 1958, Obolensky, 1959, reprinted, Fawcett (New York City), 1988.

No Longer at Ease, Heinemann, 1960, Obolensky, 1961, second edition, Fawcett, 1988.

Arrow of God, Heinemann, 1964, John Day (New York City), 1967.

A Man of the People, John Day, 1966, published with an introduction by K. W. J. Post, Doubleday (New York City), 1967.

Anthills of the Savannah, Anchor Books (New York City), 1988.

JUVENILE

Chike and the River, Cambridge University Press, 1966.

(With John Iroaganachi) *How the Leopard Got His Claws,* Nwankwo-Ifejika (Enugu, Nigeria), 1972, bound with *Lament of the Deer,* by Christopher Okigbo, Third Press, 1973.

The Flute, Fourth Dimension Publishers (Enugu, Nigeria), 1978.

The Drum, Fourth Dimension Publishers, 1978.

POETRY

Beware, Soul-Brother, and Other Poems, Nwankwo-Ifejika, 1971, Doubleday, 1972, revised edition, Heinemann, 1972.

Christmas in Biafra, and Other Poems, Doubleday, 1973.

(Editor with Dubem Okafor) *Don't Let Him Die: An Anthology of Memorial Poems for Christopher Okigbo,* Fourth Dimension Publishers, 1978.

(Coeditor) *Aka Weta: An Anthology of Igbo Poetry,* Okike (Nsukka, Nigeria), 1982.

OTHER

The Sacrificial Egg, and Other Stories, Etudo (Onitsha, Nigeria), 1962.

Girls at War, (short stories), Heinemann, 1973, Fawcett, 1988.

Morning Yet on Creation Day (essays), Doubleday, 1975.

The Trouble with Nigeria (essays), Fourth Dimension Publishers, 1983, Heinemann, 1984.

(Editor with C. L. Innes) *African Short Stories,* Heinemann, 1984.

Hopes and Impediments (essays), Heinemann, 1988.

(Editor with Innes and contributor) *The Heinemann Book of Contemporary African Short Stories,* Heinemann, 1992.

Also author of essay collection *Nigerian Topics,* 1988. Contributor to books, including *Modern African Stories,* edited by Ellis Ayitey Komey and Ezekiel Mphahlele, Faber (London), 1964; and *Africa Speaks: A Prose Anthology with Comprehension and Summary Passages,* Evans, 1970. Author of foreword, *African Rhapsody: Short Stories of the Contemporary African Experience,* 1994. Founding editor, "African Writers Series," Heinemann, 1962-72; editor, *Okike: A Nigerian Journal of New Writing,* 1971—; editor, *Nsukkascope,* a campus magazine.

Things Fall Apart has been translated into forty-five languages.

ADAPTATIONS: Things Fall Apart was adapted for the stage and produced by Eldred Fiberesima in Lagos, Nigeria; it was also adapted for radio and produced by the British Broadcasting Corporation in 1983, and for television in English and Igbo and produced by the Nigerian Television Authority in 1985.

SIDELIGHTS: Since the 1950s, Nigeria has witnessed "the flourishing of a new literature which has drawn sustenance both from traditional oral literature and from the present and rapidly changing society," writes Margaret Laurence in her book *Long Drums and Cannons: Nigerian Dramatists and Novelists.* Thirty years ago, Chinua Achebe was among the founders of this new literature and over the years many critics have come to consider him the finest of the Nigerian novelists. His achievement has not been limited to his native country or continent, however. As Laurence maintains in her 1968 study of his novels, "Chinua Achebe's careful and confident craftsmanship, his firm grasp of his material and his ability to create memorable and living characters place him among the best novelists now writing in any country in the English language."

Unlike some African writers struggling for acceptance among contemporary English-language novelists, Achebe has been able to avoid imitating the trends in English literature. Rejecting the European notion "that art should be accountable to no one, and [needs] to justify itself to nobody," as he puts it in his book of essays, *Morning Yet on Creation Day,* Achebe has embraced instead the idea at the heart of the African oral tradition: that "art is, and always was, at the service of man. Our ancestors created their myths and legends and told their stories for a human purpose." For this reason, Achebe believes that "any good story, any good novel, should have a message, should have a purpose."

Achebe's feel for the African context has influenced his aesthetic of the novel as well as the technical aspects of his works. As Bruce King comments in *Introduction to Nigerian Literature:* "Achebe was the first Nigerian writer to successfully transmute the conventions of the novel, a European art form, into African literature." In an Achebe novel, King notes, "European character study is subordinated to the portrayal of communal life; European economy of form is replaced by an aesthetic appropriate to the rhythms of traditional tribal life." Kofi Awoonor writes in *The Breast of the Earth* that, in wrapping this borrowed literary form in African garb, Achebe "created a new novel that possesses its own autonomy and transcends the limits set by both his African and European teachers."

On the level of ideas, Achebe's "prose writing reflects three essential and related concerns," observes G. D. Killam in his book *The Novels of Chinua Achebe,* "first, with the legacy of colonialism at both the individual and societal level; secondly, with the *fact* of English as a language of national and international exchange; thirdly, with the obligations and responsibilities of the writer both to the society in which he lives and to his art." Over the past century, Africa has been caught in a war for its identity between the forces of tradition, colonialism, and independence. This war has prevented many nations from raising themselves above political and social chaos to achieve true independence. "Most of the problems we see in our politics derive from the moment when we lost our initiative to other people, to colonizers," Achebe observes in his book of essays. He goes on to explain: "What I think is the basic problem of a new African country like Nigeria is really what you might call a 'crisis in the soul.' We have been subjected—we have subjected ourselves too—to this period during which we have accepted everything alien as good and practically everything local or native as inferior."

In order to reestablish the virtues of precolonial Nigeria, chronicle the impact of colonialism on native cultures, and expose present-day corruption, Achebe needed to clearly communicate these concerns to his fellow countrymen and to those outside his country. The best channel for these messages was writing in English, the language of colonialism. It is the way in which Achebe transforms language to achieve his particular ends, however, that many feel distinguishes his writing from the writing of other English-language novelists. To convey the flavor of traditional Nigeria, Achebe translates Ibo proverbs into English and weaves them into his stories. "Among the Ibo the art of conversation is regarded very highly," he writes in his novel *Things Fall Apart,* "and proverbs are the palm-oil with which words are eaten." "Proverbs are cherished by Achebe's people as tribal heirlooms, the treasure boxes of their cultural heritage," explains Adrian A. Roscoe in his book *Mother Is Gold: A Study of West African Literature.* "Through them traditions are received and handed on; and when they disappear or fall into disuse . . . it is a sign that a particular tradition, or indeed a whole way of life, is passing away." Achebe's use of proverbs also has an artistic aim, as Bernth Lindfors suggests in *Folklore in Nigerian Literature.* "Achebe's proverbs can serve as keys to an understanding of his novels," comments the critic, "because he uses them not merely to add touches of local color but to sound and reiterate themes, to sharpen characterization, to clarify conflict, and to focus on the values of the society he is portraying."

To engender an appreciation for African culture in those unfamiliar with it, Achebe alters English to reflect native Nigerian languages in use. "Without seriously distorting the nature of the English," observes Eustace Palmer in *The Growth the African Novel,* "Achebe deliberately introduces the rhythms, speech patterns, idioms and other verbal nuances of Ibo. . . . The effect of this is that while everyone who knows English will be able to understand the work and find few signs of awkwardness, the reader also has a sense, not just of black men using English, but of black Africans speaking and living in a genuinely black African rural situation." In the opinion of *Busara* contributor R. Angogo, this "ability to shape and mould English to suit character and event and yet still give the impression of an African story is one of the greatest of Achebe's achievements." The reason, adds the reviewer, is that "it puts into the reader a kind of emotive effect, an interest, and a thirst which so to say awakens the reader."

Finally, Achebe uses language, which he sees as a writer's best resource, to expose and combat the propaganda generated by African politicians to manipulate their own people. "Language is our tool," he told Anthony Appiah in a *Times Literary Supplement* interview, "and language is the tool of the politicians. We are like two sides in a very hostile game. And I think that the attempt to deceive with words is countered by the efforts of the writer to go behind the words, to show the meaning."

Faced with his people's growing inferiority complex and his leaders' disregard for the truth, the African writer cannot turn his back on his culture, Achebe believes. "A writer has a responsibility to try and stop [these damaging trends] because unless our culture begins to take itself seriously it will never . . . get off the ground." He states his mission in his essay "The Novelist as Teacher": "Here then is an adequate revolution for me to espouse—to help my society regain belief in itself and to put away the complexes of the years of denigration and self-abasement. And it is essentially a question of education, in the best sense of that word. Here, I think, my aims and the deepest aspirations of society meet."

Although he has also written poetry, short stories, and essays—both literary and political—Achebe is best known for his novels: *Things Fall Apart, No Longer at Ease, Arrow of God, A Man of the People,* and *Anthills of the Savannah.* Considering Achebe's novels, Anthony Daniels writes in the *Spectator,* "In spare prose of great elegance, without any technical distraction, he has been able to illuminate two emotionally irreconcilable facets of modern African life: the humiliations visited on Africans by colonialism, and the utter moral worthlessness of what replaced colonial rule." Set in this historical context, Achebe's novels develop the theme of "tradition versus change," and offer, as Palmer observes, "a powerful presentation of the beauty, strength and validity of traditional life and values and the disruptiveness of change." Even so, the author does not appeal for a return to the ways of the past. Palmer notes that "while deploring the imperialists' brutality and condescension, [Achebe] seems to suggest that change is inevitable and wise men . . . reconcile themselves to accommodating change. It is the diehards . . . who resist and are destroyed in the process."

Two of Achebe's novels—*Things Fall Apart* and *Arrow of God*—focus on Nigeria's early experience with colonialism, from first contact with the British to widespread British administration. "With remarkable unity of the word with the deed, the character, the time and the place, Chinua Achebe creates in these two novels a coherent picture of coherence being lost, of the tragic consequences of the African-European collision," offers Robert McDowell in a special issue of *Studies in Black Literature* dedicated to Achebe's work. "There is an artistic unity of all things in these books which is rare anywhere in modern English fiction."

Things Fall Apart, Achebe's first novel, was published in 1958 in the midst of the Nigerian renaissance. Achebe explained his motivation to begin writing at this time in an interview with Lewis Nkosi published in *African Writers Talking: A Collection of Radio Interviews:* "One of the things that set me thinking [about writing] was Joyce Cary's novel set in Nigeria, *Mr. Johnson,* which was praised so much, and it was clear to me that this was a most superficial picture . . . not only of the country, but even of the Nigerian character. . . . I thought if this was famous, then perhaps someone ought to try and look at this from the inside." Charles R. Larson, in his book *The Emergence of African Fiction,* details the success of Achebe's effort, both in investing his novel of Africa with an African sensibility and in making this view available to African readers. "In 1964, . . . *Things Fall Apart* became the first novel by an African writer to be included in the required syllabus for African secondary school students throughout the English-speaking portions of the continent." Later in that decade, it "became recognized by African and non-African literary critics as the first 'classic' in English from tropical Africa," adds Larson.

The novel tells the story of an Ibo village of the late 1800s and one of its great men, Okonkwo. Although the son of a ne'er-do-well, Okonkwo has achieved much in his life. He is a champion wrestler, a wealthy farmer, a husband to three wives, a title-holder among his people, and a member of the select *egwugwu* whose members impersonate ancestral spirits at tribal rituals. "The most impressive achievement of *Things Fall Apart* . . .," maintains David Carroll in his book *Chinua Achebe,* "is the vivid picture it provides of Ibo society at the end of the nineteenth century." He explains: "Here is a clan in the full vigor of its traditional way of life, unperplexed by the present and without nostalgia for the past. Through its rituals the life of the community and the life of the individual are merged into significance and order."

This order is disrupted, however, with the appearance of the white man in Africa and with the introduction of his religion. "The conflict in the novel, vested in Okonkwo, derives from the series of crushing blows which are levelled at traditional values by an alien and more powerful culture causing, in the end, the traditional society to fall apart," observes Killam. Okonkwo is unable to adapt to the changes that accompany colonialism. In the end, in frustration, he kills an African employed by the British, and then commits suicide, a sin against the tradition to which he had long clung. The novel thus presents "two main, closely intertwined tragedies," writes Arthur Ravenscroft in his study *Chinua Achebe,* "the personal tragedy of Okonkwo . . . and the public tragedy of the eclipse of one culture by another."

Although the author emphasizes the message in his novels, he still receives praise for his artistic achievement. As Palmer comments, "Chinua Achebe's *Things Fall Apart* . . . demonstrates a mastery of plot and structure, strength of characterization, competence in the manipulation of language and consistency and depth of thematic exploration which is rarely found in a first novel." Achebe also achieves balance in recreating the tragic consequences of the clash of two cultures. Killam notes that "in showing Ibo society before and after the coming of the white man he avoids the temptation to present the past as idealized and the present as ugly and unsatisfactory." And, as Killam concludes, Achebe's "success proceeds from his ability to create a sense of real life and real issues in the book and to see his subject from the point of view which is neither idealistic nor dishonest."

Arrow of God, the second of Achebe's novels of colonialism, takes place in the 1920s after the British have established a presence in Nigeria. The "arrow of god" mentioned in the title is Ezeulu, the chief priest of the god Ulu

who is the patron deity of an Ibo village. As chief priest, Ezeulu is responsible for initiating the rituals that structure village life, a position vested with a great deal of power. In fact, the central theme of this novel, as Laurence points out, is power: "Ezeulu's testing of his own power and the power of his god, and his effort to maintain his own and his god's authority in the face of village factions and of the [Christian] mission and the British administration." "This, then, is a political novel in which different systems of power are examined and their dependence upon myth and ritual compared," writes Carroll. "Of necessity it is also a study in the psychology of power."

In Ezeulu, Achebe presents a study of the loss of power. After his village rejects his advice to avoid war with a neighboring village, Ezeulu finds himself at odds with his own people and praised by the British administrators. The British, seeking a candidate to install as village chieftain, make him an offer, which he refuses. Caught in the middle with no allies, Ezeulu slowly loses his grip on reality and slips into senility. "As in Achebe's other novels," observes Gerald Moore in *Seven African Writers,* "it is the strong-willed man of tradition who cannot adapt, and who is crushed by his virtues in the war between the new, more worldly order, and the old, conservative values of an isolated society."

The artistry displayed in *Arrow of God,* Achebe's second portrait of cultures in collision, has drawn a great deal of attention, adding to the esteem in which the writer is held. Charles Miller comments in a *Saturday Review* article that Achebe's "approach to the written word is completely unencumbered with verbiage. He never strives for the exalted phrase, he never once raises his voice; even in the most emotion-charged passages the tone is absolutely unruffled, the control impeccable." Concludes Miller, "It is a measure of Achebe's creative gift that he has no need whatever for prose fireworks to light the flame of his intense drama."

Killam recognizes this novel as more than a vehicle for Achebe's commentary on colonialism. He suggests in his study that "Achebe's overall intention is to explore the depths of the human condition and in this other more important sense *Arrow of God* transcends its setting and shows us characters whose values, motivations, actions and qualities are permanent in humankind." Laurence offers this evaluation in her 1968 book: "*Arrow of God,* in which [Achebe] comes into full maturity as a novelist, . . . is probably one of the best novels written anywhere in the past decade."

Achebe's three other novels—*No Longer at Ease, A Man of the People,* and *Anthills of the Savannah*—examine Africa in the era of independence. This is an Africa less and less under direct European administration, yet still deeply affected by it, an Africa struggling to regain its footing in order to stand on its own two feet. Standing in the way of realizing its goal of true independence is the corruption pervasive in modern Africa, an obstacle Achebe scrutinizes in each of these novels.

In *No Longer at Ease,* set in Nigeria just prior to independence, Achebe extends his history of the Okonkwo family. Here the central character is Obi Okonkwo, grandson of the tragic hero of *Things Fall Apart.* This Okonkwo has been raised a Christian and educated at the university in England. Like many of his peers, he has left the bush behind for a position as a civil servant in Lagos, Nigeria's largest city. "*No Longer at Ease* deals with the plight of [this] new generation of Nigerians," observes Palmer, "who, having been exposed to education in the western world and therefore largely cut off from their roots in traditional society, discover, on their return, that the demands of tradition are still strong, and are hopelessly caught in the clash between the old and the new."

Many faced with this internal conflict succumb to corruption. Obi is no exception. "The novel opens with Obi on trial for accepting bribes," notes Killam, " . . . and the book takes the form of a long flashback." "In a world which is the result of the intermingling of Europe and Africa . . . Achebe traces the decline of his hero from brilliant student to civil servant convicted of bribery and corruption," writes Carroll. "It reads like a postscript to the earlier novel [*Things Fall Apart*] because the same forces are at work but in a confused, diluted, and blurred form." In *This Africa: Novels by West Africans in English and French,* Judith Illsley Gleason points out how the imagery of each book depicts the changes in the Okonkwo family and the Nigeria they represent. As she points out, "The career of the grandson Okonkwo ends not with a machete's swing but with a gavel's tap."

Here again in this novel Achebe carefully shapes language, to inform, but also to transport the reader to Africa. "It is through [his characters'] use of language that we are able to enter their world and to share their experiences," writes Shatto Arthur Gakwandi in *The Novel and Contemporary Experience in Africa.* Gakwandi adds: "Through [Achebe's] keen sensitivity to the way people express themselves and his delicate choice of idiom the author illuminates for us the thoughts and attitudes of the whole range of Nigerian social strata." The impact of Achebe's style is such that, as John Coleman observes in the *Spectator,* his "novel moves towards its inevitable catastrophe with classic directness. Nothing is wasted and it is only after the sad, understated close that one realises, once again how much of the Nigerian context has been touched in, from the prejudice and corruption of Lagos to the warm, homiletic simplicities of life."

A Man of the People is "the story of the yokel who visits the sinful city and emerges from it scathed but victorious," writes Martin Tucker in *Africa in Modern Literature,* "while the so-called 'sophisticates' and 'sinners' suffer their just desserts." In this novel, Achebe casts his eye on African politics, taking on, as Moore notes, "the corruption of Nigerians in high places in the central government." The author's eyepiece is the book's narrator Odili, a schoolteacher; the object of his scrutiny is the Honorable M. A. Nanga, Member of Parliament, Odili's former teacher and a popular bush politician who has risen to the post of Minister of Culture in his West African homeland.

At first, Odili is charmed by the politician; but eventually he recognizes the extent of Nanga's abuses and decides to oppose the minister in an election. Odili is beaten, both physically and politically, his appeal to the people heard but ignored. The novel demonstrates, according to Gakwandi, that "the society has been invaded by a wide range of values which have destroyed the traditional balance between the material and the spiritual spheres of life, which has led inevitably to the hypocrisy of double standards." Odili is a victim of these double standards.

Despite his political victory, Nanga, along with the rest of the government, is ousted by a coup. "The novel is a carefully plotted and unified piece of writing," writes Killam. "Achebe achieves balance and proportion in the treatment of his theme of political corruption by evoking both the absurdity of the behavior of the principal characters while at the same time suggesting the serious and destructive consequences of their behavior to the commonwealth." The seriousness of the fictional situation portrayed in *A Man of the People* became real very soon after the novel was first published in 1966 when Nigeria itself was racked by a coup.

Two decades passed between the publications of *A Man of the People* and Achebe's 1988 novel, *Anthills of the Savannah.* During this period, the novelist wrote poetry, short stories, and essays. He also became involved in Nigeria's political struggle, a struggle marked by five coups, a civil war, elections marred by violence, and a number of attempts to return to civilian rule. *Anthills of the Savannah* represents Achebe's return to the novel, and as Nadine Gordimer comments in the *New York Times Book Review,* "it is a work in which 22 years of harsh experience, intellectual growth, self-criticism, deepening understanding and mustered discipline of skill open wide a subject to which Mr. Achebe is now magnificently equal." It also represents a return to the themes informing Achebe's earlier novels of independent Africa. "This is a study of how power corrupts itself and by doing so begins to die," writes *Observer* contributor and fellow Nigerian Ben Okri. "It is also about dissent, and love."

Three former schoolmates have risen to positions of power in an imaginary West African nation, Kangan. Ikem is editor of the state-owned newspaper; Chris is the country's minister of information; Sam is a military man who has become head of state. Sam's quest to have himself voted president for life sends the lives of these three and the lives of all Kangan citizens into turmoil. "In this new novel . . . Chinua Achebe says, with implacable honesty, that Africa itself is to blame," notes Neal Ascherson in the *New York Review of Books,* "and that there is no safety in excuses that place the fault in the colonial past or in the commercial and political manipulations of the First World." Ascherson continues that the novel becomes "a tale about responsibility, and the ways in which men who should know better betray and evade that responsibility."

The turmoil comes to a head in the novel's final pages. All three of the central characters are dead. Ikem, who spoke out against the abuses of the government, is murdered by Sam's secret police. Chris, who flees into the bush to begin a journey of transformation among the people, is shot attempting to stop a rape. Sam is kidnapped and murdered in a coup. "The three murders, senseless as they are, represent the departure of a generation that compromised its own enlightenment for the sake of power," writes Ascherson. And, as Okri observes, "The novel closes with the suggestion that power should reside not within an elite but within the awakened spirit of the people." Here is the hope offered in the novel, hope that is also suggested in its title, as Charles Trueheart relates in the *Washington Post:* "When the brush fires sweep across the savanna, scorching the earth, they leave behind only anthills, and inside the anthills, the surviving memories of the fires and all that came before."

Anthills of the Savannah was well-received and earned Achebe a nomination for the Booker Prize. In Larson's estimation, printed in the *Tribune Books,* "No other novel in many years has bitten to the core, swallowed and regurgitated contemporary Africa's miseries and expectations as profoundly as *Anthills of the Savannah.*" It has also enhanced Achebe's reputation as an artist; as *New Statesman* contributor Margaret Busby writes, "Reading [this novel] is like watching a master carver skillfully chiselling away from every angle at a solid block of wood: at first there is simply fascination at the sureness with which he works, according to a plan apparent to himself. But the point of all this activity gradually begins to emerge—until at last it is possible to step back and admire the image created."

Despite the fact that Achebe's next book, *Hopes and Impediments,* is a collection of essays and speeches written over a period of twenty-three years, it was perceived in many ways to be a logical extension of the ideas he examined in *Anthills of the Savannah.* In this collection, however, he is not addressing the way in which Africans view themselves but rather the manner in which Africa is viewed by the outside world. The central theme of the essays is the corrosive impact of the racism that pervades the traditional Western appraisal of Africa. The collection opens with an examination of Joseph Conrad's 1902 novella *Heart of Darkness;* Achebe criticizes Conrad for projecting an image of Africa as "the other world"—meaning non-European and, therefore, uncivilized. Achebe argues that to this day, the Condradian myth persists that Africa is a dark and bestial land. The time has come, Achebe states, to sweep away the old prejudices in favor of new myths and socially "beneficent fiction" which will enable Africans and non-Africans alike to redefine the way they look at the continent.

Some reviewers are highly critical of Achebe's premise in *Hopes and Impediments.* Craig Raine, writing in the *London Review of Books,* objects to Achebe's efforts to "place art at the service of propaganda and social engineering." Other reviewers, however, are untroubled by this notion and see the collection as highly worthwhile. Observes Adam Lively in *New Statesman and Society,* "Western writers could learn much from these African visions . . . not because they radiate universal truths in a way that Europe has seen itself as doing, but precisely because they are so divergent from, so seemingly irrelevant to, our own head-down anxieties." Says Joe Wood of the *New York Times Book Review,* "Mr. Achebe aims to nudge readers to think past their stubborn preconceptions, and he succeeds marvelously."

In his writings—particularly his novels—Achebe has created a significant body of work in which he offers a close and balanced examination of contemporary Africa and the historical forces that have shaped it. "His distinction is to have [looked back] without any trace either of chauvinistic idealism or of neurotic rejection, those twin poles of so much African mythologizing," maintains Moore. "Instead, he has recreated for us a way of life which has almost disappeared, and has done so with understanding, with justice and with realism." And Busby commends the author's achievement in "charting the socio-political development of contemporary Nigeria." However, Achebe's writing reverberates beyond the borders of Nigeria and beyond the arenas of anthropology, sociology, and political science. As literature, it deals with universal qualities. And, as Killam writes in his study: "Achebe's novels offer a vision of life which is essentially tragic, compounded of success and failure, informed by knowledge and understanding, relieved by humour and tempered by sympathy, embued with an awareness of human suffering and the human capacity to endure." Concludes the critic, "Sometimes his characters meet with success, more often with defeat and despair. Through it all the spirit of man and the belief in the possibility of triumph endures."

BIOGRAPHICAL/CRITICAL SOURCES:

BOOKS

Achebe, Chinua, *A Man of the People,* introduction by K. W. J. Post, Doubleday, 1967.

Achebe, *Morning Yet on Creation Day,* Doubleday, 1975.

Achebe, *Things Fall Apart,* Fawcett, 1977.

Achebe, *Hopes and Impediments,* Heinemann, 1988.

Awoonor, Kofi, *The Breast of the Earth,* Doubleday, 1975.

Baldwin, Claudia, *Nigerian Literature: A Bibliography of Criticism,* G. K. Hall (Boston, MA), 1980.

Carroll, David, *Chinua Achebe,* Macmillan (New York City), 1990.

Contemporary Literary Criticism, Gale (Detroit, MI), Volume 1, 1973; Volume 3, 1975; Volume 5, 1976; Volume 7, 1977; Volume 11, 1979; Volume 26, 1983; Volume 51, 1988; Volume 75, 1993.

Duerden, Dennis and Cosmo Pieterse, editors, *African Writers Talking: A Collection of Radio Interviews,* Africana Publishing, 1972.

Gakwandi, Shatto Arthur, *The Novel and Contemporary Experience in Africa,* Africana Publishing, 1977.

Gikandi, Simon, *Reading Chinua Achebe: Language and Ideology in Fiction,* Heinemann, 1991.

Gleason, Judith Illsley, *This Africa: Novels by West Africans in English and French,* Northwestern University Press (Evanston, IL), 1965.

Killam, G. D., *The Novels of Chinua Achebe,* Africana Publishing, 1969.

King, Bruce, *Introduction to Nigerian Literature,* Africana Publishing, 1972.

King, *The New English Literatures: Cultural Nationalism in a Changing World,* Macmillan, 1980.

Larson, Charles R., *The Emergence of African Fiction,* Indiana University Press (Bloomington), 1972.

Laurence, Margaret, *Long Drums and Cannons: Nigerian Dramatists and Novelists,* Praeger (New York City), 1968.

Lindfors, Bernth, *Folklore in Nigerian Literature,* Africana Publishing, 1973.

McEwan, Neil, *Africa and the Novel,* Humanities Press (Atlantic Highlands, NJ), 1983.

Moore, Gerald, *Seven African Writers,* Oxford University Press (Oxford, England), 1962.

Njoku, Benedict Chiaka, *The Four Novels of Chinua Achebe: A Critical Study,* Peter Lang (New York City), 1984.

Omotoso, Kole, *Achebe or Soyinka?: A Reinterpretation and a Study in Contrasts,* Hans Zell Publishers, 1992.

Palmer, Eustace, *The Growth of the African Novel,* Heinemann, 1979.

Petersen, K. H., *Chinua Achebe: A Celebration,* Heinemann, Dangeroo Press, 1991.

Ravenscroft, Arthur, *Chinua Achebe,* Longmans, Green (Essex, England), 1969.

Roscoe, Adrian A., *Mother Is Gold: A Study of West African Literature,* Cambridge University Press (Cambridge, England), 1971.

Tucker, Martin, *Africa in Modern Literature,* Ungar (New York City), 1967.

Wren, Robert M., *Achebe's World: The Historical and Cultural Context of the Novels,* Three Continents (Washington, DC), 1980.

PERIODICALS

Afro-American and African Journal of Arts and Letters, winter, 1990.

America, June 22-29, 1991.

Boston Globe, March 9, 1988.

Busara, Volume 7, number 2, 1975.

Commonweal, December 1, 1967.

Commonwealth Essays and Studies, fall, 1990.

Economist, October 24, 1987.

English Studies in Africa, September, 1971.

Listener, October 15, 1987.

Lively Arts and Book Review, April 30, 1961.

London Review of Books, August 7, 1986; October 15, 1981; June 22, 1989, p. 16-17.

Los Angeles Times Book Review, February 28, 1988.

Massachusetts Review, spring, 1987.

Michigan Quarterly Review, fall, 1970.

Modern Fiction Studies, fall, 1991.

Nation, October 11, 1965; April 16, 1988.

New Africa, November, 1987.

New Statesman, January 4, 1985; September 25, 1987.

New Statesman and Society, July 22, 1988, p. 41-42; February 9, 1990, p. 30.

New York Review of Books, March 3, 1988.

New York Times, August 10, 1966; February 16, 1988.

New York Times Book Review, December 17, 1967; May 13, 1973; August 11, 1985; February 21, 1988; November 12, 1989, p. 55.

Observer (London), September 20, 1987.

Parabola, fall, 1992.

Publishers Weekly, February 21, 1994, p. 249.

Saturday Review, January 6, 1968.

School Library Journal, December, 1992, p. 146.

Spectator, October 21, 1960; September 26, 1987.

Studies in Black Literature: Special Issue; Chinua Achebe, spring, 1971.

Times Educational Supplement, January 25, 1985.

Times Literary Supplement, February 3, 1966; March 3, 1972; May 4, 1973; February 26, 1982; October 12, 1984; October 9, 1987.

Tribune Books (Chicago), February 21, 1988.

Utne Reader, March/April, 1990.

Village Voice, March 15, 1988.

Wall Street Journal, February 23, 1988.
Washington Post, February 16, 1988.
Washington Post Book World, February 7, 1988.
World Literature Today, summer, 1985.
World Literature Written in English, November, 1978.*

*   *   *

ADAMSON, Lesley
See GRANT-ADAMSON, Lesley

*   *   *

ADLER, Irving   1913-
(Robert Irving)

PERSONAL: Born April 27, 1913, in New York, NY; married Ruth Relis (an illustrator, writer, and teacher), 1935 (died March 30, 1968); married Joyce Sparer (a teacher and writer); children: Stephen, Peggy Adler Robohm. *Education:* City College of New York, B.S. (magna cum laude), 1931; Columbia University, M.A., 1938, Ph.D., 1961. *Avocational interests:* Gardening.

ADDRESSES: Home—R.R. 1, Box 532, North Bennington, VT 05257-9748.

CAREER: Teacher of mathematics in New York City high schools, 1932-52; writer and lecturer, 1952—; instructor at Columbia University, 1957-60, Bennington College, Bennington, VT, 1961, and Southern Vermont College, Bennington, 1983. Consultant, Educational Policies Commission of National Education Association, 1940-41; conducted courses in in-service training program of New York City Board of Education, 1947-49; chairman, Coordinating Committee of Vermont Peace Organizations, 1961-63; president, Vermont-in-Mississippi Corporation (civil rights organization), 1965-67; member, Shaftsbury School Board, 1976-82, chairman, 1979-80; member, Mount Anthony Union High School District School Board, 1981-84. Trustee of Public Funds, Town of Shaftsbury, 1990-93.

MEMBER: Mathematical Association of America, American Mathematical Society, National Council of Teachers of Mathematics, Authors League of America, Vermont Academy of Arts and Sciences (trustee, 1975-81; president, 1978-81), Phi Beta Kappa, Kappa Delta Pi, Sigma Xi.

AWARDS, HONORS: National Science Foundation fellow, 1959; recipient with first wife, Ruth Adler, of award for "outstanding contributions to children's literature," New York State Association for Supervision and Curriculum Development, 1961; "outstanding science books for

children" citations, National Science Teachers Association and the Children's Book Council, 1972, 1975, 1980, and 1990; American Association for the Advancement of Science fellow, 1982; Vermont Academy of Arts and Sciences fellow, 1985; D.Sc., St. Michael's College, 1990; Townsend Harris Medal, City College Alumni Association, 1993, for "outstanding post-graduate achievement."

WRITINGS:

FOR CHILDREN; ILLUSTRATED BY WIFE, RUTH ADLER, EXCEPT AS NOTED

The Secret of Light, illustrated by Ida Weisburd, International Publishers, 1952, published as *The Story of Light,* illustrated by Anne Lewis, Harvey House, 1971.
(With Gaylord Johnson) *Discover the Stars,* Sentinel, 1954, revised edition, 1965.
Fire in Your Life, John Day, 1955.
Time in Your Life, John Day, 1955, revised edition, 1969.
The Stars: Decoding Their Messages, John Day, 1956.
Tools in Your Life, John Day, 1956.
Monkey Business: Hoaxes in the Name of Science, John Day, 1957.
Man-Made Moons, John Day, 1957, revised edition published as *Seeing the Earth from Space,* 1959.
Magic House of Numbers, John Day, 1957, revised edition, 1977.
How Life Began, John Day, 1957, revised edition, illustrated with daughter, Peggy Adler, 1977.
Dust, John Day, 1958.
The Sun and Its Family, John Day, 1958.
Mathematics: The Story of Numbers, Symbols and Space, illustrated by Lowell Hess, Golden Press, 1958.
The Tools of Science, John Day, 1958, published as *The Changing Tools of Science: From Yardstick to Synchrotron,* John Day, 1973.
Weather in Your Life, illustrated with P. Adler, John Day, 1959, revised edition, 1975.
Hot and Cold, illustrated by P. Adler, John Day, 1959, revised edition, 1975.
The Giant Golden Book of Mathematics: Exploring the World of Numbers and Space, Golden Press, 1960.
Temperature in Your Life, illustrated by P. Adler, Dobson, 1960.
Light in Your Life, illustrated by I. Weisburd, Dobson, 1961.
(With P. Adler) *The Adler Book of Puzzles and Riddles, or, Sam Loyd Up to Date,* illustrated by P. Adler, John Day, 1962.
Mathematics Workbooks with Self-Teaching and Learning Exercises, illustrated by Dick Martin, Golden Press, 1962.
Color in Your Life, John Day, 1962.

Inside the Nucleus, John Day, 1963.
Logic for Beginners, John Day, 1964.
Electricity in Your Life, John Day, 1965.
The Wonders of Physics, illustrated by Cornelius De Witt, Golden Press, 1966.
Energy, illustrated with E. Viereck, John Day, 1970.

FOR CHILDREN; WRITTEN WITH AND ILLUSTRATED BY R. ADLER, EXCEPT AS NOTED

Numbers Old and New, illustrated by P. Adler, John Day, 1960.
Things That Spin, John Day, 1960.
Rivers, John Day, 1961.
Shadows, John Day, 1961, revised edition, 1968.
The Story of a Nail, John Day, 1961.
Why? A Book of Reasons, John Day, 1961.
Your Eyes, John Day, 1962.
Oceans, John Day, 1962.
Insects and Plants, John Day, 1962.
Air, John Day, 1962, revised edition, 1972.
Storms, John Day, 1963.
Your Ears, illustrated by P. Adler, John Day, 1963.
Why and How?, John Day, 1963.
The Earth's Crust, John Day, 1963.
Irrigation, John Day, 1964.
Numerals: New Dresses for Old Numbers, John Day, 1964.
Fibers, John Day, 1964.
Heat, John Day, 1964, published as *Heat and Its Uses,* 1973.
Houses, John Day, 1964.
Machines, John Day, 1964.
Coal, John Day, 1965, revised edition, 1974.
Evolution, John Day, 1965.
Atoms and Molecules, John Day, 1966.
Taste, Touch and Smell, John Day, 1966.
Magnets, John Day, 1966.
Tree Products, John Day, 1967.
Sets, John Day, 1967.
The Calendar, John Day, 1967.
Communication, John Day, 1967.
Directions and Angles, John Day, 1969.
Sets and Numbers for the Very Young, illustrated by P. Adler, John Day, 1969.

FOR CHILDREN; UNDER PSEUDONYM ROBERT IRVING

Hurricanes and Twisters, illustrated by R. Adler, Knopf, 1955.
Rocks and Minerals and the Stories They Tell, illustrated by Ida Scheib, Knopf, 1956.
Energy and Power, illustrated by Leonard E. Fisher, Knopf, 1958.
Sound and Ultrasonics, illustrated by L. E. Fisher, Knopf, 1959.
Electromagnetic Waves, illustrated by L. E. Fisher, Knopf, 1960.

Electronics, illustrated by R. Adler, Knopf, 1961.
Volcanoes and Earthquakes, illustrated by R. Adler, Knopf, 1962.

OTHER BOOKS FOR CHILDREN

(With second wife, Joyce Adler) *Language and Man,* illustrated by Laurie Jo Lambie, John Day, 1970.
Atomic Energy, illustrated by E. Viereck, John Day, 1971.
Integers: Positive and Negative, illustrated by L. J. Lambie, John Day, 1972.
(Editor) *Readings in Mathematics,* Ginn, 1972.
Petroleum: Gas Oil, and Asphalt, illustrated by P. Adler, 1975.
The Environment, illustrated by P. Adler, John Day, 1976.
Food, illustrated by P. Adler, John Day, 1977.
(With P. Adler) *Metric Puzzles,* F. Watts, 1977.
(With P. Adler) *Math Puzzles,* F. Watts, 1978.
The Stars: Decoding Their Messages, illustrated by P. Adler, 1980.
Mathematics, illustrated by Ron Miller, Doubleday, 1990.

FOR ADULTS

What We Want of Our Schools, John Day, 1957.
The New Mathematics, John Day, 1958, revised edition, 1969.
Thinking Machines, John Day, 1961, revised edition, 1974.
Probability and Statistics for Every Man, John Day, 1963.
A New Look at Arithmetic, John Day, 1964.
The Elementary Mathematics of the Atom, John Day, 1965.
A New Look at Geometry, John Day, 1966.
Groups in the New Mathematics, illustrated by R. Adler and E. Viereck, John Day, 1968.
Mathematics and Mental Growth, illustrated by R. Adler and E. Viereck, John Day, 1968.

OTHER

Also author of *The Impossible in Mathematics,* National Council of Teachers of Mathematics, c. 1957. Contributor of articles to periodicals, including *Nation* and *Journal of Theoretical Biology.*

Adler's books have been translated into seventeen languages, including French, German, Portuguese, Dutch, Danish, Norwegian, Swedish, Spanish, and Japanese. Adler's works are included in the Kerlan Collection at the University of Minnesota and the de Grummond Collection at the University of Southern Mississippi.

SIDELIGHTS: Irving Adler's books interpret science and mathematics for children. Though he began his career as a mathematics teacher in the 1930s, Adler has authored over 75 books for children since the early 1950s, as well as several works for adults. A number of his children's books, including those among "The Reason Why" series, were illustrated by and coauthored with his first wife, the late Ruth Adler, also a mathematics teacher. Throughout his writings, Adler has explained a wide range of scientific subjects for young readers, within areas such as astronomy, physics, atomic structure, geology, and weather phenomenon, as well as mathematics. He once told a *Horn Book* reviewer that his "primary goal is to present scientific ideas so simply that they can be followed and understood by an unsophisticated reader."

During a graduate course in atomic structure at Columbia, it occurred to Adler that the basic theories of science were simple enough to explain to children. He found it "fascinating," as he described in *Third Book of Junior Authors,* "that everything we know about the tiny atoms of which all things are made is based on coded light messages sent to us by the atoms." A few years later, while taking a course in star identification at New York City's planetarium, and reading at the same time a book on astrophysics, Adler realized a connection in how scientists likewise gather coded light messages in understanding the distant stars in the universe. "By this time," he added in *Third Book,* "there was a full-grown book in my head clamoring to be let out to explain to children how we learn about small things like atoms and big things like stars by studying the coded light messages they send us." With this impetus, Adler wrote his first children's book, *The Secret of Light,* which was published in 1952 and which explained the role of light in understanding atomic structure. Four years later, with his book *The Stars: Decoding Their Messages,* he explained the similar way that scientists use light to gain important knowledge about the stars.

After beginning his new career as a science writer, Adler went on to publish more than 75 children's books over the next four decades. He once commented to *CA* about being able to explain matters of science to a young audience: "I believe children are interested in and can understand very profound scientific truths when those truths are presented clearly in their own language. In fact many adults say they like to read my children's books because they are informative and yet not too difficult to read and follow." After the publication of Adler's first children's science book in 1952, his wife Ruth began providing illustrations for his work, and also helped him in selecting subjects and critiquing his writing. They became coauthors in 1960 with *Numbers Old and New,* the first of numerous books they wrote for "The Reason Why" series, published by John Day.

Throughout his career, Adler has also written books for adults on science and mathematics. He commented in a *Library Journal* article that his main task in being a science writer—whether for children or adults—is "transmitting to the layman an understanding of the vast, com-plex, and growing body of scientific knowledge." Adler sees a close parallel between his work and that of any artist. "Like the discovery of new scientific knowledge or the writing of poems, plays or novels, [successful science writing] requires the play of a creative imagination, which, no less than artistic constructs, illuminates the structure of reality."

In the 1970s Adler published a series of articles in the *Journal of Theoretical Biology* which recounted his research work in phyllotaxis, an area of mathematical biology. Over the years, he has lectured at numerous mathematics conventions in North America and abroad, and in 1984 spoke on a five-month university and teacher's convention circuit that took him to New Zealand, Australia, Hong Kong, Singapore, Malaysia, Thailand, and India.

BIOGRAPHICAL/CRITICAL SOURCES:

BOOKS

Third Book of Junior Authors, edited by Doris de Montreville and Donna Hill, H. W. Wilson, 1972, pp. 2-4.

PERIODICALS

Horn Book, October, 1965.
Library Journal, December 15, 1966.

*   *   *

ALEXANDER, Kate
See ARMSTRONG, Tilly

*   *   *

ALLAN, Mabel Esther 1915-
(Jean Estoril, Priscilla Hagon, Anne Pilgrim)

PERSONAL: Born February 11, 1915, in Wallasey, Cheshire, England; daughter of James Pemberton (a merchant) and Priscilla (Hagon) Allan. *Education:* Educated at private schools in England. *Avocational interests:* Book collecting.

ADDRESSES: Home—Glengarth, II, Oldfield Way, Heswall, Wirral L60 6RQ, England. *Agent*—Curtis Brown/John Farquharson Ltd., 162-168 Regent St., London W1R 5TB, England.

CAREER: Author. Served as warden of a wartime nursery for children during World War II. *Military service:* Women's Land Army, two years during World War II.

AWARDS, HONORS: Nomination for Edgar Allan Poe Award, Mystery Writers of America, 1972, for *Mystery in Wales;* *Horn Book* honor list for *An Island in a Green Sea.*

WRITINGS:

JUVENILE FICTION

The Glen Castle Mystery, Warne, 1948.

The Adventurous Summer, illustrated by Isabel Veevers, Museum Press, 1948.

Wyndhams Went to Wales, illustrated by Beryl Thornborough, Sylvan Press, 1948.

Cilia of Chiltern's Edge, illustrated by Betty Ladler, Museum Press, 1949.

Mullion, illustrated by R. Walter Hall, Hutchinson, 1949.

Jimmy John's Journey, Dent, 1949.

Trouble at Melville Manor, illustrated by I. Veevers, Museum Press, 1949.

Holiday at Arnriggs, Warne, 1949.

Chiltern Adventure, illustrated by T. R. Freeman, Blackie & Son, 1950.

School under Snowdon, Hutchinson, 1950.

Everyday Island, Museum Press, 1950.

Over the Sea to School, illustrated by W. Mackinlay, Blackie & Son, 1950.

Seven in Switzerland, illustrated by I. Veevers, Blackie & Son, 1950.

The Exciting River, illustrated by Helen Jacobs, Nelson, 1951.

Clues to Connemara, Blackie & Son, 1952.

MacIans of Glen Gillean, Hutchinson, 1952.

Return to Derrykereen, Ward, 1952.

School in Danger, illustrated by Eric Winter, Blackie & Son, 1952.

School on Cloud Ridge, Hutchinson, 1952.

School on North Barrule, Museum Press, 1952.

Lucia Comes to School, Hutchinson, 1953.

Room for the Cuckoo: The Story of a Farming Year, Dent, 1953.

The Secret Valley, illustrated by C. Instrcll, Arnold, 1953.

Strangers at Brongwerne, Museum Press, 1953.

Three Go to Switzerland, illustrated by I. Veevers, Blackie & Son, 1953.

Here We Go Round: A Career Story for Girls, Heinemann, 1954.

Adventure Royal, illustrated by C. W. Bacon, Blackie & Son, 1954.

Margaret Finds a Future, Hutchinson, 1954.

Meric's Secret Cottage, Blackie & Son, 1954.

New Schools for Old, Hutchinson, 1954.

Summer at Town's End, illustrated by Iris Weller, Harrap, 1954.

Adventures in Switzerland, Pickering & Inglis, 1955.

Changes for the Challoners, Ward, 1955.

Glenvara, Hutchinson, 1955, published as *Summer of Decision,* Abelard, 1957.

Judith Teaches, Bodley Head, 1955.

The Mystery of Derrydane, illustrated by Vera Chadwick, Schofield & Sims, 1955.

Swiss School, Hutchinson, 1955.

Adventure in Mayo, Ward, 1956.

Amber House, Hutchinson, 1956.

Balconies and Blue Nets: The Story of a Holiday in Brittany, illustrated by Peggy Beetles, Harrap, 1956.

Flora at Kilroinn, Blackie & Son, 1956.

Lost Lorrenden, Blackie & Son, 1956.

Strangers in Skye, Heinemann, 1956, Criterion, 1958.

Two in the Western Isles, Hutchinson, 1956.

Vine Clad Hill, illustrated by T. P. Freeman, Bodley Head, 1956, published as *Swiss Holiday,* Vanguard, 1957.

Ann's Alpine Adventure, Hutchinson, 1957.

At School in Skye, illustrated by Constance Marshall, Blackie & Son, 1957.

Black Forest Summer, Bodley Head, 1957, Vanguard, 1959.

Sara Goes to Germany, Hutchinson, 1957.

Blue Dragon Days, Heinemann, 1958, published as *Romance in Italy,* Vanguard, 1962.

The Conch Shell, illustrated by T. R. Freeman, Blackie & Son, 1958.

House by the Marsh, illustrated by Sheila Rose, Dent, 1958.

Rachel Tandy, Hutchinson, 1958.

Amanda Goes to Italy, Hutchinson, 1959.

Catrin in Wales, Bodley Head, 1959, Vanguard, 1961.

"On Stage, Flory!," F. Watts, 1959, published in England as *A Play to the Festival,* Heinemann, 1959.

Shadow over the Alps, Hutchinson, 1960.

Hilary's Summer on Her Own, F. Watts, 1960, published in England as *A Summer in Brittany,* Dent, 1960.

Tansy of Tring Street, illustrated by Sally Holliday, Heinemann, 1960.

Bluegate Girl, Hutchinson, 1961.

Holiday of Endurance, Dent, 1961.

Home to the Island, illustrated by Geoffrey Whittam, Dent, 1962, Vanguard, 1966.

Pendron under the Water, illustrated by T. R. Freeman, Harrap, 1962.

Schooldays in Skye, Blackie & Son, 1962.

Signpost to Switzerland, Heinemann, 1962, Criterion, 1966.

The Ballet Family, illustrated by A. R. Whitear, Methuen, 1963, Criterion, 1966.

Kate Comes to England, Heinemann, 1963, published as *Kate Goes to England,* Vanguard, 1967.

The Sign of the Unicorn: A Thriller for Young People, illustrated by Shirley Hughes, Dent, 1963, Criterion, 1963.

New York for Nicola, Vanguard, 1963, White Lion, 1977.

Mystery in Arles, Vanguard, 1964, published in England as *It Happened in Arles,* Heinemann, 1964.

The Ballet Family Again, illustrated by A. R. Whitear, Methuen, 1964, published as *The Dancing Garlands,* Criterion, 1966.

Fiona on the Fourteenth Floor, illustrated by S. Hughes, Dent, 1964, published as *Mystery on the Fourteenth Floor,* Criterion, 1965.

The Way over Windle, Metheun, 1966.

Skiing to Danger, Heinemann, 1966, published as *Mystery of the Ski Slopes,* Criterion, 1966.

In Pursuit of Clarinda, illustrated by Margaret Wetherbee, Dent, 1966.

A Summer at Sea, Dent, 1966, Vanguard, 1967.

Missing in Manhattan, illustrated by M. Wetherbee, Dent, 1967, published as *Mystery in Manhattan,* Vanguard, 1968.

The Mystery Began in Madeira, Criterion, 1967, published in England as *It Started in Madeira,* Heinemann, 1967.

The Wood Street Secret, illustrated by S. Hughes, Methuen, 1968, Abelard, 1970.

The Wood Street Group, illustrated by S. Hughes, Methuen, 1969.

The Kraymer Mystery, Criterion, 1969, Abelard, 1973.

Climbing to Danger, Heinemann, 1969, published as *Mystery in Wales,* Vanguard, 1971.

The Wood Street Rivals, illustrated by S. Hughes, Methuen, 1970.

Christmas at Spindle Bottom, illustrated by Lynette Hemmant, Dent, 1970.

Dangerous Inheritance, Heinemann, 1970.

The Secret Dancer, illustrated by Juliet Mozley, Dent, 1971.

The May Day Mystery, Criterion, 1971, Severn House, 1980.

Behind the Blue Gates, Heinemann, 1972.

An Island in a Green Sea, illustrated by Charles Robinson, Atheneum, 1972, Dent, 1973.

Time to Go Back, Abelard, 1972, Criterion, 1974.

The Wood Street Helpers, illustrated by S. Hughes, Methuen, 1973.

A Formidable Enemy, Heinemann, 1973, Thomas Nelson, 1975.

The Secret Players, illustrated by James Russell, Brockhampton, 1974.

Mystery in Rome, Vanguard, 1974, published in England as *The Bells of Rome,* Heinemann, 1975.

Ship of Danger, Criterion, 1974, Heinemann, 1974.

The Night Wind, illustrated by Charles Robinson, Atheneum, 1974, Severn House, 1982.

A Chill in the Lane, Thomas Nelson, 1974.

Crow's Nest, Abelard, 1975.

The Flash Children, illustrated by Gavin Rowe, Dodd, 1975, Brockhampton Press, 1975.

Romansgrove, illustrated by Gail Owens, Atheneum, 1975, Severn House, 1984.

Bridge of Friendship, Dent, 1975, Dodd, 1977.

Away from Wood Street, illustrated by S. Hughes, Methuen, 1976.

Trouble in the Glen, illustrated by Jutta Ash, Abelard, 1976.

The Rising Tide, Heinemann, 1976, Walker, 1978.

My Family's Not Forever, Abelard, 1977.

The View beyond My Father, Abelard, 1977, Dodd, 1978.

The Pine Street Pageant, illustrated by Rosemary Chanter, Abelard, 1978.

Tomorrow Is a Lovely Day, Abelard, 1979, published as *A Lovely Tomorrow,* Dodd, 1980.

Wood Street and Mary Ellen, illustrated by Lesley Smith, Methuen, 1979.

The Mills Down Below, Abelard, 1980, Dodd, 1981.

Pine Street Goes Camping, illustrated by Patricia Drew, Abelard, 1980.

Strangers in Wood Street, illustrated by L. Smith, Methuen, 1981.

The Horns of Danger, Dodd, 1981, Severn House, 1985.

The Pine Street Problem, illustrated by P. Drew, Abelard, 1981.

A Strange Enchantment, Abelard, 1981, Dodd, 1982.

Growing Up in Wood Street, Methuen, 1982.

Goodbye to Pine Street, illustrated by P. Drew, Abelard, 1982.

Alone at Pine Street, illustrated by P. Drew, Abelard, 1983.

The Crumble Lane Adventure, Methuen, 1983.

A Dream of Hunger Moss, illustrated by Bertram M. Tormey, Dodd, 1983, Severn House, 1985.

A Secret in Spindle Bottom, Abelard, 1984.

Friends at Pine Street, Abelard, 1984.

Trouble in Crumble Lane, Methuen, 1984.

The Flash Children in Winter, Hodder & Stoughton, 1985.

The Pride of Pine Street, Blackie & Son, 1985.

The Crumble Lane Captives, Methuen, 1986.

A Mystery in Spindle Bottom, Blackie & Son, 1986.

The Road to Huntingland, Severn House, 1986.

The Crumble Lane Mystery, Methuen, 1987.

Up the Victorian Staircase: A London Mystery, Severn House, 1987.

First Term at Ash Grove, Blackie & Son, 1988.

The Mystery of Serafina: A New York Adventure, privately printed, 1990.

Queen Rita at the High School and Other School Stories, privately printed, 1991.

UNDER PSEUDONYM JEAN ESTORIL; JUVENILE FICTION

Ballet for Drina, illustrated by Eve Guthrie and M. P. Steedman Davies, Hodder & Stoughton, 1957, Vanguard, 1958, revised edition, Scholastic, 1989.

Drina's Dancing Year, Hodder & Stoughton, 1958, Simon & Schuster, 1987.

Drina Dances in Exile, Hodder & Stoughton, 1959, Simon & Schuster, 1987, published as *Drina Dances Alone,* Scholastic, 1989.

Drina Dances in Italy, illustrated by E. Guthrie and M. P. S. Davies, Hodder & Stoughton, 1959, Vanguard, 1961, published as *Drina Dances on Stage,* Scholastic, 1989.

Drina Dances Again, Hodder & Stoughton, 1960, Simon & Schuster, 1989.

Drina Dances in New York, Hodder & Stoughton, 1961, Simon & Schuster, 1989.

Drina Dances in Paris, Hodder & Stoughton, 1962, Simon & Schuster, 1990.

Drina Dances in Madeira, Hodder & Stoughton, 1963, Simon & Schuster, 1990.

Drina Dances in Switzerland, Hodder & Stoughton, 1964, Simon & Schuster, 1990.

Drina Goes on Tour, Brockhampton, 1965, Simon & Schuster, 1990.

We Danced in Bloomsbury Square, illustrated by Muriel Wood, Heinemann, 1967, Follet, 1970, published as *The Ballet Twins,* Simon & Schuster, 1989.

Drina, Ballerina, Simon & Schuster, 1991.

UNDER PSEUDONYM PRISCILLA HAGON; JUVENILE FICTION

Cruising to Danger, illustrated by William Plummer, World Publishing, 1966, Harrap, 1968.

Dancing to Danger, illustrated by Susanne Suba, World Publishing, 1967.

Mystery at Saint-Hilaire, illustrated by W. Plummer, World Publishing, 1968.

Mystery at the Villa Bianca, illustrated by W. Plummer, World Publishing, 1969.

Mystery of the Secret Square, illustrated by Ray Abel, World Publishing, 1970.

UNDER PSEUDONYM ANNE PILGRIM; JUVENILE FICTION

The First Time I Saw Paris, Abelard, 1961.
Clare Goes to Holland, Abelard, 1962.
A Summer in Provence, Abelard, 1963.
Strangers in New York, Abelard, 1964.
Selina's New Family, Abelard, 1967.

OTHER

Murder at the Flood (adult novel), Paul, 1958.
The Haunted Valley and Other Poems, privately printed, 1981.

To Be an Author: A Short Autobiography, Charles Gill & Sons, 1982.

More about Being an Author (autobiography), Charles Gill & Sons, 1985.

The Background Came First: My Books and Places, Part I, Britain and Ireland (autobiography), privately printed, 1988.

The Background Came First: My Books and Places, Part II, Other Countries (autobiography), privately printed, 1988.

The Road to the Isles and Other Places: Some Journeys with a Rucksack, privately printed, 1989.

Chiltern School, privately printed, 1990.

The Two Head Girls and Other School Stories, privately printed, 1992.

The Way to Glen Bradan and Other Scottish, Welsh, & Irish Stories, privately printed, 1993.

Ragged Robin Began It and Other Articles about Old Girls' Books, privately printed, 1993.

Contributor of articles to periodicals, including *The Writer, Irish Travel, Women's Outlook,* and *Parent's Review.* Allan's books have been translated into numerous foreign languages, including French, German, Polish, Italian, Norwegian, Dutch, Portuguese, and Japanese. Allan's manuscript collection is housed at University of Southern Mississippi.

SIDELIGHTS: Since publishing her first book in 1948, British writer Mabel Esther Allan has written over 170 books for children and young adults. Early on Allan produced conventional books for young children, such as adventures, mysteries, school stories, and romances for adolescent girls. Later in her career Allan's books became more autobiographical in scope and delved into topics such as British life during World War II, the women's suffrage movement, and the lives of urban working-class youth. In *Twentieth-Century Children's Writers,* Alan Edwin Day remarked that the variety of Allan's themes show her to be a writer who displays "vitality, exuberance, and versatility" and who cannot be classified into a clearly-defined category.

Allan was born in Wallasey, a town on the Mersey River in England. As a young girl she suffered from poor eyesight and disliked both school and her teachers. She began to sell poetry and short stories at the age of nineteen, yet her desire to publish a children's book was interrupted by World War II. In 1944 Allan's sight suddenly dramatically improved, and the following year she sold her first novel to be published, *The Glen Castle Mystery.*

Allan often set her books in places she had visited. She once remarked to *CA* on the importance of place to her early books: "For many years *places* were all important to me as an author. The background always came first. It was partly the wish to live again experiences I had enjoyed, though formed and altered to make a story. I believe that my ability to evoke places is the thing that has given the most pleasure to readers."

Allan further told *CA* of the limitations of writing for young people in her early career: "I began to publish books during the days when there were many taboos in books for young people. It wasn't even possible to suggest that children sometimes hated their parents or that atheism was as desirable a state as being Protestant, Catholic, or a follower of any other religion. Unconsciously maybe this influenced me." However, one area in which Allan was considered unconventional was her portrayal of schools, as she told *CA:* "I believed passionately in co-education, which was unusual in Britain then and almost unknown in boarding schools. I believed in self-discipline and not in imposed discipline, and in learning for learning's sake and not for marks in class."

Throughout the 1960s Allan was firmly established as a top-selling children's writer. While her early books are today most popular among book collectors, her Drina series, originally published in the 1950s and 1960s, still enjoys a high readership. Written under the pseudonym of Jean Estoril, the Drina books focus on the experiences of a young dancer on her way to becoming an international ballet star. In 1989 and 1990, updated editions of the original books were published in both the United States and Great Britain.

Around 1970 Allan's books became more autobiographical in nature. As she commented in *CA,* she discovered that she "could be much more truthful" and "could look to the past, and write about it." Allan found herself able to address topics and concerns which she had previously avoided. "I could suggest that some people had no religious beliefs and might even be better human beings because of that. I could write about young people who disliked their parents. I could also mention sexual feelings." *An Island in a Green Sea* and *Time to Go Back* were the first of Allan's books to reflect this change in direction, and together with books such as *The View beyond My Father, A Lovely Tomorrow,* and *A Strange Enchantment,* they "go deeper than any of my earlier books." In *The Mills Down Below,* for example, Allan depicted the women's suffrage movement in Great Britain in the early part of the twentieth century, an issue of particular importance to her. "I wish I had written more about women's rights, and children's rights, too," she commented in *To Be an Author: A Short Autobiography.* "The older I get the more strongly I feel about such things. . . . I grew up as a second class citizen just because I was a girl, and I never even questioned it for a very long time."

In 1991 Allan began retracing the steps of her early career. Though she did not keep copies of the several hundred stories she wrote between 1936 and 1957, she has recovered many from the original publications and plans to publish them privately. Allan commented to *CA* that her long and varied life as a writer has been largely a satisfying one. "I had years of struggle and disappointment and I wouldn't relive them for anything, but it was all worth it in the end. . . . When aspiring authors ask me for advice, the first thing I say is: 'Don't contemplate it unless you can stand spending a large part of your life alone, shut up with a typewriter.' " Allan has repeatedly commented that she writes for herself about what she finds appealing, yet she enjoys having a positive effect on her readers. "I am glad where I have given pleasure, or have helped," she stated in *To Be an Author.* "And particularly glad if I have sent people to places I have loved."

BIOGRAPHICAL/CRITICAL SOURCES:

BOOKS

Allan, Mabel Esther, *To Be an Author: A Short Autobiography,* Charles Gill & Sons, 1982.
Allan, Mabel Esther, *More about Being an Author,* Charles Gill & Sons, 1985.
Allan, Mabel Esther, *The Background Came First: My Books and Places, Part I, Britain and Ireland,* privately printed, 1988.
Allan, Mabel Esther, *The Background Came First: My Books and Places, Part II, Other Countries,* privately printed, 1988.
Twentieth-Century Children's Writers, 3rd edition, St. James, 1989.

PERIODICALS

Bulletin of the Center for Children's Books, September, 1977; July-August, 1980; April, 1982; November, 1982; February, 1984.
Junior Literary Guild, March, 1980.

*   *   *

ALTER, Robert B(ernard) 1935-

PERSONAL: Born April 2, 1935, in New York, NY; son of Harry (a salesman) and Tillie (Zimmerman) Alter; married Judith Berkenbilt, June 4, 1961 (divorced February, 1973); married Carol Cosman (an editor and translator), June 17, 1973; children: (first marriage) Miriam, Dan; (second marriage) Gabriel, Micha. *Education:* Columbia University, B.A., 1957; Harvard University, M.A., 1958, Ph.D., 1962. *Religion:* Jewish.

ADDRESSES: Home—1475 Le Roy Ave., Berkeley, CA 94708. *Office*—Department of Comparative Literature,

University of California, Berkeley, CA 94720. *Agent*—Georges Borchardt, 136 East 57th St., New York, NY 10022.

CAREER: Columbia University, New York City, instructor, 1962-64, assistant professor of English, 1964-66; University of California, Berkeley, associate professor, 1967-69, professor of Hebrew and comparative literature, 1969-89, chair of comparative literature department, 1970-72, Class of 1937 Professor, 1989—.

MEMBER: American Academy of Arts and Sciences (fellow), Council of Scholars of Library of Congress, American Comparative Literature Association, Association for Jewish Studies, National Association of Professors of Hebrew.

AWARDS, HONORS: English Institute essay prize, 1965; Guggenheim fellow, 1966-67, 1979-80; National Endowment for the Humanities senior fellow, 1972-73; Institute for Advanced Studies, Jerusalem, fellow, 1980-83; National Jewish Book Award, 1982, for *The Art of Biblical Narrative;* Joel H. Cavior Award for religious thought, 1987, for *The Art of Biblical Poetry.*

WRITINGS:

Rogue's Progress: Studies in the Picaresque Novel, Harvard University Press, 1965.

Fielding and the Nature of the Novel, Harvard University Press, 1968.

After the Tradition: Essays on Modern Jewish Writing, Dutton, 1969.

Partial Magic: The Novel as a Self-Conscious Genre, University of California Press, 1975.

Defenses of the Imagination, Jewish Publication Society, 1978.

(With wife, Carol Cosman) *A Lion for Love: A Critical Biography of Stendahl,* Basic Books, 1979.

The Art of Biblical Narrative, Basic Books, 1981.

Motives for Fiction, Harvard University Press, 1984.

The Art of Biblical Poetry, Basic Books, 1985.

(Editor with Frank Kermode) *The Literary Guide to the Bible,* Harvard University Press, 1987.

The Invention of Hebrew Prose: Modern Fiction and the Language of Realism, University of Washington Press, 1988.

The Pleasures of Reading: In an Ideological Age, Simon & Schuster, 1989.

Necessary Angels: Tradition and Modernity in Kafka, Benjamin, and Scholem, Harvard University Press, 1991.

The World of Biblical Literature, Basic Books, 1992.

Hebrew and Modernity, Indiana University Press, 1994.

Commentary, columnist, 1965-73, contributing editor, 1973-87; contributor to *New Republic, London Review of Books,* and *New York Times Book Review.*

SIDELIGHTS: With the publication of *The Art of Biblical Narrative* in 1981, Robert Alter gained a reputation as a literary interpreter of the Bible, especially the Hebrew Bible, or Old Testament. Alter subjected the Bible to the kind of scrutiny that secular literature often receives but the Bible rarely does. Typically, the Bible is either accepted as the truth by religious believers, or it is examined for contradictions by others. Instead, Alter studied the text for the design of its narrative, structure, and technique. In *The Art of Biblical Narrative,* he discusses the strategies and literary features of its stories, including scenes, characterization, dialogue, verbal and gestural repetition, and silence. Reynolds Price, writing in *Washington Post Book World,* finds that Alter uncovers "virtually uncontestable evidence for his contention that the stories—far from being the awkwardly conflated primitive documents that so much scholarship has led us to see—are as sophisticated in their verbal and formal devices as any other ancient narratives."

Finding the Old Testament a complex fusion of history and fiction, Alter maintains that the authors of the Bible "were among the pioneers of prose fiction in the Western tradition." He notes that one common feature of biblical writing was a tendency to give the characters' speech priority over the narrator's own. Alter gives as one example David's return to Jerusalem with the Ark of the Covenant; the perspective the Bible gives is not that of the narrator but of Michal, David's first wife. Alter points out that the reader can only infer the reason for Michal's scorn. Like a modern novelist, the writer has left interpretation to the reader. *New Republic* writer Geoffrey Hartman argues that "Alter turns laconic stories, through his care for detail and nuance, into miniature novels," explaining each one "line by line, until the characters are men and women we can get to know, until their actions and passions, and their social and psychological milieu, resemble ours."

Alter's next book concentrated solely on critical analysis of modern fiction. *Motives for Fiction* is a collection of what the author calls "episodic critical writing" that originally appeared in such publications as *American Scholar, Commentary,* and the *New Republic.* In his essays Alter argues that the novel can be "an imaginative instrument for the empirical exploration of social, moral, and psychological realities." This thesis met with some criticism. In an article for the *Los Angeles Times Book Review,* Michael F. Harper imagines that Alter sees himself as "St. George galloping to . . . [readers'] aid, crucial lance at the ready." Harper criticizes the fact that the book "lumps together under the heading of 'structuralism and its aftermath' such disparate spirits as Roland Barthes, Gerard Genette, Jacques Lacan, Michel Foucault, Tzvetan Todorov, Jacques Derrida, but he gives no detailed exposition of any of their works. Instead of confronting their arguments,

Alter is content . . . to deny their claims by invoking 'experience' and 'indispensable common sense,' as if this somehow settled the matter." A reviewer for the *Journal of Modern Literature* dismisses Alter as "one of those urbane modern critics who almost never cite work by anyone else, but who seem terribly derivative nonetheless." Not all critics greeted *Motives for Fiction* with such disdain, however. Victor Brombert in the *New Republic* calls Alter a "sensible critic" who "refuse[s] to indulge in sterile exercises of ingenuity." Robert D. Spector, writing in *World Literature Today*, stresses Alter's emphasis on reality, remarking that his "aesthetic sensibility enhances a fine sense of the historical content. His flair for detail never interferes with his grasp of broader implications. There is verve, and even a sting, in his prose; but his judgments are fair."

For *The Art of Biblical Poetry* Alter returns to the language and literature of the Hebrew Bible, this time concentrating on poetic technique in the sacred text. This is a subject fraught with difficulty, because, as Peter Levi states in the *New York Times Book Review*, "It is not even agreed which bits of the Bible are in verse." Nonetheless, Levi considers Alter's achievement "admirable; he lays a strong foundation for students of the Bible." He further writes: "The analysis of the Psalms is particularly convincing. . . . I would despair of analyzing how they work as poetry. Mr Alter, using clear eyes and dogged common sense, has successfully shown how most of them work."

Frank Kermode joined Robert Alter as co-editor of *The Literary Guide to the Bible,* a collection of essays on the Bible as literature. "With one or two exceptions," writes Harold Bloom in the *New York Review of Books*, "everything of high literary critical value in this huge volume happens to be written by the two hard-working editors." However, poet Donald Davie in the *New Republic* suggests that some may think that in reading the Bible as literature "we are being either frivolous or foolish, we are decoding as literature what was never coded as literature, thus getting a wrong message and missing the right one." Davie concludes that Alter is "the wittiest" of the book's contributors and the author of "a splendidly concise and illuminating essay, 'The Characteristics of Ancient Hebrew Poetry.' "

Eugene Kennedy in the Chicago *Tribune Books* lauds *The Literary Guide to the Bible* as "a needed contribution to our appreciation of the Bible as a powerful work of literature." He added: "If this book does nothing else but restore the scriptures to their rightful place in our cultural consciousness, it will justify the honors that, on so many grounds, it richly deserves." Despite this, he finds the magic of "spontaneous literary imagination" to be missing. Likewise, Elizabeth Struthers Malbon, writing in the *New York Times Book Review*, credits the editors and authors with an "enormous and enormously important" task that "is accomplished well, if not quite flawlessly." Like other reviewers, she commends the essays contributed by the editors, but even in those she believes the "traditionalism of [the] literary outlook" may date it rather quickly.

Alter returned to contemporary literary criticism with *The Pleasures of Reading: In an Ideological Age.* This "frankly oppositional work," according to Robert Boyers of the *New York Times Book Review,* all but invites academic critics to "scoff at Mr. Alter's charming and hopeless naivete." Yet Boyers shares Alter's dismay, "fostered by deconstructionists . . . that character in fiction is a pernicious illusion." Boyers regards *The Pleasures of Reading* as a "richly inflected and only intermittently polemical" defense of character in literature and other "discarded orthodoxies." Boyers states that "Mr. Alter's assault on influential misconceptions often seems astonishing, if only because it is hard to believe that it is necessary." Jack Fuller of the Chicago *Tribune Books* reached a similar conclusion: "Add this volume to the growing list of welcome works of criticism that reassure lovers of literature that they are not fools to like a book for its characters and story and seriousness of purpose." Conversely, Jay Parini of the *Nation* rejects *The Pleasures of Reading* as "ultimately a weak book, written defensively by a critic who denies his own ideology while he points a finger at others for being 'ideological.' "

Alter's *The World of Biblical Literature,* elicits praise from E. P. Sanders in the *New York Times Book Review.* "Almost everyone would benefit from reading this book," Sanders writes, mentioning people as diverse as fundamentalists, biblical scholars, secularists, and people who read for pleasure and insight. "The exploration of individual biblical passages, which are the backbone of *The World of Biblical Literature,* are addictive," Sanders continues. Joseph Coates, writing in *Tribune Books,* commends Alter for insisting on the importance of reading the Bible "in its compelling immediacy, in the momentum of its complex continuities." He quotes Alter's observation that, however odd it may sound, "we are in fact better readers of biblical narrative because we are lucky enough to come after Flaubert and Joyce, Dante and Shakespeare." Coates adds: "And we, as readers, are lucky to come after Alter."

BIOGRAPHICAL/CRITICAL SOURCES:

BOOKS

Alter, Robert B., *Motives for Fiction,* Harvard University Press, 1984.

PERIODICALS

Commentary, April, 1969.
Georgia Review, spring, 1969.

Journal of Modern Literature, November, 1984, p. 374.

Los Angeles Times, October 19, 1979.

Los Angeles Times Book Review, May 20, 1984, p. 3; December 8, 1985.

Nation, August 7/14, 1989, pp. 179-180.

New Republic, July 4/11, 1981; July 9, 1984; April 28, 1986; October 26, 1987, pp. 28-33; June 26, 1989, pp. 36-38.

Newsweek, January 18, 1988.

New York Review of Books, March 31, 1988, pp. 23-25; November 5, 1992.

New York Times Book Review, January 26, 1969; October 7, 1979; July 19, 1981; July 24, 1983; October 20, 1985; December 20, 1987; June 25, 1989; July 14, 1991; February 9, 1992.

Times Literary Supplement, November 5, 1982; February 19, 1988; August 2, 1991.

Tribune Books (Chicago), November 8, 1987; July 16, 1989, p. 7; February 23, 1992.

Washington Post Book World, September 16, 1979; August 30, 1981; August 13, 1989; April 19, 1992.

World Literature Today, summer, 1984, pp. 479-480.

*   *   *

ANTHONY, Peter
See SHAFFER, Peter (Levin)

*   *   *

ARMITAGE, Ronda (Jacqueline) 1943-

PERSONAL: Born March 11, 1943, in Kaikoura, New Zealand; daughter of Jack (a farmer) and Beatrix (Shand) Minnitt; married David Armitage (a painter and illustrator), 1966; children: Joss, Kate. *Education:* Attended University of Auckland, 1963, 1969, and Massey University, 1965; Hamilton Teacher's College, certificate of teaching, 1962, diploma of teaching, 1969.

ADDRESSES: Home—Old Tiles Cottage, Church Lane, Hellingly, East Sussex BN27 4HA, England.

CAREER: Schoolteacher in Duvauchelles, New Zealand, 1964-66, London, England, 1966, and Auckland, New Zealand, 1968-69; Dorothy Butler Ltd., Auckland, adviser on children's books, 1970-71; Lewes Priory Comprehensive School, Sussex, England, assistant librarian, 1976-77; East Sussex County Council, East Sussex, England, member of teaching staff, 1978—. Family therapist at local family center.

AWARDS, HONORS: Esther Glen Award, New Zealand Library Association, 1978, for *The Lighthouse Keeper's Lunch.*

WRITINGS:

JUVENILE FICTION; ILLUSTRATIONS BY HUSBAND, DAVID ARMITAGE

The Lighthouse Keeper's Lunch, Deutsch (London), 1977.

The Trouble with Mr. Harris, Deutsch, 1978.

Don't Forget, Matilda!, Deutsch, 1978.

The Bossing of Josie, Deutsch, 1980, published in the United States as *The Birthday Spell,* Scholastic Book Services, 1981.

Ice Creams for Rosie, Deutsch, 1981.

One Moonlit Night, Deutsch, 1983.

Grandma Goes Shopping, Deutsch, 1984.

The Lighthouse Keeper's Catastrophe, Deutsch, 1986.

The Lighthouse Keeper's Rescue, Deutsch, 1989.

When Dad Did the Washing, Deutsch, 1990.

Watch the Baby, Daisy, Deutsch, 1991.

Looking after Chocolates, Deutsch, 1992.

A Quarrel of Koalas, Deutsch, 1992.

The Lighthouse Keeper's Picnic, Deutsch, 1993.

OTHER

Let's Talk about Drinking, Deutsch, 1982.

New Zealand, Deutsch, 1983.

*   *   *

ARMITAGE, Shelley S(ue) 1947-

PERSONAL: Born June 17, 1947, in Fort Worth, TX; daughter of Robert Allen (a banker and farmer) and Dorothy (a banker; maiden name, Dunn) Armitage. *Education:* Texas Tech University, B.A., 1969, M.A., 1971; University of New Mexico, Ph.D., 1983.

ADDRESSES: Home—P.O. Box 524, Vega, TX 79092. *Office*—Department of American Studies, University of Hawaii at Manoa, 2444 Dole Street, Honolulu, HI 96822.

CAREER: Vega Enterprise, Vega, TX, reporter and columnist, 1961-65; Tarrant County Junior College, Hurst, TX, assistant professor, 1971-74, associate professor of English, 1975-78; University of Asmara, Ethiopia, lecturer, 1974; University of Albuquerque, Albuquerque, NM, assistant professor of interdisciplinary studies, 1981-82; West Texas State University, Canyon, associate professor of English, 1982—. Fulbright scholar of American culture and literature, Universidade Nova de Lisboa, Lisbon, Portugal, 1990; Roderick Professorship, University of Texas at El Paso, 1995; visiting professor of American literature and cultural studies, Memphis State University, Memphis, TN; associate professor of American studies, University of Hawaii at Manoa. Alternate member of U.S. Olympic Women's Basketball Team, 1976; executive director of New Mexico Humanities Council, 1985.

MEMBER: Modern Language Association of America, American Studies Association, American Association of University Professors, Western Literature Association, Western Writers Association, Phi Beta Kappa.

AWARDS, HONORS: Grants from National Endowment for the Humanities, 1973-74, 1978-79; Rockefeller grant, 1985; named distinguished alumna by the English department of Texas Tech University, 1992.

WRITINGS:

(Editor, with Thomas Barrow and William Tydeman) *Reading into Photography: Essays on Photographic Criticism,* University of New Mexico Press (Albuquerque, NM), 1983.
John Held, Jr.: Illustrator of the Jazz Age (biography), Syracuse University Press (Syracuse, NY), 1987.
(Editor) Peggy Pond Church, *Wind's Trail: The Early Life of Mary Austin* (biography), Museum of New Mexico Press (Santa Fe, NM), 1990.
Peggy Pond Church (biography), Boise State University (Boise, ID), 1993.
(Editor) *That Dancing Ground of Sky: The Collected Poetry of Peggy Pond Church,* Red Crane Books (Santa Fe, NM), 1993.
Kewpies and Beyond: The World of Rose O'Neill (biography), University Press of Mississippi (Jackson, MS), 1994.
Bones Incandescent: The Nature Journals of Peggy Pond Church, University of New Mexico Press, in press.

Also contributor to *The American Self,* edited by Sam Girgus, University of New Mexico Press. Contributor of more than fifty articles and poems to magazines, including *Western Humanities Review, Paintbrush, American Transcendental Quarterly, Journal of Popular Culture, Exposure,* and *New Mexico Humanities Review.* Editor of *American Indian Quarterly,* 1974-76.

SIDELIGHTS: "For years," Shelley S. Armitage told *CA,* "I've been plagued by the notion that, because I was required to be a generalist in each of my teaching assignments, my writing would suffer. I had to teach primarily outside my major concentration, so I have conducted something like eighteen different courses over the past eleven years—courses ranging from wilderness literature to contemporary literature to advertising, feature writing, and folklore. My writing has followed these diverse teaching assignments. What I have come to write is a kind of creative nonfiction: work that may be based on scholarly research, but which is stylistically wrought. One of my challenges has been to allow ideas to emerge from form. Even approaching a piece of criticism as art, interested in

it for its own words' sake, is a preoccupation. Now my journals have taken over, and I work from these original texts.

"One recent journal entry addresses the question of the writer and her 'place,' in my case the Llano Estacado, the vast tableland whose cloth falls in a rugged border of breaks, arroyos, and canyons. Here the land appears at peace, a giant slumbering amidst its countless symbiotics. Yesterday the wheat was taken from the field. From the distance, the movement of combines creates a silvery image, like a liquid metal tracing the contours of the horizon. What is the meaning of the vertical, the horizontal? Can one go gently and upright, or was this a first rebellion? Perhaps to write is to trace one's finger over the landscape and find what dwells there.

"I hope for some Panhandle essays to emerge from such searches, in the spirit of *The Outermost House* or *A Texas Naturalist.* I am fascinated by examining a discrete space and finding what lives there, and how, and why. I am also re-working some of my historical research, for instance on a woman humorist of the nineteenth century, for fictional purposes.

"The last several years I have been teaching at the University of Hawaii and at Memphis State University, both places which have made me remember differently my Texas upbringing. Yet each is a distinctly regional place, and I sometimes call up comparatively bird or canyon, pine smell, or chamisa color due to some immediate resonance with the present landscape(s) which somehow remind. I've always liked Maxine Kumin's title of her collection, *To Make a Pasture.* Somehow in marking there is making, as Linda Connor said many years ago about the nature of photographing petroglyphs. Because I am always teaching as I am trying to write, I deal with dialogues which may disrupt what I would like to think of as lyric. Yet even these, the facts of a field, hold some connection to the deeper skein of words and feelings I like to work with. My own academic writing which used to feature non-conformist topics now feels that way in style. I see myself moving to more creative nonfiction, essays on place, what is seen, but more often not. Sometimes I go to my journals hoping they will take me away from one more review, one more article, listening. I am particularly intrigued with other avenues for words more than words: music, photographs, sports."

*   *   *

ARMSTRONG, Tilly 1927-
(Kate Alexander, Tania Langley)

PERSONAL: Born April 8, 1927, in Sutton, England; daughter of Alexander Edward (a plumber) and Florence

May (Brain) Armstrong. *Education:* Attended school in Wimbledon, England.

ADDRESSES: Home—23 Leslie Gardens, Sutton, Surrey SM2 6QU, England. *Agent*—Felicity Bryan, 2A North Parade, Baubury Rd., Oxford OX2 6PE, England.

CAREER: World Health Organization, Geneva, Switzerland, secretary, 1955-58; Glenbow Foundation, Calgary, Alberta, Canada, assistant archivist, 1959-61; British Steel Corp., London, England, secretary, 1962-72, personnel officer, 1973-81; writer, 1981—.

MEMBER: International PEN, Romantic Novelists Association, Society of Authors.

WRITINGS:

ROMANCE NOVELS

Lightly like a Flower, Collins (London), 1978.
Come Live with Me, Collins, 1979.
Joy Runs High, Collins, 1979, Dell (New York City), 1980.
A Limited Engagement, New English Library (London), 1980.
Summer Tangle, Piatkis Books (London), 1983.
Small Town Girl, Piatkis Books, 1983.
Pretty Penny, Piatkis Books, 1985.

DRAMATIC NOVELS; UNDER PSEUDONYM KATE ALEXANDER

Fields of Battle, St. Martin's (New York City), 1981.
Friends and Enemies, St. Martin's, 1982.
Paths of Peace, Macdonald Publishers (Edinburgh), 1984.
Bright Tomorrows, Macdonald Publishers, 1985.
Songs of War, Macdonald Publishers, 1987.
Great Possessions, Century, 1989.
The Shining Country, Century, 1991.
The House of Hope, Century, 1992, St. Martin's, 1994.
Voices of Song, Piatkis Books, 1994.

UNDER PSEUDONYM TANIA LANGLEY

Dawn (period novel), Fawcett (New York City), 1980 (published in England as *Mademoiselle Madeleine,* Corgi Books [London], 1981).
London Linnet, Granada Publishing, 1985.
Genevra, Grafton Books, 1987.

SIDELIGHTS: "Writing started as a hobby," Tilly Armstrong told *CA,* "became an absorbing interest, and is now my full time occupation. At one time I alternated light romantic novels with nineteenth-century period novels and strongly dramatic books, but now I concentrate on the Kate Alexander novels.

"I wrote for at least twenty years, making only occasional attempts to get published, all unsuccessful. My breakthrough came when I started sending manuscripts to women's magazines. I had two romantic serials accepted simultaneously by the sister magazines, *Woman's Weekly* and *Woman and Home.*

"After that I was launched and started getting my novels into hardback and paperback. At first I expanded my writing into other types of novels because I was faced with the possibility of what I still regard as my true career—personnel work—coming to an end with cutbacks in the steel industry. I became redundant in November, 1981, and by that time I was well-launched as a writer under my own name and my two pseudonyms.

"I particularly enjoy the research I do before starting to write a novel. This is mainly in the local public library, paying particular attention to old newspapers. For my three war novels, written under the name of Kate Alexander, I also consulted the Imperial War Museum in London. All my books are love stories, but I do like them to have an extra dimension, an interesting overseas setting for the lighter romantic novels, for instance. *Dawn* centered round the Franco-Prussian War of 1870-71, *London Linnett* deals with the London Music Hall at the end of the last century, and *Genevra* with early department stores. The Kate Alexander novels range from the tenth century to the present day. I classify myself as a storyteller rather than a writer with a message, and I try to write novels with a good, strong story line and well-defined characters."

*   *   *

ASHLEY, Steven
See McCAIG, Donald

B

BAKER, T(homas) Lindsay 1947-

PERSONAL: Born April 22, 1947, in Cleburne, TX; son of Garnell A. and Mary Lois (Miller) Baker; married Julie Philips. *Education:* Texas Tech University, B.A., 1969, M.A., 1972, Ph.D., 1977.

ADDRESSES: Home—Rio Vista, TX. *Office*—P.O. Box 507, Rio Vista, TX 76093.

CAREER: Texas Tech University, Lubbock, lecturer in history, 1970-75; Technical University of Wroclaw, Wroclaw, Poland, Fulbright lecturer, 1975-77; Texas Tech University, lecturer in history and program manager of history of engineering program, 1977-79; Panhandle-Plains Historical Museum, Canyon, TX, curator of science and technology, 1978-87; Fort Worth Museum of Science and History, Fort Worth, TX, curator of history, 1987-89; Baylor University, curator of Governor Bill and Vara Daniel Historical Village, Strecker Museum, 1989-92, director of academic programs and graduate studies, Department of Museum Studies, 1992—. Consultant to museums and historical agencies.

MEMBER: International Molinological Society (member of council, 1992—), American Association of Museums, American Historical Association, National Trust for Historic Preservation, American Association for State and Local History, Polish American Historical Association, Association for Living Historical Farms and Agricultural Museums, Western History Association, Society of Southwest Archivists, Texas Archaeological Society, Texas State Historical Association (fellow), Texas Association of Museums, Texas Folklore Society, Gamma Theta Upsilon.

AWARDS, HONORS: Scholarship recipient from Kosciuszko Foundation, 1973-74 and 1977; Coral H. Tullis Award from Texas State Historical Association and Eliza-beth Broocks Bates Award from Daughters of the Republic of Texas, both 1979, for *The First Polish Americans;* Coke Wood Award from Westerners International, 1986, for *The Survey of the Headwaters of the Red River, 1876;* Ralph Coats Roe Medal from American Society of Mechanical Engineers, 1987, for "contributions to a better understanding of the role of engineers in contemporary society"; Texas Award for Preservation of Historic Architecture from Texas Historical Commission, 1987, and Award for Excellence, Society for Technical Communication, 1988, both for *Building the Lone Star;* certificate of commendation, American Association for State and Local History, and citation from San Antonio Conservation Society, both 1993, for *Lighthouses of Texas.*

WRITINGS:

(With Steven R. Rae) *Information Summaries: Sixty Sites of Historic Engineering Works in Arizona, Colorado, New Mexico, Texas, and Utah,* Water Resources Center, Texas Tech University (Lubbock, TX), 1972.

(With Rae, Joseph E. Minor, and Seymour V. Connor) *Water for the Southwest: Historical Survey and Guide to Historic Sites,* American Society of Civil Engineers (New York City), 1973.

(Developmental editor) *Poles in Texas Resource Guide,* Ethnic Heritage Studies Program, Southwest Educational Development Laboratory, 1975.

The First Polish Americans: Silesian Settlements in Texas, Texas A & M University Press (College Station, TX), 1979.

Historia najstarszych polskich osad w Ameryce, Zaklad Narodowy im. Ossolinskich, 1981.

The Polish Texans, Institute of Texan Cultures, 1982.

The Reverend Leopold Moczygemba: Patriarch of Polonia, Polish American Priests Association, 1984.

A Field Guide to American Windmills, University of Oklahoma Press (Norman), 1985.

(Editor) *The Survey of the Headwaters of the Red River, 1876,* Panhandle-Plains Historical Society, 1985.

(With Billy R. Harrison) *Adobe Walls: The History and Archeology of the 1874 Trading Post,* Texas A & M University Press, 1986.

Building the Lone Star: An Illustrated Guide to Historic Sites, Texas A & M University Press, 1986.

Ghost Towns of Texas, University of Oklahoma Press, 1986.

Lighthouses of Texas, Texas A & M University Press, 1991.

Blades in the Sky: Windmilling through the Eyes of B. H. "Tex" Burdick, Texas Tech University Press, 1992.

(Editor with Julie P. Baker) *I Never Told Nobody 'bout This: The Oklahoma Slave Narratives,* University of Oklahoma Press, in press.

Contributor to history journals. Editor and publisher of *Windmillers' Gazette.*

SIDELIGHTS: T. Lindsay Baker once told *CA:* "I am an active participant in the 'living history interpretation' of the experiences of the people who lived in the American West. I have served as one of the founders of living history groups that portray the lives of traders on the Santa Fe Trail in the 1840s and buffalo hide hunters in Kansas in the 1870s. I also built and lived for eighteen months in a turn-of-the-century-style sod house.

"James S. French, the individual whom I portray in many of the living history presentations, was an actual person who lived on the southwestern frontier in the 1870s. A one-time whisky peddler among the Cheyenne Indians, among whom he lived for two years, he later became the camp cook and a skinner for a buffalo hide hunting crew headed by William Dixon, and as such he participated in the Battle of Adobe Walls on June 27, 1874.

"The living history programs, given alone or in company with colleagues, are usually presented at historic sites and museums on the southern Great Plains. In these programs the presenters dress in authentic historic attire and recreate a lived-in camp of the type used in the past by the people who are portrayed. The presentations are based on original research into primary source materials from the time periods portrayed, such as diaries and journals, business records, reminiscences, letters, and transcripts of interviews.

"The reason for my construction of the sod house was to give myself a better understanding of what day-to-day life on the agricultural frontier actually was like. I lived in the one-room earthen structure for eighteen months, drinking and washing in hauled water, heating and cooking with wood as fuel, lighting with kerosene, and living on a dirt floor. My nearest neighbor was two miles away and my company each evening as I drifted off to sleep was the singing of coyotes in the distance. Through such experiences I gained insights into life on the fringe of settlement that I never would have achieved in a lifetime of studying written sources."

Baker more recently told *CA:* "Today I live on a historic cotton farm beneath the live oak trees about halfway between Fort Worth and Waco in the middle of nowhere. The place is one that my great grandparents purchased as poor cotton farmers in 1900, and the office in which I write is the same room in the wood-frame farmhouse in which the wake was held for my great grandfather in 1914. When I began structural restoration of the dwelling, it was a derelict hulk half-filled with mouldy hay and a few dead animals. After a very strict two-year structural restoration, today it looks about the way that it did in 1910. Although the home does have electricity, it is heated mostly with wood fires (including a wood-burning range in the kitchen for cooking as well) and has no central heating or air conditioning. Who could ask for an atmosphere more conducive to writing? You're either melting or shivering."

BIOGRAPHICAL/CRITICAL SOURCES:

PERIODICALS

Accent West, January, 1982.
American Historical Review, April, 1980.
Journal of American History, September, 1986.
PolAmerica, summer, 1978.
South Dakota History, fall, 1985.
Western Historical Quarterly, April, 1986.

*   *   *

BAXTER, John
   See HUNT, E(verette) Howard (Jr.)

*   *   *

BEDFORD, Sybille 1911-

PERSONAL: Born March 16, 1911, in Charlottenburg, Germany; daughter of Maximilian von Schoenebeck and Elizabeth Bernard; married Walter Bedford, 1935. *Education:* Privately educated in Italy, England, and France.

ADDRESSES: Office—c/o Green and Heato, 37 Goldhank Rd., London, W12 8Q0 England.

CAREER: Writer.

MEMBER: Society of Authors, PEN (vice president, 1979), Royal Society of Literature (fellow), Reform Club.

AWARDS, HONORS: Officer of the Order of the British Empire, 1981.

WRITINGS:

NONFICTION

The Sudden View: A Mexican Journey (travel book), Gollancz, 1953, revised edition, Atheneum, 1963, (also published in England as *A Visit to Don Otavio: A Traveller's Tale from Mexico,* Collins, 1960).

The Best We Can Do: An Account of the Trial of John Bodkin Adams, Collins, 1958, published in America as *The Trial of Dr. Adams,* Simon & Schuster, 1959.

The Faces of Justice: A Traveller's Report, Simon & Schuster, 1961.

Aldous Huxley: A Biography, Collins/Chatto & Windus, Volume I, 1973, Volume II, 1974, both volumes published together, Knopf, 1974.

As It Was: Pleasures, Landscapes, and Justice, Sinclair-Stevenson, 1990.

NOVELS

A Legacy, Weidenfeld & Nicolson, 1956, Simon & Schuster, 1959.

A Favourite of the Gods, Simon & Schuster, 1963, reprinted with an introduction by Peter Vansittart, Virago, 1984.

A Compass Error, Collins, 1968.

Jigsaw: An Unsentimental Education (a biographical novel), Knopf, 1989.

Contributor to periodicals, including *Chimera, Decision, Encounter, Esquire, Harper's Bazaar, Horizon, Life, New York Review of Books, Observer, Spectator,* and *Vogue.*

ADAPTATIONS: A Legacy was televised in 1975.

SIDELIGHTS: Although best known as a novelist, Sybille Bedford has also written a two-volume biography of Aldous Huxley, a number of food and travel essays, and several celebrated accounts of trials that she attended. In his introduction to a later edition of her second novel, *A Favourite of the Gods,* Peter Vansittart talked about the varied nature of Bedford's writing, calling her "an authority on law, a connoisseur of unusual houses and families, of manners, wit, social rituals, food and drink."

Bedford's novels have been praised by such distinguished authors as Evelyn Waugh and Aldous Huxley. Yet many critics consider her novels anachronistic because of her use of the aristocracy and upper classes as the central characters and the prevailing milieus of her fiction. Despite this criticism, however, many reviewers agree that Bedford has a graceful and lucid style of writing. In a discussion of Bedford's work published in the *Voice Literary Supplement,* David Leavitt characterized Bedford's literary strengths in the following manner: "Dry wit, careful attendance to detail, dialogue in which, as Elizabeth

Bowen once wrote, there is 'more to be said than can come through,' are the hallmarks of Bedford's fiction."

Many of Bedford's novels are concerned with life in Europe from the turn of the century until the advent of World War II. Also characteristic of Bedford's writing is her extensive use of her own personal history. For example, in *A Legacy,* her first novel, Bedford tells the story of a German baron and his four sons. The basic facts of this narrative were drawn from Bedford's own family history. Reviewing the work in the *Times Literary Supplement,* Laura Marcus wrote that "the author successfully interweaves personal and political history and, although her characters are somewhat stylized, the hectic atmosphere of Edwardian Germany is convincingly portrayed." Bedford continued to draw upon her own history in her next two novels, *A Favourite of the Gods* and *A Compass Error.* Detailing the lives of three generations of European women, the works portray a lifestyle Bedford herself was part of while growing up in Europe. Commenting on these works in his *Voice Literary Supplement* essay, Leavitt said that these books were examples of Bedford's ability to portray individuals as they interact with society, a gift, said Leavitt, she shared with other writers of her generation. "If her works of fiction share a goal," he wrote, "it could probably best be stated as the determination to show the ways in which the private lives of individuals reflect the larger political life of their culture, and vice versa. . . . She portrays the evolution of Nazism and Fascism where it really took place—in living rooms, kitchens and on beaches."

In 1989 Bedford issued *Jigsaw: An Unsentimental Education.* The story of a nineteen-year-old girl named Billi, this work closely parallels Bedford's own childhood in Europe. The novel relates how, while living with her mother on the Cote d'Azur, Billi begins working on a novel. David R. Slavitt described *Jigsaw* in the *Chicago Tribune* as "a splendid book, lucid, balanced, humane and civilized, with an enchanting and depressing story of the author's mother, who is its central figure." He concluded, "This is a treasure of a book, one of the best I know about mothers and daughters."

In addition to her fiction writing, Bedford has also published a number of nonfiction titles. Notable among these is her two-volume biography of English author Aldous Huxley. Published first in two volumes, the work draws upon numerous letters and journals of Huxley and his first wife, Maria Nys, as well as Bedford's own recollection of her experiences with the couple. Bedford, who was a close friend of the Huxleys, uses the books to depict Huxley as a man rather than a writer, and she has gained much acclaim for her rendition of his life. In *Newsweek* Peter S. Prescott said that Huxley "has been well served in this vibrant and illuminating biography." The critic further noted that "Bedford knew the Huxleys intimately and brings a novelist's perceptions to her history of a novelist: Maria Huxley's death, for instance, is rendered as affectingly as any death in fiction."

Some critics, however, like R. Z. Sheppard of *Time* magazine, who said that Bedford "takes a rather protective and insular approach to her subject," felt that Bedford focuses too deeply on Huxley's personal life. Similarly, Stanley Weintraub's review of *Aldous Huxley* in the *New Republic* also criticized Bedford's highly personal approach to biography, saying that Bedford "forc[es] . . . the reader to pay a high price for her humanizing of Huxley, who—it is true—appears less than human from many of his books."

Yet, while critics were divided over Bedford's unwillingness to interpret events in Huxley's life, the biography was praised for its attention to accuracy and detail. Weintraub admitted that the work was a "crucial source of information about the man and fascinating reading in itself." And Diana Trilling, writing in the *New York Times Book Review,* said that despite Bedford's focus on the writer's private life, this book was the "first full-length study of Aldous Huxley's life and should do much to return this now little-read figure of the twenties to his proper standing in the literary history of the century." Others, like William Abrahams, admired Bedford's approach to the biography. In an essay published in the *Atlantic Monthly,* Abrahams said that "Mrs. Bedford, of course, is an artist, as anyone familiar with her novel *A Legacy* will know already. She has performed prodigies of research and mastered a staggering amount of material; *her* Aldous has indeed 'some kind of shape'; her biography is unquestionably a work of art; I admire it immensely." Prescott judged that Huxley "has been well served in this vibrant and illuminating biography."

Over the years, Bedford has also gained a reputation for writing well about both travel and legal trials. *As It Was: Pleasures, Landscapes, and Justice,* which Bedford issued in 1990, gathers her own writings from the 1950s and 1960s. The varied narratives that comprise the book range from sketches of different countries, like Denmark and Switzerland, to discussions of French cooking, to a reflection on notable court cases, including Jack Ruby's trial for murdering Lee Harvey Oswald (the man who assassinated former President John F. Kennedy). The assorted chronicles, said Peter Levi in the *Spectator,* make "the most ordinary journeys and shopping expeditions read like a crisp, unforgettable honeymoon." From her four novels to her Huxley biography to her journalistic essays, critics have noted that Bedford's ability to make characters—real or imagined—come to life is what distinguishes her work from that of other writers.

BIOGRAPHICAL/CRITICAL SOURCES:

BOOKS

Bedford, Sybille, *A Favourite of the Gods,* with an introduction by Peter Vansittart, Virago, 1984.

PERIODICALS

American Scholar, summer, 1965.
Atlantic Monthly, March, 1957; April, 1969; January, 1975.
Chicago Tribune, June 11, 1989, p. 3.
Christian Science Monitor, January 31, 1957; October 21, 1969.
Commonweal, December 6, 1974; March 28, 1975.
Encounter, March, 1963.
Guardian Weekly, September 28, 1974.
Harper's, April, 1963; April, 1969; April, 1975.
Hudson Review, summer, 1975.
Listener, November, 1968; October 17, 1974.
Manchester Guardian, March 27, 1957.
Nation, March 28, 1953; March 31, 1956; May 4, 1963; February 1, 1975; December 30, 1991.
New Criterion, April, 1994.
New Republic, June 26, 1961; November 16, 1974, pp. 24-27.
New Statesman, January 17, 1959; May 26, 1961; October 18, 1968; September 20, 1974; May 12, 1989; September 14, 1990.
Newsweek, December 9, 1974, p. 109; December 30, 1974.
New Yorker, April 27, 1957; February 17, 1975.
New York Herald Tribune Book Review, January 10, 1954; February 3, 1957.
New York Review of Books, April 24, 1969; January 23, 1975; April 27, 1989, p. 22.
New York Times, January 17, 1954; February 3, 1957.
New York Times Book Review, March 23, 1969; November 24, 1974, pp. 1, 42; May 20, 1984; December 22, 1985; May 28, 1989; December 3, 1989.
Observer, September 16, 1969; September 15, 1974; April 20, 1975; May 31, 1987; May 7, 1989; September 9, 1990; March 8, 1992; March 14, 1993.
Observer Review, October 13, 1968.
Partisan Review, spring, 1976.
Saturday Review, February 9, 1957; March 16, 1963; November 16, 1974, pp. 16-18.
South Atlantic Quarterly, summer, 1975.
Spectator, April 13, 1956; November 14, 1958; May 26, 1961; October 25, 1968; September 28, 1974; February 18, 1984; May 20, 1989; November 25, 1989; September 15, 1990.
Time, December 2, 1974, p. 107.
Times (London), February 17, 1984; March 10, 1984; May 11, 1989; September 15, 1990.
Times Educational Supplement, December 21, 1984.

Times Literary Supplement, March 13, 1953; April 20, 1956; October 24, 1968; September 20, 1974; June 1, 1984; June 22, 1984; May 12, 1989; October 26, 1990.
Voice Literary Supplement, June, 1990, pp. 9-10.
Washington Post, December 11, 1968.
Washington Post Book World, November 17, 1974; November 17, 1985; April 2, 1989.

—*Sketch by Elizabeth Judd*

*   *   *

BIBOLET, R. H.
See KELLY, Tim

*   *   *

BIDERMAN, Albert D. 1923-

PERSONAL: Born July 10, 1923, in Paterson, NJ; son of Isaac and Celia (Silberstein) Biderman; married Sumiko Fujii, November 9, 1951; children: David Taro, Joseph Shiro, Paula Kei. *Education:* New York University, A.B., 1947; University of Chicago, M.A., 1952, Ph.D., 1964.

ADDRESSES: Home—6247 North Kensington St., McLean, VA 22101. *Office*—School of Public Affairs, 216 Ward, American University, 4400 Massachusetts Ave. N.W., Washington, DC 20016.

CAREER: Illinois Institute of Technology, Chicago, instructor in sociology, 1948-52; U.S. Air Force, Maxwell Air Force Base, AL, research social psychologist, 1952-57; Bureau of Social Science Research, Washington, DC, senior research associate, 1957-86; American University, Washington, DC, research professor of justice, 1986—. Director, Crime Survey Research Consortium, 1979-86. *Military service:* U.S. Army, 1943-45.

MEMBER: American Sociological Association, American Association for Public Opinion Research, American Association for the Advancement of Science (fellow), American Statistical Association (fellow), District of Columbia Sociological Society (president, 1965-66).

AWARDS, HONORS: Stewart A. Rice Merit Award, District of Columbia Sociological Society, 1985.

WRITINGS:

(Editor with Herbert Zimmer) *The Manipulation of Human Behavior,* Wiley (New York City), 1961.
March to Calumny: The Story of American POW's in the Korean War, Macmillan (New York City), 1963.
(Coeditor) *Mass Behavior in Battle and Captivity: The Communist Soldier in the Korean War,* University of Chicago Press (Chicago), 1968.

(With Elisabeth T. Crawford) *The Political Economics of Social Research: The Case of Sociology,* Bureau of Social Science Research, 1968.
(Compiler with Crawford) *Social Scientists and International Affairs: A Case for a Sociology of Social Science,* Wiley, 1969.
(Editor with Thomas F. Drury) *Measuring Work Quality for Social Reporting,* Halsted (New York City), 1976.
(With Albert J. Reiss) *Data Sources on White-Collar Law Breaking,* U.S. National Institute of Justice, 1980.
(With James P. Lynch) *Understanding Crime Incidence Statistics: Why the UCR Diverges from the NCS,* Springer Verlag (New York City), 1991.

Also author of numerous research papers on social and economic statistical indicators, indoctrination of American prisoners of war, coercive interrogation, and captivity situations. Also contributor to numerous books, including *The New Military: Changing Patterns of Organization,* edited by Morris Janowitz, Russell Sage (New York City), 1964; *Psychological Stress,* edited by Mortimer Appley and Richard Trumbull, Appleton-Century-Crofts (East Norwalk, CT), 1966; *The Draft: A Handbook of Facts and Alternatives,* edited by Sol Tax, University of Chicago Press, 1967; *Handbook of Military Institutions,* edited by Roger W. Little, Sage Publications (Beverly Hills, CA), 1971; *Victimology: A New Focus,* edited by Israel Drapkin and Emilio Viano, Lexington Books (Lexington, MA), 1975; and *A Quarter Century of International Social Science,* edited by Stein Rokkan, Concept Publishing (New Delhi), 1979. Contributor to *International Encyclopedia of the Social Sciences.* Contributor of articles to professional journals. Member of editorial advisory board, *Information Design Journal,* 1979—.

*   *   *

BINGHAM, Carson
See CASSIDAY, Bruce (Bingham)

*   *   *

BLAKE, Judith (Kincade) 1926-1993

PERSONAL: Born May 3, 1926, in New York, NY; died of respiratory illness, April 29, 1993, in Los Angeles, CA; daughter of Forrest James and Sylvia (Blake) Kincade; married Kingsley Davis (a professor and sociologist), 1954 (marriage ended); married LeRoy Graymer; children: (first marriage) Laura Isabelle. *Education:* Columbia University, B.S., 1950, Ph.D., 1961. *Avocational interests:* Gardening.

CAREER: Columbia University, Bureau of Applied Social Research, New York City, research assistant, 1953;

Conservation Foundation of New York, New York City, research associate, 1953-57; University of California School of Nursing, San Francisco, lecturer in sociology, 1957-59; University of California, Berkeley, lecturer in department of sociology, 1957, lecturer in department of speech, 1961-62, assistant professor, then associate professor, 1962-69, professor, School of Public Health, 1969-72; University of California at Los Angeles, Fred H. Bixby Professor of Population Policy, beginning 1976, member of advisory board of Rand Graduate School.

MEMBER: American Sociological Association, American Association for Public Opinion Research, American Public Health Association, Population Association of America (president, 1980), Sociological Research Association (president, 1978), American Association for the Advancement of Science, American Academy of Arts and Sciences, Pacific Sociological Association.

AWARDS, HONORS: Population Council fellowship, 1954; Guggenheim fellowship, 1976-77; Phi Beta Kappa visiting scholarship, 1976-77; William J. Goode Award, American Sociological Association, 1989, for *Family Size and Achievement.*

WRITINGS:

(With J. Mayone Stycos and Kingsley Davis) *Family Structure in Jamaica: The Social Context of Reproduction,* Free Press of Glencoe (New York City), 1961.
(With Jerry J. Donovan) *Western European Censuses, 1960: An English Language Guide,* Institute of International Studies, University of California (Berkeley), 1971.
Family Size and Achievement, University of California Press (Berkeley), 1989.

Contributor of articles to behavioral science journals. Editor, *Annual Review of Sociology.*

OBITUARIES:

PERIODICALS

Los Angeles Times, May 13, 1993, p. A22.
New York Times, May 14, 1993, p. B7.*

*   *   *

BOWSKILL, Derek 1928-
(Pauline Edwardes)

PERSONAL: Born July 19, 1928, in Scunthorpe, England; son of Harold Fish (an engineer) and Marion (Sylvester) Bowskill; married Jill Edwards (marriage ended); married Mary Harrison (marriage ended); children: Sara Jane Bowskill Brown. *Education:* Attended University of Shef-

field, 1948-49, Birmingham College of St. Peter, 1950-52, and Rose Broford College of Speech and Drama, 1952-53. *Politics:* "Humanitarian individualist." *Religion:* Atheist.

ADDRESSES: Agent—Tessa Sayle Agency, 11 Jubilee Pl., London SW3 3TE, England.

CAREER: Worked as county drama adviser in Devonshire, England, 1954-67; University of Sussex, Brighton, England, head of department of drama, film, and television, 1967-69; writer, 1969—. Media adviser to organizations and schools. *Military service:* British Army, 1946-48.

WRITINGS:

PLAYS; ALL FIRST PRODUCED IN LONDON, ENGLAND

Action (one-act), 1969.
Re-Action (one-act), 1969.
Gambit (one-act), 1969.
Children of the Sun (one-act), 1969.
Masks and Faces (three-act), 1969.
Everybody Needs a Little Warmth (one-act), 1969.
Legends of the Seasons (two-act), 1969.
Gambetto (one-act), 1970.
Gambado; or, What Shall We Do to Caroline Fairweather? (five-act), 1970.
Woman, Angel of . . . ??? (three-act), 1970.
Gilgamesh: Hero of Babylon (one-act), Kenyon-Deane (London), 1973.
Seaventures (one-act), Kenyon-Deane, 1973.
(Under pseudonym Pauline Edwardes) *Legends of the Seasons,* Kenyon-Deane, 1973.
(Under pseudonym Pauline Edwardes) *Powers of the Earth* (one-act), Kenyon-Deane, 1973.
Lady Seeks Position (one-act), Performance Publications (West Sussex, England), 1974.
"Maker of Love" (five-act), Kenyon-Deane, 1974.
The Long Home (one-act), Samuel French (London), 1975.

Also author of *Six Short Plays,* Longman. Also author of produced plays *The Trojan War* (three-act), *Home Is* (one-act), *A Hard Sell* (one-act), *Nothing in the Telling* (one-act), and *The Third Age* (one-act), all published by Performance Publications.

OTHER

Acting and Stagecraft Made Simple, W. H. Allen (London), 1973, published as *Acting: An Introduction,* Prentice-Hall (Englewood Cliffs, NJ), 1977.
Person to Person: A Survey of the Intimate Personal Confrontation Business, Allen & Unwin (London), 1973.
All the Lonely People, Bobbs-Merrill (New York City), 1973.
Drama and the Teacher, Pitman (London), 1974.

Workshop, Volume 1: *Circus, Fairground, Zoo: Pupils' Book*, illustrations by Paul Manktelow, Dent (London), 1974.

Swingers and Swappers, Star Books (London), 1975.

Photography Made Simple, W. H. Allen, 1975.

All about Theatre, W. H. Allen, 1975.

The How and Why Wonder Book of Radio and TV, illustrations by Raymond Turvey, Transworld (London), 1976.

(Editor with Anthea Linacre) *The "Male" Menopause*, Muller (London), 1976, Brooke House (Los Angeles, CA), 1977.

Getting on . . . and Getting Off, Harwood-Smart (Blandford, England), 1976.

All about Cinema, W. H. Allen, 1976.

People Need People: A Journey through the Landscape of Loneliness, Wildwood House (London), 1977.

(With Linacre) *Men: The Sensitive Sex*, Muller, 1977.

The D.I.Y. Mind Book, Wildwood House, 1978.

Single Parents, Futura Publications (London), 1978.

Drama in Action, Hutchinson (London), 1979.

The Thames to the Wash, Imray (St. Ives, England), 1984.

Northeast Waterways: A Cruising Guide to the Rivers Witham, Trent, Yorkshire, Ouse, and Associated Waterways, Imray, 1986.

The Solent, Imray, 1989.

French Mediterranean Ports: A Cruising Guide, A&C Black, 1992.

The Medway: A Cruising Guide, Imray, 1993.

Contributor of articles and poems to magazines.

WORK IN PROGRESS: From the Channel to the Med: A Guide to the French Waterways; The Southwest: A Cruising Guide to the West Country; The River Seine: A Cruising Guide.

SIDELIGHTS: Derek Bowskill once told *CA:* "In almost all my works I hope to convince someone that there is no need for him to feel inadequate, obliged, inferior, or generally BAD—as my parents instructed me to feel from my earliest memories. It has taken me half a century to understand that they were wrong.

"Since 1978 I have been all at sea on nautical projects; being all at sea is the one place where you learn very fast not to be all at sea."

*   *   *

BRADFORD, Benjamin 1925-

PERSONAL: Born October 28, 1925, in Alexandria, LA; son of Robert Lee (in railroad work) and Edith (Turner) Bradford; married Elizabeth Wheeler, April 2, 1946; children: Alison Bradford Harrington, Megan Bradford

Hughes, Benjamin Todd. *Education:* Attended Louisiana State Northwestern University, 1942, and Mississippi College, 1943-44; Louisiana State University, M.D., 1948; postdoctoral study at Tulane University. *Politics:* Democrat. *Religion:* Episcopalian.

ADDRESSES: Home—355 Lone Oak Rd., Paducah, KY 42001. *Office*—2320 Broadway, Paducah, KY 42001. *Agent*—Earl Graham, Graham Agency, 451 West 44th St., New York, NY 10019.

CAREER: United States Public Health Service, New York City, and New Orleans, LA, internship and residence, 1948-54; private practice of medicine in Paducah, KY, 1954—. Clarion State University, visiting playwright, 1972; University of Kentucky, playwright-in-residence, 1973-75. Markethouse Theatre, founding member and former president. Member, regional arts panel and Kentucky Arts Commission. *Military service:* U.S. Navy, 1943-46. U.S. Public Health Service, 1948-54. U.S. Naval Reserve, 1954—; now commander.

MEMBER: American Medical Association, American Society of Authors, Dramatists Guild, American Guild of Authors and Composers, American Society of Composers, Authors, and Publishers, Southeastern Theatre Conference, Kentucky Medical Society, Kentucky Arts Commission Board of Governors, Kentucky Theatre Association, McCracken County Medical Society.

AWARDS, HONORS: John Gassner Memorial Award, New England Theatre Conference, 1968, for *Concentric Circles*, 1969, for *You Don't See Many Red Cars from Montana*, and 1970, for *Look Away, Look Away;* Kent Messenger Drama Award, 1969, for *Where Are You Going, Hollis Jay?;* Golden Windmill Award, Radio Nederland, 1971, for *Post Mortem;* Theatre Guild of Webster Grove Award, 1972, for *Concentric Circles;* best play and best playwright citations from *Daily Variety,* 1974, for *Lunch* and *You Don't See Many Red Cars from Montana;* Donovan Rhysinger Award, University of Missouri.

WRITINGS:

PLAYS

Segments of a Contemporary Morning (five-act; produced in New York City at Old Reliable Theatre, 1972), Holiday House, 1971.

Princess (one-act; produced in Los Angeles at Staircase Theatre, 1974), Performance Publishing, 1976.

Loving Kindness (one-act), Performance Publishing, 1976.

The Goats (one-act; produced in Los Angeles at Melrose Theatre, 1973), Performance Publishing, 1977.

Where Are You Going, Hollis Jay? (two-act; produced in Canterbury, Kent, England, at University of Kent, 1969), Samuel French, 1979.

PLAYS PRODUCED

Concentric Circles: The Scene/I, produced in New York City at Old Reliable Theatre, 1969.

The Anthropologists (one-act), produced in New York City at Stage Lights Theatrical Club, 1969.

The Ideal State (one-act), produced in New York City at Inner Theatre, 1969.

Motel (one-act), produced in New York City at Old Reliable Theatre, 1970.

A High Structure Falls Farther (three-act), produced in New York City at Old Reliable Theatre, 1970.

Post Mortem, produced in Lexington, KY, 1971.

Losing Things (one-act), produced at University of Wisconsin at Earplay Theatre, 1973.

Code Ninety-Nine (five-act), produced at University of Wisconsin, 1973.

Good Days, Bad Days (one-act), produced at University of Wisconsin at Earplay Theatre, 1973.

Lunch (one-act), produced in Los Angeles at Garden Theatre Festival, 1974.

(With Blatz Harrington) *To Make a Man* (two-act musical), produced in Lexington at University of Kentucky, 1974.

Look Away, Look Away (one-act), produced in New York City at Three Muses Theatre, 1977.

The Cowboy and the Legend, produced in Jupiter, FL, at Burt Reynolds Dinner Theatre, 1981.

Also author with Dexter Freeman of *Scoring,* produced in Lexington, KY, at the Arts Council Dinner Theater and *Love* (two-act), produced in Pennsylvania at Bucks County Playhouse. Author of *Parabus,* produced in Pennsylvania at Clarion Street College, *Geometric Progression,* produced in New York City at Theatre 13, *Rendezvous,* produced in Kentucky at Jefferson Community College, *Life and Death in a Public Place,* produced in Los Angeles at Staircase Company, *Birds of Passage* (one-act), produced in New York City at Unicorn, *A Double Fraktur L* (one act), produced in New York City at Unicorn, *Doillies,* produced in Gulfport, MS, *The Moon Bridge* (three-act), produced in New York City at Broadway Theater Guild, *Balloons and Other Ironies,* produced at the University of Kentucky, *Helping Hands* (with Blatz Harrington), produced by Kentucky State Hospital Association, *Touch and Go,* produced in Lexington by S.E.T.C., *Conversation Piece* (one-act), produced in Los Angeles at Staircase Company, *Pitfall for a Rational Man,* produced in Clarion, PA, and *You Don't See Many Red Cars from Montana.* Author of *Spartans,* "Quatre Jours," an episode, 1973; author with Dexter Freeman, *Favorite Son,* a television series, 1974; author of *Princess Reluctant,* a music book, 1975. Contributor to theater journals, including *DeKalb Literary Journal.*

WORK IN PROGRESS: A Jigsaw Puzzle Look at American Life with Several Pieces Missing, a musical in 34 scenes; *Sons,* a novel.

SIDELIGHTS: Benjamin Bradford commented to *CA:* "Why do I write? A compulsion, I think, to overachieve, to compete, to create. What else is there?"

BIOGRAPHICAL/CRITICAL SOURCES:

PERIODICALS

Show Business, February 21, 1970; July 4, 1970.
Village Voice, August 21, 1969; November 13, 1969; July 9, 1970, p. 47.*

*   *   *

BRANDI, John 1943-

PERSONAL: Born November 5, 1943, in Los Angeles, CA. *Education:* California State University, Northridge, B.F.A., 1965.

ADDRESSES: Home—P.O. Box 2553, Corrales, NM 87048.

CAREER: Poet and painter. Served as a Peace Corps volunteer in highland Ecuador and Upper Amazon Basin, 1965-68; poet in residence for the Alaska Council on the Arts, California Arts Council, Montana Arts Council, Nevada Council on the Arts, and New Mexico Arts Division, 1973—; poet-in-the-parks, Carlsbad Caverns and Guadalupe Mountains, 1979; founder and editor, Tooth of Time Books, 1978-89. Worked variously as carpenter, cannery packer, and vineyard planter. Retrospective exhibit of works held at Univeristy of New Mexico, Albuquerque, 1986; has had one-man exhibits of paintings in Houston, San Francisco, and Santa Fe.

AWARDS, HONORS: Poetry prize, Portland State University, 1972; State Arts Councils Awards to Reside as Poet-in-the-Schools: Alaska, New Mexico, Montana, Nevada, 1973—; fellowship in poetry, National Endowment for the Arts, 1980; several grants to small press awards, National Endowment for the Arts, 1981-86, for work as editor and founder of Tooth of Time Books; grant, Wittner Bynner Foundation, 1984, for translating Mexican poetry; *The Cowboy from Phantom Banks* was selected by the National Endowment for the Arts to represent American writers abroad in the Frankfurt International Book Fair, 1984; poet in residence award, Just Buffalo/Literary Center, 1988; Djerassi Foundation Residency Award, 1990; Guadalajara International Bookfair Invitational Reading, 1994; Tea & Tattered Pages Poetry Series, Paris, France, 1994.

WRITINGS:

POETRY

A Nothing Book, privately printed, 1964.

Emptylots: Poems of Venice and L.A., Nail Press, 1971.

Field Notes from Alaska, Nail Press, 1971.

Three Poems for Spring, Nail Press, 1973.

August Poem, Nail Press, 1973.

Firebook, Smokey the Bear Press, 1974.

Turning Thirty Poems, Duende Press (Oakland, CA), 1974.

In a December Storm, Tribal Press (Cable, WI), 1975.

Looking for Minerals, Cherry Valley Editions (Wheaton, MD), 1975.

In a September Rain, Copper Canyon Press (Port Townsend, WA), 1976.

Poems from Four Corners, Great Raven Press (Fort Kent, ME), 1978.

As It Is These Days, Whistling Swan Press, 1979.

Andean Town circa 1980, Tooth of Time Books (Santa Fe, NM), 1980.

Poems for the People of Coyote, Distant Longing Press, 1980.

Sky House/Pink Cottonwood, Tooth of Time Books, 1980.

That Crow that Visited Was Flying Backwards, Tooth of Time Books, 1982.

At the World's Edge, Painted Stork Editions, 1983.

Zuleikha's Book, Doggerel Press (Santa Barbara, CA), 1983.

Poems at the Edge of Day, White Pine Press (Buffalo, NY), 1983.

That Back Road In: Poems from the American Southwest 1972-1983, Wingbow Press (Berkeley, CA), 1985.

Hymn for a Night Feast: Poems, 1979-1986, Holy Cow! Press (Duluth, MN), 1988.

Shadow Play: Poems, 1987-1991, Light & Dust Books (Kenosha, WI), 1992.

Weeding the Cosmos, Selected Haiku, La Alameda Books (Albuquerque, NM), 1994.

PROSE POEMS

Poem Afternoon in a Square of Guadalajara, Maya Books, 1970.

Smudgepots: For Jack Kerouac, Nail Press, 1973.

The Phoenix Gas Slam, Nail Press, 1973.

The Guadalupes: A Closer Look, Carlsbad Caverns Natural History Association, 1978.

Rite for the Beautification of All Beings, Toothpaste Press (West Branch, IA), 1983.

SHORT STORIES

Desde Alla, Tree Books (Berkeley, CA), 1971.

One Week of Mornings at Dry Creek, Christopher's Press, 1971.

Narrowgauge to Riobamba, Christopher's Press, 1975.

The Cowboy from Phantom Banks, Floating Island Books, 1982.

In the Desert We Do Not Count the Days: Stories & Illustrations, Holy Cow! Press, 1991.

OTHER

Tehachapi Fantasy, privately printed, 1964.

Towards a Happy Solstice, Christopher's Press, 1971.

Y Aun Hay Mas, Dreams and Explorations: New and Old Mexico, Christopher's Press, 1972.

San Francisco Lastday Homebound Hangover Highway Blues, Nail Press, 1973.

A Partial Exploration of Palo Flechado Canyon, Nail Press, 1973.

Chimborazo: Life on the Haciendas of Highland Ecuador (poems, narrations, and photographs), Akwesasne Notes Press, 1976.

Memorandum from a Caribbean Isle, Blackberry Books (Bolinas, CA), 1977.

Diary from Baja California, Christopher's Press, 1978.

Diary from a Journey to the Middle of the World, Figures Press, 1980.

A Question of Journey, the Asia Journals, Light & Dust Books, 1995.

Designer and printer, with Jack Hirschman, of collage-poems *Interchange,* 1964, and *Kline Sky,* 1965; illustrator of *Tiny Talk,* a collection of poems by Laura Chester, 1972, of *Abra,* a children's story by David Meltzer, 1977, of *The Confounding,* a story by Steve Sanfield, 1981, and of *Only the Ashes,* a collection of translations by Sanfield, 1981. Author, with Barbara Szerlip, John Wilson, and Alice Karle, of *Four Dogs Mountain Songs,* 1980 and, with Steve Sanfield, of *Circling,* 1988.

SIDELIGHTS: John Brandi told *CA:* "My parents were my first teachers, encouraging me at a very early age to learn *from* the world as well as about it. They took me camping along California's coast, into the Sierra Nevada mountains, and through the Mojave to the high deserts of the Southwest. As a child I was asked to draw pictures of things remembered from these excursions and combine them with writings about people and places, a crashing wave, a giant redwood, a shelf of lichens, an encounter with a bear. These drawings and writings were stapled together into my first books. I still adhere to the writing, illustrating, and hand-illuminating of my own books; and I still journey: to Mexican cloud forests, to crowded Asian ghettos, to Arctic tundra, to the high arid reaches of Bolivia and Ladakh, to the dances and shadow-puppet plays of Java and Bali—seeking source and renewal in geographies and peoples of lands near and far. I journey to balance great with small, to face the conflicts and chaos and deep questions that travel brings; to return with a new sense of clarity and confirmation about myself, the world, my work. Poetry is a result of these travels, as is painting; but more primarily a link to inner geographies, deep-cave visions, erotic and psychic landscapes within—an individual yet archetypal vision brought forward for others to view, as well as a modest attempt toward world solidarity and peace."

Brandi also wrote that as a painter he works in the tradition of poet Kenneth Patchen, who was known for his visionary combinations of words and whimsical imagery. Brandi's major exhibits include shows at Laurel Seth Gallery, Santa Fe, NM; Houston's Moody Gallery; the Thompson Gallery, University of New Mexico, Albuquerque; Claudia Chapline Gallery, Stinson Beach, CA; Writers and Books, Rochester, NY; The Book Project, Seattle, WA; Lola Montez House, Nevada City, CA; and Cannessa Gallery, San Francisco, CA.

* * *

BRATHWAITE, Edward Kamau 1930-

PERSONAL: Original name Lawson Edward Brathwaite; born May 11, 1930, in Bridgetown, Barbados; son of Hilton Edward and Beryl (Gill) Brathwaite; married Doris Monica Welcome (a teacher and librarian), March 26, 1960; children: Michael. *Education:* Attended Harrison College, Barbados; Pembroke College, Cambridge, B.A. (honors), 1953, Diploma of Education, 1954; University of Sussex, D.Phil., 1968.

ADDRESSES: Office—New York University, Washington Square, New York, NY 10003.

CAREER: Writer, poet, playwright, and editor. Education officer with Ministry of Education of Ghana, 1955-62; University of the West Indies, Kingston, Jamaica, tutor in Department of Extra Mural Studies assigned to island of Saint Lucia, 1962-63, university lecturer, 1963-72, senior lecturer in history, 1972-76, reader, 1976-83, professor of social and cultural history, 1982-91; affiliated with New York University, New York City, 1991—. Plebiscite officer for the United Nations in the Trans-Volta Togoland, 1956-57. Visiting professor, Southern Illinois University, 1970, University of Nairobi, 1971, Boston University, 1975-76, University of Mysore (India), 1982, Holy Cross College, 1983, Yale University, 1988; visiting fellow, Harvard University, 1987.

MEMBER: Caribbean Artists Movement (founding secretary, 1966—).

AWARDS, HONORS: Arts Council of Great Britain bursary, 1967; Camden Arts Festival prize, 1967; Cholmondeley Award, 1970, for *Islands;* Guggenheim fellowship, 1972; City of Nairobi fellowship, 1972; Bussa Award, 1973; Casa de las Americas Prize for Poetry, 1976; Fulbright fellow, 1982 and 1987; Institute of Jamaica Musgrave Medal, 1983.

WRITINGS:

The People Who Came (textbooks), three volumes, Longmans, 1968-72.

Folk Culture of the Slaves in Jamaica, New Beacon, 1970, revised edition, 1981.

The Development of Creole Society in Jamaica, 1770-1820, Clarendon Press, 1971.

Caribbean Man in Space and Time, Savacou Publications, 1974.

Contradictory Omens: Cultural Diversity and Integration in the Caribbean, Savacou Publications, 1974.

Our Ancestral Heritage: A Bibliography of the Roots of Culture in the English-Speaking Caribbean, Literary Committee of Carifesta, 1976.

Wars of Respect: Nanny, Sam Sharpe, and the Struggle for People's Liberation, API, 1977.

Jamaica Poetry: A Checklist, 1686-1978, Jamaica Library Service, 1979.

Barbados Poetry: A Checklist, Slavery to the Present, Savacou Publications, 1979.

Kumina, Savacou Publications, 1982.

Gods of the Middle Passage, privately printed, 1982.

National Language Poetry, privately printed, 1982.

Afternoon of the Status Crow, Savacou Publications, 1982.

The Colonial Encounter: Language, University of Mysore, 1984.

History of the Voice: The Development of Nation Language in Angolophone Caribbean Poetry, New Beacon, 1984.

Jah Music, Savacou Publications, 1986.

Roots: Literary Criticism (essays), Casa de los Americas, 1986.

Visibility Trigger/Le detonateur de visibilite, Cahiers de Louvain, 1986.

Sappho Sakyi's Meditations, Savacou Publications, 1989.

Shar, Savacou Publications, 1990.

Middle Passages, Bloodaxe Books, 1992.

Also author of *Korabra,* 1986.

POETRY

Rights of Passage (also see below), Oxford University Press, 1967.

Masks (also see below), Oxford University Press, 1968.

Islands (also see below), Oxford University Press, 1969.

(With Alan Bold and Edwin Morgan) *Penguin Modern Poets 15,* Penguin, 1969.

Panda No. 349, Roy Institute for the Blind, 1969.

The Arrivants: A New World Trilogy (contains *Rights of Passage, Masks,* and *Islands*), Oxford University Press, 1973.

Days and Nights, Caldwell Press, 1975.

Other Exiles, Oxford University Press, 1975.

Poetry '75 International, Rotterdamse Kunstsichting, 1975.

Black + Blues, Casa de las Americas, 1976.

Mother Poem, Oxford University Press, 1977.

Soweto, Savacou Publications, 1979.

Word Making Man: A Poem for Nicolas Guillen, Savacou Publications, 1979.

Sun Poem, Oxford University Press, 1982.

Third World Poems, Longmans, 1983.

X/Self, Oxford University Press, 1987.

PLAYS

Four Plays for Primary Schools (first produced in Salt-pond, Ghana, 1961), Longmans, Green, 1964.

Odale's Choice (first produced in Saltpond, Ghana, 1962), Evans Brothers, 1967.

EDITOR

Iouanaloa: Recent Writing from St. Lucia, Department of Extra Mural Studies, University of West Indies, 1963.

New Poets from Jamaica (anthology), Savacou Publications, 1979.

Dream Rock, Jamaica Information Service, 1987.

RECORDINGS

The Poet Speaks 10, Argo, 1968.

Rights of Passage, Argo, 1969.

Masks, Argo, 1972.

Islands, Argo, 1973.

The Poetry of Edward Kamau Brathwaite, Casa de las Americas, 1976.

Poemas, Casa de las Americas, 1976.

Atumpan, Watershed, 1989.

OTHER

Contributor to *Bim* and other periodicals. Editor, *Savacou* (magazine), 1970—.

SIDELIGHTS: Edward Kamau Brathwaite is generally regarded as one of the West Indies' most prolific and talented writers. More well known for his poetry, Brathwaite often seeks to explore in his writings his past and present self while examining his identity as a black person living in the Caribbean. Andrew Motion writes in the *Times Literary Supplement* that "throughout his career Brathwaite has been concerned to define his identity as a West Indian."

It was the publication of *Rights of Passage* in 1967, *Masks* in 1968, and *Islands* in 1969, that brought Brathwaite to the attention of a larger group of critics and readers. These three books of poetry constitute an autobiographical trilogy collectively entitled *The Arrivants: A New World Trilogy* that examines a Caribbean man's search for identity. The volumes trace Brathwaite's initial encounter with white culture, his journey to Africa in search of a racial self-image, and his eventual return to his Caribbean homeland. Laurence Lieberman writes in *Poetry:* "[Brathwaite] has been able to invent a hybrid prosody which, combining jazz/folk rhythms with English-speaking meters, captures the authenticity of primitive African rituals." "In general," writes Hayden Carruth in the *Hudson Review,* "[Brathwaite] has been remarkably successful in reproducing black speech patterns, both African and Caribbean, in English syntax, using the standard techniques of contemporary poetry, and he has been equally successful in suggesting to an international audience the cultural identities and attitudes of his own people."

In 1977 Brathwaite released *Mother Poem,* the first book in a promised second trilogy. The next book of the trilogy, *Sun Poem,* was published in 1982, and the third, *X/Self,* was released in 1987. As in Brathwaite's first trilogy, *Mother Poem, Sun Poem,* and *X/Self* continue Brathwaite's exploration of his selfhood. As Andrew Motion explains in *Times Literary Supplement:* "In *Mother Poem,* [Brathwaite] provides another detailed account of his home [in the West Indies]. But in addition to exploring his complex relationship with the place, he also recounts its own efforts to find an independent and homogeneous character." David Dorsey remarks in *World Literature Today:* "Brathwaite is particularly ingenious in achieving semantic complexity through his use of assonance, enjambment, word divisions, grammatical and lexical ambiguity, puns and neologisms. This joie d'esprit occurs within a rhythm always obedient to the emphases and feelings intended. The style paradoxically reveals the author's sober, passionate and lucid perception on the beauty and pain black Barbadians are heir to."

In a *World Literature Today* review of *Sun Poem* Andrew Salkey comments that "Brathwaite writes 'performance,' 'rituals' and 'illuminations' which result in conflated portraits of persons, places and events recalled through a filter of sequential evocative poems—no ordinary creative accomplishment."

BIOGRAPHICAL/CRITICAL SOURCES:

BOOKS

Authors and Areas of the West Indies, Steck-Vaughn, 1970.

Brathwaite, Doris Monica, *A Descriptive and Chronological Bibliography (1950-1982) of the Work of Edward Kamau Brathwaite,* New Beacon, 1988.

Brathwaite, Doris Monica, *Edward Kamau Brathwaite: His Published Prose and Poetry 1948-1986,* Savacou Publications, 1986.

Caribbean Writers, Three Continents, 1979.

Contemporary Literary Criticism, Volume 2, Gale, 1979.

Contemporary Poets, St. James, 1991, pp. 93-95.
Dictionary of Literary Biography, Volume 125: *Twentieth-Century Caribbean and Black African Writers,* Gale, 1993, pp. 8-28.
West Indian Literature, Archon Books, 1979.

PERIODICALS

Ariel, April, 1990, pp. 45-57.
Books, January, 1970.
Books and Bookmen, May, 1967.
Book World, November 3, 1968.
Caribbean Quarterly, June, 1973.
Caribbean Studies, January, 1971.
Choice, June, 1976.
Critical Quarterly, summer, 1970.
Hudson Review, summer, 1974.
Jamaica Journal, September, 1968.
Library Journal, March 15, 1970.
Nation, April 9, 1988, pp. 504-507.
New Statesman, April 7, 1967.
Partisan Review, February, 1989, pp. 316-320.
Poetry, April, 1969; May, 1971.
Saturday Review, October 14, 1967.
Third World Quarterly, March, 1988, pp. 334-337.
Times Literary Supplement, February 16, 1967; August 15, 1968; January 28, 1972; June 30, 1972; November 14, 1975; January 20, 1978; February 18, 1983.
Virginia Quarterly Review, autumn, 1963; autumn, 1968; spring, 1970.
West Africa, March 16, 1987, pp. 514-515.
World Literature Today, winter, 1977; summer, 1978; summer, 1983.

* * *

BRITTON, Karl (William) 1909-1983

PERSONAL: Born October 12, 1909, in Scarborough, Yorkshire, England; died July 23, 1983; son of James Nimmo (a minister) and Elsie Clare (Slater) Britton; married Sheila Margaret Christie, September 25, 1936; children: Margaret Clare, Andrew, Kate. *Education:* Clare College, Cambridge, M.A. (first class honors), 1932; Harvard University, A.M., 1934. *Religion:* Church of England.

CAREER: University College of Wales, Aberystwyth, lecturer in philosophy, 1934-37; University College of Swansea, Swansea, Wales, lecturer in philosophy, 1937-51; University of Newscastle upon Tyne, Newcastle upon Tyne, England, professor of philosophy, 1951-75. University of Durham, public orator, 1960-62, dean of Faculty of Arts, 1961-63, 1966-69. Served in Regional Commissioner's Office, Reading, 1941-45.

MEMBER: Mind Association (secretary, 1948-60; president, 1963), Cambridge Union Society (president, 1931).

AWARDS, HONORS: Choate fellowship at Harvard University, 1932-34; D.Litt., University of Durham, 1976.

WRITINGS:

Communication: A Philosophical Study of Language, Routledge & Kegan Paul, 1939, McGrath, 1970.
John Stuart Mill: An Introduction to the Life and Teaching of a Great Pioneer of Modern Social Philosophy and Logic, Penguin, 1953, Dover, 1969.
The Paragon of Knowledge (pamphlet), University of Durham, 1954.
Philosophy and the Meaning of Life, Cambridge University Press, 1969.
Charlie Dunbar Broad, 1887-1971, British Academy, 1980.

Contributor to papers on J. S. Mill, David Hume, and on communication.

BIOGRAPHICAL/CRITICAL SOURCES:

PERIODICALS

Times Literary Supplement, September 18, 1970.

OBITUARIES:

PERIODICALS

Times (London), September 22, 1983.*

* * *

BROCK, Gavin
See LINDSAY, (John) Maurice

* * *

BROWN, Louis M(orris) 1909-

PERSONAL: Born September 5, 1909, in Los Angeles, CA; son of Emil (a business executive) and Anna Brown; married Hermione Kopp (a lawyer), 1937; children: Lawrence David, Marshall Joseph, Harold Arthur. *Education:* University of Southern California, A.B. (cum laude), 1930; Harvard University, J.D., 1933. *Religion:* Jewish.

ADDRESSES: Home—606 North Palm Dr., Beverly Hills, CA 90210. *Office*—1901 Ave. of the Stars, Ste. 850, Los Angeles, CA 90067.

CAREER: Admitted to California bar, 1933, and U.S. Supreme Court bar, 1944; attorney in Los Angeles, CA, 1933-35; Emil Brown & Co., Los Angeles, vice president, 1936-64; Dura Steel Products Co., Los Angeles, vice president, 1936-41; Reconstruction Finance Corp., Washington, DC, counsel, 1942-44; Pacht, Warne, Ross & Bernhard, Los Angeles, partner, 1944-47; Irell & Manella, Los Angeles, partner, 1947-69, counsel, 1969-72; University of Southern California, Los Angeles, lecturer in law, 1950-51, adjunct professor of law, 1960-74, academic director of program for legal-para professionals, 1970-77, professor of law, 1974-80, professor of law emeritus, 1980—. Tax Institute, planning committee member, 1948-69; Jewish Personnel Relations Bureau and Community Relations Committee, member, 1950-60; American Arbitration Association, member of national panel of arbitrators, 1956-63; founder and administrator of Emil Brown Fund for Preventive Law prize awards, 1963-85, Hermione and Louis Brown Fund, 1985—; Louis Brown Client Counseling Competition, founder and administrator, 1968-73, consultant, 1973—. Southwestern University Law School, Los Angeles, lecturer in law, 1939-41; University of California at Los Angeles, lecturer in law, 1944-46; Loyola-Marymount Law School, visiting professor, 1977-82; Whittier College Law School, distinguished visiting professor, 1980-85; Northrop University trustee, 1982; National Center for Preventive Law, board of trustees, 1987—; University of Denver College of Law, board of trustees, 1987—. Member of American Community Symphony Orchestra European Tour, 1968.

MEMBER: International Association of Jewish Lawyers and Jurists, American Bar Foundation (fellow), American Bar Association (chair of standing committee on legal assistance for servicemen, 1969-72, member of accreditation committee sect. legal education and admissions the bar, 1978-81), American Judicature Society, American Business Law Association, State Bar Association of California (committee on professional responsibility and conduct member, 1983-84), Society for Values in Higher Education, Los Angeles County Bar Association (prepaid legal services committee chairman, 1970-71), Beverly Hills Bar Association (president, 1961), Town Hall of Los Angeles, Friends of Beverly Hills Public Library (president, 1960), Order of the Coif, Masons, Harvard Club of Southern California, B'nai B'rith.

AWARDS, HONORS: An issue of *Southern California Law Review* was published in Brown's honor in 1975; LL.D., Manhattan College, 1977; merit award, University of Southern California General Alumni Association, 1979; distinguished service award, Beverly Hills Bar Association, 1980; Pacem in Terris medal, Manhattan College, 1991.

WRITINGS:

(Editor) *Major Tax Problems,* four volumes, Tax Institute, University of Southern California (Los Angeles), 1948-51, 1962.

Preventive Law, Prentice-Hall (Englewood Cliffs, NJ), 1950, revised edition (with Edward Rubin), Greenwood (Westport, CT), 1970.
How to Negotiate a Successful Contract, Prentice-Hall (Englewood Cliffs, NJ), 1955.
Legal Checkup Guides for Creditor-Debtor Relationships of a Going Business, California Continuing Education of the Bar, 1974.
Manual for Periodic Legal Checkup, California Lawyers Service, 1974.
(With Edward A. Dauer) *Perspectives on the Lawyer as Planner,* Foundation Press (Mineola, NY), 1978.
(With Edward A. Dauer) *Planning by Lawyers: Materials on a Nonadversarial Legal Process,* Foundation Press (Mineola, NY), 1978.
Lawyer-Client Counseling and Decisions: Teaching Materials, University of Southern California Law Center (Los Angeles), 1978.
Client Counseling Competition, American Bar Association (Chicago), 1979.
Lawyering Through Life: The Origin of Preventive Law, F.B. Rothman (Littleton, CO), 1986.
(With Anne O. Kandel) *The Legal Audit: Corporate Internal Investigation,* C. Boardman (New York City), 1990.

Also author of *Jurisprudence, A Seminar in the Practice of Preventive Law,* 1963, and *Planning by Lawyers: An Introductory Course in the Practice of Preventive Law,* [Los Angeles], 1972. Editor, "Legal View" column, *Los Angeles Times,* 1991—. Contributor of articles to law journals and to *Better Homes and Gardens* and *PLA.**

*   *   *

BROWN, Paula 1925-
(Paula Brown Glick)

PERSONAL: Born February 24, 1925, in Chicago, IL; married, 1948 (marriage ended); married, 1966. *Education:* University of Chicago, B.A., 1943, M.A., 1948; University of London, Ph.D., 1950.

ADDRESSES: Office—Department of Anthropology, State University of New York at Stony Brook, Stony Brook, NY 11794.

CAREER: University of London, London, England, assistant lecturer in anthropology, 1948-51; International African Institute, London, research assistant, 1951; Institute of Industrial Relations, University of California, Los Angeles, research anthropologist, 1952-55; University of Wisconsin, Madison, lecturer in sociology and anthropology, 1955-56; Australian National University, Canberra, research fellow, 1956-63, fellow, 1963-65, senior fellow in anthropology and sociology, 1965; Cambridge University, England, visiting lecturer in archaeology and anthropology, supervisor of students, and member of Senior Common Room, 1965-66; State University of New York at Stony Brook, associate professor, 1966-68, professor of anthropology, 1968—. Welfare Branch, Community Chest, Los Angeles, research consultant, 1954; Palos Verdes College, instructor, 1954-55; presentations at conferences in Nigmegen, The Netherlands and Chicago, 1987; Australian National University, University of Papua, New Guinea, visiting professor, 1987; Institute of Papua, New Guinea Studies, associate, 1987; presented lectures at Lae University of Technology, Goroka Teacher's College, University of Papua, New Guinea, American Embassy staff, all 1987; session chair, presentation, and symposium coordinator at anthropology conferences Savannah, GA, 1988. Columbia University Seminar on Ecological Systems and Cultural Evolution, associate; American Museum of Natural History, research associate.

MEMBER: American Anthropological Association (fellow), Association of Social Anthropologists, Association of Applied Anthropology, Society for Urban Anthropology, Asia Society, Association for Social Anthropology in Oceania, Royal Anthropological Association (fellow), New York Academy of Sciences (fellow).

AWARDS, HONORS: Fulbright scholar at University of London, 1949-50; Wenner-Gren Foundation award, 1984, for research on leadership; American Council of Learned Societies fellow, 1985, for Simbu research; Fulbright fellow, Papua, New Guinea, 1987.

WRITINGS:

(With I. R. Weschler) *Evaluating Research and Development,* Institute of Industrial Relations, University of California (Los Angeles) 1953.

(With H. C. Brookfield) *Struggle for Land: Agriculture and Group Territories among the Chimbu of the New Guinea Highlands,* Oxford University Press (Melbourne), 1963.

(With H. C. Brookfield) *The People of Vila,* Department of Human Geography, Research School of Pacific Studies, Australian National University (Canberra), 1969.

The Chimbu: A Study of Change in the New Guinea Highlands, Schenkman (Cambridge, MA), 1972.

(Editor with Georgeda Buchbinder, and author of introduction) *Man and Women in the New Guinea Highlands,* American Anthropological Association (Washington, DC), 1976.

Highland Peoples of New Guinea, Cambridge University Press, 1978.

The Simbu: People of Papua, New Guinea, National Cultural Council (Port Moresby, Papua, New Guinea), 1981.

(Editor with Donald Tuzin) *The Ethnography of Cannibalism,* Society for Psychological Anthropology, American Anthropology Association (Washington, DC), 1983.

Also contributor, under name Paula Brown Glick, to *Essays in Comparative Social Stratification,* edited by Leonard Plotnicov and Arthur Tuden, 1970. Contributor to *An Integrated Approach to Nutrition and Society: The Case of the Chimbu,* edited by Evan Hipsley, New Guinea Research Unit, Australian National University, 1966, *New Guinea on the Threshold,* edited by E. Fisk, Australian National University Press, 1966, *Pigs, Pearlshells, and Women,* edited by R. M. Glasse and M. J. Meggitt, Prentice-Hall, 1969, *Pacific Marketplaces,* H. C. Brookfield, Australian National University Press, 1969, *Social and Ecological Systems,* edited by Philip Burnham and Roy Ellen, Academic Press, 1979, *Ethnographic Research: A Guide to General Conduct,* edited by R. F. Ellen, Academic Press, 1984, and *Encyclopedia of Religion,* edited by Mircea Eliade and others, 1987.

WORK IN PROGRESS: *A Generation at Mindima,* with Harold Brookfield; *Fifty Years of Change in the New Guinea Highlands;* editing *Big Man—Strong Man—Culture Hero* for *Oceania Monographs,* with J. Watson.*

*　　　*　　　*

BRUCHAC, Joseph III 1942-

PERSONAL: Surname is pronounced Brew-shack; born October 16, 1942, in Saratoga Springs, NY; son of Joseph E. (a taxidermist) and Flora (Bowman) Bruchac; married Carol Worthen, June 13, 1964; children: James Edward, Jesse Bowman. *Education:* Cornell University, A.B., 1965; Syracuse University, M.A., 1966; graduate study at State University of New York at Albany, 1971-73; Union Graduate School, Ph.D., 1975. *Religion:* Animist.

ADDRESSES: Home—P. O. Box 308, Greenfield Center, NY 12833. *Office*—Greenfield Review Press, Greenfield Center, NY 12833. *Agent*—Barbara Kouts, P. O. Box 558, Bellport, NY 11713.

CAREER: Keta Secondary School, Ghana, West Africa, teacher of English and literature, 1966-69; Skidmore College, Saratoga Springs, NY, instructor in creative writing and in African and black literatures, 1969-73; teacher of creative writing at Great Meadows Institute, Comstock Prison, 1972-74; Greenfield Review Press, Greenfield Center, NY, publisher and editor of *Greenfield Review,*

1969—; director, Greenfield Review Literary Center, 1981—; founder, Good Mind Records.

MEMBER: Poetry Society of America, PEN.

AWARDS, HONORS: New York State Arts Council grant, 1972; Vermont Arts Council grant, 1972; monthly poetry prize from Poetry Society of America, February, 1972; New York State CAPS poetry fellowship, 1973, 1982; poetry fellowship, National Endowment for the Arts, 1974; editors' fellowship, Co-ordinating Council of Literary Magazines, 1980; Rockefeller Foundation humanities fellowship, 1982-83; American Book Award, Before Columbus Foundation, 1985, for *Breaking Silence: An Anthology of Asian-American Poetry.*

WRITINGS:

POETRY

Indian Mountain and Other Poems, Ithaca House, 1971.
The Buffalo in the Syracuse Zoo, Greenfield Review Press (Greenfield Center, NY), 1972.
Flow, Cold Mountain Press, 1975.
The Road to Black Mountain, Thorp Springs Press, 1977.
This Earth Is a Drum, Cold Mountain Press, 1977.
Entering Onondaga, Cold Mountain Press, 1978.
There Are No Trees inside the Prison, Blackberry Press, 1978.
(Translator from the Iroquois) *The Good Message of Handsome Lake,* Unicorn Press (Greensboro, NC), 1979.
Ancestry, Great Raven, 1980.
Translator's Son, Cross-Cultural Communications, 1981.
Remembering the Dawn, Blue Cloud, 1983.
Walking with My Sons and Other Poems, Landlocked Press, 1986.
Tracking, Ion Books, 1986.
Near the Mountains: New and Selected Poems, White Pine Press, 1987.
Long Memory and Other Poems, Wurf (Munster, IN), 1989.
(With Jonathan London) *Thirteen Moons on Turtle's Back: A Native American Year of Moons,* Philomel, 1992.

SHORT STORIES AND FOLK TALES

Turkey Brother and Other Iroquois Folk Tales, Crossing Press, 1976.
Stone Giants and Flying Heads: More Iroquois Folk Tales, Crossing Press, 1978, published as *Stone Giants and Flying Heads: Adventure Stories of the Iroquois,* 1979.
The Wind Eagle and Other Abenaki Stories, Bowman Books, 1984.
Iroquois Stories: Heroes and Heroines, Monsters and Magic, Crossing Press, 1985.

(With Michael Caduto) *Keepers of the Earth: Native American Stories and Environmental Activities for Children,* Fulcrum, 1987, paperback edition published as *Native American Stories,* 1988, selections published as *Native American Animal Stories,* 1992.
The Faithful Hunter: Abenaki Stories, Bowman Books, 1988.
Return of the Sun: Native American Tales from the Northeast Woodlands, Crossing Press, 1989.
Hoop Snakes, Hide Behinds, and Side-Hill Winders: Tall Tales from the Adirondacks, Crossing Press, 1991.
(With Michael J. Caduto) *Keepers of the Animals: Native American Stories and Wildlife Activities for Children,* Fulcrum, 1991.
Turtle Meat and Other Stories, Holy Cow! Press, 1992.
The First Strawberries, Dial, 1993.
Flying with the Eagle, Racing the Great Bear: Stories from Native North America, BridgeWater Books, 1993.
(With Gayl Ross) *The Girl Who Married the Moon: Stories from Native North America,* BridgeWater Books, 1994.
The Great Ball Game: A Muskogee Story, Dial, 1994.
Gluskabe and the Four Wishes, Cobblehill Books/Dutton, 1994.

Bruchac has also recorded many of his stories, found in *The Storytellers Collection.*.

EDITOR

(With William Witherup) *Words from the House of the Dead: An Anthology of Prison Writings from Soledad,* Greenfield Review Press, 1971.
The Last Stop: Writings from Comstock Prison, Greenfield Review Press, 1974.
(With Roger Weaver) *Aftermath: An Anthology of Poems in English from Africa, Asia, and the Caribbean,* Greenfield Review Press, 1977.
The Next World: Poems by Thirty-Two Third-World Americans, Crossing Press, 1978.
Songs from This Earth on Turtle's Back: Contemporary American Indian Poetry (anthology), Greenfield Review Press, 1983.
The Light from Another Country: Poetry from American Prisons (anthology), Greenfield Review Press, 1984.
Breaking Silence: An Anthology of Asian American Poetry, Greenfield Review Press, 1984.
(With others) *North Country: An Anthology of Contemporary Writing from the Adirondacks and the Upper Hudson Valley,* Greenfield Review Press, 1985.
New Voices from the Longhouse: An Anthology of Contemporary Iroquois Writing, Greenfield Review Press, 1989.
Returning the Gift: Poetry and Prose from the First North American Native Writers Festival, University of Arizona Press, 1994.

OTHER

The Poetry of Pop (essays), Dustbooks, 1973.

The Dreams of Jesse Brown (novel), Cold Mountain Press, 1977.

How to Start and Sustain a Literary Magazine: Practical Strategies for Publications of Lasting Value, Provision House Press, 1980.

Survival This Way: Interviews with Native American Poets, University of Arizona Press, 1987.

Dawn Land (novel), Fulcrum, 1993.

The Native American Sweat Lodge: History and Legends, Crossing Press, 1993.

Fox Song (juvenile), Philomel, 1993.

A Boy Called Slow (juvenile), Philomel, 1995.

Work is represented in numerous anthologies, including *New Campus Writing,* edited by Nolan Miller, McGraw, 1966; *Syracuse Poems, 1963-1969,* edited by George P. Elliott, Syracuse University Press, 1970; *Our Only Hope Is Humor: Some Public Poems,* edited by Robert McGovern and Richard Snyder, Ashland Poetry Press, 1972; *From the Belly of the Shark: A New Anthology of Native Americans,* edited by Walter Lowenfels, Vintage, 1973; *The Remembered Earth,* edited by Geary Hobson, University of New Mexico, 1979; *The Pushcart Prize Anthology, 1980-81,* Pushcart Press, 1981; *From A to Z: 200 Contemporary Poets,* Swallow Press, 1981; *Editors' Choice,* Spirit That Moves Us, 1981; *Peace Is Our Profession,* East River Anthology, 1981; *Earth Power Coming: Short Fiction in Native American Literature,* edited by Simon Ortiz, Navajo Community College Press, 1983.

Also author of *Peter Davis,* an album of songs. Contributor of poetry to over four hundred periodicals, including *New Letters, Paris Review, Akwesasne Notes, Hudson Review, American Poetry Review,* and *Contact/II.* Assistant editor, *Epoch,* 1964-65; contributing editor, *Nickel Review,* 1967-71, and *Studies in American Indian Literature,* 1983—; contemporary music editor, *Kite,* 1971-73; editor, *Prison Writing Review,* 1976-82.

SIDELIGHTS: "Joe Bruchac," declares Chris Carola in the *Saratogian,* "walks in two worlds, the white man's and the Indian's. In one, he's a writer, businessman, father and husband. In the other, he's a traveler, a listener, a storyteller." According to *Publishers Weekly* contributor Sybil Steinberg, Bruchac, who is half Abenaki, ranks as "perhaps the best-known contemporary Native American storyteller." Bruchac draws on his heritage for his critically acclaimed collections, including *Flying with the Eagle, Racing the Great Bear: Stories from Native North America,* and *The Girl Who Married the Moon: Stories from Native North America.* These stories also influence his novel *Dawn Wind,* about the Abenaki living in the American northeast before the arrival of Columbus. "His stories,"

Steinberg concludes, "are often poignant, funny, ironic—and sometimes all three at once."

In addition to his many written collections, Bruchac also performs his stories orally. He has recorded some of them on cassette tape for sale through his recording company, Good Mind Records. "Storytelling—sitting down and listening to someone tell a story—takes you out of time, puts you in a timeless place," Bruchac told *Glens Falls Post Star* writer Joan Patton. "And when the story's over, you kind of blink and wonder where you've been and how you got back to where you are." "In doing this," states Carola, "he carries on a tradition begun centuries ago, when Iroquois clans gathered around the longhouse fire, where . . . they listened to the 'old man or woman who knows how things came to be, why things are as they are, the stories which teach people how to live in balance.' "

"I was born in 1942 in Saratoga Springs, New York, during October, that month the Iroquois call the Moon of Falling Leaves" Bruchac told *CA.* "My writing and my interests reflect my mixed ancestry, Slovak on one side and Native American (Abenaki) and English on the other. Aside from attending Cornell University and Syracuse and three years of teaching in West Africa, I've lived all of my life in the small Adirondack foothills town of Greenfield Center in a house built by my grandfather.

"Much of my writing and my life relates to the problem of being an American. While in college I was active in civil rights work and in the anti-war movement. . . . I went to Africa to teach—but more than that, to be taught. It showed me many things. How much we have as Americans and take for granted. How much our eyes refuse to see because they are blinded to everything in a man's face except his color. And, most importantly, how human people are everywhere—which may be the one grace that can save us all.

"I write poetry, fiction and some literary criticism and have been fortunate enough to receive recognition in all three areas. After returning from Ghana in 1969, my wife Carol and I started the Greenfield Review and the Greenfield Review Press. Since 1975, I've been actively involved in storytelling, focussing on northeastern Native American tales and the songs and traditions of the Adirondack Mountains of upstate New York, and I am frequently a featured performer at storytelling gatherings. I've also done a great deal of work in teaching and helping start writing workshops in American prisons. I believe that poetry is as much a part of human beings as is breath—and that, like breath, poetry links us to all other living things and is meant to be shared.

"My writing is informed by several key sources. One of these is nature, another is the native American experience (I'm part Indian). . . . I like to work outside, in the earth-mother's soil, with my hands . . . but maintain my life as an academic for a couple of reasons: it gives me time to write (sometimes) and it gives me a chance to share my insights into the beautiful and all too fragile world of human life and living things we have been granted. Which is one of the reasons I write—not to be a man apart, but to share."

BIOGRAPHICAL/CRITICAL SOURCES:

PERIODICALS

Albany Times Union, June 1, 1980.
Glens Falls Post Star, February, 1988.
Los Angeles Times Book Review, November 1, 1992, p. 11; January 10, 1993, p. 9.
Publishers Weekly, April 26, 1976, p. 60; September 23, 1983, p. 71; December 2, 1983, p. 84; August 24, 1984, p. 78; February 10, 1992, p. 80; October 19, 1992, p. 73; March 15, 1993, p. 68.
Saratogian, January 27, 1988.

* * *

BRULLER, Jean (Marcel) 1902-1991
(Vercors, J. Bruller Vercors)

PERSONAL: Born February 26, 1902, in Paris, France; died June 10, 1991, in Paris, France; son of Louis and Ernestine (Bourbon) Bruller; married Jeanne Barusseaud, 1931 (divorced); married Rita Barisse, 1957; children: Francois, Jean-Louis, Bertrand. *Education:* Attended University of Paris and a technical college, received diploma in electrical engineering; studied art in Paris after military service.

ADDRESSES: Home—58, Quai des Orfevres, 75001 Paris, France.

CAREER: Graphic artist, 1926-40; founder with Pierre de Lescure of Editions de Minuit (publishing house for French Resistance movement), 1941; writer, 1941-91. Artwork has been exhibited worldwide, including Vienna, 1970, and Budapest and Cologne, 1971. Producer, under name J. Bruller Vercors, of *Callichromies,* reproductions of paintings based on his own process developed from silkscreen (includes works by Renoir, Van Gogh, Braque, and Picasso), 1952-58. Designed sets and costumes for Comedie Francaise, Paris, 1964. *Military service:* French Army, 1940, served in Alpine regiment in Tunis; became lieutenant.

MEMBER: PEN (vice president of French section), Comite National des Ecrivains (honorary president).

AWARDS, HONORS: Council of Europe prize, 1981, for *One Hundred Years of French History,* Volume I: *Moi, Ar-*

istide Briand; Prix de l'Union rationaliste, 1982; Commander des Arts et des Lettres; Legion d'honneur; Medaille de la Resistance.

WRITINGS:

UNDER PSEUDONYM VERCORS

Le Silence de la mer, Editions de Minuit (Paris), 1941, published as *Les Silences de la mer,* Pantheon (New York City), 1943, translation by Cyril Connolly published as *The Silence of the Sea,* Macmillan (New York City), 1944 (published in England as *Put Out the Light*), illustrated enlarged edition published as *Le Silence de la mer,* Club des Libraries de France (Paris), 1964.
La Marche a l'etoile, Editions de Minuit, 1945, Pantheon, 1946, translation by Eric Sutton published as *Guiding Star,* Macmillan, 1946.
Le Songe, Editions de Minuit, 1945.
Souffrance de mon pays, Emile-Paul, 1945.
Le Sable du temps, Emile-Paul, 1946.
Les Armes de la nuit, Editions de Minuit, 1946.
L'Imprimerie de Verdun, Bibliotheque francaise, 1947.
Les Mots, Editions de Minuit, 1947.
Les Yeux et la lumiere: Mystere a six voix, A. Michel (Paris), 1948.
Plus ou moins homme (essays), A. Michel, 1950.
La Puissance du jour, A. Michel, 1951.
Les Animaux denatures (novel), A. Michel, 1952, translation by wife, Rita Barisse, published as *You Shall Know Them,* Little, Brown, 1953 (published in England as *Borderline,* Macmillan, 1954), published as *The Murder of the Missing Link,* Pocket Books (New York City), 1958.
Portrait d'une amitie et autres morts memorables, A. Michel, 1954.
Les Pas dans la sable: L,Amerique, la Chine, et la France, A. Michel, 1954.
Coleres (novel), A. Michel, 1956, translation by Barisse published as *The Insurgents,* Harcourt (San Diego, CA), 1956, reprinted, Ayer Co., 1979.
Les Divagations d'un Francais en Chine (self-illustrated), A. Michel, 1956.
P.P.C.; ou, Le Concours de Blois, A. Michel, 1957, translation by Jonathan Griffin published as *For the Time Being,* Hutchinson, 1960.
Goetz, Musee de Poche, 1958.
Sur ce Rivage, A. Michel, Volume 1: *Le Periple,* 1958, Volume 2: *Monsieur Prousthe: Un Souvenir,* 1958, Volume 3: *La Liberte de decembre* [and] *Clementine,* 1960, translation of volumes 2 and 3 by Barisse published as *Paths of Love,* Putnam (New York City), 1961, published in England as *Freedom in December,* Hutchinson, 1961.

(Editor) *Morale chretienne et morale marxiste,* La Palatine (Paris), 1960.

Sylva (novel), B. Grasset, 1961, translation by Barisse published under same title, Putnam, 1962.

(With Paul Misraki) *Les Chemins de l'etre: Une Discussion,* A. Michel, 1965.

(With Paul Silva-Coronel) *Quota; ou, Les Plethoriens* (novel), Stock, 1966, translation by Barisse published as *Quota,* Putnam, 1966.

La Bataille du silence: Souvenirs de minuit, Presses de la Cite (Paris), 1967, translation by Barisse published as *The Battle of Silence,* Holt, 1968.

Le Radeau de la Meduse (novel), Presses de la Cite, 1969, translation by Audrey C. Foote published as *The Raft of the Medusa,* McCall, 1971.

Liberte ou fatalite? Oedipe et Hamlet, Perrin (Paris), 1970.

Contes des Cataplasmes, Editions G.P. (Paris), 1971.

Sillages (novel), Presses de la Cite, 1972.

Sept Sentiers du desert, Presses de la Cite, 1972.

Questions sur la vie a MM les biologistes, Stock, 1973.

Comme un Frere, Plon (Paris), 1973.

Tendre Naufrage (novel), Presses de la Cite, 1974.

Ce que je crois (essay), B. Grasset, 1975.

Je cuisine comme un chef (cookbook), Seghers, 1976.

Les Chevaux du temps (novel), Tchou, 1977.

Sens et non-sens de l'histoire (essay), Galilee, 1978.

Camille; ou, l'enfant double (children's book), Editions G.P., 1978.

Le Piege a loup (novella), Galilee, 1979.

(With Olga Wormser-Migot) *Assez Mentir!* (essay), Ramsay, 1979.

One Hundred Years of French History, Plon, Volume 1: *Moi, Aristide Briand,* 1981, Volume 2: *Les occasions perdues,* 1982, Volume 3: *Les nouveaux jours,* 1984.

Also author of *Anne Boleyn,* 1985, and *Le Tigre d'Anvers,* 1986. Author of introduction, *Un Homme sans l'Occident,* by Diego Brosset, Editions de Minuit, 1946.

COLLECTIONS; UNDER PSEUDONYM VERCORS

Three Short Novels (includes *Guiding Star, Night and Fog, and The Verdun Press*), Little, Brown, 1947.

La songe precede de ce jour-la, P. Seghers, 1950.

Le Silence de la mer et autres recits, A. Michel, 1951.

Les Armes de la nuit et [and] La Puissance du jour, A. Michel, 1951.

Les Animaux denatuires [and] La Marche a l'etoile (also see below), Livre de Poche, 1956.

PLAYS; UNDER PSEUDONYM VERCORS

Zoo; ou, l'Assassin philanthrope (based on *Les Animaux denatures;* first produced in Carcassonne, France, 1963), Theatre National Populaire, 1964, translation by James Clancy produced as *Zoo; or The Philanthropic Assassin by Vercors: A Judicial, Zoological,*

and Moral Comedy in Three Acts, at Cornell University (Ithaca, NY), March, 1968.

(Translator and illustrator) William Shakespeare, *Hamlet: Une Tragedie en cinq actes,* Editions Vialetay, 1965.

(Adaptor) *Oedipe-Roi* (based on work by Sophocles), first produced in La Rochelle, France, 1967, produced in Paris, France, 1970.

Le Fer et le velours, produced in Nimes, France, 1969.

(Adaptor) *Chat!* (based on Hungarian play by Istvan Orkeny), Gallimard, 1974.

Collected Theatre, Volume 1: *Zoo; ou, l'assassin philanthrope, Le Fer et le velours, [and] Le Silence de la mer,* Volume 2: *For Shakespeare (Hamlet, Macbeth),* Galilee, 1978.

COLLECTIONS OF ARTWORK; UNDER NAME JEAN BRULLER

21 Recettes de Mort Violente, 1926, published as *21 Delightful Ways of Committing Suicide for the Use of Persons Who are Discouraged or Disgusted with Life for Reasons Which Do Not Concern Us,* Covici, Friede, 1930.

Also author of artwork collections, *Hypotheses sur les amateurs de peinture* (title means "Hypotheses on Art Lovers"), 1927; *Un Homme coupe en tranches* (title means "A Man Cut Up in Slices"), 1929; *Les Releves trimestriels,* 1932-38; *Nouvelle cle des songes* (title means "A New Key to Dreams"), 1934; *L'Enfer* (title means "This Is Hell"), 1935; *Visions intimes et rassurantes de la guerre* (title means "Comforting Visions of the War"), 1936; *Silences,* 1937; *La Danse des vivants* (title means "The Dance of the Living"), 1938. Illustrator of editions of Kipling, Racine, and others, and of children's books.

SIDELIGHTS: During the Nazi occupation of France in World War II, Jean Bruller, operating under the name Vercors, co-founded an underground publishing house in order to print and distribute literary works important to the Resistance. Editions de Minuit, or Midnight Press, produced more than twenty volumes of contemporary literature in direct defiance of both the German and Vichy governments. The first of these "midnight editions" was Bruller's own *The Silence of the Sea.* This short novel was widely read and translated into over thirty languages. Its publication in the United States is said to have aroused much fervent anti-Nazi sentiment. Each copy of the original edition included the following statement: "Propaganda is not our domain. We mean to safeguard our inner life and freely serve our art. The names matter little. It is no longer a question of petty personal fame."

The Battle of Silence is the story of the *Midnight Press,* containing Bruller's personal recollections of life in Nazi-ruled Paris. The book describes the difficulty and danger under which Bruller and others were forced to publish, for such activities were potentially punishable by torture or death. *New Yorker* reviewer Naomi Bliven explains that Bruller's account is "enthralling because it is matter-of-fact; it provides the circumstantial evidence—practical details and down-to-earth descriptions—that makes it easy for readers to envision the author's fantastic activities."

BIOGRAPHICAL/CRITICAL SOURCES:

BOOKS

Konstantinovic, R.D., *Vercors ecrivain et dessinateur,* C. Klincksieck, 1969.

Vercors, *Le Silence de la mer,* Editions de Minuit (Paris), 1941, published as *Les Silences de la mer,* Pantheon, 1943, translation by Cyril Connolly published as *The Silence of the Sea,* Macmillan, 1944 (published in England as *Put Out the Light*), illustrated enlarged edition published as *Le Silence de la mer,* Club des Libraries de France (Paris), 1964.

Vercours, *La Bataille du silence: Souvenirs de minuit,* Presses de la Cite (Paris), 1967, translation by Barisse published as *The Battle of Silence,* Holt, 1968.

PERIODICALS

Atlantic, February, 1969.
New Yorker, March 9, 1946; November 8, 1969.
New York Herald Tribune Book Review, June 28, 1953.
New York Times Book Review, October 24, 1971.

OBITUARIES:

PERIODICALS

Chicago Tribune, June 12, 1991, sec. 3, p. 12.
Detroit Free Press, June 12, 1991, p. B2.
Los Angeles Times, June 16, 1991, p. A32.
New York Times, June 13, 1991, p. D24.
Times (London), June 13, 1991, p. 20.*

*   *   *

BRYAN, J(oseph) III 1904-1993

PERSONAL: Born April 30, 1904, in Richmond, VA; died of cancer, April 3, 1993, in Richmond, VA; son of Joseph St. George and Emily Page (Kemp) Bryan; married Katherine Lansing Barnes, 1930 (divorced, 1954); married Jacqueline de la Grandiere, 1960 (died, 1988); married Elizabeth Mayo Atkinson McIntosh; children: (first marriage) St. George II (deceased, 1969), Joan, Courtlandt. *Education:* Princeton University, A.B., 1927. *Religion:* Episcopalian.

CAREER: Reporter and editorial writer, *News Leader,* Richmond, VA, and *Chicago Journal,* Chicago, IL, 1928-31; associate editor, *Parade,* 1931-32; managing editor, *Town and Country,* 1933-36; associate editor, *Satur-*day *Evening Post,* 1937-40; freelance writer, 1940-93. Fellow and former trustee, Virginia Museum of Fine Arts, 1963-73; trustee of Poe Foundation. *Military service:* U.S. Army Reserve, 1927-37, became first lieutenant; U.S. Naval Reserve, 1942-53, served in Pacific, became lieutenant commander, received distinguished public service award, special assistant to secretary of U.S. Air Force, 1952-53; U.S. Air Force Reserve, 1953-64, became colonel.

MEMBER: Virginia Historical Society, Society of the Cincinnati, Society of Colonial Wars, Commonwealth Club (Richmond, VA), Buck's Club (London), Ivy Club (Princeton), Princeton Club (New York City), Racquet and Tennis Club (New York City).

WRITINGS:

(With Philip Reed) *Mission beyond Darkness,* Duell, Sloan & Pearce, 1945.
(With William F. Halsey) *Admiral Halsey's Story,* Whittlesey House, 1947.
Aircraft Carrier, Ballantine (New York City), 1954, reprinted, Bantam (New York City), 1982.
The World's Greatest Showman: The Life of P. T. Barnum (juvenile), Random House (New York City), 1956.
The Sword over the Mantel, McGraw (New York City), 1960.
The Merry Madmen of 52nd Street (booklet), Whittet & Shepperson, 1968.
(With Charles J. V. Murphy) *The Windsor Story,* Morrow (New York City), 1979.
Merry Gentlemen (and One Lady), Atheneum (New York City), 1985.
Hodgepodge, Atheneum, 1986.
Hodgepodge Two, Atheneum, 1989.

Contributor of more than one hundred articles to popular magazines, including *Reader's Digest, McCall's,* and *Holiday.*

SIDELIGHTS: The Windsor Story is a dual biography of the Duke and Duchess of Windsor. Authors J. Bryan III and Charles J. V. Murphy portray the royal couple in sometimes unflattering terms, going behind their public image of marital bliss to the true nature of their relationship. The couple's life together, according to Jean Strouse of *Newsweek,* is "a nasty, pathetic tale of selfishness, greed, weakness, and ineptitude."

In 1936, the Duke of Windsor, then King Edward VIII of England, renounced his throne because the woman he wished to marry, American divorcee Wallis Simpson, could not be named his queen. His was the shortest reign—eleven months—of any English king in over five hundred years. At the time, according to Strouse, H. L. Mencken described his abdication as "the greatest news story since the Resurrection." *The Windsor Story* primarily concentrates on the lives of the royal couple after the abdication, when they became the leading figures in cafe society. "The couple," writes a reviewer for the *New Yorker*, "appear to have lived lives compounded of frivolity and grievance, extravagance and meanness."

There are several scandalous incidents related by Bryan and Murphy to support their contention that the Windsors were not as happily married as they were often depicted. The Duchess's affair with a millionaire playboy, the Duke's sometimes ambivalent sexual orientation, and the couple's shameless use of other people's money are all examined in sensational detail, much of it supplied by their former servants and friends. But the most damning evidence of marital strife seems, to the authors, to lie in what they see as the Duchess's domination of the Duke. "[The Duke] was waiting for the woman who would dominate him," they write. "He was happiest under a despot." The Duke, writes Strouse, "never stopped worshipping his Duchess, and she never stopped punishing him." "Although the king traded his crown for the woman he insisted he could not live without," Nancy Naglin of the *Chicago Tribune Book World* states, "in both life and love, she conspired to make him the most miserable of men." As Anthony Howard of the *New York Times Book Review* puts it, "One undoubtedly became a monster and the other in no time was translated into her creature."

Bryan and Murphy also shed light on some of the reasons for the Duke's failure to receive any government work after his abdication, emphasizing his ambivalence toward Nazism as a major factor. During a visit to Germany just before World War II, the Duke was warmly greeted by government officials and was seen giving Nazi salutes in public. After the war began, the Nazis offered to position the Duke as King once they had conquered England, an offer to which the Duke apparently kept himself open. The Duke's ineffective performance during his brief stint as ambassador to the Bahamas also reflected poorly on his judgment and abilities. As ambassador, his administration was marred by an openly racist attitude, while the Windsors' frequent trips to jet-setter vacation spots abroad left him little time to deal with problems of state.

Although John Richardson of the *New York Review of Books* describes *The Windsor Story* as "a geyser of dirt and hot air," and Elizabeth Wheeler of the *Los Angeles Times Book Review* finds that "the authors don't present a lot of evidence for this portrait aside from their own observations, the comments of other Windsor friends who disliked the duke and duchess, and a few pretty shaky suppositions," other critics found the book, for all its scandal, to be well-researched and fascinating. "The authors," the *New Yorker* critic believes, "succeed in making [the Windsors] continuously interesting . . . partly by shrewd re-

porting and partly by furnishing a first-rate background, which offers a history of social change in Western society." Eve Auchincloss of the *Washington Post Book World* states, "One would have to be insensible to read the appalling but fairminded story [Bryan and Murphy] so skillfully tell without gloating fascination."

BIOGRAPHICAL/CRITICAL SOURCES:

BOOKS

J. Bryan III and Charles J. V. Murphy, *The Windsor Story*, Morrow, 1979.

PERIODICALS

Chicago Tribune Book World, December 9, 1979.
Los Angeles Times Book Review, November 11, 1979.
Newsweek, December 3, 1979.
New Yorker, November 5, 1979.
New York Review of Books, February 21, 1980.
New York Times Book Review, October 28, 1979.
Times Literary Supplement, January 4, 1980.
Village Voice, September 17, 1979.
Washington Post Book World, November 11, 1979.

OBITUARIES:

PERIODICALS

New York Times, April 6, 1993, p. B7.*

*   *   *

BUCKEYE, Donald A(ndrew) 1930-

PERSONAL: Born March 12, 1930, in Lakewood, OH; son of Andrew M. (a pattern maker) and Elizabeth (Wagner) Buckeye; married Nancy R. O'Neill, June 16, 1962; children: Pamela Jean, Karen Ann. *Education:* Ashland College, B.S.Ed., 1953; Indiana University, M.A., 1961, Ed.D., 1968.

ADDRESSES: Home—1823 Witmire Blvd., Ypsilanti, MI 48197. *Office*—Department of Mathematics, Eastern Michigan University, Ypsilanti, MI 48197.

CAREER: High school teacher, 1953-54; math instructor, Army Education Center, Sendai, Japan, 1954-56; high school mathematics teacher in public schools in Lakewood, OH, 1957-65; Eastern Michigan University, Ypsilanti, professor of mathematics, 1968—. Teaching assistant at Ohio State University, 1962-65; teaching associate at Indiana University, 1966-68. *Military service:* U.S. Army, 1954-56.

MEMBER: National Council of Teachers of Mathematics, Michigan Council of Teachers of Mathematics, Ohio Council of Teachers of Mathematics, Cleveland Council of Teachers of Mathematics (vice-president, 1960-61; president, 1962-63), Phi Delta Kappa.

WRITINGS:

Experiments in Probability and Statistics, Midwest Publications (Troy, MI), 1969.
(With William A. Ewbank and John L. Ginther) *Downpour of Math Lab Experiments,* Midwest Publications (Troy, MI), 1969.
Experiments and Puzzles in Logic, Midwest Publications (Troy, MI), 1970.
Creative Geometry Experiments, Midwest Publications (Troy, MI), 1970.
Creative Experiments in Algebra, Midwest Publications (Troy, MI), 1971.
(With Ginther) *Creative Mathematics,* Canfield Press, 1971.
(With Ginther) *Creative Mathematics Laboratory Manual,* Canfield Press, 1971.
(With Ewbank and Ginther) *Cloudburst of Math Lab Experiments,* five volumes, Midwest Publications (Troy, MI), 1971.
N.R. Math Activities, Midwest Publications (Troy, MI), Volume 1, 1972, Volume 2, 1973, Volume 3, 1974.
Experiments in Fractions, Midwest Publications (Troy, MI), 1972.
Introducing the Metric System with Activities, Midwest Publications (Troy, MI), 1972.
Primary Activities in Mathematics, Midwest Publications, 1972.
(With Ewbank and Ginther) *Cheap Math Lab Equipment,* Midwest Publications (Troy, MI), 1972.
I'm OK, You're OK, Let's Go Metric, 1974.
(With others) *School Math,* eight volumes, Rand McNally (Chicago), 1974.
Basic Math Amusements, Midwest Publications (Troy, MI), 1976.
Bottle Cap Mathematics, Midwest Publications (Troy, MI), 1976.
Cheap Metric Equipment: Activities and Games, Midwest Publications (Troy, MI), 1976.
(With Karen Buckeye) *Problem Solving Using Computers,* three volumes, Midwest Publications (Pacific Grove, CA), 1984.
(With Ginther) *Cloudburst of Creative Mathematics Activities,* two volumes, Midwest Publications (Pacific Grove, CA), 1989.
Problem Solving Using Bingo Chips, two volumes, Tricon, 1995.

BIOGRAPHICAL/CRITICAL SOURCES:

PERIODICALS

Booklist, October 15, 1974, p. 224.
Science Books & Films, December, 1971, p. 201.

BUCKINGHAM, James (William) 1932-1992
(Jamie Buckingham)

PERSONAL: Born March 28, 1932, in Vero Beach, FL; died of liver cancer, February 17, 1992, in Melbourne, FL; son of Walter S. (in business) and Elvira (Thompson) Buckingham; married Jacqueline Law, June 4, 1954; children: Bruce, Robin, Bonnie, Timothy, Sandy. *Education:* Mercer University, A.B., 1954; Southwestern Baptist Theological Seminary, B.D., 1957, postgraduate student, 1958. *Avocational interests:* Private flying, golf, fishing.

CAREER: Pastor of South Main Street Baptist Church, Greenwood, SC, 1957-65, Harbor City Baptist Church, Eau Gallie, FL, 1965-66, and Tabernacle Church, Melbourne, FL, beginning 1967. Member of publisher's board, Logos International. Member of board of directors, Logos Fellowship, beginning 1971. *Military service:* U.S. Army Reserve, chaplain, 1954-58; became captain.

MEMBER: Exchange Club, Civil Air Patrol, Lions Club.

AWARDS, HONORS: Named best columnist by Florida Press Association, 1974, and Evangelical Press Association, 1975.

WRITINGS:

UNDER NAME JAMIE BUCKINGHAM; WITH KATHRYN KUHLMAN

God Can Do It Again, Prentice-Hall (Englewood Cliffs, NJ), 1969.
Nothing Is Impossible, Prentice-Hall, 1973.
Captain LeVrier Believes in Miracles, Bethany Fellowship, 1973.
Ten Thousand Miles for a Miracle, Bethany Fellowship, 1974.
How Big Is God?, Bethany Fellowship, 1974.
Standing Tall, Bethany Fellowship, 1975.
Never Too Late, Bethany Fellowship, 1975.
Twilight to Dawn, Bethany Fellowship, 1976.
Medicine to Miracles, Bethany Fellowship, 1976.

UNDER NAME JAMIE BUCKINGHAM, EXCEPT AS NOTED

(With Nicky Cruz) *Run, Baby, Run,* Logos International (Plainfield, NJ), 1968.
(With Arthur Katz) *Ben Israel: The Odyssey of a Modern Jew,* Logos International, 1969.
(Under name James Buckingham) *Some Gall—and Other Reflections on Life,* Word Books (Waco, TX), 1969.
Coming Alive, with John Buckingham as medical consultant, illustrations by Cathy Hanley and Bob Hanley, Logos International, 1970.
One Man's Perspective, Word Books, 1970.
(With John Buckingham) *Your New Look: Junior High Age,* illustrations by Al Petrik, Logos International, 1970.

(With Cruz) *The Lonely Now,* Logos International, 1971.

(With Pat Robertson) *Shout It from the Housetops,* Logos International, 1971.

(With Aaron Johnson) *The End of Youngblood Johnson,* Chosen Books (Lincoln, VA), 1972.

O Happy Day: The Happy Goodman Story, Word Books, 1973.

Into the Glory, Logos International, 1974.

(With Corrie ten Boom) *Tramp for the Lord,* Revell (Tappan, NJ), 1974.

(With Juan Carlos Ortiz) *Call to Discipleship,* Logos International, 1975.

(With Bill Sherwood) *Let's Begin Again,* Logos International, 1975.

Risky Living: Keys to Inner Healing, Logos International, 1976.

Daughter of Destiny: Kathryn Kuhlman, Her Story, Logos International, 1976.

(With ten Boom) *Don't Wrestle, Just Nestle,* Revell, 1976.

Coping with Criticism, Logos International, 1978.

The Last Word (Published and Unpublished): For Christians—and Others Who Take Themselves Too Seriously, Logos International, 1978.

(Editor) Kathryn Kuhlman, *A Glimpse into Glory,* Logos International, 1979.

Where Eagles Soar, Chosen Books, 1980.

Jesus World: A Novel, Chosen Books, 1981.

Power for Living, second edition, revised, Power for Living (South Holland, IL), 1983.

A Way through the Wilderness, Chosen Books, 1983.

Let's Talk about Life, revised edition, Creation House (Wheaton, IL), 1987.

Ten Bible People Like Me Workbook, Paraclete (Orleans, MA), 1988.

Ten Miracles of Jesus Workbook, Paraclete, 1988.

Ten Parables of Jesus Workbook, Paraclete, 1988.

The Truth Will Set You Free, but First It Will Make You Miserable: The Wit and Wisdom of Jamie Buckingham, Creation House, 1988.

(With Bill Nelson) *Mission: An American Congressman's Voyage to Space,* Harcourt (San Diego, CA), 1988.

Armed for Spiritual Warfare (book with video), Paraclete, 1989.

The Nazarene, Servant Publications (Ann Arbor, MI), 1991.

Parables: Poking Holes in Religious Balloons, Creation House, 1991.

Summer of Miracles, Creation House, 1991.

Look out World—I'm Me, Creation House, 1993.

Contributor to books, including *Rebels in the Church,* edited by Ben Johnson, Word, Inc., 1971; and *I Laugh . . . I Cry . . . ,* by Don Paulk, Kingdom Publishers, 1987. Author of regular column, "The Last Word," *Logos Journal,* beginning 1972, and column in *Charisma;* editorial

columnist, *Vero Beach Journal* and *National Courier.* Contributor of over one hundred articles to national periodicals, including *Church Administration, Lutheran Standard,* and *Orlando Sentinel.* Roving editor, *Guideposts,* 1972-74; executive editor, *Logos Journal,* beginning 1975; editor for *Ministry Today.*

SIDELIGHTS: James Buckingham once told *CA* that he "has spent time in the Amazon jungles, behind the Iron Curtain, the islands of the South Pacific, the Orient, and into the Himalayas—collecting research for books and carrying the good news of the move of God as well."

OBITUARIES:

PERIODICALS

New York Times, February 24, 1992, p. B10.*

*   *   *

BUCKINGHAM, Jamie
    See BUCKINGHAM, James (William)

*   *   *

BUCKLEY, Anthony D.   1945-

PERSONAL: Born July 3, 1945, in Castleford, Yorkshire, England; son of John K. (a printer) and Kathleen (a teacher; maiden name, Beaumont) Buckley; married Linda J. Roberts (a teacher), July 8, 1966; children: Thomas John, Benjamin David, Samuel James Edgar, Daniel Robert Francis. *Education:* University of York, B.A. (with honors), 1967; University of Leicester, M.A., 1968; attended University of Ibadan, 1969-71, and Queen's University, Belfast, 1973-75; University of Birmingham, Ph.D., 1982. *Religion:* Atheist.

ADDRESSES: Home—4 Church Ave., Holywood, County Down, Northern Ireland. *Office*—Ulster Folk and Transport Museum, Cultra Manor, Holywood, County Down, Northern Ireland.

CAREER: History teacher at school in Isle of Sheppey, Kent, England, 1971-73; Ulster Folk and Transport Museum, Holywood, Northern Ireland, research anthropologist, 1975—. Organizer of museum exhibitions in Northern Ireland, "Brotherhoods in Ireland," 1986, and "Remembering 1690," 1990.

MEMBER: Royal Anthropological Institute, Association of Social Anthropologists, Anthropological Association of Ireland (chair, 1994—).

AWARDS, HONORS: Leverhulme scholar in Nigeria, 1969-71; Dr. John Kirk Essay Prize from Society for Folklife Studies, 1985, for article "The Chosen Few: Biblical Texts in the Regalia of an Ulster Secret Society"; Amaury Talbot Prize for African Anthropology from Amaury Talbot Trust, 1985, for *Yoruba Medicine.*

WRITINGS:

A Gentle People: A Study of a Peaceful Community in Northern Ireland, Ulster Folk and Transport Museum, 1982.
Yoruba Medicine, Oxford University Press, 1985.
(With M. C. Kenney) *Negotiating Identity: Rhetoric and Social Drama in Northern Ireland,* Smithsonian Institution Press (Washington, DC), 1995.

Contributor to anthropology, folklore, and sociology journals.

WORK IN PROGRESS: Research on the fraternal societies, the religious life, and the social structure of Northern Ireland.

SIDELIGHTS: Anthony D. Buckley once told *CA:* "My book *Yoruba Medicine* arose from research I did in Nigeria, where I spent two years discussing the opinions of a small handful of traditional healers. I found that these men employed a germ theory to explain the ailments of the body, as well as elaborate pharmacopeia to kill the germs and drive them from the body. Whereas European theory regards germs as harmful agents waiting to invade the body, Yoruba thought sees them as beneficial until, because of the bad habits of their owner, 'they overflow the bag [in the body] where God has placed them.' Though Yoruba herbalists do have 'magical' practices, their work is primarily an attempt to cure diseases that is based upon a rational understanding of the human body.

"Since 1975, I have been an anthropologist at the Ulster Folk and Transport Museum. Here I have made studies of both Protestant and Catholic communities, as well as studies of unofficial healing, fundamentalist religion, the marching tradition, and secret and fraternal societies.

"I have been struck with the way that even the most serious elements in everyday Ulster life are permeated by playfulness. This is true, for example, in the rituals of the Orange and Black Institutions which express through biblical imagery the political and religious concerns of many modern Ulster Protestants. In this strife-torn country, I have been led to doubt the reality of its so-called 'two cultural traditions.' And I have found it necessary to try to explain the paradoxical co-existence of bitter sectarian hostility with friendly good-neighborliness often across the 'sectarian divide.'"

Buckley more recently told *CA* that his book *Negotiating Identity: Rhetoric and Social Drama in Northern Ireland,* written jointly with M. C. Kenney, "concerns the way that

individuals describe and dramatize their identities through social drama including play, secular and religious ritual, rioting, etc."

BIOGRAPHICAL/CRITICAL SOURCES:

PERIODICALS

Times Literary Supplement, January 10, 1986.

*   *   *

BUECHNER, Thomas S(charman)   1926-

PERSONAL: Born September 25, 1926, in New York, NY; son of Thomas S. (an advertising executive) and Anne (Lines) Buechner; married Mary Hawkins, September 15, 1949; children: Barbara, Thomas Jr., Matthew. *Education:* Princeton University, 1944; attended Art Students League, 1946; L'Ecoles des Beaux Arts at Fontainebleau and Paris, 1947-48; Institute Voor Pictologie, 1948.

ADDRESSES: Home—11 North Road, Corning, NY 14830.

CAREER: Compania ed Formento, San Juan, PR, designer, 1946. Metropolitan Museum of Art, New York City, assistant manager of display department, 1949-50, 1975-80; Corning Museum of Glass, Corning, NY, director, 1950-60, president, 1971-86; Corning Community College, head of art department, 1958-60; Brooklyn Museum, Brooklyn, NY, director, 1960-71; Steuben Glass, New York City, vice president, 1971-73, president, 1973-82, chair, 1982-85; Corning Glass Works Foundation, chair, 1971-86; director, Corning International Corporation, 1971-75; member of board of trustees, Louis C. Tiffany Foundation, 1972—, Corning Glass Works, vice-president and director of cultural affairs, 1985-86. Portrait and landscape painter; one-man shows: Adler Gallery, 1982, 1984, Arnot Art Museum, 1985, OK Harris, 1992, 1994.

MEMBER: Royal Society of Art (fellow), American Association of Museums (member of council, 1969), National Collection of Fine Arts (member of advisory board, 1971-89), Board of Overseers of Parsons School of Design, Shelbourne Museum Board of Trustees, Lawrenceville School Board of Trustees, Save Venice Inc. Board of Trustees, The Century Association.

AWARDS, HONORS: Man of the Year award from Brooklyn College, City University of New York, 1965; Forsythia award from Brooklyn Botanic Garden, 1971; Gari Melchers Medal from American Artist Fellows, 1971.

WRITINGS:

Frederick Carder: His Life and Work, Corning Museum of Glass (Corning, NY), 1952.

(Editor with Axel Von Saldern) *Brooklyn Museum Handbook,* Brooklyn Museum, 1967.

Norman Rockwell: Artist and Illustrator, Abrams (New York City), 1970.

The Norman Rockwell Treasury, Galahad (New York), 1979.

(Illustrator) *Field Studies,* [Rockwell, NY], 1991.

(With others) *Stanislav Libensky and Jaroslava Brychtova: A 40-Year Collaboration in Glass,* Preface, 1994.

Also author of *Glass Vessels in Dutch Painting of the Seventeenth Century,* 1952, *Guide to the Collections of the Corning Museum of Glass,* 1955, *Arts of David Levine,* 1979, and *Ogden Pleissner,* 1984. Contributor to *Encyclopaedia Britannica, Hisperia, Interiorsu, Life, Museum News, Antiques, Archaeology, Art News, Connoisseur, New York Review of Books* and *Design.* Author of numerous catalogues, monographs, and histories for Corning Glass Works and Brooklyn Museums.

BIOGRAPHICAL/CRITICAL SOURCES:

PERIODICALS

American Artist, November, 1971, p. 64.
Booklist, January 15, 1971, p. 393.
Choice, February, 1971, p. 1635.
New York Herald Tribune, August 4, 1960.
New York Times Book Review, December 6, 1970, p. 2.
Time, December 14, 1970, p. 92.

*   *   *

BUELL, Lawrence   1939-

PERSONAL: Born June 11, 1939, in Bryn Mawr, PA; son of C. A. (a business executive) and Marjorie (Henderson) Buell; married Phyllis Kimber (an educational administrator), August 18, 1962; children: Denise, Deirdre. *Education:* Princeton University, B.A., 1961; Cornell University, M.A., 1963, Ph.D., 1966. *Avocational interests:* Sports, reading.

ADDRESSES: Office—Department of English, Oberlin College, Oberlin, OH 44074.

CAREER: Tunghai University, Taichung, Taiwan, instructor in English, 1963-65; Oberlin College, Oberlin, OH, assistant professor, 1966-72, associate professor, 1972-77, professor of English, 1977—. Chair of the board of trustees of Oberlin Shansi Memorial Association, 1972-74, trustee, 1974—.

WRITINGS:

Design of Literature, Pendulum Press (West Haven, CO), 1973.

Literary Transcendentalism, Cornell University Press (Ithaca, NY), 1973.

New England Literary Culture: From the Revolution to the Renaissance, Cambridge University Press (New York City), 1986, revised edition, 1989.

(Editor) *Ralph Waldo Emerson: A Collection of Critical Essays,* Prentice-Hall (Englewood Cliffs, NJ), 1992.

Contributor of articles to professional journals.*

*   *   *

BURG, Dale R(onda)   1942-

PERSONAL: Born April 27, 1942, in Valley Stream, NY; daughter of Sylvan A. (an attorney) and Miriam (an actress and writer; maiden name, Layn) Burg; married Richard Nusser; children: Alden Fitzpatrick. *Education:* Brown University, A.B., 1962; Cornell University, M.A., 1964.

ADDRESSES: Office—130 West 57th St., New York, NY 10019.

CAREER: Leo Burnett, television production assistant, 1964; Columbia Artists Management, member of press and promotion department, 1964-67; Gimbels Theatre Club, administration assistant, 1967; APA-Phoenix Repertory Co., administration assistant, 1967-70; Abby Hirsch Public Relations, publicist, 1970-72; Columbia Pictures Industries, New York City, manager of corporate communications, 1972-83, and director of television writers' workshop; freelance writer, 1983—. Instructor at New York University, 1979-81, and at the New School for Social Research, New York City, 1984.

MEMBER: Writers Guild of America (East), Women in Film.

WRITINGS:

(With Abby Hirsch) *The Great Carmen Miranda Look-Alike Contest & Other Bold-Faced Lies* (nonfiction), St. Martin's (New York City), 1974.

(With Mary Ellen Pinkham) *Mary Ellen's Help Yourself Diet Plan,* St. Martin's, 1974.

How to Help the One You Love Stop Drinking, Putnam (New York City), 1986.

Clean House!, Crown (New York City), 1994.

What's Stopped Happening To Me?, Citadel (Secaucus, NJ), 1994.

How to Mom, Dell (New York City), 1995.

Writer for Columbia Broadcasting System (CBS) and National Broadcasting Company (NBC). Author of columns with Mary Ellen Pinkham, "Mary Ellen Says," in *Woman's Day*, 1984—, and "Mary Ellen," in *Star*, 1988—. Also contributor to numerous periodicals, including *Working Woman, Cosmopolitan, Glamour, Family Circle, Ladies Home Journal, Village Voice,* and *New Woman.*

WORK IN PROGRESS: Writing nonfiction.

SIDELIGHTS: Dale R. Burg once told *CA:* "Through years of public relations work in the entertainment field (much of it prior to my long association with Columbia Pictures), I met editors who commissioned my earliest and very occasional pieces—generally humorous, first-person essays. When I observed someone reading—and laughing aloud at—my first published piece in the *Village Voice,* I had a wonderful sense of accomplishment, and I prefer writing light pieces though most of the time the words don't come easily.

"Ghost-writing for Mary Ellen Pinkham, the helpful hints expert who sold millions of her reference books, proved a breakthrough in my career. Sometimes it's odd to be ghost-writing humor (I wonder how many others have such a job!), but I love the chance to do humorous essays on a regular basis (as in the *Star*).

"I think humorists are observers of life, unlike fiction writers, who are *storytellers,* and I envy people who can spin a good yarn, while I appreciate being able to 'get the laugh' (and I enjoy collaborating with storytellers in script form). My greatest moments in front of the word processor are the ones when a joke comes so suddenly and unexpectedly it makes *me* laugh out loud. There are a very few consistently good humor writers out there, conspicuously Dave Barry, Marcelle Clements, and Wendy Wasserstein."

*   *   *

BURIAN, Richard M(artin) 1941-

PERSONAL: Born September 14, 1941, in Hanover, NH; son of Hermann M. (an ophthalmologist) and Gladys (Hart) Burian; married Linda Wilmeth, June 8, 1983 (divorced); married F. M. Anne McNabb, June 26, 1987; children: (first marriage) David, Laura; Derek McNabb (stepson). *Education:* Reed College, B.A., 1963; University of Pittsburgh, Ph.D., 1971. *Politics:* Democrat.

ADDRESSES: Home—1002 Eheart St., Blacksburg, VA 24060. *Office*—Center for the Study of Science in Society, Virginia Polytechnic Institute and State University, Blacksburg, VA 24061-0247.

CAREER: Brandeis University, Waltham, MA, assistant professor of philosophy, 1967-76, associate dean of col-

lege, 1973-76; Drexel University, Philadelphia, PA, associate professor of philosophy, 1977-83; Virginia Polytechnic Institute and State University, Blacksburg, VA, professor of philosophy and head of department, 1983-92, professor of science studies and philosophy and director of Center for the Study of Science in Society, 1992—. Assistant professor at Florida Agricultural and Mechanical University, 1968-69; research associate at Museum of Comparative Zoology, Harvard University, 1976-77; visiting associate professor at University of Pittsburgh, 1978, and University of California, Davis, 1982.

MEMBER: American Association for the Advancement of Science, American Philosophical Association (chair of program committee of Eastern Division, 1984), American Society of Zoologists (program officer, Division of History and Philosophy of Biology, 1993), Philosophy of Science Association (member of executive committee, 1984-88; chair of program committee, 1992-94), History of Science Society, Society for Social Studies of Science, Federation of American Scientists, Genetics Society of America, Society for the Study of Evolution, Society of Systematic Zoology, Sigma Xi.

AWARDS, HONORS: Fellow of American Council of Learned Societies, 1976-77, National Science Foundation, 1984, and National Humanities Center, 1991-92; grants from National Endowment for the Humanities, 1979 and 1985-87.

WRITINGS:

(Editor with Robert N. Brandon) *Genes, Organisms, Populations: Controversies over the Units of Selection,* MIT Press (Cambridge, MA), 1985.
(Editor with J. Margolis and M. Krausz) *Rationality, Relativism and the Human Sciences,* Nijhoff (Dordrecht), 1986.

Contributor to numerous books, including *The Sociobiology Debate,* edited by A. Caplan, Harper (New York City), 1978; *Scientific Discovery, Logic and Rationality,* D. Reidel, 1980; *Dimensions of Darwinism,* edited by Margorie Grene, Cambridge University Press (New York City), 1983; *The New Biology and the New Philosophy of Science,* edited by D. Depew and Bruce Weber, MIT Press, 1985; *Evolutionary Biology at the Crossroads,* Queen's College Press (Flushing, NY), 1989; *A Conceptual History of Embryology,* edited by Jean Gayon and Doris Zallen, Plenum Press (New York City), 1991; and *Keywords in Evolutionary Biology,* edited by E. F. Keller and E. A. Lloyd, Harvard University Press (Cambridge, MA), 1992.

Coeditor of monograph series "History and Philosophy of Biology," Oxford University Press (New York City). Contributor to numerous biology and philosophy journals, including *Philosophical Forum, Evolutionary Biology, Genet-*

ics, and *Biology and Philosophy.* Associate editor, *Perspectives on Science: Historical, Philosophical, Social,* 1993—. Member of editorial boards of *Biology and Philosophy, Journal of the History of Biology, History and Philosophy of the Life Sciences,* and *Philosophy of Science.*

WORK IN PROGRESS: Handling Heredity: A Century of Heredity in French Biology (with Gayon and Zallen); chapters for books, including *The Evolution of Theodosius Dobzhansky, Natural History and Evolution of an Animal Society: The Paper Wasp Case, History of Genetics,* and *New Perspectives on the History and Philosophy of Molecular Biology;* numerous papers and articles for journals.

SIDELIGHTS: Richard M. Burian once told *CA:* "My deepest interest is to develop a comparative analysis of the ways in which different sciences make progress. As a philosopher, my concern is triple. I want to learn the distinctive features (if any) of scientific knowledge; I want to understand the interaction of different traditions, a phenomenon which takes place frequently in science, though it is seldom recognized or understood; and I want to locate the particular ways of thinking that have proved important in the context of contemporary biology within a larger cultural and historical matrix."

Reviewing the book *Genes, Organisms, Populations: Controversies over the Units of Selection* for the *Times Literary Supplement,* Lary Shaffer observed that Burian and his collaborator "have edited a splendid volume" examining "the evolutionary importance of the level at which [natural selection] occurs."

BIOGRAPHICAL/CRITICAL SOURCES:

BOOKS

Callebant, Werner, *Taking the Naturalistic Turn, or How Real Philosophy of Science Is Done,* Chicago University Press, 1993.

PERIODICALS

Times Literary Supplement, January 18, 1985.

*   *   *

BURKE, David 1927-

PERSONAL: Born May 17, 1927, in Melbourne, Australia; son of John William (an accountant) and Gertrude Olive (an opera singer; maiden name, Davies) Burke; married Helen Patricia Wane (a journalist), March 5, 1957 (marriage ended February, 1985); married Catherine Stephen (a librarian), August, 1988; children: Mary, Anne, Margaret, Jane, Julia. *Education:* Attended school in South Brisbane, Queensland, Australia.

ADDRESSES: Home—Sydney, Australia. *Office*—P.O. Box 82, Mosman, New South Wales 2088, Australia.

CAREER: Worked as radio scriptwriter and production assistant, Melbourne, Australia, 1948-50; *Melbourne Herald-Sun,* Melbourne, reporter, feature writer, and sub-editor, 1950-56; *Sydney Morning Sun-Herald,* Sydney, Australia, reporter and feature writer, 1956-62; freelance author, 1965—; has also worked for Victorian Railways and in public relations.

MEMBER: Royal Australian Historical Society, Australian Railway Historical Society, Rail Transport Museum, Australian Society of Authors, Antarctic Society.

WRITINGS:

(With C. C. Singleton) *Railways of Australia,* Angus & Robertson (London), 1963.
Monday at McMurdo (novel), Muller, 1967.
Come Midnight Monday (juvenile), illustrations by J. Mare, Methuen (New York City), 1976.
Great Steam Trains of Australia, Rigby (Australia), 1978.
Darknight (novel), Methuen, 1979.
Observer's Book of Steam Locomotives of Australia, Methuen, 1979.
Full Steam across the Mountains, illustrations by Phil Belbin, Methuen, 1981.
Changing Trains, Methuen, 1982.
Kings of the Iron Horse (biography), Methuen, 1985.
Mary Ward, Then and Now (30-minute video program), Loreto, Kirribilli (Australia), 1985.
Man of Steam (biography), Iron Horse Press (Australia), 1986.
With Iron Rails (history of the New South Wales Railways), New South Wales University Press, 1988.
Road through the Wilderness, New South Wales University Press, 1991.
Moments of Terror: A History of Antarctic Aviation, New South Wales University Press, 1993.
The World of Betsey Throsby (versional history), illustrations by Anne Ferguson, Kerever Park, 1994.

ADAPTATIONS: Come Midnight Monday was adapted for television and produced as a seven-episode serial by the Australian Broadcasting Commission, first broadcast in 1982.

WORK IN PROGRESS: A social history of Sydney, Australia and its transport modes in the late nineteenth century; a musical based on the last expedition of Captain Scott to South Pole.

SIDELIGHTS: David Burke once told *CA:* "I regard myself as a general freelance writer, but my lifelong interest in railroads has led me to study the history of various Australian railways and their impact on the social and economic development of Australia. I tend to alternate between fact and fiction in my writing. I am almost constantly doing research at national and state libraries, archives, etc., and I maintain comprehensive files."

Burke explained to *CA*: "My parallel interest is studying the history of Antarctic exploration, including research accomplished during three assignments in Antarctica. My recent book *Moments of Terror: A History of Antarctic Aviation* has been published simultaneously in Australia, United States, and the United Kingdom."

*   *   *

BURNS, Hobert Warren 1925-

PERSONAL: Born October 13, 1925, in Los Angeles, CA; son of Hobert Washington and Rebecca (Price) Burns; married Patricia Rowe, 1954; children: Carol, Janifer, Charles. *Education:* Menlo Junior College (now Menlo College), A.A., 1948; Stanford University, A.B., 1950, A.M., 1951, Ed.D., 1957.

ADDRESSES: Home—1527 Waverley St., Palo Alto, CA 94301.

CAREER: History teacher in Burbank, CA, 1951-53, and in Palo Alto, CA, 1953-57; Rutgers University, New Brunswick, NJ, assistant professor of philosophy of education, 1957-60; Syracuse University, Syracuse, NY, associate professor and chairman, area of cultural foundations of education, 1960-63; Hofstra University, Hempstead, NY, professor of education and dean of School of Education, 1963-66; San Jose State University, San Jose, CA, professor of philosophy and academic vice president, 1967-83, acting president, 1969-70; Sonoma State University, Rohnert Park, CA, interim president, 1983-84. Fulbright professor of sociology, University of Chile, 1959; visiting professor at Universidad Technica de Santa Maria, 1960, University of Hawaii, 1962, University of Southern California, 1963, and University of California at Los Angeles, 1966; J. Richard Street Lecturer, Syracuse University, 1963. Advisor and consultant to numerous educational organizations.

MEMBER: Phi Beta Kappa, Phi Delta Kappa.

AWARDS, HONORS: Trustees' citation for academic excellence, Hofstra University, 1966; Distinguished Alumni Award, Menlo College, 1969.

WRITINGS:

The Critical Incident Technique as an Instrument of Educational Research: A Philosophic Analysis, School of Education and the Graduate School, Stanford University (Stanford, CA), 1957.

(Editor with C. W. Scott and C. M. Hill) *The Great Debate: Our Schools in Crisis,* Prentice-Hall (Englewood Cliffs, NJ), 1959.
(Author and editor with C. J. Brauner) *Essays in the Philosophy of Education,* Association Press (Syracuse, NY), 1961.
(Author and editor with Brauner) *Philosophy of Education: Essays and Commentaries,* Ronald, 1962.
(Editor) *Education and the Development of Nations,* Center for Development Education, Syracuse University (Syracuse), 1963.
(Editor) *Sociological Backgrounds of Adult Education,* Center for the Study of Liberal Education for Adults (Chicago), 1964.

Contributor to books, including *Education: Intellectual, Moral, Physical,* University of Pennsylvania Press, 1961; *Contemporary Issues Here and Abroad,* University of Pennsylvania Press, 1963; *Education in Comparative and International Perspectives,* Holt, 1971. Contributor to *Saturday Review, Philosophy of Science, Educational Forum,* and other periodicals. Also author of numerous pamphlets on education topics. Member of editorial board, *Studies in Philosophy and Education,* 1960-64; academic editor, Prentice-Hall "Foundations of Education" paperback series.

WORK IN PROGRESS: An Introduction to Symbolic Logic with Lucius R. Eastman, Jr.; *Language and Logic: The Art of Reasoning.*

*   *   *

BUSCHKUEHL, Matthias 1953-

PERSONAL: Surname is pronounced "bush-cool"; born April 28, 1953, in Hamburg, West Germany (now Germany); son of Hans Alfred (a teacher) and Katharina Maria (a teacher; maiden name, Mausolf) Buschkuehl. *Education:* University of Hamburg, Ph.D., 1979. *Politics:* Conservative (Christlich-Soziale Union, Bavarian Christian Democrat). *Religion:* Roman Catholic. *Avocational interests:* Jujitsu, travel, dance floor music, video clips, films not produced in Hollywood, and languages.

ADDRESSES: Home—Pfahlstrasse 17a, D-85072, Eichstaett, West Germany. *Office*—Universitaetsbibliothek Eichstaett, Am Hofgarten 1, D-85072 Eichstaett, West Germany.

CAREER: State Library of Prussian Cultural Resources, West Berlin, Germany, library assistant, 1979-81; Catholic University of Eichstaett, University Library, Eichstaett, West Germany, subject librarian and head of theology library, 1981-92, head of library of Munich branch, 1986—, head of manuscripts department, 1992—.

MEMBER: American Catholic Historical Association, Verein Deutscher Bibliothekare.

WRITINGS:

IN GERMAN

Die irische, schottische, und roemische Frage: Disraeli's Schluesselroman "Lothair" (1870) (title means "The Irish, Scottish, and Roman Question: Disraeli's Key Novel *Lothair* (1870)"), EOS (St. Ottilien, West Germany), 1980.

Heilige Schrift, Konnersreuth, Widerstand (title means "Sacred Scripture, Konnersreuth, Resistance"), University of Eichstaett, 1982.

(With Bernhard Stasiewski) *Seminar und Hochschule in Eichstaett unter dem Nationalsozialismus* (title means "Seminary and University in Eichstaett Under Nazism"), University of Eichstaett, 1984.

Franz Xaver Mayr, University of Eichstaett, 1987.

Missionsgeschichte der Oosterinsel (title means "Mission History of Easter Island"), University of Eichstaett, 1988.

Die Bibliothek Michael Glossner (title means "The Library of Michael Glossner"), Harrassowitz (Wiesbaden, West Germany), 1991.

Michael Glossner und die Theologie seiner Zeit (title means "Michael Glossner and the Theology of His Times"), University of Eichstaett, 1992.

Joseph Lechner, University of Eichstaett, 1993.

OTHER

Great Britain and the Holy See, 1746-1870, Irish Academic Press, 1982.

Contributor to *Bibliotheksforum Bayern, Catholic Historical Review, Annuarium Historiae Conciliorum.*

SIDELIGHTS: Matthias Buschkuehl once told *CA:* "During my grammar school days I had already begun to acquire a special fondness for Cardinal Newman, and during long stays in Croydon, Dublin, Oxford, and Edinburgh my interest grew to include English, Irish, and Scottish Roman Catholic theology and church history. In addition to my Jesuit education, a special influence in my academic life was my supervisor at the University of Hamburg, Professor Ludwig Borinski, who has worked on British history. My travels and my education contributed to a non-Anglo-Saxon point of view and to a conservative stand. I write in opposition to the predominant trend of historiography, which in 1994 is biased in favor of those who were in power in state and press."

BIOGRAPHICAL/CRITICAL SOURCES:

PERIODICALS

Times Literary Supplement, March 23, 1984.

BUSH, L(uther) Russ(ell III) 1944-

PERSONAL: Born December 25, 1944, in Alexandria, LA; son of Luther Russell, Jr. (a dentist) and Sara Frances (a bookseller and artist; maiden name, Warnock) Bush; married Cynthia Ellen McGraw (a teacher, floral designer, and decorative consultant), June 2, 1968; children: Joshua Russell, Bethany Charis. *Education:* Mississippi College, B.A., 1967; Southwestern Baptist Theological Seminary, M.Div., 1970, Ph.D., 1975. *Religion:* Southern Baptist.

ADDRESSES: Office—Southeastern Baptist Theological Seminary, Box 1889, Wake Forest, NC 27588.

CAREER: Southwestern Baptist Theological Seminary, Fort Worth, TX, instructor, 1973-75, assistant professor, 1975-83, associate professor of philosophy of religion, 1983-89; Southeastern Baptist Theological Seminary, Wake Forest, NC, professor of philosophy of religion, vice president for academic affairs, and dean of the faculty, 1989—.

MEMBER: American Academy of Religion, Evangelical Philosophical Society (regional president, 1983-85), Evangelical Theological Society (regional president, 1982-83; national president, 1993-94), Society of Biblical Literature, Society of Christian Philosophers.

WRITINGS:

(With Tom J. Nettles) *Baptists and the Bible* (a study in Baptist historical theology), Moody, 1980.

(Editor) *Classical Readings in Christian Apologetics, A.D. 100-1800,* Zondervan, 1983.

Style and Study (a manual), Alpha Graphics, 1978, 3rd edition, 1983.

A Handbook for Christian Philosophy, Zondervan, 1991.

Also author of *The Bible: God's Fertile Ground,* 1987. Contributor to *Southwestern Journal of Theology, Light, Criswell Theological Review,* and *Faith and Mission.*

WORK IN PROGRESS: A book discussing science and scripture; a book analyzing twentieth-century popular culture.

SIDELIGHTS: L. Russ Bush once told *CA:* "I grew up in an atmosphere of active interest in Southern Baptist affairs (my families on both sides were church leaders) and have always sought to serve my denomination with integrity and loyalty. I was conscious of denominational activities even as a young man and often attended convention meetings at the state and national levels.

"The earliest ideas for *Baptists and the Bible* trace their roots to 'talking theology' with co-author Tom Nettles and other friends during college and seminary days. We all heard statements to the effect that Baptists had never held to the theory of biblical inerrancy and that such ideas were a new innovation among Baptist theologians. We discussed the whole range of theological and biblical questions that arise in the course of a professional theological education, but underneath them all we came to realize the foundational importance of the issue of the extent of scriptural dependability. The coming of Tom Nettles to teach church history at Southwestern allowed the two of us to pursue our long interest in writing a history of the doctrine that seemed to underlie this major denominational concern.

"My interest in philosophy and apologetic reasoning has often directed my academic research, as in collecting the group of readings that make up my published work on the subject of Christian apologetics, and led to my *A Handbook for Christian Philosophy*. College work in the natural sciences fueled my interest in the relationship between science and religion, and most of my first sabbatic year was spent in Cambridge, England, studying that question. My second sabbatical in Washington, DC, focused on these same concerns. Other apologetic emphases show up in my academic papers, class lectures, and in manuscripts awaiting publication.

"Moving directly from college to seminary and from seminary into teaching as a career, I have found to my surprise that many of us do not understand the teaching profession. I always thought it was the student who had to do all the work and that the professor just magically appeared in the classroom each day full of wit, wisdom, and knowledge that somehow just overflowed from his mind. That notion, however, proved to be wrong—teaching is like swimming: you can't do much of it unless you get all the way into the water.

"I'm a busy person, but I hate routine. I love to read, and I love to write. My fear is that I will waste away my most productive years by succumbing to the depressing debilitation of academic routine and busywork. It is so easy to fail to reach the important goals in life. Somehow we must disengage ourselves from the 'urgent' and seek that which matters."

C

CALDER, Jason
See DUNMORE, John

*   *   *

CAMPTON, David   1924-

PERSONAL: Born June 5, 1924, in Leicester, England; son of David (a hairdresser) and Emily (Holmes) Campton. *Religion:* Independent.

ADDRESSES: Home—35 Liberty Rd., Glenfield, Leicester LE3 8JF, England. *Agent*—ACTAC, 15 High St., Ramsbury, Wiltshire, England.

CAREER: City of Leicester Education Department, Leicester, England, clerk, 1941-49; East Midlands Gas Board, Leicester, clerk, 1949-56; Studio Theatre Ltd., London, England, theater manager, 1959; Theatre in the Round Ltd., Scarborough, England, manager, 1963. Professional actor, 1957—, with Theatre in the Round Ltd., 1958-63. *Military service:* Royal Air Force, 1942-45; Fleet Air Arm, 1945-46.

MEMBER: League of Dramatists, Writers Guild of Great Britain.

AWARDS, HONORS: Bursary for playwriting, Arts Council of Great Britain, 1957; British Theatre Association Award, 1975, for *Everybody's Friend,* 1978, for *After Midnight, before Dawn,* and 1985, for *Mrs. Meadowsweet;* Japan Prize, 1978, for *Deep Blue Sea?*

WRITINGS:

PLAYS

Going Home (produced in Leicester, England, 1950), Abel Heywood, 1951.
Honeymoon Express (produced in Leicester, 1951), Abel Heywood, 1951.

Change Partners (produced in Leicester, 1952), Abel Heywood, 1951.
Sunshine on the Righteous (produced in Leicester, 1953), Rylee, 1952.
The Laboratory (produced in Leicester, 1954), J. Garnet Miller, 1955, Dramatic Publishing, 1975.
Dragons Are Dangerous, produced in Scarborough, England, 1955.
The Cactus Garden (produced in Reading, England, 1955), J. Garnet Miller, 1967.
Doctor Alexander, Campton, 1956.
(With Stephen Joseph) *Idol in the Sky,* produced in Scarborough, 1956.
Cuckoo Song, Campton, 1956.
Getting and Spending (also see below), produced in Scarborough, 1957.
A Smell of Burning (also see below), produced in Boston, MA, 1958.
Then . . . , (also see below), produced in Boston, 1958.
Memento Mori (also see below), produced in Boston, 1958.
Roses Round the Door (produced as *Ring of Roses* in Scarborough, 1958), J. Garnet Miller, 1967.
Frankenstein: The Gift of Fire (based on a novel by Mary Shelly; produced in Scarborough, 1959; also see below), J. Garnet Miller, 1973.
The Lunatic View: A Comedy of Menace (contains *Getting and Spending, A Smell of Burning,* and *Then . . . , Memento Mori* [also see below]), Studio Theatre, 1960, published as *'A Smell of Burning' and 'Then . . . ,'* Dramatists Play Service, 1971.
At Sea (also see below), produced in Newcastle under Lyme, England, 1960.
Four Minute Warning (includes *Little Brother, Little Sister* [also see below], *Mutatis Mutandis* [also see below], *Soldier from the Wars Returning* [also see below], and *At Sea*), four volumes, Campton, 1960.

Funeral Dance (produced in Dovercourt, England, 1960), J. Garnet Miller, 1962.

Mutatis Mutandis (produced in London, 1972; also see below), Campton, 1960.

Soldier from the Wars Returning (produced in London, 1961; also see below), Campton, 1960.

Little Brother, Little Sister (produced in London, 1966; also see below), Campton, 1960.

The Girls and the Boys, produced in Scarborough, 1961.

On Stage: Containing Seventeen Sketches and One Monologue (includes *Service* [produced, March, 1961], and *Table Talk* [produced, April, 1961]), J. Garnet Miller, 1964.

Passport to Florence (produced as *Stranger in the Family* in Scarborough, 1961), J. Garnet Miller, 1967.

Silence on the Battlefield (produced in Dovercourt, 1961; also see below), J. Garnet Miller, 1967.

Usher (based on a story by Edgar Allan Poe; produced in Scarborough, 1962; produced in London, 1974; also see below), J. Garnet Miller, 1973.

Incident (produced, 1962; also see below), J. Garnet Miller, 1967.

Comeback, produced in Scarborough, 1963, revised version produced as *Honey, I'm Home* in Leatherhead, England, 1964.

Don't Wait for Me, produced in London, 1963, published in *Worth a Hearing: A Collection of Radio Plays,* Blackie & Son, 1967.

Dead and Alive (produced in Scarborough, 1964), J. Garnet Miller, 1983.

Cock and Bull Story, produced in Scarborough, 1965.

Little Brother, Little Sister, and Out of the Flying Pan, Methuen, 1966, Dramatists Play Service, 1970.

Split down the Middle (produced in Scarborough, 1966), J. Garnet Miller, 1973.

Two Leaves and a Stalk (produced, 1967; also see below), J. Garnet Miller, 1967.

More Sketches, Campton, 1967.

Ladies Night: Four Plays for Women (contains *Two Leaves and a Stalk, Silence on the Battlefield, Incident* [also see below], and *The Manipulator* [also see below]), J. Garnet Miller, 1967.

The Manipulator (produced, 1968; shortened version produced as *A Point of View,* 1964; also see below), J. Garnet Miller, 1967.

On Stage Again: Containing Fourteen Sketches and Two Monologues, J. Garnet Miller, 1969.

The Right Place, produced, 1970, published in *Playbill One,* Hutchinson, 1969.

Laughter and Fear: 9 One-Act Plays (contains *Incident, Then . . . , Memento Mori, The End of the Picnic* (also see below), *The Laboratory, A Point of View, Soldier from the Wars Returning, Mutatis Mutandis,* and

Where Have All the Ghosts Gone?), Blackie & Son, 1969.

Resting Place (produced in London, 1969), Methuen, 1970.

The Life and Death of Almost Everybody (produced in London, 1970), Samuel French, 1972.

Wonderchick, produced in Bristol, England, 1970.

Time-sneeze: A Play (produced in London, 1970), Eyre Methuen, 1974.

A Tinkle of Tiny Bells, produced in Cumbernauld, England, 1971.

The Cagebirds (produced in Tunbridge Wells, England, 1971), Campton, 1972.

Jonah (produced in Chelmsford, England, 1971), J. Garnet Miller, 1972.

Us and Them, produced, 1972, published in *The Sixth Windmill Book of One-Act Plays,* Heinemann, 1972.

Come Back Tomorrow, Campton, 1972.

In Committee, Campton, 1972.

Angel Unwilling (produced, 1972), Campton, 1972.

Carmilla (based on a story by Joseph LeFanu; produced in Sheffield, England, 1972; also see below), J. Garnet Miller, 1973.

The End of the Picnic, produced in Vancouver, Canada, 1973.

Three Gothic Plays (contains *Frankenstein: The Gift of Fire, Usher,* and *Carmilla*), J. Garnet Miller, 1973.

Eskimos, produced in Horsham, England, 1973.

Relics (produced in Leicester, 1973), Evans, 1975.

An Outline of History, produced in Bishop Auckland, England, 1974.

Ragerbo!, produced in Peckleton, England, 1975.

George Davenport, The Wigston Highwayman, produced in Countesthorpe, England, 1975.

The Do-It-Yourself Frankenstein Outfit, produced in Birmingham, England, 1975, published in *The Eighth Windmill Book of One-Act Plays,* Heinemann, 1975, Samuel French, 1976.

Everybody's Friend (produced in Edinburgh, 1975), Evans, 1976, Samuel French, 1979.

What Are You Doing Here?, Samuel French, 1976.

No Go Area, Campton, 1976.

One Possessed, Campton, 1976.

Oh, Yes It Is, produced in Braunston, England, 1977.

Zodiac (produced in Melton Mowbray, England, 1977), Samuel French, 1979.

After Midnight, before Dawn (produced in Leicester, 1978), Samuel French, 1979.

The Great Little Tilley, produced in Nottingham, England, 1978.

Parcel, Samuel French, 1979.

Pieces of Campton Campton, 1979.

Who Calls? (produced in Dublin, Ireland, 1979), Samuel French, 1980.

Attitudes, Campton, 1980.

Dark Wings (produced in Leicester, 1980), Campton, 1981.

Starstation Freedom, produced in Leicester, 1981.

Two in the Corner, Campton, 1983.

Olympus, produced in Leicester, 1983.

But Not Here (produced in Leicester, 1983), Campton, 1984.

Mrs. Meadowsweet (produced in Ulverston, England, 1985), Samuel French, 1986.

Cards, Cups, and Crystal Ball (produced in Broadway, England, 1985), Campton, 1986.

Singing in the Wilderness, (produced in Leicester, 1985), Samuel French, 1986.

Our Branch in Brussels, Samuel French, 1986.

Can You Hear the Music?, Samuel French, 1988.

The Winter of 1917, Samuel French, 1989.

Smile, Samuel French, 1990.

Who's Been Sitting in My Chair?, Nimbus Press, 1992.

Becoming a Playwright, R. Hale, 1992.

Cuckoo Song, Nimbus Press, 1993.

Eskimos Provisioning, Nimbus Press, 1993.

Also author of plays *Come Christmas,* 1985, and *Simon Says . . . ,* 1986.

RADIO PLAYS

Kahani Apni Apni (serial), first broadcast on Radio Leicester, 1983.

Also author of other radio plays (some of which are based on or serve as the basis for his plays), including *A Tinkle of Tiny Bells,* 1963; *Don't Wait for Me,* 1963; *The Manipulator,* 1964; *Alison,* 1964; *Resting Place,* 1964; *End of the Picnic,* 1964; *Split down the Middle,* 1965; *Where Have All the Ghosts Gone?,* 1965; *Angel Unwilling,* 1967; *The Missing Jewel,* 1967; *Parcel,* 1968; *Boo!,* 1971; *Now You Know,* 1971; *Everybody's Friend,* 1974; *One Possessed,* 1977; *I'm Sorry, Mrs. Baxter,* 1977; *Our Friend Bimbo,* 1978; *Eskimos,* 1979; *Community,* 1979; *Peacock Feathers,* 1982; *Mrs. M.,* 1984; and *Cards, Cups, and Crystal Ball,* 1986. Author of scripts for *Inquiry* radio series, including *Holiday, As Others See Us, So You Think You're a Hero, We Did It for Laughs, Deep Blue Sea?, Isle of the Free, You Started It, Good Money, You're on Your Own, Mental Health, We Know What's Right, Tramps, Little Boy Lost, When the Wells Run Dry, Our Crowd, Nice Old Stick Really,* and *On the Rampage.*

OTHER

Also author of television scripts for *See What You Think, The Groves,* and *Starr Company* series, produced by the British Broadcasting Corporation. Work represented in numerous anthologies, including *Armada Sci-Fi #1,* Collins, 1975; *Space #3,* Abelard-Schuman, 1976; *Whispers*

One, Doubleday, 1977; *Space #6,* Hutchinson, 1980; *The Year's Best Horror Stories XI,* DAW Books, 1983; and *The Vampyre,* Beaver Books, 1986.

SIDELIGHTS: David Campton began his writing career, he once claimed, "shortly after I was first presented with a stick of chalk and a slate." He wrote some twenty plays before *Going Home* was accepted for publication in 1949.

In the late 1950s, Campton was one of a group of English playwrights, including Harold Pinter, Arnold Wesker, and John Arden, who were writing what became known as the Comedy of Menace. "The Comedy of Menace," David Thompson remarks in *Theatre Today,* "deals with a specific, more limited area [than does Theatre of the Absurd]. Its concern is with the kind of comic situation which makes one's nerves tingle because behind it lurks fear." Campton's plays were significantly different from those of his contemporaries, John Russell Taylor points out in *The Angry Theatre,* because they "do not only betoken a vague unease with things as they are, but show a social conscience worn unequivocally on their author's sleeve." "To my mind," Campton writes, "the Theatre of the Absurd is a weapon against complacency (which spreads like a malignant fungus)."

A primary concern of Campton's early comedies was the threat of a nuclear war. His *Then . . . ,* for example, is set after a nuclear holocaust which only two people have survived. The two survivors were the only ones to follow the government's advice to put a paper bag over their heads when the bombs exploded. Thompson finds that *Then . . . ,* captures "the sort of undefined fear which haunts our post-war world" and concludes that it "is a chilling little play, but at the same time a funny and rather touching one." Campton once told *CA* that "although not preoccupied with the Bomb to the extent that I may have appeared twenty years ago, I have by no means abandoned my social conscience. *Ragerbo!* and *Parcel,* for instance, are about the tendency to regard people as units rather than as human beings."

Since his early success with the Comedy of Menace, Campton has branched out to write plays for television, for radio, and for children and young adults. In these areas, too, he has been innovative in his approach. His *Timesneeze: A Play,* a play for young adult theater groups, stresses group involvement in the production. "The script is only the beginning," Campton writes in his introduction to the play, "and everyone—actors, producer, costume designers, scene painters, musicians, etc., etc., should add, and add, and add. If necessary, throw away the play we first thought of."

Doris M. Day comments in *Drama* that she finds Campton "a popular and prolific writer" whose "shorter one-act plays are the medium that have made a name and reputation" for him. And finally John Coleby concludes in another issue of *Drama* that "Campton is an established figure if still by no means an Establishment one."

BIOGRAPHICAL/CRITICAL SOURCES:

BOOKS

Campton, David, *Time-sneeze: A Play,* Eyre Methuen, 1974.

Driver, Christopher, *The Disarmers,* Hodder & Stoughton, 1964.

Joseph, Stephen, *Theatre in the Round,* Barrie & Rockliff, 1967.

Marowitz, Charles, and others, editors, *The Encore Reader,* Methuen, 1965.

Taylor, John Russell, *Anger and After,* Hill & Wang, 1962, revised edition published as *The Angry Theatre,* 1969.

Thompson, David, editor, *Theatre Today,* Longmans, Green, 1965.

Watson, Ian, *Conversations with Ayckbourn,* Macdonald Futura, 1981.

PERIODICALS

Drama, spring, 1967; summer, 1967; spring, 1968; winter, 1969; spring, 1970; autumn, 1972; autumn, 1974; autumn, 1976; spring, 1977; autumn, 1977; winter, 1979; January, 1980.

New York Times, April 12, 1969.

Times Literary Supplement, July 6, 1967.

*   *   *

CANIFF, Milton (Arthur)   1907-1988

PERSONAL: Surname is pronounced "can*iff* "; born February 28, 1907, in Hillsboro, OH; died of lung cancer, April 3 (one source says April 4), 1988, in New York, NY; son of John William (a printer) and Elizabeth (Burton) Caniff; married Esther Parsons, August 23, 1930. *Education:* Ohio State University, B.A. 1930.

CAREER: Journal Herald, Dayton, OH, staff artist, 1922-25; *Miami News,* Miami, OH, staff artist, summer, 1925; *Columbus Dispatch,* Columbus, OH, staff artist, 1925-32; Associated Press Feature Service, New York, NY, staff artist, 1932-34, creator of "Dickie Dare" and "The Gay Thirties" comic strips; creator of "Terry and the Pirates" comic strip, *Chicago Tribune,* and *New York News* Syndicate, 1934-46; creator of "Male Call" comic strip, syndicated in *Stars and Stripes* and other military newspapers during World War II; staff artist, and creator of "Steve Canyon" comic strip, Field Newspaper Syndicate, and King Features, 1947-1988. Artwork exhibited at institutions in the United States and abroad, including the Metropolitan Museum of Art, the Louvre Museum, and the Renoir Museum.

MEMBER: National Cartoonists Society (president, 1948-49; honorary chairman), National Press Club, National Aviation Club, Society of Illustrators, Arnold Air Society (honorary national commander), Players Club, Overseas Press Club (Palm Springs), Palm Springs Racquet Club, Dutch Treat Club.

AWARDS, HONORS: Reuben Award, National Cartoonists Society, 1946, 1972; honorary doctorate of law, Atlanta Law School, 1948; Sigma Delta Chi distinguished service award, 1950; Freedoms Foundation, award, 1950, certificate of merit, 1953, National Service Medal, 1967, for "creative editorials and cartoons which brilliantly espouse the precepts of human freedom," George Washington Honor Medal, 1969; Medal of Merit, U.S. Air Force Association, 1952; U.S. Treasury citation, 1953; Ohioana Career Medal, 1954; D.F.A., Rollins College (Florida), 1956; U.S. Air Force Exceptional Service Award, 1957; Ohio Governor's Award, 1957; Boy Scouts of America, Silver Beaver Award, 1960, Distinguished Eagle Award, 1969, Silver Buffalo Award, 1976; New York World's Fair Silver Medallion, 1964; National Cartoonists Society Golden Scroll, 1964; Goodwill Industries Award, 1965; New York Philanthropic League Award, 1965; Aerospace Education Council Award, 1966; named Man of the Year, U.S. Air Force Association, 1966; YMCA Service to Youth Award, 1966; first Elzie Segar Award, San Francisco Press Club, 1971; D.H.L., Ohio State University, 1974; Inkpot Award, 1974; Order of Constantine, Sigma Chi, 1976; Good Guy Award, American Legion, 1978; D.F.A., University of Dayton, 1979; the Milton Caniff Research Library established at Ohio State University, 1979; Spirit of American Enterprise Award, 1981; named to National Comic Strip Hall of Fame, 1981; named honorary member of the 8th Air Force Historical Society, 1987, for "Male Call" comic strip; Scroll of Merit, Dayton Art Institute; War Department citation for "Male Call"; Fourth Estate Award; received numerous awards from U.S. Air Force and other organizations for distinguished service.

WRITINGS:

April Kane and the Dragon Lady, Whitman, 1942.

Terry and the Pirates, Adapted from the Famous Comic Strip by Milton Caniff, Random House, 1946.

Milton Caniff's Steve Canyon, Golden Press, 1959.

COLLECTIONS OF COMIC STRIPS

Male Call by Milton Caniff: 112 of the GI Comic Strips by That Name, Featuring the Effortless War Activities of Miss Lace, Simon & Schuster, 1945, enlarged edition published as *Male Call: The First Complete Collection of the Uninhibited Adventures of Every GI's Dream Girl—Miss Lace,* Grosset, 1959.

Steve Canyon: Operation Convoy, Grosset, 1959.

Steve Canyon: Operation Eel Island, Grosset, 1959.

Steve Canyon: Operation Foo Ling, Grosset, 1959.

Steve Canyon: Operation Snowflower, Grosset, 1959.

Terry and the Pirates, Nostalgia Press, 1970.

Enter the Dragon Lady: From the 1936 Classic Newspaper Strip, Nostalgia Press, 1975.

Meet Burma, Nostalgia Press, 1975.

Let's See if Anyone Salutes: A Cartoon Story for New Children, Sheed & Ward, 1976.

Terry and the Pirates: The Normandie Affair, Nostalgia Press, 1977.

Terry and the Pirates: China Journey, Nostalgia Press, 1977.

The Complete Dickie Dare, Fantagraphics Books, 1986.

Welcome to China ("Terry and the Pirates" number 1), Nantier-Beall-Minoustchine, 1986.

Marooned with Burma ("Terry and the Pirates" number 2), Nantier-Beall-Minoustchine, 1986.

Male Call, 1942-1946, edited by Peter Poplaski, Kitchen Sink Press, 1987.

Damma Exile: Four Complete Steve Canyon Adventures by Milton Caniff, Kitchen Sink Press, 1991.

Also author of *The Complete Color Terry and the Pirates, The Scarlet Princess,* and *Terry and the Pirates Color Sundays.* Also artist for *Pocket Guide to China,* a U.S. Army publication of World War II. Much of Caniff's artwork is housed at the Milton Caniff Research Library at Ohio State University.

ADAPTATIONS: "Terry and the Pirates" was adapted as a radio series, 1938-39, 1942-44.

SIDELIGHTS: Milton Caniff will be best remembered as the creator of the adventure comic strips "Terry and the Pirates" and "Steve Canyon." These adventure strips, marked by their superior artwork and exciting stories, enjoyed a daily audience of some thirty million readers. The *New York Times* obituary writer explained that "Caniff's art was credited with bringing a new level of realism to cartoon drawing." A *Newsweek* reviewer once described Caniff as "the most widely aped artisan" in the comic strip field.

Caniff began drawing the Boy Scout page for a local newspaper at the age of thirteen. His first comic strips for the Associated Press were "Dickie Dare" and "The Gay Thirties," but he caught the public's imagination in 1934 with "Terry and the Pirates," an adventure strip about a boy, Terry Lee, and his tutor, Pat Ryan, who traveled throughout the exotic Orient encountering such villains as the voluptuous pirate queen known as the Dragon Lady.

New York News publisher Colonel Joseph M. Patterson had suggested to Caniff that he create an adventure series "so powerful that nobody could eat his breakfast without reading it." The strip's combination of action, romance, humor and fast pace was a success. John Steinbeck once wrote of the series: "When my grandchildren speak of their sugarplum eroticisms, I can say 'You see? This is how it was in my day. This Dragon Lady (from "Terry") with the figure of a debutante . . . was one of your old man's girlfriends.' "

By 1946, dissatisfied because he did not own the rights to "Terry," Caniff allowed George Wunder to take over the strip while he went on to create "Steve Canyon," featuring the adventures of a U.S. Air Force colonel. The strip was circulated in six hundred newspapers throughout the country. Caniff received many awards from the U.S. Air Force for "Steve Canyon," and the cartoon colonel himself was honored with a special "Steve Canyon Day" at the 1964 World's Fair.

More than once, ideas used by Caniff in "Steve Canyon" became a reality. In one adventure, Captain Shark, a woman submarine expert from a formidable foreign country, moved prefabricated submarines to warm-water ports over land. A year and a half later, it became known that the U.S.S.R. was actually transporting prefabricated submarines in much the same way. Then Canyon captured Shark in her snorkel submarine, an innovation that was, in fact, later developed. A reconnaissance plane used for guiding naval vessels was another idea preconceived by Caniff.

During World War II Caniff drew the "Male Call" comic strip for *Stars and Stripes,* the GI newspaper, and for some 2,000 military camp newspapers. Featuring the leggy Miss Lace in battles against the Axis enemy, the strip was a popular one with American soldiers around the world and was credited with helping to boost morale.

Phlebitis prevented Caniff from joining the military himself. "It was something I always wanted to do," the *Los Angeles Times* quoted Caniff as saying. "It was like a small boy who dreams of catching the game-winning touchdown or rescuing the heroine from the villain. Fortunately, the strips have allowed me to have a close association with the military."

"Terry and the Pirates," "Steve Canyon," and the other Caniff creations might never have appeared in print if Caniff had pursued a career in acting, something he once seriously considered. But he changed his mind when *Columbus Dispatch* cartoonist Billy Ireland advised him, "Stick to your inkpots, kid. Actors don't eat regularly." Caniff also remembered the advice of his high school art teacher back in Dayton, Ohio: "Unless a piece of art inspired the viewer to part with cash money to acquire it, then the drawing was not worth a hoot."

A self-professed "working stiff," Caniff spent from fourteen to sixteen hours every day at the drawing board. Unique among artists in the comic strip field at the time, Caniff used live models to pose for his drawings. He wrote the stories as he went along, sometimes trapping his characters in dangerous situations before coming up with a solution to their dilemma.

Expressing his philosophy in creating each comic strip, Caniff wrote: "I have always admonished myself to write for the man on the bus or the woman who is having her second cup of coffee after her husband and children have been sent off for the day. At these moments we are alone together, and I bring to them an uninterrupted display of my wares. The playwright can have the advantage of chain reaction emotion stemming from mutual appreciation by many people crowded together. I am happy to have my reader alone for the few minutes each day during which we rendezvous."

In addition to being a cartoonist, Caniff was also an oil painter. After viewing some of Caniff's paintings exhibited at the Julian Levy Gallery in New York, an art critic described him as a "genuine creative talent in the field of modern Americana."

BIOGRAPHICAL/CRITICAL SOURCES:

BOOKS

Adams, J. P., *Rembrandt of the Comic Strips,* McKay, 1946.
Authors in the News, Volume 1, Gale, 1976.

PERIODICALS

Life, January 6, 1941; December 7, 1959.
Los Angeles Times, April 21, 1974.
Newsweek, December 16, 1940; April 24, 1950.
New Yorker, January 8, 1944.
Time, January 13, 1947.

OBITUARIES:

PERIODICALS

Chicago Tribune, April 5, 1988.
Los Angeles Times, April 4, 1988.
New York Times, April 5, 1988.
Washington Post, April 5, 1988.*

CARAS, Roger A(ndrew) 1928-
(Roger Sarac)

PERSONAL: Born May 24, 1928, in Methuen, MA; son of Joseph Jacob (an insurance executive) and Bessie (an accountant; maiden name, Kasanoff) Caras; married Jill Langdon Barclay, September 5, 1954; children: Pamela Jill Rupert, Barclay Gordon. *Education:* Attended Northeastern University, 1948-49, and Western Reserve University (now Case Western Reserve University), 1949-50; University of Southern California, A.B. (cum laude), 1954. *Politics:* "Some." *Religion:* "Little." *Avocational interests:* Photography; dogs; collecting autographs, antiques, art, and natural history books; study of Abraham Lincoln.

ADDRESSES: Home—Thistle Hill Farm, 21108 Slab Bridge Rd., Freeland, MD 21053. *Office*—American Society for the Prevention of Cruelty to Animals (ASPCA), 424 East 92nd St., New York, NY 10128. *Agent*—Perry Knowlton, Curtis Brown Agency, 10 Astor Place, New York, NY 10003.

CAREER: Michael Myerberg Productions, New York City, director of animation, 1954-55; Columbia Pictures Corp., New York City, assistant to the vice president, 1955-56; Polaris Productions, Inc., New York City, and Hawk Films Ltd., London, England, vice president, 1965-68; Ivan Tors Productions, Los Angeles, CA, producer, 1968-69. Writer and radio and television broadcaster, 1969—; president, ASPCA, 1991—. Radio series include *Pets and Wildlife,* Columbia Broadcasting System (CBS) radio network, 1969-72, 1973-80, 1992—; *Reports from the World of Animals,* National Broadcasting Company (NBC) radio network, 1973; *Roger Caras' Mailbag,* WCBS radio, New York City, 1981-84; and *The Living World,* American Broadcasting Companies (ABC) radio network, 1981-84. Regular appearances on the *Today* show, NBC-TV, as house naturalist; under contract to ABC-TV network news, appearing on *World News Tonight, Nightline, Good Morning America,* and *20/20* as special correspondent for animals and the environment. Has been a frequent guest on *Tonight Show, Mike Douglas Show,* and *Dick Cavett Show* in addition to numerous other national and local television shows; host of several half-hour and hour television specials, including *The Frozen World,* CBS-TV. Member of advisory board, North American Wildlife Park and Arizona-Sonora Desert Museum; member of board of directors, Elsa Wild Animal Appeal; president of advisory council, Institute for Child Development. Associate curator of rare books, Cleveland Museum of Natural History. Honorary trustee, National Wildlife Health Foundation. Adjunct professor of English, Southampton College, Southampton, NY; adjunct professor of animal ecology and member of board of overseers, School of Veterinary Medicine, University of Pennsylvania. *Military service:* U.S. Army, 1946-48, 1950-51; became staff sergeant.

MEMBER: Explorers Club, Wildlife Federation, Wilderness Society, East African Wildlife Protective Society, Royal Society of Arts (fellow), Humane Society of the United States (vice president), Morris Animal Foundation, Holy Land Conservation Fund (president), Zero Population Growth (member of advisory board), Boy Scouts of America (member-at-large of national council), Wild Canid Survival and Research Center (member of board of directors), Outdoor Writers Association of America, Authors Guild, Writers Guild of America—West, Delta Kappa Alpha (president, 1953-55), American Kennel Club (delegate), American Bloodhound Club (president, 1980), Westminster Kennel Club, Grolier Club, Blue Key.

AWARDS, HONORS: Joseph Wood Krutch Medal, 1977, for "outstanding contributions to the betterment of our planet"; first recipient of Israel's Oryx Award for wildlife conservation, 1984; first recipient of Humane Award of the Year, American Veterinary Medical Association, 1985; James Herriot Award, 1988; Emmy Award, 1990; honorary doctorate degrees from Rio Grande College, Rio Grande, OH, 1979, University of Pennsylvania, School of Veterinary Medicine, 1984, and State University of New York, 1987.

WRITINGS:

Antarctica: Land of Frozen Time, Chilton, 1962.
Dangerous to Man: Wild Animals: A Definitive Study of Their Reputed Dangers to Man, with Seven Technical Appendices, Chilton, 1964, revised edition, Holt, 1976.
Wings of Gold, Lippincott, 1965.
(Under pseudonym Roger Sarac) *The Throwbacks,* Belmont, 1965.
The Custer Wolf: Biography of a Renegade, Little, Brown, 1966.
Last Chance on Earth: A Requiem for Wildlife, Chilton, 1966.
North American Mammals: Fur-Bearing Animals of the United States and Canada, Meredith Corp., 1967.
Monarch of Deadman Bay: The Life and Death of a Kodiak Bear, Little, Brown, 1969.
Panther!, Little, Brown, 1969.
Source of the Thunder: The Biography of a California Condor, Little, Brown, 1970.
Death as a Way of Life, Little, Brown, 1971.
Venomous Animals of the World, Prentice-Hall, 1974.
Roger Caras' Nature Quiz Book #1, Bantam, 1974.
Roger Caras' Nature Quiz Book #2, Bantam, 1974.
The Private Lives of Animals, Grosset, 1974.
Sockeye: The Life of a Pacific Salmon, Dial, 1975.

The Roger Caras Pet Book, Holt, 1976.
(Editor with others) *Pet Medicine: Health Care and First Aid for All Household Pets,* McGraw, 1977.
(Editor) *Dog Owner's Bible,* Stoeger Publishing, 1978.
The Forest: A Dramatic Portrait of Life in the American Wild, illustrations by Norman Arlott, Holt, 1979.
Yankee, Putnam, 1979.
The Roger Caras Dog Book, Holt, 1980, revised edition with illustrations by Alton Anderson, M. Evans, 1992.
Amiable Little Beasts, Macmillan, 1980.
A Celebration of Dogs, Times Books, 1982.
The Endless Migrations, illustrations by Kimio Honda, Dutton, 1985.
Mara Simba: The African Lion, Holt, 1985.
(Editor) *Harper's Illustrated Handbook of Cats,* photographs by Richard J. Katris and Nancy Katris, Harper, 1985.
(Editor) *Harper's Illustrated Handbook of Dogs,* photographs by John L. Ashby, Harper, 1985.
A Celebration of Cats, Simon & Schuster, 1986.
(Editor) *Roger Caras' Treasury of Great Cat Stories,* Dutton, 1987.
(Editor) *Roger Caras' Treasury of Great Dog Stories,* Dutton, 1987.
Animals in Their Places: Tales from the Natural World, Sierra Club Books, 1987.
A Cat Is Watching: A Look at the Way Cats See Us, Simon & Schuster, 1989.
(With Sue Pressman) *That Our Children May Know: Vanishing Wildlife in Zoo Portraits,* Longmeadow Press, 1990.
(Editor) *Roger Caras' Treasury of Great Horse Stories,* Dutton, 1990.
(With Rhonda Gray and Stephen T. Robinson) *Cats at Work,* photographs by Guy Powers, Abbeville Press, 1991.
(Editor) *Roger Caras' Treasury of Classic Nature Tales,* Dutton, 1992.
A Dog Is Listening: The Way Some of Our Closest Friends View Us, Summit Books, 1992.
(Editor) *Roger Caras' Treasury of Great Horse Stories,* Dutton, 1991.
The Cats of Thistle Hill, Simon & Schuster, 1994.

FOR CHILDREN

Sarang: The Story of a Bengal Tiger and of Two Children in Search of a Miracle: A Novel, Little, Brown, 1968.
(Editor) *Vanishing Wildlife,* Barre-Westover, 1970.
(Editor) *Animal Children,* Barre-Westover, 1970.
(Editor) *Animal Architecture,* Barre-Westover, 1971.
(Editor) *Birds in Flight,* Barre-Westover, 1971.
(Editor) *Protective Coloration and Mimicry: Nature's Camouflage,* Barre-Westover, 1972.

(Editor) *Animal Courtships,* Barre-Westover, 1972.

(Editor) *The Boundary: Land and Sea,* Barre-Westover, 1972.

(Editor) *Creatures of the Night,* Barre-Westover, 1972.

The Wonderful World of Mammals: Adventuring with Stamps, Harcourt, 1973.

Going to the Zoo with Roger Caras, Harcourt, 1973.

The Bizarre Animals, Barre-Westover, 1974.

The Venomous Animals, Barre-Westover, 1974.

A Zoo in Your Room, Harcourt, 1975.

Skunk for a Day, Windmill Books, 1976.

Coyote for a Day, Windmill Books, 1977.

Mysteries of Nature, Harcourt, 1980.

(With others) *Animal Families of the Wild: Animal Stories,* edited by William F. Russell, Crown, 1990.

OTHER

Author of syndicated newspaper column, "Our Only World," 1970-78; author of weekly column in *Long Island* magazine and monthly columns in *Family Circle* and *Ladies' Home Journal.* Contributor to numerous other magazines, including *National Observer, Texas Quarterly, Seventeen, Harper's Bazaar, My Weekly Reader, International Wildlife, Family Health, Science Digest, Argosy, National Wildlife, Family Circle, Geo,* and *American Cinematographer.* Former contributing editor, *Ladies' Home Journal* and *Geo.*

SIDELIGHTS: Roger A. Caras has traveled abroad more than sixty-five times, including over twenty-five photographic safaris to Africa and journeys to Antarctica and the Arctic. Active in the preservation of wildlife and wilderness areas, he researches people, places, and animals that interest him, then shares his enthusiasm with others through various media. As he once explained to *CA,* "I am in show-and-tell, professionally. I go where it is interesting to go, I talk with interesting people, sample interesting lifestyles, and, above all, observe wildlife and record the state of our environment. Then I talk about it all in my books, in my magazine articles and columns, [and] on radio and television. I know of no career that offers so many opportunities for self-indulgence and self-expansion as show-and-tell. The practitioner never has to grow up and rarely has to be as practical as people in other careers have to be. And who has as large a family? I've written more than sixty books. They are all my children."

Early in his career Caras decided never to write about a place he had not visited or a species he had not observed in the wild. The one time he tried to break this rule, under pressure to complete a book about Kodiak bears at a time when he had other major commitments, he gathered extensive research materials and went ahead with a draft of the manuscript, as he relates in *Animals in Their Places: Tales from the Natural World.* The compromise was a failure by Caras' standards; discarding the whole draft, he headed for Alaska to see the Kodiak bear for himself in its natural habitat. The resulting book was *Monarch of Deadman Bay: The Life and Death of a Kodiak Bear.*

Caras began research for *Mara Simba: The African Lion,* one of several fictionalized animal biographies, when he went to Kenya in 1971 with his wife and Joy Adamson, the author of *Born Free.* He made more than twenty return trips to Africa over the following fourteen years before he felt confident that he was prepared to write the book, which was published in 1985. After reading it, *Washington Post Book World* reviewer Alan Ryan, who declares himself up front "not fond of animal books," calls Caras "one of the best writers on the subject around today."

Caras' concern with the preservation of animal species and the natural environment is apparent in several of his books, including *Dangerous to Man: Wild Animals: A Definitive Study of Their Reputed Dangers to Man, with Seven Technical Appendices,* which addresses wildlife conservation, and *Last Chance on Earth: A Requiem for Wildlife,* in which the author makes a fervent appeal for the protection of forty animal species that are immediately threatened environmentally and in other ways. In an afterword to *The Forest: A Dramatic Portrait of Life in the Wild,* he cautions that the world's wild forests could vanish in half a century unless people make a commitment to save them.

Caras is also devoted to the care of domesticated animals. A number of his books focus on pets, among them *The Roger Caras Pet Book, The Roger Caras Dog Book, A Celebration of Dogs, A Celebration of Cats, A Cat Is Watching,* and *A Dog Is Listening.* Caras makes it clear in *A Celebration of Dogs,* as Robert R. Harris points out in the *New York Times Book Review,* that he is fond of almost all of the 130-plus breeds of dogs recognized by the American Kennel Club: "Although not above telling a shaggy dog story or two . . . Mr. Caras is capable of writing movingly and intelligently about dogs." In the *Washington Post,* E. Irving Eldredge describes the book as "enchanting, engrossing, amusing, written by a writer of stature who knows his subject inside out." Elizabeth Janeway in the *New York Times Book Review* calls *A Cat Is Watching* "as thorough and sensitive a tour of the cat's world as a human being can contrive, respectful and amused without being sentimental, and informative on what we know and don't know."

BIOGRAPHICAL/CRITICAL SOURCES:

BOOKS

Caras, Roger, *Animals in Their Places: Tales from the Natural World,* Sierra Club Books, 1987.

PERIODICALS

Best Sellers, November 1, 1968.
Books and Bookmen, March, 1976.
Catholic Library World, September, 1976.
Choice, February, 1977.
Los Angeles Times Book Review, May 6, 1984, p. 4; May 31, 1987, p. 2; November 8, 1987, p. 18.
New Republic, November 23, 1974.
New York Times, November 12, 1989.
New York Times Book Review, March 19, 1967; November 3, 1968; July 6, 1969; February 15, 1970; March 7, 1971; November 14, 1976; December 19, 1982, p. 15; March 11, 1984, p. 30; October 1, 1989, p. 13; September 2, 1990, p. 22.
Observer (London), December 7, 1969.
Saturday Review, February 13, 1971.
Washington Post, August 4, 1979; January 29, 1983.
Washington Post Book World, June 27, 1971; December 4, 1977; January 12, 1986, p. 3.

* * *

CARD, Orson Scott 1951-
(Brian Green, Byron Walley)

PERSONAL: Born August 24, 1951, in Richland, WA; son of Willard Richards (a teacher) and Peggy Jane (a secretary and administrator; maiden name, Park) Card; married Kristine Allen, May 17, 1977; children: Michael Geoffrey, Emily Janice, Charles Benjamin, Zina Margaret. *Education:* Brigham Young University, B.A. (with distinction), 1975; University of Utah, M.A., 1981. *Politics:* Moderate Democrat. *Religion:* Church of Jesus Christ of Latter-day Saints (Mormon). *Avocational interests:* Computer games.

ADDRESSES: Agent—Barbara Bova Literary Agency, 3951 Gulf Shore Blvd. North # PH1B, Naples, FL 33940.

CAREER: Volunteer Mormon missionary in Brazil, 1971-73; operated repertory theatre in Provo, UT, 1974-75; Brigham Young University Press, Provo, editor, 1974-76; *Ensign,* Salt Lake City, UT, assistant editor, 1976-78; freelance writer and editor, 1978—. Senior editor, Compute! Books, Greensboro, NC, 1983. Teacher at various universities and writers workshops, including Cape Cod Writer's Workshop, Antioch College, and Appalachian State University. Local Democratic precinct election judge and Utah State Democratic Convention delegate.

MEMBER: Science Fiction Writers of America.

AWARDS, HONORS: John W. Campbell Award for best new writer of 1977, World Science Fiction Convention, 1978; Hugo Award nominations, World Science Fiction Convention, 1978, 1979, 1980, for short stories, and 1986, for novelette *Hatrack River;* Nebula Award nominations, Science Fiction Writers of America, 1979, 1980, for short stories; Utah State Institute of Fine Arts prize, 1980, for epic poem "Prentice Alvin and the No-Good Plow"; Nebula Award, 1985, and Hugo Award, 1986, both for *Ender's Game;* Nebula Award, 1986, and Hugo Award, 1987, both for *Speaker for the Dead;* World Fantasy Award, 1987, for *Hatrack River;* Hugo Award, and Locus Award nomination, both 1988, both for novella "Eye for Eye"; Locus Award for best fantasy, Hugo Award nomination, and World Fantasy Award nomination, all 1988, all for *Seventh Son;* Mythopoeic Fantasy Award, Mythopoeic Society, 1988, for *Seventh Son;* Locus Award, 1989, for *Red Prophet;* Hugo Award, 1991, for *How to Write Science Fiction and Fantasy.*

WRITINGS:

PLAYS

(And director) *Tell Me That You Love Me, Junie Moon* (adaptation of work by Majorie Kellogg), produced in Provo, UT, 1969.
The Apostate, produced in Provo, 1970.
In Flight, produced in Provo, 1970.
Across Five Summers, produced in Provo, 1971.
Of Gideon, produced in Provo, 1971.
Stone Tables, produced in Provo at Brigham Young University, 1973.
A Christmas Carol (adapted from the story by Charles Dickens), produced in Provo, 1974.
Father, Mother, Mother, and Mom, produced in Provo, 1974, published in *Sunstone,* 1978.
Liberty Jail, produced in Provo, 1975.
Fresh Courage Take, produced in Salt Lake City, UT, 1978.
Elders and Sisters (adaptation of work by Gladys Farmer), produced in American Fork, UT, 1979.

Also author, under pseudonym Brian Green, of *Rag Mission,* published in *Ensign,* July, 1977. Author of *Wings* (fragment), produced in 1982.

SCIENCE FICTION AND FANTASY

Capitol (short stories), Ace Books (New York), 1978.
Hot Sleep: The Worthing Chronicle, Baronet, 1978.
A Planet Called Treason, St. Martin's (New York), 1979, revised edition, Dell (New York), 1980, published as *Treason,* St. Martin's, 1988.
Songmaster, Dial (New York), 1980.
(Editor) *Dragons of Darkness,* Ace Books, 1981.
Unaccompanied Sonata and Other Stories, Dial, 1980.
Hart's Hope, Berkley Publishing (New York), 1983.
(Editor) *Dragons of Light,* Ace Books, 1983.

The Worthing Chronicle, Ace Books, 1983.

Ender's Game (first novel in "Ender" series; also see below), Tor Books (New York), 1985.

Speaker for the Dead (second novel in "Ender" series; also see below), Tor Books, 1986.

Ender's Game [and] *Speaker for the Dead,* Tor Books, 1987.

(With others) *Free Lancers,* Baen Books, 1987.

Seventh Son (first novel in "The Tales of Alvin Maker" series), St. Martin's, 1987.

Wyrms, Arbor House (New York), 1987.

Red Prophet (second novel in "The Tales of Alvin Maker" series), Tor Books, 1988.

Folk of the Fringe (short stories), Phantasia Press (Huntington Woods, MI), 1989.

The Abyss (novelization of screenplay), Pocket Books (New York), 1989.

Prentice Alvin (third novel in "The Tales of Alvin Maker" series), Tor Books, 1989.

(With Lloyd Biggle) *Eye for Eye—The Tunesmith,* Tor Books, 1990.

Maps in a Mirror: The Short Fiction of Orson Scott Card (includes stories originally published under pseudonym Byron Walley), Tor Books, 1990.

Worthing Saga, Tor Books, 1990.

(Editor) *Future on Fire,* Tor Books, 1991.

Xenocide (third novel in "Ender" series), Tor Books, 1991.

The Changed Man, Tor Books, 1992.

Cruel Miracles, Tor Books, 1992.

Flux, Tor Books, 1992.

Lost Boys, HarperCollins (New York), 1992.

The Memory of Earth (first novel in "Homecoming" series), Tor Books, 1992.

The Call of Earth (second novel in "Homecoming" series), Tor Books, 1993.

Monkey Sonatas, Tor Books, 1993.

The Ships of Earth (third novel in "Homecoming" series), Tor Books, 1993.

(With Kathryn H. Kidd) *Lovelock,* Tor Books, 1994.

Earthfall (fourth novel in "Homecoming" series), Tor Books, 1994.

Also author of novelette *Hatrack River,* 1986. Contributor to *The Bradbury Chronicles: Stories in Honor of Ray Bradbury,* edited by William F. Nolan and Martin H. Greenberg, New American Library, 1991. Contributor to numerous anthologies.

OTHER

Listen, Mom and Dad, Bookcraft (Salt Lake City, UT), 1978.

Saintspeak: The Mormon Dictionary, Signature Books (Midvale, UT), 1981.

Ainge, Signature Books, 1982.

A Woman of Destiny (historical novel), Berkley Publishing, 1983, published as *Saints,* Tor Books, 1988.

Compute's Guide to IBM PCjr Sound and Graphics, Compute (Greensboro, NC), 1984.

Cardography, Hypatia Press, 1987.

Characters and Viewpoint, Writer's Digest (Cincinnati, OH), 1988.

(Author of introduction) Susan D. Smallwood, *You're a Rock, Sister Lewis,* Hatrack River Publications, 1989.

How to Write Science Fiction and Fantasy, Writer's Digest, 1990.

Also author of several hundred audio plays for Living Scriptures; co-author of animated videotapes. Contributor of regular review columns, "You Got No Friends in This World," *Science Fiction Review,* 1979-86, "Books to Look For," *Fantasy and Science Fiction,* 1987—, and "Gameplay," *Compute!,* 1988—. Contributor of articles and reviews to periodicals, including *Washington Post Book World, Science Fiction Review,* and *Destinies.*

Card's manuscripts are housed at Brigham Young University.

ADAPTATIONS: Xenocide has been adapted into two audiocassettes, read by Mark Rolston, Audio Renaissance, 1991; *Seventh Son* has been adapted into five audiocassettes, read by Card, Literate Ear, Inc., 1991.

WORK IN PROGRESS: Children of the Mind (fourth "Ender" book); and *Master Alvin,* Volumes four and five of the "Homecoming" series. Awaiting publication: *Alvin Journeyman* (volume four in "Alvin Maker" series), *Earthborn* (fifth novel in "Homecoming" series), *Pastwatch: The Redemption of Columbus.*

SIDELIGHTS: With the creation of Andrew "Ender" Wiggin, the young genius of *Ender's Game,* Orson Scott Card launched an award-winning career as a science fiction and fantasy writer. Since his debut in the field in 1977, when the short story "Ender's Game" appeared in *Analog* magazine, Card has penned more than twenty-four science fiction novels and has become the first writer to win the genre's top awards, the Nebula and the Hugo, for consecutive novels in a continuing series. These two novels— *Ender's Game* and *Speaker for the Dead*—have been described by *Fantasy Review* contributor Michael R. Collings as "allegorical disquisitions on humanity, morality, salvation, and redemption"—evaluations which many critics have applied to Card's other works, as well. Such thematic concerns, in part influenced by Card's devout Mormonism, are what critics feel set him apart from other writers in the science fiction field.

Respect did not come immediately, though, and some of Card's early works were panned by critics. *Hot Sleep: The Worthing Chronicle* and *A Planet Called Treason,* for example, encountered critical censure for employing standard science fiction elements and for containing what some reviewers considered gratuitous violence. George R. R. Martin, writing in the *Washington Post Book World*, particularly criticizes Card's 1981 work, *Unaccompanied Sonata and Other Stories,* finding it rife "with death, pain, mutilation, dismemberment, all described in graphic detail." These negative evaluations aside, Card's early work was generally considered to display imagination, intelligence, literary aptitude, and promise. "Card is a young, talented, and ambitious writer," concedes Martin.

That ambition and talent was both revealed and recognized in 1985, when Card released *Ender's Game.* This novel began as a short story, which Card describes in a *CA* interview as "still the most popular and the most reprinted of my stories, and I still have people tell me that they like it better than the novel. . . . When I started working on the novel that became *Speaker for the Dead,* a breakthrough for me in that story was realizing that the main character should be Ender Wiggin. That made it a kind of sequel, although its plot had nothing to do with the original plot; it was just using a character. . . . I told the publisher, Tom Doherty, that I needed to do a novel version of 'Ender's Game' just to set up *Speaker for the Dead.* That's the only reason 'Ender's Game' ever became a novel."

Ender's Game concerns the training of Ender Wiggin, a six-year-old genius who is the Earth's only hope for victory over invading "bugger" aliens. While this plot appears to be standard science fiction fare, *New York Times Book Review* critic Gerald Jonas observes that "Card has shaped this unpromising material into an affecting novel full of surprises that seem inevitable once they are explained." The difference, assert Jonas and other critics, is in the character of Ender Wiggin, who remains sympathetic despite his acts of violence. A *Kirkus Reviews* contributor, for example, while noting the plot's inherent weakness, admits that "the long passages focusing on Ender are nearly always enthralling," concluding that *Ender's Game* "is altogether a much more solid, mature, and persuasive effort" than the author's previous work.

Other critics, however, were less enthusiastic. Michael Lassell of the *Los Angeles Times Book Review,* for example, claims that Ender does not overcome the "uninspired notions of Ender's training." But *Analog* writer Tom Easton suggests that readers "reserve . . . skepticism of Ender's talent," for the novel "succeeds because of its stress on the value of empathy. . . . The governmental agents who rule young Ender are as guilty of despicable acts, but they are saved by their ability to bleed for the souls they mangle."

Following the success of *Ender's Game,* its sequel, *Speaker for the Dead,* was hailed as "the most powerful work Card has produced" by Michael R. Collings in *Fantasy Review.* "*Speaker* not only completes *Ender's Game* but transcends it. . . . Read in conjunction with *Ender's Game, Speaker* demonstrates Card's mastery of character, plot, style, theme, and development." Ender Wiggin, now working as a "Speaker for the Dead," travels the galaxy to interpret the lives of the deceased for their families and neighbors; as he travels, he also searches for a home for the eggs of the lone surviving "hive queen" of the race he destroyed as a child. "Like *Game, Speaker* deals with issues of evil and empathy, though not in so polarized a way," observes Easton in his review. Some critics found an extra element of complexity in the "Ender" books; *Washington Post Book World* contributor Janrae Frank, for example, sees "quasi-religious images and themes" in the conclusions of both novels.

It is this symbolic, metaphorical aspect of Card's work that some critics feel distinguishes and intensifies his writing. "It seemed that whenever Card drifted away from pure sf into the hazier realm of mythmaking, of allegory, he was far more successful," remarks Somtow Sucharitkul in the *Washington Post Book World,* "for his gift lay not in the creation of vividly viable futures but in his ability to feel and transmit a timeless anguish." The critic explains that as Card has de-emphasized elaborate settings in his fiction, he has shown "yet an ever-growing mastery of symbol, form and human emotional processes." About *Wyrms,* for example—a "traditional" quest adventure involving a deposed princess—*Los Angeles Times Book Review* contributor Ingrid Rimland asserts: "There is nothing trite . . . nothing swollen and contrived. . . . [*Wyrms*] is many things at once: a parable, a heroic adventure, a philosophical treatise, a finely crafted masterpiece of stylistically honed paragraphs, [and] a careful and smart understatement on the rebellious theme that God might be evil and needs to be slain."

With the publication of 1991's *Xenocide,* Card's reputation as an unflinching explorer of both moral and intellectual issues was firmly established. In this novel, Card picks up the story of Ender as he works feverishly with his adopted Lusitanian family to neutralize a deadly virus. Many critics venture that with *Xenocide,* Card relies more on the scientific ruminations of a multitude of contemplative characters rather than on a plot. "The real action is philosophical: long, passionate debates about ends and means among people who are fully aware that they may be deciding the fate of an entire species, entire worlds," observes Gerald Jonas in the *New York Times Book Review.*

Card's use of symbol and allegory is further displayed in the "Tales of Alvin Maker" series. "This series began as an epic poem I was writing during graduate study at the

University of Utah," Card says a *CA* interview, "when I was heavily influenced by Spenser and playing games with allegory. That epic poem won a prize from the Utah State Institute of Fine Arts, but I realized that there is very little future for an epic poem in terms of reaching an audience and telling a story to real people, so I converted it and expanded it and, I think, deepened and enriched it into something much longer and larger."

The first novel in the "Tales of Alvin Maker" series, *Seventh Son,* "begins what may be a significant recasting in fantasy terms of the tall tale in America," writes *Washington Post Book World* reviewer John Clute. Set in a pioneer America where the British Restoration never happened, where the "Crown Colonies" exist alongside the states of Appalachia and New Sweden, and where folk magic is readily believed and practiced, *Seventh Son* follows the childhood of Alvin Miller, who has enormous magical potential because he is the seventh son of a seventh son. While *Fantasy Review* contributor Martha Soukup admits that "this could easily have been another dull tale of the chosen child groomed to be the defender from evil," she believes that Card's use of folk magic and vernacular language, along with strongly realized characters, creates in *Seventh Son* "more to care about here than an abstract magical battle." Collings similarly notes in the same publication that *Seventh Son* continues Card's allegorical work, containing a re-working of the life of Joseph Smith, founder of the Mormon Church; nevertheless, comments the critic, Card depicts "this community's people in such a masterly way that their allegorical functioning does not impede our involvement with and deep caring for them. *Seventh Son* is a moving novel." "There is something deeply heart-wrenching about an America come true, even if it is only a dream, a fantasy novel," writes Clute, concluding that this first volume in *The Tales of Alvin Maker* is "sharp and clean and bracing."

"Because we know it is a dream of an America we do not deserve to remember, Orson Scott Card's luminous alternate history of the early 19th century continues to chill as it soothes," Clute explains in a review of *Red Prophet,* the second volume of Alvin's story. The novel traces Alvin's kidnapping by renegade Reds employed by "White Murderer" William Henry Harrison, who wishes to precipitate a massacre of the Shaw-Nee tribe. Alvin is rescued by the Red warrior Ta-Kumsaw, however, and learns of Native American ways even as he attempts to prevent the conflict caused by his supposed capture and murder. While "*Red Prophet* seems initially less ambitious" than its predecessor, covering a period of only one year, a *West Coast Review of Books* contributor comments that "in that year, Card creates episodes and images that stun with the power of their emotions." Sue Martin, however, believes that the setting is not enough to overcome the plot, which she de-

scribes in the *Los Angeles Times Book Review* as "yet *another* tale of Dark versus Light." She concedes, however, that while Alvin "seems almost Christlike" in his ability to heal and bring people together, the allegory is drawn "without the proselytizing." *Booklist* writer Sally Estes summarizes: "Harsher, bleaker, and more mystical than *Seventh Son,*" Card's second volume displays his strong historical background, "keen understanding of religious experience, and, most of all, his mastery of the art of story-telling."

In a *CA* interview Card explains one of the purposes for his "Alvin Maker" novels: "Each of the volumes in the 'Tales of Alvin Maker' series is keyed to a major issue in American history. *Seventh Son* is tied to the issue of religion in America. *Red Prophet* has to do with our treatment of the Indians. *Prentice Alvin . . .* deals with the treatment of blacks under slavery. The following one, *Alvin Journeyman,* will probably deal mostly with the treatment of women, but it's also Alvin's *Wanderjahr.* Each one has a theme on that level that gets wrapped up by the end of the book, while other issues remain."

In 1992 Card introduced his "Homecoming" series with *The Memory of Earth,* a novel many critics found to be a mixture of philosophy, futuristic technology, and Biblical lore. *Memory* opens on the planet Harmony, where for forty million years humans have been controlled by Oversoul, a powerful, global computer programmed to prevent humanity from destroying itself through needless wars. David E. Jones, in Chicago's *Tribune Books,* argues that "what Card gives us [in *The Memory of Earth*] is an interaction between supreme intelligence and human mental capability that is at once an intellectual exercise, a Biblical parable and a thoroughly enjoyable piece of storytelling."

Though firmly established as a successful author of science fiction, Card has not been limited to that genre, publishing throughout his career numerous works of nonfiction, drama and, most notably, historical fiction. In *A Woman of Destiny* (later published as *Saints*), for example, he returns to the subject of the life of Joseph Smith, first touched upon in *Seventh Son. Saints* offers an account of the lives of Smith, the founder of Mormonism, and Dinah Kirkham, the English woman who is converted to Mormonism and becomes Smith's polygamous wife. When Smith is murdered in 1844, Kirkham escapes with her fellow Mormons to Utah, where she becomes a staunch leader as well as one of the wives of Brigham Young, Smith's successor as president. *Los Angeles Times Book Review* critic Kristiana Gregory pronounces *Saints* an "engrossing epic," stressing that Card "is a powerful storyteller."

In *Saints,* Card explains in his *CA* interview, "I did not want to write a book where you had to decide whether you believed Mormonism was true or not. I wanted to write the story of people who *did* believe it, and once you accepted that they believed it, you would still care about what happened to them. . . . I didn't want the novel to be religious fiction: I wanted it to be fiction about religious people, which I think is a different thing entirely."

In a critique of the author's 1990 collection, *Maps in a Mirror: The Short Fiction of Orson Scott Card, Analog* reviewer Easton characterizes Card as "an intensely thoughtful, self-conscious, religious, and community-oriented writer." In spite of such critical acclaim and the numerous awards his writing has earned, Card seems to prefer a simpler description of himself; as he told *Publishers Weekly:* "I'm Kristine's husband, Geoffrey and Emily and Charlie's dad, I'm a Mormon, and I'm a science fiction writer, in that order."

For a previously published interview with this author, see *Contemporary Authors New Revision Series,* Volume 27.

BIOGRAPHICAL/CRITICAL SOURCES:

BOOKS

Contemporary Literary Criticism, Gale, Volume 44, 1987, Volume 47, 1988, Volume 50, 1988.

PERIODICALS

Analog, July, 1983, p. 103; July, 1985, p. 180; June, 1986, p.183; Mid-December, 1987; September, 1988, p. 179; August, 1989, p. 175; January, 1990, p. 305; March, 1991, p. 184; Mid-December, 1991.
Booklist, December 15, 1985, p. 594; December 15, 1987.
Economist, September 5, 1987, p.92.
Fantasy Review, April, 1986, p. 20; June, 1987; July/August, 1987.
Kirkus Reviews, December 1, 1980, p. 1542; November 1, 1984, p. 1021.
Kliatt, April, 1991, p. 15.
Library Journal, February 15, 1989, p. 179; November 15, 1990; September 1, 1991; October 15, 1991.
Locus, April, 1991, p. 15; February, 1992, pp. 17, 57.
Los Angeles Times Book Review, September 28, 1980; March 6, 1983; July 22, 1984, p. 8; February 3, 1985; August 9, 1987; February 14, 1988; July 20, 1990.
Magazine of Fantasy and Science Fiction, January, 1980, p. 35.
New York Times Book Review, June 16, 1985; October 18, 1987; September 1, 1991; March 15, 1992.
Publishers Weekly, December 4, 1978, p. 62; January 2, 1981, p. 49; January 24, 1986, p. 64; December 25, 1987, p. 65; September 16, 1988; May 19, 1989, p. 72; August 17, 1990, p. 55; November 30, 1990, p. 54; June 14, 1991, p. 48.
School Library Journal, January, 1991, p. 123; November, 1991.

Science Fiction and Fantasy Book Review, April, 1979, p. 27; December, 1979, p. 155; June, 1983, p. 21.
Science Fiction Review, August, 1979; February, 1986, p. 14.
SF Chronicle, June, 1988, p. 50.
Tribune Books (Chicago), March 1, 1990.
Voice of Youth Advocates, October, 1992, p. 236.
Washington Post Book World, August 24, 1980, p. 6; January 25, 1981, p. 11; March 27, 1983; February 23, 1986, p. 10; August 30, 1987; February 28, 1988; March 19, 1992.
West Coast Review of Books, March, 1984; July, 1986; number 2, 1987; number 4, 1988.
Writer's Digest, October, 1986, p. 26; November, 1986, p. 37; December, 1986, p. 32; May, 1989, p. 31.

*   *   *

CARLINSKY, Dan 1944-

PERSONAL: Born March 9, 1944, in Holyoke, MA; son of Louis H. and Ethel (Mag) Carlinsky; married Nancy Cooperstein, August 25, 1972. *Education:* Columbia University, B.A., 1965, M.S., 1966.

ADDRESSES: Home and office—P.O. Box 398, Bethlehem, CT 06751.

CAREER: Freelance writer and journalist.

MEMBER: American Society of Journalists and Authors, Authors Guild.

WRITINGS:

(With Edwin Goodgold) *Trivia* (also see below), Dell (New York City), 1966.
(With Goodgold) *More Trivial Trivia* (also see below), Dell, 1966.
(With Goodgold) *Rock 'n' Roll Trivia,* Popular Library, 1970.
(Compiler) *A Century of College Humor,* Random House (New York City), 1971.
(With David Heim) *Bicycle Tours in and around New York,* Hagstrom (New York City), 1975, 3rd revised edition published as *Twenty Bicycle Tours in and around New York City,* Backcountry (Woodstock, VT), 1992.
(With Goodgold) *The Compleat Beatles Quiz Book,* Warner Books (New York City), 1975.
(With Goodgold) *The World's Greatest Monster Quiz,* Berkley Publishing (New York City), 1975.
(With Goodgold) *Trivia and More Trivia* (contains *Trivia* and *More Trivial Trivia*), Castle Books, 1975.
The Complete Bible Quiz Book, Berkley Publishing, 1976.
Typewriter Art, Price, Stern (Los Angeles, CA), 1977.
The Great 1960's Quiz, Harper (New York City), 1978.

The Jewish Quiz Book, Doubleday (New York City), 1979.

Do You Know Your Husband?, Price, Stern, 1979.

Do You Know Your Wife?, Price, Stern, 1979.

The Great Bogart Trivia Book, Fawcett (New York City), 1980.

Are You Compatible?, Price, Stern, 1981.

Do You Know Your Mother?, Price, Stern, 1981.

Do You Know Your Father?, Price, Stern, 1981.

Celebrity Yearbook, Price, Stern, 1982.

College Humor, Harper, 1982.

Do You Know Your Boss?, Price, Stern, 1983.

(With Goodgold) *The Status Game,* New American Library (New York City), 1986.

Stop Snoring Now!, St. Martin's (New York City), 1987.

(With Goodgold) *Little Sports,* McGraw (New York City), 1990.

(With Goodgold) *The Armchair Conductor: How to Lead a Symphony Orchestra in the Privacy of Your Own Home,* Dell, 1991.

Author of a syndicated newspaper column. Contributor to periodicals, including *New York Times, Travel and Leisure, Playboy, Redbook, Woman's Day,* and *T.V. Guide.*

BIOGRAPHICAL/CRITICAL SOURCES:

PERIODICALS

Chicago Tribune Book World, December 19, 1982.

*   *   *

CARRICK, Burt
  See CASSIDAY, Bruce (Bingham)

*   *   *

CARTER, Nick
  See CASSIDAY, Bruce (Bingham)

*   *   *

CASADO, Pablo Gil   1931-

PERSONAL: Born August 17, 1931, in Santander, Spain; came to the United States in 1955, naturalized in 1963; son of Pablo (a musician) and Agueda (Casado) Gil Benet; married Carol Ann Schuman (a teacher), December 23, 1967. *Education:* Universidad Interamericana, M.A., 1960; University of Wisconsin, Ph.D., 1967. *Religion:* Unitarian Universalist.

ADDRESSES: Home—Wolf's Pond, Route 5, Chapel Hill, NC 27514. *Office*—Department of Romance Lan-

guages, University of North Carolina, Chapel Hill, NC 27514.

CAREER: Teacher in public schools of Ashland, WI, 1955-59, and Wauwatosa, WI, 1959-60; University of Northern Iowa, Cedar Falls, instructor in Spanish, 1960-63; University of North Carolina, Chapel Hill, assistant professor, 1967-70, associate professor of Spanish language and literature, 1970—. Evaluator of research grants, National Endowment for the Humanities, Washington, DC, 1973—.

MEMBER: Modern Language Association of America, American Association of University Professors, Pen Club Espanol.

WRITINGS:

La novela social espanola, 1942-1968 (title means "The Spanish Social Novel, 1942-68"), Seix Barral, 1968, corrected and enlarged edition published as *La Novela social espanola, 1920-1971,* 1973.

(With Doris K. Arjona and Albert Turner) *Lengua espanola* (title means "Spanish Language"), Books I and II, Scott, Foresman (Glenview, IL), 1969.

El paralelepipedo (novel), Joaquin Mortiz (Mexico), 1977.

Also contributor to *Modern Foreign Languages for Iowa Schools,* Iowa State Department of Public Instruction, 1963. Contributor to *Cuadernos Americanos* and other professional journals; associate editor of *Romance Notes,* 1971-75; member of advisory board, *Anales de la novela de posguerra,* University of Kansas, 1977—.

WORK IN PROGRESS: Preterito imperfecto (a novel); *Sotileza* (critical and study edition).*

*   *   *

CASSIDAY, Bruce (Bingham)   1920-
  (Carson Bingham, Burt Carrick, Nick Carter, Max Day, Mary Anne Drew, Robert Faraday, C. K. Fong, Lester Heath, Annie Laurie McAllister, Annie Laurie McMurdie, Con Steffanson, Michael Stratford)

PERSONAL: Born January 25, 1920, in Los Angeles, CA; son of Robert Maxwell and Persis (Bingham) Cassiday; married Doris S. Galloway, 1950; children: Bryan Galloway, Cathy Bingham. *Education:* University of California, Los Angeles, B.A. (highest honors), 1942. *Avocational interests:* Photography, music, theater.

ADDRESSES: Home and office—69 Dogwood Lane, Stamford, CT 06903.

CAREER: Popular Publications, New York City, editor, 1946-49; Farrell Publications, New York City, editor,

1950-53; *Argosy* magazine, New York City, fiction editor, 1954-73; Hill & Knowlton (public relations), New York City, account executive, 1973-80; Frederick Ungar Publishing Co., Inc., New York City, general editor of "Recognitions: Mystery Writers" book series, 1980-90. *Military service:* U.S. Air Force, 4 years, became staff sergeant; awarded battle stars.

MEMBER: International Association of Crime Writers, Authors Guild, Authors League of America, Writers Guild of America, Mystery Writers of America (former executive vice president; former vice president; member of regional board of directors), Private Eye Writers of America, Crime Writers Association (United Kingdom), Phi Beta Kappa, Theta Chi, Kap and Bells (University of California honorary drama society), California Scholarship Federation, Ephebian Society.

WRITINGS:

NOVELS

While Murder Waits, Graphic, 1957.
The Buried Motive, Ace Books, 1957.
The Brass Shroud, Ace Books, 1958.
The Floater, Abelard, 1960.
The Corpse in the Picture Window, Ace Books, 1961.
Dr. Reades's Decision, Lancer Books, 1962.
(Under pseudonym Lester Heath) *The Case of the Aluminum Critch,* Dell Books, 1963.
Blast-Off!, Doubleday, 1964.
Guerrilla Scout, Macmillan, 1965.
Live down the Shame, Pyramid Books, 1965.
Angels Ten, Pyramid Books, 1966.
Happening of San Remo, Pyramid Books, 1967.
Operation Goldkill, Award Books, 1967.
The Seventh Miracle, 1968.
The Wild One, Pyramid Books, 1969.
The Phoenician, Pyramid Books, 1970.
Iggy, Pyramid Books, 1973.
The Girl in the Trunk, Ace Books, 1973.
(Under pseudonym Annie Laurie McMurdie) *Nightmare Hall,* Lancer, 1973.
(Under pseudonym Nick Carter) *The Spanish Connection,* Award Books, 1973.
(Under author Ron Goulart's pseudonym Con Steffanson) *Flash Gordon: The Time Trap of Ming XIII,* Avon, 1974.
(Under pseudonym Michael Stratford) *Adam 12: The Sniper,* Award Books, 1974.
(Under pseudonym Mary Anne Drew) *The Diabolist,* Avon, 1975.
(Under pseudonym Burt Carrick) *The Candidate's Wife,* Playboy Press, 1976.
Murder Game, Carroll & Graf, 1991.

"MARCUS WELBY" SERIES

Rock a Cradle Empty, Ace Books, 1970.
The Acid Test, Ace Books, 1970.
The Fire's Center, Ace Books, 1971.

"GENERAL HOSPITAL" SERIES

Surgeon's Crisis, Award Books, 1972.
In the Name of Love, Award Books, 1974.

"THE BOLD ONES" SERIES

The Surrogate Womb, Manor Books, 1973.
A Quality of Fear, Manor Books, 1973.
To Get Along with the Beautiful Girls, Manor Books, 1974.

UNDER PSEUDONYM MAX DAY; NOVELS

So Nice, So Wild, Stanley Library, 1959.
Girl on the Beach, Beacon Books, 1960.
The Resort, Beacon Books, 1960.
Bachelor in Suburbia, Beacon Books, 1962.

UNDER PSEUDONYM CARSON BINGHAM; NOVELS

Gorgo, Monarch Books, 1960.
Payola Woman, Belmont Books, 1960.
Run Tough, Run Hard, Monarch Books, 1961.
It Happened in Hawaii, Monarch Books, 1961.
The Street Is My Beat, Monarch Books, 1961.
The Loves of Dr. Devere, Monarch Books, 1962.
The Gang Girls, Monarch Books, 1963.
Flash Gordon: The Witch Queen of Mongo, Avon, 1974.
Flash Gordon: The War of the Cybernauts, Avon, 1975.
The Phantom: The Assassins, Avon, 1975.

UNDER PSEUDONYM ROBERT FARADAY; NOVELS

The Anytime Rings, Dell Books, 1963.
Samax, the Gladiator, Dell Books, 1964.

UNDER PSEUDONYM C.K. FONG; NOVELS

The Year of the Ape, Manor Books, 1975.
The Year of the Cock, Manor Books, 1975.

UNDER PSEUDONYM ANNIE LAURIE McALLISTER; NOVELS

House of Vengeance, Berkley Books, 1976.
Queen of the Looking Glass, Berkley Books, 1978.

NONFICTION

Practical Home Repair for Women, Taplinger, 1966, reprinted, 1972.
Fix It Yourself!, Tower Books, 1970.
Survival Handbook, Tower Books, 1971.
The Best House for the Money, Belmont-Tower Books, 1972.
How to Choose Your Vacation House, Dodd, 1974.
Lawns and Landscaping, Harper, 1976.

(With wife, Doris Cassiday) *Fashion Industry Careers,* F. Watts, 1977.

The Complete Solar House, Dodd, 1977.

(With D. Cassiday) *Careers in the Beauty Industry,* F. Watts, 1978.

The Complete Condominium Guide, Dodd, 1979.

The Carpenter's Bible, Doubleday, 1981.

(With Dr. Yoko I. Takahashi) *The Tokyo Diet,* Morrow, 1985.

BIOGRAPHIES

Betty Ford: Woman of Courage, Dale Books, 1978.

(With Bill Adler) *R. F. K.: A Very Special Man,* Playboy Press, 1978.

Dinah!, F. Watts, 1979.

(With Adler) *The World of Jay Leno: His Life and Humor,* Carol, 1992.

EDITOR

Roots of Detection: The Art of Deduction before Sherlock Holmes, Ungar, 1983.

(With Walter Woeller) *The Literature of Crime and Detection: An Illustrated History from Antiquity to the Present,* Ungar, 1988.

(With Dieter Wuckell) *The Illustrated History of Science Fiction,* Ungar, 1989.

Modern Mystery, Fantasy, and Science Fiction Writers, Continuum, 1993.

OTHER

Author of *The Heister,* published in *Man's Magazine,* January, 1965. Contributor to books, including *The Murder Mystique,* edited by Lucy Freeman, Ungar, 1982; *Cloak and Dagger,* edited by Bill Pronzini and Martin H. Greenberg, Crown, 1986; and *Writing Mysteries,* edited by Sue Grafton, Writer's Digest Books, 1992. Contributor of short stories and articles to journals and periodicals, including *Dime Mystery, Shock, Detective Tales, Dime Detective, 15-Story Detective, 15-Story Western, Max Brand's Western Magazine, Forecast, Writer's Digest, The Writer, Argosy,* and *Mystery Writers Annual.* and *Adventure.* Also contributor of *The Waiting Knife, The Hidden Beast,* and *Deadly Illusion* (comic strips), King Features Syndicate, 1958.

Also author of radio scripts, including *Flight to Valhalla,* 1946, *Crossroads of a Dream,* 1946, *What Dreams Reveal,* 1946, and *Delusion,* 1948, for *Grand Central Station,* Columbia Broadcasting System (CBS), and *The Strange Death of Gordon Fitzroy,* for Suspense, CBS. Author of television script, *Doubled in Danger,* for "Pepsi Cola Playhouse," Revue Productions, 1954.

SIDELIGHTS: Travels have taken Bruce Cassiday to Italy, Algeria, Tunisia, Spain, the Caribbean, Mexico, Alaska, Canada, Hawaii, Ireland, Scotland, England, Sweden, and Finland. He once told *CA* that he believes travel is "essential for a writer not only to provide background and understanding of other places and other people for future work, but to interpret the universality of each human being's triumphs and tragedies in the life struggle."

Mr. Cassiday also detailed for *CA* readers some insights gleaned from his own extensive writing career, focusing on the craft of mystery writing: "I started out writing stories that were to be told by the human voice, in the form of radio drama, which seemed a felicitous return to a classic form of storytelling. A good radio writer could build up in the listener's mind marvelous images of stately grandeur, amusing scenes of delicious humor, ferocious and destructive confrontations, hideous manifestations of unbelievable terror. Never was there a medium more fortuitously developed to present the suspense tale in all its glory.

"Soon enough, however, sound alone was gone as the main medium, and sight and sound combined to form a new medium called television. There was nowhere for me to go but to the printed word, from psychological suspense to the mystery, which employed most of the same elements of plot and story. The mystery format at the time was simple: a crime was committed, the perpetrator sought and found, and the milieu of the crime returned to its status quo. It was a morality tale, updated to the twentieth century, pure and simple.

"That format, basically British, had been reinvigorated by American writers and restructured into the legend of the white knight—the arrival of a savior to rescue those subjugated by a tyrannical overlord, the eventual slaying of that dragon, and the tying up of various plot ends, with things left a little better than before. It was a morality tale without morality.

"It was easy to fall in love with the Marlowe-Spade-Archer style of writing, to adopt the wisecracking mood of the film noir and narrate events in a side-of-the-mouth manner—easy, and somehow just a little dangerous. Soon enough you knew you were simply a surrogate Chandler/Hammett/MacDonald. You were an instant parody of yourself.

"And the genre itself was shifting, escalating into bloodbaths, with characterization and style giving way to constant carnage, and story vanishing into limbo. I remember moving away from the insistence of slashing and ripping and using the basic elements of the crime story in a kind of contemporary novel that did not focus primarily on crime but *involved* crime. When the police procedural rose in popularity, it seemed to me a viable subgenre.

"It was, however, the espionage novel that really took over the mystery world, with the American novel of international intrigue pitted against the spy story produced by British greats like Eric Ambler and John le Carre. By now the plain and simple classic morality tale had vanished. It became a tale of *amorality,* and examination of the existential system of politics in which both sides were right—*and* wrong. The investigator tried the best he or she could to make some sense of the puzzling shambles of life in the free world.

"My own writing was turning more and more to factual reconstructions rather than fictional ones, and my fiction, strangely enough, was evolving into a more sedate and thoughtful presentation of the mystery puzzle and intellectual explication of the methods of solving such a puzzle. Not cozy, but comfortable.

"The genre by now has become of interest to scholars as well as readers. By examining this long-overlooked literature form, they seem to be finding in it the core of what reading is all about. Those who in the future might want to know what it was really like to live in twentieth-century America could do no better than turn to the best of today's mystery writers for guidance. It is here, even more so than in mainstream literature, that the truth of today's lifestyle is evoked in the printed word.

"Today I find the mystery genre a lasting, formidable, durable species. Its durability lies in the fact that it is the best of all showcases for comedies of manner, novels of sociopolitical relevance, novels of characterization, and novels of in-your-face contemporary drama. It is such, it has been such, and it always will be such."

*   *   *

CHALKER, Jack L(aurence) 1944-

PERSONAL: Born December 17, 1944, in Norfolk, VA; son of Lloyd Allen, Sr., and Nancy Alice (an artist; maiden name, Hopkins) Chalker; married Eva C. Whitley, 1978. *Education:* Towson State College, B.S., 1966; Johns Hopkins University, M.L.A., 1969. *Avocational interests:* Travel (including Europe and Australia), "riding every ferryboat in the world," esoteric high-fidelity audio, art auctioneering, conservation, national parks.

ADDRESSES: Home—5111 Liberty Heights Ave., Baltimore, MD 21207. *Agent*—Eleanor Wood, Blassingame, McCauley and Wood, 432 Park Ave. South, Suite 1205, New York, NY 10016. *Office*—Mirage Press Ltd., P.O. Box 28, Manchester, MD 21102.

CAREER: Mirage Press Ltd., Baltimore, MD, founding editor, 1960-72, editorial and marketing director, 1961—.

Social science, history, and geography teacher in public schools in Baltimore, MD, 1966-78; lecturer at University of Maryland and Smithsonian Institution; consultant to World Science Fiction Conventions. *Military service:* U.S. Air Force, air commando with Special Forces, 1968-71; Maryland Air National Guard, 1968-73; became staff sergeant.

MEMBER: World Science Fiction Society, Science Fiction Writers of America, American Federation of Labor—Congress of Industrial Organizations, Washington Science Fiction Association, New York Science Fiction Society, United Teachers of Baltimore, Pacific Northwest National Parks Association.

AWARDS, HONORS: Nominated for John W. Campbell Award for best new science fiction writer, by reader vote of World Science Fiction Convention, 1977.

WRITINGS:

SCIENCE FICTION AND FANTASY NOVELS

A Jungle of Stars, Ballantine, 1976.
Dancers in the Afterglow, Del Rey, 1978.
The Web of the Chosen, Del Rey, 1978.
A War of Shadows, Ace Books, 1979.
And the Devil Will Drag You Under, Ballantine, 1979.
The Devil's Voyage, Doubleday, 1981.
The Identity Matrix, Timescape, 1982.
The Messiah Choice, Bluejay, 1985.
Downtiming the Night Side, Tor Books, 1985.
The Armlet of the Gods, Ballantine, 1986.
(With Mike Resnick and George Alec Effinger) *The Red Tape War,* Tor Books, 1991.

THE WELL WORLD SERIES

Midnight at the Well of Souls, Del Rey, 1977.
Exiles at the Well of Souls, Del Rey, 1978.
Quest for the Well of Souls, Del Rey, 1978.
The Return of Nathan Brazil, Del Rey, 1979.
Twilight at the Well of Souls: The Legacy of Nathan Brazil, Del Rey, 1980.
Echoes of the Well of Souls, Del Rey, 1993.

THE FOUR LORDS OF THE DIAMOND SERIES

Lilith: A Snake in the Grass, Del Rey, 1981.
Cerebrus: A Wolf in the Fold, Del Rey, 1982.
Charon: A Dragon at the Gate, Del Rey, 1982.
Medusa: A Tiger by the Tail, Del Rey, 1983.

THE SOUL RIDER SERIES

Spirits of Flux and Anchor, Tor Books, 1984.
Empires of Flux and Anchor, Tor Books, 1984.
Masters of Flux and Anchor, Tor Books, 1985.
The Birth of Flux and Anchor, Tor Books, 1985.
Children of Flux and Anchor, Tor Books, 1986.

THE DANCING GODS SERIES

The River of Dancing Gods, Del Rey, 1984.
Demons of the Dancing Gods, Del Rey, 1984.
Vengeance of the Dancing Gods, Del Rey, 1985.
Songs of the Dancing Gods, Del Rey, 1990.

THE RINGS OF THE MASTERS SERIES

Lords of the Middle Dark, Ballantine, 1986.
Pirates of the Thunder, Ballantine, 1987.
Warriors of the Storm, Ballantine, 1987.
Masks of the Martyrs, Ballantine, 1988.

THE CHANGEWINDS SERIES

When the Changewinds Blow, Ace Books, 1987.
Riders of the Winds, Ace Books, 1988.
War of the Maelstrom, Ace Books, 1988.

THE QUINTARA MARATHON SERIES

Demons at Rainbow Bridge, Ace Books, 1989.
Run to Chaos Keep, Ace Books, 1992.
The Ninety Trillion Fausts, Ace Books, 1992.

THE G. O. D., INC., SERIES

The Labyrinth of Dreams, Tor Books, 1987.
Shadow Dancers, Tor Books, 1992.
The Maze in the Mirror, Tor Books, 1992.

OTHER

The New H. P. Lovecraft Bibliography, Mirage Press, 1961, revised edition with Mark Owings published as *The Revised H. P. Lovecraft Bibliography,* 1973.
(Editor) *In Memoriam: Clark Ashton Smith,* Mirage Press, 1963.
(Editor) *Mirage on Lovecraft,* Mirage Press, 1964.
(With Owings) *Index to the Science-Fantasy Publishers,* Mirage Press, 1966, revised edition published as *Index to the SF Publishers,* 1979.
(With Owings) *The Necronomicon: A Study,* Mirage Press, 1968.
An Informal Biography of Scrooge McDuck, Mirage Press, 1974.
Jack Chalker (autobiography), Tor Books, 1985.
Dance Band on the Titanic (short stories), Del Rey, 1988.

Contributor of stories to *Analog* and *Stellar Three.* Editor, *Mirage* magazine, 1961—. Columnist, *Fantasy Review.*

SIDELIGHTS: Jack L. Chalker once told *CA:* "As a trained historian, I am almost unique in writing science fiction. My concerns are not basically new technology or applications, but their effects on mankind. I see a certain historical universality in human nature which is essentially pessimistic, however; in my futures man is still going and still expanding—although the more things change the more they stay the same. My works strongly attack au-

thoritarianism, elitism, and dogmatic ideas whether they be political or otherwise. My general humanistic themes are contemporary; the translation to an exotic (and, of course, technically accurate) science fictional background makes it easier to illustrate and explore the human condition, for the contrast of human beings with exotic backgrounds tends to isolate the universals I wish to address. Individual themes concern alienation, loneliness, and the increasing dehumanization of people by the technology and fast changes that grow around them. The strong individual's attempt to maintain sanity and balance in such a dehumanized society (which is, after all, a reflection of trends I see today) and the social and psychological price that must be paid are common to my works."

Such themes continue to inform Chalker's novels, which are often set within alien societies or against the backdrop of strange and exotic locales. Though Orson Scott Card, writing in the *Washington Post Book World,* complains that Chalker's prose is "workmanlike, unmusical, [and] often annoyingly wrong," he is quick to point out that the author "spins a tale that strikes at the root of human identity. . . . Chalker is a powerful story teller who has not yet learned to write beautiful prose."

Chalker has earned a huge following on the strength of such science fiction and fantasy sagas as the "Well World" series, the "Four Lords of the Diamond" series, and the "Dancing Gods" series. The majority of Chalker's work explores the concept of body-switching: his characters undergo startling physical changes, or are mentally transplanted into a body of a different gender or species. Though this idea is addressed in one form or another in nearly all of his works, most critics agree that it is most successfully presented in 1982s *The Identity Matrix,* in which the psyche of the male protagonist is transferred through the course of the novel into the minds of several female characters. "The handling of the male narrator's reactions and adjustments to the female bodies he inhabits seem very real and are certainly superior to anything [Robert] Heinlein has done along similar lines," lauds a *Science Fiction Review* critic. Fredrica Bartz, writing in the *Science Fiction and Fantasy Book Review,* also considers *The Identity Matrix* to be among the author's best work: "Chalker works with several themes, all of them well developed and interesting: the dependence of the senses on the body, mass paranoia, psychological barriers, relations between the sexes, and mind theory. The latter theme makes the book well worth reading." Bartz concludes that the "strong element of intellect" present in *The Identity Matrix* makes the novel "what SF should be, a fiction of ideas, not just one of setting and action."

"Science fiction, long the stepchild of literature, has, I believe, come of age," Chalker once told *CA.* "In no other form of literature may serious questions be addressed as freely and serious issues isolated more clearly. I am, however, a strong believer in verisimilitude in creating societies and backgrounds, and a believer in the strong surface plot, often intricate, through which the themes are woven rather than dominating the work. One need not be a bore to address serious themes."

BIOGRAPHICAL/CRITICAL SOURCES:

PERIODICALS

Analog, March, 1980, p. 167; February, 1985, p. 47; May, 1991, p. 178.
Christian Science Monitor, August 7, 1987, p. B6.
Fantasy Review, June, 1984, p. 20; August, 1984, p. 8; October, 1984, p. 26; December, 1984, p. 23; November, 1985, p. 17; March, 1986, p. 16; September, 1986, p. 21; November, 1986, p. 26; May, 1987, p. 38.
Science Fiction and Fantasy Book Review, April, 1982, p. 16; October, 1982, p. 15; July, 1983, p. 28.
Science Fiction Chronicle, May, 1985, p. 36; December, 1985, p. 42; February, 1986, p. 32.
Science Fiction Review, May, 1982, p. 54; November, 1982, p. 15; May, 1983, p. 52; May, 1984, p. 23; February, 1985, p. 47; August, 1985, p. 17.
Washington Post Book World, October 25, 1987, p. 6.
West Coast Review of Books, March, 1984, p. 44.*

* * *

CHANDONNET, Ann F. 1943-

PERSONAL: Surname is pronounced "shan-doe-*nay*"; born February 7, 1943, in Lowell, MA; daughter of Leighton D. (a farmer) and Barbara (Cloutman) Fox; married Fernand Chandonnet (a radio announcer), June 11, 1966; children: Yves, Alexandre Jules. *Education:* Lowell State College, B.S. (magna cum laude), 1964; University of Wisconsin, M.S., 1965; graduate study at Boston University, 1967. *Avocational interests:* Conducting living history interviews, skindiving, backpacking, sewing, gardening, canoeing.

ADDRESSES: Home—6552 Lakeway Dr., Anchorage, AK 99502-1949.

CAREER: Dog-walker, housepainter, secretary; high school English teacher in the public schools of Kodiak, AK, 1965-66; Lowell State College, Lowell, MA, instructor in English, 1966-69; Security National Bank, Oakland, CA, secretary to manager, 1970-71; First Enterprise Bank, Oakland, administrative assistant to president, 1971-72; *Anchorage Daily News,* Anchorage, AK, food editor, beginning 1975, children's book reviewer, 1979-83; *Anchorage Times,* Anchorage, feature writer, 1982-1992;

Alaska magazine, contributing editor, 1992—; Alaska Northwest Books, publicist, 1993—.

MEMBER: Alaska Press Women, Mayflower Descendants in the State of Alaska.

AWARDS, HONORS: First place award from Alaska Press Women, 1975, for a feature article, "Keeping an Ancient Art Alive," a profile of one of the last surviving Aleut basket-weavers; Alaska Press Club feature writing award, 1992, for article on fetal alcohol syndrome.

WRITINGS:

Incunabula (poems), Quixote Press, 1967.
The Complete Fruit Cookbook, 101 Productions, 1972.
The Cheese Guide and Cookbook, Nitty Gritty Productions, 1973.
The Wife & Other Poems, privately printed, 1977, 2nd edition, 1980.
The Wife: Part 2 (poems), privately printed, 1979.
The Once & Future Village of Ikluat-Eklutna (self-illustrated), privately printed, 1979.
At the Fruit-Tree's Mossy Root, Wings Press, 1980.
Ptarmigan Valley (poems), Lightning Tree, 1980.
Auras, Tendrils (poems), Penumbra Press, 1984.
On the Trail of Eklutna, privately printed, 1991.
Chief Stephen's Parky (children's fiction), Roberts Rinehart, 1993.
The Alaska Heritage Seafood Cookbook, Alaska Northwest Books, in press.

Contributor to *California Girl, Venus, Early American Life, Anchorage Daily News, Great Lander, Women's Circle: Home Cooking, Christian Science Monitor,* and *Alaska Journal.* Food editor, *Diablo Valley Voice,* 1971-72; author of poem "Words for Shadows," part of a collaborative work commemorating the victims of the Exxon Valdez oil spill.

WORK IN PROGRESS: Chugach (poems).

* * *

CHANG, Raymond 1939-

PERSONAL: Born March 6, 1939, in Hong Kong; son of Junsheng (a banker) and Ju-fen (a homemaker; maiden name, Li) Chang; married Margaret Scrogin (a librarian and writer), August 3, 1968; children: Elizabeth Hope. *Education:* University of London, B.S. (first class honors), 1962; Yale University, M.S., 1963, Ph.D., 1966.

ADDRESSES: Home—146 Forest Rd., Williamstown, MA 01267. *Office*—Department of Chemistry, Williams College, Williamstown, MA 01267.

CAREER: Hunter College of the City University of New York, New York City, assistant professor of chemistry,

1967-68; Williams College, Williamstown, MA, assistant professor, 1968, became associate professor, professor of chemistry, 1979—, chair of department, 1982-83.

MEMBER: American Chemical Society, Sigma Xi.

AWARDS, HONORS: Speaking of Chinese was included on the New York Public Library's list of Books for the Teen Age, 1980, 1981, and 1982.

WRITINGS:

(With wife, Margaret Scrogin Chang) *Speaking of Chinese,* Norton, 1978.
(With Margaret Scrogin Chang) *In the Eye of War,* McElderry/Macmillan, 1990.
(With Margaret Scrogin Chang) *Cricket Warrior,* McElderry/Macmillan, 1994.

Author of seven chemistry textbooks.

WORK IN PROGRESS: Chemistry books.

SIDELIGHTS: Raymond Chang's wife, Margaret Scrogin Chang, told *CA:* "Chang's family moved to Hong Kong from their home in Shanghai to escape the 1937 Japanese invasion of China. Chang was born in the British Crown Colony, the youngest son of a family that already included nine children. Not long after the Japanese marched into Hong Kong on Christmas Day, 1941, the Changs moved back to Shanghai, where they lived under Japanese occupation. In 1949 they returned to Hong Kong, leaving Shanghai for good.

"Because of his family's background and the many relocations, Chang became fluent in several Chinese dialects. At home he heard his mother's dialect, Western Mandarin. He talked with his playmates in Shanghainese, while in school they all learned Peking Mandarin, the national standard for spoken language. In Hong Kong he had to learn a completely different spoken language, the Cantonese dialect of southern China. Fortunately for him, the same written language unites all of China.

"At the age of seventeen, Chang followed his sister to London for what he thought would be a few years of study in the West. He did not return to Hong Kong for seventeen years, and then it was only for a brief visit. On the boat that took him to England, Chang soon realized that the English he had learned as a Chinese schoolboy was inadequate for everyday communication and totally useless for reading the dinner menu, which was all in French! Once in London, he set about improving his English and now speaks so fluently that most people assume he was born in the United States.

"After a couple of years in preparatory school, Chang entered the University of London to study chemistry, and he graduated with first class honors. Partly because three of his sisters had married and moved to the United States, he decided to continue his education in America. He earned his Ph.D., married an American, and moved to a scenic corner of New England to become a chemistry professor at Williams College.

"Since for many years he was the only Asian on the faculty, Chang often went outside his field of chemistry to explain Chinese language and culture to curious students. For several years he taught a popular winter study course, a one-month introduction to Chinese language and calligraphy. When he tried to gather background materials for his course, he found no book on the Chinese language that was written for the general reader, the layman without a background in linguistics or Sinology.

"Though he was already the author of two chemistry books, he asked me to help him write a popular introduction to the Chinese language, one that people interested in China could read in bed without a pencil. *Speaking of Chinese* was the result. Chang drew on his boyhood experiences to select the proverbs, describe Chinese grammar, and write the calligraphy used in the text.

"In 1982 Chang led a group of Williams College students and alumni on a winter study tour of the People's Republic of China. It was his first trip home in more than thirty years. In Shanghai, he was amazed by the vast numbers of people, all so healthy and well-clothed. His old neighborhood looked far more crowded than he remembered. His childhood home, shabby but still standing, housed three families.

"Like many Chinese professionals who have returned to their native land for a visit, he found the territory familiar, but he knew that the country of his childhood was no longer his."

Chang drew on the memory of his years in Shanghai when he and his wife wrote *In the Eye of War,* a novel for children about a Chinese family in occupied Shanghai. Also with his wife he wrote *Cricket Warrior,* a retelling of a favorite childhood story.

*   *   *

CHAPPELL, Warren   1904-1991

PERSONAL: Born July 9, 1904, in Richmond, VA; died of heart failure, March 26, 1991, in Charlottesville, VA; son of Samuel M. (a railway clerk) and Mary Lillian (Hardie) Chappell; married Lydia Anne Hatfield, August 28, 1928. *Education:* University of Richmond, B.A., 1926; studied art at Art Students League, New York, NY, 1926-28, Offenbacher Werkstatt in Germany, 1931-32, and Colorado Springs Fine Arts Center, 1935-36. *Politics:* Independent. *Religion:* Protestant.

ADDRESSES: Home—500 Court Sq., Charlottesville, VA 22901. *Office*—Alderman Library, University of Virginia, Charlottesville, VA 22903.

CAREER: Art Students League, New York City, member of board of control, 1927-31, instructor, 1933-35; *Liberty* (magazine), New York City, promotional art director, 1928-31; typographic and decorative designer for numerous magazines, including *Woman's Home Companion,* 1932-35; Colorado Springs Fine Arts Center, Colorado Springs, CO, instructor, 1935-36; book designer, writer, and illustrator, 1936-1991; University of Virginia, Charlottesville, artist-in-residence, 1979-1991. Consultant to Book-of-the-Month Club, 1944-78; lecturer at New York University. Chappell's graphic work, drawings, illustrations, type, and designs have were exhibited at the University of Virginia Library, February and March, 1983.

MEMBER: Master Drawings Association, Lawn Society of University of Virginia, Chilmark Associations, Phi Beta Kappa.

AWARDS, HONORS: Spring Book Festival Award, *New York Herald Tribune,* 1943, for *Patterns on the Wall; The Quaint and Curious Quest of Johnny Longfoot, the Shoe King's Son* was named a John Newbery Award honor book by the Association for Library Services to Children, 1948; University of Richmond, D.F.A., 1968; Goudy Award, Rochester Institute of Technology, 1970.

WRITINGS:

The Anatomy of Lettering, Loring & Mussey, 1935.
They Say Stories, Knopf, 1960.
A Short History of the Printed Word: A "New York Times" Book, Knopf, 1970.
The Living Alphabet, University Press of Virginia, 1975.
(With Rick Cusick) *The Proverbial Bestiary,* Kennebec River Press, 1983.

ADAPTER AND ILLUSTRATOR

The Nutcracker (based on E. T. A. Hoffmann's adaptation of the version by Alexandre Dumas; contains musical themes from the symphony by Peter Ilyich Tchaikovsky), Knopf, 1958.
The Sleeping Beauty (based on the version by Charles Perrault; contains musical themes from the ballet by Tchaikovsky), Knopf, 1961.
(With John Updike) *The Magic Flute* (based on the opera by Wolfgang Amadeus Mozart; contains musical themes from the opera), Knopf, 1962.
Coppelia: The Girl with Enamel Eyes (based on the ballet by Clement-Philibert-Leo Delibes; contains musical themes from the ballet), Knopf, 1965.

ILLUSTRATOR

Jonathan Swift, *A Tale of a Tub,* Columbia University Press, 1930.
Leighton Barret, adapter, *Don Quixote de la Mancha* (based on the novel by Miguel de Cervantes), Little, Brown, 1939, revised edition published as *The Adventures of Don Quixote de la Mancha,* Knopf, 1960.
Sergei Prokofiev, *Peter and the Wolf,* Knopf, 1940.
John B. L. Goodwin, *The Pleasant Pirate,* Knopf, 1940.
Corrine B. Lowe, *Knights of the Sea,* Harcourt, 1941.
William Saroyan, *Saroyan's Fables,* Harcourt, 1941.
Julian David, *The Three Hanses,* Little, Brown, 1942.
Gustave Flaubert, *The Temptation of Saint Anthony,* translated by Lafcadio Hearn, Limited Editions, 1942.
Mark Twain, *A Connecticut Yankee in King Arthur's Court,* Heritage House, 1942.
Elizabeth Yates, *Patterns on the Wall,* Dutton, 1943.
Henry Fielding, *The History of Tom Jones, a Foundling,* Modern Library, 1943.
Brothers Grimm, *Hansel and Gretel,* Knopf, 1944.
William Shakespeare, *The Tragedies of Shakespeare,* Random House, 1944.
Catherine Besterman, *The Quaint and Curious Quest of Johnny Longfoot, the Shoe King's Son,* Bobbs-Merrill, 1947.
William McCleery, *Wolf Story,* Knopf, 1947.
Benjamin Crocker Clough, editor, *The American Imagination at Work: Tall Tales and Folk Tales,* Knopf, 1947.
Edward C. Wagenknecht, editor, *The Fireside Book of Ghost Stories,* Bobbs-Merrill, 1947.
(And editor with wife, Lydia Chappell) *A Gallery of Bible Stories,* Scheer and Jervis, 1947.
Babette Deutsch, adapter, *Reader's Shakespeare,* Messner, 1947.
Wagenknecht, editor, *A Fireside Book of Yuletide Tales,* Bobbs-Merrill, 1948.
Besterman, *Extraordinary Education of Johnny Longfoot in His Search for the Magic Hat,* Bobbs-Merrill, 1949.
Jane Austen, *The Complete Novels of Jane Austen,* two volumes, Random House, 1950.
Regina Z. Kelly, *Young Geoffrey Chaucer,* Lothrop, 1952.
Robert Tallant, *The Louisiana Purchase,* Random House, 1952.
Vincent Sheean, *Thomas Jefferson, Father of Democracy,* Random House, 1953.
Thomas B. Costain, *Mississippi Bubble,* Random House, 1955.
Paul Delarue, editor, *The Borzoi Book of French Folk Tales,* Knopf, 1956.
Manuel Komroff, *Mozart,* Knopf, 1956.
Walter de la Mare, *Come Hither,* Knopf, 1957.

Waverly Lewis Root, *The Food of France,* introduction by Samuel Chamberlain, Knopf, 1958.

Irving Kolodin, *Musical Life,* Knopf, 1958.

Joseph Donon, *The Classic French Cuisine,* Knopf, 1959.

Benjamin Albert Botkin, editor, *A Civil War Treasury of Tales, Legends, and Folklore,* Random House, 1960.

Henry Carlisle, editor, *American Satire in Prose and Verse,* Random House, 1960.

William Cole, editor, *Erotic Poetry,* Random House, 1963.

Updike, adapter, *Ring* (based on musical drama by Richard Wagner), Knopf, 1964.

Sid Fleischman, *The Ghost in the Noon Day Sun,* Little, Brown, 1965.

Conrad Richter, *The Light in the Forest,* Knopf, 1966.

Kate Douglas Wiggin and N. A. Smith, *The Fairy Ring,* Doubleday, 1967.

Delarue, compiler, *French Fairy Tales,* Knopf, 1968.

Geoffrey Household, *Prisoner of the Indies,* Little, Brown, 1968.

Updike, adapter, *Bottom's Dream* (based on William Shakespeare's play, *A Midsummer Night's Dream;* contains musical themes from the overture by Felix Mendelssohn) Knopf, 1969.

Charles B. Hawes, *Dark Frigate,* Little, Brown, 1971.

Charles Dickens, *A Charles Dickens Christmas: A Christmas Carol, The Chimes, The Cricket on the Hearth,* Oxford University Press, 1976.

Herman Melville, *Moby Dick,* Norton, 1976.

Swift, *A Voyage to Laputa, from Travels by Lemuel Gulliver,* Angelica Press, 1976.

Swift, *Gulliver's Travels,* introduction by Jacques Barzan, Oxford University Press, 1977.

Twain, *The Complete Adventures of Tom Sawyer and Huckleberry Finn,* Harper, 1978.

Robert Penn Warren, *All the King's Men,* Harcourt, 1981.

Rainer Maria Rilke, *Die Weise von Liebe und Tod des Cornets Christoph Rilke: The Lay of the Love and Death of Cornet Christoph Rilke* (poem; bilingual edition), translated by Stephen Mitchell, Arion Press, 1983.

Robert Frost, *Stories for Lesley,* edited by Roger D. Sell, University Press of Virginia, 1984.

Catherine Drinker Bowen, *Miracle at Philadelphia,* Little, Brown, 1986.

OTHER

Also author of *Let's Make a B for Bennett,* privately printed for the Typophiles, 1967; *Forty-odd Years in the Black Arts,* (lecture in typography), Press of the Good Mountain, 1972; and *My Life with Letters,* privately printed for the Typophiles, 1974. Contributor of articles to periodicals, including *Virginia Quarterly Review* and *Dolphin.* Contributor of illustrations and designs to periodicals. Designer and illustrator with wife, Lydia, of a limited edition of Honore de Balzac's *Jesus Christ in Flanders.*

SIDELIGHTS: Warren Chappell had a long and distinguished career as an illustrator and book designer, lending his skills to such time-honored tales as the Brothers Grimm's *Hansel and Gretel* as well as works by William Shakespeare, Jane Austen, and Miguel de Cervantes. During the 1940s and 1950s Chappell designed and illustrated numerous children's books and a series of nonfiction books. Among his own favorites of these years were two 1947 publications, Catherine Besterman's *The Quaint and Curious Quest of Johnny Longfoot, the Shoe King's Son,* a Newbery honor book, and William McCleery's *Wolf Story,* which was reissued in 1988 and described as an "underground classic" by *School Library Journal.*

In 1942 Chappell illustrated *A Connecticut Yankee in King Arthur's Court,* American writer Mark Twain's 1899 satiric novel. Diana Klemin, author of *The Illustrated Book: Its Art and Craft,* found Chappell the "perfect choice to illustrate this book," because his interpretive illustrations match Twain's wit and speak eloquently for his causes, complementing "the author's energy, invention, imagination, and verve." Klemin also applauded Chappell's comprehensive knowledge of his art. "He understands book format, does not try to go beyond its conventions, and overlooks no detail. The illustration, in live, strong line or rich, lusty watercolor, runs alongside its text, so that you are not groping for it, and fits within the type area." Klemin further exclaimed, "If only there were many other artists to do books as well as Chappell does his!"

Chappell also adapted and illustrated picture books from ballets, including *The Nutcracker* and *Sleeping Beauty.* A *New York Times Book Review* contributor commented that *Sleeping Beauty* had been weakened by attempts to make it suitable for young readers, and that Chappell's version revives many forgotten details, giving it "back some of its original style and charm." In addition, Chappell also created two original typefaces, the Lydian (named for his wife), and the Trajanus. The Lydian typeface has been used regularly in such notable publications as the book section of the *New York Times.*

Because of his expertise in the printing field, the *New York Times* asked Chappell to write a book about printing called *A Short History of the Printed Word.* The 1970 book traces the history of Western printing from the fifteenth century—when German inventor Johannes Gutenberg developed the technique of printing from movable type—to the twentieth century with its computerized composition. Chappell entertained his readers with anecdotes from his own experience in the trade and illustrations of type designs from different eras as well as abundant technical and historical information. Ray Nash in the *New York Times Book Review* called this a "fascinating book," while *New York Times Book Review* contributor Ray Walters assessed, "The brisk, knowledgeable style in which Mr. Chappell follows design, composition, and presswork through six centuries, lacing his account with personal reminiscences and anecdotes, should give pleasure to anyone who has ever fondled a book."

In an essay for *Something about the Author Autobiography Series,* Chappell lamented the changes in the publishing industry, with "auctions replacing negotiations," the fact that "taxes on books have made backlists uneconomical," and the differences in manufacturing processes. He commented, "I had chosen to try and keep alive the capacity for artists, rather than engineers, to control the design of printing types."

BIOGRAPHICAL/CRITICAL SOURCES:

BOOKS

Chappell, Warren, *A Short History of the Printed Word: A "New York Times" Book,* Knopf, 1970.
Klemin, Diana, *The Illustrated Book: Its Art and Craft,* Crown, 1970, p. 48.
Something about the Author Autobiography Series, Volume 10, Gale, 1990, pp. 57-74.

PERIODICALS

Booklist, March, 1966, p. 662.
Library Journal, October 15, 1991, p. 92.
New York Times Book Review, December 6, 1970, p. 90; July 27, 1980, p. 27.
Times Literary Supplement, September 28, 1973, p. 1121.
Washington Post Book World, December 13, 1981, p. 12.

OBITUARIES:

PERIODICALS

Chicago Tribune, March 31, 1991.
Chronicles, July, 1991.
Daily Progress (Charlottesville, VA), March 28, 1991.
New York Times, March 29, 1991.
Richmond News Leader, March 28, 1991.
Richmond Times-Dispatch, March 28, 1991.

*   *   *

CHASE, Caroline
See DuBAY, Sandra

CHEKKI, Dan(esh) A(yyappa) 1935-

PERSONAL: Born February 5, 1935, in Haveri, Karnatak, India; son of Virappa C. (a pleader) and Chenabasavva Yagati; married Sheela D. Leelavati Metgud, May 8, 1966; children: Mahantesh, Chenaviresh. *Education:* Karnatak University, B.A., 1956, Ph.D., 1966; University of Bombay, M.A., 1958, LL.B., 1959, D.Lib., 1960. *Avocational interests:* Photography, art collecting.

ADDRESSES: Home—38 Fitzgerald Crescent, Winnipeg, Manitoba, Canada R3R IN8. *Office*—Department of Sociology, University of Winnipeg, 515 Portage Ave., Winnipeg, Manitoba, Canada R3B 2E9.

CAREER: University of Bombay, Bombay, India, lecturer in sociology, 1958-61; Karnatak University, Dharwar, India, lecturer in sociology, 1961-66; University of Winnipeg, Winnipeg, Manitoba, Canada, assistant professor, 1968-71, associate professor, 1971-78, professor of sociology, 1979—, Institute of Urban Studies, faculty associate, 1983—. Reader at Karnatak University, 1967-72. Member of board of directors of Family Bureau of Greater Winnipeg, 1970-74, and Family Services of Winnipeg, 1976-81.

MEMBER: International Sociological Association (secretary, Community Research Committee, 1984—), Canadian Association of South Asian Studies, National Council of Family Relations, Academy of Research (president), American Sociological Association, Indian Sociological Society, Policy Studies Organization, American Academy of Political and Social Science, World Future Society, Hindu Society of Manitoba (member of board of directors, 1981-82).

AWARDS, HONORS: Research grants from Karnatak University, 1967-68, and from University of Winnipeg, 1970-78; *Choice* Outstanding Book Award, 1987, for *American Sociological Hegemony.*

WRITINGS:

Social Aspects of Ornaments (in Kannada language), Karnatak University, 1967.
Modernization and Kin Network, E. J. Brill, 1974.
The Social System and Culture of Modern India, Garland Publishing (New York City), 1975.
The Sociology of Contemporary India, South Asia Books (Columbia, MO), 1978.
Community Development: Theory and Method of Planned Change, Vikas Publishing House (India), 1980.
Participatory Democracy in Action: International Profiles of Community Development, Vikas Publishing House, 1980.
Citizen Attitudes toward City Services and Taxes, Institute of Urban Studies and Institute for Economic and Social Research, 1985.

Organized Interest Groups and the Urban Policy Process, Institute of Urban Studies (Arlington, TX), 1985.

Guru, Bless Me with Your Grace, University of Winnipeg, 1986.

American Sociological Hegemony, Garland Publishing, 1987.

Dimensions of Communities: A Research Handbook, Garland Publishing, 1989.

Contemporary Community: Change and Challenge, JAI Press (Greenwich, CT), 1990.

Communities in Transition, JAI Press, 1992.

A Quarter Century of Sociology, University of Winnipeg, 1993.

Also contributor to *The Family in India,* Mouton, 1974; *Main Currents in Indian Sociology,* edited by G. R. Gupta, Carolina Academic Press (Durham, NC), 1976; and *Structured Inequality in Canada,* Prentice-Hall (Englewood Cliffs, NJ), 1980. Contributor to journals. Assistant editor of *International Journal of Comparative Sociology,* 1964; associate editor of *Journal of Comparative Family Studies,* 1970—, and *Contributions to Asian Studies,* 1971-74; editor of sociology series in Reference Library of Social Sciences, 1980-94; advisory editor, *Indian Journal of Social Research,* 1982—, and *Journal of Sociological Studies;* editor of *Research in Community Sociology,* 1990—, and *Contributions in Sociology Series,* 1993—.

WORK IN PROGRESS: Urban Policy in Canada; Native Youth in the Urban Context.

SIDELIGHTS: Dan A. Chekki told *CA:* "Writing books based on social research has been a stimulating and challenging task aimed at understanding and interpreting social reality and discovering the unknown."

BIOGRAPHICAL/CRITICAL SOURCES:

PERIODICALS

Choice, May, 1988, p. 1481; April, 1990, p. 1401.
Reference & Research Book News, December, 1989, p. 17.
Social Forces, March, 1989, p. 821.

*   *   *

CHEN, Lincoln C(hih-ho) 1942-

PERSONAL: Born February 12, 1942, in China; brought to the United States, 1949; son of Samuel S. T. (a teacher) and Winifred (Wan) Chen; married Martha Alter, July 1, 1967; children: Gregory, Alexis. *Education:* Princeton University, B.A. (cum laude), 1964; Harvard University, M.D., 1968; Johns Hopkins University, M.P.H., 1973. *Politics:* Independent.

ADDRESSES: Home—302 Dean Rd., Brookline, MA 02146-4141. *Office*—Harvard School of Public Health, 665 Huntington Ave., Room 1110, Boston, MA 02115-6021.

CAREER: Massachusetts General Hospital, Boston, internal medicine intern, 1968-69, assistant resident in internal medicine, 1969-70; Harvard Medical School, Boston, clinical fellow, 1969-70; National Institute of Allergies and Infectious Diseases, National Institute of Health, clinical research associate, Washington, DC, 1970-72; Population Council, New York City, staff associate, 1972-77; Ford Foundation, program officer in Bangladesh, 1973-77, acting representative, 1976; International Centre for Diarrheal Disease Research, Bangladesh, scientific director, 1977-80; Ford Foundation, representative in India, Sri Lanka, and Nepal, 1981-86; Harvard School of Public Health, Boston, chairman of population services department, 1987, Takemi Professor of International Health, 1987—, study director of Community on Health Research, 1987—. University of Dhaka, Bangladesh, visiting professor of nutrition, 1970-80; Massachusetts Institute of Technology, visiting lecturer, 1976-81; White House Task Force on International Health, member, 1977; Bangladesh Institute for Developmental Studies, visiting scholar, 1977-78; National Institute of Health, U.S.-Japan Malnutrition Panel, member, 1979-80; Harvard University, visiting associate professor of population science and international health, 1980-81; United Nations University, global advisory commission member, 1980-83; UNICEF, advisory committee on child survival revolution, member, 1984—. *Military service:* U.S. Public Health Service, 1970-72; became lieutenant commander.

MEMBER: International Union Nutritional Sciences, International Epidemiology Association, International Center for Research for Women (member of board of directors, 1987), American Public Health Association, Population Association of America, National Council for International Health (member of board of directors, 1982-83), National Academy of Science (member of committee on international nutrition programs, 1982-84; member of subcommittee on vitamin A, 1986), Phi Beta Kappa, Alpha Omega Alpha.

AWARDS, HONORS: National Science Foundation award, 1964.

WRITINGS:

A Prospective Study of Birth Interval Dynamics in Rural Bangladesh, Ford Foundation (Dacca), 1974.

An Analysis of Per Capita Food Availability, Consumption, and Requirements in Bangladesh: A Systematic Approach to Food Planning, Ford Foundation (Dacca), 1974.

(With George T. Curlin and Sayed Babur Hussain) *Demographic Crises: The Impact of the Bangladesh Civil*

War (1971) on Births and Deaths in Rural Areas of Bangladesh, Ford Foundation (Dacca), 1975.

(With Rafiqul Huda Chowdhury) *Demographic Change and Trends of Food Production and Availabilities in Bangladesh, 1960-74,* Ford Foundation (Dacca), 1975.

(With A. K. M. Alauddin Chowdhury and Atiqur Rahman Khan) *The Effect of Child Mortality Experience on Subsequent Fertility: An Empirical Analysis of Pakistan and Bangladesh Data,* Ford Foundation (Dacca), 1975.

(With Sandra L. Huffman and Penny Satterthwaite) *Recent Fertility Trends in Bangladesh: Speculation on the Role of Biological Factors and Socioeconomic Change,* Ford Foundation (Dacca), 1976.

(With Chowdhury) *The Dynamics of Contemporary Famine,* Ford Foundation (Dacca), 1977.

EDITOR

Disaster in Bangladesh: Health Crisis in a Developing Nation, Oxford University Press, 1973.

(With Monowar Hossain and M. Aminur Rohman Khan) *Fertility in Bangladesh: Which Way Is It Going?,* Bangladesh Fertility Survey, National Institute of Population Research and Training (Dacca), 1979.

(With Nevin S. Scrimshaw) *Diarrhea and Malnutrition: Interactions, Mechanisms, and Interventions,* Plenum (New York City), 1983.

(With W. Henry Mosley) *Child Survival: Strategies for Research,* Cambridge University Press (New York City), 1984.

(With Jaime Sepulveda Amor, Sheldon J. Segal and Judith Masslo Anderson) *AIDS and Women's Reproductive Health,* Plenum (New York City), 1991.

(With Arthur Kleinman and Norma C. Ware) *Advancing Health in Developing Countries: The Role of Social Research,* Auburn House (New York City), 1992.

(With Kleinman and Ware) *Health and Social Change in International Perspective,* Oxford University Press (New York City), 1992.

(With Gita Sen and Adrienne Germain) *Population Policies Reconsidered: Health, Empowerment, and Rights,* Harvard University Press (Boston), 1994.

Contributor to books and professional journals.

WORK IN PROGRESS: Research on international health, nutrition, and population.*

*   *   *

CHERRY, Kelly

PERSONAL: Born in Baton Rouge, LA; daughter of J. Milton (a violinist and professor of music theory) and Mary (a violinist and writer; maiden name, Spooner) Cherry; married Jonathan Silver, December 23, 1966 (divorced, 1969). *Education:* Mary Washington College, B.A.; University of North Carolina at Greensboro, M.F.A., 1967; also attended New Mexico Institute of Mining and Technology, Virginia Polytechnic Institute (now Virginia Polytechnic Institute and State University), Richmond Professional Institute (now Virginia Commonwealth University), University of Richmond, and University of Tennessee.

ADDRESSES: Home—Madison, WI. *Office—* Department of English, 7179 Helen C. White Hall, University of Wisconsin—Madison, Madison, WI 53706. *Agent—* Miriam Altshuler, Russell & Volkening, Inc, 50 West 29th St., Apt. 7E, New York, NY 10001.

CAREER: Behrman House, Inc. (publishers), New York City, editor and writer, 1970-71; Charles Scribner's Sons, New York City, editor, 1971-72; John Knox Press, Richmond, VA, editor, 1973; Southwest Minnesota State College (now Southwest State University), Marshall, writer-in-residence, 1974 and 1975; University of Wisconsin—Madison, visiting lecturer, 1977-78, assistant professor, 1978-79, associate professor, 1979-82, professor, 1982—, writer-in-residence, 1977—, Romnes Professor of English, 1983-88, Evjue-Bascom Professor in the Humanities, 1993—. Western Washington University, distinguished writer-in-residence, 1981; *Book Forum,* contributing editor, 1984-88; *Anglican Theological Review,* consultant to poetry editor, 1986—; Rhodes College, distinguished visiting professor, 1985; *Shenandoah,* advising editor, 1988-92. Has taught at writers' conference workshops and presented numerous readings of her works at colleges and universities in both the U.S. and abroad, including Duke University, Bennington Writing Workshops, and Mount Holyoke Writers Conference; has also worked as editorial assistant, copy editor, and tutor, and as teacher to emotionally disturbed teenagers.

MEMBER: PEN, Poetry Society of America, Poets and Writers, Associated Writing Programs (member, board of directors, 1990-93), Authors Guild, Authors League of America, National Book Critics Circle, American Academy of Poets, Phi Beta Kappa.

AWARDS, HONORS: University of Virginia Dupont Fellow in philosophy, 1962-63; Canaras Award for fiction, St. Lawrence University Writers Conference, 1974; Bread Loaf fellow, 1975; Pushcart Prize, 1977; Yaddo fellow, 1979 and 1989; National Endowment for the Arts fellowship, 1980; first prize for book-length fiction, Wisconsin Council of Writers, 1980, for *Augusta Played,* and 1991, for *My Life and Dr. Joyce Brothers;* PEN/Syndicated Fiction Award, 1983, for "Life at the Equator," 1987, for "Acts of Unfathomable Compassion," and 1990, for

"About Grace"; Romnes fellowship, University of Wisconsin, 1983; fellowship, Wisconsin Arts Board, 1984 and 1989; Chancellor's Award, 1984; Ritz Paris Hemingway Award nomination, 1984, for *The Lost Traveller's Dream;* James G. Hanes Poetry Prize, Fellowship of Southern Writers, 1989, for distinguished body of work; Arts America Speaker Award (Republic of the Philippines), U.S. Information Agency, 1992.

WRITINGS:

FICTION

Sick and Full of Burning, Viking, 1974.
Augusta Played, Houghton, 1979.
Conversion (chapbook), Treacle Press, 1979.
In the Wink of an Eye, Harcourt, 1983.
The Lost Traveller's Dream, Harcourt, 1984.
My Life and Dr. Joyce Brothers, Algonquin, 1990.

POETRY

Lovers and Agnostics, Red Clay, 1975, revised, Carnegie Mellon University Press, forthcoming.
Relativity: A Point of View, Louisiana State University Press, 1977.
Songs for a Soviet Composer (chapbook), Singing Wind Press, 1980.
Natural Theology, Louisiana State University Press, 1988.
God's Loud Hand, Louisiana State University Press, 1993.
Benjamin John (chapbook), March Street Press, 1993.
Time out of Mind (chapbook), March Street Press, 1994.

NONFICTION

(Coauthor and associate editor) *Lessons from Our Living Past* (textbook), Behrman House, 1972.
Teacher's Guide for Lessons from Our Living Past (textbook), Behrman House, 1972.
The Exiled Heart: A Meditative Autobiography, Louisiana State University Press, 1991.

OTHER

(Translator) *Octavia,* in *Seneca: The Tragedies,* Volume 2, edited by Bovie and Slavitt, Johns Hopkins University Press, 1994.

Contributor to anthologies, including *The Girl in the Black Raincoat,* edited by George Garrett, Duell, Sloan & Pearce, 1966; *Pushcart Prize II,* edited by Bill Henderson, Avon, 1977; *Strong Measures: Recent American Poems in Traditional Forms,* edited by Philip Dacey and David Jauss, Harper, 1985; and *Prize Stories 1994: The O. Henry Awards,* Doubleday, 1994. Contributor of stories, poems, essays, and book reviews to periodicals, including *American Scholar, Atlantic Monthly, Commentary, Esquire, Fiction, Georgia Review, Gettysburg Review, The Independent on Sunday, Los Angeles Times Book Review, Ms., Made-moiselle, New Literary History, New York Times Book Review, North American Review, Parnassus, Southern Poetry Review, Southern Review,* and *Virginia Quarterly Review.*

Cherry's works have been translated into numerous foreign languages, including Chinese, Czech, Dutch, Latvian, Lithuanian, Polish, Swedish, and Ukrainian.

WORK IN PROGRESS: Novels, poems, and essays.

SIDELIGHTS: Award-winning poet and novelist Kelly Cherry is concerned with philosophy; with, as she explains it, "the becoming-aware of abstraction in real life—since, in order to abstract, you must have something to abstract from." Within her novels, the abstract notions of morality become her focus: "My novels deal with moral dilemmas and the shapes they create as they reveal themselves in time," she once told *CA.* "My poems seek out the most suitable temporal or kinetic structure for a given emotion."

Cherry's collections of poetry, including *Lovers and Agnostics,* published in 1975, *Relativity: A Point of View,* published in 1977, and 1993's *God's Loud Hand,* have been widely praised by critics. "Her poetry is marked by a firm intellectual passion," begins the citation preceding her receipt of the James G. Hanes Poetry Prize in 1989, "a reverent desire to possess the genuine thought of our century, historical, philosophical, and scientific, and a species of powerful ironic wit which is allied to rare good humor." Reviewing *Relativity,* Patricia Goedicke notes in *Three Rivers Poetry Journal* that "her familiarity with the demands and pressures of traditional patterns has resulted . . . in an expansion and deepening of her poetic resources, a carefully textured over- and underlay of image, meaning and diction."

Reviewers have praised Cherry's sense of humor and poetic language, as well as her keen observations on the human condition. In her novels, the author sometimes centers on female protagonists who cope with personal crises while searching for love, sexual fulfillment, and self-knowledge. Her first novel, *Sick and Full of Burning,* depicts the life and relationships of Mary "Tennessee" Settleworth, a newly divorced medical student facing her thirtieth birthday. On the other hand, *Augusta Played,* published five years later in 1979, explores the dynamics of marriage and money through the tempestuous relationship between a young flutist and her musicologist husband, giving equal weight to both a male and a female point of view. "Cherry's characters begin, as in high comedy, with stock types who gradually grow more and more complex," writes Robert Taylor in a review for the *Boston Globe.* "Behind them is the sad music of mortality . . . proclaiming that even our vanities possess absurd dignity and the absurd lies on the borderline of heartbreak."

The unique structure of Cherry's 1990 novel, *My Life and Dr. Joyce Brothers,* was also favorably received by critics. Subtitled "A Novel in Stories," the book relates, in the words of *Los Angeles Times Book Review* contributor Judith Freeman, "the plight of a middle-aged, unmarried woman named Nina who understands how the numbing jargon of self-help, so prevalent in our culture and epitomized by the philosophy of Dr. Joyce Brothers, can do nothing to alleviate a sense of deep-rooted alienation and loneliness." Freeman observes that the novel is "far too witty, too savvy, too lyrical and compassionate to resort to bitterness": She praises Cherry for performing "the admirable feat of taking hackneyed fates and infusing them with tremendous freshness."

The concerns Cherry addresses in her fiction are also reflected in her autobiography, *The Exiled Heart.* Having met and fallen in love with a Latvian musician named Imant Kalnin during the cold war, Cherry was separated from him and the couple prevented from marrying by the Soviet government. She contemplated the nature and meaning of both love and justice while living in England and waiting for a visa to visit Kalnin. *The Exiled Heart* was the result: "one of the richest and most thoughtful books I have ever read," notes Fred Chappell in a review of the work in *Louisiana Literature.* "The integrity of thought and courage of vision it portrays are qualities that abide in the memory, steadfast as fixed stares. One day this book will come into its own and will be recognized, along with some other works by Kelly Cherry, for the masterwork that it is."

"I'm concerned with the shape of ideas in time," Cherry told *CA* in a discussion of her writing, "the dynamic configuration a moral dilemma makes, cutting through a novel like a river through rock; the way a philosophical statement bounces against the walls of a poem, like an echo in a canyon. A writer, poet or novelist, wants to create a contained, complete landscape in which time flows freely and naturally. The *poems* are where I live. It's in poetry that thought and time most musically counterpoint each other, and I like a world in which the elements sing."

"I think that the crucial unit of the poem is the line; in the story, it's sentence, or voice; and in the novel, it's scene," the novelist explained to *CA,* going on to add some thoughts on the inspiration for her works of fiction. "The hidden model for *Augusta Played* is *The Tempest;* the hidden model for *In the Wink of an Eye* is *A Midsummer Night's Dream.* Shakespeare and Beethoven, they're the main ones; the idea of an extended developmental passage—that's the root impetus for everything I write. I grew up on those two."

BIOGRAPHICAL/CRITICAL SOURCES:

BOOKS

Authors in the News, Volume 1, Gale, 1976.
Bunge, Nancy L., "Conversation with Kelly Cherry," in *Finding the Words: Conversations with Writers Who Teach,* Swallow Press, 1985.
Cherry, Kelly, *The Exiled Heart: A Meditative Autobiography,* Louisiana State University Press, 1991.
Dictionary of Literary Biography Yearbook, Gale, 1983.

PERIODICALS

Boston Globe, March 17, 1979.
Chicago Tribune, May 20, 1984; April 17, 1990.
Library Journal, October 1, 1974.
Los Angeles Times Book Review, June 24, 1990.
Louisiana Literature, April, 1991.
New York Times Book Review, April 22, 1984; May 27, 1990; October 6, 1991.
Three Rivers Poetry Journal, March, 1977.

OTHER

"James G. Hanes Poetry Prize Convocation" (transcript), Fellowship of Southern Writers, 1989.

*   *   *

CLARK, J(onathan) C(harles) D(ouglas) 1951-

PERSONAL: Born February 28, 1951, in London, England. *Education:* Cambridge University, B.A., 1972, M.A., 1976, Ph.D., 1981. *Religion:* Church of England. *Avocational interests:* Skiing, claret.

ADDRESSES: Office—All Souls College, Oxford OX1 4AL, England; *Agent*—Michael Shaw, Curtis Brown Ltd., 162-168 Regent Street, London, W1R 5TB.

CAREER: Worked on London stock exchange, 1972-73; Cambridge University, Peterhouse, Cambridge, England, fellow, 1977-81; Eton College, Windsor, England, assistant master, 1981; Oxford University, All Souls College, Oxford, England, fellow, 1986—. Visiting professor, Committee on Social Thought, University of Chicago, 1993.

MEMBER: Royal Historical Society (fellow), The Beefsteak Club, London.

AWARDS, HONORS: Fellow of Leverhulme Trust, 1984-85.

WRITINGS:

The Dynamics of Change: The Crisis of the 1750's and English Party Systems, Cambridge University Press, 1982.

English Society, 1688-1832: Ideology, Social Structure, and Political Practice during the Ancien Regime, Cambridge University Press, 1985.

Revolution and Rebellion: State and Society in England in the Seventeenth and Eighteenth Centuries, Cambridge University Press, 1986.

(Editor) *The Memoirs and Speeches of James, 2nd Earl Waldegrave, 1742-1763,* Cambridge University Press, 1988.

(Editor) *Ideas and Politics in Modern Britain,* Macmillan, (London,) 1990.

The Language of Liberty 1660-1832: Political Discourse and Social Dynamics in the Anglo-American World, Cambridge University Press, 1993.

Samuel Johnson: Literature, Religion and English Cultural Politics from the Restoration to Romanticism, Cambridge University Press, 1994.

Contributor of articles and reviews to learned journals and newspapers.

WORK IN PROGRESS: An edition for Cambridge University Press of Edmund Burke's *Reflections on the Revolution in France;* a monograph on Burke's social and political thought; further work on British and Anglo-American history in the period 1660-1832.

BIOGRAPHICAL/CRITICAL SOURCES:

PERIODICALS

Times Literary Supplement, January 23, 1987.

*   *   *

CLARK, Ronald William   1916-1987

PERSONAL: Born November 2, 1916, in Wimbledon, England; died March 9, 1987; son of William Ernest (a banker) and Ethel Clark; married Irene Tapp, 1938 (divorced, 1953); married Pearla Doris Odden, 1953. *Education:* Attended King's College, Wimbledon, England. *Avocational interests:* Mountaineering.

ADDRESSES: Home—10 Campden St., London W8, England.

CAREER: Writer since mid-1930s; war correspondent with British United Press, 1943-45; foreign correspondent, 1945-48.

WRITINGS:

BIOGRAPHY

Splendid Hills: The Life and Photographs of Vittorio Sella, 1859-1943, Phoenix House, 1948.

Lion Boy: The Story of Cedric Crossfield, Phoenix House, 1954.

Eccentric in the Alps: The Story of W. A. B. Coolidge, the Great Victorian Mountaineer, Museum Press, 1959.

Sir John Cockroft, O.M., F.R.S., Phoenix House, 1959, Roy, 1960.

Sir Mortimer Wheeler, Roy, 1960.

Montgomery of Alamein, Roy, 1960.

Sir Julian Huxley, F.R.S., Phoenix House, 1960, Roy 1961.

Sir Winston Churchill, Roy, 1962.

Tizard, M.I.T. Press, 1965.

The Huxleys, McGraw, 1968.

J. B. S.: The Life and Work of J. B. S. Haldane, Hodder & Stoughton, 1968, Coward, 1969.

Einstein: The Life and Times, Crowell, 1973, revised edition published with illustrations, Abrams, 1984.

A Biography of the Nuffield Foundation, Longman, 1972.

Sir Edward Appleton, Pergamon, 1972.

The Life of Bertrand Russell, J. Cape, 1975, Knopf, 1976, revised edition published as *Bertrand Russell and His World,* Thames & Hudson, 1981.

The Man Who Broke Purple: The Life of Colonel William F. Friedman, Who Deciphered the Japanese Code in World War II, Little, Brown, 1977, published in England as *The Man Who Broke Purple: The Life of the World's Greatest Cryptologist, Colonel William F. Friedman,* Weidenfeld & Nicolson, 1977.

Edison: The Man Who Made the Future, Putnam, 1977.

Freud: The Man and the Cause, Random House, 1980.

Benjamin Franklin: A Biography, Random House, 1983.

The Survival of Charles Darwin: A Biography of a Man and an Idea, Random House, 1984.

The Life of Ernst Chain: Penicillin and Beyond, St. Martin's, 1985.

Lenin: The Man behind the Mask, Faber, 1988.

MOUNTAINEERING

The Early Alpine Guides, Phoenix House, 1949, Scribner, 1950.

The Victorian Mountaineers, Batsford, 1953, Branford, 1954.

Come Climbing with Me, Muller, 1955.

The Picture History of Mountaineering, Macmillan, 1956.

Six Great Mountaineers: Edward Whymper, A. F. Mummery, J. Norman Collie, George Leigh Mallory, Geoffrey Winthrop Young, Sir John Hunt, Dufour, 1956.

The True Book about Mountaineering, Muller, 1957.

(With Edward C. Pyatt) *Mountaineering in Britain: A History from the Earliest Times to the Present Day,* Phoenix House, 1957.

The Day the Rope Broke: The Story of the First Ascent of the Matterhorn, Harcourt, 1965, published in England as *The Day the Rope Broke: The Story of a Great Victorian Tragedy,* Secker & Warburg, 1965.

Men, Myths, and Mountains, Crowell, 1976.

JUVENILE

Great Moments in Mountaineering, Roy, 1956.

We Go to Switzerland, Harrap, 1958.

Great Moments in Escaping, Roy, 1958.

Great Moments in Rescue Work, Roy, 1959, published in England as *Great Moments of Rescue,* Phoenix House, 1959.

We Go to Scotland, Harrap, 1959.

We Go to Southern France, Harrap, 1960.

Great Moments in Battle, Phoenix House, 1960.

We Go to the West Country, Harrap, 1962.

Great Moments in Espionage, Phoenix House, 1963, Roy, 1964.

We Go to England, International Publications Service, 1963.

We Go to Northern Italy, Harrap, 1964.

(With wife, Pearla Clark) *We Go to Southern England,* International Publications Service, 1964.

The Air: The Story of the Montgolfiers, the Lilienthals, the Wright Brothers, Cobham, and Whittle, Parrish, 1966, Lynn, 1967.

Barney and the UFO, Dodd, 1979.

The Mystery in the Flooded Museum, Dodd, 1978.

OTHER

The Royal Albert Hall, Hamish Hamilton, 1958.

Instructions to Young Ramblers, Museum Press, 1958.

An Encounter in the Alps, Museum Press, 1959.

How to Use Your Camera, illustrated with the author's photographs, Oldbourne, 1961.

The Birth of the Bomb, Horizon Press, 1961, published in England as *The Birth of the Bomb: The Untold Story of Britain's Part in the Weapon That Changed the World,* Phoenix House, 1961.

The Rise of the Boffins, Phoenix House, 1962.

Explorers of the World, Natural History Press, 1964.

Battle for Britain: Sixteen Weeks That Changed the Course of History, Harrap, 1965, F. Watts, 1966.

Queen Victoria's Bomb: The Disclosures of Professor Franklin Huxtable (novel), J. Cape, 1967, Morrow, 1968.

The Bomb That Failed (novel), Morrow, 1969.

The Last Year of the Old World: A Fiction of History (novel), J. Cape, 1970.

The Alps, Knopf, 1973.

The Scientific Breakthrough: The Impact of Modern Invention, Putnam, 1974.

The Role of the Bomber, Crowell, 1977.

War Winners, Sidgwick & Jackson, 1979.

Wonders of the World, Arco, 1980.

The Greatest Power on Earth: The Story of Nuclear Fission, Sidgwick & Jackson, 1980, published as *The Greatest Power on Earth: The International Race for Nuclear Supremacy,* Harper, 1981.

Balmoral: Queen Victoria's Highland Home, Thames & Hudson, 1981.

Works of Man: The Discoveries, Inventions and Technological Achievements That Have Changed the Course of History, Viking, 1985.

Contributor to numerous periodicals, including the London *Times, Guardian, Cornhill,* and *Blackwood's.*

Clark's works have been translated into French.

SIDELIGHTS: Ronald William Clark was a prolific writer who began his career as a journalist. His reputation rests on the wide range of biographies he authored that illuminated the complex works of scientists, inventors, and others who changed the face of society. Clark was also a mountaineering aficionado, and his writings include several books in that field; *Mountaineering in Britain: A History from the Earliest Times to the Present Day,* written with Edward C. Pyatt, is still considered a standard reference work. In addition, Clark wrote travel books for young people, as well as several novels and other nonfiction works.

Born in Wimbledon, England, in 1916, Clark studied at King's College in Wimbledon and began his career as a magazine journalist. From 1943 to 1945 he served as a war correspondent with the British United Press and from 1945 to 1948 as a foreign correspondent. During this time, Clark also collected photographs of mountaineering that he used in articles for books and magazines. After his *Splendid Hills: The Life and Photographs of Vittorio Sella, 1859-1943* was published in 1948, Clark devoted himself to writing full time.

In a *Listener* review of *The Huxleys,* E. S. Turner stated that Clark "is never too occupied with his subjects as scientific philosophers to neglect them as people." This sentiment was echoed by other reviewers who found Clark's subsequent biographies of Sigmund Freud, J. B. S. Haldane, and Bertrand Russell to be especially successful in their treatment of their subjects' personal lives. Arthur Sheps of the *Times Literary Supplement,* for instance, in a review of Clark's biography of Benjamin Franklin noted that "Clark's interest in Franklin is that of a biographer rather than a historian." Like Clark's other biographies, *Benjamin Franklin: A Biography* was applauded as being highly detailed and lucidly written. Sheps observed that "although there is not a great deal of new information or interpretation for the specialist . . . this is a comprehensive biography which will be enjoyed by the general reader."

In a London *Times* review of *Freud: The Man and the Cause,* Richard Holmes called the work a "truly formidable intellectual biography" and "a wonderful piece of work, and worthy of the man." Holmes speculated that

Clark derived pleasure from wading through the massive documentation of Freud's life to create the book, but faulted Clark for steering "clear of any intimate portrait of Freud's domestic menage."

In the *Washington Post Book World,* Edwin M. Yoder commended Clark's biography of Charles Darwin, in which the scientist's struggle with his own theories is brought to life. Yoder wrote: "It is a brilliant literary conceit, offering Clark a handy framework for a fascinating study in intellectual history." Yoder also indicated that despite its highly technical style, *The Survival of Charles Darwin: A Biography of a Man and an Idea* was "an important contribution to the understanding of a much misunderstood subject, and deserves a survival of its own."

Clark was occasionally criticized for oversights in some of his books. In a review of *The Survival of Charles Darwin* for the *Times Literary Supplement,* Gillian Beer concluded that "the value of Clark's book lies in the directness with which he describes and interrelates all the complex work of which Darwin is still a part—even though he oversimplifies the man." Alan Saunders, who reviewed *The Life of Ernst Chain: Penicillin and Beyond,* in the *Times Literary Supplement,* praised Clark's scientific stories, but criticized the book's lack of references and its limited bibliography. Similarly, Anthony Quinton, in a London *Times* review of *Bertrand Russell and His World* found Clark to be successful in his enumeration of the details of Russell's life, but lacking in an understanding of the philosophy that drove his subject.

Clark's last biography was *Lenin: The Man behind the Mask.* Richard Holmes of the London *Times* wrote that Clark "was not a Kremlinologist, or even a political biographer. But he was a super elucidator of those men—usually scientists—whose lives were driven by a single, dominating idea." Holmes again complimented Clark's synthesis of "massive sources, or highly technical materials" into biographies that everyone could understand.

BIOGRAPHICAL/CRITICAL SOURCES:

PERIODICALS

Best Sellers, August 15, 1971, p. 223; June, 1983, p. 92.
Books and Bookmen, June, 1968; January, 1974, p. 94; April, 1978, p. 56.
Chicago Tribune Book World, July 14, 1985, p. 25.
Commonweal, January 24, 1969, p. 536.
Library Journal, March 1, 1986, p. 51; April 15, 1986, p. 74; December 1988, p. 100.
Listener, May 9, 1972; April 28, 1983, p. 25.
Los Angeles Times Book Review, July 31, 1983, p. 2; January 13, 1985, p. 9; March 16, 1986, p. 10.
Nation, October 14, 1968.
New Leader, September 9, 1968.

New Republic, August 10, 1968; June 6, 1981, p. 35.
New Statesman, November 1968; February 7, 1986, p. 30.
New Statesman & Society, August 5, 1988, p. 36.
Newsweek, June 24, 1968; January 13, 1969, p. 81.
New Yorker, January 13, 1986, p. 87.
New York Times, June 27, 1968; May 29, 1980, p. C19.
New York Times Book Review, January 21, 1968; June 30, 1968; July 16, 1969; February 6, 1983, p. 23; January 27, 1985, p. 23; February 5, 1989, p. 14.
Observer (London), October 20, 1968; May 8, 1977, p. 26.
Publishers Weekly, March 14, 1986, p. 92; September 23, 1988, p. 57.
Spectator, November 24, 1967; November 1, 1975, p. 567.
Times (London), August 7, 1980; September 1, 1983; July 30, 1987; August 4, 1988.
Times Literary Supplement, September 16, 1983, p. 984; August 2, 1985, p. 853; March 14, 1986, p. 283; August 12, 1988, p. 876.
Washington Post Book World, April 10, 1983, pp. 5, 14; January 20, 1985, p. 5; December 18, 1988, p. 6.

OBITUARIES:

PERIODICALS

Times (London), March 14, 1987.*

*   *   *

CLEMENTS, Robert John   1912-1993

PERSONAL: Born October 23, 1912, in Cleveland, OH; died of a brain hemorrhage, September 8, 1993, in Carmel, NY; son of Earl W. and Mildred (Warner) Clements; married Helen Louise Card, September 3, 1940 (divorced, 1954); married Lorna Levant, July 19, 1975; children: (first marriage) Caird Robert, Cleveland Warner; (second marriage) Erin June. *Education:* Oberlin College, B.A., 1934; University of Florence, diploma, 1935; University of Bordeaux, diploma, 1935; University of Chicago, Ph.D., 1939.

CAREER: University of Chicago, Chicago, IL, instructor, 1937-39; University of Illinois at Urbana-Champaign, instructor, 1939-40; Harvard University, Cambridge, MA, 1940-47, began as instructor, became assistant professor; Pennsylvania State University, State College, professor and chairman of department of Romance languages and literatures, 1947-54; New York University, New York City, professor of Romance languages and chairman of comparative literature department, 1954-78. Visiting lecturer, University of Madrid, 1953; Columbia University, university associate, beginning 1955, visiting professor, spring, 1966; Mellon Professor of Literature, University of Pittsburgh, 1968. Member of Fulbright screening committee for languages and literature, 1965-68; consultant to Juilliard School, 1971-84. Co-organizer, Civil Affairs Training Program, Harvard University, 1940-44; secretary of publications, Medieval Academy of America, 1940-47; modern language editor, Ginn & Co., 1944-57.

MEMBER: International Association for the Study of Italian Language and Literature (vice president; president, 1973-79), Modern Language Association of America, American Council of Learned Societies, Medieval Academy of America, American Association of Teachers of Italian (president, 1960-62), Dante Alighieri Society, Phi Beta Kappa.

AWARDS, HONORS: Cesare Barbieri Endowment grant, 1958; American Council of Learned Societies grant, 1958; Fulbright research fellow in Rome and Florence, Italy, 1960-61; Litt.D., University of Rome, 1961; H.H.D., Philathea College, 1966.

WRITINGS:

Critical Theory and Practice of the Pleiade, Harvard University Press, 1942.
(With Robert V. Merrill) *Platonism in French Renaissance Poetry,* New York University Press, 1957.
The Peregrine Muse: Studies in Comparative Renaissance Literature, University of North Carolina Press, 1959, revised edition, 1968.
Picta Poesis: Humanistic and Literary Theory in Renaissance Emblem Books, Edizioni Storia e Letteratura, 1960.
Michelangelo's Theory of Art, New York University Press, 1961.
Michelangelo: A Self-Portrait, Prentice-Hall, 1963, revised edition, New York University Press, 1968.
(Coauthor) *Michelangelo Scultore,* Curcio, 1963.
(Editor) *American Criticism on Dante,* New York University Press, 1965.
The Poetry of Michelangelo, New York University Press, 1965.
(Editor) *American Critical Essays on the Divine Comedy,* New York University Press, 1967.
(Editor with wife, Lorna Levant) *Renaissance Letters: Revelations of a World Reborn,* New York University Press, 1976.
(With Joseph Gibaldi) *Anatomy of the Novella,* New York University Press, 1977.
Comparative Literature as Academic Discipline, Modern Language Association of America, 1978.

Also coauthor of *Pennsylvania Curriculum Revision for Modern Languages,* 1952. Contributor to books, including *Dictionary of French Literature,* Philosophical Library, 1958; *Michelangelo,* translated by Frederick Street, Collier, 1962; *Memorial Volume to Professor Jean-Marie*

Carre, Association Internationale de Litterature Comparee, 1964; *Nobel Prize Reader,* Popular Library, 1965; and *A History of Italian Literature,* by Eugenio Donadoni, translation by Richard Monges, New York University Press, 1969. Author of column, "Literary Scene in Europe" in *Saturday Review,* 1964-71. Contributor of more than 150 articles and reviews to general and professional journals. North American editor of *Boletin de Filologia Espanola,* Madrid, Spain, and of *Romanistisches Jahrbuch,* Hamburg, Germany; associate editor, Gotham Library, 1962-93.

SIDELIGHTS: Robert John Clements visited Europe some twenty times since 1934; he spoke or read nine languages, including Greek and Russian.

OBITUARIES:

PERIODICALS

New York Times, September 9, 1993, p. D21.*

*   *   *

COCKS, Geoffrey (Campbell) 1948-

PERSONAL: Born November 13, 1948, in New Bedford, MA; son of James Fraser (a tax accountant) and Lillias Brown (a homemaker; maiden name, Campbell) Cocks; married Sarah Rogers (a legal secretary), August 28, 1971; children: Emily Anne. *Education:* Occidental College, A.B., 1970; University of California, Los Angeles, M.A., 1971, Ph.D., 1975. *Politics:* Liberal left.

ADDRESSES: Home—1002 South Locust Lane, Albion, MI 49224. *Office*—Department of History, Albion College, 611 East Porter St., Albion, MI 49224.

CAREER: Occidental College, Los Angeles, CA, instructor in history, 1974-75; Albion College, Albion, MI, assistant professor, 1975-82, associate professor, 1983-87, professor of history, 1987—, Royal G. Hall Professor of History, 1994—. Visiting assistant professor of history at University of California, Los Angeles, 1980.

MEMBER: American Historical Association, German Studies Association, Group for the Use of Psychology in History, International Association for the History of Psychoanalysis.

AWARDS, HONORS: Fellowships from German Academic Exchange Service (DAAD), 1973-74 and 1985, National Endowment for the Humanities, 1980, 1988-89, Fulbright, 1988, and National Library of Medicine Publication Grant, 1991-92.

WRITINGS:

Psychotherapy in the Third Reich: The Goering Institute, Oxford University Press (New York City), 1985.

(Editor with Travis L. Crosby) *Psycho/History: Readings in the Method of Psychology, Psychoanalysis, and History,* Yale University Press (New Haven, CT), 1987.

(Editor with Konrad H. Jarausch) *German Professions, 1800-1950,* Oxford University Press, 1990.

(Editor) *The Curve of Life: Correspondence of Heine Kohut, 1923-1981,* Chicago University Press (Chicago, IL), 1994.

(Co-editor) *Medicine in Modern Germany,* Cambridge University Press, 1995.

Contributor to periodicals, including *American Historical Review, Journal of Modern History, Psychoanalytic Review, Isis, Psychohistory Review, American Imago, Psyche, Journal of the History of Behavioral Sciences, Extrapolation, Political Psychology,* and *Social Science and Medicine.*

WORK IN PROGRESS: A book on the social history of illness under the Nazi dictatorship; a novel, *The Institute,* based on *Psychotherapy in the Third Reich.*

SIDELIGHTS: Geoffrey Cocks examines how Nazi totalitarianism affected the practice of psychotherapy in Germany between 1933 and 1945 in *Psychotherapy in the Third Reich: The Goering Institute.* The author contends that German psychotherapy was allowed to organize professionally despite repressive Nazi sociopolitical doctrines. "Psychotherapy underwent a process of Aryanization, disguised its psychoanalytical character, and manifested a preparedness to respond obediently to the State's requirements," explained Sidney Bloch in a review for the *Times Literary Supplement.* "So long as psychotherapy could be demonstrated as useful to the Reich, and its practitioners were prepared to meet the Reich's requirements," the critic elaborated, "it could continue to operate, even in a quasi-psychoanalytical fashion." In his study Cocks also reveals how the German Institute for Psychological Research and Psychotherapy maintained a mutually convenient relationship with the Nazi regime and provided for a continuity of professional development into both postwar German successor states.

Reviewing *Psychotherapy in the Third Reich* for the *Los Angeles Times Book Review,* Harvey Mindess called it "objective and careful," a scholarly, detailed study "that will serve as a reference work for students of the period." *New York Times* critic John Gross commended Cocks's "solid research and sound judgment" as well, thankful that "a neglected chapter in the history of the Nazi era . . . has at last received the attention it deserves." Bloch deemed the book "a fascinating account of [an] unsavoury chapter in the history of psychotherapy" that alerts practitioners to "the ease with which they can relinquish their autonomy and become subordinate to social, political and ideological forces contrary to the interests of their patients."

Cocks told *CA:* "I have long been interested in the relationships between academia and political authority—how ideas, theories, and professional practices are realized in the 'real' world. This interest underlies my continuing research into the history of medical psychology in Germany. My interest in German history has been lifelong, since I was born when the world was still perceptibly quivering from the thankfully failed assertion of German power. More recently I have expanded this interest to include the study of how Germans across the social spectrum dealt with illness as experienced and defined by themselves and by various agencies of the Nazi regime."

BIOGRAPHICAL/CRITICAL SOURCES:

PERIODICALS

Los Angeles Times Book Review, January 13, 1985.
New York Times, July 3, 1984; January 18, 1985.
Times Literary Supplement, October 4, 1985.

*   *   *

COHEN, Michael P. 1944-

PERSONAL: Born October 5, 1944, in Dallas, TX; son of Frank (a steel contractor) and Peggy (a laboratory technician; maiden name, Green) Cohen; married Valerie Mendenhall (a writer), June 22, 1968; children: Jesse Daniel. *Education:* University of California, Los Angeles, B.S., 1966; University of California, Irvine, Ph.D., 1973.

ADDRESSES: Home—P.O. Box 34, Cedar City, UT 84721. *Office*—Department of English, Southern Utah University, 351 West Center, Cedar City, UT 84720.

CAREER: Southern Utah University (formerly Southern Utah State College), Cedar City, professor of English, 1973—.

MEMBER: American Society for Environmental History, Western Literature Association, Sierra Club, Southern Utah Wilderness Alliance.

AWARDS, HONORS: Mark H. Ingraham Prize for best manuscript submitted to the University of Wisconsin Press, 1982, for *The Pathless Way: John Muir and American Wilderness;* nonfiction first prize from Utah Council on the Literary Arts, 1982, for *The Pathless Way,* and 1987, for *The History of the Sierra Club.*

WRITINGS:

The Pathless Way: John Muir and American Wilderness, University of Wisconsin Press (Madison), 1984.
The History of the Sierra Club, Sierra Books (San Francisco), 1988.

Contributor of articles on the history of conservation to *American Land Forum, Western American Literature,* and *Pacific Historian.* Author of introduction, *John Muir, The Yosemite,* University of Wisconsin Press, 1986.

SIDELIGHTS: The Pathless Way: John Muir and American Wilderness traces the philosophical life of the naturalist who helped establish the national park system and America's environmental movement. *Los Angeles Times Book Review*'s Jack Miles said that Michael P. Cohen's book was often "subtle and eloquent." In the *New York Times Book Review,* David Rains Wallace remarked that "*The Pathless Way* is the most thorough account I've read of Muir's complicated struggle toward harmony with nature."

Cohen told *CA:* "In the past years I have grown introspective, turning inland to write about the canyon lands of the Colorado Plateau and the Great Basin. I write in order to find out what I think. Since I must earn my living by teaching, I write very early in the morning, before my family is awake. I use a MacIntosh computer."

BIOGRAPHICAL/CRITICAL SOURCES:

PERIODICALS

Los Angeles Times Book Review, August 19, 1984.
New York Times Book Review, September 16, 1984.

* * *

COLE, William (Rossa) 1919-

PERSONAL: Born November 20, 1919, in Staten Island, NY; son of William Harrison (in business) and Margaret (a nurse and writer; maiden name, O'Donovan-Rossa) Cole; married Peggy Bennett (a writer), May, 1947 (divorced); married Galen Williams (a cultural administrator), July 10, 1967 (marriage ended); children: (first marriage) Cambria Bennett, Jeremy Rossa (daughters); (second marriage) Williams, Rossa (sons). *Politics:* Socialist. *Religion:* None.

ADDRESSES: Home and office—201 West 54th St., New York, NY 10019.

CAREER: Writer. Worked as a clerk in a deli and a bookstore in Rye, NY, in the 1930s; Alfred A. Knopf, Inc., New York City, publicity director, 1946-58; Simon & Schuster, Inc., New York City, publicity director and editor, 1958-61. Co-publisher, with Viking Press, of William Cole Books. *Military service:* U.S. Army, 1940-45; served in infantry in Europe; became sergeant; received Purple Heart.

MEMBER: International PEN (vice-president, American Center, 1955-56; executive board member, 1956—),

American PEN, Poetry Society of America (member of governing board, 1979-81), Authors Guild, Poets and Writers (member of executive board, 1970—).

AWARDS, HONORS: I Went to the Animal Fair: A Book of Animal Poems appeared on the American Library Association (ALA) List of Notable Children's Books of 1940-59, and was named an ALA notable book, 1958; *Beastly Boys and Ghastly Girls: Poems* was named an ALA notable book, 1964; *The Birds and the Beasts Were There: Animal Poems* was named an ALA notable book, 1965.

WRITINGS:

FOR ADULTS

(With Tomi Ungerer) *A Cat-Hater's Handbook; or, The Ailurophobe's Delight,* Dial, 1963.
Uncoupled Couplets: A Game of Rhymes, Taplinger, 1966.

Author of column "Trade Winds," *Saturday Review,* 1974-79; author of book review column for *Endless Vacation,* 1990—; book reviewer for *Prime Time.* Also contributor to *Atlantic, Harper's, New York Times Book Review,* and *New Yorker.*

FOR CHILDREN

Frances Face-Maker: A Going-to-Bed Book, illustrated by Ungerer, World Publishing, 1963.
What's Good for a Six-Year-Old?, illustrated by Ingrid Fetz, Holt, 1965.
What's Good for a Four-Year-Old?, illustrated by Ungerer, Holt, 1967.
What's Good for a Five-Year-Old?, illustrated by Edward Sorel, Holt, 1969.
Aunt Bella's Umbrella, illustrated by Jacqueline Chwast, Doubleday, 1970.
That Pest, Jonathan, illustrated by Ungerer, Harper, 1970.
What's Good for a Three-Year-Old?, illustrated by Lillian Hoban, Holt, 1974.
Knock Knocks: The Most Ever, illustrated by Mike Thaler, F. Watts, 1976.
A Boy Named Mary Jane, and Other Silly Verse, illustrated by George MacClain, F. Watts, 1977.
Knock Knocks You've Never Heard Before, illustrated by Thaler, F. Watts, 1977.
Give Up? Cartoon Riddle Rhymers, illustrated by Thaler, F. Watts, 1978.
New Knock Knocks, illustrated by Thaler, Granada, 1981.
(With Thaler) *Monster Knock Knocks,* illustrated by Thaler, Pocket Books, 1982.
Have I Got Dogs!, illustrated by Margot Apple, Viking, 1993.

Contributor to *Cricket's Choice,* Open Court, c. 1974; also contributor of introduction to *Nonsense Literature for*

Children: Aesop to Seuss, by Celia C. Anderson, Shoe String Press, 1989.

EDITOR; CARTOON ANTHOLOGIES

(With Marvin Rosenberg) *The Best Cartoons from Punch: Collected for Americans from England's Famous Humorous Weekly,* Simon & Schuster, 1952.

(With Dougles McKee) *French Cartoons,* Dell, 1954.

(With McKee) *More French Cartoons,* Dell, 1955.

(With Florett Robinson) *Women Are Wonderful! A History in Cartoons of a Hundred Years with America's Most Controversial Figure,* Houghton, 1956.

(With McKee) *Touche: French Cartoons,* Dell, 1961.

(With McKee) *You Damn Men Are All Alike: French Cartoons,* Gold Medal, 1962.

The Birds and the Beasts Were There: Animal Poems, illustrated by Helen Siegl, World Publishing, 1963.

Beastly Boys and Ghastly Girls: Poems, illustrated by Ungerer, World Publishing, 1964.

Oh, What Nonsense! Poems, illustrated by Ungerer, Viking, 1966.

(With Thaler) *The Classic Cartoons,* World Publishing, 1966.

The Sea, Ships, and Sailors: Poems, Songs, and Shanties, illustrated by Robin Jacques, Viking, 1967.

D. H. Lawrence: Poems Selected for Young People, illustrated by Ellen Raskin, Viking, 1967.

W. S. Gilbert, Poems, illustrated by Gilbert, Crowell, 1967.

A Case of the Giggles (contains *Limerick Giggles, Joke Giggles* and *Rhyme Giggles, Nonsense Giggles*), illustrated by Ungerer, World Publishing, 1967, published in England as *Limerick Giggles, Joke Giggles,* Bodley Head, 1969.

Man's Funniest Friend: The Dog in Stories, Reminiscences, Poems and Cartoons, World Publishing, 1967.

Poems of Thomas Hood, illustrated by Sam Fischer, Crowell, 1968.

A Book of Nature Poems, illustrated by Robert Andrew Parker, Viking, 1969.

Rough Men, Tough Men: Poems of Action and Adventure, illustrated by Enrico Arno, Viking, 1969.

The Punch Line: Presenting Today's Top Twenty-five Cartoon Artists from England's Famous Humor Magazine, Simon & Schuster, 1969.

Oh, How Silly! Poems, illustrated by Ungerer, Viking, 1970.

The Book of Giggles, illustrated by Ungerer, World Publishing, 1970.

The Poet's Tales: A New Book of Story Poems, illustrated by Charles Keeping, World Publishing, 1971.

Oh, That's Ridiculous! Poems, illustrated by Ungerer, Viking, 1972.

Pick Me Up: A Book of Short, Short Poems, Macmillan, 1972.

Poems from Ireland, illustrated by William Stobbs, Crowell, 1972.

A Book of Animal Poems, illustrated by Parker, Viking, 1973.

Making Fun! A Book of Verse, F. Watts, 1976.

An Arkful of Animals, illustrated by Lynn Munsinger, Houghton, 1978.

I'm Mad at You! Verses, illustrated by MacClain, Collins, 1978.

Oh, Such Foolishness! Poems, illustrated by Tomie de Paola, Lippincott, 1978.

Dinosaurs and Beasts of Yore: Poems, illustrated by Susanna Natti, Collins, 1979.

The Poetry of Horses, illustrated by Ruth Sanderson, Scribner, 1979.

Good Dog Poems, illustrated by Sanderson, Scribner, 1981.

Poem Stew, illustrated by Karen Ann Weinhaus, Lippincott, 1981.

A Zooful of Animals, illustrated by Munsinger, Houghton, 1990.

Also editor of *The Square Bears and Other Riddle Rhymers.*

EDITOR; ANTHOLOGIES FOR CHILDREN

Humorous Poetry for Children, illustrated by Ervine Metzl, World Publishing, 1955.

Story Poems, New and Old, illustrated by Walter Buehr, World Publishing, 1957.

I Went to the Animal Fair: A Book of Animal Poems, illustrated by Colette Rosselli, World Publishing, 1958.

Poems of Magic and Spells, illustrated by Peggy Bacon, World Publishing, 1960.

(With Julia Colmore) *The Poetry-Drawing Book,* Simon & Schuster, 1960.

Poems for Seasons and Celebrations, illustrated by Johannes Troyer, World Publishing, 1961.

(With Colmore) *The Second Poetry-Drawing Book,* Simon & Schuster, 1962.

EDITOR; POETRY ANTHOLOGIES FOR ADULTS

The Fireside Book of Humorous Poetry, Simon & Schuster, 1959.

Erotic Poetry: The Lyrics, Ballads, Idyls, and Epics of Love, Classical to Contemporary, foreword by Stephen Spender, decorations by Warren Chappell, Random House, 1963.

A Book of Love Poems, illustrated by Lars Bo, Viking, 1965.

Eight Lines and Under: An Anthology of Short, Short Poems, Macmillan, 1967.

Pith and Vinegar: An Anthology of Short Humorous Poetry, Simon & Schuster, 1969.

Poetry Brief: An Anthology of Short, Short Poems, Macmillan, 1971.

Half Serious: An Anthology of Short, Short Poems, Eyre Methuen, 1973.

Poems: One Line and Longer, Grossman, 1973.

EDITOR; OTHER ANTHOLOGIES

The Best Humor from Punch, illustrated by Sprod, World Publishing, 1953.

Folk Songs of England, Ireland, Scotland, and Wales, illustrated by Edward Ardizzone, Doubleday, 1961.

(With Colmore) *New York in Photographs,* Simon & Schuster, 1961.

The Most of A. J. Liebling (essays), Simon & Schuster, 1963.

A Big Bowl of Punch: A Heady Potpourri of Cartoons, Prose, and Verse from England's Famous Humorous Weekly, Simon & Schuster, 1964.

. . . And Be Merry! A Feast of Light Verse and a Soupcon of Prose about the Joy of Eating, Grossman, 1972.

(With Louis Phillips) *Sex: The Most Fun You Can Have without Laughing and Other Quotations,* St. Martin's, 1990.

Bah Humbug!: Quotes, Verses, and Stories for the Spiritual Heirs of Ebenezer Scrooge, St. Martin's, 1992.

Quotable New York: A Literary Companion, Pushcart, 1992.

(With Phillips) *Oh, What an Awful Thing to Say!: Needles, Skewers, Pricks, and Outright Nastiness,* St. Martin's, 1992.

SIDELIGHTS: William Cole is primarily known for his more than fifty anthologies for children and adults, including the collection of children's poetry *Beastly Boys and Ghastly Girls: Poems.* His anthologies vary in subject matter, reflecting his enthusiasm for poetry, humor, and folk songs. A *Horn Book* contributor, in a review of *Man's Funniest Friend: The Dog in Stories, Reminiscences, Poems and Cartoons,* described Cole as "an enthusiastic anthologist" who creates his collections with "gusto." Cole is committed to organizing distinctive books which spark children's interest in poetry and reading, stating in *Something about the Author Autobiography Series (SAAS)* that "any anthology, to serve its full purpose, should lead the reader to further books." Cole is also an author of several children's books of poetry and humor, including *What's Good for a Six-Year-Old?* and *A Boy Named Mary Jane, and Other Silly Verse.*

Cole uses many of his own ideas as organizing themes for anthologies and often draws on his own collection of books and clippings for material. He wrote in *SAAS:* "I was born with some of the natural instincts of the pack rat, who, as the dictionary puts it, is 'noted for carrying away small articles which it keeps in its nest.' The articles in my nest are poems, newspaper and magazine stories, files of miscellaneous clippings simply marked 'Interest.' And a couple of files noted as 'Poetry' and 'Light Verse.' It has been my habit, since I was a teenager, to clip and file away anything from a newspaper or magazine that struck my fancy. I had no reason for keeping all this stuff, except I felt that somebody should do it the honor. I now have a large library of books-that-interest-me, mostly poetry, humor, and quotations, and whenever I add a new one to the library, I first read it carefully, pencil in hand, and make light notations inside the back cover, indicating the page numbers of passages or poems that appeal. So, in a way, my entire library is an anthology."

Much of Cole's work has been as an anthologist of verse for young readers. Refraining from publishing a large general collection of this type of poetry, he has based all of his children's anthologies on specific themes such as animals, nature, magic, and nonsense. One such collection, published in 1967, is *Man's Funniest Friend: The Dog in Stories, Reminiscences, Poems and Cartoons.* This humorous look at canine pets features the verse of writers such as James Thurber, Ogden Nash, and P. G. Wodehouse as well as prose selections, photographs, and cartoons by other contributors. Another animal-oriented poetry anthology is *Dinosaurs and Beasts of Yore,* which a *Horn Book* contributor characterized as full of "good-humored, light-hearted" poems in which "comic speculation . . . is expressed at the thought of ancient monsters." Other gatherings of literature for children by Cole include *Poem Stew* and his 1990 *A Zooful of Animals.*

Cole summed up his profession in *SAAS:* "An anthologist is someone who has a crusading enthusiasm for his subject. He's a practitioner of literary buttonholing, and is continually exclaiming, through the medium of his compilations, 'Hey! Look at *this* one!' An anthology done without enthusiasm is like a TV dinner: frozen, tasteless, and quickly forgotten. In a way, it's a selfish art; the anthologist has the abiding conviction that, if he likes something, other people will. Or *should.* Where research is concerned, he should love his subject so much that he'd be wallowing around in it anyhow, even if he had no anthologistic purpose. His art is infinitely less important than that of the authors he gathers together. Montaigne said, 'I have gathered a posie of other men's flowers, and nothing but the thread that binds them is my own.' "

BIOGRAPHICAL/CRITICAL SOURCES:

BOOKS

Something about the Author Autobiography Series, Volume 9, Gale, 1990, pp. 89-108.

PERIODICALS

American Libraries, April, 1976, p. 210.

Horn Book, April, 1968; August, 1979, p. 431.

*   *   *

COOLEY, Peter (John) 1940-

PERSONAL: Born November 19, 1940, in Detroit, MI; son of Paul John (an insurance executive) and Ruth Esther (Hayhow) Cooley; married Jacqueline Marks, June 12, 1965; children: Nicole, Alissa, Joshua. *Education:* Shimer College, A.B., 1962; University of Chicago, M.A., 1964; University of Iowa, Ph.D., 1970. *Politics:* Democrat. *Religion:* Episcopalian.

ADDRESSES: Home—241 Harding St., Jefferson, LA 70121. *Office*—Department of English, Tulane University, New Orleans, LA 70118.

CAREER: University of Wisconsin, Green Bay, assistant professor, 1970-72, associate professor of English, 1972-75; Tulane University, New Orleans, LA, assistant professor, 1975-77, associate professor, 1978-83, professor of English, 1983—.

MEMBER: International PEN, Modern Language Association of America, Poetry Society of America, South Central Modern Language Association.

AWARDS, HONORS: Robert Frost fellowship in poetry, Bread Loaf Writers' Conference, 1981; Division of the Arts fellowship, State of Louisiana, 1982.

WRITINGS:

How to Go (poetry chapbook), G.S.S.C. Publications, 1968.
The Company of Strangers (poems), University of Missouri Press, 1975.
(With Dennis Trudell) *Voyages to the Inland Sea V: Essays and Poems,* Center for Contemporary Poetry, 1975.
Miracle, Miracles (poems), Juniper Press, 1977.
The Room Where Summer Ends (poems), Carnegie-Mellon University Press, 1979.
Nightseasons (poems), Carnegie-Mellon University Press, 1983.
Canticles and Complaints, Ford Brown, 1987.
The Van Gogh Notebooks, Carnegie-Mellon University Press, 1987.
The Astonished Hours, Carnegie-Mellon University Press, 1992.

Work represented in several anthologies, including *American Poetry Anthology, New American Poets of the '80s, New American Poets of the '90s,* and *Best American Poetry, 1993.* Contributor to publications, including *Poetry, New Yorker, Atlantic, Harper's, Sewanee Review, Yale Review,* *American Review, Esquire,* and *Southern Review.* Poetry editor of *North American Review,* 1970—.

WORK IN PROGRESS: Sacred Conversations.

SIDELIGHTS: Peter Cooley told *CA:* "I did not come from a family of artists or writers, and much of my desire to write came from my attempt to speak in response to works I had read—or to find a voice for feelings which lay outside—or inside—human relationships or relationships with objects or the natural world. I finally committed myself to writing when I entered the Program in Creative Writing at the University of Iowa. Despite the limitations of workshops, it was in them that I found a way to develop my own voice and, most of all, to be *heard.*"

*   *   *

COTTER, Richard V(ern) 1930-

PERSONAL: Born June 27, 1930, in Long Prairie, MN; son of Vernon M. and Edith Cotter; married Carolyn Van Duyn Clark, June 12, 1976. *Education:* Lewis and Clark College, B.S., 1952; University of Oregon, M.S., 1963, Ph.D. (with honors), 1965. *Avocational interests:* Amateur musician, lay leader of the Episcopal church.

ADDRESSES: Home—1455 West 26 Ave., Eugene, OR 97405. *Office*—College of Business Administration, University of Oregon, Eugene, OR 97403.

CAREER: Oregon Journal Publishing Co., Inc., Portland, OR, newsboy and station manager, 1942-43; Oregonian Publishing Co., Inc., Portland, newsboy, branch captain, clerk, night-and-weekend-office manager, 1944-48, district manager, 1948-53; Fairbanks Publishing Co., Inc., Fairbanks, AK, business manager, 1953-58; self-employed newspaper distributor and consultant, Portland, 1958-61; Oregon State System of Higher Education, Portland Continuation Center, Portland, instructor in business administration, 1962; University of Oregon, Eugene, instructor in finance, 1963-64; University of Nevada, Reno, assistant professor, 1965-67, associate professor, 1967-71, professor of managerial science, 1971-87, associate dean for graduate studies, 1971-78. Visiting professor at University of Oregon, 1967, University of Newcastle, Newcastle, Australia, 1973, University of Western Australia, 1978 and 1983, and University of Hawaii, 1980. Adjunct professor of Management and Finance, University of Oregon, 1989—. *Military service:* Oregon National Guard, 1948-53, Alaska National Guard, 1953-58.

MEMBER: Academy of International Business, American Finance Association, Association for Business Simulation and Experiential Learning, Financial Management Association, Western Finance Association, Western Economic Association, Phi Kappa Phi, Beta Gamma Sigma.

WRITINGS:

The Business Policy Game, Prentice-Hall, 1973.

(Coauthor) *Commercial Banking,* Prentice-Hall, 1976, third edition, 1984.

Modern Business Decisions: Player's Manual, Prentice-Hall, 1985.

The Business Policy Game: Player's Manual, Prentice-Hall, 1985, third edition, 1990.

Contributor to *AACSB Bulletin, Nevada Business Review, Journal of Financial and Quantitative Analysis,* and *National Banking Review.*

*   *   *

COWAN, Louise (Shillingburg) 1916-

PERSONAL: Born December 22, 1916, in Fort Worth, TX; daughter of John W. and Ouita (Pate) Shillingburg; married Donald Andrew Cowan (a professor of physics and university president), 1939; children: Bainard. *Education:* Texas Christian University, B.A., 1946, M.A., 1947; Vanderbilt University, Ph.D., 1953. *Avocational interests:* Painting.

ADDRESSES: Home—3413 Bristol Rd., Fort Worth, TX 76107. *Office*—Department of English, University of Dallas, P.O. Box 1330, Irving, TX 75060.

CAREER: Vanderbilt University, Nashville, TN, lecturer, 1947-53; Texas Christian University, Ft. Worth, 1953-59, began as assistant professor, became associate professor of English and creative writing; University of Dallas, Irving, TX, professor of English and chair of department, 1959-72, graduate dean 1972-77, university professor, 1978-80. Member of board of trustees, Hockaday School; member of advisory board, St. Paul's Hospital, Dallas; member of board, Goals for Dallas. Founding fellow, Thanks-Giving Square, Dallas.

MEMBER: Modern Language Association of America, American Studies Association, National College Teachers of English, South Central Modern Language Association, Texas Conference of College Teachers of English, Phi Beta Kappa.

AWARDS, HONORS: Piper Award for distinguished teaching, 1962.

WRITINGS:

NONFICTION

The Fugitive Group: A Literary History, Louisiana State University Press (Baton Rouge), 1959.

The Southern Critics: An Introduction to the Criticism of John Crowe Ransom, Allen Tate, Donald Davidson,

Robert Penn Warren, Cleanth Brooks, and Andrew Lytle, University of Dallas Press (Irving, TX), 1971.

EDITOR

(And author of introduction) *The Terrain of Comedy,* Dallas Institute Publications, 1984.

(With husband, Donald Cowan) *Classic Texts and the Nature of Authority: An Account of a Principals' Institute Conducted by the Dallas Institute of Humanities & Culture on the Campus of the University of Dallas, June 22-July 8, 1990,* Dallas Institute Publications, 1993.

OTHER

Contributor to books, including *Fugitive Reunion,* Vanderbilt University Press (Nashville, TN), 1956; *South,* Doubleday (New York City), 1961; *Reality and Myth: Essays in Southern Literature,* Vanderbilt University Press, 1963; *The Epic Cosmos,* edited by Larry Allums, Dallas Institute Publications, 1992; and *The Women on the Porch,* Sanders, J. S. & Company, 1993. Contributor to professional journals. Editor, *Descant,* 1955-57, *Kerygma,* 1961-66.*

*   *   *

COWEN, David L(aurence) 1909-

PERSONAL: Born September 1, 1909, in New York, NY; son of Meyer (a meat packer) and Mary (Goodstein) Cohen; married Mae Wisokolsky, January 24, 1934 (deceased); married Florence Weisberg, July 23, 1972 (deceased); children: (first marriage) Bruce R. *Education:* Rutgers College (now the State University of New Jersey), Litt.B., 1930, M.A., 1931. *Politics:* Independent. *Religion:* Hebrew.

ADDRESSES: Home—186 C Malden Lane, Rossmoor, NJ 08831. *Office*—Rutgers University, New Brunswick, NJ 08903.

CAREER: Rutgers University, New Brunswick, NJ, College of Pharmacy, instructor in history, 1933-44, and lecturer, 1953-78, University College, assistant professor, 1944-54, associate professor, 1954-60, professor of history, 1960-74, professor emeritus of history, 1974—, chairman of department of history and political science, University College, 1945-65, chairman of department of history, 1965-74. Assistant chief reader and chief reader, Foreign Service Officer Examination, Educational Testing Service, 1953-56; research associate, College of Physicians, Philadelphia, PA, 1964-66; member, history of life sciences study section, National Institutes of Health, 1966-70, 1978-79 (chairman), 1984-85; consultant, Medical Heritage Society, 1969-76.

MEMBER: International Academy of the History of Pharmacy (fellow, 1972), Internationale Gesellschaft fuer Geschichte der Pharmazie (member of council, 1969—), American Association of University Professors (chapter vice-president, 1953-54, 1961-62), American Institute of the History of Pharmacy (member of council, 1957-65; president, 1961-62; council chair, 1971-79), American Association for the History of Medicine (member of council, 1967-70), British Society for the History of Pharmacy (honorary), Medical History Society of New Jersey (vice president, 1980-82, president, 1982-84), Union mondiale des societes d'histoire pharmaceutiques (vice president, 1975-79, president, 1979-83), Deutsche Gesellschaft fuer Geschichte der Pharmazie (corresponding member), Sociedad Espanol de la Historia de la Farmacia (honorary), New Jersey Academy of Science (vice-president, 1963-65), New Jersey Historical Society (fellow), New Jersey Pharmaceutical Association (honorary), Rho Chi, Alpha Zeta Omega.

AWARDS, HONORS: Lindback Award for distinguished teaching, 1961, and faculty research fellowships, 1962-63, 1964-65, 1972-73, all from Rutgers University; Kremers Award, American Institute of the History of Pharmacy, 1965, for distinguished writing; United States Public Health Service research grant, 1965-66; Ferchl Medal, Deutsche Gesellschaft fuer Geschichte der Pharmazie, 1972; Cestoni Medal, Academia Italiano di Storia della Farmacia, 1973; fellow, New Jersey Historical Society, 1973; Rutgers Award, 1974; Gideon de Laune Lecture Award, Worshipful Society of Apothecaries of London, 1976; Rho Chi Lecture Award, 1976; Urdang Medal, American Institute of the History of Pharmacy, 1977; Schelenz Plaquette, Internationale Gesellschaft fuer Geschichte der Pharmazie, 1983; honorary degree, Rutgers University, 1984; elected to Hall of Distinguished Alumni, Rutgers University Alumni Federation, 1992; continuing lifetime achievement award, American Association for the History of Medicine, 1994.

WRITINGS:

(With Roy A. Bowers) *The Rho Chi Society,* American Institute of the History of Pharmacy, 1955, 5th revised edition, Rho Chi Society, 1988.

America's Pre-Pharmacopoeial Literature, American Institute of the History of Pharmacy (Madison, WI), 1961.

Medicine and Health in New Jersey: A History, Van Nostrand (Princeton, NJ), 1964.

Medical Education: The Queen's-Rutgers Experience, 1792-1830, The State University Bicentennial Commission (New Brunswick, NJ), 1966.

The New Jersey Pharmaceutical Association, 1870-1970, New Jersey Pharmaceutical Association (Trenton, NJ), 1970.

The Spread and Influence of British Pharmacopoeial and Related Literature, Internationale Gesellschaft fuer Geschichte der Pharmazie (Stuttgart), 1974.

Medicine in Revolutionary New Jersey, New Jersey Historical Commission, 1975.

(Editor with Alvin Segelman) *Antibiotics in Historical Perspective,* Merck Sharp (Rahway, NJ), 1981.

(With William H. Helfand) *Pharmacy: An Illustrated History,* Abrams (New York City), 1990.

(With Bowers) *The Rutgers University College of Pharmacy: A Centennial History,* Rutgers University Press (New Brunswick, NJ), 1991.

(Editor) Bernhard Naunyn, *Memories, Thoughts and Convictions,* Science History Publications (Canton, MA), 1994.

Contributor to professional journals. Book review editor, *Pharmacy in History,* 1962-84; member of editorial board for the "Opera pharmaceutica rariora" series.

Pharmacy: An Illustrated History has been translated into German and Spanish.

WORK IN PROGRESS: Biographical sketches for projected *American National Biography,* Oxford University Press.

SIDELIGHTS: David L. Cowen, who is competent in German, has done considerable research in Great Britain and Germany.

*   *   *

COX, Jeri
    See KIMES, Beverly Rae

*   *   *

COYNE, P. J.
    See MASTERS, Hilary

*   *   *

CROSS, Gilbert B. 1939-
(Jon Winters)

PERSONAL: Born in Walkden, near Manchester, England; son of Gilbert Edward Cross; married; children: two. *Education:* Manchester University, B.A., 1961; University of London, post-graduate certificate in education, 1962; University of Louisville, M.A., 1965; University of Michigan, Ph.D., 1971.

ADDRESSES: Home—1244 Ferdon, Ann Arbor, MI 48104. *Office*—Department of English Language and Literature, Eastern Michigan University, Ypsilanti, MI 48197.

CAREER: Eastern Michigan University, Ypsilanti, 1967—, currently professor of English language and literature. Writer.

WRITINGS:

(Coeditor with Alfred Nelson) *Drury Lane Journal: Selections from James Winston's Diaries, 1819-1827,* Society Theatre Research (London), 1974.

Next Week East Lynne: Domestic Drama in Performance, Bucknell University Press (Cranbury, NJ), 1976.

(Coeditor with Atelia Clarkson) *World Folktales: A Scribners Resource Collection,* Scribner (New York City), 1980.

(Coeditor with Nelson) *The Adelphi Calendar, 1806-1850,* Greenwood Press (Westport, CT), 1990.

(Coeditor with Nelson) *The Adelphi Calendar, 1850-1900,* Greenwood Press, 1993.

JUVENILE

A Hanging at Tyburn, Atheneum (New York City), 1983.
Mystery at Loon Lake, Atheneum, 1986.
Terror Train, Atheneum, 1987.
A Witch across Time, Atheneum, 1990.

UNDER PSEUDONYM JON WINTERS

The Drakov Memoranda, Avon (New York City), 1979.
The Catenary Exchange, Avon, 1983.
Berlin Fugue, Avon, 1985.

*   *   *

CROSSLEY-HOLLAND, Kevin   1941-

PERSONAL: Born February 7, 1941, in England; son of Peter Charles (a composer) and Joan Mary (Cowper) Crossley-Holland; married Gillian Cook; children: Kieran, Dominic (sons), Oenone, Eleanor (daughters). *Education:* Oxford University, B.A. (with honors), 1962. *Avocational interests:* Archaeology, opera, wine, walks.

ADDRESSES: Home—The Old Vicarage, Walsham-le-Willows, Bury St. Edmunds, Suffolk, 1P31 3BZ, England. *Agent*—c/o Rogers, Coleridge and White Literary, 20 Powis Mews, London W11 1JN, England.

CAREER: Macmillan & Co., Ltd., London, England, editor, 1962-69, poetry editor, 1964-72; British Broadcasting Corporation (BBC), London, Talks producer, 1972; Victor Gollancz Ltd., London, editorial director, 1972-77; Boydell and Brewer, editorial consultant, 1983-90; University of St. Thomas, St. Paul, MN, endowed chair in humanities and fine arts, and professor, 1991—. Lecturer in

English, Tufts-in-London Program, 1967-78, Regensburg University, Regensburg, Germany, 1978-80, and St. Olaf College, Northfield, MN, 1987-90. Arts Council, fellow in writing at the Winchester School of Art, 1983 and 1984; Eastern Arts Association, chair of literature panel, 1986-89; British Council, visiting lecturer to India, Germany, Iceland, and Yugoslavia. Freelance writer and broadcaster.

AWARDS, HONORS: Arts Council of Great Britain award for best book for children published in 1966-68, for *The Green Children;* Poetry Book Society Choice award, 1976, for *The Dream-House and Other Poems;* Carnegie Medal for outstanding book for children, British Library Association, 1985, for *Storm;* Poetry Book Society recommendation, 1986, for *Waterslain and Other Poems.*

WRITINGS:

FOR CHILDREN

Havelok the Dane, illustrated by Brian Wildsmith, Dutton, 1965.

King Horn, illustrated by Charles Keeping, Dutton, 1965.

The Green Children, illustrated by Margaret Gordon, Seabury, 1966.

(Editor) *Winter's Tales for Children 3,* Macmillan, 1967, St. Martin's, 1968.

(Editor) *Winter's Tales for Children 14,* St. Martin's, 1968.

The Callow Pit Coffer, illustrated by Gordon, Seabury, 1968.

(With Jill Paton Walsh) *Wordhoard: Anglo-Saxon Stories,* Farrar, Straus, 1969.

The Pedlar of Swaffham, illustrated by Gordon, Seabury, 1971.

The Fire-Brother, illustrated by Joanna Troughton, Heinemann, 1973, Seabury, 1975.

The Sea Stranger, illustrated by Troughton, Heinemann, 1973, Seabury, 1974.

Green Blades Rising: The Anglo-Saxons, Seabury, 1974.

The Earth-Father, illustrated by Troughton, Heinemann, 1976.

The Wildman, illustrated by Keeping, Deutsch, 1976.

(Editor) *The Faber Book of Northern Legends,* illustrated by Alan Howard, Faber, 1977.

(Editor) *The Faber Book of Northern Folk-Tales,* illustrated by Howard, Faber, 1980.

The Dead Moon and Other Tales from East Anglia and the Fen Country, Deutsch, 1982.

Beowulf, illustrated by Keeping, Oxford University Press, 1982.

(With Gwyn Thomas) *Tales from the Mabinogion* (retelling of Welsh folk tales), Gollancz, 1984, Tuttle, 1991.

Axe-Age, Wolf-Age: A Selection of Norse Myths, illustrated by Hannah Firman, Deutsch, 1985.

(With Susanne Lugert) *The Fox and the Cat: Animal Tales from Grimm,* illustrated by Susan Varley, Lothrop, 1985.

Storm, illustrated by Alan Marks, Heinemann, 1985.

British Folk Tales, illustrated by Peter Melnyczuk, Orchard, 1987.

Boo!: Ghosts and Graveyards, illustrated by Melnyczuk, Orchard, 1988.

Dathera Dad: Fairy Tales, illustrated by Melnyczuk, Orchard, 1988.

Piper and Pooka: Boggarts and Bogles, illustrated by Melnyczuk, Orchard, 1988.

(With Thomas) *The Quest for Olwen,* illustrated by Margaret Jones, Lutterworth Press, 1988.

Small-Tooth Dog: Wonder Tales, illustrated Melnyczuk, Orchard, 1988.

Wulf, illustrated by Gareth Floyd, Faber, 1988.

Sleeping Nanna, illustrated by Melnyczuk, Putnam, 1989.

Under the Sun and Over the Moon, illustrated by Ian Penney, Putnam, 1989.

Sea Tongue, illustrated by Clare Challice, BBC Publications, 1991.

Tales from Europe, illustrated by Lesley Buckingham, Phyllis Mahon, and Emma Whiting, BBC Publications, 1991.

Long Tom and the Dead Hand, illustrated by Shirley Felts, Deutsch, 1992.

The Labours of Herakles, illustrated by Peter Utton, Orion, 1993.

Norse Myths, illustrated by Gillian McClure, Simon & Schuster, 1993.

The Green Children, illustrated by Alan Marks, Oxford University Press, 1994.

Also author (with Thomas) of *The Tale of Taliesin,* 1992.

POETRY

On Approval, Outposts, 1961.

My Son, Turret, 1966.

Alderney: The Nunnery, Turret, 1968.

Confessional, Martin Booth/Sceptre, 1969.

A Dream Meeting, Sceptre, 1970.

Norfolk Poems, Academy, 1970.

More Than I Am: Broadsheet, Steam Press, 1971.

The Rain-Giver and Other Poems (collection), Deutsch, 1972.

The Wake, Keepsake, 1972.

Petal and Stone, Sceptre, 1975.

(Editor with Patricia Beer) *New Poetry 2,* Arts Council, 1976.

The Dream-House and Other Poems (collection), Deutsch, 1976.

Between My Father and My Son, Black Willow, 1982.

Time's Oriel and Other Poems (collection), Hutchinson, 1983.

Waterslain and Other Poems (collection), Hutchinson, 1986.

(Editor) *The Oxford Book of Travel Verse,* Oxford University Press, 1986.

(Editor) *Northern Lights: Legends, Sagas and Folk-Tales,* Faber, 1987.

(Editor) *Medieval Lovers: A Book of Days,* Weidenfeld & Nicolson, 1988.

The Painting Room and Other Poems (collection), Hutchinson, 1988.

East Anglian Poems (collection), Jardine, 1988.

Oenone in January, Old Stile, 1988.

(Editor) *Medieval Gardens: A Book of Days,* Rizzoli, 1990.

(Editor) *Peter Grimes: The Poor of the Borough,* Folio, 1990.

New and Selected Poems: 1965-1990, Hutchinson, 1990.

Eleanor's Advent, Old Stile, 1992.

TRANSLATOR

The Battle of Maldon, and Other Old English Poems, edited by Bruce Mitchell, St. Martin's, 1965.

Beowulf, introduction by Mitchell, Farrar, Straus, 1968.

Storm and Other Old English Riddles, Farrar, Straus, 1970.

The Exeter Book Riddles, Folio, 1978, Brewer, 1988.

(And editor) *The Anglo-Saxon World,* Boydell and Brewer, 1982, Oxford University Press, 1984.

Beowulf ("The Poetry of Legend" series), Boydell, 1987.

The Old English Elegies, Folio, 1988.

OTHER

(Editor) William Butler Yeats, *Running to Paradise: An Introductory Selection of the Poems of W. B. Yeats,* Macmillan (New York City), 1967.

Pieces of Land: A Journey to Eight Islands, Gollancz, 1972.

(Editor) *The Mirror of Britain,* ten volumes, Seabury, 1974-79.

(Editor) *The Faber Book of Northern Legends,* Faber, 1977.

The Norse Myths: A New Version, Pantheon, 1980.

(Editor) *The Faber Book of Northern Folk-Tales,* Faber, 1980.

(Editor) *The Riddle Book,* Macmillan, 1982.

(Editor) *Folk-Tales of the British Isles,* Faber, 1986, Pantheon, 1988.

The Legends of Arthur, Pantheon, 1987.

The Stones Remain: Megalithic Sites of Britain, Rider, 1989.

(With Nicola LeFanu) *The Green Children: An Opera in Two Acts* (opera), Novello, 1990.

(With LeFanu) *The Wildman: An Opera in Two Acts,* Boydell and Brewer, 1995.

Reviewer for *Sunday Times* (London), *Times Literary Supplement,* and *Spectator;* contributor to newspapers, poetry journals, and other periodicals.

SIDELIGHTS: Kevin Crossley-Holland's work has its basis in "roots, the sense of the past embodied in present, the relationship of person to place," he once told *CA.* As a poet, a translator, and a reteller of folklore, he learned his first lessons growing up with a father who sang traditional tales, accompanying himself on the Welsh harp. Crossley-Holland's original poetry, A. T. Tolley observed in *Dictionary of Literary Biography,* "shows the influence of his work in translating" folk material and "as a whole is notable for its evocation of the character of objects and scenes." Conversely, his poet's ear for the sounds and rhythms of language has enriched his retellings and translations of myth and legend, the work for which he is more widely known. His translations include *Beowulf, The Exeter Book Riddles,* and many more Old English poetic works.

Crossley-Holland wrote poetry at Oxford, where he studied English language and literature and earned a B.A. with honors in 1962. After graduation, he worked in publishing until 1977. During this time he published the work of other poets, including George MacBeth, Keith Harrison, R. S. Thomas, and Alan Brownjohn and had his own poems, translations, and children's books published.

Most of the poems from Crossley-Holland's early books of poetry were collected in *The Rain-Giver and Other Poems,* which Tolley commended for the author's "assured but unassuming style, poems that grow on one with continued reading." Tolley found especially noteworthy the set of five poems grouped under the title "My Son," which depict "a harrowing record of estrangement and emotional exclusion in which feeling comes through with discomforting directness," and he cited "clarity of diction, unostentatiously at the service of feeling," as a "feature of the best poems in *The Rain-Giver,* which include not only the personal pieces, but the many poems of place and landscape."

A second collection, *The Dream-House and Other Poems,* appeared four years later and was a Poetry Society Book Selection. In a piece written for the Poetry Society to promote the book, the author named "two main preoccupations" of the poems in the collection, which also contains some translations from Old English: "a keen interest in relating past to present" and a concern with destiny. Tolley found in this collection "poems of lyrical sensitivity" and "poems that are limpidly evocative of scene." The poet's interest in relating past to present was apparent also in his third major collection, *Time's Oriel and Other Poems,* in which Tolley identified the themes of "death, the passage of time, and the integrity of self" as Crossley-Holland as-

sociated them with memory. Tolley saw in *Time's Oriel* "a strength not always found in *The Dream-House*" and called it "a deeply satisfying collection." In the *Times Literary Supplement,* Simon Rae also compared the two books, noting that the "wilderness landscapes of the far north" had figured in the genesis of many poems in the former collection, which was "bleak . . . , touched by a discomfiting unhappiness." *Time's Oriel,* by contrast, "contains more sunlight and has a less oppressive air." Crossley-Holland's concern with landscape and history are still prominent in his fifth collection, *The Painting Room and Other Poems.* In the set of poems for which the collection was named, Crossley-Holland draws "parallels between John Constable's life and work and the poet's own life," as Jonathan Taylor observed in the *Times Literary Supplement.* Despite some praise, Taylor judged the work ultimately unsatisfying and "*The Painting Room . . .* a pleasant place, but perhaps too cosy to stay in long."

Crossley-Holland's *New and Selected Poems, 1965-1990* is a chronological arrangement of poems taken mainly from his previous collections with seventeen new poems added. Reviewing the book for the *Times Literary Supplement,* Virginia Rounding noted "no startling new departures, either in form or content," in the new poems and commented on the dominance of the marsh as a physical image and the poet's continuing concern with "making present the past, finding connections and correspondences in people or places, so that history becomes something to be experienced and lived now."

Of Crossley-Holland's retellings of folklore, one of the most widely reviewed is *The Norse Myths: A New Version,* a collection of thirty-two Viking tales that explain life on earth from creation to destruction. In the assessment of *Los Angeles Times* reviewer Lyle Rexer, "The force of these myths often lies in their terseness, but Crossley-Holland, a poet as well as a scholar and translator, may have much to do with that. . . . Not accidentally, he has also provided some of the formal pleasures of a good novel, especially of character." Karen Durbin also acknowledged Crossley-Holland's credentials and added in a *Voice Literary Supplement* review, "Working back to the forms and the language of the original, he has brought it close, melding the ancient and the contemporary until the distance between that world and this one dissolves." In the *Times Literary Supplement,* Gwyn Jones approved the poet's method with the myths: "The retellings throughout are managed with a story-teller's resourcefulness. The language is lively and fresh, the narrative has pace and sinew, there is a proper regard for the originals but no subservience—which is as it should be." For a children's version of the myths, Crossley-Holland gathered in *Axe-Age, Wolf-Age: A Selection of Norse Myths* twenty-two of the tales he had included in *The Norse Myths,* omitting the introductory and explanatory notes he had provided in the earlier volume.

Crossley-Holland has published several versions of the classic tale *Beowulf.* His verse translation "achieves his aim of providing a truly accessible version of the poem," in Tolley's view. In addition, his version for children was reviewed by Michael Dirda in the *Washington Post Book World,* who commented that the author "makes no pretense of scholarship, retelling the tale in a spooky, vaguely alliterative prose that hews close to the Old English" that has "its own music."

Other important Crossley-Holland works for children include a retelling of the Welsh cycle of myths in *Tales from the Mabinogion* (with Gwyn Thomas), and *Wulf,* a retelling of the stories told in an earlier trilogy about a seventeenth-century Anglican child. *Wulf,* said Heather O'Donoghue in the *Times Literary Supplement,* "is full of the conventional good things of children's literature," but it is "not a total success" as it is riddled with unconvincing speech and is "hard to read (especially for children)." Conversely, Juliet Townsend wrote in the *Spectator* that the book's language "catches brilliantly the flavour of Anglo-Saxon imagery, expressed in simple modern English." Ghost stories and ancient tales of the macabre are the fare in *The Dead Moon and Other Tales from East Anglia and the Fen Country,* which is unlike traditional children's literature in that the stories do not necessarily demonstrate a moral, and good conduct is often not rewarded. In her review of this collection for the *Times Literary Supplement,* Cara Chanteau wrote, "These stories are enormously refreshing, vaguely unsettling, and have a particular vigour all of their own."

BIOGRAPHICAL/CRITICAL SOURCES:

BOOKS

Dictionary of Literary Biography, Volume 40: *Poets of Great Britain and Ireland since 1960,* Gale, 1985.

PERIODICALS

Books and Bookmen, December, 1967; August, 1968.
Children's Book World, November 3, 1968.
Horn Book, December, 1969; December, 1971.
Listener, November 14, 1968.
Los Angeles Times, December 18, 1980.
New York Times Book Review, November 8, 1970.
Observer Review, February 26, 1970.
Punch, October 23, 1968.
Saturday Review, March 15, 1969.
Spectator, December 10, 1988, pp. 37-38.
Times (London), November 20, 1986.
Times Literary Supplement, January 23, 1969; October 16, 1969; December 19, 1980; April 17, 1981, p. 441; No-

vember 26, 1982, p. 1306; February 17, 1984, p. 168; May 10, 1985, p. 530; November 28, 1986, p. 1347; December 19, 1986, p. 1423; November 13-19, 1987, p. 1261; April 1, 1988, p. 371; October 21, 1988, p. 1181; December 16-22, 1988, p. 1406; March 30, 1990, p. 356; June 21, 1991, p. 18.
Voice Literary Supplement, December, 1981, p. 19.
Washington Post Book World, March 11, 1984, p. 11; April 14, 1985, p. 10; June 14, 1987, p. 10; February 14, 1988, p. 10.
Young Reader's Review, January, 1967; June, 1968; October, 1969.

* * *

CRUMP, (Stephen) Thomas 1929-

PERSONAL: Born September 26, 1929, in London, England; son of Norman Easedale and Kathleen Mary St. Patrick (Hodson) Crump; married Carolina Prakke, September 29, 1972; children: Maarten Thomas, Laura Caroline. *Education:* University of Michigan, LL.M., 1954; Trinity College, Cambridge, M.A., 1956, further study, 1966-68; University of London, Ph.D., 1976. *Politics:* "Jeffersonian." *Religion:* Agnostic.

ADDRESSES: Home—Twentestraat 4, Amsterdam, Netherlands. *Office*—Sarphatistraat 106 A, Amsterdam, Netherlands. *Agent*—A. D. Peters, 10 Buckingham Street, London W.C.2, England.

CAREER: Director of Africa Intelligence Service, 1956-64; barrister-at-law, 1958-66; University of Amsterdam, Amsterdam, Netherlands, senior lecturer in cultural anthropology, 1972—. *Military service:* British Army, Royal Signal Corps, 1948-49; became second lieutenant.

MEMBER: Royal Geographical Society (fellow), Royal Anthropological Institute, Nederlandse Sociologische-Antropologische Vereniging.

WRITINGS:

The Law for Everyman, Collins (London), 1963.
(With G. S. A. Wheatcroft) *The Law of Income Tax, Profits Tax, and Surtax,* Sweet & Maxwell, 1963.
Man and His Kind, Praeger (New York City), 1973.
The Context of European Anthropology: The Lesson from Italy, Mouton (The Hague, Netherlands), 1974.
The Phenomenon of Money, Routledge & Kegan Paul (London), 1981.
The Death of an Emperor: Japan at the Crossroads, Constable (London), 1989, Oxford University Press (New York City), 1991.
The Anthropology of Numbers, Cambridge University Press (Cambridge, England), 1990.

The Japanese Numbers Game: The Use and Understanding of Numbers in Modern Japan, Routledge (London), 1992.

SIDELIGHTS: Thomas Crump is interested in the ways in which people earn their living and the ways in which they use language. His research has centered on the use of money in traditional communities. Crump has studied people in Europe, North and Central America, and Africa; languages he has studied include Indo-European, Semitic, Maya, Bantu, and Japanese.*

* * *

CRYSTAL, David 1941-

PERSONAL: Born July 6, 1941, in Lisburn, County Antrim, Northern Ireland; son of Samuel Cyril and Mary (Morris) Crystal; married Molly Stack, April 1, 1964 (deceased, 1976); married Hilary Norman, September 18, 1976; children: (first marriage) Steven David, Susan Mary, Timothy Joseph, Lucy Alexandra; (second marriage) Benjamin Peter. *Education:* University College, London, B.A., 1962, Ph.D., 1966, F.C.S.T., 1983. *Politics:* None. *Religion:* Roman Catholic. *Avocational interests:* Music (in all forms), cinema, book collecting.

ADDRESSES: Home—Akaroa, Gors Ave., Holyhead, Gwynedd LL65 1PB, Wales. *Office*—P.O. Box 5, Holyhead, Gwynedd LL65 1RG, Wales.

CAREER: University of London, University College, London, England, research assistant, 1962-63; University of Wales, University College of North Wales, Bangor, assistant lecturer in linguistics, 1963-65, honorary professor of linguistics, 1986—; University of Reading, Reading, England, lecturer, 1965-69, reader, 1969-75, professor of linguistics, 1975-85; currently author, lecturer on language and linguistics, and general reference books editor. Director, Ucheldre Center, Holyhead.

MEMBER: International Phonetic Association, Linguistics Association of Great Britain, British Association of Applied Linguistics, Royal Society of Arts (fellow), Philological Society, Linguistic Society of America.

WRITINGS:

(With R. Quirk) *Systems of Prosodic and Paralinguistic Features in English,* Mouton & Co., 1964.
Linguistics, Language and Religion, Hawthorn, 1965.
What Is Linguistics?, Edward Arnold, 1968, 5th edition, 1985.
(With D. Davy) *Investigating English Style,* Longman, 1969.
Prosodic Systems and Intonation in English, Cambridge University Press, 1969.
Linguistics, Penguin, 1971, 2nd edition, 1985.

The English Tone of Voice, Edward Arnold, 1975.
(With Davy) *Advanced Conversational English,* Longman, 1975.
(With J. Bevington) *Skylarks,* Nelson, 1975.
(With P. Fletcher and M. Garman) *The Grammatical Analysis of Language Disability,* Edward Arnold, 1976.
Child Language, Learning and Linguistics, Edward Arnold, 1976, 2nd edition, 1987.
Working with LARSP, Edward Arnold, 1979.
(With J. Foster) *Databank Reading Series,* Edward Arnold, 1979.
A First Dictionary of Linguistics and Phonetics, Deutsch, 1980, 2nd edition published as *Dictionary of Linguistics and Phonetics,* 1985, 3rd edition, 1991.
Introduction to Language Pathology, Edward Arnold, 1980, 3rd edition (with Rosemary Varley), Whorr, 1993.
Clinical Linguistics, Springer, 1981, revised edition, Edward Arnold, 1987.
Directions in Applied Linguistics, Academic Press, 1981.
Profiling Linguistic Disability, Edward Arnold, 1982.
Who Cares about English Usage?, Penguin, 1984.
Linguistic Encounters with Language Handicap, Basil Blackwell, 1984.
Listen to Your Child, Penguin, 1986.
Rediscover Grammar, Longman, 1988.
The English Language, Penguin, 1988.
Pilgrimage, Holy Island Press, 1988.
(With J. C. Davies) *Covenant,* Holy Island Press, 1989.
Language from A to Z, Longman, 1991.
Making Sense of English Usage, Chambers, 1991.
Nineties Knowledge, Chambers, 1992.
Introducing Linguistics, Penguin, 1992.
An Encyclopedic Dictionary of Language and Languages, Basil Blackwell, 1992, Penguin, 1993.
Cambridge Encyclopedia of the English Language, Cambridge University Press, 1995.

EDITOR

(With W. Bolton) *The English Language,* Cambridge University Press, 1969.
Eric Partridge: In His Own Words, Deutsch, 1980.
Linguistic Controversies, Edward Arnold, 1982.
(With Bolton) *The English Language,* Sphere, 1987.
Cambridge Encyclopedia of Language, Cambridge University Press, 1987.
The Cambridge Encyclopedia, Cambridge University Press, 1990, 2nd edition, 1994.
Cambridge Concise Encyclopedia, Cambridge University Press, 1992.
Cambridge Paperback Encyclopedia, Cambridge University Press, 1993.
Cambridge Factfinder, Cambridge University Press, 1993.

Cambridge Biographical Encyclopedia, Cambridge University Press, 1994.

OTHER

Contributor to books, including *The Library of Modern Knowledge,* Readers Digest Press, 1978; *A Dictionary of Modern Thought,* A. Bullock, editor, John M. Fontana, 1978, 2nd edition, 1987; *Readers Digest Book of Facts,* Readers Digest Press, 1985. Editor, *The Language Library* series, Blackwell, and of *Journal of Child Language,* 1973-85, *Child Language Theory and Teaching,* 1985—, and *Linguistics Abstracts,* 1985—.

SIDELIGHTS: John Ross of the *Times Literary Supplement* comments about David Crystal's *A First Dictionary of Linguistics and Phonetics:* "What we have here are definitions and explanations covering the main areas of twentieth-century linguistic thought, presented in a language as clear and elegant as one could hope for." Ross continues, "For all the author's claims about the limitations of the work, it covers an impressive range of subjects." Observing that "Crystal maintains remarkable objectivity," Ross concludes, "probably the work's most outstanding quality—certainly the one most useful to its readers—is its resolute fair-mindedness."

BIOGRAPHICAL/CRITICAL SOURCES:

PERIODICALS

New York Times Book Review, May 10, 1981.
Times Literary Supplement, February 27, 1981; March 20, 1981.

*   *   *

CUNNINGHAM, Laura 1947-

PERSONAL: Born January 25, 1947, in New York, NY; daughter of Laurence Moore (an aviator) and Rose Weiss; married Barry Cunningham (a journalist), December 4, 1966 (separated, 1994); children: Alexandra Rose, Jasmine Sou Mei (both adopted). *Education:* New York University, B.A., 1966.

ADDRESSES: Home—New York, NY. *Agent*—Owen Laster, William Morris Agency, 1350 Avenue of the Americas, New York, NY 10019.

CAREER: Author.

AWARDS, HONORS: Nationwide journalism award for best profile, for cover story in *Newsday,* 1984; National Endowment for the Arts grant, 1987, for playwriting, and 1990, for creative nonfiction; New York Foundation of the Arts grant, 1987, for theater, and 1990, for nonfiction literature.

MEMBER: Authors League of America, Dramatists Guild, Authors Guild, Writers Guild of America, Girl Scouts of America, Poets and Writers, New Dramatists, Writer's Community.

WRITINGS:

Sweet Nothings (novel), Doubleday (New York), 1977.
Third Parties (novel), Coward, McCann, 1980.
Sleeping Arrangements (memoir), Knopf (New York), 1989.

PLAYS

Bang, first produced in Chicago, IL, by Steppenwolf Theatre Company, 1986.
Beautiful Bodies, first produced in Montclair, NJ, by Whole Theatre Company, 1987.
I Love You, Two (related one-act plays; contains *Where She Went, What She Did,* first produced at the Manhattan Punchline, 1988, and *The Man at the Door,* first produced at the Renegade Theatre, Hoboken, NJ, 1991), Samuel French (New York), 1988.

Also author of unpublished play "Cruising Close to Crazy."

OTHER

Contributor of articles, short stories, and reviews to periodicals, including *New Yorker, New York Times, Atlantic, Vogue,* and *Newsday.*

SIDELIGHTS: Laura Cunningham describes the problems faced by descendants of the very rich in her humorous novel *Third Parties.* The novel is set in Darton's Wood, an extravagant playground built by turn-of-the-century robber barons. Their third-generation descendants struggle to maintain the grand estates in spite of twentieth-century maintenance costs. Into this scene moves Isaac Katcher, a songwriter from the Bronx who finds peace in the beauty of Darton's Wood. When a corporation threatens to transform the country retreat into modern developments, Katcher, "in a hilarious show of strength, . . . musters an army of ex-wives and social misfits who share his views and, in a brilliantly engineered filibuster, literally bores the opposition into surrender," relates Elizabeth Forsythe Hailey in the *New York Times Book Review. Los Angeles Times Book Review* contributor Joan Reardon rates *Third Parties* "definitely one of a kind," and further calls it "a wonderful blend of fantasy and funk, . . . a just-right blend of snappy and sassy satire."

Sleeping Arrangements is an autobiographical novel of Cunningham's childhood in the Bronx during the 1950s. Novelist Ann Tyler, reviewing the book for the *Baltimore Sun,* notes, "*Sleeping Arrangements* is so funny and quirky, and it's written with such a deft touch, that at first you may not recognize its underlying seriousness." Young Lily—the fictional stand-in for author Cunningham—lives in circumstances most would call unusual. She is left an orphan at age eight by the death of her mother. She has never known her father; he was (according to her mother) killed while fighting the Germans, with his noble boxer Butch by his side. Into Lily's life sweep her two bachelor uncles to care for her. Uncle Gabe, a music teacher, writes love songs that rhyme "river" with "liver." Uncle Len aspires to be a detective and travels on mysterious errands with a change of clothes in a manila envelope. Together they create a surreal version of "normal" life that includes allowing Lily to decorate the living room to her own taste (orange and white stripes, like her favorite Good Humor bar).

But Cunningham's story is more than a catalog of wacky characters. Cunningham proves to be an affectionate and sharp chronicler of a time and place some might recall as lacking in excitement. In a *New York Times* review, Michiko Kakutani quotes a passage where Lily describes what it is like to live in the shadow of Yankee stadium: "To an extent, I lead a baseball-dominated life. Not only does the stadium emit strange lights and sounds—my mother and I soon become accustomed to the twilights, accept them as naturally as Norsemen must have tolerated their endless days in the land of the midnight sun—but the entire neighborhood is designed around the sport. . . . In season, the streets are clogged with fans; the entire neighborhood is redolent of frankfurter." In Kakutani's judgement, "*Sleeping Arrangements* stands as a model memoir—at once funny and sad, irreverent and generous."

Cunningham once told *CA*: "I have a typical writer's personal history, that is: atypical. I am of Jewish-Southern Baptist descent, was orphaned at age eight, and raised by two unmarried uncles (both writers). I'm a third-generation author: my grandparents also wrote stories and books. Motivation? I didn't know there was anything else to be. Had I known, I would have been a ballerina."

BIOGRAPHICAL/CRITICAL SOURCES:

PERIODICALS

Baltimore Sun, November 26, 1989.
Chicago Magazine, December, 1986.
Los Angeles Times Book Review, October 12, 1980.
New York Times, November 7, 1989.
New York Times Book Review, October 26, 1980.
San Francisco Chronicle, January 28, 1990.

CURTIS, Richard Kenneth 1924-

PERSONAL: Born January 22, 1924, in Worcester, MA; son of Albert W. and Vena (Masters) Curtis; married M. Elizabeth Fisher, July 7, 1945; children: Stephen Dana, David Alan, Laurel Elizabeth. *Education:* Northern Baptist Theological Seminary, Th.B., 1950; Purdue University, M.S., 1951, Ph.D., 1954. *Avocational interests:* Tennis, skiing, swimming, music.

ADDRESSES: Home—636 Braeside N. Dr., Indianapolis, IN 46260. *Office*—Indiana University/Purdue University at Indianapolis, 925 W. Michigan, Indianapolis, IN 46202.

CAREER: Russiville Baptist Church, Russiville, IN, pastor, 1947-52; ordained Baptist minister, 1951; Barrington College, Barrington, RI, department chairman, 1952-56; Bethel College, St. Paul, MN, department chairman, 1956-62; Immanuel Baptist Church, Kansas City, KS, pastor, 1962-67; Muskingum College, New Concord, OH, professor of speech and department chairman, 1967-69; Indiana University/Purdue University at Indianapolis, Indianapolis, IN, professor of speech and department chairman, 1969-71, professor of speech, 1971—. University of Missouri, Kansas City Campus, visiting lecturer in speech, 1963-67. Conductor of speech courses on commercial television in Providence, RI, and on educational television in St. Paul, MN. *Military service:* U.S. Army Air Forces, 1942-46; became first lieutenant and fighter pilot; received Distinguished Flying Cross.

MEMBER: American Association of University Professors, Speech Communication Association (chair of research committee on religious interest groups, 1957-62; chair of senior college-university division, 1981-82), World Future Society (president of central Indiana chapter, 1974—).

WRITINGS:

They Called Him Mister Moody, Doubleday (New York, NY), 1962.
Evolution or Extinction, the Choice before Us: A Systems Approach to the Study of the Future, Pergamon Press (New York, NY), 1982.
How to Be Your Own Literary Agent: The Business of Getting Your Book Published, Houghton (Boston, MA), 1984.*

D

DANIELS, James R(aymond) 1956-
(Jim Daniels)

PERSONAL: Born June 6, 1956, in Detroit, MI; son of Raymond J. and Mary T. (Rivard) Daniels; married Kristin Kovacic, September 28, 1985; children: Ramsey. *Education:* Alma College, B.A. (with honors), 1978; Bowling Green State University, M.F.A., 1980.

ADDRESSES: Home—3419 Parkview Ave., Pittsburgh, PA 15213. *Office*—Department of English, Carnegie-Mellon University, Pittsburgh, PA 15213.

CAREER: Bowling Green State University, Bowling Green, OH, lecturer in English, 1980-81; Carnegie-Mellon University, Pittsburgh, PA, visiting writer in residence, 1981-84, assistant professor, 1984-86, associate professor of English, 1986—. Judge of poetry competitions; gives readings at schools, libraries, and on National Public Radio.

AWARDS, HONORS: Winner of national Signpost Press chapbook contest, 1980, for *On the Line;* first prize from *Passages North* poetry contest, 1983, for "My Father Worked Late"; fellow of National Endowment for the Arts, 1985; Wisconsin/Brittingham Prize for Poetry from University of Wisconsin Press, 1985, for *Places/Everyone;* Pennsylvania Council on the Arts literature fellowships, 1987, 1990.

WRITINGS:

UNDER NAME JIM DANIELS

Factory Poems (chapbook), Jack-in-the-Box Press, 1979.
On the Line (chapbook), Signpost Press (Menomonee Falls, WI), 1981.
Places/Everyone (poems), University of Wisconsin Press (Madison), 1985.
The Long Ball (chapbook), Pig-in-a-Poke Press, 1988.

Digger's Territory (chapbook), Adastra Press (Easthampton, MA), 1989.
Punching Out (poems), Wayne State University Press (Detroit), 1990.
Hacking It (chapbook), Ridgeway Press (St. Clair Shores, MI), 1992.
M-80 (poems), University of Pittsburgh Press (Pittsburgh), 1993.
(Co-editor) *The Carnegie-Mellon Anthology of Poetry,* Carnegie-Mellon University Press (Pittsburgh), 1993.
Niagara Falls (chapbook), Adastra Press, 1994.
No Pets (screenplay), Braddock Films, 1994.
(Editor) *Letters to America: Contemporary Poetry on Race,* Wayne State University Press, 1995.

Contributor of poems to magazines, including *Paris Review, Cimarron Review, Iowa Review, Gettysburg Review, Kenyon Review,* and *Prairie Schooner.*

WORK IN PROGRESS: New poems, stories, and essays.

SIDELIGHTS: James R. Daniels once told *CA:* "Much of my poetry has focused on blue-collar life in my native Detroit. I feel that there is little poetry being written about the world that I come from and the people that I care about. I try to give a voice to those who are often shut out of poetry, to explore their lives both in and out of the workplace. If nothing else, I'm trying to say that these people are important, that their lives have value and meaning."

*   *   *

DANIELS, Jim
See DANIELS, James R(aymond)

DANIELS, Roger 1927-

PERSONAL: Born December 1, 1927, in New York, NY; son of George Roger (an author) and Eleanor (Lustig) Daniels; married Judith Marcia Mandel, October 2, 1960; children: Richard John, Sarah Elizabeth. *Education:* University of Houston, B.A., 1957; University of California, Los Angeles, M.S., 1958, Ph.D., 1961.

ADDRESSES: Office—Department of History, University of Cincinnati, Cincinnati, OH 45221.

CAREER: Wisconsin State College and Institute of Technology, Platteville (now University of Wisconsin—Platteville), assistant professor, 1961-62, associate professor of history, 1962-63; University of California, Los Angeles, assistant professor of history, 1963-68; University of Wyoming, Laramie, associate professor, 1968-71, professor of history, 1971; State University of New York College at Fredonia, professor of history, 1971-76; University of Cincinnati, Cincinnati, OH, professor of history, 1976—; Charles Phelps Taft Professor of History, 1994—. University of Alaska, Fairbanks, and University of Utah, distinguished visiting professor, 1983; University of Innsbruck, visiting professor, 1992. Statue of Liberty/Ellis Island Centennial Series, University of Illinois Press, chair, board of editors, 1986—. The Asian American Experience Series, University of Illinois Press, editor, 1992—. *Military service:* U.S. Army, 1952-54; became sergeant.

MEMBER: Organization of American Historians (executive board member, 1973-76), Public Works Historical Society (trustee, 1975-77), Immigration History Society (executive board member, 1980-83, 1987-90), Association for Asian/Pacific Studies (executive board member, 1980-85), Statue of Liberty/Ellis Island Centennial Commission and Foundation (history committee member, 1982-90), Society for Historians of the Gilded Age/Progressive Era (executive board member, 1989-91; vice-president, 1991-92; president, 1992-94), Immigration History Society (vice president, 1991-94, president, 1994-97), Midwest History Workshop (president, 1980—), Cincinnati Historical Society (trustee, 1989—).

AWARDS, HONORS: McMicken Dean's Award for Distinguished Scholarship, 1992; Ohioana Citation for Distinguished Service to Ohio in the Humanities, 1992; Rieveschl Award for Excellence in Scholarly or Creative Works, University of Cincinnati, 1993.

WRITINGS:

The Politics of Prejudice: The Anti-Japanese Movement in California and the Struggle for Japanese Exclusion, University of California Press (Berkeley and Los Angeles), 1962, enlarged edition, 1991.

(With Harry H. L. Kitano) *American Racism: Exploration of the Nature of Prejudice,* Prentice-Hall (Englewood Cliffs, NJ), 1970.

The Bonus March: An Episode of the Great Depression, Greenwood Press (Westport, CT), 1971.

Concentration Camps USA: Japanese Americans and World War II, Holt, 1972.

(Editor) *Essays in Western History in Honor of T. A. Larson,* University of Wyoming (Laramie), 1972.

(Editor with Spencer C. Olin, Jr.) *Racism in California: A Reader in the History of Oppression,* Macmillan, 1972.

(Editor) Harry L. Hopkins, *Spending to Save,* University of Washington Press (Seattle), 1972.

(Editor) Elmer C. Sandmeyer, *The Anti-Chinese Movement in California,* University of Illinois Press (Urbana), 1973, enlarged edition, 1991.

The Decision to Relocate the Japanese Americans, Lippincott (Philadelphia), 1975, 2nd edition, Robert E. Krieger (Melbourne, FL), 1986.

The Asian Experience in North America: Chinese and Japanese (47 volumes; includes *Anti-Chinese Violence in North America: An Original Anthology, Three Short Works on Japanese Americans,* and *Two Monographs on Japanese Canadians*), Arno, 1979.

Concentration Camps, North America: Japanese in the United States and Canada during World War II, Robert E. Krieger, 1981, 2nd edition, 1993.

(Editor with Sandra C. Taylor and Harry H. L. Kitano) *Japanese Americans: From Relocation to Redress,* University of Utah Press (Salt Lake City), 1986, revised edition, University of Washington Press, 1991.

(With Kitano) *Asian Americans: Emerging Minorities,* Prentice-Hall, 1987, 2nd edition, 1995.

Asian America: Chinese and Japanese in the United States since 1850, University of Washington Press, 1988.

(Editor) *American Concentration Camps: A Documentary History of the Relocation and Incarceration of Japanese Americans, 1941-1945,* nine volumes, Garland Publishing (New York City), 1989.

History of Indian Immigration to the United States: An Interpretive Essay, Asia Society (New York City), 1989.

Coming to America: A History of Immigration and Ethnicity in American Life, HarperCollins (New York City), 1990.

Prisoners Without Trial: Japanese Americans in World War II, Hill & Wang (New York City), 1993.

(Editor) Linda Tamura, *The Hood River Issei: An Oral History of Japanese Settlers in Oregon's Hood River Valley,* University of Illinois Press, 1993.

(Editor) Eileen Tamura, *Americanization, Acculturation, and Ethnic Identity: The Nisei Generation in Hawaii,* University of Illinois Press, 1994.

Consulting editor for "Recent American Immigrants," a series of books for children published by F. Watts (New York City), which includes the titles *Asian Indians,* 1990; *Chinese,* 1990; *Filipinos,* 1990; *Mexicans,* 1990; *Eastern Europeans,* 1991; *Southeast Asians,* 1991; *Cubans,* 1991; and *Koreans,* 1991. Contributor of articles and essays to journals, books, and encyclopedias.

* * *

DAVIS, Gordon
    See HUNT, E(verette) Howard (Jr.)

* * *

DAVIS, William Virgil 1940-

PERSONAL: Born May 26, 1940, in Canton, OH; son of Virgil Sanor and Anna Bertha (Orth) Davis; married Carol Ann Demske (an English teacher), July 17, 1971; children: William Lawrence. *Education:* Ohio University, A.B., 1962, M.A., 1965, Ph.D., 1967; Pittsburgh Theological Seminary, M.Div., 1965. *Avocational interests:* Painting, travel.

ADDRESSES: Home—2633 Lake Oaks Rd., Waco, TX 76710. *Office*—Department of English, P.O. Box 97404, Baylor University, Waco, TX 76798.

CAREER: Ordained Presbyterian minister, 1970. Ohio University, Athens, assistant professor of English, 1967-68; Central Connecticut State University, New Britain, assistant professor of English, 1968-71; Tunxis Community College, Farmington, CT, assistant professor of English, 1971-72; University of Illinois at Chicago, assistant professor of English, 1972-77; Baylor University, Waco, TX, associate professor, 1977-79, professor of English and writer-in-residence, 1979—. Guest professor of English and American literature at the University of Vienna, Austria, 1979-80, 1989-90; writer-in-residence at the University of Montana, 1983; visiting scholar/guest professor, University of Wales, Swansea, 1983; guest professor of American studies at the University of Copenhagen, Denmark, 1984; adjunct MFA faculty, Southwest Texas State University, 1990—; consultant to the creative writing program, Ohio University, 1992—; adjunct member of the graduate faculty, Texas Christian University, 1992—. Gives poetry readings and lectures internationally.

MEMBER: International Association of University Professors, PEN, Academy of American Poets, Modern Language Association of America, Poetry Society of America, Poets and Writers, Texas Institute of Letters (councilor), Texas Association of Creative Writing Teachers, Ohio University Board of Visitors, Phi Kappa Phi, Tau Kappa Alpha.

AWARDS, HONORS: Bread Loaf Writers' Conference scholar in poetry, 1970, and John Atherton Fellow in Poetry, 1980; graduate faculty fellow in creative writing at the University of Illinois, 1974; faculty fellow in poetry at Baylor University, 1979; Yale Series of Younger Poets award, 1979, for *One Way to Reconstruct the Scene;* Senior Fulbright fellowship for guest professorship at University of Vienna, 1979-80, 1989-90, and at the University of Copenhagen, Denmark, 1984; Lilly Foundation grant, 1979-80; Distinguished Humanities Lecturer, Southwest Conference Humanities Consortium, 1981-82; Calliope Press Chapbook Prize, 1984, for *The Dark Hours;* member, Texas Commission on the Arts, 1988-90; Outstanding Faculty Member, Baylor University, 1988-89; Outstanding Creative Artist, Baylor University, 1989; nominated for Pushcart Prizes, 1991, 1992, 1993; significant contribution award, College of Arts and Sciences, Ohio University, 1992.

WRITINGS:

(Editor and author of introduction) *George Whitefield's Journals, 1737-1741,* Scholars' Facsimiles & Reprints (Delmar, NY), 1969.
One Way to Reconstruct the Scene (poems), Yale University Press (New Haven, CT), 1980.
The Dark Hours (poems), Calliope Press (Hollywood, CA), 1984.
Understanding Robert Bly, University of South Carolina Press (Columbia), 1988.
Winter Light (poems), University of North Texas Press, 1990.
(Editor) *Critical Essays on Robert Bly,* G.K. Hall/Macmillan (New York City), 1992.
(Editor) *Miraculous Simplicity: Essays on R. S. Thomas,* University of Arkansas Press (Fayetteville, AR), 1993.
Robert Bly: The Poet and His Critics, Camden House (Columbia, SC), 1994.

Contributor to books, including *Encyclopedia of World Literature in the Twentieth Century,* Ungar, 1975, revised edition, 1986; *Dictionary of Literary Biography,* Volume 120, *American Poets Since WWII,* 3rd series, Gale (Detroit), 1992; *Critical Survey of Poetry: English Language Series,* revised edition, 1992; *The Page's Drift: R. S. Thomas at Eighty,* 1993; *Miraculous Simplicity: Essays on R. S. Thomas,* 1993; and *Writing Region and Nation,* 1994. Contributing editor, *Theodore Roethke: A Bibliography,* edited by James Richard McLeod, Kent State University Press, 1973. Contributor of more than seventy articles and more than fifty reviews to journals, including *James Joyce Quarterly, Studies in Short Fiction, Wallace*

Stevens Journal, Studies in the Novel, and *Modern Poetry Studies;* contributor of more than 800 poems to journals, including *Poetry, Atlantic Monthly, North American Review, Hudson Review, Gettysburg Review, New Criterion, Shenandoah, Southwest Review,* and *Poetry Northwest;* and of short stories to *Northeast, U. S. Catholic, Malahat Review,* and *New Orleans Review.* Poetry recorded as part of the Ruth Stephen Poetry Archive, University of Texas at Austin, 1993.

WORK IN PROGRESS: A collection of poems.

*   *   *

DAY, Max
See CASSIDAY, Bruce (Bingham)

*   *   *

DELDERFIELD, R(onald) F(rederick) 1912-1972

PERSONAL: Born February 12, 1912, in Greenwich, London, England; died June 24, 1972; married May Evans, 1936; children: one son, one daughter. *Education:* Educated in England.

CAREER: Enmouth Chronicle, Devon, England, began as reporter, became sub-editor, 1929-39, editor, 1945-47; freelance author, playwright, and journalist, 1947—. *Military service:* Royal Air Force, 1940-45, public relations officer in Europe, 1944-45.

WRITINGS:

ROMANCE AND HISTORICAL FICTION

All over the Town, Simon & Schuster (New York City), 1977.

Seven Men of Gascony, Bobbs-Merrill (Indianapolis, IN), 1949.

Farewell the Tranquil, Dutton (New York City), 1950, published in England as *Farewell the Tranquil Mind,* W. Laurie, 1950.

The Avenue Goes to War (also see below), Hodder & Stoughton (London, England), 1958, Ballantine (New York City), 1964.

The Dreaming Suburb (also see below), Ballantine, 1958.

Diana, Putnam, 1960, published in England as *There Was a Fair Maid Dwelling,* Hodder & Stoughton, 1960.

Stop at a Winner, Hodder & Stoughton, 1961, Simon & Schuster, 1978.

The Unjust Skies, Hodder & Stoughton, 1962.

Mr. Sermon, Simon & Schuster, 1963, published in England as *The Spring Madness of Mr. Sermon,* Hodder & Stoughton, 1963.

Too Few for Drums, Hodder & Stoughton, 1964, Simon & Schuster, 1971.

A Horseman Riding By, Hodder & Stoughton, 1966, Simon & Schuster, 1967.

The Green Gauntlet. Simon & Schuster, 1968.

The Avenue (previously published separately as *The Avenue Goes to War* and *The Dreaming Suburb*), Simon & Schuster, 1969, published in England as *The Avenue Story,* Hodder & Stoughton, 1964.

God Is an Englishman, Simon & Schuster, 1970.

Theirs Was the Kingdom, Simon & Schuster, 1971.

To Serve Them All My Days, Simon & Schuster, 1972.

Give Us This Day, Simon & Schuster, 1973.

Post of Honor, Ballantine, 1974.

Return Journey, Simon & Schuster, 1974, published in England as *Cheap Day Return,* Hodder & Stoughton, 1967.

Long Summer Days, Pocket Books (New York City), 1974.

Charlie Come Home, Simon & Schuster, 1976, published in England as *Come Home Charlie and Face Them,* Hodder & Stoughton, 1969.

PLAYS

Spark in Judea (produced in London, England, 1937), Baker (Boston, MA), 1951.

Twilight Call, produced in Birmingham, England, 1939.

Printers Devil, produced in London, 1939.

(With Basil Thomas) *This Is My Life* (three-act; produced in London), C. H. Fox, 1944.

The Spinster of South Street, produced in London, 1945.

The Worm's Eye View (three-act; produced in West End, London, 1945), Samuel French, 1948.

Peace Comes to Peckham (three-act; produced in London, 1946), Samuel French, 1948.

All over Town (three-act; produced in London, 1947; adapted from Delderfield's novel of the same title), Samuel French, 1948, Hodder & Stoughton, 1974, Ulverscroft, 1979.

The Queen Came By (three-act; produced in London, 1948), Baker, 1949.

Sailors Beware: An Elizabethan Improbability (one-act), H. F. W. Deane (London), 1950.

The Elephant's Graveyard, produced in Chesterfield, England, 1951.

Golden Rain (produced in Windsor, 1952) Samuel French (London), 1952.

Waggonload o' Monkeys: Further Adventures of Porter and Taffy (three-act), H. F. W. Deane, 1952.

The Old Lady of Cheadle (one-act), H. F. W. Deane, 1952.

Misow!, Misow! (one-act), Samuel French, 1952.

Made to Measure (one-act), Samuel French, 1952.

The Bride Wore an Opal Ring (one-act), Samuel French, 1952.

Absent Lover: A Plantagenet Improbability (one-act), Samuel French, 1953.

Smoke in the Valley (one-act), Samuel French, 1953.

Spark in the Juince (three-act), F. deWolfe & R. Stone, 1953.

The Testimonial (one-act), Samuel French, 1953.

The Orchard Walls (three-act; produced in Aldershod, Hampshire, 1953), Samuel French, 1954.

The Offending Hand (three-act; produces in Northampton, 1953), F. deWolfe & R. Stone, 1955.

Follow the Plough, produced in Leatherhead, Surrey, 1953.

And Then There Were None (one-act), Samuel French, 1954.

The Guinea-Pigs (one-act), H. F. W. Deane, 1954.

Home Is The Hunted (one-act), Samuel French, 1954.

Where There's a Will (three-act), Samuel French, 1954.

The Rounderlay Tradition, (one-act), H.F.W. Deane, 1954.

Ten till Five (one-act), F. deWolfe & R. Stone, 1954.

Musical Switch (one-act), F. deWolfe & R. Stone, 1954.

Uncle's Little Lapse (three-act), F. deWolfe & R. Stone, 1955.

Duty and the Beast (adapted from a work by Hans Keuls), produced in Worthing, Sussex, 1957.

The Mayerling Affair (three-act; produced in Pitlochry, 1957), Samuel French, 1958.

Flashpoint (three-act), Samuel French, 1958.

Wild Mink (one-act), Samuel French, 1962.

Once aboard a Lugger (three-act), Samuel French, 1962.

My Dearest Angel, produced in Pitlochry, 1963.

Also author of *Glad Tidings,* produced in 1953.

HISTORIES

Napoleon in Love, Hodder & Stoughton, 1959, Little, Brown (Boston, MA), 1960.

The Golden Millstones: Napoleon's Brothers and Sisters, Weidenfeld & Nicolson (London), 1964, Harper (New York City), 1965.

Napoleon's Marshals, Chilton (Philadelphia), 1966, published in England as *The March of the Twenty-Six: The Story of Napoleon's Marshals,* Hodder & Stoughton, 1962.

The Retreat from Moscow, Atheneum (New York City), 1967.

Imperial Sunset: The Fall of Napoleon, 1813-14, Chilton, 1968.

OTHER

These Clicks Made History: The Stories of Stanley ("Glorious") Devon, Fleet Street Philosopher, Raleigh Press, 1946.

Nobody Shouted Author (autobiographical), W. Laurie, 1951.

Bird's Eye View: An Autobiography, Constable (London), 1954.

The Adventures of Ben Gunn: A Story of the Pirates of Treasure Island (based on Robert Louis Stevenson's *Treasure Island*), Bobbs-Merrill, 1957, published in England (with illustrations by William Stobbs) as *The Adventures of Ben Gunn,* Hodder & Stoughton, 1956.

(Editor) *Tales Out of School: An Anthology of West Buckland Reminiscences, 1895-1963,* H. E. Warne, 1963.

Under an English Sky, Hodder & Stoughton, 1964.

Post of Honor, Ballantine, 1966.

For My Own Amusement (autobiographical), Hodder & Stoughton, 1968, Simon & Schuster, 1972.

Overture for Beginners (autobiographical), Hodder & Stoughton, 1970.

Also author of several screenplays, including (with William Fairchild) *Value for Money,* 1955, and (with Harold Beechman) *On the Fiddle,* 1961. Also wrote numerous radio plays, including *Cocklemouth Comet,* 1938, *The Happy Brood,* 1956, and *A Horseman Riding By* (adapted from Delderfield's own novel), 1967.

ADAPTATIONS: Diana was produced in a ten-episode series by the Arts and Entertainment channel (A&E), 1985; *To Serve Them All My Days* was produced by Public Television for the "Masterpiece Theater" series.

SIDELIGHTS: In a prolific writing career that began soon after World War II, R. F. Delderfield became best known for his romance and historical novels. Writing about Delderfield's work in this genre in *Twentieth-Century Romance and Historical Writers,* Mary Cadogan described Delderfield's novels as "not so much classic love stories as family sagas punctuated by strong romantic impulses." His stories, panoramic descriptions of the life and times that his characters live in, have been compared to such authors as Thomas Hardy and Charles Dickens. In an autobiographical work titled *For My Own Amusement,* Delderfield described himself as "a lineal descendent of the medieval minstrel who trudged from castle to castle telling tales for his supper. . . . I am a compulsive teller of tales, a real chronic case."

Born in a London borough in 1912, Delderfield was educated at local grammar schools and private colleges. Upon finishing his education, he began his writing career as a junior reporter with his father's paper, the *Enmouth Chronicle.* He continued writing for the paper until World War II, when he served as a public relations officer in the Royal Air Force for five years. It was after he returned from the war that Delderfield embarked on his long and fruitful career as a full-time author, launched formally with the success of his play titled *Worm's Eye View,* which opened in

London's West End in December, 1945. The play broke attendance records by running for five and a half years, for more than 2,000 performances.

Playwriting, however, did not satisfy Delderfield. Writing about this phase of his life in *For My Own Amusement,* Delderfield explained that although he enjoyed the financial affluence that came with the successful production of his plays, he "had never felt and never learned to feel at ease with theater folk." In fact, Delderfield saw playwriting as "a kind of extended journalism, better-paid certainly, but not nearly so interesting or so vital, because it was contrived and made to fit a pattern imposed on it by custom and fashion." And so, during the 1950s, the author turned to writing novels and histories. In *For My Own Amusement* he described this change as something that afforded him "a sense of liberation." "At last," he said, "I could write what I wanted to write, and not what fashion and the advice of professional actors dictated."

Over the next decade, Delderfield wrote four books about various aspects of the Napoleonic Empire. Drawing from his own life experiences, Delderfield says, "the characters . . . [he] created came to life as they grew from a few sentences on a blank sheet into three-dimensional, flesh-and-blood men and women." Though Delderfield's works are generally classified as part of the romance genre, his work is marked by "astute socio-political comment" said Cadogan. One of his earliest works was *Seven Men of Gascony,* a historical novel set during the Napoleonic wars. A *Christian Science Monitor* reviewer wrote: "Well-conceived and well-executed, Mr. Delderfield's story of Napoleon's last six years pulses with the devotion of unnamed hundreds of thousands and the horrors of a Continent at war—all expressed in realistic terms of ordinary, naturally decent men. The *New York Herald Tribune* added: "The author has achieved a war chronicle of breadth and vigor admirably more devoted to the sources of human behavior than to the mechanics of warfare."

In 1960, Delderfield wrote *Diana,* a romance about a Cockney orphan and a wealthy heroine. A reviewer for the *New York Times* said that, in this novel, Delderfield "recaptures with refreshing simplicity the awkwardness, excitement, and delights of youth . . . . This is a charming novel both in its understanding of the ironic predicaments of the lovers and in their identification with an enchanted setting." A reviewer for the *New Yorker* commented: "A very long and romantic English novel with a run-of-the-mill air that does not really detract from its pale but solid virtues; it is a carefully written work, and has not only a plot that unravels smoothly but enough logic to leave the reader without anything to wonder about." *Diana* was later adapted by the Arts and Entertainment channel and produced as a 10-part series. Writing about both the book and the series, John J. O'Connor commented in the *New*

York Times that "the underlying moral has a fairy-tale simplicity: People can become anything they want if they try hard enough. That may or may not be true, but it still makes for good reading and watching."

God Is an Englishman was one of Delderfield's last novels. A critic for the *New York Times Book Review* observed: "A cheerful anachronism in the world of letters, Mr. Delderfield writes with vigor, unceasing narrative drive and a high degree of craftsmanship. At his best he may remind one of Trollope, at his worst of Hugh Walpole. . . . He is a storyteller, which is no small thing to be. But he is not a novelist who can create characters so individual or so universal that they linger in the memory. . . . Although difficult to take seriously, [this book] provides a good bird's eye view of Victorian England and contains numerous snippets of social history . . . There is a place for the conventional, traditional, lively and amusing sort of fiction."

In addition to novels, Delderfield also wrote several historical studies of Napoleon. Included among these are such works as *Napoleon in Love,* where the author traced the French emperor's quest for love, and *Napoleon's Marshals,* a collective biography and history of Napoleon and his time. Delderfield was a successful writer, and his works have sold at least a million copies in the United States alone. According to Simon and Schuster, *God Is an Englishman* and *Theirs Was the Kingdom* have each sold over 65,000 copies in hardcover. Since his death in 1972, a number of titles from Delderfield's enormous catalog of work have returned into print.

BIOGRAPHICAL/CRITICAL SOURCES:

BOOKS

Delderfield, R. F., *Bird's Eye View: An Autobiography,* Constable, 1954.
Delderfield, *For My Own Amusement,* Simon & Schuster, 1972.
Delderfield, *Nobody Shouted Author,* W. Laurie, 1951.
Delderfield, *Overture for Beginners,* Hodder & Stoughton, 1970.
Something about the Author, Volume 20, Gale (Detroit), 1980.
Sternlicht, Sanford, *R. F. Delderfield,* Twayne (Boston, MA), 1988.
Twentieth-Century Romance and Historical Writers, St. James Press (Detroit), 1990.

PERIODICALS

Christian Science Monitor, March 3, 1949.
Kirkus Reviews, June 15, 1960.
New Yorker, September 17, 1960.
New York Herald Tribune, February 13, 1949.
New York Times, September 9, 1985.

New York Times Book Review, September 18, 1960; September 13, 1970.
Publishers Weekly, May 29, 1978, p. 40; April 30, 1979, p. 104.
Washington Post Book World, December 7, 1986, p. 5.

OBITUARIES:

PERIODICALS

National Observer, July 8, 1972.
Newsweek, July 10, 1971.
New York Times, June 7, 1972.
Publishers Weekly, July 17, 1972.
Washington Post, June 28, 1972.*

*　　　*　　　*

DEXTER, John
　See ZACHARY, Hugh

*　　　*　　　*

DIAMANO, Silmang
　See SENGHOR, Leopold Sedar

*　　　*　　　*

DIETRICH, Robert
　See HUNT, E(verette) Howard (Jr.)

*　　　*　　　*

DOERR, Harriet   1910-

PERSONAL: Born April 8, 1910, in Pasadena, CA; married Albert Edward Doerr (an engineer), November 15, 1930 (died, 1972); children: one son, one daughter. *Education:* Attended Smith College, 1927-28, Stanford University, 1928-30, and Scripps College, 1975-76; Stanford University, B.A., 1977, graduate study, 1978-84.

ADDRESSES: Home and office—494 Bradford St., Pasadena, CA 91105. *Agent*—Liz Darhansoff, 1220 Park Ave., New York, NY 10128.

CAREER: Writer.

MEMBER: PEN American Center, PEN Center U.S.A. West.

AWARDS, HONORS: Wallace Stegner fellowship to Stanford University, 1980-81; Henfield Foundation Award for short stories, *Transatlantic Review,* 1982; National En-

dowment for the Arts grant, 1983, for manuscript of *Stones for Ibarra;* American Book Award for first fiction from American Publishers Association, 1984, fiction award from Bay Area Book Reviewers Association, 1985, fiction award from PEN Center U.S.A. West, 1985, award from American Academy and Institute of Arts and Letters, 1985, and Gold Medal for fiction from Commonwealth Club of California, 1985, all for *Stones for Ibarra;* Harold D. Vursell Memorial Award for quality of prose style, American Academy and Institute of Arts and Letters, 1985; *Publishers Weekly,* best books list, 1993, for *Consider This, Senora.*

WRITINGS:

Stones for Ibarra (novel), Viking (New York City), 1984.
Under an Aztec Sun (short stories) Yolla Bolly Press (Covelo, CA), 1990.
Consider This, Senora (novel), Harcourt (New York City), 1993.

Also contributor to anthologies, including *The Writer on Her Work, Volume 2,* Norton (New York City), 1991, and *Best American Short Short Stories,* 1989. Contributor to periodicals, including the *New Yorker, Los Angeles Times Magazine, Santa Monica Review, Atlantic Monthly,* and *Epoch.*

ADAPTATIONS: Stones for Ibarra was adapted for a two-hour television movie starring Glenn Close, produced by Hallmark Hall of Fame, 1988.

WORK IN PROGRESS: A collection of stories and short pieces due to be published December, 1995, by Viking Penguin.

SIDELIGHTS: A 1984 American Book Award-winner, Harriet Doerr's *Stones for Ibarra* "is something of a miracle as novels go, a real act of creation," appraises critic Susan Slocum Hinerfeld in the *Los Angeles Times Book Review.* Although Harriet Doerr wrote this first novel at the age of seventy-three, critics agree that *Stones for Ibarra* is not dismissable as a fluke or mere novelty. "It's a very good novel," opines Anatole Broyard in the *New York Times,* "with echoes of Gabriel Garcia Marquez, Katherine Anne Porter and even Graham Greene." And Jonathan Yardley reflects in the *Washington Post Book World* that Doerr "has mastered the art of fiction to a degree that would be remarkable in almost any writer of any age . . . what really matters is what she has written, and it is very fine indeed."

Set in Mexico, the novel opens with Richard and Sara Everton en route to Ibarra, described by Doerr as "a declining village of one thousand souls." Fueled by the memories of Richard's great-aunt—who reminisces about the days prior to the revolution of 1910, when Richard's grandfather owned and operated a copper mine in Ibarra and his grandmother entertained and supervised the house and gardens—Richard and Sara set out to recapture their Mexican heritage. They are determined to reopen the mine and restore the family house, and to that end they have taken out loans, mortgaged their home in San Francisco, and abandoned a comfortable life in the United States. Their friends think the Evertons are out of their minds. And in *Stones for Ibarra,* Doerr remarks that "they have not considered that memories are like corks left out of bottles. They swell. They no longer fit."

The Evertons' project soon loses its focus. Shortly after their arrival, the couple learns that Richard has leukemia, with only six good years left to live. These six years become the frame for the novel whose central story, suggests Ann Hulbert in the *New Republic,* is that of "Sara's gradual awakening to the reigning fact in her own life as well as in the villagers' view of the world: the power of fate." As they try to understand their destiny, Richard and Sara continue with their mission, successfully refurbishing their ancestral home and restoring the mine to working order. Their work also draws them into touch with the villagers—as mysterious to the Evertons as the Evertons are to them—with Doerr interweaving their lives, reports *Ms.,* "in the best storytelling tradition."

According to Yardley, Doerr's "control of fictive technique . . . is exceptionally sure . . . she neither sentimentalizes nor romanticizes her Mexicans . . . but rather sees them simply as ordinary people who happen to inhabit a world that is not the same as ours." Neither the villagers nor the Evertons are that astute, however. The people of Ibarra initially regard the two Americans as *mediodesorientado,* or half-disoriented, because of their strange behavior—they plant cactus for aesthetic reasons, read separate books, and sometimes stare out a window at something they call "a view." Richard and Sara are no less perplexed by the world in which they find themselves. It is Sara, though, more than Richard, who probes into the mystical nature of Ibarra and its people, trying to understand a world in which people seem to believe in a "relentless providence"—a world in which a man named Jose Reyes kills two men in a cantina and then is himself stoned, a world in which Paz Acosta, the most beautiful girl in the village, is a prostitute.

The cultural differences between the Evertons and the townspeople lose significance as acceptance and respect grow on both sides. The people of Ibarra come to recognize the Evertons not just as strange, remarkable beings but as people dealing with the same kinds of losses they face. And Sara, writes Hulbert, learns that there is "some solacing wisdom in the villagers' superstitions, in the bottles and thorns they hide for good luck." After Richard dies, Sara happens upon a cross and stones marking the site of an accident and, explains Leslie Marmon Silko in

the *New York Times Book Review,* "is told that when people pass and remember, they bring stones. Each stone marks a recalling, a remembering, without which cultures of the spoken word cannot continue." *Stones for Ibarra,* concludes Slocum Hinerfeld, is just such "a work of substance. Solid as Sara's stones, it marks place."

In a *CA* interview, Doerr describes to interviewer Jean Ross the creative process which resulted in her numerous "linked stories" with connecting episodes, settings, and characters becoming the novel *Stones for Ibarra:* "I went to writing class and I began writing pieces about Mexico. At first they were simply pieces; they were description or maybe little events. Then I gradually became brave enough to try to make stories with plots. Then, after about two years of my class at Stanford, someone noticed they were all set in the same place and the characters were repeated; why didn't I turn them into a novel? Of course, it had never occurred to me I'd be able to write a novel."

Doerr told Lisa See in a *Publishers Weekly* interview that the composition of her next novel, *Consider This, Senora,* followed a similar format to that of *Stones for Ibarra,* mentioning that three stories from *Consider This, Senora* were published in periodicals prior to completion of the novel. *Consider This, Senora* also takes place in Mexico and looks at four North Americans living in a small village. The book again follows their lives as they intermingle with the local residents, with sometimes positive and sometimes negative results. "Doerr tells of four expatriates driven to seek refuge in a place so unfamiliar that its 'otherness' will be the catalyst that restores them," according to a contributor to *Kirkus Reviews.*

The main characters of *Consider This, Senora* come together when Sue Ames, a divorced artist, and Bud Loomis, an Arizona tax evader, purchase a dilapidated estate on ten acres of land in the small village of Amapolas. To help finance their payments, they subdivide the land and sell plots to a divorced travel writer, Fran Bowles, and her Mexican born mother, Ursula, who has come back home to Mexico to die. Over a course of five to six years, the characters through their interactions with the village locals grow and discover a peace and happiness that has alluded them most of their lives. *Los Angeles Times Book Review*'s Charles Bowden summarizes the novel this way: "In an understated yet almost lyrical voice, Doerr is able to describe a very circumscribed yet full world, a place where people are genteel, have money they inherit rather than earn and, despite all of life's blessings, know they are incomplete. These wealthy Americans come to back-roads places in Mexico and let poor people, who can barely read, teach them how to acknowledge their own feelings. It is a view that is perhaps almost a cliche about Americans in Mexico, and I'm happy to report that in Doerr's hands it works."

Consider This, Senora fared well with critics. "The novel captures a time and place as surely as a jeweler sets a stone," praises *New York Times Book Review*'s Sandra Scofield. A *Publishers Weekly* contributor hails the novel as "exquisitely nuanced, elegant and wise." Bowden proclaims *Consider This, Senora* should be savored "like a drink in the evening before a fine fire." Commenting on Doerr's descriptive abilities, Scofield finds that "Mrs. Doerr renders her characters and setting with stunning precision." Donna Seaman, a *Booklist* reviewer, lauds Doerr for her skill in developing characters and notes Doerr's characters are infused with "great dignity and resilience." The reviewer concludes that Doerr "bestows upon her entranced readers a deep sense of peace and wonder."

Commenting on writing *Consider This, Senora* over the decade from ages seventy-three to eighty-three, Doerr told See: "At this age, you don't delay. You simply don't get more and more energy as time passes. That doesn't mean you're going out of your mind, but that finding the words you're looking for doesn't happen as quickly." At the same time, she states that she does not want reviewers to use her age as a consideration when critiquing this book, telling See, "I don't want critics to say, 'She's 83, what else do you expect?' You know, blaming any little flaws on the passage of time." See perceives a multicultural message in the author's work, concluding that Doerr's "wish is that a reader will learn through her books to regard unfamiliar places and people with an open mind."

For a previously published interview, see *Contemporary Authors*, Volume 122, pp. 135-38.

BIOGRAPHICAL/CRITICAL SOURCES:

BOOKS

Contemporary Literary Criticism, Volume 34, Gale, 1985.
Doerr, Harriet, *Stones for Ibarra*, Viking, 1984.
Pearlman, Mickey, and Katherine U. Henderson, *Interview: Talks with America's Writing Women*, University Press of Kentucky, 1990.
York, Pat, *Going Strong*, Arcade Publishing, 1991.

PERIODICALS

Booklist, June, 1993.
Christian Science Monitor, January 6, 1984, p. B6; September 1, 1993, p. 13.
Globe & Mail (Toronto), March 17, 1984.
Kirkus Reviews, June 15, 1993, p. 739.
Los Angeles Times, March 4, 1984.
Los Angeles Times Book Review, January 1, 1984, p. 4; August 22, 1993, pp. 1, 9.
Ms., January, 1984, pp. 12-13, 15.
New Republic, January 30, 1984, pp. 40-41.
New Yorker, January 16, 1984.

New York Times, December 7, 1983.
New York Times Book Review, January 8, 1984, p. 8; January 20, 1985; August 15, 1993, p. 12.
Publishers Weekly, June 21, 1993; August 9, 1993, p. 420; July 4, 1994.
Times Literary Supplement, May 24, 1985.
Tribune Books (Chicago), August 22, 1993, p. 5.
Washington Post Book World, December 25, 1983, p. 3; February 14, 1988, p. 12.

*   *   *

DONALDSON, Gordon   1913-1993

PERSONAL: Born April 13, 1913, in Edinburgh, Scotland; died March 16, 1993; son of Magnus and Rachel Hetherington (Swan) Donaldson. *Education:* University of Edinburgh, M.A., 1935; University of London, Ph.D., 1938. *Religion:* Episcopalian.

ADDRESSES: Home—6 Pan Ha', Dysart, Fife KY1 2TL, Scotland.

CAREER: H. M. General Register House, Edinburgh, Scotland, assistant keeper, 1938-47; University of Edinburgh, Edinburgh, Scotland, lecturer, 1947-55, reader, 1955-63, professor of Scottish history and paleography, 1963-79. H. M. Historiographer in Scotland, 1979-93. Member, Royal Commission on the Ancient and Historical Monuments of Scotland, 1964-82.

MEMBER: British Academy (fellow), Royal Society of Edinburgh (fellow), Scottish Ecclesiological Society (president, 1963-65), Scottish Record Society (president, 1981-93).

AWARDS, HONORS: D.Litt., University of Edinburgh, 1954, and University of Aberdeen, 1976; named Commander of the British Empire, 1988.

WRITINGS:

The Making of the Scottish Prayer Book of 1637, University of Edinburgh Press (Edinburgh), 1954.
Shetland Life under Earl Patrick, Oliver & Boyd (Edinburgh), 1958.
Scotland: Church and Nation through Sixteen Centuries, S.C.M. Press (London), 1960, 2nd edition, Scottish Academic Press (Edinburgh), 1972.
The Scottish Reformation, Cambridge University Press (Cambridge), 1960, 2nd edition, 1972.

(With R. L. Mackie) *A Short History of Scotland,* Oliver & Boyd, 1962.

Scotland: James V to James VII, Oliver & Boyd, 1965, Praeger (London), 1966.

Northwards by Sea, John Grant (Edinburgh), 1966, 2nd edition, Paul Harris (Edinburgh), 1978.

The Scots Overseas, R. Hale (London), 1966.

Scottish Kings, Wiley (Chichester, England), 1967, 2nd edition, 1977.

The First Trial of Mary, Queen of Scots, Batsford (London), 1969, Stein & Day, 1970.

Scottish Historical Documents, Scottish Academic Press, 1970.

(With Robert S. Morpeth) *Who's Who in Scottish History,* Barnes & Noble (New York City), 1973.

Scotland: The Shaping of a Nation, David & Charles (Newton Abbot, England), 1974, 2nd edition, 1980.

Dictionary of Scottish History, John Donald (Edinburgh), 1977.

All the Queen's Men: Power and Politics in Mary Stewart's Scotland, Batsford, 1982.

Isle of Home, Paul Harris, 1983.

Scottish Church History, Scottish Academic Press, 1985.

Sir William Fraser, Edina Press (Edinburgh), 1985.

The Faith of the Scots, Batsford, 1990.

(Editor) *Court Book of Shetland, 1615-1629,* Shetland Library (Lerwick, Scotland), 1991.

Editor of the *Scottish Historical Review* and of texts for the Scottish History Society, Scottish Record Society, and Stair Society.

BIOGRAPHICAL/CRITICAL SOURCES:

BOOKS

Cowan, Ian B., and Duncan Shaw, editors, *The Renaissance and Reformation in Scotland: Essays in Honour of Gordon Donaldson,* Scottish Academic Press, 1983.

PERIODICALS

Times Literary Supplement, October 28, 1983.

OBITUARIES:

PERIODICALS

Times (London), March 23, 1993, p. 21.*

*   *   *

DONOGHUE, P. S.
See HUNT, E(verette) Howard (Jr.)

DOSKOCILOVA, Hana   1936-

PERSONAL: Born July 11, 1936, in Jihlava, Czechoslovakia (now Czech Republic); daughter of Jan (a lawyer) and Maria (Juraskova) Doskocil; married Miroslav Sekyrka (a bookseller), September 21, 1961. *Education:* Attended public schools in Znojmo, Czechoslovakia.

ADDRESSES: Home—152 00 Praha 5, Hlubocepy, 4/964 Peskova, Czech Republic. *Office*—Albatros, Na Perstyne 1, Prague I, Czech Republic.

CAREER: Clerk in coal store in Jihlava, Czechoslovakia, 1954-56; Academy of Sciences, Prague, Czechoslovakia, clerk, 1956-59; Albatros (publishers for children and young people), Prague, press editor, 1959-61, proofreader, 1961-64, editor in children's department, 1964-72; freelance writer, 1972—.

WRITINGS:

PICTURE BOOKS

Pohadky pro deti, mamy a taty (title means "Fairy Tales for Children, Mothers, and Fathers"), Statni Nakladatelstvi Detske Knihy (Prague), 1961, reprinted, Albatros (Prague), 1987.

Psanicko pro tebe—O hrackach (title means "A Letter for You—About Toys"), Statni Nakladatelstvi Detske Knihy, 1964.

Bydlim doma (title means "I Live at Home"), Statni Nakladatelstvi Detske Knihy, 1966.

Kajetan the Magician (translated from the German), Artia (Prague), 1967.

Cervena lodicka (title means "The Little Red Ship"), Mlada fronta (Prague), 1968.

Modern Czech Fairy Tales (English translation from the Czech), Artia, 1969.

Animal Tales, translations from the Czech by Eve Merriam, adapted by William Howard Armstrong, Doubleday, 1970.

Micka z trafiky a kocour Pivoda (title means "Pussy Cat from the Tobacconist's and Tomcat Pivoda"), Albatros, 1971.

Zviratka z celeho sveta (title means "The Animals from the Whole World"), Albatros, 1971.

Kudy chodi maly lev (title means "Where the Little Lion Walks"), Albatros, 1972.

Medvedi pohadky (title means "The Bear Fairy Tales"), Albatros, 1973.

Ukradeny orloj (title means "Rob of Astronomical Clock"), Materidouska (Prague), 1973.

Basama bernardyn a Vendulka (title means "St. Bernard Dog Named Basama and a Girl Vendulka"), Orbis (Prague), 1973.

Zviratka z lesa (title means "The Animals from the Wood"), Albatros, 1974.

Drak Barborak a Ztraceny kral Kulajda (title means "Dragon Barborak and the Lost King Kulajda"), Albatros, 1974.

Posledniho kousne pes: A dalsich ctyriadvacet prislovi v pohadkach (title means "The Last Will Be Bitten by the Dog: Proverbial Fairy Tales"), Albatros, 1974.

Eliska a tata Kral (title means "Elizabeth and Her Father King"), Albatros, 1977.

Dva dedecci z Dlouhe mile (title means "Two Grandfathers from Long Mile"), Albatros, 1978.

Jelen se zlatymi parohy (title means "The Hart with Golden Antlers"), Artia, 1978.

Jak se vychovava papousek (title means "How the Parrot Is Educated"), Albatros, 1979.

Fanek a Vendulka (title means "Small Francis and a Girl Vendulka"), Albatros, 1980.

Pohadky na dobry den (title means "Tales for a Good Day"), Albatros, 1982.

Krtek v sedmem nebi (title means "The Mole in Seventh Heaven"), Albatros, 1982.

Chaloupka z perniku (title means "Little Cottage of Gingerbread"), Artia, 1982.

Chaloupka z marcipanu (title means "Little Cottage of Marzipan"), Artia, 1983.

Diogenes v sudu—a dalsich dvacet znamych pribehu z doby davne a nejdavnejsi (title means "Diogenes in the Barrel and Twenty Other Well-Known Stories"), Albatros, 1985, 2nd edition in German, Swedish and Polish, 1987.

Pet prani: obrazkova knizka (title means "Five Aspirations"), Albatros, 1987.

My a Mys (title means "We and the Mouse") Albatros, 1988.

Kuba a barvy (title means "James and the Colours"), Albatros, 1988.

Kuba a pocasi (title means "James and the Weather"), Albatros, 1988.

Kuba a rozbite koleno (title means "James and the Broken Knee"), Albatros, 1989.

Pejskovani s Polynou (title means "Dog's Games with Polly"), Albatros, 1989.

Jablicko, obrazkova knizka (title means "Little Apple"), Albatros, 1990.

Krtek a potopa (title means "The Mole and the Flood") Albatros, 1992.

Krtek a medvedi (title means "Little Mole and the Bears"), Albatros, 1993.

Jak krtek uzdravil mysku (title means "How Little Mole Cured Little Mouse"), Albatros, 1993.

Golem Josef a ti druzi (title means "Golem Josef and the Other"; a story of golems), Albatros, 1994.

OTHER

Also author of *Krtek a paraplicko* (title means "The Mole and Little Gamp"), Publishing House Schulfernsehen (Cologne, Germany). Author of juvenile television scripts, 1963-73, animated cartoons, 1969-71, and of a puppet play; author of film *Krtek a hodiny* (title means "The Mole and the Watch"); author for Cartoon Pictures. Author of "Povidky o obrazech" (title means "Stories about the Pictures"), a series of twenty-four stories published in *Magazin "Ohnicek,"* 1985-86. Member of editorial council, *Materidouska* (children's monthly), 1966-72. Also creator of the *New Textbooks for Elementary Schools* and the *New Textbooks for the Educationally Subnormal* book series, Publishing House Scientia.

SIDELIGHTS: Many of Hana Doskocilova's books have been translated into Russian, German, French, Dutch, Japanese, and English.

*   *   *

DOTY, Carolyn 1941-

PERSONAL: Born July 28, 1941, in Tooele, UT; daughter of Oran Earl (an engineer) and Dorothy (a teacher; maiden name, Anderson) House; married William Doty (an analyst), February 2, 1963 (divorced, 1981); married Gardner H. Mein (a writer and teacher), June 16, 1986 (divorced, 1992); children: (first marriage) Stuart William, Margaret. *Education:* University of Utah, B.F.A., 1963; University of California, Irvine, M.F.A., 1979.

ADDRESSES: Home—1630 Barker, Lawrence, KS 66044. *Agent*—Virginia Barber Literary Agency Inc., 101 5th Ave., New York, NY 10003.

CAREER: School Testing Service, Berkeley, CA, assistant director, 1965-70; San Francisco State University, San Francisco, CA, lecturer, 1980; University of California, Irvine, lecturer, 1984-86; University of Kansas, Lawrence, began as assistant professor, 1986, currently associate professor. Prose director of Squaw Valley Community of Writers; member of board of directors of Renegade Theatre of Lawrence.

AWARDS, HONORS: Honorable mention from Joseph Henry Jackson Competition of San Francisco Foundation, 1975, for novel in progress; award for excellence from Santa Barbara Writers Conference, 1978; six Summer General Research Awards from the University of Kansas; Hall Travel Grant; Lawrence Arts Commission City Enhancement and Cultural Exchange Award, 1992; Mabel Fry Teaching Award.

WRITINGS:

NOVELS

A Day Late, Viking (New York City), 1980.
Fly Away Home, Viking, 1982.
What She Told Him, Viking, 1985.
Whisper (Literary Guild and Doubleday Book Club Selection), Scribner's (New York City), 1992.

Contributor to *Bay Guardian, Berkeley Gazette, Los Angeles Times,* and *Paris Review.*

WORK IN PROGRESS: A novel entitled *Vanishing Point.*

SIDELIGHTS: Carolyn Doty's first novel, *A Day Late,* focuses on two grief-stricken individuals—Sam, who has recently lost his fifteen-year-old daughter to brain cancer, and Katy, a seventeen-year-old girl abandoned by her lover once he discovers she is pregnant. Sam picks up Katy while she is hitchhiking, and the two spend one day together during which time their common feeling of grief initiates a bond. Anatole Broyard of the *New York Times* believes Doty "is dealing with dangerous material" in *A Day Late.* "Sam's problem, and . . . Doty's problem in this first novel, is to keep his grief from turning into sentimentality, to keep his pity for his daughter pure, safe from self-pity. . . . Almost every novelist wants to play with death, but the subject is surrounded by emotions that all too quickly putrefy." Although Broyard expresses such reservations, *Sunday Denver Post* contributor Rosemarie Stewart believes that even if "the subject matter sounds grim, it doesn't come off that way," and Richard Bradford of the *New York Times Book Review* concurs: "Despite the sadness that surrounds Sam and Katy, *A Day Late* is in no way depressing. . . . This may be a first novel, but it is the work of a gifted novelist, a writer of intelligence and style who is not afraid to probe into characters too rich and complex for the easy, labeling adjective." Broyard commends Doty for the novel's closing action, emphasizing his belief that "there are no solutions, only gestures. *A Day Late* is an interesting gesture."

Like *A Day Late,* Doty's subsequent novels are psychological dramas. *Fly Away Home* details Sally Bryan's short-term attempt to free herself from her family burdens—a thirteen-year-old severely retarded son and an indifferent husband. She returns with her precocious eight-year-old daughter to the Sun Valley of her college days as a reprieve from reality. For Evelyn Wilde Mayerson in the *Washington Post Book World,* "Doty, in exploring moral and ethical dilemmas, fulfills the novelist's responsibility to do more than entertain the reader. . . . The strength of *[Fly Away Home]* is the delicacy and thoughtfulness with which the author deals with a startling concept: That the ultimate freedom for women includes the right to detach themselves from not only husband but child, including the

severely handicapped child whose care preempts all else." *Los Angeles Times* critic Elaine Kendall, in turn, finds that *Fly Away Home* "is not inspirational, outlining the miracles to be wrought by love and dedication, nor is it a story of triumph over adversity. Such books, heartwarming as they are, cannot afford the luxuries of humor, satire or anger. Those are the novelist's prerogatives, and Doty employs them judiciously in this sensitive and candid book. The subject is an emotional mine field, negotiated without hesitation or a single false step."

Doty's third novel, entitled *What She Told Him,* explores the disturbed psyche of a young man, Cal Newkirk, after he hears rumors that his brave, World War II-hero father may have been a brutal rapist. Because his mother dies before he can establish the facts, Cal sets out in search of his parentage but ends up in jail on fraudulent rape charges. "Muddling through a disastrous marriage, then stumbling into a sexual-assault charge of which he isn't even sure whether he's guilty, Cal is warped from within by fantasies and nightmares that seem to stem from the rapist, his father, whose taint he thinks he carries," surmises Amy E. Schwartz, a *New Republic* reviewer. According to Schwartz, "Doty is at her best when exploring the shadowy areas of Cal's psyche. She goes courageously past the initial questions of rape and violence to more complicated and ambiguous sequences." In the *Los Angeles Times Book Review,* Doris Grumbach expresses dissatisfaction with *What She Told Him* because she is convinced the reader cannot care for Cal nor for his "plodding and listless" search for his roots. "In [Doty's] two earlier novels . . . [she] proved herself capable of skillful, convincing fiction. How then do we account for this toneless meander into a lymphatic mode of storytelling, into a fiction lacking intensity, suspense or, worse, credibility? My suspicion is that it was a novel born of an idea rather than sprung from character or compelling event, a thesis proposed and then requiring proof." However, for Eleanor Foa Dienstag in the *New York Times Book Review,* Doty "convincingly evokes the bleak terrors of prison, the narrow decencies and patriotism of heartland America, as well as Cal's tormented psyche; and her varied cast of characters drop clues like crumbs that finally lead Cal toward salvation."

Doty told *CA:* "While my principal area of interest in my first three novels was fiction written in the small towns of the western United States, (undoubtedly because I grew up in one of them), I have since lived in cities, and now live in the midwest. While landscape is still important to me, my last novel, *Whisper,* was set in New York City, with scenes and chapters set in other large cities. My novel in progress is set in San Francisco. In other words, I wrote country books while living in the cities, and now that I live in a university town, my writing has moved back to the city as a landscape. Probably because of a more intense life in the teaching of writing and literature, I've turned some toward metafiction in *Whisper* and in the novel in progress.

"I still enjoy teaching creative writing both on the graduate and undergraduate levels. The midwest has some enormously gifted writers—perhaps because the weather is so dramatic they have to top that—and it's a pleasure to work with them. It's challenging, but enormously rewarding when they go on to the kind of success students like Connie Fowler and Scott Heim are experiencing now as novelists who studied here."

BIOGRAPHICAL/CRITICAL SOURCES:

PERIODICALS

Boston Sunday Globe, April 27, 1980.
Christian Science Monitor, July 30, 1980.
Kansas City Star, December 6, 1992.
Los Angeles Times, April 24, 1980; March 18, 1982; February 17, 1992.
Los Angeles Times Book Review, February 3, 1985.
New Republic, May 20, 1985.
New York Times, April 16, 1980.
New York Times Book Review, May 4, 1980; February 3, 1985.
Sunday Denver Post, June 8, 1980.
Times Literary Supplement, May 29, 1981.
Washington Post, March 11, 1982; February 13, 1992.
Washington Post Book World, June 15, 1980.

*   *   *

DRACHE, Sharon (Abron) 1943-

PERSONAL: Born March 22, 1943, in Toronto, Ontario, Canada; daughter of Murray (a hotel owner, furniture store manager, and stock broker) and Edythe (a homemaker and dietician; maiden name, Levinter) Abron; married Arthur Barry C. Drache (a lawyer), December, 1965 (divorced June, 1990); children: Deborah, Ruth, Joshua, Mordecai. *Education:* University of Toronto, B.A., 1965, diploma in child study, 1966; attended Carleton University, 1974-78. *Religion:* Jewish.

ADDRESSES: Home—29 Clemow Avenue, Ottawa, Ontario, Canada K1S 2B1. *Office*—c/o The Writers' Union of Canada, 24 Ryerson Avenue, Toronto, Ontario, Canada M5T 2P3.

CAREER: Ontario Crippled Children's Centre, Toronto, psychometrician, 1966-68; freelance writer, 1976—; editor, lecturer, and reader, 1982—. *Poetry Canada Review,* Ottawa readings editor, 1980-82; *Ottawa Jewish Bulletin and Review,* book review editor, 1981—; Port Hope Public Library, writer-in-residence, 1987. Member of the Ottawa

Public Library Board of Trustees, 1985-88; Jewish Community Centre of Ottawa, literary consultant, 1990.

MEMBER: Writers' Union of Canada (Canada Council committee member, 1984-85; national executive 1989-90), PEN.

AWARDS, HONORS: Grants from Ontario Arts Council for children's literature, 1980 (for short fiction), May, 1981, and May, 1983; multiculturalism grant from Secretary of State, Multiculturalism Directorate, April, 1981 (for short fiction), February, 1984 (for novel-in-progress); grants from Canada Council, August, 1982 (for short fiction), October, 1984 (for novel-in-progress).

WRITINGS:

The Mikveh Man and Other Stories, Aya Press (Toronto), 1984.
Ritual Slaughter (novel), Quarry Press (Kingston, Ontario), 1989.
The Golden Ghetto (two novellas and seven short stories), Beach Holme Books (Victoria, British Columbia), 1993.

Also contributor to anthologies, including *The Dancing Sun,* edited by Jan Andrews, Press Porcepic, 1981; *Canadian Jewish Stories,* edited by Miriam Waddington, Oxford University Press, 1990; *Great Canadian Mysteries,* edited by Don Bailey and Daile Unruh, Quarry Press, 1991; *Written in Stone: A Kingston Reader,* edited by Mary Alice Downie and M. A. Thompson, Quarry Press, 1993. Member of editorial board, *Viewpoints* magazine, 1981-82.

Contributor to periodicals, including *Canadian Encyclopedia, Canadian Jewish News, Edmonton Journal, Glebe Report, Globe and Mail* (Toronto), *Jerusalem Post* (Israel), *Kingston Whig Standard, Ottawa Citizen, Poetry Canada Review, Toronto Star,* and *Western Jewish Bulletin* (Vancouver).

WORK IN PROGRESS: An adult novel entitled *A Guest in My House,* a juvenile novel entitled *Weekend Commute,* and a short story collection with the working title *Barbara Klein Muskrat Stories.*

SIDELIGHTS: Sharon Drache's *The Mikveh Man and Other Stories* is a collection of eight short stories whose Jewish-Canadian characters deal with universal modern problems. In the Toronto *Globe and Mail* Miriam Waddington compared Drache's use of fantasy to Isaac Bashevis Singer; Waddington wrote that while rich in humor and originality, "[Drache's] stories are full of earthy, realistic details which lend credibility to her zany and frequent flights of fantasy." The critic added that although the author's use of "slangy expressions and cliches" proves disconcerting, "we forgive her for the sake of her dialogue, her directness, her energy and the presence of an underlying narrative power that is rich, funny, individual and, above all, authentic." Writing in the *Jerusalem Post,* Lea Abramowitz contended that Drache "has an accurate ear for the idiom of her community" and "employs a rare combination of fantasy, humor and compassion" in her writing. Arnold Ages, reviewing Drache's book in the *Western Jewish Bulletin,* asserted that the stories "mark her as an outstanding talent, puckish and surrealistic with overtones of Kafka."

BIOGRAPHICAL/CRITICAL SOURCES:

PERIODICALS

Globe and Mail (Toronto), August 18, 1984.
Jerusalem Post, June 8, 1985.
Western Jewish Bulletin, October 4, 1984.
Winnipeg Jewish Post, September 20, 1984; November 21, 1985.

*   *   *

DREW, Mary Anne
See CASSIDAY, Bruce (Bingham)

*   *   *

DRURY, George H(erbert) 1940-

PERSONAL: Born March 29, 1940, in Boston, MA; son of Harold F. (an economist) and Olga (a homemaker; maiden name, Cook) Drury. *Education:* Bates College, B.S., 1961; attended University of Delaware, 1961-63; University of Denver, M.A., 1965. *Religion:* Presbyterian.

ADDRESSES: Home—4139 West McKinley Court, Milwaukee, WI 53208. *Office*—Kalmbach Publishing Co., P.O. Box 1612, Waukesha, WI 53187.

CAREER: Oregon Technical Institute, Klamath Falls, admissions counselor, 1965-66; Southern Pacific Railroad, San Francisco, CA, programmer, 1966-67; Data II, Oakland, CA, programmer, 1967-68; Fireman's Fund Insurance Co., San Francisco, technical writer, 1968-72; Kalmbach Publishing Co., Waukesha, WI, copy editor, 1972-75, librarian, 1975-92, book editor, 1992—.

MEMBER: National Railway Historical Society, Railroad Enthusiasts, Boston and Maine Railroad Historical Society, New Haven Railroad Historical and Technical Association, Lexington Group in Transportation History.

WRITINGS:

(Compiler) *The Train-Watcher's Guide to North American Railroads,* Kalmbach (Milwaukee), 1984, 2nd edition, 1992.

The Historical Guide to North American Railroads, Kalmbach, 1985.
(Compiler) *Guide to Tourist Railroads and Railroad Museums,* edited by Bob Hayden, Kalmbach, 1987, 3rd edition, 1990.
The Railfan Guide to Switzerland, [privately printed], 1987.
The Railfan Guide to Austria, [privately printed], 1990.
(Compiler) *Guide to North American Steam Locomotives,* Kalmbach, 1993.

EDITOR

Louis Marre and Jerry A. Pinkepank, *The Contemporary Diesel Spotter's Guide,* Kalmbach, 1989.
Peter Thorne, *Model Railroad Electronics: Basic Concepts to Advanced Projects,* Kalmbach, 1994.
William Middleton, *Manhattan Gateway,* Kalmbach, 1995.

OTHER

Contributor to *Trains* and *Model Railroader.*

WORK IN PROGRESS: A guide to German railways for the American rail enthusiast.

SIDELIGHTS: George H. Drury told *CA:* "I've been interested in railroads ever since I can remember. I got into writing about them in 1972, when I suddenly asked myself an obvious question: Why am I writing computer manuals for an insurance company when I could be writing for the magazines I've been reading for twenty years? I sent off a resume, and it happened to be the right time to do so.

"*The Train-Watcher's Guide* was born when Kalmbach's book editor said that what the world (or at least our portion of it) needed was a basic guide to contemporary railroads and did I think I could do one when I wasn't doing library duties, and I said I thought I could. The book got considerable impetus when others around here said that such a project was impossible, because if it weren't, someone would have done it long ago. The book editor and I accepted that challenge and we've been going full throttle since, creating our Railroad Reference Series.

"The railfan guides to Switzerland, Austria, and Germany are a way to share the information I've gathered in my travels with other rail enthusiasts and possibly make a little profit doing so."

*   *   *

DuBAY, Sandra 1954-
(Caroline Chase)

PERSONAL: Born October 6, 1954, in Battle Creek, MI; daughter of Harry Andrew (a municipal employee) and

Reatha Lenore (Bingham) DuBay. *Education:* Washtenaw Community College, A.A., 1974; University of Michigan, B.A., 1976. *Politics:* Independent. *Religion:* Catholic. *Avocational interests:* Reading, browsing in bookstores, stained glass.

ADDRESSES: Home—801 Bradfield, Bay City, MI 48706; and Beaver Island, MI 49782.

CAREER: The Other Room (crisis intervention center), Bay City, MI, counselor, 1977-78; freelance writer, 1978—.

WRITINGS:

HISTORICAL ROMANCE NOVELS

Mistress of the Sun King, Tower, 1980, published as *Crimson Conquest,* Leisure Books (Norwalk, CT), 1984.
Flame of Fidelity, Tower, 1981, Leisure Books, 1986.
The Claverleigh Curse, Zebra Books (New York City), 1982.
Fidelity's Flight, Leisure Books, 1982.
Whispers of Passion, Leisure Books, 1984.
In Passion's Shadow, Leisure Books, 1984.
Where Passion Dwells, Leisure Books, 1985.
By Love Beguiled, Leisure Books, 1986.
Burn On Sweet Fire, Leisure Books, 1987.
Scarlet Surrender, Leisure Books, 1987.
Wilder Shores of Love, Leisure Books, 1988.
Tempest, Leisure Books, 1989.
(Under pseudonym Caroline Chase) *Scoundrel's Caress,* Dell (New York City), 1989.
Quicksilver, Leisure Books, 1990.
Nightrider, Leisure Books, 1991.
By Love Betrayed, Leisure Books, 1993.

WORK IN PROGRESS: Two historical novels.

SIDELIGHTS: Sandra DuBay told *CA:* "At an early age I discovered that it was much easier for me to communicate through writing than verbally. At about the same time I was given a copy of *Forever Amber,* and it started my interest in history and historical fiction.

"I think that the most important part of any novel is an interesting cast of characters, since, regardless of how intriguing the plot may be, if the characters are dull or annoying no reader is going to care to follow them through the book. For me the characters often determine whether or not I finish a novel. I have put aside several novels after only a half-dozen chapters simply because I did not find the characters interesting. Conversely, I have occasionally come to a dead stop on a book for weeks because I was at a point where I would have to kill off a character I particularly liked.

"In writing historical novels, research is always a fascinating part of the writing. I love finding old memoirs and bi-ographies from the early to mid-nineteenth century. Today's historians seem intent on presenting only the facts, whereas their counterparts of the past had no qualms about including gossip and rumors that can be of great use to the historical romance novelist.

"As for the actual mechanics of writing, I believe in outlines. In addition to a general outline of the entire book that I made before starting the novel, I outline every chapter. These outlines tend to be very detailed, often running ten to fifteen pages for a fifteen- to twenty-page chapter. As a result, by the time I sit down to actually write the chapter it comes out in something very nearly its final form. Aside from minor corrections, my finished manuscripts are almost copies of the first drafts."

BIOGRAPHICAL/CRITICAL SOURCES:

PERIODICALS

Bay City Times, May 18, 1980; November 19, 1981; September 7, 1986.
Detroit Free Press, June 6, 1982.
Romantic Times, March/April, 1986; February/March, 1987.

*   *   *

DUGDALE, Robert
See HARDY, Henry

*   *   *

DUNMORE, John   1923-
(Jason Calder)

PERSONAL: Born August 6, 1923, in Trouville, France; son of William Ernest (a businessperson) and Marguerite (Martin) Dunmore; married Joyce Langley (a city councillor); children: Paul Vincent, Patricia Margaret. *Education:* University of London, B.A., 1950; University of New Zealand, Ph.D., 1961. *Politics:* Labour Party. *Religion:* Roman Catholic.

ADDRESSES: Home—35 Oriwa St., Waikanae, New Zealand. *Office*—Massey University, Palmerston North, New Zealand.

CAREER: Worked as school teacher, 1951-57; Massey University, Palmerston North, New Zealand, senior lecturer, 1961-66, professor of French, 1966-84. Managing editor, Heritage Press.

MEMBER: PEN, New Zealand Playwrights' Association (executive member), Australasian Language and Literature Association (president, 1980-82).

AWARDS, HONORS: Sir James Wattie Book of the Year Award, 1969, for *The Fateful Voyage of the St. Jean-*

Baptiste; named chevalier of French Legion of Honour, 1977; named officier, Academic Palms, 1986; New Zealand Medal, 1990; Massey Medal, 1993.

WRITINGS:

French Explorers in the Pacific, Oxford University Press, Volume 1, 1965, Volume 2, 1969.
Le Mystere d'Omboula (title means "The Mystery of Omboula"), Longmans, Paul, 1966.
Aventures dans le Pacifique (title means "Adventures in the Pacific"), Reeds, 1967.
Success at University, Whitcoulls (London), 1968.
Success at School, Whitcoulls, 1969, reprinted as *Step by Step Exam Success,* Cavanaun Books, 1979.
The Fateful Voyage of the St. Jean-Baptiste, Pegasus Press, 1969.
Meurtre a Tahiti (title means "Murder in Tahiti"), Longmans, Paul, 1971.
Norman Kirk: A Portrait, New Zealand Books, 1972.
The Expedition of the St. Jean-Baptiste: From Journals of Jean de Surville and Guillaume Labe, Hakluyt Society (Cambridge), 1981.
How to Succeed as an Extra-Mural Student, Dunmore Press, 1983.
Pacific Explorer: The Life of J. F. de la Perouse, Naval Institute Press, 1985.
Who's Who in Pacific Navigation, Hawaii University Press and Melbourne University Press, 1992.
A Playwright's Workbook, Heritage Press (Baltimore, MD), 1993.
The Journal of La Perouse, two volumes, Hakluyt Society (London), 1995.

EDITOR

R. R. Milligan, *The Map Drawn by the Chief Tukitahua,* Reeds, 1966.
Norman Kirk, *Towards Nationhood,* New Zealand Books, 1969.
An Anthology of French Scientific Prose, Hutchinson (London), 1973.

Le Journal de Laperouse, two volumes, Imprimerie Nationale (Paris), 1985.
The Book of Friends (published for the Child Cancer Foundation), Heritage Press, 1989.
New Zealand and the French: Two Centuries of Contact, Heritage Press, 1990.
The French and the Maori, Heritage Press, 1992.

TRANSLATOR

Gabriel Linge, *In Search of the Maori,* New Zealand Books, 1974.
Georges Pisier, *Kunie; or, The Isle of Pines,* Noumea, 1978.
R. Herve, *Chance Discovery of Australia and New Zealand,* Dunmore Press, 1983.

UNDER PSEUDONYM JASON CALDER

The Man Who Shot Rob Muldoon, Dunmore Press, 1976.
A Wreath for the Springboks, Dunmore Press, 1978.
The O'Rourke Affair, Dunmore Press, 1979.
Target Margaret Thatcher, Robert Hale (London), 1981.

OTHER

Also author of *New Zealand: The North Island* and *New Zealand: The South Island,* both 1987.

WORK IN PROGRESS: The Fabulous Pacific (provisional title), a new history of the Pacific merging Polynesian/Melanesian mythology and history with European exploration and colonization.

SIDELIGHTS: John Dunmore once told *CA:* "I have always moved freely from scholarly work to the theatre or the adventure thriller. My special field is the Pacific in the eighteenth century, in particular the work of explorers and especially the French. As an academic, I have published what academics are expected to publish; but like many academics, I have found relaxation and useful outlets in drama, thrillers, and politics (but then these three may well be synonymous)."

E

EDWARDES, Pauline
See BOWSKILL, Derek

*   *   *

EGERTON, John (Walden) 1935-

PERSONAL: Surname is pronounced "edge-er-ton"; born June 14, 1935, in Atlanta, GA; son of William Graham (in sales) and Rebecca (White) Egerton; married Ann Bleidt, June 6, 1957; children: Brooks B., March W. *Education:* Attended Western Kentucky State College, 1953-54; University of Kentucky, A.B., 1958, M.A., 1960. *Politics:* Independent. *Religion:* Unaffiliated.

ADDRESSES: Home and office—4014 Copeland Dr., Nashville, TN 37215.

CAREER: University of Kentucky, Lexington, member of public relations staff, 1958-60; University of South Florida, Tampa, member of public relations staff, 1960-65; Southern Education Report, Nashville, TN, staff writer, 1965-69; *Race Relations Reporter,* Nashville, staff writer, 1969-71; freelance writer, 1971—. Writer for Atlanta's Southern Regional Council, 1973-75. Journalist in residence at Virginia Polytechnic Institute and State University, 1977-78. Member of board of directors of Nashville's Family and Children's Services, 1975-77. *Military service:* U.S. Army, 1954-56.

AWARDS, HONORS: Weatherford Award, 1983, for *Generations: An American Family;* Lillian Smith Award, 1984, for *Generations: An American Family;* Tastemaker Award, International Association of Culinary Professionals, 1988, for *Southern Food: At Home, on the Road, in History.*

WRITINGS:

A Mind to Stay Here, Macmillan (New York City), 1970.

The Americanization of Dixie, Harper's Magazine Press, 1974.

Visions of Utopia, University of Tennessee Press (Knoxville), 1977.

Nashville: The Faces of Two Centuries, PlusMedia, 1979.

Generations: An American Family, University Press of Kentucky (Lexington), 1983.

(Author and editor) *Nissan in Tennessee,* Nissan Motor Manufacturing Corporation U.S.A. (Smyrna, TN), 1983.

(With Bill Weems) *South,* Graphic Arts Center (Portland, OR), 1987.

(With wife, Ann Bleidt Egerton) *Southern Food: At Home, on the Road, in History,* Knopf (New York, NY), 1987.

Side Orders: Small Helpings of Southern Cookery & Culture, Peachtree (Atlanta), 1990.

Shades of Gray: Dispatches from the Modern South, Louisiana State University Press (Baton Rouge), 1991.

Speak Now against the Day: The Generation before the Civil Rights Movement in the South, Knopf, 1994.

Contributor to *Tennessee, a Homecoming,* edited by John Netherton, Third National Corporation, 1985. Contributor of more than two hundred articles to magazines. Contributing editor of *Saturday Review of Education,* 1972-73, *Race Relations Reporter,* 1973-74, and *Southern Voices,* 1974-75.

SIDELIGHTS: John Egerton once told *CA:* "I have been writing since I was twelve. I never really had a choice, though I was thirty years old before I understood and accepted that. It has not been easy to make a living doing what I want to do and I couldn't in good conscience recommend it as a livelihood to beginners. It may be that survival for writers is becoming less and less possible with each passing year, and writers at the end of the twentieth century may be like blacksmiths at the beginning, or calligraphers in the age of Gutenberg. Nevertheless, people will keep on doing it because they suffer from an affliction diagnosed by Jean Stafford as *cacoethes scribendi*—the itch to write."

*   *   *

EGGERT, James (Edward) 1943-
(Jim Eggert)

PERSONAL: Born February 3, 1943, in Chicago, IL; son of Robert J. (an economist and forecaster) and Elizabeth (Bauer) Eggert; married Patricia Stock (a journalist), May 8, 1971; children: Anthony, Leslie. *Education:* Lawrence University, B.A., 1967; Michigan State University, M.A., 1968. *Religion:* Society of Friends (Quakers). *Avocational interests:* High jumping, music, natural history, astronomy.

ADDRESSES: Home—Route 3, Box 264, Colfax, WI 54730. *Office*—Department of Social Sciences, University of Wisconsin—Stout, Menomonie, WI 54751.

CAREER: U.S. Peace Corps, Washington, DC, volunteer worker in Kenya, 1964-66; University of Wisconsin—Stout, Menomonie, instructor, 1968-72, assistant professor, 1971-79, associate professor of social sciences, 1980—.

MEMBER: Thoreau Society, Nature Conservancy, Astronomical Society of the Pacific, Wisconsin Association of Environmental Educators.

WRITINGS:

UNDER NAME JIM EGGERT, EXCEPT AS NOTED

(With wife, Pat Eggert) *The No-Mortgage Home,* Bergamot Press, 1973.
What Is Economics?, William Kaufmann (Los Altos, CA), 1977, third edition, published under name James Eggert, Mayfield, 1993.
Investigating Microeconomics, William Kaufmann, 1979.
Low-Cost Earth Shelters, Stackpole (Harrisburg, PA), 1982.
Invitation to Economics, William Kaufmann, 1984, 2nd edition, Mayfield, 1991.
Milton Friedman, Thoreau, and Grandfather Pine, Winston-Derek (Nashville, TN), 1986.
(Under name James Eggert) *Meadowlark Economics,* M. E. Sharpe (Armonk, NY), 1992.

Contributor to periodicals.

WORK IN PROGRESS: A Cosmic Journey: Meditations on Meaning and Evolution.

SIDELIGHTS: In *What Is Economics?* Jim Eggert explores fundamental economic questions using diagrams, photographs, cartoons, and examples from everyday life. In addition, he presents environmental, political, and social issues that directly relate to basic economic principles. The primer has been adopted for class use in more than one hundred fifty colleges and universities across the United States. More recently, in *Milton Friedman, Thoreau, and Grandfather Pine,* Eggert makes his first attempt, through essays and poetry, to bridge standard economic notions with the values of ecology.

*   *   *

EGGERT, Jim
See EGGERT, James (Edward)

*   *   *

ELMAN, Richard 1934-
(Delmar Hawks, Michael Lasker, Fred McShane, Michael Parnell, Eric Pearl, John Howland Spyker)

PERSONAL: Born April 23, 1934, in Brooklyn, NY; son of Edward (an attorney) and Pearl (Beckerman) Elman; married Emily Schorr (an artist), June, 1956 (divorced, 1970); married Alice Goode (a writer), April 9, 1978; children: (first marriage) Margaret; (second marriage) Lila. *Education:* Syracuse University, B.A., 1955; Stanford University, M.A., 1957. *Politics:* Socialist.

ADDRESSES: Home—Tegucigalpa, Honduras.

CAREER: Writer. Pacifica Foundation, WBAI-FM, New York City, public affairs director, 1961-64; Columbia University, School of Social Work Research Center, New York City, research associate, 1965; Hunter College, New York City, lecturer in English, 1966; Bennington College, Bennington, VT, visiting writer, 1966-67; Columbia University, New York City, adjunct professor of writing, 1968-76; Bennington College Summer Writing Workshops, Bennington, director, 1976—; Department of Creative Writing, University of Pennsylvania, Philadelphia, PA, visiting lecturer, 1981-82; State University of New York at Stony Brook, visiting professor, 1983; University of Arizona, Tucson, visiting professor, 1985; University of Michigan, Ann Arbor, Hopwood visiting professor, 1988; Notre Dame University, Abrams Professor, 1990. *Military service:* Served in U.S. Army, circa late 1950s.

MEMBER: PEN, Authors Guild, National Yiddish Book Centre.

AWARDS, HONORS: National Endowment for the Arts fiction award, 1971; National Endowment for the Arts

Fellowship, 1974; Creative Artists Public Service Program (NY) Arts Fellowship, 1976; three time winner of PEN syndicated short story writers award.

WRITINGS:

NOVELS

A Coat for the Tsar, University of Texas Press (Austin), 1959.

The Twenty-eighth Day of Elul, Scribner (New York City), 1967.

Lilo's Diary, Scribner, 1968.

The Reckoning, Scribner, 1969.

An Education in Blood, Scribner, 1970.

Freddi and Shirl and the Kids, Scribner, 1972.

Taxi Driver (based on the original screenplay by Paul Schrader), Bantam (New York City), 1976.

(Under pseudonym John Howland Spyker) *Little Lives,* Grosset & Dunlap (New York City), 1978.

The Breadfruit Lotteries, Methuen (New York City), 1980.

(Under pseudonym Delmar Hawks) *Smokey and the Bandit,* Bantam, 1981.

(Under pseudonym Michael Lasker with Richard A. Simmons) *Gangster Chronicles: TV Tie In,* Jove (New York City), 1981.

The Menu Cypher, Macmillan (New York City), 1982.

Disco Frito, Peregrine Smith Books, 1988.

Tar Beach, Sun and Moon Press, 1992.

Also author, under pseudonym of Fred McShane, of the novel *The Foreskin Men,* Corgi, and under pseudonym Michael Parnell, *Shannon.*

POETRY

The Man Who Ate New York, New Rivers Press (New York City), 1976.

Homage to Fats Navarro, illustrations by Neil Greenberg, New Rivers Press, 1978.

In Chontales, Street Press (Port Jefferson, NY), 1981.

Cathedral-Tree-Train and Other Poems, Junction Press, 1992.

OTHER

The Poorhouse State: The American Way of Life on Public Assistance (reportage), Pantheon (New York City), 1966.

Ill-at-Ease in Compton (reportage), Pantheon, 1967.

(Editor with Albert Fried) *Charles Booth's London: A Portrait of the Poor at the Turn of the Century,* Pantheon, 1968.

Crossing Over and Other Tales (short stories), Scribner, 1973.

Uptight with the Rolling Stones (reportage), Scribner, 1973.

Cocktails at Somoza's: A Reporter's Sketchbook of Events in Revolutionary Nicaragua (reportage), Applewood Press (Cambridge, MA), 1981.

(Under pseudonym Michael Parnell) *Eric Linklater: A Critical Biography* (biography), John Murray (London), 1985.

(Under pseudonym Michael Parnell) *Laughter from the Dark: A Life of Gwyn Thomas* (biography), John Murray, 1988.

Occasional writer for radio and television, novelizer and adapter. Contributor of articles, stories, reviews, and poetry—sometimes under the pseudonym Eric Pearl—to magazines, including *Nation, New Republic, Commonweal, Paris Review, Evergreen Review, New York Times Book Review, Book Week, GEO* (New York and Germany), *Uno Mas Uno* (Mexico City), and *Prensa* (Nicaragua). Contributor to *All Things Considered,* National Public Radio, 1978—.

SIDELIGHTS: Poet, novelist, and critic Richard Elman once told *CA,* "[I] travel and read as much as I can, but that is really quite little. Mostly I depend upon being provoked by events—whether real or imagined—which forces me to attempt to muster the curiosity to put myself in somebody else's shoes. All my life I have admired writers who have evinced a rage against personal injustice. Not that I believe writers must all exhibit the same dreary consciences. . . . In my case, I would not know how to write of a [nonfictional] subject if I were not deeply moved by it—through rage, or compassion, or, perhaps, amazement and a sense of wonder."

The impetus to create poems came early, Elman related in *Contemporary Authors Autobiography Series (CAAS).* An indifferent student at best, Elman developed a serious interest in poetry during his senior year in high school, thanks to an attentive teacher. Though the poems he wrote "did not scan or rhyme and were regularly rejected by the academic squareheads of the student literary magazine," he discovered precedent for his style, he said, in the work of such poets as Walt Whitman, William Carlos Williams, Ezra Pound, Marianne Moore, and Hart Crane. Going on to Syracuse University, Elman continued to write, this time under the tutelage of professional writers who were teaching there. Later, in the creative writing graduate program at Stanford University, he met Yvor Winters, whose influence, Elman quipped, "was like taking chemotherapy for a bad cough" and whose "denunciations of [his] Brooklyn ear" drove Elman away from poetry and in the direction of journalism.

Following a stint in the army after graduate school, Elman supported himself by working as a freelance publicist and journalist in New York City and teaching for two years at Bennington College. During this time he had his first novel published (he has said that he pays graduate students to burn copies of it), and while he continued to build a solid reputation through his radio documentaries and interviews and through magazine articles and book reviews, he wrote some of the early books that he still considers important, including *The Poorhouse State: The American Way of Life on Public Assistance, The Twenty-eighth Day of Elul,* and *Lilo's Diary.*

For the *Poorhouse State,* Elman spent two years interviewing people on relief in New York's Lower East Side. In his review of *The Poorhouse State, Commonweal*'s James J. Graham said, "With much compassion, objectivity and insight, Elman has managed to write an exciting treatise on a very unpopular subject. His book should destroy both liberal and conservative myths about the welfare poor and those who service and oppress them. The only villain in this book is the Poorhouse State itself, which Elman describes as a 'system of inadequate payments, grudging services, petty rules tyrannies, and surveillance mechanism that, though always regarded as a temporary arrangement, has preserved all in their deprivations.' " Elman further pursued his interest in the welfare poor in a second book of reportage published the following year, *Ill-at-Ease in Compton,* a profile of a racially troubled California city near Watts with a large lower-middle-class population. For this account he won the plaudits of Edgar Z. Friedenberg, who wrote in the *New York Review of Books,* "Mr. Elman is not only an exceptionally perceptive observer, he is a competent and experienced interpreter of the dynamics of discrimination in America."

The Twenty-eighth Day of Elul was the first book of a trilogy, with *Lilo's Diary* and *The Reckoning,* about the Yagodahs, a Hungarian Jewish family, at the end of World War II. In each of the books, the same story is told from a different point of view. In this first of the three, the family promises to betray a cousin living under its protection in exchange for a possible chance to escape from Hungary but turns out otherwise. A *Times Literary Supplement* reviewer called the portrayal of the Yagodahs "remarkable, sometimes overwrought but never overplayed: an exercise in moral restraint which 'tells us more' than many head-on confrontations with the abyss, without being any dishonestly easier to bear."

Lilo's Diary is the same story related by the young woman the Yagodah family was willing to abandon in *The Twenty-eighth Day of Elul.* She is engaged to her Yagodah cousin, and she is dismal and vindictive, finding pleasure in her own unhappiness. Understanding at last that her Uncle Yagodah and her enemies are not so dissimilar, she makes her own compromise. Like the others, however, she becomes a loser in the process. Reviewing the book for *Commonweal,* Christopher Koch observed that *Lilo's Diary* "makes clear that [Elman] is not only a fine writer

but one whose ideas must be reckoned with. . . . Elman's ability to encapsulate the experience of World War II in a brief novel about one selfish girl, makes *Lilo's Diary* an important 20th Century work of fiction."

The point of view in *The Reckoning* is that of Newman Yagodah, the father of the family, as he struggles with the internal and external forces that drive his life. He is, in the words of Victor Burg in the *Christian Science Monitor,* "a moralist unable to act morally," and thus he "confronts an absence." Burg found *The Reckoning* "striking as whole; and within its historical context," he said, "far exceeds the potential banality of its immediate circumstances." In the *New York Times Book Review,* however, Thomas Lask saw it as Elman's "picking over the remains" of characters the reader had already come to know well enough in the two preceding books.

A 1972 novel, *Freddi and Shirl and the Kids,* was Elman's reckoning with his parents for the damage he felt they had done him. Discussing the book in *CAAS,* he recalled that the book was a result of what he described as his dreaming himself awake after his first marriage, and he called its style "terse and colloquial, as unliterary as I could make it"—a departure from his earlier writing. The book precipitated a break with his parents and his brother Leonard and left him feeling "utterly naked and also empty," but in some way it enabled him to return to writing poetry. A collection of poems called *The Man Who Ate New York* was published in 1976, and another, *Homage to Fats Navarro,* in 1978.

During the late 1970s, Elman went to Nicaragua to report on the Sandinista revolution. Deeply moved by the pervasive impact the Nicaraguan Revolution had on Central America, he wrote *CA:* "I felt touched by the grace and dignity of those who fought, and sacrificed, and died. I hope (and despair) that Nicaragua remains an open society, without any blinding U.S. interventions, and to the benefit of all Nicaraguans. Nicaragua brought me strongly back to poetry." Two of Elman's favorite books were borne from his experience in Nicaragua—*In Chontales,* a collection of poetry, and *Cocktails at Somoza's: A Reporter's Sketchbook of Events in Revolutionary Nicaragua.*

Cocktails at Somoza's contains vignettes, poems, and other pieces that constitute a report on the varied reactions of Nicaraguan citizens to the social effects of the revolution in which General Somoza was ousted and the Sandinistas took over the country's government. Though Elman "is not a Nicaraguan expert," Richard E. Feinberg noted in the *Washington Post Book World,* he "does have a talent for capturing moods and encapsulating the human predicament." John Leonard, writing in the *New York Times,* commented on Elman's refusal to empathize: "He is acquainted with doubt; he is a poet of confusion," Leonard added: "Edgy and eloquent, [Elman] roots for this revolution even as he combs his qualms."

In a lighter vein, Elman wrote two novels featuring the unlikely spy Robert Harmon, a middle-aged teacher of the history of ideas at Columbia University. The first of these books, *The Breadfruit Lotteries,* is filled with references to other literary spies such as Lord Byron and Malcolm Muggeridge. Stanley Ellin wished in the *New York Times Book Review* that this caper had been longer, and Leonard observed in a later *New York Times* review that "it is as if Lenny Bruce had written a James Bond. After such reading, who can look at another spy novel with a straight face?" *The Menu Cypher,* a sequel to *The Breadfruit Lotteries,* was seen by some reviewers as an unsuccessful mating of comedy and something graver. A *Los Angeles Times* reviewer concluded that "what Elman had on his mind is quite evidently not frivolity or parody but rage, or at minimum an angry satire of the real-life spy tricks . . . that have escaped into public notice." In the *Washington Post Book World,* Christopher Schemering pointed out, "Had the comic tone been sustained with Harmon turning the agency's supposed foolishness on its ear, this could have been a crackerjack satire. But Harmon settles his mid-life crisis by simply retiring. What begins as a prodigiously funny flight-of-fancy dive bombs and crashes right on the coast of Missed Opportunity."

Of the books that Elman has ghostwritten or written under pen names, perhaps the best known is *Little Lives,* published under the pseudonym John Howland Spyker. This series of vignettes depicting the eccentric and unfortunate residents of a small town in New York state during the 1800s was deemed "brilliant" by *Time* and compared by Leonard in another *New York Times* to Edgar Lee Masters's *Spoon River Anthology* and Sherwood Anderson's *Winesburg, Ohio.* Leonard declared further that "Mr. Spyker by turns is witty, irascible, lugubrious, vain and unseemly. When he reaches for a metaphor, it is almost always to be found in nature rather than a book, although we learn eventually that he considers himself a literary man."

Michael Parnell was Elman's pseudonym for a biography of the life of English writer Erik Linklater, who lived primarily in Scotland. It was described by Gerald Mangan in the *Times Literary Supplement* as "well organized, if a little pedestrian." Mangan called Elman's "enthusiasm for his subject . . . virtually unbounded, and his biography . . . critical only in the most nominal sense. . . . The effect is occasionally more amusing than the novels themselves, but it looks too much like adulation to be persuasive." In the *Spectator,* Jo Grimond was more positive, declaring that "Mr. Parnell performs the remarkable feat of leading us through Eric's huge literary output, never wea-

rying, always illuminating, and weaving together his life and his books."

In *Tar Beach,* a novel published in 1992, Elman returned to the subject of the family. The book relates the story of eight-year-old Peter Pintobasco, growing up Jewish in post-World War II Brooklyn. Supposedly the son of Brooklyn real estate attorney Sam Pintobasco and his wife, Lillian, Peter receives most of the parental warmth and affection from a longtime family friend—Izzy Berliner or Uncle Izzy to Peter. Izzy Berliner is also Peter's real father. Even though Izzy can never publicly recognize Peter as his son, Izzy—an idealistic dreamer whose life is a wreck—places all his hopes in his relationship with Peter. In the end, tragedy abounds when Sam learns who Peter's real father is.

Tar Beach received mixed reactions. According to *Los Angeles Times Book Review*'s Gerald Nicosia, "The only real flaw in *Tar Beach*—and it is unfortunately a sizable one—is that Elman has taken a heart-wrenchingly human story and attempted to tell it from an excessively clever, shifting point of view which more often obscures than clarifies the text. . . . If Elman could only get past what have become some of the tedious postmodern cliches of contemporary fiction, he might find himself one of our most powerful storytellers." In contrast *New York Times Book Review*'s John Domini described *Tar Beach* as "a meaty concoction about fatherhood, motherhood, and learning to live sanely with both." He continued: "Rarely has a slice of life been cut so thin, so elegantly."

Elman told *CA:* "I now believe I am more of a poet than a prose writer, though I still make a living writing novels and journalism. I love to write poems. I love language, and movement, and action, and despise carefulness that lacks caring. I wish somebody would ask me to teach the stuff sometime."

BIOGRAPHICAL/CRITICAL SOURCES:

BOOKS

Contemporary Authors Autobiography Series, Volume 3, Gale, 1986.

PERIODICALS

American Book Review, January, 1991, p. 17.
Booklist, November 1, 1992, p. 48.
Christian Science Monitor, October 9, 1969; August 10, 1981, p. B7.
Commentary, August, 1967.
Commonweal, January 6, 1967; January 17, 1969.
Library Journal, January, 1993, p. 121.
Life, June 25, 1971.
Los Angeles Times, July 25, 1982. p. 2.
Los Angeles Times Book Review, March 8, 1992, p. 5.

Multicultural Review, July, 1992, p. 50.

Nation, April 26, 1980, p. 504.

New York Review of Books, May 23, 1968.

New York Times, September 30, 1969; February 1, 1979; March 7, 1980; June 2, 1981.

New York Times Book Review, September 14, 1969; March 2, 1980, p. 8; January 30, 1983, p. 31; December 15, 1991, p. 18.

Observer Review, February 16, 1969.

Saturday Review, April 15, 1967.

Spectator, October 20, 1984, p. 28.

Time, March 12, 1979, p. 94.

Times Literary Supplement, September 21, 1967, p. 6; April 25, 1980, p. 469; April 26, 1985, p. 459.

Village Voice, March 2, 1967; February 12, 1979, p. 90.

Washington Post Book World, September 27, 1981; August 29, 1982, p. 6.*

*   *   *

ESTORIL, Jean
See ALLAN, Mabel Esther

F

FARADAY, Robert
See CASSIDAY, Bruce (Bingham)

*   *   *

FARWELL, Byron E.   1921-

PERSONAL: Born June 20, 1921, in Manchester, IA; son of E. L. and Nellie (Sheldon) Farwell; married Ruth Saxby, December 15, 1941; children: Joyce, Byron, Lesley. *Education:* Attended Ohio State University, 1939-41; attended University of Chicago, 1946-49, M.A., 1968.

ADDRESSES: Home—P.O. Box 81, Hillsboro, VA 22132. *Agent*—Russell & Volkening, Inc., 50 West 29th St., New York, NY 10001.

CAREER: Writer. Chrysler International, Geneva, Switzerland, director of public relations, 1959-65, director of administration, 1965-71; mayor of Hillsboro, VA, 1977-81. Has lectured and taught classes at many colleges and universities including University College of the University of Chicago, University of Detroit, and Army War College. Worked in both television and radio. Chairman of board of governors, College du Leman, Geneva, Switzerland, 1967-68; member of editorial board, Small Town Institute. *Military service:* U.S. Army, 1940-45, 1950-51; became captain.

MEMBER: Royal Society of Literature (fellow), Royal Geographic Society (fellow).

AWARDS, HONORS: MacDowell fellow, 1981; Distinguished Visiting Speaker in Battle Studies Program, Marine Corps Command and Staff College, 1984.

WRITINGS:

The Man Who Presumed: A Biography of Henry M. Stanley, Longmans, Green (London), 1953, Henry Holt, 1957, reprinted, Greenwood Press, 1974.
Let's Take a Trip (juvenile), Grosset, 1955.
Burton: A Biography of Sir Richard Francis Burton, Longmans, Green, 1963, Henry Holt, 1964, reprinted, Greenwood Press, 1975.
Prisoners of the Mahdi, Harper, 1967.
Queen Victoria's Little Wars, Harper, 1972.
The Great Anglo-Boer War, Harper, 1976, published in England as *The Great Boer War,* Allen Lane, 1977.
Mr. Kipling's Army, Norton, 1981, published in England as *For Queen and Country,* Allen Lane, 1981.
The Gurkhas, Norton, 1984.
Eminent Victorian Soldiers: Seekers of Glory, Norton, 1985.
The Great War in Africa, 1914-1918, Norton, 1986.
Armies of the Raj: From the Great Indian Mutiny to Independence, 1858-1947, Norton, 1989.
Ball's Bluff: A Small Battle and Its Long Shadow, EPM Publications, 1990.
Stonewall: A Biography of General Thomas J. Jackson, Norton, 1992.

Contributing editor to *Military History* and *World War II.* Also contributor of numerous articles to *Colliers Encyclopedia,* newspapers, and magazines.

WORK IN PROGRESS: Encyclopedia of Nineteenth-Century Land Warfare to be published by Norton.

SIDELIGHTS: Byron E. Farwell has consistently earned critical praise for his books on British history and for his biographies. In a *Detroit News* article, William Boozer says that Farwell "is a military historian and Virginian who got his own close-up look at the British military as an American Army captain of engineers with the Mediterranean Allied Air Force in the British Eighth Army area of World War II. Then and since, he has done his homework in giving us [a] captivating look at 19th-century British society."

Farwell's *The Man Who Presumed: A Biography of Henry M. Stanley* presents the life of news correspondent Henry M. Stanley who was commissioned by the New York *Herald* in 1869 to travel Africa to locate explorer David Livingstone. Stanley is best known for his greeting question—"Dr. Livingstone, I presume?"—when he finally found Livingstone. In a *Commonweal* review of Farwell's *The Man Who Presumed: A Biography of Henry M. Stanley,* John Cournos writes: "Mr. Farwell has done a splendid job. He has written a biography which is nearly always interesting and at times wildly exciting." R. W. Henderson, in a *Library Journal* article, notes that the story of this famed British explorer "is one that has enduring appeal. Although Farwell adds little, if anything new, he has handled his material expertly, presenting it with freshness and vigor." *San Francisco Chronicle* reviewer Marc Rivette feels that "Mr. Farwell makes [Stanley] live, even though Stanley was too shy to be universally appealing. He makes him a figure of respect and even love. It is a neat and telling job of illuminating the life of a man, once on the tip of fame, but who in this day and age is remembered mostly for his one immortal question."

Farwell's historical studies have been as well-received as his biographies, with reviewers particularly impressed by his ability to focus on the human side of the British military. A *Choice* contributor calls *The Great Anglo-Boer War* "by far the best general history" of that conflict. "Farwell, an American, has successfully written a history that graphically describes all elements of the war—military, political, and social—in a manner that holds the attention of the reader." Neal Ascherson, writing in the *New York Review of Books,* states that "Mr. Farwell hasn't tried to write a political history of the war, to approach it from any novel angle, or to base his book on original research. . . . He is simply concerned to tell the chronicle of the war from its start to its finish with all the human detail he can muster." In *Library Journal,* J. A. Casada points out that Farwell "captures the human rhythms of the war in all their inherent drama. He has given us the single best account of the war in its full scope."

One of Farwell's most widely reviewed books is *Mr. Kipling's Army,* an overall look at the British military during the nineteenth and early twentieth centuries. A *Choice* critic finds the book "a fascinating and often amusing portrait of life in the British Army during the reigns of Queen Victoria and King Edward VII," covering such topics as education, training, discipline, medical care, and dependent families. "It is essentially accurate," writes the reviewer, "pointing out the many idiosyncrasies of the army

without turning it into a caricature." According to Charles Champlin of the *Los Angeles Times Book Review,* the title of the book "seems absolutely appropriate. Kipling illuminates its pages; its descriptions in a real sense verify everything Kipling had to say." Champlin also feels that *Mr. Kipling's Army* "is alternately amusing and horrifying, obviously the result of an astonishing amount of digging (said to have taken 15 years)."

New Republic writer John Keegan believes "it was an excellent idea of Byron Farwell's to provide the still densely ranked host of Kipling's admirers with a documentary study of the principal institution from which he drew his cast of characters, the long-service, volunteer army of the Widow of Windsor, enlisted for drink and ruled by the lash, as the old saw had it. . . . The author knows a great deal about the regiments, the Fifth Fusiliers, the East Lancashires, the Rifle Brigade, the Scarlet Lancers, and he conveys to us something of their secret." Nicholas Best, in a *Times Literary Supplement* review, explains that "instead of war, [Farwell] looks at the army in peace, at its character, opinions, prejudices and way of life, at its methods of recruitment and training, both for officers and other ranks, and above all at its insularity at a time when Britain dominated forty per cent of the world's land mass." Best points out that although "much of the story has been told before, there is much that bears retelling," especially in light of the fact that "many of the Victorian army's customs and attitudes are very much alive today and, unfortunately, still flourishing."

In *The Gurkhas,* Farwell set himself the task of chronicling the history of the Nepalese Gurkha mercenary soldiers who fought first for the British and then the Indians. London *Times* reviewer Cyril Jarvis writes that Farwell's book is an "easy and readable . . . outline of their history since 1742, a description of the theatres of war in which they have been engaged and an account of their festivals, homes and family life." Elaine Kendall, in the *Los Angeles Times Book Review,* comments that the account will provide "anecdotes for months to come." "Highly personal and altogether fascinating," Kendall continues, "Though Farwell's prime purpose is to celebrate Gurkha bravery, loyalty and astonishing enthusiasm for the British cause, the most absorbing aspect of his book is the special insight into colonial mentality it provides." Other reviewers, however, like Jarvis, seem more concerned with the stories concerning the Gurkhas's uncanny skills. Along these lines, Richard West of the *Spectator* recalls with pleasure an anecdote Farwell relates in which a "Gurkha who escaped from the Japanese in Malaya and walked 800 miles through enemy land to India and safety, later attributed his success to a map he had bought from a British soldier. It turned out to be a map of London." Stories like this, concerning the Gurkhas's bravery, humor, toughness, intelligence, and honesty abound in the book.

Like *Mr. Kipling's Army, The Great War in Africa, 1914-1918* has been widely reviewed. Writing in the *New York Times Book Review,* Clifford D. May states that in the book Farwell "gives long overdue attention to theaters of war where wild animals were more feared than enemy soldiers." Edwin M. Yoder points out in his *Washington Post Book World* review that "the war in Africa was foreordained to be a sideshow," and that "Farwell goes to great, maybe even excessive lengths to nail down [this] point," yet he concedes that "within its limits, which are those of straightforward military history, *The Great War in Africa* is informative and often lively reading." Hew Strachen, however, in the *Times Literary Supplement,* criticizes Farwell for his "anglocentric, not even Eurocentric, let alone African" perspective, which is "entirely that of the field-commanders themselves."

Like much of his other work, Farwell's *Armies of the Raj: From the Great Indian Mutiny to Independence, 1858-1947* is full of anecdotes. Instead of focusing on war, a *Publishers Weekly* review notes, Farwell chooses to concentrate on recruitment, "relations between the colonists and the colonized, and the fluctuating state of morale." Philip Warner claims in the *Spectator* that "there is essential information" in the book "about the characteristics of Sikhs, Garhwalis, Dogras, and even the renowned Madras Sappers and Miners." Patrick Reardon assesses more broadly in the *Chicago Tribune* that Farwell "uses the Indian Army as a prism to look at British colonialism and its ultimate failure." Reardon also praises the "clarity" of Farwell's prose and "a pace to his writing that make . . . minutiae almost compelling."

BIOGRAPHICAL/CRITICAL SOURCES:

PERIODICALS

Chicago Tribune, September 12, 1989.
Choice, December, 1976; June, 1981.
Commonweal, October 18, 1957.
Detroit News, March 29, 1981.
Economist, December 21, 1963.
Harper's, March, 1964.
Library Journal, January 15, 1964; June 15, 1976.
Los Angeles Times, February 13, 1981.
Los Angeles Times Book Review, February 14, 1984.
New Republic, December 27, 1980.
New Statesman, November 22, 1963.
New York Review of Books, April 16, 1964; July 15, 1976.
New York Times, September 8, 1957.
New York Times Book Review, June 16, 1985, p. 13; August 9, 1987, p. 21.
Publishers Weekly, July 14, 1989, p. 66.
San Francisco Chronicle, September 10, 1957, p. 21.
Saturday Review, September 14, 1957.
Spectator, March 31, 1984, p. 29; March 3, 1990, pp. 37-38.
Time, September 23, 1957; February 28, 1964.
Times (London), March 22, 1984.
Times Literary Supplement, October 25, 1963; January 29, 1982; January 29, 1988, p. 104.
Washington Post Book World, February 22, 1981; June 29, 1985; March 8, 1987, p. 10.

*   *   *

FEITH, Herbert   1930-

PERSONAL: Born November 3, 1930, in Vienna, Austria; immigrated to Australia, 1939, became Australian citizen, 1944; married Betty Maynard Evans, December 29, 1953; children: David George, Anne Marie, Robert John. *Education:* University of Melbourne, B.A., 1951, M.A., 1955; Cornell University, Ph.D., 1961.

ADDRESSES: Home—40 Kyarra Rd., Glen Dris, Victoria, Australia. *Office*—Australian Council for Overseas Aid, 124 Napier St., Fitzroy, Melbourne, Australia.

CAREER: Ministry of Information, Republic of Indonesia, Jakarta, English language assistant, 1951-56 (participant in Australian "Volunteer Graduate Scheme" for Indonesia); Cornell University, Ithaca, NY, research associate, Modern Indonesia Project, 1956-57; Australian National University, Canberra, research fellow in department of history, 1960-62; Monash University, Melbourne, Australia, lecturer, department of politics, 1962-63, senior lecturer, 1963-66, reader, 1966-68, professor, 1968-75, reader, 1976-90; Australian Council for Overseas Aid, Melbourne, Australia, Human Rights Office, 1993—.

WRITINGS:

The Indonesian Elections of 1955: Interim Report, Department of Far Eastern Studies, Cornell University (Ithaca, NY), 1957.
The Wilopo Cabinet, 1952-1953: A Turning Point in Post-Revolutionary Indonesia, Department of Far Eastern Studies, Cornell University, 1958.
The Decline of Constitutional Democracy in Indonesia, Cornell University Press, 1962.
(Editor with Lance Castles) *Indonesian Political Thinking, 1945-65,* Cornell University Press, 1970.
(Editor with Rodney Tiffen) Rex Mortimer, *Stubborn Survivors: Dissenting Essays on Peasants and Third World Development,* Centre of Southeast Asian Studies, Monash University, 1984.

Also author of *Asia's Flashpoint, 1971: Bangladesh,* 1971; *The East Timor Issue since the Capture of Xanana Gus-*

mao, 1993. Contributor to books, including *Governments and Politics of Southeast Asia,* Cornell University Press (Ithaca, NY), 1959, revised edition, 1964; and *Indonesia,* edited by Ruth Thomas McVey, Human Relations Area File Press, 1963, revised edition, Yale University Southeast Asia Studies (New Haven, CT), 1967.

WORK IN PROGRESS: Conversations with Indonesian Friends; East Timor: The Search for a Settlement.

*　　*　　*

FELLOWS, Richard A(stley) 1947-

PERSONAL: Born January 21, 1947, in Dudley, England; son of Frank I. A. (a clerk) and Minnie (a homemaker; maiden name, John) Fellows; married Jane Gray (an administrator), January 25, 1975; children: Rosalind Jane, William Edward Astley. *Education:* Kingston upon Hull Regional College of Art, School of Architecture, diploma in architecture, 1972; University of York, Institute of Advanced Architectural Studies, M.Phil., 1980. *Avocational interests:* Singing, opera.

ADDRESSES: Home—4 Almondbury Close, Fenay Lane, Huddersfield, West Yorkshire HD5 8XX, England. *Office*—Department of Architecture, University of Huddersfield, Queensgate, Huddersfield, West Yorkshire, England.

CAREER: Architectural assistant in architecture firms in Leeds, West Yorkshire, Gloucester, Gloucestershire, and Bath, Avon, England; University of Huddersfield, Huddersfield, West Yorkshire, lecturer in architecture, 1974—. Halifax Civic Trust, West Yorkshire, member of executive committee, 1979-81; Open University, lecturer in history of architecture, summers, 1981-83; Architecture Workshops Ltd., Leeds, members of council of management, 1985—; Calderdale Architecture Workshop, Halifax, West Yorkshire, consultant director; West Yorkshire Society of Architects, Bedford Scholarship Panel, 1989-93; NCUK/ITM Programme, Malaysia, tutor/ lecturer.

MEMBER: Royal Institute of British Architects, Society of Architectural Historians of Great Britain.

WRITINGS:

Sir Reginald Blomfield: An Edwardian Architect, Zwemmer (London), 1985.
(With wife, Jane Fellows) *Buildings for Hospitality: Principles of Care and Design for Accommodation Managers,* Pitman (London), 1990.

Contributor to magazines, including *Period Home, Yorkshire Architect,* and *Landscape Design.*

WORK IN PROGRESS: A book about late nineteenth- and early twentieth-century British architecture; *Edwardian Architecture: Style and Technology,* 1995; contributions to *The Dictionary of Art,* Macmillan.

SIDELIGHTS: Richard A. Fellows examines the life and work of British architect Reginald Blomfield in his 1985 book, *Sir Reginald Blomfield: An Edwardian Architect.* A staunch opponent of the modern movement in architecture, Blomfield designed mainly large country houses and gardens reflecting his preoccupation with the "Grand Manner" style. Most notable among his works in civic architecture are London's Regent Street Quadrant and the fronts to Piccadilly Circus as well as the World War I memorial Menin Gate in Ypres, Belgium. According to *Times Literary Supplement* critic Andrew Saint, Fellows's book provides "a crisp, efficient and admirably succinct account" of the architect's career.

Fellows told *CA:* "My study of Blomfield was, to some extent, a vehicle for investigation into a complex and fascinating period of British architecture—an attempt to sort out the various strands of design in the late nineteenth and early twentieth centuries."

BIOGRAPHICAL/CRITICAL SOURCES:

PERIODICALS

British Book Notes, June, 1985, p. 356.
Times Literary Supplement, February 22, 1985, p. 195.

*　　*　　*

FEST, Joachim C. 1926-

PERSONAL: Born December 8, 1926, in Berlin, Germany; son of Johannes and Elisabeth (Straeter) Fest; married Ingrid Ascher, 1959; children: Alexander, Nicolaus. *Education:* Attended University of Freiburg, 1948-49, University of Frankfurt, 1949-51, University of Berlin, 1951-53. *Religion:* Roman Catholic.

ADDRESSES: Office—Gartenstrasse 11, D-61476 Kronberg, Germany.

CAREER: Editor, historian, publisher, writer. *Rundfunk im amerikanischen Sektor* (RIAS), Berlin, Germany, editor, 1953-61; *Norddeutscher Rundfunk-TV,* Hamburg, Germany, editor, 1961-63, editor in chief, 1963-68; freelance writer, Germany, 1968-73; *Frankfurter Allgemeine Zeitung,* Frankfurt am Main, Germany, publisher and editing director, 1973-93; visiting professor, University of Heidelberg, 1993.

MEMBER: Max Planck Society (senator), Deutsch Nationalstiftung (senator).

AWARDS, HONORS: Thomas Wolf Prize, 1971; Thomas Dehler Prize, 1973; Thomas-Mann-Preis award, Thomas Mann Gessellschaft, 1981; honorary doctorate degree, University of Stuttgart, 1982; Goethe Plakette Stadt Frankfurt, 1987; Premio Mediterraneo award, Palermo, 1989.

WRITINGS:

Das Gesicht des Dritten Reiches, Piper (Munich), 1963, translation by Michael Bullock published as *The Face of the Third Reich: Portraits of the Nazi Leadership,* Pantheon (New York City), 1970.
(Author of foreword) Jochen van Lang, editor, *Adolf Hitler: Gesichter eines Diktators* (title means "Adolf Hitler: Faces of a Dictator"), C. Wegner, 1968.
Hitler: Eine Biographie, Propylaeen-Verlag (Berlin), 1973, translation by Richard and Clara Winston published as *Hitler: A Biography,* Harcourt (New York City), 1974.
Aufgehobene Vergangenheit (essays), Deutsche Verlags-Anstalt, 1981.
Die unwissenden Magier. Ueber Thomas und Heinrich Mann, Siedler, 1985.
Der tanzende Tod, St. Gertrude, 1986.
Hitler, Random House (New York City), 1975.
Im Gegenlicht: eine italienische Reise, Siedler (Berlin, Germany), 1988.
Der zerstoerte Traum: vom Ende des utopischen Zeitalters, Siedler, 1991.
Die schwierige Freiheit. Ueber die offene Flanke der offenen Gesellschaft, Siedler, 1993.
Staatsstreich. Der lange Weg zum 20. Juli, Siedler, 1994.

Contributor to *Der Spiegel* and *Encounter.* Also contributor to German television and radio.

SIDELIGHTS: A reviewer for the *Virginia Quarterly Review* described German journalist Joachim C. Fest's *The Face of the Third Reich: Portraits of the Nazi Leadership* as a "profound, absorbing, and stimulating book. It is a collection of essays, psychological studies of eighteen major figures of Nazi Germany. Each of the figures, while significant in his own right, is shown to be at the same time representative of a segment of German society seduced by National Socialism. Each biography is enlightening, and together they provide a welcome addition to the literature on the Third Reich. Fest combines the best of journalism and scholarship; his book is carefully researched, well composed, and (despite occasional lapses into ponderous prose) smoothly written."

BIOGRAPHICAL/CRITICAL SOURCES:

PERIODICALS

America, November 28, 1970.
Christian Century, May 20, 1970.
New York Times Book Review, May 24, 1970.
Saturday Review, August 29, 1970.
Times Literary Supplement, March 19, 1970; September 13, 1987.
Virginia Quarterly Review, autumn, 1970.

*   *   *

FIRMIN, Charlotte 1954-

PERSONAL: Born May 2, 1954, in London, England; daughter of Peter (a writer and illustrator) and Joan (a bookbinder; maiden name, Clapham) Firmin; married Robert Herbert (a graphic designer), 1981; children: Olivia, Ruth, Georgia. *Education:* Attended Hornsey School of Art, 1972-73; Brighton Polytechnic, B.A. (with honors), 1976. *Politics:* Socialist. *Religion:* Agnostic.

ADDRESSES: Home—59 Stone St., Faversham, Kent, England.

CAREER: Author and illustrator of books for young people. Assistant at London Society of Genealogists, 1980-82.

WRITINGS:

JUVENILE; SELF-ILLUSTRATED

Hannah's Great Decision, Macmillan (London), 1978.
Claire's Secret Ambition, Macmillan, 1979.
Eggbert's Balloon, Collins (London), 1979.
The Eggham Pot of Gold, Collins, 1979.
Egglantine's Party, Collins, 1979.
The Giant Egg Plant, Collins, 1979.
Weird Windows, Deutsch (London), 1989.

JUVENILE; ILLUSTRATOR

Annabel Farjeon, *The Cock of Round Hill,* Kaye & Ward (London), 1977.
Terence Deary, *The Custard Kid,* A. & C. Black (London), 1978.
H. Rice, *The Remarkable Feat of King Caboodle,* A. & C. Black, 1979.
Birthe Alton, *The Magic of Ah,* Kaye & Ward, 1980.
Deary, *Calamity Kate,* A. & C. Black, 1980.
Mary Dickinson, *Alex's Bed,* Deutsch, 1980.
Dickinson, *Alex and Roy,* Deutsch, 1981.
Deary, *The Lambton Worm,* A. & C. Black, 1981.
Dickinson, *Alex and the Baby,* Deutsch, 1982.
Dickinson, *Alex's Outing,* Deutsch, 1983.
Dickinson, *New Clothes for Alex,* Deutsch, 1984.
Maurice Jones, *I'm Going on a Dragon Hunt,* Deutsch, 1987.
Jones, *I'm Going on a Gorilla Hunt,* Deutsch, 1988.
Evelyn de Jong, *Isn't She Clever?,* Deutsch, 1988.
Dickinson, *Alex and Roy: Best Friends,* Deutsch, 1989.
De Jong, *Aren't They Wonderful?,* Deutsch, 1990.

Kate Petty, *Being Bullied,* Barron's (New York City), 1991.

Petty, *Making Friends,* Barron's, 1991.

Petty, *Playing the Game,* Barron's, 1991.

Petty, *Feeling Left Out,* Barron's, 1991.

SIDELIGHTS: Charlotte Firmin told *CA* that her work "is all a matter of luck, observation, persistence, and optimism."

* * *

FLINT, Cort R(ay) 1915-

PERSONAL: Born March 17, 1915, in Leeday, OK; son of Corties Ray (a banker) and Kathryn Forrest (Logan) Flint; married Ilene Moore (a musician), May 28, 1938; children: Cort R., Jr.; Sue Ann. *Education:* Southwestern State College, B.A., 1935; University of Oklahoma, graduate study, 1937-39; Southern Baptist Theological Seminary, Th.M., 1943, Th.D., 1952, Ph.D., 1974. *Politics:* Democrat.

ADDRESSES: Home—Rt. 2, Box 174, Hillsville, VA 24343.

CAREER: Ordained Baptist minister, 1940; New Haven Baptist Church, KY, pastor, 1941-43; Pleasant Grove Baptist Church, Hodgenville, KY, pastor, 1942 and 1946-47; First Baptist Church, Olney, TX, pastor, 1948-50; First Baptist Church, Anderson, SC, pastor, 1955-66; Meadows of Dan Baptist Church, Meadows of Dan, VA, pastor, 1970-71. Baptist Theological Seminary, Louisville, KY, vice-president, 1952-53; Anderson College, Anderson, SC, president, 1957-58; Flint Books, International Development Corporation, president, 1966—. Consultant and author, 1966—. *Military service:* Oklahoma National Guard, 1933-35. U.S. Naval Reserve, 1943-46; became lieutenant.

MEMBER: International Platform Association, Rotary, Kiwanis, Masons, Ruritan.

AWARDS, HONORS: D.H., 1973.

WRITINGS:

(Editor) *The Quotable Billy Graham,* Droke, 1966.
Grief's Slow Wisdom, Droke, 1966.
To Thine Own Self Be True, Droke, 1968.
Better Men or Bitter Men?, Droke, 1969.
The Purpose of Love, Droke, 1973.

Also editor of *The Quotable Dr. Crane,* 1969. Also author of *The Best Is Yet to Come,* 1974, and *Discoveries for Greater Living,* 1974. Contributor to *Quote.*

WORK IN PROGRESS: Discoveries for Greater Selling; You Were Born to Win; Living at Your Best. *

FLORES, Dan Louie 1948-

PERSONAL: Born October 19, 1948, in Vivian, LA; son of Willie Clyde, Jr., and Kathryn (Hale) Flores. *Education:* Northwestern State University of Louisiana, B.A., 1971, M.A., 1972; Texas A & M University, Ph.D., 1978.

ADDRESSES: Home—RR2, Yellow House Canyon, Slaton, TX 79364. *Office*—Department of History, University of Montana, Missoula, MT 59812.

CAREER: Freelance writer, columnist, and conservation editor for various outdoor and environmental magazines, 1971—. Texas Tech University, Lubbock, professor of history, 1978-92; University of Montana, Missoula, Hammond Professor of Western History, 1992—. Visiting professor, University of Wyoming, 1986.

MEMBER: American Association for Environmental History, American Historical Association, Western History Association, Texas State Historical Association, Montana State History Association, Texas Institute of Letters.

AWARDS, HONORS: Townshend Whelen Prize, Digest Books, 1976; "best book on the West" citation, Westerners International, and "best book on Texas" citation, Texas State Historical Association, both 1984, for *Jefferson and Southwestern Exploration: The Freeman and Custis Accounts of the Red River Expedition of 1806;* Ray Allen Billington Prize, Western History Association, and H. Bailey Carroll Prize, Texas State Historical Association, both 1984, for "Ecology of the Red River in 1806."

WRITINGS:

Jefferson and Southwestern Exploration: The Freeman and Custis Accounts of the Red River Expedition of 1806, University of Oklahoma Press (Norman), 1984.
Journal of an Indian Trader: Anthony Glass and the Texas Trading Frontier, 1790-1810, Texas A & M University Press (College Station), 1985.
(With Amy Winton) *Canyon Visions: Photographs and Pastels of the Texas Plains,* Texas Tech University (Lubbock), 1989.
Caprock Canyonlands: Journeys into the Heart of the Southern Plains, University of Texas Press (Austin), 1990.
(With Eric Bolen) *The Mississippi Kite: Portrait of a Southern Hawk,* University of Texas Press, 1993.

Contributor to history journals, environmental periodicals, nature writing anthologies; associate editor of *Ethnohistory,* 1984-86.

WORK IN PROGRESS: A book on the sense of place in the American West, publication expected in 1995; a book on bison and Plains Indians, to be published by Yale University Press, 1996.

SIDELIGHTS: Dan Louie Flores once told *CA:* "My work on the history of the Southwest originates in my family's long interrelationship with the area—my French and Spanish ancestors have been in western Louisiana since the early eighteenth century—and in the strong sense of history and landscape that yet affects me. The latter is probably the reason I do what scholars now call environmental history. My discovery early in graduate school that Thomas Jefferson had dispatched into 'my' country a southwestern counterpart to the Lewis and Clark expedition and that since 1806 no one had bothered to assemble the documents and write the story of that Jeffersonian probe was tantamount to having my first book choose me to write it."

Flores more recently told *CA:* "As I look back over my work in light of current projects, I realize that the thread that strings through all of it is some instinctive (I don't think it is learned) fascination with the evolving historical relationships between human cultures and specific kinds of landscapes. To one degree or another, most of my articles and essays and all of my books have had something to do with regional ecologies (the Red River Valley, the Great Plains, the American West) and the endlessly intriguing ways that people have interacted with them across time. This approach has always involved a personal relationship with the land, as my early books were about the historical and environmental circumstances of the places where I lived. But more recently it has led me in something of an autobiographical direction, as I have explored my own reaction to place. So my recent and present work has become an experimental type of environmental and personal history, often (as with *Caprock Canyonlands* and my current project on sense of place in the American West) written in first-person. Thus my books and articles have combined the personal essay with historical research, the study of cultures with an effort to understand the ecological history of places.

"When I look at much of what I've written, I can't help but think that the country made me do it. Using words like 'sense of place' and 'continuum' makes it sound as if the environmentalist bent of my work has mystical origins; I rather think the sources lie in the concreteness of geology, landforms, skies, and the topophilic pull these have on all of us in some genetic way. Particularized environmental history related through closely observed personal essays that also feature social criticism thus seems to be my current direction."

* * *

FOLLETT, Robert J(ohn) R(ichard) 1928-

PERSONAL: Born July 4, 1928, in Oak Park, IL; son of Dwight W. (an executive) and Mildred (Johnson) Follett;

married Nancy L. Crouthamel, December 30, 1950; children: Brian L., Kathryn R., Jean A., Lisa W. *Education:* Brown University, A.B., 1950; Columbia University, graduate study, 1950-51.

ADDRESSES: Home—P.O. Box 8846, Keystone, CO 80345. *Office*—2233 West Grove Street, River Grove, IL 60171.

CAREER: Follett Publishing Co., Chicago, IL, editor, 1951-55, sales manager, 1955-58, general manager of educational division, 1958-68, president, 1968-78, president of Follett International, 1972—, chairperson and director of Follett Corp., 1979—. President, Alpine Research Institute, 1968—; member of Illinois Governor's Commission on Schools, 1972, and National Advisory Council on Educational Statistics, 1975-77; president, Alpine Guild Inc. Publishers, 1977—; chairperson, Book Distribution Task Force on the book industry, beginning 1978. Member of board of directors, Community Foundation of Oak Park and River Forest, 1959-86, Fund for Justice, 1974-77, and Fund for Character, 1982—; trustee, Institute for Educational Data Systems, 1965—. Member of Republican State Committee, Illinois Seventh Congressional District, 1982—. *Military service:* U.S. Army, Psychological Warfare School, 1951-53.

MEMBER: Association of American Publishers (director, 1972-79), Mid-America Publishers Association (founder), Chicago Publishers Association (president, 1976—), Sierra Club, Tower Club, River Forest Tennis Club.

WRITINGS:

Your Wonderful Body, Follett (Chicago), 1962.
How to Keep Score in Business (nonfiction), Follett, 1978.
What to Take Backpacking—And Why (essay), Alpine Guild (Oak Park, IL), 1978.
The Financial Side of Book Publishing (nonfiction), Association of American Publishers (Washington, DC), 1982, revised edition, Alpine Guild, 1987.
Financial Feasibility in Book Publishing (nonfiction), Alpine Guild, 1986.
Financial Report Fundamentals (nonfiction), Alpine Guild, 1987.
Essays from a Career, Follett, 1994.

Contributor to numerous professional journals.

* * *

FONER, Philip (Sheldon) 1910-

PERSONAL: Born December 14, 1910, in New York, NY; son of Abraham (a garage owner) and Mary (Smith) Foner; married Roslyn Held (a technical editor), 1939 (died, 1983); children: Elizabeth (Mrs. Robert S. Van der

Paer), Laura. *Education:* City College (now City College of the City University of New York), B.A., 1932; Columbia University, M.A., 1933, Ph.D., 1940.

CAREER: City College (now City College of the City University of New York), New York City, instructor in history, 1932-41; International Fur and Leather Workers, New York City, educational director, 1941-45; Citadel Press, New York City, 1945-67, became publisher; Lincoln University, Lincoln University, PA, professor of history, 1967-79, professor emeritus, 1980—.

MEMBER: American Historical Association, Organization of American Historians, Association for the Study of Negro Life and History, Phi Beta Kappa.

WRITINGS:

Business and Slavery: The New York Merchants and the Irrepressible Conflict, University of North Carolina Press, 1941, reprinted, Russell, 1968.

Morale Education in the American Army: War for Independence, War of 1812, Civil War, International Publishers, 1944.

The Jews in American History, 1645-1865, International Publishers, 1946.

History of the Labor Movement in the United States, International Publishers, Volume I: *From Colonial Times to the Founding of the American Federation of Labor,* 1947, Volume II: *From the Founding of the American Federation of Labor to the Emergence of American Imperialism,* 1956, 2nd edition, 1975, Volume III: *The Policies and Practices of the American Federation of Labor, 1900-1909,* 1964, Volume IV: *The Industrial Workers of the World, 1905-1917,* 1966, Volume V: *The American Federation of Labor in the Progressive Era, 1910-1915,* 1980, Volume VI: *On the Eve of America's Entrance into World War I, 1915-1916,* 1982, Volume VII: *1914-1918,* 1987, Volume VIII: *Postwar Struggles, 1918-1920,* 1988, Volume IX: *The T.U.E.L. to the End of the Gompers Era,* 1991, Volume X: *1925-1929,* 1993.

The Fur and Leather Workers Union: A Story of Dramatic Struggles and Achievements, Nordan Press, 1950.

The Life and Writings of Frederick Douglass, five volumes, International Publishers, 1950-1975.

Mark Twain: Social Critic, International Publishers, 1958, 2nd edition, 1966.

A History of Cuba and Its Relations with the United States, International Publishers, Volume I: *From the Conquest of Cuba to la Escalera, 1492-1845,* 1962, Volume II: *From the Annexationist Era to the Second War for Independence,* 1963.

Frederick Douglass: A Biography, Citadel, 1964, 2nd edition, 1969.

The Case of Joe Hill, International Publishers, 1966.

The Bolshevik Revolution: Its Impact on American Radicals, Liberals, and Labor, International Publishers, 1967.

American Labor and the Indo-China War: The Growth of Union Opposition, International Publishers, 1971, revised edition published as *U. S. Labor and the Vietnam War,* 1989.

The Spanish-Cuban-American War and the Birth of American Imperialism, 1895-1902, two volumes, Monthly Review Press, 1971.

Organized Labor and the Black Worker, 1619-1973, Praeger, 1974, new edition published as *Organized Labor and the Black Worker, 1619-1981,* International Publishers, 1981.

History of Black Americans, Volume I: *From Africa to the Emergence of the Cotton Kingdom,* Greenwood Press, 1975, Volume II: *From the Emergence of the Cotton Kingdom to the Eve of the Compromise of 1850,* 1983, Volume III: *From the Compromise of 1850 to the End of the Civil War,* 1983.

Labor and the American Revolution, Greenwood Press, 1976.

Blacks in the American Revolution, Greenwood Press, 1976.

The Democratic-Republican Societies, 1790-1800, Greenwood Press, 1976.

American Socialism and Black Americans: From the Age of Jackson to World War II, Greenwood Press, 1977.

Antonio Maceo: The 'Bronze Titan' of Cuba's Struggle for Independence, Monthly Review Press, 1977.

The Great Labor Uprising of 1877, Monad Press, 1977.

Women and the American Labor Movement, Free Press, Volume I: *From Colonial Times to the Eve of World War I,* 1979, Volume II: *From World War I to the Present,* 1980.

British Labor and the American Civil War, Holmes & Meier, 1981.

(With Josephine P. Pacheco) *Three Who Dared: Prudence Crandall, Margaret Douglass, Myrtilla Miner—Champions of Antebellum Black Education,* Greenwood Press, 1984.

The Workingmen's Party of the United States: A History of the First Marxist Party in the Americas, Marxist Educational Press, 1984.

First Facts of American Labor, Holmes & Meier, 1984.

(With Reinhard Schultz) *The Other America: Art and the Labor Movement in the United States,* Journeyman, 1986.

Militarism and Organized Labor: 1900-1914, MEP Publications, 1987.

(With David R. Roediger) *Our Own Time: A History of American Labor and the Working Day,* Greenwood Press, 1990.

William Heighton, International Publishers, 1991.

EDITOR

(And author of introduction) *Thomas Jefferson: Selections from His Writings,* International Publishers, 1943.

Basic Writings of Thomas Jefferson, University of North Carolina Press, 1944.

(And author of introduction) *Abraham Lincoln: Selections from His Writings,* International Publishers, 1944.

George Washington: Selections from His Writings, International Publishers, 1944.

(And author of introduction) *Frederick Douglass: Selections from His Writings,* International Publishers, 1945.

(And author of biographical essay, notes, and introduction) *The Complete Writings of Thomas Paine,* two volumes, Citadel, 1945, reprinted, 1969, as *The Life and Major Writings of Thomas Paine,* 1961.

Franklin Delano Roosevelt: Selections from His Writings, International Publishers, 1947.

Jack London: American Rebel, Citadel, 1947, revised edition, 1964.

The Letters of Joe Hill, Oak Publications, 1965.

(And author of introduction) *Helen Keller: Her Socialist Years,* International Publishers, 1967.

(And author of introduction) *The Autobiographies of the Haymarket Martyrs,* Humanities, 1969.

Frederick Douglass, *My Bondage and Freedom,* Dover, 1969.

The Black Panthers Speak, Lippincott, 1970.

Benjamin Brawley, *Early American Negro Writers,* Dover, 1970.

W. E. B. Du Bois Speaks: Speeches and Addresses, two volumes, Pathfinder, 1970.

(And author of commentary) *The Voice of Black America: Major Speeches by Negroes in the United States, 1797-1971,* Simon & Schuster, 1972, new edition published as *The Voice of Black America: Major Speeches by Negroes in the United States, 1797-1973,* Capricorn Books, 1973.

When Karl Marx Died: Comments in 1883, International Publishers, 1973, published as *Karl Marx Remembered,* Synthesis Publications, 1983.

The Life and Writings of Frederick Douglass, five volumes, International Publishers, 1975.

(And author of introduction) Jose Marti, *Inside the Monster: Writings on the United States and American Imperialism,* translated by Elinor Randall and others, Monthly Review Press, 1975.

American Labor Songs of the Nineteenth Century, University of Illinois Press, 1975.

Frederick Douglass on Women's Rights, Greenwood Press, 1976.

(And author of introduction and notes) *We, the Other People: Alternative Declarations of Independence by Labor Groups, Farmers, Women's Rights Advocates, Socialists, and Blacks,* University of Illinois Press, 1976.

The Formation of the Workingmen's Party of the United States, 1876, American Institute for Marxist Studies, 1976.

The Factory Girls: A Collection of Writings on Life and Struggles in the New England Factories of the 1840s, University of Illinois Press, 1977.

(And author of introduction) Marti, *Our America: Writings on Latin America and the Struggle for Cuban Independence,* translated by Randall and others, Monthly Review Press, 1977.

(With Brewster Chamberlin, and author of introduction) *Friedrich A. Sorge's Labor Movement in the United States: A History of the American Working Class from Colonial Times to 1890,* translated by B. Chamberlin and Angela Chamberlin, Greenwood Press, 1977.

Paul Robeson Speaks: Writings, Speeches, Interviews, Brunner/Mazel, 1978.

(With Ronald L. Lewis) *The Black Worker: A Documentary History from Colonial Times to the Present,* eight volumes, Temple University Press, 1978-1985, one volume edition published as *Black Workers: Selections,* 1988.

(And author of introduction) Marti, *On Education,* Monthly Review Press, 1979.

(With George Walker) *Proceedings of the Black National and State Conventions, 1840-1865,* two volumes, Temple University Press, 1979-1980.

Fellow Workers and Friends: I.W.W. Free-Speech Fights as Told by Participants, Greenwood, 1981.

(And author of introduction) *Alexander von Humboldt on Slavery in the United States,* Humboldt-Universitat zu Berlin, 1981.

(And author of introduction) Marti, *On Art and Literature,* translated by Randall and others, Monthly Review Press, 1982.

(And author of introduction) Marti, *Major Poems,* bilingual edition, translated by Randall, Holmes & Meier, 1982.

(And author of introduction) *Wilhelm Liebknecht: Letters to the Chicago Workingman's Advocate, November 26, 1870-December 2, 1871,* Holmes & Meier, 1982.

(With Sally M. Miller) *Kate Richards O'Hare: Selected Writings and Speeches,* Louisiana University Press, 1982.

(And author of introduction) *Mother Jones Speaks: Collected Speeches and Writings,* Monad Press, 1983.

(And author of introduction) Woodbey, George Washington, *Black Socialist Preacher,* Synthesis, 1983.

The Social Writings of Jack London, Carol Publishing, 1984.

Clara Zetkin, *Selected Writings,* translated by Kai Schoenhals, International Publishers, 1984.

(With Richard C. Winchester) *The Anti-Imperialist Reader,* Holmes & Meier, Volume I: *From the Mexican War to the Election of 1900,* 1984, Volume II: *The Literary Anti-Imperialists,* 1986.

May Day: A Short History of the International Workers' Holiday, 1886-1986, International Publishers, 1986.

(With James S. Allen and Herbert Shapiro) *American Communism & Black Americans: A Documentary History,* Temple University Press, Volume I: *1919-1929,* 1986, Volume II: *1930-1934,* 1991.

Marti, *Political Parties and Elections in the United States,* translated by Randall, Temple University Press, 1989.

(With Daniel Rosenberg) *Racism, Dissent, and Asian Americans: A Documentary History,* Greenwood, 1993.

OTHER

Member of board of editors, *Journal of Negro History* and *Pennsylvania History.*

SIDELIGHTS: Philip Foner is something of a "grand old man" among historians of the left. His extensive scholarship includes works on labor history, Afro-American history, Marxism and socialism, the history of women in the American labor movement, and the history of American imperialism. He has also edited selections from the works of such figures as Thomas Jefferson, Franklin Roosevelt, Frederick Douglass, and Jose Marti.

In *Women and the American Labor Movement,* which takes its subject from colonial times up to the 1970s, Foner describes the difficulties women workers faced as they attempted to improve labor conditions. Often struggling under conditions more exploitative than those of their male counterparts, women workers also had to overcome resistance to their participation in the early, male-dominated labor unions. According to Richard C. Wade in the *New York Times Book Review,* Foner's "analysis is class-based; he believes that working people—male and female—should have united against the common enemy, rapacious employers." Foner argues, Leslie Woodcock Tentler notes in the *Washington Post Book World,* that "the most ardent proponents of sexual equality in the union movement" were communists in the American unions.

The Workingmen's Party of the United States is one of Foner's several books which focus on "scenes and heroes the American mainstream has chosen to forget," as Paul Buhle phrases it in the *Voice Literary Supplement.* The Workingmen's Party, founded in 1876, was the first Marxist political organization in the United States. Although its influence was felt for less than a decade, it did succeed in electing several candidates to state legislatures. According to Buhle, Foner's study contains much interesting doc-

umentation, but its analysis relies too heavily on Marxist ideology to convey the complexity of the historical events.

Among Foner's many studies of the relationship between the American labor movement and socialism is *A History of American Labor and the Working Day,* co-authored with David R. Roediger. The battle for a forty-hour work week is described as an achievement of Eastern European immigrants and Socialist and Communist union members. According to Jo-Ann Mort in the *New York Times Book Review,* the authors point to the abandonment of Western European social democratic ideals by the AFL-CIO to explain the diminution of labor union power in the United States in recent years. They predict that the trend in Europe towards a shorter workweek will again influence American labor patterns, as the American workforce becomes more diverse in its needs.

Foner has extended his role as a presenter of leftist political history by his work as an editor. Among the several dozen books he has edited are volumes of the writings of Jose Marti, a Cuban exile who reported a critical view of American politics for Latin American newspapers in the late nineteenth century. In *Karl Marx Remembered,* a collection of memorials to Marx contemporaneous with his death, Foner reveals the sometimes conflicting threads of the early socialist, communist and anarchist communities. In *The Other America: Art and the Labor Movement in the United States,* Foner and co-editor Reinhard Schultz present artworks depicting the working class.

BIOGRAPHICAL/CRITICAL SOURCES:

PERIODICALS

Nation, May 1, 1982, pp. 535-536.
New York Times Book Review, November 11, 1979, p. 12; March 11, 1990.
Village Voice, May 29, 1983.
Voice Literary Supplement, December 1984, p. 20.
Washington Post Book World, March 1, 1981, p. 9.*

* * *

FONG, C. K.
  See CASSIDAY, Bruce (Bingham)

* * *

FORD, Edmund Brisco 1901-1988

PERSONAL: Born April 23, 1901, in Papcastle, Cumberland, England; died January 22, 1988; son of Harold Dodsworth and Gertrude Emma (Bennett) Ford. *Education:* Wadham College, Oxford, B.A., 1924, M.A., 1927, D.Sc.,

1943. *Avocational interests:* Archaeology, literature, travel.

CAREER: Geneticist, educator, and author. Oxford University, Oxford, England, researcher, 1924-27, demonstrator in zoology and comparative anatomy, then lecturer, 1928-38, reader, 1938-63, professor of ecological genetics, 1963-69, professor emeritus, 1969-88, director of Genetics Laboratory, 1952-69; All Souls College, Oxford, fellow, 1958-71, senior dean and fellow, 1958-71, fellow emeritus, 1976-77, distinguished fellow and senior dean, 1977-88. Galton Lecturer at University of London, 1939; Woodhall Lecturer at Royal Institution, 1957; Woodward Lecturer at Yale University, 1959, 1973. Past British member of International Committee of Genetics.

MEMBER: British Genetical Society (president, 1946-49), Nature Conservancy (founding member), Finnish Academy (foreign member), Somerset Archaeological Society (president, 1960-61), Travellers' Club.

AWARDS, HONORS: Fellow of the Royal Society (FRS), 1946; Darwin Medal, Royal Society, 1954; Weldon Medal, Oxford University, 1959; D.Sc., University of Liverpool, 1964; University of Helsinki Medal, 1967.

WRITINGS:

Mendelism and Evolution, Methuen (New York City), 1931, 8th edition, Halsted (New York City), 1965.

(With G. D. H. Carpenter) *Mimicry,* Methuen, 1933.

The Study of Heredity, Home University Library, 1938, 2nd edition, Oxford University Press (New York City), 1950.

Genetics for Medical Students, Chapman & Hall (London, England), 1942, 7th edition, 1973, Halsted, 1974.

Butterflies, Collins (New York City), 1945, 4th edition, 1977.

British Butterflies, Penguin (New York City), 1951.

Moths, Collins, 1955, 3rd edition, 1972.

Ecological Genetics, Chapman & Hall, 1964, 4th edition, Halsted, 1975.

Genetic Polymorphism, Faber (Winchester, MA), 1965.

Evolution Studied by Observation and Experiment, Oxford University Press, 1973.

Genetics and Adaptation, Edward Arnold (Baltimore, MD), 1976.

Understanding Genetics, Faber, 1979.

Taking Genetics into the Countryside, Weidenfeld & Nicolson (London, England), 1981.

(With J. S. Haywood) *Church Treasures in the Oxford District,* foreword by A. L. Rowse, Sutton (Gloucester, England), 1984.

(Editor with Richard Irwin Vane-Wright and Phillip Ronald Ackery) *The Biology of Butterflies* (symposium of the Royal Entomological Society of London), Academic Press (London, England), 1984.

Contributor of approximately eighty articles to scientific journals.

SIDELIGHTS: A retired professor and former director of the genetics laboratory at Oxford University, Edmund Brisco Ford's genetic research, some of which was conducted with Julian Huxley, covered topics including the evolution of dominance in wild material, the growth of genetic controllers, and the prediction of the correlation between human blood groups and disease. Ford originated the scientific process known as ecological genetics and expanded the study of evolution. Through experimentation and field research mainly with butterflies and moths, he supported Charles Darwin's theory of natural selection and demonstrated that a species' survival depends on its adaptability to the environment. Ford's highly esteemed work resulted in a number of scientific innovations, among them the discovery and defining of genetic polymorphism—a condition of variation within genes that accounts for such traits as susceptibility to disease.

Ford was one of the first scientists since the seventeenth century elected a Fellow of All Souls College.

BIOGRAPHICAL/CRITICAL SOURCES:

PERIODICALS

Times Literary Supplement, February 1, 1985, p. 131.

OBITUARIES:

PERIODICALS

Times (London), January 23, 1988.*

*   *   *

FORD, Richard 1944-

PERSONAL: Born February 16, 1944, in Jackson, MS; son of Parker Carrol (in sales) and Edna (Akin) Ford; married Kristina Hensley (a research professor), 1968. *Education:* Michigan State University, B.A., 1966; University of California, Irvine, M.F.A., 1970.

ADDRESSES: Agent—Amanda Urban, International Creative Management, 40 West 57th St., New York, NY 10019.

CAREER: Writer, 1976—. Lecturer at University of Michigan, Ann Arbor, 1974-76, and at Princeton University, Princeton, NJ, 1979-80; assistant professor of English, Williams College, Williamstown, MA, 1978-79.

MEMBER: Writers Guild (East), PEN.

AWARDS, HONORS: University of Michigan Society of Fellows, 1971-74; Guggenheim fellow, 1977-78; National Endowment for the Arts fellow, 1979-80, 1985-86; *The*

Sportswriter was chosen one of the five best books of 1986, *Time* magazine; PEN/Faulkner citation for fiction, 1987, for *The Sportswriter;* literature award, Mississippi Academy of Arts and Letters, 1987; literature award, American Academy and Institute of Arts and Letters, 1989; Literary Lion Award, New York Public Library, 1989; Echoing Green Foundation award, 1991.

WRITINGS:

FICTION

A Piece of My Heart (novel), Harper, 1976.
The Ultimate Good Luck (novel), Houghton, 1981.
The Sportswriter (novel), Vintage, 1986.
Rock Springs: Stories (includes "Children" and "Great Falls"), Atlantic Monthly Press, 1987.
Wildlife (novel), Atlantic Monthly Press, 1990.

OTHER

(Contributor) L. Rust Hills, editor, *Fifty Great Years of Esquire Fiction,* Viking, 1983.
American Tropical (play), produced at Louisville's Actors Theater, Louisville, KY, 1983.
(Editor with Shannon Ravenel) *The Best American Short Stories 1990,* Houghton, 1990.
(Author of introduction) *Juke Joint: Photographs by Birney Imes,* University Press of Mississippi, 1990.
Bright Angel (screenplay; based on Ford's short stories "Children" and "Great Falls,"), Hemdale, 1991.
(Editor) *The Granta Book of the American Short Story,* Viking Penguin, 1992.

Contributor of stories and essays to periodicals.

SIDELIGHTS: "Writing is the only thing I've done with persistence, except for being married," claimed Richard Ford in an interview with *Publishers Weekly,* "and yet it's such an inessential thing. Nobody cares if you do it, and nobody cares if you don't." The author undoubtedly believed that statement, yet numerous reviewers have demonstrated how much they do care about Ford's work by lavishing it with praise. He is "a formidably talented novelist" and "one of the best writers of his generation," according to Walter Clemons of *Newsweek;* he is also "the leading short story writer in the United States today," in the opinion of Toronto *Globe & Mail* contributor Alberto Manguel.

Ford, who was raised in Mississippi and Arkansas, turned to fiction after a brief, unsatisfying stint as a law student. He enrolled in the M.F.A. program at the University of California at Irvine, where he studied with such writers as E. L. Doctorow and Oakley Hall. Following his graduation, he worked on short stories and his first novel, the latter of which was published in 1976 under the title *A Piece of My Heart.* It was a tale of an Arkansas drifter and a Chi-

cago law student whose paths cross on an uncharted island deep in the Mississippi delta. Numerous reviewers praised Ford for his skillful evocation of the South and its people. "Faulknerian in setting and atmosphere, the novel reveals a writer with his own cadence and tone," observed Nolan Miller in *Antioch Review.*

Writing in the *New York Times Book Review,* novelist Larry McMurtry also raised comparisons between Ford and William Faulkner, but they were unfavorable. "If the vices this novel shares with its many little Southern cousins could be squeezed into one word, the word would be neo-Faulknerism. It reads like the worst, rather than the best, of Faulkner. . . . Portentousness, overwriting, pronouns drifting toward a shore only dimly seen, a constant backward tilt toward a past that hasn't the remotest causal influence on what is actually happening, plus a more or less constant tendency to equate eloquence with significance: these are the familiar qualities in which Mr. Ford's narrative abounds." Still, McMurty acknowledged that he saw a great deal of promise in Ford's first work, and concluded: "One would hope that . . . these vices won't prove incurable. [Ford's] minor characters are vividly drawn, and his ear is first-rate. If he can weed his garden of some of the weeds and cockleburrs of his tradition, it might prove very fertile."

Ford himself was very impatient with the whole subject of "Faulknerism," and, in fact, with any attempt to categorize his writing as being part of the Southern tradition—or any other school of writing, for that matter. "Personally, I think there is no such thing as Southern writing or Southern literature or Southern ethos, and I'm frankly sick of the whole subject," he declared in *Harper's.* "Categorization (women's writing, gay writing, Illinois writing) inflicts upon art exactly what art strives at its best never to inflict on itself: arbitrary and irrelevant limits, shelter from the widest consideration and judgment, exclusion from general excellence. When writing achieves the level of great literature, of great art (even good art), categories go out the window. William Faulkner, after all, was not a great Southern writer: he was a great writer who wrote about the South."

Ford went even farther south—to Mexico—for the setting of his second novel, *The Ultimate Good Luck.* It was the tale of a Vietnam veteran who, in an attempt to reclaim the affections of his ex-girlfriend, journeys to Mexico to rescue her brother from prison, where he is being held for his part in a drug deal. Gilberto Perez panned the book in the *Hudson Review,* writing that it "calls to mind a cheap action picture in which hastily collaborating hacks didn't quite manage to put a story together"; but *Newsweek* reviewer Walter Clemons differed sharply in his assessment, calling *The Ultimate Good Luck* "a tighter, more efficient book [than *A Piece of My Heart*], and a good one." Clemons did feel that Ford had "jimmied himself into the confines of the existentialist thriller with a conspicuous sacrifice of his robust gift for comedy," and noted his belief that the author had "larger capabilities" than those manifested in *The Ultimate Good Luck,* but he nonetheless declared that "sentence by sentence, *The Ultimate Good Luck* is the work of a formidably talented novelist." Toronto *Globe & Mail* reviewer Douglas Hill was even more enthusiastic, crediting Ford with creating "a thriller that is also a love story, and at its core a meditation upon the precariousness and impotence of post-Vietnam U.S. values."

The total sales of *A Piece of My Heart* and *The Ultimate Good Luck* combined were under 12,000 copies, but Ford's reputation and popularity soared with the publication of his third book, *The Sportswriter,* which sold more than 60,000 copies. Described by James Wood in the London *Times* as "a desperately moving and important book, at once tremulous and tough," *The Sportswriter* is narrated by its protagonist, Frank Bascombe. Bascombe is "deceptively amiable, easygoing and sweet natured," reports Clemons. "As he tells his story in a chipper, uncomplaining tone, we gradually learn that he's a damaged man who's retreated into cushioned, dreamy detachment to evade grief and disappointment." Once a promising novelist and short-story writer, Bascombe abandoned the difficulties of creating fiction for the simpler, more immediate gratifications of sports reporting and suburban life in New Jersey. The death of his son brings on a spiritual crisis he tries to avoid, distracting himself with extramarital affairs that eventually lead his wife to divorce him.

Although he continually asserts his happiness, Bascombe "asserts so hard that we are made to feel the hollowness," explained *Los Angeles Times* book critic Richard Eder. "Negation by assertion is the narrative's central device, in fact, giving it a flatness and a dead tone." Eder explained that "the point of 'The Sportswriter' is not the plot, but the quality of thought and feeling with which the narrator assays his life." The reviewer found it to be "a dull point" because, in his opinion, "Bascombe is not very nice and not very interesting." Clemons concurred that Bascombe's behavior was often "less than admirable," but in his view this increased Ford's literary achievement, for "only a scrupulously honest novelist could make us sympathetic to such an unheroic nature. Ford makes us feel we're more like Bascombe than we often care to admit." *New York Times* reviewer Michiko Kakutani, called the novel "powerful," and noted that while Bascombe's monologue was occasionally "long winded and overly meditative . . . his voice, as rendered by Mr. Ford, is so pliant and persuasive that we are insistently drawn into his story. . . . We come to see Frank not only as he sees himself (hurt, alienated, resigned to a future of diminishing returns) but also as he

must appear to others—essentially kind and decent, but also wary, passive and unwilling to embrace the real possibilities for happiness that exist around him."

"*The Sportswriter* . . . established a glittering reputation. The stories in *Rock Springs* confirm it," asserted a *Time* reviewer in his evaluation of Ford's first collection of short stories. Set mostly in Montana, the stories in *Rock Springs* tell of characters in transit, moving from one town or one way of life to another. The book elicited raves from most reviewers. "If the term 'perfect' still means 'thoroughly accomplished,' then *Rock Springs* is a perfect book," said Manguel. The *New York Times*' Michiko Kakutani, too, found the collection to be an impressive work. "Mr. Ford has managed to find a wholly distinctive narrative voice . . . a voice that can move effortlessly between neat, staccato descriptions and rich, lyrical passages. . . . [His] stories stand as superb examples of the storyteller's craft, providing us with both the pleasures of narrative and the sad wisdom of art." Kakutani pronounced enthusiastically: "This volume should confirm his emergence as one of the most compelling and eloquent storytellers of his generation."

Ford returned to the novel with 1990's *Wildlife.* Describing the inner workings of the Brinson family, the novel uses the central metaphor of a raging forest fire to symbolizes the uncontrolled forces sweeping through the family. Reviewers were divided in their assessment of this work. Jonathan Yardley, reviewing *Wildlife* for the *Washington Post,* was not pleased with the way the characters smoothed "each other's passage through life with pearls of pop-psychological wisdom" or with the abundance of metaphors in the narrative. "Like a puppy with a slipper, Ford sinks his teeth into those metaphors, shakes them all over the place and refuses to let them go," noted Yardley. Victoria Glendinning commented in the London *Times* that "there is something obsessional and over-tidy in the jigsaw neatness of his writing, his interlocking themes and images, his modest conclusions," but she allowed that the story is "beautifully made" and noted that Ford "has far more to teach Europeans about ordinary American life and the American psyche than have the flashier East Coast novelists."

The controversy and varied responses to Ford's work are the proof of its worth, according to Toronto *Globe & Mail* contributor Trevor Ferguson, who rated *Wildlife* "a superb novel." Ferguson concluded: "[The novel] is also, like its characters and like its vision of America, strangely contradictory—at once affirmative and self-limiting. Applaud or berate him as he assumes a position in the front rank of American letters, Ford and his stylistic decisions deserve heated debate."

BIOGRAPHICAL/CRITICAL SOURCES:

BOOKS

Contemporary Literary Criticism, Volume 46, Gale, 1988.

PERIODICALS

Antioch Review, winter, 1977, p. 124.
Boston Globe, October 19, 1987.
Chicago Tribune Book World, April 19, 1981.
Globe & Mail (Toronto), July 18, 1987; October 3, 1987; July 7, 1990.
Harper's, August, 1986, pp. 35, 42-43.
Hudson Review, winter, 1981-82, pp. 606-620.
Los Angeles Times, March 12, 1986.
Los Angeles Times Book Review, October 30, 1988, p. 10; June 30, 1991, p. 14.
National Review, November 12, 1976, pp. 1240-1241.
Newsweek, May 11, 1981, pp. 89-90; April 7, 1986, p. 82.
New York Review of Books, April 24, 1986, pp. 38-39.
New York Times, February 26, 1986, p. C21; September 20, 1987; April 10, 1988; June 1, 1990.
New York Times Book Review, October 24, 1976, p. 16; May 31, 1981, p. 13, 51; March 23, 1986, p. 14.
Publishers Weekly, May 18, 1990, pp. 66-67.
Time, November 16, 1987, p. 89.
Times (London), August 28, 1986; June 11, 1987; June 20, 1987; July 11, 1987; May 5, 1988; August 9, 1990.
Washington Post, June 20, 1990.
Washington Post Book World, February 20, 1977, p. N3; March 30, 1986, p. 3.*

—*Sketch by Joan Goldsworthy*

*   *   *

FORD, Thomas R(obert) 1923-

PERSONAL: Born June 24, 1923, in Lake Charles, LA; son of Gervais W. (a school superintendent) and Alma (Weil) Ford; married Harriet Lowrey (a librarian), August 13, 1949; children: Margaret Erin, Janet Patricia, Mark Lowrey, Charlotte Elizabeth. *Education:* Louisiana State University, B.S., 1946, M.A., 1948; Vanderbilt University, Ph.D., 1951.

ADDRESSES: Home—1107 Eldemere Rd., Lexington, KY 40502. *Office*—Department of Sociology, University of Kentucky, Lexington, KY 40506.

CAREER: Louisiana State University, Baton Rouge, instructor in sociology, 1948-49; University of Alabama, Tuscaloosa, assistant professor of sociology, 1950-53; U.S. Air Force Personnel and Training and Research Center, Maxwell Air Force Base, AL, statistical analyst in demography, 1953-56; University of Kentucky, Lexington, KY, member of faculty, 1956-60, professor of sociology,

1960-90, professor emeritus, 1990—, chairman of department, 1966-70, director of Center for Developmental Change, 1975-90. Southern Appalachian Studies, Inc., research director, 1957-62; President's National Advisory Committee on Rural Poverty, member, 1966-67; Population Council to Colombian Association of Medical Faculties, Bogota, Colombia, resident representative and senior advisor, 1970-72. *Military service:* U.S. Army Air Forces, 1943-45; became first lieutenant; received Air Medal with six oak leaf clusters.

MEMBER: International Rural Sociology Association (secretary, 1976-80), American Association for the Advancement of Science, American Sociological Association, Population Association of America, Rural Sociological Society (president, 1972-73), Southern Sociological Society (president, 1976-77), Southern Demographic Association.

AWARDS, HONORS: Guggenheim fellow, 1962; Fulbright research grant, Costa Rica, 1988-89; named distinguished professor, University of Kentucky, 1980.

WRITINGS:

Man and Land in Peru, University of Florida Press, 1955.
(Editor) *The Southern Appalachian Region: A Survey,* University Press of Kentucky (Lexington, KY), 1962.
Health and Demography in Kentucky, University Press of Kentucky, 1964.
(Editor) *The Revolutionary Theme in Contemporary America,* University Press of Kentucky, 1966.
(Editor with Gordon F. Dejong) *Social Demography,* Prentice-Hall, 1970.
(Editor) *Rural U. S. A.: Persistence and Change,* Iowa State University Press (Ames, IA), 1978.
(Editor with Joseph S. Vandiver and Man Singh Das) *A Legacy of Knowledge: Sociological Contributions of T. Lynn Smith,* Vikas Publishing House (Sahibabad, India), 1980.

Contributor to *Human Biology, Journal for the Scientific Study of Religion, Review of Religious Research, Rural Sociology,* and *Social Forces.*

WORK IN PROGRESS: Research on population change in Kentucky.

*   *   *

FOX, John
See TODD, John M(urray)

FOX, Renee C(laire) 1928-

PERSONAL: Born February 15, 1928, in New York, NY; daughter of Paul Fred and Henrietta (Gold) Fox. *Education:* Smith College, A.B. (summa cum laude), 1949; Harvard University, Ph.D., 1954.

ADDRESSES: Home—135 South 19th St., Philadelphia, PA 19103-4911. *Office*—Department of Sociology, University of Pennsylvania, Philadelphia, PA 19174.

CAREER: Columbia University, New York City, Bureau of Applied Social Research, research assistant, 1953-55, research associate, 1955-58; Barnard College, lecturer, 1955-58, assistant professor, 1958-64, associate professor of sociology, 1964-66; Universite Officielle du Congo, Lubumbashi, Congo, visiting professor of sociology, 1965; Harvard University, Cambridge, MA, lecturer in sociology, 1967-69, research fellow, Center for International Affairs, 1967-68, research associate, Program on Technology and Society, 1968-71; Sir George Williams University, Montreal, Quebec, visiting professor, summer 1968; University of Pennsylvania, Philadelphia, professor of sociology in departments of psychiatry and medicine, 1969—, Annenberg professor of social sciences, 1978—, chair of sociology department, 1972-78; Phi Beta Kappa visiting scholar, 1973-75; Katholieke Universiteir, Leuven, Belgium, visiting professor, 1976-77; University of Liege, Belgium, maitre de cours, 1976-77; Smith College, William Allen Neilson professor, 1980; Harvard University School of Medicine and Radcliffe College, Fae Golden Kass lecturer, 1983; Medical College of Pennsylvania/College of Physicians, Philadelphia, PA, Kate Hard Mead lecturer, 1990; Rush-Presbyterian-St. Luke's Medical Center, Chicago, IL, Lori Ann Roscetti Memorial lecturer, 1990; Women's Center, University of Missouri, Kansas City, MO, visiting scholar, 1990.

Scientific adviser, Centre de Recherches Sociologiques, Kinshasa, Congo, 1963-67, and Centre de Documentation et de Recherches, National School of Law and Administration, Kinshasa, 1965-66; member of board of directors, Institute for Intercultural Studies, New York City, and Institute of Society, Ethics and Life Sciences, Hastings-on-Hudson, NY, 1969—; vice chair, Social Science Research Council, 1971-74; member of board of clinical scholars program, Robert Wood Johnson Foundation, 1974-80; member of technical board, Milbank Memorial Fund, 1979-85; member of board, Medicine in the Public Interest, 1979—; member of President's Commission on the Study of Ethical Problems in Medicine and Biomedical and Behavioral Research, 1979-81; member of Overseers Committee to visit university health services, Harvard College, 1979-86; trustee, Russell Sage Foundation, 1981-87; director, human qualities of medicine program, James Picker Foundation, 1980-83; director d'Etudes Associe, Ecole des Hautes Etudes en Sciences Sociales, Paris, summer 1989; vice chair, Acadia Institute, 1990—.

MEMBER: American Academy of Arts and Sciences (fellow; director, 1977-80; chair of section K, 1986-87), American Association of University Professors, American Association of University Women, American Sociological Association (representative to Social Science Research Council, 1970-73; member of council, 1973-76 and 1979-81; chairman of medical sociology section, 1974-75; vice president, 1980-81), American Board of Medical Specialists, African Studies Association (fellow), Association of American Medical Colleges, Institute of Sociology, Ethics and Life Sciences (founder and governor), Institute of Intercultural Studies (assistant secretary, 1969-78; secretary, 1979-81, 1989—; vice president, 1987-89), National Academy of Science (Institute of Medicine, elected member, 1973; member of council, 1979-82), Social Science Research Council (past vice president and director), Society for the Scientific Study of Religion, Eastern Sociological Society (vice president, 1973-74; president, 1976-77), New York Academy of Sciences, Phi Beta Kappa (senate, 1982-87).

AWARDS, HONORS: Belgian-American Educational Foundation fellow, 1960-61; Guggenheim fellow, 1962; Social Science Research Council grant, 1964-65; E. Harris Harbison Gifted Teaching Award, Danforth Foundation, 1970; M.A., University of Pennsylvania, 1971; D.Sc., Medical College of Pennsylvania, 1974; L.H.D., Smith College, 1975; Radcliffe Graduate Society medal, 1977; Sc.D., St. Joseph's College, 1978; honorary doctorate degree, Katholieke Universiteir, 1978; Wilson Center, Smithsonian Institution fellow, 1987-88; L.H.D., La Salle University, 1988; Lindback Foundation award for teaching, University of Pennsylvania, 1989; D.Sc., Hahnemman University, 1991.

WRITINGS:

Experiment Perilous: Physicians & Patients Facing the Unknown, Free Press (New York City), 1959.

(With Willy De Craemer) *The Emerging Physician: A Sociological Approach to the Development of a Congolese Medical Profession,* Hoover Institution (Stanford, CA), 1968.

(With Kenneth Ewart Boulding, Harrison Brown and Edward Edelson) *Science, Development and Human Values* (sound recording), American Association for the Advancement of Science (Washington, DC), 1973.

(With Judith P. Swazey) *The Courage to Fail: A Social View of Transplantation and Dialysis,* University of Chicago Press (Chicago, IL), 1974, revised edition, 1978.

Essays in Medical Sociology: Journeys into the Field, Wiley (New York City), 1979.

(Special editor) *The Social Meaning of Death,* American Academy of Political and Social Science (Philadelphia, PA), 1980.

The Sociology of Medicine: A Participant Observer's View, Prentice Hall (Englewood Cliffs, NJ), 1989.

(With Swazey) *Spare Parts: Organ Replacement in American Society,* Oxford University Press (New York City), 1992.

In the Belgian Chateau: The Spirit and Culture of a European People in the Age of Change, Ivan R. Dee (Chicago), 1994.

Contributor to books, including *The Student Physician,* edited by Robert K. Merton and others, Harvard University Press (Cambridge, MA), 1957; *The Psychological Basis of Medical Practice,* edited by Harold I. Lief and others, Harper (New York), 1963; *Sociologists at Work,* edited by Philip E. Hammond, Basic Books (New York), 1964; and *Experimentation with Human Subjects,* edited by Paul A. Freund, Braziller (New York), 1970. Contributor to *International Encyclopedia of the Social Sciences* and to medical and other journals. Associate editor, *American Sociological Review,* 1963-66; regional editor, *Social Science and Medicine,* 1968-69, associate editor, 1969—; member of editorial board, *Journal of Medical Education,* 1971-74; member of editorial advisory board, *Encyclopedia of Bioethics,* 1973—, *Science,* 1982—, *Technology in Society,* 1982-83, *Men and Medicine,* and *Journal of Medicine and Philosophy;* member of editorial committee, *Annual Review of Sociology,* 1975-80; member of editorial board, *Bibliography of Bioethics,* 1979—, *Culture, Medicine and Psychiatry,* 1980-86, and *Journal of the American Medical Association,* 1981—; associate editor, *Journal of Health and Social Behavior,* 1985-87.

*   *   *

FRANCIS, Roy G. 1919-

PERSONAL: Born December 25, 1919, in Portland, OR; son of Carl and Edla M. (Olson) Francis; married Lillie Griffith McCormick, December 16, 1950; children: Roy G., Virginia Marr. *Education:* Linfield College, A.B., 1946; University of Oregon, M.A., 1948; University of Wisconsin, Ph.D., 1950; Harvard University, fellowship in mathematics, 1952-53. *Politics:* Democrat.

ADDRESSES: Home—11019 Saginaw Dr., Temple Terrace, FL 33617. *Office*—University of South Florida, Tampa, FL 33620.

CAREER: University of Wisconsin, Madison, acting instructor, 1949-50; Tulane University, New Orleans, LA, assistant professor and research associate, 1950-52; University of Minnesota, Minneapolis, started as assistant

professor, became professor of sociology and statistics, 1952-66; University of Wisconsin—Milwaukee, dean and Brittingham professor of sociology, 1966-74; University of Southern Florida, chairperson and professor of sociology, 1974-93, professor emeritus, 1993—. *Military service:* U.S. Army Air Forces, 1942-45; became staff sergeant; received Unit Citation with oak leaf cluster, eleven battle stars.

MEMBER: American Sociological Association, American Association of University Professors, American Civil Liberties Union, Midwest Sociological Society (consulting editor, *Sociological Quarterly;* president, 1969), Southern Sociological Society, Town and Gown.

AWARDS, HONORS: Social Science Research Council fellowship in mathematics, 1952-53.

WRITINGS:

(With others) *An Introduction to Social Research,* Stackpole (Harrisburg, PA), 1954, revised edition, Appleton-Century-Crofts (East Norwalk, CT), 1967.

(With R. Stone) *Service and Procedure in Bureaucracy,* University of Minnesota Press (Minneapolis, MN), 1957.

(With Thomas C. McCormick) *Research Methods in Behavioral Science,* Harper (New York City), 1958.

(Editor) *The Population Ahead,* University of Minnesota Press, 1958.

The Predictive Process, University of Puerto Rico Press (Rio Piedras, PR), 1960.

The Rhetoric of Science, University of Minnesota Press, 1961.

Beginning Social Statistics, Burgess (Minneapolis, MN), 1965.

(Author of introduction) E. A. Ross, *Social Control,* Johnson Reprint (New York City), 1970.

Crumbling Walls, Schenkman (Cambridge, MA), 1972.

Sociology in a Different Key: Essays in Non-Linear Sociology, Cap & Gown (Houston, TX), 1983.

(Author of foreword) Florian Znaniecki, *Cultural Reality,* Cap & Gown, 1983.

Editor of college textbook series; translator of Swedish poetry; writer of articles in professional journals, material for radio programs and educational television and filmmaking in the social sciences.*

*   *   *

FREDERICKS, Frohm
See KERNER, Fred

FREUND, Paul A(braham) 1908-1992

PERSONAL: Born February 16, 1908, in St. Louis, MO; died of cancer, February 5, 1992, in Cambridge, MA; son of Charles J. and Hulda (Arenson) Freund. *Education:* Washington University, St. Louis, MO, A.B., 1928; Harvard University, LL.B., 1931, S.J.D., 1932. *Religion:* Jewish.

ADDRESSES: Home—1010 Memorial Dr., Cambridge, MA 02138.

CAREER: Constitutional scholar, educator, and author. Office of Mr. Justice Brandeis, United States Supreme Court, Washington, DC, law clerk, 1932-33; U.S. Treasury and Reconstruction Finance Corporation, Washington, DC, attorney, 1933-35; U.S. Department of Justice, Washington, DC, special assistant to attorney general, 1935-39, 1942-46; Harvard University, Cambridge, MA, lecturer, 1939-40, professor of law, 1940-50, Charles Stebbins Fairchild professor, 1950-57, Royall professor, 1957-58, Carl M. Loeb University professor, 1958-76, professor emeritus, 1976-92. Cambridge University, Cambridge, England, Pitt Professor of American History and Institutions, 1957-58. Jefferson lecturer, National Endowment for the Humanities, 1975. Member of Judicial Nominating Commission, First Circuit. Member of Center for Advanced Studies in Behavioral Sciences, 1969-70.

MEMBER: American Academy of Arts and Sciences (fellow; former president), American Jewish Committee, American Judiciary Society, American Law Institute, American Philosophical Society, Massachusetts Historical society, Phi Beta Kappa, Phi Sigma Alpha, Harvard Society Fellows, St. Botolph Club (Boston).

AWARDS, HONORS: LL.D., Columbia University, 1954, University of Louisville, 1956, Washington University, 1956, University of Chicago, 1961, Boston University, 1964, Queens University (Ontario), 1970, Brown University, 1972, Yale University, 1972, Brandeis University, 1974, Williams College, 1974, Clark University, 1977, Harvard University, 1977, University of Bologna, 1981, Georgetown University, 1983; M.A., Cambridge University, 1957; Litt D., Cornell College, 1968, Bates College, 1973, Temple University, 1973, Yeshiva University, 1975; Scribes Award, 1969, for *On Law and Justice;* research award, American Bar Foundation, 1973; Learned Hand award, Federal Bar Council, 1978; Law award, Thomas Jefferson Memorial Foundation, 1979; Henry J. Friendly award, American Law Institute, 1989.

WRITINGS:

On Understanding the Supreme Court, Little (Boston, MA), 1949.

(Coeditor) *Constitutional Law: Cases and Other Problems,* Little, 1954, supplements, 1965, 1966, 4th edition, 1977.

The Supreme Court of the U.S., Its Business, Purposes and Performance, World Publishing (Cleveland, OH), 1961.

(Coauthor) *Religion and the Public Schools,* Harvard University Press (Cambridge, MA), 1965.

On Law and Justice, Belknap Press of Harvard University Press, 1968.

(Editor) *Experimentation with Human Subjects,* Braziller (New York City), 1970, edition with foreword by Donald Gould, Allen and Unwin (London), 1972.

(With Charles M. Whelan) *Legal and Constitutional Problems of Public Support for Nonpublic Schools,* President's Commission on School Finance (Washington, DC), 1971.

On Understanding the Supreme Court: A Series of Lectures Delivered Under the Auspices of the Julius Rosenthal Foundation at Northwestern University School of Law, in April 1949, Greenwood Press (Westport, CT), 1977.

(Senior editor with Dana L. Blatt and Norman S. Goldberg) *Casenote Legal Briefs—Constitutional Law: Adaptable to Courses Utilizing Freund, Sutherland, Howe, and Brown's Casebook on Constitutional Law,* Peter Tenen, managing editor, Jim Rosenthal, Terry Molloy and Sally Molloy, staff writers, Casenotes Publishing Co. (Beverly Hills, CA), 1978.

Felix Frankfurter, Harvard Law School, 1982.

Memoir (microform), Microfilming Corp. (Sanford, NC), 1982.

Contributor to legal journals and to *Encyclopaedia Britannica* and *Encyclopedia of Social Science.* Former member of editorial board, *Daedalus.*

SIDELIGHTS: Considered a major figure in the field of constitutional law, Paul A. Freund was a governmental advisor on many issues related to the Supreme Court and constitutional amendments. He worked for the Treasury Department, the Justice Department, and served as a special assistant to the Attorney General.

OBITUARIES:

PERIODICALS

Washington Post, February 6, 1992, p. B6.*

*   *   *

FULBROOK, Mary (Jean Alexandra) 1951-

PERSONAL: Born November 28, 1951, in Cardiff, Wales; daughter of Arthur James Cochran (a professor of crystallography) and Harriett Charlotte (a criminologist; maiden name, Friedeberg) Wilson; married Julian George Holder Fulbrook (a lawyer), June 28, 1973; children: Conrad Arthur, Erica Harriett, Carl Howard. *Education:* Cambridge University, B.A., 1973, M.A., 1977; Harvard University, A.M., 1975, Ph.D., 1979. *Politics:* Labour.

ADDRESSES: Office—University College, University of London, Gower St., London WC1E GBT, England.

CAREER: University of London, London School of Economics and Political Science, England, lecturer in sociology, 1977-78; Brunel University, Uxbridge, England, lecturer, 1978-79; Cambridge University, Cambridge, England, research fellow, 1979-82; University of London, research fellow at King's College, 1982-83, lecturer in German history at University College, 1983-91, reader in German History, 1991—, director, UCL Centre for European Studies, 1992—. Member of board of governors of Great Ormond Street Hospital School for Sick Children (vice chairperson, 1979-84); mayoress of London Borough of Camden, 1985-86; chair of governors, South Camden Community School, 1992—.

MEMBER: German History Society (member of executive committee, 1981—), Association for the Study of German Politics, Royal Historical Society (fellow).

WRITINGS:

Piety and Politics: Religion and the Rise of Absolutism in England, Wuerttemberg, and Prussia, Cambridge University Press (Cambridge, England, and New York City), 1983.

A Concise History of Germany, Cambridge University Press, 1990.

The Divided Nation: A History of Germany, 1918-1990, Fontana (London), 1991, Oxford University Press (New York City), 1992.

The Two Germanies 1945-1990: Problems of Interpretation, Humanities Press International (Atlantic Highlands, NJ), 1992.

(Editor) *National Histories and European History,* UCL Press (London), 1993, Westview Press (Boulder, CO), 1993.

Anatomy of a Dictatorship: Inside the GDR, 1949-89, Oxford University Press, 1995.

Contributor to various scholarly journals. Joint editor and founder of *German History,* 1984-94.

Several of Fulbrook's works have been translated into Italian, Hungarian, and Spanish.

WORK IN PROGRESS: A book on history and national identity in Germany since Hitler, to be published by Polity Press.

SIDELIGHTS: Daughter of a refugee from Nazi Germany and a conscientious objector/pacifist from Canada, Mary Fulbrook is intrigued by the complexities of German history. Fulbrook told *CA:* "Peculiarities can only be adequately comprehended by a wide-ranging, often expansive approach to social, political and cultural history."

BIOGRAPHICAL/CRITICAL SOURCES:

PERIODICALS

Canadian Journal of History, August, 1985.
History, March, 1985.
History Today, September, 1984.
International History Review, October, 1985.
Journal of British Studies, April, 1985.
Journal of Ecclesiastical History, January, 1985.
Social History, January, 1985.
Times Literary Supplement, April 6, 1984.

G

GAUR, Albertine 1932-

PERSONAL: Born April 9, 1932, in St. Poelten, Austria; daughter of Otto and Leopoldine (Vilaus) Kasser; married Ganesh Dutt Gaur, August, 1957 (died, 1965); married Denis Evelyn Hobbins Henning (an army officer and woodcarver), December, 1970. *Education:* University of Vienna, Dr.Phil., 1955; attended London School of Oriental and African Studies, London, 1956-58. *Avocational interests:* "Have become active in local politics. Feel it is time to make an active contribution."

ADDRESSES: Home—4 Kingswood Close, Surbiton, Surrey KT6 6DZ England.

CAREER: Lecturer in anthropology at Banasthali Vidyapith University of Jaipur, 1960-62; research assistant at India Office Library and Records, 1962-63; British Museum, London, England, assistant keeper of Indian collection, 1964-73; British Library, London, curator of South Indian collection, 1973-79, deputy director of Department of Oriental Manuscripts and Printed Books, 1979-90.

MEMBER: Royal Asiatic Society (fellow), Royal Society for the Encouragement of Arts, Manufacturers, and Commerce (fellow).

WRITINGS:

Die toerichten Traeume (novel), Europaeischer Verlag (Vienna), 1956.
Catalogue of Malayalam Books in the British Museum, British Museum Publications (London), 1971.
Indian Charters on Copper Plates in the Department of Oriental Manuscripts and Printed Books, British Library (London), 1975.
Writing Materials of the East, British Library, 1979.
Second Supplementary Catalogue of Tamil Books in the British Library, British Library, 1980.
Women in India, British Library, 1980.
A History of Writing, British Library, 1985, Scribner (New York City), 1986.
Supplementary Catalogue of Kannada Books in the British Library, British Library, 1985.
(Editor) *South Asian Studies,* British Library, 1986.
(Editor with Penelope Tuson) *Women's Studies: Papers Presented at a Colloquium at the British Library, 4 April 1989,* British Library, 1990.
A History of Calligraphy, British Library, 1994.

Contributor of poems to anthologies.

WORK IN PROGRESS: Political Implications of Writing Systems; A History of Iconography; and *Notitiae Indicae,* a critical edition of Engelbert Kaempfer's "Indian Journal" covering the years 1688-89.

SIDELIGHTS: In the *Times Literary Supplement,* reviewer Nicolete Gray writes that Albertine Gaur's 1985 book, *A History of Writing,* "covers a vast subject and is full of invaluable information," including "an interesting, and in this context new, discussion of the very relevant factor of modern computer technology." According to Gray, Gaur's book treats the subject of writing from many perspectives: writing as an expression of ideas, writing as the physical act of forming letters, and writing as a system for communicating with visual symbols. Gaur analyzes a wide variety of the forms and styles of writing that have evolved in various parts of the world over the ages, and she discusses the concept of writing as "information storage."

Gaur told *CA:* "I have been writing poems ever since I can remember, first in German and later in English. To me writing a poem is an adventure of the spirit, a means of glimpsing reality through a window, normally closed. In childhood and in my early teens my favorite role models were the great travelers like Richard Burton, Claudius

Rich, and Engelbert Kaempfer, and adventure and travel writers like Karl May.

"I came to India strictly by accident. My first husband was Indian and he was one of my teachers at the School of Oriental and African Studies in London. I am afraid I developed my 'expertise' (personally I distrust this term) in Oriental manuscripts in a similar way, by taking a job, first at the India Office Library and later at the British Museum, which involved looking after South Indian books and manuscripts.

"One of the highlights of my stay in India was the two years I spent at Banasthali Vidyapith, a rural university for girls forty miles outside Jaipur. The college was run on traditional Indian lines though the girls could learn flying and horse riding on the campus on top of living in mud houses. In my free time I used to go for long walks to the surrounding villages. Many of them had never been visited by a foreign woman and the curiosity I aroused was only matched by the hospitality I received. Near the college there lived a 'criminal' tribe who, until recent laws had changed, had been professional cattle thieves. For no reason at all they honored me with the gift of friendship and when I visited them we would often sit for long hours and talk.

"The idea of the history of writing was partly prompted by an uneasy irritation about the way most people, and many scholars, too, still feel that the alphabet is the only 'proper' forms of writing that sooner or later all 'proper' forms of writing must converge towards it, and that literacy as we know it will eventually solve nearly all social problems. Personally I do not think any true understanding, or any reliable peace, can come about as long as we think that all 'good' or 'educated' people automatically feel as we do, but only by accepting, respecting, and as far as possible understanding each other's difference."

BIOGRAPHICAL/CRITICAL SOURCES:

PERIODICALS

British Book Notes, July, 1985, p. 413; June, 1987, p. 363.
Canadian Literature, spring, 1991, p. 216.
Journal of American Literature, January, 1986, p. 383.
Journal of Asian Studies, February, 1988, p. 177.
Library Journal, February 15, 1986, p. 178.
Times Literary Supplement, September 20, 1985.

*   *   *

GEDO, John E. 1927-

PERSONAL: Born November 19, 1927, in Lucenec, Slovakia; immigrated to the United States, 1941, naturalized citizen, 1947; son of Mathias Stephen (a physician) and

Anna (a homemaker; maiden name Mandl) Gedo; married Mary Mathews (an art historian), 1953; children: Paul M., Andrew L., Nicholas M. *Education:* New York University, B.A., 1946, M.D., 1951.

ADDRESSES: Home—680 North Lake Shore Dr., Apt. 1201, Chicago, IL 60611.

CAREER: Presbyterian Hospital, Chicago, IL, intern, 1951-52; University of Chicago Clinics, Chicago, resident in psychiatry, 1952-53; University of Illinois Medical Center, Chicago, resident in psychiatry, 1953-54; Michael Reese Hospital, Chicago, resident in psychiatry, 1954-55; private practice of psychiatry, 1955—. Clinical professor at University of Illinois School of Medicine, 1970-91; training analyst at Chicago Institute for Psychoanalysis, 1972-91.

MEMBER: American Psychiatric Association, American Psychoanalytic Association.

WRITINGS:

(With Arnold Goldberg) *Models of the Mind: A Psychoanalytic Theory,* University of Chicago Press (Chicago, IL), 1973.
(Editor with George H. Pollock) *Freud, the Fusion of Science and Humanism: The Intellectual History of Psychoanalysis,* International Universities Press (New York City), 1976.
Beyond Interpretation: Toward a Revised Theory for Psychoanalysis, International Universities Press, 1979, revised edition, Analytic Press (Hillsdale, NJ), 1993.
Advances in Clinical Psychoanalysis, International Universities Press, 1981.
Portraits of the Artist: Psychoanalysis of Creativity and Its Vicissitudes, Guilford (New York City), 1983.
(Editor with Pollock) *Psychoanalysis: The Vital Issues,* two volumes, International Universities Press, 1984.
Psychoanalysis and Its Discontents, Guilford Press, 1984.
Conceptual Issues in Psychoanalysis, Analytic Press, 1986.
The Mind in Disorder: Psychoanalytic Models of Pathology, Analytic Press, 1988.
The Biology of Clinical Encounters: Psychoanalysis as a Science of Mind, Analytic Press, 1991.
(With wife, Mary M. Gedo) *Perspectives on Creativity: The Biographical Method,* Ablex Publishing (Norwood, NJ), 1992.
(Editor with Arnold Wilson) *Hierarchical Concepts in Psychoanalysis,* Guilford Press, 1993.
(With Mark Gehrie) *Impasse and Innovation in Psychoanalysis,* Analytic Press, 1993.

Contributor to medical and other scholarly journals.

WORK IN PROGRESS: The Artist and the Emotional World: Creativity and Personality, Cambridge University Press; a set of professional memoirs, Analytic Press, 1997.

SIDELIGHTS: John E. Gedo told *CA:* "Although I began to write scientific articles as reports on my clinical research in psychoanalysis, over the years I became increasingly passionate about the act of writing in itself. I have gradually withdrawn from patient care and have devoted more and more time to scholarly writing. In the future, I expect to turn almost exclusively to cultural topics. At present, I am most interested in writing my memoirs."

*   *   *

GENTRY, Marshall Bruce 1953-

PERSONAL: Born July 28, 1953, in Little Rock, AR; son of Robert Bruce (an owner and manager of a grocery store) and Daisy Belle (a bookkeeper and homemaker; maiden name, Stockwell) Gentry; married Alice Friman (a poet), September 24, 1989. *Education:* University of Arkansas, Fayetteville, B.A. (with high honors), 1975; University of Chicago, A.M., 1976; University of Texas at Austin, Ph.D., 1984. *Politics:* Liberal Democrat.

ADDRESSES: Home—6312 Central Ave., Indianapolis, IN 46220. *Office*—Department of English, University of Indianapolis, 1400 East Hanna Ave., Indianapolis, IN 46227.

CAREER: Texas A & M University, College Station, visiting instructor, 1982-83, visiting assistant professor of English, 1983-84; University of Indianapolis, Indianapolis, IN, assistant professor, 1985-91, associate professor of English, 1991—.

MEMBER: Modern Language Association of America, American Literature Association, American Association of University Professors, College English Association, Flannery O'Connor Society, Society for the Study of Midwestern Literature, Society for the Study of Southern Literature, Midwest American Culture Association, Indiana College English Association, Writers' Center of Indianapolis, Phi Beta Kappa (president, Alpha Association of Indianapolis, 1994-95, member of board of directors, 1992—), Phi Kappa Phi.

WRITINGS:

Flannery O'Connor's Religion of the Grotesque, University Press of Mississippi (Jackson), 1986.
(Coeditor) *Conversations with Raymond Carver,* University Press of Mississippi, 1990.

Contributor to *Flannery O'Connor: New Perspectives,* edited by Sura Rath and Mary Ann Shaw, University of Georgia Press, in press. Also contributor of articles and poetry to various periodicals, including *Contemporary Literature, CEA Critic, Flannery O'Connor Bulletin, Kansas Quarterly, Modern Fiction Studies, Realist Distances:*

Flannery O'Connor Revisited, Arts Indiana, and *Southern Quarterly;* editor of *The Flying Island, Volume 2,* the literary review of the Writers' Center of Indiana, 1993-94; member of editorial board, *Flannery O'Connor Bulletin,* 1993—.

WORK IN PROGRESS: Research on contemporary American fiction, especially the work of E. L. Doctorow.

SIDELIGHTS: Marshall Bruce Gentry once told *CA:* "In *Flannery O'Connor's Religion of the Grotesque* I argue that most O'Connor characters unconsciously use their grotesquerie to bring about their redemption. In the process they typically rival the O'Connor narrator for authority. Rather than equating the O'Connor narrator with O'Connor herself, I believe her narrators voice a religious conventionality that O'Connor's works reject.

"My work on contemporary fiction grows out of questions about gender in O'Connor. In my work on E. L. Doctorow I am interested in the politics of gender as they relate to questions of point of view."

Gentry more recently told *CA:* "Having fallen madly in love with an excellent poet and having started to try my own hand at writing poems, I am very interested in trying to write the kind of literary criticism that creative writers will not ridicule. I continue to take personally the works of Flannery O'Connor, but I'm also interested in the broader subject of women's voices in fiction by men."

*   *   *

GERSHON, Karen
See TRIPP, Karen

*   *   *

GILLIS, Everett A(lden) 1914-1989

PERSONAL: Born March 4, 1914, in Cameron, MO; died January 25, 1989; son of Earle Adrien (a postal clerk) and Pearle (Owens) Gillis; married Lizzie Mae Allen, August 14, 1943 (died May 25, 1978); married Ona Louise Hobson Cline, November 18, 1978. *Education:* Texas Christian University, B.A., 1936, M.A., 1939; University of Texas, Ph.D., 1948; University of California, Los Angeles, postdoctoral study, 1955-56. *Politics:* Republican. *Religion:* Baptist.

ADDRESSES: Home and office—3209 26th St., Lubbock, TX 79410.

CAREER: University of Texas at Austin, instructor in English, 1940-42; Texas College of Arts and Industries (now Texas A&I University), Kingsville, assistant professor of

English, 1947-49; Texas Tech University, Lubbock, associate professor, 1949-55, professor of English, 1956-79, professor emeritus, beginning 1979, chairman of department, 1964-69. Editor and publisher, Pisces Press. *Military service:* U.S. Army, Field Artillery, 1942-46; served in Pacific theater.

MEMBER: International Poetry Society, Modern Language Association of America (life member), National Council of Teachers of English, Poetry Society (London), South Central Modern Language Association, Southwestern American Literature Association (president, 1970), Texas Association of College Teachers, Poetry Society of Texas (life member; vice-president, 1951; councillor, beginning 1952), Texas Folklore Society (vice-president, 1960; president, 1961), Texas Institute of Letters, National Writers Club.

AWARDS, HONORS: Poetry Society of Texas, Alamo Prize, 1945, for "Growth of the Violin," Texas Prize, 1946, for "Parson John," and 1951, for "Ballad of Captain Bill McDonald," Critics Award Prize, 1947, for "Speech beyond Speech," and 1948, for "The Hunter: An Autumn Metaphor," Portrait Poem Prize, 1952, for "The Water Finder," Old South Prize, 1953, for "Estevanico the Black Sees Cibola," 1958, for "Seascape: Santa Monica Palisades," and 1973, for "The Door," and All State Prize, 1955, for "Memories"; Silver Spur Award, Texas Border Poets, 1949, for "Portrait of a Professor"; Ford Foundation fellowship, 1955-56.

WRITINGS:

Hello the House! (poems), Kaleidograph, 1944.
Who Can Retreat? (poems), Wagon & Star (Inglewood, CA), 1944.
Sunrise in Texas (poems), Fotolith, 1949.
Angles of the Wind (poems), Kaleidograph, 1954.
Sing Your America: Discussion Leader's Guide, Adult Education Department, Texas Tech University (Lubbock, TX), 1954.
(With Joseph Doggett and Rosa Bludworth) *A College Forum* (textbook), Odyssey, 1963.
Ballads for Texas Heroes (songs; music by John Q. Anderson), privately printed, 1963.
Oliver La Farge, Steck, 1967.
"The Waste Land" as Grail Romance: Eliot's Use of the Medieval Grail Legends, Texas Tech University Press, 1974.
Heart Singly Vowed (poems), Nortex, 1980.
South by West: A Galaxy of Southwestern and Western Scenes and Portraits (poems), Pisces Press (Lubbock), 1981.
Far beyond Distance (poems), Pisces Press, 1981.
Goldie (fiction), illustrations by Paul Gillis, Pisces Press, 1982.

Capsuled in Summer (poems), Pisces Press, 1985.
(Editor with Kenneth W. Davis) *Black Cats, Hoot Owls and Water Witches: Beliefs, Superstitions, and Sayings from Texas,* illustrations by Teel Sale, University of North Texas Press (Denton, TX), 1989.

Composer of choral work "West Texas Suite," commissioned by Lubbock Public Schools. Contributor to books, including *Builders of the Southwest,* edited by S. V. Connor, Texas Tech University Press, 1959; *Handbook of Texas,* Texas State Historical Society, 1967; *American Literature: A Critical Survey,* edited by Thomas Daniel Young and Ronald Edward Fine, American Book Co., 1968; and *Classical Mythology in Twentieth Century Thought and Literature,* edited by Wendell M. Aycock and Theodore M. Klein, Texas Tech University Press, 1980. Contributor to literature journals, including *South Atlantic Quarterly, Prairie Schooner, Western Folklore, Southwestern American Literature, Descant,* and *Publications of the Modern Language Association.*

WORK IN PROGRESS: Gillis was working on studies of cowboy songs and a five-volume study of the writings of T. S. Eliot.

BIOGRAPHICAL/CRITICAL SOURCES:

BOOKS

Anderson, John Q., Edwin W. Gaston, Jr., and James W. Lee, editors, *Southwestern American Literature: A Bibliography,* Swallow Press (Athens, OH), 1980.
Green, Lola Beth, and Dahlia Terrell, editors, *Gold Land: A Bibliography,* Texas Tech University Press, 1970.*

[Death date provided by Louise Gillis.]

*   *   *

GLICK, Paula Brown
See BROWN, Paula

*   *   *

GOLDSTEIN, Melvyn C. 1938-

PERSONAL: Born February 8, 1938, in New York, NY; son of Harold and Rae (Binen) Goldstein; children: Andre. *Education:* University of Michigan, B.A., 1959, M.A., 1960; University of Washington, Seattle, Ph.D., 1968.

ADDRESSES: Home—2258 Grandview Ave., Cleveland Heights, OH 44106. *Office*—Department of Anthropology, Mather Memorial, Case Western Reserve University, Cleveland, OH 44106.

CAREER: Case Western Reserve University, Cleveland, Ohio, assistant professor, 1968-71, associate professor,

1971-76, professor of anthropology, 1976-91, J. R. Harkness Professor, 1991—, chair of department, beginning 1976.

MEMBER: International Mountain Society, American Anthropological Association, Society of Applied Anthropology, Society of Medical Anthropology, Association for Anthropology and Gerontology, Nepal Studies Association.

AWARDS, HONORS: Grants from American Council of Learned Societies, 1973-74, National Institutes of Health, 1976-77, 1980-82, National Endowment for the Humanities, 1980-82, 1982-84, 1989-92, 1992-94, U.S. Department of Education, 1980-82, 1986-87, 1994-97, National Geographic Society, 1980-81, 1986-87, Smithsonian Institution, 1981-83, and National Academy of Sciences China Program, 1985, 1986-87; Joseph Levinson Prize Honorable Mention, Association of Asian Studies, 1989, for *A History of Modern Tibet, 1913-1951: The Demise of the Lamaist State.*

WRITINGS:

Modern Spoken Tibetan: Lhasa Dialect, University of Washington Press (Seattle), 1970.
Modern Literary Tibetan: A Grammar and Reader, University of Illinois Press (Champaign), 1973.
Tibetan English Dictionary of Modern Tibetan, Ratner Pustak Bhandar, 1975.
English Tibetan Dictionary of Modern Tibetan, University of California Press (Berkeley), 1984.
A History of Modern Tibet, 1913-1951: The Demise of the Lamaist State, University of California Press, 1989.
Nomads of Western Tibet: The Survival of a Way of Life, University of California Press, 1990.
Essentials of Modern Literary Tibetan: A Reading Course and Reference Grammar, University of California Press, 1991.
The Changing World of Mongolia's Nomads, University of California Press, 1994.

Contributor to anthropology journals. Editor of *Journal of Cross-Cultural Gerontology.*

*   *   *

GORMAN, Ginny
    See ZACHARY, Hugh

*   *   *

GRAHAM, Lawrence S(herman)   1936-

PERSONAL: Born July 12, 1936, in Daytona Beach, FL; son of Marion Webster (a savings and loan officer) and

Mary Virginia (Sherman) Graham; married Jane Sharp Merrell (a real estate broker), June 8, 1961; children: Merrell Anne, Virginia Lee, Lauren Sherman, Katherine McDonald. *Education:* Duke University, B.A., 1958; University of Wisconsin, M.A., 1961; University of Florida, Ph.D., 1965. *Politics:* Independent. *Religion:* Episcopalian.

ADDRESSES: Home—3404 Mt. Barker Dr., Austin, TX 78731-5725. *Office*—Department of Government, University of Texas, Austin, TX 78712-1037.

CAREER: University of Texas, Austin, assistant professor, 1965-69, associate professor, 1969-74, professor of political science, 1974—, associate director, Institute of Latin American Studies, 1975-80. Adviser for Institute of Public Administration in Lima, Peru, 1967-68. Exchange scientist, National Academy of Sciences with Romanian Academy, 1977-78, with Yugoslav Academy, 1980, and with Polish Academy, 1983. Director of performance management project, National Association of Schools of Public Affairs and Administration, 1987-89. Resident scholar, Rockefeller Foundation's Study and Conference Center, Bellagio, Italy, 1993.

MEMBER: International Political Science Association, American Society for Public Administration, American Political Science Association, Latin American Studies Association.

AWARDS, HONORS: Calouste Gulbenkian Foundation research award, 1971, 1972, 1979-80, and 1988; International Research and Exchanges Board, Poland, grant, 1984; Ford Foundation grant, Nicaragua, 1986; Hoover Institution grant, 1988; North Atlantic Treaty Organization (NATO) research fellowship, 1993.

WRITINGS:

The Clash between Formalism and Reality in the Brazilian Civil Service (microform), University of Florida, 1965, University Microfilms International (Ann Arbor, MI), 1982.
Civil Service Reform in Brazil: Principles versus Practice, University of Texas Press (Austin), 1968.
Politics in a Mexican Community, University of Florida Press, 1968.
Mexican State Government: A Prefectural System in Action, Institute of Public Affairs, University of Texas, 1971.
(Editor with Clarence E. Thurber) *Development Administration in Latin America,* Duke University Press, 1973.
Portugal: The Decline and Collapse of an Authoritarian Order, Sage Publications (Beverly Hills, CA), 1975.

(Editor with Harry M. Makler) *Contemporary Portugal: The Revolution and Its Antecedents,* with a foreword by Juan J. Linz, University of Texas Press, 1979.

(Editor with Eliza J. Willis) *Country Risk Analysis, Brazil: Seminar Report* Institute of Latin American Studies, 1982.

Romania: A Developing Socialist State, Westview Press (Boulder, CO), 1982.

(Editor with Douglas L. Wheeler) *In Search of Modern Portugal: The Revolution and Its Consequences,* University of Wisconsin Press (Madison, WI), 1983.

(Editor with Maria K. Ciechocinska) *The Polish Dilemma: Views from Within,* Westview Press, 1987.

(Editor with Robert H. Wilson) *The Political Economy of Brazil: Public Policies in an Era of Transition,* University of Texas Press, 1990.

The State and Policy Outcomes in Latin America, Praeger (New York City), 1990.

The Portuguese Military and the State: Rethinking Transitions in Europe and Latin America, Westview Press, 1993.

Politics and Government: A Brief Introduction, Chatham House Publishers (Chatham, NJ), 3rd edition (Graham not associated with earlier editions), 1994.

Also author of pamphlets *Latin America, Illusion or Reality?: A Case for a New Analytical Framework for the Region,* Institute of Latin American Studies, University of Texas, 1974, and *Public Personnel Dilemmas in Developing Countries: The Latin American Experience,* Institute of Latin American Studies, University of Texas, 1976. Contributor of articles to American and Latin American professional journals. Consulting editor, *Latin American Research Review,* 1970-71. Member of editorial boards, *Journal of Comparative Administration,* 1971-74, *Public Administration Review,* 1973-77, and *Administration and Society,* 1974-76. Chair of publications committee, Institute of Latin American Studies University of Texas, 1973-75.

SIDELIGHTS: Lawrence S. Graham has done field work for extended periods in Brazil, Peru, Mexico, Portugal, and Romania. Graham calls himself "a teacher rather than a writer by profession, most at home with the extended essay or short monograph."

*   *   *

GRAHAM, Peter W(illiam) 1951-

PERSONAL: Born February 11, 1951, in Manchester, CO; son of Thomas William (an insurance executive) and Marion (Barrows) Graham; married Kathryn Videon (a college teacher), December 28, 1973; children: Thomas Austin, James Dominic. *Education:* Davidson College,

A.B. (cum laude), 1973; Duke University, M.A., 1974, Ph.D., 1977.

ADDRESSES: Home—208 Sunset Blvd., Blacksburg, VA 24060. *Office*—Department of English, Virginia Polytechnic Institute and State University, Blacksburg, VA 24061.

CAREER: Virginia Polytechnic Institute and State University, Blacksburg, VA, assistant professor, 1978-84, associate professor, 1984-90, professor of English, 1990—.

MEMBER: Modern Language Association of America, Phi Beta Kappa.

AWARDS, HONORS: James B. Duke fellowship, Duke University, 1973-76, for graduate study in English; Eli Lilly fellowship, University of Florida, 1977-78, for postdoctoral work in the humanities and the professions; Mellon fellowship, Duke University, 1980-81, for postdoctoral research in English.

WRITINGS:

(Editor) *Byron's Bulldog: The Letters of John Cam Hobhouse to Lord Byron,* Ohio State University Press (Columbus, OH), 1984.

(Editor) *Literature and Medicine,* Volume 4: *Psychiatry and Literature,* Johns Hopkins University Press (Baltimore, MD), 1985.

Don Juan and Regency, University Press of Virginia (Charlottesville, VA), 1990.

(Editor with Elizabeth Sewell) *Literature and Medicine,* Volume 9: *Fictive Ills: Literary Perspectives on Wounds and Diseases,* Johns Hopkins University Press, 1990.

(With Fritz Gehlschlaeger) *Articulating the Elephant Man: Joseph Merrick and His Interpreters,* Johns Hopkins University Press, 1992.

(Editor with Lilian Furst) *Disorderly Eaters: Texts in Self-Empowerment,* Pennsylvania State University (University Park, PA), 1992.

(Editor with Duncan M. Porter) *The Portable Darwin,* Viking (New York City), 1993.

Member of board of editors of *Literature and Medicine.*

BIOGRAPHICAL/CRITICAL SOURCES:

PERIODICALS

Times Literary Supplement, May 17, 1985.

*   *   *

GRANGER, Bruce Ingham 1920-

PERSONAL: Born February 28, 1920, in Philadelphia, PA; son of Percival Harkness and Caroline (Gibbons) Granger; married Rosemary Jemme, 1944; children: Percival, Erling. *Education:* Attended Deep Springs Junior College, 1938-40; Cornell University, B.A., 1942, M.A., 1943, Ph.D., 1946.

ADDRESSES: Home—944 Chautauqua Ave., Norman, OK 73069. *Office*—Department of English, University of Oklahoma, Norman, OK 73019.

CAREER: University of Wisconsin—Madison, instructor in English, 1946-50; University of Denver, Denver, CO, assistant professor, 1950-53; University of Oklahoma, Norman, associate professor, 1953-61, professor, 1961-82, professor emeritus of English, 1982—. Fulbright lecturer, University of Vienna, 1968-69.

MEMBER: Modern Language Association of America, American Association of University Professors (president, University of Oklahoma chapter, 1960-61), South Central Modern Language Association (president, 1978-79), Phi Beta Kappa (Cornell chapter, secretary, 1945-46; Oklahoma chapter, secretary-treasurer, 1964-67, president, 1976-77).

AWARDS, HONORS: American Philosophical Society, summer grants-in-aid, 1955, 1958, 1965, 1966, and 1978; National Endowment for the Humanities summer grant, 1975.

WRITINGS:

NONFICTION

Political Satire in the American Revolution, 1763-1783, Cornell University Press, 1960.
Benjamin Franklin: An American Man of Letters, Cornell University Press, 1964.
(Editor with Martha Hartzog) *The Complete Works of Washington Irving,* Volume 6: *Oldstyle/Salmagundi,* Twayne, 1977.
(Editor and compiler) *American Essay Serials from Franklin to Irving,* University of Tennessee Press (Knoxville), 1978.
(Editor) Joseph Dennie, *The Farrago,* Scholars' Facsimiles & Reprints (Delmar, NY), 1985.
(Editor, compiler, and author of introduction) John Trumbull, *The Meddler (1769-70) and the Correspondent (1770-73),* Scholars' Facsimiles & Reprints, 1985.
(Editor) *Proteus Echo (1727-28),* Scholars' Facsimiles & Reprints, 1986.

Also contributor to *American Heritage, Books Abroad,* and other professional journals.*

GRANT, Frederick C(lifton)   1891-1974

PERSONAL: Born February 2, 1891, in Beloit, WI; died July 11, 1974, in Gwynedd, PA; son of Frank Avery and Anna Lois (Jack) Grant; married Helen McQueen Hardie, June 24, 1913; children: Robert McQueen, Eleanor Jean Grant Tombs. *Education:* Attended Lawrence College, 1907-09, and Nashotah House, 1909-11; General Theological Seminary, B.D.; Western Theological Seminary (now Seabury-Western Theological Seminary), S.T.M., Th.D. *Avocational interests:* Music, travel.

CAREER: Protestant Episcopal Church, ordained deacon, 1912, priest, 1913. Served in churches in Michigan and Illinois, 1913-21; Trinity Church, Chicago, IL, rector, 1921-24; Kenyon College, Divinity School, Gambier, OH, dean of Bexley Hall, 1924-26; Berkeley Divinity School, Middletown, CT, professor and librarian, 1926-27; Seabury-Western Theological Seminary, Evanston, IL, president, 1927-38; Union Theological Seminary, New York, NY, professor of Biblical theology, 1938-59, professor emeritus, 1959-74, director of graduate studies, 1945-54. Visiting professor, University of Chicago, 1928, 1937, and 1963; Fulbright Professor, Oxford University, 1959-60. Served as one of four observers for the Anglican Communion at the Vatican Council, 1962-63; member of Episcopal Church commission on marriage and divorce, 1928-40, commission on the hymnal, and committee on the Revised Standard Version Bible, beginning 1937.

MEMBER: Society of Biblical Literature and Exigesis (president, 1934), Men's Faculty Club (Columbia University), Kilin Club (New York), Author's Club (London).

AWARDS, HONORS: Eleven honorary doctor's degrees from American and Canadian universities, including L.H.D., University of Chicago, and D. Litt., Princeton University; Christian Literature Foundation Prize for *Ancient Judaism and the New Testament,* 1959; American Council of Learned Societies Award, 1960.

WRITINGS:

The Life and Times of Jesus, Abingdon, 1921.
The Early Days of Christianity, Abingdon, 1922, and Teachers' Manual, Abingdon, 1926.
The Way of Peace (devotional addresses), Morehouse (Wilton, CT), 1924.
The Economic Background of the Gospels, Oxford University Press (New York City), 1926.
New Horizons of the Christian Faith, Morehouse, 1928.
The Growth of the Gospels, Abingdon, 1933.
The Beginnings of Our Religion, Macmillan (New York City), 1934.
Frontiers of Christian Thinking, Willett & Clark, 1935.
The Gospel of the Kingdom, Macmillan, 1940.
The Earliest Gospel, Abingdon, 1943.

Can We Still Believe in Immortality?, Cloister Press, 1944.

The Practice of Religion, Macmillan, 1946.

An Introduction to New Testament Thought, Abingdon, 1950.

Christ's Victory and Ours, Macmillan, 1950.

Hellenistic Religions, Liberal Arts Press, 1953.

The Passion of the Kings, Macmillan, 1955.

How to Read the Bible, Morehouse, 1956.

Ancient Roman Religion, Liberal Arts Press, 1957.

The Gospels: Their Origin and Their Growth, Harper (New York City), 1957.

Ancient Judaism and the New Testament, Macmillan, 1959.

Basic Christian Belief, Methodist Church, 1960.

Translating the Bible, Seabury (New York City), 1961.

Roman Hellenism and the New Testament, Scribner (New York City), 1962.

Rome and Reunion, Oxford University Press, 1965.

The Vatican Council, Forward Movement (Cincinnati, OH), 1966.

EDITOR

(And translator) *From Criticism,* Willett & Clark, 1934, Harper, 1962.

Johannes Weiss, *History of Primitive Christianity,* two volumes, Wilson-Erickson, 1937, revised edition published as *Earliest Christianity,* two volumes, Harper, 1959.

Gospel and the Predicament of Modern Man, Protestant Episcopal Church, 1939.

Hellenistic Religions, Liberal Arts Press, 1953.

Burton S. Easton, *Early Christianity: The Purpose of the Acts, and Other Papers,* Seabury, 1954.

Edwin Hatch, *The Influence of Greek Ideas in Christianity,* Harper, 1957.

Nelson's Bible Commentary, Nelson, Volume VI: *New Testament: Matthew—Acts,* 1962, Volume VII: *New Testament: Romans—Revelation,* 1962.

(With H. H. Rowley) *Dictionary of the Bible,* revised edition, Scribner, 1963.

J. B. Bury, *History of the Papacy in the Nineteenth Century,* Schocken (New York City), 1964.

TRANSLATOR

Martin Dibelius, editor, *Message of Jesus Christ,* Scribner, 1939.

Dibelius, editor, *Jesus,* Westminister (Philadelphia, PA), 1949.

OTHER

Contributor to *Anglican Theological Review, Journal of Religion, Religion in Life,* and other publications. Editor, *Anglican Theological Review,* 1924-55, and *Witness,* 1941-45. Book review editor, *Witness,* 1945-52. Protestant advisory editor, *Encyclopedia Americana,* beginning 1943.

BIOGRAPHICAL/CRITICAL SOURCES:

BOOKS

Johnson, Sherman E., editor, *The Joy of Study* (festschrift in Grant's honor), Macmillan, 1951.

PERIODICALS

Christian Century, April 5, 1933, p. 463; September 4, 1940, p. 1079; April 3, 1946, p. 430; October 9, 1963, p. 1240; December 29, 1965, p. 1608.

Critic, April, 1965, p. 86.

Ethics, July, 1940, p. 481.

Journal of Religion, July, 1933, p. 326; July, 1940, p. 285; October, 1963, p. 332.

Saturday Review, August 29, 1959, p. 18.

Times Literary Supplement, August 19, 1965, p. 720.

OBITUARIES:

PERIODICALS

American Bookman, October 7, 1974.

New York Times, July 13, 1974, p. 26.*

* * *

GRANT, John E(rnest) 1925-

PERSONAL: Born August 28, 1925, in Newburyport, MA; son of Albert M. (a town official of Amesbury, MA) and Christine (Currier) Grant; married Mary Lynn Johnson, March 6, 1974; children: William J. *Education:* Attended Boston University, 1946-47, Hamilton College, 1947-49; Harvard University, A.B., 1951, A.M., 1954, Ph.D., 1960.

ADDRESSES: Home—407 Magowan Ave., Iowa City, IA 52240. *Office*—Department of English, University of Iowa, Iowa City, IA 52242.

CAREER: University of Connecticut, Storrs, instructor, 1956-60, assistant professor, 1960-64, associate professor of English, 1964-65; University of Iowa, Iowa City, professor of English, 1965—. Visiting professor, University of Alberta, 1968 and 1973, and Emory University, 1976. Visiting distinguished scholar, University of Adelaide, 1984. *Military service:* U.S. Army, 1943-46.

MEMBER: American Association of University Professors, Modern Language Association of America, Midwest Modern Language Association.

AWARDS, HONORS: American Council of Learned Societies fellowship to England, 1968-69; American Philosophical Society fellowship, 1971; National Endowment for the Humanities fellowship, 1977; Yale Center for British Art fellowship, 1981; Huntington Library fellowship, 1982.

WRITINGS:

(Editor) *Discussions of William Blake,* Heath (Boston), 1961.
(Editor with David V. Erdman) *Blake's Visionary Forms Dramatic,* Princeton University Press (Princeton), 1970.
(Editor with wife, Mary Lynn Johnson) *Blake's Poetry and Designs: Authoritative Texts, Illuminations in Color and Monochrome, Related Prose, Criticism,* Norton (New York City), 1979.
(Editor with Edward J. Rose and Michael J. Tolley) *William Blake's Designs for Edward Young's Night Thoughts,* Oxford University Press (New York City), 1980.

Contributor to books, including *Blake: A Collection of Critical Essays,* edited by Northrop Frye, Prentice-Hall, 1966, *William Blake: Essays for S. Foster Damon,* edited by Alvin Rosenfeld, Brown University Press, 1969, *Blake: The Artist,* edited by Robert N. Essick, Hennessey & Ingalls, 1973, *Essays on Romanticism,* edited by Morris Eaves and Michael Fischer, Cornell University Press, 1985, and *Blake's Truth,* 1986. Contributor to *Bulletin of Research in the Humanities, Yale Review, Modern Philology, Philological Quarterly, Bulletin of the New York Public Library, Modern Language Quarterly, Nation, Keats-Shelly Journal, Journal of Aesthetics and Art Criticism, Southern Review, Blake Newsletter, Blake Studies, James Joyce Quarterly, Studies in Romanticism, English Language Notes, Texas Studies in Literature and Language,* and *Essays in Criticism.**

*　　*　　*

GRANT-ADAMSON, Lesley 1942-
(Lesley Adamson)

PERSONAL: Born November 26, 1942, in London, England; daughter of Edwin (a civil servant) and Edna (a civil servant; maiden name, Puddefoot) Heycock; married Andrew Grant-Adamson (a journalist), December 12, 1968. *Education:* Attended grammar school in London, England.

ADDRESSES: Home—30 Bewdley St., Islington, London N1 1HB, England. *Agent*—c/o Clare Roberts at Rogers, Coleridge, and White, 20 Powis Mews, London W11 1JN, England.

CAREER: Leonard Hill Ltd., London, England, subeditor for trade journals *Fibres and Plastics* and *The Muck-*

shifter, 1960-63; Thomson Publications Ltd., subeditor for trade journals *Horological Journal* and *Retail Jeweller,* involved in production of technical books, 1960-63; *The Guardian,* London, feature writer, 1973-80; freelance writer for newspapers and magazines, 1980—. Former reporter and feature writer for *Palmers Green and Southgate Gazette, Citizen, Rugby Advertiser, Coventry Evening Telegraph,* and *Herts Advertiser.*

MEMBER: Society of Authors, Crime Writers Association, Yr Academi Gymreig, Welsh Union of Writers.

AWARDS, HONORS: Named among ten best young writers of 1986 by *Cosmopolitan.*

WRITINGS:

NOVELS

Death on Widow's Walk, Scribner (New York City), 1985, published in England as *Patterns in the Dust,* Faber (London), 1985.
The Face of Death, Faber, 1985, Scribner, 1986.
Guilty Knowledge, St. Martin's (New York City), 1986.
Wild Justice, St. Martin's, 1987.
Threatening Eye, St. Martin's, 1988.
Curse the Darkness, St. Martin's, 1990.
Too Many Questions, St. Martin's, 1991, published in England as *Flynn,* Faber, 1991.
A Life of Adventure, Faber, 1992.
The Dangerous Edge, Faber, 1993.
Dangerous Games, St. Martin's, 1994.

OTHER

(With husband, Andrew Grant-Adamson) *A Season in Spain* (travel), Pavilion, 1995.

Writer for television; short stories broadcast by British Broadcasting Corporation (BBC) Radio; contributor of articles (sometimes under name Lesley Adamson), stories, and poems to magazines, including *Cosmopolitan* and *Vole,* and to newspapers, including the London *Observer, Sunday Times,* and *Guardian.*

SIDELIGHTS: Lesley Grant-Adamson told *CA:* "I drew on my Fleet Street background for my earliest novels, which featured a gossip columnist, Rain Morgan, and a series of journalistic investigations. My first novel without her was *Threatening Eye,* a suspense novel set in a fictionalized village close to where I once lived in Hertfordshire. Rain Morgan made one more appearance in print—in *Curse the Darkness,* in which I married the detective story and the suspense novel and created a big modern novel about poverty and greed.

"Giving up Rain Morgan was not a deliberate act; I lost interest in her when I was ill. Recovering, I wrote *Flynn (Too Many Questions* in the U.S.), a detective story about tribal loyalties and featuring Laura Flynn, a London Irish private eye. With the exception of one poem and a short story, this is my only piece of writing in the first person.

"A new phase of my work began with the publication of *A Life of Adventure.* This introduced an incompetent con man, Jim Rush, an American inveigling his way into English society. I intended two books about him, the second story, *Dangerous Games,* taking place on a Caribbean island. Now I am planning a third.

"My career began with an English village mystery, but now I set my stories in places as diverse as the Lesser Antilles, Prague, Czechoslovakia, rural France, and Spain. Perhaps it's not surprising that I have now written a travel book. For a couple of years my husband and I lived in an olive grove in the Alpujarra region of Andalusia and we have now written a portrait of that region, *A Season in Spain.*"

*   *   *

GRAY, Alasdair (James) 1934-

PERSONAL: Born December 28, 1934, in Glasgow, Scotland; son of Alex Gray (a machine operator) and Amy (Fleming) Gray (a homemaker); children: Andrew. *Education:* Glasgow Art School, diploma, 1957. *Politics:* "Devolutionary Scottish C.N.D. [Campaign for Nuclear Disarmament] Socialist." *Religion:* None.

ADDRESSES: Home—39 Kersland St., Glasgow G12 8BP, Scotland. *Agent*—Xandra Hardy, 9 Elsworth Terrace, London NW3, England.

CAREER: Part-time art teacher in area of Glasgow, Scotland, 1958-62; theatrical scene painter in Glasgow, 1962-63; freelance playwright and painter in Glasgow, 1963-75; People's Palace (local history museum), Glasgow, artist-recorder, 1976-77; University of Glasgow, writer in residence, 1977-79; freelance painter and maker of books in Glasgow, 1979—.

MEMBER: Society of Authors, Scottish Society of Playwrights, Glasgow Print Workshop, various organizations supporting coal miners and nuclear disarmament.

AWARDS, HONORS: Three grants from Scottish Arts Council, between 1968 and 1981; award from Saltire Society, 1982, for *Lanark: A Life in Four Books;* award from Cheltenham Literary Festival, 1983, for *Unlikely Stories, Mostly;* award from Scottish branch of P.E.N., 1986; Bellhouston Travelling Scholarship; Booker Prize nomination, Book Trust (England), for *Lanark: A Life in Four Books.*

WRITINGS:

Old Negatives: Four Verse Sequences, J. Cape (London), 1962.

Lanark: A Life in Four Books (novel), self-illustrated, Harper (New York City), 1981, revised edition, Braziller (New York City), 1985.

Unlikely Stories, Mostly (short stories; includes "The Star," "The Spread of Ian Nicol," and "Five Letters from an Eastern Empire"), self-illustrated, Canongate (Edinburgh), 1983, revised, Penguin (London), 1984.

1982 Janine (novel), Viking (London), 1984, revised edition, Penguin, 1985.

The Fall of Kelvin Walker: A Fable of the Sixties (novel; adapted from his television play of the same title; also see below), Canongate, 1985, Braziller, 1986.

(With James Kelman and Agnes Owens) *Lean Tales* (short story anthology), J. Cape, 1985.

Saltire Self-Portrait 4, Saltire Society Publications (Edinburgh), 1988.

(Editor) *The Anthology of Prefaces,* Canongate, 1989.

McGrotty and Ludmilla; or, The Harbinger Report: A Romance of the Eighties, White Leaf, 1989.

Something Leather (novel), Random House (New York City), 1990.

Poor Things: Episodes from the Early Life of Archibald McCandless, M.D., Scottish Public Health Officer (novel), Harcourt (New York City), 1992.

Why Scots Should Rule Scotland, Canongate, 1992.

PLAYS

Dialogue (one-act), first produced in Edinburgh at Gateway Theatre, 1971.

The Fall of Kelvin Walker (two-act; adapted from his television play of the same title; also see below), first produced in Stirling, Scotland, at McRoberts Centre, University of Stirling, 1972.

The Loss of the Golden Silence (one-act), first produced in Edinburgh at Pool Theatre, 1973.

Homeward Bound (one-act), first produced in Edinburgh at Pool Theatre, 1973.

(With Tom Leonard and Liz Lochhead) *Tickly Mince* (two-act), first produced in Glasgow at Tron Theatre, 1982.

(With Liz Lochhead, Tom Leonard, and James Kelman) *The Pie of Damocles* (two-act), first produced in Glasgow at Tron Theatre, 1983.

RADIO PLAYS

Quiet People, British Broadcasting Corporation (BBC), 1968.

The Night Off, BBC, 1969.

Thomas Muir of Huntershill, BBC, 1970.

The Loss of the Golden Silence, BBC, 1974.

McGrotty and Ludmilla, BBC, 1976.

The Vital Witness, BBC, 1979.

Near the Driver, translation into German by Berndt Rull-kotter broadcast by Westdeutsche Rundfunk, 1983, original text broadcast by BBC, 1988.

TELEVISION PLAYS

The Fall of Kelvin Walker, BBC, 1968.

Dialogue, BBC, 1972.

Triangles, Granada, 1972.

The Man Who Knew about Electricity, BBC, 1973.

Honesty, BBC, 1974.

Today and Yesterday (series of three twenty-minute educational documentaries), BBC, 1975.

Beloved, Granada, 1976.

The Gadfly, Granada, 1977.

The Story of a Recluse, BBC, 1987.

SIDELIGHTS: After more than twenty years as a painter and a scriptwriter for radio and television, Alasdair Gray rose to literary prominence with the publication of several of his books in the 1980s. His works have been noted for their mixture of realistic social commentary and vivid fantasy, augmented by the author's own evocative illustrations. Jonathan Baumbach wrote in the *New York Times Book Review* that Gray's work "has a verbal energy, an intensity of vision, that has been mostly missing from the English novel since D. H. Lawrence." And David Lodge of the *New Republic* said that Gray "is that rather rare bird among contemporary British writers—a genuine experimentalist, transgressing the rules of formal English prose . . . boldly and imaginatively."

In his writing Gray often draws upon his Scottish background, and he is regarded as a major force in the literature of his homeland. Author Anthony Burgess, for instance, said in the London *Observer* that he considered Gray the best Scottish novelist since Sir Walter Scott became popular in the early nineteenth century. Unlike Scott, who made his country a setting for historical romance, Gray focuses on contemporary Scotland, where the industrial economy deteriorates and many citizens fear that their social and economic destiny has been surrendered to England. Critics praised Gray for putting such themes as Scotland's decline and powerlessness into a larger context that any reader could appreciate. "Using Glasgow as his undeniable starting point," Douglas Gifford wrote in *Studies in Scottish Literature,* "Gray . . . transforms local and hitherto restricting images, which limited [other] novelists of real ability, . . . into symbols of universal prophetic relevance."

As noted above, Gray became prominent as a writer only after several years of working as an artist and illustrator. Gray, however, traces his own literary and artistic development to the early years of his life, explaining to *CA* in a 1987 written interview that "as soon as I could draw and

tell stories, which was around the age of four or five, I spent a lot of time doing these or planning to do them. My parents were friendly to my childish efforts, as were most of my teachers, though they also told me I was unlikely to make a living by either of these jobs. . . . I was delighted to go to art school, because I was a maturer draftsman and painter than writer. My writings while at art school were attempts to prepare something I knew would take long to finish: though I didn't know how long."

Gray went on to say that although his first novel took years to complete, the story-line of what would become his now acclaimed first novel, *Lanark: A Life in Four Books,* had essentially been worked out in his mind by the time he was eighteen. A long and complex work that some reviewers considered partly autobiographical, *Lanark* opens in Unthank, an ugly, declining city explained in reviews as a comment on Glasgow and other Western industrial centers. As in George Orwell's *Nineteen Eighty-four,* citizens of Unthank are ruled by a domineering and intrusive bureaucracy. Lanark is a lonely young man unable to remember his past. Along with many of his fellow-citizens, he is plagued with "dragonhide," an insidious, scaly skin infection seen as symbolic of his emotional isolation. Cured of his affliction by doctors at a scientific institute below the surface of the earth, Lanark realizes to his disgust that the staff is as arrogant and manipulative as the ruling elite on the surface. Before escaping from this underworld, Lanark has a vision in which he sees the life story of a young man who mysteriously resembles him—Duncan Thaw, an aspiring artist who lives in twentieth-century Glasgow.

Thaw's story, which comprises nearly half the book, is virtually a novel within a novel. It echoes the story of Lanark while displaying a markedly different literary technique. As William Boyd explained in the *Times Literary Supplement,* "The narration of Thaw's life turns out to be a brilliant and moving evocation of a talented and imaginative child growing up in working-class Glasgow. The style is limpid and classically elegant, the detail solidly documentary and in marked contrast to the fantastical and surrealistic accoutrements of the first 100 pages." Like Gray, Thaw attends art school in Glasgow, and, as with Lanark, Thaw's loneliness and isolation are expressed outwardly in a skin disease, eczema. With increasing desperation, Thaw seeks fulfillment in love and art, and his disappointment culminates in a violent outburst in which he kills—or at least thinks he kills—a young woman who had abandoned him. Bewildered and hopeless, he commits suicide. Boyd considered Thaw's story "a minor classic of the literature of adolescence," and Gifford likened it to James Joyce's novel *A Portrait of the Artist as a Young Man.* The last part of Gray's book focuses once more on Lanark, depicting his futile struggle to improve the world around him. Readers have often remarked on the various diseases the characters in *Lanark*'s Unthank suffer from: dragon-hide, mouths, twittering rigor, softs. When *CA* asked Gray if these diseases had allegorical significance, he responded: "Probably, but I came to that conclusion after, not before, I imagined and described them. And it would limit the reader's enjoyment and understanding of my stories to fix on one 'allegorical significance' and say 'This is it.' "

Critics have generally lauded *Lanark,* although some expressed concern that it was hampered by its size and intricacy. Boyd, for instance, felt that the parallel narratives of Thaw and Lanark "do not happily cohere." *Washington Post Book World*'s Michael Dirda said that Lanark was "too baggy and bloated," but he stressed that "there are such good things in it that one hardly knows where it could be cut." Many critics echoed Boyd's overall assessment that "*Lanark* is a work of loving and vivid imagination, yielding copious riches." Moreover, Burgess featured *Lanark* in his book *Ninety-nine Novels: The Best in English Since 1939—A Personal Choice,* declaring, "It was time Scotland produced a shattering work of fiction in the modern idiom. This is it."

Although *Lanark* rapidly achieved critical recognition in Britain, it was Gray's second novel, *1982 Janine,* that was the first to be widely known in the United States. When asked why his work had now attained critical notice in the United States, Gray replied to *CA:* "*Lanark* was the first novel I had published in the U.S.A., by Harper & Row in 1981. It was speedily remaindered, because Harper & Row classified it as science fiction, only sent it to sci-fi magazines for review, and the sci-fi reviewers were not amused. . . . I suppose my books have been published in the United States because they sold well in Britain, and were praised by authors of *A Clockwork Orange* [Anthony Burgess] and *The History Man* [Malcolm Bradbury]."

1982 Janine records the thoughts of Jock McLeish, a disappointed, middle-aged Scottish businessman, during a long night of heavy drinking. In his mind Jock plays and replays fantasies in which he sexually tortures helpless women, and he gives names and identities to his victims, including the Janine of the title. Burgess spoke for several reviewers when he wrote in the *Observer* that such material was offensive and unneeded. But admirers of the novel, such as Richard Eder of the *Los Angeles Times,* felt that Jock's sexual fantasies were a valid metaphor for the character's own sense of helplessness. Jock, who rose to a managerial post from a working-class background, now hates himself because he is financially dependent on the ruling classes he once hoped to change.

As Eder observed, Jock's powerlessness is in its turn a metaphor for the subjugation of Scotland. Jock expounds on the sorry state of his homeland in the course of his drunken railings. Scotland's economy, he charges, has been starved in order to strengthen the country's political master, England; what is more, if war with the Soviet Union breaks out, Jock expects the English to use Scotland as a nuclear battlefield. As the novel ends, Jock resolves to quit his job and change his life for the better. Eder commended Gray for conveying a portrait of helplessness and the search for self-realization "in a flamboyantly comic narrator whose verbal blue streak is given depth by a winning impulse to self-discovery, and some alarming insight."

Gray's short-story collection *Unlikely Stories, Mostly* is "if anything more idiosyncratic" than *1982 Janine,* according to Jonathan Baumbach of the *New York Times Book Review.* Many reviewers praised the imaginativeness of the stories while acknowledging that the collection, which includes work dating back to Gray's teenage years, is uneven in quality. As Gary Marmorstein observed in the *Los Angeles Times Book Review,* some of the stories are "slight but fun," including "The Star," in which a boy catches a star and swallows it, and "The Spread of Ian Nicol," in which a man slowly splits in two like a microbe reproducing itself.

By contrast, "Five Letters from an Eastern Empire" is one of several more complex tales that received special praise. Set in the capital of a powerful empire, the story focuses on a talented poet. Gradually readers learn the source of the poet's artistic inspiration: the emperor murdered the boy's parents by razing the city in which they lived, then ordered him to write about the destruction. "The tone of the story remains under perfect control as it darkens and deepens," according to Adam Mar-Jones in the *Times Literary Supplement,* "until an apparently reckless comedy has become a cruel parable about power and meaning." While responding to a *CA* question about *Lanark* and the possible allegorical significance of its characters, Gray related an anecdote about the story "Five Letters from an Eastern Empire": "I wrote [the story] when writer-in-residence at Glasgow University. When I finished, it occurred to me that the Eastern Empire was an allegory of modern Britain viewed from Glasgow University by a writer-in-residence. A year ago I met someone just returned from Tokyo, who said he had heard a Chinese and a Japanese academic having an argument about my Eastern empire story. The Chinese was quite sure the empire was meant to be China, the Japanese that it was Japan. My only knowledge of these lands is from a few color prints, Arthur Waley's translation of the novel *Monkey* [by Wu Ch'eng-en] and some translated poems."

Gray's third novel, *The Fall of Kelvin Walker,* was inspired by personal experience. Still struggling to establish his career several years after his graduation from art school, Gray was tapped as the subject of a documentary by a successful friend at the British Broadcasting Corporation (BBC). Gray, who had been living on welfare, suddenly found himself treated to airline flights and limousine rides at the BBC's expense. In *Kelvin Walker* the title character, a young Scotsman with a burning desire for power, has a similar chance to use the communications media to fulfill his wildest fantasies. Though Kelvin arrives in London with few assets but self-confidence and a fast-talking manner, his persistence and good luck soon win him a national following as an interviewer on a television show. But in his pride and ambition Walker forgets that he exercises such influence only at the whims of his corporate bosses, and when he displeases them his fall from grace is as abrupt as his rise.

Kelvin Walker, which Gray adapted from his 1968 teleplay of the same title ("I sent it to a [BBC] director I know. He gave it to a producer who liked it"), is shorter and less surrealistic than his previous novels. The *Observer*'s Hermione Lee, though she stressed that Gray "is always worth attending to," felt that this novel "doesn't allow him the big scope he thrives on." By contrast, Larry McCaffery of the *New York Times Book Review* praised *Kelvin Walker* for its "economy of means and exquisite control of detail." Gray "is now fully in command of his virtuoso abilities as a stylist and storyteller," McCaffery said, asserting that Gray's first four books—"each of which impresses in very different ways—indicate that he is emerging as the most vibrant and original new voice in English fiction."

As reviewers became familiar with Gray's work, they noticed several recurring features in it: illustrations by the author, typographical eccentricities, and an emphasis on the city of Glasgow. Asked by *CA* about the illustrations, Gray explained a little about the process of creating this kind of manuscript: "The illustrations and cover designs of my books are not essential to them, being thought of after the text is complete. I add them because they make the book more enjoyable. The queer typography, in the three stories which use it, was devised in the act of writing, not added after, like sugar to porridge."

As Gray continued to write, critical reception of his work varied widely. Though most reviewers acknowledged his genius in such works as *Lanark,* books such as *Something Leather* and *McGrotty and Ludmilla; or, The Harbinger Report: A Romance of the Eighties* were criticized for lacking the intensity of his earlier work. Gray himself was remarkably candid about the quality and intent of some of these efforts. For example, he described *McGrotty and Ludmilla* as an Aladdin story set in modern Whitehall "with the hero a junior civil servant, wicked uncle Abanizir a senior one, and the magic lamp a secret government paper which gave whoever held it unlimited powers of blackmail." And works such as *Something Leather,* said

Gerald Mangan in the *Times Literary Supplement,* placed Gray in "an unfortunate tradition in Scottish fiction, whereby novelists have tended to exhaust their inspiration in the effort of a single major achievement." That *Lanark* was a major achievement Mangan had no doubt. "*Lanark* is now so monumental a Scottish landmark," he wrote, "that few readers would have reproached him if a decade of silence had followed it." Instead, Gray brought out "a good deal of inferior material that had evidently subsidized or distracted him during the composition of his epic." A *New York Times Book Review* article by John Kenny Crane further explained the circumstances under which Gray composed *Something Leather.* According to Crane, a publisher had been pushing Gray for years to produce a new novel. Getting nowhere and needing money, Gray shuffled around in his rejected short-story manuscripts and came up with one about a conventional working woman in Glasgow who decides to shave off her hair and begin dressing in leather clothing. The publisher sent Gray a substantial advance, and the tale of the bald, leather-clad Glaswegian woman became his first chapter, "One for the Album." Other unpublished stories, unstaged plays, and early radio and TV scripts were also pressed into service and ultimately published as *Something Leather.* Lamented Crane in his review, "Gray, who has published some very creditable works of fiction, shamelessly admits to absolutely everything in his epilogue." Yet, the critic added, "Taken on their own, some of the interior chapters have artistry and merit. I particularly liked the reflections on war in one titled 'In the Boiler Room' and the comical friction caused by the divergent life styles of boarders in 'Quiet People.' As short stories, some are quite fine. I would recommend the reader take them as such, even though Mr. Gray insists they are part of a novel." And despite his own criticism of *Something Leather,* Mangan said that in the five stories that comprise the work, Gray's "prose is generally notable for its refusal of second-hand definitions; and it is not surprising to find, among other consolations, a divertingly cynical diatribe on Glasgow's current status as culture-capital."

With the publication of *Poor Things: Episodes from the Early Life of Archibald McCandless, M.D., Scottish Public Health Officer,* purportedly edited by Gray, the author returns to form, suggested Philip Hensher in the *Spectator,* "after a rather sticky patch." The work drew comparisons to such authors as Daniel Defoe and Laurence Sterne, partly because of its eccentric humor and setting and partly because of Gray's skillful use of the traditions of the Victorian novel, which, according to Barbara Hardy in the *Times Literary Supplement,* "embodied their liberal notions of providence and progress in realistic narratives which often surge into optimistic or melioristic visions on the last page."

Set in Glasgow during the 1880s, the novel is narrated by Archie McCandless, a young medical student, who befriends the eccentric Godwin Baxter, another medical student. Baxter, who has been experimenting on the body of a beautiful and pregnant young suicide, has created "Bella" by transplanting the brain of the fetus into its mother's skull. Bella is sexually mature and wholly amoral, and McCandless wants to marry her. She, however, elopes with a wicked playboy whom she soon drives insane. After the death of her lover, Bella works for a time in a Parisian brothel before returning to Scotland. Here she runs into her ex-husband just as she is getting married to McCandless. A happy ending is combined with a clever final twist to produce a book that, said Hensher, becomes "a great deal more than entertaining only on finishing it. Then your strongest urge is to start reading it again."

Despite the author's success with later works, *Lanark* remains Gray's masterpiece. In the *New York Review of Books,* Gordon A. Craig summed up Gray's achievement in *Lanark,* praising its "masterful evocation . . . of an adolescence and young manhood in post-1945 Glasgow, of early friendships and first love, of the stirring of artistic genius and its frustration, and of the subtle social prejudices that had to be learned as one grew up." "In a larger sense," Craig continued, "the novel is an attempt to expose the ills that threaten modern society, an elaboration on a text in one of Gray's plates: 'Let Glasgow flourish'—any and all Glasgows—'by telling the truth.' "

BIOGRAPHICAL/CRITICAL SOURCES:

BOOKS

Burgess, Anthony, *Ninety-nine Novels: The Best in English since 1939—A Personal Choice,* Allison & Busby (London), 1984.
Contemporary Literary Criticism, Volume 41, Gale (Detroit, MI), 1987.

PERIODICALS

Christian Science Monitor, October 5, 1984.
Los Angeles Times, November 21, 1984.
Los Angeles Times Book Review, December 9, 1984.
New Republic, November 12, 1984.
New York Review of Books, April 25, 1991.
New York Times Book Review, October 28, 1984; May 5, 1985; December 21, 1986; August 4, 1991.
Observer (London), April 15, 1984; March 31, 1985.
Spectator, February 28, 1981; September 5, 1992.
Stage, November 30, 1972.
Studies in Scottish Literature, Volume 18, 1983.
Times (London), April 1, 1986.
Times Literary Supplement, February 27, 1981; March 18, 1983; April 13, 1984; March 29, 1985; May 10, 1985; July 6-12, 1990; April 3, 1992; August 28, 1992.

Village Voice Literary Supplement, December, 1984.
Washington Post Book World, December 16, 1984; August 31, 1986; June 16, 1991.*

*   *   *

GREEN, Brian
See CARD, Orson Scott

*   *   *

GREENE, Laura
See GREENE, Laura Offenhartz

*   *   *

GREENE, Laura Offenhartz 1935-
(Laura Greene)

PERSONAL: Born July 21, 1935, in New York, NY; daughter of Charles (in sales) and Ida (Katz) Offenhartz; married Victor Robert Greene (a professor of American history), February 21, 1957; children: Jessica, Geoffrey. *Education:* Boston University, B.S., 1958; University of Pennsylvania, M.A., 1963; also attended Kansas State University, 1963-72, University of Wisconsin—Milwaukee, and University of Wisconsin—Madison, 1984—.

ADDRESSES: Home and office—4869 North Woodburn St., Milwaukee, WI 53217.

CAREER: Junior high school English teacher in Yeadon, PA, 1961-62; high school English teacher in Haddonfield, NJ, 1962-63; Kansas State University, Manhattan, instructor in English, 1962-73; teacher at religious schools in Milwaukee, WI, 1973—. Member of teaching staff, University of Bremen, 1981, and University of Wisconsin—Milwaukee, 1982; speaker on writing for adults, children, and writing groups.

MEMBER: Authors Guild, Society of Children's Book Writers and Illustrators, Council for Wisconsin Writers, Chicago Reading Roundtable.

AWARDS, HONORS: National Council of the Social Studies citation, 1979, for *I Am an Orthodox Jew;* Arthur Tofte Memorial Award, Council for Wisconsin Writers, 1981, for *Sign Language: A First Book;* International Award for Exemplary Teaching, Kohl Foundation, 1985.

WRITINGS:

JUVENILE; UNDER NAME LAURA GREENE

I Am an Orthodox Jew, Holt (New York City), 1979.

I Am Somebody, Childrens Press (Chicago), 1980.

Change: Getting to Know about Ebb and Flow, illustrated by Gretchen Mayo, Human Sciences Press (New York City), 1981.

Help: Getting to Know about Needing and Giving, illustrated by Mayo, Human Sciences Press, 1981.

(With Eva Barash Dicker) *Sign Language: A First Book,* F. Watts (New York City), 1981, paperback edition published as *Discovering Sign Language,* Gallaudet University Press (Washington, DC), 1988.

Careers in the Computer Industry, F. Watts, 1983.

Computers in Business and Industry, F. Watts, 1984.

Computer Pioneers, F. Watts, 1985.

(With Dicker) *Sign Language Talk,* F. Watts, 1987, paperback edition published as *Sign Me Fine,* Gallaudet University Press, 1990.

(With Dicker) *Interpreting Sign Language,* F. Watts, 1989.

OTHER

Child Labor: Then and Now, F. Watts, 1992.
Wildlife Poaching, F. Watts, 1994.

Also author of feature articles for *Corporate Report Wisconsin,* a monthly business magazine, 1987-89.

WORK IN PROGRESS: *Eli Cohen: Israel's Spy in Syria* (working title), forthcoming from Jewish Publication Society; more children's books.

SIDELIGHTS: Laura Offenhartz Greene once told *CA:* "Children's egos are very fragile things. What children think of themselves is an important factor in forming their egos and thus their personalities. One thing that affects children's self-images is the way they perceive their differences and their unique qualities. I write about the differences among people which are often a source of pain and prejudice, but I try to look at these differences as a potential source of pride."

Greene added: "I have lived in Wisconsin for over twenty years, but I grew up in a small town in New Jersey where I lived close enough to school to be able to walk. Depending on which route I took home, I could pass a soda shop, a delicatessen, or the library.

"I preferred walking home past the library. When I chose this route, I was always alone and always stopped at the library. I liked the smell of the library even more than the smell of the delicatessen. It was easy to find a quiet corner by a window and read undisturbed until dark or until the librarian tapped me on the shoulder to say, 'Laura, your mom just called and said it's time to come home.' It was on one of these library days and on the snowy walk home that I decided I wanted to be a writer—I wanted to be the kind of person whose words made a difference to the people who read them.

"As the years went by, I continued to read and continued to learn. I realized the world was broken and in need of repair. Words help repair the world. Words make a difference."

*   *   *

GRIFFITHS, Louise
See GRIFFITHS, Louise Benckenstein

*   *   *

GRIFFITHS, Louise B.
See GRIFFITHS, Louise Benckenstein

*   *   *

GRIFFITHS, Louise Benckenstein   1907-
(Louise Griffiths, Louise B. Griffiths)

PERSONAL: Born September 18, 1907, in Cincinnati, OH; daughter of George William and Louise (Oetjen) Benckenstein; married C. Warren Griffiths (a professor of history and government), 1939; children: David, Thomas Daniel. *Education:* University of Cincinnati, A.B., 1929; Boston University, M.A., 1929; Columbia University, graduate study, summer sessions. *Religion:* Society of Friends (Quaker).

CAREER: Director of religious education at churches in Cincinnati, OH, and Madison, WI, 1929-39; Chicago Theological Seminary, Chicago, IL, instructor, 1940, 1941; Lawrence College (now University), Appleton, WI, instructor, 1941-42; First Unitarian Church, Alton, IL, educational director, 1943-48; Wilmington College, Wilmington, OH, instructor, beginning 1956; taught ceramics in 1960s. Affiliated with summer youth camp.

MEMBER: American Association of University Women, League of Women Voters.

WRITINGS:

Living Together in Today's World, Friendship (New York City), 1941, 2nd edition, 1947.

Brothertown, Friendship, 1941.

(Under name Louise Griffiths) *Becoming a Person: A Course for Grades Seven and Eight in Weekday Church Schools,* Westminster (Philadelphia, PA), 1941, revised edition published as *Becoming a Person: Teacher's Book,* 1959.

(Under name Louise B. Griffiths) *Junior High School Boys and Girls in the Church,* Pilgrim Press (Boston, MA, and Chicago, IL), 1944.

Missionary Education for the Junior School Age, Friendship, 1944, revised edition, 1948.

(Under name Louise Griffiths; with husband, Warren Griffiths) *God's World and Ours: A Course for Intermediates or Junior High School Groups in Vacation Church Schools,* Bethany Press (St. Louis, MO), 1949, revised edition published as *God's World and Ours: A Co-operative Vacation Church School Text for Use with Intermediate or Junior High School Groups,* 1956.

The Teacher and Young Teens, illustrations by Chris Pearson, Bethany Press, 1954.

Who Am I?, Bethany Press, 1955.

Wide as the World: Junior Highs and Missions, illustrations by Mine Okubo, Friendship, 1958.

Becoming Yourself, Abingdon (Nashville, TN), 1961.

Seekers Long Ago and Now, Religious Education Committee, Friends General Conference (Philadelphia), 1965.

Contributor to *Ceramics Monthly.*

WORK IN PROGRESS: A peace anthology for youth.*

*   *   *

GRIMM, Reinhold 1931-

PERSONAL: Born May 21, 1931, in Nuremberg, Germany; immigrated to United States in 1967; son of Eugen (a laborer) and Anna (Kaeser) Grimm; married Anneliese E. Schmidt, September 25, 1954; children: Ruth Sabine. *Education:* Attended University of Colorado, 1952-53; Erlangen University, Ph.D., 1956.

ADDRESSES: Home—6315 Glen Aire Ave., Riverside, CA 92506. *Office*—Department of Literatures and Languages, University of California, Riverside, CA 92506.

CAREER: Erlangen University, Germany, assistant professor of German literature, 1957-61; Frankfurt University, Germany, assistant professor of German literature, 1961-67; University of Wisconsin, Madison, Alexander Hohlfeld Professor of German, 1967-80, Vilas Professor of Comparative Literature and German, 1980-90; University of California, Riverside, professor of German and comparative literature, and Presidential Chair, 1990—. Visiting professor, New York University and Columbia University, 1967, University of Florida, 1973, University of Virginia, 1978; distinguished visiting professor, New Mexico State University, 1986, University of Nevada, Reno, 1989.

MEMBER: International PEN, Modern Language Association of America, American Association of Teachers of German (AATG; president, 1974-75).

AWARDS, HONORS: Foerderungspreis der Stadt Nuernberg, 1964; Guggenheim fellow, 1969-70; Institute for Research in the Humanities fellow, 1981; Hilldale award,

1988; honorary doctorate, Georgetown University, 1988; Honorary member of AATG, 1992.

WRITINGS:

Gottfried Benn: Die farbliche Chiffre in der Dichtung (title means "Gottfried Benn: The Color-Emblem in Literature"), H. Carl (Nuremberg), 1958, 2nd edition, 1962.

Bertolt Brecht: Die Struktur seines Werkes (title means "Bertolt Brecht: The Structure of His Work"), H. Carl, 1959, 6th edition, 1972.

Bertolt Brecht, J. B. Metzler, 1961, 3rd revised edition, 1971.

Bertolt Brecht und die Weltliteratur (title means "Bertolt Brecht and World Literature"), H. Carl, 1961.

(With Heinz Otto Burger) *Evokation und Montage: Drei Beitraege zum Verstaendnis moderner deutscher Lyrik* (title means "Evocation and Montage: Three Contributions towards an Understanding of Modern German Poetry"), Sachse & Pohl, 1961, revised edition, 1967.

Strukturen: Essays zur deutschen Literatur (title means "Structures: Essays on German Literature"), Sachse & Pohl, 1963.

(With others) *Romanticism Today: Friedrich Schlegel, Novalis, E. T. A. Hoffmann, Ludwig Tieck,* Inter Nationes (Bonn), 1973.

Nach dem Naturalismus: Essays zur modernen Dramatik (title means "Beyond Naturalism: Essays on Modern Drama"), Athenaeum Verlag, 1978.

Brecht und Nietzsche oder Gestaendnisse eines Dichters (title means "Brecht and Nietzsche or Confessions of a Poet"), Suhrkamp, 1979.

Von der Armut und vom Regen: Rilkes Antwort auf die soziale Frage (title means "Of Poverty and Rain: Rilke's Answer to the Social Question"), Athenaeum Verlag, 1981.

(With Walter Hinck) *Zwischen Satire und Utopie: Zur Komiktheorie und zur Geschichte der europaeischen Komoedie* (title means "Between Satire and Utopia: On the Theory and History of European Comedy"), Suhrkamp, 1982.

Texturen: Essays und anderes zu Hans Magnus Enzensberger (title means "Textures: Essays and Other Writings on Hans Magnus Enzensberger")‡, Peter Lang, 1984.

Love, Lust, and Rebellion: New Approaches to Georg Buechner, University of Wisconsin Press, 1985.

Echo and Disguise: Studies in German and Comparative Literature, Frankfurt, 1989.

Ein iberischer "Gegenentwurf"? Antonio Buero Vallejo, Brecht und das moderne Welttheater (title means "An Iberian 'Counter-Conception'? Antonio Buero Vallejo, Brecht and Modern World Theater"), Fink, 1991.

Versuche zur Europaeischen Literatur (title means "Essays on European Literature"), Bern, 1994.

EDITOR OR COMPILER

(With Wolf-Dieter Marsch) *Die Kunst im Schatten des Gottes: Fuer und wider Gottfried Benn* (title means "Art in the Shade of God: For and against Gottfried Benn"), Sachse & Pohl, 1962.

(With Viktor Zmegac) *Iwan Goll, Methusalem oder der ewige Buerger: Ein satirisches Drama* (title means "Methuselah or the Eternal Bourgeois: A Satiric Drama"), de Gruyter, 1966.

Episches Theater (title means "Epic Theater"), Kiepenheuer & Witsch, 1966, 3rd edition, 1972.

Zur Lyrik-Diskussion (title means "Concerning the Lyric"), Wissenschaftliche Buchgesellschaft, 1966, 2nd enlarged edition, 1974.

(And author of introduction) *Deutsche Romantheorien: Beitraege zu einer historischen Poetik des Romans in Deutschland* (title means "German Theories of the Novel: Essays towards a Historical Poetics of the Novel in Germany"), Athenaeum Verlag, 1968, 2nd edition, 1974.

Bertolt Brecht: Leben Eduards des Zweiten von England; Vorlage, Texte und Materialien (title means "Bertolt Brecht: The Life of Edward II of England; Sources, Texts and Materials"), Suhrkamp, 1968.

(With Conrad Wiedemann) *Literatur und Geistesgeschichte: Festgabe fuer Heinz Otto Burger* (title means "Literature and the History of Ideas: A Congratulatory Volume for Heinz Otto Burger"), E. Schmidt, 1968.

(With Jost Hermand and coauthor of introduction) *Deutsche Revolutionsdramen* (title means "German Dramas of Revolution"), Suhrkamp, 1969.

(With Henry J. Schmidt) *Brecht Fibel* (title means "Brecht Primer"), Harper, 1970.

(And author of introduction) *Deutsche Dramentheorien: Beitraege zu einer historischen Poetik des Dramas in Deutschland* (title means "German Theories of the Drama: Essays towards a Historical Poetics of the Drama in Germany"), Athenaeum Verlag, 1971, 3rd enlarged edition, 1981.

(With Klaus L. Berghahn) *Schiller: Zur Theorie und Praxis der Dramen* (title means "Schiller: Theory and Practice of His Plays"), Wissenschaftliche Buchgesellschaft, 1972, 2nd edition, 1981.

(With Hermand) *Methodenfragen der deutschen Literaturwissenschaft* (title means "Methodological Problems in German Literary Criticism"), Wissenschaftliche Buchgesellschaft, 1973.

(With Helene Scher) Friedrich Duerrenmatt, *Die Ehe des Herrn Mississippi: Eine Komoedie* (title means "The Marriage of Mr. Mississippi: A Comedy"), Holt, 1973.

Hans M. Enzensberger, *Critical Essays,* Continuum, 1982.

(With Peter Spycher and Richard Zipser) *From Kafka and Dada to Brecht and Beyond,* University of Wisconsin Press, 1982.

Hans Magnus Enzensberger, Suhrkamp, 1984.

Blacks and German Culture, University of Wisconsin Press, 1986.

(With Volker Duerr) *Nietzsche: Literature and Values,* University of Wisconsin Press, 1988.

Our Faust?: Roots and Ramifications of a Modern German Myth, University of Wisconsin Press, 1988.

(And co-translator) Felix Pollak, *Von Nutzen des Zweifels: Gedichte,* Fischer, 1989.

From Ode to Anthem: Problems of Lyric Poetry, University of Wisconsin Press, 1990.

From the Greeks to the Greens: Images of the Simple Life, University of Wisconsin Press, 1990.

Laughter Unlimited: Essays on Humor, Satire, and the Comic, University of Wisconsin Press, 1991.

(With Sara Pollak) Felix Pollak, *Lebenszeichen: Aphorismen und Marginalien,* [Vienna], 1992.

1914/1939: German Reflections of the Two World Wars, University of Wisconsin Press, 1992.

Re-Reading Wagner, University of Wisconsin Press, 1993.

(With Caroline Molina y Vedia and author of introduction) Gerhart Hauptmann, *Plays: Before Daybreak, The Weavers, The Beaver Coat,* Continuum, 1994.

Also editor, with Jost Hermand, of twenty-two volumes sponsored by Deutsche Abteilung of University of Wisconsin, including *Die sogenannten Zwanziger Jahre* (title means "The So-called Twenties"), Gehlen, 1970, *Die Klassik-Legende* (title means "The Myth of Classicism"), Athenaeum Verlag, 1971, *Exil und innere Emigration* (title means "Exile and Inner Emigration"), Athenaeum Verlag, 1972, and *Blacks and German Culture,* 1986. Contributor of essays and scholarly articles to numerous periodicals. Editor or coeditor of yearbooks and journals, including *Monatshefte,* 1967-90, *German Studies,* 1969-91, *Text und Kontext,* 1978—, and *PMLA,* 1982-85; translator of *German Quarterly,* 1991-94.

WORK IN PROGRESS: A book on impact of Calderon's stagecraft on Austria's greatest playwright, Franz Grillparzer.

*   *   *

GRISHAM, John 1955-

PERSONAL: Born February 8, 1955, in Jonesboro, AR; son of a construction worker and a homemaker; married Renee Jones; children: Ty, Shea (daughter). *Education:*

Received B.S. from Mississippi State and J.D. from University of Mississippi. *Religion:* Baptist.

ADDRESSES: Home—Oxford, MS. *Agent*—Jay Garon-Brooke Associates, Inc., 101 West 55th St., Suite 5K, New York, NY 10019.

CAREER: Writer. Admitted to the bar in Mississippi, 1981; lawyer in private practice in Southaven, MS, 1981-90. Served in Mississippi House of Representatives, 1984-90.

WRITINGS:

NOVELS

A Time to Kill, Wynwood, 1989.
The Firm, Doubleday (New York City), 1991.
The Pelican Brief, Doubleday, 1992.
The Client, Doubleday, 1993.
The Chamber, Doubleday, 1994.

ADAPTATIONS: The Firm was adapted as a film directed by Sydney Pollack and starring Tom Cruise, Gene Hackman, and Jeanne Tripplehorn, for Paramount Pictures, 1993; *The Pelican Brief* was adapted as a film directed by Alan J. Pakula and starring Julia Roberts and Denzel Washington, 1994; *The Client* was adapted as a film directed by Joel Schumacher and starring Susan Sarandon and Tommy Lee Jones, 1994; Ron Howard has been selected to direct the film adaptation of *The Chamber.*

WORK IN PROGRESS: The Rainmaker, for Doubleday.

SIDELIGHTS: When John Grisham began writing his first novel, he never dreamed that he would become one of America's bestselling novelists. Yet the appeal of his legal thrillers *The Firm, The Pelican Brief,* and *The Client* was so great that the reading public eagerly bought tens of millions of copies of these titles, and each was made into a major motion picture. The one-time lawyer now enjoys a celebrity status that few writers will ever know. "We think of ourselves as regular people, I swear we do," Grisham was quoted as saying of himself and his family in an *Entertainment Weekly* article by Kelli Pryor. "But then someone will drive 200 miles and show up on my front porch with books for me to sign. Or an old friend will stop by and want to drink coffee for an hour. It drives me crazy."

As a youth, Grisham had no dreams of becoming a writer, although he was an avid reader. His father traveled extensively in his job as a construction worker, and the Grisham family moved many times. Each time the family took up residence in a new town, Grisham would immediately go to the public library to get a library card. In 1967, the family moved to a more permanent home in Southaven, Mississippi. There Grisham enjoyed greater success in high school athletics than he did in English composition—a

subject in which he earned a D grade. After high school graduation, he enrolled at Mississippi State University to study accounting, with the ambition of eventually becoming a tax lawyer. By the time he earned his law degree from the University of Mississippi, however, his interest had shifted to criminal law. Therefore, he returned to Southaven to establish a practice in that field.

Although his practice was successful, Grisham was not happy and grew restless. He switched to the more lucrative field of civil law and won many cases, but a sense of personal dissatisfaction remained. Hoping to somehow make a difference in the world, he entered politics with the aim of reforming his state's educational system. Running as a Democrat, he won a post in the state legislature; four years later, he was reelected. After a total of six years in public office, Grisham, convinced that he would never be able to cut through the red tape of government bureaucracy in his effort to improve Mississippi's educational system, resigned his post in 1990.

While working in the legislature, Grisham continued to run his law office. His first book, *A Time to Kill,* was inspired by a scene he saw one day in court in which a preadolescent girl testified against her rapist. "I never felt such emotion and human drama in my life," Grisham disclosed to *People.* "I became obsessed wondering what it would be like if the girl's father killed that rapist and was put on trial. I had to write it down."

Writing his first novel, let alone publishing it, was no easy task for Grisham. "Because I have this problem of starting projects and not completing them," he revealed to *Publishers Weekly* interviewer Michelle Bearden, "my goal for this book was simply to finish it. Then I started thinking that it would be nice to have a novel sitting on my desk, something I could point to and say, 'Yeah, I wrote that.' But it didn't consume me. I had way too much going on to make it a top priority. If it happened, it happened."

Finishing the manuscript in 1987, Grisham next had to look for an agent. He was turned down by several before finally receiving a positive response from Jay Garon. Agent and author encountered a similarly difficult time trying to find a publisher; five thousand copies of the book were finally published by Wynwood Press and Grisham received a check for $15,000. He purchased one thousand copies of the book himself, peddling them at garden-club meetings and libraries and giving many of them away to family and friends. Ironically, *A Time to Kill* is now rated by some commentators as the finest of Grisham's novels. Furthermore, according to Pryor, "Those first editions are now worth $3,900 each," and after being republished, "the novel Grisham . . . couldn't give away has 8.6 million copies in print and has spent 80 weeks on the best-seller lists."

Despite the limited initial success of *A Time to Kill,* Grisham was not discouraged from trying his hand at another novel. The second time around, he decided to follow guidelines set forth in a *Writer's Digest* article for plotting a suspense novel. The result was *The Firm,* the story of a corrupt Memphis-based law firm established by organized crime for purposes of shielding and falsifying earnings. Recruited to the practice is Mitchell McDeere, a promising Harvard law graduate who is overwhelmed by the company's apparent extravagance. After learning of his employers' uncompromising methods, including relentless surveillance of its employees and their families, McDeere grows increasingly alarmed—and curious. When his criminal bosses discover that McDeere has been indulging his curiosity, he becomes an instant target of both the firm and the authorities who are monitoring the firm's activities. American agents from both the Central Intelligence Agency and the Federal Bureau of Investigation pressure McDeere to function as a spy within the firm. When he runs afoul of the ostensible good guys, McDeere finds himself in seemingly endless danger.

Grisham was not as motivated when writing *The Firm* as he had been when composing *A Time to Kill,* but with his wife's encouragement he finished the book. Before he even began trying to sell the manuscript, he learned that someone had acquired a bootlegged copy of it and was willing to give him $600,000 to turn it into a movie script. Within two weeks, Doubleday, one of the many publishers that had previously rejected *A Time to Kill,* offered Grisham a contract.

Upon *The Firm*'s publication, several reviewers argued that Grisham had not attained a high art form, although it was generally conceded that he had put together a compelling, thrilling narrative. *Los Angeles Times Book Review* critic Charles Champlin wrote that the "character penetration is not deep, but the accelerating tempo of paranoia-driven events is wonderful." Chicago *Tribune Books* reviewer Bill Brashler offered similar praise, proclaiming that *The Firm* reads "like a whirlwind." The novel was listed on the *New York Times* bestseller list for nearly a year, and it sold approximately ten times as many copies as its predecessor. By the time the film version was released, there were more than seven million copies of *The Firm* in print. This amazing success gave Grisham the means he needed to build his dream house, quit his law practice, and devote himself entirely to writing.

In a mere one hundred days, Grisham wrote his follow-up to *The Firm.* Another legal thriller, *The Pelican Brief* tells the story of a brilliant, beautiful female law student named Darby Shaw. When two Supreme Court justices are murdered, Shaw postulates a theory as to why the crimes were committed. Just telling people about her idea makes her gravely vulnerable to the corrupt law firm responsible for the killings. Soon she is running for her life—all the while bravely continuing to investigate the conspiracy. In reviewing *The Pelican Brief,* some critics complained that Grisham had followed the premise of *The Firm* far too closely. John Skow reflected this opinion in his review for *Time:* "*The Pelican Brief*. . . is as close to its predecessor as you can get without running *The Firm* through the office copier."

Despite such criticism, Grisham was also praised for creating another exciting story. Frank J. Prial, writing in the *New York Times Book Review,* observed that despite some flaws in *The Pelican Brief,* "Grisham has written a genuine page-turner. He has an ear for dialogue and is a skillful craftsman." Made into a film starring Denzel Washington and Julia Roberts, *The Pelican Brief* enjoyed success comparable to *The Firm,* selling millions of copies.

In just six months, Grisham put together yet another bestseller entitled *The Client.* This legal thriller focuses on a young boy who, after learning a sinister secret, turns to a motherly lawyer for protection from both the mob and the FBI. Like *The Firm* and *The Pelican Brief,* the book drew lukewarm reviews but became a bestseller and a major motion picture. For a time in the spring of 1993, after *The Client* came out and *A Time to Kill* was republished, Grisham was in the rare and enviable position of having a book at the top of the hardcover bestseller list and books in the first, second, and third spots on the paperback bestseller list.

In *Entertainment Weekly,* Grisham acknowledged that his second, third, and fourth books were formula-driven. He described his recipe for a bestseller in the following way: "You throw an innocent person in there and get 'em caught up in a conspiracy and you get 'em out." He also admitted to rushing through the writing of *The Pelican Brief* and *The Client,* resulting in "some damage" to the books' quality. Yet he also complained that the critical community treats popular writers harshly. "I've sold too many books to get good reviews anymore," he stated in Pryor's article. "There's a lot of jealousy, because [reviewers] think they can write a good novel or a best-seller and get frustrated when they can't. As a group, I've learned to despise them."

With his fifth novel, Grisham departed from his proven formula and proceeded at a more leisurely pace. He took a full nine months to write *The Chamber,* a book in which the "good guys" and "bad guys" are not as clearly defined as in his previous efforts. The novel tells the tale of Ku Klux Klansman Sam Cayhall, who is on death row for the murder of two young sons of a Jewish civil rights attorney.

After languishing in prison for years, Cayhall is surprised by the arrival of his estranged grandson, Adam Hall. Hall, an attorney, sets out to reverse his grandfather's death sentence, even though he considers Sam to be the family demon.

The novel is a careful study of a family's history, an examination of the relationship between lawyer and client, and a description of life on death row. It is "a curiously rich milieu for a Grisham novel," according to *Entertainment Weekly* critic Mark Harris, "and it allows the author to do some of his best writing since [*A Time to Kill.*]" Skow credited Grisham with producing a thought-provoking treatise on the death penalty. In his *Time* review, Skow noted that *The Chamber* "has the pace and characters of a thriller, but little else to suggest that it was written by the glib and cheeky author of Grisham's legal entertainments. His tough first novel, the courtroom rouser *A Time to Kill,* is a closer match. . . . Grisham may not change opinions with this sane, civil book, and he may not even be trying to. What he does ask, very plainly, is an important question: Is this what you want?" A reviewer for the London *Sunday Times* stated that "Grisham may do without poetry, wit and style, and offer only the simplest characterisation. The young liberal lawyer may be colourless and the spooky old prisoner one-dimensional; but there is no doubt that this ex-lawyer knows how to tell a story." While this book was less obviously commercial than his previous three books, Grisham had little trouble selling the movie rights to *The Chamber* for a record fee.

In the span of a few short years, Grisham has realized greater success than most writers will enjoy in a lifetime. But the former lawyer and politician remains realistic about his limitations and feels that a time may come when he will walk away from writing just as he previously abandoned both law and politics. In his interview with Bearden, he compared writers to athletes and concluded: "There's nothing sadder than a sports figure who continues to play past his prime."

BIOGRAPHICAL/CRITICAL SOURCES:

BOOKS

Authors and Artists for Young Adults, Volume 14, Gale (Detroit), 1995, pp. 115-21.
Contemporary Literary Criticism, Volume 84, Gale, 1995, pp. 189-201.

PERIODICALS

Booklist, February 1, 1993, p. 954.
Christian Science Monitor, March 5, 1993, p. 10.
Detroit News, May 25, 1994, p. 3D.
Entertainment Weekly, April 1, 1994, pp. 15-20; June 3, 1994, p. 48; July 15, 1994, p. 54.
Forbes, August 30, 1993, p. 24.

Globe and Mail (Toronto), March 30, 1991, p. C6.
Los Angeles Times Book Review, March 10, 1991, p. 7; April 5, 1992, p. 6; April 4, 1993, p. 6.
New Republic, August 2, 1993, p. 32; August 22, 1994, p. 35.
Newsday, March 7, 1993.
Newsweek, February 25, 1991, p. 63; March 16, 1992, p. 72; March 15, 1993, pp. 79-81; December 20, 1993, p. 121.
New York, August 1, 1994, pp. 52-53.
New Yorker, August 1, 1994, p. 16.
New York Times, March 5, 1993, p. C29; July 29, 1994, p. B10.
New York Times Book Review, March 24, 1991, p. 37; March 15, 1992, p. 9; October 18, 1992, p. 33; March 7, 1993, p. 18.
People, April 8, 1991, pp. 36-37; March 16, 1992, pp. 43-44; March 15, 1993, pp. 27-28; June 27, 1994, p. 24; August 1, 1994, p. 16.
Publishers Weekly, February 22, 1992, pp. 70-71; May 30, 1994, p. 37.
Southern Living, August, 1991, p. 58.
Sunday Times (London), June 12, 1994, p. 1.
Time, March 9, 1992, p. 70; March 8, 1993, p. 73; June 20, 1994, p. 67; August 1, 1994.
Tribune Books (Chicago), February 24, 1991, p. 6; September 8, 1991, p. 10; February 23, 1992, p. 4; February 28, 1993, p. 7.
Voice Literary Supplement, July-August, 1991, p. 7.
Wall Street Journal, March 12, 1993, p. A6.
West Coast Review of Books, June 15, 1989, p. 80.*

*   *   *

GROH, George W. 1922-1984

PERSONAL: Born March 23, 1922, in Emporia, KS; died after suffering a stroke, December 2, 1984, in New York, NY; son of George Sherman (a roofer) and Dorothy (Freitag) Groh; married Lynn Snowden (a journalist), December 22, 1950 (died October 6, 1983); children: Nancy, Barbara, Ellen, Susan (deceased). *Education:* Kansas State Teachers College (now Emporia State University), B.A., 1941; University of Missouri, B.J., 1946. *Politics:* Independent Democrat. *Avocational interests:* Fishing, wilderness canoeing.

CAREER: Corpus Christi Caller-Times, Corpus Christi, TX, reporter, 1948-50; *Milwaukee Journal,* Milwaukee, WI, reporter, 1950-52; free-lance writer in New York City, 1953-54; *MD* (magazine), New York City, senior staff writer, beginning 1956. *Military service:* U.S. Army, 1943-45, served in Glider Infantry and participated in

Normandy invasion and Battle of the Bulge; became corporal; received Bronze Star and Purple Heart.

AWARDS, HONORS: Western Heritage Award, National Cowboy Hall of Fame, 1966, for *Gold Fever: Being a True Account, both Horrifying and Hilarious, of the Art of Healing (So-Called) during the California Gold Rush.*

WRITINGS:

Where Is It?, illustrations by Murray Tinkelman, Collier Books (New York City), 1963.
Gold Fever: Being a True Account, both Horrifying and Hilarious, of the Art of Healing (So-Called) during the California Gold Rush, Morrow (New York City), 1966.
Land, Sea, and Sky: An Introduction to the Wonders of Natural Science, Collier Books, 1966.
The Black Migration: The Journey to Urban America, Weybright, 1972.

Contributor of about four hundred articles to magazines, including *American Heritage, Popular Mechanics, Reporter,* and *True.*

SIDELIGHTS: Groh once commented: "I grew up curious about the world and was lucky enough to make curiosity my livelihood. My chief interests are history, biography, natural history, and science."

OBITUARIES:

PERIODICALS

Mamaroneck Times, December 28, 1984.*

*   *   *

GURA, Philip F(rancis) 1950-

PERSONAL: Born June 14, 1950, in Ware, MA; son of Oswald Eugene and Stephanie R. (Koziara) Gura; married Leslie Ann Cobig, August 4, 1979; children: David Austin, Katherine Blair, Daniel Alden. *Education:* Harvard University, B.A. (magna cum laude), 1972, Ph.D., 1977.

ADDRESSES: Home—P.O. Box 163, Chapel Hill, NC 27514. *Office*—Department of English, University of North Carolina, Chapel Hill, NC 27599-3520.

CAREER: Middlebury College, Middlebury, VT, instructor in American literature, 1974-76; University of Colorado, Boulder, assistant professor, 1976-80, associate professor of English, 1980-85, director of American studies, 1978-80, director of graduate studies, 1981-85, professor of English, 1985-87; University of North Carolina, Chapel Hill, professor of English and American studies, 1987—. Fellow, Charles Warren Center for Studies in American

History, Harvard University, 1980-81; fellow, Institute of Early American History and Culture, Williamsburg, VA, 1985-86; senior fellow, National Endowment for the Humanities, 1985-86; Peterson fellow, American Antiquarian Society, 1989.

MEMBER: Modern Language Association of America; Colonial Society of Massachusetts, 1985; American Antiquarian Society, 1988.

AWARDS, HONORS: Norman Foerster Prize in American Literature from Modern Language Association of America, 1977, for "Thoreau's Maine Woods Indians: More Representative Men."

WRITINGS:

The Wisdom of Words: Language, Theology, and Literature in the New England Renaissance, Wesleyan University Press (Middletown, CT), 1981.
(Editor with Joel Myerson) *Critical Essays on American Transcendentalism,* G. K. Hall (Boston), 1982.
A Glimpse of Sion's Glory: Puritan Radicalism in New England, 1620-1660, Wesleyan University Press, 1983.
Early Nineteenth-Century Painting in Rural Massachusetts: John Howe of Greenwich and Enfield, c. 1803-1845, with a Transcription of His "Printer's Book," c. 1832, American Antiquarian Society (Worcester, MA), 1991.

Contributor to literature and history journals, including *American Literature, Virginia Quarterly, Yale Review,* and *Sewanee Review.*

SIDELIGHTS: In *The Wisdom of Words: Language, Theology, and Literature in the New England Renaissance,* Philip F. Gura examines the cultural context out of which American literary symbolism emerged in the decades before the Civil War. Gura focuses on religion and language theory in the first section of the book, while in the latter chapters he discusses the works of such writers as Ralph Waldo Emerson, Henry David Thoreau, and Herman Melville. In the *Journal of American History* Robert D. Richardson, Jr. writes that "the integrity of [Gura's] study lies in its fidelity to the issues and judgements of the period about which he is writing. Thus his work is solid and will last, and his readers are free to make their own connections with the present."

Gura continues his examination of New England history in *A Glimpse of Sion's Glory: Puritan Radicalism in New England, 1620-1660.* In this work Gura asserts that the Puritans were not as ideologically homogeneous as some historians have suggested and that there were, in fact, numerous acts of dissent committed by Puritan radicals. Divided into three sections, *A Glimpse of Sion's Glory* catalogs the various types of Puritan dissent, discusses the response of the Puritan establishment to radical thinkers, and provides case studies of three radicals: Anne Hutchinson, Samuel Gorton, and William Pynchon. In the *American Historical Review,* Theodore Dwight Bozeman states that "Gura displays the most thorough and integrated knowledge of New England dissent from 1620 to 1660 yet attained by any historian." Pauline Maier, writing in the *New York Times Book Review,* also offers praise for *A Glimpse of Sion's Glory:* "[Gura's] book is an evocative account of the 17th century; so sustained a work of intelligence and human sensitivity is always a rare achievement."

BIOGRAPHICAL/CRITICAL SOURCES:

PERIODICALS

American Anthropologist, September, 1982, p. 751.
American Historical Review, April, 1985, p. 478.
American Literature, May, 1982, pp. 296-98; May, 1985, p. 326.
Choice, January, 1982, p. 626; January, 1983, p. 704; December, 1984, p. 610.
Journal of American History, June, 1982; March, 1985, p. 855.
Journal of American Studies, August, 1983, pp. 281-83; December, 1987, p. 453.
Kirkus Reviews, November 15, 1983, p. 1194.
New England Quarterly, March, 1982, pp. 132-34; March, 1985, p. 104.
New York Times Book Review, April 1, 1984, p. 21.
Virginia Quarterly Review, winter, 1985, p. 7.*

*　　*　　*

GWYNN, Robin D(avid) 1942-

PERSONAL: Born June 5, 1942, in Newtonmore, Scotland; son of John David (a civil engineer) and Grace Lawless (a historian; maiden name, Lee) Gwynn; married Margaret Diana Rodger (a librarian), February 15, 1971; children: Jennifer Lee, David Morton. *Education:* Pembroke College, Cambridge, B.A., 1964, Certificate in Education, 1965, M.A., 1968; University of London, Ph.D., 1976. *Religion:* Anglican.

ADDRESSES: Home—158 Park Rd., Palmerston North, New Zealand. *Office*—Department of History, Massey University, Palmerston North, New Zealand.

CAREER: Trent Park College of Education, London, England, part-time lecturer in history, 1965-66; University of London, Goldsmith's College, London, part-time lecturer in history, 1966-67; Massey University, Palmerston North, New Zealand, lecturer, 1969-75, senior lecturer, 1976-86, reader in history, 1987—. Director of British Huguenot Heritage Year, 1984-85; chairman of Palmpex

'82 National Philatelic Exhibition; chairman of jury, Tarapex '86 and Royal 100 National Philatelic Exhibitions. Vice president and president of Palmerston North Christian Home Trust, 1974-81; vice president and president of New Zealand Philatelic Confederation, 1988-92; vice president and president of Royal Philatelic Society of New Zealand, 1988—.

AWARDS, HONORS: Leverhulme fellow, 1984-85.

WRITINGS:

A Calendar of the Letter Books of the French Church of London from the Civil War to the Restoration, 1643-1659, Scolar Press, 1979.
Huguenot Heritage: The History and Contribution of the Huguenots in Britain, Routledge & Kegan Paul, 1985.
Collecting New Zealand Stamps, Heinemann Reed, 1988.
Minutes of the Consistory of the French Church of London, Threadneedle Street, 1679-1692, Huguenot Society of Great Britain and Ireland, 1994.

Contributor to history and philatelic journals.

WORK IN PROGRESS: Research on Huguenot refugees, especially in Britain, and on New Zealand philately; editing Roger Merrice's *Entring Book,* an English political journal.

SIDELIGHTS: Robin D. Gwynn told *CA:* "Although I am not myself of Huguenot descent, I embarked on the study of the Huguenots through a family connection. As a university student at Trinity College in Dublin, my mother was encouraged to work on the Huguenots in Ireland. She subsequently wrote the standard work on that subject and became the first official researcher appointed by the Huguenot Society. She died in 1964, shortly before my final examinations. When I was asked if I wanted to write a doctoral thesis, I embarked on a project my mother would probably have undertaken had she lived: A history of the Huguenots in Britain. I did not know it would take twenty years to complete!

"By the end of that time I had sufficient knowledge to be invited from New Zealand to act as director of Huguenot Heritage Year in Britain. This was a memorable experience involving many aspects outside my normal academic environment, such as publicity, radio and television work, some twenty-eight museum exhibitions, English Tourist Board trails, and special church services culminating in one which filled St. Paul's Cathedral.

"The interest that the celebration evoked was itself a commentary on the significance of the Huguenots in British history. Not only do they provide an outstanding example of the successful assimilation of a large alien minority, but these French Protestants shared a steely resolve that made them particularly valuable immigrants. They made specific contributions to a wide variety of art, crafts, banking and mercantile pursuits, professions, and religious denominations. With such a broad subject the last word can never be said, but the interest is unending."

BIOGRAPHICAL/CRITICAL SOURCES:

PERIODICALS

Observer, March 3, 1985.
Times Literary Supplement, October 11, 1985.

H

HAGON, Priscilla
See ALLAN, Mabel Esther

* * *

HALBROOK, Stephen P.

PERSONAL: Education: Florida College, A.A., 1967; Florida State University B.S., 1969, Ph.D., 1972; Georgetown University, J.D., 1978.

ADDRESSES: Office—10605 Judicial Dr., Suite B-3, Fairfax, VA 22030.

CAREER: Florida State University, Tallahassee, instructor in philosophy, 1970-72; Tuskegee Institute, Tuskegee, AL, assistant professor of philosophy, 1972-74; Prince George's Community College, Largo, MD, instructor in philosophy, summer, 1975; Howard University, Washington, DC, assistant professor of philosophy, 1974-79; George Mason University, assistant professor of philosophy, 1980-81; in private practice (civil litigation and criminal defense), 1978—. Georgetown University, Law fellow and coordinator of Barristers Council, 1975-77; Virginia Bar Association, member of Public Information Committee; speaker at various symposia on Bill of Rights and the Second Amendment.

MEMBER: National Rifle Association, Fairfax Hospital Association (member of Ethics Forum), Mantua Citizens Association.

WRITINGS:

That Every Man Be Armed: The Evolution of a Constitutional Right, University of New Mexico Press (Albuquerque, NM), 1984.
(Editor with Michael K. McCabe) *Defectless Firearms Litigation,* NRA-ILA (Washington, DC), 1984.

A Right to Bear Arms: State and Federal Bills of Rights and Constitutional Guarantees, Greenwood Press (Westport, CT), 1989.

Contributor to numerous books, including *Firearms Violence: Issues of Regulation,* edited by Don B. Kates, Ballinger (Cambridge, MA), 1984; *The Economics of Liberty* (a reprint selected from *The Free Market),* edited by L. Rockwell, Ludwig von Mises Institute, 1990; *The Bill of Rights: Original Meaning and Current Understanding,* edited by E. Hickok, editor, University Press of Virginia (Charlottesville), 1991; and *Drug Law,* K. and E. Zeese, Clark Boardman Callahan, 1993. Contributor to law journals, including *Baylor Law Review, Journal of Air Law and Commerce, Journal on Firearms and Public Policy, Valparasio University Law Review, Vermont Law Review, Virginia Bar News,* and *West Virginia Law Review.* Contributor to periodicals, including *American Journal of Sports Medicine, American Rifleman, NRA Action, San Antonio Express-News, SAR Magazine, USA Today,* and the *Wall Street Journal.*

* * *

HALL, James W(illiam) 1937-

PERSONAL: Born October 14, 1937, in Chester, PA; son of James William (a technician) and Margaret (Crothers) Hall; married Wilma Bauer (a college professor), May 20, 1961; children: Laura, Janet, Carol. *Education:* Bucknell University, B. Music, 1959; Union Theological Seminary, M.S.M., 1961; University of Pennsylvania, M.A., 1964, Ph.D., 1967. *Politics:* Independent. *Religion:* Protestant.

ADDRESSES: Home—173 Phila Street, Saratoga Springs, NY 12866. *Office*—Empire State College of State

University of New York, 2 Union Ave., Saratoga Springs, NY 12866.

CAREER: Cedar Crest College, Allentown, PA, instructor in music and humanities, 1961-66; State University of New York, Albany, visiting assistant professor of American studies, 1966-71, assistant for academic personnel, 1966-68, began as assistant dean, became associate university dean of university-wide activities, 1968-70, assistant vice-chancellor for policy and planning, 1970-71; Empire State College/State University of New York, Saratoga Springs, NY, president, 1971—, professor of social sciences, 1971—, vice chancellor for educational technology, 1993—. Chair of various panels and committees, including State University of New York committee on the arts, 1976-79; American Association of Colleges and Universities task force on alternatives and innovations, 1976-79; Council for Adult and Experiential Learning, 1987-88; and State University of New York Council on Educational Technology, 1991—.

Member of numerous boards and committees, including Manpower Institute, 1977—; Lifelong Learning Project Board, Education Commission of the States, 1980—; board of trustees, Monmouth College, 1981-93; executive committee, board of overseers, Nelson A. Rockefeller Institute of Government, 1983—; executive committee, board of overseers, Nelson A. Rockefeller Institute of Government, State University of New York, 1983—; board of trustees, Fielding Institute, 1990—; National Advisory Board Institute for Research on Adults in Higher Education, 1991—, and advisory board, East-West Dynamics, United Nations, 1992—. Chair for accreditation activities for various committees, including Presidents Panel for the Council on Postsecondary Accreditation Project on Nontraditional Education, 1978-79, The New School of Music, Pennsylvania, 1983, and Curtis Institute of Music, 1993.

MEMBER: American Studies Association, Society for Values in Higher Education, American Association for Higher Education, American Historical Association, American Association of State Colleges and Universities (chair, task force on opportunities in lifelong learning, 1991—), Association of American Colleges, International Council for Distance Education.

AWARDS, HONORS: Danforth graduate fellow, 1959-67; distinguished alumni award, Bucknell University, 1975; designated as one of the hundred top young leaders of the American academy by *Change* magazine, 1978; scholar in residence, Rockefeller Foundation Conference Center, Bellagio, Italy, 1987; D.H.L., Thomas Edison College of New Jersey, 1992, and College for Lifelong Learning, NH, 1994.

WRITINGS:

(Editor) *Forging the American Character,* Holt (New York), 1971.
(Editor with Barbara Kevles) *In Opposition to Core Curriculum: Alternative Models for Undergraduate Education,* Greenwood Press (Westport, CO), 1981.
Access through Innovation: New Colleges for New Students, Macmillan (New York), 1991.

Contributor of over thirty articles, book reviews, and letters to various publications, including *American Quarterly, Change, Journal of Higher Education, Journal of Alternative Education,* and *New York Times.*

*   *   *

HALVERSON, William H(agen)   1930-

PERSONAL: Born July 28, 1930, in Sebeka, MN; son of Arthur William (a farmer) and Clara (Hagen) Halverson; married Marolyn Sortland, August 25, 1951; children: Lynn, Kay, Beth, Susan, Carol. *Education:* Augsburg Seminary (now Augsburg College), B.A., 1951, B.Th., 1955; Princeton Seminary, Th.M., 1957; Princeton University, M.A., 1959, Ph.D., 1961. *Politics:* Independent. *Religion:* Lutheran.

ADDRESSES: Home—2330 Nayland Rd., Columbus, OH 43220. *Office*—University College, Ohio State University, 1050 Carmack Rd., Columbus, OH 43210.

CAREER: Sherburn High School, Sherburn, MN, teacher of music and English, 1951-52; Princeton Theological Seminary, Princeton, NJ, instructor in philosophy, 1957-59; Augsburg College, Minneapolis, MN, assistant professor, 1959-61, associate professor, 1961-65, professor of philosophy and chairman of department, 1959-67; Ohio State University, Columbus, associate dean of University College, 1967-87; freelance writer and translator, 1987—.

MEMBER: American Philosophical Association, Mind Society.

WRITINGS:

A Concise Introduction to Philosophy (college textbook), Random House, 1967 (New York City), 4th edition, 1981.
A Concise Logic (college textbook), Random House (New York City), 1984.

EDITOR

(And author of introduction) *Concise Readings in Philosophy,* Random House (New York City), 1981.
Edvard Grieg Today, St. Olaf College (Northfield), 1994.

TRANSLATOR

(With Leland B. Sateren) Finn Benestad and Dag Schjelderup-Ebbe, *Edvard Greig: The Man and the Artist,* University of Nebraska Press (Lincoln), 1988.

(Translator of song texts) *Edvard Greig: Complete Works,* C. F. Peters Verlag (Frankfurt, Germany), Volume 14, 1990, Volume 15, 1991.

(With Sateren) Nils Grinde, *A History of Norwegian Music,* University of Nebraska Press, 1991.

Jon-Roar Bjorkvold, *The Muse Within,* HarperCollins (New York City), 1992.

OTHER

Contributor of articles to theology and philosophy journals, including *Mind, Journal of Religion,* and *Pacific Journal of Philosophy.*

WORK IN PROGRESS: Translating *Johan Svendsen: The Man and the Artist,* by Benestad and Schjelderup-Ebbe.

SIDELIGHTS: William H. Halverson told *CA:* "Scholarly writing has been an important part of my life since the beginning of my professional career. As a college professor I always planned my summers around my writing—several articles, to begin with, and then, in the summer of 1965, my first book, which was eventually published in 1967. Upon becoming a university administrator I vowed that I would continue to write, and I did. My pattern for those twenty years was to spend four evenings each week plus Saturday at my writing desk—about twenty hours per week minus unavoidable interruptions. Approximately 100,000 students have been introduced to philosophy through the several editions of *A Concise Introduction to Philosophy.* Since 1987, I have had the luxury of spending the best hours of each day at my writing desk. Meanwhile, the primary focus of my work has changed from writing books on philosophy to, primarily, translating books dealing with Norwegian music.

"My interest in Norwegian music (and the Norwegian language) was initially stimulated by a study trip to Norway in the summer of 1950, when I met the legendary musicologist O. M. Sandvik. That interest, which remained 'on the back burner' throughout much of my career, was revived during extended visits to Norway in 1976 and 1978, and since 1987 I have devoted much of my time to this previously avocational interest."

BIOGRAPHICAL/CRITICAL SOURCES:

PERIODICALS

New York Times Book Review, March 19, 1989, p. 22.

HAMBURGER, Michael (Peter Leopold) 1924-

PERSONAL: Born March 22, 1924, in Berlin, Germany; son of Richard (a physician and professor) and Lili M. (Hamburg) Hamburger; married Anne Beresford (an actress, musician, and poet), July 28, 1951; children: Mary Anne, Richard Benedict, Claire Miranda. *Education:* Christ Church, Oxford, B.A. and M.A., 1948. *Avocational interests:* Plants and animals, walking, gardening, riding, swimming, rowing, listening to music.

ADDRESSES: Home—Marsh Acres, Saxmundham, Suffolk 1P17 3NH, England. *Agent*—John Johnson Ltd., Clerkenwell House, 45/47 Clerkenwell Green EC1R OHT, England.

CAREER: Freelance writer, 1948-52; University of London, University College, London, England, assistant lecturer in German, 1952-55; University of Reading, Reading, England, 1955-64, began as lecturer, became reader in German; full-time writer, 1964—. Mount Holyoke College, South Hadley, MA, Florence Purington Lecturer, 1966-67; State University of New York, visiting professor at Buffalo, 1969, and at Stony Brook, 1971; Center for Humanities, Wesleyan University, Middletown, CT, visiting fellow, 1970; University of South Carolina, Columbia, visiting professor, 1973; University of California, San Diego, Regent's Lecturer, 1973; Boston University, Boston, MA, visiting professor, 1975-77; University of Essex, Essex, England, temporary professor, 1978. *Military service:* British Army, Infantry, 1943-47; became lieutenant.

MEMBER: Royal Society of Literature (fellow), Akademie der Kuenste, Deutsche Akademie fuer Sprache und Dichtung (corresponding member), Bayerische Akademie der Schoenen Kuenste.

AWARDS, HONORS: Bollingen Foundation fellowship, 1959-61, 1965-66; Cultural Committee of German Industrialists award, 1963, for translations from German; West German Deutsche Akademie fuer Sprache und Dichtung prize, 1964, for translation; Schlegel-Tieck Prize for poetry, London, 1967, 1981; Arts Council of Great Britain translation prize, 1967; Levinson Prize, 1970; gold medal, Institute of Linguistics, 1976; Inter Nationes arts prize, 1976; Wilhelm Heinse Prize for critical essays, 1978; European Poetry Translation Prize, London, 1985; Goethe Medal, 1986, for translations; Austrian State Prize for Literary Translation, 1988; honorary Litt.D., University of East Anglia, 1988; European Translation Prize, Glasgow, 1990; Order of the British Empire, 1992; Hoelderlin Prize, 1992; Petrarca Prize, 1993.

WRITINGS:

POETRY

Later Hogarth, Cope & Fenwick (London), 1945.

Flowering Cactus: Poems, 1942-49, Hand & Flower Press (Aldington, England), 1950.

Poems, 1950-51, Hand & Flower Press, 1952.

The Dual Site, Dodd, Mead (New York), 1958.

Weather and Season, Atheneum (New York), 1963.

In Flashlight, Northern House (Leeds, England), 1965.

In Massachusetts, Ox Head Press (Menomonie, WI), 1967.

Feeding the Chickadees, Turret (London), 1968.

Travelling, Fulcrum Press (London), 1969.

(With Charles Tomlinson and Alan Brownjohn) *Penguin Modern Poets 14,* Penguin (Baltimore, MD), 1969.

Travelling I-V, Agenda Editions (London), 1972.

Ownerless Earth: New and Selected Poems, Dutton (New York), 1973.

Travelling VI, I. M. Imprimit (London), 1975.

Travelling VII, [Erpeldange, Luxembourg], 1976.

Real Estate, Carcanet (Manchester), 1977.

Moralities, Morden Tower (Newcastle-upon-Tyne), 1977.

In Suffolk, Five Seasons Press (Hereford, England), 1981.

Variations, Black Swan (Redding Ridge, CT), 1981.

Collected Poems, 1941-1983, Carcanet (New York), 1984, corrected edition, 1985.

Heimgekommen, Hanser, 1984, revised edition, Thames & Hudson, 1984.

Selected Poems, Carcanet, 1988.

Roots in the Air, Anvil Press (London), 1992.

Collected Poems, 1941-1994, Anvil Press, 1995.

NONFICTION

Reason and Energy: Studies in German Literature (critical essays), Grove (New York), 1957, enlarged edition, Weidenfeld & Nicolson (London), 1970, also published as *Contraries,* Dutton (New York), 1970.

Hugo Von Hofmannsthal: Zwei Studien (criticism), Sachse & Pohl, 1964, published in the United States as *Hofmannsthal: Three Essays,* Princeton University Press (Princeton, NJ), 1972.

From Prophecy to Exorcism: The Premises of Modern German Literature (criticism), Longmans, Green (London), 1965.

The Truth of Poetry: Tensions in Modern Poetry from Baudelaire to the 1960s (criticism), Weidenfeld & Nicolson, 1969, Harcourt (New York), 1970.

A Mug's Game: Intermittent Memoirs, 1924-1954 (autobiography), Carcanet (Manchester), 1973, revised edition published as *A String of Beginnings,* Skool Books (London), 1991.

Art as Second Nature: Occasional Pieces, 1950-74 (criticism), Carcanet (Manchester), 1975.

Literarische Erfahtungen (essays), Luchterhand, 1981.

A Proliferation of Prophets: Essays on German Writers from Nietzsche to Brecht (criticism), Carcanet, 1983, St. Martin's (New York), 1984.

After the Second Flood: Essays on Post-War German Literature, St. Martin's, 1986.

Testimonies: Selected Shorter Prose, 1950-1987, St. Martin's, 1989.

TRANSLATOR

(And author of introduction) Friedrich Hoelderlin, *Poems of Hoelderlin* (bilingual edition), Nicholson & Watson (London), 1943, 2nd edition published as *Hoelderlin: His Poems,* Harvill Press (London), 1952, Pantheon (New York), 1953.

Charles Baudelaire, *Twenty Prose Poems of Baudelaire,* Editions Poetry (London), 1946, City Lights (San Francisco, CA), 1988.

(And editor and author of introduction) *Beethoven: Letters, Journals, and Conversations,* Thames & Hudson (London), 1951, Pantheon (New York), 1952.

Georg Trakl, *Decline: Twelve Poems,* Latin Press (St. Ives, England), 1952.

Albrecht Goes, *The Burnt Offering,* Pantheon, 1956.

(Editor, co-translator, and author of introduction) Hugo von Hofmannsthal, *Poems and Verse Plays,* Pantheon (New York), 1961.

(And editor and author of introduction) Hoelderlin, *Selected Verse,* Penguin, 1961.

(Editor and author of introduction with Christopher Middleton, and co-translator) *Modern German Poetry, 1910-1960,* Grove (New York), 1963.

(Editor, co-translator, and author of introduction) Hofmannsthal, *Selected Plays and Libretti,* Pantheon (New York), 1963.

(With Middleton) Guenter Grass, *Selected Poems,* Harcourt (New York), 1966.

Friedrich Hoelderlin: Poems and Fragments (bilingual edition), Routledge & Kegan Paul (London), 1966, University of Michigan Press (Ann Arbor, MI), 1967, enlarged edition, Anvil Press, 1994.

(With others) Nelly Sachs, *O the Chimneys* (selected poems and the verse play *Eli*), Farrar, Straus, 1967.

Hans Magnus Enzensberger, *Poems,* Northern House, 1967.

Peter Bichsel, *And Really Frau Blum Would Very Much Like to Meet the Milkman,* Delacorte, 1968.

Guenter Eich, *Journeys: The Rolling Sea at Setubal and The Year Lacertis,* J. Cape (London), 1968.

(With Jerome Rothenberg) Enzensberger, *Poems for People Who Don't Read Poems,* Atheneum (New York), 1968.

(With others) Sachs, *Selected Poems,* J. Cape, 1968.

(With others) Georg Trakl, *Selected Poems,* J. Cape, 1968.

Bichsel, *There Is No Such Place as America,* Delacorte, 1970, published in England as *Stories for Children,* Calder & Boyars, 1970.

Georg Buechner, *"Leonce and Lena," "Lenz," "Woyzeck,"* University of Chicago Press, 1972.

Paul Celan, *Nineteen Poems,* Carcanet, 1972.

Selected Poems, Penguin, 1972, enlarged bilingual edition, Persea (New York), 1980.

(And editor) *East German Poetry* (bilingual anthology), Dutton (New York), 1972.

Peter Huchel, *Selected Poems,* Carcanet (Manchester), 1974.

(And editor) *German Poetry, 1910-1975* (bilingual anthology), Urizen (New York), 1976, corrected edition, Persea, 1977, revised edition, 1981.

(With others) Bertolt Brecht, *Poems, 1913-1966,* Eyre Methuen, 1976, 2nd edition, Methuen, 1979.

(With Andre Lefevere) Philippe Jaccottet,

Seedtime, New Directions, 1977.

(With Middleton) Grass, *In the Egg and Other Poems,* Harcourt (New York), 1977, published in England as *Selected Poems,* Penguin, 1980.

Helmut Heissenbuttel, *Texts,* Marion Boyars (London and Boston), 1977.

Franco Fortini, *Poems,* Arc (Todmorden, England), 1978.

Paul Celan: Poems, Persea, 1980.

Rainer Maria Rilke, *An Unofficial Rilke,* Anvil Press (London), 1981, published as *Rilke: Poems 1912-1926,* Black Swan, 1981.

Johann Wolfgang von Goethe, *Goethe: Poems and Epigrams,* Anvil Press, 1983, published as *Goethe: Roman Elegies and Other Poems,* Black Swan, 1983.

Huchel, *The Garden of Theophrastus and Other Poems,* Carcanet (Manchester), 1983.

Martin Sorescu, *Selected Poems,* Bloodaxe (Newcastle-upon-Tyne), 1983.

(With Marlis Zeller Cambon) Adolph Muschg, *The Blue Man and Other Stories,* Carcanet, 1983.

Paul Celan, *Thirty-Two Poems,* Embers Handpress (Norwich, England), 1985.

(With Middleton and others) Gottfried Benn, *Primal Vision: Selected Writings,* Marion Boyars, 1985.

(With Middleton and Ralph Manheim) Grass, *Etchings and Words, 1972 to 1982,* Harcourt, 1985.

Hoelderlin, *Hoelderlin: Selected Verse,* Anvil Press Poetry (Dover, NH), 1986.

(With Hunter Hannum and David Luke) *Johann Wolfgang von Goethe: Collected Works,* Volume 8: *Verse Plays and Epic,* International Book Import, 1987.

(With Robert M. Browning, Cyrus Hamlin, and Ryder) Goethe, *Collected Works,* Volume 7: *Early Verse Drama and Prose Plays,* International Book Import, 1988.

(And author of introduction) *Poems of Paul Celan,* Persea, 1989, enlarged and corrected edition, Anvil, 1995.

Eich, *Pigeons and Moles: Selected Writings of Guenter Eich* (selected writings), Camden House (Columbia, SC), 1990.

OTHER

Poetry of Michael Hamburger (sound recording), J. Norton (New York), 1966.

Zwischen den Sprachen: Essays und Gedichte (essays and poems), S. Fischer, 1966.

Contributor to anthologies and numerous periodicals.

SIDELIGHTS: Michael Hamburger is "one of the few really first-rate poets writing in England today," according to David Miller in *Agenda. Poetry* contributor John Matthias affirms that Hamburger's poems "can and must be . . . taken as manifestations of the moral consciousness of the modern European Jew." Hamburger is also known for his work as a translator of poetry and as a writer of critical essays. His translations of the German poet Hoelderlin have helped to establish the 19th century author among English-language readers.

A *Times Literary Supplement* reviewer writes of Hamburger's critical 1957 work *Reason and Energy,* "It is the combination of poet and critic which makes the special interest.... It is a poet's preoccupation with [the] characteristic use of language which provides the insight and the illumination." E. M. Fleissner considers *Zwischen den Sprachen,* a 1966 collection of essays and poems, "truly impressive." Hamburger here and elsewhere in his essays, he contends, has bridged the gap between Germany and England, "linked the two idioms, and become one of those all-too-rare representatives of German and English literature capable of doing equal justice to both. His German style actually has gained in the process; it is more lucid and precise in dealing with intricate and subtle issues than that of many German critics."

His firmly established place among contemporary poets and critics notwithstanding, Hamburger remains most esteemed for his diligence and proficiency in resurrecting German authors for English readers. His collected translations of Friedrich Hoelderlin and Hugo von Hofmannsthal are considered definitive. In a review of *Friedrich Hoelderlin: Poems and Fragments,* John Mander writes that in Hamburger's introductory essay he "too modestly conceals the truth that it was his own translation, first published in 1943 (when he was still in his teens)," that caused England to regard Hoelderlin as a modern author. "Lacking Mr. Hamburger's mediation, Hoelderlin would have remained—as most of the German classics remain—on the outer fringe of literary acceptance in Britain and America. As it is, Hoelderlin is as much a part of the English-writing poet's awareness as any poet of the modern era. It is a remarkable and—for all the support of his fellow-poets—almost a one-man achievement. How was it done? [Principally] there was a very personal passion informing Mr. Hamburger's advocacy. The Englishing of Hoelderlin was a re-assertion, a rescuing of the language of [Hamburger's] childhood and of the values of an older Germany."

In the view of another writer for the *Times Literary Supplement,* "No other versions have ever come so close to the essential Hoelderlin, or have ever read so well. . . . Hamburger's translations are at the furthest possible remove from the now fashionable 'recreations' or 'meta-phrases' of foreign-language poems. . . . [Instead he] retains faithfully the classical metres of which Hoelderlin made such odd use." In *Poetry Nation,* Joyce Crick observes that "in Michael Hamburger we have the mediating translator at his best, one who has lived his life between two languages, between two literary skills, between two cultural traditions, and devoted long years . . . to a series of attempts, raids upon the articulate, at making available to the English tradition [Hoelderlin], this least accessible of German poets."

New York Times Book Review contributor Rika Lesser states of Hamburger's work with the poetry of Paul Celan, "[His] literary translations, his tough-minded, clear-sighted readings, are often as deeply ambiguous as the German poems given *en face.*" In the opinion of R. J. Hollingdale in the *Times Literary Supplement,* Hamburger was successful in his translation *An Unofficial Rilke* because his "decision to imitate the form has also given him scope to render the meaning of some of the individual words more precisely." Also in the *Times Literary Supplement,* Sean O'Brien adds to the praise of Hamburger's work: "Readers of more than one generation owe a debt to Michael Hamburger as a translator. Few can have done more to enhance (and in many cases create) the appreciation of German poetry among an Anglophone audience. . . . In comparison with his renown in [translation and criticism], Hamburger the poet has sometimes been overshadowed."

Hamburger's poetry treats such topics as war and those lost in it, the Holocaust, being Jewish in the postwar era, love and hate, and other personal experiences. Miller contends in *Agenda,* "Hamburger's fine intelligence, his sensitivity, his feeling for the craft of poetry, his seriousness, and his pleasantly grumpy humour and satiric ingenuity, are all qualities which should have won him a far greater audience than that which he actually has." John Matthias argues in *Poetry,* "If Michael Hamburger writes with an outraged moral consciousness, and he often does, he is also a connoisseur of the chaos that outrages him and threatens to destroy his world."

Hamburger spent his early childhood in Berlin. Although his family was predominantly of German-Jewish stock, they were not religious Jews, and, as Peter Schmidt explains in *Dictionary of Literary Biography,* "it was not until Hamburger's schoolteachers in Berlin began forming the student handball players into 'Aryan' and 'Jewish' teams that he learned he was Jewish as well as German." After Hitler came into full power in 1933, the family immigrated to Edinburgh and, a year later, moved to London. In the United Kingdom Hamburger's father, a doctor, had to go through another long process of certification to practice medicine. Hamburger was nine when he left Germany, and it was not until his year in Scotland that he began to emerge from what he has described as the extreme introversion he had developed as a child of busy and distracted parents. He later went to Oxford, where he began translating German poets and earned both a B.A. and an M.A. degree in modern languages in 1948.

Schmidt remarks that Hamburger's poetry "shows at all points an interest in experimental techniques and psychological intensities. His poetic style has changed sharply over the course of four decades, evolving from a formal, symbolist, Yeatsian style to more colloquial work in free verse which celebrates evolving rather than fixed patterns of meaning. Despite such stylistic changes, however, his work consistently contrasts art's desire for order and unity with life's sometimes gentle and sometimes violent disruption of those values." Schmidt names as "the pivotal volume in Hamburger's . . . gradual move from formal to free verse" the 1963 collection *Weather and Season,* in which the poet writes in a "newer and more various music . . . both stately and filled with the content and rhythms of contemporary speech."

Donald Davie declares in the *New York Times Book Review,* "Michael Hamburger is a contemporary poet whom I respect without reservations and an English poet who will be read and remembered long after more flashy and quarrelsome talents have burned themselves out." M. L. Rosenthal of the *New York Times Book Review* refers to Hamburger as "an exquisitely perceptive lyric poet." Robin Skelton considers his verse accomplished and notes that "the reflective poems have both delicacy and passion, and the lyrics subtlety and strength. Occasionally [Hamburger] speaks a little too easily of great matters, and sometimes his symbols have a faint smell of the study about them, but usually his craftsmanship and sensibility are successfully directed at presenting with wit, poignancy, and control the most serious problems of our divided days."

A *Times Literary Supplement* reviewer considers the poems in *The Dual Site* "often at first glance rather flat in their verbal surface, [but they] grow in interest on rereading, because of the complexity of their thought." The same reviewer, however, calls Hamburger's diction "dignified but unexciting," not commensurate with his "imaginative inventiveness or the subtlety of his insights into life." In Lawrence Norfolk's opinion, also in the *Times Literary Supplement,* Hamburger's poetry "seems to induce an anxiety of homelessness, of not belonging." Some critics find Hamburger's poetry lacking at times in feeling or drama. John Fuller, reviewing *Travelling* for the *Listener,* finds many of the poems "simply dull," though he comments that the book is saved by the "moving poems" such as "Observer," "The Cello," and "For a Family Album," in which "feelings are . . . powerfully conveyed by the images." William Scammell, in the *Times Literary Supplement,* faults Hamburger in *Variations* for leaving one "throughout the book . . . groping for substance and direction," describes a passage about a love affair as "altogether sunk by its approximation to Eliot's *Four Quartets,*" and notes unfavorably echoes of Wordsworth and Hardy, neither of whom, Hamburger told *CA,* influenced him as a poet.

In another *Times Literary Supplement* review, Terry Eagleton considers how the work in *Collected Poems 1941-1983* demonstrates Hamburger's increasing maturity as a poet. "As Hamburger evolves from . . . too generalized, rhetorical, inflexibly iambic pieces towards the leaner notations of his mature style, that contrast grows accordingly more complex," Eagleton points out. "His own poetic language . . . , neither ripely sensuous nor self-consciously chaste, neither formal nor colloquial, . . . seeks that point at which the poem refuses either to overwhelm its object or efface itself before it." In his *Contemporary Authors Autobiography Series* article, Hamburger relates, "If my real and essential life is registered anywhere, it is in my poems. . . . When I put together my collected poems for my sixtieth birthday, I had to reject most of those in my first and second collections. Those were poems that did not catch the live moments; and the reason is that I was literarily precocious long before I was anything like emotionally mature. . . . In my introversion I had not yet learned to trust my senses, least of all my eyes."

In the same essay Hamburger acknowledges being recognized by many readers more for his translations than for his poems, ironic in that the translations are work he considers generally to have a "very limited life span, so that for them not even the possibility of 'permanent value' can be entertained." Musing about the "wonderment and outrage" that are the source of poetry, he reasons, "it is not my business to ask why or how I go on, how or why my work appeals or does not appeal to those who read such work. . . . My business is to remain true to the wonderment and outrage as long as they recur, always unexpectedly, always in a way I can neither plan nor choose; and

to keep quiet when there is nothing that wants to use me to make itself heard."

BIOGRAPHICAL/CRITICAL SOURCES:

BOOKS

Contemporary Authors Autobiography Series, Volume 4, Gale, 1986.
Contemporary Literary Criticism, Gale, Volume 5, 1976, Volume 14, 1980.
Davie, Donald, *Under Briggflatts: A History of Poetry in Great Britain 1960-1988,* Carcanet, 1989.
Dictionary of Literary Biography, Volume 27: *Poets of Great Britain and Ireland, 1945-1960,* Gale, 1984, pp. 130-138.
Schmidt, Michael, editor, *Fifty Modern British Poets,* Pan, 1979.

PERIODICALS

Agenda, autumn-winter, 1973-74, pp. 139-148.
Books Abroad, summer, 1967; spring, 1970; spring, 1971.
Book Week, December 29, 1963.
Encounter, November, 1971.
Listener, March 23, 1967; February 26, 1970, pp. 413-414; October 13, 1977.
London Magazine, May, 1970.
Los Angeles Times, May 15, 1985.
Manchester Guardian, May 16, 1958; April 5, 1973.
Modern Language Review, July, 1972.
Nation, August 27, 1971.
New Statesman, March 10, 1967; September 30, 1977.
New York Review of Books, April 11, 1968.
New York Times Book Review, December 22, 1963; April 28, 1974, p. 31; April 26, 1981, p. 22.
Poetry, May, 1967; May, 1971; April, 1974.
Poetry Nation, number 3, 1974.
Saturday Review, February 1, 1964.
Sewanee Review, fall, 1977.
Times (London), February 11, 1989.
Times Literary Supplement, May 31, 1957; May 2, 1958; March 9, 1967; February 12, 1982, p. 166; April 30, 1982, p. 476; April 20, 1984, p. 434; April 27, 1984, p. 454; March 13, 1987; December 30, 1988, p. 1450; March 13, 1992, p. 25.

*   *   *

HAMILTON, John Maxwell 1947-

PERSONAL: Born March 28, 1947, in Evanston, IL; son of M. M. (in business) and Elizabeth (a social worker; maiden name, Carlson) Hamilton, married Regina Nalewajek (an attorney), September 19, 1975; children: Maxwell. *Education:* Marquette University, B.A., 1969;

graduate study at University of New Hampshire, 1971-73; Boston University, M.S., 1974; Spanish language study at Instituto de Idiomas, Cochabamba, Bolivia, 1976; George Washington University, Ph.D., 1983.

ADDRESSES: Home—567 LSU Ave., Baton Rouge, LA 70808. *Office*—Manship School of Mass Communication, Louisiana State University, Baton Rouge, LA 70803. *Agent*—(literature) Peter Shepherd, Harold Ober Associates, Inc., 425 Madison Ave., New York, NY 10017; (speaking and lecturing) Phyllis Corbitt McKenzie, Capital Speakers Inc., 655 National Press Building, Washington, DC 20045.

CAREER: Milwaukee Journal, Milwaukee, WI, reporter, 1967-69; free-lance journalist in Washington, DC, 1973-75; free-lance foreign correspondent in Latin America, Africa, and Middle East and radio correspondent for American Broadcasting Companies (ABC) in Peru and Bolivia, 1976-78; U.S. Agency for International Development (USAID), Washington, special assistant to assistant administrator, 1978-81; U.S. House of Representatives, Foreign Affairs Committee, Subcommittee on International Economic Policy and Trade, Washington, staff associate, 1981-82; International Reporting Information System, Washington, chief U.S. foreign policy correspondent, 1982-83; World Bank, Washington, North American adviser on public affairs, 1983-85, senior counsellor, 1987-92; Sigma Delta Chi Foundation, Washington, director of Main Street America and the Third World project, 1985-87; Manship School of Mass Communication, Louisiana State University, Baton Rouge, LA, director, 1992-94, dean, 1994—.

Instructor in communication at American University, Washington, 1974-75; professorial lecturer in American civilization at George Washington University, Washington, 1982; visiting professor of journalism at Northwestern University, 1985-87. Member of board of directors, Center for Foreign Journalists Selection Committee, 1989—; member of board of directors, Arthur F. Burns Fellows, 1990—; member of board of directors, European Commodity Journalism Fellowships, 1993—. American Public Radio, commentator on *MarketPlace* program, 1991—. Gives speeches and makes frequent radio and television appearances. *Military service:* U.S. Marine Corps, 1969-73; served in infantry; became captain.

MEMBER: Society of Professional Journalists, Association for Education and Journalism and Mass Communications, Association of Schools of Journalism and Mass Communication, Louisiana Press Association.

AWARDS, HONORS: Grants from Carnegie Corporation, Ford Foundation, Benton Foundation, German Marshall Fund of the United States, Rockefeller Foundation and Radio Television News Directors Foundation;

Frank Luther Mott-Kappa Tau Research Award, 1989, for *Edgar Snow: A Biography;* Journalism By-Line Award, Marquette University, 1993.

WRITINGS:

Main Street America and the Third World, foreword by Peter Jennings, Seven Locks Press, 1986, revised and enlarged edition, 1989.
Edgar Snow: A Biography, Indiana University Press, 1989.
Entangling Alliance: How the Third World Shapes Our Lives, Seven Locks Press, 1990.

Contributor to books, including Liu Ligun, editor, *In Memory of Edgar Snow,* New China Press, 1985; Joseph F. Pilat, editor, *The Nonproliferation Predicament,* Transaction Books, 1985; Rosabeth Moss Kanter, Barry A. Stein and Todd J. Jick, editors, *The Challenge of Organization Change,* Free Press, 1992; Stuart S. Nagel and Vladimir Rukavishnikov, editors, *Eastern European Development and Public Policy,* St. Martin's, 1994.

Contributor to periodicals, including *Baltimore Sun, Boston Globe, Bulletin of the Atomic Scientists, Christian Science Monitor, Columbia Journalism Review, Dallas Morning News, Des Moines Register, Europe, Freedom Forum Media Studies Journal, International Herald Tribune, Korean Herald, Lima Times, Los Angeles Times, Maryknoll, Miami Herald, Missouri Historical Review, Nation, New York Times, Newsday, Nieman Reports, Pacific Historical Review, People, Pittsburgh Press, Quill, Society, Wall Street Journal, Washington Post,* and *World Monitor Magazine.* Hamilton's *Edgar Snow: A Biography* has been translated into Chinese and Japanese.

SIDELIGHTS: A journalist interested in the interdependence of the U.S. and Third World economies—an issue given scant attention in most American newspapers—John Maxwell Hamilton was working for the World Bank in the early 1980s when he decided "to demonstrate to newspaper editors across the country that there are good local stories with third-world angles," writes David R. Francis in the *Christian Science Monitor.* Hamilton took a leave of absence from his job and arranged to do a series of six articles for the *Hattiesburg American* on the ways in which Third World issues directly affected the inhabitants of Hattiesburg, Mississippi. Though Frank Sutherland, editor of the *American* was initially skeptical about the project, the series proved quite effective. Hamilton turned up connections between a local soybean farmer's profits and the Brazilian economy, revealed that Miller-Picking, the Hattiesburg air conditioning manufacturer, depends on Third World countries to buy 90 percent of its exports, and linked a nearby pulp manufacturer's profits to a new compulsory education law in Indonesia. At the conclusion of the series, polls showed that the articles had increased local awareness about interdependence, supporting Hamilton's belief that Americans would read articles about Third World issues.

The series attracted national attention. It also inspired Hamilton to write a book, *Main Street America and the Third World,* in which he expands his approach to show the relationships between other average American towns and Third World economic developments. As Bruce Stokes states in the *National Journal,* Hamilton, "probably more than any other single journalist . . . is helping to shape public opinion about the complexity of U.S. trade and lending policy toward the Third World."

Hamilton told *CA:* "Ever since the founding of the American republic—indeed, well before—Americans have paid scant attention to international affairs. Without a doubt this has caused serious damage. The life of Edgar Snow, author of *Red Star over China* and the foreign correspondent who anticipated the Chinese Communist revolution as well as the emergence of a new world of decolonized nations after World War II, speaks volumes about the way Americans have ignored events overseas only to be overtaken by them later. Snow's case is all the more poignant because his reward for seeing ahead so clearly was to be driven into exile in Europe during the Cold War.

"Yet, as dramatic as such episodes are, it is equally significant that Americans have managed to prosper so greatly without paying serious attention to foreign affairs. That part of our history has led us to think that we can truly distance ourselves from other countries. Nothing could be more perilous. Today, as a result of changing circumstances, the United States is no longer self-sufficient. Seemingly isolated events in other countries have a daily impact on average Americans—on what they do for work (or even if they work at all); on what they do for fun; on their environment and their health; on virtually every aspect of their lives.

"In my historical writing I try, as best as I can, to explain how we have perceived the world in the past and what the pitfalls have been. In my journalism, including regular commentary on American Public Radio, I try to report objectively both foreign and domestic events, and often the way they intertwine. But it all comes down to one thing, making a modest contribution to an enormously complicated debate about the hard choices that lie ahead for Americans."

BIOGRAPHICAL/CRITICAL SOURCES:

PERIODICALS

Christian Science Monitor, November 16, 1984.
Editor and Publisher, January 10, 1987.
Evening Sun (Baltimore, MD), January 3, 1985.
National Journal, March 1, 1986.
Washington Journalism Review, January, 1985.

HANN, C. M. 1953-

PERSONAL: Born August 4, 1953, in Cardiff, Wales; married; children: two. *Education:* Oxford University, B.A., 1974; Cambridge University, Ph.D., 1979.

ADDRESSES: Office—Department of Sociology and Social Anthropology, University of Kent at Canterbury, Canterbury, England.

CAREER: New Hungarian Quarterly, Budapest, Hungary, language editor, 1979-80; Cambridge University, Corpus Christi College, Cambridge, England, research fellow, 1980-84, lecturer in social anthropology, 1984-92; University of Kent at Canterbury, Canterbury, England, professor of social anthropology, 1992—.

WRITINGS:

Tazlar: A Village in Hungary, Cambridge University Press, 1980.
A Village without Solidarity: Polish Peasants in Years of Crisis, Yale University Press, 1985.
Tea and the Domestication of the Turkish State, Eothen Press, 1990.
(Editor) *Socialism: Ideals, Ideologies and Local Practice,* Routledge, 1993.

WORK IN PROGRESS: Research on the anthropology of Eastern Europe; research on Turkish, Chinese, and Central Asian anthropology.

SIDELIGHTS: C. M. Hann told *CA:* "The anthropologist who carries out long-term fieldwork in small communities is in many ways better able to understand them and the larger social processes affecting them than are other specialists. My earlier work was concerned with an understanding of socialist societies in Eastern Europe, and this region remains at the center of my interests as its peoples cope with post-communist dilemmas."

*   *   *

HARDY, C. Colburn 1910-

PERSONAL: Born January 13, 1910, in Boston, MA; son of Charles A. (a corporate executive) and Gladys M. (an engineer; maiden name, Blake) Hardy; married Ruth E. Hart (a public relations director), June 27, 1942; children: Dorcas Ruth. *Education:* Yale University, A. B., 1931; Columbia University, additional study, 1934. *Religion:* Unitarian-Universalist.

ADDRESSES: Office—C. Colburn Hardy & Associates, 2542 Canterbury Dr. S., West Palm Beach, FL 33407.

CAREER: Republican representative in New Jersey Assembly, 1942-43; Carl Byoir & Associates (public relations firm), New York City, 1948-59, began as staffer, became vice-president; Jones Brakeley & Rockwell (public relations firm), New York City, executive vice-president, 1960-64; Federal Pacific Electric Co., Newark, NJ, director of public relations, 1965-67; General Dynamics Co., New York City, public relations, 1967-76; C. Colburn Hardy & Associates (public relations firm), West Palm Beach, FL, president, 1972—. President of Social Welfare Council and Community Service Council of New Jersey, 1967-69; member of board of directors, United Way, 1967-70, JET Corp., 1981-85, Florida Council on Aging/Adult Services, and Florida Association of American Retired Persons (AARP) State Legislative Committee. *Military service:* U. S. Naval Reserve, 1943-46; became lieutenant commander; received seven battle stars.

MEMBER: Public Relations Society of America, Phi Beta Kappa.

WRITINGS:

(With John Winthrop Wright) *Q-V-T: The Three Keys to Stock Market Profits,* Prentice-Hall (Englewood Cliffs, NJ), 1970.
Personal Money Management, Funk (New York City), 1976.
ABC's of Investing Your Retirement Funds, Medical Economics (Oradell, NJ), 1978, 2nd edition, 1982.
Investor's Guide to Technical Analysis, McGraw (New York City), 1978.
Your Money and Your Life, American Management Association (Saranac Lake, NY), 1979, 2nd edition, 1982.
Safe in Retirement, Bantam (New York City), 1980.
Guide to Financially Secure Retirement, Harper (New York City), 1982.
Facts of Life, American Management Association, 1984.
Blue Chip Investing, F. Watts (New York City), 1987.
How To Retire Prosperously, Simon & Schuster (New York City), 1989.
(With daughter, Dorcas R. Hardy) *Social Insecurity,* Villard Books, 1991.
Florida Caregivers Handbook, Creston Nelson-Morrill, 1993.
Pension Plans for Professionals, PMIC, 1994.

Contributor, sometimes under undisclosed pseudonyms, to periodicals such as *Physician's Management, Dental Management, Golden Years,* and *New Choices.* Also editor of Dun & Bradstreet's annual publication, *Guide to Your Investments,* 1974-84.

WORK IN PROGRESS: A book on pension plans warning of severe problems ahead with some viable solutions.

SIDELIGHTS: C. Colburn Hardy told *CA:* "After taking early retirement, as a public relations executive with an international defense contractor, I started a second career

as a writer. I began with articles to trade publications and newsletters, then I wrote books on investment and money management for major publishers. Later, as the result of volunteer activity in Aging Programs in Florida and nationally, I wrote on retirement. With my daughter, Dorcas, who was U.S. Commissioner of Social Security under Presidents Reagan and Bush, I wrote *Social Insecurity.*"

*   *   *

HARDY, Henry 1949-
(Robert Dugdale)

PERSONAL: Born March 15, 1949, in London, England; son of Richard Henry (a physician) and Elizabeth (Harris) Hardy; married Anne Wilkinson (a research historian), June 23, 1979; children: Ellen Elizabeth, Michael Henry Dugdale. *Education:* Corpus Christi College, Oxford, B.A., 1971, M.A., 1974; Wolfson College, Oxford, B.Phil., 1974, D.Phil., 1976. *Politics:* None. *Religion:* None.

ADDRESSES: Home—Oxford, England. *Office*—Wolfson College, Oxford OX2 6UD, England. *Agent*—Curtis Brown Ltd., Fourth Floor, Haymarket House, 28/29 Haymarket, London SW1Y 4SP, England.

CAREER: Robert Dugdale (publisher), Oxford, England, proprietor, under pseudonym Robert Dugdale, 1974—; Oxford University Press, Oxford, editor of paperbacks, 1977-80, senior editor of general books, 1980-83, joint acting chief editor of general books, 1983-85, senior editor of political and social studies, 1985-90; Wolfson College, Oxford University, Oxford, research fellow, 1990—. Editorial manager of Open Books Publishing Ltd., 1975-76; editor of Roxby Press, 1976-77. Member of Common Room at Wolfson College, 1976-90, and Senior Common Room at Corpus Christi College, Oxford, 1980—.

WRITINGS:

(Editor) Arnold Mallinson, *Quinquagesimo Anno,* Robert Dugdale (Oxford, England), 1974, revised edition published as *Under the Blue Hood: A Hotchpotch, 1923-1985,* 1985.
(Editor) Isaiah Berlin, *Selected Writings,* Volume 1: *Russian Thinkers,* Viking (New York), 1978, Volume 2: *Concepts and Categories: Philosophical Essays,* Hogarth Press (London), 1978, Viking, 1979, Volume 3: *Against the Current: Essays in the History of Ideas,* Hogarth Press, 1979, Viking, 1980, Volume 4: *Personal Impressions,* Hogarth Press, 1980, Viking, 1981.
(Editor) Berlin, *The Crooked Timber of Humanity: Chapters in the History of Ideas,* Knopf (New York City), 1991.
(Editor) Berlin, *The Magus of the North: J. G. Hamann and the Origins of Modern Irrationalism,* Farrar, Straus (New York City), 1994.

Editor of "Past Masters" series, Oxford University Press, 1980-85.

SIDELIGHTS: Henry Hardy once told *CA:* "I got to know Isaiah Berlin while I was a graduate student at Wolfson College, Oxford, and he was President. My admiration for him as a person led me to his writings, which I found deeply sympathetic. By then I was already involved in book and magazine publishing and had edited and published a collection of writings by an eccentric Oxford clergyman, Arnold Mallinson. My love for creative editorial work and my enthusiasm for Berlin's work, too little known at the time, led me to propose a collection of his scattered essays under my editorship. To my surprise and delight, he agreed.

"My interest in Berlin's work is the leading example of a general absorption in and commitment to the challenge of publishing the kind of material that would perhaps not see the light of day without active, midwifely editorial intervention. In Berlin's case it was a question of putting together and editing previously published material—something he would never have done himself, and a process which required persistent and detailed work over a number of years. My work for Oxford University Press until 1985 was more a matter of commissioning and editing books that make accessible to a wider readership the fruits of academic inquiry. The leading example here is the 'Past Masters' series—short paperbacks on principle intellectual originators of the past—that I founded in the late 1970s. Publication began in 1980, and the series is still active. The theme of the series arose directly from my work on Berlin's writings. From 1985 to 1990 I commissioned original works of scholarship, primarily in the field of politics."

Hardy more recently added: "In 1990 I left Oxford University Press to take up a research fellowship at Wolfson College which enables me to work full-time on the editing of Isaiah Berlin's unpublished papers, including letters. One volume, *The Magus of the North: J. G. Hamann and the Origins of Modern Irrationalism,* appeared in 1993; others will follow."

BIOGRAPHICAL/CRITICAL SOURCES:

PERIODICALS

British Book News, January, 1978.
New York Times Book Review, March 24, 1991, p. 1.
Times Literary Supplement, October 5, 1990, p. 1053.

*   *   *

HARRIS, T George 1924-

PERSONAL: Born October 4, 1924, in Simpson County, KY; son of Garland (a farmer) and Luna (Byrum) Harris;

married Sheila Hawkins, October 31, 1953 (died January 27, 1977); married Ann Rockefeller Roberts, March 3, 1979; children: (first marriage) Amos, Anne, Crane, Gardiner; (second marriage) Clare, Joseph, Mary Louise, Rachel Pierson. *Education:* Attended University of Kentucky, 1946; Yale University, B.A., 1949. *Politics:* Independent. *Religion:* Episcopalian.

ADDRESSES: Home—8336 Paseo Del Ocaso, La Jolla, CA 92037.

CAREER: Clarksville Leaf-Chronicle, Clarksville, TN, reporter, 1942-43; *Time,* New York City, correspondent in New York City, Chicago, IL, and Atlanta, GA, 1949-55, Chicago bureau chief, 1955-58, contributing editor, 1958-60; Time-Life-Fortune, San Francisco bureau chief, 1960-62; *Look,* New York City, senior editor, 1962-68; *Psychology Today,* Del Mar, CA, then New York City, editor, 1969-76, 1988-90; *New York,* New York City, consulting editor, 1976-77; Addison-Wesley Publishing Co., Reading, MA, consulting editor for *Aware, Industry Week, Modern Maturity, Next, Participaction, Psychologie Heute, Runner, Somatics,* and *US,* 1976—; *American Health,* New York City, cofounder and editor in chief, 1981-90; *Harvard Business Review,* Boston, MA, editor, 1992-93; University of California at San Diego, editor in residence. Public Broadcasting Service, "Bodywatch" commentator; notable journalism work included coverage of civil rights movement. Institute for the Advancement of Health, member of board of science advisers; *20/20,* consultant; American Broadcasting Co.; member of board of directors of American Health Foundation, National Volunteer Centers, Rockefeller Brothers Fund; Young Men's Christian Association (YMCA), national medical advisory committee. *Military service:* U.S. Army, served during World War II; became second lieutenant, receiving commission on battlefield of Bastogne, Belgium; received Bronze Star and Air Medal with cluster.

MEMBER: American Fitness Leader Association (vice president, 1993), Church Society for College Work (director), Phi Beta Kappa, Yale Club (New York City), Chicago Club (Chicago).

AWARDS, HONORS: School Bell Award, 1963, for *Look* articles on segregation struggles in schools; National Conference of Christians and Jews, award for coverage of riots, 1964, Brotherhood Award, 1973 and 1985; first award for excellence in economic reporting from University of Missouri, 1965; National Magazine Award for excellence in specialized journalism, 1973, for *Psychology Today;* Magazine of the Year editing award, Columbia University, 1983, for *American Health;* American Psychology Federation Award, 1983; FMI-Esther Peterson Award for nutrition education, 1990; Centennial Award, American Psychological Association, 1992.

WRITINGS:

Romney's Way: A Man and an Idea, Prentice-Hall (Englewood Cliffs, NJ), 1968.

(Editor with Paul Chance) *The Best of "Psychology Today,"* McGraw (New York City), 1990.

Contributor of articles and interviews to *Psychology Today, Ms., Industry Week, Fortune,* and other magazines.

SIDELIGHTS: Known for turning the ailing *Psychology Today* magazine into "a *Popular Mechanics* of human behavior—eminently readable, visually stimulating and worth more than $2 million a year in net profit," according to a *Time* magazine report, T George Harris installed a Ping-Pong table at the editorial offices of *PT* and is known to have said "we have created the ultimate sweatshop, one where we have eliminated the difference between work and play."

BIOGRAPHICAL/CRITICAL SOURCES:

PERIODICALS

New Republic, January 13, 1968, pp. 26-27.
Time, May 17, 1976.
Trenton Times, February 8, 1976.
Washington Post, May 15, 1976.

*   *   *

HARTEL, Klaus Dieter
See VANDENBERG, Philipp

*   *   *

HASTINGS, Adrian 1929-

PERSONAL: Born June 23, 1929, in Kuala Lumpur, Malaya; son of William George (a barrister) and Hazel Mary (Daunais) Hastings; married Elizabeth Ann Spence, 1979. *Education:* Oxford University, B.A., 1949, M.A., 1953; Propaganda Fide, Rome, Italy, D.D., 1958; Cambridge University, postgraduate certificate of education, 1958; *Politics:* Liberal.

ADDRESSES: Home—3 Hollin Hill House, 219 Oakwood Ln., Leeds LS8 2PE, England.

CAREER: Ordained Roman Catholic priest, Rome, Italy, 1955; worked in Africa, principally Uganda, Tanzania, and Zambia, 1958-72; University of London, School of Oriental and African Studies, London, England, research officer and fellow of St. Edmund's House, 1973-76; University of Aberdeen, Aberdeen, Scotland, lecturer, 1976-80, reader, 1980-82; University of Zimbabwe, Ha-

rare, professor of religious studies, 1982-85; University of Leeds, Leeds, England, professor of theology and head of department of theology and religious studies, 1985-94. Visiting professor of theology, University of Lovanium (now Universite Nationale du Zaire), Kinshasa, Zaire, 1963-64. Editor of *The Journal of Religion in Africa,* 1985—.

AWARDS, HONORS: Honorary D.D., 1992, from Edinburgh University.

WRITINGS:

Prophet and Witness in Jerusalem, Helicon (La Jolla, CA), 1958.
One and Apostolic, Sheed, 1963.
The World Mission of the Church, Paulist Press (Ramsay, NJ), 1964.
Church and Mission in Modern Africa, Fordham University Press (Bronx, NY), 1967.
A Guide to Vatican II, two volumes, Darton, Longman, and Todd, 1968-69.
Mission and Ministry, Sheed, 1971.
Church and Ministry, Gaba, 1972.
Christian Marriage in Africa, S.P.C.K., 1973.
Wiriyamu, Orbis (Los Angeles, CA), 1974.
The Faces of God, Orbis, 1976.
African Christianity, Seabury, 1976.
In Filia! Disobedience, Mayhew-McCrimmon, 1978.
A History of African Christianity, 1950-1975, Cambridge University Press (New York City), 1979.
In the Hurricane, Collins (Cleveland, OH), 1986.
The Theology of a Protestant Catholic, Trinity Press International (Winona, MN), 1990.
A History of English Christianity, 1920-1990, Trinity Press International (Philadelphia, PA), 1991.
Robert Runcie, Trinity Press International, 1991.
The Church in Africa, 1450-1950, Oxford University Press (New York City), 1994.

EDITOR

The Church and the Nations, Sheed, 1959.
Bishops and Writers: Aspects of the Evolution of Modern English Catholicism, Anthony Clarke, 1977.
Modern Catholicism: Vatican II and After, Oxford University Press (New York City), 1991.

SIDELIGHTS: Adrian Hastings told *CA:* "Throughout most of my adult life my concerns have been for Africa but also for England and Europe, for the Catholic Church but also for ecumenical Christianity, for history but also for theology, for being academically accurate but also for being involved in the public struggle for truth and justice. For the last few years much of my struggle has been focused on Bosnia, a country appallingly betrayed by Britain, Europe, the U.S., *and* the United Nations—yet it is in Bosnia that the central contemporary struggle for tolerant, pluralist society, democratically structured, has been clearest and most anguishing."

*   *   *

HAWKES, John (Clendennin Burne, Jr.) 1925-

PERSONAL: Born August 17, 1925, in Stamford, CT; son of John Clendennin Burne and Helen (Ziefle) Hawkes; married Sophie Goode Tazewell, September 5, 1947; children: John Clendennin Burne III, Sophie Tazewell, Calvert Tazewell, Richard Urguhart. *Education:* Harvard University, A.B., 1949; Brown University, M.A., 1962.

ADDRESSES: Home—18 Everett Ave., Providence, RI 02906. *Agent*—Lynn Nesbit, International Creative Management, 40 West 57th St., New York, NY 10019.

CAREER: Harvard University Press, Cambridge, MA, assistant to production manager, 1949-55; Harvard University, Cambridge, visiting lecturer, 1955-56, instructor in English, 1956-58; Brown University, Providence, RI, assistant professor, 1958-62, associate professor, 1962-67, professor of English, 1967-88, T. B. Stowell University Professor, beginning in 1973, professor emeritus, 1988—. Visiting assistant professor of humanities, Massachusetts Institute of Technology, 1959; leader of novel workshop, Utah Writers' Conference, Salt Lake City, summer, 1962; special guest, Aspen Institute for Humanistic Studies, summer, 1962; staff member, Bread Loaf Writers' Conference, summer, 1963, writer in residence, University of Virginia, April, 1965; visiting professor of creative writing, Stanford University, 1966-67; visiting distinguished professor of creative writing, City College of the City University of New York, 1971-72. Member of Panel on Educational Innovation, Washington, DC, 1966-67. *Wartime service:* American Field Service, 1944-45.

MEMBER: American Academy of Arts and Sciences, American Academy and Institute of Arts and Letters.

AWARDS, HONORS: Guggenheim fellowship, 1962-63; American Academy and Institute of Arts and Letters grant, 1962; Ford Foundation fellowship in theater, 1964-65; Rockefeller Foundation grant, 1966; Prix du Meilleur Livre Etranger, 1973; Prix Medicis Etranger for best foreign novel translated into French, 1986, for *Adventures in the Alaskan Skin Trade.*

WRITINGS:

Fiasco Hall (poems), Harvard University Printing Office, 1949.

(Editor with Albert J. Guerard and others) *The Personal Voice: A Contemporary Prose Reader,* Lippincott, 1964.

Innocent Party: Four Short Plays (contains *The Questions,* first produced in Stanford, CA, January 13, 1966; produced by National Broadcasting Company (NBC-TV), 1967; produced Off-Broadway at Players Workshop, January 14, 1972; *The Wax Museum,* first produced in Boston, MA, April 28, 1966; produced Off-Broadway at Brooklyn Academy of Music, April 4, 1969; *The Undertaker,* first produced at Theatre Company of Boston, March 28, 1967; and *The Innocent Party,* first produced at Theatre Company of Boston, February, 1968; produced Off-Broadway at Brooklyn Academy of Music, April 4, 1969), New Directions, 1967.

(Editor with others) *The American Literary Anthology I: The First Annual Collection of the Best from the Literary Magazines,* Farrar, Straus, 1968.

Lunar Landscapes: Stories and Short Novels, 1949-1963 (includes *The Owl, The Goose on the Grave,* and *Charivari*), New Directions, 1969.

Humors of Blood & Skin: A John Hawkes Reader (autobiographical notes), introduction by William H. Gass, New Directions, 1984.

Hawkes Scrapbook: A New Taste in Literature, edited by C. W. Tazewell, Dawson (Virginia Beach, VA), 1990.

NOVELS

The Cannibal, New Directions, 1949.
The Beetle Leg, New Directions, 1951, reprinted, 1967.
The Goose on the Grave: Two Short Novels (contains *The Goose on the Grave* and *The Owl;* also see below), New Directions, 1954.
The Lime Twig, New Directions, 1961.
Second Skin, New Directions, 1964.
The Blood Oranges, New Directions, 1971.
Death, Sleep, and the Traveler, New Directions, 1974.
Travesty, New Directions, 1976.
The Owl, New Directions, 1977.
The Passion Artist, Harper, 1979.
Virginie: Her Two Lives, Harper, 1982.
Adventures in the Alaskan Skin Trade, Simon & Schuster, 1985.
Innocence in Extremis (novella), Burning Deck, 1985.
Whistlejacket, Random House, 1988.
Sweet William: A Novel of Old Horse, Simon & Schuster (New York City), 1993.

OTHER

Contributor to anthologies, including *New Directions in Prose and Poetry II; The World of Black Humor: An Introductory Anthology of Selections and Criticism,* edited by Douglas M. Davis, 1967; *Write and Rewrite: A Story of the*

Creative Process, edited by John Kuehl, 1967; *Flannery O'Connor,* edited by Robert E. Reiter; *The American Novel since World War II; Writers as Teachers, Teachers as Writers; Montpellier: Centre de'etude et de recherches sur les ecrivains du Sud sur Etats-Unis de L'Universite Paul Valery,* edited by Pierre Gault. Contributor of short stories, poems, articles, and reviews to periodicals, including *Audience, Voices: A Journal of Poetry, Sewanee Review, Massachusetts Review,* and *Tri-Quarterly.*

SIDELIGHTS: John Hawkes is most often characterized as an avant-garde writer. Hawkes's own declarations about his work and methods in an interview for *Wisconsin Studies in Contemporary Literature* support this assessment: "I began to write fiction on the assumption that the true enemies of the novel were plot, character, setting, and theme, and having once abandoned these familiar ways of thinking about fiction, totality of vision or structure was really all that remained. And structure—verbal and psychological coherence—is still my largest concern as a writer." Hawkes's rejection of traditional novelistic methods results in books that critics call nightmarish and dreamlike. S. K. Oberbeck remarks: "Flannery O'Connor has said that one 'suffers [*The Lime Twig*] like a dream.' This is true of each of Hawkes's novels. His narratives move with the pace and color of a dream. Something in the dream reassures us; something either draws us on or repels us. Attraction or repulsion: these two violent reactions become suddenly mixed in the narrative as Hawkes writes it." Similarly, W. M. Frohock believes that "Hawkes's specialty is weaving little bits of authentic reality into a fabric of deep-textured nightmare." David Littlejohn adds that "the writer, since Kafka, who most purely offers a 'distortion of real experience in the manner of dreams'—our basic definition of anti-realism—is the . . . American John Hawkes."

Each of Hawkes's works has been attacked by critics who object to his unconventional methods. Alexander Klein, writing in the *New Republic,* contends that in *The Cannibal* "John Hawkes presents a 'surrealistic novel' which manages for long stretches to make dullness and surrealism appear practically synonymous. Actually the book is a series of related images (some fresh and sharp) and fragmentary sketches (a few vividly effective), gimcracked together with a semblance of plot and allegory." In like manner, a *New Yorker* reviewer finds that *The Lime Twig* "is struck through with bright flashes of emotion and imagery, but they do not compensate for the general murkiness of his prose, and they are not well enough balanced with the proportion and perspective that it very badly needs." In the *New York Times Book Review,* Jack Beatty called *Adventures in the Alaskan Skin Trade* "the most accomplished meaningless novel I have ever read."

Yet many critics find both method and purpose in the seeming madness of Hawkes's novels. Charles Matthews argues that the "essence of Hawkes's technique is to destroy the conventional linkages and unifying forces of narrative. . . . For Hawkes, the destruction of the unity of perception is a particularization of that greater sense of destruction, deracination, decomposition, and dissolution which modern man feels when confronted with all those former sources of meaning: church, state, science, art, in short, all human institutions, ideals, and ideologies. The reader of Hawkes faces the abyss indeed, but it is the abyss which he must face every day." Robert Scholes feels that "Hawkes means to use conscious thought and art to illuminate the unconscious, to show us things about ourselves which may be locked in our own unconscious minds, avoiding the scrutiny of our consciousness."

In an interview with Scholes, Hawkes's remarks about the nightmares evinced in his writing echo the contentions of Matthews and Scholes: "We can't deny the essential crippling that is everywhere in life. I don't advocate crippling; I'm an opponent of torture. I deplore the nightmare; I deplore terror; I happen to believe that it is only by traveling those dark tunnels, perhaps not literally but psychically, that one can learn in any sense what it means to be compassionate." "My fiction," Hawkes concludes in the interview, "is generally an evocation of the nightmare or terroristic universe in which sexuality is destroyed by law, by dictum, by human perversity, by contraption, and it is this destruction of human sexuality which I have attempted to portray and confront in order to be true to human fear and to human ruthlessness, but also in part to evoke its opposite, the moment of freedom from constriction, constraint, death."

In addition to discussing the psychological elements in his novels, Hawkes has also commented on his concern with structure. "My novels are not highly plotted," he observes in *Wisconsin Studies,* "but they're elaborately structured." Donald J. Greiner points out that "structure often holds the key to Hawkes's difficult fiction. . . . Structure in his work is based upon cross-references, parallels, and contrasts, rather than upon the development of plot and character. It is this technique that enriches the nightmarish overtones of the novels and gives them their poetic quality." Scholes also notes the novels' meticulously wrought structures; *The Lime Twig,* for example, "which seems so foggy and dreamlike, is actually as neatly put together as the electrical circuitry of the human nervous system." Scholes stresses the careful interweaving of recurring images and verbal patterns. In a discussion of *The Beetle Leg,* Lucy Frost also emphasizes Hawkes's use of images: "Images become crucial. . . . In the image the power of the novel resides."

Whistlejacket is typical in its reliance on structural and thematic parallels. On the surface the novel is a murder mystery; it details the lives of the Van Fleet family, which devotes itself to uppercrust hobbies and trying to hide its dirty secrets. Yet as Patrick McGrath notes in the *New York Times Book Review,* "Questions of representation, of the layers of meaning that come to light when surfaces are peeled back to expose the dark structures within, are central to *Whistlejacket.*" McGrath calls the novel a "brilliantly sustained reflection on surface and depth, illusion and exposure, and the construction of meaning." Not all critics, however, praise the elaborate structures of Hawkes's writing. Randall Green, for example, calls *The Lime Twig* "an academic exercise." For John Clute in the *Washington Post Book World,* Hawkes's novel *Whistlejacket* is "like spindrift," written "in a style whose haste too often approaches the slovenly."

Reviewers also point to a pictorial quality in Hawkes's work. David Dillon feels that Hawkes is "at his best when he is closest to the spirit of the grotesque painters—Bosch to Brueghel. . . . The juxtaposed incongruities and monstrosities and enigmatic figures in the paintings have the same effect that Hawkes has, in his earlier writing, where he delights and thoroughly disconcerts his reader all at the same time." Earl Ganz makes a similar comment: "If you wish to understand John Hawkes, a painter friend once told me, think of Brueghel. . . . As with Brueghel, there is a beauty in this terrible world, a beauty the painter expresses in color and that Hawkes is able to do through description, his ability to describe painfully vivid scenes and, at certain moments, even to share that ability with his characters." Hawkes describes in a *Massachusetts Review* interview the centrality of visual images to his creative method: "I write out of a series of pictures that literally and actually do come to mind, but I've never seen them before. It is perfectly true that I don't know what they mean, but I feel and know that they have meaning. *The Cannibal* is probably the clearest example of this kind of absolute coherence of vision of anything I have written, when all the photographs do add together or come out of the same black pit."

Another element of Hawkes's work is its humor. As Greiner shows, many reviewers are disconcerted by Hawkes's "black humor" and the bleakness of his comedy, but other critics see the humor as a central, important part of the novels. Greiner, for instance, finds that Hawkes "daringly mixes a horror with humor, the grotesque with the heroic, creating a complex tone which some readers find hard to handle." Greiner contends that Hawkes rejects traditional comedy, which usually aims to mock aberrant behavior and assert a "benevolent social norm." Hawkes's characters, "while they perform ridiculous acts and reveal absurd personal defects in the manner of tradi-

tional comedy, rarely discover their faults in time so as to be safely reestablished with society." In fact, Hawkes dismisses orthodox social norms. Fiction, he says, "should be an act of rebellion against all the constraints of the conventional pedestrian mentality around us. Surely it should destroy conventional morality."

While Hawkes spurns conventional morality, his "contemporary humor," Greiner argues, "maintains faith in the invulnerability of basic values: love, communication, sympathy. Given a world of fragmentation, self-destruction, and absurdity, Hawkes tries to meet the terrors with a saving attitude of laughter so as to defend and celebrate these permanent values." In the *Massachusetts Review* interview, Hawkes insists on his comic intentions: "I have always thought that my fictions, no matter how diabolical, were comic. I wanted to be very comic—but they have not been treated as comedy. They have been called 'black, obscene visions of the horror of life' and sometimes rejected as such, sometimes highly praised as such."

In addition to considering particular elements in his fiction, Hawkes has examined the relationship between fiction and life: "I think that we read for joy, for pleasure, for excitement, for challenge. It would seem pretty obvious, however, that fiction is its own province. Fiction is a made thing—a manmade thing. It has its own beauties, its own structures, its own delights. Its only good is to please us and to relate to our essential growth. I don't see how we could live without it. It may be that the art of living is no more than to exercise the act of imagination in a more irrevocable way. It may be that to read a fiction is only to explore life's possibilities in a special way. I think that fiction and living are entirely separate and that the one could not exist without the other." Furthermore, when asked by Scholes to comment on W. H. Auden's belief that the world would be no different if Shakespeare and Dante had never lived, Hawkes replies: "I don't agree with the idea. It seems obvious that the great acts of the imagination are intimately related to the great acts of life—that history and the inner psychic history must dance their creepy minuet together if we are to save ourselves from total oblivion. I think it's senseless to attempt to talk as Auden talked. The great acts of the imagination create inner climates in which psychic events occur, which in themselves are important, and also affect the outer literal events in time and space through what has occurred in the act of reading."

With the 1984 publication of *Humors of Blood & Skin: A John Hawkes Reader,* a collection of short stories and excerpts from his novels, critics took the opportunity to comment on the body of Hawkes's work. Writing in the *New York Times Book Review,* Arthur C. Danto concludes: "Mr. Hawkes has the power to do, gorgeously and as art, what most of us can at best do drably and as dream—transform incident into phantasm. For connoisseurs of this rare craft, the refined rewards are frequent and the pleasures subtle and the charms undeniable." In the volume's introduction, William H. Gass offers this assessment: "I hope that the book which you are holding now will provide . . . exhilaration, for these lines are alive as few in our literature are; it is a prose of great poetry; it is language linked like things in nature are—by life and by desire; it is exploratory without being in the least haphazard or confused. . . . [I]t shows me how writing should be written, and also how living should be lived. It is a prose that breathes what it sees."

BIOGRAPHICAL/CRITICAL SOURCES:

BOOKS

Bellamy, Joe David, editor, *The New Fiction: Interviews with Innovative American Writers,* University of Illinois Press, 1974.

Busch, Frederick, *Hawkes: A Guide to His Works,* Syracuse University Press, 1973.

Contemporary Literary Criticism, Gale, Volume 1, 1973, Volume 2, 1974, Volume 3, 1975, Volume 4, 1975, Volume 7, 1977, Volume 9, 1978, Volume 14, 1980, Volume 15, 1980, Volume 27, 1984, Volume 49, 1988.

Dictionary of Literary Biography, Gale, Volume 2: *American Novelists since World War II,* 1978, Volume 7: *Twentieth-Century American Dramatists,* 1981.

Dictionary of Literary Biography Yearbook: 1980, Gale, 1981.

Greiner, Donald J., *Comic Terror: The Novels of John Hawkes,* Memphis State University Press, 1973.

Hawkes, John, *Humors of Blood & Skin: A John Hawkes Reader,* introduction by William H. Gass, New Directions, 1984.

Hryciw, Carol A., *John Hawkes: An Annotated Bibliography,* Scarecrow, 1977.

Kuehl, John, *John Hawkes and the Craft of Conflict,* Rutgers University Press, 1975.

Littlejohn, David, *Interruptions,* Grossman, 1970.

Malin, Irving, *New American Gothic,* Southern Illinois University Press, 1962.

Moore, Harry T., editor, *Contemporary American Novelists,* Southern Illinois University Press, 1964.

Santore, Anthony C., and Michael Pocalyko, editors, *A John Hawkes Symposium: Design and Debris,* New Directions, 1977.

Scholes, Robert, *The Fabulators,* Oxford University Press, 1967.

PERIODICALS

American Scholar, summer, 1965.

Audience, spring, 1960.

Book Week, September 26, 1965.

Chicago Tribune Book World, September 16, 1979.

Commonweal, July 2, 1954.

Contemporary Literature, Volume 2, number 3, 1970.

Critique: Studies in Modern Fiction, Volume 6, number 2, 1963; Volume 14, number 3, 1973.

Daedalus, spring, 1963.

Encounter, June, 1966.

Globe and Mail (Toronto), September 17, 1988.

Harvard Advocate, March, 1950.

Life, September 19, 1969.

Listener, July 18, 1968; May 5, 1970.

Los Angeles Times Book Review, May 9, 1982.

Massachusetts Review, summer, 1966.

Mediterranean Review, winter, 1972.

Minnesota Review, winter, 1962.

Nation, September 2, 1961; November 16, 1985.

National Observer, June 19, 1971.

New Leader, December 12, 1960; October 30, 1961.

New Republic, March 27, 1950; November 10, 1979; November 18, 1985.

New Statesman, March 11, 1966; November 10, 1967; May 1, 1970.

Newsweek, April 3, 1967.

New Yorker, April 29, 1961.

New York Review of Books, July 13, 1967; June 10, 1982.

New York Times, September 15, 1971.

New York Times Book Review, May 14, 1961; May 29, 1966; September 19, 1971; April 21, 1974; March 28, 1976; September 16, 1979; June 27, 1982; November 25, 1984; September 29, 1985; November 25, 1985; August 7, 1988.

Saturday Review, August 9, 1969; October 23, 1971.

Southwest Review, winter, 1965; October 23, 1971.

Time, February 6, 1950; September 24, 1979.

Times Literary Supplement, February 17, 1966; October 15, 1971; February 14, 1975; February 18, 1986; March 31, 1989.

Village Voice, April 10, 1969; May 23, 1974; September 3, 1979; May 18, 1982; September 17, 1985.

Washington Post, October 1, 1969.

Washington Post Book World, October 14, 1979; May 30, 1982, pp. 1-2; September 29, 1985; July 24, 1988, pp. 1, 7.

Wisconsin Studies in Contemporary Literature, summer, 1965.*

*   *   *

HAWKS, Delmar
See ELMAN, Richard

HAYES, Penny [a pseudonym] 1940-

PERSONAL: Born February 10, 1940, in Johnson City, NY. *Education:* State University of New York at Buffalo, B.S., 1969, M.S., 1970. *Avocational interests:* Hiking, mountain climbing, singing, reading, and gardening.

ADDRESSES: c/o Naiad Press, P.O. Box 10543, Tallahassee, FL 32302.

CAREER: Worked as typist and keypunch operator for six years before attending college; special education teacher, 1970—; writer, 1981—.

MEMBER: Forty-sixers (mountain-climbing group), Cayuga Chimes (women's barbershop chorus; vice president).

WRITINGS:

LESBIAN FEMINIST NOVELS

The Long Trail, Naiad Press (Tallahassee, FL), 1986.
Yellowthroat, Naiad Press, 1988.
Montana Feathers, Naiad Press, 1990.
Grassy Flats, Naiad Press, 1992.
Kathleen O'Donald, Naiad Press, 1994.

Contributor to anthologies, including *Of the Summits,* Adirondack Forty-Sixers, 1991; *The Erotic Naiad,* Naiad Press, 1992; *The Romantic Naiad,* Naiad Press, 1992; and *The Mysterious Naiad,* Naiad Press, 1994.

SIDELIGHTS: Penny Hayes told *CA:* "I have taught special education for twenty-four years with four and a half of those years spent in West Virginia schools, deep in the coal mining areas. There coal dust collected so quickly and so thick overnight that it was necessary to dust chairs, desks and tables before the children and I could begin our school day.

"I've always been interested in writing, but it wasn't until I was thirty-nine—with the full intention of being published by the time I was forty—that I took my quest seriously. A great motivating factor in disciplining myself for writing came from watching athletes on television. It took a couple of years to decide that if those men and women could drive themselves day after day, year after year, to gain what they wanted, I could do the same. It wasn't easy to sit down daily the first few months. It took every bit of discipline I had. Five years passed before my first manuscript was accepted for publication. Writing is now something that I must do. It has become an important part of my daily routine and my life.

"Originally, there were no major circumstances surrounding the creation of my plots. My purpose for writing a book was the enjoyment of spinning a good old yarn; nothing necessarily political, nothing deep or earth shaking; just a little interesting bit of history characterizing the way

things were and the way they might have been for women at that time. Other purposes were to depict strong women, mostly lesbian feminists, presenting how they might have adjusted to and overcome difficulties they encountered.

"I've since made modifications in my philosophy of writing, having picked up important views from friends and critics. Heeding their advice has made each book I've completed more meaningful, more challenging and much more difficult than when I first began writing.

"I like to add historical information to my narratives, making them as factual as possible. I use antique dictionaries, newspapers, magazines, encyclopedias, and authors from yester-year. I also glean information from modern-day writers. Films, talk shows and notes from people who live or once lived areas in which the story takes place may become part of the plot or background. I am uncomfortable sending out any manuscript without first having visited the locale of each novel.

"I write twelve months of the year—seven days a week during the winter months and four or five during the more pleasant weather. Some days I will write for only a couple of hours; other days I may spend as many as ten or twelve hours writing. There are times when it is extremely difficult to compose because the day's school activities have left me with little energy. However, a book was never completed without its author helping it along."

*			*			*

HEATH, Lester
See CASSIDAY, Bruce (Bingham)

*			*			*

HEAT-MOON, William Least
See TROGDON, William (Lewis)

*			*			*

HEDGES, Ursula M. 1940-

PERSONAL: Born January 9, 1940, in Lucknow, Uttar Pradesh, India; daughter of Vere (a clergyman) and Gwen (Carrau) Wood-Stotesbury; married Allan George Hedges (a teacher), January 12, 1961; children: Kenneth Allan, Dwane Robert, Linelle Ursula. *Education:* Longburn College, New Zealand, diploma for secretarial course, diploma in Bible instructor's course, and certificate of theological normal training, 1958; diploma in interior design (with honors), 1978. *Religion:* Seventh-Day Adventist.

ADDRESSES: c/o Seventh-Day Adventist Conference, 119 Eagle Terrace, 4000 Brisbane, Queensland, Australia.

CAREER: Seventh-Day Adventist Conference of Northern New Zealand, Auckland, secretarial work and Bible instructor, 1959-60; Price Waterhouse & Co., Auckland, secretary-receptionist, 1960; leader and teacher of youth groups in Australia, New Zealand, and New Guinea; freelance interior decorator; Auckland Adventist High School, Auckland, New Zealand, teacher; Brisbane Adventist High School, Brisbane, Queensland, Australia, teacher; teacher of creative art in adult education programs, 1971—.

WRITINGS:

Sasa Rore: Little Warrior (juvenile), Review & Herald (Washington, DC), 1966.
Carol and Johnny Go to New Guinea (juvenile), Review & Herald, 1967.
Down Under with Carol and Johnny (juvenile), Review & Herald, 1973.

Editor of monthly, *Adventist School Journal,* printed in Warburton, Australia. Author of plays for young people, and stories and poems for religious periodicals. Author of the plays *The Graduates, The Search, The Eternal Flame,* and *What Then?,* all of which have been performed in Auckland, New Zealand.

WORK IN PROGRESS: Birth of a School, a book about her experiences in helping start a boarding school in the New Guinea jungles; *Panim Appointment* and *Something Out of Nothing* for Review and Herald.

*   *   *

HEFTER, Richard   1942-

PERSONAL: Born March 20, 1942, in New York, NY; son of Joseph (a translator) and Pauline (a bookkeeper; maiden name, Cohen) Hefter; married Olivia McLaren (executive vice-president of Optimum Resource, Inc.), October 23, 1967; children: Christopher, Nicholas, Gillian, Johnathan. *Education:* Pratt Institute, B.F.A., 1964.

ADDRESSES: Home—6 Flotilla, Hilton Head, SC 29928. *Office*—Optimum Resource, Inc., 5 Hiltech Lane, Hilton Head, SC 29926.

CAREER: Worked variously as painter, printmaker, graphic designer, publisher, and author. One Strawberry, Inc. (publishing company), New City, NY, president, 1975-90; Hefter, Johnson & Associates, Princeton, NJ, partner, 1977-81, also editor, art director, and creator of *WOW Magazine;* Euphrosyne, Inc. (licensing and publishing firm), New York City, vice president, 1977—; Optimum Resource, Inc. (computer software), Hilton Head, SC, president, 1980—.

MEMBER: Authors Guild, Authors League of America, Software Publishers Association.

AWARDS, HONORS: Fulbright fellowship, 1965; Parents' Choice Award for excellence in media for children, for years 1983-93, for *Stickybear's Early Learning Activities, Stickybear Word Scramble, Stickybear ABC, Stickybear Numbers, Stickybear Bop, Stickybear Basketbounce, Stickybear Opposites, Stickybear Shapes, Stickybear Town Builder, Car Builder, Stickybear Parts of Speech, Vocabulary Development, The New Talking Series, The New Talking Stickybear Alphabet, The New Talking Stickybear Shapes,* and *The New Talking Stickybear Opposites;* Software Showcase Award at Consumer Electronics Show, 1983-84, for *Stickybear ABC, Chivalry,* and *Stickybear Opposites,* and 1985, for *Stickybear Math;* Outstanding Software Award and Gold Medal for Education, *Creative Computing,* 1984, for *Stickybear Opposites;* Best of the Best Award, Electronic Learning, 1985, for *Stickybear Reading;* Annual Guide to the Highest Rated Software Award, Preschool through Grade 12, *Educational News Service,* 1985-86, 1989-91, and 1993, for *The New Talking Stickybear Alphabet, Stickybear Word Problems, The New Talking Stickybear Shapes, The New Talking Stickybear Opposites, Map Skills, Math Word Problems, Stickybear Math 2, Car Builder, Stickybear Town Builder, Stickybear Math, Stickybear Typing, Stickybear Reading, Stickybear ABC, Stickybear Numbers, Stickybear Shapes,* and *Stickybear Opposites.*

Second Annual A+ Readers' Choice Award, *A+ Magazine,* 1986, for *Stickybear ABC;* Critics' Choice Award for Best Educational Software, *Family Computing,* 1986, for *Stickybear Town Builder* and *Car Builder;* Nibble Software Excellence Award, *Nibble: The Reference for Apple Computing,* 1987, for "Stickybear" Series; Best Software for Apple II Computers, *A+ Magazine,* 1987, for *Stickybear ABC;* Evanston Educators' Award for Excellence, *Evanston Educators' Newsletter,* for *Stickybear ABC, Stickybear Numbers, Chivalry, Stickybear Basketbounce, Stickybear Opposites, Stickybear Shapes, Stickybear Math, Stickybear Reading, Stickybear Town Builder,* and *Stickybear Printer;* Editors' Choice Award from *inCider Magazine,* 1987, and Outstanding Reading Program Award, 1988, both for *Stickybear Reading Comprehension;* Top of the CLAS Award, *The CLAS Report,* 1988, for *Car Builder* and *Stickybear Typing;* Computer Programs for Elementary Education Award, *Northwestern Regional Educational Laboratory,* 1988, for *Stickybear Numbers, Stickybear Math,* and *Stickybear Math 2;* Publishers of Educational Software Award, *Northwest Regional Educational Laboratory,* 1988, for *Weekly Reader Software;* Media & Methods Awards Portfolio, for years 1988-91, and 1993, for *Stickybear's Reading Room, The New Talking Stickybear Opposites, The New Talking Stickybear Shapes*

(Apple IIGS), The New Talking Stickybear Alphabet, Reading Comprehension, Stickybear Parts of Speech, Stickybear Math, and *Sentence Fun;* Product All-Star Award, *A+ Magazine,* 1989, for *Car Builder;* Excellence in Software Award for best early education program, Software Publishers' Association, 1989, for *The New Talking Stickybear Alphabet;* Annual California Children's Media Award, *L.A. Parent Magazine,* 1992, for *Stickybear's Reading Room;* Pre-Miere Award for Design Excellence, *Pre Magazine,* 1992, for *Endangered Wildlife Shufflebook;* MacUser 100 Award, *MacUser Magazine,* 1993, for *Stickybear's Early Learning Activities;* Directors' Choice Award, *Early Childhood News,* Exemplary Rating Award, and District Choice Award, *Curriculum Product News,* all 1993, all for *Stickybear's Reading Room;* District Choice Award, 1994, for *Stickybear's Math Town;* Software Hits Award, *Mac Computing Magazine,* 1994, for *Stickybear's Reading Room.*

WRITINGS:

EDITOR

(With Martin Moskof) *Everything: An Alphabet, Number, Reading, Counting, and Color Identification Book,* Parents' Magazine Press (New York City), 1971.
(With Moskof) *Christopher's Parade,* Parents' Magazine Press, 1972.
(With Moskof) *The Great Big Alphabet Picture Book with Lots of Words,* Grosset, 1972.
A B C Coloring Book, Dover Books (New York City), 1973.
The Strawberry Mother Goose (verse), illustrated by Lawrence Di Fiori, One Strawberry (New City, NY), 1975.
(With Ruth Lerner Perle and Jacquelyn Reinach) *The Sweet Pickles Get to Know the World Dictionary,* illustrated by Hefter, sixteen volumes, Time-Life Books (Alexandria, VA), 1982.

"SHUFFLEBOOK" SERIES; SELF-ILLUSTRATED; WITH MOSKOF

A Shufflebook (story in phrases on cards), Western Publishing (New York City), 1970.
An Animal Shufflebook, Western Publishing, 1971.
The Endangered Wildlife Shufflebook, Optimum Resource (New York City), 1991.
The Unicef World Shufflebook, Optimum Resource, 1991.
The New Original Shufflebook, Optimum Resource, 1993.
The Dinosaur Shufflebook, Optimum Resource, 1993.
The Animals of the Americas Shufflebook, Optimum Resource, 1993.

"WOW" SERIES; WITH PHILIP JOHNSON

The Great Wow Toy Book, Scholastic (New York City), 1982.

The Great Wow Game Book, Scholastic, 1982.

"STICKYBEAR" SERIES; SELF-ILLUSTRATED

Bears at Work, Optimum Resource, 1983.
The Stickybear Book of Weather, Optimum Resource, 1983.
Jobs for Bears, Optimum Resource, 1983.
Watch Out! The Stickybear Book of Safety, Optimum Resource, 1983.
Lots of Little Bears, Optimum Resource, 1983.
Bears Away from Home, Optimum Resource, 1983.
Where Is the Bear?, Optimum Resource, 1983.
Neat Feet, Optimum Resource, 1983.
Babysitter Bears, Optimum Resource, 1983.
Fast Food, Optimum Resource, 1983.
The Stickybear's Scary Night, Optimum Resource, 1984.

"STRAWBERRY BOOK" SERIES; SELF-ILLUSTRATED

An Animal Alphabet, One Strawberry, 1974.
A Noise in the Closet, One Strawberry, 1974.
Noses and Toes, One Strawberry, 1974.
One White Crocodile Smile, One Strawberry, 1974.
The Strawberry Picture Dictionary, One Strawberry, 1974.
The Strawberry Word Book, One Strawberry, 1974.
The Strawberry Book of Colors, One Strawberry, 1975.
Things That Go, One Strawberry, 1975.
Yes and No: A Book of Opposites, One Strawberry, 1975.
The Strawberry Book of Shapes, One Strawberry, 1976.
Bruno Bear's Bedtime Book, One Strawberry, 1976.
One Bear Two Bears: The Strawberry Number Book, Strawberry/McGraw, 1980.
The Strawberry Look Book, Strawberry/McGraw, 1980.

"SWEET PICKLES" SERIES; SELF-ILLUSTRATED

Hippo Jogs for Health, Holt (New York City), 1977.
Lion Is Down in the Dumps, Holt, 1977.
Moody Moose Buttons, Holt, 1977.
Stork Spills the Beans, Holt, 1977.
Very Worried Walrus, Holt, 1977.
Yakety Yak Yak Yak, Holt, 1977.
Zip Goes Zebra, Holt, 1977.
Kiss Me—I'm Vulture, Holt, 1978.
No Kicks for Dog, Holt, 1978.
Pig Thinks Pink, Holt, 1978.
Turtle Throws a Tantrum, Holt, 1978.
Who Can Trust You—Kangaroo?, Holt, 1978.
Xerus Won't Allow It, Holt, 1978.
The Great Race, Euphrosyne, 1981.
Quick Lunch Munch, Euphrosyne, 1981.
Robot S.P.3, Euphrosyne, 1981.
Wet All Over, Euphrosyne, 1981.
The Secret Club, Euphrosyne, 1981.
Some Friend, Euphrosyne, 1981.

SOFTWARE; ILLUSTRATED AND DESIGNED BY HEFTER; PUBLISHED BY OPTIMUM RESOURCE

(With Jane Worthington, Steve Worthington, and Spencer K. Howe), *Stickybear ABC,* 1982.

(With J. Worthington and S. Worthington) *Stickybear Numbers,* 1982.

(With Jack Rice) *Old Ironsides,* 1982.

(With Rice) *Stickybear Bop,* 1982.

(With S. Worthington) *Chivalry,* 1983.

(With S. Worthington) *Stickybear Basketbounce,* 1983.

(With J. Worthington and S. Worthington) *Stickybear Opposites,* 1983.

(With J. Worthington and S. Worthington) *Stickybear Shapes,* 1983.

(With S. Worthington) *Fat City,* 1983.

(With Susan Dubicki) *Beach Landing,* 1984.

(With S. Worthington) *Run for It,* 1984.

(With Dubicki) *Stickybear Math,* 1984.

(With S. Worthington) *Stickybear Reading,* 1984.

(With S. Worthington) *Stickybear Spellgrabber,* 1984.

(With Dave Lusby) *Stickybear Town Builder,* 1984.

(With Dubicki) *Stickybear Typing,* 1984.

(With Dubicki) *Stickybear Math 2,* 1985.

(With Dave Cunningham) *Car Builder,* 1985.

(With Cunningham and Dubicki) *Codes and Cyphers,* 1985.

(With Lusby) *Stickybear Printer,* 1985.

(With Cunningham) *Stickybear Drawing,* 1986.

(With V. R. Swami) *Math Word Problems,* 1986.

(With S. Worthington) *Stickybear Basic,* 1986.

(With Lusby) *Stickybear Music,* 1986.

(With S. Worthington) *Stickybear Reading Comprehension,* 1986.

(With Swami) *Map Skills,* 1987.

(With Swami) *Stickybear Word Problems,* 1987.

(With Gary Doody) *Reading Comprehension,* 1987.

(With Cunningham and Dubicki) *Stickybear Parts of Speech,* 1987.

(With Doody) *Spelling Rules,* 1988.

(With Dubicki) *Vocabulary Development,* 1988.

(With Dubicki) *Punctuation Rules,* 1988.

(With Dubicki) *Stickybear Math 3,* 1988.

(With Swami) *Problems with Fractions and Decimals,* 1988.

(With S. Worthington) *Stickybear Writer,* 1988.

(With Dubicki) *Sentence Fun,* 1989.

(With James Yuan) *Stickybear Parts of Speech,* 1990.

(With Cunningham) *Stickybear Word Scramble,* 1991.

(With Yuan) *Stickybear's Reading Room,* 1992.

(With Cunningham and Yuan) *Stickybear Preschool* (interactive CD), 1992.

(With Yuan) *Stickybear's Early Learning Activities,* 1993.

(With Bertelli) *Stickybear's Math Town,* 1993.

(With Allison) *Team NFL 1993* (interactive CD), 1993.

(With Cunningham) *Stickybear Reading,* 1993.

(With Cunningham) *Stickybear Reading, English/Spanish* (interactive CD), 1993.

(With Cunningham) *Stickybear Math* (interactive CD), 1994.

(With Cunningham) *Stickybear Reading, English/Italian* (interactive CD), 1994.

(With John Scott) *Stickybear Pre-School, English/Spanish* (interactive CD), 1994.

(With Yuan) *Tickeo,* 1994.

(With Stanley Ralph Ross) *Hilarious* (CD-ROM), 1994.

(With Ross) *More Hilarious* (CD-ROM), 1994.

(With Ross) *Even More Hilarious* (CD-ROM), 1994.

(With Cunningham) *Team NFL 1994* (interactive CD), 1994.

(With Philips Media) *Stickybear Family Fun* (interactive CD), 1994.

OTHER

Illustrator for numerous books, including *The Scaredy Book,* by Edith Adams, Random House, 1983; and *Sweet Pickles A through Z,* Cherry Lane, 1985, and *Songs with Giggles and Tickles and Pickles,* Cherry Lane, 1985, both by Jacquelyn Reinach; and

ADAPTATIONS: The Strawberry Book of Colors was adapted into a filmstrips with guide and records or cassettes, 1976. Many of the "Stickybear" works have been published in talking versions.

SIDELIGHTS: Richard Hefter told *CA* that he thoroughly enjoys his role as writer, illustrator, and software designer: "My company, Optimum Resource, has been an industry leader in bringing quality educational programming to children and adults throughout the world. The 'Sweet Pickles' books have appeared in three languages, the 'Strawberry Book' series in more than seven, and two of the 'Stickybear' [software] programs have been released in French. Absolute delight in the work that I do attends every day, and I am grateful to [be] able to reach so many children."

BIOGRAPHICAL/CRITICAL SOURCES:

PERIODICALS

Publishers Weekly, July 22, 1983.

*   *   *

HEIFNER, Jack 1946-

PERSONAL: Born March 31, 1946, in Corsicana, TX; son of Lee (a car dealer) and Naomi G. (in sales; maiden name,

Norris) Heifner. *Education:* Southern Methodist University, B.F.A., 1968.

ADDRESSES: Home—77 West 85th St., Apt. 5A, New York, NY 10024. *Agent*—Scott Hudson Writers and Artists Agency, 19 West 44th. St., Suite 1000, New York, NY 10036.

CAREER: Playwright, 1975—. Has worked in costume shops, as room clerk, and as market researcher; worked in technical and design jobs for American Shakespeare Festival, Juilliard School, and American Opera Theatre. Actor with American Shakespeare Festival, in summer stock, and in Broadway and Off-Broadway productions, in plays including *Othello,* 1970, and *Twelfth Night.* Founding member of Lion Theatre Company, New York City. Co-producer of play *Das Lusitania Songspiel,* 1979; director of plays including *Issue? I Don't Even Know You,* produced by the Acting Company, 1984-85, his *Vanities,* produced in New York City for the Hyde Park Summer Theatre, 1984, and *Old Oysters,* produced in New York City at West Bank Cafe, 1985.

MEMBER: American Society of Composers, Authors, and Publishers (ASCAP); Actor's Equity; Dramatists Guild; Writers Guild of America.

AWARDS, HONORS: Playwriting grants from Creative Artists Public Service Program (CAPS), 1977, for *Tornado,* and from National Endowment for the Arts, 1978, for *Music-Hall Sidelights;* American Society of Composers, Authors and Publishers (ASCAP) Award, 1978, for lyrics of *Music-Hall Sidelights;* Best Play of the Year nomination, New York Drama Critics Poll, for *Vanities;* five Dramalogue Awards including best play and best writing, 1992, for *Heartbreak.*

WRITINGS:

PLAYS

Casserole, first produced in New York City at Playwrights Horizons, 1975, produced in Houston at Stages, 1982.

Vanities (three-act; first produced in New York City at Playwrights Horizons, 1976, produced Off-Broadway, 1976), Samuel French (New York City), 1976.

Porch (radio play; also see below), first produced on National Public Radio, 1977-78, produced in Scotland with *Twister* (also see below), 1986.

Music-Hall Sidelights (adapted from *L'envers du music-hall* by Colette), first produced in New York City at Lion Theatre, 1978.

Patio/Porch (two one-acts; first produced in New York City at Century Theatre, 1978), Dramatists Play Service (New York City), 1978.

Loveland (teleplay), Columbia Broadcasting System (CBS-TV), 1979.

Star Treatment, first produced in New York City at Lion Theatre, 1980.

Running on Empty (first produced in New York City at New Dramatists, 1982, produced in Houston at Stages, 1986), Dramatists Play Service, 1987.

Smile (musical; based on film of same title), music by Marvin Hamlisch, lyrics by Carolyn Leigh, produced in New York City, 1983 (not associated with 1986 Broadway production of *Smile.*)

Tornado, first produced in Houston at Stages, 1983.

Twister (one-act; also see below), produced in New York City at West Bank Cafe, 1984, produced in Scotland with *Porch,* 1986.

Tropical Depression (one-act; also see below), produced in Houston at Stages, 1984.

Natural Disasters (contains *Tropical Depression* and *Twister;* produced in New York City at West Bank Cafe, 1985), Dramatists Play Service, 1985.

(Author of music and lyrics with Ellie Greenwich) *Leader of the Pack* (musical; produced on Broadway, 1985), Samuel French, 1987.

Bargains (produced in one act in Dallas, 1987, and in two acts in San Diego at the Old Globe Theatre, 1992), Dramatists Play Service, 1992.

American Beauty (musical), music by Michael Rice, produced in Little Rock at Arkansas Repertory Theatre, 1988.

Boys' Play (one-act), first produced in New York City at West Bank Cafe, 1989.

Home Fires, first produced in Montana at Bigfork Performing Arts Center, 1990.

Heartbreak (comedy), produced in Los Angeles, 1992.

(With Don Jones) *Sing Baby Sing* (musical), produced in Little Rock, 1993.

OTHER

Also author of plays *The Lemon Cookie,* 1993, and *Clara Period,* (one-act), 1994. Author of screenplays *Crowning Glory,* Apple/Rose Films, and *A Wide Place in the Road* (unproduced), both 1994. Author of scripts for television programs *Guiding Light, Another World, Steel Magnolias,* and *Designing Women.* Work included in anthologies *The Best Short Plays of 1980,* edited by Stanley Richards, Chilton, 1980; *Contemporary Scenes for Student Actors,* edited by Michael Schulman and Eve Mekler, Penguin, 1980; and *Short Pieces from the New Dramatists,* Broadway Play Publishing, 1985.

ADAPTATIONS: A sound recording of *Porch* was made in 1977; *Vanities* was produced as a television pilot for American Broadcasting Company (ABC-TV) in 1977 and as a Home Box Office cable television production in 1980; *Bargains* was produced as a television pilot for Columbia Broadcasting System (CBS) in 1992.

WORK IN PROGRESS: Beauty Shop Bop, an original musical with music and lyrics by Evan Huss; *Peeping* (screenplay), a psychological thriller examining voyeurism; *There She Is,* a series of sketches about beauty scheduled for production in Los Angeles in 1995; *Comfort and Joy,* a play scheduled for production at Portland Center Stage, December, 1995.

SIDELIGHTS: Playwright Jack Heifner's *Vanities,* which opened in 1976, became the longest-running production in Off-Broadway history. Heifner explained to *CA* how he became a playwright: "I'd done every kind of work in the theater. I didn't like stage managing and I wasn't particularly good as an actor and I figured they would always need someone to hang a light or sew a hem so I sat down and wrote a play. There wasn't anything left to do."

Heifner began writing seriously when his father died. Amazed by American funerals and fascinated by the amount of food consumed at wakes, the playwright wrote a black comedy about the subjects in 1975. "The first play [*Casserole*] was real hard," he revealed, "but I did the draft of *Vanities* in a couple of days." *Casserole* premiered at the 1982 Texas Playwrights Festival, held at the Stages Repertory Theatre in downtown Houston. The play is set in a small Texas place like Heifner's own hometown to which Jackie Lee, an actor, returns for his father's funeral. A *Texas Monthly* reviewer noted: "The monster relatives complain in perfect small-town small talk, griping about the coleslaw and lamenting the lack of a single meat dish at the wake. (They have to settle for casserole.)" Comparing *Casserole* to Heifner's later works, the *Texas Monthly* critic found that the first play's "faults . . . stem from its ambition and its commitment, two qualities conspicuously absent from Heifner's later efforts," and added that although "*Casserole* lacks the workmanlike neatness of *Vanities,* it does have that play's more endearing virtues: a zippy way with words and a fine sense of comedy."

Margo Jefferson of *Newsweek* described *Vanities,* which traces the lives of three women from their high school days to adulthood, as "an astute, snapshot-sharp chronicle" of three rites of passage. In high school the girls are clones of each other. They look alike, talk alike, and think alike. Kathy, Joanne, and Mary are preoccupied with the opposite sex, football, and popularity. While in college, the girls become sorority sisters, undaunted by the numerous significant political events of the 1960s. After graduation, Joanne marries her high school sweetheart, Kathy becomes a physical education teacher, and Mary tours Europe. When the women are reunited in 1974, Joanne remains the happy wife while Mary is the curator of a pornographic artifacts gallery. Kathy, the organizer in high school, has given up teaching and questions what she is to do with her future.

Heifner once explained to *CA:* "The women I used as models for the three women in *Vanities* included more than just three girls in my high school. I chose another three girls from college and from my later years in New York. The characters are composites. It is not a piece of fact . . . but of fiction. The only relation to the three women I grew up with are the names. I did not know what happened to these women until after the play had been written. In fact, I've never seen or heard from them since high school."

"Heifner's fast-moving, sneakily stinging dialogue and economical staging . . . ingeniously balance caricature and realism" in *Vanities, Newsweek* reviewer Jefferson noted. Critic Alan Rich also praised the play's power in *New York* magazine: "There is nothing new, or especially startling" in *Vanities,* and yet the play "is uncommonly attractive, not a second overlong, and—excepting the author's tendency to fall back on gag lines—splendidly observant of speech and thought."

Likened to Mary McCarthy's *The Group* and Dorothy Parker's *The Big Blonde, Vanities,* said Jules Aaron of the *Educational Theatre Journal,* is "a penetrating examination of contemporary mores." Thematically, the play criticizes the dream world of college life. More importantly, *Vanities* is a comment on the way society molds people. "What this play is about," Heifner explained, "is three little golden girls who are talking about nothing." As Aaron noted, "The play deals with the *facades* of the American Dream and asks if it is enough to be 'popular' and 'accepted.' "

After four years and 1,785 performances, *Vanities* became the longest running non-musical in the history of Off-Broadway theatre. The play, whose original production costs totaled only $200, enjoyed more professional productions (280) by 1980 than any other play in America, including 200 productions by repertory companies. Home Box Office (HBO), a pay television network, offered a $400,000 production of *Vanities* as the first theatrical program for its subscribers, and the American Broadcasting Company (ABC-TV) created a pilot for a television series based on the play.

When Heifner's package of two, one-act plays entitled *Patio/Porch* opened at Broadway's Century Theater in 1978, critic Rex Reed wrote in the *New York Daily News,* "If you're one of the thousands who have seen *Vanities* (and who in his or her right mind hasn't?) you'll also cotton to this latest gift from the same playwright." *Home News* theater critic Ernest Albrecht explained the significance of the plays' titles: "The patio is an escape from a world that is empty. The porch is a spot from which one can watch the emptiness pass by." Mitch Owens found the 1986 production of *Patio/Porch* at Theatre Three in Dallas a vivid experience, saying in a *Dallas Observer* review that he was "amazed at its dead-accurate presentment of the Southern women at whose knees I spent my childhood." As Pearl, who's husband abandoned her, frets about how to furnish the patio and her beautician friend Jewel dreams of escaping the boredom, Heifner draws the audience in. "Nothing much happens in *Patio*," wrote Owens, "but our involvement in Jewel's and Pearl's humdrum lives is complete." He also praised *Porch*, in which Heifner, "mixing just the right amounts of humor, religion, and pathos, and the stars, with wondrous performances, have the audience in the palms of their hands."

Running on Empty was given its world premier at the 1986 Texas Playwrights Festival, held at Stages in Houston; Heifner also directed the production. A *TWT Theatre* contributor called the play "a sort of bird's eye view of such complexities as the conservation of natural resources, the politics of humanity, the value (if any) of various sexual roles and the necessity of proper dress during catastrophe."

Set in an austere, destitute America of the future, the play centers around Lilly and Stephen, a "platonic" married couple preparing for a party. Because commodities of all kinds are in such short supply, wrote reviewer Everett Evans in the *Houston Chronicle*, "Lilly is burning her designer originals to provide some warmth" and "Stephen is preparing imaginary food and drink in empty plates and glasses." Their guest is David, "the one great love" of both of their lives. David, who left them but still is thought of as a friend, shows up with his two new lovers. "Some chatty passages are redundant and should be trimmed," Evans noted, yet he still found the dialogue "generally good, with the comic lines cattily punchy and funny." In the end, commented Evans, *Running on Empty* "may be a bit unwieldy at times, a bit unpredictable at others. But Heifner's view of a world winding down with a whimper rather than a bang is full of ideas, humor and feeling."

Heifner once told *CA:* "If there's any common thread in my works, it would be my interest in the kind of society that creates the type of people shown in *Vanities* or *Patio/Porch*. I don't think the plays are judgmental. . . . The characters are judging each other, but the play really just presents the argument.

"I believe all my plays have been about social issues. *Patio/Porch* examines the same small town that created the women in *Vanities*, but *Patio/Porch* concerns another class structure. *Vanities* is a play about friendship. It is not a play about women since the same events could happen to three football players or fraternity brothers. *Patio/Porch* is a study of family relationships. The people in both plays are small town creations. *Star Treatment* examines a love relationship between a woman and three men. *Tor-*

nado is about the way such an event can suddenly change beliefs and alter lives.

"The people in all the plays are ordinary. I don't write about great, gifted artists or 'thinkers.' My concern is with the world of the ordinary person, and I mean 'ordinary' as a compliment—those who are trying to figure out how to get through this life."

BIOGRAPHICAL/CRITICAL SOURCES:

BOOKS

Contemporary Literary Criticism, Volume 11, Gale, 1979.
Hughes, Catharine, editor, *American Theatre Annual,* Gale, *1978-1979,* 1980, *1979-80,* 1981.
Hughes, editor, *New York Theatre Annual,* Gale, Volume 1, 1978, Volume 2, 1978.

PERIODICALS

Dallas Observer, May 15, 1986.
Educational Theatre Journal, May, 1977.
Home News, April 14, 1978, p. 12.
Houston Chronicle, July 22, 1977; January 18, 1986.
Houston Post, July 23, 1977.
Los Angeles Times, February 25, 1983.
Miami Herald, February 9, 1977.
Nation, November 13, 1976.
Newsweek, April 5, 1976.
New York, April 5, 1976; May 1, 1978; March 24, 1980.
New York Daily News, April 21, 1978.
New Yorker, April 19, 1976.
New York Post, April 14, 1978.
New York Theatre Review, June, 1978.
New York Times, March 23, 1976; June 4, 1976; August 15, 1976; August 27, 1976; April 14, 1978; September 9, 1979; February 8, 1980; March 7, 1980; July 30, 1980; August 17, 1980; November 5, 1980.
Poughkeepsie Journal, July 6, 1984, p. 44; July 13, 1984, p. 13.
Texas Monthly, July, 1982, p. 149.
Times Herald Record, July, 12, 1984, p. 72.
TWT Theatre, January 31-February 6, 1986.

*   *   *

HEILBRONER, Robert L(ouis) 1919-

PERSONAL: Born March 24, 1919, in New York, NY; son of Louis and Helen (Weiller) Heilbroner; married Joan Knapp (divorced); married Shirley E. T. Davis; children: (previous marriage) Peter, David. *Education:* Harvard University, B.A., 1940; New School for Social Research, Ph.D. *Avocational interests:* Playing the piano, painting, bird watching.

ADDRESSES: Home and office—830 Park Ave., New York, NY 10021.

CAREER: Practicing economist in government and business; New School for Social Research, New York City, Norman Thomas Professor of Economics, 1972—. Lecturer to various university, business and labor groups; Town School, chair of board, New York City, 1963-73. Member of editorial board for *Social Research, Dissent,* and other publications. *Military service:* U.S. Army, Intelligence, during World War II; served in Far East interviewing Japanese prisoners of war; became first lieutenant; received Bronze Star.

MEMBER: American Economic Association (member of executive committee, 1972; vice president, 1985), Council on Economic Priorities (member of executive committee), Phi Beta Kappa.

AWARDS, HONORS: Guggenheim fellow, 1983; LL.D., La Salle College, Ripon College, Long Island University, New School for Social Research, and Wagner College.

WRITINGS:

The Worldly Philosophers, Simon & Schuster, 1953 (published in England as *The Great Economists,* Eyre & Spottiswoode, 1955), 6th edition, 1986.
The Quest for Wealth, Simon & Schuster, 1956.
The Future as History, Harper, 1960.
The Making of Economic Society, Prentice-Hall, 1962, 9th edition, 1993.
The Great Ascent, Harper, 1963.
(With P. L. Bernstein) *A Primer on Government Spending,* Random House, 1963, 2nd edition, 1971.
Understanding Macroeconomics, Prentice-Hall, 1965, 9th edition (with James Galbraith), 1990.
The Limits of American Capitalism, Harper, 1966.
The Economic Problem, Prentice-Hall, 1968, 9th edition (with Galbraith), 1990.
Understanding Microeconomics, Prentice-Hall, 1968, 9th edition (with Galbraith), 1990.
(Editor and author of introduction) Adolph Lowe and others, *Economic Means and Social Ends* (essays), Prentice-Hall, 1969.
Between Capitalism and Socialism: Essays in Political Economics, Random House, 1970.
(Editor with A. M. Ford) *Is Economics Relevant?,* Goodyear Publishing, 1971.
(With others) *In the Name of Profit,* Doubleday, 1972.
(Editor with Paul London) *Corporate Social Policy,* Addison-Wesley, 1975.
An Inquiry into the Human Prospect, Norton, 1975, 3rd revised edition, 1991.
Business Civilization in Decline, Norton, 1976.
(Compiler with Ford) *Economic Relevance: A Second Look,* Goodyear Publishing, 1976.

(With Aaron Singer) *The Economic Transformation of America,* Harcourt, 1977, 3rd revised edition, 1994.
Beyond Boom and Crash, Norton, 1978.
Marxism: For and Against, Norton, 1980.
(With Lester C. Thurow) *Five Economic Challenges,* Prentice-Hall, 1981.
(With Thurow) *Economics Explained,* Prentice-Hall, 1982, 3rd revised edition, Simon & Schuster, 1994.
The Nature and Logic of Capitalism, Norton, 1985.
(Editor) *The Essential Adam Smith,* Norton, 1986.
Beyond the Veil of Economics, Norton, 1988.
Twenty-First Century Capitalism, Norton, 1993.

Contributor of numerous articles to national magazines.

SIDELIGHTS: In *An Inquiry into the Human Prospect,* Robert L. Heilbroner outlines a view of the future written, according to Melville J. Ulmer of the *New Republic,* "in the spirit of a new public malaise bordering on desperation." Ulmer writes that Heilbroner "sustains [his] argument with a dazzling farrago of sociology, psychoanalysis, economics and political science that few others can match." According to Ulmer, the author's forecast is grim. Quoting Heilbroner, Ulmer notes that "even though populations are huge and increasing, production will be circumscribed everywhere since man 'will be unable to sustain growth [because of diminishing resources] and unable to tolerate it [because of pollution] if he did.'" A *New Yorker* critic finds Heilbroner's soberness appropriate, asserting that "Mr. Heilbroner is as learned and eloquent an economist as John Kenneth Galbraith," and that "though he lacks Galbraith's sardonic playfulness [it] would be rather out of place in a work as grave and troubled as this one."

Raymond Williams of the *New York Times Book Review* suggests that readers of Heilbroner's 1980 book, *Marxism: For and Against,* keep *An Inquiry into the Human Prospect* in mind in order to recall the "sense of crisis" Heilbroner evoked in that earlier book. Williams contends that in both works, "it is because he cares so much, because he is contemptuous of the moods of resignation, cynicism and indulgence that are now fashionable responses to a crisis already too well known, that Mr. Heilbroner lays his mind open, explores, tests, wants to get arguments right." Williams feels that *Marxism* is "genuinely open-minded and inquiring" and that it "strains to set out arguments and objections fairly." Christopher Lehmann-Haupt of the *New York Times* also praises *Marxism* as a "wonderfully concise and lucid summary of Karl Marx's ideas, and a trenchant examination of both their usefulness and limitations."

"Marxism worn with a difference" is what Heilbroner offers in *The Nature and Logic of Capitalism,* writes Alan Ryan in the *Times Literary Supplement.* Distinctive to

Heilbroner's analysis, notes Ryan, is this "marxisant" foundation, with its "insistence that it is worth classifying social systems in the kind of way Marx did." *Los Angeles Times Book Review* contributor Milton Moskowitz emphasizes Heilbroner's depiction of capitalism in concurrence with Marxist theory "as a regime characterized by an insatiable drive to convert money into commodities and commodities into money in an endless loop . . . by extraction of profit, which Heilbroner identifies [and which Marx had earlier identified] as 'the life blood of capitalism.' " But even with his employment of Marxist theory and terminology, "Heilbroner," Moskowitz guarantees, "is not a Marxist determinist," for he is aware of the 'richness' and 'creativity' of capitalism and of its "far greater tolerance for dissent and skepticism than government." In the same vein, Ryan, among others, focuses on Heilbroner's surety that "political freedom in modern times . . . has only appeared in capitalist states."

Kenneth E. Boulding describes Heilbroner as a kind of "Unitarian Marxist" and maintains in the *New York Times Book Review* that "there is a slight air of an apologia about [*The Nature and Logic of Capitalism*] and some ambiguity about whether it is for capitalism or against it." Boulding sees some fallacies in Heilbroner's arguments "and indeed in his gentler and more liberal version of Marxism," but nevertheless asserts that "Heilbroner's book may well be more important for . . . [the 'hard thinking' that] it stimulates than for what it says, and this is no small merit." John Kenneth Galbraith, too, considers the book important, noting in the *Washington Post Book World* that although Heilbroner's essay on contemporary capitalism "must be read with the greatest attention . . . its full value . . . is very great." And Moskowitz concludes that *The Nature and Logic of Capitalism* is "probably more important than the armada of business books being landed today by publishers on how to improve management or how to make a million dollars or how to beat back the Japanese economic threat," because Heilbroner has tried to "get at the central ideas of a society."

Several of Heilbroner's books have become standard introductions to college economics courses. One such book, *The Worldly Philosophers,* has also appeared in over twenty foreign editions.

BIOGRAPHICAL/CRITICAL SOURCES:

PERIODICALS

Commonweal, June 9, 1967.
Los Angeles Times, April 8, 1982.
Los Angeles Times Book Review, November 3, 1985.
Nation, May 22, 1967.
New Republic, March 30, 1974; September 23, 1978.
New Statesman, August 24, 1979.

New Yorker, April 22, 1974.
New York Times, March 24, 1980.
New York Times Book Review, April 13, 1980; October 20, 1985.
Partisan Review, fall, 1967.
Saturday Review, January 23, 1971.
Time, April 1, 1974.
Times Literary Supplement, May 16, 1986.
Washington Post Book World, October 15, 1978; May 3, 1981; October 13, 1985.

*   *   *

HELPRIN, Mark 1947-

PERSONAL: Born June 28, 1947, in New York, NY; son of Morris (a motion picture executive) and Eleanor (Lynn) Helprin; married Lisa Kennedy (a tax attorney and banker), June 28, 1980; children: Alexandra Morris, Olivia Kennedy. *Education:* Harvard University, A.B., 1969; A.M., 1972; postgraduate study at Magdalen College, University of Oxford, 1976-77. *Religion:* Jewish. *Politics:* "Roosevelt Republican."

ADDRESSES: Agent—Harcourt Brace Jovanovich, Inc., 15 East 26th St., New York, NY 10010.

CAREER: Writer. Hudson Institute, senior fellow; Harvard University, former instructor. *Military service:* Israeli Infantry and Air Corps, field security, 1972-73; British Merchant Navy.

AWARDS, HONORS: PEN/Faulkner Award, National Jewish Book Award, and American Book Award nomination, all 1982, all for *Ellis Island and Other Stories;* American Academy and Institute of Arts and Letters Prix de Rome, 1982; Guggenheim fellow, 1984.

WRITINGS:

A Dove of the East and Other Stories, Knopf (New York City), 1975.
Refiner's Fire: The Life and Adventures of Marshall Pearl, a Foundling (novel), Knopf, 1977.
Ellis Island and Other Stories, Seymour Lawrence/ Delacorte (New York City), 1981.
Winter's Tale (novel), Harcourt (San Diego, CA), 1983.
(Adaptor) *Swan Lake* (children's book), illustrated by Chris Van Allsburg, Houghton (Boston), 1989.
A Soldier of the Great War (novel), Harcourt, 1991.
Memoir from Antproof Case, Harcourt, 1995.

Editor, with Shannon Ravenel, of *The Best American Short Stories, 1988.* Contributor of numerous short stories and articles to the *New Yorker, Esquire,* and *New York Times Magazine;* contributing editor, *Wall Street Journal.*

SIDELIGHTS: Mark Helprin is a writer whose fiction is marked by language "more classical than conversational," as Michiko Kakutani observed in the *New York Times,* and who shapes his short stories and novels "less to show my place in the world than to praise the world around me." Explaining his artistic distance from the sparse, clean prose of writers such as American author Ernest Hemingway, Helprin told Jon D. Markman of the *Los Angeles Times,* "My models are the *Divine Comedy,* and the *Bible* and Shakespeare—where they use language to the fullest." Helprin's political concerns (he pursued Middle Eastern studies in graduate school and later served in the Israeli Infantry and Air Corps) figure in his newspaper and magazine articles; his books, he has often said with little elaboration, are religious.

Helprin has told several interviewers that he became serious about writing at the age of seventeen, when, staying at a hotel in Paris, he wrote a description of the Hagia Sophia in Istanbul, which he had never seen. In a 1981 interview with Sybil S. Steinberg for *Publishers Weekly,* he gave this account of his early practice in storytelling: "My father wouldn't let me eat unless I could earn my way to the table. He would always make me stand away from the table and would say: 'Tell me a story.' Every night I would have to tell another story. Sometimes the story wasn't good enough, and my father would say, 'That's not convincing,' and cut himself another slice of steak." Questioned on this tale by Kakutani, Helprin conceded, "I do tend to exaggerate. The truth of it was that I was speaking in a metaphor for my relation to my father. He retired early and devoted all his energy towards me and sometimes it was too much. . . . I gave the courtroom truth a twist to make it a better story. . . . That's my profession—to change one thing into another."

Majoring in English as an undergraduate at Harvard, Helprin wrote short stories and sent them to the *New Yorker*—with no luck until 1969, when the magazine accepted two at the same time. These became part of his first book, the collection *A Dove of the East and Other Stories,* in which critics have noted the author's grand depictions of nature as a source of strength and healing and his concern with characters who survive loss, particularly that of loved ones.

Some critics were impressed with the wide range of settings and the graceful prose of *A Dove of the East.* In the *Saturday Review,* Dorothy Rabinowitz described the stories as "immensely readable," some "quite superb." She wrote, "Mr. Helprin's old-fashioned regard shines through all his characters' speeches, and his endorsement gives them eloquent tongues. Now and again the stories lapse into archness, and at times, too, their willed drama bears down too heavily. But these are small flaws in works so estimably full of talent and—the word must out—of

character." Amanda Heller, however, complained in the *Atlantic Monthly* that, as a result of what she called Helprin's "dreamy, antique style," she was fatigued by the "sameness of tone" throughout the stories. "It appears that Helprin is striving for loveliness above all else," she commented, "a tasteful but hardly compelling goal for a teller of tales."

Duncan Fallowell allowed in the *Spectator* that some of the stories were "unbeatably vague," but praised Helprin for "recognising the intrinsic majesty" of seemingly meaningless events, because, as Fallowell wrote, "he is also a seeker after truth. Bits of it are squittering out all over the place, sufficiently to fuse into a magnetic centre and make one recognise that the book is not written by a fool." Dan Wakefield, even more appreciative of Helprin's work, observed, "The quality that pervades these stories is love—love of men and women, love of landscapes and physical beauty, love of interior courage as well as the more easily obtainable outward strength. The author never treats his subjects with sentimentality but always with gentleness of a kind that is all too rare in our fiction and our lives."

Helprin's first novel, the rambling, picaresque *Refiner's Fire: The Life and Adventures of Marshall Pearl, a Foundling,* further delighted critics. A *New Yorker* reviewer found that Helprin described the protagonist's boyhood "lyrically and gracefully" and proved himself to be "a writer of great depth and subtle humor." For Joyce Carol Oates the problem was "where to begin" in admiring the novel she described as a "daring, even reckless, sprawling and expansive and endlessly inventive 'picaresque' tale." She wrote, "At once we know we are in the presence of a storyteller of seemingly effortless and artless charm; and if the exuberant, extravagant plotting of the novel ever becomes tangled in its own fabulous inventions, and its prodigy of a hero ever comes to seem more allegorical than humanly 'real,' that storytelling command, that lovely voice is never lost."

With *Ellis Island and Other Stories,* Helprin secured his place among contemporary writers, winning for this work a PEN/Faulkner Award, the National Jewish Book Award, and an American Book Award nomination—a rare feat for a collection of short stories. Though some critics, such as Anne Duchene in the *Times Literary Supplement,* found that Helprin's language sometimes overwhelmed his intent, the greater critical response was laudatory. In the *Washington Post Book World,* Allen Wier observed, "Beautifully written and carefully structured, Mark Helprin's *Ellis Island and Other Stories* is one of the best collections of short fiction I've read in a long time. . . . His rich textures alone would be enough to delight a reader, but there is more: wonderful *stories,* richly plotted, inventive, moving without being sentimental, humorous without being cute."

Harry Mark Petrakis stated in the *Chicago Tribune,* "In this fine collection of stories, Mark Helprin reveals range and insight whether he is writing of children or adults, of scholars, tailors, and lovers. His eye is precise and his spirit is compassionate, and when we finish the stories we have been rewarded, once more, with that astonishing catalyst of art." Reynolds Price, writing for the *New York Times Book Review,* cited as particularly memorable "The Schreuderspitze," in which a photographer who has lost his wife and son in a car accident risks his life to climb a mountain in an effort to regain his spirit; the first half of the title novella ("before a lapse into whimsy"); and "North Light," which Price described as "a brief and frankly autobiographical recollection of battle nerves among Israeli soldiers, a lean arc of voltage conveyed through tangible human conductors to instant effect."

Winter's Tale, Helprin's second novel, held a place on the *New York Times* bestseller list for four months. Seymour Krim, writing for *Washington Post Book World,* described the allegorical novel as "the most ambitious work [Helprin] has yet attempted, a huge cyclorama" with a theme "no less than the resurrection of New York from a city of the damned to a place of universal justice and hope." In his view, however, which was one of several negative critical responses to the book, it turned out to be "a self-willed fairy tale that even on its own terms refuses to convince." In the *Chicago Tribune Book World,* Jonathan Brent called the book "a pastiche of cliches thinly disguised as fiction, a maddening welter of earnest platitudes excruciatingly dressed up as a search for the miraculous." In the opinion of *Newsweek*'s Peter S. Prescott, "Helprin fell into the fundamental error of assuming that fantasy can be vaguer than realistic fiction."

In the view of Benjamin De Mott of the *New York Times Book Review,* however, not through the unique and compelling characters or "merely by studying the touchstone passages in which description and narrative soar highest" can the reader "possess the work": "No, the heart of this book resides unquestionably in its moral energy, in the thousand original gestures, ruminations, . . . writing feats that summon its audience beyond the narrow limits of conventional vision, commanding us to see our time and place afresh." *Detroit News* reviewer Beaufort Cranford found that the book "fairly glows with poetry. Helprin's forte is a deft touch with description, and he has as distinct and spectacular a gift for words an anyone writing today." Further, Cranford noted, "Helprin's fearlessly understated humor shows his comfort with a narrative that in a less adroit grasp might seem too much like a fairy tale."

Openers editor Ann Cunniff, who also caught the humor in *Winter's Tale,* wrote about "the beautiful, dreamlike quality" of some of Helprin's passages and "frequent references to dreams in the book." "All my life," Helprin explained to Cunniff, "I've allowed what I dream to influence me. My dreams are usually very intense and extremely detailed and always in the most beautiful colors. . . . Frequently, I will dream, and simply retrace that dream the day after when I write. It's just like planning ahead, only I do it when I'm unconscious."

Helprin later collaborated with illustrator Chris Van Allsburg on a retelling of *Swan Lake.* Michael Dirda wrote in the *Washington Post Book World,* "The book is so attractive—in its story, illustrations and general design—that by comparison the original ballet almost looks too ethereal." In the *Chicago Tribune,* Michael Dorris raved, "This is one of those rare juvenile classics that will keep you awake to its conclusion . . . [and] will become, I predict, among those precious artifacts your grownup children will someday request for their own children."

In *A Soldier of the Great War,* which Shashi Tharoor described in the *Washington Post Book World* as "marvelously old-fashioned, . . . a mammoth, elegiac, moving exegesis on love, beauty, the meaning of life and the meaninglessness of war," Helprin seemed to have overcome some of the critical complaints about much of his earlier work. According to John Skow in *Time,* in this tale of the old Italian soldier Alessandro, Helprin has "simplified his language, though he still works up a good head of steam, and he has moderated his enthusiasm for phantasmagoric set pieces. He has also picked themes—war and loss, youth and age—that suit a large, elaborate style." Ted Solotaroff commented in the *Nation* that "In *A Soldier,* Helprin has to take his penchant for life's heightened possibilities and transcendent meanings down into the vile trenches and nightmarish forests and jammed military prisons of the Italian sector of the war."

Regarding the scenes in *A Soldier of the Great War* in which war and mountain climbing (a past hobby of Helprin's) are combined, *Village Voice* interviewer Geoffrey Stokes remarked, "the language is muted—at least when compared to the roistering excesses of *Winter's Tale* or *Refiner's Fire.* Is this too a function of aging?" he asked Helprin. "No," the writer responded. "That's a corrective function, a kind of self-criticism. There are areas in those books where I now see a kind of weakness, a kind of self-indulgence because I was having too much fun. So there were areas that dissolved into mysticism. I just don't do that—that much—anymore." Tharoor concluded: "Clearly a writer of great sensitivity, remarkable skill and capacious intellect, Helprin relishes telling stories in the grand manner, supplying details so complete as to leave the reader in no doubt about the texture of each place and the feelings of each character in it."

BIOGRAPHICAL/CRITICAL SOURCES:

BOOKS

Contemporary Literary Criticism, Gale, Volume 7, 1977, Volume 10, 1979, Volume 22, 1982, Volume 32, 1985.
Dictionary of Literary Biography Yearbook: 1985, Gale, 1986.

PERIODICALS

Atlantic Monthly, October, 1975.
Chicago Tribune, March 29, 1981; November 12, 1989.
Chicago Tribune Book World, March 29, 1981; October 9, 1983; October 23, 1988; November 12, 1989.
Detroit News, February, 23, 1982; March 14, 1982; October 9, 1983.
Globe and Mail (Toronto), January 7, 1984; October 6, 1984.
Harper's, November, 1977.
Los Angeles Times, November 8, 1984.
Los Angeles Times Book Review, September 25, 1983; May 5, 1991.
Nation, June 10, 1991.
New Statesman, February 13, 1976.
Newsweek, September 19, 1983.
New Yorker, October 17, 1977.
New York Review of Books, February 23, 1978; August 15, 1991.
New York Times, January 30, 1981; March 5, 1981; September 2, 1983.
New York Times Book Review, November 2, 1975; January 1, 1978; March 1, 1981; September 4, 1983; March 25, 1984; May 5, 1991.
Openers, fall, 1984.
Publishers Weekly, February 13, 1981.
Saturday Review, September 20, 1975.
Spectator, April 24, 1976.
Time, July 6, 1981; October 3, 1983; November 13, 1989; May 20, 1991.
Times Literary Supplement, March 13, 1981; November 25, 1983.
Village Voice, May 28, 1991.
Washington Post Book World, February 22, 1981; September 25, 1983; November 5, 1989; May 5, 1991.

*   *   *

HEMINGWAY, Maggie   1946-1993

PERSONAL: Born March 17, 1946, in Orford, Suffolk, England; died due to defective functioning of blood-forming organs, May 9, 1993; daughter of John (a doctor) and Elizabeth (Johnston) Hemingway; married, 1967 (divorced, 1977); companion of David Matthews (a composer), beginning in 1983; children: two daughters. *Education:* University of Edinburgh, M.A., 1967.

CAREER: Held production, editorial, and home and foreign rights posts in publishing trade, 1976-86; full-time writer, 1987-93.

AWARDS, HONORS: Winifred Holtby Prize, Royal Society of Literature, 1987, for *The Bridge.*

WRITINGS:

The Bridge (novel), Atheneum (New York City), 1986.
Stop House Blues (novel), Hamish Hamilton (London), 1988.
The Postmen's House (novel), Sinclair-Stevenson (London), 1990.

Also author of the short story collection *Eyes,* 1993. Contributor of reviews to *Times Educational Supplement.*

ADAPTATIONS: The Bridge was adapted for film in 1992.

SIDELIGHTS: Maggie Hemingway, in her first novel, *The Bridge,* portrays an actual British impressionist painter, Philip Wilson Steer, whose sensual and creative art abruptly and significantly diminished in quality after 1891. Hemingway's book provides a fictional explanation for this decline. In the summer of 1887, at the seaside Suffolk village of Walberswick, England, Steer falls in love with Isobel Heatherington, the lonely wife of a London stockbroker. Due to the impropriety of their romance, the two are agonizingly separated, and their missed happiness renders the once artistically inspirational village unbearable for the painter. Although *Washington Post* critic Brigitte Weeks defined Hemingway's plot as "fragile," unable to bear the burden of a responsibility as great as ruining an artist's career, she commended the novel: "As a prose poem, in the 19th-century summer among the upper middle classes made up of evocative descriptions linked by a tenuous plot, this novel is worth reading." A "cerebral and suggestive writer," Hemingway, wrote Weeks, "knows how to evoke a scene; she can probe her characters' minds; she has a flair for detail."

Departing from the romanticism of *The Bridge,* Hemingway's later works focus on tormented individuals and address darker themes. *Stop House Blues* chronicles the life of a youth who, after being turned out of his home and raised by a cruel aunt, is wrongly convicted of a crime and sent to a prison, in which his father is a warder, to await execution. *The Postmen's House* concerns the efforts of a husband and wife to escape postwar Czechoslovakia. In *Eyes,* which was published posthumously, Hemingway addressed what a writer for the London *Times* called "the morality of non-intervention in the face of evil. The 'eyes' here are the watchers in life—people who see evil going on around them, but do nothing to stop it." The four interconnecting stories are set in Venice, nineteenth-century France, interwar London, and 1950s Devon.

Hemingway once told *CA:* "If I were to be asked what preoccupies me principally in my writing, I would say that the central subject in my novels is freedom—how people handle the various freedoms they possess and those to which they have potential access. I am perpetually surprised and eternally curious, after years of observation, about the way that if people are not 'everywhere in chains,' then those without start to manufacture them, either real or imaginary. It is a subject with such infinite variations of tragedy and comedy that it could fascinate me forever."

BIOGRAPHICAL/CRITICAL SOURCES:

PERIODICALS

Washington Post, February 17, 1987.

OBITUARIES:

PERIODICALS

New York Times, May 17, 1993, p. B8.
Times (London), May 14, 1993, p. 17.*

*   *   *

HENRIOD, Lorraine 1925-

PERSONAL: Surname is accented on first syllable; born May 12, 1925, in Los Angeles, CA; daughter of David Clark and Afton (Jones) Stephens; married Joseph L. Henriod (a lawyer), November 7, 1947; children: Stephen L., Jane (Mrs. Stuart Wise), Paul E., Joseph R., Matthew C., Marianne. *Education:* University of Utah, B.A., 1946. *Politics:* Democrat. *Religion:* Church of Jesus Christ of Latter-Day Saints (Mormon).

ADDRESSES: Home—2262 East 17th S., Salt Lake City, UT 84108.

CAREER: Writer of children's books; has worked as a newspaper reporter.

WRITINGS:

JUVENILE; PUBLISHED BY PUTNAM (NEW YORK CITY)

I Know a Postman, 1967.
I Know a Zoo Keeper, 1969.
I Know a Grocer, 1970.
Marie Curie, 1970.
Peter and the Desert, 1970.
I Know a Newspaper Reporter, 1971.
The Rock Hunters, 1972.

OTHER JUVENILE

Ancestor Hunting, illustrated by Janet Potter D'Amato, Messner (New York City), 1979.
Special Olympics and Paralympics, Watts (New York City), 1979.
Grandma's Wheelchair, illustrated by Christa Chevalier, A. Whitman (Chicago), 1982.

*   *   *

HERBERT, Gilbert 1924-

PERSONAL: Born June 22, 1924, in Johannesburg, South Africa; son of Benjamin (a merchant) and Sophia (a musician; maiden name, Miller) Herbert; married Valerie Ryan (a teacher), June 18, 1953; children: Barry (deceased), Margaret. *Education:* University of the Witwatersrand, B.Arch., 1947, Diploma in Town Planning, 1951, M.Arch., 1955; University of South Africa, D.Litt. et Phil., 1969. *Religion:* Jewish.

ADDRESSES: Home—8 Eder St., Haifa, Israel 34752. *Office*—Faculty of Architecture and Town Planning, Technion: Israel Institute of Technology, Haifa, Israel.

CAREER: University of the Witwatersrand, Johannesburg, South Africa, lecturer in architecture, 1947-61; University of Adelaide, Adelaide, Australia, reader in architecture and town planning, 1961-68; Technion: Israel Institute of Technology, Haifa, Israel, associate professor, 1968-72, professor of architecture, 1972-74, dean of faculty of architecture and town planning, 1973-74, Mary Hill Swope Professor of Architecture, 1974-93, professor emeritus, 1993—. Adjunct professor at Bezalel Academy of Art and Design, 1970-72, 1976-78. Architectural consultant, 1947-68.

MEMBER: Israel Institute of Engineers and Architects, South African Institute of Architects, Royal Australian Institute of Architects (fellow), Royal Institute of British Architects (fellow), Society of Architectural Historians.

AWARDS, HONORS: Architectural Critics and Writers Award from Institute of South African Architects, 1980, for outstanding contribution in the fields of architectural history and criticism, and for *Martienssen and the International Style;* Joseph H. Hazen Award for Literature of Twentieth Century Art from Israel Museum, 1982, for "Gropius, Hirsch, and the Saga of the Copper Houses" and "The Packaged House: Dream and Reality"; D.Arch., University of the Witwatersrand, 1986.

WRITINGS:

The Synthetic Vision of Walter Gropius, Witwatersrand University Press, 1959.
Martienssen and the International Style, Balkema, 1975.

Pioneers of Prefabrication, Johns Hopkins University Press, 1978.

The Dream of the Factory-Made House: Walter Gropius and Konrad Wachsmann, MIT Press, 1984.

(With Silvina Sosnovsky) *Bauhaus-on-the-Carmel and the Crossroads of Empire,* Yad Ben-Zvi, 1993.

OTHER

Ben (short story), broadcast by BBC World Service, 1988.

Contributor to numerous books, including *Dialogue in Development,* edited by Gershon Von Schwarze, Association of Engineers and Architects in Israel, 1970; *New Trends in Urban Planning,* edited by Dan Soen, Pergamon, 1979; *Improving the Human Condition: Quality and Stability in Social Systems,* edited by R. F. Ericson, Springer-Verlag, 1979; *Contemporary Architects,* edited by Muriel Emanuel, Macmillan, 1980; *Ethics in an Age of Pervasive Technology,* edited by Marvin Kranzberg, Westview, 1980; *International Handbook of Contemporary Developments in Architecture,* edited by Warren Sanderson, Greenwood Press, 1981; *Creating Livable Cities,* edited by N. Pressman, Contact, 1981; *Haifa and Her Sites,* edited by E. Schiller, Ariel Press, 1985; *The Development of Haifa, 1918-48,* edited by Y. Ben Artzi and M. Naor, Yad Ben-Zvi, 1989; and *International Dictionary of Architects and Architecture,* edited by R. J. Van Vynekt, St. James Press, 1993.

Also contributor to *Encyclopedia of Building Technology,* edited by H. J. Cowan, and *Encyclopedia of Modern Architecture.* Contributor to architecture journals in England, the United States, Australia, Canada, Israel, Germany, and South Africa. Contributor of poetry to *Voices.* Associate editor of *South African Architectural Record,* 1949-60; corresponding editor of *Australian Planning Institute Journal,* 1965-68; member of editorial advisory committee, *Architectural Science Review,* 1977—; member of review board, *Plan SA,* 1986—; chairperson of editorial advisory committee, *Documentation Unit Publications,* 1987—.

SIDELIGHTS: Gilbert Herbert once told *CA:* "First and foremost I am a teacher, and my writing deals with theories, and the facts uncovered by historical research. It tends, therefore, to be didactic in purpose, and, at times, didactic in tone. When a critic complained of one of my early articles that it was heavy going, he was rapped over the knuckles by Walter Gropius who said: 'Gilbert Herbert is a serious scholar, and his work is not intended to be merely entertaining.' Nevertheless, I took the criticism to heart, for there is no need for scholarship to be dull, obscure, or pretentious. Least of all, a work of architectural history.

"The cultural historian is, in his own way, something of a detective. In his attempt at reconstructing a true mosaic of past events, he searches for clues, for fragments of information, and for logical connections, cohesive patterns. He is guided as much by intuition as knowledge. He is baffled by obscure facts, frustrated by missing evidence; and sometimes he is rewarded by flashes of insight, revelations of the truth, which must be later substantiated by evidence, and properly documented. The pursuit of historical knowledge is therefore charged, as is a detective story, with an underlying element of tension, with the excitement of the chase, with the drama of the denouement. Moreover, a study of architectural history deals not only with artifacts, physical objects, sticks and stones, not only with dry dates and chronologies—important as these may be—but with a rich cast of characters, whose complex personalities must be understood, whose motivations, ambitions and dreams are vital to an interpretation of events. Then, there is the broad sweep of historical context: cultural and technological change, ideologies and politics, the inexorable pressures of economics. The broad panorama, the human drama, the piquant incident, are all germane to the writing of history, as is the hard core of solid fact."

An exhibition based on *Bauhaus-on-the Carmel and the Crossroads of Empire* was displayed in 1994 in Tel Aviv and at the Haifa Museum of Modern Art.

BIOGRAPHICAL/CRITICAL SOURCES:

PERIODICALS

Times Literary Supplement, June 21, 1985.

* * *

HIBBERD, Jack 1940-

PERSONAL: Born April 12, 1940, in Warracknabeal, Australia; son of James George (a plumber) and Moira (a singer; maiden name, Richardson) Hibberd; married first wife, Jocelyn, February 8, 1969 (divorced, 1976); married Evelyn Krape (an actress and singer), January 3, 1978; children: (first marriage) Lillian Margaret, James Benjamin; (second marriage) Samuel Spike Mendel. *Education:* University of Melbourne, M.B.B.S., 1964.

ADDRESSES: Home—87 Turner St., Abbotsford, Victoria 3067, Australia. Agent—Almost Managing, P.O. Box 34, Carlton, Victoria 3053, Australia.

CAREER: Writer. Physician in general practice in Australia, 1965-66, 1970-73, 1986—; registrar, St. Vincent's Hospital, Department of Social Medicine, Melbourne, Australia, 1967. Member of Australian Performing Group; Australia Council, member of Theatre Board, 1977-79; Melbourne Writers' Theatre, president, 1984-86.

WRITINGS:

Brain Rot (also see below), first produced in Carlton, Australia, 1967.

White with Wire Wheels, first produced in Melbourne, Australia, 1970.

(Coauthor) *Marvelous Melbourne,* first produced in Melbourne, 1970.

Klag, first produced in Melbourne, 1970.

Customs and Excise, first produced in Carlton, 1970, produced as *Proud Flesh* in Carlton, 1972.

Aorta, first produced in Melbourne, 1971.

Flesh, first produced in Carlton, 1972.

Women! (adaptation of a play by Aristophanes), first produced in Carlton, 1972.

A Stretch of the Imagination (first produced in Carlton, 1972), Currency Press, 1973.

Captain Midnight VC (first produced in Carlton, 1973; music by Lorraine Milne), foreword by Humphrey McQueen, Yackandandah, 1984.

The Les Darcy Show (first produced in Adelaide, Australia, 1973; also see below), Scribe, 1979.

The Architect and the Emperor of Assyria (adaptation of a play by Fernando Arrabel), first produced in Carlton, 1974.

Dimboola: A Wedding Reception Play (first produced in Carlton; bound with *The Last of the Knucklemen*), Penguin, 1974.

Peggy Sue (first produced in Carlton, 1974; revised version produced in Melbourne, 1983), Yackandandah, 1982.

A Toast to Melba (also see below), first produced in Adelaide, Australia, 1976.

Three Popular Plays (contains *One of Nature's Gentlemen, A Toast to Melba,* and *The Les Darcy Show*), Outback Press, 1976.

The Overcoat (adaptation of a story by Nikolai Gogol), first produced in Carlton, 1976.

(Translator) Charles Baudelaire, *Le Vin des amants: Poems from Baudelaire,* Gryphon Books, 1977.

Mothballs, first produced in Melbourne, 1981.

(With Garrie Hutchinson) *The Barracker's Bible,* illustrated by Noel Counihan and Barry Dickens, McPhee Gribble (Melbourne), 1983.

(With John Timlin) *Goodbye Ted,* Yackandandah, 1983.

Liquid Amber (also see below), first produced in Melbourne, 1984.

A Country Quinella with Damboola (includes *Liquid Amber*) Penguin, 1984.

Squibs (a collection of microplays from *Brain Rot* and short plays; includes *Asian Oranges, A League of Nations, The Three Sisters* [a parody of Anton Chekhov's story of the same title], and *Death of a Traveller* [a parody of Arthur Miller's play *Death of a Salesman*]), Phoenix (Brisbane, Australia), 1984.

(Adapter) Guy de Maupassant, *Odyssey of a Prostitute,* Outrider, 1985.

Memoirs of an Old Bastard: Being a Portrait of a City, an Epicurean Chronicle, Fantasia and Search, McPhee Gribble, 1989.

Perdita, McPhee Gribble, 1992.

Also author of unpublished and unproduced plays, including *The Last Days of Epic J. Remorse,* 1969; *A Man of Many Parts,* 1980; *Smash Hit!,* 1980; and *The Old School Tie,* 1983. Work represented in anthologies, including *Buzo, Hibberd, Romeril: Four Australian Plays* (includes *White with Wire Wheels* and *Who*), Penguin, 1970. Works published in periodicals include: *Memoirs of a Carlton Bohemian,* published in *Meanjin 3,* 1977; *Sin,* 1978, and *Glycerine Tears* and *Malarky Barks,* 1982, all published in *Meanjin 4; Lavender Bags,* published in *Aspect,* number 25, 1982; and *Death Warmed Up,* published in *Scripsi,* Volume 2, number 4, 1984. Editor of special performing arts edition of *Meanjin 4,* 1984. Author of wine column for *Age,* 1986—.

Hibberd's manuscripts are housed in the Australian Collection, Australian National Library, Canberra, Australian Capital Territory; Melbourne University Archives; La Trobe Library, Melbourne; and Eunice Hanger Collection, Fryer Library, University of Queensland.

WORK IN PROGRESS: Two plays: "Silver Threads among the Gold" and "Is Tonight the Night?"; and "Tall Tales," a six-part television comedy.

SIDELIGHTS: Jack Hibberd once told *CA:* "My plays are non-autobiographical and generally anti-naturalistic. My ambition is to write bizarre comedies that depict the sad, mad paradoxes of contemporary existence within and without Australia. Major influences on my work are vaudeville and popular demotic comedy, the theatre of the absurd, Bertolt Brecht, German expressionism, Baudelaire, and the French symbolists."

Hibberd remarked in 1986: "Over the last ten years I have been less concerned to write specifically of Australian experience but more sweepingly of human conduct in a context of comico-tragic formal experiment, especially in my monodramas and other theatrical sorties into the actor-audience farce."

BIOGRAPHICAL/CRITICAL SOURCES:

BOOKS

Contemporary Australian Drama, Currency Press, 1981.

Fitzpatrick, Peter, *After the Doll,* Edward Arnold (London), 1979.

McGillick, Paul, *Jack Hibberd,* Rodopi, 1988.*

HICKMAN, Hoyt L(eon)   1927-

PERSONAL: Born May 22, 1927, in Pittsburgh, PA; son of Leon Edward (an attorney) and Mayme (a homemaker; maiden name, Hoyt) Hickman; married Martha Whitmore (a writer), December 16, 1950; children: Peter, John, Stephen, Mary (deceased). *Education:* Haverford College, A.B. (magna cum laude), 1950; Yale University, M.Div. (cum laude), 1953; Union Theological Seminary, S.T.M., 1954. *Politics:* Democrat. *Avocational interests:* Music, genealogy, antique automobiles, travel (Europe and Israel).

ADDRESSES: Home—2034 Castleman Dr., Nashville, TN 37215.

CAREER: Ordained United Methodist minister; pastor of Methodist churches in Windber, PA, 1954-57, Claysville, PA, 1957-59, Beaver Falls, PA, 1959-64, and Erie, PA, 1964-72; General Board of Discipleship of the United Methodist Church, Nashville, TN, member of staff, 1972-93. Executive secretary of United Methodist General Commission on Worship, 1968-72; president of Erie County Council of Churches, 1970-71; member of Commission on Worship of the World Methodist Council, 1971-81; member of board of directors of Liturgical Conference, 1973-80. *Military service:* U.S. Navy, 1945-46; became seaman first class.

MEMBER: North American Academy of Liturgy (member of board of directors, 1976-77, 1986-88, 1992—), Societas Liturgical, Liturgical Conference (member of board of directors, 1973-80), Phi Beta Kappa.

WRITINGS:

Ritual in a New Day, Abingdon (Nashville, TN), 1977.
At the Lord's Table, Abingdon, 1981.
United Methodist Altars, Abingdon, 1984.
A Primer for Church Worship, Abingdon, 1984.
The Acolyte's Book, Abingdon, 1985.
Handbook of the Christian Year, Abingdon, 1986.
Holy Communion, Abingdon, 1987.
A Companion to the Book of Services, Abingdon, 1988.
The Worship Resources of the United Methodist Hymnal, Abingdon, 1989.
United Methodist Worship, Abingdon, 1991.
New Handbook of the Christian Year, Abingdon, 1992.

WORK IN PROGRESS: Worshiping with United Methodists, for Abingdon, 1996.

SIDELIGHTS: Hoyt L. Hickman told *CA:* "For twenty-one years I was the director of resource development in the section on worship for the general board of discipleship of the United Methodist Church. In retirement I continue to write and edit worship resources needed by the United Methodist Church. My interest in writing was prompted by my involvement in liturgical reform and my conviction that worship is crucial to the life and renewal of the church. Some of my books are intended for clergy, and others are intended for lay readers. While writing is supervised by a board that sees that all the diverse practices and views of our denomination are taken account of in our denominational resources, I have no difficulty in expressing my personal views and values in these books. My prime value in writing them is that our denomination has resources adequate to the fullness and diversity of our heritage, presented so clearly and persuasively that both clergy and laity can find there the resources they need for their worship."

*   *   *

HILL, Archibald A(nderson)   1902-1992

PERSONAL: Born July 5, 1902, in New York, NY; died March 27, 1992; son of Archibald Alexander (a social worker) and Mary Dorsey (a teacher; maiden name, Anderson) Hill; married Muriel Louise Byard, August 27, 1928. *Education:* Pomona College, A.B., 1923; Stanford University, M.A., 1924; Yale University, Ph.D., 1927. *Politics:* Liberal Democrat. *Religion:* "Not regular churchgoer."

CAREER: University of Michigan, Ann Arbor, instructor, 1926-29, assistant professor of English, 1929-30; University of Virginia, Charlottesville, associate professor, 1930-39, professor of English philology, 1939-50, professor of English language, 1950-53; Georgetown University, Washington, DC, vice-director of Institute of Languages and Linguistics, 1953-55; University of Texas, Austin, professor of English and linguistics, 1955-72, professor emeritus, 1972-92. *Military service:* U.S. Naval Reserve, active duty, 1942-46; became commander.

MEMBER: Linguistic Society of America (secretary-treasurer, 1951-68; president, 1969), Modern Language Association of America, American Anthropological Association, American Association for the Advancement of Science, Linguistic Association of the Southwest (president, 1973), Phi Beta Kappa.

WRITINGS:

(Editor and contributor) *Humanistic Studies in Honor of John Calvin Metcalf,* University of Virginia (Charlottesville, VA), 1941.
Introduction to Linguistic Structures: From Sound to Sentence in English, Harcourt (New York City), 1958.
Essays in Literary Analysis (collection of essays for student use), privately printed, 1965.
(Editor, author of preface, and contributor) *Linguistics Today* (based on Voice of America "Forum" series),

Voice of America, 1969, distributed overseas as *Linguistics: Voice of America Forum Lectures.*
(Editor with E. Bagby Atwood, and contributor) *Studies in Language, Literature, and Culture of the Middle Ages and Later* (volume in honor of Rudolph Willard), University of Texas Press (Austin, TX), 1969.
Constituent and Pattern in Poetry, University of Texas Press, 1976.

Contributor to books, including *Understanding Other Cultures,* edited by William A. Parker, American Council of Learned Societies, 1954; *First Perspectives on Language,* edited by William C. Doster, American Book Co. (New York City), 1963; *Applied English Linguistics,* 2nd edition, edited by Harold B. Allen, Appleton (East Norwalk, CT), 1964; *Essays on the Language of Literature,* edited by Seymour Chatman and Samuel Levin, Houghton (Burlington, MA), 1967; *A Various Language: Perspectives on American Dialects,* edited by Juanita V. Williamson and Virginia M. Burke, Holt (New York City), 1971. Writer of courses in English for adults. Contributor of articles, essays, and reviews to journals.

SIDELIGHTS: Archibald A. Hill once told *CA:* "I have been the recipient of a Festschrift, *Linguistic and Literary Studies in Honor of Archibald A. Hill.* The volume contains a bibliography of my writings to 1972 and an address I delivered to the College of Liberal Arts, University of Texas, in 1972."

BIOGRAPHICAL/CRITICAL SOURCES:

BOOKS

Jazayery, Mohammad Ali, Edgar C. Polome and Werner Winter, editors, *Linguistic and Literary Studies in Honor of Archibald A. Hill,* four volumes, Mouton [Peter de Ridder Press] (The Hague), 1976-79.

*   *   *

HILL, James
   See JAMESON, Storm

*   *   *

HIMMELSTEIN, Jerome L(ionel)   **1948-**

PERSONAL: Born July 3, 1948, in Philadelphia, PA; son of Harry Eli (in business) and Bertha (Baram) Himmelstein; married Evelyn Katherine Bogen (a lawyer), July 4, 1982. *Education:* Attended London School of Economics and Political Science, London, 1968-69; Columbia University, B.A. (cum laude), 1970; University of California, Berkeley, M.A., 1972, Ph.D., 1979.

ADDRESSES: Home—42 Hitchcock Rd., Amherst, MA 01002. *Office*—Department of Anthropology and Sociology, Box 2226, Amherst College, Amherst, MA 01002.

CAREER: New York City Department of Health, New York City, health research trainee, summers, 1970-72; University of California, Berkeley, lecturer in sociology, 1976-80; University of Michigan, Ann Arbor, fellow at Center for Research on Social Organization, 1980-82, instructor in Residential College, 1982; Amherst College, Amherst, MA, assistant professor, 1982-88, associate professor of sociology, 1988—, department chairperson, 1989—. Research associate and technical writer for National Institute on Drug Abuse, 1977; guest on radio programs.

MEMBER: American Sociological Association, Phi Beta Kappa.

AWARDS, HONORS: Fellowships from National Institute of Mental Health, 1980-82, and from National Endowment for the Humanities, 1983.

WRITINGS:

The Strange Career of Marijuana: Politics and Ideology of Drug Control, Greenwood Press (Westport, CT), 1983.
To the Right: The Transformation of American Conservatism, University of California (Berkeley, CA), 1990.

Contributor to books, including *The New Christian Right,* edited by Robert Wuthnow and Robert Liebman, Aldine (Hawthorne, NY), 1983. Contributor of articles and reviews to sociology and drug research journals, including *Contemporary Drug Problems, Contemporary Sociology, Journal for the Scientific Study of Religions, Public Opinion Quarterly, Social Forces, Society,* and *Sociological Inquiry.*

Editor of *Berkeley Journal of Sociology,* 1974-75.

WORK IN PROGRESS: Research on the changing role of the corporation in American politics.

SIDELIGHTS: Jerome L. Himmelstein told *CA:* "Four interests have animated my writing. First, a concern with ideology in the broadest sense; that is, with how our conceptions of the world are shaped by social structure and how in turn they shape our actions. Second, an interest in the social bases of politics and the conditions under which political movements emerge. Third, a concern with the history of sociological theory, especially the various images of individual and society that have been generated by the intellectual effort to come to terms with modern Western society. Fourth, an interest in the distinctive features of American social structure and culture.

"Coming of age in the late 1960s, I became interested in marijuana because of the political controversy of which it was part. *The Strange Career of Marijuana: Politics and Ideology of Drug Control* examines the historical development of marijuana laws, especially the movement for reform in the 1960s and 1970s. It traces the changing terms in which the drug and laws against it have been discussed as well. One of the more interesting issues I cover is the transformation of the public image of marijuana in the 1960s from a 'killer weed,' which made its users violent, to a 'drop-out drug,' which rendered its users apathetic and passive.

"*To the Right: The Transformation of American Conservatism* examines how the Right became a central force in American politics. It traces the transformation of conservative ideology and the construction of a conservative movement in the 1950s and 1960s. Then it looks at the impact of corporate conservatism, the religious Right, and the Republican Party on politics in the 1970s and 1980s."

BIOGRAPHICAL/CRITICAL SOURCES:

PERIODICALS

Contemporary Sociology, March, 1984.

*   *   *

HOLLAND, Isabelle 1920-

PERSONAL: Born June 16, 1920, in Basel, Switzerland; daughter of Philip (a U.S. Foreign Service officer) and Corabelle (Anderson) Holland. *Education:* Attended University of Liverpool; Tulane University of Louisiana, B.A., 1942. *Avocational interests:* "All things Spanish—music, fiestas, the sound of the language; cats."

ADDRESSES: Home—1199 Park Ave., New York, NY 10028. *Agent*—JCA Literary Agency Inc., 242 West 27th St., New York, NY 10001.

CAREER: Freelance author of novels and short stories for adults, young adults, and children. Worked for various publications, including *McCall's*, New York City, until 1956; Crown Publishers, Inc., New York City, publicity director, 1956-60; J. B. Lippincott Co., New York City, publicity director, 1960-66; *Harper's*, New York City, assistant to publisher, 1967-68; G. P. Putnam's Sons, New York City, publicity director, 1968-69.

MEMBER: Authors Guild, Authors League of America, PEN.

AWARDS, HONORS: National Book Award nomination, 1976, for *Of Love and Death and Other Journeys;* Ott Award, Church and Synagogue Library Association, 1983, for *Abbie's God Book* and *God, Mrs. Muskrat, and Aunt Dot.*

WRITINGS:

BOOKS FOR CHILDREN AND YOUNG ADULTS

Cecily, Lippincott, 1967.
Amanda's Choice, Lippincott, 1970.
The Man without a Face, Lippincott, 1972.
The Mystery of Castle Rinaldi, American Educational Publications, 1972.
Heads You Win, Tails I Lose, Lippincott, 1973.
Journey for Three, illustrated by Charles Robinson, Xerox Family Education Services, 1974.
Of Love and Death and Other Journeys, Lippincott, 1975, published in England as *Ask No Questions,* Macdonald and Jane's, 1978.
Alan and the Animal Kingdom, Lippincott, 1977.
Hitchhike, Lippincott, 1977.
Dinah and the Green Fat Kingdom, Lippincott, 1978.
Now Is Not Too Late, Lothrop, 1980.
Summer of My First Love, Fawcett, 1981.
Abbie's God Book, illustrated by James McLaughlin, Westminster, 1982.
A Horse Named Peaceable, Lothrop, 1982.
After the First Love, Fawcett, 1983.
The Empty House, Lippincott, 1983.
God, Mrs. Muskrat, and Aunt Dot, illustrated by Beth and Joe Krush, Westminster, 1983.
Perdita, Little, Brown, 1983.
Kevin's Hat, illustrated by Leonard Lubin, Lothrop, 1984.
Green Andrew Green, Westminster, 1984.
The Island, Little, Brown, 1984.
Jennie Kiss'd Me, Fawcett, 1985.
Henry and Grudge, illustrated by Lisa Chauncy Guida, Walker & Co., 1986.
The Christmas Cat, illustrated by Kathy Mitchell, Western Publishing, 1987.
Love and the Genetic Factor, Fawcett, 1987.
Toby the Splendid, Walker & Co., 1987.
Thief, Fawcett, 1988.
The Easter Donkey, Golden, 1989.
Bump in the Night, Fawcett Book Group, 1990.
The Journey Home, Scholastic, 1990.
The Unfrightened Dark, Little, Brown, 1990.
The House in the Woods, Little, Brown, 1991.
Search, Fawcett Book Group, 1991.
Behind the Lines, Scholastic, 1994.

NOVELS FOR ADULTS

Kilgaren, Weybright, 1974.
Trelawny, Weybright, 1974.
Moncrieff, Weybright, 1975.
Darcourt, Weybright, 1976.
Grenelle, Rawson Wade, 1976.
The deMaury Papers, Rawson Wade, 1977.
Tower Abbey, Rawson Wade, 1978.

The Marchington Papers, Rawson Wade, 1980.
Counterpoint, Rawson Wade, 1980.
The Lost Madonna, Rawson Wade, 1981.
A Death at St. Anselm's, Doubleday, 1984.
Flight of the Archangel, Doubleday, 1985.
A Lover Scorned, Doubleday, 1986.
Bump in the Night, Doubleday, 1988.
A Fatal Advent, Fawcett, 1989.
The Long Search, Thorndike, 1990.
Love and Inheritance, Thorndike, 1991.

OTHER

Contributor of short stories to periodicals, including *Collier's* and *Country Gentleman.* Holland's papers are kept in the Kerlan Collection at the University of Minnesota, Minneapolis, and in the deGrummond Collection at the University of Southern Mississippi, Hattiesburg.

SIDELIGHTS: Isabelle Holland is a respected author of books for a wide-range of readers. Her work for children and young adults is known internationally and is cited for its realism. In this genre, she deals with topics that, while common to the average teenager, are often seen by critics as controversial. Characters in these books deal with social ostracization, parental neglect, and sexual awakenings. As a mystery writer, Holland has also created novels that have been described as well-written gothic fiction. Despite the inclusion of often sensational material— haunted houses, murder, and drugs—these volumes for adults, like Holland's young adult fiction, have been praised for their realistic characters. Some reviewers of her books have speculated that the author's primary concern is with creating believable protagonists. Holland confirmed this in *Speaking for Ourselves,* stating that "all my books, whatever the category or form, deal, most importantly, with the inner journey of the central character."

"I think of myself as a storyteller," Holland wrote in *Speaking for Ourselves,* "and for this I am indebted to my mother." Holland's mother was often faced with the task of keeping her daughter entertained. To this end she turned to storytelling, creating tales that held Holland in rapt attention. As she grew older, Holland discovered that many of her mother's stories had roots in history and legend. She also found that in addition to being exciting and entertaining, these stories provided insight regarding real life situations. Holland was attracted to creating stories that could address genuine problems while simultaneously regaling a reader. This became an important goal in her writing. As she declared in *Speaking for Ourselves,* "stories, however long . . . should above all be interesting."

Using her experiences in English boarding schools, Holland created her first novel, 1967's *Cecily.* One of the two key characters is Elizabeth, a young woman who teaches at the Langley School, a prestigious English boarding academy. While the emphasis at Langley is on academics, proper feminine etiquette is also a priority, and there is an unspoken ideal that determines a student's success. The most accomplished girls at the school are the ones who are tall, good-looking, and cheerful. Into this environment comes thirteen-year-old Cecily. Cecily is awkward, overweight, and miserable; the opposite of the perfect Langley girl. This unhappy young girl's presence has a devastating effect on Elizabeth.

At the time *Cecily* appeared, most publishers did not have a separate category for young adults, the genre with which the book is most closely identified. As a result, the semi-autobiographical tale was published as an adult novel. Critics, however, had no trouble discerning the book as a valuable addition to the growing library of literature for young adults. *Horn Book* reviewer Ruth Hill Viguers describes *Cecily* as "a beautifully polished gem of a novel." Edith C. Howley writes in *Best Sellers* that the book is "tightly knit and plausible," cited the characters as clearly defined, and appraised the book overall as "well done."

Holland's next book, *Amanda's Choice,* was written for children but addresses problems that are universal to people in relationships. Amanda is an unhappy young girl whose father has recently remarried. Preoccupied with his new wife and other matters, her father does not pay enough attention to her. In an attempt to amend this situation, Amanda adopts vulgar language and mischievous behavior. This tactic earns her father's attention, but it is not the positive recognition that she craves. Alice Low writes in the *New York Times Book Review* that Holland "understands child-rearing, psychological nuances and social problems, but she uses her characters to carry messages rather than to tell their flesh and blood stories." Reviewing *Amanda's Choice* in the *Bulletin of the Center for Children's Books,* Zena Sutherland lauds the book for its "memorable characterization" and "good style."

Holland's third novel, 1972's *The Man without a Face,* was appraised as "deeply affecting" by *Children's Literature in Education* contributor Corine Hirsch, who calls the book Holland's "most interesting novel to date." The book is one of Holland's best known, primarily because of its controversial subject matter. Charles is a fourteen-year-old whose father has died. Since that time, his mother has remarried and divorced four times. He lives with her and his sisters. Viewing his mother's marriages as a betrayal to his father, Charles's attitude toward women in general is misogynistic. Having loved and lost his father, he is also fearful of close relationships.

As the story begins, Charles and his family are spending their summer on an upper-class resort island. Because his grades have slipped considerably, Charles must enlist the aid of a tutor to gain entrance to an exclusive boarding school. He seeks the help of Justin McLeod, a reclusive native of the island. Justin's restrained manner poses little threat to Charles's fear of close emotional ties. With the tutor's positive influence, Charles begins to face his own feelings and becomes sensitive to the needs of others. The crucial and controversial event in the story, however, comes when Charles's cat is kicked to death by the delinquent boyfriend of one of his sisters. He goes to Justin for comfort and ends up spending the night in his tutor's bed. Holland implies that an act of homosexual love occurs between Charles and Justin. Soon after, Justin dies of a heart attack, leaving all of his possessions to Charles. Charles grieves his mentor's passing, but he realizes that his relationship with Justin has helped him face his life and has enabled him to be open with others.

The inclusion of the homosexual element in *The Man without a Face* often sparked more discussion among critics than the novel's narrative quality. Many reviewers commented on Holland's motives, speculating on the novel's moral lessons. Sheryl B. Andrews writes in *Horn Book* that "the author handles the homosexual experience with taste and discretion; the act of love between Justin and Charles is a necessary emotional catharsis for the boy within the context of his story, and is developed with perception and restraint." In an adverse response to the book, Frances Hanckel and John Cunningham, writing in the *Wilson Library Bulletin,* complain of potential anti-gay sentiment. Hanckel and Cunningham felt that "in light of such limited coverage of the gay experience in YA [young adult] fiction, the possible identification of such a major character as a corrupter of children is grossly unfair." While Hirsch disagreed with Holland's stance on parenting, complaining that "character and plot are manipulated in order to illustrate the dangers of permissiveness and the value of discipline," she praises the author's use of homosexual themes, writing that "the novel's strength lies . . . in the development of [Justin and Charles's] intense emotional relationship and the corresponding enrichment of Charles' sensibilities." *Lion and the Unicorn* contributor Kate Fincke sees a deeper meaning in *The Man without a Face:* "Holland seems to have a twofold purpose. One is to speak some psychological truth on the matter of homosexuality; the other is to alleviate anxiety and to absolve guilt in the young adolescent reader about his own homosexual inclinations or acts." Comparing the fates of Justin and Charles at the novel's end, Fincke further interprets that "what Holland implies is that the transient adolescent homosexual is acceptable, but the mature homosexual is doomed."

Holland states in the *Horn Book* that she "didn't set out to write about homosexuality" in *The Man without a Face.* "I started this book with only the idea of a fatherless boy who experiences with a man some of the forms of compan-

ionship and love that have been nonexistent in his life." Holland writes that the character of Justin possesses "qualities that mythologically as well as psychologically have always been the archetypes of fatherhood." These qualities, which include masculinity and kindness, filled a void in Charles and eventually helped the boy lead a better life. This, Holland states, was more important "than the almost incidental fact that the book is about love between two people of the same sex."

Holland returned to writing novels for young adults in 1975, producing the National Book Award nominee *Of Love and Death and Other Journeys.* The central character, Meg Grant, is a teenager who is coming to a crossroads in her life. She is at an age where the adulthood she so desperately craves is within her reach, but she is also repeatedly reminded of her proximity to childhood. Her priorities change significantly when she learns that her mother has cancer. When her mother dies, Meg must learn how to deal with her grief. She falls in love with a boy named Cotton but is rejected by him. Oddly, Cotton's rejection triggers a realization in Meg that, although her mother is gone, she can survive on her own and lead a happy life.

Holland was praised for accurately evoking teenage emotion in *Of Love and Death.* "What makes the book really entertaining is Isabelle Holland's ability to capture all the precarious qualities of teenhood," lauds Anne Marie Stamford in *Best Sellers.* Stamford also admires Holland's skill in depicting real life. She concludes her review by stating that "the author's straightforward sense of humor when describing people and situations made me laugh out loud, a response rare indeed to novels these days." A critic for *Kirkus Reviews* praises the novel as "genuinely moving," and assesses *Of Love and Death* as containing "real emotion . . . that can't be ignored."

Holland wrote another children's book in 1982, *Abbie's God Book,* in which twelve-year-old Abbie conveys her thoughts on God, her family, and friends. In 1983 Holland published a related volume, *God, Mrs. Muskrat, and Aunt Dot.* The story centers around young Rebecca, a recent orphan. After the loss of her parents, Rebecca has come to live with her aunt and uncle. Told through a letter to God, Rebecca relates how her relationship with her imaginary friend, Mrs. Muskrat, has helped her adjust to her new life and surroundings. *Abbie's God Book* and *God, Mrs. Muskrat, and Aunt Dot* were jointly honored with the Church and Synagogue Library Association Ott Award in 1983.

Holland's career as a writer spans more than twenty-five years. Beginning with the publication of *Cecily* in 1967, she has received considerable praise from critics, teachers, librarians, and readers. Holland's handling of often sensitive material has been continually praised, as has her distinct portrayals of young people. As Sutherland states in the *Bulletin of the Center for Children's Books,* "it is . . . in insight into motivations and relationships that the author excels." Kaye echoes this sentiment in *Booklist,* opining that "Holland writes with compassion and a sensitive understanding of human nature and its idiosyncracies."

"My books have always dealt with the relationship between the child or adolescent and the adult or adults who live in and dominate the young person's portrait of self," Holland states in *Literature for Today's Young Adults.* She continues: "It is that struggle between the child and the adult in the creating of that self-portrait, that often preoccupies my writing." Holland believes that parents or other adults will often unintentionally inflict mental damage on a young person, damage that can scar the child for many years. While Holland's books criticize the mistreatment of young people, she also views them as a means to make people aware of, and hopefully address and correct, these problems. She summarized by stating, "if my books are about the wounds given . . . they are also about the healing that can take place, given the right adult at the right time."

BIOGRAPHICAL/CRITICAL SOURCES:

BOOKS

Contemporary Literary Criticism, Volume 21, Gale, 1982.
Gallo, Donald R., editor, *Speaking for Ourselves,* National Council of Teachers of English, 1990, pp. 97-98.
Nilsen, Pace, *Literature for Today's Young Adults,* Scott, Foresman, 1980.

PERIODICALS

Best Sellers, April 1, 1967, p. 7; December 1, 1974, pp. 382-383; May, 1975, p. 33; January, 1976, pp. 306-307; September, 1977, p. 174; June, 1979, pp. 111-112.
Booklist, January 1, 1980, p. 667.
Bulletin of the Center for Children's Books, September, 1970, pp. 9-10; April, 1979, p. 138; March, 1980, p. 135.
Children's Literature in Education, spring, 1979, pp. 25-34.
Horn Book, June, 1967, p. 353; August, 1972, pp. 375-376; June, 1973, pp. 299-305; June, 1980, p. 297.
Christian Science Monitor, June 12, 1974, p. F5; August 3, 1977, p. 23.
Junior Bookshelf, June, 1980, pp. 143-144.
Kirkus Reviews, April 1, 1975, pp. 383-384; March 15, 1977, p. 285.
Lion and the Unicorn, winter, 1979-80, pp. 86-95.
New York Times Book Review, May 3, 1970, p. 23; October 30, 1977, pp. 34, 36.
School Library Journal, September, 1977, p. 145.
Washington Post Book World, June 12, 1977, p. E4.

Wilson Library Bulletin, March, 1976.

*   *   *

HOLLY, Michael Ann 1944-

PERSONAL: Born July 19, 1944, in Alton, IL; daughter of George L. and Peggy J. Mueller; children: Lauren, Nicholas, Alexander. *Education:* William Smith College, B.A., 1973; Cornell University, M.A., 1976, Ph.D., 1981.

*ADDRESSES: Home—*101 Adams St., Rochester, NY 14627. *Office—* Department of Art and Art History, University of Rochester, Rochester, NY 14627.

CAREER: Hobart and William Smith Colleges, Geneva, NY, instructor in history, 1978-80, assistant professor, 1980-83, associate professor of history and art history, beginning 1984; University of Rochester, Rochester, NY, associate professor of art and art history and chair of department, 1986—. Director of National Endowment for the Humanities Summer Institute "Theory and Interpretation of the Visual Arts," 1987, 1989.

MEMBER: American Historical Association, College Art Association of America.

AWARDS, HONORS: Fellow of National Endowment for the Humanities, 1983, 1986-87; grant from American Council of Learned Societies, 1983; Mellon faculty fellow, Hobart and William Smith Colleges, 1983; Guggenheim fellow, 1991-92.

WRITINGS:

Panofsky and the Foundations of Art History, Cornell University Press (Ithaca, NY), 1984.
(Editor with Norman Bryson and Keith Moxey) *Visual Theory: Painting and Interpretation,* Harper (New York City), 1991.
Iconography and Iconology, Jaca (Milan, Italy), 1992.
(Editor with Bryson and Moxey) *Visual Culture: Images and Interpretation,* Wesleyan, 1994.

Contributor to books, including *Interpreting the Humanities,* 1987, *Theory between the Disciplines,* 1990, *The Johns Hopkins Guide to Literary Theory and Criticism,* 1994, and *The Point of Theory,* 1994. Contributor of essays and reviews to newspapers and scholarly journals.

WORK IN PROGRESS: Meanings and Methods: Art Historiography in the 1990s, anthology edited with Mark Cheetham, for Cambridge University Press, 1995.

SIDELIGHTS: According to critic Arthur C. Danto, Michael Ann Holly's *Panofsky and the Foundations of Art History* represents the author's attempt to incorporate the structures, discipline, and philosophy of art history as an integral part of the larger history of art. The subject of her study, the American art historian Erwin Panofsky, also attempted to place the history of art on a solid philosophical base, and Holly provides her own interpretation of Panofsky's effort in this direction. Danto wrote in the *Times Literary Supplement:* "No better first step than bringing the history of art to historical self-consciousness can be imagined . . . and in this Michael Ann Holly has rendered a great service and written a fascinating study."

BIOGRAPHICAL/CRITICAL SOURCES:

PERIODICALS

American Historical Review, February, 1986.
Art in America, July, 1985.
Choice, June, 1985.
History and Theory, Volume 25, 1986.
Journal of Aesthetics and Art Criticism, fall, 1985.
Times Literary Supplement, August 2, 1985.

*　　*　　*

HOLMES, Jeffrey 1934-

PERSONAL: Born August 16, 1934, in Bradford, Yorkshire, England; son of Frederick (a house painter and decorator) and Gertrude (a homemaker) Holmes; married Diane Matheson (an alderman), June 1, 1963; children: Bryn, Ian, Thane. *Education:* Attended University of Toronto, 1964-66. *Politics:* None. *Religion:* Protestant.

ADDRESSES: Home—224 Cooper St., Apt. 1, Ottawa, Ontario, Canada K2P OG4. *Office*—Parliamentary Centre, 275 Slater St., Ottawa, Ontario, Canada K1P 5H9.

CAREER: Daily Gleaner, Frederiction, New Brunswick, journalist, 1958-59; *Mail-Star,* Halifax, Nova Scotia, journalist, 1959-60; *Sunday Express,* London, England, journalist, 1960; United Press International, Montreal, Quebec, journalist, 1960-61; *Marketing,* Toronto, Ontario, journalist 1961-64; *Financial Post,* Toronto, journalist in Toronto and Ottawa, Ontario, 1964-67; Association of Universities and Colleges of Canada, Ottawa, director of information and secretary of board of directors, 1967-71; Association of Atlantic Universities, Halifax, executive director, 1971-78; Statistics Canada, Ottawa, director of Education, Science, and Culture Division, 1978-82, and acting director general of marketing and communications; Canadian Conference of the Arts, Ottawa, national director, 1982-83; Social Sciences and Humanities Research Council of Canada, Ottawa, director of information, 1983-87; Parliamentary Centre, Ottawa, associate, 1987—. Member of board of directors of Social Science Federation of Canada, 1981-83; member of Canadian delegation to UNESCO, 1983; vice president of Council for the Arts in Ottawa, 1985-87. Speaker at national and international conferences; guest on radio and television programs; consultant to Organization for Economic Cooperation and Development. *Military service:* British Army, 1952-57, served in Nigeria; became lieutenant. Royal Canadian Air Force, 1957-58; pilot officer.

MEMBER: Canadian Authors Association (life member; president, 1981-82; executive director, 1991-93; president, 1993—).

WRITINGS:

Farewell to Nova Scotia (novel), Lancelot Press, 1974.
Shakespeare Was a Computer Programmer (novelette), Brunswick, 1975.
The Hijacking of the P.E.I. Ferry (novel), Brunswick, 1976.
The Symons Report, Book and Periodical Development Council (Toronto), 1976.
A Little Applebert/Le Petit Applebert, Canadian Conference of the Arts, 1983.
20/20 Planning, Society for College and University Planning, 1985.

Also editor of *Spirit of Saskatoon* (video), 1987, and researcher, writer and interviewer for *Reconciliation* (video), 1992. Contributor to journals, including *Thalia.* Editor of *University Affairs,* 1967-71, and *Planning,* 1978-80.

SIDELIGHTS: Jeffrey Holmes told *CA:* "I'm still trying to return to writing fiction—for the pleasure of it—after a decade when writing for pleasure took fifth place to the demands of my job, association activities, speeches, and family. I've failed to cut back severely on associations and speeches, since I still have to earn a living. I can't do it by writing the kinds of fantasy that I enjoy (but that major publishers do not).

"I tend to think of titles first. Then I have to write a novel to fit. I have trilogies in rough for *Shakespeare Was a Computer Programmer* and *The Hijacking of the P.E.I. Ferry,* but they've been there for years. I also have six more titles-in-waiting, some of which may prove to have withered in the womb. I've put too much energy and imagination into speeches, for instance 'One Mann's Mead Is Another Porson's Poisson,' which I gave to the 1985 meeting of the Western Humour and Irony Membership Conference in Phoenix, Arizona, and published in the University of Ottawa's journal *Thalia.*"

*　　*　　*

HOMBERGER, Eric (Ross) 1942-

PERSONAL: Born May 30, 1942, in Philadelphia, PA; son of Alexander and Marilyn (Glick) Homberger; married Judy Jones, June 2, 1967; children: Martin Joshua, Margaret Alissa, Charles Michael. *Education:* University of California, Berkeley, B.A., 1964; University of Chicago, M.A., 1965; Cambridge University, Ph.D., 1972. *Politics:* Socialist. *Religion:* None.

ADDRESSES: Home—74 Clarendon Rd., Norwich NR2 2PW, England.

CAREER: University of Exeter, Exeter, England, temporary lecturer in American literature, 1969-70; University of East Anglia, Norwich, England, lecturer, 1970-88, reader in American literature, 1988—. University of Minnesota, visiting member of faculty, 1977-78; University of New Hampshire, visiting professor of American literature, 1991-92.

MEMBER: British Association for American Studies.

AWARDS, HONORS: Leverhulme fellowship in European studies, 1978-79.

WRITINGS:

(Editor with William Janeway and Simon Schama) *The Cambridge Mind: Ninety Years of the "Cambridge Review," 1879-1969,* Little, Brown (Boston, MA), 1970.

(Editor) *Ezra Pound: The Critical Heritage,* Routledge & Kegan Paul (Boston), 1972.

The Art of the Real: Poetry in England and America since 1939, Rowman & Littlefield (Totowa, NJ), 1977.

(Editor with Holger Klein and John Flower) *The Second World War in Fiction,* Salem House (Boston), 1984.

Scenes from the Life of a City: Corruption and Conscience in Old New York, Yale University Press (New Haven, CT), 1984.

John le Carre, Methuen, 1986.

American Writers and Radical Politics, 1900-1939: Equivocal Commitments, Macmillan, 1987.

(Editor with John Charmley) *The Troubled Face of Biography,* Macmillan, 1987.

John Reed, Manchester University Press (Manchester, England), 1990, St. Martin's (New York City), 1992.

(Editor with John Biggart) *John Reed and the Russian Revolution: Uncollected Articles, Letters and Speeches in Russia, 1917-1920,* St. Martin's, 1992.

Contributor to magazines and newspapers, including *Times Literary Supplement, Nation, Economist,* and *Journal of American Studies.*

SIDELIGHTS: Eric Homberger once told *CA:* "Living in England since 1965 has enabled me to confront the historical experience of my family (as emigrants, within living memory, from Europe) and of America itself. It has been hard to wave the flag; and I haven't really tried to do so. In partial consequence, I have become interested in fugi-tive areas of experience, of alienated sensibilities, whether ethnic or political, whose experience may in some way stand for the larger tendency of a society and a way of life.

"I would like to write the kind of literary criticism which is on the brink of becoming history, with its confident and unthinking grasp of the real. Criticism now has almost wholly surrendered that ambition, to its impoverishment, I think; it has the willingness to address a nonspecialist reading public. In England fifteen years ago critics still hoped to speak to such an audience. But that has mostly gone and has been replaced by a more vigorous hunger for theorization. The end result: critics only able to speak to each other, inmates, really, in a crumbling and neglected ward, trying to persuade each other that the discipline advances. I want to write a stronger, more political sort of thing. Maybe the form ought to be different. In *Scenes from the Life of a City: Corruption and Conscience in Old New York* I have tried to combine biography, social history, and some techniques of literary criticism in studies of figures, largely forgotten, who were in their day— nineteenth century—scandalous. I can imagine writing, quite consciously, to reach a wider audience, or at least a different one; the only problem is that the audience I would like to address may no longer exist."

*   *   *

HOOPER, Meredith (Jean) 1939-

PERSONAL: Born October 21, 1939, in Adelaide, Australia; daughter of Clifford (an educationist) and Jean (Hosking) Rooney; married Richard Hooper (a consultant), March, 1964; children: Rachel, Thomas, Benjamin. *Education:* University of Adelaide, B.A. (with honors), 1960; Lady Margaret Hall and Nuffield College, Oxford, M.Phil., 1964.

ADDRESSES: Home—4 Western Rd., London N2 9HX, England.

CAREER: University of Adelaide, Adelaide, Australia, tutor in history, 1961; Voluntary Service Overseas, London, administrator, 1964-65; freelance writer, 1968—. Royal Institution, visiting research fellow in the history of science, 1988—.

MEMBER: Association of British Science Writers.

AWARDS, HONORS: Tinline Prize and Overseas Scholarship, 1960; Walter Frewin Lord Prize, 1964; Beit Prize, University of Oxford, 1966; Children's Book of the Year Award commendation, Children's Book Council of Australia, 1973, for *Everyday Inventions; A for Antarctica* was shortlisted for the Environment Prize; *The Journal of the Watkin Stench* was shortlisted for the Carnegie Medal.

WRITINGS:

JUVENILE NONFICTION

Land of the Free: The United States of America, Blond Educational, 1968.

Gold Rush in Australia, Hulton Educational Publications, 1969.

Everyday Inventions, Angus & Robertson, 1972, Taplinger (New York City), 1976.

The Story of Australia, illustrated by Elaine Haxton, Angus & Robertson, 1974, Taplinger, 1976.

More Everyday Inventions, Angus & Robertson, 1976.

Dr. Hunger and Captain Thirst: Stories of Australian Explorers, Methuen, 1982.

(With Manning Clark) *History of Australia,* illustrated by Sue Ferrier, Lutterworth, 1988.

How High Is the Sky?, Simon & Schuster (New York City), 1990.

Earth and Space, Ginn, 1990.

A for Antarctica, Pan Piccolo, 1991.

I for Invention, Pan Piccolo, 1992.

The Lost Purse, Ginn, 1994.

Monkeys, Collins, 1994.

Balls, Bangs and Flashes: Great Scientific Experiments, David Bennett Books, 1994.

Germs, Jabs and Laughing Gas: Great Medical Discoveries, David Bennett Books, 1994.

The Feast, Ginn, 1994.

Looking after the Eggs, Ginn, 1994.

JUVENILE FICTION

Seven Eggs, illustrated by Terry McKenna, Harper (New York City), 1985.

The Journal of Watkin Stench, Lutterworth (Cambridge, England), 1988.

Evie's Magic Lamp, Simon & Schuster, 1990.

The Great Stone Circle, Creative Edge, 1992.

OTHER

Kangaroo Route: The Development of Commercial Flight between England and Australia, Angus & Robertson, 1985.

God 'elp All of Us: Three Great Flights, Methuen, 1986.

Cleared for Take-Off: International Flight beyond the Passenger Cabin, Angus & Robertson, 1986.

Contributor to books, including *Story Chest: 100 Bedtime Stories,* edited by Barbara Ireson, Viking Kestrel, 1986. Contributor of stories to *Puffin Post.* Member of the editorial board of *Round Table: The Commonwealth Journal of International Affairs.*

WORK IN PROGRESS: *The Pebble in My Pocket,* for Frances Lincoln, and numerous titles for Cambridge University Press Reading Scheme and Ginn Reading Scheme.

SIDELIGHTS: Meredith Hooper told *CA:* "I have specialized in books which appeal to all ages. I bring considerable research skills to bear on each subject, believing that each audience deserves the best and the general nonspecialist audience, whether children or adult, should be given access to the latest thinking. Many of my books written for children are read by adults. I have specialized in making two areas accessible and interesting to a wide audience: science and technology, and history. I have written on aviation, including an account of passenger flying on 747s, and the development of the longest air route in the world. I have also written several general histories of Australia, including the major children's history for the bicentenary with Manning Clark."

*   *   *

HOPE, Christopher (David Tully) 1944-

PERSONAL: Born February 26, 1944, in Johannesburg, South Africa; son of Dudley Mitford (a banker) and Kathleen Margaret (a bookkeeper; maiden name, McKenna) Hope; married Eleanor Marilyn Margaret Klein (a music administrator), February 18, 1967; children: Jasper Antony, Daniel Clement. *Education:* University of Witwatersrand, B.A., 1965, M.A., 1971; University of Natal, B.A. (with honors), 1970. *Avocational interests:* Travel, walking, cross-country skiing.

ADDRESSES: *Home*—9 Southwood Hall, Wood Lane, Highgate, London N6 5UF, England. *Agent*—A. P. Watt Ltd., 20 John St., London WC1N 2DL, England.

CAREER: Author of novels, short stories, children's fiction, poetry, and nonfiction. South British Insurance, Johannesburg, underwriter, 1966; Nasionale Pers (publishers), Cape Town, editor, 1966-67; *Durban Sunday Tribune,* reviewer, 1968-69; Lintas, copywriter in Durban, 1967-69, and in Durban and Johannesburg, 1973-75; Lindsay Smithers, Durban, copywriter, 1971; Halesowen Secondary Modern School, English teacher, 1972; *Bolt,* Durban, editor, 1972-73; Gordonstoun School, Elgin, Scotland, writer in residence, 1978. *Military service:* South African Navy, 1962.

MEMBER: International PEN, Authors League of America, Society of Authors.

AWARDS, HONORS: Pringle Award from the English Academy of Southern Africa, 1972, for creative writing; Cholmondeley Award for poetry from British Society of Authors, 1977; Professor Alexander Petrie Award from Convocation of the University of Natal, 1981, for "outstanding contribution to the arts and humanities"; David Higham Prize for Fiction from National Book League of Great Britain, 1981, for *A Separate Development;* Silver

Pen Award from International PEN, 1982, for *Private Parts and Other Tales;* Mother Goose Award runner-up (with Yehudi Menuhin), 1984, for *The King, the Cat, and the Fiddle;* Whitbread Book of the Year for Fiction from the Booksellers Association of Great Britain and Ireland, 1985, for *Kruger's Alp;* CNA Award from the Booksellers Association of South Africa, 1989, for *White Boy Running.*

WRITINGS:

NOVELS, EXCEPT AS INDICATED

A Separate Development, Ravan Press, 1980, Scribner, 1981.

Private Parts and Other Tales (short stories), Bateleur Press, 1981.

Kruger's Alp, Heinemann, 1984, Viking, 1985.

Black Swan (novella), illustrated by Gillian Barlow, Hutchinson, 1987, Harper, 1988.

The Hottentot Room, Heinemann, 1986, Farrar, Straus, 1987.

My Chocolate Redeemer, Minerva, 1989.

Serenity House, Macmillan, 1992.

POETRY

(With Mike Kirkwood) *Whitewashes,* [privately printed], 1971.

Cape Drives, London Magazine Editions, 1974.

In the Country of the Black Pig, London Magazine Editions, 1981.

Englishmen: A Poem, Heinemann, 1985.

NONFICTION

(Editor) Yehudi Menuhin, *The Compleat Violinist,* Summit, 1986.

White Boy Running (memoir), Anchor Books, 1988.

Moscow! Moscow! (travelogue), General, 1990.

JUVENILE FICTION

(With Yehudi Menuhin) *The King, the Cat, and the Fiddle,* illustrated by Angela Barrett, Benn, 1983, Holt, 1984.

The Dragon Wore Pink, illustrated by Barrett, A. & C. Black, 1985, Atheneum, 1986.

PLAYS

Ducktails, South African Television, 1976.

Bye-Bye Booysens, South African Television, 1977.

An Entirely New Concept in Packaging, South African Television, 1978.

Englishmen (poem for voices), BBC Radio, 1986.

Box on the Ear, BBC Radio, 1987.

Better Halves, BBC Radio, 1988.

OTHER

Work anthologized in *On the Edge of the World,* Donker, 1974; *A World of Their Own,* Donker, 1976; *A New Book of South African Verse in English,* Oxford University Press, 1979; *Modern South African Stories,* Donker, 1980; *Theatre Two,* Donker, 1981; *Best British Short Stories,* Heinemann, 1986; and *Colour of a New Day,* Lawrence & Wishart, 1990. Contributor to periodicals, including *London Magazine, Times Literary Supplement, Poetry Review, New Yorker, Transatlantic Review, Los Angeles Times, New Republic,* and *New Statesman.*

SIDELIGHTS: Born and raised in South Africa, Christopher Hope has made the wrenching racial politics of his native land the subject of his poetry, fiction, and dramas. He has lived in England since the time when, according to George Packer in *Nation,* he "felt his existence in South Africa anchored by so little substance and buoyed by so much 'incorrigible lightness' [as he wrote in *White Boy Running*] that in 1974, at age 30, caught between the nationalisms of Afrikaners and blacks, he floated off to exile in London." From there, Hope has produced writings that have won favor with critics and the public for their searing (though often funny) portrayal of the politics of hate. Hope once told *CA,* "Most of my work, I think, has been an attempt to explore the effects of discrimination, particularly racial discrimination, as exemplified by apartheid in South Africa, the injustice of which and the misery it causes are widely known; less well understood, perhaps, is the richly bizarre existence of the various population groups who must live under enforced segregation in a society obsessed with skin color. A tiny minority operate a system of racial separation everyone knows to be crazy."

Hope first received recognition with the publication of *Cape Drives,* a book of poetry, in 1974. Of the poems on South Africa (including "At the Country Club," "African Tea Ceremony," and "In the Middle of Nowhere") in *In the Country of the Black Pig,* published in 1981, Douglas Dunn writes in the *Times Literary Supplement:* "It is heartening . . . to read a poet who can balance conscience and compassion with literary good taste, distributing powerful ironies and pictures with discretion as well as concern." Of *Englishmen: A Poem,* published in 1985, Simon Rae writes in the *Times Literary Supplement* that it "dips back into history to seek out the roots of the Afrikaner identity." Finding much to praise in its economy and its chilling characterizations, Rae asserts: "The poem marks a new and exciting departure for this extremely versatile writer." Hope designated *Englishmen* a "poem for voices"; its fourteen parts were read aloud in an English Radio 3 production in 1986. Hope is also the author of several plays and children's books, but has probably achieved his greatest measure of fame for his works of prose for adults, including the novels *A Separate Develop-*

ment, Kruger's Alp, and *The Hottentot Room,* as well as the memoir *White Boy Running.*

Hope's first novel, *A Separate Development,* was awarded the David Higham Memorial prize for its story of a dark-skinned Caucasian boy, Harry Moto, who leaves his white neighborhood to live in a black township called Koelietown. There, passing as "colored," Harry encounters the world of apartheid from the opposite side, hounded by police for 'interracial' relations (with his old girlfriend). *A Separate Development* was banned in South Africa. Darryl Pinckney of the *New York Times Book Review* calls it "a wildly funny novel," but is careful to point out its seriousness: "The jaunty manner of Harry's narration is in striking contrast to the bitter experiences he relates. *Times Literary Supplement* contributor Anthony Delius asserts that Hope "has taken to prose to give us an exuberant view of the painfully funny side of apartheid." Judith Chettle of the *Washington Post Book World* also admires the novel's humor "despite the gravity of its concerns." In her opinion, *A Separate Development,* with its realistic characters, is just as effective as books that are "relentlessly grim, . . . that appear to edit their characters' speech and thinking so that they seem to resemble candidates for canonization rather than the actual participants in a real drama." Hope once commented to *CA,* "*A Separate Development* (the official euphemism for apartheid) is a kind of joke-book, because if apartheid is cruel it is also ridiculous, and the most cheering thing about its victims is their well-nourished sense of the ridiculous. It is something the guardians of racial purity find more disconcerting than earnest moralizing."

Kruger's Alp makes a departure from the more straightforward storytelling of *A Separate Development.* Ron Loewinsohn, writing in the *New York Times Book Review,* describes *Kruger's Alp* as "a novel in the form of a dream allegory, a very literary genre that we usually associate with Chaucer, Langland and Bunyan—the exotic domain of the literary antiquarian." The Whitbread-Prize-winning novel takes its shape from John Bunyan's *Pilgrim's Progress,* following a group of men who served as altar boys to a politically rebellious priest as they each come to terms with their South African heritage. Among them is Theodore Blanchaille, who has himself become a priest and who sets out from South Africa on a quest for the fabled Swiss mountain retreat built by exiled Boer leader Paul Kruger. In the allegorical narrative, the author "is telling the story of present-day South Africa," David Guy wrote in a 1985 *Washington Post* review. "This is not a book to be taken up lightly. It is a difficult, complicated, often brilliant and sometimes hilariously funny novel." *Los Angeles Times* reviewer Richard Eder described *Kruger's Alp* as "a parable of considerable wit and uneven texture. At its best, it is a rich weave of telling ab-

surdities. Sometimes, though, and particularly toward the end, the parabolic mechanics become obtrusive as the author maneuvers each one of his allegorical chickens back to its roost." Loewinsohn, however, excuses what he sees as "minor flaws, given the importance of what [Hope] has to say to us—about South Africa in particular, but also about authoritarian power everywhere."

The tale of a London pub where ex-South Africans gather to drink and remember their homeland, *The Hottentot Room* exhibits "touches of brilliant writing here and there, and stretches of compelling madness and tragedy," but it is ultimately too heavy and predictable, according to Stephen Franklin in the Chicago *Tribune Books.* In Joel Conarroe's opinion, expressed in the *Washington Post Book World, The Hottentot Room* is many things, the "All of the above" answer to the questions "Is this short, densely written work a novel? A collection of self-contained essays? A love letter to a lost homeland? A hate letter to London? A treatise on racism?" The *New York Times Book Review*'s Edward Hoagland describes it as a "fevered, obsessive portrait of a refugee community of aging, baffled revolutionaries, defrocked academics and assorted, forlorn misfits who hang about a strange after-hours pub . . . mopping imaginary equatorial sweat off their brows and batting imaginary mosquitoes." Going on to note that "this is not a commercial book in any sense of the word," Conarroe asserts, "The pleasures of Christopher Hope's text, and they are legion, are those that come from following the unexpected twists and turns of an intelligent (and troubled) writer's mind as he confronts a number of serious subjects."

White Boy Running is Hope's memoir, the story of his return to South Africa from a self-imposed exile of thirteen years on the eve of President P. W. Botha's 1987 call for elections on reforming the apartheid system. However, Carolyn Slaughter notes in the *Los Angeles Times Book Review,* "it is clear from this memoir that Hope felt himself an exile even before he left South Africa. He was a Catholic at school in the Protestant Afrikaner fortress of Pretoria; he saw the country as a place without reality and was unable to locate himself within it. He began to write because the quality of South African life had a fictional character." In the *Village Voice,* Melvyn A. Hill sees the writing of the book as mirroring its author's emotional state: "Hope's text exposes various layers of his origins, so that you experience something like his own confusion as the narrative meanders through personal and familial anecdotes, historical episodes and political commentary." J. M. Coetzee describes *White Boy Running* in the *New Republic:* "Partly reportage and political analysis, partly autobiography, partly satire, it is in essence a diagnosis of the condition of white South Africa today." Stephen Watson, writing in the *Times Literary Supplement,* notes Hope's dilemma as "a member of the English-speaking minority within South Africa, incapable of identifying with either black or white nationalism, remaining committed to a liberalism long proven impotent in this context," one who "would inevitably end up a stranger in his own country. . . . There is no disguising his sense of loss. Quite as much as his sharp eye for the absurdities of South Africa, it is the constant pressure of this sense of bereavement that makes this book as good as any of his novels." In the opinion of *Newsweek* writer Jim Miller, *White Boy Running* "lays bare, as few books have before, the follies and fears of South Africa's ruling white minority." "At the end of a book as eloquent and wise as this," Slaughter concludes, "all one can suggest is, perhaps the time has come for the white boy to stop running."

BIOGRAPHICAL/CRITICAL SOURCES:

BOOKS

Contemporary Literary Criticism, Volume 52, Gale, 1989.

PERIODICALS

Atlantic Monthly, February, 1982, p. 86; June, 1988, p. 106.
Chicago Tribune Book World, December 29, 1985, p. 30.
English in Africa, October, 1989, p. 91.
Globe and Mail (Toronto), September 8, 1990.
Los Angeles Times, May 1, 1985; August 19, 1987.
Los Angeles Times Book Review, December 20, 1981; May 22, 1988, p. 2; August 13, 1989, p. 14.
Nation, December 26, 1988, p. 724.
New Republic, June 13, 1988, p. 37.
Newsweek, December 7, 1981; June 27, 1988, p. 61.
New Yorker, December 14, 1981.
New York Times, June 25, 1987.
New York Times Book Review, December 20, 1981, p. 10; March 20, 1983, p. 39; May 5, 1985, p. 9; July 19, 1987, p. 7; November 8, 1987, p. 26.
Spectator, October 6, 1984, p. 33; December 6, 1986, p. 36; April 7, 1990, p. 33.
South, March, 1985, p. 94.
Times (London), March 30, 1989; January 27, 1990.
Times Educational Supplement, July 2, 1982, p. 21.
Times Literary Supplement, January 8, 1982, p. 38; November 5, 1982, p. 1231; September 28, 1984, p. 1085; November 29, 1985, p. 1359; June 6, 1986, p. 616; September 19, 1986, p. 1028; June 26, 1987, p. 697; March 11, 1988, p. 270; April 7, 1989, p. 363; September 11, 1992, p. 22.
Tribune Books (Chicago), June 7, 1987, p. 7; July 10, 1988, p. 6.
Village Voice, August 30, 1988, p. 54.
Wall Street Journal, May 27/28, 1988, p. 7.
Washington Post, June 11, 1985; June 6, 1988.

Washington Post Book World, January 3, 1982, p. 7; July 29, 1986; July 26, 1987, p. 8; August 13, 1989, p. 12.

*   *   *

HUBBELL, Sue 1935-

PERSONAL: Born January 28, 1935, in Kalamazoo, MI; daughter of B. LeRoy (a landscape architect) and Marjorie (a homemaker; maiden name, Sparks) Gilbert; married Paul Hubbell (an engineer), October 31, 1955 (divorced, 1983); married Arne Sieverts (spokesperson for the U.S. Senate Foreign Relations Committee), 1988; children: (first marriage) Brian; stepchildren: (second marriage) Michael, Lisa. *Education:* Attended Swarthmore College, 1952-54, and University of Michigan, 1954-55; University of Southern California, A.B., 1956, Drexel Institute, M.S., 1963.

ADDRESSES: Home—Missouri and Washington, DC. *Agent*—Liz Darhansoff, 1220 Park Ave., New York, NY 10128.

CAREER: The Book Shelf, Moorestown, NJ, manager, 1960-63; Trenton State College, Trenton, NJ, acquisitions librarian, 1963-67; elementary school librarian in Peacedale, RI, 1967-68; Brown University, Providence, RI, serials librarian, 1968-72; commercial beekeeper in Missouri, 1973—; writer, 1985—.

AWARDS, HONORS: Nomination for Walter Sullivan prize, 1991, for "Earthquake Fever" (magazine piece).

WRITINGS:

A Country Year: Living the Questions, illustrated by Lauren Jarrett, Random House (New York City), 1986.
A Book of Bees: . . .and How to Keep Them, illustrated by Sam Potthoff, Random House, 1988.
On This Hilltop, Ballantine (New York City), 1991.
Broadsides from the Other Orders: A Book of Bugs, illustrated by Dimitry Schidlovsky, Random House, 1993.
Far Flung Hubbell (collected essays and articles), Random House, 1995.

Contributor to magazines and newspapers, including *New Yorker, Smithsonian, New York Times Magazine, Time, Harper's, Sports Illustrated,* and *Discover.* Contributor to anthologies, including *Best Essays of the Year,* 1990. Author's works have been translated into French and Japanese.

WORK IN PROGRESS: Research for a book on North Africa; magazine articles.

SIDELIGHTS: Sue Hubbell has lived alone in the Ozark Mountains in southern Missouri for more than twelve years, earning a living from her eighteen million honeybees. She now splits her time between the Ozarks, where her bees are, and Washington, DC, where her husband works.

A Country Year: Living the Questions is a collection of forty-one essays describing Hubbell's reflections on life and her experiences with nature over the course of one year. Lauded by critics for her vivid descriptions of nature, Hubbell tells about trips to her beehives in her thirty-year-old pickup truck and about making her own shingles before shingling a barn. Doris Betts, writing in the *Los Angeles Times Book Review,* called *A Country Year* "a record of mysteries questioned, then embraced."

"Wild things and wild places pull me more strongly than they did a few years ago, and domesticity, dusting and cookery interest me not at all," Hubbell writes in her book, as quoted in *New York Times Book Review.* And, according to Jeremiah Tax in *Sports Illustrated,* the essays in *A Country Year* "are filled with the wonders and surprise that the diligent, empathetic observer finds in the behavior of wild things." He added that "one's reaction when finishing many of the essays is likely to be an entrancement brought on by the softness and innocence of Hubbell's prose." Betts also praised Hubbell's writing, declaring that "like a pane of glass, her prose reveals without distortion or sentimentality."

With *A Book of Bees: . . .and How to Keep Them* and *Broadsides from the Other Orders: A Book of Bugs,* Hubbell earned a reputation as "one of the two or three best writers-about-bugs now living," in the words of Noel Perrin, writing in the *Washington Post Book World. A Book of Bees* can be read as a primer in beekeeping: Hubbell tells the reader how hive frames are built to let the beekeeper get at the honey, how to calm angry bees, and how to peacefully integrate two warring colonies with just a piece of newspaper. But as David Quammen notes in *New York Times Book Review,* even readers who have no interest in taking up beekeeping can appreciate her fascinating account of her mutually dependent relationship with the bees. He quotes Hubbell: "Strictly speaking, one never 'keeps' bees—one comes to terms with their wild nature."

The appeal of *Broadsides from the Other Orders,* according to Christopher Lehmann-Haupt in his *New York Times* review, is that while many writers would not be able to describe thirteen insect orders without falling into numbing repetition, Hubbell takes a refreshingly wide variety of approaches in her thirteen chapters. She goes to California to learn about the multi-million-dollar ladybug business; she recounts the mating activities of camel crickets observed in her home terrarium; she explains the hundred-year history of humankind's attempts to eradicate the destructive gypsy moth. Hubbell is at times an amateur naturalist, and at times a wry observer of our efforts to benefit from or control the insect world. Lehmann-Haupt concludes that "given Ms. Hubbell's graceful prose and observant eye, she makes an excellent ambassador from [the insect] world to us."

BIOGRAPHICAL/CRITICAL SOURCES:

PERIODICALS

Los Angeles Times Book Review, April 13, 1986.
New York Review of Books, February 16, 1989.
New York Times, June 24, 1993.
New York Times Book Review, April 13, 1986; October 30, 1988; July 11, 1993.
Sports Illustrated, April 21, 1986.
Washington Post Book World, April 27, 1986; August 8, 1993.

*   *   *

HUBENKA, Lloyd J(ohn) 1931-1982

PERSONAL: Born January 1, 1931, in Omaha, NE; died August 18, 1982; son of Lloyd John (a dentist) and Emma (Dobrovolny) Hubenka; married Beverly Ann Conkling, February 14, 1953; children: Jayne, Evan, Naomi, Sara. *Education:* Creighton University, B.A., 1952, M.A., 1959; University of Nebraska, Ph.D., 1966; United States Army Command and General Staff College, graduate; attended United States Army War College. *Religion:* Roman Catholic.

CAREER: Creighton University, Omaha, NE, instructor, 1958-61, assistant professor, 1961-66, associate professor, 1966-68, professor of English, beginning 1968, chairperson of department, beginning 1966. Past president, Harcum Junior College. Director of Nebraska U.S. Office of Education Conference on Improving Higher Education, 1967; codirector of Nebraska U.S. Office of Education Conference on Modern Writers, 1970; curriculum consultant and member of secondary level inspection team for Omaha Public School System, both 1970; director of Nebraska Program for the Development of Secondary Teachers, 1971. Conference director, codirector, and participant, beginning 1967. *Military service:* U.S. Army, 1952-54; served in Korea; received Commendation Medal and Bronze Star. U.S. Army Reserve, beginning 1954; served to lieutenant colonel.

MEMBER: Modern Language Association of America, American Association of University Professors (president of Nebraska State Conference, 1969-70), National Council of Teachers of English, Association of Departments of English, Victorian Periodical Society, Reserve Officers Association of the United States, Association of the United States Army.

AWARDS, HONORS: Nebraska U.S. Office of Education Council grant, 1967, 1968; National Endowment for the Humanities fellow, 1968; research council grants, Creighton University, 1968, 1970.

WRITINGS:

(Editor) John Ruskin, *Unto This Last: Four Essays on the First Principles of Political Economy,* University of Nebraska Press (Lincoln), 1967.
(Editor with Reloy Garcia) *The Design of Drama: An Introduction,* McKay (New York City), 1973.
(Editor with Garcia) *The Narrative Sensibility: An Introduction to Fiction,* McKay, 1976.
(Editor) George Bernard Shaw, *Practical Politics: Twentieth-Century Views on Politics and Economics,* University of Nebraska Press, 1976.

Served as a reader for Ohio University Press and *Victorian Studies,* both 1970; consultant, University of Nebraska Press, 1969-71.*

*   *   *

HUEY, F. B., Jr. 1925-

PERSONAL: Born January 12, 1925, in Denton, TX; son of F. B. (in insurance) and Gwendolyn (Chambers) Huey; married Nonna Turner, December 22, 1950; children: Mary Anne, Linda Kaye, William David. *Education:* University of Texas, B.B.A., 1945; Southwestern Baptist Theological Seminary, M.Div., 1958, Th.D., 1961, Ph.D., 1979.

ADDRESSES: Home—6128 Whitman, Fort Worth, TX 76133. *Office*—Department of Old Testament, Southwestern Baptist Theological Seminary, 2001 West Seminary, Fort Worth, TX 76122.

CAREER: Security National Life Insurance Co., Bolivar and Denton, TX, accountant, 1947-55; ordained Baptist minister, 1956; pastor of Baptist churches in Bolivar, TX, 1956-61; Southern Baptist Convention, Foreign Mission Board, Richmond, VA, missionary in Rio de Janeiro, Brazil, 1962-65; South Brazil Baptist Theological Seminary, professor of Old Testament, 1962-65; Southwestern Baptist Theological Seminary, Fort Worth, TX, professor of Old Testament, 1965-90, adjunct professor, 1990—, associate dean for Ph.D. degree, 1983-90.

MEMBER: National Association of Baptist Professors of Religion, Society of Biblical Studies, Theta Xi, Delta Sigma Pi, Beta Gamma Sigma.

WRITINGS:

Exodus: A Study Guide Commentary, Zondervan (Grand Rapids, MI), 1977.
Yesterday's Prophets for Today's World, Broadman (Nashville, TN), 1980.
Jeremiah: Bible Study Commentary, Zondervan, 1981.
Numbers: Bible Study Commentary, Zondervan, 1981.
Ezekiel-Daniel, Broadman, 1983.
(Coauthor) *A Student's Dictionary for Biblical and Theological Studies,* Zondervan, 1983.
Helps for Beginning Hebrew Students, Scripta, 1990.
Obedience: The Biblical Key to Happiness, Broadman, 1990.
Jeremiah-Lamentations, Broadman, 1993.

Contributor to books, including *Crises in Morality,* edited by C. W. Scudder, Broadman, 1964; *The Genesis Debate,* edited by Ron Youngblood, Nelson, 1986; *Mercer Dictionary of the Bible,* Mercer, 1990; *Holman Bible Dictionary,* Holman, 1991; *Holman Bible Handbook,* Holman, 1992; *Zondervan Pictorial Encyclopedia of the Bible; Mighty Works of Grace.* Contributor to theology journals. Cotranslator of *New American Standard Bible, New International Version,* and *International Children's Bible.*

*   *   *

HUFSCHMIDT, Maynard Michael 1912-

PERSONAL: Original surname, Hufschmid; name legally changed in 1939; born September 28, 1912, in Catawba, WI; son of John Jacob (a lumber worker) and Emma Lena (Von Arx) Hufschmid; married Elizabeth Louise Leake (a librarian), July 5, 1941; children: Emily Ann, Mark Andrew. *Education:* University of Illinois, B.S., 1939; Harvard University, M.P.A., 1955, D.P.A., 1964.

ADDRESSES: Home—19191 Harvard Ave., Apt. 107-E, Irvine, CA 92715.

CAREER: Illinois State Planning Commission, Chicago, planning technician, 1939-41; U.S. National Resources Planning Board, Washington, DC, engineer in public works programs, 1941-43; U.S. Bureau of the Budget, Washington, DC, budget examiner in public investment program, 1943-49; U.S. Department of the Interior, Office of the Secretary, Washington, DC, member of program and technical review staffs in natural resource program, 1949-55; Harvard University, Cambridge, MA, research associate and director of research for Harvard water program, 1955-65; University of North Carolina at Chapel Hill, professor of planning and environmental sciences and engineering, and research professor of Institute for Research in Social Science, 1965-79.

Environment and Policy Institute, East-West Center, Honolulu, research fellow, 1979-85, acting director, 1985-86, senior consultant, 1986-89, senior fellow, 1990-93, senior consultant to Program on Environment, 1993-94. Consultant to Resources for Future, 1955, 1956, 1972-74, U.S. Bureau of Budget, 1961, Council of Economic Advisors, 1965-67, National Academy of Sciences, 1967, 1969-70, Pan-American Health Organization, 1967, 1970, and World Health Organization 1970, 1971, 1976, 1977. Member of board of directors and technical committee of North Carolina Water Resources Research Institute;

MEMBER: American Society for Public Administration, Regional Science Association (vice president), Elisha Mitchell Scientific Society, Cosmos Club, Sigma Xi, Tau Beta Pi.

AWARDS, HONORS: Clemens Herschel Award from Boston Society of Civil Engineers, 1959; National Science Foundation senior postdoctoral research fellowship, 1970-71; Kenan Research Professor, 1970-71; *Environment, Natural Systems, and Development: An Economic Valuation Guide* was named one of the outstanding academic books and nonprint materials by *Choice,* 1983; Friend of the Universities Council on Water resources, 1990; public service award, U.S. Department of the Interior, 1994.

WRITINGS:

(With Robert W. Hartley, Eleanor Wolkind, and Sidney Jaffe) *America's Capital Requirements,* Twentieth Century Fund (New York City), 1950.

(With Arthur Maass, Robert Dorfman, Harold A. Thomas, Jr., Stephen A. Marglin, and Gordon M. Fair) *Design of Water-Resource Systems,* Harvard University Press (Cambridge, MA), 1962.

(With Myron B. Fiering) *Simulation Techniques for Design of Water-Resource Systems,* Harvard University Press, 1966.

(With David E. James, Anton D. Meister, Blair T. Bower, and John A. Dixon) *Environment, Natural Systems, and Development: An Economic Valuation Guide,* Johns Hopkins University Press (Baltimore, MD), 1983.

EDITOR

Regional Planning: Challenge and Prospects, Praeger (New York City), 1969.

(With Eric J. Hyman) *Economic Approaches to Natural Resource and Environmental Quality Analysis,* Tycooly (Riverton, NJ), 1982.

(With Dixon) *Economic Valuation Techniques for the Environment: A Case Study Workbook,* Johns Hopkins University Press, 1986.

(With K. William Easter and Dixon) *Watershed Resources Management: An Integrated Framework with Studies from Asia and the Pacific,* Westview Press (Boulder, CO), 1986, revised edition, ASEAN Economic Research Unit, Institute of Southeast Asian Studies (Singapore), 1991.

(With Michael Bonnell and John S. Gladwell) *Hydrology and Water Management in the Humid Tropics: Hydrological Research Issues and Strategies for Water Management,* Cambridge University Press, 1993.

OTHER

Contributor to various publications, including *America's Needs and Resources,* Twentieth Century Fund, 1947; *Resources Development: Frontiers for Research,* edited by Franklin L. Pollack, University of Colorado Press (Boulder, CO), 1960; *Symposium on Simulation Models: Methodology and Applications to the Behavioral Sciences,* edited by Austin C. Hoggatt and Frederick E. Balderston, Southwestern Publishing, 1963; *Readings in Resource Management and Conservation,* edited by Robert Kates and Ian Burton, University of Chicago Press, 1965; *Water Resources and Economic Development in the South,* Agricultural Policy Institute, North Carolina State University (Raleigh), 1965; *The Analysis of Public Output,* edited by Julius Margolis, Columbia University Press (New York City), 1970; *Economic Analysis of Environmental Problems,* edited by Edwin S. Mills, Columbia University Press, 1975; and *Water for Sustainable Development in the Twenty-first Century,* edited by Asit K. Biswas, Mohammed Jellali, and Glen Stout, Oxford University Press (Delhi), 1993. Also contributor to numerous professional journals.

*   *   *

HUGHES, Elizabeth
See ZACHARY, Hugh

*   *   *

HUGHES, Shirley   1927-

PERSONAL: Born July 16, 1927 (some sources say 1929), in Hoylake, near Liverpool, England; daughter of Thomas James and Kathleen (Dowling) Hughes; married John Sebastian Papendiek Vulliamy, 1952; children: two sons, one daughter. *Education:* Attended Liverpool Art School and Ruskin School of Drawing and Fine Arts, Oxford. *Avocational interests:* Looking at paintings, dressmaking.

ADDRESSES: c/o Random House, 20 Vauxhale Bridge Road, London, England, SW1V 2SA.

CAREER: Author and illustrator of books for children. Visiting tutor in illustration, Ruskin School of Drawing and Fine Arts, Oxford University. Member of Registrar's Advisory Committee of Public Lending Right, 1984-88, and Library and Information Services Council, 1989-92. Lecturer to colleges, universities, libraries, and conferences on children's literature.

MEMBER: Society of Authors (member of management committee, 1983-86; chairperson of Childrens Writers and Illustrators Group, 1994—).

AWARDS, HONORS: Esther Glen Award, 1973, for *The First Margaret Mahy Story Book;* Children's Rights Workshop, 1976, for *Helpers;* Kate Greenaway Medal, British Librarians Association, 1978, for *Dogger;* Eleanor Farjeon Award, Children's Book Circle, 1984, for distinguished service to children's literature; *Horn Book* honor list citation, 1986, for *Bathwater's Hot.*

WRITINGS:

JUVENILES; SELF-ILLUSTRATED

The Trouble with Jack, Bodley Head (London), 1970.
Sally's Secret, Bodley Head, 1973, Merrimack Book Service, 1980.
Helpers, Bodley Head, 1975, published as *George the Babysitter,* Prentice-Hall (Englewood Cliffs, NJ), 1977.
Dogger, Bodley Head, 1977, published as *David and Dog,* Prentice-Hall, 1978.
It's Too Frightening for Me!, Hodder & Stoughton (London, England), 1977, published as *Haunted House,* Prentice-Hall, 1978.
Moving Molly, Bodley Head, 1978, Prentice-Hall, 1979.
Clothes, Merrimack Book Service (Topsfield, MA), 1979.
Up and Up, Prentice-Hall, 1979.
(Editor) *Over the Moon: A Book of Sayings,* Merrimack Book Service, 1980.
Here Comes Charlie Moon, Bodley Head, 1980, Lothrop, 1986.
Charlie Moon and the Big Bonanza Bust Up, Bodley Head, 1982, Merrimack Book Service, 1984.
Chips and Jessie, Lothrop (New York City), 1983.
When We Went to the Park, Lothrop, 1985.
Noisy, Lothrop, 1985.
Bathwater's Hot, Lothrop, 1985.
All Shapes and Sizes (nursery collection), Lothrop, 1986.
Colors (nursery collection), Lothrop, 1986.
Two Shoes, New Shoes (nursery collection), Lothrop, 1986.
Another Helping of Chips, Bodley Head, 1986, Lothrop, 1987.
Out and About, Walker Books, 1988, Lothrop, 1988.
Angel Mae, Walker Books, 1989, Lothrop, 1989.
The Big Concrete Lorry, Walker Books, 1989, Lothrop, 1989.
The Snow Lady, Walker Books, 1990, Lothrop, 1990.
Wheels, Walker Books, 1991, Lothrop, 1991.

Stories by Firelight, Bodley Head, 1993, Lothrop, 1993.
Bouncing, Walker Books, 1993.
Giving, Walker Books, 1993.
Hiding, Walker Books, 1994.
Chatting, Walker Books, 1994.

"LUCY AND TOM" SERIES; SELF-ILLUSTRATED

Lucy and Tom's Day, David & Charles (North Pomfret, VT), 1960.
Lucy and Tom Go to School, Gollancz (London), 1973.
Lucy and Tom at the Seaside, Gollancz, 1976.
Lucy and Tom's Christmas, Gollancz, 1981.
Lucy and Tom's A.B.C., Gollancz, 1984.
Lucy and Tom's 1-2-3, Gollancz, 1987.

"ALFIE" SERIES; SELF-ILLUSTRATED

Alfie Gets in First (also see below), Bodley Head, 1981, Lothrop, 1982.
Alfie's Feet (also see below), Bodley Head, 1982, Lothrop, 1984.
Alfie Gives a Hand (also see below), Bodley Head, 1983, Lothrop, 1984.
An Evening at Alfie's (also see below), Lothrop, 1984.
The Big Alfie and Annie Rose Storybook, Bodley Head, 1988.
The Big Alfie Out-of-Doors Storybook, Bodley Head, 1992.
The Alfie Collection (contains *Alfie Gets in First, Alfie's Feet, Alfie Gives a Hand,* and *An Evening at Alfie's*), Morrow (New York City), 1993.

"A TALE OF TROTTER STREET" SERIES; SELF-ILLUSTRATED

Angel Mae, Lothrop, 1989.
The Snow Lady, Lothrop, 1990.
The Big Concrete Lorry, Lothrop, 1990.
Wheels, Lothrop, 1991.

OTHER

Illustrator of books in series, Dorothy Edwards, "Naughty Little Sister" series, Methuen, 1962-91, and Martha Ester Allan, "Wood Street" series, Methuen, 1970-75. Also illustrator of over 110 books, including Louisa May Alcott, *Little Women,* Puffin Books, 1953; Dorothy Rust, *All Sorts of Days,* Faber, 1955; Dorothy Clewes, *The Singing Strings,* Collins, 1961; Helen Morgan, *A Dream of Dragons, and Other Tales,* Faber, 1965; Ruth Ainsworth, *The Ruth Ainsworth Book,* Heinemann, 1970; Margaret Mahy, *The First Margaret Mahy Story Book,* Dent, 1972; Marjorie Lloyd, *Fell Farm Campers,* Puffin Books, 1975; Mary Welfare, *Witchdust,* John Murray, 1980; Frances Hodgson Burnett, *The Secret Garden,* Viking, 1988; and Mahy, *The Girl with the Green Ear: Stories about Magic in Nature,* Knopf, 1992.

WORK IN PROGRESS: Rhymes for Annie Rose, for Bodley Head and Lothrop, 1995.

SIDELIGHTS: Shirley Hughes is one of England's most respected and popular authors of picture books for young children. Although she started her career as an illustrator of other authors' works in 1953, Hughes wrote and illustrated her first book, *Lucy and Tom's Day,* in 1960. "I drew the pictures for other people's stories for a long time before trying to write my own," explains Hughes in the *Fifth Book of Junior Authors and Illustrators.* "Like most illustrators, I started by learning to draw in an art school. But I think [I] differ from other artists by having a narrative turn of mind, with strong theatrical overtones. Designing a picture-book, after all, is like being a whole company of actors, producer, stage designer, and lighting manager, all in one. That's why it's so enjoyable."

As author and illustrator of over 150 books, Hughes has received numerous awards and honors, including the Eleanor Farjeon Award for distinguished service to children's literature. Aidan Chambers describes Hughes in *Horn Book* as "an illustrator who inspires affection as well as admiration." Chambers observes further: "Essentially a dramatist—she has said that she thinks of the words in her picture books as being the captions for silent films—Hughes does the kind of illustrations that make you smile because the artist so clearly loves people and possesses that best of all gifts, the ability to show what is extraordinary and absorbing about everyday life."

In her works for preschool-age youngsters, such as the "Lucy and Tom" and "A Tale of Trotter" series, Hughes is known and admired for creating books which vividly capture the universal fears and joys of childhood. Hughes accomplishes this task by realistically and humorously depicting average preschool children and their families going about their everyday routines. Reviewers have praised Hughes for accurately presenting such real-life situations as the first day of school, adjusting to a new babysitter, suffering through a disastrous birthday party, the loss of a favorite toy, and many other situations that can cause anxiety and confusion for young children. "No one explores the comedy of ordinary life more accurately and more hilariously than Shirley Hughes," stresses Marcus Crouch in *Junior Bookshelf,* "and the fun and the truth spring from the same source. She is a great observer, and also one of those rare artists who write as well as they draw."

Critics credit Hughes's understanding and sensitive manner with its ability to reassure young readers as they see other children dealing with problems similar to their own. Edward Hudson reports in his review of *Lucy and Tom Go to School* for *Children's Book Review* that "there are many anxieties and fears which all children share and which once overcome, remain so for always. . . . One hurdle which all children have to overcome is their first day at school and in writing about Lucy and Tom's experiences at this critical time, Shirley Hughes has produced a book which should render every mother with this approaching problem, eternally grateful to her. It is not just the subject, but the way she handles it that makes this sequel to *Lucy and Tom's Day,* an attractive, immensely practical aid for mothers and teachers at playgroup and infant school level. Shirley Hughes's healthy, cherubic children with their mussy hair, rolled down socks and untidy clothes are drawn straight from life, with an authenticity which instantly communicates with the reader."

Hughes has also written and illustrated many story books for primary-grade readers that combine delightful and cheerful text with endearing illustrations. In such Hughes books as *Helpers* (published in the United States as *George the Babysitter*), *Dogger* (published in the United States as *David and Dog*), *Out and About,* and *Here Comes Charlie Moon,* Hughes exhibits the same loving, honest, sensitive, and humorous approach to the concerns and feelings of juvenile readers as in her writings for younger children. "Shirley Hughes has the enviable gift of capturing childhood in her text and illustrations," proclaims E. Colwell in a review of *An Evening at Alfie's* published in the *Junior Bookshelf.* "She does not indulge in sentimentality for her boys and girls are down-to-earth, sometimes naughty, always full of life. . . . The background of the story is one most children know, the home. It is a home where there is affection and neighbours are kind. The adventures are those which a child reader understands and can share in imagination. . . . Needless to say the illustrations are delightful, a celebration of childhood."

Barbara Ann Kyle further discusses Hughes's ability to touch her young readers with her delightful prose and enchanting illustrations. In a *Babbling Bookworm* review of *Dogger,* Kyle suggests that "with a great deal of care and concern, Shirley Hughes has written and illustrated a story about a lost toy. . . . With simple prose and detailed pictures that every child will wish to explore, Ms. Hughes has skillfully dealt with a real family situation that evokes sympathy from the reader. She is as good a storyteller as she is an artist. . . . It's a touching book and well worth keeping a special place in one's library. One of the best of 1978."

Kicki Moxon Browne observes in the *Times Literary Supplement* that "Hughes's books [are] totally irresistible, with her crumpled, lived-in people and relaxed prose," while Julia Eccleshare, also in the *Times Literary Supplement,* adds that "underneath the pleasant appearance of her illustrations she has always shown a remarkable ability to see things from a child's perspective."

Hughes once shared some of her feelings about her work in children's literature: "I think that I was lucky to have the experience of illustrating a lot of other people's stories before somebody suggested that I should do a book of my own. This was when my own children were very young, at an age of being read to, so I knew how important the text in a picture book is however sparse the words. But, of course, the pictures aren't just the icing on the cake, they are crucial to the way the reader perceives the story, a first introduction to fiction. The characterization, the setting of the scene and a lot of the humor goes into the pictures. It is a shared entertainment, with two people pointing things out to one another and enhancing their responses; a particularly rewarding audience to work for.

"I draw all my characters out of my head (I rarely use models) although for story ideas I do rely on real experiences. Whenever possible I lurk about in children's playgrounds with a sketchbook, to get the right feeling of movement. Now my own family is grown-up, but fortunately I'm invited to meet lots of children in schools and libraries up and down the country, and find their reactions endlessly refreshing and a great spur to invention."

BIOGRAPHICAL/CRITICAL SOURCES:

BOOKS

Children's Literature Review, Volume 15, Gale, 1988, pp. 118-134.

Holtze, Sally Holmes, *Fifth Book of Junior Authors and Illustrators,* H. W. Wilson, 1983.

MacCann, Donnarae, and Olga Richard, *The Child's First Books: A Critical Study of Pictures and Texts,* H. W. Wilson, 1973, pp. 109-110.

PERIODICALS

Babbling Bookworm, March, 1979, p. 1.

Books for Your Children, spring, 1979, p. 3.

Bookshelf, December, 1984, p. 247; December, 1985, pp. 258-259.

Children's Book Review, December, 1973, p. 107.

Growing Point, January, 1978, p. 3250; January, 1979, p. 3449.

Horn Book, April, 1980, pp. 211-214; June, 1984, p. 320.

Junior Bookshelf, February, 1976, p. 16; February, 1978, p. 16; February, 1980, pp. 15-16.

New York Times Book Review, June 24, 1984, p. 33; July 17, 1988, p. 30.

Punch, December 2, 1981, pp. 1023-24.

School Librarian, June, 1974, p. 204; December, 1984, pp. 308-309; March, 1986, p. 46; May, 1987, pp. 135-136.

Times Literary Supplement, September 28, 1973, p. 1120; November 20, 1981, p. 1359; September 17, 1982, p. 1002; June 15, 1984, p. 677; September 27, 1985, p. 1079.

HUGHES, Thomas Parke 1923-

PERSONAL: Born September 13, 1923, in Richmond, VA; son of Hunter Russell (a lumber merchant) and Mary (Quisenberry) Hughes; married Agatha Chipley, August 7, 1948; children: Thomas P. (deceased), Agatha H., Lucian P. *Education:* University of Virginia, B.M.E., 1947, M.A., 1950, Ph.D., 1953.

ADDRESSES: Home—8330 Millman St., Philadelphia, PA 19118. *Office*—Department of History and Sociology of Science, University of Pennsylvania, 3440 Market Street, Suite 500, Philadelphia, PA 19104-3325.

CAREER: University of Virginia, Charlottesville, instructor in engineering, 1951-54; Sweet Briar College, Sweet Briar, VA, assistant professor of modern European history, 1954-56; Washington and Lee University, Lexington, VA, assistant professor, 1956-59, associate professor of history, 1959-63; Massachusetts Institute of Technology (MIT), Cambridge, associate professor of history, 1963-66; Johns Hopkins University, Baltimore, MD, visiting associate professor of history, 1966-69; Southern Methodist University, Institute of Technology, Dallas, TX, professor of history of technology, 1969-73; University of Pennsylvania, Department of History and Sociology of Science, Philadelphia, professor, 1973—.

University of Wisconsin, visiting professor, 1963; University Center of Virginia, visiting scholar, 1966; Johns Hopkins University, fellow of Center for Recent American History, 1966-69; Smithsonian Institution, research associate, 1968-69; Torsten Althin professor, Royal Institute of Technology, Stockholm, Sweden; Wissenschaftszentrum, founding research professor, Berlin, Germany, 1988; MIT, visiting professor, 1991 and 1993. Smithsonian Institution, member of advisory council, 1984-90. *Military service:* U.S. Navy, 1943-46; became lieutenant junior grade. U.S. Naval Reserves; became lieutenant commander.

MEMBER: Society for the History of Technology (vice-president, 1977-79), American Historical Association, History of Science Society (member of council), Johns Hopkins Society of Scholars, Swedish Royal Academy of Engineering Sciences, Phi Beta Kappa.

AWARDS, HONORS: Fulbright post-doctoral fellow in Germany, 1958-59; Social Science Research Council grant, 1971; Rockefeller Humanities Grant, 1976; Institute of Advances Studies fellow, Berlin, 1983; Leonardo da Vinci Medal, 1984; Guggenheim fellow, 1986; Bernal Prize, Society of Social Studies Science, 1990; Dexter Prize, for *Elmer Sperry: Inventor and Engineer* and for *Networks of Power: Electrification in Western Society, 1880-1930;* Pulitzer Prize nomination, Columbia University, for *American Genesis: A Century of Invention and Technological Enthusiasm.*

WRITINGS:

Medicine in Virginia, 1607-1699, Virginia 350th Anniversary Celebration Corp., 1957.
(Editor), *Development of Western Technology since 1500,* Macmillan (New York City), 1964.
(Editor and author of introduction), *Lives of Engineers: Selections from Samuel Smiles,* MIT Press (Cambridge, MA), 1966.
Elmer Sperry: Inventor and Engineer, Johns Hopkins Press (Baltimore, MD), 1971.
Edison: Professional Inventor, Science Museum (London, England), 1976.
Networks of Power: Electrification in Western Society, 1880-1930, Johns Hopkins University Press, 1983.
(Editor with Wiebe E. Bijker and Trevor J. Pinch), *The Social Construction of Technological Systems: New Directions in the Sociology and History of Technology,* MIT Press, 1987.
(With Renate Mayntz), *The Development of Large Technical Systems,* Max-Planck Institute (Frankfurt, Germany), 1988.
American Genesis: A Century of Invention and Technological Enthusiasm, Viking, 1989, Penguin (New York City), 1989.
(With wife, Agatha Hughes), *Lewis Mumford: Public Intellectual,* Oxford University Press (New York City), 1990.

Contributor to *Dictionary of American Biography, Dictionary of Scientific Biography,* and to various history, business, and technology journals.*

*   *   *

HUGHES, Zach
  See ZACHARY, Hugh

*   *   *

HUGHES, Zachary
  See ZACHARY, Hugh

*   *   *

HUNT, E(verette) Howard (Jr.)   1918-
  (Howard Hunt; John Baxter, Gordon Davis, Robert Dietrich, P. S. Donoghue, David St. John, pseudonyms)

PERSONAL: Born October 9, 1918, in Hamburg, NY; son of Everette Howard and Ethel Jean (Totterdale) Hunt;

married Dorothy L. Wetzel, September 7, 1949 (died, 1972); married Laura E. Martin, 1977; children: (first marriage) Lisa Tiffany, Kevan Totterdale (daughter), Howard, David; (second marriage) Austin, Hollis. *Education:* Brown University, A.B., 1940.

ADDRESSES: Home—10115 Biscayne Blvd., Miami Shores, FL 33138. *Agent*—Scott Meredith Literary Agency, 845 Third Ave., New York, NY 10022.

CAREER: Movie screenwriter and editor of *March of Time,* 1942-43; war correspondent for *Life* magazine, 1943; screenwriter, 1947-48; worked in various capacities for the Central Intelligence Agency (CIA) of the United States Government in Paris, France, Tokyo, Japan, Montevideo, Uruguay, Vienna, Austria, Madrid, Spain, and Mexico City, Mexico, 1949-70; vice president and director of Robert R. Mullen & Co. (public relations firm), 1970-71; consultant to U.S. President Richard Nixon, 1971-72; writer and lecturer on national security. *Military service* U.S. Naval Reserve, 1940-42. U. S. Army Air Forces, 1943-46; became first lieutenant.

MEMBER: Army and Navy Club, Miami Shores Country Club.

AWARDS, HONORS: Guggenheim fellowship in creative writing, 1946-47.

WRITINGS:

NOVELS

Undercover: Memoirs of an American Secret Agent, Berkley (New York City), 1974.
The Hargrave Deception, Stein & Day (Briarcliff Manor, NY), 1980.
The Gaza Intercept, Stein & Day, 1981.
Cozumel, Stein & Day, 1985.
The Kremlin Conspiracy, Stein & Day, 1985.
Guadalajara, Stein & Day, 1987.
Murder in State, St. Martin's Press (New York City), 1990.
Chinese Red, St. Martin's Press, 1992.
Body Count, St. Martin's Press, 1992.
Mazatlan: A Jack Novak Thriller, Donald I. Fine, 1993.
Ixtapa, Donald I. Fine, 1994.

NOVELS; UNDER NAME HOWARD HUNT

East of Farewell, Knopf (New York City), 1942.
Limit of Darkness, Random House (New York City), 1944.
Stranger in Town, Random House, 1947.
Maelstrom, Farrar, Straus (New York City), 1948.
Bimini Run, Farrar, Straus, 1949.
The Violent Ones, Fawcett (New York City), 1950.
Give Us This Day, Arlington House (New Rochelle, NY), 1973.

The Berlin Ending: A Novel of Discovery, Putnam (New York City), 1973.

NOVELS; UNDER PSEUDONYM JOHN BAXTER

A Foreign Affair, Avon (New York City), 1954.
Unfaithful, Avon, 1955.
A Gift for Gomala, Lippincott (Philadelphia), 1962.

NOVELS; UNDER PSEUDONYM GORDON DAVIS

I Came to Kill, Fawcett, 1953.
House Dick, Fawcett, 1961, published under real name as *Washington Payoff,* Pinnacle Books (New York City), 1975.
Counterfeit Kill, Fawcett, 1963, published under real name, Pinnacle Books, 1975.
Where Murder Waits, Fawcett, 1965.

NOVELS; UNDER PSEUDONYM ROBERT DIETRICH

The Cheat, Pyramid Books (New York City), 1954.
Be My Victim, Dell (New York City), 1956.
Murder on the Rocks, Dell, 1957.
The House on Q Street, Dell, 1958.
End of a Stripper, Dell, 1959.
Mistress to Murder, Dell, 1960.
Murder on Her Mind, Dell, 1960.
Angel Eyes, Dell, 1961.
Calypso Caper, Dell, 1961.
Curtains for a Lover, Lancer, 1962.
My Body, Lancer, 1963.
Ring around Rosy, Fawcett, 1964.

NOVELS; UNDER PSEUDONYM P. S. DONOGHUE

The Dublin Affair, Donald I. Fine, 1988.
The Sankov Confession, Donald I. Fine, 1992.
Evil Time, Donald I. Fine, 1992.

NOVELS; UNDER PSEUDONYM DAVID St. JOHN

Hazardous Duty, Signet (New York City), 1965.
Return from Vorkuta, Signet, 1965.
The Towers of Silence, Signet, 1966.
Festival for Spies, Signet, 1966.
The Venus Probe, Signet, 1966.
The Mongol Mask, Weybright & Talley (New York City), 1968.
The Sorcerers, Weybright & Talley, 1969.
Diabolus, Weybright & Talley, 1971.
One of Our Agents Is Missing, Signet, 1972.
The Coven, Weybright & Talley, 1972.

OTHER

(Under Baxter pseudonym) *Hollywood in the Thirties,* A. S. Barnes (New York City), 1968.
The Gangster Film, A. S. Barnes, 1970.

Also author of play *The Calculated Risk,* c. 1948. Contributor to political and foreign affairs journals.

SIDELIGHTS: The author of several dozen spy/adventure novels published throughout the 1940s, 1950s, and 1960s, E. Howard Hunt achieved widespread notoriety during the early 1970s—for his role in the Watergate scandal rather than for his literary accomplishments. A former CIA officer with some twenty years' experience in conducting undercover work, Hunt was hired by the administration of President Richard Nixon in 1971 as a part-time "consultant." Working for G. Gordon Liddy, Hunt helped organize the break-in at the offices of Daniel Ellsberg's psychiatrist (Ellsberg was suspected of leaking to the *New York Times* the classified information that was eventually published as *The Pentagon Papers*) and, somewhat later, the infamous bugging and burglary operation at Democratic National Headquarters in the Watergate office complex. For his part in the conspiracy, Hunt pleaded guilty and served three years in federal prison.

Drawing on his own experience as a CIA officer, as well as on his general knowledge of government operations, Hunt managed to write at least one novel a year while working for that agency during the 1950s and 1960s. Each manuscript had to be submitted to his superiors for approval before being sent to the publisher—and in many cases his works were published under one of several pseudonyms. Hunt received a certain amount of literary recognition as a result of Watergate; the regular appearance of his name in the news prompted a publisher to reprint several of his novels, leading to a reassessment of Hunt's work.

Gore Vidal offers his evaluation of Hunt's novels in the *New York Review of Books:* "[Hunt] demonstrates the way a whole generation of writers ordered words upon the page in imitation of what they took to be [Ernest] Hemingway's technique. . . . Yet unwary imitators are apt to find themselves (as in [Hunt's] *Limit of Darkness*) slipping into aimless redundancies. . . . Had [Hunt] not chosen a life of adventure I think he might have made a good second string to O'Hara's second string to Hemingway. . . . Throughout his life's work there is a constant wistful and, finally, rather touching identification with the old American patriciate."

Leaving memories of the Watergate era behind him, Hunt has continued to add to his long list of published spy novels. His 1981 novel, *The Gaza Intercept,* is the story of a radical Arab splinter group that plans to risk World War III by acquiring neutron bombs made by the United States, annihilating Tel Aviv, Israel, and placing its own leader at the center of all Arab/Israeli negotiations. Described as a "macho thriller" by Robert Lekachman in the *New York Times Book Review, The Gaza Intercept* boasts a team of Mossad heroes who eventually save Tel Aviv from destruction. Writes Lekachman: "To give Mr. Hunt his due, the caper has its moments. The action is swift if not always believable." Maude McDaniel, reviewing *The Gaza Intercept* for the *Washington Post Book World,* notes that "faithful readers may feel a sense of *deja vu* for they have undoubtedly read it all before, though perhaps less concisely." Commenting on the predictable nature of Hunt's plot lines, McDaniel adds that Jay Black, the hero of *The Gaza Intercept,* "can hardly be told from any other thriller hero."

In response to his critics, Hunt once told *CA:* "Whatever niche I may occupy as a writer will not be found among the Hate America, pacifist, social-consciousness group whose views dominate literary America and whose spokesmen view me through prisms of political and social prejudice. Widespread opprobrium attached to the CIA and the Nixon administration has had a damaging effect on my ability to publish successfully under my own name. And reviewers in general have chosen to criticize my life rather than professionally appraise my work."

BIOGRAPHICAL/CRITICAL SOURCES:

BOOKS

Authors in the News, Volume 1, Gale (Detroit), 1976.
Contemporary Literary Criticism, Volume 3, Gale, 1975.
Szulc, Tad, *Compulsive Spy: The Fated Career of E. Howard Hunt,* Viking, 1974.

PERIODICALS

Guardian Weekly, February 15, 1981.
Harper's, December, 1974.
Los Angeles Times Book Review, June 10, 1990, p. 11.
New York Review of Books, December 13, 1973; November 28, 1974.
New York Times Book Review, August 30, 1981, p. 10.
New York Times Magazine, June 3, 1973.
Saturday Review, November 16, 1974.
Time, January 29, 1973; June 11, 1973.
Times Educational Supplement, February 20, 1981.
Tribune Books (Chicago), December 15, 1991, p. 6.
Washington Post Book World, August 2, 1981, p. 10; September 22, 1985, p. 6.*

*   *   *

HUNT, Howard
   See HUNT, E(verette) Howard (Jr.)

HUNTER, Joan
   See YARDE, Jeanne Betty Frances

*   *   *

HURT, James (Riggins)   1934-

PERSONAL: Born May 22, 1934, in Ashland, KY; son of Joe (a farmer) and Martha Clay (Riggins) Hurt; married Phyllis Tilton (a professor of music), June 5, 1958; children: Christopher, Ross, Matthew. *Education:* University of Kentucky, A.B., 1956, M.A., 1957; Indiana University, Ph.D., 1965.

ADDRESSES: Home—1001 West William, Champaign, IL 61821. *Office*—325 English Bldg., 608 South Wright St., University of Illinois at Urbana-Champaign, Urbana, IL 61801.

CAREER: University of Illinois at Urbana-Champaign, assistant professor, 1966-69, associate professor, 1969-73, professor of English, 1973—. *Military service* U.S. Army, 1957-59.

MEMBER: Illinois State Historical Society.

AWARDS, HONORS: Illinois Center for Advanced Study fellow, 1979-80, 1986-87.

WRITINGS:

Aelfric, Twayne (Boston, MA), 1972.
Catiline's Dream: An Essay on Ibsen's Plays, University of Illinois Press (Champaign, IL), 1972.
(Editor) *Focus on Film and Theatre,* Prentice-Hall (Englewood Cliffs, NJ), 1974.
(Editor with Brian Wilkie) *Literature of the Western World,* Volume I: *The Ancient World through the Renaissance,* Volume II: *Neoclassicism through the Modern Period,* Macmillan (New York City), 1984, 2nd edition, in press.
Writing Illinois: The Prairie, Lincoln, and Chicago, University of Illinois Press, 1993.
(Editor) *Literature: A Contemporary Introduction,* Macmillan, 1994.

Also author of plays *Angel Band, Walden: A Ceremony,* and *Abraham Lincoln Walks at Midnight,* 1980.

*   *   *

HUSS, Roy (G.)   1927-1983(?)

PERSONAL: Born June 26, 1927, in New Orleans, LA; presumed murdered in Sumatra, Indonesia, in January, 1983; declared legally dead in 1987; son of Joseph J. and Adeline (Guerchoux) Huss. *Education:* Tulane University, B.A., 1947, M.A., 1949; University of Chicago, Ph.D., 1959. *Politics:* Democrat. *Religion:* None.

CAREER: Chicago City Junior College, Wilson Branch, Chicago, IL, instructor in English literature, 1951-56; Wayne State University, Detroit, MI, instructor in English literature, 1957-59, 1960-62; Queens College of the City University of New York, Flushing, NY, instructor, 1962-66, assistant professor, 1967-72, associate professor of English, 1972-83, founder of film studies department. Fulbright Professor at Athens College, Athens, Greece, 1956-57, and University of Messina, Sicily, 1959-60; lecturer on film at New York Community College, 1966-67.

MEMBER: American Federation of Film Societies, Modern Language Association, American Civil Liberties Union, National Psychological Association for Psychoanalysis (member-in-training), Association for Applied Psychoanalysis, Joint Council on Mental Health, Phi Beta Kappa.

WRITINGS:

(With Norman Silverstein) *The Film Experience: Elements of Motion Picture Art,* Harper (New York City), 1968.
(Editor) *Focus on Blow-Up,* Prentice-Hall (Englewood Cliffs, NJ), 1971.

(Editor with T. J. Ross) *Focus on the Horror Film,* Prentice-Hall, 1972.
The Mindscapes of Art: Dimensions of the Psyche in Fiction, Drama and Film, Fairleigh Dickinson University Press (East Brunswick, NJ), 1986.

Contributor to scholarly publications, including *Theatre Notebook* and *Dalhousie Review.* Member of editorial staff, *Psychoanalytic Review.*

SIDELIGHTS: Roy Huss was conducting research in Indonesia with his colleague James Dresser Allen when the two men vanished while taking a short cut through a forest near their hotel. A hotel employee at first confessed to murdering the two men but, when police led him to the area where he claimed to have buried the victims, the man changed his story. Indonesian police were unable to charge the man with a crime without evidence of foul play. In 1987, relatives of Huss and Allen had the two men declared legally dead by a New York court.

BIOGRAPHICAL/CRITICAL SOURCES:

PERIODICALS

New York Times, September 18, 1987, p. B3.*

I

INGLIS, Brian (St. John)   1916-1993

PERSONAL: Born July 31, 1916, in Dublin, Ireland; died February 11, 1993; son of Claude Cavendish (an engineer) and Vera (Blood) Inglis; married Ruth Langdon (a journalist), December 23, 1958 (divorced, 1972); children: Diana Eleanor, Neil Langdon. *Education:* Magdalen College, Oxford, B.A. (honors), 1939; University of Dublin, Ph.D., 1950.

ADDRESSES: Home—Garden Flat, 23 Lambolle Rd., London N.W. 3, England. *Agent*—Curtis Brown Ltd., 162 Regent St., London W1R 5TA, England.

CAREER: Irish Times, Dublin, Ireland, columnist, 1946-48, parliamentary correspondent, 1950-53; University of Dublin, Trinity College, Dublin, assistant to professor of modern history, 1949-53, lecturer in economics, 1951-53; *Spectator,* London, England, assistant editor, 1954-59, editor, 1959-62, director, 1962-93. Television commentator on a number of programs, including *What the Papers Say,* 1956-59, and *All Our Yesterdays,* 1961-73. *Military service:* Royal Air Force, 1940-46; became squadron leader; mentioned in dispatches.

WRITINGS:

The Freedom of the Press in Ireland, Faber (London), 1954.

The Story of Ireland, Faber, 1956.

Emotional Stress and Your Health, Criterion Press (Torrance, CA), 1958, published in England as *Revolution in Medicine,* Hutchinson (London), 1958.

West Briton, Faber, 1962.

The Case for Unorthodox Medicine, Putnam (New York), 1964, published in England as *Fringe Medicine,* Faber, 1964.

Private Conscience, Public Morality, Deutsch (London), 1964.

Doctors, Drugs, and Disease, Deutsch, 1965.

A History of Medicine, Weidenfeld & Nicolson (London), 1965.

Abdication, Macmillan (New York City), 1966.

Men of Conscience, Macmillan (New York City), 1971, published in England as *Poverty and the Industrial Revolution,* Hodder & Stoughton (London), 1971.

Roger Casement, Harcourt (New York City), 1974.

The Forbidden Game: A Social History of Drugs, Scribner (New York City), 1975.

The Opium War, Hodder & Stoughton, 1976.

Natural and Supernatural, Hodder & Stoughton, 1978.

Natural Medicine, Collins (London), 1979.

The Diseases of Civilisation, Hodder & Stoughton, 1981.

Science and Parascience: A History of the Paranormal, 1914-1939, Hodder & Stoughton, 1984.

The Paranormal, Granada Publishing (London), 1985.

The Hidden Power, J. Cape (London), 1986.

The Power of Dreams, Grafton Books (London), 1987.

The Unknown Guest, Chatto & Windus (London), 1987.

Trance: A Natural History of Altered States of Mind, Grafton Books, 1989.

Downstart: The Autobiography of Brian Inglis, Chatto & Windus, 1990.

Also author of *Coincidences,* 1990.

BIOGRAPHICAL/CRITICAL SOURCES:

PERIODICALS

Times, March 22, 1984.

OBITUARIES:

PERIODICALS

Times (London), February 13, 1993, p. 17.*

INNES, Michael
 See STEWART, J(ohn) I(nnes) M(ackintosh)

*   *   *

IRVING, Robert
 See ADLER, Irving

J

JACKSON, Christine E(lisabeth) 1936-

PERSONAL: Born March 6, 1936, in Huddersfield, Yorkshire, England; daughter of Arthur (an engineering plant designer) and Helen Jane (Rowland) Adams; married Andrew Bairstow Jackson (a librarian), September 16, 1960. *Education:* Manchester Polytechnic, A.L.A., 1959. *Politics:* Conservative. *Religion:* Protestant.

ADDRESSES: Home—Amberley, Hare St., near Buntingford, Hertfordshire SG9 0EQ, England.

CAREER: Huddersfield Public Library, Huddersfield, England, reference librarian, 1953-60; College of Further Education, Bedford, England, librarian, 1960-65; Hertfordshire County Library, Radlett, England, branch librarian, 1967-69.

MEMBER: Royal Society for the Protection of Birds, Society for the History of Natural History, National Trust.

AWARDS, HONORS: Bronze Medal, British Philatelic Exhibition, 1978, for *Collecting Bird Stamps.*

WRITINGS:

British Names of Birds, H., F. & G. Witherby (London), 1968.
Bird Illustrators: Some Artists in Early Lithography, H., F. & G. Witherby, 1975.
Collecting Bird Stamps, H., F. & G. Witherby, 1977.
Wood Engravings of Birds, H., F. & G. Witherby, 1978.
Bird Etchings: The Illustrators and Their Books, 1655-1855, Cornell University Press (Ithaca, NY), 1985.
Prideaux John Selby: A Gentleman Naturalist, Spredden Press (London), 1992.
Great Bird Paintings, Antique Collectors' Club (Woodbridge, Suffolk, England), Volume 1: *The Old Masters,* 1993, Volume 2: *The Eighteenth Century,* 1994, Volume 3: *The Nineteenth Century,* 1995.

Contributor to *George Lodge: Artist Naturalist,* edited by John Savory, Croom Helm (London), 1986. Also author of pamphlets on local history; and author of introductions to art catalogues. Contributor to periodicals, including *Journal of the Society for the Bibliography of Natural History, Archives of Natural History, Naturae, Bird Observer,* and *Northumbrian.*

WORK IN PROGRESS: Dictionary of Bird Painters of the World: The Twentieth Century, Volume 4 of *Great Bird Paintings,* for publication in 1996; and *The Oriental Masters,* Volume 5 of *Great Bird Paintings,* for publication in 1997.

SIDELIGHTS: Christine E. Jackson once told *CA:* "My books about bird illustrations combine my interests in art, birds, and people in their historical settings. Having retired from librarianship, I had the opportunity to read widely in my chosen subjects and to search for primary material that would elucidate the methods of illustration employed by bird artists working in England from the seventeenth through the nineteenth centuries—that is, prior to the introduction of photographic reproduction of illustrations in books.

"Having traced new and original information from diverse sources, I wrote three volumes in order to encourage both an awareness and an appreciation of the achievements of early book producers.

"I used my own collection [of bird stamps] as the basis for my book *Collecting Bird Stamps.* I find that topical stamp collecting is less popular in Great Britain than it is in the United States."

The author more recently added: "From 1990 my interest in bird art changed from illustrators of bird books to bird artists who painted pictures in oils, watercolours, pastels, etc."

JACKSON, Keith
See KELLY, Tim

*   *   *

JAMESON, (Margaret) Storm 1891-1986
(James Hill, William Lamb)

PERSONAL: Born January 8, 1891, in Whitby, Yorkshire, England; died of natural causes, September 30, 1986, in Cambridge, England; daughter of William Storm (a sea captain) and Hannah Margaret (Gallilee) Jameson; married second husband, Guy Patterson Chapman (a writer and historian), February 1, 1926 (died June 20, 1972); children: (first marriage) C. W. Storm Clark. *Education:* Leeds University, B.A. (first-class honors), 1912; King's College, London, M.A., 1914.

ADDRESSES: Office—c/o Macmillan & Co., 4 Little Essex St., London WC2, England.

CAREER: Novelist, playwright, literary critic, and publishing administrator. *New Commonwealth,* London, England, editor, 1919-21; Alfred A. Knopf, Inc., New York City, English representative and later comanager of London office, 1925-28; *New English Weekly,* London, reviewer, 1934. Also worked as a copywriter for the Carlton Agency, London.

MEMBER: English Centre of International PEN (president, 1938-45).

AWARDS, HONORS: John Ruteau fellowship, 1912-13; D. Litt., Leeds University, 1948; English Centre of International PEN award, 1974, for *There Will Be a Short Interval.*

WRITINGS:

FICTION

The Pot Boils, Constable, 1919.
The Happy Highways, Century, 1920.
The Clash, Little, Brown, 1922.
The Pitiful Wife, Constable, 1923, Knopf, 1924.
Lady Susan and Life: An Indiscretion, Chapman & Dodd, 1924.
Three Kingdoms, Knopf, 1926.
The Lovely Ship (also see below), Knopf, 1927.
Farewell to Youth, Knopf, 1928.
The Voyage Home (also see below), Knopf, 1930.
A Richer Dust (also see below), Knopf, 1931.
The Triumph of Time: A Trilogy (includes *The Lovely Ship, The Voyage Home,* and *A Richer Dust*), Heinemann, 1932.
That Was Yesterday, Knopf, 1932.
The Single Heart (also see below), Benn, 1932.
A Day Off (also see below), Nicholson & Watson, 1933.

Women against Men (includes *A Day Off, Delicate Monster,* and *The Single Heart*), Knopf, 1933.
Company Parade, Knopf, 1934.
Love in Winter, Knopf, 1935.
In the Second Year, Macmillan, 1936.
None Turn Back, Cassell, 1936.
Delicate Monster (also see above), Nicholson & Watson, 1937.
(Under pseudonym William Lamb) *The World Ends,* Dent, 1937.
(Under pseudonym James Hill) *Loving Memory,* Collins, 1937.
The Moon Is Making, Cassell, 1937, Macmillan, 1938.
(Under pseudonym James Hill) *No Victory for the Soldier,* Collins, 1938.
Here Comes a Candle, Cassell, 1938, Macmillan, 1939.
The Captain's Wife, Macmillan, 1939, published in England as *Farewell, Night; Welcome, Day,* Cassell, 1939.
Europe to Let: The Memoirs of an Obscure Man, Macmillan, 1940.
Cousin Honore, Cassell, 1940, Macmillan, 1941.
The Fort, Macmillan, 1941.
Then Shall We Hear Singing: A Fantasy in C Major, Macmillan, 1942.
Cloudless May, Macmillan (London), 1943, Macmillan (New York City), 1944.
The Journal of Mary Hervey Russell, Macmillan, 1945.
The Other Side, Macmillan, 1946.
Before the Crossing, Macmillan, 1947.
The Black Laurel, Macmillan (London), 1947.
The Moment of Truth, Macmillan, 1949.
The Green Man, Macmillan (London), 1952, Harper, 1953.
The Hidden River, Harper, 1955, published serially under title *The House of Hate.*
The Intruder, Macmillan/St. Martin's Press (London), 1956.
A Cup of Tea for Mr. Thorgill, Harper, 1957.
One Ulysses Too Many, Harper, 1958, published in England as *A Ulysses Too Many,* Macmillan, 1958.
Last Score: Or, The Private Life of Sir Richard Ormston, Harper, 1961, published serially under title *The Lion and the Dagger.*
The Road from the Monument, Harper, 1962.
A Month Soon Goes, Harper, 1963.
The Blind Heart, Harper, 1964, published in England as *The Aristide Case,* Macmillan, 1964.
The Early Life of Stephen Hind, Harper, 1966.
The White Crow, Harper, 1968.
There Will Be a Short Interval, Harper, 1973.

NONFICTION

Modern Drama in Europe, Collins, 1920.

The Georgian Novel and Mr. Robinson, Morrow, 1929.

The Decline of Merry England, Bobbs-Merrill, 1930.

No Time Like the Present (autobiography), Knopf, 1933.

The Soul of Man in the Age of Leisure, Nott, 1935.

The Novel in Contemporary Life, The Writer (Boston), 1938.

The End of This War, Allen & Unwin, 1941.

The Writer's Situation and Other Essays, Macmillan (London), 1950.

Morley Roberts: The Last Eminent Victorian, Unicorn Press, 1961.

Journey from the North: Autobiography of Storm Jameson, Collins, two volumes, 1969-70, Harper, 1970.

Parthian Words (literary criticism), Collins, 1970, Harper, 1971.

Speaking of Stendhal, Gollancz, 1979.

TRANSLATOR

Guy de Maupassant, *Mont-Oriol,* Knopf, 1924.

de Maupassant, *Yvette and Other Stories,* Knopf, 1924.

de Maupassant, *Horla and Other Stories,* Knopf, 1925.

(With Ernest Boyd) de Maupassant, *Eighty-Eight Short Stories,* Knopf, 1930.

EDITOR

Challenge to Death: A Symposium on War and Peace, Constable, 1934, Dutton, 1935.

Rebecca West and others, *London Calling: A Salute to America,* Harper, 1942.

A Kind of Survivor: The Autobiography of Guy Chapman, Gollancz, 1975.

OTHER

Full Circle (one-act play), Basil Blackwell, 1929.

Civil Journey (essays), Cassell, 1939.

A Day Off: Two Short Novels and Some Stories, Macmillan (London), 1959.

Author of television plays, including *William the Defeated* (published in *The Book of the PEN,* edited by Hermon Ould, Barker, 1950), and *The Commonplace Heart,* 1953; contributor of short stories, articles, introductions, and prefaces to numerous publications, including introduction to *Tale without End* by Lilo Linke, Knopf, 1934.

SIDELIGHTS: At a dinner meeting with Storm Jameson to discuss the manuscript of her first novel, the amused publisher said to his wife, "She is the first author I ever knew to let herself be hacked to pieces without a murmur." But, as Jameson explained in her autobiography, "What he took for submissiveness or timidity was nothing of the sort. It was a deep unrealized contempt for novel-writing as a serious use for energy and intellect." Despite this attitude and the fact that the ten-pound advance Constable gave her on *The Pot Boils* "meant that their loss on the book was precisely ten pounds heavier than it would have been," Jameson had more than forty-five books of fiction to her credit by the time of her death at the age of ninety-five. Literary criticism, translations of de Maupassant, articles, short stories, and plays added further to the large body of work she produced in more than fifty years of writing.

Jameson's fiction was popular in England during the 1930s and 1940s. Several of her novels reflect feminist views. In an obituary in the *Chicago Tribune,* it was recalled that Jameson, "with writer Rebecca West . . . was a vigorous supporter of women's independence in the 1920s and was a friend of H. G. Wells, who supported the feminist movement." It was also noted in the article that Tim Farmiloe, a Macmillan director, said just after Jameson's death that "if she had been a young feminist writing now, she would have been all the rage."

Wary all her life of settled domesticity, Jameson said in *Journey from the North: Autobiography of Storm Jameson,* "Writing is only my second nature. I would infinitely rather write than cook, but I would rather run around the world, looking at it, than write." She traveled extensively in Europe, especially in France, a country for which she felt a fondness "peculiarly English, a sort of humble love." In the years preceding World War II, her work as a PEN official with exiled writers took her to Germany, Austria, Poland, Hungary, and Czechoslovakia. Returning to Poland and Czechoslovakia in 1945, she observed Warsaw in ruins and the internment camps which then housed German prisoners of war, but she also observed a strong spirit of renaissance among the artists of those countries. Jameson's travels for PEN, according to the *Times* obituary, "provided invaluable raw material for what may come to be regarded as her most successful novels: *Cousin Honore* and *Europe to Let* . . . and *Cloudless May.*" Of these, *Cousin Honore,* a story set in Alsace from 1918 to 1939, enjoyed particular acclaim, and it was one of the author's favorites among her own works.

In 1948, teaching positions at Pittsburgh University brought Jameson and her husband, Guy Chapman, to the United States. Although Jameson found the country "oppressively large," she described Pittsburgh, to the surprise of many Americans, as a "splendid city" that still retained its European elements. With a small group of friends there, she experienced a rare sense of community in which she was "perfectly at ease, perfectly light-hearted."

Ambitious from childhood, James seemed to be driven to write the novels she herself described as "too many," sometimes recording personal family details for later use in her fiction. A sequence of Jameson's novels, including *The Lovely Ship, The Voyage Home,* and *A Richer Dust,* was inspired by the author's Yorkshire family's history of shipbuilding and seafaring. Of her own ties to the area in which she grew up, Jameson told a *Times* interviewer in 1984, after she had lived in Cambridge for many years, "I carry North Yorkshire around with me, the unkindness of the people, their severity but also their honesty." Though most of her fiction received mixed critical attention, throughout her career she commanded the sort of respect V. S. Pritchett paid her in the *Christian Science Monitor:* "Miss Jameson is one of the intelligent novelists. She can always be relied upon not to outrage our judgment. She is shrewd and is intensely interested in character not only for its own amusing or tragic sake but because of a very pleasant seriousness of temperament." Twenty-four years later, W. S. White said in a review of *The Road from the Monument,* "The present, mature Storm Jameson is a social satirist of a keen perception, a skillful writer, who has an ability to comment with ironic detachment, a figure of literary distinction and integrity which makes the merely angry young British writers seem pallid and puerile."

In *Parthian Words,* a collection of historical and critical essays on the novel, Jameson took much modern fiction to task for its lack of clarity and its emphasis on pornography, which she distinguished from eroticism. In *Journey from the North* she said, "I am genuinely puzzled by the indifference, even hostility, so many writers (critics and others) feel for clear writing. I am prepared to work hard and loyally to find my way in the deeper, less readily intelligible levels in a work, but only if I can believe in the writer's good faith. Only if I can believe that he at least tried to be accessible."

In an article for *Writer,* Jameson quoted a remark of Coleridge as advice to the aspiring novelist: "Never pursue literature as a trade." She wrote of the "intolerable anguish of being forced to succeed, year in year out, as a public entertainer, spinning my verbal webs, going through my tricks, perhaps with diminishing intellectual and financial returns, again and again and again, with the agility of a street acrobat." She would wait, she said further, until her early thirties before attempting a novel: "Not too long, not so long that the terrible sharpness of young senses—like the sharpness of sensual excitement which makes a traveller's first moments in a foreign country worth more to him in insight and emotion than a year's stay—had lost their acuteness, but long enough to be able to see myself with a margin of detachment . . . and long enough for my relationship with my fellowmen to begin, at least to begin, to be unclouded by vanity, diffidence, greed."

BIOGRAPHICAL/CRITICAL SOURCES:

BOOKS

Dictionary of Literary Biography, Volume 36: *British Novelists, 1890-1929, Modernists,* Gale, 1985.

Jameson, Storm, *Journey from the North,* Harper, 1970.

PERIODICALS

Best Sellers, April 1, 1971.
Books, April, 1970.
Books and Bookmen, May, 1970.
Bookseller, September 19, 1970.
Christian Science Monitor, September 29, 1937; July 19, 1969.
New Republic, March 13, 1971.
New York Herald Tribune Books, April 8, 1962.
New York Times Book Review, May 9, 1971; January 12, 1986, p. 34.
Spectator, October 25, 1969.
Times (London), March 2, 1984.
Writer, April, 1971.

OBITUARIES:

BOOKS

Contemporary Authors, Volume 120, Gale, 1987.

PERIODICALS

Chicago Tribune, October 12, 1986.
Los Angeles Times, October 13, 1986.
Times (London), October 7, 1986.*

*   *   *

JONES, Charles Edwin 1932-

PERSONAL: Born June 1, 1932, in Kansas City, MO; son of Dess Dain (a streetcar and bus operator) and Dove (Barnwell) Jones; married Beverly Anne Lundy (a librarian), May 30, 1956; children: Karl Laurence. *Education:* Bethany-Peniel College, B.A., 1954; University of Oklahoma, summer graduate study, 1954; University of Michigan, M.A.L.S., 1955; University of Wisconsin, M.S., 1960, Ph.D., 1968; Episcopal Divinity School, additional study, 1975-76. *Politics:* Democrat.

ADDRESSES: Home—12300 Springwood Dr., Oklahoma City, OK 73120.

CAREER: Nazarene Theological Seminary, Kansas City, MO, head librarian, 1958-59; Park College, Parkville, MO, head librarian, 1961-63; University of Michigan, Ann Arbor, manuscript curator of Michigan Historical Collections, 1965-69; Houghton College, Houghton, NY, associate professor of history, 1969-71; Brown University, Providence, RI, catalog librarian, 1971-76; Westlake Nursing Center, Oklahoma City, OK, chaplain in residence, 1989—; ordained deacon, Reformed Episcopal Church, 1990. Visiting professor, Tuskegee Institute, 1968-69, and Clarion State College, 1979. Consultant,

Billy Graham Evangelistic Association, 1972. *Military service:* U.S. Army, 1956-58.

MEMBER: American Theological Library Association, Canadian Church Historical Society.

WRITINGS:

Jonathan Edwards and Politics, 1727-1750, University of Wisconsin Press (Madison), 1960.
Perfectionist Persuasion: The Holiness Movement and American Methodism, 1867-1936, Scarecrow (Metuchen, NJ), 1974.
A Guide to the Study of the Holiness Movement, Scarecrow, 1974.
A Guide to the Study of the Pentecostal Movement, two volumes, Scarecrow, 1983.
Black Holiness, Scarecrow, 1987.
The Charismatic Movement, two volumes, Scarecrow, 1995.

Contributor to books, including *Critical Essays on Jonathan Edwards,* edited by W. J. Scheick, G. K. Hall (Boston), 1980; *Rethinking Methodist History,* edited by R. E. Richey and K. E. Rowe, Kingswood (London), 1985; *Dictionary of Christianity in America,* edited by D. G. Reid, Inter-Varsity Press (Leicester, England), 1990; and *America's Alternative Religions,* edited by Timothy Miller, State University of New York Press (Albany), 1995. Contributor to periodicals, including *Journal of Church and State, Journal of the Canadian Church Historical Society, New England Quarterly, Wesleyan Theological Journal, Missouri Historical Review, New York History,* and *Methodist History.*

WORK IN PROGRESS: The Holiness Movement, a revision of *A Guide to the Study of the Holiness Movement,* for Scarecrow.

*   *   *

JOSIPOVICI, Gabriel   1940-

PERSONAL: Born October 8, 1940, in Nice, France; son of Jean (a writer) and Sacha (Rabinovitch) Josipovici. *Education:* Studied at Victoria College, Cairo, Egypt, 1950-56, and Cheltenham College, 1956-57; St. Edmund Hall, Oxford, B.A., 1961.

ADDRESSES: Home—60 Prince Edwards Rd., Lewes, Sussex, England. *Office*—Arts Building, University of Sussex, Falmer, Brighton, Sussex BN1 9RH, England. *Agent*—John Johnson, Clerkenwell House, 45-7 Clerkenwell Green, London EC1R OHT, England.

CAREER: University of Sussex, Falmer, Brighton, England, lecturer in English and comparative literature,

1963-74, reader in English, 1974-84, professor of English, 1984—; University College, London, Northcliff Lecturer, 1981-82; University of Oxford, Weidenfeld Professor of Comparative Literature, 1996-97.

AWARDS, HONORS: Sunday Times award, 1970, for *Evidence of Intimacy;* South East Arts Literature Prize, 1978, for *The Lessons of Modernism and Other Essays.*

WRITINGS:

NOVELS

The Inventory, M. Joseph, 1968.
Words, Gollancz, 1971.
The Present, Gollancz, 1975.
Migrations, Harvester, 1977.
The Echo Chamber, Harvester, 1980.
The Air We Breathe, Harvester, 1981.
Conversations in Another Room, Methuen, 1984.
Contre-Jour: A Triptych after Pierre Bonnard, Carcanet, 1986.
The Big Glass, Carcanet, 1991.
In a Hotel Garden, Carcanet, 1993.
Moo Pak, Carcanet, 1994.

CRITICISM

The World and the Book: A Study of Modern Fiction, Macmillan, 1971, 2nd edition, 1978.
The Lessons of Modernism and Other Essays, Macmillan, 1977.
Writing and the Body (Northcliff Lectures), Harvester, 1982.
The Mirror of Criticism: Selected Reviews, 1977-1982, Harvester, 1983.
The Book of God: A Response to the Bible, Yale University Press, 1988.
Text and Voice: Essays 1981-1991, Carcanet, 1992.

OTHER

Mobius the Stripper (stories and short plays), Gollancz, 1974.
(Author of introduction) *Portable Saul Bellow,* Viking, 1974.
(Editor) *The Modern English Novel: The Reader, the Writer, and the Work,* Harper, 1976.
Four Stories, Menard, 1977.
Vergil Dying (play), Span, 1979.
(Editor and author of introduction) Maurice Blanchot, *The Siren's Song: Selected Essays,* translated by Sacha Rabinovitch, Harvester, 1982.
In the Fertile Land (short stories), Carcanet, 1987.
Steps: Selected Fiction and Drama, Carcanet, 1990.

Also author of plays *Evidence of Intimacy, Dreams of Mrs. Fraser, Marathon, Playback, A Life, AG, Flow, The Seven,* and *Kin.* Contributor to *Adam International Review, Criti-*

cal Quarterly, Encounter, European Judaism, Jewish Quarterly (London), *Nouvelle Revue Francaise, Transatlantic Review, Tempo, Listener, London Review of Books, New York Review of Books, Times Literary Supplement, Independent,* and *Salmagundi.*

SIDELIGHTS: "Gabriel Josipovici is a born writer not afraid of the dark," asserts *Listener* critic John Mellors. "He asks questions, mainly in dialogue, both in his stories and short plays, about identity, truth, memory, death and the relationships between mind and body and writer and words." "Novelist and literary theorist, playwright and university lecturer, short-story writer and critic: Gabriel Josipovici is all of these," *Dictionary of Literary Biography* contributors Linda Canon and Jay L. Halio remark. "His erudition is surpassed only by his sensitivity to language and artistic form, making him one of the leading experimentalists writing fiction in Britain today."

Josipovici's first novel, *The Inventory,* was "an impressive debut," according to a *Times Literary Supplement* reviewer, a book "at once complex (in its implications) and lucid (in its style)" with a "fugue-like" structure and "barely a superfluous line." *The Inventory* follows a young man as he takes inventory of a dead man's belongings and becomes involved with acquaintances and relatives of the deceased. *New Statesman* reviewer Gillian Tindall finds that *The Inventory,* "though slight, suggests such an interesting view of reality and memory that one is eager for the next attempt."

Josipovici's second novel, *Words,* attracted less, and generally less favorable, notice than his first. In a book composed "entirely of smalltalk . . . frequently too small to struggle to the right-hand margin," *Listener* reviewer John Carey believes the author intends his readers "to imagine vast emotional problems wallowing around under the dribble of dialogue." *Words* tells the story of a couple who are visited by his former lover and her daughter. "Beyond this," a *Times Literary Supplement* reviewer maintains, "most of . . . [*Words*] is mystery; to be elucidated (which is the point of things) only through close reading of the constant dialogue in which the book is almost entirely couched. The situation emotionally is indeed obscure." The reviewer allows that "the final outcome, and message, of *Words* is cleverly achieved," but hopes for "evidence in future books that something more substantial and more clearly located in recognizable living will prove Mr. Josipovici's abilities beyond doubt."

Canon and Halio find *Migrations* the best example of Josipovici's application to his own work of "the principles of fragmentation and discontinuity, of repetition and spiralling, which we found underlying the works of Kafka, Eliot, Stevens, Proust, Robbe-Grillet, Virginia Woolf, and Beckett" which he discussed in an address to the National

Association of Teachers of English in 1972. *Times Literary Supplement* reviewer Blake Morrison acknowledges that readers may find *Migrations* difficult to follow, yet he asserts that "those who are familiar with . . . Josipovici's previous novels, and with the theories promulgated in his critical study *The World and the Book,* will accept that the frustrations experienced in reading *Migrations* are Mr. Josipovici's means of making us share his protagonist's struggle to articulate a sense of life's purpose." Nonetheless, Morrison adds, "even patient readers will be disappointed by the latter part of the novel."

The Echo Chamber, Peter Lewis comments in the *Times Literary Supplement,* "is more immediately enjoyable and accessible than much of [Josipovici's] previous fiction." The action follows a young man as he leaves the hospital after a breakdown and attempts to regain his memory of the traumatic event that prompted his illness. The book "returns to the style of *Words* but with a significant difference," Canon and Halio observe: "like a mystery thriller (the genre it parodies), it builds up suspense concerning an event and reaches its climax and epiphany only on the last page." In the *Spectator,* Paul Ableman describes *The Echo Chamber* as "a book without qualities. It employs considerable literary skill to say precisely nothing about anything."

The Air We Breathe, Josipovici's sixth novel, is another "technical *tour de force,*" says Peter Lewis in the *Times Literary Supplement.* But Lewis finds that the author's "preoccupation with expanding the possibilities of the novel is leading him towards a formal and stylistic sophistication operating in a vacuum." In *The Air We Breathe,* suggests Lewis, "technique comes perilously close to being an end in itself; the artistry of *The Echo Chamber* seems to have given way to artiness." Kathleen Fullbrook, writing in *British Book News,* is more positive, describing *The Air We Breathe* as "a novel which analyses language and silence and the nature of the gaps that occur in the attempt to think about and to communicate experience through words. It is a distinguished addition to the shelf of postmodernist fiction."

Josipovici's nonfiction has also received critical attention. In *The World and the Book* he extols the virtues of such authors as T. S. Eliot, Marcel Proust, and Vladimir Nabokov, comparing their unorthodox approaches to literature with the innovative techniques of Francois Rabelais and Miguel de Cervantes. Reviewing *The World and the Book,* David Lodge remarks in *Critical Quarterly:* "Mr. Josipovici is intelligent, eloquent and formidably well-read. He cares passionately about literature and can communicate his enthusiasm infectiously to the reader. . . . [His] stimulating and educative voice comes like a current of cool and invigorating air." A reviewer for the *Times Literary Supplement* says, "Great literary criticism is the most evasive of achievements. Gabriel Josipovici seems blessed with all the gifts: a lucid style, vast imaginative energy, a huge storehouse of reading, a living concern for art, as well as a certain self-conscious humility at this whole buzz and fuzz in the face of aesthetic experience."

Josipovici's second book of criticism, *The Lessons of Modernism,* appeared in the same year as *Migrations.* David Lodge, who had applauded the earlier *The World and the Book,* asserts in the *New Statesman* that the author is "capable of beautifully phrased, brilliantly illuminating observations on particular texts." Yet the critic has reservations about *The Lessons of Modernism,* especially Josipovici's blanket rejection of realism. Lodge argues that "criticism should surely account for the continuing vitality of realistic modes of artistic presentation, and refine its methods of 'reading' them, rather than just wishing them away." Other critics believe that Josipovici is correct in his dismissal of traditional forms. Alan Wilde, writing in the quarterly *Contemporary Literature,* finds that modernism "is made to extend seamlessly and commodiously from 1880 to the present, and the book neglects the case . . . for a distinctively postmodernist literature. Nevertheless, . . . this is a particularly exhilarating and engaging work, fused finally by its passionate unity of point and purpose."

Two more books of literary criticism followed publication of *The Air We Breathe. Writing and the Body* is the somewhat expanded text of the Northcliffe Lectures for 1981 which Josipovici delivered at University College in London. The author states in the first lecture that his purpose is "to examine the role which language, writing and books play in our lives, the lives we live with our bodies." Denis Donoghue begins his *Times Literary Supplement* review by commenting, "I congratulate anyone who made head or tail of the Lectures on a first hearing." Yet Donoghue discovers much that is perceptive and enlightening, though sometimes digressive, in the book, including Josipovici's lecture on Shakespeare. However, the critic also considers many of the author's judgments untenable. "Josipovici's meditations have their own exaltation," Donoghue concludes, "but not enough, by way of an enabling or persuasive context, to make the reader complete for himself the meaning Josipovici has hardly begun to incite." *International Fiction Review* contributor Harold E. Lusher concludes: "Quite apart from the degree of disappointment that the general reader may feel over the possibility of ever coming in terms with so impenetrable a topic," the book "is nevertheless a valiant and fascinating effort to widen our understanding and sharpen our awareness of how close the relationship is between the process and the organism. If that relationship is ultimately inexplicable, one must nevertheless give high marks to a writer who ad-

dresses the question anew with such courage and intelligence."

The second critical work after *The Air We Breathe* was *The Mirror of Criticism,* in which Josipovici's "analysis of C. H. Sisson's shoddy translation of Dante is wonderfully clever and learned, and his discussions of Chaucer are excellent," Tom Paulin notes in the *Observer.* Malcolm Bowie, in the *London Review of Books,* is similarly affirmative, calling *The Mirror of Criticism* "the travel diary of a perceptive and generous-minded explorer, going where the reviewing road takes him and inventing his notions as the journey demands."

After two more novels that attracted limited but respectful attention, *Conversations in Another Room* and *Contre-Jour,* Josipovici wrote a book that, while hardly a bestseller, gained widespread critical recognition. In *The Book of God: A Response to the Bible,* a work that examines the Bible as literature, Josipovici dissects the various translations of the first words of Genesis, the story of Joseph and his brothers, the instructions for building the Tabernacle, the Book of Judges, the questions of prose or verse, and the use and significance of dialogue. He also raises questions of interpretation, discusses the viewpoints of others, and gives his own reasoned opinions. Denis Donoghue, writing in the *Times Literary Supplement,* regards Josipovici's response to the Bible as "not only highly intelligent but considerate. His 'personalism' is at every point honorable, thoughtful, decent and exacting in an entirely justified cause." Piers Paul Read, reviewing *The Book of God* for the *Spectator,* finds it "exceeds the hopes I had of a book of this kind. It is erudite yet lucid, impassioned yet impartial, and filled with insights gained from Josipovici's familiarity with European literature—with Dante, Proust or Joyce."

BIOGRAPHICAL/CRITICAL SOURCES:

BOOKS

Contemporary Literary Criticism, Gale, Volume 6, 1976, Volume 43, 1987.
Dictionary of Literary Biography, Volume 14: *British Novelists since 1960,* Gale, 1983.

PERIODICALS

British Book News, April, 1982, p. 259.
Contemporary Literature, summer, 1979, pp. 369-376.
Critical Quarterly, summer, 1972, pp. 171-185.
Criticism, winter, 1974.
International Fiction Review, winter, 1984, pp. 69-71.
Listener, November 4, 1971, pp. 624-625; January 9, 1975; September 29, 1977.
London Review of Books, July 5, 1984, pp. 22-23.
Nation, December 24, 1983, p. 676.

New Statesman, October 4, 1968, p. 435; December 17, 1971; August 26, 1977, pp. 279-280.
New York Times Book Review, April 10, 1988, p. 18.
Observer, February 5, 1984, p. 53.
Spectator, March 22, 1980, p. 21; January 7, 1989, p. 23; November 25, 1989, p. 44.
Times Literary Supplement, October 31, 1968; November 12, 1971, p. 1409; February 25, 1972; March 24, 1978, p. 361; March 21, 1980, p. 312; November 13, 1981, p. 1330; January 7, 1983, p. 6; November 30, 1984, p. 1392; July 25, 1986, p. 819; May 13, 1988, p. 533; March 31, 1989, p. 331; March 8, 1991, p. 19; August 14, 1992, p. 7.
Washington Post Book World, April 19, 1992, p. 1.

*   *   *

JUENGER, Ernst 1895-
(Ernst Junger)

PERSONAL: Born March 29, 1895, in Heidelberg, Germany; son of Ernst (a chemist and pharmacist) and Lily (Lampl) Juenger; married Gretha von Jeinsen, August 3, 1925 (died, 1960); married Liselotte Lehrer, March 3, 1962; children: Ernstel (died November, 1944), Alexander J. (died April, 1993). *Education:* Attended University of Leipzig, 1923-25.

ADDRESSES: Home—88515, Langenenslingen-Wilflingen, Germany.

CAREER: Writer. Honorary member, International Nomenclature Committee—Division of Literature, 1982; honorary president, Societe allemande-togolaise, 1985. *Military service:* German Army, 1914-23; became lieutenant; wounded seven times; received Pour le merite; German Army, 1939-44; became captain.

MEMBER: Society for Bloy Studies (honorary member).

AWARDS, HONORS: Literary awards from cities of Bremen and Goslar, West Germany, both 1955; Grand Order of Merit, Federal Republic of Germany, 1959; Federal League of German Industry Literature Prize, 1960; Immermann Prize, City of Duesseldorf, 1965; Freiherr vom Stein Gold Medal, 1970; Schiller Gedaechtnispreis, 1974; Star of the Grand Cross of Merit, Federal Republic of Germany, 1977; Golden Eagle, City of Nice, 1977; Medaille de la Paix, City of Verdun, 1979; Order of Merit, Baden-Wuerttemberg, 1980; Prix Europa-Litterature, Fondation Internationale pour le Rayonnement des Arts et des Lettres, 1981; Prix Mondial Cino-del-Duca, 1981; Goethe Prize, City of Frankfurt, 1982; Diplome d'Honneur et Medaille, city of Montpellier, 1983; Premio Circeo, Association for Italian-German Friendship, 1983; Schulterband, highest distinction of Grand Cross of

Merit, 1985; Premio Mediterraneo, Center of Mediterranean Culture (Palermo), 1986; Bayerischer Maximiliansorden fuer Wissenschaft und Kunst, 1986; Prix international Dante Alighieri, Accademia Casentinese, 1987; Premio Internazionale Tevere (Rome), 1987; honorary doctorate, University of Bilbao, 1989; Oberschwaebischer Kunstpreis, 1990; Robert Schuman Prize, F.V.S. Foundation, 1993; Gran Premio Cultura, Venice Biennial, 1993.

WRITINGS:

IN ENGLISH TRANSLATION

In Stahlgewittern: Aus dem Tagebuch eines Strosstruppfuehrers (personal narrative), E. S. Mittler & Sohn, 1922, published as *In Stahlgewittern: Ein Kriegstagbuch,* [Hamburg, Germany], 1934, translation by Basil Creighton published as *Storm of Steel: From the Diary of a German Storm-Troop Officer on the Western Front,* Doubleday, 1929, reprinted, H. Fertig, 1975.
Das Waeldchen 125: Eine Chronik aus den Grabenkaempfen 1918 (personal narrative), E. S. Mittler & Sohn, 1925, translation by Creighton published as *Copse One Hundred Twenty-Five: A Chronicle from the Trench Warfare of 1918,* Chatto & Windus, 1930.
Afrikanische Spiele (personal narrative), Hanseatische Verlagsanstalt, 1936, reprinted, E. Klett, 1965, translation by Stuart Hood published as *African Diversions,* 1954.
Auf den Marmorklippen (novel), [Hamburg], 1939, translation by Hood published as *On the Marble Cliffs,* New Directions, 1947, reprinted, Penguin, 1970.
Der Friede: Ein Wort an die Jugend Europas, ein Wort an die Jugend der Welt (essay), [West Germany], 1945, translation by Hood published as *The Peace,* Regnery, 1948.
Glaeserne Bienen (novel), E. Klett, 1957, translation by Louise Bogan and Elizabeth Mayer published as *The Glass Bees,* Noonsday Press, 1960.
Eumeswil, E. Klett, 1977, translation by Joachim Neugroschel published under same title, Marsilio Publishers Corp. (New York), 1993.
Aladin's Problem, Klett-Cotta, 1983, translation by Neugroschel published as *Aladdin's Problem,* Marsilio Publishers Corp., 1992.
Eine Gefuehrliche Begegnung, Klett-Cotta, 1985, translation by Hilary Barr published as *A Dangerous Encounter,* Marsilio Publishers Corp., 1993.

IN GERMAN; HISTORY

Der Kampf als inneres Erlebnis (title means "Struggle as Inner Experience"), E. S. Mittler & Sohn, 1922.
Feuer und Blut: Ein kleiner Ausschnitt aus einer grossen Schlacht, Stahlhelm Verlag, 1925, 5th edition, Hanseatische Verlagsanstalt, 1941.

Gaerten und Strassen: Aus den Tagebuechern von 1939 und 1940 (personal narrative), E. S. Mittler & Sohn, 1942.

(With Armin Mohler) *Die Schleife: Dokumente zum Weg,* Verlag der Arche, 1955.

Jahre der Okkupation (personal narrative; title means "Years of Occupation"), E. Klett, 1958.

IN GERMAN; TRAVEL

Atlantische Fahrt, [London; first edition appeared under the auspices of the YMCA for German prisoners of war], 1947, 2nd edition, Verlag der Arche, 1948.

Ein Inselfruehling: Ein Tagebuch aus Rhodes, Verlag der Arche, 1948.

Myrdun: Briefe aus Norwegen, 3rd edition (earlier limited editions appeared in 1943 restricted to members of the German Army in Norway), Verlag der Arche, 1948, reprinted, E. Klett, 1975.

Am Kieselstrand, V. Klostermann, 1951.

Am Sarazenenturm, V. Klostermann, 1955, 2nd edition, 1955.

Zwei Inseln: Formosa, Ceylon, Olten, 1968.

Also author of travel books *Dalmatinischer Aufenthalt,* 1934, *Aus der goldenen Muschel,* 1948, *Serpentara,* 1957, and *San Pietro,* 1957.

IN GERMAN; ESSAYS

Der Arbeiter: Herrschaft und Gestalt, Hanseatische Verlagsanstalt, 1932.

Blaetter und Steine (title means "Leaves and Stones"), Hanseatische Verlagsanstalt, 1934.

Geheimnisse der Sprache: Zwei Essays, Hanseatische Verlagsanstalt, 1939, reprinted, V. Klostermann, 1963.

Ueber die Linie (title means "Across the Line"), V. Klostermann, 1950.

Der Waldgang, V. Klostermann, 1951.

Der gordische Knoten, V. Klostermann, 1953.

Das Sanduhrubuch, V. Klostermann, 1954.

An der Zeitmauer (title means "At the Time Barrier"), E. Klett, 1959.

Der Weltstaat: Organismus und Organisation, E. Klett, 1960.

Essays, E. Klett, 1960.

Sgraffiti, E. Klett, 1960.

Typus, Name, Gestalt, E. Klett, 1963.

Grenzgaenge, Olten, 1965.

Grenzgaenge: Essays, Reden, Traeume, E. Klett, 1966.

Zahlen und Goetter, Philemon und Baucis: Zwei Essays, E. Klett, 1974.

(With Wolf Jobst Sieder) *Baeume: Gedichte und Bilder,* Propylaeen Verlag, 1976.

IN GERMAN; EDITOR

Die Unvergessenen, W. Andermann, 1928.

Der Kampf um das Reich (title means "The Struggle for the Empire"), Rhein & Ruhr, c. 1929.

Das anlitz des Weltkrieges, Neufeld & Henius, 1930.

Franz Schauwecker, *Der feurige Weg,* Frundsberg Verlag, 1930.

Krieg und Krieger, Junker & Duennhaupt, 1930.

Antoine Rivarol, *Rivarol,* V. Klostermann, 1956.

IN GERMAN; OTHER

Das abenteuerliche Herz: Aufzeichnungen bei Tag und Nacht, Frundsberg Verlag, 1929, 2nd edition published as *Das abenteuerliche Herz: Figuren und Capriccios,* Hanseatische Verlagsanstalt, 1938.

Luftfahrt ist not!, W. Andermann, 1930.

Sprache und Koerperbau, Verlag der Arche, 1947.

Heliopolis: Rueckblick auf eine Stadt (novel), Heliopolis Verlag, 1949.

Strahlungen (personal narrative; title means "Radiations"), Heliopolis Verlag, 1949, three-volume edition, Deutscher Taschenbuch Verlag, 1964.

Besuch auf Godenholm (stories; title means "Visit in Godenholm"), V. Klostermann, 1952.

Capriccios: Eine Auswahl, Reclam Verlag, 1953.

Erzaehlende Schriften, E. Klett, 1960.

Werke (title means "Works"), ten volumes, E. Klett, 1960.

(Compiler with Klaus Ulrich Leistikow) *Mantrana: Ein Spiel,* E. Klett, 1964.

Subtile Jagden (memoirs; title means "The Subtle Chase"), E. Klett, 1967.

Ad hoc, E. Klett, 1970.

Annaeherungen: Drogen und Rausch, E. Klett, 1970.

Sinn und Bedeutung: Ein Figurenspiel, E. Klett, 1971.

Die Zwille (semi-autobiographical; title means "The Slingshot"), E. Klett, 1973.

Ausgewaehlte Erzaehlungen, E. Klett, 1975.

(With Alfred Kubin) *Eine Begegnung* (correspondence), Propylaeen Verlag, 1975.

Saemtliche Werke (collected works), eighteen volumes, Klett-Cotta, 1978-83.

Siebzig verweht, two volumes, Klett-Cotta, 1980-81.

Autor und Autorschaft (title means "Author and Authorship"), Klett-Cotta, 1984.

Zwei Mal Halley (title means "Halley Revisited"), Klett-Cotta, 1987.

Zeitspruenge (title means "Time-Fissures"), Klett-Cotta, 1990.

Die Schere (title means "The Shears"), Klett-Cotta, 1990.

Siebzig verweht III, Klett-Cotta, 1993.

OTHER

Coeditor of *Standarte, Arminius, Widerstand, Der Vormarsch* and *Die Kommenden* magazines, late 1920s-early 1930s. Coeditor and cofounder, *Antaios: Zeitschrift fuer eine freie Welt,* 1959. Some of Juenger's work has appeared in French and Swiss editions.

ADAPTATIONS: Edgardo Cozarinsky's film *One Man's War* is based on Juenger's Parisian diaries.

SIDELIGHTS: One of modern Germany's foremost men of letters, Ernst Juenger is best known for his *In Stahlgewittern: Aus dem Tagebuch eines Strosstruppfuehrers,* translated as *Storm of Steel: From the Diary of a German Storm-Troop Officer on the Western Front.* He has also published highly-acclaimed travel books, diaries, and essays. Speaking of the diversity of Juenger's accomplishment, Carl Steiner writes in the *Dictionary of Literary Biography:* "The soldier-philosopher, a combination with which ancient civilizations such as those of Greece and Rome were quite comfortable, has become a rarity in the modern age of progressive overspecialization. If one adds the categories of naturalist, writer, and essayist, one moves into even more rarified circles. Ernst Juenger, blending the courage of the soldier with the curiosity of the student of life forms, the skill and imagination of the literary stylist with the probing intellect of the researcher, is such an exceptional individual. What makes him even more special is the fact that he was still writing in his ninety-first year. He is the oldest German writer of stature, and his represents the longest life span of any major figure in the annals of German literature. To call him the doyen of twentieth-century German letters is indeed no exaggeration."

As a young man, Juenger was fascinated by warfare and the military life. His longing to experience battle firsthand asserted itself at the age of sixteen when he ran away from home to join the French Foreign Legion. Juenger's father did not share his son's enthusiasm, however, and with the help of the authorities, located and returned the underaged boy to his home. But when World War I erupted, Juenger immediately enlisted in the German Army. He distinguished himself on the Western Front, received Germany's highest military honor, and was wounded seven times. From his World War I experiences came his first book, *In Stahlgewittern: Aus dem Tagebuch eines Strosstruppfuehrers,* translated into English as *Storm of Steel: From the Diary of a German Storm-Troop Officer on the Western Front* and based on the diaries he kept at the time. The book was praised across the United States as a significant and revealing insight into the mind of a German officer.

In his introduction to *Storm of Steel,* R. H. Mottram asserts that the work was profound and meaningful because the author did not shy away from depicting events and feelings exactly as they occurred; he censored nothing. Mottram's description of Juenger reveals much of the tone of the work: "He was no middle-aged civilian, unwillingly taking up arms and finding all his worst preconceptions

abundantly fulfilled. He was nearly as good a specimen as ever worshipped Mars [the Roman god of war], and to what did he come? To that unescapable doom that brings to meet violence precisely such resistance as shall cancel and annul it." Mottram concludes that "on this point the strength and finality of the testimony cannot be missed."

Juenger does not apologize in *Storm of Steel* for the bloodshed and violence of warfare, but rather revels in the glories of battle. As he writes in the book: "War means the destruction of the enemy without scruple and by any means. War is the harshest of all trades, and the masters of it can only entertain humane feelings as long as they do no harm." A reviewer for *New Statesman* declares: "Herr Juenger has a remarkable gift for describing certain emotions, complex and hard of analysis, which beset, and still have power to bewilder, the man of even average sensibility who was brought by war into abrupt contact with the most primitive of human experiences."

In addition to recommending it to the general public, several reviewers consider *Storm of Steel* a book imperative for pacifists to read and study. As F. Van de Water of the *New York Evening Post* observes, the book "presents a view of battle not generally recognized, yet too logical to be overlooked." A reviewer for *Spectator* also advises pacifists to heed "this fine book," commenting, "It is even better propaganda than [Erich M. Remarque's] *All Quiet on the Western Front,* for there is a certain horrible lure in the completeness of that work of genius, whereas this is a ghastly, gripping story whose truth and whose horror stand out all the plainer for the author's psychic blindness."

After the war, Juenger attended the University of Leipzig where he studied both philosophy and zoology, becoming interested particularly in entomology, the study of insects. Hilary Barr, translator of Juenger's *A Dangerous Encounter,* told *CA* that "the [German] term 'Subtiler Jagd,' which Juenger uses throughout his works, refers to his entomological excursions (primarily beetle-chasing) as well as to his practice (more a second vocation) of observing close-up the wonders of the animal and plant kingdoms. He is also a passionate collector and renowned entomologist (coleopterist)." Numerous reviewers, in fact, attribute his probing and analytical approach in writing to his university training in the sciences. It was at this time that he first became politically active and participated in radical organizations. His political views maintained that a democracy of all the people could never retain order in the world. He looked forward to the rise of the new "Federation" and the coming of the new man, an industrial individual who would take responsibility to restore order to the chaotic world. He defined and explained these ideas in his 1932 work, *Der Arbeiter: Herrschaft und Gestalt,* or "The Worker."

When Hitler came to power, Juenger dropped out of the political scene due to his disillusionment with the Nazi party. Although the Nazis were striving for totalitarianism, he felt that their interpretation was a mockery of the "true system" he advocated. With this in mind, in 1939 he wrote *Auf den Marmorklippen,* an allegorical novel based on Nazi practices and later translated as *On the Marble Cliffs.* A major turning point in his literary career, he first offered in this work a more humanistic and, some insist, almost Christian point of view.

On the Marble Cliffs depicts the annihilation of a peaceful and gentle country by "barbarian hordes." Quickly recognized as anti-Nazi when released to English-speaking audiences, the book miraculously escaped the censor's eye when published in Germany in 1939. By the time the German government realized the novel's true meaning and halted further publication, tens of thousands of copies were already in circulation. Juenger's honor was not seriously questioned, however, for he was loyally serving with the German Army at the time.

Alfred Werner of the *New York Times* praises the book, but complains that "despite its poetical merits and its unmistakable challenge to Hitlerism, [*On the Marble Cliffs*] fails to uplift the reader because of its impotent hopelessness." A reviewer for the *New Yorker* claims that "Mr. Juenger's allegory, which is full of the same sort of hobgoblinism that the Nazis themselves went in for—skulls, torches, midnight revels, and so on—is so murky that most readers are likely to miss the point."

As an appeal for humanist values, Juenger wrote *Der Friede: Ein Wort an die Jugend Europas, ein Wort an die Jugend der Welt,* translated as *The Peace,* in late 1941. Barr told *CA* that "he drafted the essay in the fall and winter of '41-'42, when German arms were most successful, and kept it hidden in a reinforced safe so that the Gestapo, who had him under continual observation, should not get hold of it. Copies were passed from hand to hand in secret; [it was] finally published in 1945." Dedicated to the memory of his son Ernstel, who was killed in action in 1944, the work is an acknowledgement of Germany's guilt and a plea for world peace to end the senseless sacrifice of human life. Although he still repudiated liberalism, Juenger called for a renunciation of nationalism and the affirmation of the individual. Barr also told *CA* that Juenger "pleaded for a politically united Europe, a new and legitimate order analogous to the Holy Roman Empire." Erik von Kuehnelt-Leddihn of *Catholic World* observes that *The Peace* "is not only a highly prophetic piece of writing in the finest literary style . . . but it is also a blueprint for the sound peace which should have followed this terrible massacre."

Juenger employed a fantastic and dream-like style of writing in his next book, *Glaeserne Bienen,* published in English translation as *The Glass Bees.* This allegorical novel tells of a former cavalryman, Captain Richard, who must perform extensive feats of strength and endurance in the magical garden of political dictator Zapparoni in order to secure employment. The garden is filled with thousands of glass bees, tiny mechanized robots able to lay waste to all civilization if summoned. According to E. S. Pisko of the *Christian Science Monitor,* the glass bees symbolize "the destruction Juenger sees modern technology wreaking upon human society." Siegfried Mandel of the *New York Times Book Review* commends the novel as "harrowing and thought-disturbing," asserting that it "contributes not only to prophetic and nihilistic literature but also to an understanding of the inner and outer forces that shape many a man's attitude toward tyranny."

BIOGRAPHICAL/CRITICAL SOURCES:

BOOKS

Arnold, Heinz Ludwig, editor, *Wandlung und Wiederkehr: Festschrift zum 70. Geburtstag Ernst Juenger,* Georgi (Aachen), 1965.
Arnold, H. L., *Ernst Juenger,* Steglitz (Berlin), 1966.
Baumer, Franz, *Ernst Juenger,* Colloquium (Berlin), 1967.
Bohrer, Karl Heinz, *Die Asthetik des Schreckens: Die pessimistische Romantik und Ernst Juengers Fruehwerk,* Hanser (Munich), 1978.
Brock, Erich, *Ernst Juenger und die Problematik der Gegenwart,* Schwabe (Basel), 1943.
Decombis, Marcel, *Ernst Juenger: L'homme et l'oeuvre jusqu'en 1936,* Aubier (Paris), 1943.
Dictionary of Literary Biography, Volume 56: *German Fiction Writers, 1914-1945,* Gale, 1987.
Hietala, Marjatta, *Der neue Nationalismus in der Publizistik Ernst Juengers und des Kreises um ihn 1920-1933,* Suomalaison Tiedeakatemian Toimituksia (Helsinki), 1975.
Juenger, Ernst, *Storm of Steel: From the Diary of a German Storm-Troop Officer on the Western Front,* translation by Basil Creighton, Doubleday, 1929, reprinted, H. Fertig, 1975.
Katzmann, Volker, *Ernst Juengers magischer Realismus,* Olms (Hildesheim), 1975.
Kerker, Arnim, *Ernst Juenger—Klaus Mann: Gemeinsamkeit und Gegensatz in Literatur und Politik,* Bouvier (Bonn), 1974.
Konrad, Helmut, *Kosmos: Politische Philosophie im Werk Ernst Juengers,* Blasaditsch (Vienna), 1972.
Loose, Gerhard, *Ernst Juenger,* Twayne (New York), 1974.

Martin, Alfred von, *Der heroische Nihilismus und seine Uberwindung: Ernst Juengers Weg durch die Krise,* Scherpe (Krefeld), 1948.

Mohler, Arnim, editor, *Die Schleife: Dokumente zum Weg von Ernst Juenger,* Arche (Zurich), 1955.

Muehleisen, H., and H. P. des Coudres, *Bibliographie der Werke Ernst Juengers,* Klett-Cotta, 1985.

Mueller-Schwefe, Hans-Rudolf, *Ernst Juenger,* Barmen (Wuppertal), 1951.

Nebel, Gerhard, *Ernst Juenger und das Schicksal des Menschen,* Marees (Wuppertal), 1948.

Paetel, Karl O., *Ernst Juenger: Eine Bibliographie,* Lutz & Meyer, 1953.

Paetel, K. O., *Ernst Juenger in Selbstzeugnissen und Bilddokumenten,* Rowohlt (Hamburg), 1962.

Schwartz, Hans Peter, *Der konservative Anarchist: Politik und Zeitkritik Ernst Juengers,* Rombach (Freiburg), 1962.

Stern, Joseph Peter, *Ernst Juenger: A Writer of Our Time,* Yale University Press, 1953.

Woods, Roger, *Ernst Juenger and the Nature of Political Commitment,* Heinz (Stuttgart), 1982.

PERIODICALS

Atlantic, May, 1961.

Catholic World, November, 1948.

Christian Science Monitor, March 2, 1961.

Nation, March 27, 1948.

New Statesman, August 17, 1929.

New Yorker, March 20, 1948.

New York Evening Post, September 28, 1929.

New York Times, April 4, 1978.

New York Times Book Review, February 19, 1961.

Spectator, June 22, 1929.

Texas Studies in Literature and Language, winter, 1965.

Yale Review, June, 1961.

*   *   *

JUNGER, Ernst
   See JUENGER, Ernst

K

KAISER, Christopher B(arina) 1941-

PERSONAL: Born October 16, 1941, in Greenwich, CT; son of Herbert John (a businessperson) and Olga Rita (a musician; maiden name, Barina) Kaiser; married Martha Mercaldi (a primary school teacher), June 27, 1970; children: Justin Barina, Matthew Emerson, Patrick Ellwood. *Education:* Harvard University, A.B. (cum laude), 1963; University of Colorado at Boulder, Ph.D., 1968; Gordon-Conwell Theological Seminary, M.Div. (summa cum laude), 1971; University of Edinburgh, Ph.D., 1974.

ADDRESSES: Home—246 Norwood Ave., Holland, MI 49424. *Office*—Western Theological Seminary, Holland, MI 49423-3696.

CAREER: Gordon College, Wenham, MA, part-time lecturer in physics and astronomy, 1968-71; University of Edinburgh, Edinburgh, Scotland, lecturer in Christian dogmatics, 1973-75; QEI, Inc., Bedford, MA, computer scientist, 1975-76; Western Theological Seminary, Holland, MI, visiting professor, 1976-77, assistant professor, 1977-82, associate professor, 1982-88, professor of historical and systematic theology, 1988—. Hope Reformed Church, elder, 1979—; Reformed Church in America (RCA), ordained minister, 1980, member of the commission on theology of the General Program Council, 1988-1992, RCA ecumenical delegate to theology committee of the Caribbean and North American Area Council of the World Alliance of Reformed Churches (WARC), 1988—; RCA ecumenical delegate to Official Dialogue between WARC and the Oriental Orthodox churches, 1994—. Center of Theological Inquiry, resident member, 1984, 1987; participant in the Official Dialogue between WARC and the Eastern Orthodox Church, 1988-94;

MEMBER: Institute for Theological Encounter with Science and Technology, American Scientific Affiliation, American Society of Church History, Calvin Studies Society, Conference on Faith and History, Society for the History of Technology, Institute for Global Ethics.

WRITINGS:

The Doctrine of God: An Historical Survey, Crossway (Westchester, IL), 1982.
Creation and the History of Science, (third volume in "History of Christian Theology" series), Eerdmans Publishing (Grand Rapids, MI), 1991.

Contributor to books, including *One God in Trinity,* edited by Peter Toon and James D. Spiceland, Samuel Bagster (London), 1980. Contributor to various theology and science journals, including *Calvin Theological Journal, Calviniana, Horizons in Biblical Theology, Reformed Review, Scottish Journal of Theology, Astrophysical Journal, Asbury Theological Journal, Crux, Convivium, Religious Studies,* and *Science, Technology, and Society;* book review editor of *Reformed Review,* 1977—; member of publications committee of Western Theological Seminary, 1977—.

SIDELIGHTS: Christopher B. Kaiser told *CA:* "Personally I have moved from a position of skeptical scientist to that of Christian humanist. Much of my work is motivated by a desire to understand the meaning of Christian faith in relation to the development of science and technology. As a theologian my task is to test and reform the traditional expressions of faith on the basis of past history and also the needs of an emerging world culture in which science and technology will play a prominent role. Take, for example, the two most fundamental doctrines of the Christian faith, the Trinity and creation *ex nihilo.* The Trinity has come down to us as a mind-boggling idea that has no apparent relation to life or history. But the emergence of evolutionary explanations of life and the tendencies in a technological society towards individualism and isolation have turned our attention to the question of the meaning of our own personhood. From this perspective, it becomes possible to rediscover neglected aspects of the traditional doctrine of the Trinity, in particular, as I explain in my book *Doctrine of God,* those that stress the ultimate nature of reality (anterior to evolution) as personal, where personhood is relational or interpersonal.

"If this is so, we may take our own experiences in intimacy and the excitement of building relationships as intimations of the ultimate and anticipations of some future perfection towards which we now strive. The doctrine of the Trinity thus gives structure to the experience of modernity even as the problems of modernity elicit new depths of meaning from the doctrine.

"A corollary of the interpersonal understanding of ultimate reality is a new sense of what it means to be created in the image of God. That image resides, not in our individual natures, but in our relatedness to others. The image of the Trinity is ultimately the composite of all possible interpersonal relationships, and the defacing of that image can be seen in the alienation that springs from poverty and injustice wherever they occur, at home or abroad.

"If the doctrine of the Trinity establishes the nature of the Ultimate and the goal towards which we strive, the doctrine of creation assures us that the present condition of things—depersonalizing as it is—can and will be changed. In the beginning God created what is out of nothing, *ex nihilo.* There are no constraints built into the cosmos other than his (or her) will. Moreover, in the incarnation of the Word and the outpouring of the Spirit, God is imbuing humans with all the powers and all the responsibilities that he himself normally shoulders. In the early Church people actually believed this, and as I discuss in *Creation and the History of Science,* much of the impetus towards modern science and technology grew out of such faith. A rediscovery of the meaning of faith in God the Triune Creator can thus bring a sense of direction and help establish ethical priorities in our lives as we manage the development of technology and recreate the world in which we and our children will live."

BIOGRAPHICAL/CRITICAL SOURCES:

PERIODICALS

Calvin Theological Journal, 1985, pp. 287-88.
Journal of the Evangelical Theological Society, September, 1984, pp. 359-60.
Scottish Journal of Theology, 1984, pp. 386-87.

*   *   *

KAMENETZ, Rodger 1950-

PERSONAL: Born January 20, 1950, in Baltimore, MD; son of Irvin and Miriam Kamenetz; married Moira Crone

(a fiction writer), October 15, 1979; children: Anya Miriam, Kezia Vida. *Education:* Yale University, B.A., 1970; Johns Hopkins University, M.A., 1972; Stanford University, M.A., 1975.

ADDRESSES: Home—2343 Terrace Ave., Baton Rouge, LA 70806. *Office*—Department of English, Louisiana State University, Baton Rouge, LA 70803.

CAREER: Louisiana State University, Baton Rouge, associate professor, 1985-90, professor of English, 1990—, director of creative writing program, 1983-86, director of Jewish Studies minor, 1993—.

WRITINGS:

The Missing Jew (poems), Dryad (Takoma Park, MD), 1980.
Nympholepsy (poems), Dryad, 1985.
Terra Infirma (autobiographical essays), University of Arkansas Press (Fayetteville), 1985.
The Missing Jew: New and Selected Poems, Time Being Books, 1992.
The Jew in the Lotus: A Poet's Rediscovery of Jewish Identity in Buddhist India, Harper (San Francisco), 1994.

Poetry represented in various anthologies, including *Voices within the Ark,* Avon (New York City), 1980. Also contributor to numerous periodicals, including *Antioch Review, Missouri Review, New England Review, Pennsylvania Review, Ploughshares, Grand Street, New Republic, North American Review, Southern Review,* and *Tikkun.*

WORK IN PROGRESS: Stuck, a book of poems, for Time Being Books, 1996.

SIDELIGHTS: Writing in the *Sewanee Review,* Paul Ramsey praised Rodger Kamenetz's *The Missing Jew,* noting that the author "is a wonderfully pensive, able writer, sprucely rhythmical. The rhythms and Jewish speech-patterns remarkably blend. The patterns of development are many and satisfying: narrative, argument, thoughtful surprises, dialogue, questions and answers." And Andrei Codrescu commented in the *San Francisco Review of Books* that the "ear at work here is as good as W[illiam] C[arlos] Williams' in the early poems."

Kamenetz once told *CA:* "*The Missing Jew* started as poems I wrote in the voice of my dead grandfather. I soon came to realize, by studying Jewish texts, particularly the Talmud, that I could hear echoes of his voice in those works, so I came to enlarge the scope of the book to include larger chunks of Jewish history and literature. I did not intend to be an exclusively ethnic writer. I think the specialization of Jewish literature in the West is absurd since so much of Western thought is Jewish thought. The title was partly inspired by a remark of a friend that the word 'Jew' was impossible to use in a poem, partly by the death of my grandfather, and partly by my own search for the Jew that was missing in me.

"In *Terra Infirma* I chose prose as a way of deepening my exploration of a difficult terrain: the death of my mother. I felt I wanted to lay bare everything in this book without the constriction of the formal considerations of poetry. I found, however, that prose offered formal challenges of its own so that I became equally fascinated with the process and the content. I call these writings essays, but in the radical sense." The book describes the author's ambiguous relationship with his mother, a strong-willed woman who loved her children possessively. *Newsweek* reviewer Gene Lyons commented that the combination "is an oddly haunting book—as impossible to summarize as it is to forget."

Kamenetz more recently told *CA*: "*The Jew in the Lotus: A Poet's Rediscovery of Jewish Identity in Buddhist India* . . . is a spiritual adventure travelogue—an account of my trip to India accompanying a group of rabbis to a meeting with the Dalai Lama. It also describes the convergence of mystical Judaism and Tibetan Buddhism and includes interviews with prominent Jewish Buddhists and Jewish Hindus including Ram Dass and Allen Ginsberg."

BIOGRAPHICAL/CRITICAL SOURCES:

PERIODICALS

Baltimore Jewish Times, February 16, 1979.
Entertainment Weekly, October 7, 1994.
Forward, December 11, 1992; June 3, 1994.
Newsweek, May 19, 1986.
New York Times Book Review, July 24, 1994.
Poetry Flash, April, 1981.
San Francisco Review of Books, December, 1980.
Sewanee Review, fall, 1980.
Southern Review, spring, 1986.

*   *   *

KANE, Pablo
See ZACHARY, Hugh

*   *   *

KANTO, Peter
See ZACHARY, Hugh

*   *   *

KAPLAN, Benjamin   1911-

PERSONAL: Born April 9, 1911, in New York, NY; son of Morris and Mary (Berman) Kaplan; married Felicia Lamport, April 16, 1942; children: James Lamport, Nancy Lamport. *Education:* City College (now City College of the City University of New York), A.B., 1929; Columbia University, LL.B., 1933.

ADDRESSES: Home—2 Bond St., Cambridge, MA 02138-2308. *Office*—Harvard Law School, Cambridge, MA 02138.

CAREER: Admitted to New York State Bar, 1934, and Bar of Massachusetts, 1950. Greenbaum, Wolff & Ernst (law firm), New York, NY, began as associate, became a member, 1934-42, 1946; Harvard University, Cambridge, MA, visiting professor of law, 1947-48, professor of law, 1948-61, Royall professor of Law, 1961-72, Royall Professor emeritus, 1972—; Supreme Judicial Court of Massachusetts, Boston, associate justice, 1972-81. National Association for the Advancement of Colored People, director of Legal Defense and Educational Fund, Inc.; Copyright Society of U.S.A., trustee; Columbia Law School, member of executive committee on project for effective justice; Judicial Conference of United States, reporter to advisory committee on civil rules, 1960-66, member, 1966-70; co-reporter of restatement of law judgments to American Law Institute, 1970-73. *Military service:* U.S. Army, 1942-46, became lieutenant colonel; awarded Legion of Merit and Bronze Star.

MEMBER: American Law Institute, Bar Association of City of New York, Phi Beta Kappa.

AWARDS, HONORS: A.M., Harvard University, 1948; LL.D., Suffolk University, 1974, Harvard University, 1981, and Northwestern University, 1981.

WRITINGS:

(Editor with Richard H. Field) *Materials for a Basic Course in Civil Procedure,* Foundation Press (Brooklyn), 1950, sixth edition, 1990.
(Editor with Livingston Hall) *Judicial Administration and the Common Man,* American Academy of Political and Social Science (Philadelphia), 1953.
(With Ralph S. Brown, Jr.) *Cases on Copyright, Unfair Competition, and Other Topics Bearing on the Protection of Literary, Musical, and Artistic Works,* Foundation Press, 1960.
An Unhurried View of Copyright, Columbia University Press (New York), 1967.
(With Field and Kevin M. Clermont) *Teacher's Manual to Accompany Materials for a Basic Course in Civil Procedure,* Foundation Press, 1979.
(Editor with Norman S. Goldenberg and Robert J. Switzer) *Casenote Legal Briefs—Copyright: Adaptable to Courses Utilizing Kaplan and Brown's Casebook in Copyright,* Casenotes Publishing Company (Beverly Hills, CA), 1979.

Also contributor to legal journals.*

* * *

KAPLAN, Sidney 1913-1993

PERSONAL: Born March 1, 1913, in New York, NY; died of heart disease, June 15, 1993, in Northampton, MA; son of Henry and Dora (Kuhl) Kaplan; married Emma Nogrady (a librarian), May 6, 1933; children: Cora Lotte Kaplan Lushington, Paul H. D. *Education:* City College (now of the City University of New York), B.A., 1940; Boston University, M.A., 1947; Harvard University, Ph.D., 1960.

CAREER: University of Massachusetts, Amherst, instructor, 1946-51, assistant professor, 1951-56, associate professor, 1956-60, professor of American literature and black studies, 1960-78; writer. Fulbright lecturer and visiting lecturer at University of Thessaloniki, Greece, University of Zagreb, Yugoslavia, and University of Kent, England; *Massachusetts Review*, founder and editor, 1959-63; *Gehenna Press*, editor. Consultant to National Portrait Gallery, Smithsonian Institution, and Public Broadcasting System for *The Civil War* and *Africans in America. Military service* U.S. Army, 1942-45; became first lieutenant.

MEMBER: American Studies Association.

AWARDS, HONORS: Bancroft Award, Association for the Study of Negro Life and History, 1950, for article "The Miscegenation Issue of the Election of 1864."

WRITINGS:

(Editor) Edgar Allan Poe, *The Narrative of A. Gordon Pym*, Hill & Wang (New York City), 1960.
(Editor) Herman Melville, *Battle-Pieces and Aspects of the War*, Scholar's Facsimiles & Reprints (Delmar, NY), 1960, revised edition, University of Massachusetts Press (Amherst), 1972.
The Portrayal of the Negro in American Painting, Bowdoin College Museum of Art (Brunswick, ME), 1964.
(Editor) Samuel Sewall, *The Selling of Joseph: A Memorial*, Gehenna Press, 1968.
(Editor with Jules Chametzky, and contributor) *Black and White in American Culture: An Anthology from the Massachusetts Review*, University of Massachusetts Press, 1969.
(With wife, Emma Nogrady Kaplan) *The Black Presence in the Era of the American Revolution, 1770-1800*, New York Graphic Society (Boston, MA), 1973, revised edition, University of Massachusetts Press, 1989.

American Studies in Black and White: Selected Essays, 1949-1989, edited by Allan D. Austin, University of Massachusetts Press, 1991.

Contributor to *The Image of the Negro in American Literature*, edited by J. E. Hardy and S. L. Gross, University of Chicago Press (Chicago), 1967. Contributor of about forty articles and reviews to history, literature, and black studies journals.

SIDELIGHTS: Sidney Kaplan once commented: "The interrelationships of society, literature, and art in the United States have been my continuing scholarly concern."

OBITUARIES:

PERIODICALS

New York Times, June 19, 1993, p. 10.
Washington Post, June 21, 1993, p. D8.*

* * *

KAUFMAN, Gloria Joan Frances (Shapiro) 1929-

PERSONAL: Born April 5, 1929, in Danbury, CT; daughter of Harry Louis (in business) and Philma (in business; maiden name, Goldfracht) Kaufman; married Samuel Shapiro (a professor), June 19, 1959; children: Leslie Viktora, David. *Education:* Russell Sage College, B.A., 1950; Brooklyn College (now of the City University of New York), M.A., 1952; Brandeis University, Ph.D., 1961.

ADDRESSES: Home and office—305 Wakewa, South Bend, IN 46617.

CAREER: Oakland University, Rochester, MI, instructor, 1960-62, assistant professor of English, 1962-63; self-employed, 1963-65; Indiana University, South Bend, assistant professor, 1965-71, associate professor, 1971-84, professor of English, 1984-93. Member of Women's Shelter Advisory Committee, 1976-80, and policy board, 1977-80; alternate delegate from Indiana to the National Women's Conference, 1977.

MEMBER: National Women's Health Network, National Women's Studies Association, Association of Independent Video and Filmmakers, Center for New Television, Women's Caucus of the Modern Language Association of America, SANE, Shakespeare Association, Union of Concerned Scientists, Women's Action for Nuclear Disarmament (WAND), Women's Institute for Freedom of the Press.

AWARDS, HONORS: Elected to New York Academy of Sciences, 1952, for master's thesis on time in twentieth-century science, philosophy, and literature; Fulbright grant to study philosophy of science at University of Munich, 1956-57; Medal of Honor, Centro Studi Scambi Internazionale, Rome, Italy, 1966, for promoting international poets in the United States.

WRITINGS:

(With Mary Laporte, composer) *Which Witch Is Which?,* Willis Music Co., 1953.
(Editor with Mary Kay Blakely) *Pulling Our Own Strings: Feminist Humor and Satire,* Indiana University Press (Bloomington, IN), 1980, reprint, 1994.
In Stitches: A Patchwork of Feminist Humor & Satire, Indiana University Press, 1991.

Also producer and director of various feminist videotapes, including *Marge Piercy: Poet,* 1979; *Clothes* and *Women, Ritual, and Religion,* both 1983; *The Politics of Humor: A Feminist View, Pornography: Legal Issues and Beyond,* and *Alice Neel,* all 1986.

WORK IN PROGRESS: A novel and a film.

BIOGRAPHICAL/CRITICAL SOURCES:

PERIODICALS

Washington Post, October 14, 1980.

*　　*　　*

KAYE, Harvey J(ordan)　1949-

PERSONAL: Born October 9, 1949, in Englewood, NJ; son of Murray N. (a contractor) and Frances A. (a sales clerk; maiden name, Sehres) Kaye; married Lorna C. Stewart (a secretary), May 5, 1973; children: Rhiannon, Fiona. *Education:* Attended National University of Mexico, 1970; Rutgers University, B.A., 1971; University of London, M.A., 1973; Louisiana State University, Ph.D., 1976. *Politics:* "Democratic socialist." *Religion:* Jewish.

ADDRESSES: Home—523 Larscheid St., Green Bay, WI 54302. *Office*—Department of Social Change and Development, University of Wisconsin—Green Bay, Green Bay, WI 54301.

CAREER: Louisiana State University, Baton Rouge, instructor in social science and assistant director of summer school in Mexico City, 1974, 1975; St. Cloud State University, St. Cloud, MN, assistant professor of social science, 1977-78; University of Wisconsin—Green Bay, assistant professor, 1978-83, associate professor, 1983-85, professor of social change and development, 1985-88, Rosenberg Professor of Social Change and Development, 1990—, chair of department of social change and development, 1985-88, director of Center for History and Social Change, 1990—. Visiting fellow at Institute for Advanced

Research in the Humanities, University of Birmingham, 1986-87. Executor of George Rude's literary estate, 1993—.

MEMBER: American Sociological Association, American Historical Association, Organization of American Historians, American Studies Association, William Morris Society, Wisconsin Labor History Society (vice-president, 1984-86).

AWARDS, HONORS: Wisconsin Humanities Council grant, 1979-80; Lilly Endowment fellow, 1978-79; National Endowment for the Humanities fellow, 1981, 1983; Isaac Deutscher Memorial Prize, 1993, for *The Education of Desire: Marxists and the Writing of History.*

WRITINGS:

The British Marxist Historians: An Introductory Analysis, Basil Blackwell/Polity Press (Oxford, England), 1984.
(Editor and author of introduction) *Selected Writings of V. G. Kiernan,* Volume 1: *History, Classes and Nation-States,* Polity Press/Basil Blackwell, 1988, Volume 2: *Poets, Politics and the People,* Verso (New York City), 1989, Volume 3: *Imperialism and Its Contradictions,* Routledge & Kegan Paul (New York City), 1995.
(Editor and author of introduction) *The Face of the Crowd: Selected Essays of George Rude,* Humanities (Atlantic Highlands, NJ), 1988.
(Editor with Keith McClelland, and contributor) *E. P. Thompson: Critical Perspectives,* Temple University Press (Philadelphia, PA), 1990.
The Powers of the Past: Reflections on the Crisis and the Promise of History, University of Minnesota Press (Minneapolis, MN), 1991.
The Education of Desire: Marxists and the Writing of History, Routledge & Kegan Paul, 1992.
(Editor with Mari Jo Buhle and Paul Buhle, and contributor) *The American Radical,* Routledge & Kegan Paul, 1994.
(Editor) George Rude, *Ideology and Popular Protest,* University of North Carolina Press (Chapel Hill), in press.

Contributor to books, including *After the End of History,* edited by J. Gardner, Collins & Brown (London, England), 1992; *Protest and Survival: Essays for E. P. Thompson,* edited by J. Rule and R. Malcolmson, New Press (New York City), 1993; and *Writing and Reading Arguments: A Rhetoric and Reader,* edited by R. P. Batteiger, Allyn & Bacon (Boston, MA), 1994. Contributor to encyclopedias. Editor with Elliott J. Gorn of "American Radicals" series, Routledge & Kegan Paul, 1994—. Contributor to numerous periodicals, including *Politics and Society, Canadian Review of Sociology and Anthropology, Times Higher Education Supplement, Chronicle of Higher Edu-*

cation, *Radical History Review, Contemporary Sociology,* and *American Historical Review.* Member of editorial board, *Marxist Perspectives,* 1978-80, *Wisconsin Sociologist,* 1985-87, 1991-93, and *Review of Education, Pedagogy and Cultural Studies,* 1993—.

The British Marxist Historians: An Introductory Analysis has been published in Japanese, Spanish, and Chinese.

SIDELIGHTS: Harvey J. Kaye once told *CA:* "All of my writings are concerned with history: historical perspective, historical consciousness, and historical imagination. I attribute this to the influence of my grandfather, a lawyer and student of history. The words of Antonio Gramsci well state the feeling for the past he instilled in me: 'I think you must like history as I did when I was your age, for it deals with men and women as they unite together in society and work and struggle and make a bid for a better life.' Remembrance can contribute to liberation.

"My interest in the British Marxist historians—Maurice Dobb, Rodney Hilton, Christopher Hill, Eric Hobsbawm, George Rude, E. P. Thompson, and Victor Kiernan (along with others)—can be understood in these terms: they have contributed more than any other group of historians to the development of the approach to studying the past known as history from below or from the bottom up; recovering the lives, struggles, and aspirations of the common people, peasants, and workers."

Kaye more recently added: "Increasingly, I find myself exploring the American radical tradition. Co-editing *The American Radical,* for which I wrote the chapter on Tom Paine, I was impressed by the diversity and pluralism which have characterized the history of American radicalism. And I have come to understand America's revolutionaries, rebels and reformers as 'the prophetic memory of American democracy.' Truly a 'tradition,' every generation of American radicals has found inspiration in the struggles and aspirations of its predecessors, and this experience, or process, has regularly transcended lines of race, ethnicity, and gender. That is the subject of my next writing project."

BIOGRAPHICAL/CRITICAL SOURCES:

PERIODICALS

New Republic, February 10, 1986.
Times Literary Supplement, May 23, 1986.

*　　*　　*

KAYMOR, Patrice Maguilene
    See SENGHOR, Leopold Sedar

KELLEY, True (Adelaide) 1946-

PERSONAL: Born February 25, 1946, in Cambridge, MA; daughter of Mark E. (an illustrator) and Adelaide (an artist; maiden name, True) Kelley; married Steven Lindblom (a writer and illustrator); children: Jada Winter Lindblom. *Education:* University of New Hampshire, B.A., 1968; attended Rhode Island School of Design, 1968-71.

ADDRESSES: Home—Old Denny Hill, Warner, NH 03278.

CAREER: Freelance illustrator, 1971—; writer, 1978—.

MEMBER: Society of Childrens' Book Writers and Illustrators, Authors Guild, Authors League of America, Audubon Society, Warner Raconteur's Association.

AWARDS, HONORS: "Children's Choice" book, International Reading Association, 1982, for *A Valentine for Fuzzboom.*

WRITINGS:

JUVENILE; SELF-ILLUSTRATED

(With husband, Steven Lindblom) *The Mouses' Terrible Christmas,* Lothrop, 1978.
(With Lindblom) *The Mouses' Terrible Halloween,* Lothrop, 1980.
A Valentine for Fuzzboom, Houghton, 1981.
Buggly Bear's Hiccup Cure, Parents' Magazine Press, 1982.
(With Lindblom) *Let's Give Kitty a Bath,* Addison-Wesley, 1982.
The Mystery of the Stranger in the Barn, Dodd, 1986.
Look, Baby! Listen, Baby! Do, Baby!, Dutton, 1987.
Let's Eat!, Dutton, 1989.
Day Care Teddy Bear, Random House (New York), 1990.
(With Christine Kleitsch) *It Happened at Pickle Lake,* Dutton, 1993.
I've Got Chicken Pox, Dutton, 1994.
Hammers and Mops, Pencils and Pots, Crown (New York), 1994.

ILLUSTRATOR

Ann Cole, Carolyn Haas, Faith Bushnell, and Betty Weinberger, *I Saw a Purple Cow,* Little, Brown, 1972.
Franklyn Branley, *Sun Dogs and Shooting Stars: A Skywatcher's Calendar,* Houghton, 1980.
Michael Pellowski, *Clara Cow Joins the Circus,* Parents Magazine Press, 1981.
Cole, Haas, and Weinberger, *Purple Cow to the Rescue,* Little, Brown, 1982.
Branley, *Water for the World,* Crowell, 1982.
Gilda Berger and Melven Berger, *The Whole World of Hands,* Houghton, 1982.

Joanne Oppenheim, *James Will Never Die,* Dodd, 1982.

Sunshine and Snowflakes: The Scribblers Play Book, Western Publishing (New York), 1982.

Ben Schneideman, *Let's Learn BASIC,* Little, Brown, 1984.

Branley, *Shivers and Goose Bumps: How We Keep Warm,* Crowell, 1984.

Joyce S. Mitchell, *My Mommy Makes Money,* Little, Brown, 1984.

Joanna Cole, *Cuts, Breaks, Bruises, and Burns: How Your Body Heals,* Harper (New York), 1985.

Eric Arnold and Jeff Loeb, *Lights Out!: Kids Talk about Summer Camp,* Little, Brown, 1986.

Branley, *What the Moon Is Like,* Crowell, 1987.

Patricia Lauber, *Get Ready for Robots,* Crowell, 1987.

Riki Levinson, *Touch! Touch!,* Dutton, 1987.

Branley, *It's Raining Cats and Dogs,* Houghton, 1987.

J. Cole, *Mixed-Up Magic,* Scholastic (New York), 1987.

James Deem, *How to Find a Ghost,* Houghton, 1988.

Philip Balestrino, *The Skeleton Inside You,* Crowell, 1989.

Debra Meryl, *Baby's Peek-a-Boo Album,* Putnam (New York), 1989.

A. F. Bauman, *Guess Where You're Going, Guess What You'll Do,* Houghton, 1989.

(With Lindblom) Gregory Niles and Douglas Eldredge, *The Fossil Factory,* Addison-Wesley, 1989.

Susan Breslow and Sally Blakemore, *I Really Want a Dog,* Dutton, 1989.

Branley, *Superstar,* Crowell, 1990.

Paul Showers, *How Many Teeth?,* Harper, 1991.

Deem, *How to Catch a Flying Saucer,* Houghton, 1991.

Michaela Morgan, *Dinostory,* Dutton, 1991.

Judy Donnelly, *All around the World,* Grosset & Dunlap, 1991.

Showers, *Look at Your Eyes,* Harper, 1992.

Wendy Lewison, *Where's Baby?,* Scholastic, 1992.

Lewison, *Uh-Oh Baby,* Scholastic, 1992.

Lewison, *Bye-Bye Baby,* Scholastic, 1992.

Stephanie Calmenson, *Rollerskates!,* Scholastic, 1992.

Deem, *How to Hunt Buried Treasure,* Houghton, 1992.

Spider on the Floor: A Raffi Song Book, Crown, 1993.

Deem, *How to Read Your Mother's Mind,* Houghton, 1993.

Deem, *How to Make Your Mummy Talk,* Houghton, 1995.

Patricia Brennan Demuth, *In Trouble with Teacher,* Dutton, 1995.

Also illustrator of numerous textbooks.

OTHER

It's Raining Cats and Dogs has been published in Dutch.

KELLY, Robert 1935-

PERSONAL: Born September 24, 1935, in Brooklyn, NY; son of Samuel Jason and Margaret Rose (Kane) Kelly; married Joan Elizabeth Laskin, 1955 (divorced, 1969), married Helen Belinky, April, 1969 (divorced, 1978), married Charlotte Mandell, 1993. *Education:* City College (now City College of the City University of New York), A.B., 1955; attended Columbia University, 1955-58.

ADDRESSES: Office—Department of English, Bard College, Annandale-on-Hudson, NY 12504.

CAREER: Continental Translation Service, New York City, translator, 1955-58; Wagner College, New York City, lecturer in English, 1960-61; Bard College, Annandale-on-Hudson, NY, assistant professor of English, 1961-68, professor of English, 1974—; Milton Avery Graduate School of the Arts, Annandale-on-Hudson, NY, codirector of writing program, 1974—. Cofounder, with George Economou, *Chelsea Review,* 1957-60, and *Trobar,* 1960—; editor, *Matter,* 1963—; State University of New York at Buffalo, Buffalo, NY, assistant professor of English, 1964; Tufts University, Medford, MA, visiting lecturer in modern poetry, 1966; New York City Writers Conference, Staten Island, conducted fiction workshop, summer, 1967. Poet-in-residence at California Institute of Technology, Pasadena, 1971-72; University of Kansas, 1975; Dickinson College, 1976; and Naropa Institute, 1977—.

AWARDS, HONORS: Los Angeles Times First Annual Book Award, 1980, for *Kill the Messenger Who Brings Bad News.*

WRITINGS:

POETRY

Armed Descent, Hawk's Well Press, 1961.

Her Body against Time (English and Spanish editions), Ediciones El Corno Emplumado, 1963.

Tabula, Dialogue Press, 1964.

Enstasy, Matter, 1964.

Matter/Fact/Sheet/1, Matter, 1964.

Matter/Fact/Sheet/2, Matter, 1964.

Round Dances, illustrated by Josie Rosenfeld, Trobar, 1964.

(With Jerome Rothenberg) *Lunes/Sightings,* Hawk's Well Press, 1964.

Lectiones, Duende, 1965.

Song XXIV, Pym-Randall Press, 1966.

Weeks, Ediciones El Corno Emplumado, 1966.

Words in Service, Robert Lamberton, 1966.

Devotions, Salitter, 1967.

Twenty Poems, Matter, 1967.

Axon Dendron Tree (long poem), Matter, 1967.

Crooked Bridge Love Society, Salitter, 1967.

A Joining: A Sequence for H.D., Black Sparrow Press, 1967.

Alpha, J. Fisher, 1967.

From the Common Shore, Book V, Minkoff, 1968.

Songs I-XXX, Pym-Randall Press, 1968.

Statement, Black Sparrow Press, 1968.

Sonnets, Black Sparrow Press, 1968.

Finding the Measure, Black Sparrow Press, 1968.

The Common Shore, Books I-V: A Long Poem about America, Black Sparrow Press, 1969.

We Are the Arbiters of Beast Desire, MBVL, 1969.

A California Journal, Big Venus, 1969.

Kali Yuga, Grossman, 1970.

Flesh, Dream, Book, Black Sparrow Press, 1971.

Ralegh, Black Sparrow Press, 1972.

The Pastorals, Black Sparrow Press, 1972.

Reading Her Notes, Salisbury Press, 1972.

The Tears of Edmund Burke, privately printed, 1973.

The Mill of Particulars, Black Sparrow Press, 1973.

Whaler Frigate Clippership, Tansy, 1973.

The Belt, University of Connecticut Library, 1974.

The Loom, Black Sparrow Press, 1975.

Sixteen Odes, Black Sparrow Press, 1976.

The Lady Of, Black Sparrow Press, 1977.

The Convections, Black Sparrow Press, 1977.

The Book of Persephone, Treacle Press, 1978.

Kill the Messenger Who Brings Bad News, Black Sparrow Press, 1979.

Sentence, Station Hill Press, 1980.

Spiritual Exercises, Black Sparrow Press, 1981.

The Alchemist to Mercury: An Alternate Opus, edited by Jed Rasula, North Atlantic, 1981.

Mulberry Women, illustrated by Matt Phillips, Hiersoux, 1982.

Under Words, Black Sparrow Press, 1983.

Thor's Thrush, Coincidence Press, 1984.

Not This Island Music, Black Sparrow Press, 1987.

The Flowers of Unceasing Coincidence, edited by George Quasha, Station Hill Press, 1988.

Oahu, St. Lazaire Press, 1988.

Ariadne, St. Lazaire Press, 1991.

Manifesto for the Next New York School, Leave Press, 1991.

A Strange Market, Black Sparrow Press, 1992.

Selected Poems, 1960-1992, in press.

PROSE

The Well wherein a Deer's Head Bleeds (play; produced in New York, 1964), Black Sparrow Press, 1968.

The Scorpions (novel), Doubleday, 1967.

Eros and Psyche (play; music by Elie Yarden), produced in New York, 1971.

In Time (essays and manifestos), Frontier Press, 1971.

Cities (fiction), Frontier Press, 1972.

Sulphur, privately printed, 1972.

A Line of Sight (fiction), Black Sparrow Press, 1974.

Wheres, Black Sparrow Press, 1978.

The Cruise of the Pnyx, Station Hill Press, 1979.

How Do I Make Up My Mind, Lord?: Story Devotions for Boys, (juvenile), illustrated by Tom Maakestad, Augsburg, 1982.

A Transparent Tree (short fiction), McPherson, 1985.

The Mail of Mann: The Story of the Isle of Man Post Office, Manx Associated Publications, 1988.

Doctor of Silence (short stories), McPherson, 1988.

Cat Scratch Fever, McPherson, 1990.

Queen of Terrors (fiction), in press.

EDITOR

(With Paris Leary, and contributor) *A Controversy of Poets: An Anthology of Contemporary American Poetry,* Doubleday, 1965.

Paul Blackburn, *The Journals,* Black Sparrow Press, 1975.

Contributor to a variety of literary magazines, including *Chelsea Review, Trobar, Caterpillar,* and *Sulfur.*

A collection of Kelly's manuscripts are housed at the Lockwood Memorial Library, State University of New York at Buffalo.

WORK IN PROGRESS: Parsifal, a novel.

SIDELIGHTS: "The literary task Robert Kelly has set for himself is succinctly stated in his 1975 book of poetry, *The Loom:* 'Say it all / over again, / but say it all. / Write everything,' " noted Larry McCaffery in the *New York Times Book Review.* A prolific poet, short story writer, essayist, novelist, and editor, Kelly has accomplished his ambitious undertaking: he has produced a large body of work, much of which is experimental and which focuses on different modes of expression. In addition, he has promoted the works of other writers of experimental poetry and fiction through developing writing courses, holding workshops, and as cofounder of several literary magazines, including *Chelsea Review* in 1957, *Trobar* in 1960, *Matter,* and *Sulfur.*

"My life's concern is to be instrumentality of utterance, that is, to be of the everlasting human maker—with the sense of continuous song or declaration," Kelly once told *CA.* "I am consequently concerned with all forms of transmutation and the sciences that compel them: linguistics, theology, magic, alchemy, politics, biology, cinema, painting, dance, music, medicine, archeology, geology, anthropology. There is no history."

In an interview with David Ossman published in *The Sullen Art,* Kelly explained his conception of the "poetry of images": "When I speak of Image Poetry, I'm speaking both of a way of looking at all poetry, and also, in our own time, of a particular stance of the poet as regards his material; that stand generates a kind of poetry not necessarily dominated by the images which form the dominant movement of the poem. . . . The poetic Image is not a thing. It is a process and a discovered identity. It discovers its being in its function. . . . Image is the rhythm of poetry." Kelly is considered one of the co-inventors of the term "deep image," according to Robert Atwan in the *Los Angeles Times Book Review.*

Kelly's 1964 *Lunes/Sightings* introduces and defines a poetic form of his own invention—the lune. He wrote in the book's foreword: "Lunes are small poems that spend half their lives in darkness and half in light. Each lune has thirteen syllables, one for each month of the moon's year. Along about the middle, the dark of the moon comes. The full moon is the approximate splendor of the whole lune, provided the clouds do not fall too heavily on that poem. The lune is a form. Each lune is a separate poem." A. R. Ammons said of these poems: "The method for . . . Kelly . . . is to make minimal means reverberate to the maximum. This can seem like straining both ways. But in enough cases the reverberations asked for are generated."

Kelly's 1967 novel *The Scorpions* seemed to thoroughly mystify critics. Eliot Fremont-Smith compared both the novel's style and content to the works of such writers as Wilhelm and Jacob Grimm, J. R. R. Tolkien, C. S. Lewis, William Golding, Carl Jung, J. P. Donleavy, Ray Bradbury, and Vladimir Nabokov in his review for the *New York Times,* but agreed with many critics that Kelly's work cannot effectively be defined by comparisons. Fremont-Smith observed: "I suppose it should be noted, too, that the author, a teacher and a poet, makes frequent reference to the fact that scorpions attack in reverse, as it were, over their backs; so perhaps we are supposed to read backwards from the closing page. Or something."

Although Albert Mobilio found *A Transparent Tree,* Kelly's first collection of novellas and short stories, challenging, he suggested that the author successfully renders his work interpretable, perhaps because of its obscurity. "All possible readings," wrote Mobilio in the *Village Voice Literary Supplement,* "are encouraged here. These 11 stories are 'trying to be everything,' Kelly admits in his afterword; his ambition energizes the collection, inspiring us to join the creative fray." McCaffery compared Kelly's experimental prose style to the writing of poetry: "Such an approach places many of the same demands on the reader as poetry does; he must focus on each word and image and observe the way patterns emerge and different resonances of meaning and feeling are created. The result is often a sense of ambiguity, even obscurity, but this seems to be part of Mr. Kelly's effort to break down our usual associations and express life's confusion."

In her review of Kelly's short fiction collection *Cat Scratch Fever,* Bertha Harris praised the author's nerve. She observed in the *New York Times Book Review* that his works are "full of signs and wonders," and called him "the joker in the deck of post-modernist writing." Many of Kelly's stories, which at first seem simple and even stock, are, according to Harris, misleading and complex. Harris described Kelly as "a dexterous strategist. When he waxes prosaic, slightly off-center, he is often concealing one or more of his preoccupations—which include sheltered boyhoods, mythology, sex and demonology—and he is inviting the reader into interpretive folly." Jonathan Yardley, writing in the *Washington Post Book World,* compared some of the shorter stories in *Cat Scratch Fever* to the fables of Jorge Luis Borges and Italo Calvino. Yet Yardley maintained that "that doesn't mean he's impossible to read, only that he is restless and versatile." Harris concluded that Kelly deserves greater critical attention than he has received. "While they are uneven," she said, "all the stories are displays of the extraordinary range of his imagination and his imperatives as a writer."

BIOGRAPHICAL/CRITICAL SOURCES:

BOOKS

Ossman, David, *The Sullen Art,* Corinth, 1963.

PERIODICALS

Antioch Review, winter, 1989.
Atlantic Monthly, February, 1961.
Kulchur, autumn, 1962.
Los Angeles Times Book Review, December 18, 1983, p. 2; January 13, 1991, p. 10.
New York Times, January 11, 1967.
New York Times Book Review, January 8, 1961; September 15, 1985, p. 18; January 19, 1992; May 31, 1992.
Poetry, June, 1966; September, 1966.
Saturday Review, February 4, 1961.
Village Voice Literary Supplement, October, 1985.
Washington Post Book World, June 23, 1991, p. 12.*

*   *   *

KELLY, Tim 1935-
(R. H. Bibolet, Keith Jackson, J. Moriarity, Vera Morris, Robert Swift)

PERSONAL: Born October 2, 1935, in Saugus, MA; son of Francis Seymour and Mary-Edna (Furey) Kelley. *Education:* Emerson College, B.A., 1956, M.A., 1957; Yale University, graduate study, 1966.

ADDRESSES: Home and office—8730 Lookout Mountain Ave., Hollywood, CA 90046.

CAREER: Playwright. Drama critic, *Arizona Republic,* c. 1965; theater editor, *Points West* magazine.

MEMBER: Dramatists Guild, Writers Guild West.

AWARDS, HONORS: Fendrich Playwriting Award, 1963, for *Not Far from the Giaconda Tree;* American Broadcasting Company fellow, Yale University, 1965-66; Sergel Drama Prize, University of Chicago, 1973, for *Yankee Clipper;* Bicentennial Playwriting Award, University of Utah, 1975, for *Beau Johnny;* playwriting award, International Thespian Society, 1976, for *The Tale that Wagged the Dog;* creative writing award, National Endowment for the Arts, 1976; Weisbroad Playwriting Award, 1980, for *The Lalapalooza Bird;* Nederlander Playwriting Award, 1980, for *Bloody Jack;* San Diego Opera House Award, 1981, for *Dark Deeds at Swan's Place;* Elmira College Playwriting Award, 1991, for *Crimes at the Old Brewery;* Northern Kentucky Playwriting Award, 1991, for *Don't Be Afraid of the Dark;* Columbia Entertainment Theatre Award, 1992, for *Renfield.*

WRITINGS:

PLAYS

Road Show, first produced in Martha's Vineyard, MA, 1957.

O'Rourke's House, first produced by National Broadcasting Co. Matinee Theater, 1958.

Widow's Walk (first produced in Scottsdale, AZ, at Stagebrush Theater, 1959), Harper, 1963.

Not Far from the Giaconda Tree (one-act; first produced at Stagebrush Theater, 1961), Pioneer Drama Service, 1964.

The Burning Man (two-act; first produced at Stagebrush Theater, 1962), Samuel French, 1962.

A Darker Flower, first produced Off-Broadway at Pocket Theater, 1963.

The Trunk and All that Jazz, first produced in Boston at Image Theater, 1963.

The Floor Is Bright with Toys, first produced in Phoenix, AZ, at Arizona Repertory Theater, 1963.

Song of the Dove, first produced at Stagebrush Theater, 1964.

Murder on Ice, first produced at Stagebrush Theater, 1964.

The Natives Are Restless (long one-act; first produced in Seattle, WA, at Theater Northwest, 1965), Pioneer Drama, 1969.

Welcome to the Casa, first produced in Fairfield, CT, at Meadowbrook Playhouse, 1965.

(Adaptor) John Ruskin, *King of the Golden River,* Pioneer Drama Service, 1966.

Everything's Jim Dandy (two-act; first produced by American Broadcasting Company, 1966), I. E. Clark, 1981.

Bluebeard Had a Wife, Dramatic Publishing, 1967.

The Marvelous Playbill, Dramatic Publishing, 1967.

While Shakespeare Slept (one-act), Baker's Plays, 1967.

Late Blooming Flowers, first produced in Los Angeles at Ivar Theater, 1968.

Two Fools Who Gained a Measure of Wisdom (adaptation of *Nothing to Choose Between Them* by Anton Chekhov), Dramatic Play Service, 1968.

The Timid Dragon, Dramatic Publishing, 1968.

The Eskimos Have Landed, Pioneer Drama Service, 1969.

If Sherlock Holmes Were a Woman (one-act), Baker's Plays, 1969.

How to Get Rid of a Housemother (one-act), Baker's Plays, 1969.

Always Marry a Bachelor (one-act), Baker's Plays, 1970.

It's a Bird! It's a Plane! It's Chickenman!, Pioneer Drama Service, 1970.

The Last of Sherlock Holmes (one-act), Baker's Plays, 1970.

Second Best Bed, Dramatists Play Service, 1970.

The Silk Shirt (one-act), Samuel French, 1970.

Up the Rent (one-act), Dramatic Publishing, 1970.

(Stage adaptor) *The Deceitful Marriage,* Baker's Plays, 1971.

Alias Smedley Pewtree, Pioneer Drama Service, 1971.

The Mouse and the Raven, Pioneer Drama Service, 1971.

West of the Pecos, Dramatic Publishing, 1971.

Ladies of the Tower, Dramatic Publishing, 1971.

(Under pseudonym R. H. Bibolet) *Barrel of Monkeys,* Performance Publishing, 1972.

The Keeping Place, Pioneer Drama Service, 1972.

No Opera at the Opr'y House Tonight, or, Too Good to Be True, Dramatic Publishing, 1972.

Merry Murders at Montmarie, Performance Publishing, 1972.

Lemonade Joe Rides Again, Performance Publishing, 1972.

The Witch Who Wouldn't Hang, Performance Publishing, 1972.

The Yankee Doodle (musical; music and lyrics by George M. Cohan), Performance Publishing, 1972.

W. C. Fieldworthy: Foiled Again, Performance Publishing, 1973.

Creeps by Night (one-act), Baker's Plays, 1973.

(Under pseudonym R. H. Bibolet) *Navajo House,* Baker's Plays, 1973.

The Gift and the Giving (one-act), Samuel French, 1973.

Yankee Clipper, produced at Back Alley Theater, Los Angeles, 1973.

(Stage adaptor) *M*A*S*H* (full-length version), Dramatic Publishing, 1973.

(Stage adaptor) *M*A*S*H* (one-act), Dramatic Publishing, 1973.

The Brothers O'Toole (also see below), Pioneer Drama Service, 1973.

Seven Wives for Dracula, Pioneer Drama Service, 1973.

The Remarkable Susan, Dramatists Play Service, 1973.

Tap Dancing in Molasses (one-act), Baker's Plays, 1973.

Memorial, Pioneer Drama Service, 1974.

(Stage adaptor) Mary Shelley, *Frankenstein* (two-act; produced in Paris), Samuel French, 1974.

Virtue Victorious; or, Only a Mother's Love Could Save Him, Dramatic Publishing, 1974.

Frankenstein Slept Here, Pioneer Drama Service, 1974.

Reunion on Gallows Hill, Pioneer Drama Service, 1974.

(Stage adaptor, with S. Carle) Conrad Aiken, *Silent Snow, Secret Snow,* Dramatic Publishing, 1974.

Monster Soup, Pioneer Drama Service, 1974.

Egad, the Woman in White (adapted from *The Woman in White* by Wilkie Collins), Samuel French, 1975.

Young Dracula, Pioneer Drama Service, 1975.

Happily Ever After, Pioneer Drama Service, 1975.

Sherlock Meets the Phantom, Pioneer Drama Service, 1975.

Bride of Frankenstein, Pioneer Drama Service, 1976.

Dirty Work in High Places, Baker's Plays, 1976.

(Stage adaptor) *Hawkshaw The Detective,* Pioneer Drama Service, 1976.

(Stage adaptor) Sir Arthur Conan Doyle, *The Hound of the Baskervilles* (two-act), Samuel French, 1976.

Beau Johnny, produced at Pioneer Memorial Theater, Salt Lake City, UT, 1976.

Lizzie Borden of Fall River (two-act), Pioneer Drama Service, 1976.

(Stage adaptor) Oscar Wilde, *The Canterville Ghost,* Performance Publishing, 1976.

(Stage adaptor) Anton Chekhov, *Masha,* Pioneer Drama Service, 1976.

Sherlock Holmes' First Case, Performance Publishing, 1976.

The Butler Did It, Baker's Plays, 1977.

The Cave (one-act), Dramatists Play Service, 1977.

Crazy Mixed-Up Island of Dr. Moreau (adaptation of *The Island of Dr. Moreau* by H. G. Wells), Baker's Plays, 1977.

Cry of the Banshee (also see below), Pioneer Drama Service, 1977.

The Invisible Man, Pioneer Drama Service, 1977.

Jocko; or, The Monkey's Husband, I. E. Clark, 1977.

(Stage adaptor) *Case of the Curious Moonstone,* Performance Publishing, 1977.

Loco-Motion, Commotion, Dr. Gorilla, and Me, Baker's Plays, 1977.

Country Gothic, Performance Publishing, 1977.

Mark Twain in the Garden of Eden, Baker's Plays, 1977.

The Convertible Teacher, Performance Publishing, 1977.

Sherlock Holmes, Pioneer Drama Service, 1977.

(Stage adaptor) H. G. Wells, *The Time Machine,* Pioneer Drama Service, 1977.

(Stage adaptor) Frank L. Baum, *The Wonderful Wizard of Oz,* Pioneer Drama Service, 1977.

The Tale that Wagged the Dog, Dramatic Publishing, 1977.

(Stage adaptor) *Dracula: The Vampire Play,* I. E. Clark, 1978.

It's Bigfoot, Pioneer Drama Service, 1978.

Enter Pharoah Nussbaum (three-act), Baker's Plays, 1978.

(Stage adaptor) Lewis Carroll, *Alice's Adventures in Wonderland,* Pioneer Drama Service, 1978.

The Great All-American Musical Disaster (three-act), Baker's Plays, 1978.

A Marriage Proposal—Western Style, Pioneer Drama Service, 1978.

(Stage adaptor) *Sweeney Todd: Demon Barber of the Barbary Coast,* I. E. Clark, 1978.

Victoria at 18, Dramatic Publishing, 1978.

Nashville Jamboree (musical), Performance Publishing, 1978.

Whatever This Is, We're All In It Together, Performance Publishing, 1978.

Captain Fantastic: A Wild Farce about Comic Books, Baker's Plays, 1979.

Pecos Bill and Slewfoot Sue Meet the Dirty Dan Gang, Pioneer Drama Service, 1978.

(Stage adaptor) Edgar Allan Poe, *The Fall of the House of Usher,* I. E. Clark, 1979.

Captain Nemo and His Magical Marvelous Submarine Machine, Pioneer Drama Service, 1979.

Toga! Toga! Toga!, Pioneer Drama Service, 1979.

Lost in Space and the Mortgage Due, Eldridge Publishing, 1979.

The Soapy Murder Case (three-act), Baker's Plays, 1979.

(Stage adaptor) Dorothy Macardle, *The Uninvited* (three-act), Dramatists Play Service, 1979.

The Incredible Bulk at Bikini Beach, Pioneer Drama Service, 1980.

The Frankensteins Are Back in Town, I. E. Clark, 1980.

Lady Dracula, Pioneer Drama Service, 1980.

Lantern in the Wind, I. E. Clark, 1980.

Krazy Kamp, Pioneer Drama Service, 1980.

Murder in the Magnolias, Baker's Plays, 1980.

The Green Archer, Baker's Plays, 1980.

Unidentified Flying High School, Meriwether, 1980.

A'Haunting We Will Go, Dramatic Publishing, 1980.

The Shame of Tombstone, Pioneer Drama Service, 1980.

Airline, Pioneer Drama Service, 1980.

(Stage adaptor) *Sherlock Holmes and the Adventure of the Speckled Band,* I. E. Clark, 1981.

Dark Deeds at Swan's Place; or, Never Trust a Tattooed Sailor, Samuel French, 1981.

Bloody Jack: A Thriller Based on the Murders of Jack the Ripper, I. E. Clark, 1981.

Lumberjacks and Wedding Belles (musical), Pioneer Drama Service, 1981.

Toby Tyler, Pioneer Drama Service, 1981.

The Lalapalooza Bird, I. E. Clark, 1981.

Terror by Gaslight, Dramatists Play Service, 1981.

Under Jekyll's Hyde, Pioneer Drama Service, 1981.

First on the Rope, I. E. Clark, 1982.

Mrs. Wiggs of the Cabbage Patch (three-act), I. E. Clark, 1982.

Don't Rock the Boat, Eldridge Publishing, 1983.

(Stage adaptor) *Tom Sawyer: A Comedy in Two Acts,* I. E. Clark, 1983.

The Zombie (three-act), Samuel French, 1983.

Murder Takes a Holiday, I. E. Clark, 1984.

The Dracula Kidds: The House on Blood Pudding Lane, I. E. Clark, 1986.

The Butler Did It, Singing (musical), music by Arne Christiansen, Baker's Plays, 1986.

The Face on the Barroom Floor, or, Glimpsed through the Sawdust; An Astonishing Theatrical Event Illustrating in Words and Action the Evil of Greed and the Triumph of True Love, Samuel French, 1986.

Time and Time Again (two-act musical), music by Bill Francoeur and Jack Sharkey, Pioneer Drama Service, 1987.

(Stage adaptor) Wilkie Collins, *The Woman in White* (musical), music by Sharkey, Samuel French, 1987.

Cinderella Meets the Wolfman: A Howlingly Funny Musical Spoof, music by Sharkey, Samuel French, 1988.

It Was a Dark and Stormy Night, Baker's Plays, 1988.

Spring Break, Pioneer Drama Service, 1989.

Follow that Rabbitt, Pioneer Drama Service, 1989.

The Amazing Adventures of Dan Daredevil: A Musical Spoof of Radio's Golden Age (music by Christiansen and O. Kittleson), Baker's Plays, 1989.

The Picture that was Turned to the Wall; or, She May Have Seen Better Days, Samuel French, 1989.

Small Wonder (two-act), Baker's Plays, 1989.

Calling the Hawk, Pioneer Drama Service, 1990.

Rumpelstiltskin, Pioneer Drama Service, 1990.

Yours Truly, Jack Frost, Pioneer Drama Service, 1990.

The Empty Chair, Pioneer Drama Service, 1990.

Fog on the Mountain, Dramatists Play Service, 1990.

It's a Howl (two-act musical), music and lyrics by Larry Nestor, Eldridge Publishing, 1990.

The Omelet Murder Case, Dramatists Play Service, 1990.

Snow White, Pioneer Drama Service, 1990.

Curse You, Otis Crummy, Pioneer Drama Service, 1990.

(Stage adaptor) John Polidori, *The Vampyre* (two-act), Dramatists Play Service, 1990.

Varney the Vampire; or, "The Feast of Blood" (two-act), Samuel French, 1990.

Krazy Kamp—The Musical, Pioneer Drama Service, 1991.

Song of the Mounties, Pioneer Drama Service, 1991.

Jack and the Magic Beans (musical), Pioneer Drama Service, 1991.

Night of Living Terror, Pioneer Drama Service, 1991.

Mountain Fever, Pioneer Drama Service, 1991.

Live a Little, Pioneer Drama Service, 1991.

If These Walls Could Talk, Pioneer Drama Service, 1991.

Hello from Mongo, Pioneer Drama Service, 1991.

Great Ghost Chase, Pioneer Drama Service, 1991.

Hollywood Hotel, Contemporary Drama Service, 1991.

Don't Be Afraid of the Dark (two-act), Baker's Plays, 1991.

Wagon Wheels West (musical), Pioneer Drama Service, 1991.

Spell of Sleeping Beauty, Pioneer Drama Service, 1992.

Meet the Creeps, Pioneer Drama Service, 1992.

Wolf at the Door, Contemporary Drama Service, 1992.

Jack and the Giant (musical), Pioneer Drama Service, 1992.

Santa's Big Trouble, Pioneer Drama Service, 1992.

The Jungle Book, Pioneer Drama Service, 1992.

Crimes at the Old Brewery, I. E. Clark, 1992.

The Hunchback of Notre Dame, I. E. Clark, 1992.

Night of the Living Beauty Pageant, Baker's Plays, 1992.

Aladdin and the Magical, Wonderful Lamp (musical), Pioneer Drama Service, 1993.

You Ain't Nothin' But a Werewolf, Pioneer Drama Service, 1993.

Funny Bones, Contemporary Drama Service, 1993.

Lagooned, Eldridge Plays, 1993.

Hooray for Hollywood, Pioneer Drama Service, 1993.

Internal Teen Machine, Pioneer Drama Service, 1993.

Dirty Work on the Trail, Pioneer Drama Service, 1993.

Bang! Bang! You're Dead, Pioneer Drama Service, 1993.

Street Story, Pioneer Drama Service, 1993.

That's the Spirit, Baker's Plays, 1993.

Also author of *Our Indian Heritage,* 1974; *Saratoga,* 1978; (adaptor) *Nicholas Nickleby, Schoolmaster,* 1981; *Tumbleweeds,* 1982; *Oliver Twisted,* 1982; (adaptor) *Little Miss Christie,* 1982; *The Mystery of the Black Abbot,* 1982; *Horror High,* 1982; *Lucky, Lucky Hudson,* 1982; *The 12th Street Gang,* 1982; *Love Is Murder,* 1982; *Charming Sally,* 1982; *Zorro's Back in Town,* 1983; *Hospital,* 1983; *The Clods of Hopper,* 1983; *Videomania,* 1983; *The Omelet Murder Case,* 1983; *What's News at the Zoo,* 1983; *The Comedian,* 1984; *Beast of the Baskervilles,* 1984; (adaptor) Mark Twain, *A Connecticut Yankee in King Arthur's Court,* 1984; *Squad Room,* 1984; *Never Trust a City Slicker,* 1984; *Laffing Room Only,* 1984; *How Santa Got His Christmas Tree,* 1985; *Destiny,* 1985; *Money, Power, Murder, Lust, Revenge, and Marvelous Clothes* (musical), 1985; *Murder by Natural Causes,* 1985; *Life on the Bowery,* 1985; *The Secret of Skull Island,* 1986; *The Ghostchasers,* 1986; *Belle of Bisbee,* 1986; *Murder Game,* 1986;

Hurricane Smith and the Garden of the Golden Monkey, 1986; *Hurricane Smith—The Musical,* 1986; *Tied to the Tracks,* 1986; *Slambo,* 1986;*Who Walks in the Dark,* 1987; *Dog Eat Dog,* 1987; (adaptor) *The Three Musketeers* (musical), 1987; *Sherlock Holmes and the Giant Rat of Sumatra,* 1987; (adaptor) Victor Hugo, *Les Miserables,* 1987; *18 Nervous Gumshoes,* 1987; *The Incredible Day Christmas Disappeared from Evergreen Town,* 1987; *Perils of Pumpernickel Pass,* 1988; *Help! I'm Trapped in a High School,* 1988; *Victor Hugo . . . In Rehearsal,* 1989; *My Gypsy Robe,* 1989; *Robin Hood,* 1989; *Those Wedding Bells Shall Not Ring Out,* 1989; *Luncheonette of Terror,* 1989; *The Phantom of the Op'ry,* 1989; *Renfield,* 1992; *Charley's Charmers,* Performance Publishing; *Ten Weeks with the Circus,* Pioneer Drama Service; *Raggedy Dick and Puss,* produced at Seattle Repertory Theater, Seattle, WA; *Pictures from the Walls of Pompeii,* produced at South Coast Repertory Theater; *The Adventure of the Clouded Crystal.*

Work sometimes published under various pseudonyms, including R. H. Bibolet, J. Moriarity, Vera Morris, Keith Jackson, and Robert Swift. Many of Kelly's plays have been translated into French and German.

The Tim Kelly Theatre Collection is housed at the University of Wyoming.

SCREENPLAYS

Cry of the Banshee, American International Pictures, 1972.
The Brothers O'Toole, American National, 1973.
Sugar Hill, American International Pictures, 1974.
Bogard, Lester-Traynor Films, 1975.
Get Fisk, 1975.

Also author of screenplays *Black Streetfighter,* Centaur Films, and *Black Fist,* Worldwide Films.

NOVELS

Ride of Fury (western), Ace Books, 1964.

Also author of the "Cos Fury" series of western novels.

OTHER

Also author of scripts for television series, including *Bonanza, Hec Ramsey, Here Come the Brides, The High Chaparral, Khan, Kojak, Matinee Theater, Nakia, Name of the Game,* and *Powderkeg.*

Contributor of articles and drama criticism to magazines and journals, including *Arizona Highways Magazine* and *Mystery.* Author's works have been translated into foreign languages, including French.

SIDELIGHTS: A tremendously prolific dramatist, Tim Kelly is the author of many plays intended for larger theaters as well as works suitable for performances on civic stages and in schools as children's theater presentations. Kelly's works cover a wide variety of subjects and styles, ranging from comedy and farce to mystery and horror. "I write many plays that are 'cross-overs'," Kelly asserted in an interview in *Secondary School Theater Journal.* "That is, they can be performed by any level theater group— from community theater to university stage; from off-Off-Broadway to Equity Companies." Kelly's motivation in writing numerous works for children over the years has been to develop an interest in theatre among his young audiences: "I want their initial experience with live theater to be *happy.*"

Kelly's work ranges from detective thrillers to musical comedies, with horror one of his favorite genres. "I suppose if I were starting out all over again, I would write certain types of material under one name, other types under another," Kelly commented to *CA.* "I find people are a bit disturbed if a playwright displays interest in more than one form. I guess it's a little like discovering Agatha Christie writing a television sitcom. Anyway, it's too late to change now. I enjoy the considerable success I have with my plays . . . there's no doubt about it—I'm a workaholic. However, I'm fortunate. I love the stage, I love my work, and I love seeing it in print."

BIOGRAPHICAL/CRITICAL SOURCES:

PERIODICALS

Arizonian, January 30, 1964.
Detroit Free Press, March 22, 1981.
Drama-Logue, January, 1991.
Footlights, April, 1978.
Los Angeles Times, November 29, 1984.
Secondary School Theater Journal, winter, 1981.
University of Utah Review, April, 1976.
Washington Post, September, 1993.

*   *   *

KENNEDY, Michael   1926-

PERSONAL: Born February 19, 1926, in Manchester, England; son of Hew Gilbert and Marian Florence (Sinclair) Kennedy; married Eslyn May Durdle, May 16, 1947. *Education:* Attended Berkhamsted School, 1939-41. *Politics:* Conservative. *Religion:* Church of England.

ADDRESSES: Home—3 Moorwood Dr., Sale, Cheshire M33 4QA, England.

CAREER: Daily Telegraph, London, England, member of editorial staff, Manchester office, 1941—, staff music critic, 1951—, northern editor, 1960-86, chief music critic *Sunday Telegraph,* 1989—. Royal Manchester College of Music, member of council, honorary member, 1971;

Royal Northern College of Music, member of council, 1972-89, fellow, 1981, member of board of governors, 1989—. *Military service:* Royal Navy, 1943-46.

MEMBER: Athenaeum, Lancashire County Cricket Club.

AWARDS, HONORS: Officer of the Order of the British Empire, 1981.

WRITINGS:

The Halle Tradition: A Century of Music, Manchester University Press (Manchester, England), 1960.
The Works of Ralph Vaughan Williams, Oxford University Press (Oxford, England), 1964.
Portrait of Elgar, Oxford University Press, 1968, 4th edition, 1993.
Portrait of Manchester, R. Hale (London, England), 1970.
Elgar Orchestral Works, BBC Publications (London, England), 1970.
History of Royal Manchester College of Music, Manchester University Press, 1971.
Barbirolli: Conductor Laureate, MacGibbon & Kee (London, England), 1971.
(Editor) *Autobiography of Charles Halle,* Elek (London, England), 1973, revised edition, 1991.
Mahler, Dent (London, England), 1974.
Richard Strauss, Dent, 1976.
Concise Oxford Dictionary of Music, Oxford University Press, 1980.
Britten, Dent, 1981, revised edition, 1993.
The Halle: 1858-1983, Manchester University Press, 1983.
Strauss Tone Poems, BBC Publications, 1984.
The Oxford Dictionary of Music, Oxford University Press, 1985, 2nd edition, 1994.
Adrian Boult, Hamish Hamilton (London, England), 1987.
Portrait of Walton, Oxford University Press, 1989.
Music Enriches All: Twenty-one Years of the RNCM, Carcanet Press (Manchester, England), 1994.

Contributor to *Musical Times, Listener, Gramophone,* and *BBC Record Review.*

*   *   *

KENYON, Kate
 See RANSOM, Candice F.

*   *   *

KERMODE, (John) Frank   1919-

PERSONAL: Born November 29, 1919, in Douglas, Isle of Man, England; son of John Pritchard and Doris (Ken-

nedy) Kermode; married Maureen Eccles, 1947 (divorced, 1970); children: Mark, Deborah. *Education:* Liverpool University, B.A., 1940, M.A., 1947. *Avocational interests:* Music.

ADDRESSES: Home—27 Luard Road, Cambridge CB2 2PJ, England. *Office*—King's College, Cambridge University, Cambridge CB2 1ST, England.

CAREER: King's College, University of Durham, lecturer, 1947-49; University of Reading, lecturer, 1949-58; University of Manchester, professor, 1958-65; University of Bristol, Winterstoke Professor of English, 1965-67; University College, London, Lord Northcliffe Professor of modern English literature, 1967-74; King's College, Cambridge, King Edward VII Professor of English literature and fellow, 1974-82. Visiting professor, Harvard University, summer, 1961; Warton Lecturer, British Academy, 1962; Mary Flexner Lecturer, Bryn Mawr College, 1965; Gauss Lecturer, Princeton University, 1970; Charles Eliot Norton Professor, Harvard University, 1977-78; visiting professor, Columbia University, 1983, 1985. *Military service:* Royal Navy, 1940-46; became lieutenant.

MEMBER: Royal Society of Literature (fellow), British Academy (fellow), American Academy of Arts and Sciences (honorary member), Officier de l'Ordre des Arts et des Sciences (France).

AWARDS, HONORS: Fellowship, Wesleyan University Center for Advanced Studies, 1963-64 and 1969-70; knighted by Queen Elizabeth of England, 1991; honorary degrees include D.H.L., University of Chicago; D. Litt., University of Liverpool; Dr., University of Amsterdam; and D. Litt, University of Newcastle.

WRITINGS:

CRITICISM

Romantic Image, Routledge & Kegan Paul, 1957, Macmillan, 1958.
John Donne, Longmans, Green, 1957.
Wallace Stevens, Oliver & Boyd, 1960, Grove Press, 1961, revised edition, 1967.
Puzzles and Epiphanies: Essays and Reviews, 1958-1961, Chilmark, 1962.
William Shakespeare: The Final Plays, Longmans, Green, 1963.
The Patience of Shakespeare, Harcourt, 1964.
On Shakespeare's Learning, Wesleyan University Press, 1965.
The Sense of an Ending: Studies in the Theory of Fiction, Oxford University Press, 1967.
Continuities, Random House, 1968.
Modern Essays, Collins, 1971.

Shakespeare, Spenser, Donne: Renaissance Essays, Viking, 1971, published as *Renaissance Essays: Shakespeare, Spenser, Donne,* Fontana Books, 1973.

Novel and Narrative, University of Glasgow Press, 1972.

D. H. Lawrence, Viking, 1973.

(Contributor) Seymour Chatman, editor, *Approaches to Poetics,* Columbia University Press, 1973.

The Classic: Literary Images of Permanence and Change, Viking, 1975, reissued with foreword, Harvard University Press, 1983.

How We Read Novels, University of Southampton Press, 1975.

The Genesis of Secrecy, Harvard University Press, 1979.

The Art of Telling: Essays on Fiction, Harvard University Press, 1983.

Forms of Attention, Chicago University Press, 1985.

History and Value: The Clarendon Lectures and the Northcliffe Lectures, 1987, Oxford University Press, 1988.

An Appetite for Poetry, Harvard University Press, 1989.

Poetry, Narrative, History, Blackwell, 1990.

The Uses of Error, Harvard University Press, 1991.

EDITOR

English Pastoral Poetry: From the Beginnings to Marvell, Barnes & Noble, 1952.

William Shakespeare, *The Tempest,* Methuen, 1954.

Seventeenth-Century Songs, Oxford University Press, 1956.

The Living Milton: Essays by Various Hands, Routledge & Kegan Paul, 1960, Macmillan, 1961.

Discussions of John Donne, Heath, 1962.

Spenser: Selections from the Minor Poems and the Fairie Queene, Oxford University Press, 1965.

Four Centuries of Shakespearean Criticism, Avon, 1965.

The Metaphysical Poets: Essays on Metaphysical Poetry, Fawcett, 1969.

King Lear: A Casebook, Macmillan, 1969.

(With Richard Poirier) *The Oxford Reader: Varieties of Contemporary Discourse,* Oxford University Press, 1971.

(With John Hollander and others) *The Oxford Anthology of English Literature* (two volumes), Oxford University Press, 1973.

Selected Prose of T. S. Eliot, Harcourt, 1975.

Henry James, *The Figure in the Carpet, and Other Stories,* Penguin, 1986.

(With Robert Alter) *The Literary Guide to the Bible,* Harvard University Press, 1987.

(With Keith Walker) *Andrew Marvell,* Oxford University Press, 1990.

Coeditor, *Encounter,* 1966-67; general editor, "Modern Masters" series, Fontana, 1970—, and "Oxford Authors" series, 1984—.

OTHER

Contributor to periodicals, including *Encounter, London Review of Books, New Statesman, New Republic, New York Review of Books, Partisan Review,* and *Review of English Studies.*

SIDELIGHTS: Frank Kermode, widely-respected as a literary critic and scholar, has written on a range of topics, from the Bible and Shakespeare to deconstructionist theory and the value of the review essay. He is perhaps best known for his ability to assess and explain arcane subjects for layperson and academic alike. Stephen Logan, writing in the *Spectator,* praised *The Uses of Error,* a collection of Kermode's reviews published in 1991, for its even-handed treatment of different scholarly factions and of literary debate. Wrote Logan, "[Kermode's book] gracefully attests the workings of a critical intelligence at once tentative and assured, in a style in which lucidity ministers to subtlety, and terseness entails no sacrifice of precision." And critic Walter Kendrick noted in the *New York Times Book Review,* "Erudite yet undogmatic, Kermode smoothly bridges the abyss between professors and common readers. And he never fails to do his readers the honor of assuming that their intelligence and generosity equal his own."

For Kermode, the possibility of being endlessly interpreted and reinterpreted is a prerequisite for a work's inclusion into the literary canon. In an age of skepticism, the indeterminacy of certain works is what makes them endure. Kermode's argument, put forth in the three lectures constituting *Forms of Attention,* is described by John Bayley in the *Times Literary Supplement:* "A tolerant orthodoxy is based on the fact that we know nothing for certain: hence *Hamlet* and *Ulysses* are perpetually discussable—and it is because classes can and will conveniently discuss them that they are in the canon. Critical uncertainty makes them immortal, and it is the attention of the critic that gives them perpetual value."

1979's *The Genesis of Secrecy* brings the Bible, one of the most enduring and widely-discussed canonical texts in the Western world, under Kermode's scrutiny. Although Biblical scholars have demonstrated an interest in employing the methods of literary criticism, Kermode notes that few secular scholars had included what he terms sacred texts among the focuses of their attention. In the *Times Literary Supplement,* C. H. Sisson commented upon the appeal that the Bible holds for Kermode: "As [Kermode] remarks, 'the scholarly quality and discipline of the best biblical study is high enough to be, in many ways, exemplary' for literary critics." Sisson pointed out, however, that Kermode's belief that scholars themselves determine what is permitted in terms of interpretation leads to the interpretation or criticism mattering more than the text itself, an idea that scholars should—but would not necessarily—

reject. "The best critics," contended Sisson, "disappear before the work; the worst hold the stage."

Many of Kermode's essays have been concerned with the problems inherent in the interpretation process, especially between the adherents of avant-garde literary theories and their more conservative counterparts. Kermode argues for establishing a middle ground between what he calls "the catastrophe theorists," those deconstructionists who believe that every literary text carries within it the seeds of its own subversion, and the "panic-stricken reactionaries" who refuse to acknowledge that there is anything to literature beyond the conventional elements of characterization, plot, and theme. Speaking of Kermode's *The Art of Telling: Essays on Fiction,* Gregory A. Schirmer wrote in the *Los Angeles Times:* "Here is that badly needed voice of reason." However, critic Valentine Cunningham was not so easily persuaded by Kermode's arguments. Reviewing Kermode's *Essays on Fiction 1971-82* in the *Times Literary Supplement,* Cunningham faulted Kermode for failing to back up his assertions. "The theories of post-structuralism," the critic noted, "offend Kermode's sense of history and so he seeks to handle them with the precisions of historical assurance thus displayed. They also offend his sense of morality. . . . Nowhere in this collection, however, is Kermode very precise about where the amorality, let alone immorality, of the new criticism really resides." Nevertheless, Cunningham praised Kermode for his sensible argument against post-structuralism.

By 1990, when Kermode published *An Appetite for Poetry,* his position had become more resolute, a response to the escalating battle between the opposing camps of literary interpretation. "In 1983, Mr. Kermode was tolerantly witty about the academic vogue of structuralism and its more 'frightening' offshoot, deconstructionism," wrote Nina Auerbach in the *New York Times Book Review.* "Today he writes defensively, as a beleaguered believer within a profession avid to dismantle the inheritance it is our business to preserve." Although Auerbach pointed out that some of Kermode's comments about his scholarly opponents are perhaps too negative and thus unfair, she believed that his celebration of the literary canon is an important reminder of the glorious possibilities of literature. As Auerbach observed, "*An Appetite for Poetry* is among Mr. Kermode's most compact, accessible and intense books, one whose eloquence will remind many teachers and scholars of the magnitude of what we do."

BIOGRAPHICAL/CRITICAL SOURCES:

PERIODICALS

Book World, February 23, 1969.
Commonweal, December 1, 1967; December 2, 1983; April 6, 1990.

Guardian Weekly, September 11, 1988; October 15, 1989; March 17, 1991.
Kenyon Review, September, 1967.
Listener, June 29, 1967; May 19, 1983; November 14, 1985; August 25, 1988.
Los Angeles Times, December 8, 1983.
New Republic, July 20, 1974.
New Statesman, August 4, 1967; May 27, 1983; February 15, 1991.
New Yorker, November 10, 1975.
New York Review of Books, March 12, 1970; October 5, 1972; March 1, 1990; August 15, 1991.
New York Times, October 1, 1971.
New York Times Book Review, August 17, 1969; July 14, 1985; December 20, 1987, p. 1; July 17, 1988; October 1, 1989, p. 12; April 28, 1991; May 5 1991; June 9, 1991.
Observer, December 6, 1981; May 15, 1983; June 26, 1988; December 2, 1990; February 10, 1991.
Partisan Review, winter, 1968.
Saturday Review, March 2, 1963.
Spectator, November 11, 1960; February 23, 1991.
Times (London), December 24, 1987.
Times Educational Supplement, June 17, 1983; August 15, 1986; December 15, 1989; May 24, 1991; March 13, 1992.
Times Literary Supplement, March 13, 1969; January 11, 1980; July 22, 1983; November 22, 1985; February 19, 1988; July 1, 1988; September 1, 1989; January 26, 1990; February 8, 1991, p. 19.
Tribune Books, November 8, 1987, p. 12.
Virginia Quarterly Review, winter, 1984; winter, 1986.
Washington Post Book World, April 7, 1985; April 19, 1992, p. 1.
Yale Review, June, 1958; autumn, 1967.

—*Sketch by Elizabeth Judd*

*   *   *

KERN, E. R.
See KERNER, Fred

*   *   *

KERNER, Fred 1921-
(Frohm Fredericks, E. R. Kern, Frederick Kerr, M. N. Thaler)

PERSONAL: Born February 15, 1921, in Montreal, Quebec, Canada; son of Sam and Vera (Goldman) Kerner; married second wife, Sally Dee Stouten, May 18, 1959; children: (first marriage) Jon; (second marriage) David,

Diane. *Education:* Sir George Williams University (now Concordia University), B.A., 1942.

ADDRESSES: Home—25 Farmview Crescent, Willowdale, Ontario, Canada M2J 1G5. *Office*—Publishing Projects, Inc., 55014 Fairview Mall, Willowdale, Ontario, Canada M2J 5B9.

CAREER: Saskatoon Star-Phoenix, editorial writer, 1942; *Montreal Gazette,* Montreal, Quebec, assistant sports editor, 1942-44; worked variously as newsperson, editor, and news executive for the Canadian Press in Montreal, Toronto, and New York City, 1944-50; Associated Press, New York City, assistant night city editor, 1950-56; Hawthorn Books, Inc., New York City, editor, 1957-58, president and editor-in-chief, 1964-68; Fawcett Publications, Inc., New York City, editor-in-chief of Crest and Premier Books, 1958-64; Hall House, Inc., Greenwich, CT, editor, 1963-64; Centaur House Publishers, Inc., New York City, president and editor-in-chief, 1964-75; Publishing Projects, Inc., New York City and Toronto, president, 1968—; Book and Educational Division, Reader's Digest Association (Canada), publishing director, 1968-75; Communications Unlimited, Toronto, president, 1969—; Harlequin Books Ltd., Don Mills, Ontario, vice president and publishing director, 1975-83, editor emeritus and senior consulting editor, 1983—. Lecturer at Long Island University, 1968; editor-in-residence at several writers' conferences in the United States and Canada. Judge, Cobalt National Poetry Contest; trustee, Canadian Authors Association Literary Awards, Benson & Hedges Awards, Gibson Awards, Sir George Williams University journalism awards, and Rothman Literary Award of Merit; director, Publitex International Corp., Peter Kent, Inc., Pennorama Crafts, Inc., Disque Design, Inc., National Mint, Inc., and Personalized Services, Inc.; member of board of governors, Concordia University, Montreal, 1973-77, Canadian Writers' Foundation, and Academy of Canadian Writers; vice-chair, Federal Public Lending Right Commission and Canadian Copyright Institute; member of local school boards in New York City and Westmount, Quebec, Canada.

MEMBER: International Platform Association, Canadian Authors Association (president of Montreal branch, 1972-75; vice president, 1973-80; national president, 1982-83), Organization of Canadian Authors and Publishers (founding member; member of board of governors, 1977-83), Canadian Book Publishers' Council (honorary life member), CAA Fund to Develop Canadian Writers (founding president, 1983), Canadian Association for the Restoration of Lost Positives (president, 1969—), Mystery Writers of America (editor of *The Third Degree*), Overseas Press Club (chair of election committee, 1960-64; chair of library and book-night committee, 1961), Word on the Street (founding member), Canadian

Society of Professional Journalists, Writer's Union of Canada, Periodical Writers' Association of Canada, Authors Guild, Authors League of America, American Academy of Political and Social Science, European Academy of Arts, Sciences and Humanities, American Management Association, Edward R. Murrow Fund (chair of publisher's committee), Advertising Club of New York, Association of Alumni of Sir George Williams University (president of New York branch, 1959-64; president, 1973-75), Authors' Club (London, England), Toronto Men's Press Club (founding director), Canadian Society (New York), Dutch Treat Club (New York), Deadline Club (New York), Sigma Delta Chi.

AWARDS, HONORS: Montreal YMCA Literature Award, 1938, 1939, and 1940; Crusade for Freedom Award, American Heritage Foundation, 1954; Queen's Silver Jubilee Medal, 1979, for contributions to international publishing; Air Canada Literary Award, 1979, for contributions to Canadian writing; Allan Sangster Award, Canadian Authors Association, 1982; Apex Award, 1992, for newsletter editing; *Toronto Star* short fiction award, 1988; Lyn Harrington Diamond Jubilee Award, 1989; Mercury Award, 1990, for outstanding achievement in professional communications.

WRITINGS:

(With Leonid Kotkin) *Eat, Think, and Be Slender,* Hawthorn, 1954, new edition, Wilshire, 1960.
(With Walter Germain) *The Magic Power of Your Mind,* Hawthorn, 1956.
(With Joyce Brothers) *Ten Days to a Successful Memory,* Prentice-Hall, 1957.
Stress and Your Heart, Hawthorn, 1961.
(Under pseudonym Frederick Kerr) *Watch Your Weight Go Down,* Pyramid Publications, 1963.
(With Germain) *Secrets of Your Supraconscious,* Hawthorn, 1965.
(With David Goodman) *What's Best for Your Child—and You,* Hawthorn, 1966.
(With Jesse Reid) *Buy High, Sell Higher!,* Hawthorn, 1966.
(Under pseudonym M. N. Thaler) *It's Fun to Fondue,* Centaur Press, 1968.
(With Ion Grumeza) *Nadia,* Hawthorn, 1977.
Mad About Fondue, Irwin, 1986.
Careers in Writing, CAA, 1986.
(With Andrew Willman) *Prospering Through the Coming Depression,* Fitzhenry & Whiteside, 1988.
Home Emergency Handbook, McClelland & Stewart, 1990.

Contributor to books, including *Successful Writers and How They Work,* edited by Larston Farrar, Hawthorn, 1958; *Words on Paper,* edited by Roy Copperud, Hawthorn, 1960; *The Overseas Press Club Cookbook,* edited by Sigrid Schultz, Doubleday, 1962; *The Seniors' Guide to Life in the Slow Lane,* Eden Press, 1986; *The Writer's Essential Desk Reference,* edited by Glenda Tennant Neff, Writer's Digest Books, 1991; *Lifetime: A Treasury of Uncommon Wisdoms,* Macmillan Canada, 1992. Author of several columns, including "A Word to the Wise" in *Canadian Author & Bookman.* Contributor to periodicals, including *American Weekly, Maclean's, Science Digest, Reader's Digest, Best Years, Weight Watchers,* and *True.* Editor, *Third Degree* and *National Newsline.* Also scriptwriter for Joyce Brothers's television program for two years. Ghostwriter for columns by actress Anita Colby and publisher Enid Haupt of *Seventeen* magazine; sometimes writes under pseudonyms Frohm Fredericks and E. R. Kern.

Many of Fred Kerner's books have been translated into French, Spanish, German, Portuguese, Italian, and Japanese.

EDITOR

Love Is a Man's Affair, Fell, 1958.
A Treasury of Lincoln Quotations, Doubleday, 1965.
The Canadian Writer's Guide, Fitzhenry & Whiteside, 11th edition, 1992.

WORK IN PROGRESS: Canadian English usage; *1001 Ways to Have Good Luck; Public Speaking for Fun and Profit;* children's books on word-play.

SIDELIGHTS: Fred Kerner gave *CA* his advice to aspiring writers: "If you wish to develop your style, you must first learn to love the basic tools of the writer's craft: *words.* Learn to love them for their color, their texture, their weight, their sound—even their visual impact. Learn to fully appreciate them as your tools. English is the most flexible language and its use—properly and appropriately—is the most important aspect of being a competent and capable writer."

* * *

KERR, Frederick
  See KERNER, Fred

* * *

KERSH, Cyril 1925-1993

PERSONAL: Born February 24, 1925, in London, England; died May 13, 1993; son of Hyman (a master tailor) and Leah (Miller) Kersh; married Suzanne Fajner, June

25, 1956. *Education:* Attended high school in Essex, England. *Religion:* Jewish.

CAREER: The People, reporter, news and features editor, 1943-54; *Illustrated,* features editor, 1954-59; *London Evening Standard,* features writer, 1959-60; *Men Only,* editor, 1960-63; *Sunday Mirror,* features editor, became senior features executive, 1963-76; *Reveille,* editor, 1976-79; *Sunday Mirror,* assistant editor, 1979-84, managing editor, 1984-86. *Military service:* Royal Navy, 1943-47.

MEMBER: Our Society, Scribes, Paternosters.

WRITINGS:

NOVELS

The Aggravations of Minnie Ashe, M. Joseph (London, England), 1970.
The Diabolical Liberties of Uncle Max, M. Joseph, 1973.
The Soho Summer of Mr. Green, W. H. Allen (London, England), 1974.
The Shepherds Bush Connection, W. H. Allen, 1975.
Minnie Ashe at War, W. H. Allen, 1979.

OTHER

A Few Gross Words: The Street of Shame, and My Part in It, (autobiography), Simon & Schuster (New York City), 1990.

Contributor to magazines.

SIDELIGHTS: Cyril Kersh once told *CA:* "I am the brother of Gerald Kersh (an infinitely finer writer). I was encouraged by a piece I wrote in *Queen* magazine about my mother. It had enough material in it for five short stories, so I wrote five. Then I realized nobody (more or less) prints short stories, so I started a novel. Offered a generous advance, I finished it. It topped the British best-seller lists for several weeks. Since I didn't want to be known as a one-novel author, others followed."

OBITUARIES:

PERIODICALS

Times (London), May 17, 1993, p. 19.*

* * *

KEYES, Ralph 1945-

PERSONAL: Surname rhymes with "eyes"; born January 12, 1945, in Cincinnati, OH; son of Scott (a regional planner) and Charlotte Esther (a writer; maiden name, Shachmann) Keyes; married Muriel Gordon (a college administrator), February 13, 1965; children: David Gordon, Scott Michael. *Education:* Antioch College, B.A., 1967; London

School of Economics and Political Science, graduate study, 1967-68.

ADDRESSES: Home—690 Omar Circle, Yellow Springs, OH 45387. *Agent*—Colleen Mohyde, Doe Coover Agency, 58 Sagamore Ave., Medford, MA 02155.

CAREER: Newsday, Long Island, NY, assistant to publisher and feature writer, 1968-70; Prescott College, visiting assistant professor, 1971 and 1974; Temple University, Philadelphia, PA, lecturer, 1979; Widener University, Chester, PA, lecturer, 1983. Center for Studies of the Person, La Jolla, CA, fellow, 1970-79. Has also taught at Antioch College. Frequent speaker and leader of workshops and seminars on behavioral topics.

MEMBER: Authors Guild, Authors League of America, Antioch Writer's Workshop (board of directors).

AWARDS, HONORS: Woodrow Wilson Fellow; San Diego Press Club Headliner of the Year for Literature, 1976; citation for non-fiction from the *Athenaaeum* (Philadelphia, PA).

WRITINGS:

We, the Lonely People: Searching for Community, Harper (New York City), 1973.
Is There Life after High School?, Little, Brown (Boston, MA), 1976.
The Height of Your Life, Little, Brown, 1980.
Chancing It: Why We Take Risks, Little Brown, 1985.
Timelock: How Life Got So Hectic and What You Can Do about It, HarperCollins (New York City), 1991.
"Nice Guys Finish Seventh": False Phrases, Spurious Sayings, and Familiar Misquotations, HarperCollins, 1992.
(Editor) *Sons on Fathers: A Book of Men's Writing* (anthology), HarperCollins, 1992.

Contributor of articles to magazines, including *Newsweek, Nation, Playboy, Mademoiselle, Human Behavior, Popular Psychology, Car and Driver, Change, West, Parade, Esquire, New York, Reader's Digest, Publishers Weekly, Cosmopolitan, Antioch Review, Family Weekly, Gentlemen's Quarterly, Village Voice*, and others. Also contributor to newspapers, including the *New York Times, Los Angeles Times, Philadelphia Inquirer*, and many others.

ADAPTATIONS: Is There Life after High School? was adapted for the stage as a musical comedy and opened on Broadway in 1982.

WORK IN PROGRESS: The Courage to Write, Henry Holt, due 1995.

SIDELIGHTS: In his writings, Ralph Keyes has explored obstacles ranging from learning how to deal with loneliness in an increasingly dehumanized and mobile society to the obvious (and not so obvious) difficulties associated with being unusually tall or short. Relying on statistical information, results from questionnaires, and comments obtained during personal interviews, the author blends a touch of humor and occasional sadness with his factual findings to come up with highly readable and entertaining "studies" of various insecurities which plague countless American adults. But why, he is often asked, does he choose to dwell almost exclusively on the negative aspects of human existence? The answer, notes Keyes, is simple: "Failure is more universal than success and I'm looking for universal subjects. I'm much more interested in exploring areas where I feel room for growth."

One of Keyes's most popular endeavors in this field focuses on what he believes to be the ultimate American experience—high school. *Is There Life after High School?* features Keyes's customary blend of facts and humor, and a certain nostalgia as well, as he recounts the trials and tribulations of adolescence as seen through the eyes of various celebrities and non-celebrities. According to some reviewers, this method is especially appealing when it is applied to a subject such as high school, for it always comes as a relief to the reader to know that Henry Kissinger was the fat kid nobody would eat lunch with and that the bully who used to push Mike Nichols's head under water and stand on it is now a used-car salesman.

Taking into account these stories and other types of information, Keyes concludes that being included in or rejected from the popular group in high school is integral to shaping a person's future. He distinguishes between high school "innies" and "outies," with the "in" group consisting of male jocks and their female equivalents—cheerleaders—and the "out" group consisting of everyone who is *not* a jock or a cheerleader. In short, he offers some comfort to the "outies" of the world: he claims that they are better off in the long run. Writing about the book in the *Chicago Tribune Book World*, Susan Brownmiller points out, "The winners of the high school celebrity sweepstakes are not necessarily the ones who sail from success to success in the afterlife . . . The standards of conformity by which they judge themselves and the rest of us do not prepare them completely for the varied games of individual achievement that adult persons play."

Lois Gould, commenting in the *New York Times Book Review*, calls *Is There Life after High School?* a "painstaking—and pain-inducing—autopsy on high school." Gould also remarks, "High school, like youth itself, is best appreciated from a safe distance—say, 20 years. Even then, it hurts when you laugh. And if you stop laughing, it hurts worse. Ralph Keyes knows all this only too well. He is, like most of us, a lifelong sufferer from high school disease. . . . Painful as it is to revive these horrors by publishing them, it is, for some, the only thing that helps. . . .

Keyes is fond of quoting rock star Frank Zappa, to the effect that 'high school isn't a time or place; it's a state of mind.' And in Keyes's mind, the state remains peopled by raunchy Doby Gillises, Archies and Jugheads, all wearing letter sweaters, and by Gidgets doing maddeningly sexy cartwheels knowing full well their underpants are showing."

For Francis H. Curtis writing in *Best Sellers*, the book falls somewhat short of expectations, for "while [it] does make a valid point or two, Keyes has tried to capitalize on research to give it authenticity and on sex and foul language to make it a seller. This turns an interesting topic and a valuable contribution to the literature into a treatise that fails to be much of either." In the *Christian Science Monitor*, R. J. Cattani criticizes Keyes for being "a high school fan, a reunion buff " who "writes more with nostalgia than irony," but the reviewer concludes that *Is There Life after High School?* "roars with adolescent enthusiasm and apprehension. . . . [The author] should find many readers among those who now and then take out their senior yearbooks." Writing in the *Washington Post Book World*, L. J. Davis observes, "Reading this thoroughly engaging little study is like finding our adoption papers; we always knew it was true. High school in America is a universal but singularly worthless social experience that spectacularly rewards the meaningless skills of a few, traumatizes the majority, and marks us for life. . . . Keyes doesn't tell us what to do about it, but it is nice to know that we aren't alone."

Keyes dealt with the social ramifications of height in his 1980 book, *The Height of Your Life*, which, as John Leonard explains in the *New York Times*, "has to do with the war between the talls and the smalls; how our own height relative to someone else's affects our perceptions of ourselves, our self-esteem; what it feels like to be abnormal on either end of the scale . . . how always having to look up at other people is, literally, a pain in the neck." In addition to trivia such as heights of well-known people (Julia Child is six feet two inches, for example) and general facts (we all shrink an inch or two after age thirty), Keyes provides thoughts about how height breeds stereotype and even discrimination. Leonard finds this effort "an odd, breezy book, quick to record a joke, occasionally rueful, that gathers a kind of sadness as it moves along. . . . I am made to realize how crucial size is in social dynamics, and how cruel those dynamics are."

Keyes's next book, *Chancing It: Why We Take Risks*, was prompted, Lee Powell reports in *People Magazine*, by "a feeling of restlessness—one he believed others of his generation were sharing." The author explained: "People were talking the way I felt . . . wanting to take more risks." The questions, Powell says, were why "and what constituted a risk in the first place?" More than five hundred interviews later, with an assortment of subjects as diverse as nuns and go-go dancers, policemen and drug dealers, Keyes wrote *Chancing It*, in which he set forth his finding that there are two kinds, or levels, of risk—one that poses physical excitement and danger and another that involves personal chance-taking, such as revealing private emotions or making long-term commitments. The two levels of risk are usually mixed within any individual, though most people tend to prefer one kind to the other. Humiliation, Keyes elaborates to Powell, is "the universal risk," the one we are willing to avoid by taking other serious— even potentially fatal—risks. For example, Keyes tells Powell, "high-wire walker Philippe Petit, who denies taking risks, told me he once worked on a cable that was dangerously loose just to avoid the embarrassment of walking away." Keyes suggests that we analyze our own risk-taking styles with the goals of finding productive outlets for our preferred risk-taking method (such as finding a job driving an ambulance or washing windows on a high-rise building for physical risk-takers) and taking some carefully chosen risks from the level we are less comfortable with to provide a "balanced diet of risks," Zick Rubin quotes Keyes as saying in the *New York Times Book Review*.

John Urquhart, writing for the *Philadelphia Inquirer*, labels *Chancing It* "an entertaining, insightful tour through the psychology of risk-taking, with all its paradoxes and contradictions." Urquhart adds that the book "helps readers recognize the contradictions in their own risk-taking behavior, and it makes the case that accepting risk is an essential part of a full and healthy life." However, Rubin calls Keyes "an entertaining writer with a light touch" but takes exception to his analysis of the psychology of risk taking, which he considers "too loose and facile to be truly enlightening." He believes that the author "overemphasizes the role of personality and underemphasizes the role of situational factors in determining the risks we take." Despite Urquhart's objection that the book lacks "practical pieces of information about risks in today's life," such as health risks associated with smoking and drunken driving, he notes that "what you get from *Chancing It* . . . is a richly exampled, well-written account of the diversity of human judgment and behavior in the face of choices involving the fear of possible loss."

In 1992, Keyes saw the publication of two books, *"Nice Guys Finish Seventh": False Phrases, Spurious Sayings, and Familiar Misquotations*, and *Sons on Fathers: A Book of Men's Writing*, an anthology which he edited. *Sons on Fathers* includes almost eighty essays and poems which Keyes collected for about twenty years. The selections are by men who have written strongly emotional pieces about their fathers. The contributions are from such luminaries as former President Jimmy Carter, Ernest Hemingway's son Patrick, and writer Robert Bly as well as other authors, poets, novelists, and journalists. Mary Carroll writing for *Booklist* observes, "*Sons on Fathers* is a celebration, a meditation, a plaint, and a eulogy," and the work was deemed an "important collection" by a reviewer for the *Library Journal.*

"*Nice Guys Finish Seventh*" is a volume of research dedicated to clarifying the origin and wording of such common expressions as "Winning isn't everything, it's the only thing," "There ain't no such thing as a free lunch," "Play it again, Sam," and hundreds of others. The book's title has its roots in the saying "Nice guys finish last," which has been attributed to Brooklyn Dodger manager Leo Durocher speaking of rival team the New York Giants. Keyes offers that Durocher actually said, as he waved to the Giants' dugout, "The nice guys are all over there. In seventh place." In addition, Keyes points out, seventh place wasn't even last. A reviewer for the *Wilson Library Bulletin* says that the work is "basic to reference collections," and Mary Carroll in *Booklist* also notes Keyes' "interesting, often surprising facts about who said what when . . . deserves a place in most quotation collections."

Keyes told *CA:* "For most of my adult life I have been a free-lance writer. Like so many who do it for a living, I don't enjoy writing as such. (Peter De Vries once said, 'I love being a writer. What I can't stand is the paperwork.') Yet I do like much that surrounds the writing process: developing story ideas, interviewing subjects, doing research. Creating a whole from these parts can be quite satisfying. There are few types of work with more tangible evidence of how you've spent your time than writing. Nor is there a better shot at immortality.

"Because so much of my writing gets onto 'touchy' ground, I nearly always try to soften it with humor. Just as the smoothest Scotch can pack the hardest punch, heavy messages are best conveyed with light prose. Although I don't see my work as a tool for righting social wrongs, I do hope it gives aid and comfort to readers by suggesting that they're not alone in having reactions to life which may feel embarrassing. Confronting 'negative' thoughts and feelings directly can have positive outcomes. (Unburdening myself with *Is There Life after High School?* made it possible for me to attend my twentieth class reunion, and enjoy it immensely).

"The longer I write, the simpler I'd like my writing to be; a well-cleaned piece of glass through which the reader can see clearly to the content inside. The ideal would be prose so transparent that readers wouldn't even be aware of my fingers at the keyboard. . . . The hardest work of writing, I find, is concealing how much effort it takes, and beating down the urge to show off."

BIOGRAPHICAL/CRITICAL SOURCES:

PERIODICALS

Best Sellers, September, 1976.
Booklist, January 1, 1985, p. 604; October 1, 1992; May 15, 1992, p. 1646.
Chicago Tribune Book World, June 13, 1976.
Christian Science Monitor, July 21, 1976.
Library Journal, May 15, 1976; June 15, 1992.
Los Angeles Times, May 8, 1980.
Newsweek, May 19, 1980.
New York Daily News, September 8, 1985.
New York Times, April 14, 1980, p. C17.
New York Times Book Review, June 13, 1976, p. 8; February 3, 1985, p. 7.
People Magazine, May 13, 1985.
Philadelphia Inquirer, February 17, 1985.
Washington Post Book World, May 30, 1976.
Wilson Library Bulletin, January, 1993.

*　　*　　*

KIMES, Beverly Rae 1939-
(Jeri Cox, Cullen Thomas)

PERSONAL: Born August 17, 1939, in Aurora, IL; daughter of Raymond Lionel (a locomotive engineer) and Grace (a homemaker; maiden name, Perrin) Kimes; married James H. Cox (president of an automotive restoration company), July 6, 1984. *Education:* University of Illinois at Urbana-Champaign, B.S., 1961; Pennsylvania State University, M.A., 1963.

ADDRESSES: Home and office—215 East 80th St., New York, NY 10021.

CAREER: Mateer Playhouse, Neffs Mills, PA, publicity director, 1962; Pavillion Theatre, University Park, PA, publicity director, 1963; Automobile Quarterly Publications, New York City and Princeton, NJ, assistant editor, 1963-64, associate editor, 1965-66, managing editor, 1967-74, editor, 1975-81; executive editor, Classic Car Club of America, 1981—. Lecturer on automotive history at educational institutions and professional and civic organizations; conducts historical and architectural lecture-tours for Outdoors Clubs of New York City.

MEMBER: International Motor Press Association, National Automotive History Collection at Detroit Public Library (member of board of trustees), National Automotive Journalism Association, Society of Automotive Historians (past board member, chairperson of publications committee, and president), Milestone Car Society (past board member), Auburn-Cord-Duesenburg Museum (member of national advisory board), Museum of Transportation (Brookline, MA; member of board), Second-Third East 80th Street Block Association (member of board of directors), Theta Sigma Phi.

AWARDS, HONORS: Cugnot Award from Society of Automotive Historians, 1978, for article "The Nash Story," 1979, for *Packard: A History of the Motor Car and the Company,* 1984, for *My Two Lives: Race Driver to Restaurateur,* and 1985, for *Standard Catalog of American Cars, 1805-1942;* Thomas McKean Trophy from Antique Automobile Club of America, 1984, for *My Two Lives,* 1985, for *Standard Catalog of American Cars, 1805-1942,* and 1986, for *The Star and the Laurel: The Centennial History of Daimler, Mercedes, and Benz;* Moto Award from National Association of Automotive Journalism, 1984, for *My Two Lives,* 1985, for *Standard Catalog of American Cars, 1805-1942,* and 1986, for *The Star and the Laurel;* Friend of Automotive History Award from Society of Automotive Historians, 1985; citation for distinguished service, Classic Car Club of America, 1991; citation for distinguished service, Automotive Hall of Fame, 1993; Benz Award, 1993, for article "Ken Purdy: King of the Road."

WRITINGS:

NONFICTION

The Classic Tradition of the Lincoln Motorcar, Automobile Quarterly (Kutztown, PA), 1968.

(With Richard M. Langworth) *Oldsmobile: The First Seventy-five Years,* Automobile Quarterly, 1972.

The Cars That Henry Ford Built: A Seventy-fifth Anniversary Tribute to America's Most Remembered Automobiles, Princeton Publishing (Princeton, NJ), 1978.

(With Rene Dreyfus) *My Two Lives: Race Driver to Restaurateur,* Aztex (Tucson, AZ), 1983.

(With Robert C. Ackerson) *Chevrolet: A History From 1911,* Princeton Publishing, 1984.

Standard Catalog of American Cars, 1805-1942, Krause Publications (Iola, WI), 1985, second edition, 1989.

The Star and the Laurel: The Centennial History of Daimler, Mercedes, and Benz, Mercedes-Benz of North America, 1986.

The Classic Car: The Ultimate Book about the World's Grandest Automobiles, Classic Car Club of America (Madison, NJ), 1990.

EDITOR

(And author of introduction) *Automobile Quarterly's Great Cars and Grand Marques,* Dutton (New York City), 1976.

Packard: A History of the Motor Car and the Company, Princeton Publishing, 1979.

Automobile Quarterly's Complete Handbook of Automotive Hobbies, Princeton Publishing, 1981.

OTHER

Contributor to magazines, occasionally under pseudonyms Cullen Thomas or Jeri Cox. U.S. editor of *Enciclopedia dell' Automobile;* contributing editor of automobile sections of *World Book Encyclopedia.*

WORK IN PROGRESS: Anecdotal history of the automobile in America for Crown.

SIDELIGHTS: Beverly Rae Kimes once told *CA:* "Becoming an automobile historian was never in my plans. It happened simply because I arrived in New York City fresh from college and in need of a job—and the most promising job offered was with a new automobile history magazine. I had two degrees in journalism and a portfolio of published writing (theatre-related stories mostly), but my only other qualification for my new job was possession of a driver's license. I knew nothing about cars. But as soon as I began to learn, I became hooked.

"The fascination of automotive history is its social and cultural universality. No other invention of the modern age has so profoundly changed the way in which we live. In large measure, the automobile remade society in its image. Just imagine a world without cars today—hard to do, though admittedly some of the automobile's more severe critics would like to. Granted, the advent of the horseless age brought social and ecological problems in its wake, but I daresay the automobile will be with us until that distant day when we are molecularly beamed from place to place 'Star Trek' style. That makes the study of the automobile ever enthralling. And likewise do the people involved in making automobile history, not only the manufacturers, designers, engineers, race car drivers, and others, but those on the periphery, from Rudyard Kipling, who was a turn-of-the-century auto enthusiast, to Adolf Hitler, who strove to conquer the world of Grand Prix years before taking on the rest of the world, to contemporary oil-rich sheiks with Rolls-Royces and Ferraris by the dozens.

"Recognition in a field dominated by men might have been difficult save for a decision of my parents. Beverly can be a masculine name, and for some time most readers assumed I was a man. Letters from Europe were routinely addressed to Herr Kimes, M. Kimes, Sr. Kimes, etc.; when a British publisher with whom I'd corresponded for months unexpectedly appeared in my office one day, he initially assumed I was my secretary. Admittedly, early on I did not discourage the notion that I was a man because to ballyhoo my gender then would have been counterproductive. Establishing credentials as a historian was uppermost. By the time the word was generally out that I was not a man, I had published more than one hundred articles on automobile history and my reputation could easily survive the fact that I was writing about something women were not supposed to know anything about. Even today, two decades later, people who've been reading me for years but are meeting me for the first time often admit to astonishment on learning my true gender. I find this quite charming.

"Hopefully, the foregoing will indicate my approach to the writing of automobile history. I pride myself on being a student of the automobile. The more I know about its history the more aware I am of how much more I have to learn."

*   *   *

KINCAID, Jamaica 1949-

PERSONAL: Born Elaine Potter Richardson, May 25, 1949, in St. John's, Antigua, West Indies; daughter of a carpenter/cabinet maker and Annie Richardson; married Allen Shawn (a composer and teacher at Bennington College); children: Annie Shawn and Harold. *Education:* Studied photography at the New School for Social Research in New York; attended Franconia College, NH. *Religion:* Methodist.

ADDRESSES: Home—284 Hudson, New York, NY, and Bennington, VT. *Office*—*New Yorker,* 25 West 43rd St., New York, NY 10036.

CAREER: Writer. *New Yorker,* New York City, staff writer, 1976—. Lecturer, Bennington College, VT.

AWARDS, HONORS: Morton Dauwen Zabel Award, American Academy and Institute of Arts and Letters, 1983, for *At the Bottom of the River;* Lila Wallace-*Reader's Digest* Fund annual writer's award, 1992.

WRITINGS:

At the Bottom of the River (short stories), Farrar, Straus (New York City), 1983.
Annie John (novel), Farrar, Straus, 1985.
A Small Place (essays), Farrar, Straus, 1988.
Annie, Gwen, Lilly, Pam and Tulip, illustrations by Eric Fischl, Knopf (New York City) and Whitney Museum of American Art, 1989.
Lucy (novel), Farrar, Straus, 1990.

Also contributor to periodicals.

SIDELIGHTS: Jamaica Kincaid gained wide acclaim with her first two works, *At the Bottom of the River* and *Annie John.* In these books about life on the Caribbean island of Antigua, where she was born, Kincaid employs a highly poetic literary style celebrated for its rhythms, imagery, characterization, and elliptic narration. As Ike Onwordi wrote in *Times Literary Supplement:* "Jamaica Kincaid uses language that is poetic without affectation. She

has a deft eye for salient detail while avoiding heavy symbolism and diverting exotica. The result captures powerfully the essence of vulnerability."

"Everyone thought I had a way with words, but it came out as a sharp tongue. No one expected anything from me at all. Had I just sunk in the cracks it would not have been noted. I would have been lucky to be a secretary somewhere," Kincaid told Leslie Garis in the *New York Times Magazine.* When she was seventeen, Kincaid, whose given name was Elaine Potter, left the rural island to become an *au pair* in New York City. By the time she returned, almost twenty years later, she had become a successful writer for the *New Yorker* magazine under her chosen name.

In her first collection of stories, *At the Bottom of the River,* Kincaid shows an imposing capacity for detailing life's mundane aspects. This characteristic of her writing is readily evident in the oft-cited tale "Girl," which consists almost entirely of a mother's orders to her daughter: "Wash the white clothes on Monday and put them on the stone heap; wash the color clothes on Tuesday and put them on the clothesline to dry; don't walk barehead in the hot sun; cook pumpkin fritters in very hot sweet oil . . .; on Sundays try to walk like a lady, and not like the slut you are so bent on becoming." Anne Tyler, in a review for *New Republic,* declared that this passage provides "the clearest idea of the book's general tone; for Jamaica Kincaid scrutinizes various particles of our world so closely and so solemnly that they begin to take on a nearly mystical importance."

"The Letter From Home," also from *At the Bottom of the River,* serves as further illustration of Kincaid's style of repetition and her penchant for the mundane. In this tale a character recounts her daily chores in such a manner that the story resembles an incantation: "I milked the cows, I churned the butter, I stored the cheese, I baked the bread, I brewed the tea," Kincaid begins. In *Ms.,* Suzanne Freeman cited this tale as evidence that Kincaid's style "is . . . akin to hymn-singing or maybe even chanting." Freeman added that Kincaid's "singsong style" produces "images that are as sweet and mysterious as the secrets that children whisper in your ear."

With the publication of *At the Bottom of the River,* Kincaid was hailed as an important new voice in American fiction. Edith Milton wrote in the *New York Times Book Review* that Kincaid's tales "have all the force of illumination, and even prophetic power," and David Leavitt noted in the *Village Voice* that they move "with grace and ease from the mundane to the enormous." He added that "Kincaid's particular skill lies in her ability to articulate the internal workings of a potent imagination without sacrificing the rich details of the external world on which that imagination thrives." Doris Grumbach expressed similar praise in a review for the *Washington Post Book World.* She declared that the world of Kincaid's narrators "hovers between fantasy and reality" and asserted that Kincaid's prose "results not so much in stories as in states of consciousness." Grumbach also noted that Kincaid's style, particularly its emphasis on repetition, intensifies "the feelings of poetic jubilation Kincaid has . . . for all life."

That exuberance for life is also evident in Kincaid's second book, *Annie John,* which contains interrelated stories about a girl's maturation in Antigua. In *Annie John* the title character evolves from a young girl to an aspiring nurse and from innocent to realist: she experiences her first menstruation, buries a friend, gradually establishes a life independent of her mother, and overcomes a serious illness. She is ultimately torn by her pursuit of a career outside her life in Antigua, and Kincaid renders that feeling so incisively that, as Elaine Kendall noted in her review for the *Los Angeles Times,* "you can almost believe Kincaid invented ambivalence."

Critically acclaimed as a coming-of-age novel, *Annie John* was praised by a number of reviewers for expressing qualities of growing up that transcend geographical locations. "Her work is recollections of childhood," Paula Bonnell remarked in the *Boston Herald.* "It conveys the mysterious power and intensity of childhood attachments to mother, father and friends, and the adolescent beginnings of separation from them." Susan Kenney, writing in *The New York Times Book Review,* noted Annie John's ambivalence about leaving behind her life in Antigua and declared that such ambivalence was "an inevitable and unavoidable result of growing up." Kenney concluded that Kincaid's story is "so touching and familiar . . . so inevitable [that] it could be happening to any of us, anywhere, any time, any place. And that's exactly the book's strength, its wisdom, and its truth."

Kincaid's second novel, *Lucy,* is a first-person narrative in which nineteen-year-old Lucy expresses not only feelings of rage, but struggles with separation from her homeland and especially her mother. *Lucy* is about a young woman from Antigua who comes to an unnamed American city to work as an *au pair* girl. She is employed by a wealthy, white couple—Mariah and Lewis—to take care of their four young daughters. In the *Washington Post Book World,* Susanna Moore commented: "Lucy is unworldly. She has never seen snow or been in an elevator. . . . Written in the first person, [the novel] is Lucy's story of the year of her journey—away from her mother, away from home, away from the island and into the world." Richard Eder mused in the *Los Angeles Times Book Review* that "The anger of Lucy . . . is an instru-

ment of discovery, not destruction. It is lucid and cool, but by no means unsparing."

The novel ends with Lucy writing in a journal given to her by Mariah, the woman for whom she works, and weeping over the very first line: " 'I wish I could love someone so much that I would die from it.' And then as I looked at this sentence a great wave of shame came over me and I wept and wept so much that the tears fell on the page and caused all the words to become one great blur." Eder ended his review saying, "she will turn the page and go on writing."

Derek Walcott, a West Indian poet, talked with Garis in the *New York Times Magazine* about Kincaid's identification with issues that thread through all people's lives: "That relationship of mother and daughter—today she loves her mother, tomorrow she hates her, then she admires here—that is so true to life, without any artificiality, that it describes parental and filial love in a way that has never been done before. [Kincaid's] work is so full of spiritual contradictions clarified that it's extremely profound and courageous."

Thulani Davis, writing in the *New York Times Book Review* said, "Ms. Kincaid is a marvelous writer whose descriptions are richly detailed; her sentences turn and surprise even in the bare context she has created, in which there are few colors, sights or smells and the moments of intimacy and confrontation take place in the wings, or just after the door closes. . . . Lucy is a delicate, careful observer, but her rage prevents her from reveling in the deliciousness of a moment. At her happiest, she simply says, 'Life isn't so bad after all.' "

Henry Louis Gates, Jr., a distinguished critic and black studies scholar, told Emily Listfield in *Harper's Bazaar* that he felt comfortable comparing Kincaid's work to that of Tony Morrison and Wole Soyinka: "There is a self-contained world which they explore with great detail. Not to chart the existence of that world, but to show that human emotions manifest themselves everywhere." Gates said that an important contribution of Kincaid is that "she never feels the necessity of claiming the existence of a black world or a female sensibility. She assumes them both. I think it's a distinct departure that she's making, and I think that more and more black American writers will assume their world the way that she does. So that we can get beyond the large theme of racism and get to the deeper themes of how black people love and cry and live and die. Which, after all, is what art is all about."

BIOGRAPHICAL/CRITICAL SOURCES:

BOOKS

Black Literature Criticism, Volume 2, Gale, 1991.

Contemporary Literary Criticism, Gale, Volume 43, 1987, Volume 68, 1991.

Cudjoe, Selwyn, "Jamaica Kincaid and the Modernist Project: An Interview," *Caribbean Women Writers: Essays from the First International Conference.* Callaloo, 1990.

Dance, D. Cumber, editor, *Fifty Caribbean Writers,* Greenwood, 1986.

Ferguson, Moira, *Jamaica Kincaid: Where the Land Meets the Body,* University Press of Virginia, 1994.

Kincaid, Jamaica, *At the Bottom of the River,* Farrar, Straus, 1983.

Kincaid, Jamaica, *Lucy,* Farrar, Straus, 1990.

PERIODICALS

Atlantic, May, 1985.
Boston Herald, March 31, 1985.
Christian Science Monitor, April 5, 1985.
Harper's Bazaar, October, 1990.
Listener, January 10, 1985.
Library Journal, December 1, 1989.
Los Angeles Times, April 25, 1985.
Los Angeles Times Book Review, October 21, 1990.
Maclean's, May 20, 1985.
Ms., January 1984.
Nation, June 15, 1985.
New Republic, December 31, 1983.
New Statesman, September 7, 1984.
New York Times Book Review, January 15, 1984; April 7, 1985; July 10, 1988; October 28, 1990.
New York Times Magazine, October 7, 1990.
Times Literary Supplement, November 29, 1985.
Village Voice, January 17, 1984.
Virginia Quarterly Review, summer, 1985.
Voice Literary Supplement, April 1985.
Washington Post, April 2, 1985.
Washington Post Book World, October 7, 1990.
World Literature Today, autumn, 1985.

OTHER

Interview with Jamaica Kincaid conducted by Kay Bonetti, recorded for American Audio Prose Library (Bennington, VT), 1991.

*   *   *

KIRK, Donald R.   1935-

PERSONAL: Born April 19, 1935, in Canon City, CO; married; wife's name Janice E. (a musician and artist); children: Ned, Amy. *Education:* Shasta College, A.A.; University of Oregon, B.S. and M.S. *Politics:* Democrat. *Religion:* Protestant.

ADDRESSES: Home—Box 190, Palo Cedro, CA 96073. *Office*—Department of Biology, Shasta College, Redding, CA 96001.

CAREER: Boise Junior College (now Boise State College), Boise, ID, assistant professor of biology, 1963-65; Shasta College, Redding, CA, professor of biology, 1965—.

MEMBER: American Nature Study Society, Natural Wildlife Federation, Audubon Society.

WRITINGS:

Wild Edible Plants of the Western United States, Naturegraph, 1970.

(With wife, Janice E. Kirk) *Cherish the Earth: The Environment and Scripture,* Herald Press, 1993.

*   *   *

KIRK, Michael
See KNOX, William

*   *   *

KITCHEN, Helen (Angell)

PERSONAL: Born in Fossil, OR; daughter of Lloyd Steiwer and Hilda (Miller) Angell; married Jeffrey C. Kitchen, August 12, 1944 (divorced, 1985); children: Jeffrey Coleman, Jr., Erik L., Lynn W. *Education:* University of Oregon, B.A. (with honors), 1942.

ADDRESSES: Home—4309 Embassy Park Dr. N.W., Washington, DC 20016. *Office*—Director of African Studies, Center for Strategic and International Studies, 1800 K St. N.W., Washington, DC 20006.

CAREER: Reader's Digest, Pleasantville, NY, member of editorial staff, 1942-44; political researcher in Cairo, Egypt, 1944-46; *Middle East Journal,* Washington, DC, assistant editor, 1948; U.S. Department of State, Washington, DC, review officer in Division of Research for Near East, South Asia, and Africa, 1950-58; *Africa Report,* Washington, DC, editor, 1960-68; director of Africa Area Study, Rockefeller Commission on Critical Choices for Americans, 1974-76; executive director, United States-South Africa Leader Exchange Program, 1978-81; Center for Strategic and International Studies (CSIS), Washington, DC, director of African Studies, 1981—. Member of board of public advisers, Bureau of African Affairs, U.S. Department of State, 1963-70; member of board, African Development Foundation, 1985-92; member, Ford Foundation Study Group on South Africa, 1984-91, and Council on Foreign Relations; U.S. Africanist member, United States-Soviet Task Force on Regional Conflict, 1988-92.

Consultant to RAND Corp., 1962-68, and Secretary of State's Advisory Committee on South Africa, 1985-86.

MEMBER: African Studies Association of the United States (trustee, 1964-67), Phi Beta Kappa.

AWARDS, HONORS: Award for Outstanding Service, U.S. Secretary of State, 1957; honorary Ph.D., Lafayette College (PA), 1990.

WRITINGS:

The Press in Africa, Ruth Sloan Associates, 1956.
(Editor) *The Educated African: A Country-by-Country Survey of Educational Development in Africa,* Praeger (New York City), 1962.
(Editor) *A Handbook of African Affairs,* Praeger, 1964.
(Editor) *Footnotes to the Congo Story: An Africa Report Anthology,* Walker & Co. (New York City), 1967.
Africa: From Mystery to Maze, Lexington Books (Lexington, MA), 1976.
(Editor) *Options for U.S. Policy toward Africa,* American Enterprise Institute for Public Policy Research (Washington, DC), 1979.
U.S. Interests in Africa, Praeger, 1983.
(With Michael Clough) *The United States and South Africa: Realities and Red Herrings,* Center for Strategic and International Studies (Washington, DC), 1984.
Angola, Mozambique, and the West, Praeger, 1987.
Some Guidelines on Africa for the Next President, Center for Strategic and International Studies, 1988.
South Africa: In Transition to What?, Praeger, Volume 1, 1988, Volume 2, 1994.

Contributor to periodicals. Editor, *African Index,* 1978-82, and *CSIS Africa Notes,* 1982—.

*   *   *

KLIEVER, Lonnie D(ean)   1931-

PERSONAL: Born November 18, 1931, in Corn, OK; son of David R. (a mechanic) and Amanda (Warkentine) Kliever; married Arthiss Laughman, August 14, 1964; children: Launa Deane, Marney Marie. *Education:* Hardin-Simmons University, B.A. (magna cum laude), 1955; Union Theological Seminary, New York, NY, B.D. (cum laude), 1959; Duke University, Ph.D.,1963. *Avocational interests:* Politics, woodworking, camping.

ADDRESSES: Home—9549 Spring Branch, Dallas, TX 75238. *Office*—Department of Religion, Southern Methodist University, Dallas, TX 75275.

CAREER: University of Texas, El Paso Campus, assistant professor, 1962-63, associate professor of philosophy, 1963-65; Trinity University, San Antonio, TX, associate

professor of religion, 1965-69; University of Windsor, Windsor, Ontario, Canada, associate professor, 1969-71, professor of theology, 1971-75; Southern Methodist University, Dallas, TX, professor of religion and chairman of department, 1975—.

MEMBER: American Academy of Religion, American Association of University Professors, Society for the Scientific Study of Religion, Canadian Society for the Study of Religion, American Cultural Association.

WRITINGS:

(With John H. Hayes) *Radical Christianity: The New Theologies in Perspective,* Droke, 1968.
H. Richard Niebuhr, Word Books, 1977.
The Shattered Spectrum: A Survey of Contemporary Theology, John Knox Press (Atlanta, GA), 1981.
(Editor) *The Terrible Meek: Religion and Revolution in Cross-Cultural Perspective,* Paragon House, 1987.
(Editor) *Dax's Case: Essays in Medical Ethics and Human Meaning,* Southern Methodist University Press (Dallas, TX), 1989.

Contributor to *Journal of Religion, Harvard Theological Review, Religion in Life, Religious Studies Review, Journal for the Scientific Study of Religion, Studies in Religion, Journal of the American Academy of Religion* and *Christian Century.*

SIDELIGHTS: Lonnie D. Kliever has traveled in the former Soviet Union as well as in Western Europe, Korea and Mexico.

BIOGRAPHICAL/CRITICAL SOURCES:

PERIODICALS

Choice, December, 1981, p. 518.
Kirkus Review, December 1, 1980, p. 1556.
Library Journal, February 15, 1981, p. 460.
Religious Studies Review, January, 1983, p. 54.

*   *   *

KNIFFEN, Fred B(owerman)   1900-1993

PERSONAL: Born January 18, 1900, in Britton, MI; died May 19, 1993; son of Samuel Bradshaw and Mary Ingersoll (Bowerman) Kniffen; married Virginia Arp, 1927; children: Samuel James, Donald Avery, Nancy Rabalais, Anthony G. *Education:* University of Michigan, A.B. (with high distinction), 1922; University of California, Ph.D., 1929; University of Munich, postdoctoral student, 1938-39. *Religion:* Presbyterian.

ADDRESSES: Home—Baton Rouge, LA.

CAREER: Louisiana State University, Baton Rouge, assistant professor and professor, 1924-66, Boyd Professor of Geography and Anthropology, 1966-70, Emeritus Boyd Professor, 1970 onwards.

MEMBER: Association of American Geographers (councillor and member of executive committee, 1959-62; honorary president, 1964-65), American Anthropological Association, American Association for the Advancement of Science, Sigma Xi, Phi Beta Kappa, Masons.

AWARDS, HONORS: University of Munich, Rosenwald Fellow, 1938-39; Naval Reserve fellow, 1950-51; National Park Service fellow, 1955-56; National Science Foundation fellow, 1960-62; distinguished faculty fellow, Louisiana State University Foundation, 1966-67.

WRITINGS:

Achomawi Geography, University of California Press (Berkeley, CA), 1928.

The Natural Landscape of the Colorado Delta, University of California Press, 1932.

Pomo Geography, University of California Press, 1939.

The Indians of Louisiana, illustrated by Mildred Compton, Louisiana State University Press (Baton Rouge, LA), 1945.

(With Richard Joel Russell and Evelyn Lord Pruitt) *Culture Worlds,* Macmillan (New York City), 1951.

(With Henry Glassie) *Building in Wood in the Eastern United States: A Time-Place Perspective,* American Geographical Society, 1966.

Louisiana: Its Lands and People, Louisiana State University Press, 1968.

(With Malcolm L. Comeaux) *The Spanish Moss Folk Industry of Louisiana,* Museum of Geoscience, Louisiana State University Press, 1979.

(With Hiram F. Gregory and George A. Stokes) *Historic Indian Tribes of Louisiana: From 1542 to the Present,* Louisiana State University Press, 1987.

Cultural Diffusion and Landscapes, edited by H. Jesse Walker and Randall A. Detro, Geoscience Publications, Department of Geography and Anthropology, Louisiana State University Press, 1990.

Contributor to books and publications, including *Walapai Ethnography,* edited by A.L. Kroeber, Krause Reprint Corporation, 1964; and *American Folklife,* edited by Don Yoder, University of Texas Press, 1976. Has also contributed to such journals as *Landscape, Western Folklore,* and *World Book.*

BIOGRAPHICAL/CRITICAL SOURCES:

BOOKS

H. J. Walker and W. G. Haag, editors, *Men and Cultural Heritage: Papers in Honor of Fred B. Kniffen,* Louisiana State University Press, 1974.

PERIODICALS

American Antiquity, January, 1990, p. 202.
American Historical Review, February, 1989, p. 201.
Journal of Southern History, February, 1989, p. 106.
Pioneer America Society, (special issue honoring Fred Kniffen), July, 1971.
Western Historical Quarterly, November, 1988, p. 456.*

*   *   *

KNOX, Bill
See KNOX, William

*   *   *

KNOX, William   1928-
   (Michael Kirk, Bill Knox, Robert MacLeod,
   Noah Webster)

PERSONAL: Born February 20, 1928, in Glasgow, Scotland; son of Robert (a journalist) and Rhoda (maiden name, MacLeod) Knox; married Myra Ann McKill, March 31, 1950; children: Susan Elizabeth, Michael Craig, Marian Ailsa (deceased). *Education:* Attended schools in Scotland. *Religion:* Church of Scotland.

ADDRESSES: Home and office—Thanemoss, 55 Newtonlea Ave., Newton Mearns, Glasgow G77 5QF, Scotland.

CAREER: Full-time writer and broadcaster. *Evening Citizen,* Glasgow, Scotland, copy boy, 1944-45; *Evening News,* Glasgow, reporter and deputy news editor, 1945-57; *Empire News,* London, England, Scottish news editor, 1957-59; Scottish Television, Glasgow, news editor, 1959-61; *Evening Citizen,* Glasgow, motoring correspondent, 1962-67. Host of "Crime Desk" weekly television program, 1976-88.

MEMBER: Mystery Writers of America, Crime Writers Association, Scottish Motoring Writers Association (past president), Royal Naval Volunteer Reserve Club (Scotland), Eastwood Rotary Club (past president).

AWARDS, HONORS: Paul Harris Rotary International Fellow, 1990; U.K. Police Review award for crime novel which gave the best portrayal of police procedures for *Crossfire Killings.*

WRITINGS:

FICTION; UNDER NAME BILL KNOX

Deadline for a Dream, John Long (London, England), 1957, published as *In at the Kill,* Doubleday (New York City), 1961.
Cockatoo Crime, John Long, 1958.
Death Department, John Long, 1959.
Leave It to the Hangman, John Long, 1960. Doubleday, 1961.
Death Calls the Shots, John Long, 1961.
Die for Big Betsy, John Long, 1961.
Little Drops of Blood, Doubleday, 1962.
Sanctuary Isle, John Long, 1962, published as *The Grey Sentinels,* Doubleday, 1963.
The Man in the Bottle, John Long, 1963, published as *The Killing Game,* Doubleday, 1963.
The Drum of Ungara, Doubleday, 1963, published in England as *Drum of Power,* John Long, 1964.
The Scavengers, John Long, 1964.
The Taste of Proof, Doubleday, 1965.
Devilweed, Doubleday, 1966.
The Ghost Car, Doubleday, 1966, published in England as *The Deep Fall,* John Long, 1966.
Blacklight, Doubleday, 1967.
Justice on the Rocks, John Long, 1967, Doubleday, 1968.
Figurehead, Doubleday, 1968, published in England as *The Klondyker,* John Long, 1968.
The Tallyman, Doubleday, 1969.
Blueback, Doubleday, 1969.
Who Shot the Bull?, Doubleday, 1970, published in England as *Children of the Mist,* John Long, 1970.
Seafire, Doubleday, 1971.
To Kill a Witch, Doubleday, 1971.
Stormtide, Doubleday, 1972.
Draw Batons, Doubleday, 1973.
(With Edward Boyd) *The View from Daniel Pike,* St. Martin's (New York City), 1974.
Whitewater, Doubleday, 1974.
Rally to Kill, John Long, 1975, Doubleday, 1976.
Hellspout, Doubleday, 1975.
Pilot Error, Doubleday, 1977.
Witchrock, John Long, 1977, Doubleday, 1978.
Live Bate, John Long, 1978, Doubleday, 1979.
Bomb Ship, Doubleday, 1980.
A Killing in Antiques, Doubleday, 1981.
Bloodtide, Doubleday, 1982.
The Hanging Tree, Doubleday, 1984.
Wavecrest, Doubleday, 1985.
The Crossfire Killings, Doubleday, 1986.
Dead Man's Mooring, Doubleday, 1987.
The Interface Man: A Colin Thane, Scottish Crime Squad Case, Doubleday, 1989.
The Drowning Nets, Doubleday, 1991.

FICTION; UNDER PSEUDONYM ROBERT MacLEOD

Cave of Bats, John Long, 1964, Holt, 1966.
Lake of Fury, John Long, 1966, Holt, 1968.
Isle of Dragons, John Long, 1967.
Place of Mists, John Long, 1969, McCall, 1970.
Path of Ghosts, John Long, 1971.
Nest of Vultures, John Long, 1973.

FICTION; UNDER PSEUDONYM NOAH WEBSTER

Flickering Death, Doubleday, 1970, published in England under pseudonym Robert MacLeod as *A Property in Cyprus,* John Long, 1970.
A Killing in Malta, Doubleday, 1972, published in England under pseudonym Robert MacLeod, John Long, 1972.
A Burial in Portugal, Doubleday, 1974, published in England under pseudonym Robert MacLeod, John Long, 1973.
A Witchdance in Bavaria, Doubleday, 1975, published in England under pseudonym Robert MacLeod, John Long, 1975.
A Pay-Off in Switzerland, Doubleday, 1977, published in England under pseudonym Robert MacLeod, John Long, 1977.
An Incident in Iceland, Doubleday, 1980, published in England under pseudonym Robert MacLeod, Hutchinson (London, England), 1980.
A Problem in Prague, Doubleday, 1982, published in England under pseudonym Robert MacLeod, Hutchinson, 1982.
A Legacy from Tenerife, Doubleday, 1984, published in England under pseudonym Robert MacLeod, Hutchinson, 1984.
A Flight from Paris, Doubleday, 1987.
The Money Mountain, Doubleday, 1987.
Witchline: An Andrew Laird Marine Insurance Investigation, Doubleday, 1988, published in England as *Witchline* under pseudonym Robert Macleod, Century, 1988.
The Spanish Maze Game, Doubleday, 1991, published in England under pseudonym Robert MacLeod, Century, 1991.

FICTION; UNDER PSEUDONYM MICHAEL KIRK

All Other Perils, Doubleday, 1974, published in England under pseudonym Robert MacLeod, John Long, 1974.
Dragonship, Doubleday, 1977, published in England under pseudonym Robert MacLeod, John Long, 1976.
Salvage Job, Doubleday, 1979, published in England under pseudonym Robert MacLeod, John Long, 1978.

Cargo Risk, Doubleday, 1981, published in England under pseudonym Robert MacLeod, Hutchinson, 1981.
Mayday from Malaga, Doubleday, 1983, published in England under pseudonym Robert MacLeod, Hutchinson, 1983.
A Cut in Diamonds, Doubleday, 1985, published in England under pseudonym Robert MacLeod, Century, 1985.

NONFICTION; UNDER NAME BILL KNOX

(With Robert Colquhoun) *Life Begins at Midnight,* John Long, 1961.
(With David Murray) *Ecurie Ecosse,* Stanley Paul, 1962.
(With John Glaister) *Final Diagnosis,* Hutchinson, 1964.
Court of Murder, Hutchinson, 1968.
The Thin Blue Line, John Long, 1973.
Scottish Tales of Crime, Mainstream (Edinburgh, Scotland), 1983.

Honorary editor, *Scottish Lifeboat* magazine of Royal National Lifeboat Institution, 1984—.

SIDELIGHTS: William Knox once told *CA* that "having a newspaper and TV background as a 'fact' man in crime and feature writing and as a TV presenter saves a lot of research time when it comes to novel writing. In fact, work is a circle pattern. Research for, say, a real-life TV piece has its spin-off in terms of ideas for a possible novel. The additional research to tidy the novel often sparks off a fresh, future 'real-life' piece.

"Again, any writer will agree it can be a pretty lonely business [but] the TV and media world is exactly the opposite and so one background compensates for the other. Not to mention that travel abroad as a journalist means someone else picks up the tab!"

A prolific writer, Knox's writing is "refreshing" in its "quiet competence" and skillful plotting, writes Newgate Callendar in the *New York Times Book Review.* Under his own name and pseudonyms, Knox has created several series detectives, the best of whom do their sleuthing at sea. *Blacklight* and *Bloodtide* are two of the books published under the name Bill Knox that feature First Officer Webb Carrick of the Fisheries Protection Service. Writing as Michael Kirk in another series, Knox relates the exploits of Andrew Laird, a marine-claims investigator. *Mayday from Malaga* is one such fast-paced book that shows Laird in action. Newgate Callendar notes that *Mayday from Malaga,* like all of Knox's books, is "cleanly, smoothly written . . . with intelligent characterization." Under his Noah Webster pen name, Knox makes Scottish Treasury investigator Jonathan Gault into a world traveler, involving him in such cases as *A Killing in Malta, An Incident in Iceland,* and *A Legacy from Tenerife.* Callendar, reviewing *A Problem in Prague* in the *New York Times Book*

Review, calls Knox-as-Webster "a fine pro" at mixing murder, action, and suspense. The detective about whom Knox has written most often (and under his own name), however, is Superintendent Colin Thane of the Scottish Crime Squad in Glasgow. Thane, along with his ulcerated sidekick, Phil Moss, solves crimes in works such as *Pilot Error, The Tallyman,* and *The Hanging Tree.* Callendar assesses that Knox is "a master of his backgrounds and police methods."

Knox's books have been translated into German, French, Italian, Dutch, Portuguese, and other languages. A collection of his manuscripts was established at Boston University in 1969.

BIOGRAPHICAL/CRITICAL SOURCES:

PERIODICALS

Books & Bookmen, February, 1968; July, 1973.
Book World, February 20, 1977.
New Yorker, September 16, 1974.
New York Times Book Review, October 24, 1976; January 1, 1978; October 3, 1982, p. 16; May 22, 1983, p. 49; January 8, 1984, p. 27.
Observer, August 20, 1972.
Saturday Review, April 26, 1969.
Times Literary Supplement, October 29, 1971.

*   *   *

KNUDSEN, James 1950-

PERSONAL: Surname is pronounced Ka-*newd*-sen; born December 7, 1950, in Geneva, IL; son of Willard R. (a manager) and Lorraine (a teacher; maiden name, Olson) Knudsen; married Jeanne Cunningham (a teacher and writer), January 6, 1979; children: Seth, Celeste. *Education:* Attended University of Missouri, 1969-71; University of Iowa, B.A., 1973; University of Massachusetts—Amherst, M.F.A., 1976.

ADDRESSES: Office—Department of English, University of New Orleans, New Orleans, LA 70148.

CAREER: University of New Orleans, New Orleans, LA, instructor, 1977-86, assistant professor, 1986-89, associate professor of English, 1989—.

MEMBER: Authors Guild, Authors League of America.

WRITINGS:

Just Friends (young adult novel), Avon, 1982.
Playing Favorites (young adult novel), Avon, 1987.

BIOGRAPHICAL/CRITICAL SOURCES:

PERIODICALS

Booklist, April 15, 1987, p. 1275.

Kliatt, spring, 1987, p. 12.
Library Journal, September 15, 1982.
Publishers Weekly, January 16, 1987, p. 75.

*   *   *

KOPPER, Philip (Dana) 1937-

PERSONAL: Born June 2, 1937, in New York, NY; son of William Conrad (a genealogist) and Florine (a psychologist; maiden name, Dana) Kopper; married Mary Carll (a writer), August 21, 1979; children: Timothy; stepchildren: Christopher, Andrew, Jonathan Hallett. *Education:* Yale University, B.A., 1959. *Religion:* Episcopalian.

ADDRESSES: Home—3515 Leland St., Chevy Chase, MD 20815. *Agent*—John Hawkins, Paul R. Reynolds Inc., 71 West 23rd St., New York, NY 10010.

CAREER: Look magazine, New York City, member of promotion staff, 1959; *Baltimore Sun,* Baltimore, MD, police reporter, 1960-61; *Washington Post,* Washington, DC, reporter, editor, and critic, 1961-66. Freelance writer, 1966—. Assistant to the Chair of National Endowment for the Arts, 1975. Adjunct professor of literature, American University.

MEMBER: Authors Guild, Washington Independent Writers.

AWARDS, HONORS: First prize, American Medical Writers Association, for "distinguished medical writing"; second prize for film, National Association of Government Communicators; two working fellowships to Bread Loaf Writers Conference.

WRITINGS:

The Wild Edge: Life and Lore of the Great Atlantic Beaches, Times Books (New York City), 1979, 2nd edition, Globe Pequot (Chester, CT), 1991.
The National Museum of Natural History, Abrams (New York City) and Smithsonian Institution (Washington, DC), 1982.
A Christmas Testament, Stewart, Tabori (New York City), 1982.
(With Thomas B. Allen and Karen Jensen) *Earth's Amazing Animals,* National Wildlife Federation (Washington, DC), 1983.
Colonial Williamsburg, Abrams (New York City) and Colonial Williamsburg (Williamsburg, VA), 1986.
(With others) *The Smithsonian Book of North American Indians: Before the Coming of the Europeans,* Smithsonian Books (Washington, DC), 1986.
National Gallery of Art: A Gift to the Nation, National Gallery of Art (Washington, DC), 1991.
Washington: Seasons of the Capital, Elliott & Clark (Washington, DC), 1992.

Contributor to Time-Life Books and *Encyclopaedia Britannica.* Contributor to periodicals, including *New York Times, Quest, Smithsonian, American Scholar,* and *National Geographic.*

BIOGRAPHICAL/CRITICAL SOURCES:

PERIODICALS

Chicago Tribune Book World, December 5, 1982, p. 10.
Los Angeles Times Book Review, December 12, 1982, p. 7.
Washington Post Book World, August 12, 1979, p. 7; November 28, 1982, p. 3; December 5, 1982, p. 1; December 7, 1986, p. 12.*

*   *   *

KORN, Henry (James) 1945-

PERSONAL: Born September 19, 1945, in New York, NY; son of Samuel Henry and Ruth (Beck) Korn; married Joan Willner (an educator), December 22, 1968 (divorced, 1977); married Donna Stein, February 14, 1982; children: (second marriage) Sophie. *Education:* Johns Hopkins University, A.B., 1968. *Politics:* Democrat. *Religion:* Jewish. *Avocational interests:* Baseball.

ADDRESSES: Office—158 Main Street, East Hampton, NY 11937.

CAREER: Brooklyn Museum, Brooklyn, NY, assistant administrator and project writer, 1969-71; Staten Island Institute, Staten Island, NY, administrative coordinator, 1971-74; Jewish Museum, New York City, administrator, 1975-78; executive director, Lower Manhattan Cultural Council, 1978-80; Santa Monica Art Commission Foundation, Santa Monica, CA, executive director, 1986-89; City of Irvine, Irvine, CA, manager of cultural affairs, 1990-93; Guild Hall of East Hampton/John Drew Theatre, president, 1993—. Founder and editor, Assembling Press, Brooklyn, NY, 1970-79. Member of board of directors of arts and cultural organizations; member of advisory board, Franklin Furnace Archive; member of international council, Participation Project Foundation. Consultant to numerous arts organizations and museums.

MEMBER: American Association of Museums, National Arts Club, Poets and Writers.

AWARDS, HONORS: Best small press titles award, *Library Journal,* 1974, for *Exact Change;* city livability award, U. S. Conference of Mayors, 1989; best municipal art program, *L. A. Weekly,* 1989; award of excellence, California Parks and Recreation Society, 1991.

WRITINGS:

Exact Change (short fiction), Assembling (Brooklyn, NY), 1974.

Pontoon Manifesto (novel), Assembling, 1975.
Proceedings of the National Academy of the Avant Garde: Administering the Coup de Grace to the American Reality Consensus (short fiction), Assembling, 1975.
Muhammad Ali Retrospective (collection of stories, essays, and articles), Assembling, 1976.
Inside Thirteen Flags (short fiction), Gegenstein, 1981.
A Difficult Act to Follow: Stories and Essays 1969-1979 (short fiction), Assembling, 1981.

EDITOR

(With Richard Kostelanetz) *First Assembling*, Assembling, 1970.
(With Kostelanetz and Mike Metz) *Second Assembling*, Assembling, 1971.
(With Kostelanetz and Metz) *Third Assembling: A Collection of Otherwise Unpublishable Manuscripts*, Assembling, 1972.
(With Kostelanetz and Metz) *Fourth Assembling*, Assembling, 1973.
(With Kostelanetz and Metz) *Fifth Assembling: A Collection of Otherwise Unpublishable Manuscripts*, Assembling, 1974.
(With Kostelanetz and Metz) *Sixth Assembling*, Assembling, 1975.
(With Kostelanetz) *Seventh Assembling*, Assembling, 1977.
(With Kostelanetz) *Eighth A-K Assembling*, Assembling, 1978.
(With Kostelanetz) *Eighth K-Z Assembling*, Assembling, 1978.

OTHER

Contributor to periodicals, including *Connoisseur, Art and Auction, American Book Review, Metropolis, L. A. Weekly, Santa Monica Outlook*. Short fiction has been published in anthologies published by Prentice-Hall, Ballantine, Bantam, and American Library Association. Editor of *Ninth Assembling;* contributor to numerous books.

BIOGRAPHICAL/CRITICAL SOURCES:

BOOKS

Kostelanetz, Richard, *The End of Intelligent Writing*, Sheed & Ward, 1973.
Montag, Thomas, *Learning to Read Again*, Cat's Pajamas, 1976.

PERIODICALS

Los Angeles Times, June 25, 1988; May 17, 1990; July 8, 1993.
Margins, summer, 1975.
Newsday, November 22, 1993.
New York Times, July 8, 1993.
Smithsonian Press, June 30, 1994.

KOUTOUKAS, H. M.   1947-

PERSONAL: Born June 4, 1947, in Endicott, NY; son of Harilabie and Agnes (Dailey-Ogden) Koutoukas; married Theodora Sangree (a countess), June 1, 1964; married H. K. Klein (a critic), June 11, 1968; children: Antigone, Medea, Linn, Christopher-Swan. *Education:* Attended Harper College, Binghamton, NY; attended New School for Social Research, 1962-65, and Middleton College, 1964-65; Universalist Life Church, Modesto, CA, Ph.D. *Religion:* Greek Orthodox.

ADDRESSES: Office—c/o Judson Church, Washington Square, New York, NY 10012. *Agent*—Nino Karlweis, 250 East 65th St., New York, NY 10021.

CAREER: Dramatist and director. Pioneer in Off-Off Broadway movement; chairperson of drive to build Caffe Cino, New York City; founder of Chamber Theatre Group, New York City, and Supper Theatre concepts. Associated with Electric Circus and other theatre groups in New York City.

MEMBER: New York Playwrights Strategy.

AWARDS, HONORS: National Arts Club Award, 1962; Obie Award, *Village Voice*, 1965; Professional Theatre Wing Award.

WRITINGS:

The Compleat Anthology of Lesbian Humour, Beau Rivage (New York City), 1983.

PLAYS

The Last Triangle, produced in New York City, 1965.
Tidy Passions; or, Kill, Kaleidoscope, Kill, produced in New York City, 1965.
All Day for a Dollar; or, Crumpled Christmas, produced Off-Off Broadway at Caffe Cino, 1966.
The Laundromat Medea, produced in New York City, 1966.
Only a Countess May Dance When She's Crazy (also see below), produced in New York City, 1966.
Pomegranada, produced in New York City, 1966.
With Creatures Make My Way, produced in New York City, 1967.
(And director) *When Clowns Play Hamlet,* produced in New York City, 1967.
View from Sorrento, produced in New York City, 1967.
Howard Kline Trilogy, produced in New York City, 1968.
A Letter from Colette, produced Off-Off Broadway at Judson Poets' Theatre, 1969.
Christopher at Sheridan Squared, produced Off-Off Broadway at Performance Garage, 1971.
Grandmother Is in the Strawberry Patch, produced Off-Off Broadway at La Mama Experimental Theatre, 1974.

(With others) *French Dressing* (revue), produced in New York City, 1974.

One Man's Religion, produced Off-Off Broadway at La Mama Experimental Theatre, 1975.

The Pinotti Papers, produced Off-Off Broadway at La Mama Experimental Theatre, 1975.

(And director) *Star Followers in an Ancient Land,* produced Off-Off Broadway at La Mama Experimental Theatre, December, 1975.

The Legend of Sheridan Square, produced in New York City, 1976.

(And director) *Turtles Don't Dream,* produced in New York City, 1977.

(And director) *Too Late for Yogurt,* produced in New York City, 1978.

The Butterfly Encounter, produced in New York City, 1978.

When Lightning Strikes Twice (two-play performance containing *Awful People Are Coming Over So We Must Be Pretending to Be Hard at Work and Hope They Will Go Away* and *Only a Countess May Dance When She's Crazy*), produced in New York City at Charles Ludlam Theater, January, 1991.

OTHER

Work is represented in anthologies, including *The Off-off Broadway Playbook,* Bobbs-Merrill (Indianapolis, IN), 1972; and *More Plays from Off-off Broadway,* edited by Michael T. Smith, Bobbs-Merrill, 1972. Also the author of *Pope Jean.*

SIDELIGHTS: H. M. Koutoukas once told *CA:* I "have learned from strangers and wish to wander and report on the darker side of life's areas."

Writing in *Vogue,* John Gruen explained that "Koutoukas is deeply involved in assaulting the theatrical traditions and conventions of Off-off-Broadway. He had invented Chamaber Theater—theater that takes place in people's living rooms. Koutoukas wishes to return to the eighteenth century when theatricals in great private halls were taken for granted. He goes to extreme lengths to assure a proper milieu for his productions, usually a large living room. His patrons, or hosts, give him complete freedom, carte blanche in the way he stages his plays. Koutoukas also exercises complete control over his audiences. The *Howard Klein Trilogy* was staged in a private room that allowed only twelve persons in the audience . . . by choice. Koutoukas sends out a questionnaire to all persons wishing to see his plays. Potential guests must answer 60 per cent of these questions on theater lore correctly in order to gain admittance. Only a small percentage gets to see a Koutoukas play."

BIOGRAPHICAL/CRITICAL SOURCES:

PERIODICALS

New York Times, January 14, 1991.
Show Business, August 30, 1969.
Vogue, March 1, 1969, pp. 114, 116.*

*   *   *

KRAKEL, Dean (Fenton) 1923-

PERSONAL: Born July 3, 1923, in Ault, CO; son of Eldon A. (an automobile mechanic) and Gretta (Cross) Krakel; married Iris Moneta Lesh, June 27, 1947; children: Ira Dean, Susan E. (deceased), Jennie Lynn, Jack Remington. *Education:* Colorado State College of Education (now University of Northern Colorado), A.B., 1950; University of Denver, M.A., 1952; University of Colorado Extension Center, graduate study, 1959. *Politics:* Republican. *Religion:* First Christian Church. *Avocational interests:* Art appraisal.

CAREER: Colorado State Historical Society, Denver, assistant curator, 1950-52; University of Wyoming, Laramie, assistant professor of library science and archivist in library, 1952-56; U.S. Air Force Academy, Colorado Springs, CO, deputy director of museum and fine arts program, 1956-61; Thomas Gilcrease Institute of American History and Art, Tulsa, OK, executive director, 1961-64; National Cowboy Hall of Fame and Western Heritage Center, Oklahoma City, OK, managing director and executive vice president, beginning 1964, trustee and assistant secretary of executive committee, beginning 1969, director of Royal Western Watercolor Competition, beginning 1973. Director, Anti Metric Society, 1976—; member of board of trustees, Oklahoma City University. *Military service:* U.S. Naval Reserve, Air Corps, active duty, 1943-46; served in European theater.

MEMBER: Cowboy Artists of America (honorary member), Association of Sports Halls of Fame and Museums (vice president, 1974-75), National Academy of Western Art (trustee, 1971—), Rodeo Historical Society (honorary life member of board of directors), American Association of Museums, Society of Western Art Appraisers (director, 1974-75), Western Historians, Zoological Society of Oklahoma (honorary member of board of directors), Oklahoma Westerners.

AWARDS, HONORS: Mountain Plains Seven Library Award, Mountain Plains Library Association, 1955, for outstanding literary contributions; Outstanding Nonfiction Book Award, Southwest Library Association, c. 1972, for *Tom Ryan: A Painter in Four Sixes Country;* Trustees' Gold Medal Award, National Cowboy Hall of

Fame, 1975, for contributions to art; D.H.L., University of Colorado, 1976; American Heritage Award, Northern Colorado University, 1978; Gari Melcher Medal for Arts, New York Art Society, 1985; inducted into National Cowboy Hall of Fame.

WRITINGS:

The Saga of Tom Horn: The Story of a Cattlemen's War, with Personal Narratives, Newspaper Accounts, and Official Documents and Testimonies, Powder River Publishers (Laramie, WY), 1954.
South Platte Country: A History of Old Weld County, Colorado, 1739-1900, Powder River Publishers, 1954.
James Boren: A Study in Discipline, Northland Press (Flagstaff, AZ), 1968.
Tom Ryan: A Painter in Four Sixes Country, Northland Press, 1971.
End of the Trail: The Odyssey of a Statue, University of Oklahoma Press (Norman, OK), 1973.
Adventures in Western Art, Lowell Press (Kansas City, MO), 1977.
Mitch, on the Tail End of the Old West: A Personal Biography of Arthur Roy Mitchell, Western Artist, introduction by Harold Von Schmidt, Powder River Book Co. (Oklahoma City, OK), 1981.
Conrad Schwiering: Painting on the Square, photographs by Dean Krakel II, Powder River Book Co., 1981.

Also author of introductions for books on the American West. Contributor to periodicals, including *Art in America, U.S. News and World Report,* and *Saturday Evening Post.* Editor, *Persimmon Hill Magazine,* 1972-75.

BIOGRAPHICAL/CRITICAL SOURCES:

BOOKS

Ainsworth, E. M., editor, *The Cowboy in Art,* World Publishing, 1968.

PERIODICALS

Empire Magazine (of *Denver Post*), October 16, 1955.
Publishers Weekly, July 17, 1954.
Saturday Evening Post, fall, 1972.*

*   *   *

KRAMER, Jack
    See KRAMER, Jack N.

*   *   *

KRAMER, Jack N.   1923-1983
    (Jack Kramer)

PERSONAL: Born February 24, 1923, in Lynn, MA; died December 13, 1983; son of Charles and Sarah (Lipschitz)

Kramer. *Education:* Attended School of the Museum of Fine Arts, Boston (studied with Karl Zerbe), 1941-43, 1945-49, and University of Reading (studied with J. Anthony Betts), 1950; studied privately with artist Oskar Kokoschka, London, 1950; studied in Europe, 1950-53; Rhode Island School of Design, B.F.A., 1954.

CAREER: University of Illinois at Urbana-Champaign, instructor in art, 1955-56; Boston University, Boston, MA, assistant professor, 1957-64, associate professor, 1964-71, professor of art, beginning 1971. School of Vision, assistant to Oskar Kokoschka and instructor, summers, 1955-58; Artists Studio Co-op, Fenway Studios Inc., president, 1982. Exhibitions and solo shows at numerous galleries, including Boston Psychoanalytic Society and Institute, 1977, Cambridge Art Association, 1978, Gallery of World Art, Newton, MA, 1979, Attleboro Museum, Attleboro, MA, 1981, Kingston Gallery, 1981, and Wenniger Graphics Gallery, Boston, 1981; collections exhibited at William Gurlitt Museum, Linz, Austria, Addison Gallery of American Art, and Phillips Academy, Andover, MA, and in private collections. *Military service:* U.S. Army Air Forces, 1943-45.

MEMBER: Copley Society of Boston.

AWARDS, HONORS: Thomas B. Clarke Award, National Academy of Design, 1982; retrospective, catalog of paintings and drawings, and establishment of scholarship fund in his honor, all Boston University, 1985; numerous other awards for painting and drawing.

WRITINGS:

Human Anatomy and Figure Drawing: The Integration of Structure and Form, Van Nostrand (New York City), 1972, 2nd edition published as *Human Anatomy and Figure Drawing: The Integration of Structure and Perspective,* 1984.
(Under name Jack Kramer) *Painting on Glass,* Van Nostrand, 1977.
The Jefferson Image, Museum of Westward Expansion (St. Louis), 1978.

Contributor of illustrations to *Audience, Drawing,* and *Liberal Context.* Portfolios of his drawings appeared in *Audience* magazine, 1961, and *Liberal Context,* 1965.*

[Death information provided by June E. Mendelson, executor of Kramer's estate]

*   *   *

KRAUSS, Ruth (Ida)   1911-1993

PERSONAL: Born July 25, 1911, in Baltimore, MD; died July 10, 1993, in Westport, CT; daughter of Julius and Blanche (Rosenfeld) Krauss; married David Johnson

Leisk (a writer and illustrator under pseudonym Crockett Johnson), c. 1940 (died July 11, 1975). *Education:* Attended Peabody Institute of Music, New School for Social Research, Maryland Institute of Art, and Columbia University; Parsons School of Fine and Applied Art, bachelor's degree.

CAREER: Writer; also conducted poetry workshops.

MEMBER: Authors League of America, PEN.

WRITINGS:

FOR CHILDREN

A Good Man and His Good Wife, illustrated by Ad Reinhardt, Harper (New York City), 1944, revised edition, illustrated by Marc Simont, 1962.
The Carrot Seed, illustrated by Crockett Johnson, Harper, 1945.
The Great Duffy, illustrated by Richter, Harper, 1946.
The Growing Story, illustrated by Phyllis Rowand, Harper, 1947.
Bears, illustrated by Rowand, Harper, 1948.
The Big World and the Little House, illustrated by Simont, H. Schuman (New York City), 1949.
The Happy Day, illustrated by Simont, Harper, 1949.
The Backward Day, illustrated by Simont, Harper, 1950.
I Can Fly (verse), illustrated by Mary Blair, Simon & Schuster (New York City), 1950.
The Bundle Book, illustrated by Helen Stone, Harper, 1951.
A Hole Is to Dig: A First Book of First Definitions, illustrated by Maurice Sendak, Harper, 1952.
A Very Special House, illustrated by Sendak, Harper, 1953.
How to Make an Earthquake, illustrated by Johnson, Harper, 1954.
I'll Be You and You Be Me, illustrated by Sendak, Harper, 1954.
Charlotte and the White Horse, illustrated by Sendak, Harper, 1955.
(With Johnson) *Is This You?,* illustrated by Johnson, W. R. Scott (New York City), 1955.
I Want to Paint My Bathroom Blue, illustrated by Sendak, Harper, 1956.
The Birthday Party, illustrated by Sendak, Harper, 1957.
Monkey Day, illustrated by Rowand, Harper, 1957.
Somebody Else's Nut Tree, and Other Tales from Children, illustrated by Sendak, Harper, 1958.
A Moon or a Button: A Collection of First Picture Ideas, illustrated by Remy Charlip, Harper, 1959.
Open House for Butterflies, illustrated by Sendak, Harper, 1960.
Mama, I Wish I Was Snow; Child, You'd Be Very Cold, illustrated by Ellen Raskin, Atheneum (New York City), 1962.

A Bouquet of Littles (verse), illustrated by Jane Flora, Harper, 1963.
Eyes, Nose, Fingers, Toes, illustrated by Elizabeth Schneider, Harper, 1964.
The Little King, The Little Queen, The Little Monster; And Other Stories You Can Make up Yourself, self-illustrated, Albert Whitman (Chicago), 1966.
The Happy Egg, illustrated by Johnson, Scholastic (New York City), 1967.
This Thumbprint: Words and Thumbprints, self-illustrated, Harper, 1967.
What a Fine Day For . . . (verse), music by Al Carmines, illustrated by Charlip, Parents Magazine Press (New York City), 1967.
I Write It (verse), illustrated by Mary Chalmers, Harper, 1970.
Everything under a Mushroom (verse), illustrated by Margot Tomes, Four Winds Press (New York City), 1973.
Little Boat Lighter Than a Cork, illustrated by Esther Gilman, Magic Circle Press (Connecticut), 1976.
Somebody Spilled the Sky (verse), illustrated by Eleanor Hazard, Greenwillow (New York City), 1979.
Poems for People, Morrow, 1979.
Minestrone: A Ruth Krauss Selection (verse), self-illustrated, Greenwillow, 1981.
Big and Little, illustrated by Mary Szilagyi, Scholastic, 1987.

Also author of *Love Poems for Children,* 1986. Contributor to textbooks and anthologies.

POEM-PLAYS FOR ADULTS

The Cantilever Rainbow, illustrated with woodcuts by Antonio Frasconi, Pantheon (New York City), 1965.
There's a Little Ambiguity over There among the Bluebells, and Other Theatre Poems, illustrated by Marilyn Harris, Something Else Press (New York City), 1968.
If Only (produced Off-Off Broadway at Judson Poets' Theatre), Toad Press (Eugene, OR), 1969.
Under Twenty, Toad Press, 1970.
Love and the Invention of Punctuation, Bookstore Press (Lenox, MA), 1973.
This Breast Gothic, Bookstore Press, 1973.
Under Thirteen, Bookstore Press, 1976.
If I Were Freedom, produced in Annandale-on-Hudson, NY, at Bard College, 1976-77.
Re-examination of Freedom (produced in Boston at Boston University, 1976-77), Toothpaste Press (West Branch, IA), 1981.
When I Walk I Change the Earth, Burning Deck (Providence, RI), 1978.
Small Black Lambs Wandering in the Red Poppies, produced in New York City, 1982.
Ambiguity 2nd, produced in Boston, 1985.

Also author of *A Beautiful Day,* produced Off-Off Broadway at Judson Poets' Theatre, *Newsletter, In a Bull's Eye, Pineapple Play, Quartet, A Show, a Play—It's a Girl!, Onward, Duet; or, Yellow Umbrella,* and *Drunk Boat.*

OTHER

Contributor of poetry to periodicals, including *Harper's, New World Writing, Plumed Horn, Kulchur, Locus Solus,* and *Chelsea Review.*

A collection of Krauss's manuscripts is at Dupont School, Wilmington, DE.

SIDELIGHTS: Widely known as a children's book author, Ruth Krauss was also an illustrator and an author of poem-plays for the theater. She once wrote: "The work in the poetry and the theater are fusing into one with the books for young people. Things that were considered far-out, like my 'news items,' are accepted by children now. They are attuned to it. Still there are some things that children don't have the background for understanding the allusions and references contained. A lot of my poems have been produced on stage as part of musicales, such as at the Judson Poets' Theatre. Some of the poems that were considered so advanced have been included in the Ginn & Co. textbooks and anthologies collected by David Kerdian. . . . *The Cantilever Rainbow* was considered too sophisticated for kids. My work has a lot of humor in it, I hope, whereas most modern poets are so serious."

BIOGRAPHICAL/CRITICAL SOURCES:

BOOKS

Barbara Bader, *American Picturebooks from "Noah's Ark" to "The Beast Within,"* Macmillan, 1976.
Dictionary of Literary Biography, Volume 52: *American Writers for Children since 1960: Fiction,* Gale (Detroit), 1986, pp. 228-32.
Twentieth-Century Children's Writers, 3rd edition, St. James Press (Chicago), 1989, pp. 546-47.

PERIODICALS

Christian Science Monitor, May 13, 1954.
Nation, August 25, 1969.
New York Herald-Tribune Book Review, May 30, 1954; November 14, 1954.
New York Times Book Review, April 29, 1979.
Saturday Review, July 16, 1960.

OBITUARIES:

PERIODICALS

New York Times, July 15, 1993, p. D22.*

KUBICEK, Robert V(incent)   1935-

PERSONAL: Born November 19, 1935, in Drumheller, Alberta, Canada; son of Frederick and Roxanna (MacKenzie) Kubicek; married, 1970, wife's name, Mila; children: Brett Booth. *Education:* University of Alberta, B.Ed., 1956, M.A., 1958; London School of Economics and Political Science, graduate study, 1958-59; Duke University, Ph.D., 1964.

ADDRESSES: Home—3755 West 13th, Vancouver, British Columbia, Canada V6R 2S7. *Office*—University of British Columbia, 2075 Westbrook Pl., Vancouver, British Columbia Canada V6T 1W5.

CAREER: Edmonton Journal, reporter, Edmonton, Alberta, 1956-58; teacher, 1959-60, University of British Columbia, Vancouver, instructor, 1963-65, assistant professor, 1965-69, associate professor of history, 1969-78, professor of history, 1978—, head of history department, 1979-85, associate dean, faculty of arts, 1990—.

MEMBER: Canadian Association of African Studies, Canadian Association of University Teachers, Canadian Historical Association.

AWARDS, HONORS: Canada Council summer research grants, 1966 and 1970, fellowships, 1968-69 and 1973-74.

WRITINGS:

The Administration of Imperialism: Joseph Chamberlain at the Colonial Office, Duke University Press (Durham, NC), 1969.
Economic Imperialism in Theory and Practice: The Case of South African Gold Mining Finance 1886-1914, Duke University Press, 1979.

Contributor to history journals.*

*   *   *

KUHSE, Helga   1940-

PERSONAL: Surname is pronounced *Coo*-sa; born March 26, 1940, in Hamburg, Germany; immigrated to Australia, 1962, naturalized citizen, c. 1978; daughter of Peter (a merchant) and Klara (Witten) Zietan; married Bill Kuhse (an engineer), July 8, 1961; children: Martina. *Education:* Monash University, B.A. (with honors), 1978, Ph.D., 1983. *Religion:* None.

ADDRESSES: Home—Lot 1, Bowman Rd., Upper Beaconsfield 3808, Australia. *Office*—Centre for Human Bioethics, Monash University, Wellington Rd., Clayton, Victoria 3168, Australia.

CAREER: Monash University, Centre for Human Bioethics, Clayton, Victoria, Australia, deputy director, 1981-90, director, 1991—.

MEMBER: World Federation of Right to Die Societies (treasurer and secretary, 1986-92; president, 1992-94), Voluntary Euthanasia Society of Victoria (committee member, 1980-91; president, 1991—).

WRITINGS:

(With Peter Singer) *Should the Baby Live? The Problems of Handicapped Infants,* Oxford University Press, 1985.

Sanctity of Life in Medicine, Oxford University Press, 1987.

(With Singer and others) *Embryo Experimentation,* Cambridge University Press, 1991.

(With Singer) *Individuals, Humans, Persons: Questions of Life & Death,* Academia Verlag, 1994.

Willing to Listen—Wanting to Die, Penguin (New York City), 1994.

Editor of *Bioethics News,* 1981—; coeditor of *Bioethics,* 1986—.

WORK IN PROGRESS: Research on the role of the nurse.

SIDELIGHTS: Should the Baby Live? The Problems of Handicapped Infants, which Helga Kuhse wrote with Peter Singer, is a philosophical examination of the issues involved in allowing severely handicapped infants to die. The book's starting point is the Baby Doe case of 1982, controversial because of a court ruling that implies that parents have the right to choose between two medical opinions, even when the choice will result in their infant's death. Kuhse and Singer declare themselves in favor of this ruling. By attacking some traditional moral assumptions, such as the distinction between allowing a hopelessly crippled infant to die by withholding treatment and killing it more actively by lethal injection, and the belief that all human life is of equal value, the authors assert that infanticide is acceptable in some situations. To them, the potential quality of existence should be the prime consideration when making life and death medical decisions. Allaying concerns about the possibility of initially merciful infanticide spreading to unwanted healthy babies or to whole social classes or ethnic groups, Kuhse and Singer provide some guidelines for policy formation. *Should the Baby Live?,* concluded R. G. Frey, reviewer for the *Times Literary Supplement,* "is a sensitive, thoughtful, and rigorously argued book."

Helge Kuhse once told *CA:* "I am motivated to use philosophy (that is, rational thought) to help us solve some of the complex and daunting dilemmas raised by new developments in the biomedical sciences."

BIOGRAPHICAL/CRITICAL SOURCES:

PERIODICALS

New Republic, February 17, 1986.
Times Literary Supplement, April 18, 1986.

L

LADERMAN, Carol (C.)

PERSONAL: Born in New York, NY; daughter of Philip (an engineer) and Sylvia (a singer; maiden name, Sugarman) Ciavati; married Gabriel Laderman (an artist); children: Raphael, Michael. *Education:* Hunter College of the City University of New York, B.A. (with honors), 1972; Columbia University, M.A., 1974, M.Phil., 1975, Ph.D. (with distinction), 1979. *Religion:* Jewish. *Avocational interests:* Travel (more than a dozen countries in Asia and Europe), music (playing piano).

ADDRESSES: Home—760 West End Ave., New York, NY 10025. *Office*—Department of Anthropology, City College, City University of New York, New York, NY 10031.

CAREER: City University of New York, New York City, adjunct assistant professor of anthropology at Hunter College, 1978-80, adjunct assistant professor of anthropology at Brooklyn College, 1979-80, professor of anthropology and chair of department at City College, 1990—; Yale University, New Haven, CT, visiting lecturer in anthropology, 1980-82; Fordham University, Bronx, NY, assistant professor, 1982-88, associate professor of anthropology, 1988-90, acting chair of department of anthropology, 1982-88. Visiting research scholar, Institute for Social and Policy Studies, 1980-81; resident scholar, Bellagio Center of Rockefeller Foundation, 1989. Associate, Columbia University Seminar on South and Southeast Asia, 1982—; research affiliate in anthropology, Yale University, 1982-84. Has delivered lectures and papers at conferences, annual meetings, and colleges and universities, 1977—; has conducted anthropological research throughout the world. Manuscript or proposal reviewer for numerous periodicals, publishers, and foundations. Anthropological consultant to North American Conference on Ethiopian Jewry, 1982—.

MEMBER: International Association for the Study of Traditional Asian Medicine (secretary-general), American Anthropological Association, American Ethnological Association, Council on Nutritional Anthropology (member of executive board, 1985-89), Association for Asian Studies (member of executive committee of Women in Asian Studies), Society for Medical Anthropology, Royal Asiatic Society (Malaysian branch), New York Women's Anthropological Conference, Metropolitan Medical Anthropology Society.

AWARDS, HONORS: Danforth Foundation fellowship, 1972-75, summer language study grant, 1975, and award, 1978; National Institute for Mental Health fellowship, 1975-78; Social Science Research Council foreign area fellowship, 1975-77, and stipend, 1978; National Endowment for the Humanities translation program grant, 1982-85; Fordham University faculty research award, 1984 and 1985, summer research grant, 1987, and faculty fellowship, 1989-90; National Endowment for the Humanities award for interpretive research, 1987-90; honorable mention, Stirling Award, 1987; John Simon Guggenheim Memorial Foundation fellowship, 1987-88; travel grants, Smithsonian Institution, 1990, and American Council of Learned Societies, 1990; honorable mention, Victor Turner Award for Ethnographic Writing, 1991; City College of New York grant, 1991; PSC City University of New York research grant, 1993.

WRITINGS:

Wives and Midwives: Childbirth and Nutrition in Rural Malaysia, University of California Press (Berkeley, CA), 1983.

(Editor with Penny Van Esterik) *Techniques of Healing in Southeast Asia,* Pergamon Press (Oxford, England), 1988.

Taming the Wind of Desire: Psychology, Medicine and Aesthetics in Malay Shamanistic Performance, University of California Press, 1991.
Main Peteri: Malay Shamanism, [Kuala Lumpur], 1991.

Contributor to books, including *Anthropology of Human Birth,* edited by Margarita A. Kay, F. A. Davis (Philadelphia, PA), 1980; *Women in Southeast Asia,* edited by Van Esterik, Center for Southeast Asia Studies, Northern Illinois University (DeKalb, IL), 1982; *Diet and Domestic Life in Society,* edited by Anne Sharman, Janet Theophano, Ellen Messer, and Karen Curtis, Temple University Press (Philadelphia, PA), 1991; and *Embodiment and Experience,* edited by Thomas Csordas, Cambridge University Press (New York City), 1994. Contributor to scholarly journals and popular magazines, including *American Ethnologist, Social Science and Medicine, Medical Anthropology, Asia, Journal of Asian Studies, Studies in Third World Societies,* and *Science Digest.* Member of editorial board, *Anthropology and Humanism* and *Birth.*

WORK IN PROGRESS: Editing, with Marina Roseman, and contributing to *The Performance of Healing;* a book chapter; a journal article.

SIDELIGHTS: Carol Laderman once told *CA:* "My interest in doing research in Malaysia proceeds directly from my previous research in the Hispanic community of New York City. While working with a nutritionist connected with Mount Sinai Hospital on a possible connection between anemia of adolescent mothers and ethnic eating patterns (as it turned out, there was no connection), I was struck by the flexibility with which people who believe in a humoral system interpret their beliefs into behavior. Humoral systems—beliefs that foods, medicines, diseases, and so on are inherently 'hot' or 'cold'—had been discussed previously by anthropologists working in Latin America and the Caribbean, China, India, and parts of Southeast Asia, but their accounts presented these systems as taxonomies whose categories seemed frozen like flies in amber, rather than dynamic, variable, and subject to manipulation. Malaysia seemed an ideal place to study a humoral system in action. A port of call for Chinese and Indian traders from ancient times, first Hinduized and later converted to Islam, Malaysia received humoral philosophy from three different sources.

"Another important reason for choosing Malaysia was that my research site was sponsored by the Malaysian Ministry of Health. This allowed me to combine ethnographic research with biomedical tests (blood, urine, diet) which gave my conclusions a force that they otherwise would have lacked. In order to gather the material for these tests, I was trained to collect blood in the General Hospital at Kuala Trengganu, the state capital of the east

coast state of Trengganu, where my family and I were to spend two years, from 1975 to 1977, and to return in 1982.

"My research focused on childbirth and nutrition but encompassed the traditional Malay medical system as it adapted to cosmopolitan medicine, Malay sex roles, marriage and childrearing, religious beliefs (both Islamic and other), social and economic life, and the local ecology. My family and I lived in a typical Malay house-on-stilts, dressed like our neighbors (in my case, in a sarong), ate the same food, celebrated with them, and mourned at their funerals. We all became fluent in Malay. I became apprenticed to a village midwife, assisted dozens of women giving birth, and learned to give the soothing and invigorating massages that all new Malay mothers receive. Malay midwives' duties require them to be adept at obstetrics, nursing, and rituals that allow them to operate effectively in the world of pragmatic experience and in confrontations with the invisible world peopled with spirits who may endanger their patients. My teacher, Sapiah, was a veteran midwife who had never lost a patient in over thirty years.

"I was also fortunate enough to become apprenticed to a local shaman, Pak Long Awang (who became my foster father), and his partner, Pak Daud. I became a regular member of Pak Long's entourage, attending numerous ceremonies, where I learned that Malay shamans effected their cures through a coherent method of non-projective psychotherapy as well as by the use of exorcism. My speculations about the biomedical effects of these rituals have become standard reading in many college courses. I transcribed and translated three complete ceremonies chosen from among the many I tape-recorded. I was able to return to Malaysia in 1982, with the support of the National Endowment for the Humanities, to confer with Malay ritual specialists and to complete the annotations of these ceremonies.

"My interests range from an appreciation of the poetic quality of the shamanic rituals and the analysis of their symbolic content to an appreciation of their psychological, physiological, and biochemical effects. My aim has been to integrate ethnology and 'hard' science and to bridge the gap between 'culture' and 'practical reason.' I believe that the publication of my work in journals ranging from those aimed at the general literate public, those meant for undergraduates, those read by anthropologists, and, particularly, those read by 'hard' as well as social scientists has had an impact on the thinking of those who are now concerned with the implementation of public policy and those who may be in that position in the future."

LAMB, William
    See JAMESON, Storm

*   *   *

LANGLEY, Tania
    See ARMSTRONG, Tilly

*   *   *

LASKER, Michael
    See ELMAN, Richard

*   *   *

LAUGHLIN, James   1914-

PERSONAL: Born October 30, 1914, in Pittsburgh, PA; son of Henry Hughart and Marjory (Rea) Laughlin; married Margaret Keyser, March 13, 1942 (divorced, 1952); married Ann Clark Resor, May 19, 1956; children: (first marriage) Paul, Leila; (second marriage) Robert, Henry. *Education:* Harvard University, A.B., 1939. *Politics:* Republican. *Religion:* Presbyterian.

ADDRESSES: Home—Mountain Rd., Norfolk, CT 06058. *Office*—New Directions Publishing Corp., 80 Eighth Ave., New York, NY 10011.

CAREER: New Directions (now New Directions Publishing Corporation), New York City, founder, 1936, editor and publisher, 1936—; Intercultural Publications, Inc., New York City, president, 1952-69. Alta Lodge Co., vice-president, 1948-58, president, 1958-59; Alta Ski Lifts Co., vice-president, 1950—. University of Iowa, Iowa City, Ida Bean Visiting Lecturer, 1981-82; Brown University, Providence, RI, adjunct professor of English, 1983. Lecturer at over twenty colleges and universities, including University of California, Los Angeles, 1974; member of visiting committee to department of German at both Princeton University and Harvard University. Consultant to Indian Southern Languages Book Trust, Madras, 1956-58; member of U.S. National Commission for UNESCO, 1962-63, and U.S. National Commission for International Cooperation Year, 1966. Trustee, Merton Legacy Trust; agent, Ezra Pound Literary Property Trust and estate of William Carlos Williams.

MEMBER: PEN, American Academy of Arts and Sciences, Authors League of America, Century Association, Salt Lake City Winter Sports Association, Harvard Club.

AWARDS, HONORS: American Academy of Arts and Letters Award, 1977, for distinguished service to the arts;

Carey-Thomas citation, *Publishers Weekly,* 1978; award from PEN, 1979; National Arts Club Medal of Honor for Literature, 1984; prize for short story published in *Atlantic;* decorated Chevalier, Legion of Honor, for cultural service in publishing translations of French literature; recipient of various honorary degrees, including D.Litt., Hamilton College, 1970, and Colgate University, 1973, and D.H.L., Duquesne University, 1981, and Yale University, 1982.

WRITINGS:

The River, New Directions (New York City), 1938.
Some Natural Things (poems), New Directions, 1945.
Skiing East and West, with photographs by Helen Fischer and Emita Herran, Hastings House (New York City), 1946.
Spearhead: Ten Years' Experimental Writing in America, New Directions, 1947.
Report on a Visit to Germany, Henri Held (Lausanne), 1948.
A Small Book of Poems, New Directions, 1948.
The Wild Anemone and Other Poems, New Directions, 1957.
Selected Poems, New Directions, 1959 (published in England as *Confidential Report, and Other Poems,* Gaberbocchus, 1959).
The Pig (poems), Perishable Press, 1970.
In Another Country: Poems 1935-1975, City Lights Books (San Francisco, CA), 1978.
Gists and Piths: A Memoir of Ezra Pound, Windhover Press (New York City), 1982.
The Deconstructed Man (poems), Windhover Press, 1985.
Stolen and Contaminated Poems, Turkey Press (Isla Vista, CA), 1985.
The House of Light, woodcuts by Vanessa Jackson, Grenfell Press (New York City), 1986.
The Master of Those Who Know: Ezra Pound, City Lights Books, 1986.
James Laughlin: Selected Poems, 1935-1985, City Lights Books, 1986.
Tabellae (poems), Grenfell Press, 1986.
The Owl of Minerva: Poems, Copper Canyon Press (Port Townsend, WA), 1987.
Pound as Wuz: Essays and Lectures on Ezra Pound, Graywolf Press (St. Paul, MN), 1987.
The Bird of Endless Time: Poems, Copper Canyon Press, 1989.
Random Essays: Recollections of a Publisher, Moyer Bell (Mt. Kisco, NY), 1989.
William Carlos Williams and James Laughlin: Selected Letters, Norton, 1989.
Random Stories, with an introduction by Octavio Paz, Moyer Bell, 1990.

Kenneth Rexroth and James Laughlin: Selected Letters,
edited by Lee Bartlett, Norton, 1991.
Collected Poems of James Laughlin, Moyer Bell, 1992.
Delmore Schwartz and James Laughlin: Selected Letters,
edited by Robert Phillips, Norton, 1993.
The Man in the Wall: Poems, foreword by Guy Davenport, New Directions, 1993.

Translator of other books of poetry for publication abroad. Contributor of short stories to periodicals, including *Atlantic,* and skiing articles to *Town and Country, Harper's, Ski, Sports Illustrated, Ski Annual,* and other periodicals.

EDITOR

(And commentator) *Poems from the Greenberg Manuscripts: A Selection from the Work of Samuel B. Greenberg,* New Directions, 1939.
(With Albert M. Hayes) *A Wreath of Christmas Poems by Virgil, Dante, Chaucer and Others,* New Directions, 1942.
(With U. Myat Kyaw) *Perspective of Burma,* Intercultural Publications, 1958.
(With Hayden Carruth) *A New Directions Reader,* New Directions, 1964.
(With Naomi Burton and Patrick Hart) *The Asian Journal of Thomas Merton,* New Directions, 1975.

Also editor of *New Directions in Prose and Poetry* series, forty-five volumes, New Directions, 1936—; and various numbers of *Perspectives USA* and "Perspectives" supplements to *Atlantic,* 1952-58.

SIDELIGHTS: While a sophomore on leave of absence from Harvard University, James Laughlin met Ezra Pound in Rapallo, Italy, and was invited to attend the "Ezuversity"—Pound's term for the private tutoring he gave Laughlin over meals, on hikes, or whenever the master paused in his labors. "I stayed several months in Rapallo at the 'Ezuversity,' learning and reading," recalls Laughlin in an interview with Linda Kuehl for the *New York Times Book Review,* "until Pound said it was time for me to go back to Harvard and do *something useful.* Being useful meant that I should publish books, because at the time publishing was still suffering from the Depression and none of [Pound's] friends, except Hemingway, had steady publishers." "Never has advice been better followed," surmises poet and critic Donald Hall in the *New York Times Book Review,* for after returning to Harvard from Italy, Laughlin founded New Directions, a company dedicated to publishing quality works with little regard to their chances for commercial success.

With his own money (Laughlin's well-to-do father had given him $100,000 when he graduated from college), Laughlin initially set out to publish and thereby recognize experimental and avant-garde writers of merit. His first New Directions book, an anthology containing the work of such authors as Pound, Gertrude Stein, E. E. Cummings, William Carlos Williams, Elizabeth Bishop, and Henry Miller, appeared in 1936. "At the time," reports Hall, "the 22-year-old editor-publisher . . . loaded his Buick with 600 unpaginated copies [of *New Directions in Prose and Poetry*], became a traveling salesman, and persuaded bookstores to stock a few volumes—out of pity, he believes."

During the 1940s, according to Hall, Laughlin's company provided the first lengthy publication of Randall Jarrell, John Berryman, Karl Shapiro, Tennessee Williams, Paul Goodman, Jean Garrigue, John Frederick Nims, and Eve Merriam. The list of New Directions authors eventually grew to include George Oppen, Carl Rakosi, Charles Reznikoff, Robert Creeley, Lawrence Ferlinghetti, Gregory Corso, Gary Snyder, Kenneth Rexroth, Denise Levertov, Thomas Merton, and Robert Duncan. "For the most part," writes Hall, "the list represented the new," which initially meant limited commercial success. "When I started doing the books," Laughlin told Edwin McDowell of the *New York Times Book Review,* "they were way out ahead of the public taste. Nobody could understand them and nobody wanted to buy them. . . . But a younger generation of professors matured and became interested in using them in college courses, and that's what put us on our feet."

Though, as Hall points out, New Directions "started in the service of verbal revolution," it made other, equally impressive contributions to literature in print. It published F. Scott Fitzgerald's *The Crack Up* when other publishers would not; when *The Great Gatsby* was out of print, New Directions brought it back; the company also reprinted the works of Henry James, E. M. Forster, Ronald Firbank, and Evelyn Waugh when no one else would. Hall believes that in these instances, the decision to publish established authors was governed by the same assumptions underlying the publication of new writers: "the assumption of quality and the assumption that these books would not sell in the marketplace."

But New Directions may have made its most important contribution, suggests Hall, in bringing foreign authors to American readers in translation: "not only the obvious Rimbaud, Baudelaire, Rilke, Valery, Kafka and Cocteau, but the less known and the unknown: Montale, Neruda, Queneau, Cardenal, Lorca, Pasternak, Paz, Borges, Mishima, Lihn, Vittorini, Parra, Guillevic." The first American publisher of Vladimir Nabokov, New Directions made available Nabokov's critical work on Gogol, a group of short stories, and some translations of classic Russian poetry, as well as his second novel in English, *The Real Life of Sebastian Knight.*

After years of being subsidized by the money of Laughlin's family, New Directions eventually became a profit-making venture. Aided by the million-copy sale of Lawrence Ferlinghetti's *Coney Island of the Mind,* the hundreds of thousands of reprints of Herman Hesse's *Siddharta,* the academic acceptance of writers like Pound, and the popularity of younger authors like Gary Snyder, Denise Levertov, and John Hawkes, the company started to make money. Laughlin, who emphasized in the *New York Times Book Review* that New Directions has always been an intimate group venture and that the profits have been "small," modestly gave others credit for the company's critical and commercial success: "I am only a happenstance catalyst who started publishing because Ezra said I had to 'do something useful.' The credit, whatever there may be, belongs to the writers we published and to the long-suffering people who actually saw that the books got printed, proofread, and sold. Without all of them, New Directions would have been just an amateur's hobby."

While Laughlin is most often recognized for his work as a publisher, he is also a writer and poet. In a laudatory review of his writing career in the *Dictionary of Literary Biography,* John A. Harrison and Donald W. Faulkner propose that Laughlin "is perceived as a minor poet, in part because he has chosen to publish so little. . . . That [he] continues to apologize for his poetry is unfortunate, for it has been recognized as fresh, concise, full of wit, of impeccable quality, lucid, ironic, and often intense." Laughlin himself, relate Harrison and Faulkner, described his poetry as " 'an arbitrary visual pattern against the sound pattern of a colloquial cadence to get tension and surprise.' " Harrison and Faulkner respond by saying that "The short lines, unhindered by punctuation, seem to have an impact that makes [Laughlin's] . . . work more memorable." The *Dictionary of Literary Biography* article also quotes poet Denise Levertov, who calls Laughlin's poems "free of bombast and of any pretentiousness. . . . Emotion is disciplined in the precision of his diction and the strictness of his idiosyncratic form. . . ." Through the years, Laughlin has published various collections of his work, including such works as *The House of Light, The Pig,* and *James Laughlin: Selected Poems, 1935-1985.*

Also included in Laughlin's list of writing credits are various essay collections. Notable among these is a 1987 work, *Pound as Wuz: Essays and Lectures on Ezra Pound.* As the title suggests, the work is a compilation of essays and lectures, where, drawing on memories of his own relationship with Pound, Laughlin investigates the sources the noted author used for his writings over the years. Writing in the *New York Times Book Review,* Robert Minkoff praises the book, calling Laughlin "an enthusiastic guide to favorite Pound topics, from Provencal poetry to monetary theory." Laughlin's experiences with other authors also led him to issue his 1989 work, *Random Essays: Recollections of a Publisher,* a collection of talks and essays composed over the years. Reviewing the work for the *Los Angeles Times,* Richard Eder says, "Laughlin's literary opinions are gentlemanly; they range between sensible and silly. What shines through is his kindness and civility, his individuality, and the joy he took in his authors." Eder goes on to say that "the time . . . [Laughlin] spent with Pound, Williams and Gertrude Stein allows him to add some nicely provocative touches to their well-established images."

In 1990 Laughlin expanded the list of his writings to include *Random Stories,* a collection of short stories written mainly before he graduated from Harvard. John Litweiler opens his review of the work in the *Chicago Tribune* by quoting critic Kenneth Rexroth, who praised Laughlin's work as a publisher, adding that, " 'He is [also] an excellent and original poet, and might have been writing his own poems.' " Litweiler continues this praise to include Laughlin's work as a short-story writer: "His own fiction, too, it's now clear from Laughlin's collection of so-called 'Random Stories.' " In discussing this collection, Litweiler feels that Laughlin "seldom presents description—it would only get in the way of the particulars of existence that reveal his people, places, feelings. . . . With Laughlin's fiction, despite its usual absence of overt drama, action is constant. Life, indeed, flows."

Over the years, Laughlin has issued some twenty books, including poetry, short stories, and essay collections. Despite this impressive list of writings and the mostly favorable critical reception it has received, Laughlin's greatest achievements are most readily and most often acknowledged in his work as a publisher. Laughlin himself, as quoted in the *Dictionary of Literary Biography,* described his writing thus: " 'It's very light; it's sentimental, it deals with no great subjects, no great thoughts.' " To which, responds Hall, " 'perhaps, if the poet pretends that he does not take his work seriously, he is free to continue it.' "

BIOGRAPHICAL/CRITICAL SOURCES:

BOOKS

Dictionary of Literary Biography, Volume 48: *American Poets: 1880-1945,* Gale, 1986.
Henderson, Bill, editor, *The Art of Literary Publishing: Editors on Their Craft,* Pushcart Press, 1980.

PERIODICALS

American Poetry Review, November/December, 1981, p. 19.
Chicago Tribune, December 24, 1990.
Conjunctions, winter, 1981-82.
Los Angeles Times, July 13, 1989; March 8, 1991, p. E2.
Newsweek, May 1, 1967.

New York Review of Books, June 2, 1988, p. 14.
New York Times Book Review, February 25, 1973; August 23, 1981, p. 13; February 28, 1982; November 2, 1986, p. 28; June 12, 1988, p. 23.
Publishers Weekly, November 22, 1985, p. 24.
Times Literary Supplement, February 8, 1990, p. 11.
Washington Post Book World, January 3, 1988, p. 5.*

* * *

LEE, Martin A. 1954-

PERSONAL: Born January 17, 1954, in New York, NY; son of Goodwin (in business) and Silva (a library director; maiden name, Jelinek) Lee. *Education:* University of Michigan, B.A., 1975.

ADDRESSES: Agent—Elaine Markson Literary Agency, Inc., 44 Greenwich Ave., New York, NY 10011.

CAREER: Assassination Information Bureau, Washington, DC, co-director, and co-editor of bimonthly newsletter *Clandestine America,* 1977-79; Foundation for National Progress, San Francisco, CA, visiting fellow, 1980-81; Institute for Social Justice, New York, NY, director, 1986—; co-founder, Fairness and Accuracy In Reporting (FAIR); editor, *Extra!,* 1987-89. Guest teacher-in-residence, University of Illinois, and lecturer at Harvard University, Columbus University, Johns Hopkins University, and other schools.

MEMBER: Phi Beta Kappa.

AWARDS, HONORS: Avery and Jule Hopwood Awards from the University of Michigan, 1971, for essay, 1972, for short story, 1974, for essay, and 1975, for essay; Pope Foundation Award for investigative journalism, 1994.

WRITINGS:

(With Bruce Shlain) *Acid Dreams: The CIA, LSD, and the Sixties Rebellion,* Grove, 1986, revised edition published as *Acid Dreams: The Complete Social History of LSD, the CIA, the Sixties and Beyond,* with introduction by Andrei Codrescu, 1992.
(With Norman Solomon) *Unreliable Sources: A Guide to Detecting Bias in News Media,* Lyle Stuart, 1990.

Contributor to *Dictionary of Literary Biography,* Volume 16: *The Beats: Literary Bohemians in Postwar America,* 1983, and to such periodicals as *Rolling Stone, Village Voice, Mother Jones, Nation, National Catholic Reporter, Christian Science Monitor, Interview, The Progressive, Newsday,* and the *San Francisco Chronicle.* Lee's writings have also been translated into French, Dutch, Danish, and Swedish.

WORK IN PROGRESS: A nonfiction book about the resurgence of fascism in Europe for Little, Brown.

SIDELIGHTS: Acid Dreams: The CIA, LSD, and the Sixties Rebellion reveals controversial evidence that links certain U.S. government officials to the widespread use and availability of the mind-expanding drug lysergic acid diethylamide (LSD) during the 1960's psychedelic revolution. Making use of previously classified Central Intelligence Agency (CIA) documentation, authors Martin A. Lee and Bruce Shlain expose massive experimentation with LSD and other hallucinogenic substances by various CIA and military personnel. The extent of this involvement ranges from a 1950's conspiracy by CIA agents to mix LSD into the refreshments at one of the agency's annual Christmas parties to the collusion between the CIA and the military in developing and deploying superhallucinogens as a weapon against Vietcong soldiers during the Vietnam War. The authors also present information suggesting that black market distribution of several drugs, including LSD, resulted from illicit transactions conducted by some government personnel. Under suspicion are CIA dealings with informant Ronald Stark, a chemist who produced vast quantities of illegal psychedelics for public consumption. In addition, a former head of the Federal Narcotics Bureau, Harry Anslinger, is revealed as having sheltered the CIA's secret testing of LSD on unsuspecting American citizens.

In tracing the emergence and dissemination of LSD, the book also chronicles the drug-oriented counterculture that evolved during the era. Such events as the Berkeley Free Speech Movement and the Haight-Ashbury Love-In, both in the San Francisco area, as well as the militant political rebellions of 1968 and 1969 are highlighted along with such period notables as LSD advocate Timothy Leary, Beat poets Ken Kesey and Allen Ginsberg, and popular rock groups of the 1960's.

The book *Unreliable Sources,* on the other hand, addresses a current "dangerous trend" problem within the news media. Lee and Solomon assert that the news media is the spokesperson for American big business and "enshrines an elitist expression of conservative ideology," as Richard J. Holmes writes in *Bloomsbury Review.* Using numerous examples, the authors reveal how the media-owning corporations manipulate the objective presentation of the news by the selection of particular guests and certain topics. Furthermore, there is the news media's deliberate misuse of language. Lee and Solomon call the practice "linguicide" and maintain that it "occurs [for example] when journalists say 'tax reform' but actually mean huge giveaways to the wealthy . . . or when building new weapons of mass destruction is called 'modernization' of a 'deterrent.' As Holmes points out, it is Lee and Solomon's "intent . . . for the consumer of news to [be able to] read and understand the 'story behind the story'—the elite conservatism, media congames, 'media cartels,' policy-driven source journalism, 'ad-itorial' campaigns, important 'under-reported' stories, FBI/CIA smear tactics, calculated avoidance of complexity, absence of historical or cultural context, media myth-making, . . . media taboos, . . . and press and hiring prejudice, . . . [so that the consumer can] develop . . . skills in 'detecting bias in the news media'."

BIOGRAPHICAL/CRITICAL SOURCES:

PERIODICALS

American Book Review, November, 1989, p. 7.
Bloomsbury Review, September, 1991, p. 6.
Booklist, June 15, 1990, p.1934.
Journal of American History, March, 1987, p. 1078.
Los Angeles Times Book Review, May 18, 1986, p. 12.
Library Journal, April 1, 1986, p. 150; May 1, 1990, p. 96.
Nation, November 8, 1986, p. 492.
Publishers Weekly, February 7, 1986, p. 69; April 20, 1990, p. 63; April 13, 1992, p. 55.
Tribune Books (Chicago), September 22, 1991, p. 8.
Washington Post Book World, May 25, 1986, p. 12; September 30, 1990, p. 13.

*   *   *

LEONARD, Lawrence 1928-

PERSONAL: Born August 22, 1928, in London, England; son of Lawrence (a musician) and Florence (a musician; maiden name, Hampson) Leonard; married Josephine Duffy (deceased); married Katharine Wolpe (a musician); married Rose Walker (an art historian); children: (first marriage) Jenifer, Simon. *Education:* Attended Royal Academy of Music and l'Ecole Normale de Musique. *Politics:* Liberal. *Religion:* Church of England. *Avocational interests:* Chess, mountain walking.

ADDRESSES: Home—Boxhurst, Old Reigate Rd., Nr. Dorking, Surrey RH4 1NT, England.

CAREER: Symphonic conductor and teacher of conducting at Morley College, London, England; guest conductor throughout the world. Earlier positions included one year as assistant conductor, British Broadcasting Corporation (BBC) Northern Orchestra, five years as assistant conductor, Halle Orchestra, and five years as music director, Edmonton Symphony Orchestra (Alberta, Canada). *Military service:* British Army; musician in Irish Guards.

MEMBER: Royal Academy of Music (fellow), Composers' Guild of Great Britain (chairperson, 1977), Performing Rights Society, Guildhall School of Music (fellow).

WRITINGS:

The Horn of Mortal Danger (children's novel), Julia MacRae Books (London), 1983.

MUSICAL COMPOSITIONS

(Arranger) Modest Petrovich Moussorgsky, *Pictures at an Exhibition,* (for solo piano and orchestra), Boosey & Hawkes (Oceanside, NY), 1980.
(Lyricist) *What the Waiter Saw: A Music Theatre Piece,* music by David Sutton-Anderson, performed October, 1986.

Also arranger for Saint-Saens's *The Carnival of Animals* for symphony orchestra.

OTHER

Also author of *Jason's Will* (children's novel), *Heroin for Heroes* (novel), *Trotsky* (play), *What the Waiter Saw* (play), *1812 and All That* (humor), and short stories; also composer of *Mezoon,* a tone-poem commissioned for the birthday of the Sultan of Oman, performed by Royal Philharmonic Orchestra, recorded and videotaped at Abbey Road; also composer of pieces for orchestra; also arranger of music. Also conductor on numerous recordings, including *Francesca Da Rimini, Sleeping Beauty Suite,* Bach's *Complete Harpsichord Concerti,* and *Telemann Flute Suite.*

SIDELIGHTS: Lawrence Leonard told *CA:* "As a conductor, I was for five years assistant to Sir John Barbirolli with the Halle Orchestra; I premiered *West Side Story* in London and have conducted opera and ballet at the Royal Opera House, at the Volksoper in Vienna, and at the National Opera in Ankara [Turkey]. I have conducted all the major British orchestras and guested widely in Europe. For five years I was music director of the Edmonton Symphony Orchestra in Canada.

"I now conduct at Morley College in London, where I also teach conducting. I decided some years ago to devote myself to writing music and words in order to explore my talents as a creative—as opposed to a re-creative—artist."

*   *   *

LEVINSON, Nancy Smiler 1938-

PERSONAL: Born November 5, 1938, in Minneapolis, MN; daughter of Paul (an attorney) and Minnie (Meleck) Smiler; married Irwin Levinson (a cardiologist), June 1, 1966; children: Matthew, Danny. *Education:* University of Minnesota, B.A., 1960. *Politics:* Democrat. *Religion:* Jewish.

ADDRESSES: Home—1139 Coldwater Canyon Dr., Beverly Hills, CA 90210.

CAREER: Port Chester Daily Item, Westchester, NY, reporter, 1960-61; *Time* magazine, researcher, 1962-63; Bantam Books, Inc., New York City, associate editor,

1963-66; teacher in Head Start program in Los Angeles, CA, 1967-68; freelance writer and editor, 1974—.

MEMBER: Society of Children's Book Writers, Southern California Council on Literature for Children and Young People.

AWARDS, HONORS: I Lift My Lamp: Emma Lazarus and the Statue of Liberty, Christopher Columbus: Voyager to the Unknown, and *Snowshoe Thompson* were selected "distinguished works of fiction" by the Southern California Council on Literature for Children and Young People in 1986, 1991, and 1993 respectively; *Christopher Columbus: Voyager to the Unknown* was also selected as a Notable Children's Book of 1990 by the American Library Association.

WRITINGS:

JUVENILE

Contributions of Women: Business (biography), Dillon (Minneapolis), 1981.
World of Her Own (novel), Harvey House (New York City), 1981.
Silent Fear (novel), Crestwood (Mankato, MN), 1981.
The First Women Who Spoke Out (biography), Dillon, 1982.
Make A Wish (novel), Scholastic Inc. (New York City), 1983.
The Ruthie Greene Show (novel), Lodestar (New York City), 1985.
(Coauthor) *Getting High in Natural Ways* (nonfiction), Hunter House (Claremont, CA), 1986.
I Lift My Lamp: Emma Lazarus and the Statue of Liberty (biography), Lodestar, 1986.
The Man Who Broke the Sound Barrier (biography), Walker & Co. (New York City), 1988.
Clara and the Bookwagon (historical fiction), HarperCollins (New York City), 1988.
Your Friend, Natalie Popper (novel), Lodestar, 1990.
Christopher Columbus: Voyager to the Unknown (nonfiction), Lodestar, 1990.
Snowshoe Thompson (historical fiction), HarperCollins, 1992.
Sweet Notes, Sour Notes (fiction), Lodestar, 1993.
Turn of the Century: Our Nation One Hundred Years Ago (nonfiction), Lodestar, 1994.

Contributor to periodicals, including *Los Angeles Times, Los Angeles Herald Examiner, Writer's Digest, Newsday, Seventeen, American Girl,* and *Highlights for Children.*

SIDELIGHTS: Nancy Smiler Levinson told *CA:* "Writing for the young reader is the most joyous and challenging work I have ever done. I feel that writing, both fiction and nonfiction, deals with feelings and emotions. It is rewarding to be able to draw a reader into caring about my char-

acters and connect with what they are experiencing. In regard to writing nonfiction, I am especially interested in exploring history. I like to write nonfiction so that it reads like a story."

*   *   *

LINDBERG, Carter (Harry)   1937-

PERSONAL: Born November 23, 1937, in Berwyn, IL; son of Harry and Esther (Bell) Lindberg; married Alice Knudsen, 1960; children: Anne, Erika, Matthew. *Education:* Augustana College, B.A., 1959; Lutheran School of Theology, Chicago, IL, M.Div., 1962; University of Iowa, Ph.D., 1965.

ADDRESSES: Home—113 Whitney St., Northboro, MA 01532. *Office*—School of Theology, Boston University, 745 Commonwealth Ave., Boston, MA 02215.

CAREER: Susquehanna University, Selinsgrove, PA, assistant professor of philosophy and religion, 1965-67; College of the Holy Cross, Worcester, MA, assistant professor of theology, 1967-72; Boston University, MA, assistant professor, 1972-76, associate professor, 1976-79, 1982-85, professor of theology, 1986—; Centre d'Etudes Oecumeniques, Strasbourg, France, research professor of theology, 1979-82. Lecturer at Assumption College, Worcester, 1969-72; visiting lecturer at St. Francis Xavier University, Antigonish, Nova Scotia, summer, 1972; volunteer professor at Norfolk State Prison; lecturer at New England churches; member of New England Lutheran Social Ministry Committee, 1968-71, chairperson, 1971; member of Council of Theologians, 1972-79, and New England Lutheran-Catholic Dialogue, 1978-79.

MEMBER: American Society of Church History, American Society for Reformation Research, Luther-Gesellschaft, Society for Sixteenth-Century Studies (vice president, 1977-78; president, 1978-79).

WRITINGS:

(Editor, translator, and contributor) *Luther's Ecumenical Significance,* Fortress (Philadelphia), 1983.
The Third Reformation?: Charismatic Renewal and Lutheran Tradition, Mercer University Press (Macon, GA), 1983.
(Editor) *Piety, Politics, and Ethics: Reformation Studies in Honor of George Wolfgang Forell,* Sixteen Century Journal Publishers, Northeast Missouri State University (Kirksville), 1984.
Martin Luther, Graded Press, 1988.
(With H. C. Kee, and others) *Christianity: A Social and Cultural History,* Macmillan (New York City), 1991.

(Editor with Emily Albu Hanawalt) *Through the Eye of a Needle: Judeo-Christian Roots of Social Welfare,* Thomas Jefferson University Press (Kirksville), 1993.
Beyond Charity: Reformation Initiatives for the Poor, Fortress, 1993.

Contributor to several books, including *Sixteenth-Century Essays and Studies,* edited by Carl Meyer, Foundation for Reformation Research, 1970; *Disguises of the Demonic,* edited by Alan Olsen, Association Press, 1975; *Les Dissidents du seizieme siecle entre l'humanisme et le catholicisme,* edited by Marc Lienhard, Koerner, 1983; *Oekumenische Erschliessung Martin Luthers,* edited by Peter Manns and Harding Meyer, Paderborn, 1983; and *Tainted Greatness: Antisemitism and Cultural Heroes,* edited by Nancy A. Harrowitz, Temple University Press (Philadelphia), 1994. Also contributor of over eighty articles and reviews to various theology journals.

*   *   *

LINDBLOM, Steven (Winther) 1946-

PERSONAL: Born March 29, 1946, in Minneapolis, MN; son of Charles Edward (a writer and professor of political science) and Rose Catherine Lindblom; married True Kelley (a writer and illustrator); children: Jada Winter. *Education:* Attended St. John's College, Annapolis, MD, 1964-65; Rhode Island School of Design, B.F.A., 1972. *Avocational interests:* Old bicycles and machinery, flying, diving.

ADDRESSES: Home—Old Denny Hill, Warner, NH 03278.

CAREER: Freelance illustrator and writer.

AWARDS, HONORS: How to Build a Robot was selected as one of the "Best Books of the Year" by the Bank Street College of Education, 1985.

WRITINGS:

JUVENILE

(With wife, True Kelley) *The Mouse's Terrible Christmas,* illustrated by Kelley, Lothrop (New York City), 1978.
The Fantastic Bicycles Book, Houghton (Boston), 1979.
(With Kelley) *The Mouse's Terrible Halloween,* illustrated by Kelley, Lothrop, 1980.
Let's Give Kitty a Bath, illustrated by Kelley, Addison-Wesley (Reading, MA), 1982.
How to Build a Robot, Crowell (New York City), 1985.
Let's Go Shopping, Western Publishing (New York City), 1988.
Tiny Dinosaurs, Western Publishing, 1988.
Snakes and Reptiles, Western Publishing, 1989.

Airplanes and Other Things That Fly, Western Publishing, 1990.
Flying Dinosaurs, Western Publishing, 1990.
Fly the Hot Ones, Houghton, 1991.

ILLUSTRATOR

Bernie Zubrowski, *Messing around with Water Pumps and Siphons: A Children's Museum Activity Book,* Little, Brown (Boston), 1981.
Ross Olney, *The Internal Combustion Engine,* Lippincott (Philadelphia), 1982.
Seymour Simon, *Computer Sense, Computer Nonsense,* Lippincott, 1984.
(With Kelley) Niles, Gregory, and Douglas Eldredge, *The Fossil Factory,* Addison-Wesley, 1989.

WORK IN PROGRESS: A book about diving; an adult science fiction novel.

SIDELIGHTS: Steven Lindblom once told *CA:* "While I have written more fiction than nonfiction at this point, nonfiction writing is my first love. I think there are two very negative forces at work on our children today. One is television, which is turning children into drones who are only observers and who have been convinced that experiences seen on television are somehow as valid as the real thing. (I think a child who neither read nor watched television might be happier and more constructive than one who did both!) The other is that modern technology has become so complex and remote that we begin to see ourselves as its victims rather than its masters and cease accepting any responsibility for the future.

"There are two things good children's nonfiction can do about this: encourage kids to get out and do things for themselves and reduce the world that surrounds them to manageable terms, restoring to them the feeling that they can comprehend it, and therefore control it.

"It's important that kids realize that whenever someone tells them, 'It's too complicated for you to understand,' the person probably is just covering up his own lack of understanding."

*   *   *

LINDSAY, (John) Maurice 1918-
(Gavin Brock)

PERSONAL: Born July 21, 1918, in Glasgow, Scotland; son of Matthew (an insurance manager) and Eileen Frances (Brock) Lindsay; married Aileen Joyce Gordon (a teacher), August 3, 1946; children: Seona Morag, Kirsteen Ann, Niall Gordon Brock, Morven Morag Joyce. *Education:* Attended Glasgow Academy, 1926-36, Scottish National Academy of Music, 1936-39. *Politics:* Liberal.

ADDRESSES: Home—7 Milton Hill, Milton, Dumbarton G82 2TS, Scotland.

CAREER: Scottish Daily Mail, Edinburgh, Scotland, drama critic, 1946-47; *Bulletin,* Glasgow, Scotland, music critic, 1946-60; British Broadcasting Corp., Glasgow, freelance broadcaster, 1946-61; Border Television, Carlisle, England, program controller, 1961-62, production controller, 1962-64, features executive and senior interviewer, 1964-67; Scottish Civic Trust, Glasgow, director, 1967-83, consultant, 1983—. Historic Buildings Council for Scotland, member, 1976-87; National Heritage Memorial Fund, trustee, 1980-84; Europa Nostra, honorary secretary-general, 1983-91; New Lanark Conservation, trustee, 1987-94. *Military service:* British Army, World War II; became captain.

MEMBER: Association for Scottish Literary Studies (president, 1988-91), Saltire Society (honorary publications secretary, 1948-52), Royal Incorporation of Architects in Scotland (honorary fellow).

AWARDS, HONORS: Rockefeller Atlantic Award, 1946, for *The Enemies of Love: Poems, 1941-1945;* Commander, Order of the British Empire, 1979; Doctor of Letters, University of Glasgow, 1982; holder of Territorial Decoration.

WRITINGS:

POETRY

The Advancing Day, privately printed, 1940.
Perhaps To-morrow, privately printed, 1941.
Predicament, Alden Press, 1942.
No Crown for Laughter, Fortune Press (London), 1943.
The Enemies of Love: Poems, 1941-1945, Maclellan, 1946.
Selected Poems, Oliver & Boyd (Edinburgh, Scotland), 1947.
Hurlygush: Poems in Scots, introduction by Hugh Mac-Diarmid, Serif Books, 1948.
At the Woods Edge, Serif Books, 1950.
Ode for St. Andrew's Night, and Other Poems, New Alliance Press, 1951.
The Exiled Heart: Poems, 1941-1956, edited and introduced by George Bruce, R. Hale (London), 1957.
Snow Warning, and Other Poems, Linden Press (Sussex, England), 1962.
One Later Day, and Other Poems, Brookside Press (London), 1964.
This Business of Living, Akros Publications (Nottingham, England), 1969.
Comings and Goings, Akros Publications, 1971.
Selected Poems, 1942-1972, R. Hale, 1973.
The Run from Life: More Poems, 1942-1972, Cygnet Press (Oxford, England), 1975.

Walking without an Overcoat: Poems, 1972-1976, R. Hale, 1977.
Collected Poems, edited with introduction by Alexander Scott, Paul Harris Publishing (Edinburgh), 1979.
A Net to Catch the Wind, and Other Poems, R. Hale, 1981.
The French Mosquitoes' Woman and Other Diversions and Poems, R. Hale, 1985.
Requiem for a Sexual Athlete, R. Hale, 1988.
Collected Poems 1940-1990, Mercat Press (Edinburgh), 1990.
On the Face of It: Collected Poems Volume II, R. Hale, 1993.

EDITOR

Sailing To-morrow's Seas: An Anthology of New Poems, introduction by Tambimuttu, Fortune Press, 1944.
Poetry-Scotland, Volume I, Maclellan, 1944, Volume II, Maclellan, 1945, Volume III, Maclellan, 1947, Volume IV (with Hugh MacDiarmid) Serif Books, 1949.
(And contributor) *Modern Scottish Poetry: An Anthology of Scottish Renaissance, 1920-1945,* Faber (London), 1946, 4th edition published as *Modern Scottish Poetry: An Anthology of Scottish Renaissance, 1925-1985,* R. Hale, 1986.
(And contributor, with Fred Urquhart) *No Scottish Twilight: New Scottish Short Stories* (includes "Boxing Match"), Maclellan, 1947.
Selected Poems of Alexander Gray, Maclellan, 1948.
Poems by Sir David Lyndsay of the Mount, Oliver & Boyd, 1948.
(With Helen B. Cruickshank; and author of introduction) *Selected Poems by Marion Angus,* Serif Books, 1950.
(And author of introduction) *John Davidson: A Selection of His Poems,* preface by T. S. Eliot, Hutchinson, 1961.
(With Edwin Morgan and George Bruce) *Scottish Poetry,* Aldine (Hawthorne, NY), Volume I, 1966, Volume II, 1966, Volume III, 1968, Volume IV, 1969, Volume V, 1970, Volume VI, 1972, Volume VII, 1974, Volume VIII, 1976, Volume IX, 1977.
(Editor with Robert Laird Mackie) *A Book of Scottish Verse,* 2nd edition, Oxford University Press (Oxford, England), 1967, 3rd edition, St. Martin's (New York City), 1983.
(Consultant editor) *Voices of Our Kind: An Anthology of Contemporary Scottish Verse for Schools,* Saltire Society (Edinburgh), 1971.
(And contributor) *Scotland: An Anthology,* R. Hale, 1974, St. Martin's, 1975, revised edition, R. Hale, 1989.
As I Remember: Ten Scottish Writers Reflect How Writing for Them Began, R. Hale, 1979.
Scottish Comic Verse 1425-1980, R. Hale, 1981.

(With Alexander Scott) *The Comic Poems of William Ten-nant,* Association for Scottish Literary Studies (Aberdeen, Scotland), 1989.

(With Joyce Lindsay) *The Scottish Dog: An Anthology,* Mercat Press, 1989.

Thomas Hamilton's "The Youth and Manhood of Cyril Thornton," Association for Scottish Literary Studies, 1990.

(With J. Lindsay) *Pleasure of Gardens: A Literary Companion,* Mercat Press, 1991.

(With J. Lindsay) *The Scottish Quotation Book: A Literary Companion,* R. Hale, 1991, Barnes & Noble (New York City), 1992.

(With J. Lindsay) *The Music Quotation Book,* R. Hale, 1992.

(With J. Lindsay) *The Theatre and Opera Lovers' Quotation Book,* R. Hale, 1993.

(With J. Lindsay) *The Robert Burns Quotation Book,* R. Hale, 1994.

Also editor, with Douglas Young, of Oliver & Boyd's "Saltire Modern Poets" series, 1947.

OTHER

A Pocket Guide to Scottish Culture, Maclellan, 1947, University Distributors, 1947.

The Scottish Renaissance, Serif Books, 1948.

The Lowlands of Scotland, R. Hale, Volume I: *Glasgow and the North,* 1953, Volume II: *Edinburgh and the South,* 1956, both volumes, International Publications Service (New York City), 1956.

Robert Burns: The Man, His Work, the Legend, MacGibbon & Kee, 1954, Dufour (Chester Springs, PA), 1963, 4th edition, St. Martin's, 1994.

Dunoon: The Gem of the Clyde Coast (guidebook), Town Council of Dunoon, 1954.

Clyde Waters: Variations and Diversions on a Theme of Pleasure, R. Hale, 1958.

The Burns Encyclopaedia, Hutchinson, 1959, 4th edition, R. Hale, 1991.

(With David Somervell) *Killochan Castle, Ayrshire* (guidebook), Pilgrim Press (Derby, England), 1960.

By Yon Bonnie Banks: A Gallimaufry, Hutchinson, 1961.

The Discovery of Scotland, Based on Accounts of Foreign Travellers from the Thirteenth to the Eighteenth Centuries, R. Hale, 1964, Roy, 1965.

The Eye Is Delighted: Some Romantic Travellers in Scotland, Muller, 1971, Transatlantic (Albuquerque, NM), 1972.

Portrait of Glasgow, R. Hale, 1972, revised edition published as *Glasgow,* 1989.

Robin Philipson, Edinburgh University Press (Edinburgh), 1977.

History of Scottish Literature, R. Hale, 1977, revised edition, 1992.

Francis George Scott and the Scottish Renaissance, Paul Harris Publishing, 1980.

(With Anthony Kerssting) *The Buildings of Edinburgh,* Batsford (London), 1981, 2nd edition, 1987.

Thank You for Having Me: A Personal Memoir, R. Hale, 1983.

(With Denis Hardley) *Unknown Scotland,* Batsford, 1984.

The Castles of Scotland, Constable (London), 1986, revised edition, 1994.

Count All Men Mortal: A History of Scottish Provident 1837-1937, Scottish Provident, 1987.

Victorian and Edwardian Glasgow, Batsford, 1987.

Illustrated Guide to Glasgow, 1837, R. Hale, 1989.

(With David Bruce) *Edinburgh: Past and Present,* R. Hale, 1990.

Author of librettos for two operas, *The Abbot of Drimmock,* 1957, and *The Decision,* music by Thea Musgrave, J. & W. Chester, 1967. Author of commentaries for two films. Contributor to *Grove's Dictionary of Music and Musicians.* Contributor under pseudonym Gavin Brock to journals such as *Scottish Field* and *Scottish Review.* Editor, *Scots Review,* 1949-50, and *Scottish Review,* 1975-85.

WORK IN PROGRESS: "A final volume, *News of the World,* which includes a fairly coruscating sonnet sequence on modern ills, 'The Inept Joiner,' a humorous/satirical commentary on the copycat cases following the United States's Lorena Bobbitt trial, and a sequence of children's poems about a dog, Spruff."

SIDELIGHTS: Maurice Lindsay told *CA:* "Poetry, so far as I am concerned, starts with whatever brings into being 'the lyric cry,' though satire and humor have increasingly taken over as the initial urge in later years. Most of my poems have begun as unrelated images. A phrase in a newspaper or from a conversation has been set down in my notebook and has come together with other phrases or related images, eventually being sorted out by 'anvil work,' to use Graves's description. I have been a poet of 'dailyness,' my material being the stuff of ordinary life. 'He makes the mundane marvellous,' wrote Christopher Rush, reviewing my 1979 *Collected Poems* in *Scottish Literary Journal,* or, as Iain Crichton Smith said in the *Scotsman,* 'He has always been a poet of the quotidian, of the random sparkle of the every day.'

"My earliest influences were MacNeice and MacDiarmid, the one for his humanity, the other for his passionate—but ultimately Marxist and so self-defeating—concern for Scotland. Although I have written on Scotland and its history and cultural traditions, music, painting, and architecture, my main interest has been as a poet; and although I sometimes employ free verse, I have more often striven to revivify formal verse forms for effective modern use.

"I do not have any advice to give to young aspiring writers other than that which I used to give to aspiring t.v. performers or writers when I was running the programs of the U.K. Independent Border Television Station: 'Don't, unless you really can't help it.' You need the stamina of a prize fighter to survive unscathed, and imagination isn't a commodity much valued in our dogma-ridden violent modern world."

BIOGRAPHICAL/CRITICAL SOURCES:

BOOKS

Kinsley, James, editor, *Scottish Poetry: A Critical Survey,* Cassell (London), 1955.

PERIODICALS

Observer Review, July, 1968.
Scotsman, June 1, 1991.
Scottish Literary Journal Supplement, summer, 1980.
Scottish Review, Number 16, 1979.
Times Literary Supplement, June 26, 1981.

*   *   *

LOCHTE, Dick
  See LOCHTE, Richard S(amuel)

*   *   *

LOCHTE, Richard S(amuel) 1944-
  (Dick Lochte)

PERSONAL: Born October 19, 1944, in New Orleans, LA; son of Richard Samuel (an insurance investigator) and Eileen (a musician; maiden name, Carbine) Lochte. *Education:* Tulane University, B.A., 1966.

ADDRESSES: Home—P.O. Box 5413, Santa Monica, CA 90409. *Agent*—William Morris Agency, 1350 Avenue of the Americas, New York, NY 10019.

CAREER: Playboy, Chicago, IL, publicist and writer, 1966-73; freelance writer, 1973—. *Military service:* U.S. Coast Guard Reserve, 1962-69; became lieutenant commander.

MEMBER: International PEN, International Crime Writers Association, Writers Guild of America, Mystery Writers of America, National Book Critics Circle, American Crime Writers League, Private Eye Writers of America.

AWARDS, HONORS: Nero Wolfe Award, Rex Stout Society, and special award, Mystery Writers of America, both 1985, both for *Sleeping Dog;* Theatre Los Angeles Governors Award, 1989, for body of work in theatre criticism.

WRITINGS:

The Playboy Writer (nonfiction), HMH Publications, 1968.
(Coauthor) *Escape to Athena* (screenplay), ITC/Associated Film Distribution, 1979.
(Under name Dick Lochte) *Sleeping Dog* (mystery novel), Arbor House (New York City), 1985.
(Under name Dick Lochte) *Philip Strange* (screenplay), Michael Laughlin Productions, 1985.
(Under name Dick Lochte) *Laughing Dog* (sequel to *Sleeping Dog*), Arbor House, 1987.
(Under name Dick Lochte) *Blue Bayou,* Simon & Schuster (New York City), 1992.
(Under name Dick Lochte) *The Neon Smile* (sequel to *Blue Bayou*), Simon & Schuster, 1995.

Also author of screenplay *Sleeping Dog,* based on his novel of the same title. Theatre critic, *Los Angeles,* 1974—; columnist, *Los Angeles Times,* 1975-85.

WORK IN PROGRESS: A novel, *Devil Dog.*

SIDELIGHTS: Richard S. Lochte once told *CA:* "It has been said that young writers today are interested in writing The Great American Film instead of The Great American Novel. If true, it is because they are unfamiliar with the differences—make that perils—the two media hold for the writer. As a novelist, the writer is in total control of the material and as such is responsible for research, accuracy, clarity of thought, and so on. As a screenwriter, he or she prepares a blueprint and thereafter is responsible only for cashing the check for services rendered.

"Writing pulled me through schools and college. If I hadn't been interested in it, I'd probably still be stuck back there trying to figure out why $E = mc^2$. When I didn't know an answer, which was often, I made one up. I did some of my most creative writing in college. Later, it was a way of getting away from a nine-to-five job."

BIOGRAPHICAL/CRITICAL SOURCES:

PERIODICALS

Los Angeles Times Book Review, November 24, 1985.
New York Times Book Review, November 17, 1985.

*   *   *

LOPEZ, Barry Holstun 1945-

PERSONAL: Born January 6, 1945, in Port Chester, NY; son of Adrian Bernard and Mary (Holstun) Lopez; married Sandra Landers (a bookwright), June 10, 1967. *Education:* University of Notre Dame, A.B. (cum laude), 1966, M.A.T., 1968; University of Oregon, graduate study, 1969-70.

ADDRESSES: Home—Oregon. *Agent*—Peter Matson, Sterling Lord Literistic, Inc., One Madison Ave., New York, NY 10010.

CAREER: Full-time writer, 1970—. Columbia University, New York City, associate at Gannett Foundation Media Center, 1985—; Eastern Washington University, Cheney, WA, Distinguished Visiting Writer, 1985; University of Iowa, Iowa City, Ida Beam Visiting Professor, 1985; Carleton College, Northfield, MN, Distinguished Visiting Naturalist, 1986; University of Notre Dame, Notre Dame, IN, W. Harold and Martha Welch Visiting Professor of American Studies, 1989. Sino-American Writers Conference in China, delegate, 1988. Correspondent, *Outside,* 1982—.

MEMBER: PEN American Center, Authors Guild, Poets and Writers.

AWARDS, HONORS: John Burroughs Medal for distinguished natural history writing, Christopher Medal for humanitarian writing, and Pacific Northwest Booksellers award for excellence in nonfiction, all 1979, and American Book Award nomination, 1980, all for *Of Wolves and Men;* Distinguished Recognition Award, Friends of American Writers, 1981, for *Winter Count;* National Book Award in nonfiction (formerly American Book Award), Christopher Book Award, Pacific Northwest Booksellers award, National Book Critics Circle award nomination, *Los Angeles Times* book award nomination, American Library Association notable book citation, *New York Times Book Review* "Best Books" listing, and American Library Association "Best Books for Young Adults" citation, all 1986, and Francis Fuller Victor Award in nonfiction from Oregon Institute of Literary Arts, 1987, all for *Arctic Dreams: Imagination and Desire in a Northern Landscape;* Award in Literature from American Academy and Institute of Arts and Letters, 1986, for body of work; Guggenheim fellow, 1987; L.H.D., Whittier College, 1988; Parents' *Choice* Award, 1990, for *Crow and Weasel;* Lannan Foundation Award in nonfiction, 1990, for body of work; Governor's Award for Arts, 1990; Best Geographic Educational Article, National Council for Geographic Education, 1990, for "The American Geographies."

WRITINGS:

Desert Notes: Reflections in the Eye of a Raven (fictional narratives), Andrews & McMeel, 1976.
Giving Birth to Thunder, Sleeping with His Daughter: Coyote Builds North America (Native American trickster stories), Andrews & McMeel, 1978.
Of Wolves and Men (nonfiction), Scribner, 1978.
River Notes: The Dance of Herons (fictional narratives), Andrews & McMeel, 1979.
Desert Reservation (chapbook), Copper Canyon Press, 1980.
Winter Count (fiction), Scribner, 1981.
Arctic Dreams: Imagination and Desire in a Northern Landscape (nonfiction), Scribner, 1986.
Crossing Open Ground (essays), Scribner, 1988.
Crow and Weasel (fable), illustrated by Tom Pohrt, North Point Press, 1990.
The Rediscovery of North America (essay), University Press of Kentucky, 1991.

OTHER

Contributor to numerous books, including *Wonders: Writings and Drawings for the Child in Us All,* edited by Jonathan Cott and Mary Gimbel, Rolling Stone Press, 1980; *Resist Much, Obey Little: Some Notes on Edward Abbey,* edited by James Hepworth and Gregory McNamee, Dream Garden, 1985; *Before and After: The Shape and Shaping of Prose,* edited by D. L. Emblen and Arnold Solkov, Random House, 1986; *Best American Essays,* edited by Gay Talese and Robert Atwan, Ticknor and Fields, 1988; *Bighorse the Warrior,* by Tiana Bighorse, University of Arizona Press, 1990; *Helping Nature Heal: A Whole Earth Catalogue,* edited by Richard Nilson, Ten Speed Press, 1991; *Contemporary Voices,* edited by Rick Bass, Texas A & M University Press, 1992.

Contributor to numerous periodicals, including *Harper's, North American Review, New York Times, Orion Nature Quarterly, Antaeus, National Geographic,* and *Outside.* Contributing editor, *North American Review,* 1977—, and *Harper's,* 1981-82, 1984—; guest editor of special section, "The American Indian Mind," for *Quest,* September/October, 1978; advisory editor, *Antaeus,* autumn, 1986.

Lopez's books have been translated into Chinese, Dutch, Finnish, French, German, Italian, Japanese, Norwegian, Portuguese, Russian, Spanish, and Swedish.

ADAPTATIONS: Composer John Luther Adams consulted with Lopez and others to create a stage adaptation of *Giving Birth to Thunder,* which was performed in Juneau, Alaska, in 1987; three stories from *River Notes* have been recorded with accompanying music by cellist David Darling; portions of *Desert Notes* and *Arctic Dreams* have been adapted for the stage by modern dance companies.

WORK IN PROGRESS: A work of fiction, set on the northern plains in the eighteenth century; a work of nonfiction about landscapes remote from North America; essays, articles, and short fiction for magazines.

SIDELIGHTS: Barry Holstun Lopez's early magazine articles and books established his reputation as an authoritative writer on the subjects of natural history and the environment. He has been favorably compared to such distinguished naturalist/authors as Edward Hoagland, Peter

Matthiessen, Edward Abbey, Sally Carrighar, and Loren Eiseley. Lopez's later works are praised for their philosophical content as well, for in such works as *Of Wolves and Men* and *Arctic Dreams: Imagination and Desire in a Northern Landscape* the author uses natural history as a metaphor for discussing some larger moral issues. "A writer has a certain handful of questions," Lopez explained to Nick O'Connell in a *Seattle Review* interview. "Mine seem to be the issues of tolerance and dignity. You can't sit down and write directly about those things, but if they are on your mind and if you're a writer, they're going to come out in one form or another. The form I feel most comfortable with, where I do a lot of reading and aimless thinking, is in natural history."

Lopez spent most of his first ten years in Southern California—"before it became a caricature of itself," he told *Western American Literature* interviewer Jim Aton. By the time the family moved back to Lopez's birthplace in New York, he had formed a strong emotional attachment to the West Coast, and so he returned to live there when he was twenty-three years old. Lopez's graduate studies in folklore led him to write his first book, a retelling of Native American stories featuring the coyote as a trickster figure. It was published some time later as *Giving Birth to Thunder, Sleeping with His Daughter: Coyote Builds North America.* Deciding that life as a writer was preferable to life as a scholar, Lopez left the university in 1970, settled with his wife on the McKenzie River in western Oregon, and devoted himself to writing full-time.

A 1974 assignment for *Smithsonian* magazine led to Lopez's first major book, *Of Wolves and Men.* His research for that article "catalyzed a lot of thinking about human and animal relationships which had been going on in a vague way in my mind for several years," he said in a *CA* interview. "I realized that if I focused on this one animal, I might be able to say something sharp and clear." In his book, Lopez attempts to present a complete portrait of the wolf. He includes not only scientific information but also wolf lore from aboriginal societies and an overview of the animal's role in literature, folklore, and superstition.

The result, say many critics, is a book that succeeds on several levels. First, Lopez has gathered "an extraordinary amount of material," writes a contributor to the *New York Review of Books,* making *Of Wolves and Men* one of the most comprehensive sources of information on these animals ever published. Second, in showing readers the many diverse images of the wolf, the author reveals how man "creates" animals by projecting aspects of his own personality onto them. Third, Lopez illustrates how undeserved is Western civilization's depiction of the wolf as a ruthless killer. His observations showed him that the Eskimos' conception of the wolf is much closer to the truth; among them, wolves are respected and emulated for their intelli-

gence and strong sense of loyalty. What society thinks about the wolf may reveal something about itself, concludes Lopez, for while Western man has reviled the wolf as a wanton killer, he himself has brutally and pointlessly driven many animals to extinction. Whitley Streiber, writing for the *Washington Post,* believes that *Of Wolves and Men* is "a very important book by a man who has thought much on his subject. Above all he has listened to many people who claim to know about wolves. In coming to terms with the difference between what we know and what we imagine about the wolf, Lopez has shed light on some painful truths about the human experience. By laying no blame while facing the tragedy for what it is, he has made what we have done to the wolf a source of new knowledge about man."

Lopez found that he was strongly drawn to the Arctic even after *Of Wolves and Men* was completed. Over the next four years he made several more trips there, and in 1986 he published an account of his travels entitled *Arctic Dreams: Imagination and Desire in a Northern Landscape.* While the book provides a wealth of factual information about the Arctic region, it is, says the *New York Times*'s Michiko Kakutani, "a book about the Arctic North in the way that 'Moby-Dick' is a novel about whales." In *Arctic Dreams* Lopez restates the deeper themes found in *Of Wolves and Men,* but while *Of Wolves and Men* focused tightly on man's relationship with a specific animal, *Arctic Dreams*'s scope is wider, exploring man's relationship with what Lopez refers to as "the landscape." He explained to Jim Aton, "By landscape I mean the complete lay of the land—the animals that are there, the trees, the vegetation, the quality of soils, the drainage pattern of water, the annual cycles of temperature, the kinds of precipitation, the sounds common to the region."

Arctic Dreams drew many favorable reviews, both for its vivid descriptions of the North and for the questions it raises about man's place in nature. "The writing, at times, is luminous, powerful and musical. Lopez infuses each sentence with grace," asserts George Tombs in the Toronto *Globe & Mail.* "It is a lyrical geography and natural history, an account of Eskimo life, and a history of northern explorations," finds *Los Angeles Times Book Review* contributor Richard Eder. "But mainly, it is a . . . reflection about the meaning of mankind's encounter with the planet. . . . Its question, starting as ecology and working into metaphysics, is whether civilization can find a way of adapting itself to the natural world, before its predilection for adapting the natural world to itself destroys self and world, both." Lopez elaborated on the feelings that prompted him to write *Arctic Dreams* in his interview with Aton: "I think if you can really see the land, if you can lose your sense of wishing it to be what you want it to be, if you can strip yourself of the desire to order and to name and see the land entirely for itself, you see in the relationship of all its elements the face of God. And that's why I say the landscape has an authority."

Man's interactions with "the landscape" are often highlighted in Lopez's fiction as well as in his nonfiction. His short story collections are praised by many reviewers. For example, in a *Detroit News* review of *River Notes: The Dance of Herons,* David Graber writes: "Lopez delicately surveys the terrain of shared experience between a man and place, in this case a river in the Pacific Northwest. . . . [The author] has an unsentimental naturalist's knowledge combined with profound love-of-land. . . . [His] writing has a dreamlike quality; the sensuality of his words, his . . . playful choice of simile serve as counterpoint to his precisely accurate portrayals of salmon spawning and herons fishing, of Douglas fir falling to the chainsaw and willow crowding the riverbank." Edith Hamilton of the *Miami Herald* says that in *River Notes* "Lopez transmogrifies the physical characteristics of the river—the bend, the falls, the shallows, the rapids—into human experience: the bend as a man seriously ill for a long time who suddenly, for no reason as the river bends for no reason, decides he will recover. The falls is a strangely gothic convolution of the original fall from grace, brought up to date by a vagabond with mythic yearnings who ends his search at the high brink of the river's falls. . . . Lopez's nice shallows become deep reflecting mirrors, their images multiplying beyond ease. . . . Not since Ken Kesey's drastically different novel, *Sometimes a Great Notion,* has a writer so caught and pinned the mossy melancholy of Oregon." In his *Progressive* review, David Miller makes the point that, despite the book's deceptively simple title, it is no mere study of herons. He writes that *River Notes* "is about a small world of relationships among people, herons, salmon, cottonwoods—and all creatures drawn to this rushing, tumbling, powerful, and endangered emblem of natural life, the river. . . . [The book] is a thing of beauty in itself, as tantalizingly real and yet as otherworldly as your own reflection on a river's surface. . . . It is a rare achievement; perhaps—I've never said this before and know that only time will tell—it is a work of genius."

Saturday Review writer Alan Cheuse believes that *Winter Count,* another collection of short fiction, is the book that will win for Lopez "recognition as a writer who like, say, Peter Matthiessen or Edward Hoagland, goes to the wilderness in order to clarify a great deal about civilization." Cheuse commends Lopez for weaving "a style reminiscent of some important contemporary Latin American magical realists" and for turning "the sentiments of a decade's worth of ecology lovers into a deeply felt and unnervingly powerful picture of reality." *Los Angeles Times* reviewer Elaine Kendall writes: "There's a boundary, no wider than a pinstripe, where fact and fiction barely touch. With so much room on either side and assorted areas where overlap is expected, few writers choose to confine themselves to that fine line where the two simply meet. Lopez is one of those few. He makes that delicate border his entire territory. *Winter Count* is a small and perfectly crafted collection of just such encounters between imagination and reality. . . . Lopez's observations are so acute the stories expand of their own accord, lingering in the mind the way intense light lingers on the retina." Finally, David Quammen, in a *New York Times Book Review* article, says that *Winter Count* is "full of solid, quiet, telling short works. Each of the stories . . . is as economical in design, as painstakingly crafted and as resonant as a good classical guitar." Quammen concludes that Lopez's fiction "is as spare, as pared down and elemental as the lives it describes, the values it celebrates. One of his characters says, 'I've thrown away everything that is no good,' and this perilously righteous algorithm seems a key part of the author's own epic."

Discussing his fiction with Aton, Lopez commented: "My interest in a story is to illuminate a set of circumstances that bring some understanding of human life, enough at least so that a reader can identify with it and draw some vague sense of hope or sustenance or deep feeling and in some way be revived. . . . It's important to me . . . to go into a story with a capacity for wonder, where I know I can derive something 'wonder-full' and then bring this into the story so that a reader can feel it and say, 'I am an adult. I have a family, I pay bills, I live in a world of chicanery and subterfuge and atomic weaponry and inhumanity and round-heeled politicians and garrulous, insipid television personalities, but still I have wonder. I have been brought to a state of wonder by contact with something in a story.'"

BIOGRAPHICAL/CRITICAL SOURCES:

BOOKS

Lopez, Barry Holstun, *Arctic Dreams: Imagination and Desire in a Northern Landscape* (nonfiction), Scribner, 1986.

Lueders, Edward, editor, *Writing Natural History: Dialogues with Authors,* University of Utah Press, 1989.

O'Connell, Nicholas, *At the Field's End: Interviews with Twenty Pacific Northwest Writers* (excerpted in *Seattle Review*), Madrona, 1987.

Paul, Sherman, *Hewing to Experience: Essays and Reviews on Recent American Poetry and Poetics, Nature and Culture,* University of Iowa Press, 1989.

PERIODICALS

Bloomsbury Review, January/February, 1990.
Chicago Tribune, November 5, 1978; March 30, 1986.

Chicago Tribune Book World, November 23, 1979.
Christian Science Monitor, February 12, 1979.
Detroit News, November 4, 1979.
English Journal, April, 1989.
Environmental Journal, January/February, 1991.
Globe & Mail (Toronto), May 31, 1986.
Harper's, December, 1984.
Los Angeles Times, November 12, 1978; May 9, 1981.
Los Angeles Times Book Review, March 2, 1986; February 14, 1988.
Miami Herald, September 30, 1979; March 29, 1986.
Missouri Review, Volume 11, number 3, 1988.
Nation, November 11, 1978.
New Republic, June 30, 1979.
Newsweek, October 16, 1978.
New Yorker, February 26, 1979; March 17, 1986; November 26, 1990.
New York Review of Books, October 12, 1978.
New York Times, January 4, 1979; February 12, 1986; March 29, 1986.
New York Times Book Review, November 19, 1978; June 14, 1981; February 16, 1986; April 24, 1988; November 25, 1990.
North Dakota Quarterly, winter, 1988.
Observer, June 24, 1979.
Orion Nature Quarterly, summer, 1990.
Pacific Northwest, March/April, 1980.
Progressive, May, 1980.
Publishers Weekly, October 11, 1985; June 23, 1989; July 27, 1990.
Saturday Review, April, 1981.
Seattle Review, fall, 1985.
Time, March 10, 1986.
Times Literary Supplement, December 7, 1979; August 8, 1986.
Washington Post, November 27, 1978; November 18, 1986; November 24, 1986.
Washington Post Book World, March 9, 1986.
Western American Literature, spring, 1986.*

*   *   *

LOWE, David
See LOWE, David Garrard

*   *   *

LOWE, David Garrard 1933-
(David Lowe)

PERSONAL: Born January 9, 1933, in Baltimore, MD; son of Martin Vogel (an equestrian) and Grace (Garrard) Lowe. *Education:* Oberlin College, B.A., 1955; University

of Michigan, M.A., 1958. *Politics:* Republican. *Religion:* Episcopalian.

ADDRESSES: Home—225 East 79th St., New York, NY 10021. *Office*—New York School of Interior Design, 170 East 70th St., New York, NY 10021. *Agent*—Carl Brandt, Brandt & Brandt Literary Agents Inc., 1501 Broadway, New York, NY 10036.

CAREER: Look (magazine), New York City, editor and writer, 1960-64; *American Heritage* (magazine), New York City, editor and writer, 1964-69; *McCall's* (magazine), New York City, editor and writer, 1969-71; Chanticleer Press, New York City, editor and writer, 1971-75; Dover Publications, New York City, staff writer, 1975-80; New York School of Interior Design, New York City, professor of architectural history, 1980—, director of gallery, 1987—. Newberry Library, research associate, 1975-80; Cooper-Hewitt Museum, lecturer, 1982—; visiting professor, Metropolitan Museum of Art, 1983, and Columbia University Graduate School of Business Administration; New York Academy of Art, director of gallery and special projects, 1986-87; American Academy, Rome, visiting scholar, 1992. Assistant to Muriel Gardiner, psychiatrist and founder of the New-Land Foundation, 1977-85; WNYC-Radio, architecture and urban affairs critic, 1980—; Canadian Broadcasting Corp. (CBC), broadcaster, 1980-82.

MEMBER: Victorian Society of America (member of board of directors), Writers Room (founding member of board of directors), Century Association, Coffee House.

AWARDS, HONORS: Avery Hopwood Award, University of Michigan, 1950s; grant, Graham Foundation for Advanced Studies in the Fine Arts, 1974; Cliff Dwellers Arts Foundation and Society of Midland Authors awards, both 1975, both for *Lost Chicago.*

WRITINGS:

UNDER NAME DAVID LOWE, EXCEPT AS NOTED

(Editor) *New York, N.Y.: A Study of a City,* American Heritage Publishing (New York City), 1968.
(Editor with Douglas Cooper) *Braque: The Great Years,* Art Institute of Chicago (Chicago), 1972.
Lost Chicago, Houghton (Boston), 1975.
Postcard Views of Old Chicago, Dover (New York City), 1976.
Postcard Views of Old Boston, Dover, 1976.
Postcard Views of Old London, Dover, 1977.
The Great Chicago Fire, Dover, 1979.
Chicago Interiors: Views of a Splendid World, Contemporary Books (Chicago), 1979.
St. Bartholomew's: An Architectural History of a Church, Victorian Society, 1982.

Paris in the Belle Epoque: Historical Photographs from the Archives of Roger-Viollet, New York School of Interior Design (New York City), 1992.

(Under name David Garrard Lowe) *Stanford White's New York,* edited by Jacqueline Onassis, Doubleday (New York City), 1992.

Beaux-Arts New York, New York School of Interior Design, 1993.

Contributor of numerous articles to periodicals, including *New York Times, Wall Street Journal, Esquire, Travel and Leisure, Horizon, Prairie Schooner,* and *Commonweal.*

WORK IN PROGRESS: A social history of America in the Gilded Age.

SIDELIGHTS: David Garrard Lowe once told *CA:* "Beginning in 1959 I was an editor and writer for Cowles Communications in New York City. I specialized in the field of urban news and worked closely with stringers in London and Rome and with the Washington bureau of *Look* and *Christian Science Monitor.* Then I was with *American Heritage,* where I worked closely with such writers as Bruce Catton, James Flexner, and John Brooks. As senior editor with *McCall's,* in charge of architecture and conservation, I commissioned and edited pieces by Marcia Davenport, Josephine Johnson, and Kurt Vonnegut, as well as other leading writers.

"From 1972 to 1975 I was under contract to write *Lost Chicago,* on the vanished architecture of that city. My interest in America's historic architecture has led me to become an activist in preserving that architecture. Through testimony before bodies such as New York City's Landmarks Preservation Commission and by means of lectures and articles I have tried to make my knowledge a force for saving this country's great heritage."

Chicago Tribune Book World contributor Paul Gapp describes Lowe's *Chicago Interiors* as "a rollicking but scholarly Chicago picture book that will appeal to the nostalgia crowd, architecture buffs, popular history addicts, or anyone who has ever been in love with this city."

BIOGRAPHICAL/CRITICAL SOURCES:

PERIODICALS

Chicago Tribune Book World, November 25, 1979.
Historic Preservation, January/February, 1993.
Library Journal, August, 1992, p. 96.

*　　　　*　　　　*

LUSTIG, Arnost 1926-

PERSONAL: Born December 21, 1926, in Prague, Czechoslovakia (now Czech Republic); immigrated to the United States in 1970; son of Emil and Therese (Lowy) Lustig; married Vera Weislitz, July 24, 1949; children: Josef, Eva. *Education:* College of Political and Social Sciences, Prague, Czechoslovakia, M.A., 1951, Ing. degree, 1954.

ADDRESSES: Home—4000 Tunlaw Rd. NW Apt. 825, Washington, DC 20007. *Office*—Department of Literature, American University, Washington, DC 20016.

CAREER: Radio Prague, Prague, Czechoslovakia, Arab-Israeli war correspondent, 1948-49; Czechoslovak Radio Corp., correspondent in Europe, Asia, and North America, 1950-68; Barrandov Film Studios, Prague, screenwriter, 1960-68; writer in Israel, 1968-69; Jadran Film Studio, Zagreb, Yugoslavia, screenwriter, 1969-70; University of Iowa, Iowa City, member of International Writers Program, 1970-71, visiting lecturer, 1971-72; American University, Washington, DC, professor of literature, 1973—. Head of the Czechoslovak film delegation to the San Sebastian Film Festival, 1968; member of the jury, Karlovy Vary International Film Festival, 1968; visiting professor, Drake University, 1972-73; guest of the Biennale in Venice, Italy, 1977; member of the jury, International Neustadt Prize for Literature, 1980. Lecturer in film and literature at universities in Czechoslovakia, Israel, Japan, Canada, and the United States.

MEMBER: Authors Guild, Authors League of America, PEN, Film Club (Prague).

AWARDS, HONORS: First prize, Mlada fronta publishing house, 1962, for *Diamonds of the Night;* best short story, University of Melbourne, 1962, for "Lemon"; first prize, Czechoslovak Radio Corp., 1966, for radio play *Prague Crossroads;* first prize, Monte Carlo Film Festival, 1966, for television film *A Prayer for Katerina Horovitzova;* Klement Gotwald State Prize, 1967, nomination for National Book Award, 1974, and B'nai B'rith Award, 1974, all for *A Prayer for Katerina Horovitzova;* first prize, Czechoslovak Radio Corp., 1967, for radio play *A Man the Size of a Postage Stamp;* second prize, San Sebastian Film Festival, 1968, for *Dita Saxova;* Jewish National Book Award, 1980, for *Dita Saxova,* and 1987, for *The Unloved: From the Diary of Perla S.;* Emmy Award, outstanding screenplay, 1985, for documentary *Precious Legacy;* D. of Hebrew Letters, Spertus College, 1986.

WRITINGS:

Ulice ztracenych bratri, Mlada fronta, 1949.
Muj znamy Vili Feld (novel), Mlada fronta, 1949.
Dita Saxova (novel), Ceskoslovensky spisovatel, 1962, Harper (New York City), 1980, translation by Theiner published as *Dita Sax,* Hutchinson (London), 1966.
Nikoho neponizis, Nase vojsko, 1963.

Modlitba pro Katerinu Horovitzovou (novel), Ceskoslovensky spisovatel, 1964, translation by Nemcova published as *A Prayer for Katerina Horovitzova,* Harper, 1973, Overlook Press (New York City), 1985.

Bile brizy na podzim, Ceskoslovensky spisovatel, 1966.

Horka vune mandli, Mlada fronta, 1968.

Milacek, Ceskoslovensky spisovatel, 1969.

Z deniku sedmnactilete Perly Sch. (novel), Sixty-Eight Publishers, 1979, translation by Vera Kalina-Levine published as *The Unloved: From the Diary of Perla S.,* Arbor House (New York City), 1985.

Indecent Dreams (three novellas), Northwestern University Press (Evanston, IL), 1988.

Street of Lost Brothers (short stories), with a foreword by Jonathan Brent, Northwestern University Press, 1990 (also see below).

Tma nema stin, Ceskoslovensky spisovatel, 1991.

(With Milan Kundera and Josef Skvorecky) *Velka trojka,* Galaxie, 1991.

COLLECTED WORKS

Noc a nadeje (short stories), Nase vojsko, 1958, translation by George Theiner published as *Night and Hope* (also see below), Dutton (New York City), 1962.

Demanty noci (short stories), Mlada fronta, 1958, translation by Iris Urwin published as *Diamonds of the Night* (also see below), Artia, 1962, new translation by Nemcova, Inscape, 1977.

Darkness Casts No Shadow, translation by Jeanne Nemcova, Inscape, 1977.

Night and Hope, Inscape, 1977, translation by Theiner, Northwestern University Press, 1985.

SCREENPLAYS

Transport from Paradise (adapted from *Night and Hope*), Studio Barrandov (Prague), 1963.

Diamonds of the Night (adapted from *Darkness Casts No Shadow*), Studio Barrandov, 1964.

Dita Saxova, Studio Barrandov, 1968.

OTHER

Author of television scripts *The Blue Day,* T.V. Prague, 1960; *A Prayer for Katerina Horovitzova,* T.V. Prague, 1965; (with Ernest Pendrell) *Terezin,* American Broadcasting Companies (ABC-TV), 1965; *Stolen Childhood,* TV-Rome, 1966. Author of radio scripts for Radio Prague, including *Prague Crossroads,* 1966, and *A Man the Size of a Postage Stamp,* 1967. Also author of text for Otmar Macha's symphonic poem, "Night and Hope," 1961, and of texts for cantatas, "The Beadl from Prague," 1984, "Precious Legacy," 1984, and "The Street of Lost Brothers," 1991; also author of the short filmscript *Bit to Eat,* 1962, and of commentary to documentary *The Triumph of Memory,* 1989. Correspondent for literary magazines in Czechoslovakia, 1950-58; editor, *Mlady svet* (magazine), 1958-60.

Lustig's works have been translated into more than twenty languages, including German, Spanish, Japanese, Polish, Hebrew, Hindi, Esperanto, French, Estonian, Italian, Norwegian, and Yiddish.

SIDELIGHTS: According to Johanna Kaplan in the *New York Times Book Review,* Czechoslovak author Arnost Lustig is "the too-little-known author of over half a dozen works of fiction," including the critically acclaimed *A Prayer for Katerina Horovitzova,* which was nominated for a National Book Award in 1974. *Dita Saxova* and *The Unloved: From the Diary of Perla S.,* both won Lustig the National Jewish Book Award in addition to his honors for his film and television scripts. Elizabeth Kastor, writing in the *Washington Post* pronounced the author's body of work "grim fables of concentration camps and World War II," yet noted that Lustig's friends consider the survivor of Theresienstadt, Auschwitz, and Buchenwald an optimist. This optimism is one of the qualities that has distinguished Lustig among writers of Holocaust literature; the *Los Angeles Times Book Review* asserts that "in Arnost Lustig's works, it's the courage, dignity and bravery of characters in the foreground that one remembers." Discussing the nature of Lustig's characters in the *Washington Post Book World,* Curt Leviant says: "Under the sentence of death, his people freeze time, preserve [decency]. They luminesce like light crystals in the dark."

Lustig once told *CA:* "Every writer has a duty to be as good as he can as a writer, to tell stories he likes in the best way he can. . . . I like stories about brave people, about how they survived under the worst circumstances. I like people who are fighting for their fate, and who are better in the end, richer, in a sense, than they were in the beginning. I think that each writer has a certain duty—to imagine himself in theory as perhaps the last human being alive under certain circumstances and that perhaps his testimony will be the last one. He is obliged to deliver that testimony."

Lustig's novels and stories often deliver the testimony of the Holocaust's arguably saddest victims: children—usually adolescent girls—who, unlike their creator, do not survive the camps. According to Kastor, the "bleak, hallucinatory *Darkness Casts No Shadow*" is Lustig's "most autobiographical book," the story of two young boys who briefly escape their fate during a train wreck on their way to being transferred from one camp to the next. The similarity to Lustig's own experience ends with the boys' eventual recapture and death. Kaplan calls the novel "a harsh, suspenseful anti-fairy tale . . . [that] must surely be counted a hidden classic."

Dita Saxova is the story of a young survivor of Nazi death camps who tries to come to grips with living, after having expected to die for so long. Stephen Goodwin, writing in the *Washington Post,* calls the book "a meditative novel." Though Goodwin admitted that he often found Dita's thoughts difficult to follow and often too much like Lustig's, he said that "when Dita's voice does sound, there is no mistaking its ring of truth, [wisdom] and felt experience. At such moments I don't have to understand Dita; she is mysterious and she is real, and I have only to listen." Goodwin's criticism of what Kastor calls the "elliptical puzzle" of Lustig's writing is not uncommon; *Los Angeles Times* book critic Richard Eder expressed a similar opinion about the writing in *The Unloved.* In defense of Lustig's style, Kastor asserted that "the confusion is endemic to the material: With a subject like Lustig's, narrative sense cannot always be maintained."

A Prayer for Katerina Horovitzova concerns another young woman thrust into the Holocaust. Katerina is a nineteen-year-old Polish dancer who becomes embroiled in a scheme to escape the fate of being sent to a concentration camp. Soon it becomes apparent that her rescuers are really only after the money of the captives and have no intention of sparing them or her from the atrocities of the death camps. Jasper Rees of the London *Times* maintained that the story "has the hard and fast simplicity of a parable." Furthermore, Rees continued, "The world Lustig has recreated is a pure vision of the inferno." Lustig's worlds often evoke hellish imagery. Joseph Coates, critic for the Chicago *Tribune Books,* wrote of Lustig's collection of stories *Street of Lost Brothers:* "It is Lustig's achievement not merely to bring the reader into the various special hells of the Holocaust but also to make them seem commonplace, as indeed they were and are to those who inhabit them."

Lustig's *The Unloved* is the testimony of a seventeen-year-old girl imprisoned at Theresienstadt who sells her body for whatever small tokens the prisoners can amass. Ursula Hegi said in the *New York Times Book Review* that Lustig "has written a stunning and unsentimental novel, celebrating moments of normality amid corruption and death." Lawrence L. Langer sounded a similar note in the *Washington Post Book World:* "Part of the emotional intensity of the narrative derives from the clinical detachment with which the potential victims themselves discuss the prospects of survival." Jonathan Brent of the Chicago *Tribune Books* declared that "Perla's diary is a dreamily erotic, desultory record of [the] process of inward brutalization." He described *The Unloved* as "an eloquent and moving

testament to the enduring worth of the individual and the inexhaustible human need to realize this worth in action."

The protagonist of each of the three novellas in *Indecent Dreams* is again a young woman; according to Richard Lourie in the *Washington Post Book World,* "The tales are also strongly united by their structure and atmosphere. In each a mood is built, gathering like a storm, and only in the final moments is that energy discharged in the lightning of violence." Kaplan summarized the artistry of Lustig's work as a whole: "A world so entirely bound by suffering can be painful to enter, but Mr. Lustig, searching out a code of honor in this most defiled, inhuman sphere, has come upon a maximalist human canvas. His view is oddly invigorating and his work invites a maximal audience: it will quarrel, it will recognize, it will marvel and yes, of course, sometimes it will have to look away."

Lustig had been a prominent writer in Prague, Czechoslovakia, before the Soviet invasion of 1968. As he once told *CA:* "Once everything was lost, when the country was invaded, I was declared by the last congress of the Communist party an 'enemy of the state,' and an 'imperialist agent,' a 'Zionist.' They said all my books and films were paid for by some world conspiracy." When conditions in Czechoslovakia became intolerable and writing was no longer possible, Lustig and his family moved to the United States in an effort "to be outside and keep writing, and to be free, and to keep some hope."

BIOGRAPHICAL/CRITICAL SOURCES:

PERIODICALS

Best Sellers, October 15, 1973.
Booklist, November 1, 1973.
Choice, fall, 1974.
Kirkus Reviews, August 1, 1973.
Los Angeles Times, October 23, 1985.
Los Angeles Times Book Review, December 29, 1985, p. 9.
New York Times Book Review, October 21, 1973; March 18, 1979, p. 21; January 19, 1986, p. 20; June 19, 1988, p. 1; July 22, 1990, p. 32.
Proteus, spring, 1974.
Publishers Weekly, February 21, 1977; March 13, 1987.
Southwest Review, winter, 1974.
Times (London), November 1, 1990.
Tribune Books (Chicago), November 24, 1985, p. 40; December 16, 1990, p. 3.
Washingtonian, May, 1977.
Washington Post, January 11, 1980; August 9, 1988.
Washington Post Book World, June 12, 1977, p. 1; January 12, 1986, p. 10; June 19, 1988, p. 10.

M

MacDONALD, Dennis Ronald 1946-

PERSONAL: Born July 1, 1946, in Chicago, IL; son of James Ronald (a minister) and Mildred (Friend) Mac-Donald; married Diane Louise Prosser (a campus minister), June 9, 1973; children: Katya Louise, Julian Peter. *Education:* Bob Jones University, A.B., 1968; McCormick Theological Seminary, M.Div., 1974; Harvard University, Ph.D., 1978.

ADDRESSES: Home—5319 South Telluride Court, Aurora, CO 80015. *Office*—Department of Biblical Interpretation, Iliff School of Theology, 2201 South University Blvd., Denver, CO 80210.

CAREER: Goshen College, Goshen, IN, assistant professor of the Bible, 1977-80; Iliff School of Theology, Denver, CO, associate professor of the *New Testament* and Christian Origins, 1980—; visiting professor, Harvard University, 1985-86.

MEMBER: Society of Biblical Literature (vice president of Rocky Mountain region, 1983-84, president, 1984-85).

AWARDS, HONORS: Grant from Indiana Council on the Humanities, 1978; Clarence G. Campbell fellow, Harvard University, 1975-76; younger scholar of Association of Theological Schools, 1983; grant from National Endowment for the Humanities, 1983.

WRITINGS:

The Legend and the Apostle: The Battle for Paul in Story and Canon, Westminster (Philadelphia), 1983.
There Is No Male or Female: The Fate of a Dominical Saying in Paul and Gnosticism, Fortress (Philadelphia), 1986.
(Editor) *Apocryphal Acts of the Apostles,* Scholars Press (Chico, CA), 1986.

The Acts of Andrew and the Acts of Andrew and Matthias in the City of the Cannibals, Scholars Press, 1990.
Christianizing Homer: The Odyssey, Plato, and the Acts of Andrew, Oxford University Press, 1994.

Contributor to *Mennonite Quarterly Review, Reformed Journal* and numerous theological journals.

SIDELIGHTS: Dennis Ronald MacDonald commented: "I am intrigued by the light the New Testament Apocrypha can shed on Christian Origins. *The Legend and the Apostle* uses folklore theory to study the Acts of Paul, a second-century apocryphal Acts, dependent on stories about Paul probably told by women. At the moment, I am writing a book on the apocryphal Acts of Andrew, which will include an original translation of Greek, Latin, and Coptic fragments of the now dismembered book. In part, my motivation for study of this literature is my curiosity concerning popular, officially disapproved traditions, perspectives, and practices of early Christians."*

*   *   *

MacLEOD, Robert
See KNOX, William

*   *   *

MacMAHON, Bryan (Michael) 1909-

PERSONAL: Born September 29, 1909, in Listowel, County Kerry, Ireland; son of Patric Mary (a land clerk) and Joanna (a teacher; maiden name, Caughlin) Mac-Mahon; married Kathleen Ryan, November 4, 1936; children: Patrick Gerald, James, Bryan, Maurice, Eoin. *Education:* Attended St. Michael's College, Listowel, 1921-28, and St. Patrick's College, Dromcondra, Dublin, 1928-30; qualified as national teacher, 1930. *Politics:* Eclectic. *Religion:* Roman Catholic.

ADDRESSES: Home and office—38 Church St., Listowel, County Kerry, Ireland. *Agent*—Curtis Brown Ltd., 575 Madison Ave., New York, NY 10022; and A. P. Watt & Son, Literary Agents, 20 John St., London WC1N 2DR, England.

CAREER: Writer, folklorist, balladmaker, and lecturer. Teacher at parochial primary school in Dublin, 1930-31; Scoil Realta na Maidine 2 (Morning Star School No. 2), Listowel, County Kerry, Ireland, 1942-75, began as teacher, became principal teacher. Producer and author of plays and pageants; shareholder of Abbey Theatre. Past proprietor of bookstore with wife, Joanna. Initiated series *The Balladmaker's Saturday Night* for Radio Eireann; has done other broadcasting for Radio Eireann, British Broadcasting Corp. (BBC), Channel Four Brittain, Yugoslav TV, WSUI (United States), and various stations on the west coast of the United States. Represented Ireland in the humanities at Harvard International Seminar, 1963; visiting lecturer at Writers' Workshop at University of Iowa, 1965; opening speaker at National Council of Teachers of English conference in Colorado Springs, CO, 1968; founded first Irish Short Story Workshop, in conjunction with Writers' Week in Listowel, 1972; also has lectured in Germany and throughout Ireland.

MEMBER: Irish Academy of Letters, Irish PEN (president, 1972), Aosdana (artists' group organized by the Irish Arts Council), Listowel Drama Group (founding member).

AWARDS, HONORS: Bell Magazine Award for best short story, 1945; Catholic Press Award for best short story in a Catholic magazine in the United States, 1961, and runner-up (to Flannery O'Connor), 1962; honorary LL.D., National University of Ireland, 1972, for services to Irish literature; Kerryman of the Year, 1987; literary award, American Ireland Fund, 1993.

WRITINGS:

The Lion Tamer and Other Stories, Macmillan (London), 1948, Dutton (New York City), 1949.
Jackomoora and the King of Ireland's Son (juvenile), Dutton, 1950.
Children of the Rainbow (novel), Dutton, 1952.
The Red Petticoat and Other Stories, Dutton, 1955.
The Honey Spike (novel), Dutton, 1967.
Brendan of Ireland (juvenile), photographs by W. Suschitzky, Hastings House (New York City), 1967.
Patsy-O and His Wonderful Pets (juvenile), Dutton, 1970.
Here's Ireland (nonfiction), Dutton, 1971, revised edition, Butler Sims (Dublin), 1982.

(Translator) Peig Sayers, *Peig,* Syracuse University Press (Syracuse, NY), 1973.
The End of the World and Other Stories, Poolbeg (Dublin), 1976.
The Sound of Hooves and Other Stories, Bodley Head (London), 1985.
Patsy-O Goes to Spain (juvenile), Poolbeg, 1989.
Mascot Patsy-O (juvenile), Poolbeg, 1992.
The Master (autobiography), Poolbeg, 1992.
The Tallystick (short story collection), Poolbeg, 1994.

PLAYS

The Bugle in the Blood, produced in Dublin at Abbey Theatre, 1949.
Song of the Anvil (produced in Dublin at Abbey Theatre for International Theatre Festival, 1960; later produced in California by Ria Mooney of Abbey Theatre), published in *Seven Irish Plays, 1946-1964,* edited by Robert Hogan, University of Minnesota Press (Minneapolis), 1967.
The Honey Spike, produced in Dublin at Abbey Theatre, 1961.
The Gap of Life, produced in Dublin at Peacock Theatre by Society of Irish Playwrights, 1972.

Also author of one-act play *The Master,* produced by his son Eoin, broadcast on Radio Eireann, and produced in Limerick at Belltable Theatre, and of other one-act plays, including *The Time of the Whitethorn* and *Jack Furey;* also author of other plays for Listowel Drama Group and of radio and television plays for adults and children; also author of historical pageants for national occasions in Ireland, including *Seachtar Fear, Seach La* (produced in Croke Park and Casement Park, Dublin, and later televised), four teleplays for children, and a radio feature, all in commemoration of the 1916 Easter Rebellion.

OTHER

Also contributor to Irish and German short story anthologies. Has recorded his stories for Lamont Library, 1963. Contributor to periodicals, including *Natural History, Kenyon Review, Irish Writing, Icarus, Sports Illustrated, Woman's Day,* and *Partisan Review.*

Some of MacMahon's work has been published in German and other European languages.

ADAPTATIONS: MacMahon's novel *Children of the Rainbow* and his translation of Peig Sayers's *Peig* have been serialized by Radio Eireann; *Children of the Rainbow* was broadcast in a dramatized version by Canadian Broadcasting Co. (CBC); *The Master* was serialized by Radio Eireann and read by MacMahon in national broadcast.

WORK IN PROGRESS: Short stories, national pageants, and a longer untitled experimental work.

SIDELIGHTS: Initial recognition of Bryan MacMahon's work came in *Bell* magazine, where he was welcomed as a poet of merit by Frank O'Connor and as a short story writer by editor Sean O'Faolain. MacMahon's first published collection, *The Lion Tamer and Other Stories,* received a cover note in the *Saturday Review* and such a cordial reception from American critics that it quickly went through four printings. The author's stories and poems have been published in magazines in Ireland, England, the United States, and Germany, and are included in most anthologies of modern Irish writing. His plays have enjoyed periodic revivals as well. Some of his work has also appeared under undivulged pseudonyms.

MacMahon likes "people, people, people," and lives in a small town because it affords him the unique opportunity to meet neighbors in all their moods. He credits the tradespeople of the town for his most valuable education and "reckons a visit to the saddler's shop essential in every day."

A lifelong collector of native music, MacMahon told *CA* that as a relief from serious work, he "often writes ballads which are published in his native town by his friend the printer and are sung later in the pubs of Ireland." His work on the Radio Eireann series, *The Balladmaker's Saturday Night,* helped pave the way for Ireland's current revival of native balladry. A "fluent speaker of Irish," he says that he "draw[s] much sustenance from a Gaelic background." One of the few "outsiders" who can speak Shelta, the secret language of the Irish traveling people, he considers these people the "final free" and the "outer palisades of human liberty."

MacMahon considers Ireland one of the last places where a human being is valued and looks forward to his return after a stint of lecturing in America. He prefers to read short stories and novels in translation from other languages and cultures, chiefly those of Africa, the Philippines, and South America. He finds life exciting and the day too short for his many interests and activities, which include beagling, fishing, and wandering in Ireland.

BIOGRAPHICAL/CRITICAL SOURCES:

BOOKS

Journal of Irish Literature, Proscenium (Newark, DE), 1971.
MacMahon, Bryan, *The Master* (autobiography), Poolbeg, 1992.

PERIODICALS

Atlantic, May, 1952.
Best Sellers, March 1, 1967.

Library Journal, January 1, 1952; January 1, 1955; January 1, 1967.
New Statesman, September 15, 1967.
New Yorker, March 15, 1952; March 12, 1955.
New York Times, January 30, 1955; February 26, 1967.
Saturday Review, March 25, 1967.
Times (London), May 2, 1985.
Times Literary Supplement, May 23, 1952.

*   *   *

MARKS, Alfred H(arding) 1920-

PERSONAL: Born July 18, 1920, in Farmingdale, NY; son of Theodore Augustus (a merchant and farmer) and Greta (Boettiger) Marks; married Herta Mattler, December 20, 1942; children: Thea Welch, Christina Haley, Stuart. *Education:* Potsdam State College (now State University of New York College at Potsdam), B.Ed., 1946; Syracuse University, M.A., 1949, Ph.D., 1953. *Politics:* Democrat. *Religion:* Dutch Reformed.

ADDRESSES: Home—10 Bruce Ave., New Paltz, NY 12561. *Office*—State University of New York College at New Paltz, New Paltz, NY 12561.

CAREER: U.S. Department of Defense, Washington, DC, research analyst, 1946-47; Syracuse University, Syracuse, NY, instructor, 1949-53; Ohio State University, Columbus, instructor, 1953-56; Ball State Teachers College (now Ball State University), Muncie, IN, 1956-63, began as assistant professor, became associate professor of English; State University of New York College at New Paltz, professor of English, 1963-85, emeritus professor of American literature, 1985—. Senior Fulbright lecturer, Kanazawa University, Japan, 1965-66; visiting professor, University of Hawaii, 1973-74; participant, National Endowment for the Humanities Institute on Japanese Literature, Princeton University, summer, 1979. Historian, town/village of New Paltz, 1992—. Director, Carl Carmer Center for Catskill Mountain and Hudson River Studies, 1975-85. President, John Burroughs Association, Inc., 1985-90. *Military service:* U.S. Army, 1942-46; became first lieutenant.

MEMBER: Modern Language Association of America, American Federation of Teachers, Association of Teachers of Japanese, Japan Society, Haiku Society of America.

WRITINGS:

(Translator) Yukio Mishima, *Forbidden Colors,* Knopf (New York City), 1968.
(Translator) Mishima, *Thirst for Love,* Knopf, 1969.
(With Barry D. Bort) *Guide to Japanese Prose,* G. K. Hall (Boston), 1975, 2nd edition, 1984.

(Translator with Thomas Kondo) Ihara Saikaku, *Tales of Japanese Justice,* University of Hawaii Press (Honolulu), 1979.

(With Edythe Polster) *Surimono: Prints by Elbow,* Lovejoy Press, 1981.

(Compiler) *What Shall I Read on Japan: An Introductory Guide,* 12th edition (Marks was not associated with earlier editions), Japan Society (New York City), 1982.

(Translator of poems) Cynthia Bogel and Israel Goldman, editors, *Hiroshige: Birds and Flowers,* Braziller (New York City), 1988.

(Translator with Takashi Kodaira) *The Essence of Modern Haiku: Three Hundred Poems by Seishi Yamaguchi,* Mangajin (Atlanta), 1993.

Also author of *Literature of the Mid-Hudson Valley,* 1974. Contributor to periodicals, including *American Literature* and *PMLA. Literature East and West,* editor, 1961-66, editor-in-chief, 1966—; editor, *John Burroughs Review,* 1985—.

WORK IN PROGRESS: Translating, with Harue and Travis Summersgill, *The Geisha's Day: Yoshitoshi's Twenty-four Hours at Shinbashi and Yanagibashi;* translating Yasuhiko Murai's *Recollections of Iwojima.*

* * *

MARMUR, Dow   1935-

PERSONAL: First name is pronounced "dov"; born February 24, 1935, in Sosnowiec, Poland; son of Maksymilian and Cecylia (Solewicz) Marmur; married Fredzia Zonabend, May 20, 1956; children: Viveca, Michael, Elizabeth. *Education:* Attended University of Stockholm, 1955-57; Leo Baeck College, London, rabbinical ordination, 1962. *Religion:* Jewish.

ADDRESSES: Home—297 Hillhurst Blvd., Toronto, Ontario, Canada M6B 1M9. *Office*—Holy Blossom Temple, 1950 Bathurst St., Toronto, Ontario, Canada M5P 3K9.

CAREER: Rabbi of Southwest Essex Reform Synagogue, Ilford, Essex, England, 1962-69, and Northwest Reform Synagogue, London, 1969-83; senior rabbi of Holy Blossom Temple, Toronto, Ontario, 1983—.

WRITINGS:

Reform Judaism (essays), Reform Synagogues of Great Britain (London), 1975.

A Genuine Search (essays), Reform Synagogues of Great Britain, 1979.

Beyond Survival: Reflections on the Future of Judaism, Darton, Longman & Todd (London), 1983.

Walking toward Elijah, Welch Publishing (Burlington, Ontario), 1988.

The Star of Return, Greenwood, 1991.

Contributor to periodicals. Editor, *Living Judaism,* 1966-71.

WORK IN PROGRESS: A collection of essays gleaned from published material in the 1980s.

SIDELIGHTS: Dow Marmur wrote *Beyond Survival: Reflections on the Future of Judaism* in response to post-Holocaust Jewish literature, which almost without exception expresses concern for the survival and future of the Jewish tradition. According to Geza Vermes in the *Times Literary Supplement,* Marmur contends that the future of Judaism depends on "a return to the true spirit of prophecy," a spiritual reawakening to the wellsprings of the religion itself. Whereas the three factions of Judaism—orthodox, progressive, and Zionist—have each claimed to champion the cause of Jewish life, Marmur holds that "if Judaism is to have a future, its factions much join together to form a 'greater Israel.' " In addition, Marmur argues that this "greater Israel" will comprise Jews and non-Jews alike, including Christians and, perhaps, Muslims and communists. Vermes concludes that *Beyond Survival* "will appeal primarily to Jews who look for a renewal of Judaism. . . . This is an honest, tactful and thoughtful book that deserves careful study by a wide readership."

BIOGRAPHICAL/CRITICAL SOURCES:

PERIODICALS

Times Literary Supplement, January 28, 1983.

* * *

MARSDEN, Peter (Richard Valentine)   1940-

PERSONAL: Born April 29, 1940, in London, England; son of Sidney L. V. and Emily Sylvia (Lynde) Marsden; married Frances Elizabeth McKerrell; children: (previous marriage) Paul Stephen Valentine, Mark Richard Valentine; Katie-May McKerrell (stepdaughter). *Education:* Attended Kilburn Polytechnic, 1957. *Politics:* Liberal. *Religion:* Church of England. *Avocational interests:* Planetary geology ("including Earth") and family history.

ADDRESSES: Home—21 Meadow Lane, Lindfield, Sussex RH16 2RJ, England. *Office*—Museum of London, London Wall, London EC2Y 5HN, England.

CAREER: Museum of London, London, England, archaeologist, 1959—. Director and secretary, Nautical Museums Trust (creators of Shipwreck Heritage Centre), Hastings, East Sussex, England.

MEMBER: Society of Antiquaries (fellow), Institute of Field Archaeologists, Society for Nautical Archaeology (member of committee), Society for Nautical Research, Committee for Nautical Archaeology (member of committee).

WRITINGS:

The Wreck of the Amsterdam, Hutchinson (London), 1974, Stein & Day (Briarcliff Manor, NY), 1975.
Roman London, Thames & Hudson (New York City), 1980.
The Marsden Family of Paythorne and Nelson, 1666-1981, privately printed, 1981.
The Historic Shipwrecks of South-East England, Jarrold Colour Publications (Norwick, England), 1987.
The Roman Forum Site in London, Her Majesty's Stationery Office (HMSO; London), 1987.

Contributor to magazines and newspapers.

WORK IN PROGRESS: A book on the ancient ships and shipwrecks of London.

SIDELIGHTS: Reviewing Peter Marsden's *Roman London,* Philip Howard of the London *Times* notes that the author "stands back from his excavations to give a broad historical reconstruction of Roman London for the general reader, with 160 photographs, plans, and drawings." Howard concludes that "Peter Marsden's piecing together of the ancient jig-saw is punctilious and persuasive." Marsden told *CA* that his interest in old ships, archaeology, exploration, and discovery is motivated by "extreme curiosity and the challenge of the unknown. Also," he adds, "writing books while commuting forty miles by train each day is a worthwhile use of the journey time."

BIOGRAPHICAL/CRITICAL SOURCES:

PERIODICALS

Times (London), December 11, 1980.*

* * *

MARTIN, Graham Dunstan 1932-

PERSONAL: Born October 21, 1932, in Leeds, England; son of Edward Dunstan (a schoolmaster) and Margaret (Lightbody) Martin; married Ryllis Daniel, August 21, 1954 (divorced); married Anne Moone Crombie (a social worker), June 14, 1969; children: Jonathan, Stefan, Juliet, Lewis, Aidan. *Education:* Oriel College, Oxford, B.A., 1954; Victoria University of Manchester, graduate certificate, 1955; Linacre College, Oxford, B.Litt., 1965.

ADDRESSES: Office—Department of French, University of Edinburgh, 60 George Sq., Edinburgh 8, Scotland.

CAREER: Writer. Teacher of French and English in secondary schools in England, 1956-65; University of Edin-

burgh, Scotland, lecturer in French, 1965—. Lecturer in English at University of Paris, 1976-77.

MEMBER: Society of Authors, British Society of Aesthetics.

WRITINGS:

(Translator with John H. Scott) *In the Year of the Strike* (poetry), Rapp & Whiting, 1968.
(Editor and translator) Paul Valery, *Le Cimetiere marin,* Edinburgh University Press, 1971.
(Translator with Scott) *Love and Protest* (poetry), Harper (London), 1972.
(Editor and translator) *Anthology of Contemporary French Poetry,* Edinburgh University Press, 1972.
(Translator) Louise Labe, *Sonnets,* edited by Peter Sharratt, Edinburgh University Press, 1973.
Language, Truth, and Poetry: Notes towards a Philosophy of Literature, Edinburgh University Press, 1975.
(Translator with others) Jean-Claude Renard, *Selected Poems,* Oasis Press, 1978.
Giftwish (novel), Allen & Unwin (London), 1980, Houghton (Boston), 1981.
The Architecture of Experience: The Role of Language and Literature in the Construction of the World, Edinburgh University Press, 1981.
Catchfire (novel), Allen & Unwin, 1981, Houghton, 1982.
The Soul Master (novel), Allen & Unwin, 1984.
Time-Slip (novel), Allen & Unwin, 1986.
The Dream Wall (novel), Allen & Unwin, 1987.
Half a Glass of Moonshine, Unwin Hyman, 1988.
Shadows in the Cave: Mapping the Conscious Universe, Penguin Arkana (London), 1990.

WORK IN PROGRESS: Historical fiction set in Scotland in the sixth century, dealing with the confrontation of Christianity and pagan druidism.

SIDELIGHTS: Graham Dunstan Martin once told *CA:* "My academic work is based on a love of poetry, a love of teaching, a detestation of 'conventional wisdom,' and a belief in the relevance of literature to life. Nor is anything more relevant than fantasy, my essays in this genre having arisen out of reading fairy tales to my small sons. I have on two occasions spent a year working in France (my favorite place, along with Scotland), and of course speak French (a physical pleasure, like food or folksinging)."

* * *

MARTIN, Michael William 1946-
(Mike W. Martin)

PERSONAL: Born November 6, 1946, in Salt Lake City, UT; son of Theodore R. and Ruth (Lochhead) Martin;

married Shannon Snow, August 1, 1968; children: Sonia Renee, Nicole Marie. *Education:* University of Utah, B.S. (magna cum laude), 1969, M.A., 1972; University of California, Irvine, Ph.D., 1977.

ADDRESSES: Home—22842 Via Octavo, Mission Viejo, CA 92691. *Office*—Department of Philosophy, Chapman University, 333 North Glassell St., Orange, CA 92666.

CAREER: Chapman College (now University), Orange, CA, instructor, 1976-78, assistant professor, 1978-82, associate professor, 1982-86, professor of philosophy, 1986—, chairperson of department, 1979-81, 1982-84, and 1989-91, chairperson of faculty, 1986-87. Member of graduate faculty, extension, California State Polytechnic University, Pomona, 1979 and 1981, and at University of California, Los Angeles, 1990-94; University of California, Irvine, visiting assistant professor, 1981, 1983, visiting scholar, 1981-82.

MEMBER: American Philosophical Association, Phi Beta Kappa, Phi Kappa Phi.

AWARDS, HONORS: National Endowment for the Humanities fellow, 1978-80, 1981-82; Graves Award, 1983, for outstanding teaching in the humanities; Association of American Colleges grant, 1986; Institute of Electrical and Electronics Engineers award, 1992, for "Distinguished Literary Contributions Furthering Engineering Professionalism."

WRITINGS:

UNDER NAME MIKE W. MARTIN

(With Roland Schinzinger) *Ethics in Engineering,* McGraw (New York City), 1983, new edition, 1989.
(Editor) *Self-Deception and Self-Understanding,* University Press of Kansas (Lawrence), 1985, new edition, 1989.
Self-Deception and Morality, University Press of Kansas, 1986.
Everyday Morality, Wadsworth, 1989, new edition, 1995.
Virtuous Giving: Philanthropy, Voluntary Service, and Caring, Indiana University Press (Bloomington), 1994.

Contributor to *Business and Professional Ethics,* edited by Wade L. Robison, Michael S. Pritchard, and Joseph Ellin, Humana, 1982; *The Contemporary Turn in Applied Philosophy,* edited by Michael Bradie, Thomas Attig, and Nicholar Rescher, Bowling Green State University Press, 1983; *The American Classics Revisited: Recent Studies in American Literature,* edited by P. C. Kar and D. Ramakrishna, American Studies Research Centre, 1985; *Wissen und Gewissen,* edited by Otto Neumaier, University of Salzburg, 1986; and *The Philosophy of Laughter and Humor,* edited by John Morreall, State University of New York Press, 1986.

Also contributor of more than fifty essays and articles to philosophy, engineering, and literature journals.

WORK IN PROGRESS: Love's Virtues, a study of the virtues that contribute to long-term personal relationships.

SIDELIGHTS: Michael William Martin told *CA:* "My primary interests are interdisciplinary—finding ways to link literatures and approaches of different fields as they jointly illuminate moral and intellectual issues that sprawl across any tidy academic boundaries, keeping in mind that interdisciplinary work is linking rather than dissolving disciplines. I have two favorite quotations about writing. One is from Ludwig Wittgenstein: 'It is only the attempt to write down your ideas that enables them to develop.' The other is Moliere's counsel to 'humanize your talk, and speak to be understood.' "

*   *   *

MARTIN, Mike W.
    See MARTIN, Michael William

*   *   *

MASTERS, Hilary   1928-
    (P. J. Coyne)

PERSONAL: Born February 3, 1928, in Kansas City, MO; son of Edgar Lee (a writer) and Ellen Frances (maiden name, Coyne) Masters; married Polly Jo McCulloch, March 5, 1955 (divorced, 1986); married Kathleen E. George, June 7, 1994; children: Joellen, Catherine, John D. C. *Education:* Attended Davidson College, 1944-46; Brown University, A.B., 1952.

ADDRESSES: Agent—Christina Ward, P.O. Box 515, North Scituate, MA 02060.

CAREER: Bennett & Pleasant (press agents for concert and dance artists), New York City, member of staff, 1952; self-employed theatrical press agent for Off-Broadway and summer theaters, 1953-56; *Hyde Park Record* (newspaper), Hyde Park, NY, editor and publisher, 1956-59. Visiting faculty member, University of North Carolina at Greensboro, 1974; visiting writer-in-residence, Drake University, 1975-77; also affiliated with Clark University, 1978, Ohio University, 1979, University of North Carolina at Greensboro, 1980-81, and University of Denver, 1982; Fulbright lecturer to Finland, 1983; professor of English and creative writing and director of creative writing program at Carnegie-Mellon University. Former Democratic Candidate for New York's 100th Assembly District, 1965-66; member of advisory committee to speaker of New York Assembly, 1967-68. Freelance photographer for Image Bank and exhibits. *Military service:* U.S. Navy, 1946-47; naval correspondent.

MEMBER: Associated Writing Programs, Authors Guild, Authors League of America, PEN.

AWARDS, HONORS: Recipient of Yaddo writers' colony fellowship, 1980, 1982; short stories cited for honorable mention by *Best Short Stories* and *Pushcart Prize* anthologies.

WRITINGS:

NOVELS

The Common Pasture, Macmillan (New York City), 1967.
An American Marriage, Macmillan, 1969.
Palace of Strangers, World Publishing, 1971.

"THE HARLEM VALLEY TRIO" NOVELS

Clemmons, Godine, David (Boston), 1985.
Cooper, St. Martin's (New York City), 1987.
Strickland, St. Martin's, 1989.

OTHER

Last Stands: Notes from Memory (biography), David Godine (Boston), 1982.
Hammertown Tales (short stories), Wright (Winston-Salem, NC), 1986.
Manuscript for Murder (a "Ned Spearbroke" mystery), Dodd (New York City), 1987.
Success: New and Selected Short Stories, foreword by George Garrett, St. Martin's, 1992.

Contributor to anthologies, including *Brand X Anthology of Fiction,* edited by William Zaranka, Apple Wood (Cambridge, MA), 1983; *Ohio Review Anthology,* edited by Wayne Dodd, Ohio Review (Athens), 1983. Contributor of stories and essays to *Greensboro Review, Kenyon Review, Massachusetts Review, Michigan Quarterly, Ohio Review, Prairie Schooner, Sports Illustrated, Texas Review, Virginia Quarterly Review,* and other journals.

WORK IN PROGRESS: Montezuma's Revenge, a novel; *Body of Work,* a "Ned Spearbroke" mystery; *Disorderly Conduct,* a collection of essays.

SIDELIGHTS: Novelist and short story writer Hilary Masters is the son of poet Edgar Lee Masters, who wrote the acclaimed *Spoon River Anthology,* and the grandson of Indian Wars veteran Tom Coyne. Masters recalls these men, and other members of his family, in his book *Last Stands: Notes from Memory.* But the work "is much more than a documentation of [the author's ancestral history]," notes *Chicago Tribune Book World* critic Ross Talarico.

"It is a beautifully written rendering of no less than a century of American life—more specifically, of the myths and realities of family life in America as we pass from Fort Custer, after the massacre, to the burial of Masters's colorful, adventurous grandfather . . . in Arlington in 1954."

Edgar Lee Masters was sixty years old, and long past his artistic prime, when his son was born. "The aging writer needed peace and quiet to salvage his dwindling reputation," recounts Paul Gray in a *Time* review of *Last Stands.* "His wife, nearly 30 years his junior, insisted on working toward a graduate degree at Columbia University. A child, however welcome, did not fit in with their plans." Young Masters was regularly shuttled between his parents's residences in New York and his grandfather's home in Kansas City. He remembers in the book: "The arrangement gave me the best of two different worlds, for a time; moreover, no one told me it was unusual." And although the memoir mainly focuses on the relationship between the author and his father and grandfather, *New York Times Book Review* critic Donald Hall observes that "by the end [of the work], in a gradual, convincing shift, the book finds its hero—and it is not the old Indian fighter . . . or the famous writer living out neglect. It is the author's mother. She determines to live her own life against her husband's discouragement, determines to rule and remain herself despite a famous husband and a powerful father. She manages to make a career, to remain helpful, to raise her son and take care of old parents and a husband almost her parents' age. She *manages:* Ellen Coyne Masters is an admirable creature of true dignity."

Last Stands "is a fitting title, alluding to Custer, to [Coyne's] last visits to another era, [to Edgar Lee Masters's] last attempt at being a writer in the heroic, romantic tradition—to Hilary Masters's last chance to assimilate it all, to record it, to give it the truth and honor of the written word," says Talarico. Concludes Jonathan Yardley of the *Washington Post Book World:* "[Masters] has not written a narrative but woven a tapestry, in which he moves back and forth in time without any warning to the reader yet without ever creating confusion. He pays loving tribute to his forebears but declines to sentimentalize them. And he never loses sight of the essential truth that we can never know the past, that it can only and always be a mystery, that the most we can hope to do is reinvent it for whatever meaning it offers to the present. This Hilary Masters has done in his small, luminous, consequential book."

Masters followed up his memoir with "The Harlem Valley Trio," a well received trilogy of novels made up of *Clemmons, Cooper,* and *Strickland.* Like *Last Stands, Clemmons* wins praise for its unusual structure as well as its compelling tale. "A major pleasure of Hilary Masters' latest novel [his earlier novels are *The Common Pasture, An*

American Marriage, and *Palace of Strangers*]," writes James McConkey in the *Washington Post Book World,* "comes from the reader's page-to-page involvement in the altering moods of the fiction [Masters] has created; he is a deft craftsman, capable of moving from a sardonic insight to compassion, from satire to rowdy comedy, from sexual passion to a wish for, perhaps even a glimpse of, an order or unity beyond our splintered and violent world." In the *New York Times Book Review,* William Ferguson describes *Clemmons* as a "well-told chronicle."

Where George Core sees *Clemmons* as "a wonderful comic novel that celebrated life," the critic informs readers of the *Washington Post Book World* that "*Cooper* is forged in a darker spirit." According to Core, the novel is no less appealing than its predecessor despite its difference in tone. In reference to the many characters obsessed either literally or metaphorically with flying, Core concludes: "By novel's end everyone has had his flight . . . The metaphors of flying and falling are beautifully sustained throughout the action of a memorable book worth rereading, as I have done with relish."

Gordon M. Henry, critic for the *New York Times Book Review,* characterizes *Strickland,* the final novel in the "Harlem Valley" trilogy, as attempting to go beyond those Vietnam tales that try to depict the stages of a soldier's journey, from the difficulty of leaving home for war to the bittersweet feelings upon returning after a tour of duty. Masters "takes this process a step further by examining the life lived by a veteran war correspondent years after he has ostensibly reintegrated himself into American Society," Henry asserts. For the critic, however, the attempt is unsuccessful; while conceding that *Strickland* is not lacking in conviction, Henry concludes that its hero is ultimately unconvincing.

Masters is also the author of two acclaimed collections of short stories. Of the first, *Hammertown Tales,* Carol Ames writes in the *New York Times Book Review:* "This book of fine stories traces its lineage to Sherwood Anderson's [*Winesburg, Ohio*] and beyond to [*Spoon River Anthology*]." In a later *New York Times Book Review* article, Constance Decker Thompson praises Masters's *Success: New and Selected Short Stories,* describing the book as "erudite, engaging and lovingly detailed." The stories in *Success* are "cagey, lucid, and rock-solid tales to engage, challenge, instruct, and delight," according to *Harvard Review*'s Susan Dodd. Comparing Master's selection with the short fiction of Alice Munro and Peter Taylor, she concludes: "The stories of *Success* yield the depth and comlexity of novels. Hilary Masters writes, always, of place and memory, of time and change. His homeground is the rocky yet fertile soil of human connection and the soul's persistent striving toward it, a striving that on this earth's terms must pass, for now, for salvation.

Noting that he has never written or publically discussed the fate that made him a famous poet's son, Masters wrote *CA:* "Since my first novel *The Common Pasture,* I have endeavored to keep the chance 'acquaintance' with my father [Edgar Lee Masters], the poet of *Spoon River Anthology,* off of book flaps and out of publisher's blurbs. This insistence has been the bane of book publicists and marketers, but I did not wish to be looked at as a curio, if not a freak; certainly, my intention was not to claim special privilege or attention. But Cecil Scott, bless him, was then the editor-in-chief at Macmillan, and he insisted this biographical fact appear on this decent, little novel. I had little to say about it. And so the damage, if you will, was done.

"Nor have I written specifically about my father as I could have—another book for the list. He does appear as one of the four characters in my family biography, *Last Stands: Notes from Memory;* he could hardly be omitted. However, he is by no means the most important character in the book, and as Donald Hall points out in his review, this post was gradually assumed in the course of the narrative by the mother.

"If this relationship has helped me, I will never know, though I worry sometimes that it might have given my work an undeserved interest. It is clear some writers or reviewers have used it to dismiss my work. The most flagrant but amusing attack in this line was the review of my last collection of stories in an important trade weekly in which the writer 'explored' the supposed oedipal relationship, emphasizing for evidence of my particular hang-up, that I called the collection *Success.* Not a line of description or evaluation was given to any of the stories. A. Dumas, fils, had little trouble with this identity apparently; the salons of Paris welcomed him and his work. As for me, and aside from the respect and tenderness I hold for my father's memory, I think of the 'title' as a mark to be borne with dignity and grace, as any child would want to honor any parent."

BIOGRAPHICAL/CRITICAL SOURCES:

BOOKS

Masters, Hilary, *Last Stands: Notes from Memory,* Godine, 1982.

PERIODICALS

Booklist, April 15, 1987, p. 1249; November 15, 1989, p. 640; March 15, 1992, p. 1337.
Chicago Tribune, September 2, 1986; May 18, 1987.
Chicago Tribune Book World, October 31, 1982.
Harvard Review, June, 1992.
Los Angeles Times, February 20 1985.
Newsweek, December 20, 1982.

New York Times Book Review, December 19, 1982; January 22, 1984, p. 30; February 24, 1985, p. 22; April 20, 1986, p. 22; September 13, 1987, p. 34; February 11, 1990, p. 18; May 10, 1992, p. 16.
Time, November 29, 1982.
Washington Post Book World, November 14, 1982; March 17, 1985, p. 8; June 28, 1987, p. 14.

*   *   *

MATTINGLEY, Christobel (Rosemary) 1931-

PERSONAL: Born October 26, 1931, in Brighton, South Australia, Australia; daughter of Arthur Raymond (a civil engineer) and Isabelle Margaret (Provis) Shepley; married Cecil David Mattingley (a teacher), December 17, 1953; children: Rosemary Christobel, Christopher Jonathan David, Stephen Michael. *Education:* University of Tasmania, B.A. (with honors), 1951; Public Library of Victoria Training School, certificate of proficiency, 1952; Library Association of Australia, registration certificate (associate), 1971. *Religion:* Anglican. *Avocational interests:* Nature study (especially birdwatching), reading, music, gardening, exploring the Australian bush (especially in wilderness areas), camping, swimming, beachcombing, travel (New Zealand, England, Europe, Papua New Guinea, Japan, Korea, India, and Bangladesh), flying in light aircraft, people-watching.

ADDRESSES: Home—316 Wynyard Grove, Wattle Park, South Australia 5066, Australia. *Agent*—A. P. Watt & Son, 20 John St., London WC1N 2DR, England.

CAREER: Department of Immigration, Canberra, Australia, librarian, 1951; Latrobe Valley libraries, Latrobe Valley, Australia, regional librarian, 1953; teacher and librarian in England, 1954-55; Prince Alfred College, Adelaide, Australia, librarian, 1956-57; St. Peter's Girls' School, Adelaide, librarian, 1966-70; Wattle Park Teachers College, Adelaide, acquisitions librarian, 1971, reader services librarian, 1972; Murray Park College of Advanced Education, Adelaide, lecturer and reader education librarian, 1973-74; writer, 1974—; writer in residence, West Australian College of Advanced Education, Churchlands, 1982; editor/researcher of Aboriginal history volume for official 1986 sesquicentenary publications, South Australian Sesquicentenary Board, 1983-88.

Presenter of *Children's Books to Enjoy,* a weekly television program, 1973-74. Cofounder of South Australian section of Community Aid Abroad, 1964; citizen member of Burnside City Council Library, 1971-84; South Australia chairperson of National Book Council of Australia, 1979-83; member of Public Lending Right Committee, 1984-88.

MEMBER: Australian Society of Authors, Australian Conservation Foundation, National Trust, Australian Refugee Association, Tandanya National Aboriginal Cultural Institute, South Australia Writers' Centre.

AWARDS, HONORS: Commendations, Children's Book Council of Australia, 1972, for *Windmill at Magpie Creek* and *Worm Weather;* Australian Library Promotion Council, commendation, 1973, public relations award, 1974; fellowships, Australia Council Literature Board, 1975, 1983; scholarship for study in Munich, International Youth Library, 1976-77; Inaugural Medal for Outstanding Book for Junior Readers, Children's Book Council of Australia, 1982, for *Rummage;* New South Wales Writers Award, National Parks and Wildlife Services, 1983; Australian Christian Book of the Year Children's Award, 1986, for *The Miracle Tree;* Advance Australia Award, 1990, for Outstanding Contribution to Literature.

WRITINGS:

Women Artists of Australia (screenplay), South Australian Film Corp., 1980.
Come to the Party!: Children's Libraries (screenplay), South Australian Film Corp., 1980.
(Editor) *Survival in Our Own Land: "Aboriginal" Experiences in "South Australia" since 1836,* Wakefield Press, 1988.

JUVENILE

The Picnic Dog, Hamish Hamilton (London), 1970.
Windmill at Magpie Creek, Brockhampton (Leicester), 1971.
Worm Weather, Hamish Hamilton, 1971.
Emu Kite, Hamish Hamilton, 1972.
Queen of the Wheat Castles, Brockhampton, 1973.
The Surprise Mouse, Hamish Hamilton, 1974.
Tiger's Milk, Angus & Robertson (Sydney, Australia), 1974.
The Battle of the Galah Trees, Brockhampton, 1974.
Show and Tell, Hodder & Stoughton (Sydney), 1974.
Lizard Log, Hodder & Stoughton, 1975.
The Great Ballagundi Damper Bake, Angus & Robertson, 1975.
The Long Walk, Thomas Nelson (Melbourne, Australia), 1976.
New Patches for Old, Hodder & Stoughton, 1977.
The Special Present and Other Stories, Collins (Sydney), 1977.
The Big Swim, Thomas Nelson, 1977.
Budgerigar Blue, Hodder & Stoughton, 1978.
The Jetty, Hodder & Stoughton, 1978.
Black Dog, Collins, 1979.
Rummage, Angus & Robertson, 1981, HarperCollins (New York City), 1992.
Brave with Ben, Hamish Hamilton, 1982.

Lexl and the Lion Party, Hodder & Stoughton, 1982.

The Magic Saddle, Hodder & Stoughton, 1983.

Duck Boy, Angus & Robertson, 1983, Atheneum (New York City), 1986.

Southerly Buster (novel for adolescents), Hodder & Stoughton, 1983.

The Angel with a Mouth Organ, Hodder & Stoughton, 1984, Holiday House (New York City), 1985.

Ghost Sitter, Patrick Hardy (London), 1984.

The Miracle Tree, Hodder & Stoughton, 1985, Harcourt (San Diego, CA), 1986.

McGruer and the Goat, Angus & Robertson, 1986.

The Butcher, the Beagle, and the Dog Catcher, Hodder & Stoughton, 1990.

Tucker's Mob, Omnibus (Adelaide, Australia), 1992.

The Sack, Puffin (Melbourne), 1993.

No Gun for Asmir, Puffin, 1993.

OTHER

Also author of television filmscripts *The Long Walk,* 1978, and *Rummage,* 1983, based on her books of the same titles. Also contributor to several anthologies, including *A Taste of Cockroach,* Australian Association for the Teaching of English (Adelaide), 1974; *A Swag of Australian Stories,* Ward, Lock (London), 1977; *Spooks and Spirits,* Hodder & Stoughton, 1978; *Early Dreaming,* Jacaranda Press, 1980; *Dreamtime,* Viking Kestrel (Melbourne), 1989; and *Eerie Tales,* Hodder & Stoughton, 1991. Contributor to proceedings of professional organizations. Contributor of stories, articles, and poems to library journals and literature periodicals for adults and children, including *Australian Library Journal, New Zealand Libraries, Reading Time, Cricket, Classroom, Australian Author,* and *Landfall.* Some of Mattingley's books have been recorded on tape and serialized on radio and television programs in Australia and abroad.

Some of Mattingley's books have been published in Danish, German, French, and several Aboriginal languages, and have been transcribed in Braille. The Canberra University Library houses the bibliography *Published Work of Christobel Mattingley* in the Lu Rees Archives Collection.

WORK IN PROGRESS: Picture books *The Race* for Ashton/Scholastic Inc. and *Big Sister, Little Sister* and *Poppy Peeker* for Puffin; junior novels *The Secret* for Puffin and *Dance with Didgeridoo* for Omnibus; *Memoirs of Tasmanian Ruby Paul: Trowutta—That's the Truth,* for HarperCollins; a biography, *King of the South West,* for Random House; *Muris Survives Sarajevo,* a sequel to *No Gun for Asmir.*

SIDELIGHTS: Australian author Christobel Mattingley has been writing acclaimed children's books since 1970. Though primarily creating picture books such as *Rum-*

mage and *The Magic Saddle* and middle-grade novels like *Windmill at Magpie Creek* and *The Miracle Tree,* she has also authored novels for young adults, such as *New Patches for Old* and *Southerly Buster.* Mattingley is also the editor of a nonfiction book for adults, *Survival in Our Own Land: "Aboriginal" Experiences in "South Australia," since 1836* shortlisted in two major awards, and has contributed stories for adults and children to periodicals.

Mattingley was born Christobel Rosemary Shepley in 1931, in Brighton, South Australia. "I lived the first eight years of my life in a house perched on a sandhill," she once told *CA.* "The freedom of the sandhills, the mystery of the sea, and the joys of a fresh-washed beach with new possibilities of discoveries each day contributed, I now believe, to my evolution as a writer." From an early age, she was encouraged in her literary efforts. She recalled to *CA:* "Our home was well supplied with books of all kinds, and my parents always read to and made up stories for my sister and me, so that by the time I went to school it was natural for me to write my own. I wrote poems in my mother's recipe book, and some of my first story pieces were published in the children's pages of the newspaper."

Mattingley also spent time putting on plays of fairy tales with her sister, and listening to radio shows. "We followed certain serials very keenly, which must have helped to develop my ear for the cadence of the spoken word and my sense of story," she commented. "Now I always hear the words I write, and I read my work aloud because I believe that if stories read aloud easily, they will also read well silently." Moreover, she added, "The power of language caught my imagination very early and before I was eight I had begun teaching myself Latin and French. By the time I was twelve I was trying German and Swedish, also self-taught."

Her father's civil engineering position required her family to move frequently; consequently Mattingley grew up in several different areas of Australia. After eight years in Brighton, she lived for a time in Sydney, and then moved to Tasmania. Mattingley linked this experience to her writings: "Wonderful opportunities for sailing, skiing, and bush walking in the wilderness areas strengthened the affinity I had always felt with nature. At the same time a growing understanding of my father's work as a civil engineer led me to appreciate the need for man's harmony with his environment. This has since come through, quite subconsciously, in my writing. Animals and birds feature in almost all of my books, not because I set out to write stories about animals, but because for me they have always been a natural part of life."

Her years working with children as a teacher and librarian and her experiences with her own children inspired her writing, said Mattingley. "I perceived vividly the drama and conflict in the world of the child and the stories which are all around us in everyday things, events, and places. I wrote my first story, 'The Special Present,' after our daughter lost her first tooth. *The Picnic Dog* was written because our dog was run over. An onion growing in a glass of water gave me the idea for *Show and Tell,* and our older son's jar of pet worms started me on *Worm Weather.* When our younger son gave me a mouse in a box for a surprise early birthday present he also gave me two stories, *The Surprise Mouse* and *Budgerigar Blue.*"

Mattingley's earlier works were primarily realistic portrayals of ordinary children in Australian settings. Often, such as in *Windmill at Magpie Creek,* the child protagonist has to learn to face up to his or her fears. But Mattingley's writing took a different bent after her mid-1970s trips to Europe; she was able to write fantasy for the first time. As she recounted: "Visiting Bremen in 1974 for the Loughborough Conference and living in Munich during the snowy winter of 1976 had spontaneously brought forth stories, the seeds of which had been sown early in my childhood, when my father read me 'Androcles and the Lion,' 'The Town Musicians of Bremen,' and many other folk and fairy tales. In *Lexl and the Lion Party, The Magic Saddle,* and [the story] 'Katzenfell,' I found myself writing with a strain of fantasy in a way that would not have been possible for me in Australia."

Similarly, a trip to Japan to visit her daughter, who had a postgraduate scholarship there, inspired Mattingley to write her later work *The Miracle Tree.* Though a picture book, it deals with mature subject matter—a Japanese couple separated for twenty years by the atomic bombing of Nagasaki. Another of Mattingley's picture books, *The Angel with a Mouth Organ,* also deals with the horrors of war, this time following the trials of a European refugee family during World War II. War also led to *No Gun for Asmir,* the author told *CA,* which "is based on the true story of two families of Bosnian refugees our son helped to escape. . . . The families had just arrived when we met them and I was deeply touched by their courage and dignity. I was especially moved by the vulnerability of seven-year-old Asmir, suddenly trying to be responsible for his mother and baby brother, in place of his father, Muris, who had not been allowed to leave Sarajevo." Mattingley told *CA* that the family's plight compelled her to help. "I supported the family's campaign to obtain permission for Muris to leave Sarajevo and enlisted ready help from the Australian, British and German publishers [of *No Gun for Asmir*], as well as many readers. The book played a significant part in obtaining an approved safe exit visa for him and a limited entry visa to Austria." Mattingley plans two more books about the family's experiences, entitled *Muris Survives Sarajevo* and *Asmir in Vienna.*

Many of Mattingley's books for young adults deal with contemporary problems. *New Patches for Old* tells the story of a young girl whose family immigrates to Australia after her father loses his job; she struggles to make new friends in a peer group that makes fun of her poverty. *Southerly Buster* concerns another teenage girl whose parents are suddenly having another child—the protagonist must deal with her feelings about her parents' sexuality and her own. *The Sack* shows a family struggling with the effects of unemployment. "I found myself writing this book quite spontaneously early in 1992," Mattingley told *CA.* "Heartwrenching stories of hardship and distress in the severe unemployment crisis in Australia and our church's commitment to help alleviate misery for some families by weekly grocery contributions were in my consciousness. But the trigger came, I believe, from deep in my subconscious memories of growing up in the Great Depression of the 1930s, when my grandmother's weekly food baskets from the country kept our family going." In the story Shane's father "gets the sack" (loses his job), and Shane finds his life changed in many uncomfortable ways. Eventually he realizes that, although the family has had to give up luxuries like designer jeans and even the most basic of necessities like the house and car, Shane still has what matters most—a loving family. "There has been a strong response to this book as it reflects a situation in which many families sadly find themselves today," Mattingley remarked.

In addition to her books for children, Mattingley has served as the editor for an adult nonfiction work, *Survival in Our Own Land: "Aboriginal" Experiences in "South Australia" since 1836.* She commented about the project: "This book does not celebrate the coming of the white settlers, but seeks to tell some of the story of displacement and loss of culture, language and lifestyle which most Aboriginal people have suffered. It breaks new ground in presenting the Aboriginal point of view and contains statements from over 120 Aboriginal people." She later added, "*Tucker's Mob,* which I wrote in 1979-80 after visiting an Aboriginal community in the Northern Territory, was not published until 1992, reflecting the lack of interest in indigenous peoples. I deliberately did not use the word 'Aboriginal' in the story, choosing an Ezra Jack Keats approach, just presenting the family as people. I also deliberately included some Kriol, the authentic language of the community, to create awareness of other languages besides mainstream English. Dynamic illustrations by Jeanie Adams point up the Aboriginal characters and setting. The Aboriginal Education Unit of South Australia has approved the book and two others with Aboriginal content I have since written. The Unit has undertaken to translate *Tucker's Mob* into Aboriginal languages."

BIOGRAPHICAL/CRITICAL SOURCES:

BOOKS

Children's Literature Review, Volume 24, Gale, 1989.
Oral History, National Library of Australia, 1981, new edition, 1990.
Something about the Author, Autobiography Series, Volume 18, Gale, 1994.

PERIODICALS

Children's Literature in Education, Volume 18, number 2, 1987, pp. 97-104.
New Zealand Libraries, December, 1979.
Reading Time, April, 1977; October, 1979; July, 1982; October, 1982; October, 1983; October, 1986.

* * *

MAYNE, Seymour 1944-

PERSONAL: Born May 18, 1944, in Montreal, Quebec, Canada. *Education:* McGill University, B.A. (with honors), 1965; University of British Columbia, M.A., 1966, Ph.D., 1972.

ADDRESSES: Office—University of Ottawa, Department of English, 175 Waller, Ottawa, Ontario, Canada K1N 6N5.

CAREER: Poet. Jewish Institute, Montreal, Quebec, lecturer in Jewish Canadian literature, 1964; Very Stone House, Vancouver, British Columbia, cofounder and managing editor, 1966-69; Ingluvin Publications, Montreal, cofounder and literary editor, 1970-73; University of British Columbia, Vancouver, lecturer in English, 1972; University of Ottawa, Ottawa, Ontario, assistant professor, 1973-78, associate professor, 1978-85, professor of English, 1985—; Mosaic Press/Valley Editions, Oakville, Ontario, cofounder and editor, 1974-83. Visiting professor, Hebrew University of Jerusalem, 1979-80, 1983-84, and Concordia University, 1982-83. Writer-in-residence, Hebrew University, 1987-88.

AWARDS, HONORS: Canada Council arts grants, 1969, 1973, 1977, 1979, and 1984; Ontario Arts Council grants, 1974, 1976, 1983, 1985, 1987, and 1992; J. I. Segal Prize in English-French Literature, 1974, and York Poetry Workshop Award, 1975, both for *Name;* Canada Council senior arts grant, 1984; American Literary Translators Association (ALTA) Poetry Translation Award, 1990; Multiculturalism and Citizenship Canada Award, 1991.

WRITINGS:

POETRY

That Monocycle the Moon, Catapult, 1964.

Tiptoeing on the Mount, McGill Poetry Series, 1965, 2nd revised edition, Catapult, 1965.
From the Portals of Mouseholes, Very Stone House, 1966.
Touches, University of British Columbia, 1966.
I Am Still the Boy (broadside), Western Press, 1967.
Anewd, Very Stone House, 1969.
earseed (broadside), Very Stone House, 1969.
the gigolo teaspoon (broadside), Very Stone House, 1969.
Manimals (poetry and prose), Very Stone House, 1969.
Mutetations, Very Stone House, 1969.
ticklish ticlicorice (broadside), Very Stone House, 1969.
Mouth, Quarry Press, 1970.
Face, Blackfish, 1971.
For Stems of Light, Very Stone House, 1971, revised edition, Mosaic Press/Valley Editions, 1974.
Name, Press Porcepic, 1975, 2nd edition, Mosaic Press/Valley Editions, 1976.
Begging (broadside), Valley Editions, 1977.
Diasporas, Mosaic Press/Valley Editions, 1977.
Racoon (broadside), Valley Editions, 1979.
Abel and Cain (broadside), Sifrei HaEmek (Jerusalem), 1980.
The Impossible Promised Land: Poems Selected and New, Mosaic Press/Valley Editions, 1981.
Seven Poems, League of Canadian Poets, 1983.
Neighbour Praying (broadside), Sifrei HaEmek, 1984.
Vanguard of Dreams: New and Selected Poems, Sifriat Poalim (Tel Aviv), 1984.
Crazy Leonithas (broadside), Valley Editions, 1985.
Children of Abel, Mosaic Press, 1986.
Diversions, Noovo Masheen (Ottawa), 1987.
Down Here (broadside), Tree, 1990.
Simple Ceremony, Hakibbutz Hameuchad, 1990.
Ha'arava Le'sinai (broadside), Sifrei Hamek, 1992.
Killing Time, Mosaic Press, 1992.
Arbeh Ha'dmamah, Iton 77 Editions, 1993.

EDITOR

(With Patrick Lane) *Collected Poems of Red Lane,* Very Stone House, 1968.
(With Victor Coleman) *Poetry of Canada,* Intrepid Press, 1969.
(With Dorothy Livesay) *Forty Women Poets of Canada,* Ingluvin Publications, 1971.
Engagements: The Prose of Irving Layton, McClelland & Stewart, 1972.
Cutting the Keys, Writing Workshop of the University of Ottawa, 1974.
(And author of introduction) *The A. M. Klein Symposium,* University of Ottawa Press, 1975.
Splices, Writing Workshop of the University of Ottawa, 1975.
(And author of introduction) *Choice Parts,* Writing Workshop of the University of Ottawa, 1976.

(And author of introduction) *Irving Layton: The Poet and His Critics,* McGraw, 1978.

(And cotranslator) Rachel Korn, *Generations: Selected Poems,* Mosaic Press, 1982.

(And author of introduction) *Essential Words: An Anthology of Jewish Canadian Poetry,* Oberon Press, 1985.

(And cotranslator) Moshe Dor, *Crossing the River: Selected Poems,* Mosaic Press, 1989.

(And contributor) *Six Ottawa Poets,* Mosaic Press, 1990.

TRANSLATOR

(With Catherine Leach) Jerzy Harasymowicz, *Genealogy of Instruments,* Valley Editions, 1974.

Burnt Pearls: Ghetto Poems of Abraham Sutzkever, Mosaic Press, 1981.

(With Laya Firestone-Seghi and Howard Schwartz) Dan Jaffe, editor, *Jerusalem as She Is: New and Selected Poems of Shlomo Vinner,* BkMk Press, 1991.

Melech Ravitch, *Night Prayer and Other Poems* (contains both Yiddish and English), Mosaic Press, 1993.

OTHER

Contributor to various anthologies, including *The Penguin Book of Canadian Verse,* edited by Ralph Gustafson, Penguin, 1975; *Aurora: New Canadian Writing 1979,* edited by Morris Wolfe, Doubleday, 1979; *Voices within the Ark: Modern Jewish Poets,* edited by Anthony Rudolf and Howard Schwartz, Avon, 1980; *The New Oxford Book of Canadian Verse,* edited by Margaret Atwood, Oxford University Press, 1982; *The Lyric Paragraph: Canadian Prose Poems,* edited by R. Allen, Quadrant Editions, 1986; *Relations,* edited by Kenneth Sherman, Mosaic Press, 1986; *Ghosts of the Holocaust,* edited by S. Florsheim, Wayne State University Press, 1989; *The Other Language: English Poetry of Montreal,* edited by E. Farkas, Muses' Co., 1989.

Also contributor of poetry and prose to journals, including *Canadian Forum, Fiddlehead, Jewish Dialog, Prism International,* and *West Review.* Coeditor of *Cataract,* 1961-62; poetry editor of *Forge,* 1961-62, and *Viewpoints,* 1990—; editor of *The Page,* 1962-63, *Catapult,* 1964, *Jewish Dialog,* 1974-81, *Stoney Monday,* 1978, and *Parchment,* 1991—; contributing editor at *Viewpoints,* 1982-90, and *Tel Aviv Review,* 1989—; consulting editor of *Bywords,* 1990—, and *Poet Lore,* 1992—. Some of Mayne's poetry has been translated into French, Hebrew, Polish, and Spanish.

ADAPTATIONS: Mayne's poetry and criticism have been broadcast on Canadian Broadcasting Corp. (CBC-Radio) programs, including *New Canadian Writing, Anthology, Critics on Air,* and *The Arts in Review.*

WORK IN PROGRESS: Translations of Yiddish and Hebrew poetry.

SIDELIGHTS: The predominant theme of Seymour Mayne's poetry is death, a point illustrated by Kenneth Sherman's description of Mayne in *Canadian Literature* as a "poet of lamentations" with an "uncanny ability to capture the essential, singular qualities of the departed and to render that humanness in vivid and sympathetic terms, making the reader forcefully aware of the loss." However, Mayne's works offer more than sadness and pain. In the *Dictionary of Literary Biography* David Staines wrote that although "a bleak, even pessimistic, vision of life permeates his powerful verse, . . . Mayne finds hope in his steadfast commitment to his Jewish traditions and in man's awareness and acceptance of the cyclic pattern of life."

Even though Staines called Mayne's early works *That Monocycle the Moon* and *Tiptoeing on the Mount* "light-hearted explorations of human passion and sensuality," he acknowledged that in *Mouth,* which *Contemporary Poets* contributor John Robert Colombo called Mayne's "central publication," the poet "begins to examine the body in mystical rather than merely sensual terminology." Writing in *Canadian Literature,* Joseph Pivato remarked that even Mayne's earlier poems had "the added perspective of painful separations, sickness and death, and [were] thus saved . . . from being simply titillating juvenilia." Staines asserted that Mayne was influenced early on by professor Louis Dudek and poetry instructor Irving Layton, but also acknowledged that "Mayne is the direct literary descendant of A. M. Klein, the disciplined control of his verse reminiscent of Klein's poetry and the increasing emphasis on Jewish characters, idiom, and traditions reminiscent of Klein's early writings."

Some of Mayne's works focus on the Holocaust, including those in the collection *The Impossible Promised Land: Poems Selected and New,* which emphasize "remembering, bringing back to life for a moment the many who have been erased by the Holocaust and its fallout," observed John Oughton in *Books in Canada.* Oughton also commented that while "death negated the being of many, . . . Mayne is determined to replace that negation with some affirmation of their continuation in the collective memory of culture or the individual recall of the poet."

BIOGRAPHICAL/CRITICAL SOURCES:

BOOKS

Contemporary Poets, 5th edition, St. James, 1991.

Dictionary of Literary Biography, Volume 60: *Canadian Writers since 1960, Second Series,* Gale, 1987.

PERIODICALS

Books in Canada, March, 1982, p. 15; April, 1982, p. 34; November, 1985, p. 26; March, 1987, p. 27.

Canadian Forum, October, 1965, p. 164; March, 1968, p. 282; November, 1970, p. 310.

Canadian Literature, spring, 1964; winter, 1968; spring, 1972; summer, 1975; spring, 1979; winter, 1982.

Choice, July, 1979, p. 667; July, 1982, p. 1560; March, 1986, p. 1060.

Quill & Quire, December, 1978.

*   *   *

McALLISTER, Annie Laurie
See CASSIDAY, Bruce (Bingham)

*   *   *

McCAIG, Donald   1940-
(Snee McCaig; Steven Ashley, a pseudonym)

PERSONAL: Born 1940, in Butte, MT; married; wife's name, Anne (a breeder of Rambouillet sheep). *Education:* Montana State University, B.A.; attended various graduate schools.

ADDRESSES: Home—Williamsville, VA. *Agent*—Knox Burger Associates Ltd., 39 1/2 Washington Sq. S., New York, NY 10012.

CAREER: Writer. Teacher of philosophy at Wayne State University, Detroit, MI, and University of Waterloo, Waterloo, Ontario, in the mid-1960s; copywriter and copy chief for advertising agencies in Detroit and New York City, including Gilbert Advertising and Young & Rubicam; producer of "Murray the K" 's *Radio Free Toronto* radio show, 1965; commentator on *All Things Considered* program, National Public Radio. Sheep and hay crop farmer in Highland County, VA. Organizer of the Bath Highland volunteer fire department in Highland County. Writing instructor, Dabney S. Lancaster Community College, Clifton Forge, VA.

MEMBER: PEN, United States Border Collie Club, Virginia Border Collie Association (president).

WRITINGS:

NOVELS

(Under pseudonym Steven Ashley) *Caleb, Who Is Hotter than a Two-Dollar Pistol,* McKay (New York City), 1975.

(Under pseudonym Steven Ashley) *Stalking Blind,* Dial (New York City), 1976.

The Butte Polka, Rawson, Wade (New York City), 1980.

Nop's Trials, Crown (New York City), 1984.

The Man Who Made the Devil Glad, Crown, 1986.

The Bamboo Cannon, Crown, 1989.

Nop's Hope, Crown, 1994.

OTHER

(Under name Snee McCaig) *Last Poems,* Alternative Press, 1975.

Eminent Dogs, Dangerous Men (nonfiction), E. Burlingame Books, 1991, published as *Eminent Dogs, Dangerous Men: Searching through Scotland for a Border Collie,* HarperCollins (New York City), 1991.

An American Homeplace: The Real World of Rural America (nonfiction), Crown, 1992.

Also author of numerous novels under undisclosed pseudonyms. Contributor to periodicals, including *Atlantic, Blair and Ketchum's Country Journal, Gentleman's Quarterly, Harper's, New York Times, Outside, Sports Illustrated,* and *Washington Post.*

SIDELIGHTS: With "a face the color of beefsteak, hands like knots on a tree, and blond-turning-gray sideburns that [remind] you of honeysuckle patches clamoring to be cut back," Donald McCaig looks more like a backwoods farmer than a New York City adman-turned-novelist, according to Isaac Rehert in the Baltimore *Sun.* McCaig did indeed abandon a "fast lane" advertising career to farm and write on his eighteenth-century homestead in mountainous western Virginia where he and his wife, Anne, raise Rambouillet sheep and harvest alfalfa for hay. It wasn't until the publication of *Nop's Trials* that McCaig found relative fame and prosperity. Before the release of the book, James Conaway in a *Washington Post* article predicted that the novel "could make [McCaig] famous . . . if the prepublication reviews and the publicity people are right. It could be one of the most dramatic reversals of fortune in recent publishing history, making McCaig the richest subsistence farmer in Highland County."

Called a classic by *Publishers Weekly*'s Sybil Steinberg, *Nop's Trials* concerns the dognapping, subsequent tribulations, and eleventh-hour rescue of a working Border collie named Nop. While a *People* magazine writer characterizes the book as "a kind of *Lassie* meets *Watership Down,*" combining an old-fashioned dog story with the anthropomorphism associated with Richard Adams's work, other critics comment that McCaig has brought his canine and human characters up to date, creating an animal story that deals with more complex personalities and issues than those usually embraced by the genre. Dannye Romine declares in the *Charlotte Observer* that *Nop's Trials* is more than he expected, calling it "a man-loves-dog, man-loses-dog, man-gets-dog-back novel that's surprisingly irresistible." After two crooks steal the basically trusting dog, his gentle, stoic nature is tested as he passes through the hands of a rodeo roustabout, a bag lady, animal shelter employees, and an assortment of villains. Nop's heroism, unlike that of Lassie or Rin Tin Tin, stems from his drive and talent for survival. He performs no spectacular acts of bravery, such as saving children from burning buildings. Instead, he adapts to the sometimes horrible situations he finds himself in, looks for the good in the people he encounters, and is prepared, always, to do that for which he was bred—to work for humans.

Discussing McCaig's techniques of applying human characteristics to the canines in the book, Edmund Fuller of the *Wall Street Journal* contends that "the central problem of all animal stories is the inescapable element of anthropomorphism. In the psychology of his dogs, as seen in the thoughts attributed to them, Mr. McCaig is convincing." The author tells Conaway that he "wanted to have [the dogs] talk in the book, because they do talk. But it's hard to make a language out of shrugs and eye movements. These are very ritualistic, formal dogs. If they spoke, they might use something like mandarin Chinese, or Elizabethan English." So McCaig set the animal speech apart from that of humans by giving his dogs a very proper-sounding vocabulary filled with "thees" and "thous." "One reason his canine speeches work is simply that McCaig has put dogs' non-verbal, usually ritual and entirely natural communication with each other and other animals into words," writes Beaufort Cranford in the *Detroit News.* "It's easy, for example, to imagine one dog greeting another by bragging about himself, as they often do here, because dogs obviously do that."

Critics praise the way the book handles human characters as well. States the *Detroit News*'s Bruce Cook, "What Donald McCaig has done so well here is to intertwine Nop's story with that of his master, Louis Burkholder, a stock farmer in the Blue Ridge country of Virginia." Pitting Burkholder's loyalty to his dog against his love and responsibilities toward his family gives the novel an added dimension, as several reviewers note. Cook continues, "[Burkholder's] are ordinary problems, but very real human problems, and [the author] handles them in a realistic, respectful way that says he knows something about the devious indirections of the human psyche. All his characters ring true."

McCaig admits that Nop is based, at least in part, on his own Border collie, Pip. However, McCaig worries that his portrayal of Nop's finer qualities will encourage readers to buy Border collies as pets. He offers a caution at the back of book: "Border collies are very bright, quick and more than a little weird. They are not suitable for most city apartments. Their working instincts are strong and their self-esteem comes from working well. A bored, mishandled Border collie can get into awful trouble."

Writing for the *Washington Post Book World,* Garret Epps compares McCaig's next novel, *The Man Who Made the Devil Glad,* to the crime novels of Elmore Leonard, deeming it "mostly convincing, sexy enough, and readable indeed." Epps calls the book "a tightly written thriller about murder, corruption and drugs in the highlands of West Virginia," noting that McCaig "has a good ear for the clipped, twangy speech of the eastern mountains" and that "he's also very good at describing the chaotic, ruined countryside of the mountains." Sybil Steinberg in *Publisher's Weekly* asserts, "McCaig's rendition of country talk is perfect. In spare, laconic dialogue, he conveys the archaic flavor of southern rural speech." In concluding, Epps lauds the novel as a "quick, hard-hitting read."

Although the story and setting are different, *The Bamboo Cannon,* a Caribbean adventure featuring a struggling pilot, a spoiled, upper-class pill-popper, and a political revolution, generates similar compliments from critics. In another *Publishers Weekly* review, Steinberg points out that McCaig has a "fine ear for West Indian patois" and labels the book an "entertaining odd-couple adventure," while *New York Times Book Review*'s Vicki Weissman says *The Bamboo Cannon* "cracks along at a roaring pace" as the author "conjures up perfectly every feeling evoked by exotic ads for Caribbean vacations: fantasy, adventure and a happy ending." A *Kirkus Reviews* contributor commends the novel for its "bright pastel local color and characters, . . . and a plot that calypsoes from one high note to the next," and deems the work "a literary pina colada, sweet but packing a giddy punch."

McCaig returns to tales of Border collies in *Eminent Dogs, Dangerous Men: Searching through Scotland for a Border Collie,* a nonfiction account of his own search for a new canine in Scotland. Christopher Lehmann-Haupt in the *New York Times* declares that the book "is rich in dog lore and by no means poor as a study of human behavior." Border collies also play a part in McCaig's *An American Homeplace: The Real World of Rural America,* a collection of stories about the delight rural life can bring. As Chris Goodrich states in the *Los Angeles Times Book Review,* "You'll encounter many dogs and sheep and trainers here, to be sure, but the best parts . . . have to do with crops and trucks and floods and community service." A *Kirkus Reviews* contributor calls the essays "lyrical and timely," and concludes, "McCaig brings a kind of loving humility to his subjects, a rare quality. His collection is uneven, but, at its best, pure and moving."

BIOGRAPHICAL/CRITICAL SOURCES:

PERIODICALS

Atlantic, October, 1980, p. 101; February, 1981; May, 1984, p. 22; January, 1987, p. 90.
Charlotte Observer, April 23, 1984.
Chicago Tribune, May 15, 1984.
Detroit News, April 8, 1984; May 2, 1984.
Kirkus Reviews, September 1, 1986, p. 1315; December 1, 1988, p. 1698; June 15, 1992, p. 764.

Library Journal, March 1, 1980, p. 637.
Los Angeles Times Book Review, June 3, 1984, p. 8; March 24, 1991, p. 6; September 20, 1992, p. 6.
National Review, September 5, 1980, p. 1096.
New Yorker, October 13, 1980; p. 191.
New York Times, April 12, 1984, p. 22; March 14, 1991, p. C19.
New York Times Book Review, January 16, 1977; April 15, 1984, p. 22; March 26, 1989, p. 12.
People, June 4, 1984.
Publishers Weekly, June 13, 1980, p. 68; April 6, 1984, pp. 76-77; September 5, 1986, p. 91-92; August 28, 1987, p. 74; November 25, 1988, p. 57; June 22, 1992, p. 52; August 24, 1992, p. 76.
Sun (Baltimore), April 8, 1984.
Wall Street Journal, April 17, 1984, p. 32.
Washington Post, March 26, 1984; January 11, 1989.
Washington Post Book World, November 9, 1986, p. 5; September 13, 1992, p. 12.

—*Sketch by Geri J. Speace*

*　　　*　　　*

McCAIG, Snee
See McCAIG, Donald

*　　　*　　　*

McCLOSKEY, (John) Robert   1914-

PERSONAL: Born September 15, 1914, in Hamilton, OH; son of Howard Hill and Mable (Wismeyer) McCloskey; married Margaret Durand (a children's librarian), November 23, 1940; children: Sarah, Jane. *Education:* Attended Vesper George Art School, Boston, MA, 1932-36, and National Academy of Design, 1936-38. *Politics:* Democrat.

ADDRESSES: Home—Little Deer Isle, ME 04650.

CAREER: Writer and illustrator of children's books. Bas relief artist for municipal building, Hamilton, OH, 1935; mural painter for four years; also worked as commercial artist. *Military service:* U.S. Army, 1942-45; became technical sergeant.

MEMBER: American Academy in Rome (fellow), PEN, Authors League of America.

AWARDS, HONORS: Prix de Rome, 1939; Caldecott Medal, 1942, for *Make Way for Ducklings,* and 1958, for *Time of Wonder;* Caldecott Medal honor book award, 1949, for *Blueberries for Sal,* and 1953, for *One Morning in Maine;* D.Litt., Miami University, Oxford, OH, 1964; D.Let., Mount Holyoke College, 1967; Catholic Library

Association's Regina Medal, 1974, for "continued distinguished contribution to children's literature"; D.Litt., University of Maine, 1990; *Make Way for Ducklings, Homer Price, Blueberries for Sal, One Morning in Maine,* and *Time of Wonder* have been selected as notable books by the American Library Association.

WRITINGS:

SELF-ILLUSTRATED

Lentil, Viking, 1940.
Make Way for Ducklings, Viking, 1941.
Homer Price, Viking, 1943.
Blueberries for Sal, Viking, 1948.
Centerburg Tales, Viking, 1951.
One Morning in Maine, Viking, 1952.
Time of Wonder, Viking, 1957.
Burt Dow, Deep-Water Man: A Tale of the Sea in the Classic Tradition, Viking, 1963.

ILLUSTRATOR

Anne Burnett Malcolmson, *Yankee Doodle's Cousins,* Houghton, 1941.
Robert Hobart Davis, *Tree Toad,* Stokes, 1942.
Claire Huchet Bishop, *The Man Who Lost His Head,* Viking, 1942.
Tom Robinson, *Trigger John's Son,* Viking, 1949.
Ruth Sawyer, *Journey Cake, Ho!,* Viking, 1953.
Anne H. White, *Junket,* Viking, 1955.
Keith Robertson, *Henry Reed, Inc.,* Viking, 1958.
Keith Robertson, *Henry Reed's Journey,* Viking, 1963.
Keith Robertson, *Henry Reed's Baby-Sitting Service,* Viking, 1966.
Robertson, *Henry Reed's Big Show,* Viking, 1970.

ADAPTATIONS: Weston Woods filmed versions of *Make Way for Ducklings,* 1955, *Lentil,* 1957, *Time of Wonder,* 1961, *The Doughnuts* (based on *Homer Price*), 1963, *Blueberries for Sal,* 1967, *The Case of the Cosmic Comic* (based on *Homer Price*), 1976; and *Burt Dow: Deep-Water Man,* 1983. *One Morning in Maine* was made into a filmstrip and cassette with teacher's guide, Viking, 1979; the film *Homer Price* was produced by Miller Brody.

SIDELIGHTS: Robert McCloskey is a highly-regarded author and illustrator of children's books who has blended interests in music, engineering, and art to create an original, satirical style with a distinctly "Americana" flavor. His boy characters, Homer Price and Lentil, have been compared by critics like *Twentieth-Century Children's Writers* contributor James E. Higgins to Mark Twain's Tom Sawyer. Higgins comments that, like Sawyer, "McCloskey's boys have the knack of getting themselves into and out of fantastic adventures and misadventures. The incidents in these books are authentically shaped out of actual experience and touched with the gentle humor of a grown-up's remembrance." The unforgettable duck family in McCloskey's Caldecott Medal-winning *Make Way for Ducklings* has also warmed the hearts of several generations of readers.

As a child, McCloskey was encouraged by his parents to follow his interests. This he did, learning to play a succession of instruments: the piano, harmonica, percussion, and finally oboe. Later he became fascinated with how mechanical and electrical things work. "I built trains and cranes with remote controls, my family's Christmas trees revolved, lights flashed and buzzers buzzed, fuses blew and sparks flew," he related in the autobiographical film *Robert McCloskey*. McCloskey also discovered art. He contributed drawings to his high school yearbook and newspaper and taught soap carving at the local Young Men's Christian Association (YMCA). By his senior year, McCloskey was skilled enough in art to win a scholarship to Boston's Vesper George School of Art through a woodcut engraving in a contest sponsored by *Scholastic* magazine. During the summers McCloskey returned to his hometown of Hamilton, Ohio, where he worked as a YMCA boys' camp counselor.

At the camp McCloskey ventured into new forms of art, such as carving a totem pole. "It had eyes as big as saucers," he recalled in *Robert McCloskey*. "I was carving larger and larger things, from bars of soap to trunks of trees. The chips were larger, too," he added. As a result of this work, in 1934 McCloskey was asked by an architect to create over twenty bas reliefs in stone for the municipal building in his hometown. Eventually the children's section of the library in this building was named after him.

While at school in the Back Bay section of Boston, McCloskey went through an idealistic period. "My mind in those days was filled with odd bits of Greek mythology, with accent on Pegasus, Spanish galleons, Oriental dragons, and all the stuff that really and truly great art is made of," he remembered in *Caldecott Medal Books: 1938-1957*. It therefore didn't occur to him that the ducks he sometimes fed in a public garden might be interesting subjects. But a visit with a children's book editor in New York brought McCloskey back down to earth. She suggested he toss out some of his grandiose ideas and begin to focus more on the natural world around him, advice he followed back in Boston.

In 1936 McCloskey returned to New York City, this time to study at the National Academy of Design. During the summers he continued to study art under Jerry Farnsworth in Provincetown, Cape Cod. While he won several awards for his work at the school of design, it became clear he could not live on the proceeds from sales of his paintings. So McCloskey reluctantly accepted a job in commercial art, which he worked at until he decided to go back to Ohio in 1938.

In Ohio McCloskey amassed a new portfolio of paintings and drawings based on local scenes. The artist soon returned to New York and, on the strength of these works, was hired, with Francis Scott Bradford, to create murals in Cambridge, Massachusetts, for the Lever Brothers Building. In 1939 he received the Prix de Rome, which granted him funds to study in Europe, but because of World War II McCloskey was unable to take advantage of the prize until ten years after he received it.

Also in 1939, McCloskey published his first children's book, *Lentil*, a story about a young harmonica player. The double-spread sepia artwork helped make this humorous hometown story a classic for children of all ages. Writing in the *Dictionary of Literary Biography*, Alice Fannin finds that "Lentil's world is one which contains no real threats and only minor upsets, where an energetic young boy . . . can learn to use the talents he has instead of lamenting those he does not have and can rise to at least momentary fame, living out the American dream." Marguerite P. Archer praises *Lentil* in *Elementary English*: "Both Lentil and the town of Alto, Ohio (circa 1912) seem completely authentic. Every detail counts as the boy, the town and its people are so masterfully caricatured."

In 1942 McCloskey's *Make Way for Ducklings* appeared and won the Caldecott Medal. The author/illustrator put much effort into the study of mallard ducks before creating the drawings for the book. After observing preserved ducks at New York City's American Museum of Natural History, McCloskey discovered interesting facts about the habits of mallards from books in the museum's library. He gleaned further information from an ornithologist and went so far as to purchase four live ducks from a poultry dealer. In *Caldecott Medal Books* McCloskey explains that when he brought the birds back to his apartment, his artist roommate "didn't even bat an eye." He adds, "I spent the next weeks on my hands and knees, armed with a box of Kleenex and a sketch book, following ducks around the studio and observing them in the bathtub."

According to Fannin, "for children, the pleasure of [*Make Way for Ducklings*] lies in pictures and in theme. Executed in soft charcoal, then lithographed, the pictures of the ducks—so beautifully accurate—and the drawings of Boston from a duck's-eye view provide much of the story's attraction. . . . The message is comforting: parents provide care and safety, helped when necessary by the proper authority, and ducklings who learn the proper duck behavior find security and end sleepily in a pleasant haven." Since the late 1980s, larger-than-life-size bronze replicas of the mother duck and her ducklings have stood in the Boston Public Garden, the setting for McCloskey's tale.

After serving as a visual aids technical sergeant in the U.S. Army during World War II, in 1943 McCloskey came out with *Homer Price,* six stories that relate events in the hero's life. *Homer Price* is praised by James Daugherty in *Horn Book* for McCloskey's artistic prowess and sense of humor: "The way these boys fit into their pants, wear their shirts, and the way the folds of their clothes pull with every movement is all there to intensify vivid humor and real character. This humorous reality pervades even the objects in each scene so that you get the full delicious flavor out of every detail of Homer's room and the unforgettable barber shop." Archer remarks, "The stories in *Homer Price* are obviously fictional, but the enthralled reader has a feeling that they *could* be true (maybe)." She also describes Homer Price as "a classic hero to American children." McCloskey continued the escapades of Homer Price in *Centerburg Tales.*

McCloskey has written several stories set on an island off the coast of Maine where he and his family spent their summers. One of these stories is *Blueberries for Sal,* whose lead character is based on McCloskey's daughter, Sarah. In this charming, simple tale, a mother and her daughter go berry picking in the Maine woods at the same time that a mother bear and her cub are out for a walk. Mothers and babies get mixed up for a brief, surprising, but harmless moment. According to Helen W. Painter, writing in *Elementary English,* "Young children adore the story and read the large pictures easily. The excellent line drawings and even the print are done in the deep color of blueberries." The reviewer for the *New York Herald Tribune Book Review* calls it "a delight to the eye," while *Horn Book* reviewer Anne Carroll Moore comments, "Mr. McCloskey has done some of his best drawing—as true to the life line of the Maine coast as to the living child and her mother in their search for blueberries on their island. Beauty, truth and the sure line of an artist who has thoroughly mastered his technique set this book apart."

By the time McCloskey wrote *One Morning in Maine,* his second daughter, Jane, had been born. She appears in the book along with her older sister. As described by Painter, *One Morning in Maine* is "a warm family story which also is full of homey details and affection. There are pictures of Sal squeezing toothpaste on Jane's brush, Sal patting the dog as mother explains that a loose tooth means that she has become a big girl, . . . Sal telling animals and birds about her tooth and then getting her father to help look for it in the mud where they had dug clams. . . . Beautiful dark blue double-page spreads give a reader a feeling of the island, the water, and the coast in a most impressionable way." Norah Smaridge called the book "a tragi-comic experience with which young readers quickly identify." Mary Gould Davis showed admiration for *One Morning in Maine* in *Saturday Review:* "As we follow the story of Sal and her lost tooth we feel as refreshed as though we had spent a day with [the characters] on their island. Beauty and humor and the integrity of an artist who is always close to the thing that he dramatizes make this one of the outstanding picture books of this year—and perhaps of many years."

With *Time of Wonder,* McCloskey became the first artist to receive the Caldecott Medal twice. The illustrations for *Time of Wonder* were a departure from his usual artistic style; this simple story of a Maine island is told in watercolors. As Painter describes it: "[*Time of Wonder*] is a slight but rhythmic story . . . of the beauty of the island during changes of season and tide, and of the coming of the storm. . . . A safe, familiar world meets the hurricane but with the security of close family relationships. Children can see beauty in the paintings. The forest quiet with the sound of growing ferns, the soft greens of slowly unfurling fiddleheads, the spreading rain-rings on water, the ghostly gray and yellow fog, the bright stars and their reflections, the lighted window as the dark winds of the hurricane close in on house and forest." As Margaret Sherwood Libby sees it in the *New York Herald Tribune Book Review,* "*Time of Wonder* is a paean in words and lovely water colors of youth, of summer holidays, and of the beauties of Penobscot Bay. The great sweeping pictures have the luminous quality that is the peculiar charm of this medium. The bright almost unreal colors of a 'blue Maine day' contrast with soft and subtler shades, abstract patterns mingle with scenes of realism."

McCloskey staunchly advocates making the study of art more widespread. In *Newbery and Caldecott Medal Books: 1956-1965,* the artist points out the important roles played by form, rhythm, texture, space relationships, color, and repetition in good design. "It is important," he argues, "that we develop people who can make worthwhile pictures, and it is important that we teach people to 'read' these pictures. That is why, in my opinion, every child, along with learning to read and write, should be taught to draw and to design."

McCloskey said in an autobiographical sketch written for the *Junior Book of Authors:* "It is just sort of an accident that I write books. I really think up stories in pictures and just fill in the pictures with a sentence or a paragraph or a few pages of words." When putting together artwork for a book, McCloskey considers what the printing process can best reproduce. It can take him two or three years to come up with a new story, partly because he is a meticulous researcher and observer of the world around him.

Summing up McCloskey's reputation, Fannin notes: "A first-rate illustrator, in his books McCloskey provides art that is an added attraction—always well done and sometimes exquisite." Speaking of his humor, Painter finds that "this quality, plus the ability to portray facets of ordinary but real living which are familiar to all of us, creates a kind of magnet that draws us together. . . . Perhaps seldom has an individual in his representation of reality verging on the comic made greater use of his own background and personal characteristics in his work than has Robert Mc-Closkey."

BIOGRAPHICAL/CRITICAL SOURCES:

BOOKS

Arbuthnot, May Hill, *Children and Books,* 3rd edition, Scott, Foresman, 1964.

Bader, Barbara, *American Picture Books from Noah's Ark to the Beast Within,* Macmillan, 1976, p. 140.

Children's Literature Review, Volume 7, Gale, 1984, p. 189.

Contemporary American Illustrators of Children's Books, Rutgers University Press, 1974.

Dictionary of Literary Biography, Volume 22: *American Writers for Children, 1900-1960,* Gale, 1983, p. 259.

Hopkins, Lee Bennett, editor, *Books Are by People,* Citation, 1969.

Huck, Charlotte S., and Doris Young Kuhn, *Children's Literature in the Elementary School,* Holt, 1968, pp. 95, 331.

Kingman, Lee, editor, *Newbery and Caldecott Medal Books: 1956-1965,* Horn Book, 1965.

Kunitz, Stanley J., and Howard Haycroft, *Junior Book of Authors,* Wilson, 1951, p. 203.

Lanes, Selma, *Down the Rabbit Hole,* Atheneum, 1971.

Larrick, Nancy, *A Parent's Guide to Children's Reading,* 3rd edition, Doubleday, 1969.

MacCann, Donnarae, and Olga Richard, *The Child's First Books,* Wilson, 1973.

Miller, Bertha Mahony, and Elinor Whitney Field, editors, *Caldecott Medal Books: 1938-1957,* Horn Book, 1957, p. 307.

Smaridge, Norah, *Famous Author-Illustrators for Young People,* Dodd, Mead, 1973, p. 106.

Smith, Dora V., *Fifty Years of Children's Books 1910-1960: Trends, Backgrounds, Influences,* National Council of Teachers of English, 1963, p. 48.

Twentieth-Century Children's Writers, St. James Press, 1989, p. 655.

Viguers, Ruth Hill, and others, *A Critical History of Children's Literature,* Macmillan, 1953, p. 567.

Viguers, R. H., *Illustrators of Children's Books: 1946-1956,* Horn Book, 1958.

PERIODICALS

Elementary English, May, 1954, p. 251; May, 1958, p. 287; March, 1960, p. 143; February, 1968, p. 145.

Horn Book, September/October, 1941, p. 380; November/December, 1941, p. 445; July/August, 1942, p. 277;

November/December, 1943, pp. 408, 425; January/February, 1948; November/December, 1948, p. 434; March/April, 1951, p. 94; May/June, 1951, p. 179; July, 1957; December, 1957, p. 480; December, 1963, p. 592; January/February, 1989, p. 106.

Language Arts, April, 1979, p. 375.

New York Herald Tribune Book Review, October 3, 1948, p. 8; May 13, 1951, p. 17; May 11, 1952, p. 7; December 15, 1957, p. 9.

New York Herald Tribune Books, April 28, 1940, p. 8; August 31, 1941, p. 6.

New York Times Book Review, May 19, 1940, p. 10; October 19, 1941, p. 10; November 14, 1943, p. 6; May 6, 1951, p. 22; October 6, 1963, p. 42.

Publishers Weekly, June 27, 1942.

Saturday Review, May 10, 1952, p. 48.

OTHER

Robert McCloskey (film), Western Woods, 1964.

*   *   *

McCORMACK, Arthur Gerard   1911-1992

PERSONAL: Born August 16, 1911, in Liverpool, England; died December 11, 1992; son of Francis and Elizabeth (Ranard) McCormack. *Education:* Studied at St. Francis Xavier College, Liverpool, England, and colleges of St. Joseph's Missionary Society in England and Holland; University of Durham, B.A. (first class honors), 1939, M.A., 1942. *Avocational interests:* Reading, driving his scooter.

CAREER: Member of St. Joseph's Missionary Society, Mill Hill, London, England. Ordained priest, 1936; missionary priest in British Cameroons, West Africa (now West Cameroun, Cameroun Republic), 1940-48, served as principal of St. Joseph's College, 1945-46, and Training College for Teachers, 1946-48; invalided to England in 1948; mainly light parish duties and experimental work as teacher, 1956-63; St. Joseph's College, Mill Hill, London, staffmember, 1963-92; Populations and Development Office, Rome, Italy, director, 1973-86.

Attended Second Vatican Council as expert on population and development of developing countries, 1963-65; special advisor to the Secretary General, World Population Conference, Bucharest, 1974; consultant to United Nations Fund for Population Activities, beginning 1975; co-founder and staff member for seven years, Vatican Commission for Justice and Peace. Member of Research Center for International Social Justice, University of Louvain, and Secretariat de Liaison et Recherche pour les Problemes de Population (Louvain).

WRITINGS:

People, Space, Food, Sheed (London), 1960.

Population Explosion and World Hunger, Hawthorn (Gloucestershire), 1963.

(Editor) *Christian Responsibility and World Poverty,* Newman (London), 1963.

World Poverty and the Christian, Hawthorn, 1963.

Poverty and Population, Catholic Social Guild (Oxford), 1964.

(Editor) *Leon Joseph Suenens: The Church in Dialogue,* Fides, 1965.

Cardinal Vaughan (biography), Burns & Oates (Kent, England), 1966.

Christian Initiation, Hawthorn (New York City), 1968.

The Population Problem, Crowell (New York City), 1970.

The Population Explosion: A Christian Concern (originally written as a pamphlet for the International Justice and Peace Commission of England and Wales), Harper (New York City), 1973.

Also author of *Multinational Investment: Boon or Burden for the Developing Countries,* 1980. Contributor to *Blackfriars, Commonweal, Tablet,* and other periodicals. Coeditor, *World Justice.*

WORK IN PROGRESS: Commentary on the Vatican Council document "The Church in the Modern World," for Benziger; studies on population, underdeveloped nations, marriage, sex, birth control, international social justice, pastoral sociology, freedom from hunger.

SIDELIGHTS: Population expert and author Arthur Gerard McCormack, a Roman Catholic priest whose views on population control conflicted with Catholic doctrine, earned international respect for his work to address the problem of world poverty. An adviser on population and developing countries to the Second Vatican Council in the 1960s, McCormack was instrumental in drafting the Church's plan to encourage progress and social justice throughout the world. He remained in Rome to work for the Pontifical Commission for Justice and Peace, but his support of artificial birth control as a means of curbing poverty in Third World countries caused him to lose favor with some Church officials, and he resigned his post in the 1970s. McCormack continued to focus on population issues, serving as a consultant to the World Population Congress in Bucharest from 1971 to 1975 and as a delegate to the 1984 non-governmental population conference in Mexico City, where he gave the concluding address.

OBITUARIES:

PERIODICALS

Times (London), January 2, 1993, p. 15.*

McCOY, Kathleen 1945-
(Kathy McCoy)

PERSONAL: Born April 25, 1945, in Dayton, OH; daughter of James Lyons (an engineer) and Caron (a nurse; maiden name, Curtis) McCoy; married Robert Miles Stover (a district manager of manufacturing), May 28, 1977. *Education:* Northwestern University, B.S., 1967, M.S., 1968; Pacific Western University, Ph.D., 1991; Antioch University, M.A., 1995.

ADDRESSES: Home and office—25665 Rancho Adobe Rd., Valencia, CA 91355. *Agent*—Susan Ann Protter, 110 West 40th St., Suite 1408, New York, NY 10022.

CAREER: Freelance writer, 1965-68, 1977—; *'Teen* magazine, Los Angeles, CA, feature editor, 1968-77; coordinator of clinical Ph.D. program, California School of Professional Psychology, 1992—. Adjunct member of faculty, Antioch College (West), 1973; guest lecturer, California State University, Los Angeles, 1974. Guest on radio and television talk shows.

MEMBER: Society of Professional Journalists, Women in Communications (Central Area representation, 1975-76), Screen Actors Guild.

AWARDS, HONORS: Eddie Award, Western Magazine Association, 1975, for a sex education/body awareness article in *'Teen* magazine; Maggie Award, 1984, for sex education column in *Seventeen* magazine; selection as one of "Best Books for Young Adults," American Library Association, 1980, for *The Teenage Body Book.*

WRITINGS:

UNDER NAME KATHY McCOY

Discover Yourself, Petersen Publishing (Los Angeles), 1976.

Discover Yourself II, Petersen Publishing, 1978.

(With Charles Wibbelsman) *The Teenage Body Book,* Pocket Books (New York City), 1979, revised edition, Simon & Schuster (New York City), 1984, new and revised edition published as *The New Teenage Body Book,* Body Press/Perigee (New York City), 1992.

The Teenage Survival Guide, Simon & Schuster, 1981.

Coping with Teenage Depression: A Parent's Guide, New American Library (New York City), 1982.

The Teenage Body Book Guide to Sexuality, Simon & Schuster, 1983.

The Teenage Body Book Guide to Dating, Simon & Schuster, 1983.

(With Wibbelsman) *Growing and Changing: A Handbook for Pre-teens,* Perigee (New York City), 1986.

Solo Parenting: Your Essential Guide, How to Find the Balance between Parenthood and Personhood, New American Library, 1987.

Changes and Choices: A Junior High Survival Guide, Perigee, 1989.

(With Wibbelsman) *Crisis-Proof Your Teenager,* Bantam (New York City), 1991.

Understanding Your Teenager's Depression: Issues, Insights, and Practical Guidance for Parents, Berkley Publishing (New York City), 1994.

Am I Crazy for Feeling So Bad?, Berkley Publishing, 1995.

Also author of educational scripts for Walt Disney Studios. Contributor to *Make the Good Things Happen,* edited by Judith D. Houghton, Bonnie Piedmonte, and Judy Thomas, Abelard-Schuman (New York City), 1976. Also contributor to numerous periodicals, including *Glamour, Mademoiselle, Redbook, Clinical Child Psychology,* and *TV Guide.* Contributing editor, *'Teen* magazine, 1978; columnist for *Seventeen* magazine, 1983-90.

WORK IN PROGRESS: Past Forgiving, nonfiction; *Leave or Stay,* nonfiction; *The Crocodiles Will Arrive Later,* a novel.

*　　　*　　　*

McCOY, Kathy
　　See McCOY, Kathleen

*　　　*　　　*

McMURDIE, Annie Laurie
　　See CASSIDAY, Bruce (Bingham)

*　　　*　　　*

McNAUGHTON, Colin 1951-

PERSONAL: Born May 18, 1951, in Wallsend-upon-Tyne, England; son of Thomas (a pattern maker) and May (Dixon) McNaughton; married Francoise (Julie), June 27, 1970; children: Ben, Timothy. *Education:* Central School of Art and Design, B.A., 1973; Royal College of Art, M.A., 1976.

ADDRESSES: Home—C 29 Odhams Walk, Covent Garden, London W.C. 2, England.

CAREER: Taught at Cambridge School of Art; freelance author and illustrator in London, England, 1976—.

AWARDS, HONORS: First Prize for Didactic Literature from the Cultural Activities Board of the city of Trento in association with the Children's Literature Department of the University of Padua, Italy, 1978, for *C'era una volta* (Italian edition of combined volumes *Colin McNaughton's*

ABC and Things and *Colin McNaughton's 1, 2, 3 and Things;* British Book Design and Production Award, 1989, for *Jolly Roger and the Pirates of Abdul the Skinhead,* and 1993, for *Who's That Banging on the Ceiling? A Multistory Story;* Kurt Maschler Award, 1991, for *Have You Seen Who's Just Moved in Next Door to Us?*

WRITINGS:

JUVENILE FICTION; SELF-ILLUSTRATED

Colin McNaughton's ABC and 1, 2, 3: A Book for All Ages for Reading Alone or Together, Doubleday, 1976, published in England in two volumes as *Colin McNaughton's ABC and Things* and *Colin McNaughton's 1, 2, 3 and Things,* Benn, 1976, also published in England in two volumes as *ABC and Things* and *1, 2, 3 and Things,* Macmillan, 1989.

(With Elizabeth Attenborough) *Walk, Rabbit, Walk,* Viking, 1977.

The Great Zoo Escape, Heinemann, 1978, Viking, 1979.

The Rat Race: The Amazing Adventures of Anton B. Stanton, Doubleday, 1978, Walker Books, 1988.

Anton B. Stanton and the Pirats, Doubleday, 1979, published in England as *The Pirats: The Amazing Adventures of Anton B. Stanton,* Benn, 1979.

Football Crazy, Heinemann, 1980, published in the U.S. as *Soccer Crazy,* McElderry Book, 1981.

King Nonn the Wiser, Heinemann, 1981.

If Dinosaurs Were Cats and Dogs, verses adapted by Alice Low, Four Winds Press, 1981, revised edition with verses by McNaughton, 1991.

Fat Pig (also see below), Benn, 1981, Puffin, 1987.

Crazy Bear, Holt, 1983.

"There's an Awful Lot of Weirdos in Our Neighborhood" and Other Wickedly Funny Verse, Simon & Schuster, 1987, published in England as *There's an Awful Lot of Weirdos in Our Neighbourhood: A Book of Rather Silly Verse and Pictures,* Walker Books, 1987.

Santa Claus Is Superman, Walker Books, 1988.

Jolly Roger and the Pirates of Abdul the Skinhead, Simon & Schuster, 1988.

Who's Been Sleeping in My Porridge? A Book of Silly Poems and Pictures, Ideals Children's Books, 1990.

Watch Out for the Giant-Killers!, Walker Books, 1991.

Guess Who Just Moved In Next Door?, Random House, 1991, published in England as *Have You Seen Who's Just Moved In Next Door to Us?,* Walker Books, 1991.

Who's That Banging On the Ceiling? A Multistory Story, Candlewick Press, 1992.

Making Friends with Frankenstein, Walker Books, 1993, Candlewick Press, 1994.

"BOOKS OF OPPOSITES" SERIES; JUVENILE; SELF-ILLUSTRATED

At Home, Philomel Books, 1982, published in England as *Long-Short: At Home,* Methuen/Walker Books, 1982.

At Playschool, Philomel Books, 1982, published in England as *Over-Under: At Playschool,* Methuen/Walker Books, 1982.

At the Party, Philomel Books, 1982, published in England as *Hide-Seek: At the Party,* Methuen/Walker Books, 1982.

At the Park, Philomel Books, 1982, published in England as *In-Out: At the Park,* Methuen/Walker Books, 1982.

At the Stores, Philomel Books, 1982, published in England as *Fat-Thin: At the Shops,* Methuen/Walker Books, 1982.

"VERY FIRST BOOKS" SERIES; JUVENILE; SELF-ILLUSTRATED

Spring, Methuen/Walker Books, 1983, Dial Books, 1984.

Summer, Methuen/Walker Books, 1983, Dial Books, 1984.

Autumn, Methuen/Walker Books, 1983, Dial Books, 1984.

Winter, Methuen/Walker Books, 1983, Dial Books, 1984.

ILLUSTRATOR

James Reeves, compiler, *The Springtime Book: A Collection of Prose and Poetry,* Heinemann, 1976.

Reeves, compiler, *The Autumn Book: A Collection of Prose and Poetry,* Heinemann, 1977.

Jenny Hawkesworth, *A Handbook of Family Monsters* (juvenile wit and humor), Dent, 1980.

Andrew Lang, compiler, *The Pink Fairy Book* (fairy tales), edited by Brian Alderson, revised edition (McNaughton was not associated with previous edition), Viking, 1982.

Robert Louis Stevenson, *Treasure Island,* Holt, 1993.

ILLUSTRATOR; JUVENILE FICTION

Hester Burton, *A Grenville Goes to Sea,* Heinemann, 1977.

Reeves, *Eggtime Stories,* Blackie & Son, 1978.

Mary McCaffrey, *The Mighty Muddle,* Eel Pie Publishing, 1979.

Wendy Wood, *The Silver Chanter: Traditional Scottish Tales and Legends* (juvenile), Chatto & Windus, 1980.

Emil Pacholek, *A Ship to Sail the Seven Seas,* Kestrel Books, 1980.

Allan Ahlberg, *Miss Brick the Builder's Baby,* Kestrel Books, 1981, Golden Press, 1982.

Ahlberg, *Mr. and Mrs. Hay the Horse,* Kestrel Books, 1981.

Russell Hoban, *The Great Fruit Gum Robbery,* Methuen/Walker Books, 1981, published as *The Great Gum Drop Robbery,* Philomel Books, 1982.

Hoban, *They Came from Aargh,* Philomel Books, 1981.

Hoban, *The Flight of Bembel Rudzuk,* Philomel Books, 1982.

Hoban, *The Battle of Zormla,* Philomel Books, 1982.

Ahlberg, *Mrs. Jolly's Joke Shop,* Kestrel Books, 1988.

ILLUSTRATOR; "RED NOSE READERS" SERIES BY ALLAN AHLBERG; JUVENILE

Help!, Random House, 1985.

Jumping, Random House, 1985.

Make a Face, Random House, 1985.

Big Bad Pig, Random House, 1985.

Fee Fi Fo Fum, Random House, 1985.

Happy Worm, Random House, 1985.

Bear's Birthday, Random House, 1985.

So Can I, Random House, 1985.

Shirley's Shops, Random House, 1986.

Push the Dog, Random House, 1986.

Crash, Bang, Wallop!, Random House, 1986.

Me and My Friend, Random House, 1986.

Blow Me Down, Random House, 1986.

Look Out for the Seals, Random House, 1986.

One Two Flea, Random House, 1986.

Tell Us a Story, Random House, 1986.

ILLUSTRATOR; "FOLDAWAYS" SERIES BY AHLBERG; JUVENILE

Circus, Granada/Collins, 1984, Derrydale Books, 1988.

Zoo, Granada/Collins, 1984, Derrydale Books, 1988.

Families, Granada/Collins, 1984, Derrydale Books, 1988.

Monsters, Granada/Collins, 1984, Derrydale Books, 1988.

ADAPTATIONS: Fat Pig was adapted for the stage as a rock musical in 1983 and has been produced in France, Germany, Austria, Great Britain, the United States, Finland, and Norway.

SIDELIGHTS: Since the mid-1970s, Colin McNaughton has charmed countless children with his cartoon-like illustrations for the books of popular authors such as Allan Ahlberg (*Mr. and Mrs. Hay the Horse*) and Russell Hoban (*The Great Gum Drop Robbery*). An interviewer in *Books for Keeps* says of McNaughton's native England that "there can be scarcely a child in the land who hasn't identified with his tumbling anthropomorphic animals and boisterous, chubby humans." With the publication of books such as *There's an Awful Lot of Weirdos in This Neighborhood, Jolly Roger and the Pirates of Abdul the Skinhead, Who's Been Sleeping in My Porridge? A Book of Silly Poems and Pictures,* and *Guess Who Just Moved in Next Door?,* children have been treated to McNaughton's own witty, rhyming tales and poems as well.

The *Books for Keeps* contributor also notes that Mc-Naughton's illustrations take their style from the comics of the artist's childhood and from Christmas annuals like *Beano* and *Dandy,* among others. McNaughton remarks in *Books for Keeps* that comics have been "rejected, looked down on, scorned, thought of as being cheap" but have seen a revival of late; "not only is [the comic format] a wonderful way of telling stories," he comments, "but it's the modern way for today's children: it's about movement, the step between film and the book."

"There's an Awful Lot of Weirdos in Our Neighborhood" and Other Wickedly Funny Verse marked McNaughton's first real movement into the giddy poetry that distinguishes his writings. Previously, financial constraints had McNaughton illustrating books one after another—fifty in ten years of work. In an interview with Scott Steedman for the Society for Young Publishers' *Inprint,* McNaughton explains that *"There's an Awful Lot of Weirdos in Our Neighborhood"* was the first book after nearly a decade to which he was able to devote any real time. Thus, Mc-Naughton tells Steedman, he considers *Weirdos* his "first book really," and adds, "I finally thought I was getting somewhere, doing what I wanted to do with books." Steedman also appreciates *Jolly Roger and the Pirates of Abdul the Skinhead,* calling it "hilarious . . . full of verbal and historical word-play, a clever parody of the pirate stories we all read and saw at the cinema as kids."

Brian Alderson in the London *Times* also lauds Mc-Naughton's work. He calls *Who's Been Sleeping in My Porridge?* a "dandified beano of a book," and praises the author's range, writing, "[McNaughton] can travel from limericks to lists, from puns to ballads, and all the time he finds the natural illustration." Of *Watch Out for the Giant-Killers!,* a story that takes up the popular ecology theme, Alderson writes that it is far more subtle—hence, successful—than most of its ilk. Alderson states that McNaughton's warning about the Amazonian rainforest "has none of the plonking didacticism that comes from less thoughtful artists."

As Hilary Macskill points out in *Nursery World,* the author "has been drawing abnormal beings—monsters, aliens, and giants—since he was a boy," and those monsters appear in his books, including *Making Friends with Frankenstein.* "He sees himself in a sense competing with comics, not just deriving inspiration from them," explains Macskill. "He says he would really like to see comic-readers poring over his books instead." She quotes Mc-Naughton as saying, "It's a bit of a crusade in my life to get children of seven and over reading picture books."

BIOGRAPHICAL/CRITICAL SOURCES:

BOOKS

Moss, Elaine, *Picture Books for Young People 9-13* (bibliography), Thimble, 1981.

PERIODICALS

Books for Keeps, Number 8, May, 1981; Number 37, March, 1986.
Inprint, April, 1989.
Nursery World, October 8, 1992, p. 14.
Times, June 2, 1990; June 1, 1991, p. 22.
Times Literary Supplement, November 22, 1991, p. 23.

*   *   *

McSHANE, Fred
See ELMAN, Richard

*   *   *

McSHERRY, Frank D(avid), Jr. 1927-

PERSONAL: Born December 18, 1927, in McAlester, OK; son of Frank D. (an attorney) and Mary (a teacher; maiden name, Clinton) McSherry. *Education:* Attended Texas A & M University, 1946, University of Oklahoma, 1947-48 and 1949-53, and University of Santo Tomas, 1948.

ADDRESSES: Home—314 West Jackson, McAlester, OK 74501.

CAREER: Commercial artist, 1953-74. Member of McAlester Friends of the Library, 1981-82, and McAlester Arts and Humanities Council. *Military service:* U.S. Army Air Forces, 1945-47.

MEMBER: McAlester Writers Guild (past president), Baker Street Irregulars (honorary member).

WRITINGS:

EDITOR; EXCEPT AS INDICATED

(With Martin H. Greenberg and Charles G. Waugh, and author of preface) *Baseball Three Thousand,* Elsevier (New York City)/Nelson, 1981.
(With Greenberg and Waugh, and author of preface) *A Treasury of American Horror Stories,* Crown (New York City)/Bonanza, 1985.
(With Greenberg and Waugh, and author of preface) *Detectives A-Z,* Crown/Bonanza, 1985.
(With Greenberg and Waugh) *Strange Maine,* Tapley, 1986.
(With Greenberg and Waugh, and author of preface) *Nightmares in Dixie,* August House (Little Rock, AR), 1987.

(With Carol-Lynn Roessel Waugh and Greenberg) *Murder and Mystery in Boston,* Dembner (New York City), 1987.

(With Waugh and Greenberg, and author of introduction) *Sunshine Crime,* Rutledge Press (New York City), 1987.

(With Roessel Waugh and Greenberg) *Murder and Mystery in Chicago,* Rutledge Press, 1987.

(With Waugh and Greenberg) *Cinemonsters,* TSR, Inc., 1987.

(With Waugh and Greenberg, and author of preface) *Dixie Ghosts,* Rutledge Press, 1988.

(With Waugh and Greenberg, and author of preface) *Yankee Witches,* Tapley, 1988.

(With Waugh and Greenberg) *Haunted New England,* Yankee Books (Dublin, NH), 1988.

(With Greenberg and Waugh, and author of preface) *Red Jack,* DAW Books (New York City), 1988.

(With Waugh and Greenberg) *Civil War Children,* August House, 1988.

(With Waugh and Greenberg, and author of preface) *Pirate Ghosts of the American Coast,* August House, 1988.

(With Waugh and Greenberg, and author of preface) *Mississippi River Tales,* August House, 1988.

(With Greenberg and Waugh, and author of introduction) *The Best Horror Stories of Arthur Conan Doyle,* Academy Chicago (Chicago), 1989.

(With Waugh and Greenberg) *Murder and Mystery in Maine,* Dembner, 1989.

(With Waugh and Greenberg, and author of preface) *A Treasury of American Mystery Stories,* Crown/Bonanza, 1989.

(With Waugh and Greenberg) *East Coast Ghosts,* Middle Atlantic, 1989.

(With Greenberg and Waugh) *The Fantastic World War II,* Baen, 1990.

(With Waugh and Greenberg, and author of preface) *Ghosts of the Heartlands,* Rutledge Press, 1990.

(With Waugh and Greenberg) *New England Ghosts,* Rutledge Press, 1990.

(With Waugh and Greenberg) *Eastern Ghosts,* Rutledge Press, 1990.

(With Waugh and Greenberg, and author of preface) *Western Ghosts,* Rutledge Press, 1990.

(Author of preface) Greenberg and Waugh, editors, *Devil Worshippers,* DAW Books, 1990.

(With Waugh) *Spooky Sea Stories,* Yankee Books, 1991.

(With Greenberg and Waugh, and author of preface) *Civil War Ghosts,* August House, 1991.

(With Waugh and Greenberg, and author of preface) *Hollywood Ghosts,* Rutledge Press, 1991.

(With Waugh and Greenberg) *The Fantastic Civil War,* Baen, 1991.

(With Waugh and Greenberg, and author of preface) *Great American Ghost Stories,* Rutledge Press, 1991.

(With Greenberg and Waugh, and author of preface) *Confederate Battle Stories,* August House, 1992.

(With Waugh and Greenberg, and author of preface) *More Dixie Ghosts,* Rutledge Press, 1994.

Studies in Scarlet, Borgo (San Bernardino, CA), in press.

Blink of an Eye, Borgo, in press.

Also author of *A Study in Black.* Contributor to numerous anthologies, including *Popular Culture and the Expanding Consciousness,* edited by Ray B. Browne, Wiley (New York City), *A Mystery Reader,* edited by Nancy Ellen Talburt and Lyna Lee Montgomery, Scribner (New York City), and *Villains, Detectives, and Heroes,* edited by Michael L. Cook, Greenwood Press (Westport, CT). Contributor of articles and stories to periodicals, including *Armchair Detective, Mike Shayne Mystery Magazine, Zane Grey Western, Mystery Fancier,* and *Mystery Reader's Newsletter.*

WORK IN PROGRESS: A Study in War, a psychoanalytic study of war and analysis of battle tactics by means of mass psychology; *The Vanishers in Fact and Fiction,* a study of people who mysteriously disappear; reference books on mystery, film, and science fiction (with Greenberg and Waugh), for Garland Publishing.

SIDELIGHTS: Frank D. McSherry, Jr., once told *CA:* "I am extremely interested in the use of psychoanalysis as a basis for the formation of an overall theory of both criminal behavior and military tactics. I hope the theory formed will explain past and future criminal behavior and permit prediction of the future and explanation of past military tactical actions. The basic theme of my writing is that intelligent use of the scientific method will solve our problems."

*   *   *

MEWSHAW, Michael 1943-

PERSONAL: Born February 19, 1943, in Washington, DC; son of John Francis and Mary Helen (Murphy Dunn) Mewshaw; married Linda Kirby, June 17, 1967; children: Sean, Marc. *Education:* University of Maryland, B.A., 1965; University of Virginia, M.A., 1966, Ph.D., 1970. *Religion:* Roman Catholic.

ADDRESSES: Home—Charlottesville, VA. *Agent*—Owen Laster, William Morris Agency, 1350 Sixth Ave., New York, NY 10019.

CAREER: University of Virginia, Charlottesville, instructor in English, 1970, visiting writer, 1989-91; University of Massachusetts, Amherst, assistant professor of English, 1970-71; University of Texas at Austin, began as assistant professor, became associate professor of English, 1973-83. American Academy, Rome, Italy, visiting artist, 1975-76, writer in residence, 1977-78.

MEMBER: PEN, Society of Fellows of the American Academy in Rome, Texas Institute of Letters, U.S. Tennis Writers Association, Phi Beta Kappa.

AWARDS, HONORS: Fulbright fellowship in creative writing, 1968-69; William Rainey fellowship to Bread Loaf Writers Conference, 1970; National Endowment for the Arts fellowship, 1974-75; Carr Collins Award for Best Book of Nonfiction, 1980 and 1983; Guggenheim Foundation grant, 1981-82; Book of the Year award from *Tennis Week*, 1993.

WRITINGS:

NOVELS

Man in Motion, Random House (New York City), 1970.
Waking Slow, Random House, 1972.
The Toll, Random House, 1974.
Earthly Bread, Random House, 1976.
Land without Shadow, Doubleday (New York City), 1979.
Year of the Gun, Atheneum (New York City), 1984.
Blackballed, Atheneum, 1986.
True Crime, Poseidon (New York City), 1991.

NONFICTION

Life for Death, Doubleday, 1980.
Short Circuit, Atheneum, 1983.
Money to Burn: The True Story of the Benson Family Murders, Atheneum, 1987.
Playing Away: Roman Holidays and Other Mediterranean Encounters, Atheneum, 1988.
Ladies of the Court: Grace and Disgrace on the Women's Tennis Tour, Crown (New York City), 1993.

OTHER

Contributor of short stories, poetry, articles, and reviews to various periodicals, including *Sewanee Review, London Magazine, New Statesman, Texas Monthly, Nation, European Travel and Life, Washington Post, Playboy, Travel Holiday, Los Angeles Times, Dallas Morning News, Architectural Digest,* and *New York Times Book Review.*

ADAPTATIONS: *Year of the Gun,* starring Andrew McCarthy and Sharon Stone, was adapted for film by director John Frankenheimer, 1991.

SIDELIGHTS: Michael Mewshaw has published varied works in several genres, including investigations of professional sports, travel essays, mystery novels, and nonfiction

accounts of highly-publicized murder cases. He finished his first novel, *Man in Motion,* while in Europe on a Fulbright fellowship. "Strictly speaking," he comments in a *Library Journal* article, "[*Man in Motion*] is not autobiographical, but it obviously partakes of my own experience and of what I have observed of others. . . . [It is] the story of a man who flees and returns, and who may flee again, but who for once recognizes his limitations and realizes the absolute necessity of coming to grips with what he has tried to leave, but which refuses to leave him."

Reviewing *Man in Motion* for the *Washington Post,* Larry McMurtry compares it to Jack Kerouac's *On the Road:* "Both are picaresques; both record journeys across America; both wear themselves out in Mexico." The similarity, he finds, ends there. Kerouac's book is more romantic as it "records the exhilaration of a generation at finding it could move." Mewshaw's hero, however, discovers that "moving is finally just tiring." McMurtry believes that along with "the requisite novelistic skills . . . [Mewshaw] has something more important, and rarer: an instinct for subjects in which something human and crucial is at stake."

In many of his novels, Mewshaw combines an adventure story with questions of moral responsibility. *Nation* reviewer Alan Cheuse remarks: "Mewshaw, unlike many of our contemporaries, focuses as much on problems of conscience as on problems of consciousness. . . . [He] creates first-rate adventure narrative about believable characters set in an atmosphere of moral rigor." Yet Mewshaw refrains from didacticism. *New York Times Book Review* critic Jerome Charyn commends the author's restraint in *Land without Shadow,* saying that the book is remarkable because "it does not create a simplified scheme of good guys and bad guys. It is a novel of dangling men and women, brittle causes and fears. . . . [It] disturbs without preaching to us."

Several critics acknowledge *The Toll* as Mewshaw's best work up to that point. Writing in the *New York Times Book Review,* James R. Frakes calls it "one of the most thoroughgoing strippings-away of man's pretensions to humanity since *Last Exit to Brooklyn*—but this time on the level of pure action and impure motives, noble rhetoric curdled into yellow bile, idealism boiled down to gut-survival, flower children rotting on a compost heap." The novel's protagonist, Ted Kuyler, becomes involved with five American hippies who need his help in freeing their friend from a Moroccan jail. A rivalry between Kuyler and the group's pseudorevolutionary leader develops, creating conflicts which lead the group to bribery, deceit, betrayal, and murder. Frakes remarks that "these middle-class freedom fighters stink with deception and self-indulgence and doom themselves by refusing to acknowledge the existence of limits."

Best Sellers critic V. A. Salamone states that although *The Toll* is "another contemporary novel loaded with violence . . . [it] is definitely a spellbinder. . . . Among all this violence and decay many human values are interwoven which gives some moral worth." *New Statesman*'s Peter Straub compares the novel to Roman Polanski's film *Chinatown*: "Value is invented and local and the world a primal disorder. . . . As in that film, good intentions, experience, passion and foresight, the qualities which should create cases of order, come to nothing."

Life for Death, Mewshaw's first nonfiction book, tells the story of Wayne Dresbach, Mewshaw's childhood friend, who at the age of fifteen shot and killed his socially prominent, adoptive parents one morning in January 1961. Dresbach was given a one-day trial, convicted in twelve minutes, and sentenced to life in prison. In 1978 Mewshaw began his own investigation by interviewing the paroled Dresbach and others connected with the case. His probing uncovered a bizarre tale of child abuse, alcoholism, and sexual experimentation as the motivating force behind the murders. The community and criminal justice system had conspired to conceal this information from the jury, and fear and shame prevented the boy from revealing it.

In the *New York Times Book Review,* contributor Tom Buckley calls the book "a modest, scrupulous rendering of a story of a boy's multiple betrayals that is almost Dickensian in its intensity." *Dictionary of Literary Biography* writer Jean Wyrick comments, "Once more, Mewshaw's powers of description not only enable him to recreate the tragic series of events leading to the murders but also to dramatize accurately and expose the facade of propriety surrounding the case—a facade which silenced witnesses and cost an abused child twenty years of his life."

Following the completion of *Life for Death,* Mewshaw shifted gears and began a six-month chronicle of the men's professional tennis tour entitled *Short Circuit.* After conducting countless interviews with various players, tour officials, and agents, Mewshaw quickly concluded that the sport was riddled with financial corruption. In his book, he asserts that illegal activities, such as the awarding of bonus money for big-name players to participate in tournaments and the frequent "tanking" of matches, existed and became an accepted practice as the tour increased in popularity. The impact of *Short Circuit*'s publication in 1983 was felt immediately, as tennis star Guillermo Vilas was heavily fined and suspended for one year after it was discovered that he had accepted large sums of participation money from tournament organizers.

Although many critics applaud Mewshaw's investigative abilities and results in *Short Circuit,* others ultimately fail to see much point in conducting the expose. Art Seidenbaum argues in the *Los Angeles Times Book Review* that,

despite his impressive "detective" work, Mewshaw exposes nothing new: "Most of the abuses [Mewshaw] chronicles can be reduced to a few simple facts: Sports is often more entertainment than competition, big money and corruption are rarely strangers to each other, overpaid and pampered youngsters are often selfish. Perhaps I've been too long at the fair, but this information comes as no surprise." Charles Leerhsen, writing in *Newsweek,* agrees: "Mewshaw sometimes seems in danger of swooning over rumors and allegations that have been known to the pretzel vendors at Forest Hills for years."

Playing Away: Roman Holidays and Other Mediterranean Encounters, a collection of short travel essays first published in *European Travel and Life* magazine, offers a realistic portrait of Italy, France and North Africa. In the *New York Times Book Review,* Tim Cahill attempts to capture the feeling of the essays, quoting from Mewshaw's examination of the Roman autumn: "If the streets are the Romans' real home, then during these first wet, chill days, the city has the haunted look of a home abandoned. Grass sprouts in the cracks between the cobblestones, and white marble slabs become veined with green moss. Metal flanges and bolts that help hold together the classical antiquities bleed rust. A vast loneliness settles over the city, and nothing is more forlorn than the empty piazzas where puddles swell slowly into lakes, and tables and chairs are stacked haphazardly outside of cafes like jetsam tossed up by high tide."

Mewshaw once told *CA:* "In some ways *Man in Motion* is more than the title of my first novel. I've spent most of my adult life traveling, sometimes out of curiosity, sometimes out of boredom, more often a combination of both." In an article for the *Nation,* Mewshaw explains: "Personally I would prefer to go to places where at first I don't speak the language or know anybody, where I easily lose my direction and have no delusions that I'm in control. Feeling disoriented, even frightened, I find myself awake, alive, in ways I never would at home. All my senses suddenly alert, I can hear again, smell, see—and afterward, if I'm lucky, I can write."

BIOGRAPHICAL/CRITICAL SOURCES:

BOOKS

Contemporary Literary Criticism, Volume 9, Gale, 1978.
Dictionary of Literary Biography Yearbook: 1980, Gale, 1981.
Garrett, George, editor, *The Writer's Voice: Conversations with Contemporary Writers,* Morrow, 1973.

PERIODICALS

Best Sellers, March 1, 1974.
Chicago Tribune Book World, June 17, 1979.
Chronicle of Higher Education, October 18, 1976.

Library Journal, June 15, 1970.
Los Angeles Times Book Review, October 12, 1980; September 4, 1983; February 26, 1984; July 21, 1991.
Nation, June 3, 1978; June 7, 1979.
New Statesman, August 23, 1974.
Newsweek, August 8, 1983.
New Yorker, September 13, 1976.
New York Times, September 12, 1976.
New York Times Book Review, March 24, 1974; June 17, 1979; August 24, 1980; August 7, 1983; October 2, 1983; May 20, 1984; November 30, 1986; September 13, 1987; June 10, 1990; June 30, 1991.
Publishers Weekly, April 12, 1993.
Times Literary Supplement, June 17, 1977.
Village Voice, August 9, 1983.
Washington Post, October 3, 1970.
Washington Post Book World, July 19, 1987; June 9, 1991.

*   *   *

MEYENDORFF, John 1926-1992

PERSONAL: Born February 17, 1926, in Neuilly-sur-Seine, France; died of pancreatic cancer, July 22, 1992, in Montreal, Quebec, Canada; son of Theophile (a painter) and Catherine (Schidlovsky) Meyendorff; married Marie Mojaysky, January 26, 1950; children: Paul, Serge, Elizabeth, Anna. *Education:* University of Paris, B.Ph., B.D., and Licencie-es-Lettres, 1948, Diplome d'etudes superieres, 1949, Diplome de l'Ecole Partique des Hautes Etudes, 1954, and Docteur-es-Lettres, 1958.

CAREER: Priest of Eastern Orthodox Church. Orthodox Theological Institute, Paris, 1950-59, began as lecturer, became assistant professor of church history; St. Vladimir's Orthodox Theological Seminary, Tuckahoe, NY, professor of church history and patristics, 1959-84, dean emeritus, 1984-92. Harvard University, Dumbarton Oaks Research Library and Collection, lecturer in Byzantine theology, 1959-67, and acting director of studies, 1977. Adjunct professor in department of religion, Columbia University, 1962-67; professor of Byzantine history, Fordham University, 1967. Centre National de la Recherche Scientique, research fellow, 1953-56. World Council of Churches, former chair of Faith and Order Commission, was member of central committee; Syndesmos, cofounder and first general secretary; U.S. Committee of Byzantine Studies, was member of executive committee.

MEMBER: Orthodox Theological Society of America, American Patristics Association, British Academy (fellow).

AWARDS, HONORS: LL.D., University of Notre Dame, 1966; National Endowment for the Humanities fellow, 1977-78; Guggenheim fellow, 1981.

WRITINGS:

Introduction a l'etude de Gregoire Palamas, Editions du Seuil, 1959, translation by George Lawrence published as *A Study of Gregory Palamas,* Faith Press, 1964.
St. Gregoire Palamas et la mystique orthodoxe, Editions du Seuil, 1959, translation published as *St. Gregory Palamas and Orthodox Spirituality,* St. Vladimir's Seminary Press (Crestwood, NY), 1974.
(Editor and author of commentary and critical notes) *Gregory Palamas, Defense des saints hesychastes,* two volumes, [Louvain], 1959, 2nd edition, 1974, translation published as *Gregory Palamas,* Paulist Press (Ramsey, NJ), 1983.
L'Eglise Orthodoxe hier et aujourd'hui, Editions du Seuil, 1960, 2nd edition, 1969, translation by John Chapin published as *The Orthodox Church: Its Past and Its Role in the World Today,* Pantheon (New York City), 1962, revised edition with additions by author, Darton, Longman, & Todd, 1962.
Orthodoxie et catholicite, Editions du Seuil, 1965, translation published as *Orthodoxy and Catholicity,* Sheed, 1966.
Le Christ dans la theologie byzantine, Editions du Cerf, 1969, translation published as *Christ in Eastern Christian Thought,* Corpus Books, 1969, 2nd edition, St. Vladimir's Seminary Press, 1975.
Marriage: An Orthodox Perspective, St. Vladimir's Seminary Press, 1970.
Byzantine Hesychasm: Historical and Theological Problems, Variorum, 1973.
(Editor with Joseph McLelland) *The New Man: An Orthodox and Reformed Dialogue,* Agora Books, 1973.
Byzantine Theology, Fordham University Press (Bronx, NY), 1974.
Living Tradition, St. Vladimir's Seminary Press, 1976.
The Legacy of Byzantium in the Orthodox Church, St. Vladimir's Seminary Press, 1981.
Byzantium and the Rise of Russia: A Study of Byzantino-Russian Relations in the Fourteenth Century, Cambridge University Press (New York City), 1981.
Catholicity and the Church, St. Vladimir's Seminary Press, 1983.
(Editor with Bernard McGinn and Jean Leclercq) *Christian Spirituality: Origins to the Twelfth Century,* Crossroad (New York City), 1985.
Vvedenie v sviatootecheskoe bogoslovie: konspekty lektsii, RBR (New York City), 1985.
(Editor with Jill Raitt and McGinn) *Christian Spirituality: High Middle Ages and Reformation,* Crossroad, 1987.
The Vision of Unity, St. Vladimir's Seminary Press, 1987.
Witness to the World, St. Vladimir's Seminary Press, 1987.

(Editor with Louis Dupre and Don E. Saliers) *Christian Spirituality: Post-Reformation and Modern,* Crossroad, 1989.

Imperial Unity and Christian Divisions: The Church, 450-680 AD, St. Vladimir's Seminary Press, 1989.

(Editor with John Breck and E. Silk) *The Legacy of St. Vladimir: Byzantium, Russia, America,* St. Vladimir's Seminary Press, 1990.

(With N. B. Artamonova) *Vizantiia i Moskovskaia Rus': ocherk po istorii tserkovnykh i kul'turnykh sviazei v XIV veke,* YMCA-Press (Paris), 1990.

(Editor and author of introduction with Robert Tobias) *Salvation in Christ: A Lutheran-Orthodox Dialogue,* Augsburg (Minneapolis, MN), 1992.

The Primacy of Peter: Historical and Ecclesiological Studies, St. Vladimir's Seminary Press, 1992.

(With Aristeides Papadakis) *The Christian East and the Rise of the Papacy: The Church 1071-1453 A.D.,* St. Vladimir's Seminary Press, 1994.

St. Vladimir's Seminary Quarterly, editor, 1959-84; editorial advisor and contributor, *Encyclopaedia Britannica.*

The Orthodox Church has also been published in Italian, Spanish, Dutch, and German editions.

BIOGRAPHICAL/CRITICAL SOURCES:

PERIODICALS

Times Literary Supplement, March 13, 1981.

OBITUARIES:

PERIODICALS

Chicago Tribune, July 26, 1992, section 2, p. 6.
New York Times, July 24, 1992, p. D16.*

*　　　*　　　*

MILLER, Barbara S(toler)　1940-1993

PERSONAL: Born August 8, 1940, in New York, NY; died of cancer, April 19, 1993, in New York, NY; daughter of Louis O. (a business executive) and Sara (Cracken) Stoler; married James Robert Miller (divorced); married Max Greenwood; children: Gwenn Alison. *Education:* Barnard College, A.B. (magna cum laude), 1962; Columbia University, M.A., 1964; University of Pennsylvania, Ph.D. (with distinction), 1968.

CAREER: Columbia University, Barnard College, New York City, assistant professor, 1968-72, associate professor, 1972-77, professor of Oriental studies, 1977-93, Samuel R. Milbank Professor, 1987-93, chair of department, 1972-74, 1979-87. American Council of Learned Societies-Social Science Research Council, member of Joint Com-

mittee on South Asia, 1982-87, member of Joint Committee on International Programs, 1988-93. Director of a summer seminar for college teachers, National Endowment for the Humanities, 1981. Member of publication board, Columbia University Press, 1973-79; faculty representative, Barnard College Board of Trustees, 1976-79; cochair, Barnard Studies in the Humanities, 1978-93; Columbia University Society of Fellows in the Humanities, member of governing board, 1978-93, chair, 1986-88; member of executive committee, Southern Asia Institute, Columbia, 1979-93; board member, American Council of Learned Societies, 1988. Member of advisory committee, Princeton University Press, 1980-86; member of advisory council on archaeology, anthropology, and related disciplines, Smithsonian Institution, 1983-85. Scholarly adviser to Peter Brooks on *The Mahabharata,* 1988-89.

MEMBER: PEN (member of translation committee), American Oriental Society (director-at-large, 1981-83), Association for Asian Studies (president, 1990-91), American Numismatic Society, Phi Beta Kappa.

AWARDS, HONORS: Avery and Jule Hopwood Award for writing, University of Michigan, 1959; Woodrow Wilson fellow, 1962; National Defense Foreign Language fellow, 1962-63; American Institute of Indian Studies, senior fellow, 1974-75, 1981-82, travel grant, summer, 1977; Guggenheim fellow, 1974-75; Mellon fellow, 1976; National Council of Women award, 1979, for work in higher education; Social Science Research Council, South Asia fellow, 1981-82; L.H.D., Mount Holyoke College, 1989. Also recipient of a number of grants or stipends from American Association of University Women, 1965-66, National Endowment for the Humanities, summer, 1971, American Philosophical Society, summer, 1971, National Endowment for the Humanities, 1971, 1981, 1986, and 1988, American Council of Learned Societies, 1973 and 1978, Smithsonian Institution, 1981.

WRITINGS:

(Translator from the Sanskrit) D. D. Kosambi, editor, *Bhartrihari: Poems,* Columbia University Press (New York City), 1967.

(Editor and translator from the Sanskrit) *Phantasies of a Love-Thief: The Caurapancasika Attributed to Bilhana,* Columbia University Press, 1970.

(With Leonard Gordan) *A Syllabus of Indian Civilization,* Columbia University Press, 1971.

(Contributor) Jaroslav Prusek, editor, *The Dictionary of Oriental Literatures,* Basic Books (New York City), 1973.

(Editor and translator from the Sanskrit) *Love Song of the Dark Lord: Jayedeva's Gitagovinda,* Oxford University Press (New York City), 1977.

The Hermit and the Horse-Thief: Sanskrit Poems of Bhartrihari and Bilhana, Columbia University Press, 1978.

(Translator from the Spanish) Agueda Pizzaro, *Sombraventadora/Shadowinnower,* Columbia University Press, 1979.

(Editor and author of biographical essay) *Exploring India's Sacred Art: Selected Papers of Stella Kramrisch,* University of Pennsylvania Press (Philadelphia, PA), 1983.

(Contributor) *Essays in Gupta Culture,* Motilal Banarsidas (Delhi, India), 1983.

(Editor and translator from the Sanskrit) *Theatre of Memory: The Plays of Kalidasa,* Columbia University Press, 1984.

(Editor with Mildred Archer) William G. Archer, *Songs for the Bride: Wedding Rites of Rural India,* Brooklyn College Press (Brooklyn, NY), 1985.

(Translator from the Sanskrit) *The Bhagavadgita: Krishna's Counsel in Time of War,* Columbia University Press, 1986.

(Editor) *The Powers of Art: Patronage in Indian Culture,* Oxford University Press, 1992.

(Editor) *Masterworks of Asian Literature in Comparative Perspective: A Guide for Teaching,* M. E. Sharpe (Armonk, NY), 1994.

Also contributor to *The Divine Consort,* 1982. Contributor to numerous journals. Guest editor, *Journal of South Asian Literature,* 1971. Member of editorial board, *Translations from the Oriental Classics,* Columbia University Press, 1975-93.

SIDELIGHTS: Barbara S. Miller once told *CA:* "My close rereading of works of American and European literature in the context of Asian works has stimulated me to return to a major preoccupation of my student years: the writing of poetry and fiction. I am currently at work on a novel, tentatively entitled *A Nest of Mothers.* In it I am examining the relationships among an orphaned young Russian woman, her brother (an air force pilot 'lost' in the Himalayan foothills while flying a transport plane from India to China in 1944), her two aunts (one a poet, the other a physician), and her foster mother (an eccentric collector of Oriental art). The characters are modeled on various members of my family, partly based on diaries, poems, and other documents that have recently come into my possession.

"I feel that the novel is the most appropriate form in which to express the range of my ideas about the 'encounter' with Asia. Rather than conflicting with my scholarly work, the long and highly disciplined sessions of analyzing my fictional characters are helping me to 'flesh out' the personalities of the elusive kings, priests, and poets of ancient India."

Miller was competent in French, Spanish, Hindi, Sanskrit, Pali, and Prakrits. She traveled extensively in India and also in other parts of Asia, Europe, South America, and Africa.

BIOGRAPHICAL/CRITICAL SOURCES:

PERIODICALS

Antioch Review, spring, 1980.
Times Literary Supplement, December 23, 1983.

OBITUARIES:

PERIODICALS

New York Times, April 20, 1993, p. B8.*

*   *   *

MOHLER, James A(ylward) 1923-

PERSONAL: Born July 22, 1923, in Toledo, OH; son of Edward Francis (a teacher and writer) and Gertrude (Aylward) Mohler. *Education:* Xavier University, Cincinnati, OH, Litt.B., 1946; Bellarmine School of Theology, Ph.L., 1949, S.T.L., 1956; Loyola University, Chicago, M.S.I.R., 1960; University of Ottawa, Ph.D., 1964; University of St. Paul, S.T.D., 1965. *Avocational interests:* Photography, horticulture, viticulture, fishing, the outdoors.

ADDRESSES: Office—John Carroll University, University Heights, Cleveland, OH 44118.

CAREER: Entered Society of Jesuits, 1942, ordained Roman Catholic priest, 1955. St. Ignatius High School, Chicago, IL, teacher, 1949-52; Jesuit Indian Mission, Sault Sainte Marie, MI, teacher, 1954-56; John Carroll University, Cleveland, OH, instructor, 1960-65, assistant professor, 1965-69, associate professor, 1969-74, professor of religious studies, 1974-94, professor emeritus, 1994—, director of Bernet Hall, 1960-62. Member of Pastoral Ministry, Catholic Diocese of Cleveland. Visiting scholar, Union Theological Seminary, New York City, 1966; research fellow at institutes, colleges, and universities in the United States and abroad, including Institute Saint Serge, Paris, 1968, Tien Educational Institute, People's Republic of China, 1972, St. Xavier's College, Bombay, 1974, and Yale University, 1978. Spiritual and retreat director. Consulting theologian.

MEMBER: Catholic Theological Society of America, American Academy of Religion, College Theology Society, American Association of University Professors, Association for Asian Studies.

WRITINGS:

Man Needs God: An Interpretation of Biblical Faith, John Carroll University Press (Cleveland), 1966.

(With others) *Speaking of God,* edited by D. Dirscherl, Bruce Publishing, 1967.

The Beginning of Eternal Life: The Dynamic Faith of Thomas Aquinas, Origins and Interpretation, Philosophical Library (New York City), 1968.

Dimensions of Faith, Yesterday and Today, Loyola University Press (Chicago), 1969.

The Origin and Evolution of the Priesthood, Alba House (Staten Island, NY), 1970.

The Heresy of Monasticism: The Christian Monks, Types and Anti-Types, Alba House, 1971.

The School of Jesus: An Overview of Christian Education, Yesterday and Today, Alba House, 1973.

Cosmos, Man, God, Messiah: An Introduction to Religion, John Carroll University Press, 1973.

Dimensions of Love, East and West, Doubleday (New York City), 1975.

Sexual Sublimation and the Sacred, John Carroll University Press, 1978.

The Sacrament of Suffering, Fides/Claretian (Chicago), 1979.

Dimensions of Prayer, John Carroll University Press, 1981.

Love, Marriage, and the Family, Yesterday and Today, Alba House, 1982.

Paradise: Gardens of the Gods, Satya Press, 1984.

Health, Healing, and Holiness: Medicine and Religion, Satya Press, 1986.

Late Have I Loved You: Augustine on Human and Divine Relationships, An Interpretation, New City Press (Brooklyn, NY), 1991.

A Speechless Child Is the Word of God: Augustine on the Trinity, Christ, Mary, Church and Sacraments, Prayer, Hope and the Two Cities, New City Press, 1992.

Contributor to various religion journals.

WORK IN PROGRESS: Books on suffering, the theology of work, abortion, confession, modern mystics, hope and the Eucharist.

SIDELIGHTS: James A. Mohler is competent in Latin, Greek, French, Italian, German, Spanish, and Chinese.

*　　　*　　　*

MONTAGUE, Jeanne
See YARDE, Jeanne Betty Frances

*　　　*　　　*

MORIARITY, J.
See KELLY, Tim

MORRIS, Vera
See KELLY, Tim

*　　　*　　　*

MORSE, Roger A(lfred) 1927-

PERSONAL: Born July 5, 1927, in Saugerties, NY; son of Grant D. (a superintendent of schools) and Margery A. (a teacher; maiden name, Saxe) Morse; married Mary Lou Smith, October 6, 1951; children: Joseph G., Susan A., Mary Ann. *Education:* Cornell University, B.S., 1950, M.S., 1953, Ph.D., 1955. *Politics:* Republican. *Avocational interests:* Farming; cutting emeralds, rubies, and sapphires.

ADDRESSES: Home—278 Lower Creek Rd., Ithaca, NY 14850. *Office*—Department of Entomology, Comstock Hall, Cornell University, Ithaca, NY 14853.

CAREER: State Plant Board of Florida, Gainesville, apiculturist (beekeeper), 1955-57; University of Massachusetts, Field Station, Amherst, assistant professor of horticulture, 1957; Cornell University, Ithaca, NY, assistant professor, 1957-64, associate professor, 1964-70, professor of apiculture, 1970—, chairman, department of entomology, 1986-89. Visiting professor of apiculture, University of the Philippines, 1968, University of Sao Paulo, 1978, and University of Helsinki, 1989; guest lecturer at colleges and universities. Member, Tompkins County Fair Board, 1970-77, and Tompkins County Board of Representatives, 1975; former volunteer fire chief. Advisor on bee disease control and management programs in numerous countries; consultant to the Food and Agriculture Organization of the United Nations and to private companies. *Military service:* U.S. Army, 1944-47; became staff sergeant.

MEMBER: International Union for the Study of Social Insects, International Bee Research Association (vice-chair of council; chair of American committee), Rotary International (president of Ithaca section, 1979-80), Entomological Society of America (fellow; president of Eastern branch, 1989; member of numerous committees), American Association for the Advancement of Science (fellow), Philippine Association of Entomologists, Eastern Apicultural Society, Florida Entomological Society, New York Academy of Science, Sigma Xi, Delta Sigma Rho, Phi Kappa Tau.

AWARDS, HONORS: Fifteen travel and research grants from National Science Foundation, beginning 1961; research grant from U.S. Army, 1966; three research grants from National Institute of Health; five research grants from U.S. Department of Agriculture; two research grants from Environmental Protection Agency; two grants from New York State Department of Agriculture and Markets;

Apimondia Gold Medal, 1979, for *Honey Bee Pests, Predators, and Diseases;* Apimondia Silver Medal, 1981, for *Making Mead;* honorary doctorate degree, Akademia Rolnicza, Poland, 1989.

WRITINGS:

The Complete Guide to Beekeeping, Dutton (New York), 1972, 5th edition published as *The New Complete Guide to Beekeeping,* Countryman Press (Woodstock, VT), 1994.
Bees and Beekeeping, Cornell University Press (Ithaca, NY), 1975.
(Editor) *Honey Bee Pests, Predators, and Diseases,* Cornell University Press, 1978, 3rd edition, A. I. Root (Medina, OH), 1995.
Comb Honey Production, Wicwas Press, 1979.
Rearing Queen Honey Bees, Wicwas Press, 1980, revised edition, 1994.
(Editor of English edition) Henrik Hanson, *Honey Bee Brood Diseases,* Danish State Bee Disease Committee, 1980.
Making Mead, Wicwas Press, 1981.
A Year in the Beeyard, Scribner (New York), 1983.
(Editor with Ted Hooper) *The Illustrated Encyclopedia of Beekeeping,* Dutton, 1984.
(With William L. Coggshall) *Beeswax: Production, Harvesting, Processing and Products,* Wicwas Press, 1985.
ABC and XYZ of Bee Culture, 40th edition (Morse was not associated with earlier editions), A. I. Root, 1990.

Contributor to *Honey,* edited by Eva Crane, Bee Research Association, 1975. *Annals of the Entomological Society of America,* member of editorial board, 1972-76, chair of editorial board, 1976. Contributor of hundreds of articles to conservation, natural history, and beekeeping journals. Research editor of *Gleanings in Bee Culture,* 1959—.

Some of Morse's books have appeared in Russian, Italian, Romanian, Portuguese, and Vietnamese editions.

WORK IN PROGRESS: Honey and Pollen Plants of North America; Pollination of Commercial Agricultural Crops and *Pollination of All Agricultural Crops,* both for A. I. Root; *Honey: Processing and Packaging; An Updated History of the Empire State Honey Producers Association; A History of American Beekeeping; A History of Cornell University Entomology.*

SIDELIGHTS: Regarding *The Illustrated Encyclopedia of Beekeeping,* edited by Roger A. Morse and Ted Hooper, Dorothy Galton writes in the *Times Literary Supplement* that "every possible subject connected with honey-bees and bee-keeping (excluding bumble and other solitary bees) is covered in language as simple as the subject allows. . . . The *Encyclopedia* will answer practically every question the amateur and specialist may ask, and it can be recommended as replacement for all existing books on the subject written for readers using modern methods of beekeeping."

Morse has spent a total of a year studying bees in Asia and has made numerous study trips to Europe, Africa, and South America. He also holds a U.S. patent on a method of making wine from honey.

BIOGRAPHICAL/CRITICAL SOURCES:

PERIODICALS

Times Literary Supplement, August 23, 1985.

*   *   *

MUNN, Geoffrey C(harles) 1953-

PERSONAL: Born April 11, 1953, in Hastings, Sussex, England; son of Stewart Hayden (in British Navy) and Heather Rosemary (a homemaker; maiden name, Hollingworth) Munn; married Caroline Teresa Watney (a homemaker), April 9, 1983; children: Alexander, Edward. *Politics:* None. *Religion:* Church of England.

ADDRESSES: Home—2 Palace Grove, Fox Hill, London SE19 2XD, England. *Office*—Wartski Ltd., 14 Grafton St., London W1X 4DE, England.

CAREER: Wartski Ltd., London, England, managing director, 1973—.

MEMBER: Society of Antiquaries (fellow), Worshipful Company of Goldsmiths (freeman).

WRITINGS:

Castellani and Giulano: Revivalist Jewellers of the Nineteenth Century, Rizzoli International, 1984.
(With Charlotte Gere) *Artists' Jewellery: Pre-Raphaelite to Arts and Crafts Monuments,* Antique Collectors Club, 1989.
The Triumph of Love: Amatory Jewelry from the Renaissance to Art Deco, Thames & Hudson, 1993.

Contributor to art journals and newspapers.

*   *   *

MYERS, R(obert) E(ugene) 1924-

PERSONAL: Born January 15, 1924, in Los Angeles, CA; son of Harold Eugene and Margaret (Anawalt) Myers; married Patricia A. Tazer, August 17, 1956; children: Edward E., Margaret A., Hal R., Karen I. *Education:* University of California, Berkeley, A.B., 1955; Reed College, M.A., 1960; University of Minnesota, additional study,

1960-63; University of Georgia, Ed.D., 1968. *Politics:* Democrat. *Religion:* Protestant.

ADDRESSES: Home—1457 Meadow Ct., Healdsburg, CA 95448.

CAREER: Elementary school teacher in Oregon, California, and Minnesota, 1954-61; Augsburg College, Minneapolis, MN, assistant professor of education, 1962-63; University of Oregon, Eugene, assistant professor of education, 1963-66; elementary school teacher in Eugene, 1966-67; University of Victoria, British Columbia, associate professor of education and associate director of teacher education, 1968-70; associate research professor of education in Teaching Research Division, Oregon State System of Higher Education, 1970-73; Northwestern, Inc., Portland, OR, filmmaker, 1973-74; University of Portland, Portland, OR, associate professor of education, 1974-75; freelance film producer, 1975-77; Oregon State Department of Education, Salem, learning resources specialist, 1977-81; Linn-Benton Education Service District, Albany, OR, curriculum coordinator, 1981-87. Visiting professor, San Diego State University, Northeastern Louisiana University, Winona State University, Oregon College of Education, University of Victoria, Paine College, and Texas Tech University. Has appeared on various television programs. *Military service:* U.S. Merchant Marines, 1943-45.

MEMBER: International Reading Association, National Association for Gifted Children (member of board of directors, 1974-77), Mid-Valley Reading Council (member of board of directors).

AWARDS, HONORS: Outstanding book award, Pi Lambda Theta, 1972, for *Creative Learning and Teaching;* Golden Eagle, Council on International Nontheatrical Events, 1973, for film *Feather.*

WRITINGS:

(With E. Paul Torrance) *Creative Learning and Teaching,* Dodd (New York City), 1970.

JUVENILE

(With Torrance) *Invitations to Thinking and Doing* (with teacher's guide), Ginn (Needham, MA), 1965.
(With Torrance) *Invitations to Speaking and Writing Creatively* (with teacher's guide), Ginn, 1965.
(With Torrance) *Can You Imagine?* (with teacher's guide), Ginn, 1965.
(With Torrance) *Plots, Puzzles, and Ploys* (with teacher's guide), Ginn, 1966.
(With Torrance) *For Those Who Wonder* (with teacher's guide), Ginn, 1966.
(With Torrance) *Stretch* (with teacher's guide), Perceptive, 1968.

It's a Butterfly! (with audio cassette), United Learning, 1977.
It's a Dolphin! (with audio cassette), United Learning, 1977.
It's a Squirrel! (with audio cassette), United Learning, 1977.
It's a Toad! (with audio cassette), United Learning, 1977.
It's an Alligator! (with audio cassette), United Learning, 1977.
Wondering, Creative Learning Press (Mansfield Center, CT), 1984.
Imagining, Creative Learning Press, 1985.
What Next?, Zephyr Press (Somerville, MA), 1994.
Facing the Issues, Zephyr Press, 1995.

JUVENILE FILMSTRIPS

Animal Friends, A.I.M.S. Instructional Media, 1974.
Exploring the Unexplained, United Learning, 1974.
Investigating the Unknown, United Learning, 1974.
Sing along with Animals, United Learning, 1975.
Hand Tools: An Introduction to Working with Wood and Plastic, A.I.M.S. Instructional Media, 1975.

FILMS

Feather (juvenile), ACI Media, 1973.
Flexibility, Teaching Research, 1973.
Learning Sets, Teaching Research, 1973.
Perseveration, Teaching Research, 1973.
Inducing a Creative Set: The Magic Net, Teaching Research, 1973.
Elephants (juvenile), ACI Media, 1974.

OTHER

Contributor to *Rewarding Creative Behavior,* edited by Torrance, Prentice-Hall (Englewood Cliffs, NJ), 1965.

Creative Learning and Teaching has been published in Spanish.

WORK IN PROGRESS: Writing booklets involving creative thinking about the future and social problems.

SIDELIGHTS: R. E. Myers once told *CA:* "My motivation for writing has always had two sides: self-expression and professional reasons. The latter generally deal with helping young people become more creative. I am interested in intelligence, learning, instructional materials and techniques, motivation, and personality. I've done research in all of these areas."

Myers adds: "In the past few years I've been involved in organizing, and giving workshops in, young authors festivals. Writing for today's teachers and students is a challenge. On the one hand, the situations confronting teachers have changed in variety and seriousness since I started teaching and writing about teaching in the 1950s. On the other hand, although young people aren't motivated by all of the same things, they still basically are excited about learning. It's inherent in human nature. I try to pique their intellectual sensibilities, and I try to engage their senses of humor.

"With regard to tickling the funny bones of young people, my approach is to cause *them* to discover the improbable, the quirky, the anomalous, and the ridiculous. *They* put the ideas together to create some humorous notion. I've

always been influenced by James Thurber, and I suppose the materials I write reflect that fact; but I am not a disciple nor has anyone ever proved to be.

"*Creative Learning and Teaching,* the book Paul Torrance and I wrote so long ago, continues to be sold in the Spanish translation. I'm not sure why.

"I'm constantly humbled by my wife and children—all of whom seem to write better than I can."

N

NAISMITH, Robert J. 1916-

PERSONAL: Born March 4, 1916, in Edinburgh, Scotland; son of Robert James Sinclair (an office manager) and Ann (Smith) Naismith. *Education:* Edinburgh College of Art, Diploma in Art, 1941, Diploma in Town Planning, 1942. *Politics:* "None." *Religion:* Protestant.

ADDRESSES: Home—14 Ramsay Garden, Royal Mile, Edinburgh EH1 2NA, Scotland. *Office*—Scottish Arts Club, 24 Rutland Sq., Edinburgh EH1 2BW, Scotland.

CAREER: Sir Frank Mears & Partners, Edinburgh, Scotland, architect and town planning and landscape consultant, 1943-85; architectural consultant and writer, 1985—. Lecturer at Heriot Watt University and Edinburgh College of Art, 1958-84. Architect for burghs of Penicuik, 1945-75, Dalkeith, 1950-75, and Tranent, 1957-71; planning consultant to city of Perth. Has exhibited watercolors at galleries in the United Kingdom. Lecturer throughout the world on architectural topics; guest on various television and radio programs.

MEMBER: Royal Institute of British Architects (fellow), Royal Incorporation of Architects in Scotland (fellow), Society of Antiquaries of Scotland (fellow), Scottish Arts Club.

AWARDS, HONORS: Civic Trust Award, 1971, for Selkirk Town Centre; Civic Trust Commendation, 1984, for Dalkeith High Street.

WRITINGS:

Scotland's Towns Are Centuries New, IPC Business Press (Surrey, England), 1971.
Buildings of the Scottish Countryside, Gollancz (London), 1985.
The Story of Scotland's Towns, John Donald (Edinburgh), 1989.

Contributor to periodicals, including *Scotsman.*

SIDELIGHTS: Robert J. Naismith once told *CA:* "My interest in cities and towns was inspired by Sir Patrick Geddes—I now live in his house—and by Sir Frank Mears, my former partner. I believe Scottish architecture and towns of the past have significant relevance to future building. I also believe that the reflection of national character and spirit is essential to towns and buildings in all countries. Internationalism is destructive to civic life.

"Another interest is the arts. I have exhibited watercolors of architectural and landscape works at the Royal Academy, the Royal Scottish Academy, the Royal Hibernian Gallery, and the Fine Arts Society in Glasgow. I have traveled to Europe, Africa, America, and the Far East to lecture on buildings and towns."

BIOGRAPHICAL/CRITICAL SOURCES:

PERIODICALS

Times Literary Supplement, August 23, 1985.

*   *   *

NANDA, B(al) R(am) 1917-

PERSONAL: Born October 11, 1917, in Rawalpindi, India (now in Pakistan); son of P. D. and Shrimati Maya (Devi) Nanda; married Janak Khosla, May 24, 1946; children: Naren and Biren (sons). *Education:* Attended Government College, Lahore, 1935-39. *Religion:* Hindu. *Avocational interests:* Visiting universities and institutions in India and abroad.

ADDRESSES: Home—S-174 Panchshila Park, New Delhi 110017, India.

CAREER: Indian Railways, New Delhi, India, joint director, Ministry of Railways, 1962-64; Indian Institute of

Public Administration, New Delhi, project director, 1964; Nehru Memorial Museum and Library, New Delhi, director, 1965-79.

AWARDS, HONORS: Rockefeller fellow, 1964; Indian Council of Social Science Research national fellow, 1979-80; Dadabhai Naoroji Memorial Award, 1981, for *Gokhale: The Indian Moderates and the British Raj;* Padma Bhushan Award, 1988.

WRITINGS:

Mahatma Gandhi: A Biography, Allen & Unwin (London), 1958, abridged edition, 1965, reprint of original edition, Oxford University Press, 1981.
The Nehrus: Motilal and Jawaharlal, Allen & Unwin, 1962, Oxford University Press, 1985.
Motilal Nehru, Publications Division, Government of India (New Delhi), 1964.
Gandhi: A Pictorial Biography, Publications Division, Government of India, 1972.
Gokhale, Gandhi and the Nehrus: Studies in Indian Nationalism, St. Martin's (New York City), 1974.
Gokhale: The Indian Moderates and the British Raj, Princeton University Press (Princeton, NJ), 1977.
(With P. C. Joshi and Raj Krishna) *Gandhi and Nehru,* Oxford University Press, 1979.
Jawaharlal Nehru: A Pictorial Biography, Publications Division, Government of India, 1980.
The Moderate Era in Indian Politics, Oxford University Press, 1981.
Gandhi and His Critics, Oxford University Press, 1985.
Gandhi, Pan-Islamism, Imperialism and Nationalism in India, Oxford University Press, 1989.
In Gandhi's Footsteps: The Life and Times of Jamnalal Bajaj, Oxford University Press, 1990.
Jawaharlal Nehru: Rebel and Statesman, Oxford University Press, in press.

EDITOR

Socialism in India, Vikas Publications (Delhi), 1972.
Indian Foreign Policy: The Nehru Years, International Book Distributors (New York City), 1976.
Science and Technology in India, Vikas Publications, 1977, Advent Books (New York City), 1986.
Essays in Modern Indian History, Oxford University Press, 1980.
Selected Works of Govind Ballabh Pant, Oxford University Press, Volumes 1-4, 1993-94, Volumes 5 and 6, in press.

WORK IN PROGRESS: Gandhi: The Strategy of Non-Violence; Indian Nationalism: The Historical Perspective; Selected Works of Govind Ballabh Pant, Volume 7 and onwards, for Oxford University Press.

SIDELIGHTS: B. R. Nanda once told *CA:* "I have been trying to reconstruct the story of the Indian nationalist movement and the lives of some of its outstanding leaders who combined intense nationalism with a wide world view. I am fascinated by the subtle interplay of personalities and politics, and the insights such studies can yield for the understanding of political history. Though I have drawn largely on primary sources and written in a scholarly framework, my object has been to interest not only fellow historians but the general reader in India and abroad. Several of my books have been simultaneously published in India, Britain and U.S.A., and have been translated into Indian and European languages."

BIOGRAPHICAL/CRITICAL SOURCES:

PERIODICALS

Times Literary Supplement, November 23, 1962; February 3, 1978; February 6, 1987.

*　　　*　　　*

NEWHALL, Beaumont 1908-1993

PERSONAL: Born June 23, 1908, in Lynn, MA; died of complications from a stroke, February 26, 1993, in Santa Fe, NM; son of Herbert William (a physician) and Alice Lilia (Davis) Newhall; married Nancy Wynne Parker (a writer), July 1, 1936 (died, 1974); married Christi Weston, 1975 (divorced, February, 1985); children: Theo Christopher Newhall (stepson). *Education:* Harvard University, A.B. (cum laude), 1930, A.M., 1931; graduate study at Institut d'Art et d'Archeologie, University of Paris, 1933, and Courtauld Institute of Art, London, 1934. *Avocational interests:* Gastronomy—historical, theoretical, and practical.

CAREER: Philadelphia Museum of Art, Philadelphia, PA, lecturer, 1931-32; Metropolitan Museum of Art, New York City, assistant, department of decorative arts, 1932-33; Museum of Modern Art, New York City, librarian, 1935-42, curator of photography, 1940-42, 1945-46; International Museum of Photography, George Eastman House, Rochester, NY, curator, 1948-58, director, 1958-71, trustee, beginning 1962, named honorary trustee, 1980; University of New Mexico, visiting professor of art, 1971-84, professor emeritus, beginning 1984. Lecturer at Black Mountain College, 1946-48, University of Rochester, 1954-55, Rochester Institute of Technology, 1956-68, and Salzburg Seminar in American Studies, Salzburg, Austria, 1958, 1959; State University of New York at Buffalo, visiting professor of art, 1969-71. Wolfe Publications, food editor, 1956-65; Rochester Civic Music Association, director, 1962-71. *Military service:* U.S. Army Air Forces, 1942-45, served in European theater; became major.

MEMBER: Royal Photographic Society of Great Britain (honorary fellow), Photographic Society of America (fellow), Professional Photographers of America (honorary master of photography), Deutsche Gesellschaft fuer Photographie (honorary), American Academy of Arts and Sciences (fellow).

AWARDS, HONORS: Guggenheim Foundation fellowship, 1947, 1975; Kulturpreis, Deutsche Gesellschaft fuer Photographie, 1970; D.Art, Harvard University, 1978; MacArthur Foundation fellow, 1984-89; D.F.A., State University of New York—Brockport, 1986; Progress Medal, Photographic Society of America.

WRITINGS:

Photography: A Short Critical History (originally written as illustrated catalog of an exhibition, "Photography, 1839-1937"), Museum of Modern Art (New York City), 1938, revised edition published as *The History of Photography, from 1839 to the Present Day*, 1949, revised and enlarged edition published as *The History of Photography: From 1839 to the Present*, 1982.

(Editor) *On Photography: A Source Book of Photo History in Facsimile*, Century House (Watkins Glen, NY), 1956.

(Editor and author of introduction with wife, Nancy Newhall) *Masters of Photography*, Braziller (New York City), 1958.

The Daguerreotype in America, Duell (New York City), 1961, 3rd revised edition, Dover (New York City), 1976.

Frederick H. Evans, George Eastman House (Rochester, NY), 1964.

(With Nancy Newhall) *T. H. O'Sullivan, Photographer: With an Appreciation by Ansel Adams*, George Eastman House, 1966.

Latent Image: The Discovery of Photography, Doubleday (Garden City, NY), 1967.

(Editor) *Dorothea Lange Looks at the American Country Woman*, George Ritchie (San Francisco), 1968.

Airborne Camera: The World from the Air and Outer Space, Hastings House (New York City), 1969.

(With Diana E. Edkins) *William H. Jackson*, Morgan & Morgan (Dobbs Ferry, NY), 1974.

(Editor) *Photography, Essays and Images: Illustrated Readings in the History of Photography*, Museum of Modern Art, 1980.

In Plain Sight: The Photographs of Beaumont Newhall, foreword by Ansel Adams, G. M. Smith (Salt Lake City), 1983.

Photography and the Book: Delivered on the Occasion of the Eighth Bromsen Lecture, May 3, 1980, Trustees of the Public Library of the City of Boston, 1983.

(Editor with Amy Conger) *Edward Weston Omnibus: A Critical Anthology*, Peregrine Smith (Salt Lake City), 1984.

Focus: Memoirs of a Life in Photography, Bulfinch Press (Boston), 1993.

Contributor to books, including *Bauhaus, 1919-1928*, edited by Herbert Bayer, Walter Gropius, and Ilse Gropius, Museum of Modern Art, 1938; and *Photographs*, by Henri Cartier-Bresson, Grossman, 1963. *Art in America*, contributing editor, 1957-65.

Newhall's written archives are kept at the John Paul Getty Museum, Los Angeles, CA.

BIOGRAPHICAL/CRITICAL SOURCES:

BOOKS

Contemporary Photographers, 2nd edition, St. James Press, 1988.

OBITUARIES:

PERIODICALS

Chicago Tribune, February 28, 1993, section 2, p. 6.
Los Angeles Times, February 27, 1993, p. A24.
New York Times, February 27, 1993, p. 27.*

*   *   *

NICHOLLS, Judith (Ann) 1941-

PERSONAL: Born December 12, 1941, in Westwoodside, Lincolnshire, England; daughter of Ernest Leonard (an education officer) and Joyce (a hairdresser; maiden name, Kelsey) Sharman; married John Richard Nicholls (a university lecturer), September 9, 1961; children: Dominique, Guy, Tracey. *Education:* Bath College of Higher Education, B.Ed. (with first class honors), 1984. *Avocational interests:* Family, walking, swimming, art lessons, cooking (mainly vegetarian food).

ADDRESSES: Home—Church View, Churchyard, Westbury, Wiltshire BA13 3DA, England.

CAREER: Modern Woman (magazine), London, England, secretary and assistant, 1960-61; Calne and Westbury Comprehensive Schools, Wiltshire, England, English teacher, 1976-79; Holt Primary School, Wiltshire, teacher, 1979-85; writer, 1985—. Gives poetry readings and workshops for children and teachers; has judged in national poetry competitions; has appeared on poetry programs for school broadcast.

MEMBER: Society of Authors.

WRITINGS:

POETRY FOR CHILDREN

Magic Mirror and Other Poems for Children (also see below), Faber & Faber (Boston), 1985.

Midnight Forest and Other Poems (also see below), Faber & Faber, 1987.

Popcorn Pie (contains *What's in the Parcel?, Who's Missing?, Sounds Good!,* and *I Don't Know How;* also see below), illustrations by Tessa Richardson-Jones, Mary Glasgow Publications (London), 1988.

Dragonsfire and Other Poems, illustrations by Shirley Felts, Faber & Faber, 1990.

Higgledy-Humbug (contains *What's the Time, Mr. Dandelion?, I Want My Mum!, O'Grady Says, Blue Wellies, Yellow Wellies, Jelly for the King,* and *Sticky Song;* also see below), Mary Glasgow Publications, 1990.

Wish You Were Here?, Oxford University Press (Oxford, England), 1992.

Midnight Forest [and] *Magic Mirror,* Faber & Faber, 1993.

Wiggle Waggle, Longman (Harlow, Essex, England), 1994.

Snail Song, Longman, 1994.

Ben Biggins' House, Longman, 1994.

Not Yet! Ben Biggins Said, Longman, 1994.

Ben Biggins' Tummy, Longman, 1994.

Ben Biggins' Socks, Longman, 1994.

Storm's Eye, Oxford University Press, 1994.

What's in the Parcel?, HarperCollins (London), 1994.

Who's Missing?, HarperCollins, 1994.

Sounds Good!, HarperCollins, 1994.

I Don't Know How, HarperCollins, 1994.

What's the Time, Mr. Dandelion?, HarperCollins, 1994.

I Want My Mum!, HarperCollins, 1994.

O'Grady Says, HarperCollins, 1994.

Blue Wellies, Yellow Wellies, HarperCollins, 1994.

Jelly for the King, HarperCollins, 1994.

Sticky Song, HarperCollins, 1994.

Otherworlds, Faber & Faber, 1995.

EDITOR

Wordspells (anthology), illustrations by Alan Baker, Faber & Faber, 1988.

What on Earth . . . ? (anthology), Faber & Faber, 1989.

Sing Freedom! (anthology), Faber & Faber, 1991.

Earthways, Earthwise (anthology), Oxford University Press, 1993.

A Trunkful of Elephants, Methuen (London), 1994.

OTHER

Seeing and Doing (television broadcast), Thames Television, 1989.

Three Poets in a Zoo (television broadcast), Middle English Programme, Channel 4 (England), 1992 and 1993.

Also author of Poetry Society Resource Packs for primary and secondary schools; creator of *Zig-Zag,* BBC-TV, and two radio programs for *Pictures in Your Mind,* 1987 and 1988. Work represented in more than one hundred anthologies, including *The Oxford Book of Story Poems,* edited by Michael Harrison and Christopher Stuart-Clark, Oxford University Press, 1990; *This Poem Doesn't Rhyme,* edited by Gerard Benson, Viking, 1990; and *All in the Family,* edited by John Foster, Oxford University Press, 1994; poems broadcast regularly on BBC Schools' Radio. Contributor of articles and reviews to periodicals, including *Times Educational Supplement, Education Guardian, Junior Education,* and *Child Education.*

WORK IN PROGRESS: Two small books for young children.

SIDELIGHTS: Judith Nicholls told *CA:* "I'm particularly interested in where poems come from, how they get from 'airy nothing' onto the page, and how we can help children (or adults) find ideas and develop them into poems. My own ideas seem to come from all kinds of different sources, which I can usually pinpoint in retrospect, but this is never a process that guarantees a 'recipe' for the next poem! After their first appearance, the poems go through several pages of drafts over a period of some days, during which the various words or lines or even punctuation nag at me until they're removed, added to, reworded, and transferred until finally I'm reasonably satisfied.

"Working in schools gives valuable feedback if you are writing for children. If you go into schools as a poet, rather than a teacher, the important thing is to offer something 'extra' to promote enjoyment and understanding of poetry, something which perhaps wouldn't be on offer in the normal school day. I also like to show all the drafts that precede a typical poem: it's important for children to know that adults, too, struggle with words.

"Though I really enjoy children's books, I didn't set out initially to write for children. I'm only consciously aware of writing for a particular age-group when I write for very *young* children. Maybe it's the same with many authors of children's books. It's not so much that the books are written for children, but that the authors have at least a little part of themselves that has never quite left childhood behind."

NORDHAM, George Washington 1929-

PERSONAL: Born February 22, 1929, in Waldwick, NJ; son of George (an architect) and Florence (Rockett) Nordham; married Jean Andrews, April 7, 1956 (died October 13, 1969); children: John Andrews. *Education:* George Washington University, B.A., 1949; University of Pennsylvania Law School, LL.B., 1952.

ADDRESSES: Home—67 East Prospect St., Waldwick, NJ 07463.

CAREER: Admitted to the Bar of New York State, 1959; Morgan Guaranty Trust Co., New York City, trust administrator, 1955-60; Richardson-Vicks, Inc., New York City, assistant treasurer, 1960-66; Binney & Smith, Inc., New York City, corporate secretary, 1966-71; Prentice-Hall, Inc., Englewood Cliffs, NJ, legal editor, 1971-73; legal administrator for private law firms in New Jersey, 1973-77; Prentice-Hall, Inc., Englewood Cliffs, legal editor, 1977-90. *Military service:* U.S. Army, Finance Corps, 1952-55; became second lieutenant.

MEMBER: New York State Bar Association, Elks.

WRITINGS:

George Washington: Vignettes and Memorabilia, Dorrance, 1977.
George Washington's Women: Mary, Martha, Sally, and 146 Others, Dorrance, 1977.
George Washington and Money, University Press of America, 1982.
George Washington and the Law, Adams Press, 1982.
George Washington: A Treasury (short stories), Adams Press, 1983.
George Washington's Religious Faith, Adams Press, 1986.
George Washington, President of the Constitutional Convention, Adams Press, 1987.
The Age of Washington: George Washington's Presidency, Adams Press, 1989.
Happy-Blessed: Assurances of God's Love, Professional Press, 1993.
Miracles of Jesus, Adams Press, 1993.
Mary the Mother of Jesus, Adams Press, 1993.
Sin, Adams Press, 1994.

Contributor of articles to periodicals, including *Daughters of the American Revolution* and *New York State Bar Journal.*

SIDELIGHTS: Sharing both birthday and moniker with the first president of the United States, George Washington Nordham has built a lifelong avocation around his namesake. A collector of Washington memorabilia, he was encouraged in his hobby by his father, who, in 1932, purchased the first item for his son's collection—a replica of Jean-Antoine Houdon's life-sized bust of George Washington, finished in gold and weighing forty pounds. Since that time Nordham's collection has grown to include more than twenty-five busts, one hundred paintings, prints, and wall plates, hundreds of commemorative coins and stamps, paper currency, and a library of more than five hundred books on the founding father, now permanently located at the Sons of the American Revolution in Louisville, Kentucky. Some of the items Nordham has acquired date back to the early 1800s.

Since the publication of his books on Washington, Nordham's expertise has been sought out by historical societies, and he has exhibited his Washington paraphernalia in several New Jersey cities. Since retiring from Prentice-Hall, Nordham has written on religious topics and his books are popular in Bible study groups and church libraries.

BIOGRAPHICAL/CRITICAL SOURCES:

PERIODICALS

Americana, February, 1983.
GW Times, February, 1982.
New Jersey Monthly, February, 1986.
New York, February 25, 1980.

*   *   *

NOSSITER, Bernard D(aniel) 1926-1992

PERSONAL: Born April 10, 1926, in Manhattan, NY; died of lung cancer, June 24, 1992, in Manhattan, NY; son of Murry (a businessperson) and Rose (Weingarten) Nossiter; married Jacqueline Robinson, December 6, 1950; children: Daniel, Joshua, Adam, Jonathan. *Education:* Dartmouth College, B.A., 1947; Harvard University, M.A., 1948.

CAREER: New York Telegram and Sun, New York City, journalist, 1952-55; *Washington Post,* Washington, DC, beginning 1955, served as national economics reporter and European economics correspondent, London correspondent, 1971-79; *New York Times,* New York City, chief of United Nations (U.N.) bureau, 1979-83. *Military service:* U.S. Army, 1944-46, 1951-52, served in infantry; became second lieutenant.

MEMBER: Phi Beta Kappa.

AWARDS, HONORS: Award from Hillman Foundation, 1965, for *The Mythmakers;* Overseas Press Club Award, 1966; Polk Award for national reporting, 1969.

WRITINGS:

The Mythmakers, Houghton, 1964.
Soft State: A Newspaperman's Chronicle of India, Harper, 1970.
Britain: A Future That Works, Houghton, 1978.

The Global Struggle for More, Harper, 1987.
Fat Years and Lean: The American Economy since Roosevelt, HarperCollins, 1990.

BIOGRAPHICAL/CRITICAL SOURCES:

PERIODICALS

New York Times, November 22, 1970.
Washington Post, October 24, 1970.

OBITUARIES:

PERIODICALS

Los Angeles Times, June 27, 1992, p. A26.
New York Times, June 25, 1992, p. D26.
Times (London), July 4, 1992, p. 21.*

*   *   *

NOVACK, George (Edward) 1905-1992
(William F. Warde)

PERSONAL: Born August 5, 1905, in Boston, MA; died July 30, 1992, in New York, NY; son of Israel and Ada (Marcus) Novack; married Evelyn Andreas Reed, June 22, 1942 (died, 1979). *Education:* Attended Harvard University, 1922-27. *Politics:* Socialist.

CAREER: Writer and lecturer. Fund for the Republic, Santa Barbara, CA, research associate, 1958; associate editor, *International Socialist Review,* 1965-74. Socialist Workers Party, member of National Committee, 1940-72, treasurer of national campaign committee, 1968, secretary, 1972. Served on several civil liberties defense committees and was national secretary of the Socialists' Civil Rights Defense Committee.

WRITINGS:

An Introduction to the Logic of Marxism, Merit Publishers, 1942, 5th edition, 1969.
The Irregular Movement of History (essays; originally published in three issues of *Labour Review*), New Park Publications, 1957.
(Under pseudonym William F. Warde) *The Long View of History,* Merit Publishers, 1958, Pioneer Publishers, 1960.
Who Will Change the World?, YSF Publication (Toronto), 1961.
Moscow versus Peking, Pioneer Publishers, 1963.
(Editor with Isaac Deutscher) *Leon Trotsky, The Age of Permanent Revolution,* Dell (New York City), 1964.
The Origins of Materialism, Merit Publishers, 1965.
(Author of introduction under pseudonym William F. Warde; with Joseph Hansen) *Leon Trotsky, In Defense of Marxism,* Merit Publishers, 1965.

(With Robert Vernon) *Watts and Harlem: The Rising Revolt in the Black Ghettos,* Pioneer Publishers, 1965.
(Editor and author of introduction) *Existentialism versus Marxism: Conflicting Views on Humanism,* Dell, 1966.
(With Lawrence Stuart and Derrick Morrison) *The Black Uprisings,* Merit Publishers, 1967.
The Understanding of History (two essays), Merit Publishers, 1967, new edition, 1974.
(With George Breitman) *Black Nationalism and Socialism,* Merit Publishers, 1968.
(With Paul Boutelle and others) *Murder in Memphis: Martin Luther King and the Future of the Black Liberation Struggle,* Merit Publishers, 1968.
Black Slavery and Capitalism: The Rise and Fall of the Cotton Kingdom, National Education Dept., Socialist Workers Party, 1968.
Empiricism and Its Evolution: A Marxist View, Merit Publishers, 1968.
How Can the Jews Survive: A Socialist Answer to Zionism, Merit Publishers, 1969.
(With Ernest Mandel) *The Revolutionary Potential of the Working Class,* Merit Publishers, 1969, new edition, Pathfinder Press (New York City), 1974.
(With Pierre Frank and Ernest Mandel) *Key Problems of the Transition from Capitalism to Socialism,* Merit Publishers, 1969.
Genocide against the Indians: Its Role in the Rise of U.S. Capitalism, Pathfinder Press, 1970.
Marxism versus Neo-Anarchist Terrorism, Pathfinder Press, 1970.
Revolutionary Dynamics of Women's Liberation, Pathfinder Press, 1970.
(With Ernest Mandel) *The Marxist Theory of Alienation,* Pathfinder Press, 1970, 2nd edition, 1973.
Democracy and Revolution, Pathfinder Press, 1971.
(Compiler with Joseph Hansen) *The Transitional Program for Socialist Revolution,* Pathfinder Press, 1973.
Humanism and Socialism, Pathfinder Press, 1973.
Pragmatism versus Marxism: An Appraisal of John Dewey's Philosophy, Pathfinder Press, 1975.
(Editor and author of introduction) *America's Revolutionary Heritage: Marxist Essays,* Pathfinder Press, 1976.
(Compiler and author of introductory essays with Hansen) *The Transitional Program for Socialist Revolution: Including "The Death Agony of Capitalism and the Tasks of the Fourth International," by Leon Trotsky,* Pathfinder Press, 1977.
Polemics in Marxist Philosophy, Monad Press (New York City), 1978.

Contributor to *Marxist Essays in American History,* edited by Robert Himmel, Merit Publishers, 1966; contributor and author of introduction, *Their Morals and Ours,* Merit Publishers, 1966. Contributor to numerous newspapers and periodicals, including *Militant, New International,* and *Intercontinental Press.*

SIDELIGHTS: George Novack was actively engaged in socialist causes from 1932 until his death in 1992. In 1937 he was a prime mover in organizing the International Commission of Inquiry into the Moscow Trials headed by philosopher John Dewey.

OBITUARIES:

PERIODICALS

Los Angeles Times, August 1, 1992, p. A24.*

O

O'BRIEN, Conor Cruise 1917-
(Donat O'Donnell)

PERSONAL: Surname listed in some sources as Cruise O'Brien; born November 3, 1917, in Dublin, Ireland; son of Francis Cruise (a journalist and literary critic) and Katherine (Sheehy) O'Brien; married Christine Foster, 1939 (divorced, 1962); married Maire MacEntee, January 9, 1962; children: Donal, Fedelma (Mrs. Nicholas Simms), Kathleen (Mrs. Joseph Kearney), Sean Patrick, Margaret. *Education:* Trinity College, Dublin, B.A. (modern literature), 1940, B.A., 1941, Ph.D., 1953. *Avocational interests:* Travel.

ADDRESSES: Home—Whitewater, Howth Summit, Dublin, Ireland.

CAREER: Entered Irish Civil Service, 1942, member of Department of Finance, 1942-44, Department of External Affairs, member of staff, 1944-61, Information and Cultural Section, department head and managing director of Irish News Agency, 1948-55, counsellor to Irish Embassy, Paris, France, 1955-56, delegate and head of United Nations Irish section, 1955-61, assistant secretary of Department of External Affairs, 1960, named member of executive staff of United Nations secretariat, 1961, served as representative of United Nations Secretary-General in Katanga (now Shaba, Zaire), 1961; Labour Party Member of Dail Eireann representing Dublin North-East, 1969-77; Minister for Posts and Telegraphs, 1973-77; member of Senate, Republic of Ireland, 1977-79. University of Ghana, vice-chancellor, 1962-65; New York University, Albert Schweitzer Chair in the humanities, 1965-69; Nuffield College, Oxford, visiting fellow, 1973-75; University of Dublin, pro-chancellor, 1973—; Dartmouth College, visiting professor of history and Montgomery Fellow, 1984-85. Editor-in-chief, *Observer* (London) 1979-81; contributing editor, *The Atlantic,* 1986—.

MEMBER: Royal Irish Academy, Royal Society of Literature, Athenaeum Club.

AWARDS, HONORS: D.Litt. from University of Bradford, 1971, University of Ghana, 1974, University of Edinburgh, 1976, University of Nice, 1978, University of Coleraine, 1981, and Queen's University, Belfast, 1984; Valiant for Truth Media Award, 1979.

WRITINGS:

(Under pseudonym Donat O'Donnell) *Maria Cross: Imaginative Patterns in a Group of Modern Catholic Writers,* Oxford University Press, 1952.

Parnell and His Party: 1880-90, Oxford University Press, 1957.

To Katanga and Back: A U.N. Case, Hutchinson, 1962, Simon & Schuster, 1963.

Conflicting Concepts of the United Nations, Leeds University Press, 1964.

Writers and Politics (essays), Pantheon, 1965.

(With Northrop Frye and Stuart Hampshire) *The Morality of Scholarship,* edited by Max Black, Cornell University Press, 1967.

The United Nations: Sacred Drama, illustrated by Feliks Topolski, Simon & Schuster, 1968.

Conor Cruise O'Brien Introduces Ireland, edited by Owen Dudley Edwards, Deutsch, 1969, McGraw, 1970.

Albert Camus of Europe and Africa, Viking, 1970, published as *Camus,* Fontana, 1970.

(With wife, Maire MacEntee O'Brien) *The Story of Ireland,* Viking, 1972, published as *A Concise History of Ireland,* Thames & Hudson, 1972.

The Suspecting Glance, Faber, 1972.

States of Ireland, Pantheon, 1972.

Herod: Reflections on Political Violence, Hutchinson, 1978.

Neighbours: Four Lectures, edited by Thomas Pakenham, Faber, 1980.

The Press and the World, Birkbeck College (London), 1980.

Edmund Burke: Master of English, English Association, 1981.

Religion and Politics, New University of Ulster, 1984.

The Siege: The Saga of Israel and Zionism, Simon & Schuster, 1986.

Passion and Cunning: Essays on Nationalism, Terrorism and Revolution, Simon & Schuster, 1988.

God Land: Reflections on Religion and Nationalism, Harvard University Press, 1988.

The Great Melody: A Thematic Biography of Edmund Burke, University of Chicago Press, 1993.

Conor: An Anthology, selections by Donald H. Akenson, Cornell University Press, 1994.

EDITOR

The Shaping of Modern Ireland, Routledge & Kegan Paul, 1960.

Edmund Burke, *Reflections on the Revolution in France,* Penguin, 1969.

(With William Dean Vanech) *Power and Consciousness,* New York University Press, 1969.

CONTRIBUTOR

Irving Howe, editor, *The Idea of the Modern in Literature and the Arts,* Horizon, 1968.

Arthur I. Blaustein and R. R. Woock, editors, *Man Against Poverty: World War III,* introduction by John W. Gardner, Random House, 1968.

George A. White and C. H. Newman, editors, *Literature in Revolution,* Holt, 1972.

Teilhard de Chardin: In Quest of the Perfection of Man, Fairleigh Dickinson University Press, 1973.

Speeches Delivered at the 35th Annual Dinner of the Anglo-Israel Association, Anglo-Israel Association, 1983.

(Author of forward) Andrew Malraux, *The Walnut Trees of Altenburg,* University of Chicago Press, 1992.

PLAYS

King Herod Explains, produced in Dublin, 1969.

Murderous Angels: A Political Tragedy and Comedy in Black and White (produced in Los Angeles and New York City, 1970), Little, Brown, 1968.

OTHER

Contributor of articles to periodicals, including *Atlantic, Nation, New Statesman,* and *Saturday Review.*

SIDELIGHTS: Conor Cruise O'Brien has distinguished himself as a literary critic, diplomat, dramatist, biographer, historian, and politician. He rose to world prominence as Irish delegate to the United Nations and as spe-cial representative of U.N. Secretary-General Dag Hammarskjold. A *New Statesman* writer stated that "In so far as a civil servant can, [O'Brien] became a minor national hero; the Irish independent, asserting his country's independence along with his own." The article went on to describe O'Brien as "a modern version of that 19th-century radical phenomenon, the Only White Man the Natives Trust."

It has been suggested that Hammarskjold's knowledge of and admiration for *Maria Cross,* a volume of critical essays that O'Brien published in 1952 under the pseudonym of Donat O'Donnell, was influential in his decision to ask O'Brien to serve on his executive staff. Under Hammarskjold, O'Brien was assigned to oversee U.N. operations at Katanga in the Congo in 1961, a time of violent political upheavals. Later that year he was relieved of these duties at his own request and resigned from the foreign service altogether. Following his resignation, O'Brien made public his intention to publish a book about the difficulties he had encountered in the service of the U.N. in the Congo—shortly thereafter, he received a letter from then acting Secretary-General U Thant advising him that unauthorized disclosure of United Nations affairs was prohibited by regulation. Thant's letter serves as the preface of *To Katanga and Back,* an autobiographical narrative of the crisis in the Congo, which O'Brien published in 1963 despite U.N. censure.

Although his ties with the United Nations were officially broken, O'Brien remained concerned with the intricate workings of the U.N. organization. In 1968's *The United Nations: Sacred Drama,* O'Brien portrays the United Nations as both temple and stage, with the U.N. Secretary-General serving as a kind of high priest with a spiritual authority. As John Osborne explained in the *New Republic,* "A profanation occurs . . . when [the Secretary-General] 'steps down from the religious level of politics, to the level of applied politics.' " Critic Albert Bremel commented favorably on O'Brien's conception of the dramatic aspects of the United Nations. "Theater is an art. If it is to be good theater, it requires the exercise of imagination," he noted in the *New York Times Book Review.* "That is what Mr. O'Brien is really concerned with. Imaginative participants will recognize (some have already recognized) the U.N. as a superb arena for dramatizing the threats to survival."

As an extension of his conception of the U.N. as drama, O'Brien drew on his experiences in Katanga to write the play *Murderous Angels: A Political Tragedy and Comedy in Black and White.* The play provoked controversy even before it was staged due to O'Brien's reworking of historical events in the Congo. The author did not intend *Murderous Angels* to be viewed as a documentary drama or as 'theatre of fact,' but rather as a tragedy, as its subtitle implies. "While the historian must hesitate, lacking absolute proof, the dramatist may present the hypothesis which he finds most convincing," O'Brien writes as an introduction to his work, justifying his dramatic license.

In *States of Ireland*, O'Brien again courts controversy through his views on the Irish conflict in which he was actively involved as a left-wing Irish Labour Party deputy. Wrote Vivian Mercier in the *Nation*, "The most unpopular statement in the whole book is probably this: 'While two communities are as bitterly antagonistic as are Catholics and Protestants [in Northern Ireland] now, it is not merely futile but actually mischievous to talk about uniting Ireland.' What he means is that in a united Ireland Catholics would outnumber Protestants by at least three to one." In *States of Ireland*, O'Brien argues that the two distinct Catholics and Protestant communities are a reality, the existence of which makes any goal of Irish unification impractical, if not impossible. O'Brien, a Catholic by upbringing, whose first wife, Christine Foster, was a Protestant, examines the situation from both a historical and an autobiographical perspective. "To Conor," Mercier observed, "Irish history came first of all as the history of his family."

A reviewer for the *Times Literary Supplement* described the contents of *States of Ireland* as sometimes confusing because of the breadth of O'Brien's undertaking: "some general history, fragments of literary criticism, spasms of autobiography, an extract from Dr. Cruise O'Brien's political diary for the ominous summer of 1970, an extended account of the developing situation in Northern Ireland and, by way of appendix, a splendid diatribe against Sinn Fein which was intended to flatten the President of that organization . . . in public debate and by all accounts did just that." In the *New York Review of Books*, John Horgan summed up a widely held view of what *States of Ireland* achieved: "Dr. O'Brien's great contribution to the Irish situation can be easily and quickly stated: he has forced people to face up to the fact that the tradition of the majority of people living in Ireland is a sectarian and a nationalist one, and that the link between its sectarian and its nationalist aspects will not be dissolved simply by wishful thinking."

Several reviewers of *The Siege: The Saga of Israel and Zionism* have echoed the same question: Why would an Irish historian chose to write the history of Zionism, from its pre-Herzl days to the state of Israel in the post-Begin era? "The answer," noted Walter Reich in the *Washington Post Book World*, "lies in [O'Brien's] past—in his identity as a member of a nationality, Irish Catholic, that has experienced stigmatization, and in his identity as the son of a lapsed Catholic growing up in a southern Irish sea of disapproving believers. These identities, he says, helped him form a bond with the story of a people whose stigmatiza-

tion has been profound and whose experience with disapproval has been catastrophic."

At least one reviewer was less convinced about O'Brien's qualifications for the task. Milton Viorst, writing in the *Chicago Tribune Book World*, complained that "O'Brien is an Irishman, which scarcely disqualifies him from writing about Jews, but he comes to the subject as a researcher, with no discernible 'feel.' " On the other hand, in the *New Republic* Walter Laqueur argued that O'Brien's critical distance proves an advantage. He noted, "But his vantage point—he is the detached but friendly outsider—gives his work a freshness lacking in most of the committed literature on the subject." Although Patrick Seale disagreed with O'Brien's position in the *Spectator*, he praised O'Brien's ability as a writer; "He is almost incapable of writing a dull sentence. He is also an immensely persuasive advocate, clear, master of his sources, able to marshall his arguments, skilled at demolishing his adversaries with slur and innuendo." And Abba Eban, who reviewed *The Siege* in the *Los Angeles Times Book Review*, noted that the strengths of the work reflect well on its author. The book, Eban observed, "bears the mark of a restless, original idiosyncratic mind and—more surprisingly—a talent for the patient toil required by meticulous research."

BIOGRAPHICAL/CRITICAL SOURCES:

BOOKS

Hughes, Catherine, *Plays, Politics, and Polemics,* Specialist Publications, 1973.
O'Brien, Conor Cruise, *Murderous Angels: A Political Tragedy and Comedy in Black and White,* Little, Brown, 1968.
Weightman, John, *The Concept of the Avant-Garde,* Open Court, 1973.

PERIODICALS

Chicago Tribune Book World, March 9, 1986, p. 39.
Commentary, September, 1965.
Commonweal, December 2, 1988.
Guardian Weekly, April 27, 1986; March 27, 1988, p. 28; December 4, 1988.
Listener, May 30, 1968.
Los Angeles Times Book Review, March 16, 1986.
Nation, December 20, 1965, p. 502; February 23, 1970; March 27, 1972; March 12, 1973.
New Republic, September 11, 1965; September 7, 1968; March 3, 1986; September 12, 1988.
New Statesman, December 6, 1968.
Newsweek, October 17, 1966; March 24, 1986.
New York Review of Books, September 8, 1966; July 31, 1969; May 3, 1973.
New York Times, September 15, 1961; February 25, 1986; May 13, 1986; February 22, 1991.

New York Times Book Review, October 31, 1965; August 4, 1968; February 11, 1973; March 2, 1986; February 15, 1987, p. 38; July 24, 1988.

Observer (London), January 26, 1969; June 1, 1986; July 20, 1986; November 30, 1986; February 28, 1988, p. 26; March 13, 1988, p. 42; February 2, 1990.

Partisan Review, Number 2, 1988.

Spectator, June 17, 1978; January 3, 1981; June 14, 1986; December 6, 1986, p. 32; March 12, 1988; May 7, 1988.

Time, April 21, 1986.

Times Educational Supplement, June 10, 1988.

Times Literary Supplement, December 23, 1965; June 27, 1968; July 17, 1969; January 29, 1970; July 7, 1972; November 10, 1972; August 11, 1978; November 14, 1980; October 10, 1986; March 18, 1988, p. 298; August 5, 1988; April 13, 1990.

Washington Post Book World, February 16, 1986, p. 1; October 23, 1988, p. 13; February 25, 1990.*

*   *   *

O'DONNELL, Donat
    See O'BRIEN, Conor Cruise

*   *   *

O'HANLON, Daniel John   1919-1992

PERSONAL: Born May 10, 1919, in Wallsend-on-Tyne, England; died from injuries sustained in a car accident, June 17, 1992, in Berkeley, CA; immigrated to the United States, 1920; son of Dan (in insurance and real estate) and Margaret Alice (Cottam) O'Hanlon. *Education:* Loyola University, Los Angeles, CA, B.A. (summa cum laude), 1939; Gonzaga University, M.A., 1946; Milltown Park, Dublin, Ireland, S.T.L., 1953; Gregorian University, S.T.D., 1958; also studied at Universities of Fribourg and Tuebingen, and at Harvard University and Syracuse University. *Avocational interests:* Sailing.

CAREER: Entered Society of Jesus (Jesuits), 1939; Loyola University, Los Angeles, CA, instructor in philosophy, 1946-49; ordained Roman Catholic priest, 1952, completed Jesuit training in Port Townsend, WA, 1953-54; Alma College, Los Gatos, CA, associate professor, 1959-64, professor of fundamental theology, 1964-65; Graduate Theological Union, Berkeley, CA, professor of systematic theology at Jesuit School of Theology, 1965-89. Staff member and interpreter for Vatican Secretariat for Christian Unity, 1964-65; visiting professor at Stanford University, 1965, and University of California, Santa Barbara, winter, 1969; member of U.S. Bishops Committee on

Education for Ecumenism, 1965-92; member of board of directors of North American Liturgical Conference, 1966-69, Institute for Ecumenical and Cultural Research, 1967-71, and Divinity School of St. Louis University, beginning 1969.

MEMBER: Catholic Theological Society of America, Society for Religion in Higher Education, Pacific Coast Theological Society, Catholic Biblical Association.

WRITINGS:

The Influence of Schelling on the Thought of Paul Tillich, Gregorian University Press, 1958.

(Editor with Daniel J. Callahan and Heiko Oberman) *Christianity Divided,* Sheed, 1961.

(Editor with Hans Kueng and Yves Congar) *Council Speeches of Vatican II,* Paulist/Newman, 1965.

What's Happening to the Church, St. Anthony Messenger Press, 1974.

Correspondent for *America,* summer, 1963. Contributor to scholarly theological journals and to popular magazines, including *America, Commonweal,* and *Saturday Review.* O'Hanlon's books have been published in Dutch, Spanish, French, and German.

SIDELIGHTS: Daniel John O'Hanlon was known for his work in Roman Catholic theology and his distinguished teaching career. He was a leading proponent of unity among the world's religions, a cause that is commonly referred to as the ecumenical movement. O'Hanlon once wrote: "I spent many years working in the Protestant-Catholic ecumenical movement, and now I have begun to enlarge my horizons and see how bridges can be built between East and West, especially between Christianity and Hinduism and Buddhism. But that puts it too abstractly. What I want to do first of all, while remaining a Christian, is bring these elements to a living unity in my own life, and in doing that, help others to do the same." O'Hanlon studied Hinduism and Buddhism in India, Sri Lanka, Thailand, Burma, and Japan, in 1973 and 1974.

BIOGRAPHICAL/CRITICAL SOURCES:

PERIODICALS

National Catholic Reporter, July 18-September 19, 1975.

OBITUARIES:

PERIODICALS

Chicago Tribune, June 20, 1992, section 2, p. 17.
New York Times, June 19, 1992.*

ORIGO, Iris (Margaret Cutting) 1902-1988

PERSONAL: Born August 15, 1902, in Birdlip, Gloucestershire, England; died June 28, 1988, in Siena, Italy; daughter of William Bayard (a diplomat) and Sybil Marjorie (Cuffe) Cutting; married Antonio Origo (an agriculturist), 1924 (died, 1976); children: Gian Clemente Bayard (deceased), Benedetta, Donata. *Education:* Educated privately in Florence, Italy.

ADDRESSES: Home—La Foce, Chianciano Terme 53042, Siena, Italy.

CAREER: Biographer; lecturer in medieval history at Harvard University, Cambridge, MA, 1958; vice-president of International Social Service.

MEMBER: Royal Society of Literature (fellow).

AWARDS, HONORS: Gold Medal, Italian Red Cross; honorary doctorate from Wheaton College, 1960, and Smith College, 1964; Isabella d'Este Medal, 1966; Dame Commander, Order of the British Empire, 1978.

WRITINGS:

BIOGRAPHIES

Gianni, privately printed, 1933.
Leopardi: A Biography, foreword by George Santayana, Oxford University Press, 1935, revised edition published as *Leopardi: A Study in Solitude,* Hamish Hamilton, 1953.
Allegra, Hogarth, 1935.
Tribune of Rome: A Biography of Cola di Rienzo, Hogarth, 1938.
The Last Attachment: The Story of Byron and Teresa Guiccioli as Told in Their Unpublished Letters and Other Family Papers, Scribner, 1949, revised edition, Collins, 1962.
A Measure of Love, J. Cape, 1957, Pantheon, 1958.
The Merchant of Prato: Francesco di Marco Datini, J. Cape, 1956, Knopf, 1957, published with foreword by Barbara Tuchman as *The Merchant of Prato, Francesco di Marco Datini, 1335-1410,* Godine, 1986.
The World of San Bernardino, Harcourt, 1962.
A Need to Testify: Portraits of Lauro de Bosis, Ruth Draper, Gaetano Salvemini, Ignazio Silone and an Essay on Biography, Harcourt, 1984.
Un'amica: Rittrato di Elsa Dallolio, Passigli, 1988.

OTHER

War in Val d'Orcia: A Diary (autobiography), J. Cape, 1947, published with an introduction by Denis Mack Smith as *War in Val d'Orcia, 1943-1944: A Diary,* Godine, 1984.
Giovanna and Jane (a story for children), J. Cape, 1950.

(Editor and translator, with John Heath-Stubbs) Giacomo Leopardi, *Selected Prose and Poetry,* Oxford University Press, 1966, New American Library, 1967.
Images and Shadows: Part of a Life (autobiography), J. Murray, 1970, Harcourt, 1971.
(Compiler) *The Vagabond Path* (poems and prose), Scribner, 1972.

Author of introduction to *Sunset and Twilight,* by Bernard Berenson, Hamish Hamilton, 1964. Contributor of articles to periodicals, including *Atlantic Monthly, Times Literary Supplement, History Today,* and *Speculum.*

SIDELIGHTS: Iris Origo has been described by numerous critics as one of the finest writers in English about things Italian. Born of Anglo-Irish and American parents, she was raised in Italy and tutored by a noted classical scholar, Solone Monti. Origo traveled widely in her youth and made Italy her permanent home when she married Marchese Antonio Origo in 1924. Her books reflect this background; the subjects of most of her biographies have been Italians, many of whom lived in the Middle Ages and the nineteenth century.

Origo's first published biography was a life of the nineteenth-century poet Giacomo Leopardi. In a review of *Leopardi: A Biography* a writer for the *Times Literary Supplement* pronounced the book "wise and illuminating," and Stark Young of the *New Republic* called it "excellent . . . balanced, sane and on the whole distinguished." Some critics faulted Origo for restricting herself to Leopardi's life and attempting no thorough critical assessment of his work. "The literary aspect of the biography is not its strongest claim to our admiration," remarked Peter Quennell of *New Statesman and Nation,* who nonetheless called the book "well written, nicely balanced, carefully documented." When a new edition was published eighteen years later, Foscarina Alexander wrote of Origo in the *Spectator:* "Sympathetic and discerning, devoted to her subject yet recognizing his considerable faults of character, expert at sifting evidence and settling old controversies, she is the ideal biographer."

Leopardi was followed by a study of Allegra Clairmont, Lord Byron's illegitimate daughter. After one more book, a biography of fourteenth-century Roman patriot Cola di Rienzo, World War II brought a hiatus in Origo's writing. The author devoted herself to work with the Red Cross and established a home for refugee children on her estate, La Foce. She and her husband also aided the anti-Fascist resistance, hiding partisans and escaped prisoners of war in La Foce's woods. La Foce was bombed and shelled, and the Origos were turned out of their home by German soldiers and forced to walk, with twenty-three small children, twelve miles to the nearest village. Iris Origo's diary of those years was published in 1947 as *War in Val d'Orcia: A Diary.*

Returning to biography in 1949, Origo examined the poet Lord Byron's love affair with the Contessa Teresa Guicciolo in *The Last Attachment: The Story of Bryon and Teresa Guicioli as Told in Their Unpublished Letters and Other Family Papers.* Origo persuaded Teresa's great-nephew to grant her access to Byron's love letters and many other documents, a favor he had denied to several would-be biographers. This was a challenge since he was quite deaf, and, as Origo remarked, "It is difficult to be persuasive or reassuring at the top of one's voice." The book was hailed as a "first-rate biography with a dash of mystery" by Clive Bell in the *Spectator,* and a reviewer remarked in the *San Francisco Chronicle* that "no previous biographer . . . has probed so deeply into the period of . . . [Byron's] Italian residence." A writer for the *Times Literary Supplement* found the new material, which included the complete Italian text of 149 of Byron's letters, "overcrowded" by Origo's retelling of previously known facts. "A briefer view of the story," the reviewer suggested, "would have left more room for the author's fine imaginative and interpretative talent." In a later edition of the *Times Literary Supplement* another critic described *The Last Attachment* as "still our fullest, most balanced, and most perceptive account of the relationship."

Origo's books continued to win critical acclaim. *A Measure of Love,* containing five biographical essays on British and Italian figures of the nineteenth century, was applauded by a critic in the *Manchester Guardian* as a "fascinating expose of nineteenth century attitudes." And Quennell wrote in the *New York Times* that "Origo is a biographer who understands the heart. Her personages move and speak." In *The Merchant of Prato: Francesco di Marco Datini,* Origo drew from the many documents left by Francesco di Marco Datini, reconstructing his domestic, social, and business life. Sidney Painter of the *New York Times* observed that the biography is "both a scholarly monograph . . . and a literary work of art. . . . Origo's characters live and breathe, hate, love and believe."

Origo's biography of San Bernardino was also well received. The Tuscan saint, who was canonized only six years after his death in 1444, was one of the most popular preachers of his time. *The World of San Bernardino* quotes many of his sermons. In a review of the book in *Critic,* a writer noted that the quotes "are filled with the life of his day and often, judged by the standards of our day, have the abrasive quality of sandpaper." A writer for the *Economist* called *The World of San Bernardino* "a vivid and lively picture not only of the saint and his work, but also of the world in which he lived and the people to whom he preached. . . . It is a brilliant idea, brilliantly carried out;

it combines scholarship with fine writing and vivid narrative."

Origo also won praise when she wrote of her own life in *Images and Shadows: Part of a Life.* This autobiography tells of her childhood in Italy, Ireland, and America; of her studies with Monti, who provided an education in the fifteenth-century humanist tradition; and of the Origos' work in reclaiming the eroded, exhausted farmland of the estate they had chosen to buy in Tuscany. Many critics found Origo's portraits of her parents especially memorable. Her father, "an intense, many-sided, and sane young man" who encouraged her to read and to exercise her intellect, died before she was eight; nevertheless, he "casts the longest shadow across this book," remarked William Archer of *Best Sellers.* Origo writes of her three years in "society"—which she considered a waste of time—with "refreshing wit and merciless precision," a reviewer in *Listener* observed. Origo writes also of the gardens she created at La Foce and of the problems of biography, concluding in *Images and Shadows* that "only by discovering what life 'felt like,' to our subject . . . can we become aware of him as a *person* at all." *Images and Shadows,* wrote Anne Fremantle in the *New York Times Book Review,* is "a book nourishing from every point of view, filled with relations, friends, family, travel, work and war, but, above all, with love and learning."

A second hiatus in Origo's writing began around 1972, the year her poetry and prose compilation *The Vagabond Path* was published, when her husband had a stroke that left him half paralyzed; he died in 1976. Origo's next book was *A Need to Testify: Lauro de Bosis, Ruth Draper, Gaetano Salvemini, Ignazio Silone and an Essay on Biography,* published in 1984. It was a mix of biography and autobiography, noted H. Stuart Hughes in the *New York Times Book Review,* in the sense that her written impressions of the figures she portrayed in it were based partly on her memories of them as friends. "They all knew one another as well as the author; their lives were intertwined," Hughes explained. All had in various ways actively opposed Benito Mussolini's Fascist rule in the years surrounding World War II. Origo's other sources for her account were her subjects' letters and published writings. P. N. Furbank, reviewing *A Need to Testify* for the *Times Literary Supplement,* faulted Origo for being "a bit reverential, in the manner more often reserved for royalty" and for holding the reader "at a certain distance" from her friends, unlike Boswell and Carlyle, whom she named as her biographer heroes in the essay that begins the book. But Furbank nevertheless called Origo "a masterly narrator" and her account of her subjects "absorbing." Hughes particularly applauded her portrayal of Silone and said in summary that "her protagonists loom up heroic, larger than life."

The same year *A Need to Testify* was published, Origo's *War in Val d'Orcia* was released in the United States. Published with a new introduction, the historian Denis Mack Smith acclaimed the book's importance as a depiction of rural destruction wrought by war, rare in comparison to portrayals of urban bombing. *Newsweek* reviewer Peter S. Prescott wondered "why this extraordinary book should have been ignored by American publishers for 37 years," praising Origo for her reportorial account of daily happenings. "Wisely, . . . she did not seek to rewrite her story as a memoir," he said. "Cast as a diary, the most temporary of literary forms, [*War in Val d'Orcia*] retains a sense of immediacy and suspense, her hopes and fears of each moment, and so is likely to endure."

Origo's brief last book, *Un'amica: Rittrato di Elsa Dallolio*—her only book written in Italian—was published in 1988, the year she died of undisclosed causes. Another biography, it treated the life of Origo's friend Elsa Dallolio, whom reviewer Harvey Sachs described in the *Times Literary Supplement* as a fighter "for humane causes in Italy" and "a peripheral but much esteemed figure in the lives of Gaetano Salvemini, Bernard Berenson, Benedetto Croce, Jacques Maritain . . . and many others in the public eye." Though he found Origo remiss for not disclosing whether or not Dallolio was ever in love, Sachs concluded by calling the book, "like its immediate predecessor, *A Need to Testify,* a refreshingly unobjective yet unsentimentalized tribute to [Origo's] adoptive country, as well as Origo's valedictory gift to her readers."

In his review of *A Need to Testify* and *War in Val d'Orcia,* Hughes described Origo and her work in words that could stand as a tribute for her life. She was, he wrote, "a cosmopolitan in the pre-jet-set style of dignity and unintimidating ease in a variety of settings," and her books bore "her characteristic stamp of learning tempered with modesty, and enthusiastic participation in the lives of her fellow human beings, present and past."

BIOGRAPHICAL/CRITICAL SOURCES:

BOOKS

Origo, Iris, *War in Val d'Orcia: A Diary* J. Cape, 1947, published as *War in Val d'Orcia, 1943-1944: A Diary,* Godine, 1984.
Origo, Iris, *Images and Shadows: Part of a Life,* Harcourt, 1971.

PERIODICALS

Atlantic Monthly, July, 1971.
Best Sellers, May 15, 1971.
Commonweal, March 15, 1963.
Critic, December, 1962-January, 1963.
Economist, April 6, 1963.
Listener, December 24, 1970.

Manchester Guardian, October 22, 1957.
New Republic, August 21, 1935; May 8, 1971.
New Statesman and Nation, July 6, 1935.
Newsweek, April 2, 1984, p. 76.
New York Times, April 28, 1957; November 10, 1957; May 29, 1984.
New York Times Book Review, May 23, 1971; July 1, 1984, p. 10.
San Francisco Chronicle, November 20, 1949.
Saturday Review, May 8, 1971.
Spectator, September 16, 1949; November 27, 1953.
Times Literary Supplement, June 20, 1935; September 16, 1949; October 2, 1953; November 13, 1970; July 16, 1971; April 20, 1984, p. 428; October 7, 1988, p. 1094.
Washington Post, June 18, 1984.

OBITUARIES:

BOOKS

Burgess, Patricia, editor, *The Annual Obituary 1988,* St. James Press, 1990.*

*   *   *

OZ, Amos 1939-

PERSONAL: Given name Amos Klausner; born May 4, 1939, in Jerusalem, Israel; son of Yehuda Arieh (a writer) and Fania (Mussman) Klausner; married Nily Zuckerman, April 5, 1960; children: Fania, Gallia, Daniel. *Education:* Hebrew University of Jerusalem, B.A., 1963; St. Cross College, Oxford, M.A., 1970.

ADDRESSES: Office—Ben Gurion University Negev, Beer Sheva, Israel. *Agent*—Mrs. D. Owen, 28 Narrow St., London E. 14, England.

CAREER: Writer, 1962—. Visiting fellow, St. Cross College, Oxford University, 1969-70; writer in residence, Hebrew University of Jerusalem, 1975, and Colorado College, 1985; professor, Ben Gurion University Negev, Beer Sheva, Israel, 1986—. Has worked as tractor driver, youth instructor, school teacher, and agricultural worker at Kibbutz Hulda, Israel. *Military service:* Israeli Army, 1957-60; also fought as reserve soldier in the tank corps in Sinai, 1967, and in the Golan Heights, 1973.

MEMBER: PEN.

AWARDS, HONORS: Holon Prize for Literature, 1965; Israel-American Cultural Foundation award, 1968; B'nai B'rith annual literary award, 1973; Brener Prize, 1978; Bialik Prize, 1986; Prix Femina, 1988; Wingate Prize, 1988; International Peace Prize, German Publishers Association, 1992.

WRITINGS:

Artzot ha' tan (short stories), Massada (Tel Aviv), 1965, translation by Nicholas de Lange and Philip Simpson published as *Where the Jackals Howl, and Other Stories,* Harcourt (New York City), 1981.

Makom acher (novel), Sifriat Po'alim (Tel Aviv), 1966, translation by de Lange published as *Elsewhere, Perhaps,* Harcourt, 1973.

Michael sheli (novel), Am Oved (Tel Aviv), 1968, translation by de Lange in collaboration with Oz published as *My Michael,* Knopf (New York City), 1972.

Ad mavet (two novellas), Sifriat Po'alim, 1971, translation by de Lange in collaboration with Oz published as *Unto Death,* Harcourt, 1975.

Laga'at ba'mayim, laga'at ba'ruach (novel), Am Oved, 1973, translation by de Lange in collaboration with Oz published as *Touch the Water, Touch the Wind,* Harcourt, 1974.

Anashim acherim (anthology; title means "Different People"), Ha'Kibbutz Ha'Meuchad (Tel Aviv), 1974.

Har he'etza ha'raah (three novellas), Am Oved, 1976, translation by de Lange in collaboration with Oz published as *The Hill of Evil Counsel,* Harcourt, 1978.

Soumchi (juvenile), Am Oved, 1978, translation by Oz and Penelope Farmer published as *Soumchi,* Harper (New York City), 1980.

Be' or ha'tchelet he'azah (essays; title means "Under This Blazing Light"), Sifriat Po'alim, 1979.

Menucha nechonah (novel), Am Oved, 1982, translation by Hillel Halkin published as *A Perfect Peace,* Harcourt, 1985.

Po ve'sham b'eretz Yisra'el bistav 1982 (nonfiction), Am Oved, 1983, translation by Maurie Goldberg-Bartura published as *In the Land of Israel,* Harcourt, 1983.

(Editor with Richard Flantz and author of introduction) *Until Daybreak: Stories from the Kibbutz,* Institute for the Translation of Hebrew Literature, 1984.

Mi-mordot ha-Levanon, Am Oved, 1987, translation by Goldberg-Bartura published as *The Slopes of Lebanon* (essays), Harcourt, 1989.

Black Box (novel), translation by de Lange, Harcourt, 1988.

La-dat Ishah, Keter (Yerushalayim, Israel), 1989.

To Know a Woman, Harcourt, 1991.

Ha-Matsav Ha-Selishi, Keter, 1991.

Fima, Harcourt, 1993.

Shetikat Ha-Shamayim, Keter, 1993.

Al Tagioi Laila, Keter, 1994.

Editor of *Siach lochamium* (translated as "The Seventh Day"). Contributor of essays and fiction to periodicals in Israel, including *Davar.* Also contributor to such journals as *Encounter* and *Partisan Review.*

ADAPTATIONS: My Michael and *Black Box* have been adapted into films of the same titles in Israel.

SIDELIGHTS: Through fiction and nonfiction alike, Israeli author Amos Oz describes a populace under emotional and physical siege and a society threatened by internal contradictions and contention. According to Judith Chernaik in the *Times Literary Supplement,* Oz writes books that are "indispensable reading for anyone who wishes to understand . . . life in Israel, the ideology that sustains it, and the passions that drive its people." Immensely popular in his own country, Oz has also established an international reputation. Translations of his books have appeared in more than fifteen languages, including Japanese, Dutch, Norwegian, and Rumanian. In a *New Republic* assessment of the author's talents, Ian Sanders notes: "Amos Oz is an extraordinarily gifted Israeli novelist who delights his readers with both verbal brilliance and the depiction of eternal struggles—between flesh and spirit, fantasy and reality, Jew and Gentile. . . . His carefully reconstructed worlds are invariably transformed into symbolic landscapes, vast arenas where primeval forces clash." *Times Literary Supplement* contributor and novelist A. S. Byatt observes that in his works on Israel, Oz "can write with delicate realism about small lives, or tell fables about large issues, but his writing, even in translation, gains vitality simply from his subject matter." *New York Review of Books* correspondent D. J. Enright calls Oz Israel's "most persuasive spokesman to the outside world, the literary part of it at least."

"In a sense Amos Oz has no alternative in his novels but to tell us what it means to be an Israeli," writes John Bayley in the *New York Review of Books.* Oz is a sabra, or native-born Israeli, who has seen military service in two armed conflicts—the Six Day War and the Yom Kippur War—and has lived most of his adult life as a member of Kibbutz Hulda, one of Israel's collective communities. His fictional themes arise from these experiences and are often considered controversial for their presentations of individuals who rebel against the Israeli society's ideals.

The kibbutz provides Oz with a powerful symbol of the nation's aspirations, as well as a microcosm of the larger Jewish family in Israel, suffocatingly intimate and inescapable, yet united in defense against the hostile forces besieging its borders. *New York Times Book Review* contributor Robert Alter declares that nearly all of Oz's fiction "is informed by the same symbolic world picture: a hemmed-in cluster of fragile human habitations (the kibbutz, the state of Israel itself) surrounded by dark, menacing mountains where jackals howl and hostile aliens lurk." According to *Jewish Quarterly* contributor Jacob Sonntag, the people of Oz's fiction "are part of the landscape, and the landscape is part of the reality from which there is no escape." If the landscape is inescapable, the bonds of family also offer little relief. *New York Times Book Review* correspondent Morris Dickstein writes: "The core of feeling in Oz's work is always some sort of family, often a family being torn apart." *Los Angeles Times* correspondent Elaine Kendall similarly observes that Oz's fiction "confronts the generational conflicts troubling Israel today; emotional rifts intensified by pressure and privation. In that anguished country, the usual forms of family tension seem reversed; the young coldly realistic; the elders desperately struggling to maintain their belief in a receding ideal."

Alter contends that Oz's work is "symptomatic of the troubled connection Israeli writers increasingly feel with the realities of the Jewish state." Chernaik elaborates on this submerged "interior wilderness" that Oz seems compelled to explore: "The overwhelming impression left by his fiction is of the precariousness of individual and collective human effort, a common truth made especially poignant by a physical landscape thoroughly inhospitable to human settlement, and given tragic dimensions by the modern history of the Jews and its analogues in Biblical history." Oz himself told the *New Republic* that he tries to tap his own turmoil in order to write. His characters, he said, "actually want two different things: peace and excitement, excitement and peace. These two things don't get along very easily, so when people have peace, they hate it and long for excitement, and when they have excitement, they want peace."

A central concern of Oz's fiction is the conflict between idealistic Zionism and the realities of life in a pluralistic society. As a corollary to this, many of his sabra characters have decidedly ambivalent feelings towards the Arab population, especially Palestinians. *Commentary* essayist Ruth R. Wisse writes that in book after book, "Oz has taken the great myths with which modern Israel is associated—the noble experiment of the kibbutz, the reclamation of the soil, the wars against the British and the Arabs, the phoenix-like rise of the Jewish spirit out of the ashes of the Holocaust—and shown us their underside: bruised, dazed, and straying characters who move in an atmosphere of almost unalleviated depression." Nehama Aschkenasy offers a similar assessment in *Midstream:* "The collective voice is suspiciously optimistic, over-anxious to ascertain the normalcy and sanity of the community and the therapeutic effect of the collective body on its tormented member. But the voice of the individual is imbued with a bitter sense of entrapment, of existential boredom and nausea, coupled with a destructive surrender to the irrational and the antinomian." Dickstein notes that the author often "takes the viewpoint of the detached participant, the good citizen who does his duty, shares his family's ideals but remains a little apart, wryly skeptical, unable to lose himself in the communal spirit."

"Daytime Israel makes a tremendous effort to create the impression of the determined, tough, simple, uncomplicated society ready to fight back, ready to hit back twice as hard, courageous and so on," Oz told the *Partisan Review*. "Nocturnal Israel is a refugee camp with more nightmares per square mile I guess than any other place in the world. Almost everyone has seen the devil." The obsessions of "nocturnal Israel" fuel Oz's work, as Mark Shechner notes in *Nation.* "In [Oz's] fiction," Shechner writes, "the great storms that periodically descend on the Jews stir up strange and possessed characters who ride the gusts as if in a dream: raging Zionists, religious fanatics poised to take the future by force, theoreticians of the millennium, strategists of the end game, connoisseurs of bitterness and curators of injustice, artists of prophecy and poets of doctrine."

This is not to suggest, however, that Oz's work is unrelentingly somber or polemical. According to Dickstein, the "glow of Oz's writing comes from the spare and unsentimental warmth of his own voice, his feeling for atmosphere and his gallery of colorful misfits and individualists caught in communal enterprises." Bayley likewise concludes: "One of the admirable things about Oz's novels is the humor in them, a humor which formulates itself in having taken, and accepted, the narrow measure of the Israeli scene. Unlike much ethnic writing his does not seek to masquerade as Weltliterature. It is Jewish literature acquiescing amusedly in its new militantly provincial status."

My Michael, a novel about the psychological disintegration of a young Israeli housewife, was Oz's first work translated and published in English. *New Republic* contributor Lesley Hazleton calls the book "a brilliant and evocative portrait of a woman slowly giving way to schizoid withdrawal" and "a superb achievement, . . . the best novel to come out of Israel to date." In *Modern Fiction Studies,* Hana Wirth-Nesher expresses the view that Oz uses his alienated protagonist "to depict the isolation and fear that many Israelis feel partially as a country in a state of siege and partially as a small enclave of Western culture in a vast area of cultures and landscapes unlike what they have known." Alter praises *My Michael* for managing "to remain so private, so fundamentally apolitical in its concerns, even as it puts to use the most portentous political materials."

Paul Zweig claims in the *New York Times Book Review* that when *My Michael* was published in Israel shortly after the Six Day War, it proved "extremely disturbing to Israelis. At a time when their country had asserted control over its destiny as never before, Oz spoke of an interior life which Israel had not had time for, which it had paid no heed to, an interior life that contained a secret bond to the Asiatic world beyond its border." Disturbing though it was, *My Michael* was a best-seller in Israel; it established Oz's reputation among his fellow Israelis and gave him entree into the international world of letters.

Oz's first novel, *Elsewhere, Perhaps,* was his second work to be translated and published abroad. Most critics feel that the book is the best fictional representation of kibbutz life to emerge from Israel; for instance, *Jewish Quarterly* reviewer Jacob Sonntag writes: "I know of no other book that depicts life in the Kibbutz more vividly, more realistically or with greater insight." In the *Nation,* William Novak notes that the story of sudden violent events in the lives of three kibbutz families "engages our sympathies because of the compelling sincerity and moral concerns of the characters, and because of the extent to which this is really the story of an entire society." *New York Times Book Review* correspondent A. G. Mojtabai stresses the realistic sense of conflict between military and civilian values portrayed in *Elsewhere, Perhaps.* According to Mojtabai, two perceptions of "elsewhere" are active in the story: "elsewhere, perhaps, the laws of gravity obtain—not here; elsewhere, perhaps in some kingdom by the sea exists the model which our kibbutz imperfectly reflects, a society harmonious, healthful, joyful, loving—not here, not yet." Novak concludes that the novel's publication in the United States "should help to stimulate American appreciation of contemporary Israeli literature and society."

Oz's novel *A Perfect Peace,* published in Israel in 1982 and the United States in 1985, revolves around two young kibbutzniks—one rebellious after a lifetime in the environment, the other an enthusiastic newcomer—and an aging politician, founder of the collective. According to Alter, the novel is "a hybrid of social realism and metaphysical brooding, and it gains its peculiar power of assertion by setting social institutions and political issues in a larger metaphysical context. There is a vivid, persuasive sense of place here . . . but local place is quietly evoked against a cosmic backdrop." *Times Literary Supplement* reviewer S. S. Prawer observes that the work holds the reader's attention by providing a "variety of boldly drawn characters who reveal themselves to us in and through their speech. . . . Oz's storytelling, with its reliance on journals and inner monologues, is pleasantly old-fashioned." In a *New York Times Book Review* piece, Grace Schulman contends that it is "on a level other than the documentary that this novel succeeds so well. It is concerned with inner wholeness, and with a more profound peace than respect between generations and among countries. . . . The impact of this novel lies in the writer's creation of characters who are outwardly ordinary but inwardly bizarre, and at times fantastic."

"As a seamstress who takes different pieces of cloth and sews them into a quilt, Amos Oz writes short pieces of fiction which together form a quilt in the reader's conscious-

ness," notes J. Justin Gustainis in *Best Sellers.* "Just as the quilt may be of many colors but still one garment, Oz's stories speak of many things but still pay homage to one central idea: universal redemption through suffering." Oz began his literary career as an author of short fiction. He has since published several volumes of stories and novellas, including *Where the Jackals Howl and Other Stories, Unto Death,* and *The Hill of Evil Counsel.*

Aschkenasy suggests that the stories in *Where the Jackals Howl* "are unified by an overall pattern that juxtaposes an individual permeated by a sense of existential estrangement and subterranean chaos with a self-deceiving community collectively intent upon putting up a facade of sanity and buoyancy in order to deny—or perhaps to exorcise—the demons from without and within." Chernaik notes of the same book that the reader coming to Oz for the first time "is likely to find his perception of Israel permanently altered and shaped by these tales."

The novellas in *Unto Death* "take as their theme the hatred that surrounds Jews and that destroys the hated and the haters alike," to quote Joseph McElroy in the *New York Times Book Review. Midstream* contributor Warren Bargad finds this theme one manner of expressing "the breakdown of the myth of normalcy which has been at the center of Zionist longing for decades: the envisioned State of Israel, with its promise of autoemancipation, which would make of the Jewish people a nation among nations. For Oz it is still an impossible dream."

In the Land of Israel, a series of interviews Oz conducted with a wide variety of Israelis, is his best-known work of nonfiction. Shechner claims that the book "provoked an outcry in Israel, where many saw the portraits of Jews as exaggerated and tailored to suit Oz's politics." The study does indeed present a vision of a pluralistic, creatively contentious society, "threatened as much by the xenophobia and self-righteous tribalism within as by enemies without," according to Gene Lyons in *Newsweek.* Christopher Lehmann-Haupt offers a similar opinion in the *New York Times:* "All together, the voices of *In the Land of Israel* serve to elucidate the country's complex ideological crosscurrents. And conducted as they are by Mr. Oz, they sing an eloquent defense of what he considers a centrist position, though some of his critics might call it somewhat left-of-center." Lyons feels that the work is most valuable for what it shows the reader about Oz and his positions about his country's future. Lyons concludes: "Eloquent, humane, even religious in the deepest sense, [Oz] emerges here—and I can think of no higher praise—as a kind of Zionist Orwell: a complex man obsessed with simple decency and determined above all to tell the truth, regardless of whom it offends."

In an assessment of Oz's nonfiction, Shechner describes what he calls the "two Amos Ozes." One, Shechner writes, is "a fiction writer with an international audience, the other an Israeli journalist of more or less hometown credentials. . . . Oz's journalism would seem to have little in common with the crepuscular world of his fiction. A blend of portraits and polemics, it is straightforward advocacy journalism, bristling with editorials and belonging to the world of opinions, ideologies and campaigns." Despite his fiction's sometimes bleak portrayal of Israel, Oz believes in his homeland and expresses strong opinions on how he feels it should be run. Alter notes: "In contrast to the inclination some writers may feel to withdraw into the fastness of language, the Oz articles reflect a strenuous effort to go out into Israeli society and sound its depth." Furthermore, according to Roger Rosenblatt in the *New York Times Book Review,* as a journalist, Oz establishes "that he is no ordinary self-effacing reporter on a quest, but a public figure who for years has participated in major national controversies and who regularly gives his views of things to the international press, 'ratting' on his homeland." Schulman suggests in the *Washington Post Book World* that Oz's journalism "may be the way to an esthetic stance in which he can reconcile the conflicting demands of artistic concern and political turbulence."

Critics find much to praise in Oz's portraits of the struggling nation of Israel. "Mr. Oz's words, his sensuous prose and indelible imagery, the people he flings living onto his pages, evoke a cauldron of sentiments at the boil; yet his human vision is capacious enough to contain the destruction and hope for peace," writes Richard R. Lingeman in the *New York Times.* "He has caught a welter of fears, curses and dreams at a watershed moment in history, when an uneasy, restless waiting gave way to an upsurge of violence, of fearsome consequences. The power of his art fuses historical fact and symbol; he makes the ancient stones of Jerusalem speak, and the desert beyond a place of jackals and miracles." Kendall concludes: "This land of Oz is harsh and unfamiliar, resisting interpretation, defying easy solutions. His Israel is a place few tourists ever see and visiting dignitaries rarely describe." In the *Saturday Review,* Alfred Kazin states that Oz's effect on him is always to make him realize "how little we know about what goes on inside the Israeli head. . . . To the unusually sensitive and humorous mind of Amos Oz, the real theme of Jewish history—especially in Israel—is unreality. When, and how can a Jew attain reality in the Promised Land, actually touch the water, touch the wind?" Chernaik feels that Oz is "without doubt a voice for sanity, for the powers of imagination and love, and for understanding. He is also a writer of marvelous comic and lyric gifts, which somehow communicate themselves as naturally in English as in Hebrew."

Oz is an unusual Israeli writer in that he has chosen to stay at the kibbutz throughout his career, even though the income from his royalties is substantial. Even when he was younger, he said in *Partisan Review,* the kibbutz "evoked and fed my curiosity about the strange phenomenon of flawed, tormented human beings dreaming about perfection, aching for the Messiah, aspiring to change human nature. This perpetual paradox of magnanimous dream and unhappy reality is indeed one of the main threads in my writing." Furthermore, he told the *Washington Post,* his fellow kibbutzniks react to his works in fascinating ways: "It's a great advantage, you know, to have a passionate, immediate milieu and not a literary milieu—a milieu of real people who tell me straight in my face what they think of my writing."

Hebrew is the language in which Oz chooses to write; he calls it a "volcano in action," still evolving rapidly into new forms. Oz likes to call himself the "tribal storyteller," as he explained in the *New York Times:* "I bring up the evil spirits and record the traumas, fantasies, the lunacies of Israeli Jews, natives and those from Central Europe. I deal with their ambitions and the powderbox of self-denial and self-hatred." In a *Washington Post* interview, he maintained that Israel would always be the source from which his inspiration would spring. "I'm fascinated," he said of his homeland. "Yes, indeed, I'm disgusted, appalled, sick and tired sometimes. Even when I'm sick and tired, I'm there. . . . It's my thing, if you will, in the same sense that William Faulkner belonged in the Deep South. It's my thing and my place and my addiction."

Married and the father of three children, Oz continues to live and work at Kibbutz Hulda. He also speaks and travels frequently, bringing his personal thoughts to television and lecture audiences in Israel and abroad. Describing his creative impulses, Oz told the *New York Times:* "Whenever I find myself in total agreement with myself, then I write an article—usually in rage—telling the government what to do. But when I detect hesitation, more than one inner voice, I discover in me the embryo of characters, the seeds of a novel."

BIOGRAPHICAL/CRITICAL SOURCES:

BOOKS

Contemporary Literary Criticism, Gale, Volume 5, 1976, Volume 8, 1978, Volume 11, 1979, Volume 27, 1981, Volume 33, 1985, Volume 54, 1989.

PERIODICALS

Atlantic, December, 1983; May, 1988.
Best Sellers, October, 1978.
Chicago Tribune, December 7, 1989.
Commentary, July, 1974; April, 1984.
Jewish Quarterly, spring-summer, 1974.

Los Angeles Times, May 21, 1981; June 24, 1985; December 25, 1989.

Los Angeles Times Book Review, December 11, 1983; May 29, 1988, p. 3; May 12, 1991, p. 2.

Midstream, November, 1976; January, 1985.

Modern Fiction Studies, spring, 1978.

Nation, September 7, 1974; June 8, 1985; June 4, 1988, p. 796.

National Review, April 20, 1984.

New Leader, January 6, 1975.

New Republic, November 29, 1975; October 14, 1978; June 27, 1981; July 29, 1985; October 28, 1991, p. 36-40.

Newsweek, November 21, 1983; July 29. 1985.

New Yorker, November 18, 1974; August 7, 1978; August 19, 1985.

New York Review of Books, February 7, 1974; January 23, 1975; July 20, 1978; September 26, 1985; August 18, 1988, p. 30.

New York Times, May 19, 1978; July 18, 1978; May 22, 1981; October 31, 1983; November 11, 1989.

New York Times Book Review, May 21, 1972; November 18, 1973; November 24, 1974; October 26, 1975; May 28, 1978; April 26, 1981; March 27, 1983; November 6, 1983; November 25, 1984, p. 44; June 2, 1985; April 24, 1988, p. 7; March 19, 1989, p. 32; February 4, 1990; January 24, 1991, p. 32; June 9, 1991, p. 32; July 26, 1992, p. 24; October 24, 1993, p. 12.

Observer (London), July 7, 1985, p. 21; July 13, 1986, p. 27; June 26, 1988, p. 42; July 17, 1988, p. 42; February 4, 1990, p. 61; February 3, 1991, p. 54; September 12, 1993, p. 53.

Partisan Review, Number 3, 1982; Number 3, 1986.

Publishers Weekly, May 21, 1973; September 6, 1993, p. 84.

Saturday Review, June 24, 1972; November 2, 1974; May 13, 1978.

Spectator, January 9, 1982; December 17, 1983; August 10, 1985.

Studies in Short Fiction, winter, 1982.

Time, January 27, 1986.

Times (London), August 1, 1985.

Times Literary Supplement, July 21, 1972; February 22, 1974; March 21, 1975; October 6, 1978; September 25, 1981; July 27, 1984; August 9, 1985; June 24, 1988, p. 697; December 2, 1988, p. 1342; March 2, 1990.

Village Voice, February 14, 1984.

Washington Post, December 1, 1983.

Washington Post Book World, May 28, 1972; May 31, 1981; June 14, 1981; November 13, 1983; July 14, 1985.

World Literature Today, spring, 1982; spring, 1983; summer, 1984; autumn, 1986.

P

PAOLUCCI, Anne (Attura)

PERSONAL: Born in Rome, Italy; naturalized United States citizen; daughter of Joseph and Lucy (Guidoni) Attura; married Henry Paolucci. *Education:* Barnard College, B.A.; Columbia University, M.A., Ph.D.; also attended University of Perugia and the University of Rome.

ADDRESSES: Office—St. John's University, Jamaica, NY 11349.

CAREER: Rye Country Day school, Rye, NY, English teacher, 1955-57; The Brearly School, New York City, English teacher, 1957-59; City College of the City University of New York, New York City, assistant professor of English and comparative literature, 1959-69; St. John's University, Jamaica, NY, university research professor, 1969—, professor of English, 1975—, department chair, 1982—, director of Doctor of Arts program in English. Queens College of the City University of New York, distinguished (adjunct) visiting professor, 1982. Special lecturer, universities of Bologna, Catania, Messina, Palermo, Milan, Innsbruck, and Pisa, 1965-67, University of Bari, 1967, University of Urbino, summers, 1966 and 1967, Renaissance Institute at the Ashland Shakespeare Festival (Oregon), summers, 1974 and 1975, Chinese University of Hong Kong, 1979, Australian National University, Monash University, Deakin University, University of Adelaide, University of Queensland (St. Lucia), Flinders University, and Latrobe University, Australia, 1979; Fulbright lecturer in American drama at University of Naples, 1965-67; visiting fellow, Humanities Research Centre, Australian National University, 1979; guest speaker (with Edward Albee), Ohio Northern University, 1990.

Member of American Commission to Screen Fulbright Applicants for the United States, 1966, 1967; founder of American Playwrights' and Producers' Showcase (Na-

ples), 1967; special guest of Yugoslav Ministry of Culture, 1972; member of board of directors, World Centre for Shakespeare Studies, 1972—; founder and executive director, Council on National Literatures, 1974—; consultant to National Endowment for the Humanities, 1977—; member of advisory board, UNESCO's Commission of Technological and Cultural Transformation, 1978—; member of North American advisory council, Shakespeare Globe Theatre Center, 1981—; member of fellowship board, National Graduate Fellows Program (appointed by President Reagan), 1985-86; member of National Council on Humanities, 1986—. Organized and hosted television series *Magazines in Focus,* NYC-Television, 1972-73, and *Successful Women: Before, During, and After Women's Lib,* American Broadcasting Corporation, 1973; theatrical producer and director.

MEMBER: International Shakespeare Association, International Comparative Literature Association, Renaissance Institute of Japan, Byron Society of America and England (founding member of advisory board, 1973—), American Institute of Italian Studies (board of advisors, 1977—), American Society of Italian Legions of Merit (board of directors; chairman of cultural committee, 1990—), American Comparative Literature Association, PEN American Center, Renaissance Society of America, Modern Language Association of America (member of executive committee, 1975-77), Shakespeare Association of America, Hegel Society of America, Dante Society of America (member of council, 1974-76; vice president, 1976-77), Pirandello Society of America (founding member and vice president, 1968-79; president, 1979—), American Society of Italian Legions of Merit (board of directors, 1990—), National Society of Literature and the Arts, Alpha Psi Omega, Barnard Alumni Association, Andiron Club of New York (honorary member).

AWARDS, HONORS: Fulbright scholar at University of Rome, 1951-52; Artemesia award from *Quicksilver* (literary magazine), 1961, for "Poetry Reading"; Woodbridge honorary fellow, Columbia University, 1961-62; New York State grants, 1963, 1964, 1964-65; writer in residence at Yaddo colony, 1965; voted one of the ten best teachers, City College of the City University of New York, 1969; award from Italian-American Women of Achievement, 1970; drama award from Medieval and Renaissance Conference at Western Michigan University, 1972, for play *Minions of the Race;* received notable rating, *New York Times,* 1972, for *Magazines in Focus* television series; Woman of the Year award from Herman Henry Scholarship Foundation, 1973; Woman of the Year award, Woman's Press Club of New York, 1974; American Council of Learned Societies grant, 1978; City-Wide Italian Week Award, 1982; leadership award, Association of Teachers of New York, 1983; honored by Pirandello Society of America's 25th anniversary awards dinner, 1983; named one of ten outstanding Italian ambassadors in Washington, 1986; named Cavaliere of the Italian Republic, 1986; Gold Medal, National Italian American Foundation, 1990; award from Consortium of Italian-American Associations, 1991; award from American-Italian History Association, 1991; Columbus Award, Catholic Charities, 1991.

WRITINGS:

NONFICTION

(Translator) *Machiavelli's "Mandragola,"* Liberal Arts Press, 1957.
(Translator) Henry Paolucci and James Brophy, *Pierre Duhem on Galileo,* Twayne (Boston, MA), 1962.
Hegel on Tragedy, Anchor Books (New York City), 1962.
A Short History of American Drama, University of Urbino Press, (Italy), 1966.
Eugene O'Neill, Arthur Miller, Edward Albee, University of Urbino Press, 1967.
Commenti critici sur Giulio Cesare, Macbeth, Amleto, Otello, (title means "Critical Commentary on Julius Caesar, Macbeth, Hamlet, Othello"), University of Urbino Press, 1967.
From Tension to Tonic: The Plays of Edward Albee, Southern Illinois University Press (Carbondale, IL), 1972.
Pirandello's Theater: The Recovery of the Modern Stage for Dramatic Art, Southern Illinois University Press, 1974.
(Editor and author of introduction) *Canada,* Griffon House (Whitestone, NY), 1977.
(Editor and author of introduction) *Dante's Influence on American Writers,* Griffon House, 1977.
(Editor with Ronald Warwick) *India: Review of National Literatures,* Bagehot Council, 1979.

(With husband, H. Paolucci) *Dante and the "Quest for Eloquence" in India's Vernacular Languages,* Griffon House, 1984.
(Editor with Jennifer Stone) Mary Reynolds, *Pirandello: Annual Volume of Review of National Literature Essays on the Fiction and Plays of Luigi Pirandello, Nobel Laureate,* Bagehot Council, 1986.
(Editor) *Contemporary Literary Theory: An Overview,* Bagehot Council, 1987.
(Editor with H. Paolucci) *Columbus; Modern Views of Columbus and his Time: Essays, Poems, Reprints,* Griffon House, 1990.

Also editor, with Donald Puchala, of *Problems in National Literary Identity and the Writer as Social Critic: Selected Papers of the Fourth Annual NDEA Seminar on Foreign Area Studies, Columbia University, February 28-29, 1980,* Bagehot Council.

PLAYS

The Short Season (three acts), first produced in New York City at Cubiculo, 1970.
Minions of the Race, (one act), first produced in Kalamazoo, MI, at Western Michigan University, 1972.
(Translator) Mario Appollonio, *The Apocalypse According to J. J. [Rousseau]* (three acts), first produced in New York City at Classic Theater, 1976.
Incidents at the Great Wall, (one act), first produced with *Minions of the Race* in New York City at The Churchyard Theater, 1976.
In the Green Room with Machiavelli (first produced as a reading at Ashland Shakespeare Festival, 1974), Griffon House, 1980.
Cipango!: A One-Act Play in Three Scenes about Christopher Columbus (produced in New York City, 1987), Griffon House, 1985.
The Actor in Search of His Mask (one act; produced in Italian translation, Genoa, Italy, 1987), Griffon House, 1987.

SOUND RECORDINGS

Political Idealism and Political Realism: Dante and Machiavelli, Everett/Edwards Co., 1975.
Classical and Modern Tragedy: From Aeschylus to Shakespeare and Beyond, Everett/Edwards Co., 1975.
Masks in Focus: Dissolution of Character in Pirandello's Plays, Everett/Edwards Co., 1975.
Toward a New Theory of Comparative Literature, Everett/Edwards Co., 1975.

Also editor of forty-cassette series on China, for Everett/Edwards Co.

POEMS

Poems Written for Sbek's Mummies, Marie Menken, and Other Important Persons, Places and Things, Griffon House, 1977.
Riding the Mast Where It Swings, Griffon House, 1980.
Tropic of the Gods, Griffon House, 1980.
Gorbachev in Concert (and Other Poems), Bagehot Council, 1991.

FICTION

Eight Short Stories, Griffon House, 1977.
Sepia Tones: Seven Short Stories, Rimu Publishing/ Griffon House, 1986.
(With Nishan Paolucci) *Grandma, Pray for Me,* Bagehot Council, 1990.

OTHER

Contributor of numerous poems, stories, articles, and reviews to magazines, including *American Pen, Ararat, Literature East and West, Poem, South Carolina Review, Kenyon Review, Quicksilver, Shakespeare Quarterly,* and *Pacific Quarterly.* Founder and editor of *Review of National Literatures* and *CNL/Report,* both 1970—, and *CNL/Quarterly World Report,* both 1978—; member of editorial board of *Barnard Alumnae,* 1969-71, and *Pirandello Newsletter,* 1972; member of advisory board of *Italian-Americana,* 1973—, *America-Latina,* 1975—, and *Gradiva,* 1977—.

SIDELIGHTS: Though she became a United States citizen in her youth, Anne Paolucci has remained an amazingly energetic participant in civic, scholarly, educational, and media events which celebrate the Italian heritage. Commenting on her busy schedule in a *New York Daily News* profile, Paolucci admitted to sometimes writing around the clock without realizing it. "I just wish I had thirty hours in the day," she said of her hectic lifestyle. "It's a lot of work, but I enjoy it. I have fun."

In 1979 Paolucci's travels took her to Australia, where in addition to lecturing at a number of universities she found inspiration for her second book of poems, *Riding the Mast Where It Swings.* The centerpiece of this collection is a ten-page sequence entitled "Tropic of the Gods" which is dedicated "to my Australian friends." The poem attempts to capture the brooding presence of the Australian landscape, the American speaker's response to it, and echoes of the world culture from ancient Egypt through the Renaissance to such modernist poets as Ezra Pound and T. S. Eliot. It concludes: "Oblivion is a large silence / Beyond art." Other sequences in the collection deal with the Italian-American experience through the medium of bilingual poetry.

Italian-American experiences surface once again in Paolucci's 1986 volume of short stories, *Sepia Tones.* While the title refers to the brown-and-white tint of old photographs which accompany the stories, it also expresses a dominant tone of nostalgia in the stories themselves. Set in New York City and in the farm country of southern Italy, the stories are partially linked by recurring characters and setting. Reviewing the volume for the *New York Times Book Review,* Nancy Forbes praised the quality of "Rara," the story of a terminally ill priest, and "The Oracle Is Dumb or Cheat," a tale of two young lovers choosing between heritage and freedom. However, some of the other stories, Forbes felt, suffered from the author's unwillingness to give away the characters' unpleasant secrets; but the volume as a whole, she comments, "helps dispel the silence" about the Italian-American experience.

BIOGRAPHICAL/CRITICAL SOURCES:

BOOKS

Paolucci, Anne, *Riding the Mast Where It Swings,* Griffon House, 1980.

PERIODICALS

New York Daily News, November 22, 1978.
New York Times Book Review, February 16, 1986, p.16.*

*   *   *

PAPPAS, Lou Seibert 1930-

PERSONAL: Born August 1, 1930, in Corvallis, OR; daughter of Emil E. (a wholesale grocer) and Norma (Helgesson) Seibert; married Nicholas Pappas (a consultant), November 21, 1956 (divorced July, 1983); children: Derek, Alexis, Christian, Niko. *Education:* Oregon State University, B.S., 1952. *Avocational interests:* Travel, daily swimming, gardening.

ADDRESSES: Home—1201 Bryant St., Palo Alto, CA 94301.

CAREER: Sunset magazine, Menlo Park, CA, staff home economist, 1952-58, 1964-71; De Anza College, Cupertin, CA, instructor in home economics, 1972-78; food editor of *Peninsula Time Tribune,* 1978-91. Consultant to western food firms and to Ortho Books.

MEMBER: Home Economists in Business, Kappa Kappa Gamma.

AWARDS, HONORS: Hope Chamberlain Award, Oregon State University, 1975; R. T. French C. Tastemaker Award, 1983, for *Vegetable Cookery.*

WRITINGS:

Crossroads of Cooking, George Ritchie (San Francisco), 1973.
Greek Cooking, Harper (New York City), 1973.
Party Menus, Harper, 1974.
Bread Baking, Nitty Gritty Productions (Concord, CA), 1975.
Crockery Pot Cookbook, Nitty Gritty Productions, 1975.
Egg Cookery, 101 Productions (San Francisco), 1976.
Casseroles/Salads, Nitty Gritty Productions, 1977.
Gourmet Cooking the Slim Way, Addison-Wesley (Reading, MA), 1977.
International Fish Cookery, 101 Productions, 1979.
Entertaining the Slim Way, Addison-Wesley, 1979.
Cookies, Nitty Gritty Productions, 1981.
Entertaining in the Light Style, 101 Productions, 1982.
Vegetable Cookery, H.P. Books, 1982.
Creative Soups and Salads, Nitty Gritty Productions, 1983.
New American Chefs, 101 Productions, 1986.
(With Jane Horn) *Winemakers Cookbook,* Chronicle Books (San Francisco), 1986.
15-Minute Meals, Nitty Gritty Productions, 1991.
The Working Cook, Bristol, 1990.
Biscotti, Chronicle Books, 1992.
Cheesecake, Chronicle Books, 1993.
Holiday Feasts, Chronicle Books, 1993.
Pesto, Chronical Books, 1994.
Cinnamon, Chronicle Books, 1994.

SIDELIGHTS: Lou Seibert Pappas told *CA:* "Writing cookbooks, for me, is a great joy, an outpouring and sharing of great culinary discoveries. It is an intensive, well-disciplined time, brimming with working with great zeal. It is a way to consummate so many pleasures of travel and dining in one small compact volume. I write because I hope to bring pleasure to others with simple, sophisticated, delectable dishes."

*   *   *

PARNELL, Michael
    See ELMAN, Richard

*   *   *

PATON, David Macdonald   1913-1992

PERSONAL: Born September 9, 1913, in Hendon, England; died July 18, 1992, in England; son of William (a minister) and Grace Mackenzie (Macdonald) Paton; married Alison Georgina Stewart, September 12, 1946; children: William Stewart, John Mackenzie, David Michael Macdonald. *Education:* Brasenose College, Oxford, B.A., 1936, M.A., 1939.

CAREER: Ordained priest of Church of England, 1941; Student Christian Movement, Birmingham, England, secretary, 1936-39; Church of England missionary in China, 1940-44; Cambridge University, Westcott House, Cambridge, England, chaplain and librarian, 1945-46; Church of England missionary in China, 1947-50; vicar of Yardley Wood, Birmingham, 1952-56; Student Christian Movement Press (now SCM Press Ltd.), London, England, editor, 1956-59; Council for Ecumenical Co-operation of Church Assembly, London, secretary, 1959-63; Missionary and Ecumenical Council of Church Assembly, London, secretary, 1964-69; St. Mary de Crypt and St. John the Baptist Church of England, Gloucester, rector, 1970-81. Honorary Canon of Canterbury Cathedral, 1966-80, canon emeritus, beginning 1980. Chaplain to Queen Elizabeth II, 1972-83; vicar of Christ Church, Gloucester, 1979-81. Chairman of Churches' China Study Project, 1972-79, and Gloucester Civic Trust, 1972-77.

AWARDS, HONORS: Fellow of Selly Oak Colleges, 1981.

WRITINGS:

Christian Missions and the Judgment of God, SCM Press, 1953.
(With John T. Martin) *Paragraphs for Sundays and Holy Days,* SCM Press, 1957.
(Editor) *Essays in Anglican Self-Criticism,* SCM Press, 1958.
(Editor) *The Ministry of the Spirit,* World Dominion Press, 1960.
Anglicans and Unity, Mowbray, 1962.
(Editor) *Reform of the Ministry: A Study in the Work of Roland Allen,* Lutterworth, 1968.
(With Robert O. Latham) *Point of Decision,* Society for Promoting Christian Knowledge/Epworth Press, 1968.
(Editor) *Breaking Barriers,* World Council of Churches, 1976.
(Editor with C. W. Long) *The Compulsion of the Spirit: A Roland Allen Reader,* Eerdmans, 1983.

Also author of *The Life and Times of Bishop Ronald Hall of Hong Kong,* 1985. Contributor to religious journals.

OBITUARIES:

PERIODICALS

Times (London), August 22, 1992, p. 13.*

PEARL, Eric
See ELMAN, Richard

*   *   *

PEKIC, Borislav 1930-1992

PERSONAL: Surname pronounced "pekitch"; born February 4, 1930, in Podgorica, Yugoslavia (now Montenegro); died July 2, 1992, in London, England; immigrated to England, 1971; son of Vojislav Dusan (a lawyer) and Ljubica (an economist; maiden name, Petrovic) Pekic; married Liliana Glisic (an architect), May 11, 1958; children: Alexsandra. *Education:* Attended University of Belgrade, 1954-58. *Politics:* "Do not belong to any political party; by conviction social democrat." *Religion:* Serbian Orthodox.

ADDRESSES: Agent—Prince & Prince, Postbus 5400, Amsterdam, Holland.

CAREER: Lovcen Film, Titograd, Yugoslavia, dramaturge, 1959-64; free-lance writer, 1964-92.

MEMBER: PEN, Association of Yugoslav Writers, Association of Film Artists of Yugoslavia.

AWARDS, HONORS: First prize in film competition, 1958, for two filmscripts; *Hodocasce Arsenija Njegovana: Portret,* named best Yugoslav novel, 1970; *The Generals* named best Yugoslav comedy, 1972.

WRITINGS:

Vreme cuda, Prosveta (Belgrade), 1965, 2nd edition, Luca (Titograd), 1961, translation by Lovett Edwards published as *Time of Miracles,* Harcourt, 1976, reissued, Northwestern University Press, 1994.
Hodocasce Arsenija Njegovana: Portret, Prosveta, 1970, 2nd edition, 1971, translation by Bernard Johnson published as *Arsenie Negovan's Pilgrimage,* Harcourt, 1977, reissued, Northwestern University Press, 1994.
Uspon i pad Ikara Gubelkijana (title means "The Rise and Fall of Icarus Gubelkiyan"), Slovo Ljubve (Belgrade), 1975.
Odbrana i poslednji dani (title means "The Defense and Last Days"), Slovo Ljubve, 1977.
Zlatno runo (title means "The Golden Fleece"; parts one and two of tetralogy), Prosveta, 1977.
Pisma iz tu ine, Biblioteka Moderne, 1987.
Novi Jerusalim, Beograd, 1988.
Sentimentalna povest britanskog carstva, Beograd, 1992.
Atlantida, Biblioteka Moderne, 1988.

PLAYS

Generali ili Bratsvo po oruzju (title means "The Generals; or, a Kinship in Arms"), first produced in Belgrade at Atelje 212 Theatre, 1971.

Kako zabaviti gospodina Martina? (title means "How Can Mr. Martin Be Amused?"), first produced in Belgrade at Serbian National Theatre, 1970.
U Edenu na Istoku (title means "Eastwards, in Eden"), first produced in Belgrade at Atelje 212 Theatre, 1971.
Kako upokojiti vampira (title means "How To Get Rid of a Vampire"), first produced in Belgrade at Students Theatre, 1977.
Kategoricki zahtev (title means "Categorical Demand"), first produced in Titograd at Montenegrian National Theatre, 1977.

RADIO PLAYS

The Generals, first broadcast in Germany, 1969.
Goodby, Comrade, Goodby, first broadcast in Germany, 1970.
How Can Mr. Martin Be Amused?, first broadcast in Germany, 1971.
Theseus, Did You Kill the Minotaur?, first broadcast in Germany, 1972.
Eastwards, in Eden, first broadcast in Germany, 1973.
The Destruction of Speech, first broadcast in Germany, 1973.
Who Killed Lilly Schwarzkopf?, first broadcast in Germany, 1973.
The Case of One Commercial Traveller, first broadcast in Germany, 1974.
Categorical Demand, first broadcast in Germany, 1974.
How To Get Rid of a Vampire, first broadcast in Germany, 1974.
Who Killed My Immortal Soul?, first broadcast in Germany, 1974.
The Bad Day on the Stock Exchange, first broadcast in Germany, 1974.
Judah Triptych (includes *The Miracle in Jerusalem, The Miracle in Ghadara,* and *The Miracle in Jabnel*), first broadcast in Germany, 1975.

FILMSCRIPTS

The Fourteenth Day, Lovcen Film, 1961.
Don't Touch Into the Luck, Lovcen Film, 1963.
The Man, Lovcen Film, 1965.
The Generals, first broadcast by TV-Belgrade, 1973.

OTHER

Also adaptor of numerous works into filmscripts. Contributor to Yugoslav periodicals, including *Knjizevne Novine, Scena, Borba, Vidici,* and *Knjizevnost.* Editorial board member of journal *Knjizevne Novine,* 1968-69. Author of *The Years the Locust Devoured,* published in 1990.

SIDELIGHTS: Borislav Pekic once told *CA:* "My main interest is to study the relationship between man and various forms of power, from ownership to political power;

the main aim being to reveal all aspects of possession from which spiritual and moral deterioration derives and to denounce all forms of totalitarianism.

"History speaks for itself. The possession of property and power over people, namely all aspects of power over someone or something, in the end, results in oneself being possessed and overcome by one's own property, and the power which one enforces. I believe this to be the direct consequence of a wrongly orientated civilization, where the occasional regulators such as religion, morality and humanitarianism are helpless. Under these circumstances no revolutions except revolutions of an objective make any valid sense. The only hope lies in the realization of the vital necessity to utterly change one's angle on the view of life. Unfortunately such a conduct would seem as hopeless as a desperate attempt of a man to draw himself out of the mud, by pulling his own hair."

During his exile in Great Britain, Pekic maintained his Yugoslav passport and did not consider himself to be an emigrant. "Being temporarily away from my country will enable me to view the present situation there from an objective distance, and therefore obtain a clearer picture of socialism. Socialism is directly or indirectly linked with the theme of my writing, and it is necessary to prevent the manifestation of any one opinion."

Before his exile, Pekic was imprisoned for six years of a fifteen-year sentence at hard labor. He had been accused of organizing a Yugoslav social democratic student conspiracy against the state in 1948 while a student at the University of Belgrade. Pekic stated: "My six years of imprisonment as well as the lack of freedom to which I have been exposed for the best part of my life have influenced my work a great deal."

Regarding the lack of literary freedom, he said: "If any work is declared as unsuitable for publication for either ideological or political reasons, in the majority of the cases the work contains an undesirable truth. In that context the prohibition takes the form of a paradoxical compliment to the work. Thinking rationally, I accept it in this way. Emotionally however, it deeply disturbs me, as it is depriving me of an audience in my own country and therefore the freedom to express my opinion. This incapacity is in most cases only momentary. Literary work is virtually impossible to destroy and the temporarily buried works eventually come to life again. Almost like vampires, dating back to the folktales, the works seek revenge.

"Censorship is undoubtedly one of the most repulsive aspects of enforcing power in the intellectual sphere. Although in the long run it does not achieve the desired effect nor prevent the further development and exchange of ideas, it is unfortunately able to, in the short run, slow down the mentioned progress. The effect is multilateral.

The cases where the censorship reaches the threat of the author's banishment, it becomes, through the achieved fear and insecurity of the victims, a weapon of prevention as it forces the author into author-censorship and compromise. On the other hand it provides the people in power with the comfortable and peaceful feeling of everyone being in complete agreement."

OBITUARIES:

PERIODICALS

Times (London), July 9, 1992, p. 19.*

*   *   *

PETRAS, James Frank   1937-

PERSONAL: Born January 17, 1937, in Lynn, MA; married Elizabeth L. McLean, 1959; children: two. *Education:* Boston University, B.A. (cum laude), 1958; University of California, Berkeley, M.A., 1963, Ph.D., 1967.

ADDRESSES: Home—50 Dogwood Ln., Swarthmore, PA. *Office*—Department of Sociology, State University of New York, Binghamton, NY 13901.

CAREER: Pennsylvania State University, University Park, assistant professor, 1967-69, associate professor of political science, 1969-72, research associate at Institute of Public Administration, 1967-72, project director of public administration and agrarian reform program in Chile and Peru; State University of New York at Binghamton, professor of sociology, 1973—. Resident scholar, Center for the Study of Democratic Institutions, 1967; visiting lecturer, Torcuato Di Tella Institute, Center of Development Studies Caracas, Venezuela, Universidad Nacional, Montevideo, Uruguay, and Universidad San Andres; lecturer at colleges and universities in the United States and Europe.

MEMBER: American Sociological Association, American Political Science Association, Latin American Studies Association (member of executive council, 1971-72).

AWARDS, HONORS: Doherty Foundation Latin American studies research fellowship, 1965-66, for field research in Chile; Social Science Research Council grant, summers, 1970, 1975; Ford Foundation faculty fellowship, 1970-71.

WRITINGS:

Chilean Christian Democracy (monograph), Institute of International Studies, University of California, Berkeley, 1967.
(Editor with Maurice Zeitlin) *Latin America: Reform or Revolution?*, Fawcett (New York), 1968.
Political and Social Forces in Chilean Development, University of California Press, 1969.

(Editor with Martin Kenner) *Fidel Castro Speaks,* Grove (New York), 1969.

(With Zeitlin) *El Radicalismo politico de la clase trabajadora chilena* (title means "Chilean Working Class Radicalism"), Centro Editor de America Latina, 1970.

Politics and Structure in Latin America, Monthly Review Press (New York), 1970.

(With Robert LaPorte) *Cultivating Revolution: The United States and Agrarian Reform in Latin America,* Random House (New York), 1971.

Los Militares peruanos: Modernizadores o revolucionarios? (title means "Peruvian Military: Modernizers or Revolutionaries?"), Amorotu, 1971.

America latina: Politica y economia (title means "Latin America: Politics and Economy"), Editorial Periferia, 1972.

(With Hugo Zemelman) *Peasants in Revolt,* University of Texas Press (Austin), 1973.

Latin America: Dependence or Revolution, Wiley (New York), 1973.

Puerto Rico and the Puerto Rican Experience, Schenkman (Cambridge, MA), 1974.

(Editor with Adalberto Lopez) *The United States and Chile,* Monthly Review Press, 1975.

(With Morris Morley) *U.S. Imperialism and the Overthrow of Allende,* Monthly Review Press, 1975.

(Coauthor) *The Nationalization of Venezuelan Oil,* Praeger (New York), 1977.

Critical Perspectives on Imperialism and Social Class in the Third World, Monthly Review Press, 1979.

(Coauthor) *Class, State and Power in the Third World,* Allanheld, Osmun (Totowa, NJ), 1981.

Capitalist and Socialist Crises in the Late Twentieth Century, Rowman & Allanheld (Totowa), 1984.

Latin America: Bankers, Generals, and the Struggle for Social Justice, Rowman & Littlefield (Totowa), 1986.

The Reagan Administration and Nicaragua, Institute for Media Analysis, 1987.

(With Morley) *Latin America in the Time of Cholera,* Routledge & Kegan Paul (Boston), 1993.

(With Fernando Leiva) *Democracy and Poverty in Chile,* Westview (Boulder, CO), 1994.

(With James Kurth) *Mediterranean Paradoxes,* Berg Oxford, 1994.

OTHER

Contributor to books, including *Apolitical Politics,* Cromwell, edited by John Playford and Charles A. McCoy, 1967; *Trends and Tragedies in American Foreign Policy,* edited by Michael Parenti, Little, Brown (Boston), 1971; and *Revolution and Counter-Revolution in Chile,* edited by Paul Sweezy, Monthly Review Press, 1974. Contributor to anthologies, including *The New Cuba: An Anthology of*

Critical Evaluation, edited by Ronald Radosh, Crowell (New York), 1975. Contributor of articles and reviews to scholarly journals.

*   *   *

PEYREFITTE, (Pierre) Roger 1907-

PERSONAL: Born August 17, 1907, in Castres, France; son of Jean (a landowner) and Eugenie (Jamme) Peyrefitte. *Education:* University of Toulouse, diplome d'etudes lange et de litterature francaise, 1925; School of Political Studies, Paris, diplome, 1930. *Religion:* Catholic. *Avocational interests:* Antiques (the sale of his Greek and Roman coin collection in 1974 was the largest auction of its kind ever held in France), erotic art, rare books.

ADDRESSES: Home—9 avenue du Marechal-Maunoury, Paris 75016, France.

CAREER: French Ministry of Foreign Affairs, attache in Paris, 1931-33, secretary in French Embassy in Athens, Greece, 1933-38, attache in Paris, 1938-40, 1943-45. Writer, 1944—.

AWARDS, HONORS: Prix Theophraste Renaudot, 1945, for *Les Amities particulieres;* prize from the city of Palermo, Italy, 1953, for *Du Vesuve a l'Etna.*

WRITINGS:

NOVELS IN ENGLISH TRANSLATION

Les Amities particulieres, J. Vigneau, 1945, translation by Felix Giovanelli published as *Special Friendships,* Vanguard, 1950, translated by Edward Hyams, Secker & Warburg, 1958.

Les Ambassades, Flammarion (Paris), 1951, translation by Hyams published as *Diplomatic Conclusions,* Thames & Hudson, 1954.

Les Cles de Saint Pierre, Flammarion, 1955, translation by Hyams published as *The Keys of St. Peter,* Criterion, 1957.

Chevaliers de Malte, Flammarion, 1957, translation by Hyams published as *Knights of Malta,* Criterion, 1959.

L'Exile de Capri, Secker & Warburg, 1961.

La Nature du prince, 1963, translation by Peter Fryer published as *The Prince's Person,* Secker & Warburg, 1964, Farrar, Straus, 1965.

Les Juifs, Flammarion, 1965, revised edition, 1968, translation by Bruce Lowery published as *The Jews: A Fictional Venture into the Follies of Anti-Semitism,* Bobbs-Merrill, 1967.

OTHER

Mademoiselle de Murville (novel), J. Vigneau, 1947.

L'Oracle (novel), Flammarion, 1947.
Les Amours singulieres (short stories), Flammarion, 1949.
Jeunes Proies (short stories), Flammarion, 1956.
Les Fils de la lumiere (novel), Flammarion, 1961.
Les Americains (novel), Flammarion, 1968.
Des Francais (satire), Flammarion, 1970.
La Coloquinte (novel), Flammarion, 1971.
Roy (novel), Albin Michel, 1974.
L'illustre Ecrivain (novel), Albin Michel, 1982.
La Soutane rouge (novel), Le Mercure, 1983.

PLAYS

Le Prince des neiges (three act; first produced in Paris at Hebertot Theatre, 1946), Flammarion, 1947.
Le Spectateur nocturne (three act), Flammarion, 1960.

NONFICTION

La Mort d'une mere (autobiography), Flammarion, 1950.
Du Vesuve a l'Etna, Flammarion, 1952, translation by J. H. F. McEwen published as *South from Naples,* Thames & Hudson, 1954.
Les Secrets des conclaves, Flammarion, 1964.
Lettre ouverte a Monsieur Francois Mauriac, Editions Dynamo, 1964.
Notre Amour (auto-confessions), Flammarion, 1967.
L'Enfant amour, Flammarion, 1969.
(With Paul Xavier Giannoli) *Roger Peyrefitte; ou, Les Cles du scandale,* Fayrad, 1970.
Manouche (biography of Germaine Germain), Flammarion, 1972, translation by Derek Coltman published under same title, Hart-Davis (London), 1973, translation by Sam Flores published under same title, Grove (New York City), 1974.
Tableaux de chasse; ou, La vie extraordinaire de Fernand Legros (biography), Albin Michel, 1976.
Propos secrets (biography), Albin Michel, 1977.
La jeunesse d'Alexandre, Albin Michel, 1977.
L'Enfant de coeur, Albin Michel, c. 1978.
Les Conquetes d'Alexandre, Albin Michel, c. 1979.
Alexandre le Grand, Albin Michel, 1981.

EDITOR

Un Musee de l'amour, Editions du Rocher (Monaco), 1972.

(And translator) *Straton of Sardis and Lucian of Samosata, La Muse garconniere et les amours,* Flammarion, 1973.

OTHER

Also author of *Henry de Montherlent-Roger Peyrefitte correspondence,* 1983; *Voltaire, sa Jeunesse et son temps,* 1985; *L'Innominato, nouveaux propos secrets,* 1989; and *Reflexion sur de Gaulle,* 1992.

ADAPTATIONS: Les Ambassades was adapted for the stage in 1961, and *Les Amities particulieres* was made into a film in 1964.

SIDELIGHTS: Roger Peyrefitte has been both denounced as a "mere scandalmonger and sly pornographer" and vindicated as a "moralist of genuine indignation" for his satirical parodies of European society—criticisms that have resulted in several legal suits. In 1958 he accepted amnesty from a suit filed by the Italian Government in response to an article about Pope Pius XII. Another suit was filed involving the book *L'Exile de Capri* in 1959. In 1965 he defeated an attempt by members of the Rothschild family to stop the sale of *Les Juifs,* although a few lines of the book had to be changed in later printings. In 1970 actress Marlene Dietrich sued over *Des Francais* and sensation spread far beyond the borders of Italy when Peyrefitte wrote a magazine article accusing Pope Paul VI of maintaining a homosexual relationship before he rose to the papacy.

Out of court Peyrefitte's work has sparked confrontation between artists and other writers. During the filming of *Les Amities particulieres* in 1964 a protest occurred which divided the Paris literary world nineteen years after the book's original publication. Critics have been equally divided in their opinions of Peyrefitte's books. Panning *Les Juifs* (published in the United States as *The Jews: A Fictional Venture into the Follies of Anti-Semitism*), Renee Winegarten concluded: "Peyrefitte, who has been called an industrialist of scandal, has merely seized yet another opportunity to exercise his talent as backbiter and mischief-maker royal."

Other critics have pointed out his elegant style and upheld his right as an artist to choose subject matter without having to anticipate reader prejudice. In a review of *The Prince's Person,* a book heavily impugning the Catholic

Church of the Renaissance, Laurent LeSage asserted: "To tell a tale so bawdy Peyrefitte deploys all the graces of his style. Nuance, delicate thrust, allusion, humorous understatement, and the strictest propriety of language keep the story from foundering in its offensiveness. He is an artist, not a pornographer. A historian, too, if you will, of impressive erudition—but still an artist, who makes fact and document cast their own spell within a most terse narration." LeSage's only regret is "that such art is not put to nobler uses."

In *Manouche,* the biography of Germaine Germain, the famous paramour of Mistinguett and Paul-Bonaventure Carbone, a *Newsweek* writer observed the apt parallel of the woman to the times in which she lived. "As Roger Peyrefitte implies in his book, a best seller in Europe, she was symptomatic both of France's frenetic gaiety during the early 1930s and of the nation's moral deterioration during Nazi occupation. . . . If this book is nominally a biography of a colorful, raunchy personality, it is equally an evocation of France's most ignominious era." In this book, he evokes bitter memories of occupied France and revives some accusations of alleged collaboration.

BIOGRAPHICAL/CRITICAL SOURCES:

PERIODICALS

Commentary, January, 1968.
Kenyon Review, summer, 1962.
Newsweek, July 19, 1965; January 1, 1967; September 30, 1974.
New York Times Book Review, October 14, 1965; February 25, 1968.
Punch, November 29, 1967.
Saturday Review, May 8, 1965; November 2, 1968.
Time, July 16, 1965.
Times Literary Supplement, July 13, 1967.
Variety, July 8, 1970.*

*   *   *

PHELPS, Gilbert (Henry, Jr.) 1915-1993

PERSONAL: Born January 23, 1915, in Gloucester, England; died June 15, 1993, in Finstock, Oxfordshire, England; son of Gilbert Henry (a clerk) and Mary (Wilks) Phelps; married Dorothy Elizabeth Coad, April 11, 1939 (divorced); married Dorothy Kathleen Batchelor, 1972; children: (first marriage) John David, Jean Hazel; (second marriage) Sebastian Barnes, Bartholomew Barnes, Julian Wesley (stepsons). *Education:* Fitzwilliam College, Cambridge, B.A. (first class honors), 1937, St. John's College, Cambridge, M.A., 1941. *Politics:* Progressive. *Religion:* Anglican.

ADDRESSES: Agent—Elaine Green Ltd., 31 Newington Green, Islington, London N16 9PU, England.

CAREER: British Institute, Lisbon, Portugal, British Council lecturer in English, 1940-42; Blundell's School, Tiverton, Devon, England, senior English master, 1943-45; British Broadcasting Corp., producer in Bristol, England, 1945-50, supervisor of educational talks in London, England, 1950-52, chief instructor of staff training, 1953-60; full-time writer, lecturer, and broadcaster on travel, history, and literature. Lecturer to British Armed Forces, 1943-50. Guest lecturer at numerous universities and colleges throughout Great Britain and the United States. Made numerous appearances on BBC network for Home, World, European, and Far Eastern Services. Judge for various literary awards. *Military service:* Royal Air Force, 1940-43.

MEMBER: International PEN, Royal Society of Literature (fellow), Society of Authors, Royal Commonwealth Society, Southern Arts Association (former chairman of literature panel).

AWARDS, HONORS: Poetry award, University of Pennsylvania, 1950; Arts Council Award, 1965; Arts Council bursary, 1968.

WRITINGS:

The Dry Stone (novel), Barker, 1953, published as *The Heart in the Desert,* John Day, 1954.
A Man in His Prime (novel), John Day, 1955.
The Russian Novel in English Fiction, Hutchinson, 1956, reprinted, Scholarly Press, 1971.
Latin America, British Broadcasting Corp., 1956.
The Centenarians (novel), Heinemann, 1958.
The Love before the First, Heinemann, 1960.
The Winter People (novel), Bodley Head, 1962, Simon & Schuster, 1964, abridged edition, Chatto & Windus, 1965.
A Short History of English Literature, Folio, 1962, revised and enlarged edition published as *A Survey of English Literature: Some of the Main Themes and Developments from Beowulf to 1939,* Pan Books, 1965.
The Green Horizons: Travels in Brazil, Simon & Schuster, 1964 (published in England as *The Last Horizon: Travels in Brazil,* Bodley Head, 1964, 2nd edition published as *The Last Horizon: A Brazilian Journey,* Knight, 1971).
The Tenants of the House (novel), Barrie & Jenkins, 1971.
Mortal Flesh (novel), Random House, 1973 (published in England as *The Old Believer,* Barrie & Jenkins, 1973).
The Low Roads (novel), Barrie & Jenkins, 1975.
The Tragedy of Paraguay, St. Martin's, 1975.
Squire Waterton (biography), EP Publishing, 1976.
Story of the British Monarchy, Nile & Mackenzie, 1977.

A Reader's Guide to Fifty British Novels, 1600-1900, Barnes & Noble, 1979 (published in England as *An Introduction to Fifty British Novels, 1600-1900,* Pan Books, 1979).

From Myth to Modernism: A Short Survey of World Fiction, Folio, 1987.

EDITOR

Living Writers, Sylvan Press, 1950.

(And author of introduction and notes) William Makepeace Thackery, *Vanity Fair,* Pan Books, 1967.

Question and Response: A Critical Anthology of English and American Poetry, Cambridge University Press, 1969.

(And author of introduction and notes) Laurence Sterne, *Tristram Shandy,* Folio, 1970.

The Byronic Byron: A Selection from the Poems of Lord Byron, Longman, 1971.

(And author of introduction and notes) H. G. Wells, *Tono-Bungay,* Pan Books, 1972.

(And author of introduction and notes) Charlotte Bronte, *Villette,* Pan Books, 1973.

(And author of introduction and notes) E. M. Forster, *Howard's End,* Folio, 1973.

(And author of introduction) Charles Waterton, *Wanderings in South America, the North-West of the United States, and the Antilles in the Years 1812, 1816, 1820, 1824,* abridged edition, Knight, 1973, Transatlantic, 1974.

(Author of introduction) *The Rare Adventures and Painful Peregrinations of William Lithgow,* Folio, 1974.

(And author of introduction) *Byron: An Autobiographical Anthology,* Grasshopper Press, 1974.

(And author of introduction and notes) William Makepeace Thackeray, *Henry Esmond,* Pan Books, 1974.

(And author of introduction and notes) Samuel Johnson, *The History of Rasselas,* Folio, 1975.

Arlott and Trueman on Cricket, British Broadcasting Corp., 1977.

(And author of introduction and notes) Stendhal, *The Charterhouse of Parma,* Folio, 1977.

(With son, John Phelps) James Herriot and others, *Animals Tame and Wild,* Sterling, 1979, published as *Between Man and Beast,* Bonanza Books, 1979, reissued, 1989.

(And author of introduction and notes) Henry James, *The Europeans,* Folio, 1982.

(And author of introduction and notes) Virginia Woolf, *To the Lighthouse,* Folio, 1988.

CONTRIBUTOR

Life under the Tudors, Falcon Press, 1950.
Life under the Stuarts, Falcon Press, 1951.
Explorers Remember, Hodder & Stoughton, 1967.

Collected Articles on George Gissing, Cassell, 1967.
Notes on Literature, British Council, 1973.
John D. Jump, editor, *A Byron Symposium,* Macmillan, 1975.
Pelican Guide to English Literature, eight volumes, Penguin, 1981-82.
A History of British Culture, nine volumes, Folio, 1988.

OTHER

Work represented in anthologies, including: Malcolm Elwin, editor, *Faber Book of West County Stories,* Macdonald & Co., 1947; *Poetry Awards,* University of Pennsylvania Press, 1950; *PEN New Poems,* M. Joseph, 1953. Author of radio plays, including *The Tide Comes In,* 1960, *The Spanish Cave* (based on novel by Geoffrey Household), 1960, *The Winter People* (based on Phelps's novel of same title), 1964, *Deliberate Adventure,* 1968, and *The Tankerdown Skull;* also author of television features. Contributor of fiction, poetry, and articles on education to London periodicals, including *Observer, Spectator, Listener, New Statesman,* and *Poetry Review.* Editor of an edition of William Shakespeare's *Romeo and Juliet* and of *The Cambridge Guide to Arts and Literature.* Contributor to *A Guide to English Literature,* Cassell.

BIOGRAPHICAL/CRITICAL SOURCES:

PERIODICALS

Atlantic, October, 1964.
Books, October, 1971.
Book Week, December 6, 1964.
Commonweal, June 18, 1954.
New York Times, May 16, 1954, May 16, 1955.
Saturday Review, May 22, 1954, June 4, 1955, October 10, 1964.
Spectator, March 11, 1955.
Times Literary Supplement, March 25, 1955.

OBITUARIES:

PERIODICALS

Times (London), June 29, 1993, p. 15.*

*   *   *

PILGRIM, Anne
  See ALLAN, Mabel Esther

*   *   *

PLAYFAIR, Guy Lyon 1935-

PERSONAL: Born April 5, 1935, in Quetta, India; son of I.S.O. (a military officer) and Jocelyn (Malan) Playfair.

Education: Pembroke College, Cambridge, B.A. (with honors), 1959.

ADDRESSES: Office—7 Earls Court Sq., London SW5 9BY, England.

CAREER: Freelance writer and photographer in Brazil, 1961-75; U.S. Agency for International Development, Information Office, Rio de Janeiro, Brazil, writer, 1967-71.

MEMBER: Society for Psychical Research, Society of Authors, College of Psychic Studies.

WRITINGS:

The Unknown Power, Pocket Books (New York City), 1975.
The Indefinite Boundary, St. Martin's (New York City), 1977.
(With Scott Hill) *The Cycles of Heaven,* St. Martin's, 1978.
This House Is Haunted: The True Story of a Poltergeist, Stein & Day (New York City), 1980.
If This Be Magic, J. Cape (London), 1985.
The Haunted Pub Guide, Harrap (London), 1985.
(With Uri Geller) *The Geller Effect,* Henry Holt (New York City), 1987.
(With David Berglas) *A Question of Memory,* J. Cape, 1988.
The Evil Eye: The Unacceptable Face of Television, J. Cape, 1990.

Contributor to *The Unexplained,* Orbis, 1980-82.

SIDELIGHTS: Guy Lyon Playfair told *CA:* "I am interested in border areas of human experience and in anomalous phenomena of all kinds. I find the influence of sunspots as interesting as the behavior of poltergeists or psychic surgeons, and I strongly object to finding my books classified as 'occult.' I am not concerned with the 'supernatural' but with unexplored areas of nature that are by definition natural."

Playfair is an amateur musician who has played trombone in several orchestras and jazz groups. He admits to having almost become a professional jazz musician, "but the life was too hectic." Now he owns a concert harpsichord, "which I keep meaning to learn to play properly. But however badly I play, it's better than watching television, which I gave up several years ago after reading Jerry Mander's *Four Arguments for the Elimination of Television.*"

* * *

POLITI, Leo 1908-

PERSONAL: Born November 21, 1908, in Fresno, CA; married Helen Fontes, 1938; children: Paul, Suzanne. *Ed-*

ucation: Studied at National Art Institute, Monza, Italy, for six years.

ADDRESSES: Home—Los Angeles, CA. *Office*—c/o Macmillan Publishing Co., Inc., 866 Third Ave., New York, NY 10022.

CAREER: Artist, author, and illustrator. Worked as an artist for *Script,* Los Angeles, CA.

AWARDS, HONORS: Caldecott Honor Book, American Library Association (ALA), 1947, for *Pedro, the Angel of Olvera Street,* and in 1949, for *Juanita;* Herald Tribune Spring Book Festival Honor Award, 1948, for *Juanita,* and 1949, for *At the Palace Gates;* Caldecott Medal for best illustrated book of the year, American Library Association, 1950, for *Song of the Swallows;* Herald Tribune Spring Book Festival Award for picture books, 1952, for *Looking-for-Something: The Story of a Stray Burro in Ecuador;* Southern California Council on Literature for Children and Young People Award, for significant contribution to children's literature in the field of illustration, 1961, for *Moy Moy;* Regina Medal, Catholic Library Association, 1966, for "continued distinguished contribution to children's literature"; Friends of Children and Literature Award, 1980, for "excellence in children's literature with a California theme."

WRITINGS:

SELF-ILLUSTRATED; FOR CHILDREN

Little Pancho, Viking (New York City), 1938.
Pedro, the Angel of Olvera Street (ALA Notable Book), Scribner (New York City), 1946.
Young Giotto, Horn, 1947.
Juanita, Scribner, 1948.
Song of the Swallows (Junior Literary Guild selection), Scribner, 1951.
Little Leo (Junior Literary Guild selection), Scribner, 1951.
The Mission Bell (ALA Notable Book), Scribner, 1953.
The Butterflies Come, Scribner, 1957.
Saint Francis and the Animals, Scribner, 1959.
A Boat for Peppe, Scribner, 1960.
Moy Moy, Scribner, 1960.
All Things Bright and Beautiful, Scribner, 1962.
Lito and the Clown, Scribner, 1962.
Rosa, Scribner, 1963.
Piccolo's Prank, Scribner, 1965.
Mieko, Golden Gate Books (San Carlos, CA), 1969.
Emmet, Scribner, 1971.
The Nicest Gift, Scribner, 1973.
Three Stalks of Corn, Scribner, 1976.
Mr. Fong's Toy Shop, Scribner, 1978.

Contributor to *Expectations 1980* (braille anthology), published by Braille Institute Press.

SELF-ILLUSTRATED; FOR ADULTS

Bunker Hill, Los Angeles: Reminiscences of Bygone Days, Desert Southwest (Palm Desert, CA), 1964.
Tales of the Los Angeles Parks, Best West (Palm Desert, CA), 1966.
The Poinsettia, Best West, 1967.

ILLUSTRATOR

Ruth Sawyer, *The Least One,* Viking, 1941.
Margarita Lopez, *Aqui se habla espanol,* Heath, 1942.
Helen Garrett, *Angelo, the Naughty One,* Viking, 1944.
Frank Henius, editor, *Stories from the Americas,* Scribner, 1944.
Catherine Blanton, *The Three Miracles,* Day, 1946.
Louis Perez, *El Coyote, the Rebel,* Holt, 1947.
Helen Rand Parish, *At the Palace Gates,* Viking, 1949.
M. Lopez de Mestos and Esther Brown, *Vamos a Habla Espanol,* Heath, 1949.
Ann Nolan Clark, *Magic Money,* Viking, 1950.
Clark, *Looking-for-Something: The Story of a Stray Burro in Ecuador* (Junior Literary Guild selection), Viking, 1952.
Alice Dalgliesh, *The Columbus Story* (ALA Notable Book), Scribner, 1955.
Elizabeth Coatsworth, *The Noble Doll,* Viking, 1961.
Edith Parker-Hinckley, *Two Girls and a Kite,* Moore Historical Foundation, 1984.
Dolores S. Lisica, editor, *Around the World, Around Our Town: Recipes from San Pedro,* R. & E. Miles, 1986.
Tony Johnston, *Lorenzo, the Naughty Parrot,* Harcourt, 1992.

Also contributor of numerous illustrations to children's magazines.

ADAPTATIONS: Song of the Swallows was adapted for a filmstrip with record or cassette, and was also released as a cassette with an accompanying book and teacher's guide, Miller-Brody.

SIDELIGHTS: Leo Politi is best known for his works depicting life in the historic Spanish section of Los Angeles, surrounding Olvera Street. His warm, earthy pictures have helped to preserve the area's culture for children of all backgrounds to enjoy. Politi has also written and illustrated books about the same area for adults. Although he was born in Fresno, California, Politi's family returned to his mother's hometown in Italy when he was seven years old. It was here, for the most part, that he spent the rest of his youth and adolescence. Politi liked to draw from an early age, and as Rosemary Livsey reported in her article for *Horn Book,* in Italy "he spent happy days playing, studying and drawing everything that he saw, on scraps of paper, in his books, wherever he could find space." Politi and his family also spent a year in London, England,

where, as Livsey revealed, he "went often to St. Martin's Lane to watch the artists draw on the sidewalks." Politi told Livsey that he was deeply impressed by "the deftness of the lines and the speed with which the colored chalk pictures appeared on the pavements."

After the Politi family returned to Italy, the author's mother, convinced of her son's talent, encouraged him to enter a scholarship competition. He won a place at the National Art Institute at Monza, near Milan, Italy, and studied there for six years. Politi left the institute qualified to be an art teacher, but he chose instead to begin creating on his own. With a friend he experimented with textile and tapestry design; he also did his first book illustrations.

Politi eventually returned to California via the Panama Canal, falling in love with the Latin American countries he visited along the way. As Livsey explained: "The gentleness and beauty of the Latin Americans filled him with a desire to learn more of these people for whom he felt great admiration and kinship." After Politi married, he and his wife settled in the Hispanic section of Los Angeles, on Olvera Street. In his book for adults, *Bunker Hill, Los Angeles: Reminiscences of Bygone Days,* Politi recalled attempting to make a living through his artwork; "It was during the depression, and many a night my wife sat patiently at my side as I did water colors in front of the El Paseo Cafe. I might sketch the woman making tortillas in the puesto across from us, or the three Mexican musicians singing near us, or the little urchins running up and down the street. Sometimes, with just a knife, I carved on discarded blocks of wood I found. And many a cold night we waited for customers who never came." Times got better when Politi began doing illustrations for the magazine *Script.* He published his first children's book, *Little Pancho,* in 1938. Eventually Politi's work came to the attention of Alice Dalgliesh, an editor at Scribner, and he began illustrating the works of other children's authors and eventually creating his famous California stories for children. Politi also met with success writing and illustrating books for adults during the 1960s, including *Bunker Hill, Los Angeles* and *Tales of the Los Angeles Parks.*

BIOGRAPHICAL/CRITICAL SOURCES:

BOOKS

Arbuthnot, May Hill, *Children and Books,* 3rd edition, Scott, Foresman, 1964.
Politi, Leo, *Bunker Hill, Los Angeles: Reminiscences of Bygone Days,* Desert Southwest, 1964.

PERIODICALS

Catholic Library World, February, 1966.
Horn Book, March-April, 1949, pp. 97-108; July-August, 1950; April, 1966, pp. 218-22.

PORTER, Laurence M(inot) 1936-

PERSONAL: Born January 17, 1936, in Ossining, NY; son of Fairfield and Anne Elizabeth (Channing) Porter; married Elizabeth Johnson Hart (an architect), June 9, 1960 (divorced, 1979); married Laurel Melinda Cline (a social worker and writer), January 17, 1980 (divorced, 1992); children: Leon Fairfield, Sarah Elizabeth, John Carl Fairfield. *Education:* Harvard University, A.B. (cum laude), 1957, A.M., 1959, Ph.D., 1965. *Politics:* "For human rights and human services." *Religion:* Agnostic. *Avocational interests:* Singing in madrigal groups, running (including the Boston Marathon).

ADDRESSES: Home—723 Collingwood Dr., East Lansing, MI 48823-3416. *Office*—Department of Romance and Classical Languages and Literatures, Michigan State University, 341 Old Horticulture Building, East Lansing, MI 48824-1112.

CAREER: Michigan State University, East Lansing, instructor, 1963-65, assistant professor, 1965-69, associate professor, 1969-73, professor of French and comparative literature, 1973—. Codirector of National Colloquium on Nineteenth-Century French Studies, 1978; University of Pittsburgh, Andrew W. Mellon Distinguished Visiting Professor of Comparative Literature, 1980. *Military service:* U.S. Army Reserve, 1957-63.

MEMBER: International Comparative Literature Association, Modern Language Association of America, American Association of University Professors, American Comparative Literature Association, American Association of Teachers of French, Phi Kappa Phi, Sierra Club, Appalachian Mountain Club.

AWARDS, HONORS: Ford Foundation grant, 1966; National Endowment for the Humanities travel grant, 1989; United States Information Agency grant, 1991.

WRITINGS:

(Editor and translator, with Elisha Greifer) Joseph de Maistre, *On God and Society,* Regnery, 1959.
The Renaissance of the Lyric in French Romanticism, French Forum Monographs, 1978.
The Literary Dream in French Romanticism, Wayne State University Press (Detroit, MI), 1979.
(Editor with wife, Laurel Porter) *Aging in Literature,* International Book Publishers, 1984.
(Editor) *Critical Essays on Gustave Flaubert,* G. K. Hall (Boston, MA), 1986.
The Interpretation of Dreams: Freud's Theories Revisited, Twayne (Boston), 1987.
The Crisis of French Symbolism, Cornell University Press (Ithaca, NY), 1990.

(Editor with Eugene F. Gray) *Approaches to Teaching "Madame Bovary,"* Modern Language Association of America (New York City), 1995.

Contributor to books, including *A Critical and Selective Bibliography of French Literature,* Volume 5: *The Nineteenth Century,* Syracuse University Press, 1994. Contributor to professional journals. Member of editorial boards of *Degre Second,* 1976-92, *Nineteenth-Century French Studies,* 1982—, and *Studies in Twentieth-Century Literature,* 1990—.

WORK IN PROGRESS: Beyond Our Control: Redefining the Fantastic in Literature; The Marginal Muse: French Women Authors from the Middle Ages to the Present.

SIDELIGHTS: Laurence M. Porter told *CA:* "As a critic and professor, I try to teach people to read and write better. To me, this means helping people to overcome the unreasoning prejudices that impoverish their experience and to recognize the nuance, hidden coherence, and significant detail which disclose the richness of artistic creation. I encourage people to articulate their own perceptions in a way which allows them to discover the wealth of their own individualities and to profit from the unlimited second chances which reading and writing, unlike life, can offer."

*   *   *

PORTER, Michael E. 1947-

PERSONAL: Born May 23, 1947, in Ann Arbor, MI; son of Howard Eugene (an army officer) and Stana (in retail sales; maiden name, von Werner) Porter; married Deborah Zylberberg, October 26, 1985; children: Ilana, Sonia. *Education:* Princeton University, B.S.E. (with high honors), 1969; Harvard University, M.B.A. (with high distinction), 1971, Ph.D., 1973. *Avocational interests:* Athletics, the music industry (as manager of aspiring recording artists).

ADDRESSES: Office—School of Business, Harvard University, Aldrich 200, Boston, MA 02163.

CAREER: Harvard University, School of Business, Boston, MA, assistant professor, 1973-77, associate professor, 1977-82, professor of business administration, 1982-1990, C. Roland Christensen professor of business administration, 1990—. Member of board of directors of Alpine, Inc., Anatar Investments, Council on Competitiveness, Hyatt Legal Plans, Lotus Development Corporation, Alpha-Beta Technologies, and President's Commission on Industrial Competitiveness, 1983-85; Governor's Council on Economic Growth and Technology, MA, 1991, chair, 1994; Basque government of Spain, special advisor, 1991—; consultant on competitive strategy to U.S. and overseas firms and to government agencies; member of editorial advisory board, *Antitrust Law and Economics Review, European Management Journal, Journal of Economics and Management Strategy, Long Range Planning, Technology Analysis and Strategic Management;* director of Strategic Management Society; member of visiting boards of Bunker Hill Community College, Weatherhead School of Management at Case Western University. *Military service:* U.S. Army Reserve, 1969-77; became captain.

MEMBER: American Economic Association, American Marketing Association, Phi Beta Kappa, Sigma Xi, Tau Beta Pi.

AWARDS, HONORS: Member of National Collegiate Athletic Association Golf All-American Team, 1968; David A. Wells Prize in Economics, Harvard University, 1973-74, for outstanding doctoral research; McKinsey Foundation award, 1979, 1987, for year's best *Harvard Business Review* article; Graham and Dodd Award, Financial Analysts Federation, 1980, for outstanding research; outstanding academic book citation, *Choice,* 1980-81, for *Competitive Strategy;* International Academy of Management fellow, 1985; George F. Terry award, Academy of Management, 1985, for *Competitive Advantage;* Academy of Management fellow, 1988; distinguished professional award, Society of Competitor Intelligence Professionals, 1989, for outstanding contributions to the field of competitive intelligence; class of 1969 distinguished service award, Princeton University, 1989; Foreign Member, Royal Academy of Engineering Sciences, 1991; Charles Coolidge Parlin Award, American Marketing Association, 1991; Irwin Award, Academy of Management, 1993; honorary doctorates from Stockholm School of Economics, 1989, Johnson & Wales University, 1991, Erasmus University, 1993, and Universidada Tecnica de Lisbon, 1994.

WRITINGS:

Interbrand Choice, Strategy, and Bilateral Market Power, Harvard University Press (Cambridge, MA), 1976.
(With A. M. Spence, R. E. Caves, and J. M. Scott) *Studies in Canadian Industrial Organization,* Canadian Royal Commission on Corporate Concentration, 1977.
Competitive Strategy: Techniques for Analyzing Industries and Competitors, Free Press (New York City), 1980.
(With A. M. Spence and R. E. Caves) *Competition in the Open Economy,* Harvard University Press, 1980.
Cases in Competitive Strategy, Free Press, 1982.
Competitive Advantage: Creating and Sustaining Superior Performance, Free Press, 1985.
(With C. R. Christensen, K. R. Andrews, R. L. Hammermesch, and J. L. Bower) *Business Policy: Text and Cases,* 6th edition, Irwin, 1986.

(Editor) *Competition in Global Industries,* Harvard Business School Press (Cambridge, MA), 1986.
Michael Porter on Competitive Strategy (videotape), Harvard Business School Video Series (Cambridge, MA), 1988.
The Competitive Advantage of Nations, Free Press, 1990.
(With Graham T. Crocombe and Michael J. Enright) *Upgrading New Zealand's Competitive Advantage,* Oxford University Press, 1991.
(Editor with Cynthia A. Montgomery) *Strategy: Seeking and Securing Competitive Advantage,* Harvard Business School Press, 1991.
(With Orjan Solbell and Ivo Zander) *Advantage Sweden,* Norstedts Forlag AB (Stockholm), 1991.
(With Silvio Borner, Rolf Weder, and Michael J. Enright) *Internationale Wettbewerbsvorteile: Ein Strategisches Konzept fur die Schweiz* (title means "International Competitive Advantage: A New Strategic Concept for Switzerland"), Campus Verlag (Frankfurt/New York), 1991.
(Editor) *Capital Choices: Changing the Way America Invests in Industry,* Harvard Business School Press, 1992.

Also author of *Canada at the Crossroads;* contributor to economic journals, popular magazines, and newspapers, including *Harvard Business Review, Fortune* and *Wall Street Journal.* Contributing editor of *Journal of Business Strategy;* associate editor of *Review of Economics and Statistics.*

ADAPTATIONS: The Competitive Advantage of Nations was adapted for video by the Harvard Business School Video Series, 1993.

SIDELIGHTS: Michael E. Porter once told *CA:* "My long-term research thrust has been to build a conceptual bridge between the business strategy field and applied microeconomics, two areas that had been largely independent. This broad intersection is the subject of the great majority of my writings. *Competitive Strategy: Techniques for Analyzing Industries and Competitors* is the first comprehensive statement of this research in a form accessible to the practicing manager and has opened up a whole new area in the business strategy field. The book *Competitive Advantage: Creating and Sustaining Superior Performance* extended the thinking from analyzing the competitive environment to a rigorous approach of creating and sustaining competitive advantage in the industrial firm. *Competition in Global Industries* has developed the unique competitive issues in international strategy. My newest research addresses the competitiveness of countries and the implications for both firms and governments."

BIOGRAPHICAL/CRITICAL SOURCES:

PERIODICALS

Antitrust Bulletin, spring, 1991.
European Management Journal, fall, 1991.

R

RALPH, Margaret Nutting 1941-

PERSONAL: Born March 23, 1941, in Lincoln, NE; daughter of Charles B. (a professor of law) and Mary Agnes (a Latin teacher; maiden name, Flanagan) Nutting; married Donald E. Ralph (a psychologist), July 20, 1963; children: Daniel, John, Anthony, Kathleen. *Education:* St. Mary's College, Notre Dame, IN, B.A. (magna cum laude), 1963; University of Massachusetts at Amherst, M.A., 1970; University of Kentucky, Ph.D., 1980. *Religion:* Roman Catholic.

ADDRESSES: Home—431 Dudley Rd., Lexington, KY 40502. *Office*—Office of Catholic Education, 1310 Leestown Rd., Lexington, KY 40502.

CAREER: Teacher at Roman Catholic school in Hyattsville, MD, 1963-64; religion teacher at Roman Catholic high school in Lexington, KY, 1974-83; University of Kentucky, Lexington, instructor in English and religious studies, 1980—. Presenter of *The Bible as Literature,* a monthly program on WJMM Radio, 1976-79; Roman Catholic Diocese of Lexington, director of RCIA and Evangelization and secretary of educational ministries, 1988—; Lexington Theological Seminary, director of two master of arts tracks for Roman Catholics, 1988—; consultant in adult faith development to Office of Catholic Education.

WRITINGS:

Choose Life: Reflections on the Death Penalty Study Guide, Catholic Conference of Kentucky, 1984.
"And God Said What?": An Introduction to Biblical Literary Forms for Bible Lovers, Paulist Press (Ramsey, NJ), 1986.
Willie of Church Street, Paulist Press, 1989.
Plain Words about Biblical Images, Paulist Press, 1989.

Discovering the Gospels: Four Accounts of the Good News, Paulist Press, 1990.
Discovering the First Century Church: The Acts of the Apostles, Letters of Paul and the Book of Revelation, Paulist Press, 1991.
Discovering Old Testament Origins, Paulist Press, 1992.
Discovering Prophecy and Wisdom, Paulist Press, 1993.

"And God Said What?": An Introduction to Biblical Literary Forms for Bible Lovers was released on videocassette by American Video Cassette Educational Library, 1987. Contributor of articles to magazines, including *Christian Adulthood, Today's Parish, Living Light,* and *Catechism Magazine.*

SIDELIGHTS: Margaret Nutting Ralph told *CA:* "My primary goal is to enable adults to grow in their knowledge and love of Scripture. I see a gulf between the faith life of adults and the academic pursuits of Scripture scholars, but I find these two worlds are totally compatible. I would like to present the work of Scripture scholars to adults in such a way that the growth of knowledge and the growth in faith go hand in hand."

*   *   *

RANSOM, Candice F. 1952-
(Kate Kenyon)

PERSONAL: Born July 10, 1952, in Washington, DC; daughter of Thomas Garland and Irene Dellinger (Lightfoot) Farris; married Frank Wesley Ransom (a satellite engineer), February 14, 1979. *Education:* Attended high school in Oakton, VA.

ADDRESSES: Home—14400 Awbrey Patent Dr., Centreville, VA 22020. *Office*—P.O. Box 936, Centreville, VA 22020.

CAREER: Writer. Worked as a secretary.

MEMBER: Society of Children's Book Writers and Illustrators, Children's Book Guild of Washington, DC.

WRITINGS:

JUVENILE

The Silvery Past, Scholastic Inc. (New York City), 1982.
Amanda, Scholastic Inc., 1984.
Susannah, Scholastic Inc., 1984.
Breaking the Rules, Scholastic Inc., 1985.
Emily, Scholastic Inc., 1985.
Kathleen, Scholastic Inc., 1985.
Blackbird Keep, Silhouette Books (New York City), 1986.
Cat's Cradle, Silhouette Books, 1986.
Nicole, Scholastic Inc., 1986.
Sabrina, Scholastic Inc., 1986.
Thirteen, Scholastic Inc., 1986.
(Under pseudonym Kate Kenyon) *The Day the Eighth Grade Ran the School,* Scholastic Inc., 1987.
Fifteen at Last, Scholastic Inc., 1987.
Fourteen and Holding, Scholastic Inc., 1987.
Kaleidoscope, Crosswinds, 1987.
Going on Twelve, Scholastic Inc., 1988.
My Sister, the Meanie, Scholastic Inc., 1988.
Millicent the Magnificent, Scholastic Inc., 1989.
My Sister, the Traitor, Scholastic Inc., 1989.
(With Carrie Randall) *The Secret,* Scholastic Inc., 1989.
Today Fifth Grade, Tomorrow the World, Willowisp Press, 1989.
Almost Ten and a Half, Scholastic Inc., 1990.
My Sister, the Creep, Scholastic Inc., 1990.
There's One in Every Family, Scholastic Inc., 1990.
Funniest Sixth Grade Video Ever, Willowisp Press, 1991.
Ladies and Jellybeans, Bradbury Press (Scarsdale, NY), 1991.
The Love Charm, Willowisp Press, 1991.
Sixth Grade High, Scholastic Inc., 1991.
Hocus-Pocus after School, Willowisp Press, 1992.
Shooting Star Summer, Boyds Mills Press (Honsedale, PA), 1992.
The Big Green Pocketbook, HarperCollins (New York City), 1993.
Listening to Crickets: A Story about Rachel Carson, Carolrhoda (Minneapolis, MN), 1993.
So Young to Die: The Story of Hannah Senesh, Scholastic Inc., 1993.
Third Grade Stars: Tales from the Third Grade, Troll (Mahwah, NJ), 1993.
We're Growing Together, Bradbury Press, 1993.
Who Needs Third Grade?, Troll, 1993.
Between Two Worlds, Scholastic Inc., 1994.
Jimmy Crack Corn, Carolrhoda, 1994.
The Man on Stilts, Philomel Books, 1994.

The Spitball Class, Archway/Minstrel, 1994.
Third Grade Detectives, Troll, 1994.
Why Are Boys So Weird?, Troll, 1994.
One Christmas Dawn, BridgeWater, 1995.

OTHER

Contributor of articles and stories to magazines, including *Seventeen, Rural Living, Writer's Digest, Single Parent, Highlights for Children,* and *Lutheran Women.*

WORK IN PROGRESS: *When the Whippoorwill Calls,* a picture book; *Searching for Poppa Bear* and *Fire in the Sky,* two novels for younger readers; and *Voice from the Grave, Haunted Homeroom,* and *Creepy Cousin,* a supernatural series for middle grades.

SIDELIGHTS: Candice F. Ransom told *CA:* "My first novel, penciled on the long bus ride home from school at the age of seven, began with the immortal lines, 'It was dark. Everything was silent. Then in rustling leaves. . . .' The books I wrote in elementary school were feeble imitations of Nancy Drew and of *Lassie Come Home,* in which I was always the main character. As a lonely child growing up in rural Fairfax County, I wrote to while away long evenings, and who else would I rather have read about having wonderful adventures than myself?

"During the sixth grade, my best friend and I spent recess periods tunneling out tangles of honeysuckle and wisteria that were wrapped thick around dogwood trees growing along the perimeter of the playground. Hidden in the Honeysuckle Hideout, we spied on an old man's house high on the hill, scratched our poison ivy, and collaborated on a mystery novel. Those were the golden years, when writing was fun, effortless.

"In high school, I worried that I had a severe case of arrested development. While other kids were passing around *The Green Berets,* with page 388 marked, I was still reading *The Borrowers.* My English teacher set me straight. 'You're going to be a children's writer,' she said. Relieved that I was not living my life in reverse like Merlin in *The Once and Future King,* I set out to fulfill her prophecy. The summer I was sixteen, I wrote a children's novel on my new typewriter and mailed poetry off to the *New Yorker,* a writer at last. That same year, my first poem was published (alas, not in the *New Yorker*), but the novel was lost in the mail, en route to Harper & Row, who never realized how lucky they were.

"After high school, I went to work as a secretary, but I still yearned to be a children's writer. Whenever I walked into the children's room of a library, memories of myself at nine, wide-eyed and thrilled to be in a roomful of books, overpowered me to the point where I thought I'd faint. I had to write, and I did.

"Now that my dream has come true, I often reflect what a strange world I inhabit, trapped between the floors of childhood and adulthood—not really *there*, but not really *here* either.

"Much of my material comes from within, drawn from my own past, which I remember vividly, and a lot of my childhood interests have carried over into my profession. It came as no great surprise to me that my first published novel was a mystery, since I had devoured dozens as a child. A grown-up love for history has led to the discovery of a new passion, writing historical novels for young people.

"Best of all, I am able to recapture that shivery feeling of anticipation I once had whenever I turned to the first page of a new library book. Only now the pages are blank, waiting for me to fill them."

*   *   *

RAY, David (E.) 1932-

PERSONAL: Born May 20, 1932, in Sapulpa, OK; son of Dowell Adolphus and Katherine (Jennings) Ray; married first wife, Florence (divorced); married second wife, Ruth, c. 1964 (marriage ended); married third wife, Judy, 1970; children: (first marriage) Winifred Catherine; (second marriage) Wesley (adopted stepdaughter), Samuel Cyrus David (deceased); (third marriage) Sapphina (stepdaughter). *Education:* University of Chicago, B.A., 1952, M.A., 1957.

ADDRESSES: Home—5517 Crestwood Dr., Kansas City, MO 64110. *Office*—Department of English, University of Missouri—Kansas City, Kansas City, MO 64110.

CAREER: Instructor in English, Wright Junior College, Chicago, IL, 1957-58, Northern Illinois University, DeKalb, 1958-60, and Cornell University, Ithaca, NY, 1960-64; Reed College, Portland, OR, assistant professor of humanities, 1964-66; University of Iowa, Iowa City, lecturer at Writers' Workshop, 1969-70; Bowling Green State University, Bowling Green, OH, visiting associate professor of English, 1970-71; University of Missouri—Kansas City, associate professor, 1971-74, professor of English, 1974-92, professor emeritus, 1992—. Visiting associate professor of English, Syracuse University, 1978-79; visiting professor of English, University of Rajasthan, 1981-82, and to universities in Australia and New Zealand, 1991-92; exchange professor, University of Otago, 1987. Founding editor and producer of weekly radio program *New Letters on the Air*, broadcast on National Public Radio. Has lectured or given poetry readings at more than one hundred colleges and universities in the United States, Canada, and England.

MEMBER: Poetry Society of America (member of regional committee, 1979), Coordinating Council of Literary Magazines (member of grants committee, 1975 and 1979), Modern Language Association of America, PEN, Authors Guild, National Writers Union, American Association of University Professors, Friends Association for Higher Education, Phi Kappa Phi.

AWARDS, HONORS: Academy of American Poets honorable mention, 1955 and 1956; Young Writers Award, *New Republic*, 1958; Abraham Woursell fellowship, University of Vienna, 1966-71; poetry award, *Kansas City Star*, 1974; William Carlos Williams Prize, Poetry Society of America, 1979, for *The Tramp's Cup*; Coordinating Council of Literary Magazines editorial fellowship, 1979; Nelson-Atkins Museum Poetry Contest award, 1980; Indo-United States fellowship, Council for International Exchange of Scholars, 1981-82; N. T. Veatch Award, University of Missouri—Kansas City, 1982, for distinguished research and creative activity; PEN Syndicated Fiction Award, 1982, for "The Hijacking," 1983, for "Ram Ram," 1984, for "A Pitcher of Orange Juice," 1985, for "Sanctuary," 1986, for "With Loss of Eden", and 1987, for "At Aunt Tina's"; Associated Writing Programs Poetry Contest winning finalist, 1982 and 1983, second prize, 1985; National Endowment for the Arts fellowship in creative writing, 1983; Thorpe Menn Award for Literary Achievement, American Association of University Women, 1983, for *The Touched Life: Poems Selected and New;* Sotheby's/Arvon International Poetry Award, 1983, for "The Roadmenders"; faculty fellowship, University of Missouri—Kansas City, 1984; Weldon Springs Humanities Seminar fellowship, University of Missouri—Kansas City, 1986; Stanley Hanks Memorial Contest, St. Louis Poetry Center, second place award, 1986, for "Stupid Animal Tricks," first prize awards, 1990 and 1991; Washington Prize, *Word Works*, 1987, for poem "The Place"; art criticism award, *Forum* magazine, 1988; Emily Dickinson Award, Poetry Society of America, 1988; Maurice English Poetry Award, 1988, for *Sam's Book;* Dale Djerassi fellowship in Literature, Djerassi Foundation, 1988; award for poetry, *Nebraska Review*, 1989, for "To Pliny the Roman" and "Sonnet"; national poetry award, Passaic Community College, 1989; first prize for fiction, *Kansas City View*, 1990, for "First Ice of Winter"; first prize award, Stanley Hanks Memorial Contest, St. Louis Poetry Center, 1990 and 1991; first prize in fiction and first prize in poetry, H. G. Roberts Foundation Award, both 1993; Kossuth Award, Hungarian Freedom Fighters.

WRITINGS:

POETRY

X-Rays: A Book of Poems, Cornell University Press (Ithaca, NY), 1965.

Dragging the Main and Other Poems, Cornell University Press, 1968.

A Hill in Oklahoma, BkMk Press (Kansas City, MO), 1972.

Gathering Firewood: New Poems and Selected, Wesleyan University Press (Middletown, CT), 1974.

Enough of Flying: Poems Inspired by the Ghazals of Ghalib, Writers' Workshop (Calcutta, India), 1977.

The Tramp's Cup, Chariton Review (Kirksville, MO), 1978.

The Farm in Calabria and Other Poems, Spirit That Moves Us (Iowa City, IA), 1979.

The Touched Life: Poems Selected and New, Scarecrow (Metuchen, NJ), 1982.

On Wednesday I Cleaned Out My Wallet, Pancake Press (San Francisco), 1985.

Elysium in the Halls of Hell: Poems about India, Nirala Publications (Jaipur, India), 1986.

Sam's Book, Wesleyan University Press, 1987.

The Maharani's New Wall and Other Poems, Wesleyan University Press, 1989.

Wool Highways and Other Poems, Helicon Nine Editions, 1993.

EDITOR

The Chicago Review Anthology, University of Chicago Press (Chicago), 1959.

From the Hungarian Revolution: A Collection of Poems (adapted from the Hungarian *Fuveskert*), Cornell University Press, 1966.

(With Robert Bly) *A Poetry Reading against the Vietnam War,* American Writers against the Vietnam War, 1966.

(With Robert M. Farnsworth) *The Life and Work of Richard Wright, Including Haiku and Unpublished Prose,* University of Missouri—Kansas City, New Letters (Kansas City), 1971, published as *Richard Wright: Impressions and Perspectives,* University of Michigan Press (Ann Arbor), 1973.

(With Gary Gildner) *Since Feeling Is First: An Anthology of New American Poetry,* University of Missouri—Kansas City, New Letters, 1976.

(With wife, Judy Ray) *New Asian Writing: A New Letters Anthology,* Writers' Workshop, 1979.

(With Jack Salzman) *A Jack Conroy Reader,* Burt Franklin, 1980.

E. L. Mayo, *Collected Poems,* Swallow Press (Athens, OH), 1981.

From A to Z: 200 Contemporary American Poets; 200 Poets from New Letters Magazine, Swallow Press, 1981.

(With Amritjit Singh) *India: An Anthology of Contemporary Writing,* Ohio University Press and Swallow Press, 1983.

New Letters Reader One: An Anthology of Contemporary Writing, Ohio University Press and Swallow Press, 1983.

New Letters Reader Two: An Anthology of Contemporary Writing, Ohio University Press and Swallow Press, 1984.

New Letters: A Book of Translations, University of Missouri—Kansas City, New Letters, 1985.

OTHER

The Mulberries of Mingo and Other Stories (short stories), Cold Mountain Press, 1978.

(Translator) *Not Far from the River* (transcreations from the *Gatha-saptasati*), Prakrit Society (New Delhi, India), 1983, Copper Canyon Press (Port Townsend, WA), 1990.

Work is represented in numerous anthologies, including *New Poets of England and America,* edited by Donald Hall and Robert Pack, Meridian, 1962; *Where Is Vietnam?: American Poets Respond,* edited by Walter Lowenfels, Anchor-Doubleday, 1967; *The Creative Voice,* edited by Ken Lawless, Holt, 1971; *Fifty Contemporary Poets,* edited by Alberta Turner, Longman, 1977; *Norton Introduction to Literature,* 3rd edition, edited by Bain, Beatty, and Hunter, Norton, 1981; and *Divided Light: Father and Son Poems,* edited by J. Shinder, Sheep Meadow, 1984. Also contributor of essays, poetry, fiction, criticism, and reviews to more than one hundred periodicals, including *Nation, New Republic, Reporter, Poetry* (Chicago), *Accent, Critic, Odyssey, Paris Review, Chelsea, London Magazine, Saturday Review, Harper's, New Yorker, New American Review, Yale Review, Quarterly Review of Literature,* and *Atlantic Monthly. Chicago Review,* editor, 1956-57, advisory editor, 1963—; *Epoch,* associate editor, 1960-64; *New Letters,* editor, 1971-85.

ADAPTATIONS: The Orphans of Mingo, an unpublished novel by Ray, was adapted as a play by Willard Manus and produced at the Group Repertory Theatre, 1985.

SIDELIGHTS: A *Prairie Schooner* reviewer declares that "David Ray's poetry seems an extension of personality, a telling of private experience to a public world. . . . [He] owns a precise and piercing imagination that captures human sentiment without ever lapsing into pathos." Helen Vendler of the *New York Times Book Review* regards "Ray's stance [as] that of the clumsy truthteller, his honesty guaranteed by a stammer here, a childish phrase there, embarrassment somewhere else."

Deno Trakas, writing in *Dictionary of Literary Biography,* describes Ray's poetry as "unpretentious and unembellished," reflecting the influence of William Carlos Williams, who once praised Ray's work. Trakas notes too that "from the consistent autobiographical background of

Ray's poetry, the reader can piece together a characterization of the author," from the primarily rural scenes of his difficult childhood in *X-Rays: A Book of Poems* and other books through his political concerns and his travels associated with teaching positions in several foreign countries. In the *Iowa Review,* Valerie Trueblood explains that "the poem is not an act of wresting meaning from the past for [Ray]; it is a *return* to the past, where scalding moments existed, the essence of life was tasted, the self was born."

These views of Ray's work are more or less echoed in a *Chicago Review* critic's assessment of *X-Rays,* the poet's first published collection. In this review, the critic remarks that "no book was ever better titled, for in piece after deeply personal piece there is the feel of the x-ray, an excoriated quality. The volume must be one of the most honest—to the point of violent self-deprecation—to appear in a long time."

Nation's Elliott Coleman, who sees evidence of "a wit both mordant and vivacious" in *X-Rays,* believes that "the extraordinary life of [*Dragging the Main and Other Poems*] goes deeper [than mere wit]. Pictures cannot quite be taken of it. And it is ultra-sonic; one cannot quite hear it, but only feel its effects. . . . This is a dragnet of a book, catching what is priceless." Robert D. Spector of the *Saturday Review* finds that the collection contains poems in which "emotion is never forced [and] the language [is] always appropriate to the feeling." But a *Choice* critic characterizes Ray's work in *Dragging the Main and Other Poems* as being marked by "flat conversational tones and a somewhat tired attitudinizing toward a range of subjects."

Another *Choice* critic describes *The Tramp's Cup* as "pleasantly readable poetry" that is "also quite forgettable." Hayden Carruth, however, comments in *Harper's:* "Toughness and flatness and even sometimes boredom are the verbal qualities of David Ray's poems, chosen deliberately to make bearable the outrage and pain of his poetic vision. . . . No one should begrudge an artist's methods . . . provided he or she can come up with enough successes to justify our admiration. . . . David Ray does."

In a review of *The Touched Life: Poems Selected and New,* Trueblood writes in the *Iowa Review* that she believes that these poems, especially those about childhood, demonstrate that "pathos . . . has a nourishing power for Ray," but she sees in them too a "salve": Ray's "delight in his portion of love, his readiness for what is or might be good." Ann Struthers proclaims in the *Greenfield Review:* "Here are poems that transcend grief, the corporate grief of living in a murderous century and the personal grief of the abandoned child. . . . Ray writes with compassion and understanding."

Several of Ray's books of poetry grew out of his travels. These include *The Tramp's Cup, Enough of Flying: Poems Inspired by the Ghazals of Ghalib, The Farm in Calabria and Other Poems, Elysium in the Halls of Hell: Poems about India,* and *The Maharani's New Wall and Other Poems.*

Sam's Book is a memorial to Ray's son, who died in the fall of 1984 in what Ray has described as "a senseless alcohol-related accident." Andy Brumer, writing in the *New York Times Book Review,* considers *Sam's Book* remarkable for "the direct manner in which Mr. Ray faces both his son's life and death." Since his son died, Ray relates in *Contemporary Authors Autobiographical Series* (*CAAS*): "I have been aware that I am engaged in a long process of mourning, for Samuel Cyrus David Ray . . . certainly, but also for my childhood and for friends lost and for many glories passed from this earth." He continues to explore some of these feelings not only in poems but also in short stories, a genre in which he has won several PEN fiction awards since 1982. He resolves, as he wrote in *CAAS,* to give thanks "for this healing that has begun in me," in the words of a Quaker prayer, and "not to waste this remaining time in depression and anxiety, in trivial conflict and futile causes."

In his recollections for *CAAS,* Ray describes growing up in Oklahoma during the Depression, spending his early years with unloving parents whose behavior toward him and his sister, Mary Ellen, ranged from inattentive to actively abusive. After attempts at farming and barbering, Ray's father deserted the family; his mother eventually remarried, but the children were in and out of foster homes and, at one point, an orphanage. Ray has described this last experience in his poem "Orphans" and other works. He recalls in *CAAS:* "When parents die, they are mourned. The wound heals over the sacred introject, a stone near the heart. But when they live on, mourning can be even more intense, awakened again and again, enraged by new reunions that don't work out."

Ray once told *CA:* "Someone asked me one time if it feels good to get a fan letter. I guess it does, but it's also a rather abstract experience. But once in a while something happens that makes a writer feel that it's all worth it. I was up at Yaddo, just walking in the woods one day. And a few days later the director mentioned that he had been showing people around and he had casually pointed out, just like a birdwatcher, 'Oh there goes a poet, David Ray.' And a women in the group said, 'Oh, he wrote a poem which moved me to tears.' Well, that's sort of what it's all about. I never met that woman; I didn't get her name. It's a totally abstract experience in a way. She wasn't going to communicate with me. But that's a very meaningful kind of thing. You expressed something and someone understood it and was moved by it. That's what it's all about: the poet in the forest, the song attended now and then."

BIOGRAPHICAL/CRITICAL SOURCES:

BOOKS

Contemporary Authors Autobiographical Series, Volume 7, Gale (Detroit), 1988, pp. 135-153.
Dictionary of Literary Biography, Volume 5: *American Poets since World War II,* Gale, 1980, pp. 175-180.

PERIODICALS

Chicago Review, Volume 18, number 2, 1965.
Choice, April, 1969; March, 1975; October, 1979.
Greenfield Review, spring, 1986, pp. 137-140.
Harper's, May, 1979, p. 89.
Iowa Review, winter, 1985, pp. 139-144.
Nation, March 17, 1969, pp. 345-346.
New York Times Book Review, April 6, 1975; January 17, 1988, p. 30.
Prairie Schooner, spring, 1977.
Saturday Review, March 15, 1969.

*   *   *

REAGAN, Ronald (Wilson) 1911-

PERSONAL: Born February 6, 1911, in Tampico, IL; son of John Edward (in shoe sales) and Nelle (Wilson) Reagan; married Jane Wyman (an actress), January 24, 1940 (divorced, 1948); married Nancy Davis (an actress), March 4, 1952; children: (first marriage) Maureen Elizabeth, Michael Edward; (second marriage) Patricia Ann, Ronald Prescott. *Education:* Eureka College, B.A., 1932. *Politics:* Republican.

ADDRESSES: Home—668 St. Cloud Rd., Bel Air, Los Angeles, CA 90077. *Office*—Fox Plaza Tower, 34th Fl., Century City, Los Angeles, CA.

CAREER: WOC-Radio, Davenport, IA, sports announcer; 1932-33; WHO-Radio, Des Moines, IA, sports announcer and editor, 1932-37; actor in more than fifty feature films, 1937-64, including *Love Is on the Air,* 1937, *Accidents Will Happen,* 1938, *Hell's Kitchen,* 1939, *Dark Victory,* 1939, *Angels Wash Their Faces,* 1939, *Knute Rockne—All American,* 1940, *Brother Rat and a Baby,* 1940, *Santa Fe Trail,* 1940, *Kings Row,* 1941, *International Squadron,* 1941, *Nine Lives Are Not Enough,* 1941, *Juke Girl,* 1942, *Desperate Journey,* 1942, *This Is the Army,* 1943, *Stallion Road,* 1947, *That Hagen Girl,* 1947, *The Voice of the Turtle,* 1947, *Night unto Night,* 1948, *John Loves Mary,* 1949, *The Hasty Heart,* 1950, *Storm Warning,* 1950, *Louisa,* 1950, *Bedtime for Bonzo,* 1951, *She's Working Her Way through College,* 1952, *Hong*

Kong, 1952, *Prisoner of War,* 1954, *Law and Order,* 1954, *Tennessee's Partner,* 1955, *Hellcats of the Navy,* 1957, and *The Killers,* 1964; *General Electric Theater* television program, actor and production supervisor, and speaker throughout the United States for General Electric's personnel relations program, 1954-62; *Death Valley Days* television series, host and actor, 1962-65.

Governor of the state of California, 1967-74; host of a nationally syndicated radio commentary program and author of a nationally syndicated weekly newspaper column, 1975, 1977—; Republican candidate for U.S. presidential nomination, 1976; President of the United States of America, 1981-89.

Chairman, Republican Governors Association, 1969; presidential appointee to advisory commission on intergovernmental relations, 1970; member of human resources committee of National Governors' Conference, 1972; presidential appointee to commission investigating the Central Intelligence Agency (CIA), 1974-75; member of board of directors of Committee on Present Danger, 1977—; member of board of directors of *National Review* magazine, 1989—, and Committee on Fundamental Education, St. John's Hospital; served on board of trustees, Eureka College; member of California Republican State Central Committee and national advisory board of Young Americans for Freedom. Lecturer and public speaker. Owner and operator of a horse breeding and cattle ranch. *Military service:* U.S. Army Air Forces, 1942-46; became captain.

MEMBER: Academie des sciences morales et politiques (foreign associate member), Screen Actors Guild (member of board of directors, 1946-60; president, 1947-52, 1959-60), Motion Picture Industry Council (former president and member of board of directors), American Federation of Radio and Television Artists, California Thoroughbred Breeders Association, Young Men's Christian Association (YMCA), Friars Club, Rancheros Visitadores, Bohemian Club, Tau Kappa Epsilon.

AWARDS, HONORS: Recipient of numerous awards, including National Safety Council Public Interest Award, 1954; National Humanitarian Award, National Conference of Christians and Jews, 1962; George Washington Honor Medal Award, Freedoms Foundation, 1971, for a public address, and 1973, for a published article; Medal of Valor (Israel), 1971; Knight of the Grand Cross of the Most Honorable Order of Bath (G.C.B.), 1989; Grand Cordon, Supreme Order of the Chrysanthemum (Japan), 1989; Honorary Citizen of Berlin, 1992; Presidential Medal of Freedom, 1993; Matsunaga Medal of Peace, 1993.

WRITINGS:

(With Richard G. Hubler) *Where's the Rest of Me?* (autobiography), Duell, Sloan & Pearce, 1965, published as *My Early Life,* 1981.

(With Charles Hobbs) *Ronald Reagan's Call to Action,* Warner Books (New York City), 1976.

Ronald Reagan Talks to America, Devin, 1982.

Speaking My Mind: Selected Speeches, Simon & Schuster (New York City), 1989.

An American Life (autobiography), Simon & Schuster, 1990.

Ronald Reagan: The Great Communicator (collected speeches), edited by Kurt Ritter and David Henry, Greenwood Press (Westport, CT), 1992.

Actor, Ideologue, Politician: The Public Speeches of Ronald Reagan, edited by Davis W. Houck and Amos Kiewe, Greenwood Press, 1993.

Also author of *Abortion and the Conscience of the Nation,* 1984. The U.S. Government Printing Office has published the public papers of the Reagan presidency. Columnist and contributor to periodicals.

SIDELIGHTS: The first actor and union member to be elected president of the United States, Ronald Reagan served two terms during the 1980s. His presidency was marked by a sharp increase in defense spending, an aggressive policy towards totalitarian countries like the Soviet Union, a growing economy, and what many observers called a renewed sense of American patriotism. Despite, or perhaps because of, his frequent battles with congressional Democrats and such scandals as the Iran-Contra affair, Reagan ranks as the most popular living American president. Former British prime minister Margaret Thatcher, writing in *National Review,* found that Reagan "achieved the most difficult of all political tasks: changing attitudes and perceptions about what is possible."

Reagan was raised in Illinois where his father owned a series of shoe stores. After graduating from Eureka College in 1932 with a degree in economics and sociology, Reagan took his first job as a sports announcer for radio station WOC in Davenport, Iowa. Later he moved to a sister station, WHO in Des Moines. In 1937, while in Los Angeles covering the Chicago Cubs spring training, Reagan secured his first movie role in a Warner Bros. film, *Love Is on the Air.*

For the next twenty years Reagan appeared in over fifty films, including such popular and critical successes as *Dark Victory, Knute Rockne—All American* (in which Reagan uttered the famous line "Win one for the gipper."), *Santa Fe Trail,* and *Kings Row.* Concurrent with his career as an actor Reagan became involved in film industry politics and was elected president of the Screen Actors Guild, the union for film actors. During his tenure as

president, he testified before the House Committee on Un-American Activities in its investigation into alleged Communist infiltration into the motion picture industry. At least one Hollywood union had been controlled by the Communist Party during the 1930s. Although he appeared as a cooperative witness, Reagan did admonish the Committee: "I hope that we are never prompted by our own fear of Communism into compromising any of our democratic principles." In 1959 he led a Guild strike to win salary increases and medical benefits for its members and a share of royalties for movies shown on television.

By the 1950s Reagan had turned to television as host of *General Electric Theater* and later as host of *Death Valley Days.* As part of the promotional campaign for the *General Electric Theater,* Reagan made appearances at General Electric plants across the country speaking on current events. In the years following World War II, Reagan, who then considered himself a New Deal Democrat, was active in liberal causes. He wrote about the era in his autobiography *Where's the Rest of Me?:* "I was a near-hopeless hemophiliac liberal. I bled for causes: I had voted Democratic, following my father, in every election. . . . I was blindly and busily joining every organization I could find that would guarantee to save the world." Although he supported Harry S Truman for president in 1948 and the liberal senatorial candidate Helen Gahagan Douglas (who lost the election to Richard Nixon) in 1950, Reagan's politics became increasingly conservative during the 1950s. He campaigned for Dwight Eisenhower in 1952 and 1956 and for Nixon in 1960. It wasn't until 1962, however, that he officially switched to the Republican party.

Reagan attributed his conversion to conservatism to the speeches he gave as personnel relations speaker for General Electric. From 1954 to 1962 he toured all 135 General Electric plants and spoke to an estimated quarter of a million employees about public issues, especially the disastrous effects of big government. Reagan related how his political orientation shifted during this period: "Eventually what happened to me was because I always did my own speeches and did the research for them, I just woke up to the realization one day that I had been going out and helping to elect the people who had been causing the things I had been criticizing. So it wasn't any case of some mentor coming in and talking me out of it. I did it in my own speeches."

Reagan burst onto the national political scene when his fund-raising speech for Republican presidential candidate Barry Goldwater was nationally televised in October of 1964. "A Time for Choosing"—a conservative analysis of government bureaucracy—"drew more contributions than any other single speech in political history," the *New York Times* stated. Buoyed by his success and urged by friends and advisers to pursue a career in politics, Reagan announced his candidacy for the governorship of California the next year.

Billing himself as a "citizen politician," Reagan based his campaign on such issues as slashing taxes and welfare expenses and halting bureaucratic growth and the student revolt at the University of California. An effective speaker and campaigner, Reagan beat incumbent Edmund G. "Pat" Brown, Sr., by over one million votes and was elected governor in 1966. Simplicity was to be the cornerstone of Reagan's term of office, and he set the tone in his inaugural address. He told the people of California: "For many years now, you and I have been shushed like children and told there are no simple answers to the complex problems which are beyond our comprehension. Well, the truth is, there *are* simple answers."

In 1971, what some regard as Reagan's outstanding accomplishment as governor was passed into law—the Welfare Reform Act of 1971. Reagan had referred to welfare as "this cancer eating at our vitals" and had made reform a top priority. The success of the welfare reform bill is still hotly disputed; admirers claim it saved the state $2 billion, while critics claim it cost the state $100 million in its first full year of operation.

So successful was he as governor of California, one of the nation's most populous states and among the largest economies in the world, that by 1976 Reagan was being touted in Republican circles as a possible presidential candidate. That year he ran for his party's nomination and won more primary votes than did the Republican incumbent, President Gerald Ford. Reagan's campaign was nominally based on a program of "creative federalism," but its real strength lay in his deftness as an orator. This skill would become the issue detractors returned to throughout his career. Reagan wrote in the foreword to *Speaking My Mind: Selected Speeches*, "Some of my critics over the years have said that I became president because I was an actor who knew how to give a good speech. I suppose that's not too far wrong. Because an actor knows two important things—to be honest in what he's doing and to be in touch with the audience. That's not bad advice for a politician either."

Although Ford won the party's nomination on the first convention ballot, with 1,187 votes to Reagan's 1,070, the campaign had established Reagan as a viable candidate and a strong campaigner. Four years later, he arrived at the 1980 Republican Convention as the party's unopposed candidate. In his acceptance speech as Republican presidential nominee, Reagan supported a conservative platform calling for increased defense spending, tax cuts to spur the economy, a rollback in government regulation, voluntary prayer in public schools, and tuition credits for private schooling, and voiced strong opposition to school busing, abortion, and the Equal Rights Amendment. In the November general election, Reagan overwhelmed the incumbent Jimmy Carter with 51 percent of the popular vote to Carter's 41 percent. In the electoral college he garnered 489 votes to Carter's 49. In the 1984 election, the Reagan/George Bush ticket easily outdistanced the Democratic ticket of Walter Mondale and Geraldine Ferraro with nearly 60 percent of the popular vote and an electoral margin of 525 to 13.

Inheriting an economy that was plagued by double-digit inflation, declining wages, and slow growth, Reagan called for government policy favorable to entrepreneurial growth. By cutting taxes and lessening federal regulations, Reagan helped spur what Thatcher described as "the longest period of peacetime economic growth in U.S. history." George Gilder, writing in *National Review,* listed some of the economic achievements of the Reagan presidency: the creation of 15 million new jobs, a doubling of the stock market, growth in industrial production, investment, and productivity, and an increase in per-capita income. In addition, inflation was brought to manageable levels and mortgage rates were cut in half. "Defying a worldwide siege of economic stagnation," wrote Gilder, "the Reagan boom was unique in the postwar era."

One of the keystone policies of the Reagan administration was a renewed aggressive stance against the Soviet Union. Speaking before the Berlin Wall, for example, Reagan called upon Soviet premier Mikhail Gorbachev to "tear the wall down." In a speech delivered at Moscow University, under a bust of communist theorist Vladimir Lenin, Reagan expounded on the benefits of a free market economy and a democratic political system, urging the students in his audience to work for reform within their communist country. In more concrete terms, the Reagan administration supported freedom fighters in Afghanistan, who were fighting against Soviet troops occupying their country, and the contras waging a guerrilla war against the Marxist Nicaraguan government. As Lou Cannon of the *Washington Post* explained it, as quoted in *National Review,* "Reagan's principal idea is that individuals and nations prosper when they are allowed maximum freedom."

A rebuilding of national defense, brought to low levels following the Vietnam War in the 1970s, was another top Reagan priority. He hoped that an arms race would bankrupt an already weak Soviet economy. When Reagan introduced the Strategic Defense Initiative, a controversial research program designed to produce a space-based missile defense system utilizing high-powered laser beams, political opponents called the idea preposterous and expensive. But some observers have argued in retrospect that the SDI program was primarily a bluff to draw the Soviets into an arms race they could not afford. The resulting economic pressures pushed the Soviets, these observers argue, to make peaceful overtures to the United States.

One of the major triumphs of the second Reagan term was a lessening of tension between the United States and the Soviet Union, the result of meetings between Reagan and Gorbachev in Geneva, Switzerland, in 1985 and in Reykjavik, Iceland, in 1986. By 1990, the Soviet Union's communist government had collapsed, its Eastern European satellites were free, and the threat of nuclear war between the two superpowers was ended.

During Reagan's second term attention also focused on two major scandals: apparent trading of arms for hostages in Iran and covert aid to Nicaraguan contra rebels. The controversy surrounding these issues continued to follow Reagan even after he left the White House. It was during this second term also that press accounts and books written by former administration officials began to raise serious questions about Reagan's detached executive style and its effect on how the nation's affairs were conducted. As the second term drew to a close at least 110 Reagan Administration officials had been accused or convicted of unethical or illegal conduct. Reagan continued to remain high in popular opinion, while political observers were very sharply divided in assessing the impact of his presidency.

In 1990, Reagan's book *An American Life* was published. It had been preceded the year before by *Speaking My Mind,* a collection of his speeches beginning with a 1951 address to a national Kiwanis convention and ending with his 1989 farewell address. Of *An American Life,* Jonathan Yardley wrote in the *Washington Post Book World,* "It tells us nothing about the man who wrote it, save that which we are able to extract by painful and time-consuming inference. . . . Certainly it is difficult to imagine *An American Life* will be of any real use to those who, now and in the future, attempt to make sense of Ronald Reagan and the era to which his name has been given." Maureen Dowd, a *New York Times* White House correspondent, suggested that a better title for the memoirs would be "The Mannequin Speaks." After summarizing the portrait painted by others in recent books of "a President preternaturally disengaged and passive, of a man who forgot about assignments once he had completed them and people once they had passed out of sight," she wrote: "And yet, through omission, selective choice of facts and a cozy yet commanding prose style deftly devised by Mr. Reagan's ghostwriter, the former *New York Times* correspondent Robert Lindsey, the book attempts to counter those other accounts by presenting Mr. Reagan as an astute and active Chief Executive, a compassionate boss and family man, a leader with only enough guilelessness to make him charming."

New York Times reviewer Christopher Lehmann-Haupt offered a more positive review of *An American Life,* commenting that Reagan "comes across as an unpretentious and likable man. . . . Despite its longueurs and other deficiencies, what *An American Life* conveys is that Ronald Reagan was both a consummate actor and a man of considerable substance. It was not with mirrors that despite the Iran-contra scandal, he recovered his prestige and left office the most popular President of modern times. If this book is any evidence, the American people were not entirely mistaken in admiring him so avidly."

BIOGRAPHICAL/CRITICAL SOURCES:

BOOKS

Bestsellers 90, Issue 1, Gale (Detroit), 1990, pp. 64-65.

Boskin, Michael J., *Reagan and the Economy: The Successes, Failures and Unfinished Agenda,* ICS Press (San Francisco), 1989.

Boyer, Paul, editor, *Reagan as President: Contemporary Views of the Man, His Politics, and His Policies,* Ivan R. Dee, 1990.

Brown, Edmund G., and Bill Brown, *The Political Chameleon,* Praeger (New York City), 1976.

Hogan, Joseph, *The Reagan Years: The Record in Presidential Leadership,* St. Martin's (New York City), 1990.

Kiewe, Amos, and Davis W. Houck, *A Shining City on a Hill: Ronald Reagan's Economic Rhetoric, 1951-1989,* Greenwood Press (Westport, CT), 1991.

Kimzey, Bruce W., *Reaganomics,* West Publishing (St. Paul, MN), 1983.

Kirkpatrick, Jeanne J., *The Reagan Doctrine and U.S. Foreign Policy,* Heritage Foundation (Washington, DC), 1985.

Mannaford, Peter, and Charles D. Hobbs, *Remembering Reagan,* Regnery (Chicago), 1994.

Metzger, Robert P., *Reagan: American Icon,* University of Pennsylvania Press (Philadelphia), 1989.

Noonan, Peggy, *What I Saw at the Revolution: A Political Life in the Reagan Era,* Random House (New York City), 1990.

Reagan, Maureen, and Dorothy Herrmann, *First Father, First Daughter: A Memoir,* Little, Brown (Boston), 1989.

Salamon, Lester M., and Michael S. Lund, editors, *The Reagan Presidency and the Governing of America,* Urban Institute (Washington, DC), 1984.

Schweizer, Peter, *Victory: The Reagan Administration's Secret Strategy That Caused the Collapse of the Soviet Union,* Grove (New York City), 1994.

Thomas, Tony, *The Films of Ronald Reagan,* Carol Publishing, 1982.

Thompson, Kenneth W., editor, *Leadership in the Reagan Presidency,* University Press of America (Lanham,

MD), Part 1: *Seven Intimate Perspectives,* 1992, Part 2: *Eleven Intimate Perspectives,* 1993.

Wills, Garry, *Reagan's America,* Doubleday (New York City), 1987.

PERIODICALS

American Spectator, August, 1988, pp. 16-19.
Chicago Tribune, June 16, 1989.
Esquire, March, 1976.
Globe and Mail (Toronto), November 24, 1990.
Harper's, February, 1976; November, 1976.
Los Angeles Times, November 21, 1975; August 17, 1988.
Nation, June 22, 1974; January 10, 1976.
National Review, August 5, 1988, pp. 35-38; December 30, 1988, pp. 22-24.
New Republic, June 12, 1976.
Newsweek, May 17, 1976; August 9, 1976; August 16, 1976; August 30, 1976.
New Yorker, October 18, 1976; October 25, 1976.
New York Times, June 9, 1966; January 3, 1967; January 1, 1988; April 14, 1988; January 26, 1989; June 6, 1989; June 14, 1989; November 5, 1990; November 7, 1990.
New York Times Book Review, August 15, 1976; November 18, 1990.
New York Times Magazine, November 14, 1965; October 16, 1966; February 22, 1976; June 6, 1976.
Time, August 2, 1976; August 9, 1976; August 30, 1976; April 28, 1980.
Times (London), December 8, 1990, p. 26.
Times Literary Supplement, December 21, 1990, p. 1370.
U.S. News and World Report, February 9, 1976; August 9, 1976.
Washington Post, February 28, 1989; June 2, 1989; October 24, 1989.
Washington Post Book World, November 4, 1990.*

—*Sidelights by Thomas Wiloch*

*   *   *

REES, David Bartlett 1936-1993

PERSONAL: Born in 1936 in London, England; died of an AIDS-related disease, May 22, 1993; son of Gerald (a civil servant) and Margaret (Healy) Rees; married Jenny Lee Watkins (a teacher), July 23, 1966 (divorced); children: Stephen, Adam. *Education:* Queen's College, Cambridge, B.A., 1958. *Avocational interests:* Travel, classical music, attending concerts, surfing, tracing his family tree.

CAREER: Schoolmaster at secondary schools in London, England, 1960-65, and in Ickenham, England, 1965-68; St. Luke's College, Exeter, England, lecturer, 1968-73, senior lecturer, 1973-77; University of Exeter, Exeter, lec-

turer in education, 1977-83; freelance writer, beginning 1984; California State University, San Jose, CA, visiting professor, beginning 1984.

AWARDS, HONORS: Carnegie Medal from Library Association, 1978, for *The Exeter Blitz;* Other Award from Children's Rights Workshop, 1980, for *The Green Bough of Liberty.*

WRITINGS:

Storm Surge, Lutterworth, 1975.
Quinton's Man, Dobson, 1976, Elsevier Nelson, 1979.
The Missing German, Dobson, 1976.
Landslip (juvenile), Hamish Hamilton, 1977.
The Ferryman, Dobson, 1977.
The Spectrum, Dobson, 1977.
Risks, Heinemann, 1977, Thomas Nelson, 1978.
The Exeter Blitz, Hamish Hamilton, 1978, Elsevier Nelson, 1980.
The House That Moved (juvenile), Hamish Hamilton, 1978.
In the Tent, Dobson, 1979.
Silence, Dobson, 1979, Elsevier Nelson, 1981.
The Green Bough of Liberty, Dobson, 1980.
The Lighthouse, Dobson, 1980.
The Marble in the Water (essays on children's writers), Horn Book, 1980.
The Night before Christmas Eve (juvenile), Wheaton, 1980, Pergamon, 1982.
Miss Duffy Is Still with Us, Dobson, 1980.
A Beacon for the Romans (juvenile), Wheaton, 1981.
Holly, Mud, and Whisky (juvenile), Dobson, 1981.
The Milkman's on His Way, Gay Men's Press, 1982.
The Flying Island (juvenile), Dobson, 1982.
The Mysterious Rattle (juvenile) Hamish Hamilton, 1982.
Waves, Longman, 1983.
The Estuary, Gay Men's Press, 1983.
Out of the Winter Gardens, Olive Press, 1984.
Painted Desert, Green Shade (essays on writers for children and young adults), Horn Book, 1984.
A Better Class of Blond, Olive Press, 1985.
Islands (short stories), Knights Press, 1985.
Watershed, Knights Press, 1986.
The Hunger, Gay Men's Press, 1986.
The Burglar (juvenile), Arnold/Wheaton, 1986.
Friends and Neighbours (juvenile) Arnold/Wheaton, 1986.
(Editor and contributor, with Peter Robins) *Oranges and Lemons: Stories by Gay Men,* Third House, 1987.
Twos and Threes, Third House, 1987.
Flux (short stories), Third House, 1988.
Quince, Third House, 1988.
The Wrong Apple, Knights Press, 1988.
The Colour of His Hair, Third House, 1989.
Letters to Dorothy (essays and stories), Third House, 1990.

What Do Draculas Do? (essays on writers for children and young adults), Third House, 1990.
(With Robins) *Fabulous Tricks,* Inbook, 1991.
Dog Days, White Nights (essays), Third House, 1992.
Not for Your Hands (autobiography), Third House, 1992.
Packing It In (travel guide), Millivres Books, 1992.

OTHER

Work represented in anthologies, including: *Remember Last Summer?,* edited by John Foster, Heinemann, 1980; *Cracks in the Image,* Gay Men's Press, 1981; *School's OK,* edited by Josie Karavasil, Evans, 1982; *Messer Rondo and Other Stories,* Gay Men's Press, 1983; *Knockout Short Stories,* Longman, 1988; *The Freezer Counter,* Third House, 1989. Author of column in *Gay News.* Regular contributor of book reviews to *Times Literary Supplement* and contributor to literature and library journals. The University of Exeter, England, owns Rees's manuscript collection.

SIDELIGHTS: David Bartlett Rees once commented: "I'm not sure why I write, but I hope my books will make teenagers and children happier than I was. I see connections between bits of my life and other people's lives and try to work them into a coherent, meaningful shape. I write a lot about disasters, ancestors, and landscape—place is very important to me—particularly Devonshire and Exeter, but also London, Greece, America, and Ireland."

OBITUARIES:

PERIODICALS

Times (London), May 26, 1993, p. 19.*

*   *   *

RHUE, Morton
See STRASSER, Todd

*   *   *

RICE, Edward 1918-

PERSONAL: Born October 23, 1918, in New York; son of Edward and Elsie Rice; married Margery Hawkinson (a television executive), 1947 (divorced, 1967); married Susanna Lee Franklin (a member of the Bear clan of the Seneca Nation of the Iroquois Federation), 1985 (died, 1993); children: (first marriage) Edward III, Christopher. *Education:* Attended Columbia University, 1940. *Politics:* "Philosophical anarchist." *Religion:* Catholic.

ADDRESSES: *Office*—Box 381, Sagaponack, NY 11962.

CAREER: Writer, artist, photographer. Editor, *Collier's* and *Look* magazines. Pathe News, New York City, writer of documentary films, 1947-53; *Jubilee* magazine, New York City, founder and editor in chief, 1953-67.

AWARDS, HONORS: *Mother India's Children: Meeting Today's Generation in India* was chosen as "One of the Outstanding Books of the Year," *New York Times,* 1971.

WRITINGS:

The Man in the Sycamore Tree: The Good Times and Hard Life of Thomas Merton, Doubleday (New York City), 1970.
Mother India's Children: Meeting Today's Generation in India, illustrated with own photographs, Pantheon (New York City), 1971.
(Editor) Pagal Baba, *Temple of the Phallic King,* Simon & Schuster (New York City), 1973.
The Five Great Religions, illustrated with own photographs, Four Winds (Bristol, FL), 1973.
John Frum He Come: A Polemical Work about a Black Tragedy, Doubleday, 1974.
The Ganges: A Personal Encounter, illustrated with own photographs, Four Winds, 1974.
Journey to Upolu: Robert Louis Stevenson, Victorian Rebel, Dodd (New York City), 1974.
Marx, Engels and the Workers of the World, Four Winds, 1977.
Eastern Definitions, Doubleday, 1978.
Ten Religions of the East, Four Winds, 1978.
Babylon, next to Nineveh: Where the World Began, Four Winds, 1979.
Margaret Mead: A Portrait, Harper (New York City), 1979.
American Saints and Seers: American-Born Religions and the Genius behind Them, Four Winds, 1982.
Captain Sir Richard Francis Burton: The Secret Agent Who Made the Pilgrimage to Mecca, Discovered the Kama Sutra, and Brought the Arabian Nights to the West, Scribner (New York City), 1990.

Also author of scripts for television documentaries and motion pictures. Contributor of articles to periodicals.

SIDELIGHTS: Edward Rice once wrote: "I have had a lifelong interest in India, going back to my childhood. One of my favorite uncles, a kind of 'Delinquent Cha-cha,' went out at the age of eighteen for a ten-year stint on the rubber plantations and was a great influence on me. I have made ten trips to India and many trips to Bangladesh, Pakistan, Nepal, the Middle East, and Vietnam, Cuba, and East Africa. Such travel led me to write often about Asia—most of my books have themes dealing with India or with the Orient—religion, philosophy, history, etc.

"I get into some odd and interesting places. I have gone up the Essequibo River in Guyana, for example, and to Wadi Ram on the Saudi Arabian border, and have spent a few days in a Tibetan refugee camp. I have seen Mount Everest twice and met a man in Tunisia who wants to cover the world with trees the way other men want to pave it with asphalt and macadam. I have eaten fresh caviar right out of the sturgeon, and I have been told by an astrologer in Benares, India, that in a previous life I was a Persian prince but was reborn an American because of my sins. I have been told the secrets of meditation by the Dalai Lama's guru.

"In Jordan some Bedouin nomads threatened to shoot me for photographing an old shepherd woman, and a few hours later the Jordanian Army said I was to be shot for photographing a secret military installation. I thought it was a garage. The only real accident I've had was in Benares when a cyclist ran into my rickshaw. What is good about my work is that I travel a lot and write about and photograph interesting subjects. It's tough physically, but it's always exciting. Now my children—both sons—are interested in a similar way of life."

Rice's curiosity about what it would be like to grow up in a country like India led to his 1971 book, *Mother India's Children: Meeting Today's Generation in India.* "What pleased me most was discovering how 'real' the young Indians are," he wrote. "Even with the lack of facilities that we take for granted, their lives are, in most cases, full, varied, and interesting. Sometimes they are held back by custom and the caprices of history. But still they have spirit and life. The same life force that animates and excites young Americans is present but in a different context.

"I have special feelings about India. We seem to be cross-fertilizing each other: American technology, freedom, concern for social justice on the one hand; and on the other, the ancient, cosmic Indian soul, the third eye and the inner ear which tie India to the ancient primordial past. Several astrologers told me that America and India have compatible horoscopes and are the two great nations most suited to each other, being halves of the same whole."

By the time he was 71 years old, Rice had written a number of books, founded and edited a magazine, *Jubilee,* that published works by writers and public figures such as Jack Kerouac, W. H. Auden, and Mother Teresa, written hundreds of magazine articles, and traveled extensively throughout the world. But however rich and satisfying his life had been, he had never achieved fame or written a best-seller. Then, at an age when many writers might end their careers, Rice penned a biography of his boyhood hero—and found himself on the *New York Times* best-seller list for ten weeks.

"Eventually I realized that there was no good work on Richard Burton (the explorer, not the actor), and began research," Rice once explained. "Burton was a kind of

'James Bond of the 1840s'—involved in a plot to overthrow the Shah of Persia, seeking out new lands for the English to colonize, making extensive notes for himself about native languages, ethnology, religions, as well as archeology, economic conditions and trade opportunities. . . . He was very dark and could pass himself off as an Asian, an Afghan or a Gypsy in particular, and made the pilgrimage to Mecca. One of the few Europeans to do so without being exposed as a stranger and beheaded. He also was the first European to enter Somalia. He explored central Africa, made the overland trip to California during the great immigrant period, was British consul in Brazil, Damascus, and finally at Trieste, then a part of Austro-Hungary. He is best known, perhaps, for his sixteen-volume translation of the *Arabian Nights.*"

Rice's book, entitled *Captain Sir Richard Francis Burton: The Secret Agent Who Made the Pilgrimage to Mecca, Discovered the Kama Sutra, and Brought the Arabian Nights to the West,* was not expected to do well when it was first brought out. Its publisher, Scribner, issued the biography in an extremely small first printing—only five thousand copies. Initially, reviewers offered the biography only modest praise. Then novelist Anthony Burgess wrote an enthusiastic essay on the front page of the *New York Times Book Review,* and sales quickly rose. Within weeks, the book had sold an additional forty thousand copies.

Rice's own reaction to his book's success was mixed. "It feels good," he told Mervyn Rothstein in the *New York Times,* but he added, "I worked hard on all those other books, too, as hard on some of them as I did on the Burton book, though the Burton book took longer." In another sense, Rice told Rothstein, "everything I did was a preparation for Burton"—that is, Rice felt his own travels and love of adventure prepared him to write about an adventurer of a previous era.

Captain Sir Richard Francis Burton portrays Burton as a swashbuckling nineteenth-century explorer and spy. "He could do everything," Rice told Rothstein. "He was a great hero." Burton's travels to the Middle East resulted in his classic translation of the *Arabian Nights,* and his experiences in India led to his bringing the *Kama Sutra*—a long-lost Indian sex manual—to the West. In his own day, his was a household name, although his fame faded in the twentieth century. But as Rice told Rothstein, "people love to read about a hero," and part of the appeal of Rice's book was that it offered a chance to do so.

Burgess's review, enticingly titled "Living for Sex and Danger," praised Rice's book for its gripping depiction of Burton's adventures. "Rice's telling of the tale—an odyssey really, of the travail and travels of [Burton] and of the unquenchable urge to get at the truth of life that rode above the tale—is first-class." Jonathan Kirsch, writing in the *Los Angeles Times,* found the book "so full of fascinating historical scholarship and yet so exotic and exciting that I read late into the night and started again at dawn."

A few critics offered minor reservations. "Although this is not the definitive biography, it is an amazing story and Burton and Rice combine to tell it very well," wrote Robert Irwin in the *Washington Post Book World.* "But one should not believe absolutely all of what they tell you." And though *Newsweek* reviewer David Gates dubbed Rice "a good storyteller," he expressed frustration with Rice's lack of psychoanalytic insight, feeling that Rice's view of Burton was ultimately a relatively superficial one.

Rice himself rejects previous biographies of Burton as *too* psychoanalytic. "Previous biographers made the claim that Burton wasn't sure of his identity, that he was always searching for the real Burton," the author told Rothstein. "But he knew who Richard Francis Burton was. You can't go to any of the dangerous places he went to, embark on any of the adventures he undertook, without being sure of yourself. He knew he was going to be better than the other guy—stronger, smarter, more courageous."

BIOGRAPHICAL/CRITICAL SOURCES:

BOOKS

Bestsellers 90, Issue 4, Gale (Detroit), 1990, pp. 58-60.

PERIODICALS

Atlantic Monthly, July, 1990, p. 105.
Christian Science Monitor, August 9, 1990, p. 14.
Los Angeles Times, May 23, 1990.
New York, July 1, 1991, p. 126.
New York Times, July 4, 1990; September 18, 1990.
New York Times Book Review, May 20, 1990, pp. 1, 24, 26.
Newsweek, May 21, 1990, p. 94.
Tribune Books (Chicago), June 10, 1990, p. 6.
Virginia Quarterly Review, autumn, 1990, p. 129.
Wall Street Journal, June 6, 1990, p. A14.
Washington Post Book World, May 20, 1990, pp. 3, 6.

*   *   *

RICKS, Christopher (Bruce) 1933-

PERSONAL: Born September 18, 1933, in London, England; son of James Bruce and Gabrielle (Roszak) Ricks; married Kirsten Jensen, 1956 (divorced, 1975); married Judith Aronson, 1977; children: (first marriage) David, Julia, Laura, William; (second marriage) Alice, James, Sophie. *Education:* Balliol College, Oxford, B.A., 1956, B.Litt., 1958, M.A., 1960. *Religion:* Atheist.

ADDRESSES: Home—39 Martin St., Cambridge, MA 02138. *Office*—Boston University, Boston, MA 02215;

Lasborough College, Lasborough Park, Tetbury GL8 8UF, England.

CAREER: Oxford University, Oxford, England, fellow and tutor at Worcester College and university lecturer, 1958-68; University of Bristol, Bristol, England, professor of English, 1968-75; Cambridge University, Cambridge, England, professor of English, 1975-86; Boston University, Boston, MA, professor of English, 1986—; affiliated with Lasborough College. Visiting professor, Stanford University and University of California, Berkeley, 1965, Smith College, 1967, Harvard University, 1971, Wesleyan University, 1974, and Brandeis University, 1977, 1981, and 1984. *Military service:* British Army, 1951-53; became lieutenant in the Green Howards.

MEMBER: American Academy of Arts and Sciences (fellow), British Academy (fellow), Tennyson Society (vice-president).

WRITINGS:

EDITOR

(And author of introduction with Harry Carter) Edward Rowe Mores, *Dissertation upon English Typographical Founders and Foundries, 1788,* Oxford University Press (Oxford, England), 1962.

(And author of introduction) *Poems and Critics: An Anthology of Poetry and Criticism from Shakespeare to Hardy,* Collins (London), 1966, Harper (New York City), 1972.

A. E. Housman: A Collection of Critical Essays, Prentice-Hall (Englewood Cliffs, NJ), 1968.

Alfred Tennyson, *Poems, 1842,* Collins, 1968.

John Milton, *Paradise Lost and Paradise Regained,* New American Library (New York City), 1968.

The Poems of Tennyson, Longmans, Green (Harlow, England), 1969, revised edition, 1987.

(And author of introduction) *The Brownings: Letters and Poetry,* Doubleday (New York City), 1970.

English Poetry and Prose, 1540-1674, Barrie & Jenkins (Covent Garden, England), 1970.

English Drama to 1710, Sphere (London), 1971.

(And author of introduction) *Selected Criticism of Matthew Arnold,* New American Library, 1972.

(With Leonard Michaels) *The State of the Language,* University of California Press (Berkeley, CA), 1980.

The New Oxford Book of Victorian Verse, Oxford University Press, 1987.

(With Michaels) *The State of the Language: 1990 Edition,* Faber (London), 1990.

OTHER

Milton's Grand Style, Clarendon Press (Oxford), 1963.
Tennyson, Macmillan, 1972, revised edition, 1987.
Keats and Embarrassment, Clarendon Press, 1974.

The Force of Poetry, Oxford University Press, 1984.
Eliot and Prejudice, Faber, 1988.
Beckett's Dying Words, Oxford University Press, 1993.

General editor, "English Poets" series, Penguin. Contributor of articles to professional journals. Coeditor, *Essays in Criticism.*

SIDELIGHTS: In *The Force of Poetry,* the highly respected English critic Christopher Ricks sheds new light on twelve poets by examining their techniques. Described by *Los Angeles Times Book Review* contributor Douglas Sun, as "a critical miniaturist," Ricks "enlarges our understanding by presenting some aspect or facet of the poet's language we may have missed," according to Helen Bevington. Her article in the *New York Times Book Review* lists the poets under scrutiny as A. E. Housman, William Empson, Stevie Smith, Robert Lowell, Philip Larkin, and Geoffrey Hill from the twentieth century, and John Gower (a friend of Geoffrey Chaucer), Andrew Marvell, John Milton, Ben Johnson, William Wordsworth, and Thomas Lovell Beddoes from prior times, the earliest being Gower from the fourteenth century. "In each poet the marvelous resources of language appeal to [Ricks], and as critic and scholar he calls tremendously on his knowledge of literature past and present to provide new insights, aspects, and illuminations," Bevington observes. Ricks augments these essays, written over a period of twenty years, with essays on cliches, falsehoods, misquotations (particularly those of Walter Pater and Matthew Arnold), and the correspondence between slang and rapid change in America. Bevington deems Ricks "a lively critic, who assures us through clarifying analysis of [poetry's] power and force in our lives."

BIOGRAPHICAL/CRITICAL SOURCES:

PERIODICALS

Chicago Tribune Book World, May 24, 1981.
Los Angeles Times Book Review, February 10, 1980; March 17, 1985.
New York Times Book Review, January 6, 1980; March 17, 1985.
Times (London), July 9, 1987.
Times Literary Supplement, February 22, 1980.
Washington Post Book World, February 17, 1980; May 10, 1981.

*   *   *

RIDGE, Martin 1923-

PERSONAL: Born May 7, 1923, in Chicago, IL; son of John and Ann (Lew) Ridge; married Marcella Jane VerHoef, March 17, 1948; children: John Andrew, Curtis Cordell, Wallace Karsten, Judith Lee. *Education:* Chicago Teacher's College (now Northeastern Illinois University), B.A., 1943; Northwestern University, M.A., 1949, Ph.D., 1951. *Politics:* Democrat.

ADDRESSES: Home—533 West Coolidge, San Gabriel, CA 91775. *Office*—Henry E. Huntington Library, San Marino, CA 91109; and Department of History, California Institute of Technology, 1201 East California Blvd., Pasadena, CA 91125.

CAREER: Westminster College, New Wilmington, PA, began as instructor, became assistant professor of American history, 1951-55; San Diego State College (now University), San Diego, CA, assistant professor of history, 1955-66; Indiana University, Bloomington, professor of history, 1966-77; Henry E. Huntington Library, San Marino, CA, senior research associate, 1977—; California Institute of Technology, Pasadena, CA, professor of history, 1981—. Visiting professor at Northwestern University, summer, 1959, and University of California, Los Angeles, summer, 1963. Member of board of directors of California Historical Landmarks Commission, 1954-64; consultant to San Diego City and County Schools, 1962-65, and Los Angeles County Museum, 1979—; member of Indiana Hospital and Health Planning Facilities Council, 1974-75; member of numerous prize committees, including Pulitzer Prize juries, 1978, 1979, 1981, and 1985. *Wartime service:* U.S. Merchant Marine, 1943-45.

MEMBER: American Historical Association, Organization of American Historians, Agricultural History Society, Social Science History Association, Southern Historical Association, Western History Association (vice president, 1985-86; president, 1986-87), Historical Society of Southern California, New Mexico Historical Association.

AWARDS, HONORS: Fellow of William Randolph Hearst Foundation, 1950, Social Science Research Council, 1950, American Council of Learned Societies, 1960, Newberry Library, 1962, Baker Library (Harvard School of Business), 1964, Guggenheim Foundation, 1965-66, Henry E. Huntington Library, 1973-74, American Antiquarian Society, 1982, and Historical Society of Southern California, 1992; Annenberg scholar at University of Southern California, 1979-80; Best Book awards, American Historical Association and Phi Alpha Theta, both 1963, for *Ignatius Donnelly: The Portrait of a Politician;* participant in British Academy Exchange, 1986; Gilberto Espinosa Prize, *New Mexico Historical Review,* 1989; Ray Allen Billington Prize for best article on western history, 1990-91.

WRITINGS:

Ignatius Donnelly: The Portrait of a Politician, University of Chicago Press (Chicago), 1962, revised edition, Minnesota Historical Society (St. Paul), 1991.

(With Vanza Devereau) *California Work and Workers*, Wagnar, Harr (San Francisco), 1963.

(With Walker D. Wyman) *The American Adventure: A History*, Lyons & Carnahan (Chicago), 1964.

(Editor with Ray Allen Billington) *America's Frontier Story: A Documentary History of Western Expansion*, Holt (New York City), 1969.

(With Raymond J. Wilson and George Spiero) *Liberty and Union: A History of the United States* (juvenile), two volumes, Houghton (Boston), 1973.

(With Billington) *American History after 1865*, 9th edition, Littlefield, (Totowa, NJ), 1981.

(Editor) *The New Bilingualism: An American Dilemma*, University of Southern California Press (Los Angeles), 1981.

(With Billington) *Westward Expansion: A History of the American Frontier*, 5th edition, Macmillan (New York City), 1982.

Atlas of American Frontiers, Rand McNally (Chicago), 1992.

EDITOR AND AUTHOR OF INTRODUCTION

Francis Parkman, *The Oregon Trail*, Folio Society (London), 1974.

Oliver Johnson, *A Home in the Woods*, Indiana University Press (Bloomington), 1978.

Frederick Jackson Turner: Wisconsin's Historian of the Frontier, University of Wisconsin Press (Madison), 1986.

Billy Bryant, *Children of Ol' Man River*, R. R. Donnelly (Chicago), 1988.

Westward Journeys: Memoirs of Jesse A. Applegate and Vainia Honeywell Porter Who Traveled the Overland Trail, R. R. Donnelly, 1989.

Frederick Jackson Turner: Three Essays, University of New Mexico Press (Albuquerque), 1993.

OTHER

Contributor to books, including *The Significance of the Frontier in American History*, by Francis Jackson Turner, University of Wisconsin Press, 1985; and *Incidents of a Voyage to California, 1849*, Arthur Clark (Glendale, CA), 1987. Member of editorial boards of *Encyclopedia Americana*, 1968—, and *Encyclopedia of the American West*. Coeditor of "Histories of the American Frontier" and "West in the Twentieth Century" series. *Southern California Quarterly*, associate editor, 1963-69, acting editor, 1964; *Journal of American History*, editor, 1966-77. Member of editorial boards, *Historian*, 1952-58, *Agricultural History*, 1957-75, *Pacific Historical Review*, 1961-64,

Southern California Quarterly, 1962-65, *Prologue*, 1971-74, *America: History and Life*, 1973-93, *Arizona and the West*, 1977-81, *American West*, 1977-80, *New Mexico Historical Review*, 1987-92, and *Montana, the Magazine of Western History*, 1989—.

WORK IN PROGRESS: A social history of silver.

*   *   *

RISJORD, Norman K(urt) 1931-

PERSONAL: Born November 25, 1931, in Manitowoc, WI; son of Norman Edmund (an attorney) and Ireme F. (Kubista) Risjord; married Constance M. Winter, 1959; children: Mark, Eric. *Education:* College of William and Mary, A.B., 1953; Johns Hopkins University, graduate study, 1953-54; University of Virginia, M.A., 1957, Ph.D., 1960.

ADDRESSES: Home—5901 South Highlands, Madison, WI 53705. *Office*—History 3211 Humanities Bldg., University of Wisconsin—Madison, 455 North Park St., Madison, WI 53706-1483.

CAREER: DePauw University, Greencastle, IN, assistant professor of history, 1960-64; University of Wisconsin—Madison, began as assistant professor, 1964, became associate professor, then became professor of history, 1969. *Military service:* U.S. Army, 1954-56.

MEMBER: Phi Beta Kappa.

AWARDS, HONORS: William H. Kiekhofer Prize for best teacher, University of Wisconsin, 1965.

WRITINGS:

The Old Republicans, Columbia University Press (New York City), 1965.

Forging the American Republic, 1760-1815, Addison-Wesley (Reading, MA), 1973.

People and Our Country, Holt (New York City), 1978, third edition, 1986.

Chesapeake Politics, 1781-1800, Columbia University Press, 1978.

Representative Americans: The Revolutionary Generation, Heath (Lexington, MA), 1980.

Representative Americans: The Colonists, Heath, 1981.

America: A History of the United States, Prentice-Hall (Englewood Cliffs, NJ), 1985.

Jefferson's America, 1760-1815, Madison House, Inc., 1991.

Thomas Jefferson, A Biography, Madison House, Inc., 1994.

WORK IN PROGRESS: Liability Insurance Cases, twenty volumes, Risjord Publications (Atlanta, GA); *Wis-*

consin, the Story of the Badger State; a biography of Patrick Creagh.

SIDELIGHTS: After retiring from the University of Wisconsin, Norman K. Risjord purchased a house in the historic district of Annapolis, Maryland, where he continues to focus on the history of Maryland and Virginia. Among future projects is a biography of Patrick Creagh, a self-made merchant of Annapolis, and the "Creagh House," built in 1735, which Risjord owns.

*   *   *

ROBERTS, Willo Davis 1928-

PERSONAL: Born May 28, 1928, in Grand Rapids, MI; daughter of Clayton R. and Lealah (Gleason) Davis; married David W. Roberts (a building supply company manager, photographer, and writer), May 20, 1949; children: Kathleen, David M., Larrilyn (Lindquist), Christopher. *Education:* Graduated from high school in Pontiac, MI. *Religion:* Christian. *Avocational interests:* Travel, playing the organ.

ADDRESSES: Home—12020 West Engebretsen Rd., Granite Falls, WA 98252. *Agent*—Curtis Brown, 10 Astor Place, New York, NY 10019.

CAREER: Writer. Has worked in hospitals and doctors' offices; past co-owner of dairy farm. Lecturer and workshop leader at writers' conferences and schools; consultant to the executive board of Pacific Northwest Writers' Conference.

MEMBER: Mystery Writers of America, Society of Children's Book Writers, Authors Guild, Authors League of America, Seattle Freelancers, Eastside Writers.

AWARDS, HONORS: Notable Children's Trade Book citation, National Council for the Social Studies/Children's Book Council, 1977, Young Hoosier Book Award, Association for Indiana Media Educators, 1980, West Australian Young Readers Award, 1981, and Georgia Children's Book Award, University of Georgia, 1982, all for *Don't Hurt Laurie!;* Mark Twain Award, Missouri Library Association/Missouri Association of School Librarians, 1983, and California Young Readers Medal, California Reading Association, 1986, both for *The Girl with the Silver Eyes;* Pacific Northwest Writers Conference Achievement Award, 1986, for body of work; *Eddie and the Fairy Godpuppy* was named a West Virginia Children's Book Award honor book, 1987; Edgar Allan Poe Award, Mystery Writers of America, 1989, for *Megan's Island;* Washington State Governor's Award for contribution to the field of children's literature, 1990, for body of work; Mark Twain Award, Young Hoosier Book Award, South Caro-

lina Children's Book Award, and Nevada Young Reader's Award, all for *Baby-Sitting is a Dangerous Job;* Outstanding Science Trade Book for Children citation, National Science Teachers Association/Children's Book Council, for *Sugar Isn't Everything.*

WRITINGS:

THE "BLACK PEARL" SERIES; ALL PUBLISHED BY POPULAR LIBRARY

The Dark Dowry, 1978.
The Stuart Strain, 1978.
The Cade Curse, 1978.
The Devil's Double, 1979.
The Radkin Revenge, 1979.
The Hellfire Heritage, 1979.
The Macomber Menace, 1980.
The Gresham Ghost, 1980.

JUVENILE FICTION

The View from the Cherry Tree, Atheneum, 1975.
Don't Hurt Laurie!, illustrated by Ruth Sanderson, Atheneum, 1977.
The Minden Curse, illustrated by Sherry Streeter, Atheneum, 1978.
More Minden Curses, illustrated by Streeter, Atheneum, 1980.
The Girl with the Silver Eyes, Atheneum, 1980.
House of Fear, Scholastic, 1983.
The Pet-Sitting Peril, Atheneum, 1983.
No Monsters in the Closet, Atheneum, 1983.
Eddie and the Fairy Godpuppy, illustrated by Leslie Morrill, Atheneum, 1984.
Elizabeth, Scholastic, 1984.
Caroline, Scholastic, 1984.
Baby-Sitting is a Dangerous Job, Atheneum, 1985.
Victoria, Scholastic, 1985.
The Magic Book, Atheneum, 1986.
Sugar Isn't Everything Atheneum, 1987.
Megan's Island, Atheneum, 1988.
What Could Go Wrong? Atheneum, 1989.
Nightmare, Atheneum, 1989.
To Grandmother's House We Go, Atheneum, 1990.
Scared Stiff, Atheneum, 1991.
Dark Secrets, Fawcett/Juniper, 1991.
Jo and the Bandit, Atheneum, 1992.
What Are We Going to Do About David?, Atheneum, 1993.

FICTION

Murder at Grand Bay, Arcadia House, 1955.
The Girl Who Wasn't There, Arcadia House, 1957.
Murder is So Easy, Vega Books, 1961.
The Suspected Four, Vega Books, 1962.
Nurse Kay's Conquest, Ace Books, 1966.
Once a Nurse, Ace Books, 1966.

Nurse at Mystery Villa, Ace Books, 1967.
Return to Darkness, Lancer Books, 1969.
Devil Boy, New American Library, 1970.
Shroud of Fog, Ace Books, 1970.
The Waiting Darkness, Lancer Books, 1970.
Shadow of a Past Love, Lancer Books, 1970.
The Tarot Spell, Lancer Books, 1970.
The House at Fern Canyon, Lancer Books, 1970.
Invitation to Evil, Lancer Books, 1970.
The Terror Trap, Lancer Books, 1971.
King's Pawn, Lancer Books, 1971.
The Gates of Montrain, Lancer Books, 1971.
The Watchers, Lancer Books, 1971.
The Ghosts of Harrel, Lancer Books, 1971.
The Secret Lives of the Nurses, Pan, 1971, published in the
     United States as *The Nurses,* Ace Books, 1972.
Inherit the Darkness Lancer Books, 1972.
Nurse in Danger, Ace Books, 1972.
Becca's Child, Lancer Books, 1972.
Sing a Dark Song, Lancer Books, 1972.
The Face of Danger, Lancer Books, 1972.
Dangerous Legacy, Lancer Books, 1972.
Sinister Gardens, Lancer Books, 1972.
The M.D., Lancer Books, 1972.
Evil Children, Lancer Books, 1973.
The Gods in Green, Lancer Books, 1973.
Nurse Robin, Lennox Hill, 1973.
Didn't Anyone Know My Wife?, Putnam, 1974.
White Jade, Doubleday, 1975.
Key Witness, Putnam, 1975.
Expendable, Doubleday, 1976.
The Jaubert Ring, Doubleday, 1976.
Act of Fear, Doubleday, 1977.
Cape of Black Sands, Popular Library, 1977.
The House of Imposters, Popular Library, 1977.
Destiny's Women, Popular Library, 1980.
The Search for Willie, Popular Library, 1980.
The Face at the Window, Raven Press, 1981.
A Long Time to Hate, Avon, 1982.
The Gallant Spirit, Popular Library, 1982.
Days of Valor, Warner Books, 1983.
The Sniper, Doubleday, 1984.
Keating's Landing, Warner Books, 1984.
The Annalise Experiment, Doubleday, 1985.
Different Dream, Different Lands, Worldwide, 1985.
My Rebel, My Love, Pocket Books, 1986.
To Share a Dream, Worldwide, 1986.
Madawaska, Worldwide, 1988.

SIDELIGHTS: "Seconds before the windshield shattered into a crazed, opaque spider web pattern, Nick saw the terrified face that would remain forever imprinted on his mind: eyes wide and unseeing, mouth stretched in a grimace of horror. Nick didn't hear the scream, but he knew there had to be one. . . . Not that it mattered. The man who had fallen from the overpass onto the hood of Nick's old, blue Pinto was already dead, his neck broken when he struck the car."

In this, the opening to *Nightmare,* Willo Davis Roberts delivers immediate horror and surprise of the kind that few would like to feel in real life, but which many may love to experience vicariously through fiction. Who could imagine the horror of such a thing happening to them? And how can one put down the book until there is an explanation for why it did happen? How will things turn out? As a writer of suspense thrillers and mysteries for both young readers and adults, Roberts wastes no words in getting right at the action, a device, she suggests, that is imperative to the genre. "The opening is the most important part of the novel. This applies to almost every work of fiction, but particularly suspense novels," she writes in *The Writer* magazine. Roberts continues, "The opening has to have that narrative hook, that grabber that makes a reader turn the page and become immediately absorbed in the story."

As readers become absorbed in *Nightmare,* they find Nick's suspicions of foul play confirmed when he takes off on an interstate trip in the family motorhome to visit his brother and finds that he and his stowaway passenger, Daisy, are being followed by two menacing bad guys who must be daringly eluded until the teen-aged pair can unravel the mystery of the "accident" at the overpass. Roberts explains in *The Writer* that she usually doesn't know in advance exactly how things will turn out in her mysteries: "It's more fun for me to write if the action develops out of the characters, when I say 'What would I do if I were confronted by this problem?' What I would actually do would be to get hysterical and call the cops, but one's protagonist must have more fortitude than that. What I want is for the characters to develop to the stage where they are 'real' people, and then act as sensibly or courageously as they can." Though *Nightmare*'s ending was deemed "a bit farfetched" by reviewer Ethel R. Twichell in *Horn Book,* the novel carries the kind of building suspense that is common to most of Roberts's work for young people.

A productive author with over eighty books to her credit, Roberts began her writing career with adult mystery novels, the first of which was published in 1955 (a time when she was working to raise and help support, with her husband David, her four children). From there—though mystery writing is the core of her work—she followed a genre writing path that led to "nurse novels," Gothics, and historical fiction and, beginning with *The View from the Cherry Tree,* to writing for kids.

The latter is something Roberts says she never intended to do. In various accounts, Roberts explains that though

Cherry Tree was written as an adult suspense novel, her editor and agent felt it would fare better as a children's book. After about a year, Roberts relented and reworked it for a prospective audience of younger readers. Now, many critics consider the book a classic of its kind. "I hadn't anticipated the non-monetary rewards of writing for kids, such as the volume of fan mail," Roberts comments in an essay for the *Something About the Author Autobiography Series* (*SAAS*). "Adults write to an author primarily to tell her what she [or he] did wrong. Kids write to you for that, too, but more often they tell you what they love about your books. Their letters are warm and funny and poignant and wonderful." She continues, "I never had any trouble switching from adult to kids' books; I think in essence I've remained about eleven myself."

Roberts's books for young people now number over twenty; more than half of them are mysteries. Other Roberts tomes deal with the problems that many children face, things like divorce, abuse, isolation, physical problems, or moving to a new town. As Roberts further explains in *SAAS:* "Children are still vulnerable; they have little control over their lives and the adults around them are not always aware of nor responsive to their fears and problems. They feel inadequate, awkward, shy, frightened, and they still respond to encouragement and love. I know about those things."

Roberts was born and raised in Michigan, spending winters in various towns in the lower part of the state, and most summers further north along Lake Michigan, where she developed a love for the woods and water. She demonstrated her storytelling ability at an early age: "I began to write as soon as I could put the stories on paper; before that I just made them up and told them to my younger sisters," she remarks in an essay for the *Fifth Book of Junior Authors and Illustrators.* Her father, whom she describes in *SAAS* as a man with "a quick mind and a quick tongue" and quite a storyteller in his own right, supported the family by doing various kinds of jobs, including truck driving and running trolling boats. "We always ate, but we never had anything in a material sense. It didn't bother him if his family lived in a shack as long as we were warm and had food in the house," Roberts recalls in *SAAS.*

The family never stayed in one town for long and the frequent moves—Roberts attended as many as six schools during her fourth grade year—resulted in a number of difficulties for the author. Not only were there gaps in her education—such as never fully learning the multiplication tables—but it was also hard to make and maintain friendships with other kids her age.

For the young Roberts, reading and writing were both a joy and a refuge. In *SAAS,* she cites *Black Beauty, Heidi, Anderson's* and *Grimm's Fairy Tales,* and *Hans Brinker,*

or the Silver Skates as early favorites; later on she enjoyed the "Nancy Drew" and "Hardy Boys" series, as well as murder mysteries that her parents had on hand. Libraries were a treasure trove for her. Roberts writes in *SAAS* that by age ten, she had read every juvenile book in the libraries of two towns: "When adults assured me that these school days were the best ones of my life, I nearly despaired. It's possible, though, that if school hadn't been so miserable, and moving around so traumatic as it was, I wouldn't have spent nearly as much time writing. . . . I was writing my own stories for two basic reasons at that point. They entertained me when I couldn't find enough books to read, and they took me out of the real world when other people around me made me feel inadequate and without worth."

At age seventeen, Roberts conceived of and began writing a historical novel, and even though she eventually decided that she wasn't yet up to the task, she didn't give up on that early, original idea. Some thirty-five years later, she sold a proposal based on it to a publisher, and, because of the story's length, it was eventually published as two books: *The Gallant Spirit* and *Days of Valor.*

Once she graduated from high school, Roberts began to seriously consider writing as a way to eventually earn a living. It was at this time that she met David Roberts, who had just spent three years in the Navy and was on his way to the West Coast. The couple's courtship was unusual in that they did not go out on as much as one single date; but after five months of letter writing, Roberts joined her husband-to-be in Oregon where he had found a job, and the two were married. Roberts writes in *SAAS* that though "we would never recommend our methods to anyone else (especially not our kids!) we are still happily married . . . and we're still best friends."

The Robertses would have to draw on that friendship for strength during some of the hard times ahead of them. With a family of four children—Kathleen, David, Larrilyn, and Christopher—to raise, Roberts found little time for her writing. For twelve years, the family operated a dairy farm in California's San Joaquin Valley. Despite long days spent in hard work, the farm fell into debt, largely because of factors the Robertses could not control, like destructive weather conditions and livestock illnesses. In the midst of the family's struggles, however, Roberts's had her first publishing success: she sold a mystery for adults, *Murder at Grand Bay,* for $150. Soon after, however, Roberts made the realization—a devastating one at the time—that she couldn't yet earn enough money with her writing to help support the family.

Roberts got a job at a small local hospital where, as she tells C. Herb Williams in *Writer's Digest,* "I did everything from dispatching the ambulance to processing paper work in the emergency room." She also managed to sell several more mysteries to publishers. In a "side" benefit, while working at the hospital, Roberts became familiar with "nurse novels," which were essentially Gothic-like suspense stories that featured young aides as their heroines. Using some of her newly gained knowledge about the workings of hospitals, Roberts wrote and sold several tales for $1,000 advances before the demand for the genre dried up and publishers stopped buying them.

After the Robertses left the dairy farm, both worked at full-time jobs, he as a manager of a building supply company and she in doctors' offices. Undaunted by circumstances that left her with little creative time, Roberts continued to produce saleable novels by writing at night. "I used to come home from work exhausted, feed the kids, and lie down for an hour, setting the timer so I wouldn't pass out for the night. I got up around 8:30 or 9 and worked until 11 every night. It got to the place where I told my family, 'Don't bother me unless you're bleeding,' " she tells Williams.

Roberts's long list of published books indicates that her hard work paid off: in the 1970s alone, she had more than forty books published. "I was lucky that my husband, David, was always supportive. Without that, everything would have been so much harder," she admits in *SAAS.* Once the children were grown and on their own and Roberts had enough book contracts to support them for a time, her husband retired from his job and the two of them began travelling. When not on the road, they spent time at home on their country place in Washington. Looking back, Roberts says in *SAAS,* she has few regrets about her life. In fact, she indicates her struggles were opportunities to learn and grow and that she doesn't feel shortchanged that she never got a college education. "I urge young people to get as much education as they can manage. But I would also say to those for whom college is not an option that they needn't despair over that," she advises in *SAAS.* "Learning can be done anywhere, through reading and through life's experiences. It's possible to have multiple degrees, for instance, and have no understanding of what other people go through, how they struggle just to survive and to cope with the mishaps life dishes out."

In fact, some of Roberts's life experiences, particularly those from family life, have made their way into her books. Sometimes it's in the small details, like the Robertses' Airedales Susie and Rudy, who show up as book characters' pets. Sometimes those experiences become the basis for plots themselves. A good example is Roberts's first book for young people, *The View from the Cherry Tree,* which is about Rob, an eleven-year-old boy who climbs to his favorite hiding place high up in the crook of a cherry tree limb in order to get away from the household brouhaha created by preparations for his sister's wedding. While in the tree, he witnesses the mysterious murder of

the cranky old woman next door, with whom his past encounters have nearly always gotten him into trouble. When Rob tries to tell various family members and friends that the old woman's death was no accident, no one believes him—except for the actual murderer, who is among them. Rob must then summon up all the courage he can in order to outwit and expose the murderer on his own. Roberts writes in *SAAS* that she got the idea for *Cherry Tree* while her own daughter, Larrilyn, was preparing for her wedding: "The book was based largely on things that really happened (exaggerated, naturally) and my kids said I should be ashamed to take money for the book because they provided all the material."

It took Roberts only two weeks to write *The View from the Cherry Tree.* She says the only other book that came to her as easily was *Nightmare,* and, again, in this book one can detect the connection to the author's own experiences: Roberts and her husband—who does freelance photography and writing on outdoors and wildlife subjects—do their extensive travelling in a motorhome like the one described in careful detail in *Nightmare* (theirs, however, is equipped with an office and computer so that they can write while on the road). And while they have had some adventures during their travels (like the grizzly bear that attacked the trailer in Alaska), the couple have not experienced any adventures like the dark one that Nick has while driving his interstate nightmare. As in all fiction, the author's imagination picks up where real life experiences leave off.

Roberts's books for young readers bear a great many similarities to each other. They feature young characters (many of them red-headed) in unfamiliar surroundings. Either the young protagonists have just moved to a new town or have come to stay with grandparents or other relatives whom they don't know well. They soon find themselves thrust, quite unexpectedly, into difficult—and in the mysteries, usually dangerous—circumstances. Adults either can't be relied upon for action or can only be helpful to a point, so the kids use their own gumption and ingenuity to find a way out of their predicaments. Many of the stories feature big, old houses, the kind that are likely to be haunted, ones with towers or turrets that figure prominently in the youngsters' attempts to thwart crooks.

But the most common and more general element of all Roberts's books is the suspense they create, that mixed feeling of anxiety and uncertainty that a reader gets, which grows steadily in anticipation of a story's resolution. When one picks up a mystery, one expects suspense, and reviewers recommend Roberts's mysteries most often because they are solidly constructed and sustain a high level of suspense (regardless of how believable the plots may or may not be). Along the way, Roberts provides clues and motives that both create question marks and make it possible for alert readers to try to figure out the mystery. In *Nightmare,* for instance, what might a chain of soda can tabs Nick absently picks up off the ground at the scene of the accident have to do with his being followed later on? Why, in *More Minden Curses,* would two old ladies with few resources see to it that their many cats be decked out in glittery collars? How does picking up a discarded newspaper in an airport make three children kidnapping victims in *What Could Go Wrong?*

"These days many so-called mysteries are not mysteries at all, in the sense that you have a puzzle to solve," Roberts explains in her *The Writer* article. Her mysteries, in which she provides puzzles aplenty, range in their intensity levels. On the "high" end are books like *Cherry Tree* and *Nightmare,* in which kids' accidental involvement in a mystery or crime actually puts them in peril. In *Baby-Sitting is a Dangerous Job,* thirteen-year-old Darcy takes a baby-sitting job for the children in a wealthy family. She soon finds there is more to the job than she bargained for. Not only are the three kids a handful, but they are also being watched by two suspicious men who turn out to be kidnappers. Darcy and her charges are kept prisoners-for-ransom in a remote old house until they can come up with a scheme to both alert the police to their location and foil their captors. A reviewer for *School Library Journal* deemed the novel "a solid suspense story" in which Roberts gives "a very resourceful young girl plenty of chances to show her mettle."

Megan's Island also features resourceful young characters, but ones who are in a different kind of pinch. Megan and her younger brother Sandy begin their summer vacation before school is even out when they are abruptly packed up one night by their single-parent mother and taken on an all-night drive to their grandfather's lake cottage in Minnesota. The children's mother, who gives no reason for the family's sudden departure and seems afraid, makes arrangements for their household things to be put in storage, and goes away to look for a job and a place for them to live in a new town. Though the family's past moves from town to town did not make Megan suspicious, it becomes clear to her now that the trio have been—and still are—on the run. A mysterious situation becomes more so when one by one, Megan begins discovering clues that indicate there are secrets about her family's past. Then strange men come poking around the place, with one even asking questions about red-haired kids like Megan and Sandy. With the help of a newly made friend, Ben, the children claim one of the lake's many islands, where they build a tree house for fun and end up using it as a hiding place when their pursuers threaten their safety.

In a *Junior Literary Guild* article, Roberts explains that she got the idea for *Megan's Island* while she and her husband were on a 1986 research trip to Canada that took them through the area of the St. Lawrence River's Thousand Islands. It reminded her of childhood days in northern Michigan. "I was so enchanted by these islands," she writes, "some of them barely large enough for a person to stand on, many the size to hold a house, that I asked my husband to take pictures of them." (The photos were later used by illustrator Leslie Morrill to create the book's cover.) According to a review of *Megan's Island* by Zena Sutherland in the *Bulletin of the Center for Children's Books,* "fluid writing style, the excitement of the action," and "solidity of the characterization" make up for an "occasionally turgid" plot.

In some of her mysteries, Roberts uses a lighter touch, incorporating humor and creating mysteries that unfold within the ordinary routines of daily life, rather than ones that interrupt or occur outside those normal circumstances. In *The Minden Curse,* young Danny Minden comes to stay with his grandfather and aunt in a small lake town while his father is overseas. He and Gramps seem to be cursed with the "ability" to always be on the scene when accidents or strange things happen, and in this case, it's a bank robbery and dog-napping. The follow-up book, *More Minden Curses,* is described by a critic in *Booklist* as the "more cohesive tale" of the two, in which Danny starts school, after having been tutored for years while on the road with his photographer father. In the book, Danny becomes involved with the town's elderly Caspitorian sisters (the "Cat Ladies"), whom someone is trying to force out of their home because the family treasure is supposedly hidden there; he also has to try to kidnap the sisters' nasty cat "Killer" as a rite of initiation into his new friends' secret club. In addition to the mystery action it provides, the book delves into the difficulties of making friends and settling into a new place.

Roberts uses a similar formula—children who must prove themselves after being uprooted and sent to stay with relatives—in *Jo and the Bandit,* but puts a twist on it by giving it a historical setting. The story takes place in 1860s Texas, when the grandmother who is raising Josephine and her little brother Andrew dies, and the children are sent to stay with their rough-edged bachelor Uncle Matthew until they can be taken in by an aunt. On their way, their stagecoach is ambushed by bandits, including a young redheaded one who mysteriously returns Josephine's stolen locket once she and her brother are settled in at Uncle Matthew's. Jo uses her artistic abilities to draw wanted posters of the bandits and becomes involved in a potentially dangerous scheme to trick and catch the outlaws; she must also find a way to keep the kind young bandit from being convicted along with them. Reviewer Jeanette Larson, writing in *School Library Journal,* suggested that though the story's pace may be slow in spots, "it is refreshing to find a strong-minded, independent female protagonist in a genre [Westerns] usually overwhelmed by bonnets and gingham."

Other "lighter" mysteries by Roberts have supernatural elements to them. Most notable is *The Girl with the Silver Eyes,* winner of the Mark Twain Award and the California Young Reader Medal. Roberts says in a *Junior Literary Guild* article that, like *Cherry Tree, The Girl with the Silver Eyes* was also first imagined as an adult suspense novel: "At first, editors (of adult books) felt that my young characters were too precocious, their vocabularies too advanced, etc. for their ages. I finally convinced them that these were the only kinds of children I knew, and that there were such kids, like my own, and eventually these were accepted."

Katie, the girl with the silver eyes, is a good example of an advanced child who is not readily accepted by her peers. Aside from her strange eyes, she is set apart from other children her age by her above-average intelligence, her ability to communicate in a telepathic way with animals, and her telekinetic powers, which allow her to move objects without touching them. Almost everyone finds her unsettling, including her own divorced mother, with whom she's just been reunited after living for a time with a stern grandmother. She makes friends with Mrs. Michaelmas, an eccentric older woman in the apartment building, who lends her books and has no trouble believing in Katie's special powers. She consoles Katie: "Seems to me you're better than most folks. And maybe that's it; they don't want anyone to be better, or smarter, or more powerful in any way. They're afraid of people who are different, so they make fun of them. Attack them. It's foolish, but it's the way people are." Another new friend—the paper boy Jackson Jones—later comes to Katie's aid when a new neighbor, Mr. Cooper, starts asking too many questions and the young heroine begins to think that she might be in danger. Katie later learns of a drug that her mother and other women took while they were pregnant; she also finds there are other kids like her. When all of these kids come together to help Katie, they discover, for the first time, how it feels not to be the only one.

Like her character Mrs. Michaelmas, Roberts expresses an empathy for those who are different, perhaps because as a youngster she too felt set apart from her peers. In *SAAS,* she writes about "underdogs": "Such people are everywhere, though they don't wear labels on their foreheads so you would notice them. They tend not to push themselves forward, not to create a fuss to win you over to their side. But oh! how lovely it is for them when anyone expresses understanding or sympathy. I often write from the viewpoint of the underdog because it comes so naturally. I've been there. Plain. Poor. Bright, but too timid to claim any honors or recognition for that. Dreaming so many dreams, and all of them, it seemed, unattainable." In

her second book for young people, *Don't Hurt Laurie!,* Roberts takes on the difficult subject of child abuse by writing about a bright girl with a few simple dreams that are, quite literally, beaten down by her mother, Annabelle. Laurie's father walked out when she was very young. Because Laurie reminds Annabelle of him, whenever her mother gets angry or has one of her migraines, she takes it out on her daughter by beating, burning or cutting her. When hospital or school personnel get suspicious about Laurie's frequent injuries or Annabelle's explanations about how clumsy her daughter is, Annabelle and Laurie move to a new place.

The abuse continues even after Annabelle remarries. And although she is able to keep the secret from her travelling salesman husband, it's not long before Laurie's new stepbrother Tim and her next-door friend George figure out what is going on. In the past, Laurie has been afraid that no adult would believe her story. But when things get so out of hand that Annabelle beats Laurie in Tim's presence, the children flee to the safety of Tim's grandmother's home, where the truth finally comes out. Annabelle is confronted and is taken away for psychiatric help. The ending implies that they will someday be able to be rejoined as a family. "I was not an abused child, but my father was, and I had several friends who were, also," Roberts writes in *SAAS.* "*Don't Hurt Laurie!* came out of their experiences."

The book elicited varying responses from critics. Judith Viorst, writing in *The New York Times Book Review,* says that "its subject matter is inevitably lurid, sadistic, and violent" and deemed it ultimately not "necessary" for young readers. A reviewer for *Horn Book,* however, claims that "the book's strength lies in the realistic and believable portrayal of the young girl's frustration and helplessness." And a reviewer for the *Bulletin of the Center for Children's Books* cites the novel for its "excellent characterization" and an approach that "is both realistic about the problem and realistically encouraging about its alleviation." According to Roberts, the book is still popular with kids. "Librarians have told me it is among the most stolen books in their libraries, presumably by battered kids who can't afford to own it but want to read and re-read it," she explains.

Roberts's most recent book for kids is *What Are We Going to Do About David?*. Marilyn Long Graham, writing in *School Library Journal,* calls it the "fine story" of "an introspective, keenly sensitive child" with a plot that "unfolds at a brisk pace, with the concerns of a preadolescent boy convincingly portrayed." When David's parents decide to separate, he gets sent to stay with his grandmother, Ruthie, who lives in a small town along the Washington coast. There, with Ruthie's nurture and the companionship of her energetic dog and a new friend—who is disfigured and has problems of his own to confront—David begins to overcome his feelings of loneliness, homesickness, and worry about his family situation. He is even able to stand up for himself before his parents when the time comes for him to make a decision about his future.

"One way to hold your readers is to make them care what happens to the protagonist," Roberts explains in *The Writer*. "Make them fear for her, laugh with her, cry for her. Make the reader identify with your characters, feel the sorrow, the pain, the fear, the thumping heart and the labored breathing." She continues, "A character not only can, but should, have flaws that make him human."

The young characters in Roberts's novels ultimately find their own ways of overcoming their personal limitations and obstacles. For several of them—David included—books and writing provide a good way to cope. For Roberts, who has persevered through many obstacles throughout her life using her natural love of those very things for both pleasure and profit, the writing life has proved to be a good one. Her advice to would-be writers is also about practice and perseverance. In *SAAS,* she writes, "I do think it's very important to write regularly and to set priorities that allow this, if you ever want to be published. It's also essential to develop such a strong belief in what you want to do that you get thick-skinned about criticism of your dreams." With her own children also writing and having work published and her grandchildren showing promise, it seems that it is possible to pass on the love of a writing life. As the author tells Williams, "If you reach a point where you can make a living doing something you really enjoy, you're ahead of 99 percent of the rest of the world."

BIOGRAPHICAL/CRITICAL SOURCES:

BOOKS

Roberts, Willo Davis, *Nightmare,* Atheneum, 1989.
Roberts, Willo Davis, *The Girl with the Silver Eyes,* Atheneum, 1980.
Roberts, Willo Davis, essay in *Fifth Book of Junior Authors and Illustrators,* edited by Sally Holmes Holtze, Wilson, 1983.
Something About the Author Autobiography Series, Volume 8, Gale, 1989.

PERIODICALS

Booklist, June 15, 1980.
Bulletin of the Center for Children's Books, June, 1977; April, 1988.
Horn Book, August, 1977; November, 1989.
Junior Literary Guild, September, 1980; April-September, 1988.
New York Times Book Review, April 17, 1977.

School Library Journal, May, 1985; July, 1992; April, 1993.
Writer, February, 1990.
Writer's Digest, August, 1981.

—*Sketch by Tracy J. Sukraw*

*   *   *

ROEMER, Milton I(rwin) 1916-

PERSONAL: Born in 1916 in Paterson, NJ; married; children: two. *Education:* Cornell University, B.A., 1936, M.A., 1939; New York University, M.D., 1940; University of Michigan, M.P.H., 1943.

ADDRESSES: Office—School of Public Health, University of California, Los Angeles, CA 90024.

CAREER: Barnert Memorial Hospital, Paterson, NJ, rotating intern, 1940-41; New Jersey State Department of Health, Trenton, medical officer in Venereal Disease Control Division, 1941-42; U.S. Public Health Service, 1943-51, served as assistant to chief medical officer in War Food Administration, 1943-45, associate in medical care administration to chief of the States Relations Division, 1945-47, and director of West Virginia Public Health Training Center and Monongalia County Health Department, 1948-49, became senior surgeon; Yale University, New Haven, CT, assistant professor, 1949-50, associate professor of public health, 1950-51; World Health Organization, Geneva, Switzerland, chief of social and occupational health section, 1951-53; Saskatchewan Department of Public Health, Regina, director of medical and hospital services, 1953-56; Yeshiva University, Albert Einstein College of Medicine, New York City, lecturer in medicine, 1956-57; Cornell University, Ithaca, NY, associate research professor, 1957-60, research professor of administrative medicine, 1960-62, director of research at Sloan Institute of Hospital Administration, 1957-62; University of California, Los Angeles, professor of health services and preventative medicine, beginning 1962, head of Division of Medical Care Organization, 1962-64, head of Division of Medical and Hospital Administration, 1965-67, head of Division of Health Administration, 1967-70.

Member, U.S. National Subcommittee on Medical Care Statistics, Institute of Medicine (of National Academy of Sciences), California State Health Department committees on medical care for children, seasonal agricultural workers, and hospital utilization, California Center for Health Services Research (member of policy board, 1968-72), Los Angeles Psychiatric Service (member of board of directors), and Los Angeles County Committee on Affairs of the Aging; diplomate, National Board of Medical Examiners, 1941, and American Board of Preventative Medicine and Public Health; fellow, Institute of European Health Services Research. Consultant to state and federal government agencies and to international organizations.

MEMBER: International Epidemiological Association, American Public Health Association (fellow; member of governing council, 1967—), American Sociological Association, American College of Preventive Medicine, California Academy of Preventive Medicine (president, 1972—), Phi Beta Kappa, Sigma Xi, Phi Kappa Phi, Alpha Omega Alpha, Delta Omega.

WRITINGS:

Social Factors Influencing American Medical Practice, Cornell University (Ithaca, NY), 1939.

A System for Quantitative Appraisal of Voluntary Hospitalization Insurance Plans, University of Michigan (Ann Arbor), 1942.

(With F. D. Mott) *Rural Health and Medical Care,* McGraw (New York City), 1948.

A Health Demonstration Area in Ceylon, World Health Organization (Geneva), 1951.

A Health Demonstration Area in El Salvador, World Health Organization, 1951.

(With Ethel A. Wilson) *Organized Health Services in a County of the United States,* Federal Security Agency, Public Health Service (Washington, DC), 1952.

Medical Care in Relation to Public Health: A Study of Relationships between Preventive and Curative Health Services throughout the World, World Health Organization, 1956.

(With Max Shain) *Hospital Utilization under Insurance,* American Hospital Association (Chicago), 1959.

(Editor) *Henry E. Sigerist on the Sociology of Medicine,* M.D. Publications (New York City), 1960.

Medical Care Administration: Content, Positions, and Training in the United States, University of California School of Public Health (Los Angeles), 1963.

Medical Care in Latin America, Pan American Union (Washington, DC), 1963.

Health Services in the Los Angeles Riot Area, University of California, Los Angeles, 1965.

(With Olive Manning) *The Rural Health Services Scheme in Malaysia,* Office for the Western Pacific, World Health Organization, 1969.

The Organisation of Medical Care under Social Security: A Study Based on the Experience of Eight Countries, International Labour Office (Geneva), 1969.

(Editor with Donald M. DuBois and Shirley W. Rich) *Health Insurance Plans: Studies in Organizational Diversity,* University of California School of Public Health, 1970.

(With Jay W. Friedman) *Doctors in Hospitals: Medical Staff Organization and Hospital Performance,* Johns Hopkins Press (Baltimore), 1971.

Evaluation of Community Health Centres, World Health Organization, 1972.

Health Insurance Effects: Services, Expenditures, and Attitudes under Three Types of Plan, School of Public Health, University of Michigan, 1972.

(Editor) *Health Service Organization: A Collection of Readings,* Division of Health Administration, School of Public Health, University of California, 1972.

(With R. F. Bridgman) *Hospital Legislation and Hospital Systems,* World Health Organization, 1973.

(With Foline E. Gartside and C. E. Hopkins) *Medicaid Services in California under Different Organizational Modes: A Comparative Study of Organizational Characteristics and Their Relationships to the Volume, Costs, Quality and Outcomes of Services to Medicaid Beneficiaries,* School of Public Health, University of California, 1973.

(With Ruth Roemer) *Health Manpower in Four Countries: An Annotated Bibliography,* U.S. Department of Health, Education, and Welfare, Public Health Service, Health Resources Administration, Bureau of Health Manpower, Division of Medicine (Rockville, MD), 1974.

(With Robert W. Hetherington, Carl E. Hopkins, and others) *Health Insurance Plans: Promise and Performance,* Wiley (New York City), 1975.

Health Care Systems in World Perspective, Health Administration Press (Ann Arbor), 1976.

Rural Health Care, Mosby (St. Louis, MO), 1976.

Comparative National Policies on Health Care, Dekker (New York City), 1977.

Social Medicine: The Advance of Organized Health Service in America, Springer Publishing (New York City), 1978.

(With R. Roemer) *Health Care Systems and Comparative Manpower Policies,* Dekker, 1981.

Ambulatory Health Services in America: Past, Present, and Future, Aspen Systems Corporation (Rockville), 1981.

(With T. Fulop) *International Development of Health Manpower Policy,* World Health Organization, 1982.

An Introduction to the U.S. Health Care System, Springer Publishing, 1982, 2nd edition, 1986.

National Strategies for Health Care Organization: A World Overview, University of Michigan Health Administration Press, 1985.

National Health Systems of the World, Oxford University Press (New York City), Volume 1: *Countries,* 1991, Volume 2: *Issues,* 1993.

Contributor of about three hundred eighty articles on social and organizational aspects of health services to professional journals.

SIDELIGHTS: Milton I. Roemer once told *CA:* "Work in public health service, research, and teaching since 1941 has enabled me to learn a great deal about the diverse health care systems of the United States and some sixty other countries on all the continents. This experience has inspired my writing."

*　　*　　*

ROOT, Deane L(eslie) 1947-

PERSONAL: Born August 9, 1947, in Wausau, WI; son of Forrest Kent (a manufacturer's representative) and Marguerite (a financial secretary; maiden name, Fleenor) Root; married Doris Jane Dyen (an ethnomusicologist), August 27, 1972; children: Jessica Edith, Melanie Elizabeth. *Education:* New College, B.A., 1968; University of Illinois, N.Mus., 1971, Ph.D., 1977.

ADDRESSES: Office—Stephen Foster Memorial, University of Pittsburgh, Pittsburgh, PA 15260.

CAREER: University of Wisconsin—Madison, lecturer in music history, 1973; Macmillan Publishers Ltd., London, editor of popular music and text editor of *The New Grove Dictionary of Music and Musicians,* 1974-76; University of Illinois at Urbana-Champaign, general editor of "Resources of American Music History" project, 1976-80; University of Pittsburgh, curator of Stephen Foster Memorial and Foster Hall and adjunct assistant professor of music, 1982—, administrator of Heinz Memorial Chapel, 1983—. Lecturer and instructor, Lake City Community College, 1981-82; visiting research associate, Florida State University, 1981-82. Adjudicator, South Carolina Arts Commission, 1981-83; historian and museum curator, Blue-Gray Army, Inc., 1982; conductor of musical activities, Columbia County Council on Aging, 1982; manager of Suwannee River Bicycle Tours, 1980-81. Founding chairperson, Historic Preservation Board of Lake City and Columbia County, 1982; chairperson, Fine Arts Council of Lake City/Columbia County, 1982; chairperson of public relations, Lake City Playshop, 1981-82.

MEMBER: International Association for the Study of Popular Music, American Studies Association, American Musicological Society (member of council, 1989-92), Center for Black Music Research, Society for Ethnomusicology, Sonneck Society for American Music (member of board of directors, 1979-80; president, 1989-93), Music Library Association, Florida Folklore Society (founding member of board of directors, 1982), Columbia County Historical Society, Community Concert Association,

Greater Pittsburgh Museum Council (president, 1987-89), Pi Kappa Lambda.

AWARDS, HONORS: Woodrow Wilson fellow, 1968.

WRITINGS:

(General editor and contributor) *Resources of American Music History: A Directory of Source Materials from Colonial Times to World War II,* University of Illinois Press (Champaign), 1981.
American Popular Stage Music, 1860-1880, UMI Research Press (Ann Arbor, MI), 1981.
Music of Florida Sites (monograph), Florida State University (Tallahassee), 1983.
(Coeditor) *The Music of Stephen C. Foster: A Critical Edition,* Smithsonian Institution Press (Washington, DC), 1990.
(General editor) *Nineteenth-Century American Musical Theater,* 16 volumes, Garland Publishing (New York City), 1994.

Contributor to *Yearbook for Inter-American Music Research,* 1972; *The New Grove Dictionary of Music and Musicians,* 1981; and *The New Grove Dictionary of American Music,* 1986. Also contributor to music journals. Editor, *Music of the American Theater,* special issue of *American Music,* winter, 1984.

SIDELIGHTS: Deane L. Root once told *CA:* "My work is motivated by the need to strengthen performing arts organizations at the local level, to provide access to information about our cultural history, and to promote awareness and participation in historic preservation.

"Throughout my career I have sought to direct scholarly attention toward the enduring qualities and customs of everyday life in America, especially as they are represented in so-called 'popular' and 'ephemeral' media. I have enjoyed musical performance as a trumpet player and later as a tenor and conductor. As a historian, I have been most concerned with seeing beyond other historians' delineations and labelings of 'firsts' and 'great men' to discover the full richness of context in which historical figures operated. I have sought to provide accurate reference information for students and scholars of American music, to help demonstrate the abundant variety of musical activity in American life."

*　　*　　*

ROSENBERG, Jane 1949-

PERSONAL: Born December 7, 1949, in New York, NY; daughter of Abner Emmanuel (a real estate developer) and Lily (Quittman) Rosenberg; married Michael B. Frankel, February 17, 1974 (divorced, 1978); married

Robert F. Porter (a writer), May 30, 1982; children: (second marriage) Melo (stepdaughter), Ava Hermine, Eloise Pearl. *Education:* Attended City of London College and Sir John Cass College of Art, 1970; Beaver College, B.F.A., 1971; New York University, M.A., 1973.

ADDRESSES: Agent—Susan Cohen, Writers House Inc., 21 West 26th St., New York, NY 10010.

CAREER: Daniel & Charles Associates, New York City, commercial artist, 1973; Ethical Culture School, New York City, art teacher, 1974-75; freelance illustrator and designer, 1975-81; art director of *New York News for Kids,* 1979-80; set illustrator for Metropolitan Opera Guild, 1986. Exhibitions at galleries in New York City, including Master Eagle Gallery, 55 Mercer Gallery, and Judith Christian Gallery.

MEMBER: Authors Guild.

WRITINGS:

JUVENILES

(Self-illustrated) *Dance Me a Story: Twelve Tales from the Classic Ballets,* Thames & Hudson, 1985.
(Self-illustrated) *Sing Me a Story: The Metropolitan Opera's Book of Opera Stories for Children,* Thames & Hudson and the Metropolitan Opera, 1989.
(Self-illustrated) *Play Me a Story: A Child's Introduction to Classical Music Through Stories and Poems,* Knopf, 1994.

ILLUSTRATOR

Gloria Rothstein, *A Scholastic Skills Program: Vocabulary Skills,* Scholastic, 1980.
Rose Beranbaum, *Romantic and Classic Cakes,* Irena Chalmers, 1981.

Also illustrator of *Technology of the City,* edited by David Jacobs, for Abrams; contributor of illustrations to magazines.

WORK IN PROGRESS: Writing and illustrating *The Memoirs of Harlequin,* the story of the clowns of the commedia dell'arte, and *They Say the Balloon Has Gone Up to the Moon.*

SIDELIGHTS: Jane Rosenberg told *CA:* "Trained as a fine artist in New York City and exhibiting my paintings in downtown galleries, I turned to freelance illustration for income. I preferred illustrating to teaching or full-time commercial art, both of which demanded too much time away from the studio. The more my work appeared in magazines, newspapers, and books, the more appealing the notion of illustrating a project of my own became. Turning to a lifelong interest—the ballet—I retold the stories of the great classical ballets in the manner of fairy tales, attempting to offer the reader more than a program synopsis.

"Since childhood, illustrated books have held an irresistible attraction for me. Now I find myself painting and writing for children, telling tales of the ballet, opera, or the programmatic classical musical repertory; combining my art with my love of the performing arts into one of the most satisfying of all forms, the illustrated book. As parents face budget cutbacks in public schools and music programs are abandoned, it is more important than ever to expose young children to classical music. I attempt, in my books to convey the delights of great music through stories, poems and art."

BIOGRAPHICAL/CRITICAL SOURCES:

PERIODICALS

Opera Quarterly, Volume 9, number 2, 1993.
Times Educational Supplement, April 11, 1986.

* * *

ROTHSCHILD, Kurt Wilhelm 1914-

PERSONAL: Name indexed as Kurt William Rothschild in some sources; born October 21, 1914, in Vienna, Austria; son of Ernst (in sales) and Phillipine (Hollub; a homemaker) Rothschild; married Valerie Kunke (a secretary), August 10, 1938; children: Thomas, Elisabeth Rothschild Menzel. *Education:* University of Vienna, Dr. Juris, 1938; University of Glasgow, M.A. (with honors), 1940. *Politics:* Socialist. *Religion:* None. *Avocational interests:* Walking, climbing, theatre, film, and reading novels.

ADDRESSES: Home—Doblinger Hauptstrasse 77A, A1190 Vienna, Austria.

CAREER: University of Glasgow, Glasgow, Scotland, lecturer in economics, 1940-47; Austrian Institute for Economic Research, Vienna, Austria, senior member of research staff, 1947-66; University of Linz, Linz, Austria, professor of economics, 1966-85, professor emeritus, 1985—. Member of Austrian Supreme Cartel Court, 1975-80; consultant to Austrian Institute for Economic Research.

MEMBER: American Economic Association, Royal Economic Society, Gesellschaft fuer Sozial- und Wirtschaftswissenschaften, Gesellschaft fuer National-oekonomie, Club of Rome.

AWARDS, HONORS: Award from city of Vienna, 1980, for distinguished work in the social sciences; science award from city of Linz, 1982; honorary doctorates from University of Rachen, 1987, University of Augsburg, 1990, and University of Bremen, 1994.

WRITINGS:

Austria's Economic Development between the Two World Wars, Muller, 1947.

The Austrian Economy since 1945, Royal Institute of International Affairs, 1950.

The Theory of Wages, Basil Blackwell, 1954.

Lohntheorie (title means "Wage Theory"), F. Vahlen, 1963.

Marktform, Loehne und Aussenhandel (title means "Market Forms, Wages, and Foreign Trade"), Europa-Verlag, 1966.

Wirtschaftsprognose (title means "Economic Forecasting"), Springer-Verlag, 1969.

Development of Income Distribution in Western Europe, Organization for Economic Cooperation and Development, 1971.

(Editor) *Power in Economics,* Penguin, 1971.

(With Ewald Nowotny) *Bestimmungsgruende der Lohnbewegung* (title means "Determinants of Money Wage Movements"), Springer-Verlag, 1972.

(With H. J. Schmahl) *Beschleunigter Gerdwertschwund* (title means "The Decline in the Value of Money"), Weltwirtschaftliches Institut, 1973.

(With others) *The Utilization of Social Sciences in Policy Making,* Organization for Economic Cooperation and Development, 1977.

Arbeitslosigkeit in Oesterreich, 1955-1975 (title means "Unemployment in Austria, 1955-1975"), Institute for Labour Market Studies, 1977.

Einfuehrung in die Ungleichgewichts theorie (title means "Introduction to Disequilibrium Theory"), Springer-Verlag, 1981.

(Editor with H. Krupp) *Wege zur Vollbeschaeftigung* (title means "Roads to Full Employment"), Rombach-Verlag, 1986.

Theorien der Arbeitslosigkeit, Oldenburg, 1988.

Ethics and Economic Theory, Edward Elgar, 1993.

Employment, Wages and Income Distribution: Critical Essays in Economics, Routledge, 1994.

Also contributor to economic journals.

SIDELIGHTS: Kurt Wilhelm Rothschild told *CA:* "I always felt and still feel that economic theory, in spite of its weaknesses, can help to alleviate some of the pressing problems in this world. Unfortunately, too much of the present work is purely formal, career-oriented and often dealing with minor problems. I think that a greater drive for relevancy is the main task in economic science."

Rothschild also wrote: "I have a strong interest in economic, social, and political development. I want to improve the economic situation of less privileged groups. I am critical of entrenched interest groups. On all these matters economic theory could make a greater contribution if it did not get lost—too often—in unrealistic problems and sophisticated detail. In my writings I hope to find ways of turning research toward relevant questions and extracting usable answers from theoretical results."

BIOGRAPHICAL/CRITICAL SOURCES:

BOOKS

Laski, K. and others, editors, *Beitraege zur Diskussion und Kritik der Neoklassischen Oekonomie: Festschrift fuer K. W. Rothschild und V. Steindl,* Springer-Verlag, 1979.

* * *

RUBIN, Larry (Jerome) 1930-

PERSONAL: Born February 14, 1930, in Bayonne, NJ; son of Abraham Joseph and Lillian (Strongin) Rubin. *Education:* Attended Columbia University, 1949-50; Emory University, B.A., 1951, M.A., 1952, Ph.D., 1956. *Religion:* Jewish.

ADDRESSES: *Home*—Box 15014, Druid Hills Branch, Atlanta, GA 30333. *Office*—Department of English, Georgia Institute of Technology, Atlanta, GA.

CAREER: Georgia Institute of Technology, Atlanta, instructor in English, 1956-58, assistant professor, 1958-65, associate professor, 1965-1973, professor of English, 1973—. Visiting professor, Jagiellonian University, Krakow, Poland, 1961-62, University of Bergen, Norway, 1966-67, Free University of West Berlin, 1969-70, and University of Innsbruck, Austria, 1971-72.

MEMBER: Poetry Society of America, College English Association, South Atlantic Modern Language Association, Phi Beta Kappa, Omicron Delta Kappa.

AWARDS, HONORS: Reynolds Lyric Award, Poetry Society of America, 1961, for "Instructions for Dying"; Georgia Writer's Association Literary Achievement Award, 1963, for *The World's Old Way;* Sidney Lanier Award, Oglethorpe University, 1964, for *The World's Old Way;* John Holmes Memorial Award, 1965, for "For Parents, Out of Sight"; Georgia Poet of the Year award, Dixie Council of Authors and Journalists, 1967, for *Lanced in Light,* and 1975, for *All My Mirrors Lie;* Poetry Society of America annual award, 1973, for "The Bachelor, as Professor."

WRITINGS:

POETRY

The World's Old Way, University of Nebraska Press, 1962.

Lanced in Light, Harcourt, 1968.

All My Mirrors Lie, David Godine (Boston), 1975.

Poems also appear in anthologies, including *The Golden Year: The Poetry Society of America Anthology, 1910-1960,* Fine Editions, 1960; *La Poésie contemporaine aux Etats-Unis,* Editions de la Revue Moderne, 1962; *Southern Poetry Today,* Impetus Press, 1962; *The New Orlando Poetry Anthology,* Volume II, New Orlando Publications, 1963; *Anthology of Southern Writing,* edited by Miller Williams and John W. Carrington, Louisiana State University Press, 1967; *The Norton Introduction to Literature,* Norton, 1975, 1991; *A Geography of Poets,* Bantam, 1979; *Contemporary Southern Poetry,* Louisiana State University Press, 1979; and *The Mode Thing: An Anthology of Contemporary Southern Poetry,* University of Arkansas Press, 1987. Contributor to periodicals and poetry journals, including *American Scholar, Antioch Review, Commonweal, Epoch, Harper's, Kenyon Review, London Magazine, New Yorker, New York Times, Poetry, Prairie Schooner, Quarterly Review of Literature, Saturday Review, Sewanee Review, Transatlantic Quarterly, Virginia Quarterly Review,* and *Yale Review.*

WORK IN PROGRESS: Unanswered Calls.

SIDELIGHTS: A poet whose work has been published in a wide variety of anthologies and magazines, both popular and literary, Larry Rubin is known for writing structured poems that are influenced by formal conventions. On the dust jacket of Rubin's *Lanced in Light,* which was published in 1968, Emily Dickinson was said to be his mentor, and F. H. Griffin Taylor, writing in the *Sewanee Review,* noticed echoes of her work in Rubin's poems. In *Georgia Review,* Robert L. Hull commented: "It is not surprising that *Lanced in Light* succeeds as a fine collection of poetry. Mr. Rubin's first volume, *The World's Old Way . . .* clearly indicates the talent and promise of a gifted poet. The second collection provides even more evidence of that talent."

The virtues of *Lanced in Light,* according to Samuel French Morse's *Virginia Quarterly Review* article, are "those of a writer who is unintimidated by conventional structures." On the other hand, Morse found fault with the collection's "solemnity," and suggested that Rubin is more impressive in individual poems than in a book-length volume. Stanley Cooperman of *Prairie Schooner,* lodged a similar complaint, stating that Rubin's reliance on poetic conventions too often renders his work "a *low-risk* poetry." However, Cooperman also pointed out that Rubin sometimes creates memorable verse with his conservative form. Wrote Cooperman: "There are, however, lyrics that do have a certain rolling nobility to them—a quality which many readers may find attractive precisely because so few contemporary poets attempt to achieve it. And there are moments when Mr. Rubin's insistence on careful shaping, and holding back, deliberately, seems at once old-fashioned and surprisingly new."

BIOGRAPHICAL/CRITICAL SOURCES:

PERIODICALS

Atlanta Journal-Constitution, April 28, 1963.
Georgia Review, winter, 1968.
Georgia Tech Alumnus, March, 1961.
Prairie Schooner, fall, 1968.
Sewanee Review, April, 1969.
Southern Review, April, 1978.
Virginia Quarterly Review, summer, 1968; autumn, 1976.

*   *   *

RUBIN, Louis D(ecimus), Jr. 1923-

PERSONAL: Born November 19, 1923, in Charleston, SC; son of Louis D. (an electrical contractor) and Janet (Weinstein) Rubin; married Eva Redfield (a professor), June 2, 1951; children: Robert, William. *Education:* Attended College of Charleston, 1940-42; Yale University, 1943-44; University of Richmond, B.A., 1946; Johns Hopkins University, M.A., 1949, Ph.D., 1954. *Politics:* Democrat. *Religion:* Jewish (Reform). *Avocational interests:* Music, boating and sleeping.

ADDRESSES: Home and office—702 Gimghoul Rd., Chapel Hill, NC 27514.

CAREER: Bergen Evening Record, Hackensack, NJ, reporter, 1946-47; *News Leader,* Staunton, VA, city editor, 1947-48; *Associated Press* staff writer, 1948; Johns Hopkins University, Baltimore, MD, instructor in English, 1948-54; *Morning News,* Wilmington, DE, assistant telegraph editor, 1949; University of Pennsylvania, Philadelphia, assistant professor of American civilization, executive secretary of the American Studies Association, 1954-55; *News Leader,* Richmond, VA, associate editor, 1956-57; Hollins College, Hollins College, VA, associate professor, 1957-59, professor, 1960-67, chairman of English department, 1959-67; University of North Carolina at Chapel Hill, professor of English, 1967-72, University Distinguished Professor of English, 1972-89. President, Algonquin Books of Chapel Hill, 1982-88; editorial director, 1989-91. Visiting professor at Louisiana State University, summer, 1957, University of North Carolina, spring, 1965, University of California, Santa Barbara, summer, 1966, and Harvard University, summer, 1969; Fulbright professor, University of Aix-Marseilles (Nice, France), summer, 1960; lecturer, American studies summer seminars, Kyoto, Japan, 1980; lecturer under the auspices of U.S. State Department in Austria and Germany, 1981. Editor of *Hopkins Review,* 1949-53, *Provincial,* 1956-57, *Hollins Critic,* 1963-69, *Southern Literary Studies* series, Louisiana State University Press, 1964-73, 1975-93, and *Southern Literary Journal,* 1969-89. Advisory editor, University of North Carolina Press; member of editorial advisory board, *Mississippi Quarterly,* 1973-75. Coordinator, U.S. Information Agency Forums, 1973-74, 1976-78. *Military service:* U.S. Army, Army Specialized Training Division, 1943-46.

MEMBER: South Atlantic Modern Language Association, Society for the Study of Southern Literature (member of executive council, 1968-76; president, 1974-76), Fellowship of Southern Writers (chancellor, 1991-93), Phi Beta Kappa.

AWARDS, HONORS: Sewanee Review fellowship, 1953; Guggenheim fellowship, 1956; American Council of Learned Societies fellowship, 1964; Distinguished Virginian Award, 1972; Litt. D., University of Richmond, 1974; Mayflower Society award, 1978; Jules F. Landry Award, Louisiana State University Press, 1978; D. Litt., Clemson University, 1986; South Carolina Academy of Authors, 1987; O. Max Gardner Medal, 1989; D. Litt., College of Charleston, 1989; North Carolina Award, 1992; D. Litt., University of The South, 1992; D. Litt., University of North Carolina at Asheville, 1993.

WRITINGS:

Thomas Wolfe: The Weather of His Youth, Louisiana State University Press (Baton Rouge), 1955.

No Place on Earth: Ellen Glasgow, James Branch Cabell, and Richmond-in-Virginia, University of Texas Press (Austin), 1959.

The Golden Weather (novel), Atheneum (New York City), 1961.

The Faraway Country: Writers of the Modern South, University of Washington Press (Seattle), 1963, published as *Writers of the Modern South: The Faraway Country,* 1966.

The Curious Death of the Novel: Essays in American Literature, Louisiana State University Press, 1967.

The Teller in the Tale, University of Washington Press, 1967.

George W. Cable: The Life and Times of a Southern Heretic, Pegasus (Indianapolis), 1969.

The Writer in the South, University of Georgia Press (Athens), 1972.

(With Blyden Jackson) *Black Poetry in America: Two Essays in Interpretation,* Louisiana State University Press, 1974.

William Elliott Shoots a Bear: Essays on the Southern Literary Imagination, Louisiana State University Press, 1976.

Virginia: A Bicentennial History, Norton (New York City), 1977.

The Way Fugitives: Four Poets and the South, Louisiana State University Press, 1978.

The Boll Weevil and the Triple Play (fiction), Tradd Street Press (Charleston), 1979.

Surface of a Diamond, (novel), Louisiana State University Press, 1981.

A Gallery of Southerners, Louisiana State University Press, 1982.

(With photographs by Scott Mylin) *Before the Game,* Taylor Publishing, 1988.

The Edge of the Swamp: A Study in the Literature and Society of the Old South, Louisiana State University, 1989.

Small Craft Advisory: A Book About the Building of a Boat, Atlantic Monthly Press, 1991.

The Mockingbird in the Gum Tree: A Literary Gallimaufry, Louisiana State University Press, 1991.

EDITOR

(With R. D. Jacobs) *Southern Renascence: The Literature of the Modern South,* Johns Hopkins Press (Baltimore), 1953.

(With J. J. Kilpatrick) *The Lasting South,* Regnery, 1957.

Teach the Freeman: Correspondence of Rutherford B. Hayes and the Slater Fund for Negro Education, 1881-1893, two volumes, Louisiana State University Press, 1959.

(With Jacobs) *South: Modern Southern Literature in Its Cultural Settings,* Doubleday (New York City), 1961.

(With J.R. Moore) *The Idea of an American Novel,* Crowell (New York City), 1961.

The Hollins Poets, University Press of Virginia (Charlottesville), 1967.

A Biographical Guide to the Study of Southern Literature, Louisiana State University Press, 1969.

The Yemassee Lands: The Poems of Beatrice Ravenel, University of North Carolina Press (Chapel Hill), 1969.

(With R. B. Davis and C. H. Holman) *Southern Writing, 1585-1920,* Odyssey, 1970.

Thomas Wolfe: A Collection of Critical Essays, Prentice-Hall, 1973.

The Comic Imagination in American Literature, Rutgers University Press (New Brunswick, NJ), 1973.

(With Holman) *Southern Literary Study: Prospects and Possibilities,* University of North Carolina Press, 1975.

The Literary South, Wiley (New York City), 1979, Louisiana State University Press, 1986.

(With Robert Bain and Joseph N. Flora) *Southern Writers: A Biographical Dictionary,* Louisiana State University Press, 1979.

The American South: Portrait of a Culture, Voice of America, 1979, revised edition, 1993.

(With Jackson, Rayburn S. Moore, Lewis P. Simpson, and Thomas Daniel Young) *The History of Southern Literature,* Louisiana State University Press, 1985.

(With J. L. Idol, Jr.) Thomas Wolf, *Mannerhouse: A Play with a Prologue and Four Acts,* Louisiana State University Press, 1985.

An Apple for My Teacher: Twelve Authors Tell about Teachers Who Made the Difference, Algonquin Books of Chapel Hill, 1987.

The Algonquin Library Quiz Book, Algonquin Books of Chapel Hill, 1990.

Contributor to magazines and professional journals. Editor of *Hopkins Review,* 1949-53, *Provincial,* 1956-57, *Hollins Critic,* 1963-69, and *Southern Literary Journal,* 1969-89; member of editorial advisory board, *Mississippi Quarterly;* advisory editor, University of North Carolina Press, 1973-75.

BIOGRAPHICAL/CRITICAL SOURCES:

PERIODICALS

Kenyon Review, Volume 30, number 4, 1968.
New Republic, March 3, 1982.
New York Times, March 7, 1968.
New York Times Book Review, March 25, 1979; December 1, 1985.
Sewanee Review, winter, 1969.
Times Literary Supplement, January 8, 1982.
Village Voice, December 23, 1981.
Washington Post, December 2, 1981.

*   *   *

RUCHLIS, Hy(man)   1913-1992

PERSONAL: Born April 6, 1913, in Brooklyn, NY; died of kidney failure and a cardiac disorder, June 30, 1992, in West Palm Beach, FL; son of Morris and Kate (Zelevyansky) Ruchlis; married Elsie Kardonsky (an actuary), August 25, 1934; children: Carol Lee Ember, Michael Lewis. *Education:* Brooklyn College (now Brooklyn College of the City University of New York), B.S., 1933; Columbia University, M.A., 1935.

CAREER: New York Board of Education, New York City, teacher, 1934-50, department chairman, 1950-55; Science Research Associates, Chicago, IL, designer of educational materials, 1955-56; A. C. Gilbert, New Haven, CT, designer, 1956-57; Basic Books, Science Materials Center, New York City, vice-president, 1957-62; Allis-Chalmers, Science Materials Center, Milwaukee, WI, general manager, 1962-64; Harcourt, Brace & Jovanovich, Inc., New York City, director of educational technology, 1964-66; Fairleigh Dickinson University, New York City, adjunct professor and director of Educational Media Center, 1966-70; Book-Lab, Inc., New York City, president,

1970-75. Consultant, Dave Garroway's program *Exploring the Universe,* 1962.

MEMBER: Federation of Science Teachers Associations (president, 1948-49), United Community Organization.

AWARDS, HONORS: Received honorable mention as best science book, New York Academy of Science, 1969, for *Invitations to Investigate.*

WRITINGS:

(With M. Eidinoff) *Atomics for the Millions,* Whittlesey House, 1947.
Exploring Physics, Harcourt, 1950.
What Makes Me Tick, Harvey House, 1957.
Thank You, Mr. Sun, Harvey House, 1957.
Story of Mathematics, Harvey House, 1957.
Orbit, Harper, 1957.
Wonder of Light, Harper, 1959.
Wonder of Heat Energy, Harper, 1960.
(With Don Herbert) *Beginning Science with Mr. Wizard,* Doubleday, 1961.
Clear Thinking, Harper, 1962, reprinted, Prometheus, 1990.
Discovering Scientific Method, Harper, 1963.
Your Changing Earth, Harvey, 1963.
Wonder of Electricity, Harper, 1965.
Concepts in Science Classroom Laboratories, Harcourt, 1965.
Bathtub Physics, Harcourt, 1967.
(With Paul F. Brandwein) *Invitations to Investigate* (based on the card set entitled "100 Invitations to Investigate"), Harcourt, 1968.
Phonic Word Builder, Book-Lab, 1972.
Guidelines to Education of Non-readers, Book-Lab, 1973.
How a Rock Came to Be on a Fence on a Road near a Town, Walker, 1973.
(With Belle Sharefkin) *Reality-Centered Learning,* Scholastic Book Services, 1975.
How Do You Know It's True, Prometheus Books, 1991

OTHER

Also editor and designer of the "Science Book-Labs" series and editor of *The Hip Reader.*

OBITUARIES:

PERIODICALS

New York Times, July 2, 1992, p. D19.*

*   *   *

RULE, James B(ernard)   1943-

PERSONAL: Born March 30, 1943, in San Jose, CA; son of Calvin J. (a banker) and Ruth (a secretary; maiden name, Lambert) Rule. *Education:* Brandeis University, B.A., 1964; Harvard University, Ph.D., 1969.

ADDRESSES: Home—205 High St., Port Jefferson, NY 11777. *Agent*—Berenice Hoffman, 215 West 75th St., #16A, New York, NY 10023. *Office*—Department of Sociology, State University of New York at Stony Brook, Stony Brook, NY 11794.

CAREER: State University of New York at Stony Brook, associate professor, 1973-79, professor of sociology, 1979—. Research fellow, Nuffield College, Oxford, 1969-71; associate, Clare Hall, Cambridge, 1972-73. Consultant to Privacy Protection Study Commission.

MEMBER: American Sociological Association.

AWARDS, HONORS: Fulbright fellowship, 1971-72; C. Wright Mills Award from Society for the Study of Social Problems, 1973, for *Private Lives and Public Surveillance;* Rockefeller humanities fellowship, 1976-77; Guggenheim fellowship, 1977-78; fellow of Center for Advanced Study in the Behavioral Sciences, 1977-78.

WRITINGS:

Private Lives and Public Surveillance, Schocken, 1974.
Value Choices in Electronic Funds Transfer Policy, U.S. Government Printing Office, 1975.
Insight and Social Betterment, Oxford University Press, 1978.
The Politics of Privacy, Elsevier, 1981.
Theories of Civil Violence, University of California Press, 1988.

Editorial board member, *Dissent,* 1983, and *Social Problems,* 1992.

S

SACHS, Marilyn (Stickle) 1927-

PERSONAL: Born December 18, 1927, in New York, NY; daughter of Samuel and Anna (Smith) Stickle; married Morris Sachs (a sculptor), January 26, 1947; children: Anne, Paul. *Education:* Hunter College (now Hunter College of the City University of New York), B.A., 1949; Columbia University, M.S. in L.S., 1953. *Politics:* "Changing constantly." *Religion:* Jewish. *Avocational interests:* Walking, reading, and good company.

ADDRESSES: Home—733 31st Ave., San Francisco, CA 94121.

CAREER: Writer of children's books. Brooklyn Public Library, Brooklyn, NY, librarian, 1949-60; San Francisco Public Library, San Francisco, CA, part-time children's librarian, 1962-67.

AWARDS, HONORS: Notable Children's Book Award, American Library Association, 1968, for *Veronica Ganz,* 1973, for *A Pocket Full of Seeds,* 1987, for *Fran Ellen's House,* and 1991, for *The Big Book for Peace; School Library Journal* Best Books of the Year citation, 1971, for *The Bears' House,* and 1973, for *The Truth about Mary Rose; New York Times* Outstanding Books of the Year citation, 1971, for *The Bears' House,* and 1973, for *A Pocket Full of Seeds;* National Book Award nomination, 1972, for *The Bears' House;* Silver Pencil Award (Holland), 1974, for *The Truth about Mary Rose,* and 1977, for *Dorrie's Book;* Jane Addams Children's Book Honor Award, 1974, for *A Pocket Full of Seeds,* and 1990, for *The Big Book for Peace;* Austrian Children's Book Prize, 1977, for *The Bears' House;* Garden State Children's Book Award for Younger Fiction, 1978, for *Dorrie's Book;* Association of Jewish Libraries Award, 1983, for *Call Me Ruth;* Best Books for Young Adults citation, American Library Association, 1984, for *The Fat Girl;* Christopher Award, 1986, for *Underdog;* Bay Area Book Reviewers Associa-

tion (BABRA) Award, 1988, for *Fran Ellen's House;* Recognition of Merit Award, George C. Stone Center for Children's Books, 1989, for *The Bears' House* and *Fran Ellen's House.*

WRITINGS:

Amy Moves In, Doubleday, 1964.
Laura's Luck, Doubleday, 1965.
Amy and Laura (also see below), Doubleday, 1966.
Veronica Ganz, Doubleday, 1968.
Peter and Veronica, Doubleday, 1969.
Marv, Doubleday, 1970.
The Bears' House, Doubleday, 1971.
Reading between the Lines (play), Children's Book Council, 1971.
The Truth about Mary Rose, Doubleday, 1973.
A Pocket Full of Seeds, Doubleday, 1973.
Matt's Mitt (also see below), Doubleday, 1975.
Dorrie's Book, Doubleday, 1975.
A December Tale, Doubleday, 1976.
A Secret Friend, Doubleday, 1978.
A Summer's Lease, Dutton, 1979.
Bus Ride, Dutton, 1980.
Class Pictures, Dutton, 1980.
Fleet-footed Florence (also see below), Doubleday, 1981.
Hello . . . Wrong Number, Dutton, 1981.
Beach Towels, Dutton, 1982.
Call Me Ruth, Doubleday, 1982.
Fourteen, Dutton, 1983.
The Fat Girl, Dutton, 1984.
Thunderbird, Dutton, 1985.
Underdog, Doubleday, 1985.
Baby Sister, Dutton, 1986.
Almost Fifteen, Dutton, 1987.
Fran Ellen's House, Dutton, 1987.
Just Like a Friend, Dutton, 1989.
Matt's Mitt [and] *Fleet-Footed Florence,* Dutton, 1989.

At the Sound of the Beep, Dutton, 1990.
(Editor with Ann Durell) *The Big Book for Peace,* Dutton, 1990.
Circles, Dutton, 1991.
What My Sister Remembered, Dutton, 1992.
Thirteen Going on Seven, Dutton, 1993.
Ghosts in the Family, Dutton, 1995.

Amy and Laura was included in *Best-Selling Apples,* Scholastic, Inc., 1985. Sachs is also author of reviews for *New York Times* and *San Francisco Chronicle.* A collection of Sachs's works is held in the Kerlan Collection at the University of Minnesota.

ADAPTATIONS: Veronica Ganz was adapted as a filmstrip and released by Insight Media Programs, 1975.

SIDELIGHTS: With the publication of her first book *Amy Moves In* in 1964, Marilyn Sachs helped launch a publishing trend in realistic fiction. Her protagonists often do not fit into mainstream teenage life; distanced from their peers by circumstance or choice, they struggle to find solutions to dilemmas that will still allow them to be true to themselves. Sachs has been praised by critics for her knack for realistically portraying relationships and has also been commended for incorporating relevant social issues in her works.

Many of these elements appear in *Amy Moves In.* Laura Stern, although two years older than her sister Amy, has to share her bedroom with her sibling. In addition to normal teenage problems, the girls cope with the fact that their father is unemployed. A reviewer for *Virginia Kirkus' Service* deems it a funny book that "offers readers valid insights into people and their behavior." Its depression-era setting, notes the reviewer, "is true to its time and true to the unchanging conditions of childhood."

"By today's standards," Sachs tells Marguerite Feitlowitz in an interview for *Something about the Author,* "*Amy Moves In* is a very mild book. But back then [the 1950s], apparently it wasn't mild enough. Amy's perfectly nice father doesn't work, and that was one problem. Editors asked that I find him some suitable employment. They wanted all the other 'loose ends' tied up. As though life were neat and tidy. I couldn't make changes I didn't believe in, so the manuscript sat in my desk drawer for ten years." Sachs also features the Stern sisters in *Laura's Luck* and *Amy and Laura.*

Sachs drew on her own family history for a later book. "*Call Me Ruth,*" she tells Feitlowitz, "is a book that owes a lot to my immigrant heritage. My grandmother came to this country from Russia at the turn of the century. As with the father in the novel, my grandfather had come over first to earn the money to bring over the rest of his family. My mother, like Ruth, was born on the other side.

Fanny, who in the novel is Ruth's mother, is based in part on my grandmother. The struggle between Fanny and Ruth is essentially their conflict over what it means to be an American."

Sachs also involved her newly Americanized characters in events from American history. "Because the characters in [*Call Me Ruth*] worked in textile sweatshops, I needed to know a great deal about the details of that life," Sachs related to Feitlowitz. "I spent days and days reading about early textile strikes, many of which were led by women. I was also able to talk with a very elderly woman who had participated in some of those strikes and had written a monograph on early efforts to organize textile workers. The 1911 strike figures largely in *Call Me Ruth.*" Ruth, who wants to adopt what she considers an American way of life, finds herself constantly at odds with her mother's desire to preserve her European Jewish heritage. A *Publishers Weekly* reviewer calls it a moving story that "typifies the gap between two people who have loved each other unreservedly" until differences test their relationship, while Denise M. Wilms observes in *Booklist* that even Ruth's very American teacher "will never see her as more than a poor little immigrant girl" and calls the story "bittersweet" and "thought-provoking."

The European Jewish heritage and the Holocaust figure in another of Sachs's novels. "*A Pocket Full of Seeds,*" Sachs explains to Feitlowitz, "is based on an interval in the life of Fanny Krieger, a friend of mine. Fanny, a French Jew, was trapped in France during World War II. Her family was rounded up by the Gestapo while Fanny was out visiting friends and [they] eventually died in Auschwitz. Fanny lived in hiding and then was brought to America by a cousin." Fanny's story in the book is given to a girl named Nicole who, states Zena Sutherland in the *Bulletin of the Center for Children's Books,* "changes from a blithe eight-year-old to a mature adolescent." "Mrs. Sachs's depiction of life in a small, peaceful French town highlights the tragic intrusion of war," writes Jennifer Farley Smith in the *Christian Science Monitor;* "and her characters are sharply and sympathetically drawn."

Sachs presents quite a different situation in *The Fat Girl*—"an unusual, cross-generational study in the corruptions of power—with strongly limned if poisonously weak adults, and fuzzier stand-in teens," according to a writer for *Kirkus Reviews.* Jeff, a high-school senior, seemingly has many advantages; he's good-looking, confident, and popular. "But at home," reveals Kicki Moxon Browne in the *Times Literary Supplement,* "he lives in a tense, uneasy atmosphere with his self-denying and embittered mother, haunted by his father's treacherous departure and by his own recurring night terrors." At a ceramics class he befriends Ellen, an overweight girl who has a crush on him. When she admits that she harbors thoughts of suicide, Jeff takes over her life: "Like some latter-day Henry Higgins, he chooses her clothes, . . . her makeup, her hair style and even her perfume," explains *New York Times Book Review* contributor Barbara Cutler Helfgott. Eventually Ellen breaks away from Jeff's obsessive controlling and learns to live her own life. "Though they part bitterly," Helfgott remarks, "each has been helped through a troubled time."

"I feel very lucky to be a writer of books for children and young adults," Marilyn Sachs told *CA.* "So far I have written twenty-eight published books (and some others that we don't need to talk about), and hope I can keep on writing for the rest of my life. Each book I write is new territory for me, new research, new daydreams. I may get irritated and frustrated, but seldom bored.

"And I write for the choicest group of readers. They send me letters. Sometimes they don't like my books and they let me know why. Often they tell me their problems and identify with a character in one of my stories. Books brought me great comfort as a child, and still do. It makes me feel proud that a book of mine can comfort someone as books have always comforted me."

BIOGRAPHICAL/CRITICAL SOURCES:

BOOKS

Contemporary Literary Criticism, Volume 35, Gale, 1985.
de Montreville, Doris, and Elizabeth D. Crawford, editors, *Fourth Book of Junior Authors and Illustrators,* H. W. Wilson, 1978.
Something about the Author, Volume 52, Gale, 1988, pp. 141-46.

PERIODICALS

Booklist, September 1, 1982, p. 48.
Bulletin of the Center for Children's Books, March, 1974, p. 117.
Christian Science Monitor, May 1, 1974, p. F1.
Kirkus Reviews, March 1, 1984.
Library Journal, June 15, 1970; September, 1970.
Los Angeles Times Book Review, December 28, 1980.
New York Times Book Review, November 7, 1971; March 11, 1973; August 19, 1979; September 20, 1981; April 1, 1984, p. 29; March 18, 1990.
Publishers Weekly, January 8, 1973; August 6, 1982, p. 69; August 25, 1989; July 27, 1990, p. 234; February 1, 1991, p. 80.
Times Literary Supplement, October 16, 1969; August 30, 1985, p. 958; May 29, 1987, p. 589.
Virginia Kirkus' Service, May 1, 1964, p. 453.
Voice of Youth Advocates, October, 1992, p. 230.
Washington Post Book World, July 12, 1981.
Wilson Library Bulletin, September, 1990, p. 100.

St. JOHN, David
See HUNT, E(verette) Howard (Jr.)

*   *   *

SARAC, Roger
See CARAS, Roger

*   *   *

SCOTT, James F(razier)   1934-

PERSONAL: Born July 9, 1934, in Atchison, KS; son of James B., Jr., and Helen (Frazier) Scott; married Carolyn Davis (a communications teacher), June 17, 1961; children: Adrienne T., James Davis. *Education:* Rockhurst College, B.S., 1955; University of Kansas, M.A., 1957, Ph.D., 1960.

ADDRESSES: Home—7567 Cornell, St. Louis, MO 63130. *Office*—Department of English, St. Louis University, St. Louis, MO 63103.

CAREER: University of Kentucky, Lexington, instructor in English, 1960-62; St. Louis University, St. Louis, MO, assistant professor, 1962-65, associate professor, 1965-69, professor of English, 1969-72; Ruhr University, Bochum, Germany, guest professor, 1972-76; St. Louis University, professor of English, 1976—, chairman of department, 1982-85. Optical Illusions, Inc. (video production company), owner and manager, 1985—; photographer.

MEMBER: Modern Language Association of America, American Association of University Professors, Phi Beta Kappa.

AWARDS, HONORS: Alexander von Humboldt Foundation fellowship, 1974-76; grants from Missouri Committee for the Humanities, Missouri Humanities Council, Missouri Arts Council, St. Louis Regional Arts Commission, Arts and Education Council of Greater St Louis, and Committee of Access and Local Origination Programming of University City, Missouri.

WRITINGS:

FILMS

(And director) *Stanley Elkin: First Person Singular* (video documentary), Warner/Amex Cable Television, 1982.
(And director) *Trova* (video documentary), Warner/ Amex Cable Television, 1983.
(And producer-director) *Music of Stillness: The World of Sara Teasdale* (video documentary), Continental Cablevision, 1984.

(And producer-director) *Worlds of Bright Glass: The Ravenna Mosaic Company* (video documentary), KETC-TV (St. Louis, MO), 1992.

Also scripted documentaries *Marine Meteorology, Sound in the Sea,* and *Marine Mammals;* scripted and directed the documentaries *Grandeur in Granite,* 1986, and *The Business of Export* (eight-part series), 1987-91; and participated in production of documentary *First Person Singular,* 1982.

OTHER

Film: The Medium and the Maker, Holt (New York City), 1975.

Contributor to journals, including *American Quarterly, Arcadia, Journal of Aesthetics and Art Criticism, Literatur in Wissenschaft und Unterricht, Nineteenth-Century Fiction, Philological Quarterly,* and *Victorian Studies.*

SIDELIGHTS: James F. Scott writes: "I am interested chiefly in the social dimension of the arts, with considerable emphasis upon the newer mass media (film, television, etc.). My work in video documentary, which includes work on literature, sculpture, and architecture, is designed to make material in the traditional art forms accessible to audiences largely oriented to electronic communications. I continue to consider teaching an important means of maintaining the critical perspectives necessary for good writing."

*   *   *

SELF, Peter J(ohn) O(tter) 1919-

PERSONAL: Born June 7, 1919, in Brighton, England; son of Albert Henry (a public servant) and Rosalind Self; married Diana Mary Pitt, 1950 (divorced); married Elaine Rosenbloom Adams, 1959 (divorced); married Sandra Guerita Moiseiwitsch Gough (a librarian), 1981; children: (second marriage) Jonathan Otter, William Woodard. *Education:* Attended Harvard University, 1952-53; Balliol College, Oxford, B.A., 1941, M.A., 1956. *Politics:* "Environmentalist and egalitarian." *Religion:* Anglican. *Avocational interests:* Walking, golf and storytelling.

ADDRESSES: Home—7 Hobbs St., O'Conner, Canberra, Australian Capital Territory, Australia. *Office*—Research School of Social Science, Australian National University, P.O. Box 4, Canberra, Australian Capital Territory 2600, Australia.

CAREER: Economist, London, England, member of editorial staff, 1944-62; University of London, London, professor of public administration, 1965-83, professor emeritus, 1983—; Australian National University, Canberra,

senior research fellow, 1982-84, visiting fellow, 1985—. Extramural lecturer at University of London, 1944-49; London School of Economics and Political Science, London, lecturer, 1947-61, reader in political science, 1961-65, member of Greater London Group, 1968-81; visiting professor at Cornell University, 1958 and 1967; director of administrative studies at British Civil Service College, 1969-70; visiting fellow at Australian National University, 1976 and 1980-81; lecturer at University of Alabama, 1978; Osborn Memorial Lecturer at Royal Society of Arts, 1981; chairman of Joint University Council Public Administration Committee, 1968-71. Member of South-East Region Economic Planning Council, 1965-79; member of British Treasury Working Party on Research in Government, 1970; chairman of Australian Government Inquiry Into Local Government Finance, 1984-85; consultant on administrative reform to Organization for Economic Cooperation and Development, and Glasgow Corporation on Urban Renewal.

MEMBER: European Consortium of Political Research (member of council, 1973-80), British Town and Country Planning Association (chairman of executive committee, 1961-69; chairman of council, 1979-83), Royal Institute of Public Administration (member of council and research board, 1978—), Royal Town Planning Institute (honorary member), Carr Society, Reform Club.

WRITINGS:

Cities in Flood: The Problems of Urban Growth, Faber (London), 1957.
(With Herbert Storing) *The State and the Farmer,* Allen & Unwin (London), 1962.
Administrative Theories and Politics, Allen & Unwin, 1972.
Econocrats and the Policy Process: The Politics and Philosophy of Cost-Benefit Analysis, Macmillan, 1976.
Planning the Urban Region: A Comparative Study of Policies and Organisations, University of Alabama Press, 1982.
Political Theories of Modern Government, Allen & Unwin, 1985.
Government by the Market? The Politics of Public Choice, Macmillan (London), 1993, Westview Press, 1993.

Also contributor to anthologies, including *Essays in Reform,* edited by Bernard Crick, Oxford University Press, 1967; *The Quality of Urban Life,* edited by H.J. Schmandt and Walter Bloomberg, Jr., Sage Publications, 1969; *Nature and Conduct,* edited by R.S. Peters, Macmillan, 1975; and *Public Spending Decisions,* edited by Maurice Wright, Allen & Unwin, 1980. Contributor to public administration, political science, and planning journals. Past editor of *Town and Country Planning;* member of editorial boards of *Political Quarterly* and *Urban Affairs Annual.*

WORK IN PROGRESS: "A book on the general theme of the future of public policy in modern societies, intended for a wide audience; also the history of London planning."

SIDELIGHTS: Peter J. O. Self once told *CA:* "I started my career on the editorial staff of *The Economist,* London, writing on subjects that no other staff member wanted to handle. The subjects I got in this manner included Town and Country Planning, Agricultural Policy and Local Government, and I wrote on these subjects in *The Economist* for over fifteen years and also wrote a book on each of them. Thus is one's career shaped by chance situations.

"My academic career has been spent mainly at The London School of Economics and Political Science, but after retiring from there I have been based for the last eleven years at The Australian National University. I have taught and written about many aspects of public policies, but I have always believed that anyone who does this should get practical experience of how governments work. I have done this in a number of ways: as a member of official committees, as a temporary public official, as a consultant to OECD and public authorities and as chairman for many years of a voluntary organisation.

"I have always been fascinated by how cities work and by urban planning. After World War II in Britain, I was a strong supporter of new towns, countryside protection, regional development and the creation of more humane and habitable cities. I wrote my first book, *Cities in Flood* on this theme. Interestingly at that time my publisher thought that no-one would be interested in the problems of cities; today there is a book a day on the subject! However, alas, our cities have not improved as a consequence. I continued to be active in urban affairs as a writer and teacher and occasional consultant, and I have been able to continue with these interests since I came to Australia. My wife and I enjoy living in Canberra, which was built as an attractive garden city.

"In recent decades I have become increasingly interested in theories of politics and public policy. I criticise the claims of economists to quantify almost everything in money terms in my book, *Econocrats and the Policy Process.* I discuss different theories of how the political system works in my book, *Political Theories of Modern Government.* My latest book, *Government by the Market* fires a broadside at the idea that the market system on its own will produce a good society and that governments are inefficient and incapable of pursuing broad social goals. I feel sadly that we are much too acquiescent towards the social inequalities and environmental degredation committed in the name of economic growth, and that we need to recover our collective capacity to solve social problems.

"I have tried to address my academic books to subjects of general interest and to make them as clear and readable as possible. I think much academic writing today is unnecessarily abstruse. My current intention is to write a book on the state of modern politics and the economy which will have a wider general appeal and be addressed to a popular rather than academic audience. I like writing articles for newspapers which helps one to concentrate on essentials."

BIOGRAPHICAL/CRITICAL SOURCES:

PERIODICALS

Times Literary Supplement, October 8, 1976.

*   *   *

SENELICK, Laurence P(hilip) 1942-

PERSONAL: Born October 12, 1942, in Chicago, IL; son of Theodore (a purchasing agent) and Evelyn (Marder) Senelick. *Education:* Northwestern University, B.A., 1964; Harvard University, A.M., 1968, Ph.D., 1972. *Avocational interests:* Cooking, collecting.

ADDRESSES: Home—117 Mystic St., West Medford, MA 02155. *Office*—Department of Drama, Tufts University, Medford, MA 02155.

CAREER: Emerson College, Boston, MA, assistant professor of English, 1968-72; Tufts University, Medford, MA, assistant professor, 1972-76, associate professor, 1976-83, professor of drama and oratory, 1987—. Professional actor and director, 1963—; director of Proposition Cabaret, 1968-69, and Summer School Theatre Workshop at Harvard University, 1974-75. Member of Russian Research Center at Harvard University. Member of subcommittee on theatre and dance, ACLS-Soviet Ministry of Culture commission on arts and arts research. Honorary curator of Russian Drama and Theatre, Harvard Theatre Collection, 1991—; McGregor Visiting Scholar/Artist, Wabash College, 1992.

MEMBER: International Federation for Theatre Research, American Society for Theatre Research, Actors' Equity Association, Society for Cultural Relations with the U.S.S.R., British Music Hall Society, British Theatre Institute.

AWARDS, HONORS: Woodrow Wilson fellow, 1964 and 1965; grant from National Endowment for the Humanities, 1977; Guggenheim fellow, 1979, 1987; Institute for Advanced Studies (West Berlin) fellow, 1984-85; George Freedley Award, Theatre Library Association, for *Gordon Craig's Moscow Hamlet;* Salzburg Seminar fellow, 1988; National Theatre Translation Fund award, 1993.

WRITINGS:

(Editor and translator) Anton Chekhov, *The Seagull [and] The Cherry Orchard,* AHM Publishing, 1977.

(With David Brownell) *Tchaikovsky's Sleeping Beauty,* Bellerophon Books, 1978.

A Cavalcade of Clowns, Bellerophon Books, 1978.

(Editor and translator) *Russian Dramatic Theory from Pushkin to the Symbolists: An Anthology,* University of Texas Press (Austin), 1981.

(With D. F. Cheshire and Ulrich Schneider) *British Music Hall, 1840-1923,* Shoe String (Hamden, CT), 1981.

Gordon Craig's Moscow Hamlet, Greenwood Press (Westport, CT), 1982.

Dead Souls (two-act play; adapted from the novel by Nikolai Gogol), first produced in Medford, MA, at Tufts University, May, 1982.

Serf Actor: A Biography of Mikhail Shchepkin, Greenwood Press, 1984.

Anton Chekhov, Macmillan/Grove, 1985.

(With P. Haskell) *The Cheese Book,* Simon & Schuster (New York City), 1985.

(Translator) Klaus Mann, *The Pious Dance,* PAJ Press, 1987.

Humpty Dumpty: The Age and Stage of G. L. Fox, University Press of New England (Hanover, NH), 1988.

Cabaret Performance: Europe, 1890-1940, PAJ Press, 1988.

(Editor) *National Theatre in Northern and Eastern Europe, 1746-1900,* Cambridge University Press (New York City), 1991.

Cabaret Performance, Volume 2: *Europe, 1920-1940,* Johns Hopkins University Press (Baltimore), 1992.

(Editor) *Wandering Stars: Russian Emigre Theatre, 1905-1940,* University of Iowa Press (Iowa City), 1992.

(Editor) *Gender in Performance: The Presentation of Difference in the Performing Arts,* University Press of New England, 1992.

Also editor and contributor, *Sources and Documents of Western Theatre,* Volume XII, Cambridge University Press. Contributor to *McGraw-Hill Encyclopedia of World Drama, Oxford Companion to the Theatre, Academic American Encyclopedia, International Encyclopedia of Dance, Cambridge Guide to World Theatre, Cambridge Guide to American Theatre, International Dictionary of the Theatre, Journal of the History of Sexuality,* and *McGill's Critical Survey of Drama.* Contributor to periodicals, including *Russian Review, New Boston Review, Call Boy, After Dark, History of Photography, Cuisine, Theater, Poetics Today, Theatrephile, American Speech, 19th Century Theatre Research, Theatre Studies,* and *Theatre Quarterly.* Editor of *Dickens Studies,* 1965-69.

WORK IN PROGRESS: An edition of the 1840 and 1850 diaries of Charles Rice; a history of production in Chekhov's plays; a documentary history of Soviet theatre.

SIDELIGHTS: Laurence P. Senelick told *CA:* "It is immensely important to inform one's scholarship and research by practical experience in the field. I maintain an active life as an actor, director, playwright, and screenwriter as an adjunct to my investigations of the theatre of the past. The traffic works both ways: the practical experience illuminates the historical study."

*   *   *

SENGHOR, Leopold Sedar 1906- (Silmang Diamano, Patrice Maguilene Kaymor)

PERSONAL: Born October 9, 1906, in Joal, Senegal (part of French West Africa; now Republic of Senegal); son of Basile Digoye (a cattle breeder and groundnut planter and exporter) and Nyilane (Bakoume) Senghor; married Ginette Eboue, September, 1946 (divorced, 1956); married Collette Hubert, October 18, 1957; children: (first marriage) Francis-Aphang, Guy-Waly (deceased); (second marriage) Philippe-Maguilen (deceased). *Education:* Baccalaureate degree from Lycee of Dakar, 1928; University of Paris, Sorbonne, agregation de grammaire, 1933, studied African languages at Ecole des Hautes Etudes, Paris, 1929-32.

ADDRESSES: Home—Corniche Ouest, Dakar, Senegal Republic; 1 square de Tocqueville, 75017 Paris, France.

CAREER: Lycee Descartes, Tours, France, instructor in Greek and Latin classics, 1935-38; Lycee Marcelin Berthelot, St. Maur-des-Fosses, France, instructor in literature and African culture, 1938-40 and 1943-44; Ecole Nationale de la France d'Outre Mer, professor, 1945; French National Assembly, Paris, France, and General Council of Senegal, Dakar, Senegal, elected representative, beginning in 1946; Bloc Democratique Senegalais, Dakar, founder, 1948; French Government, Paris, delegate to United Nations General Assembly in New York City, 1950-51, Secretary of State for scientific research, and representative to UNESCO conferences, 1955-56, member of consultative assembly, 1958, minister-counsellor to Ministry of Cultural Affairs, Education, and Justice, 1959-60, advisory minister, beginning in 1960; City of Thies, Senegal, mayor, beginning in 1956; Senegalese Territorial Assembly, elected representative, beginning in 1957; founder and head of Union Progressiste Senegalaise, beginning in 1958; Mali Federation of Senegal and Sudan, president of Federal Assembly, 1959-60; Republic of Senegal, President of the Republic, 1960-80, Minister of Defense, 1968-69; Socialist Inter-African, chair of executive bureau, 1981—; Haut Conseil de la Francophonie, vice president, 1985—. Cofounder, with Lamine Gueye, of Bloc Africain, 1945; representative for Senegal to French Constituent Assemblies, 1945 and 1946; official grammarian for writing of French Fourth Republic's new constitution, 1946; sponsor of First World Festival of Negro Arts, Dakar, 1966; chair of Organisation Commune Africaine et Malgache, 1972-74; established West African Economic Community, 1974; chair of ECONAS, 1978-79. *Military service:* French Army, infantry, 1934-35; served in infantry battalion of colonial troops, 1939; prisoner of war, 1940-42; participated in French Resistance, 1942-45; received serviceman's cross, 1939-45.

MEMBER: Comite National des Ecrivains, Societe des Gens de Lettres, Societe Linguistique de France.

AWARDS, HONORS: Numerous awards, including corresponding membership in Bavarian Academy, 1961; International French Friendship Prize, 1961; French Language Prize (gold medal), 1963; International Grand Prize for Poetry, 1963; Dag Hammarskjoeld International Prize Gold Medal for Poetic Merit, 1963; Marie Noel Poetry Prize, 1965; Red and Green International Literature Grand Prix, 1966, German Book Trade's Peace Prize, 1968; associate membership in French Academy of Moral and Political Sciences, 1969; Knokke Biennial International Poetry Grand Prix, 1970; membership in Academy of Overseas Sciences, 1971; membership in Black Academy of Arts and Sciences, 1971; Grenoble Gold Medal, 1972; Haile Selassie African Research Prize, 1973; Cravat of Commander of Order of French Arts and Letters, 1973; Apollinaire Prize for Poetry, 1974; Prince Pierre of Monaco's Literature Prize, 1977; Prix Eurafrique, 1978; Alfred de Vigny Prize, 1981; Aasan World Prize, 1981; election to Academie Francaise, 1983; Jawaharlal Nehru Award, 1984; Athinai Prize, 1985.

Also recipient of Grand Cross of French Legion of Honor, Commander of Academic Palms, Franco-Allied Medal of Recognition, membership in Agegres de Grammaire and American Academy of Arts and Letters. Numerous honorary doctorates, including those from Fordham University, 1961, University of Paris, 1962, Catholic University of Louvain (Belgium), 1965, Lebanese University of Beirut, 1966, Howard University, 1966, Laval University (Quebec), 1966, Harvard University, 1971, Oxford University, 1973, and from the universities of Ibadan (Nigeria), 1964, Bahia (Brazil), 1965, Strasbourg (France), 1965, Al-Azan (Cairo, Egypt), 1967, Algiers (Algeria), 1967, Bordeaux-Talence (France), 1967, Vermont, 1971, California at Los Angeles, 1971, Ethiopia Haile Selassie I, 1971, Abidjan (Ivory Coast), 1971, and Lagos (Nigeria), 1972.

WRITINGS:

POETRY

Chants d'ombre (title means "Songs of Shadow"; includes "Femme noire" and "Joal"; also see below), Seuil, 1945.

Hosties noires (title means "Black Sacrifices"; includes "Au Gouverneur Eboue," "Mediterranee," "Aux Soldats Negro-Americains," "Tyaroye," and "Priere de paix"; also see below), Seuil, 1948.

Chants pour Naeett (title means "Songs for Naeett"; also see below), Seghers, 1949.

Chants d'ombre [suivi de] *Hosties noires* (title means "Songs of Shadow" [followed by] "Black Sacrifices "), Seuil, 1956.

Ethiopiques (includes "Chaka," poetic adaptation of Thomas Mofolo's historical novel *Chaka;* "A New York"; and "Congo"), Seuil, 1956, critical edition with commentary by Papa Gueye N'Diaye published as *Ethiopiques: Poemes,* Nouvelles Editions Africaines, 1974.

Nocturnes (includes *Chants pour Naeett,* "Elegie de minuit," and "Elegie a Aynina Fall: Poeme dramatique a plusieurs voix" [title means "Elegy for Aynina Fall: Dramatic Poem for Many Voices"]), Seuil, 1961, translation by John Reed and Clive Wake published as *Nocturnes,* Heinemann Educational, 1969, with introduction by Paulette J. Trout, Third Press, 1971.

Elegie des Alizes, original lithographs by Marc Chagall, Seuil, 1969.

Lettres d'hivernage, illustrations by Marc Chagall, Seuil, 1973.

Paroles, Nouvelles Editions Africaines, 1975.

Oeuvre Poetique, Editions du Seuil, 1990, translation and introduction by Melvin Dixon published as *Leopold Sedar Senghor: The Collected Poetry,* University Press of Virginia, 1991.

Contributor of poems to periodicals, including *Chantiers, Les Cahiers du Sud, Les Lettres Francaises, Les Temps Modernes, Le Temp de la Poesie, La Revue Socialiste, Presence Africaine,* and *Prevue.*

CRITICAL AND POLITICAL PROSE

(With Robert Lemaignen and Prince Sisowath Youteyong) *La Communaute imperiale francaise* (includes "Views on Africa; or, Assimilate, Don't Be Assimilated"), Editions Alsatia, 1945.

(With Gaston Monnerville and Aime Cesaire) *Commemoration du centenaire de l'abolition de l'esclavage,* introduction by Edouard Depreux, Presses Universitaires de France, 1948.

Rapport sur la doctrine et le programme du parti, Presence Africaine, 1959, translation published as *Report on the Principles and Programme of the Party,* Presence

Africaine, 1959, abridged edition edited and translated by Mercer Cook published as *African Socialism: A Report to the Constitutive Congress of the Party of African Federation,* American Society of African Culture, 1959.

Rapport sur la politique generale, [Senegal], 1960.

Nation et voie africaine du socialisme, Presence Africaine 1961, new edition published as *Liberte 2: Nation et voie africaine du socialisme,* Seuil, 1971, translation by Mercer Cook published as *Nationhood and the African Road to Socialism,* Presence Africaine, 1962, abridged as *On African Socialism,* translation and introduction by Cook, Praeger, 1964.

Rapport sur la doctrine et la politique generale; ou, Socialisme, unite africaine, construction nationale, [Dakar], 1962.

(With Pierre Teilhard de Chardin) *Pierre Teilhard de Chardin et la politique africaine* [and] *Sauvons l'humanite* [and] *L'Art dans la ligne de l'energie humaine* (the first by Senghor, the latter two by Teilhard de Chardin), Seuil, 1962.

(With others) *Le Racisme dans le monde,* Julliard, 1964.

Theorie et pratique du socialisme senegalais, [Dakar], 1964.

Liberte 1: Negritude et humanisme, Seuil, 1964, selections translated and introduced by Wendell A. Jeanpierre published as *Freedom 1: Negritude and Humanism,* [Providence, RI], 1974.

(In Portuguese, French, and Spanish) *Latinite et negritude,* Centre de Hautes Etudes Afro-Ibero-Americaines de l'Universite de Dakar, 1966.

Negritude, arabisme, et francite: Reflexions sur le probleme de la culture (title means "Negritude, Arabism, and Frenchness: Reflections on the Problem of Culture"), preface by Jean Rous, Editions Dar al-Kitab Allubmani (Beirut), 1967, republished as *Les Fondements de l'Africanite; ou, Negritude et arabite,* Presence Africaine, 1967, translation by M. Cook published as *The Foundations of "Africanite"; or, "Negritude" and "Arabite,"* Presence Africaine, 1971.

Politique, nation, et developpement moderne: Rapport de politique generale, Imprimerie Nationale (Rufisque), 1968.

Le Plan du decollage economique; ou, La Participation responsable comme moteur de developpement, Grande Imprimerie Africaine (Dakar), 1970.

Pourquoi une ideologie negro-africaine? (lecture), Universite d'Abidjan, 1971.

La Parole chez Paul Claudel et chez les Negro-Africains, Nouvelles Editions Africaines, 1973.

(With others) *Litteratures ultramarines de langue francaise, genese et jeunesse: Actes du colloque de l'Universite du Vermont,* compiled by Thomas H. Geno and Roy Julow, Naaman (Quebec), 1974.

Paroles (addresses), Nouvelles Editions Africaines, 1975.

Pour une relecture africaine de Marx et d'Engels (includes "Le socialisme africain et la voie senegalaise"), Nouvelles Editions Africaines, 1976.

Pour une societe senegalaise socialiste et democratique: Rapport sur la politique generale, Nouvelles Editions Africaines, 1976.

Liberte 3: Negritude et civilisation de l'universel (title means "Freedom 3: Negritude and the Civilization of the Universal"), Seuil, 1977.

(With Mohamed Aziza) *La Poesie de l'action : Conversations avec Mohamed Aziza* (interviews), Stock (Paris), 1980.

Ce que je crois: Negritude, francite, et la civilisation de l'universel, Bernard Grasset, 1988.

Also author of *L'Apport de la poesie negre,* 1953; *Langage et poesie negro-africaine,* 1954; *Esthetique negro-africain,* 1956; and *Liberte 4: Socialisme et planification,* 1983. Author of four technical works on Wolof grammar. Contributor to books, including *Cultures de l'Afrique noire et de l'Occident,* Societe Europeenne de Culture, 1961; and *La Senegal au Colloque sur le liberalisme planifie et les voies africaines vers le socialisme, Tunis, 1-6 juillet 1975,* Grand Imprimerie Africaine (Dakar), 1975. Author of lectures and addresses published in pamphlet or booklet form, including *The Mission of the Poet,* 1966; *Negritude et germanisme,* 1968; *Problemes de developpement dans les pays sous-developpes,* 1975; *Negritude et civilisations mediterraneennes,* 1976; and *Pour une lecture negro-africaine de Mallarme,* 1981. Contributor, sometimes under the pseudonyms Silmang Diamano or Patrice Maguilene Kaymor, of critical, linguistic, sociological, and political writings to periodicals and journals, including *Journal de la Societe des Africanists, Presence Africaine,* and *L'Esprit.*

OTHER

(Editor) *Anthologie de la nouvelle poesie negre et malgache de langue francaise* [precede de] *Orphee noir, par Jean Paul Sartre* (poetry anthology; title means "Anthology of the New Negro and Malagasy Poetry in French [preceded by] Black Orpheus, by Jean-Paul Sartre"), introduction by Sartre, Presses Universitaires de France, 1948, fourth edition, 1977.

(With Abdoulaye Sadji) *La Belle Histoire de Leuk-le-Lievre* (elementary school text; title means "The Clever Story of Leuk-the-Hare"), Hachette, 1953, reprinted as *La Belle Histoire de Leuk-le-Lievre: Cours elementaire des ecoles d'Afrique noir,* illustrations by Marcel Jeanjean, Hachette, 1961, British edition (in French) edited by J. M. Winch, illustrations by Jeanjean, Harrap, 1965, adaptation published as *Les Aventures de Leuk-le-Lievre,* illustrations by G. Lorofi, Nouvelles Editions Africaines, 1975.

(Author of introductory essay) *Anthologie des poetes du seizieme siecle* (anthology), Editions de la Bibliotheque Mondiale, 1956.

Le diaslogue des cultures, Seuil (Paris), 1993.

Also author of prose tale *Mandabi* (title means "The Money Order"). Translator of poetry by Mariane N'Diaye. Contributor of selected texts to books, including *Afrique Africaine* (photography), photographs by Michel Huet, Clairfontaine, 1963; *Terre promise d'Afrique: Symphonie en noir et or* (poetry anthology), lithographs by Hans Erni, Andre et Pierre Gonin (Lausanne), 1966; and *African Sojourn* (photography), photographs by Uwe Ommer, Arpel Graphics, 1987. Founder of journals, including *Condition Humaine,* with Aime Cesaire and Leon Gontran Damas, *L'Etudiant Noir,* and, with Alioune Diop, *Presence Africaine.*

OMNIBUS VOLUMES

Leopold Sedar Senghor (collection of prose and poems; with biographical-critical introduction and bibliography), edited by Armand Guibert, Seghers, 1961, reprinted as *Leopold Sedar Senghor: Une Etude d'Armand Guibert, avec un choix de poemes [et] une chronologie bibliographique, "Leopold Sedar Senghor et son temps,"* Seghers, 1969.

(In English translation) *Selected Poems,* edited and translated by John Reed and Clive Wake, introduction by Reed and Wake, Atheneum, 1964.

Poemes (includes *Chants d'ombre, Hosties noires, Ethiopiques, Nocturnes,* and "poemes divers"), Seuil, 1964, fourth edition, 1969, reprinted 1974, new edition, 1984.

L. S. Senghor: Poete senegalais, commentary by Roger Mercier, Monique Battestini, and Simon Battestini, F. Nathan, 1965, reprinted, 1978.

(In English translation) *Prose and Poetry,* selected and translated by Reed and Wake, Oxford University Press, 1965, Heinemann Educational, 1976.

(In French with English translations) *Selected Poems/ Poesies choisies,* English-language introduction by Craig Williamson, Collings, 1976.

(In French) *Selected Poems of Leopold Sedar Senghor,* edited, with English-language preface and notes, by Abiola Irele, Cambridge University Press, 1977.

Elegies majeures [suivi de] *Dialogue sur la poesie francophone,* Seuil, 1979.

(In English translation) *Poems of a Black Orpheus,* translated by William Oxley, Menard, 1981.

ADAPTATIONS: Senghor's *Mandabi* was adapted for film by Ousmane Sembene.

SIDELIGHTS: President of the Republic of Senegal from the proclamation of that country's independence in 1960 until he stepped down in 1980, Leopold Sedar Senghor is considered, according to *Time,* "one of Africa's most respected elder statesmen." Yet until 1960 Senghor's political career was conducted primarily in France rather than in Africa. He is a product of the nineteenth-century French educational system, a scholar of Greek and Latin, and a member of the elite Academie Francaise, but he is best known for developing "negritude," a wide-ranging movement that influenced black culture worldwide. As the chief proponent of negritude, Senghor is credited with contributing to Africa's progress toward independence from colonial rule and, according to Jacques Louis Hymans in his *Leopold Sedar Senghor: An Intellectual Biography,* with "setting in motion a whole series of African ideological movements." Senghor first gained widespread recognition, however, when his first collection of poetry was published in 1945; he followed that volume with a highly esteemed body of verse that has accumulated numerous prestigious honors, most notably consideration for the Nobel Prize in Literature. Senghor, thus, seems to be, as Hymans suggests, "the living symbol of the possible synthesis of what appears irreconcilable: he is as African as he is European, as much a poet as a politician, . . . as much a revolutionary as a traditionalist."

From the outset, disparate elements comprised Senghor's life. He was born in 1906 in Joal, a predominantly Moslem community established by Portuguese settlers on the Atlantic coast south of Dakar, a major Senegalese port and capital of what was then known as French West Africa. Senghor's mother was a Roman Catholic, and through maternal or paternal lines Senghor was related to the Fulani ethnic group, the Mandingo tribe, and the Serer ethnic group—said to provide a connection between Senghor and Serer royalty. His early childhood afforded contact with traditional customs and beliefs, with indigenous poetry, and with the surrounding natural setting. These contacts, critics note, strongly influenced Senghor's later life. As Sebastian Okechukwu Mezu explained in his 1973 study, *The Poetry of Leopold Sedar Senghor:* "This early childhood gave Senghor the material for his lyric poems. . . . Despite the splendours of political life, perhaps because of the excess of its paraphernalia, [Senghor] comes back to these memories of childhood . . . in his poems, events evoked several times in his public speeches and television interviews, images that have become a kind of obsession, romanticized during the years of his absence from Senegal, and because of this process of nostalgic remembrance, taken to be reality itself. Poetic life for Senghor as a result of this becomes a continual quest for the kingdom of childhood, a recovery, a recapture of this idyllic situation."

As a child Senghor demonstrated a lively intelligence and an early ambition to become a priest or a teacher, and was accordingly enrolled in a Catholic elementary school in

1913. The following year he began living in a boarding house four miles from Joal at N'Gasobil, where he attended the Catholic mission school operated by the Fathers of the Holy Spirit. There Senghor was encouraged to forsake his ancestral culture while he learned Latin and studied European civilization as part of a typical nineteenth-century French teaching program. In 1922 he entered Libermann Junior Seminary in Dakar. In his four years there Senghor acquired a sound knowledge of Greek and Latin classics. Obliged to leave the seminary when he was deemed ill-suited to the priesthood, Senghor, disappointed, entered public secondary school at a French-style lycee in Dakar. There he earned numerous scholastic prizes and distinction for having bested white pupils in academic performance. Senghor obtained his secondary school degree with honors in 1928 and was awarded a half scholarship for continued study in France.

In Paris Senghor boarded at the Lycee Louis-le-Grand, where top-ranking French students study for entrance exams to France's elite higher education programs. One of Senghor's classmates was Georges Pompidou, later prime minister and, eventually, president of France. Pompidou exposed Senghor to the works of French literary masters Marcel Proust, Andre Gide, and Charles Baudelaire. During this time Senghor was also influenced by the writings of Paul Claudel, Arthur Rimbaud, and Maurice Barres. Senghor's lycee education in Paris emphasized a methodology for rigorous thought and instilled habits of intellectual discipline, skills that Senghor embraced. He meanwhile continued to observe Roman Catholicism and expressed support for a restoration of the French government to monarchical rule. According to Hymans, Senghor in his student days was considered fully assimilated into Paris's intellectual milieu, which began including political and social liberation movements such as socialism, rationalism, humanism, and Marxism.

Europe was also reassessing African cultural traditions. European writers, artists, and musicians were exploring Africa's cultural wealth and incorporating what they discovered into their own creations. Paris of the late 1920s was permeated with Europe's new cultural appreciation of Africa, and in this atmosphere an exciting period of discovery began for Senghor. He began meeting with black students from the United States, Africa, and the Caribbean, and soon a friendship grew between Senghor and Aime Cesaire, a writer from the French West Indian territory of Martinique. Another of Senghor's acquaintances was Paulette Nardal, a West Indian and the editor of a journal, *La Revue du Monde Noir*. Published in French and English, the journal was intended to provide a forum for black intellectuals writing literary and scientific works, to celebrate black civilization, and to increase unity among blacks worldwide. Through its editor Nardal,

Senghor met West Indian writers Etienne Lero and Rene Maran and read the poetry of black Americans.

In *The New Negro,* an anthology published in 1925, Senghor encountered the works of prominent writers such as Paul Laurence Dunbar, W. E. B. Du Bois, Countee Cullen, Langston Hughes, Claude McKay, Zora Neale Hurston, James Weldon Johnson, and Jean Toomer. The anthology's editor, Alain Locke, was a professor of philosophy at Harvard University and a contributor to *La Revue du Monde Noir;* Senghor met him through Nardal as well. When Senghor, Cesaire, and Leon-Gontran Damas, a student from French Guiana, sought a name for the growing francophone interest in African culture, they borrowed from the title of Locke's anthology and dubbed the movement "neo-negre" or "negre-nouveau." These labels were later replaced by "negritude," a term coined by Cesaire. Senghor credits Jamaican poet and novelist Claude McKay with having supplied the values espoused by the new movement: to seek out the roots of black culture and build on its foundations, to draw upon the wealth of African history and anthropology, and to rehabilitate black culture in the eyes of the world. With Cesaire and Damas, Senghor launched *L'Etudiant Noir,* a cultural journal.

In exalting black culture and values, Senghor emphasized what he perceived as differences between the races. He portrayed blacks as possessing intuitive and artistic natures, seeing in them an essential and exuberant emotionalism that whites tend to suppress with reason and intellect. Europe he saw as alien, dehumanized, and dying; in stark contrast, he considered Africa vital, nourishing, and thriving. As racism and fascism swept through Europe in the 1930s, Senghor's attitudes hardened. For a brief period he became disillusioned with Europe and abandoned his religious faith. However, as Hymans has suggested, Senghor began to see that "the same Romantic anti-rationalism that fathered racism among the Fascists of the 1930s underlay his early reaction against the West." Thus, as Senghor observed the increasing turmoil in Europe caused by Fascist regimes in Italy and Germany and witnessed the dangers of racism, he began to modify his position.

Senghor nevertheless continued to cite what he considered to be differences between the races, such as an intuitive African way of understanding reality. But more importantly, as negritude evolved, he emphasized racial pride as a way of valuing black culture's role in a universal civilization. In this vein, he published an essay in 1939 titled "What the Negro Contributes." Themes that Senghor introduced to negritude at this time included a humanism based on the solidarity of all races, a moderate position that gave primacy to culture and maintained respect for other values. As Senghor told an audience he addressed in Dakar in 1937: "Assimilate, don't be assimilated." He later developed negritude further, however, by working to insure not only that African cultural identity became accessible to blacks worldwide, but that the unique aspects of African life were accorded status in the cultural community of society as a whole. Once African modes of thought and artistic expression are restored to their proper place among the world's cultures, Senghor proposed, then a sort of cultural cross-breeding can occur. This mixing of the races, according to Mezu, was conceived as "a symbiotic union where blacks will bring to the rendezvous of the races their special . . . talents." Hymans examined this development of negritude since its inception in the 1930s and quoted Senghor's retrospective assessment of the movement: "Like life, the concept of negritude has become historical and dialectical. It has evolved."

Much of what later informed negritude had yet to be developed when in 1933 Senghor became the first African to obtain the coveted agregation degree from the Sorbonne in Paris. This distinction led to his first teaching position, at the Lycee Descartes in Tours, France. Senghor's new appreciation for Africa, coupled with his estrangement from his homeland, created an internal conflict that found resolution when he began writing poetry. Influenced by the works of Andre Breton and other surrealist writers, Senghor drew on surrealist techniques for his poetic style. Surrealism, with its emphasis on the irrational, depended on a creative process that tapped latent energies and subconscious sources of imagination without drawing a distinction between the fantastic and the real. Senghor found this process similar to traditional African modes of thought and employed it in his poetry. "By adopting the surrealist techniques," Mezu explained, "he was at the same time modern and African: educated and modernist from the white European viewpoint, traditional and faithful to the motherland from the African viewpoint. This dualism, or rather ambivalence, is ever present in Senghor's theories, poetry and actions." Nevertheless, Mezu noted, "there is a difference between the surrealist norm and the Senghorian philosophy. The difference is basically one of degree. For the surrealists, their effort, and an effort only, was to discover the point where reality and dream merge into one. For Senghor . . . this principle is already possessed, already a part of the ancestral culture."

The poems Senghor wrote in the late 1930s were later published in the collection *Chants d'ombre*. For the most part, these poems express Senghor's nostalgia for Africa, his sense of exile, estrangement, and cultural alienation, and his attempt to recover an idealized past. In a style based on musical rhythms, the poet evokes the beauty of the African landscape and peoples, the richness of Africa's past and the protecting presence of the dead, and the innocence and dignity inherent in his native culture. These poems, critics note, celebrate an Africa Senghor knew as a child, one transformed by nostalgia into a paradise-like simplic-

ity. In some of the volume's other poems Senghor laments the destruction of the continent's culture and the suffering of its people under colonial rule. One of the collection's frequently cited pieces, "Femme noir," employs sensual yet worshipful language intended to glorify all black women. In "Joal" Senghor returns to his native village, revisiting places and inhabitants he had once known very well; it is, according to Mezu, "easily one of the most beautiful poems created by Senghor." When *Chants d'ombre* was published in 1945 it was well received in Paris and brought Senghor to public attention as a voice of black Africa. "In recreating the distant continent by verse," Hymans observed, "Senghor helped blaze the trail that led to the phenomenon of negritude."

World War II intervened between the writing of the poems collected in *Chants d'ombre* and their eventual publication. Germany invaded Poland in September, 1939, and Senghor was immediately called to active duty to protect France at the German border. While the holder of a high academic degree is usually made a commissioned officer, Senghor as a black man was made a second-class soldier in the Colonial Infantry. France fell to the German assault in June, 1940, the same month Senghor was captured and interned in a German prison camp. At the time of his capture he was almost shot along with some other Senegalese prisoners, but a French officer interceded on his behalf. While in prison Senghor met African peasants who had been recruited into the French Army, and began to identify with their plight. He wrote a number of poems that he sent by letter to his old classmate and friend Georges Pompidou; they were hand-delivered by a German guard who had been a professor of Chinese at the University of Vienna before the war. These poems later formed the core of Senghor's second published collection, *Hosties noires,* which appeared in 1948.

Hosties noires documents Senghor's realization that he was not alone in his exile from Africa, explores his increasing sense of unity with blacks as an exploited race, and elucidates the positive meaning Senghor finds in the sacrifices blacks have made. In poems such as "Au Gouveneur Eboue," which treats a black man's willingness to die for the salvation of the white world, Senghor memorializes blacks fighting for Europe. Elsewhere in *Hosties noires,* Senghor protests the exploitation of black soldiers and attacks western sources of power and violence. In other poems, such as "Mediterranee" and "Aux Soldats Negro-Americains," he rejoices in the common bonds formed with fellow soldiers and with American blacks. And with "Priere de paix" and "Tyaroye" Senghor hopes for unity and peace; while denouncing colonialism, he calls for an end to hatred and welcomes the new life that succeeds death. The collection, according to Mezu, is "the most homogeneous volume of Senghor's poetry, from the point of view not only of theme but also of language and sentiment."

Through the influence of West Indian colleagues Senghor was released from prison in June, 1942, and resumed teaching at the lycee in suburban Paris where he had earlier served as instructor of literature and African culture. He joined a Resistance group and also participated in activities involving colonial students. During the war, negritude had gained momentum, and when *Chants d'ombre* appeared in 1945, a new group of black intellectuals eagerly embraced Senghor's poetry and cultural theories. That year he published the influential essay "Views on Africa; or, Assimilate, Don't Be Assimilated." In the 1930s Senghor had concentrated on cultural rather than political issues; after the war, encouraged by colonial reforms extended to French West Africans, he decided to run for election as one of Senegal's representatives in the French National Assembly. With Lamine Gueye, Senghor formed the Bloc Africain to involve the Senegalese people in their political fate. France was forming a new constitution, and in recognition of his linguistic expertise, France's provisional government appointed Senghor the document's official grammarian. Senghor founded the Bloc Democratique Senegalais (BDS) in 1948; throughout the 1950s the BDS dominated Senegalese politics.

Senghor's literary activities also continued. In 1947 he founded, with Alioune Diop, the cultural journal *Presence Africaine.* Along with a publishing house of the same name, *Presence Africaine* became under Diop's direction a powerful vehicle for black writing worldwide. As editor of *Anthologie de la nouvelle poesie noire et malgache de langue francaise,* published in 1948, Senghor brought together contemporary poetry written by francophone blacks. An essay titled "Orphee noir" ("Black Orpheus"), by French philosopher and writer Jean-Paul Sartre, introduced the anthology. Sartre's essay outlined the cultural aims of black peoples striving to recapture their heritage. In the process Sartre defined and gained notoriety for the philosophy of negritude, portraying negritude as a step toward a united society without racial distinction. Many consider "Black Orpheus" to be the most important document of the negritude movement.

After 1948 Senghor became increasingly active politically, serving as France's delegate to the 1949 Council of Europe and as a French delegate to the United Nations General Assembly in 1950 and 1951; also in 1951, he was resoundingly reelected to the French National Assembly. In 1955 and 1956 Senghor served in the cabinet of French president Edgar Faure as secretary of state for scientific research and attended UNESCO conferences as a representative of France. While some French-held territories sought independence from colonial rule, often with accompanying violence, Senghor pushed for an arrangement

giving French overseas territories equal status in a federation relationship facilitating economic development. He constantly modified his stance while avoiding violence and making small gains. In Dakar in 1953, according to Hymans, Senghor defined politics as "the art of using a method which, by approximations that are constantly corrected, would permit the greatest number to lead a more complete and happy life."

A collection of poems Senghor had been working on since 1948 was published as *Ethiopiques* in 1956. These poems reflect Senghor's growing political involvement and his struggle to reconcile European and African allegiances through crossbreeding, both figurative and literal. The year *Ethiopiques* was published Senghor divorced his African wife to marry one of her friends, a white Frenchwoman; critics have suggested that Senghor's views on cross-breeding represent an attempt to resolve his personal conflict by eliminating the divisive social elements that divided his loyalties. One of *Ethiopiques*'s poems, "Chaka," is a dramatic adaptation of Thomas Mofolo's novel about a Zulu hero who forged and ruled a vast domain in the early nineteenth century. Mezu called "Chaka" Senghor's "most ambitious piece." Others have drawn parallels between Senghor's life and the poem's attempt to combine in the character of Chaka both the poet and politician. In "Chaka" Senghor applied his theories about the combination of music, dance, and poetry found in native African art forms. As Mezu noted, "Senghor aimed to illustrate what he considered an indigenous form of art where music, painting, theatre, poetry, religion, faith, love, and politics are all intertwined." In addition to musical and rhythmic elements, native plants and animals also figure prominently in *Ethiopiques,* whose other poems include "A New York," and "Congo."

When France's Fourth Republic collapsed in 1958 and France began to form a new constitution—along with new policies toward Africa—Senghor joined the advocates of independence for African territories. The French government under Charles de Gaulle appointed Senghor to the consultative assembly that would formulate the new constitution and policies. De Gaulle's proposed constitution, which was adopted in late 1958, accorded French West African territories autonomy within the French Community. At the same time De Gaulle warned Senghor that complete independence for West Africa would mean a cessation of technical and financial aid. In 1959 Senghor countered with the Mali Federation, linking Senegal and the Sudan (now Mali). The Mali Federation proclaimed its independence in June, 1960, but two months later Senegal withdrew and reproclaimed its independence. A Senegalese constitution was drawn up in August, 1960, and the following month Senghor was elected to a seven-year term as president of the new Republic of Senegal. Almost twenty-five years later Senghor told *Time,* "The colonizing powers did not prepare us for independence."

Poems Senghor wrote during the tumultuous years leading up to his election as president of Senegal were published in the 1961 collection *Nocturnes,* which featured a group of love poems previously published as *Chants pour Naeett* in 1949. In *Nocturnes* Senghor ponders the nature of poetry and examines the poetic process. Critics have noted that in this volume, particularly in poems such as "Elegie de minuit," Senghor reveals his regret for time spent in the empty pomp of political power, his nostalgia for his youth, and his reconciliation with death. Mezu called "Elegie de minuit" the poet's " 'last' poem."

After 1960, Senghor wrote mainly political and critical prose, tied closely to the goals, activities, and demands of his political life. During this time he survived an attempted coup d'etat staged in 1962 by Senegal's prime minister, Mamadou Dia. The following year Senghor authorized the Senegalese National Assembly to draw up a new constitution that gave more power to the president, elected to five-year terms. Known for his ability to hold factions together, he remained in power, reelected in 1968 and 1973, despite more coup attempts, an assassination plot in 1967, and civil unrest in the late 1960s. Much of Senghor's writing from this era outlines the course to which he feels Africa must hold. Commenting on the instability suffered after African nations achieved independence, Senghor told *Time:* "The frequency of coups in Africa is the result of the backwardness in civilization that colonization represented. . . . What we should all be fighting for is democratic socialism. And the first task of socialism is not to create social justice. It is to establish working democracies."

According to Hymans, Senghor's brand of socialism, often called the African Road to Socialism, maps out a middle position between individualism and collectivism, between capitalism and communism. Senghor sees socialism as a way of eliminating the exploitation of individuals that prevents universal humanism. Some of Senghor's writings on this topic were translated by Mercer Cook and published in 1964 as *On African Socialism.* Appraising *On African Socialism* for *Saturday Review,* Charles Miller called its selections "exquisitely intellectual tours de force." Senghor's important political writings include *Liberte 1: Negritude et humanisme,* of which portions are available in translation; a work translated by Cook as *The Foundations of "Africanite": or, "Negritude" and "Arabite"; Politique, nation, et developpement moderne; Liberte 3: Negritude et civilization de l'universel;* and *Liberte 4: Socialisme et planification.* In a collection of interviews with Mohamed Aziza published in 1980, Senghor discussed his poetry, his politics, and his life. Senghor "comes across in these interviews as a brilliant, sincere, and steadfast leader who has

yet managed to retain a sense of humility," wrote Eric Sellin, reviewing the collection for *World Literature Today.* Sellin continued: "His unswerving fidelity to personal and national programs is more readily understandable in light of his autobiographical introspections about his youth and education." Published as *La Poesie de l'action: Conversations avec Mohamed Aziza,* the volume, Sellin concluded, is "an important and interesting book." Later in 1980, Senghor stepped down from Senegal's presidency when his protege, Prime Minister Abdou Diouf, took office.

Senghor is revered throughout the world for his political and literary accomplishments and a life of achievement that spans nearly six decades. He was widely thought to have been under consideration in 1962 for the Nobel Prize in Literature in recognition of his poetic output. When a major English-translation volume devoted to Senghor's body of poetry appeared in 1964, *Saturday Review* likened Senghor to American poet Walt Whitman and determined that the poems represented were "written by a gifted, civilized man of good will celebrating the ordinary hopes and feelings of mankind." The *Times Literary Supplement* called Senghor "one of the best poets now writing in [French]" and marveled at his "astonishing achievement to have combined so creative a life with his vigorous and successful political activities." Senghor was elected to one of the world's most prestigious and elite intellectual groups, the Academie Francaise, in 1983.

When a new collected edition of Senghor's poetry appeared in 1984, Robert P. Smith, Jr., writing in *World Literature Today* identified Senghor as a "great poet of Africa and the universe." Praising the masterly imagery, symbolism, and versification of the poetry, Smith expressed particular admiration for Senghor's "constant creation of a poetry which builds up, makes inquiries, and expands into universal dimensions," and cited an elegy Senghor wrote for his deceased son as "one of the most beautiful in modern poetry." Critics characterize Senghor's poetic style as serenely and resonantly rhetorical. While some readers detect a lack of tension in his poetry, most admire its lush sensuality and uplifting attitude. Offered as a means of uniting African peoples in an appreciation of their cultural worth, Senghor's poetry, most agree, extends across the chasm that negritude, at least in its early form, seemed to have created in emphasizing the differences between races. "It is difficult to predict whether Senghor's poetry will excite the same approbation when the prestige of the President and that of the idealist no longer colour people's view of the man," Mezu acknowledged. "The Senegalese poet will certainly survive in the history of the Black Renaissance as the ideologist and theoretician of negritude." Writing in the *Washington Post Book World,* K. Anthony Appiah sees Senghor's poetry as "an integral part of his political and intellectual career rather than as a free-standing accomplishment demanding separate literary treatment."

Senghor's negritude in its more evolved form refuses to choose between Africa and Europe in its quest for worldwide national, cultural, and religious integration. Himself a synthesis of disparate elements, Senghor, in his role as reconciler of differences, holds to negritude as a median between nationalism and cultural assimilation. "Politically, philosophically, Senghor has been a middle-of-the-roader, a man of conciliation and mediation," Mezu declared, adding: "Negritude should . . . be seen as a stage in the evolution of the literature of the black man. . . . The contemporary trend in African poetry seems to be away from the negritude movement as the racism and colonialism that inspired this literature dies out or becomes less barefaced." Senghor's life, according to Hymans, "might be summarized as an effort to restore to Africa an equilibrium destroyed by the clash with Europe." For those who see contradictions in Senghor's effort over more than five decades, Hymans observed that "one constant in his thought appears to surmount the contradictions it contains: universal reconciliation is his only goal and Africa's only salvation."

BIOGRAPHICAL/CRITICAL SOURCES:

BOOKS

Blair, Dorothy S., *African Literature in French,* Cambridge University Press, 1976.
Bureau de Documentation de la Presidence de la Republique, *Leopold Sedar Senghor: Bibliographie,* second edition, Fondation Leopold Sedar Senghor, 1982.
Contemporary Literary Criticism, Volume 54, Gale, 1989.
Crowder, Michael, *Senegal: A Study in French Assimilation Policy,* Oxford University Press, 1962.
Guibert, Armand, *Leopold Sedar Senghor: L'Homme et l'oeuvre,* Presence Africaine, 1962.
Hymans, Jacques Louis, *Leopold Sedar Senghor: An Intellectual Biography,* University Press, Edinburgh, 1971.
Kesteloot, Lilyan, *Comprendre les poemes de Leopold Sedar Senghor,* Saint Paul Classiques Africain, 1987.
Markovitz, Irving Leonard, *Leopold Sedar Senghor and the Politics of Negritude,* Atheneum, 1969.
Mezu, Sebastian Okechuwu, *The Poetry of Leopold Sedar Senghor,* Fairleigh Dickinson University Press, 1973.
Moore, Gerald, *Seven African Writers,* Oxford University Press, 1962.
Neikirk, Barend van Dyk Van, *The African Image (Negritude) in the Work of Leopold Sedar Senghor,* A. A. Balkema 1970.
Nespoulous Neuville, Josiane, *Leopold Sedar Senghor: De la tradition a l'universalisme,* Seuil, 1988.
Rous, Jean, *Leopold Sedar Senghor,* J. Didier, 1968.

Saint Cheron, Francoid de, *Senghor et la terre,* Sang de la Terre, 1988.
Saravaya, Gloria, *Langage et poesie chez Senghor,* L'Harmattan, 1989.
Vaillant, Janet G., *Black, French and African: A Life of Leopold Sedar Senghor,* Harvard University Press, 1990.

PERIODICALS

Black World, August 14, 1978.
Callaloo, winter, 1990.
Ebony, August, 1972.
Essence, September, 1987.
French Review, May, 1982.
Maclean's, February 24, 1986, p. 22.
New York Review of Books, December 20, 1990, p. 11.
Saturday Review, January 2, 1965.
Time, June 9, 1978; January 16, 1984.
Times Literary Supplement, June 11, 1964.
Washington Post Book World, July 5, 1992, p. 2.
World Literature Today, spring, 1965; autumn, 1978; summer, 1981; winter, 1985; summer, 1990, p. 540.

*　　*　　*

SENNHOLZ, Hans F. 1922-

PERSONAL: Born February 3, 1922, in Brambauer, Germany; immigrated to United States, 1949, naturalized citizen, 1955; married Mary Homan (an editor), July 25, 1954; children: Robert. *Education:* University of Marburg, M.A., 1948; University of Cologne, Ph.D. (political science), 1949; New York University, Ph.D. (economics), 1955.

ADDRESSES: 30 South Broadway, Irvington, NY 10533.

CAREER: White & Weld, New York City, accountant, 1951-54; Iona College, New Rochelle, NY, assistant professor of economics, 1954-56; Grove City College, Grove City, PA, professor of economics, 1956-92. Foundation for Economic Education, trustee, 1969—, chairman of the board, 1982-85, president, 1992—.

WRITINGS:

How Can Europe Survive?, Van Nostrand (New York City), 1955.
The Great Depression, Bramble Minibooks, 1969.
Inflation, or Gold Standard?, Bramble Minibooks, 1973.
(Editor and contributor) *Gold Is Money,* Greenwood Press (Westport, CO), 1975.
Death and Taxes, Heritage Foundation (Washington, DC), 1976, 2nd edition, Libertarian Press, 1982.
Age of Inflation, Western Islands (Belmont, MA), 1979.
Money and Freedom, Libertarian Press (Holland, IL), 1985.

Debts and Deficits, Libertarian Press, 1987.
The Politics of Unemployment, Libertarian Press, 1987.
The Savings and Loan Bailout, Libertarian Press, 1989.

Also author of pamphlets on economic issues. Translator of three volumes of *Capital and Interest,* 1956, by Eugen von Boehm-Bawerk, and *A Critique of Interventionism,* 1977, by Ludwig von Mises.

SIDELIGHTS: Hans F. Sennholz told *CA:* "As a private pilot, I like to fly to my speaking engagements in my Grumman Tiger airplane, accompanied by my favorite co-pilot, my wife."

*   *   *

SERVICE, Pamela F. 1945-

PERSONAL: Born October 8, 1945, in Berkeley, CA; daughter of Forrest Leroy (a dentist) and Floy (Flemming) Horner; married Robert Gifford Service, July 8, 1967; children: Alexandra Floyesta. *Education:* University of California, Berkeley, B.A., 1967; University of London, M.A., 1969. *Politics:* Democrat. *Religion:* Methodist.

ADDRESSES: Home—419 North Washington, Bloomington, IN 47408. *Office*—Monroe County Museum, 202 East Sixth, Bloomington, IN 47408.

CAREER: Indiana University—Bloomington, publicist for Art Museum, 1970-72; Monroe County Museum, Bloomington, curator, 1978—. Member of Bloomington City Council, 1979—.

MEMBER: Society of Children's Book Writer's, American Association of Museums, American Association of State and Local History, Sierra Club, Humane Society, Monroe County Historical Society, Monroe County Civic Theatre, Bloomington Town Theatre.

WRITINGS:

Winter of Magic's Return, Atheneum (New York City), 1985.
A Question of Destiny, Atheneum, 1986.
When the Night Wind Howls, Atheneum, 1987.
Tomorrow's Magic, Atheneum, 1987.
Stinker from Space, Scribner (New York City), 1988.
The Reluctant God, Atheneum, 1988.
Vision Quest, Atheneum, 1989.
Wizard of Wind and Rock, Atheneum, 1990.
Under Alien Stars, Atheneum, 1990.
Being of Two Minds, Atheneum, 1991.
Weirdos of the Universe, Unite!, Atheneum, 1992.
Stinker's Return, Scribners, 1993.
All's Faire, Atheneum, 1993.
Phantom Victory, Scribners, 1994.
Storm at the Edge of Time, Walker, 1994.

A regular columnist on history for the *Bloomington Herald Times,* 1980—.

WORK IN PROGRESS: Will Power, a Shakespearean time-slip, and *Wizard Boy: A Legend of Merlin,* a play version of *Wizard of Wind and Rock.*

SIDELIGHTS: Pamela F. Service once told *CA:* "I write for children because it is there that fiction writers can make a real difference in shaping reader's interests and attitudes. And I write science fiction and fantasy because these genres give us greater freedom to explore the human condition in ways that are not too tedious nor too painfully close. In my books I try to convey some of my own concern for humanity's past and for our future, and to incorporate some of my own experiences in politics, theater and archaeology, as well as a feel for various places I have traveled and lived."

*   *   *

SHAFFER, Peter (Levin) 1926-
(Peter Anthony, a joint pseudonym)

PERSONAL: Born May 15, 1926, in Liverpool, England; son of Jack (a real estate agent) and Reka (Fredman) Shaffer. *Education:* Trinity College, Cambridge, B.A., 1950. *Politics:* Conservative anarchist. *Religion:* Humanist. *Avocational interests:* Music, architecture.

ADDRESSES: Home—173 Riverside Dr., New York, NY 10024. *Agent*—c/o McNaughton-Lowe Representation, 200 Fulham Road, SW10, England.

CAREER: Playwright and critic. Worked in the New York Public Library, New York City, 1951-54, and for Bosey & Hawkes (music publishers), London, England, 1954-55; literary critic for *Truth,* 1956-57; music critic for *Time and Tide,* 1961-62. *Wartime service:* Served as a conscript in coal mines in England, 1944-47.

MEMBER: Royal Society of Literature (fellow), Dramatists Guild, Garrick Club (London).

AWARDS, HONORS: Evening Standard Drama Award, 1958, and New York Drama Critics Circle Award, 1960, both for *Five Finger Exercise;* Antoinette Perry Award (Tony), Outer Critics Circle Award, and New York Drama Critics Circle Award, all 1975, all for *Equus;* Tony Award, 1980, and best play of the year award from *Plays and Players,* both for *Amadeus;* New York Film Critics Circle Award, 1984, Los Angeles Film Critics Association Award, 1984, and Academy Award of Merit (Oscar) from the Academy of Motion Picture Arts and Sciences, 1985, all for screenplay adaptation of *Amadeus;* named Commander of the British Empire, 1987; *Evening Standard* Drama Award for Best Comedy, 1988, for *Lettice and*

Lovage: A Comedy; Hamburg Shakespeare Prize, 1989; William Inge Award for Distinguished Achievement in the American Theatre, 1992.

WRITINGS:

PLAYS

Five Finger Exercise (produced on the West End at the Comedy Theatre, July 16, 1958; produced on Broadway at the Music Box Theater, December 2, 1959; also see below), Hamish Hamilton, 1958, Harcourt, 1959.

The Private Ear [and] *The Public Eye* (two one-acts; produced on the West End at the Globe Theatre, May 10, 1962; produced on Broadway at the Morosco Theatre, October 9, 1963; also see below), Hamish Hamilton, 1962, Stein & Day (Briarcliff Manor, NY), 1964.

The Merry Rooster's Panto, produced on the West End at Wyndham's Theatre, December, 1963.

The Royal Hunt of the Sun: A Play Concerning the Conquest of Peru (produced by the National Theatre Co. at the Chichester Festival, July 7, 1964; produced on Broadway at the ANTA Theatre, October 26, 1965), Samuel French (London), 1964, Stein & Day, 1965.

A Warning Game, produced in New York City, 1967.

Black Comedy (one-act; produced by the National Theatre Co. at the Chichester Festival, July 27, 1965; also see below; produced on Broadway at the Ethel Barrymore Theatre with *White Lies* [also see below], February 12, 1967; produced on the West End at the Lyric Theatre as *Black Comedy* [and] *The White Liars* [also see below], 1968), Samuel French, 1967.

The White Liars, Samuel French, 1967.

Black Comedy [and] *White Lies,* Stein & Day, 1967, published in England as *The White Liars* [and] *Black Comedy,* Hamish Hamilton, 1968.

It's about Cinderella, produced in London, 1969.

Equus (produced by the National Theatre Co. on the West End at the Old Vic Theatre, July 26, 1973; produced on Broadway at the Plymouth Theater, October 24, 1974; also see below), Deutsch, 1973, Samuel French, 1974.

Shrivings (three-act; produced on the West End at the Lyric Theatre as *The Battle of Shrivings,* February 5, 1970; also see below), Deutsch, 1974.

Equus [and] *Shrivings,* Atheneum (New York City), 1974.

Three Plays (contains *Five Finger Exercise, Shrivings,* and *Equus*), Penguin (New York City), 1976.

Four Plays, Penguin, 1981.

Amadeus (produced on the West End by the National Theatre Co. at the Olivier Theatre, November 2, 1979; produced on Broadway at the Broadhurst Theater, December 17, 1980; also see below), Deutsch, 1980, Harper (New York City), 1981.

Collected Plays of Peter Shaffer, Crown, 1982.

Yonadab: The Watcher, produced on the West End by the National Theatre Co. at the Olivier Theatre, December 4, 1985, published as *Yonadab: A Play,* Harper, 1988.

Lettice and Lovage: A Comedy (produced on the West End at the Globe Theatre, 1987; produced on Broadway at the Ethel Barrymore Theater, March 25, 1990), HarperCollins, 1990.

The Gift of the Gorgon: A Play, (produced at the Barbican, 1992), Pantheon Books (New York City), 1994.

NOVELS; WITH BROTHER, ANTHONY SHAFFER

(Under joint pseudonym Peter Anthony) *Woman in the Wardrobe,* Evans Brothers, 1951.

(Under joint pseudonym Peter Anthony) *How Doth the Little Crocodile?,* Evans Brothers, 1952, published under names Peter Shaffer and Anthony Shaffer, Macmillan (New York City), 1957.

Withered Murder, Gollancz, 1955, Macmillan, 1956.

SCREENPLAYS

(With Peter Brook) *Lord of the Flies,* Walter Reade, 1963.

The Pad (and How to Use It) (adaptation of *The Private Ear*), Universal, 1966.

Follow Me!, Universal, 1971.

The Public Eye (based on Shaffer's play of the same title), Universal, 1972.

Equus (based on Shaffer's play of the same title), United Artists, 1977.

Amadeus (based on Shaffer's play of the same title), Orion Pictures, 1984.

TELEVISION PLAYS

The Salt Land, Independent Television Network, 1955.

Balance of Terror, British Broadcasting Corp., 1957.

RADIO PLAYS

The Prodigal Father, British Broadcasting Corp., 1955.

OTHER

(Editor) *Elisabeth Frink Sculpture: Catalogue Raisonne,* Trafalger Square, 1988.

Whom Do I Have the Honor of Addressing?, Deutsch, 1990.

Contributor of articles to periodicals, including *Theatre Arts, Atlantic, Encore,* and *Sunday Times.*

ADAPTATIONS: Five Finger Exercise was filmed by Columbia in 1962; *The Royal Hunt of the Sun: A Play Concerning the Conquest of Peru* was filmed by CBS's Cinema Center Films.

SIDELIGHTS: "Whatever else Peter Shaffer may lack, it isn't courage, it isn't derring-do. His plays traverse the centuries and the globe, raising questions that have perplexed minds from Job to Samuel Beckett," Benedict Nightingale writes in the *New York Times*. Shaffer examines the conflict between atheism and religion in *The Royal Hunt of the Sun: A Play Concerning the Conquest of Peru;* the nature of sanity and insanity in modern society in *Equus;* the role of genius in *Amadeus;* and Old Testament ethics in *Yonadab: The Watcher*. These epic plays are always a visual spectacle, but some critics feel that Shaffer's spectacles mask superficial stories. *Newsweek* contributor Jack Kroll characterizes the typical Shaffer play as "a large-scale, large-voiced treatment of large themes, whose essential superficiality is masked by a skillful theatricality reinforced by . . . extraordinary acting." Despite such criticism, Shaffer's plays are enormously popular—both *Equus* and *Amadeus* had Broadway runs of more than one thousand performances each.

Shaffer's first major success was *The Royal Hunt of the Sun,* based on Francisco Pizarro's sixteenth-century expedition to the Incan Empire of Peru. To force the Incan people to give him the gold he desired, Pizarro took their leader, Atahuallpa, prisoner. But Atahuallpa refused to concede defeat and the resulting battle between Pizarro's forces and the Incan Indians proved disastrous for his people. In the ensuing battle, Atahuallpa is killed. But Pizarro had befriended the Incan leader. When Atahuallpa dies, Pizarro renounces Catholicism to adopt the Incan religion.

The Royal Hunt of the Sun is considered unique because of its historical subject and its stylized theatrical techniques, including mime and adaptations of Japanese Kabuki theater. To enhance the visual spectacle of the play, Shaffer specified that the Indians wear dramatic Incan funeral masks during Atahuallpa's death scene; many in the audience later claimed to have seen the masks change expression during the production. "They hadn't, of course," Shaffer told Richard Schickel in *Time*. "But the audience invested so much emotion in the play that it looked as if they had."

Despite this positive emotional response from audiences, some critics feel the play's language and theatrical devices are not effective. *Drama*'s Ronald Hayman thinks that Shaffer borrows from so many different traditions and uses so many theatrical devices that "instead of unifying to contribute to the same effect, the various elements make their effects separately and some of them are superfluous and distracting." Warren Sylvester Smith in the *Dictionary of Literary Biography* indicates that the language "sometimes fail[s] to achieve the magnitude of the characters or to match the scope of the events." And Hayman faults the dialogue for being "lustreless, tumbling into cliches and even pleonasms like 'trapped in time's cage' when nothing less than poetry would take the strain Shaffer is putting on it."

But other critics, and many playgoers, had a more generous response to *The Royal Hunt of the Sun*. These reviewers mention that the elaborate sets and costumes, the epic story, and the innovative rendition of history were exciting additions to the contemporary dramatic scene. John Russell Taylor writes in *Peter Shaffer* that as a "piece of sheer theatrical machinery the play is impeccable." He concludes that *The Royal Hunt of the Sun* is "at once a spectacular drama and a thinkpiece."

In Shaffer's 1973 play, *Equus,* he confronts the question of sanity in the modern world. Despite its morbid focus, *Equus* was so well-liked that the opening-night Broadway audience gave it a five-minute standing ovation. "It's never happened to me before," Shaffer told Schickel. "I cry every time I think about it." *Equus* is based on a newspaper report of a boy who blinded several horses in a north England stable. The play revolves around psychiatrist Martin Dysart's treatment of the boy, Alan Strang, for the offense he committed.

During his examination of the boy, Dysart discovers that Strang is a pagan who believes that horses are gods. Therefore, when a stable girl attempts to seduce him in front of the horses, Strang is impotent. In frustrated rage that they have seen his failure, Strang blinds the horses. Dysart tries to treat him in a conventional manner, but eventually finds that he prefers Strang's primitive passion to his own rational, controlled personality. Brendan Gill notes in the *New Yorker* that Dysart "poses questions that go beyond the sufficiently puzzling matter of the boy's conduct to the infinitely puzzling matter of why, in a world charged with insanity, we should seek to 'cure' anyone in the name of sanity."

Equus brought complaints from some reviewers who argue that it superficially portrays insanity and psychoanalysis. *Equus,* John Simon suggests in *New York,* "falls into that category of worn-out whimsy wherein we are told that insanity is more desirable, admirable, or just saner than sanity." *Commentary* contributor Jack Richardson states that *Equus* seems to be a "perfect case-study in the mediocrity of insight necessary nowadays for a play to enjoy a popular reputation for profundity." Simon concludes that no "amount of external embellishment can overcome the hollowness within."

Other reviewers feel that because of the enthusiastic audience response to the play, *Equus* may be depicting a significant trend in modern society. Gerald Weals reports in *Commonweal* that *Equus* "clearly touches a nerve in the New York audience, as it did earlier in London, which means that it is something more serious . . . than the effectively theatrical play it so obviously is. . . . *Equus,* it seems, is more than a highclass melodrama. It is a cry for the power of irrationality. Or an echo."

Shaffer's next play, *Amadeus,* is based on the life of eighteenth-century composer Wolfgang Amadeus Mozart. Richard Christiansen of the *Chicago Tribune* believes that the characters in *Amadeus* and *Equus* are similar, remarking that "here again, as in 'Equus,' an older, learned man of the world is struck and amazed by the wild inspiration of a much younger man who seemingly is possessed with divine madness." The older man in *Amadeus* is Antonio Salieri, portrayed as a second-rate composer who is consumed by jealousy because of the young Mozart's greater talent.

Shaffer became interested in the rivalry between Mozart and Salieri upon reading material about Mozart's mysterious death. Shaffer at first suspected that Salieri may have murdered the composer, but further research proved this to be wrong. "But by then the cold eyes of Salieri were staring at me," Shaffer tells Roland Gelatt in the *Saturday Review.* "The conflict between virtuous mediocrity and feckless genius took hold of my imagination, and it would not leave me alone."

In *Amadeus,* Salieri has made a bargain with God. He is to remain pious in return for being made the most popular composer of his time. As court composer in Vienna, Salieri is satisfied that his bargain with God has been kept. But then Mozart arrives at the court, playing music Salieri considers to be the finest he has ever heard. And in contrast to Salieri's piety, Mozart is a moral abomination—a bastard, a womanizer, and an abrasive man with a scatological sense of humor. Salieri feels cheated and angry, and begins to sabotage Mozart's budding career by spreading rumors about him. These rumors, along with Mozart's contentious personality, serve to ostracize him from polite society and cause him to lose his pupils. Eventually Mozart becomes ill and dies, and the play asks whether he was killed by Salieri or died from natural causes.

"*Amadeus* . . . is about the ravaging of genius by mediocrity," Robert Brustein writes in the *New Republic.* Some critics believe Shaffer handled his material in much the same manner, charging him with a superficial portrayal of Mozart's life. Brustein argues that "at the same time that the central character—a second-rate kapellmeister named Antonio Salieri—is plotting against the life and reputation of a superior composer named Wolfgang Amadeus Mozart, a secondary playwright named Peter Shaffer is reducing this genius, one of the greatest artists of all time, to the level of a simpering, braying ninny."

Despite complaints from reviewers, audiences received *Amadeus* enthusiastically, and it played in many European cities. Bernard Levin, writing in the London *Times,* sums up the feelings of many theatergoers by writing that "those who go to [*Amadeus*] prepared to understand what

it is about will have an experience that far transcends even its considerable value as drama." Impressed with the play's serious intentions, Gelatt writes that "*Amadeus* gives heartening evidence that there is still room for the play of ideas."

Perhaps Shaffer's most famous work is the screenplay adaptation of *Amadeus,* written in collaboration with director Milos Forman and producer Saul Zaentz. This 1984 film won several Academy Awards, including best screenplay adaptation and best picture of the year.

For the movie, Shaffer and his collaborators kept the basic story of the play, but changed several key points. For example, Shaffer tells Michiko Kakutani that in the play, Salieri had been "too much the observer of the calamities he should have been causing." In the movie, Salieri takes a more active role in Mozart's death. Vincent Canby comments in the *New York Times* that this new version of Salieri's character "may not be history, but it's the high point of this drama."

Another difference between the play and film is the way music is used. Shaffer and Forman thought music was very important to the film. Shaffer remarks to Kakutani: "In a way, Milos and I, as it were, met on that middle ground—he from film, I from the stage; he from the visual, I from the verbal. We met on ground that is neither visual nor verbal, but acoustic and abstract—we met there in music." The movie incorporated staged sequences from some of Mozart's operas and used Mozart's music in the entire soundtrack—things that were impossible to do in the play. The result, writes David Denby in *New York,* is "perhaps the juiciest dramatization in movie history of the emotional power of classical music."

Amadeus was filmed with Shaffer's characteristic visual spectacle in the centuries-old cathedrals and churches of Prague, Czechoslovakia. Geoff Brown comments in the London *Times* on the ambience of the production, writing that "so many films lie on the screen today looking shrivelled or inert; *Amadeus* sits there resplendent, both stately and supple, a compelling, darkly comic story of human glory and human infamy."

Critics voiced many of the same complaints with the movie that they had with the play, particularly attacking the supposed pretentiousness of the story. Jascha Kessler, for example, says in a radio broadcast for KUSC-FM, Los Angeles, that *Amadeus* offers us "a heavy dose of pseudo-profundities, in a formulation composed of nothing but worn-out truisms. . . . I think everyone who had anything to do with making [*Amadeus*], an example of cultural pretentiousness at its intellectual best today, ought to be ashamed."

Critic Richard A. Blake, however, writes in *America* that *Amadeus* was "the most powerful film I have seen in a long time" and praises the characters, setting, and music. In contrast to Kessler's finding, Blake believes that in the conflict between Salieri and Mozart "rests the plight of the human condition, that furious tension between what might be and what really is. For believers, there remains the question: Why is the Incarnation so capricious? Why does the spark of divinity glow in such unlikely crevices: dissolute artists, unbearable saints? . . . Salieri could not answer those questions, and they drove him to murder and insanity. Neither could Shaffer, and they drove him to drama."

In December of 1985, Shaffer's play *Yonadab: The Watcher* opened to mixed reviews. Based on the Old Testament account of King David's reign in ancient Jerusalem, the play focuses on court hanger-on Yonadab, who believes an ancient superstition that incest committed between members of the royal family promotes wisdom in government. He convinces Amnon, King David's son, to rape his own sister, Tamar. Commenting on the strikingly different subject matter of this play, Shaffer tells Higgins: "I never want to repeat myself, so it is essential to come up in a different place every time."

Although some critics express many of the same complaints about *Yonadab: The Watcher* that they have about previous Shaffer plays—historical inaccuracies, superficial treatment of theme, lack of character development—Shaffer remains undaunted. Dan Sullivan reports in the *Los Angeles Times* that Shaffer told Associated Press's Matt Wolf: "Audiences are very excited by the play; that's the main thing."

Audience reaction to 1987's *Lettice and Lovage: A Comedy* was also positive. Wolf writes in the *Chicago Tribune* that the play, "an overtly commercial, out-and-out comedy," was winning "nightly bravos and may even get an award or two." Shaffer wrote the play as a gift for actress Maggie Smith, who starred in his earlier work *Black Comedy* and plays the lead role of Lettice.

The fact that audiences are excited by Shaffer's plays is a testament to his popularity and staying power. Smith concludes that though Shaffer is sometimes slighted by critics, "none of [his] imputed failings has inhibited the lines at the box office or deterred serious theatergoers from expressing gratitude for the revitalization [he] has brought to contemporary drama."

BIOGRAPHICAL/CRITICAL SOURCES:

BOOKS

Brustein, Robert, *The Third Theatre,* Knopf, 1969.
Contemporary Literary Criticism, Gale, Volume 5, 1976, Volume 14, 1980, Volume 18, 1981, Volume 37, 1986.
Dictionary of Literary Biography, Volume 13: *British Dramatists since World War II,* Gale, 1982.
Lumley, Frederick, *New Trends in Twentieth-Century Drama,* Oxford University Press, 1967.
McCrindle, J. F., editor, *Behind the Scenes,* Holt, 1971.
Taylor, John Russell, *Anger and After,* Methuen, 1962.
Taylor, John Russell, *Peter Shaffer,* Longman, 1974.

PERIODICALS

America, October 13, 1984.
American Imago, fall, 1974.
Chicago Tribune, March 7, 1983; September 19, 1984; November 15, 1987.
Commentary, February, 1975.
Commonweal, April 25, 1975.
Drama, autumn, 1970; January, 1980.
Encounter, January, 1975.
Film Comment, September/October, 1984; January/February, 1985.
Globe and Mail (Toronto), June 13, 1987.
Guardian, August 6, 1973.
Harper's, July, 1981.
Hudson Review, summer, 1967.
Listener, February 12, 1970; December 12, 1985.
Los Angeles Times, December 10, 1982.
Modern Drama, September, 1978; March, 1985.
Monthly Film Bulletin, January, 1985.
Nation, February 27, 1967; January 17, 1981.
National Review, October 19, 1984.
New Leader, February 27, 1967.
New Republic, January 17, 1981; October 22, 1984.
New Statesman, February 13, 1970.
Newsweek, February 20, 1967; November 4, 1974; December 29, 1980.
New York, November 11, 1974; September 24, 1984.
New Yorker, February 25, 1967; November 4, 1974; March 10, 1980; December 29, 1980.
New York Times, September 29, 1968; December 23, 1979; December 18, 1980; September 16, 1984; September 19, 1984; December 22, 1985; February 13, 1987; March 26, 1990.
New York Times Magazine, August 17, 1973; October 25, 1974; October 27, 1974; April 13, 1975.
Observer, February 25, 1968; December 8, 1985.
Partisan Review, spring, 1966.
Plays and Players, November, 1979; February, 1980.
Punch, February 28, 1968.
Reporter, March 9, 1967.
Saturday Review, February 25, 1967; February, 1981.
South Atlantic Quarterly, autumn, 1980.
Spectator, March 1, 1968.
Time, November 11, 1974; December 29, 1980.

Times (London), January 9, 1985; January 18, 1985; November 28, 1985; December 6, 1985; November 17, 1988.

Vogue, March 15, 1967.

Washington Post, July 5, 1979; November 9, 1980; November 13, 1980; November 23, 1980; March 26, 1990.

OTHER

Kessler, Jascha, *Peter Shaffer: 'Amadeus,'* broadcast on KUSC-FM, Los Angeles, CA, October 12, 1984.

*   *   *

SHAH, (Sayed) Idries   1924-

PERSONAL: Born June 16, 1924, in Simla, India; son of Ikbal (a professor) and Saira (Khanum) Ali-Shah; married Cynthia Kabraji; children: Saira, Safia, Tahir. *Education:* Privately educated.

ADDRESSES: Office—c/o C. Hoare and Co., 37 Fleet St., London EC4P 4D6, England. *Agent*—c/o Collins-Knowleton-Wing, Inc., 575 Madison Ave., New York, NY; A. P. Watt Ltd., 20 John Street, London WC1NDR, England.

CAREER: International Press Agency Service, president, 1953-65; Institute for Cultural Research, London, director of studies, 1966—. Visiting professor, University of Geneva, 1972-73, and University of California, 1976; professor ad honorem, National University, La Plata, Argentina, 1974, and University of the Savior, Buenos Aires, Argentina, 1976. Patron, Cambridge Poetry Festival, 1975. Life member, National Trust; life governor, Royal Hospital and Royal National Life Boat Institution. Producer of films. Advisor to heads of state and to educational authorities in several countries.

MEMBER: Royal Economic Society (fellow), Royal Society for the Arts, Royal Commonwealth Society, Society of Authors, Folklore Society, PEN, British Association for the Advancement of Science, Athenaeum Club, Garrick Club, Club of Rome.

AWARDS, HONORS: Six first prizes, UNESCO International Book Year, 1972; Gold Medal from Cambridge University poetry festival, 1973, for services to poetry; International Community Service Award, 1973; award from Institute for the Study of Human Knowledge, 1976, for distinguished services to knowledge.

WRITINGS:

Oriental Magic, forward by Louis Martin, Rider, 1956, Philosophical Library (New York City), 1957, revised edition with illustrations by Pauline O'Donovan and Shah, Octagon Press (New York City), 1968.

Destination Mecca, Rider, 1957, 2nd edition, Octagon Press, 1969.

The Secret Lore of Magic: Books of the Sorcerers, F. Muller, 1957, 2nd edition, 1970.

The Sufis, introduction by Robert Graves, Doubleday (New York City), 1964.

The Exploits of the Incomparable Mulla Nasrudin, illustrations by Richard Williams, J. Cape, 1966.

Special Problems in the Study of Sufi Ideas, London Society for Understanding Fundamental Ideas, 1966, 2nd edition, Turnbridge Wells (Kent) Society for the Understanding of the Foundation of Ideas, 1968.

Tales of the Dervishes: Teaching Stories of the Sufi Masters over the Past Thousand Years, J. Cape, 1967.

Caravan of Dreams, Octagon Press, 1968.

Reflections, Zenith Books, 1968, 2nd edition, Octagon Press, 1969.

The Way of the Sufi, J. Cape, 1968.

The Pleasantries of the Incredible Mulla Nasrudin, illustrations by Williams and Errol LeCain, J. Cape, 1968.

The Book of the Book, Octagon Press, 1969.

Wisdom of the Idiots, Octagon Press, 1969, 2nd edition, 1970.

The Dermis Probe, J. Cape, 1970.

Thinkers of the East: Studies in Experimentalism, J. Cape, 1971, published as *Thinkers of the East,* Penguin (New York City), 1972.

The Magic Monastery: Analogical and Action Philosophy of the Middle East and Central Asia, Dutton, 1972.

The Subtleties of the Inimitable Mulla Nasrudin, illustrations by Richard Purdum, Dutton (New York City), 1973.

Graphic Sayings, Kindersley & Skelton, 1973.

The Elephant in the Dark, Octagon Press, 1974.

A Veiled Gazelle, Octagon Press, 1977.

Special Illumination: The Sufi Use of Humor, Octagon Press, 1977.

(Translator from the Persian) *Three Hundred Tales of Wisdom: Life, Teachings and Miracles of Jalaludin Rumi from Aflaki's "Munaqib," Together with Certain Important Stories from Rumi's Works,* Octagon Press, 1978.

Learning How to Learn: Psychology and Spirituality in the Sufi Way, Octagon Press, 1978.

A Perfumed Scorpion: The Way to the Way, Octagon Press, 1978.

World Tales: The Extraordinary Coincidence of Stories Told in All Times in All Places, (Book-of-the-Month Club selection), Harcourt (San Diego, CA), 1979.

Letters and Lectures of Idries Shah, compiled and edited by Adam Musa, Octagon Press, 1981.

Seeker after Truth: A Handbook, Octagon Press, 1982.

Kara Kush: A Novel, Stein & Day (Briarcliff Manor, NY), 1986.
Darkest England, Octagon Press, 1987.
The Natives Are Restless, Octagon Press, 1989.
The Commanding Self, Octagon Press, 1994.

Also contributor to *The Diffusion of Sufi Ideas in the West: An Anthology of New Writings by and about Idries Shah,* edited by Leonard Lewin, Keysign Press (Boulder, CO), 1972, 2nd edition published as *The Elephant in the Dark, and Other Writings on the Diffusion of Sufi Ideas in the West,* (also see below), Dutton, 1976. Also author of material for animated film lecture series "Contentions." Editor of monographs published by Institute for Cultural Research. Contributor of short stories and articles on Middle East topics to journals and newspapers.

ADAPTATIONS: Several films have been made from Shah's works, including *The Dermis Probe,* which was selected for showing at the New York and London film festivals, *Magnificent Idiot,* which was based on the Mulla Nasrudin books, and *Reflections.*

WORK IN PROGRESS: Adventures in the Known World and *Nail Soup,* in press.

SIDELIGHTS: Idries Shah, known as The Sayed as was his father before him, traces his descent from the Prophet Mohammed and the Emperors of Persia through the Caliph Musa al-Kasim. Following a centuries-old tradition, Shah became leader of the Sufis, or Islamic mystics, upon his father's death in 1969. He is now widely-recognized in academic and religious circles as the world's foremost expert on and proponent of the Sufi philosophy. In 1970, Shah and Sufism were the subjects of a British Broadcasting Corporation television documentary entitled *The Dreamwalkers.*

In a recent summarization of his work, Shah told *CA:* "Freeing Sufism from cultish accretions, weirdness and oriental quaintness has taken twenty-five years. The books are now fully established in academia (over 300 universities) and have a huge general readership in the East and West. Coinciding with the 1960's upsurge of interest in 'higher consciousness' made the effort doubly difficult. Both Eastern and Western students had based their opinions in this area on seriously distorted traditions. Some, including a few respected academics, still do. Essentially, Sufic thought rejects indoctrination, authority-figures and mechanical ritual as practiced in cults. Yet these are the elements which, knowingly or not, many people crave. Unfamiliarly, it is the elimination of negative features which, Sufis assert, leads to enlightenment. Several million copies on this theme, seen from various viewpoints, (and with abundant primary classical references) have now been sold. All titles are still in print, and are constantly reprinted. Extensively paperbacked and translated

into twelve languages, they are used in orientalism, literary, anthropological, sociological, religious and psychological studies, and have been widely acclaimed as general reading. The wide variety of fields invaded by this material has caused great surprise—though not to me. As a mainstream specialist, I was merely at the right place at the right time, and have made this task my avocation."

BIOGRAPHICAL/CRITICAL SOURCES:

BOOKS

Anasari, H., *Books by Idries Shah,* Key Press, 1974.
Archer, N.P., *Idries Shah: Printed Word International,* Designist Communications, 1977.
Dervish, B., *Journeys with a Sufi Master,* Octagon Press, 1982.
Easterling, R., and Kamil Hanafy, compilers, *Evenings with Idries Shah: Sufi Discussions,* Octagon Press, 1981.
Fergusson, C.R., *Idries Shah: Reviews and Comments,* Key Press, 1973.
Ghali, H., *Shah International Press Review Collection,* Octagon Press, 1979.
Griffiths, L., *Idries Shah: Published Bio-Source Materials,* Designist Communications, 1981.
Hosain, Seyyed N., *Persian, Arabic, Turkish and Urdu Profiles of Idries Shah,* Key Press, 1974.
Jazairi, A.A., *Idries Shah: What the Critics Say,* Designist Communications, 1976.
Lewin, Leonard, editor, *The Diffusion of Sufi Ideas in the West: An Anthology of New Writings by and about Idries Shah,* Keysign Press (Boulder, CO), 1972, 2nd edition published as *The Elephant in the Dark, and Other Writings on the Diffusion of Sufi Ideas in the West,* Dutton, 1976.
Martinez, C., *Idries Shah: Hispanic Critiques,* Designist Communications, 1973.
Rushbrook-Williams, L. F., editor, *Sufi Studies: East and West,* Dutton, 1973.
Yar, M., *Idries Shah: Reviews in Britain, Pakistan, South Africa,* Key Press, 1973.

PERIODICALS

Los Angeles Times Book Review, August 24, 1986.
New York Times Book Review, May 7, 1972; June 15, 1986.

*   *   *

SHAHA, Rishikesh 1925-

PERSONAL: Born May 16, 1925, in Tansen, Nepal; son of Tarak Buhadur (in government service) and Madan Divyeshvari (Rana) Shaha; married Siddhanta Rana, July

12, 1946; children: Shri Prakash (son). *Education:* Patna University, B.A., 1943, M.A. (English), 1945; Allahabad University, M.A. (political science), 1954. *Politics:* Democratic socialism. *Religion:* "Non-practicing Hindu." *Avocational interests:* Reading, writing, big game hunting, swimming.

ADDRESSES: Home and office—Shri Nivas, Kamal Pokhari, Kathmandu, Nepal.

CAREER: Tri-Chandra College, Kathmandu, Nepal, teacher of English and Nepali, 1945-48; Nepal Democratic Congress, Calcutta, India, later Kathmandu, founding member, 1948-49, leader, 1950-52; Nepal Advisory Assembly, Kathmandu, leader of the opposition, 1952; Nepali Congress, Kathmandu, general secretary, 1953-55; United Nations representative from Nepal and first residential ambassador to the United States, both 1956-60; Nepali minister of finance, 1960-62, minister of foreign affairs, 1962; chairman of Royal Commission for the Drafting of the 1962 Constitution of Nepal; special ambassador at large with cabinet rank, 1962-63; chairman of standing committee of the King's Council, 1963-64; East-West Center, Honolulu, Hawaii, senior fellow, 1965-66, alumni fellow, 1984; member of Nepal's national legislature (from graduates' constituency), 1967-71; imprisoned in solitary confinement, 1969-70; School of International Studies of Jawaharlal Nehru University, visiting professor, 1971; University of California, Berkeley, regents' professor in the department of political science, 1971-72; president of Nepal Council of World Affairs, 1973-75; arrested December, 1974; Smithsonian Institution, Washington, DC, fellow of Woodrow Wilson International Center for Scholars, 1976—; arrested May, 1977, released, 1989; campaigned for restoration of multi-party democracy before 1980 referendum; president of Human Rights Organization of Nepal, 1988—.

MEMBER: Amnesty International (president of Nepal chapter, 1973-75), Nepal Nature Conservation Society (president, 1973-75), All-Nepal College and University Teachers Association (past chairman), Nepali Literary Society (past chairman).

WRITINGS:

Nepal and the World, Khoj Parisad, Nepali Congress, 1954.
Heroes and Builders of Nepal, Oxford University Press, 1965.
Notes on Hunting and Wild Life Conservation in Nepal, privately printed, 1970.
Nepali Politics: Retrospect and Prospect, Oxford University Press (New York City), 1975.
An Introduction to Nepal, Ratna Pustak Bhandur (Kathmandu), 1976.

Essays in the Practice of Government in Nepal, Manohar (New Delhi), 1982.
(With others)*Future of South Asia,* Macmillan (India), 1986.
Modern Nepal: A Political History, 1769-1955 (two volumes), Manohar, 1990.
Three Decades and Two Kings (1960-1990): Eclipse of Nepal's Partyless Monarchic Rule, Sterling (New Delhi), 1990.
Politics in Nepal, 1980-1990: Referendum, Stalemate, and the Triumph of People Power, Manohar, 1990, third revised edition, 1993.
Ancient and Medieval Nepal, Manohar, 1992.

IN NEPALI

Igbal and Nazrul (translations of poems), Pakistan Embassy (Kathmandu), 1969.
Sarbajanik Suraksha Kanoon Ra Bandi Pratyakshikaran (title means "Public Security Act and Habeas Corpus"), privately printed, 1970.
Dalabihin Panchayati Prajatantrayek Adhikarik Prarup (title means "Partyless Panchayat Democracy: An Authoritative Outline"), privately printed, 1970.
Nepal: Rajanitik vyavastha evam pararashtra niti, Konarka (Varanasi), 1982.

Contributor to international journals, in English and Nepali.

SIDELIGHTS: Rishikesh Shaha's work with the United Nations has included many memorable experiences. In the second emergency session of the United Nations General Assembly held in October, 1956, Shaha was the first among the Asian non-aligned nations to declare support on behalf of his country for the resolution condemning Russian action in Hungary. Burma and Ceylon followed in agreement. Shaha was critically stabbed in New York City's Central Park on the opening day of the September, 1957, General Assembly. He maintained, however, that hoodlums are hoodlums everywhere in the world and that it could have happened to him even in his own capital. He won acclaim by confronting Kruschev in the General Assembly of 1960, sometimes called "the session of the shoe and the broken gavel." Shaha said that "new members of the United Nations are not likely to be bullied or blackmailed by a show of force into accepting a super power's line of thought, because they value their freedom of judgement and action." In 1961, Shaha was elected chairman of the international commission set up by the General Assembly to investigate the circumstances leading to the death of Dag Hammarskjoeld.

Shaha has been imprisoned several times in connection with his agitation for human rights and the rule of law in Nepal. In May, 1977, he was arrested for the publication of his article "Recent Amendments to the Constitution of

Nepal," published in the *India Left Review* in August, 1976. In addition, Shaha has participated in international conferences of lawyers and jurists, and he has traveled widely in Europe, India, China, Japan, and Africa.

*   *   *

SHATTUCK, Charles H(arlen)   1910-1992

PERSONAL: Born November 23, 1910, near Belvidere, IL; died following a long illness, September 21, 1992, in Urbana, IL; son of D. H. and Katherine (Hines) Shattuck; married Susan Deuel, 1936; children: Kate, Judith. *Education:* University of Illinois, A.B., 1932, M.A., 1934, Ph.D., 1938.

CAREER: University of Illinois at Urbana-Champaign, assistant in English, beginning 1934, professor of English, 1958-79, professor emeritus, beginning 1979, director in the University Theatre, 1943-63, member of Center for Advanced Study, 1965-66. Henry Noble MacCracken Professor of English and director of experimental theater, Vassar College, 1948-49; visiting professor, University of Colorado, 1964, University of Tennessee, 1979, and State University of New York College at Plattsburgh, 1980.

MEMBER: Shakespeare Association of America (president, 1979-80).

AWARDS, HONORS: Folger Shakespeare Library fellow, 1959, 1961, 1974, and 1978; Guggenheim fellow, 1961-62 and 1968-69; George Freedley Award for best book on theater, 1969, for *The Hamlet of Edwin Booth,* 1976, for *Shakespeare on the American Stage,* Volume 1, and 1987, for *Shakespeare on the American Stage,* Volume 2; Barnard Hewitt Award for outstanding research in theater history, 1987, for *Shakespeare on the American Stage,* Volume 2.

WRITINGS:

(Editor with Kerker Quin) *Accent Anthology,* Harcourt (New York City), 1946.
Bulwer and Macready: A Chronicle of the Early Victorian Theatre, University of Illinois Press (Champaign), 1958.
Mr. Macready Produces "As You Like It," Beta Phi Mu (Pittsburgh), 1962.
(Editor) *William Charles Macready's "King John,"* University of Illinois Press, 1962.
The Shakespeare Promptbooks: A Descriptive Catalogue, University of Illinois Press, 1965.
Merry Wives of Windsor: Six Episodes in the Life of a Play, Dell (New York City), 1966.
The Hamlet of Edwin Booth, University of Illinois Press, 1969.

(Contributor) Joseph Donohue, editor, *The Theatrical Manager in England and America,* Princeton University Press (Princeton, NJ), 1971.
(Contributor) Oscar Brockett, editor, *Studies in Theatre and Drama,* Mouton (Hawthorne, NY), 1972.
(Coeditor) *Accent: An Anthology, 1940-1960,* University of Illinois Press, 1973.
John Philip Kemble Promptbooks, eleven volumes, Folger Shakespeare Library (Cranburynswick, NY), 1974.
(Contributor) G. B. Evans, editor, *The Riverside Shakespeare,* Houghton (Boston), 1974.
Shakespeare on the American Stage, Folger Books, Volume 1, 1976, Volume 2, 1987.

Contributor of reviews and articles to *Journal of English and Germanic Philology, Shakespeare Quarterly, Theatre Notebook, Theatre Survey, Nineteenth-Century Theatre Research,* and other drama and theater journals. Coeditor, *Accent: A Quarterly of New Literature,* 1940-60.

OBITUARIES:

PERIODICALS

Chicago Tribune, September 23, 1992, section 3, p. 13.
New York Times, September 23, 1992, p. B7.*

*   *   *

SHATTUCK, Roger (Whitney)   1923-

PERSONAL: Born August 20, 1923, in New York, NY; son of Howard F. (a physician) and Elizabeth (Colt) Shattuck; married Nora Ewing White (a dancer), August 20, 1949; children: Tari Elizabeth, Marc Ewing, Patricia Colt, Eileen Shepard. *Education:* Yale University, B.A., 1947.

ADDRESSES: Office—Boston University, University Professors Program, 745 Commonwealth Ave., Boston, MA 02215-1401.

CAREER: UNESCO, Paris, France, information officer in film section, 1947-48; *Chicago Daily News,* Chicago, IL, reporter in Paris, 1948-49; Harcourt, Brace & Co. (publishers), New York, NY, assistant trade editor, 1949-50; Harvard University, Cambridge, MA, member of Society of Fellows, 1950-53, instructor in French, 1953-56; University of Texas at Austin, assistant professor, 1956-59, associate professor of romance languages, 1959-62, professor of French and English, 1962-71, chairman of department of French and Italian, 1968-71; free-lance writer, 1971-74; University of Virginia, Charlottesville, Commonwealth Professor of French, 1974-88; Boston University, university professor and professor of modern languages, 1988—. Lecturer at various universities, museums, and art galleries. Provediteur general, College de Pataphysique, 1961—; National Translation Center, member of advisory board, 1964-69, chairman, 1966-69; member of National Humanities Faculty, 1972-73. *Military service:* U.S. Army Air Forces, 1942-45; served as pilot in Southwest Pacific; became captain.

AWARDS, HONORS: Guggenheim fellow, 1958-59; Fulbright research fellow, 1958-59; American Council of Learned Societies research fellow, 1969-70; decorated Ordre des Palmes Academiques; National Book Award, 1975, for *Marcel Proust;* National Book Critics Circle Award nomination for *The Innocent Eye,* 1984; the American Academy and Institute of Arts and Letters award, 1987; elected to American Academy of Arts and Sciences, 1990; Doctorat honoris causa, Universite d'Orleans, France, 1990.

WRITINGS:

NONFICTION

The Banquet Years: The Origins of the Avant-Garde in France, 1885 to World War One, Harcourt, 1958, revised edition, Vintage Books, 1968.
Proust's Binoculars: A Study of Memory, Time & Recognition in A La Recherche du Temps Perdu, Random House, 1963.
Marcel Proust, Viking, 1974.
The Forbidden Experiment: The Story of the Wild Boy of Aveyron, Farrar, Straus, 1980.
The Innocent Eye: On Literature and the Arts, Farrar, Straus, 1984.
(And author of introduction) *The History of Surrealism,* Harvard University Press, 1989.
Henri Rousseau, Abrams, 1991.

EDITOR

(And translator) Rene Daumal, *Mount Analogue: A Novel of Symbolically Authentic Non-Euclidean Adventures in Mountain Climbing,* Pantheon, 1960.
(With William Arrowsmith) *The Craft and Context of Translation,* University of Texas Press, 1961.
(And translator) *The Selected Writings of Guillaume Apollinaire,* New Directions, 1963, revised edition, New Directions, 1971.
(With Simon W. Taylor) *Selected Writings of Alfred Jarry: Ubu Cuckolded, Exploits & Opinions of Dr. Faustroll, Pataphysician, & Other Writings,* Grove, 1966.
(And translator with Frederick Brown) Paul Valery, *Occasions,* Princeton University Press, 1970.

OTHER

Half Tame (poetry; illustrated by Naoko Matusubara), University of Texas Press, 1964.
(Translator) Daumal, *A Fundamental Experiment* (short stories and essays), Hanuman Books, 1987.

Also author of introduction, *Nights as Day, Days as Night* by Michel Leiris, translated by Richard Sieburth, (French title, *Nuit sans Nuit*), Marsilio Publishers, 1988, and *Exploits & Opinions of Dr. Faustroll, Pataphysician* by Alfred Jarry, translated by Simon W. Taylor, Exact Change, 1993. Contributor to *Best Short Stories of 1953* and *Two Lives—Georgia O'Keefe and Alfred Stieglitz: A Conversation in Paintings and Photographs* (essays), edited by Alexandra Arrowsmith and Thomas V. West, Callaway Editions, 1992. Contributor of short stories to *Harper's, Discovery,* and other publications; contributor of poetry to *New Republic, Virginia Quarterly Review, Hudson Review, Poetry, New Yorker,* and other publications. Advisory editor, *Texas Quarterly,* 1958-60, *Delos, International Drama, Texas Studies in Literature and Language, Teaching Language through Literature,* and *Texas Observer;* member of editorial board, *PMLA,* 1977-78.

SIDELIGHTS: In his book *The Forbidden Experiment,* author Roger Shattuck, a noted Marcel Proust scholar, recounts the story of the so-called "Wild Boy of Aveyron." The story begins on January 9, 1800, when a frightened, half-naked boy was captured in the woods near Saint-Sernin, France, a village in a region known as Aveyron. Victor, as he eventually came to be called, appeared to be about twelve years old but was just over four feet tall, was not housebroken, and could not speak; his only interests seemed to be food and sleep. No one knew where, when, or why he had been abandoned, though the many scars on his body hinted at the possibility of earlier abuse or a long life of hardship in the forest.

During most of the early part of his captivity, Victor was cared for by a succession of intelligent and scientifically curious people who treated him with kindness. Meanwhile, reports of his existence—many of which contained wildly exaggerated descriptions of his appearance and behavior—proliferated to the point where Lucien Bonaparte, brother of Napoleon and minister of the interior, summoned the child to the Paris Institute for Deaf-Mutes so that he might be examined by members of the newly formed Society of the Observers of Man. The Society, seeing in Victor the opportunity to study a person who had been relatively untouched by civilization, hoped to find in him the answers to questions philosophers had pondered for centuries: What is Man's basic nature and what has civilization imposed upon him? Is his behavior learned or innate? Is he by nature an aggressive beast who requires the rigid controls of society or a "noble savage" who should be allowed to develop freely? The idea of deliberately separating a child from human society for experimental purposes was unthinkable; here was a boy, however, who seemed to represent the best alternative.

After several months, disappointed members of the Society were forced to conclude that Victor was either an incurable imbecile or a deaf-mute and therefore not worthy of further study, mostly because he was not able to tell them what they wanted to know. But one medical student at the Institute disagreed with his superiors and eventually received permission to take the young boy into his care. Dr. Jean-Marc Gispard Itard, a solitary man in his mid-twenties who devoted much of his time to research, was determined to communicate with Victor and to teach him to communicate with others. Unlike his colleagues, Itard felt that Victor was a prime example of John Locke's *tabula rasa,* the "blank slate" upon which could be "written" everything that would help to bring him to life and then to a civilized state. The doctor thus took it upon himself to expose Victor to all of the experiences and sensations deemed appropriate to bring about this awakening. He arranged a variety of outings and visits to leading salons of the day; he introduced Victor to mirrors, hot baths, and numerous games designed to develop his intelligence; he taught him to say a few words (mostly dealing with food) and to associate objects with their visual representations. Victor also learned to cry and to demand and to show affection.

Itard worked with Victor for five years until the onset of puberty caused the boy to experience bursts of uncontrollable curiosity, rage, desire, and frustration. Disturbed and discouraged by the changes in his pupil, Itard gave up all hope of civilizing Victor and finally turned him over to his foster mother, a benevolent and affectionate woman named Madame Guerin. (She had been caring for him almost since the day of his arrival in Paris.) Victor lived with Madame Guerin until he died (of unknown causes) in 1928. Itard later became famous for his pioneering work in educating the deaf.

Drawing his material from several previous studies, especially Dr. Itard's own papers, Shattuck, according to *Newsweek's* Jean Strouse, "goes beyond these sources in his superb account of the wild boy of Aveyron. Erudite but never showy, he pieces the full story together, places it in scientific and social context, and animates his narrative with lively asides. . . . Shattuck assesses but sees no need to pass judgment on this remarkable story. . . . [His] careful reconstruction of [Victor's] experiences—with the twentieth century's perspectives on psychology, history, philosophy, and linguistics—adds a rich new chapter to the interesting debate about nature vs. nurture."

"Roger Shattuck has done a beautiful job of re-creating the story, skillfully using a wealth of known documents and discovering a few new ones," notes Howard E. Gruber in the *New York Times Book Review.* "Although there have been other good books about the wild child, Mr. Shattuck's has the merits of conciseness, completeness, humanity and just enough detachment." Anthony Storr of the *Spectator* agrees, describing *The Forbidden Experi-*

ment as "an admirably written, thoughtful, and movingly perceptive account of the Wild Boy and his mentors" that "will appeal to a wider readership" than previous studies. The *Los Angeles Times's* Robert Kirsch praises Shattuck's "insight and compassion" as well as his ability to be "objective and critical where necessary," while the *New York Times's* John Leonard declares that "no one has ever addressed the issues—of freedom, humanity, culture, doubt and wonder—with more intelligence and grace than Mr. Shattuck."

On the other hand, Rodney Needham, commenting in the *Washington Post Book World,* feels that "there is something of a puzzle that [*The Forbidden Experiment*] should have been put into print" considering the number of times other people have written books on the same subject. Still, the critic goes on to note, "within its limits the book comes off perhaps well enough: it provides a chronological description of the events (divided by Itard according to theoretical interests), together with useful incidental materials. Inspired by the intrinsic poignancy of the tale, it makes a convenient introduction to an adventitious but inexhaustibly interesting experiment."

Robert Darnton of the *New York Review of Books* also wonders why Shattuck decided to contribute yet another volume to the collection of wild boy literature. He finds *The Forbidden Experiment* "thin by comparison" to an earlier work, Harlan Lane's *The Wild Boy of Aveyron,* stating that "it contains no new finding, and it goes over the old ground so lightly as to read in places like a parody of a textbook." He also has reservations that *The Forbidden Experiment* represents just one more interpretation of Itard's interpretation of Victor's unfathomable behavior; in other words, it's not exactly the "straightforward narrative" Shattuck prefers to call it.

Yet, like Needham, even Darnton admits that "to dismiss *the Forbidden Experiment* as inadequate history—too little too late in the marketplace of ideas—would be to miss its point. It deserves to be read as a story. . . . This is no anthropological exhibit but a fellow human speaking to us from across two centuries of time. The aura of experimentation fades, and we are left with a picture of the lonely scientist and his dumb companion at the end of their day's work." "It is a beautiful story," concludes Darnton, "and we feel grateful to Shattuck for telling it so well."

In his 1984 work, *The Innocent Eye,* Shattuck offers his opinions on modern literature and the arts. The book includes essays and reviews written between 1960 and 1983 on subjects ranging from artists Claude Monet and Marcel Duchamp to authors Charles-Pierre Baudelaire and Honore de Balzac to Dada and Surrealism. "Culturally, [Shattuck's] concerns are France (primary) and the United States (secondary); chronologically, he is mainly interested in 'middle-distance' modernism," states Robert M. Adams in the *Washington Post Book World*. He adds that "Shattuck sets forth his subjects with the lucidity and order of a good teacher; he is at the same time a stiff polemicist, who does not hesitate to make known his own point of view toward the topics under discussion." Germaine Bree, writing in the *New York Times Book Review*, observes that "Shattuck's is a fast-paced, interesting book spun out of a wealth of intimately assimilated culture. There is no question in his mind as to the value of that culture in forging an art of living both privately and collectively as civilized human beings. What concerns him is the role of the teacher and critic in discerning amid the welter of theories and facts those nodes, or active centers, of human creativity that keep a culture alive."

BIOGRAPHICAL/CRITICAL SOURCES:

PERIODICALS

Detroit News, December 13, 1984.
Listener, August 14, 1980.
Los Angeles Times, April 7, 1980.
Los Angeles Times Book Review, May 5, 1985, p. 10.
Nation, March 16, 1985, p. 309.
New Republic, April 12, 1980.
Newsweek, April 28, 1980.
New York Review of Books, May 15, 1980.
New York Times, April 22, 1980; December 17, 1984, p. 21; April 8, 1987.
New York Times Book Review, July 27, 1980; October 3, 1982; February 3, 1985, p. 14.
Spectator, August 23, 1980.
Times Literary Supplement, October 31, 1980; May 23, 1986, p. 573.
Washington Post Book World, July 20, 1980; December 30, 1984, p. 4.

* * *

SHERIFF, John K(cith) 1944-

PERSONAL: Born April 10, 1944, in McPherson, KS; son of Albert Edward (a minister) and Veda Marie (a homemaker; maiden name, Holcomb) Sheriff; married Elsie Mae Bacon (director of sales and customer service for a press); children: John Kent, Karen Malee. *Education:* Greenville College, B.A., 1966; University of Illinois at Urbana-Champaign, M.A., 1967; University of Oklahoma, Ph.D., 1972.

ADDRESSES: Home—P. O. Box 154, 315 East 24th St., North Newton, KS 67117. *Office*—Department of English, Bethel College, North Newton, KS 67117.

CAREER: Bethel College, North Newton, KS, instructor in English, 1967-69; University of Oklahoma, Norman, in-

structor in English, 1971-72; Bethel College, North Newton, assistant professor, 1972-75, associate professor, 1975-81, professor of English, 1981-89, E. E. Leisy Distinguished Professor of English, 1990—. Visiting fellow at University of Kansas, 1979.

MEMBER: American Association of University Professors, National Council of Teachers of English, Midwest Modern Language Association, Midwestern American Society for Eighteenth-Century Studies.

AWARDS, HONORS: Andrew Mellon postdoctoral senior fellowship from University of Kansas, 1979; Lilly Foundation grant from University of Denver, 1981; National Endowment for the Humanities research fellowship, 1983-84; David H. Richert Distinguished Scholar Award, Bethel College, 1988.

WRITINGS:

The Good-Natured Man: The Evolution of a Moral Ideal, 1660-1800, University of Alabama Press (University, AL), 1982.
The Fate of Meaning: Charles Peirce, Structuralism, and Literature, Princeton University Press (Princeton, NJ), 1989.
(Editor) *A Drink from the Stream,* Bethel College (North Newton, KS), 1991.
Charles Peirce's Guess at the Riddle: Grounds for Human Significance, Indiana University Press (Bloomington), 1994.

Also contributor to *Semiotic Themes,* edited by Richard T. DeGeorge, University of Kansas Publications, 1981.

WORK IN PROGRESS: The Scarlet A: The Study of a Sign, in press.

SIDELIGHTS: John K. Sheriff once told *CA:* "My writing is almost always related to philosophical issues in the context of literary studies. My first book was a study of eighteenth-century fiction in its philosophical context, and *The Fate of Meaning* is a critique of the treatment of meaning in contemporary literary theory. This penchant for tackling big issues is also reflected in my most recent book, *Charles Peirce's Guess at the Riddle: Grounds for Human Significance.* Nathan Houser says in the foreword to this work, 'This is a book about human meaning—not in the technical and analytical sense, but as an answer to the human predicament. Sheriff writes for those whose interest in Peirce is rooted in the humanities: in theology, semiotics, literary theory, and esthetics. He expounds Peirce's original unified theory of the universe—from cosmology to semiotic—and develops Peirce's message for human life: there is no need for resignation or for despair, for there is a real 'possibility of unlimited intellectual and moral growth and *of unlimited survival* for the human community.' "

SICHEL, Werner 1934-

PERSONAL: Born September 23, 1934, in Munich, Germany; son of Joseph and Lilly (Greenwood) Sichel; married Beatrice Bonne, February 22, 1959; children: Lawrence, Linda. *Education:* New York University, B.S., 1956; Northwestern University, M.A., 1960, Ph.D., 1964.

ADDRESSES: Home—123 Merriweather Lane, Kalamazoo, MI 49006. *Office*—Department of Economics, Western Michigan University, Kalamazoo, MI 49008.

CAREER: Roosevelt University, Chicago, IL, assistant professor, 1959-60; Western Michigan University, Kalamazoo, instructor, 1960-64, assistant professor, 1964-66, associate professor, 1966-72, professor of economics, 1972—, chairperson of department, 1985—. Instructor, Lake Forest College, 1959-62; Fulbright senior lecturer, University of Belgrade, 1968-69; visiting scholar, Hoover Institution, Stanford University, 1984-85.

MEMBER: American Economic Association, Midwest Business Economics Association (president, 1989-90), Midwest Economics Association (president, 1994-95).

WRITINGS:

(Editor) *Industrial Organization and Public Policy: Selected Readings,* Houghton (Boston), 1967.

(Editor) *Antitrust Policy and Economic Welfare,* Bureau of Business Research, University of Michigan (Ann Arbor), 1970.

(With Peter Eckstein) *Basic Economic Concepts: An Aid to the Study of Economic Problems,* Volume 1: *Microeconomics,* Volume 2: *Macroeconomics,* Rand McNally (Chicago), 1974, 2nd edition, 1977.

(Editor with Thomas G. Gies) *Public Utility Regulation: Change and Scope,* Heath (Lexington, MA), 1975.

(Editor) *The Economic Effects of Multinational Corporations,* Bureau of Business Research, University of Michigan, 1975.

(Editor) *Salvaging Public Utility Regulation,* Lexington Books (Lexington, MA), 1976.

(Editor) *Economic Advice and Executive Policy: Recommendations from Past Members of the Council of Economic Advisers,* Praeger (New York City), 1978.

(Editor) *Public Utility Rate Making in an Energy Conscious Environment,* Westview (Boulder, CO), 1979.

(Editor with Gies) *Applications of Economic Principles in Public Utility Industries,* Division of Research, Graduate School of Business Administration, University of Michigan, 1981.

(Editor with Gies) *Deregulation: Appraisal before the Fact,* Division of Research, Graduate School of Business Administration, University of Michigan, 1982.

(With Martin Bronfenbrenner and Wayland Gardner) *Economics,* Volume I: *Macroeconomics,* Volume II: *Microeconomics,* with study guide, instructor's manual, and test bank, Houghton, 1984, 3rd edition, 1990.

(With wife, Beatrice Sichel) *Economic Journals and Serials: An Analytical Guide,* Greenwood Press (Westport, CT), 1986.

(Editor) *The State of Economic Science: The Views of Six Nobel Laureates,* W. E. Upjohn Institute for Employment Research, 1989.

Contributor of articles to professional journals, including *Journal of Risk and Insurance, St. John's Law Review, Antitrust Bulletin, Antitrust Law and Economic Review,* and *Journal of Economic Issues.*

*   *   *

SILVERSTEIN, Shel(by) 1932-
(Uncle Shelby)

PERSONAL: Born in Chicago, IL; divorced; children: one daughter.

ADDRESSES: Office—c/o Grapefruit Productions, 106 Montague St., Brooklyn, NY 11201.

CAREER: Cartoonist, composer, lyricist, folksinger, writer, and director. *Playboy,* Chicago, IL, writer and cartoonist, 1956—. Appeared in film, *Who Is Harry Kellerman and Why Is He Saying Those Terrible Things about Me?,* 1971. *Military service:* Served with U.S. forces in Japan and Korea during 1950s; cartoonist for Pacific *Stars and Stripes.*

AWARDS, HONORS: New York Times Outstanding Book Award, 1974, Michigan Young Readers' Award, 1981, and George G. Stone Award, 1984, all for *Where the Sidewalk Ends: The Poems & Drawings of Shel Silverstein; School Library Journal* Best Books Award, 1981, Buckeye Award, 1983 and 1985, George G. Stone Award, 1984, and William Allen White Award, 1984, all for *A Light In the Attic;* International Reading Association's Children's Choice Award, 1982, for *The Missing Piece Meets the Big O.*

WRITINGS:

SELF-ILLUSTRATED

Now Here's My Plan: A Book of Futilities, foreword by Jean Shepherd, Simon & Schuster (New York City), 1960.

Uncle Shelby's ABZ Book: A Primer for Tender Young Minds (humor), Simon & Schuster, 1961.

Playboy's Teevee Jeebies (drawings), Playboy Press (Chicago), 1963.

Uncle Shelby's Story of Lafcadio, the Lion Who Shot Back (juvenile), Harper (New York City), 1963.

The Giving Tree (juvenile), Harper, 1964.

Uncle Shelby's Giraffe and a Half (verse; juvenile), Harper, 1964, published in England as *A Giraffe and a Half,* J. Cape (London), 1988.

Uncle Shelby's Zoo: Don't Bump the Glump! (verse; juvenile), Simon & Schuster, 1964.

(Under pseudonym Uncle Shelby) *Who Wants a Cheap Rhinoceros!,* Macmillan (New York City), 1964.

More Playboy's Teevee Jeebies: Do-It-Yourself Dialog for the Late Late Show (drawings), Playboy Press, 1965.

Where the Sidewalk Ends: The Poems & Drawings of Shel Silverstein (poems), Harper, 1974.

The Missing Piece (juvenile), Harper, 1976.

Different Dances (drawings), Harper, 1979.

A Light in the Attic (poems), Harper, 1981.

The Missing Piece Meets the Big O (juvenile), Harper, 1981.

PLAYS

The Lady or the Tiger Show (one-act; from the short story by Frank Stockton), first produced in New York City at Ensemble Studio Theatre, May, 1981.

(And director) *Gorilla,* first produced in Chicago, 1983.

Wild Life (contains *I'm Good to My Doggies, Nonstop, Chicken Suit Optional,* and *The Lady or the Tiger Show*), first produced in New York City, 1983.

Remember Crazy Zelda?, first produced in New York City, 1984.

The Crate, first produced in New York City, 1985.

The Happy Hour, first produced in New York City, 1985.

One Tennis Shoe, first produced in New York City, 1985.

Little Feet, first produced in New York City, 1986.

Wash and Dry, first produced in New York City, 1986.

The Devil and Billy Markham (drama; produced in New York City at Lincoln Center, December, 1989, with David Mamet's *Bobby Gould in Hell* under the collective title *Oh, Hell*) published in *Oh, Hell!: Two One-Act Plays,* Samuel French (New York City), 1991.

(Contributor) Billy Aronson, editor, *The Best American Short Plays 1992-1993: The Theatre Annual since 1937,* Applause (Diamond Bar, CA), 1993.

OTHER

(Contributor) Myra Cohn Livingston, editor, *I Like You, If You Like Me: Poems of Friendship,* Margaret McElderry Books (New York City), 1987.

(With David Mamet) *Things Change* (screenplay), Grove Press (New York City), 1988.

Also composer and lyricist of songs, including "A Boy Named Sue," "One's on the Way," "The Unicorn," "Boa Constrictor," "So Good to So Bad," "The Great Conch Train Robbery," and "Yes, Mr. Rogers." Albums of Silverstein's songs recorded by others include *Freakin' at the Freakers Ball,* Columbia, 1972; *Sloppy Seconds,* Columbia, 1972; *Dr. Hook,* Columbia, 1972; and *Bobby Bare*

Sings Lullabys, Legends, and Lies: The Songs of Shel Silverstein, RCA Victor, 1973. Albums of original motion picture scores include *Ned Kelly,* United Artists, 1970, and *Who Is Harry Kellerman and Why Is He Saying Those Terrible Things about Me?* Columbia, 1971. Other recordings include *Drain My Brain,* Cadet; *Dirty Feet,* Hollis Music, 1968; *Shel Silverstein: Songs and Stories,* Casablanca, 1978; *The Great Conch Train Robbery,* 1980; and *Where the Sidewalk Ends,* Columbia, 1984. *The Giving Tree* has been translated into French.

ADAPTATIONS: The film version of *Things Change* was directed by Mamet and released by Columbia Pictures in 1988.

SIDELIGHTS: Shel Silverstein is best known for his collections of children's poetry *Where the Sidewalk Ends: The Poems & Drawings of Shel Silverstein* and *A Light in the Attic,* both of which enjoyed extended stays on the *New York Times* Bestseller List. Silverstein is also the author of the children's classic *The Giving Tree.* In addition to his writings for children, Silverstein has served as a longtime *Playboy* cartoonist, has written several plays for adults, and has penned and recorded such country and novelty songs as Johnny Cash's "A Boy Named Sue."

As Edwin McDowell reported in the *New York Times Book Review,* Silverstein "for several years now . . . has refused interviews and publicity tours, and he even asked his publisher not to give out any biographical information about him." It is, however, known that Silverstein was born in Chicago in 1932, is divorced, and has one daughter. In one of the few interviews he has granted, a 1975 *Publishers Weekly* interview with Jean F. Mercier, Silverstein discussed his earliest literary beginnings: "When I was a kid—12, 14, around there—I would much rather have been a good baseball player or a hit with the girls. But I couldn't play ball, I couldn't dance. . . . So, I started to draw and to write. I was . . . lucky that I didn't have anyone to copy, be impressed by. I had developed my own style, I was creating before I knew there was a Thurber, a Benchley, a Price and a Steinberg. I never saw their work till I was around 30."

Silverstein's talents were well-developed when he joined the U.S. armed forces in the 1950s. Stationed in Japan and Korea, he worked as a cartoonist for the Pacific edition of the military newspaper *Stars and Stripes.* After his release, Silverstein became a cartoonist for *Playboy* in 1956, and his work for that magazine resulted in such collections as *Playboy's Teevee Jeebies* and *More Playboy's Teevee Jeebies: Do-It-Yourself Dialog for the Late Late Show.*

Silverstein's career as a children's author began with the 1963 publication of *Uncle Shelby's Story of Lafcadio, the Lion Who Shot Back.* He confided to Mercier: "I never planned to write or draw for kids. It was Tomi Ungerer, a friend of mine, who insisted . . . practically dragged me, kicking and screaming, into (editor) Ursula Nordstrom's office. And she convinced me that Tomi was right, I could do children's books." *Lafcadio* concerns a lion who obtains a hunter's gun and practices until he becomes a good enough marksman to join a circus. A *Publishers Weekly* reviewer called the book "a wild, free-wheeling, slangy tale that most children and many parents will enjoy immensely."

Although *Lafcadio* and *Uncle Shelby's Giraffe and a Half* met with moderate success, it was not until *The Giving Tree* that Silverstein first achieved widespread fame as a children's writer. The story of a tree that sacrifices its shade, fruit, branches, and finally its trunk to a little boy in order to make him happy, *The Giving Tree* had slow sales initially, but its audience steadily grew. As Richard R. Lingeman reported in the *New York Times Book Review*, "Many readers saw a religious symbolism in the altruistic tree; ministers preached sermons on *The Giving Tree;* it was discussed in Sunday schools." Despite its popularity as a moral or fable, the book was on occasion attacked by feminist critics for what they perceived as its inherent sexism; Barbara A. Schram noted in *Interracial Books for Children:* "By choosing the female pronoun for the all-giving tree and the male pronoun for the all-taking boy, it is clear that the author did indeed have a prototypical master/slave relationship in mind . . . How frightening that little boys and girls who read *The Giving Tree* will encounter this glorification of female selflessness and male selfishness."

In 1974 Silverstein published the collection of poems titled *Where the Sidewalk Ends.* Earning Silverstein favorable comparisons to Dr. Seuss and Edward Lear, *Where the Sidewalk Ends* contained such humorous pieces as "Sarah Cynthia Sylvia Stout / Would Not Take the Garbage Out," "Dreadful," and "Band-Aids." The collection and its 1981 successor, *A Light in the Attic,* continue to be popular with both children and adults; *Publishers Weekly* called the latter book "a big, fat treasure for Silverstein devotees, with trenchant verses expressing high-flown, exhilarating nonsense as well as thoughts unexpectedly sober and even sad."

Silverstein's 1976 *The Missing Piece*, like *The Giving Tree*, has been subject to varying interpretations. The volume chronicles the adventures of a circle who, lacking a piece of itself, goes along singing and searching for its missing part. But after the circle finds the wedge, he decides he was happier on the search—without the missing wedge—than he is with it. As Anne Roiphe explained in the *New York Times Book Review, The Missing Piece* can be read in the same way as "the fellow at the singles bar explaining why life is better if you don't commit yourself to anyone

for too long—the line goes that too much togetherness turns people into bores—that creativity is preserved by freedom to explore from one relationship to another. . . . This fable can also be interpreted to mean that no one should try to find all the answers, no one should hope to fill all the holes in themselves, achieve total transcendental harmony or psychic order because a person without a search, loose ends, internal conflicts and external goals becomes too smooth to enjoy or know what's going on. Too much satisfaction blocks exchange with the outside." Silverstein published a sequel, *The Missing Piece Meets the Big O,* in 1981. This work is told from the missing piece's perspective, and as in the original, the book's protagonist discovers the value of self-sufficiency.

Since 1981, Silverstein has concentrated on writing plays for adults. One of his best known, *The Lady or the Tiger Show,* has been performed on its own and with other one-act works collectively entitled *Wild Life.* Updating a short story by American novelist and fiction writer Frank Stockton, *The Lady or the Tiger Show* concerns a game show producer willing to go to extreme lengths to achieve high ratings. Placed in a life-or-death situation, the contestant of the show is forced to choose between two doors; behind one door lies a ferocious tiger while the girl of his dreams is concealed behind the other. The play was characterized in *Variety* as "a hilarious harpooning of media hype and show biz amorality."

Silverstein has also collaborated with American playwright, scriptwriter, director, and novelist David Mamet on several projects. The two cowrote the screenplay for Mamet's 1988 film *Things Change,* which starred Joe Mantegna and Don Ameche. Silverstein's play *The Devil and Billy Markham* and Mamet's *Bobby Gould in Hell* have also been published and produced together under the collective title *Oh, Hell.* Performed as a monologue, *The Devil and Billy Markham* relates a series of bets made between Satan and a Nashville songwriter and singer. Although the work received mixed reviews, William A. Henry III noted in *Time* that "Silverstein's script, told in verse with occasional bursts of music, is rowdy and rousing and raunchily uproarious, especially in a song about a gala party where saints and sinners mingle."

BIOGRAPHICAL/CRITICAL SOURCES:

BOOKS

Children's Literature Review, Volume 5, Gale (Detroit), 1983, pp. 208-213.
Twentieth-Century Children's Writers, 3rd edition, St. James Press (Detroit), 1989, pp. 886-887.

PERIODICALS

Book Week, March 21, 1965.
Detroit News, November 4, 1979.

Interracial Books for Children, Volume 5, number 5, 1974.
Nation, January 29, 1990, pp. 141-44.
New Republic, January 29, 1990, pp. 27-8.
Newsweek, December 7, 1981.
New York, May 30, 1983, p. 75; December 18, 1989, pp. 105-07.
New Yorker, November 14, 1988, p. 89; December 25, 1989, p. 77.
New York Times, May 29, 1981; October 11, 1981.
New York Times Book Review, September 24, 1961; September 9, 1973; November 3, 1974; May 2, 1976; April 30, 1978; November 25, 1979; November 8, 1981; March 9, 1986, pp. 36-37.
People, August 18, 1980.
Publishers Weekly, October 28, 1963; February 24, 1975; September 18, 1981.
Saturday Review, November 30, 1974; May 15, 1976.
Time, December 18, 1989, p. 78.
Variety, May 11, 1983, p. 112; December 13, 1989, p. 89.
Washington Post Book World, April 12, 1981.
Wilson Library Bulletin, November, 1987, p. 65.*

*   *   *

SMITH, Duane A(llan) 1937-

PERSONAL: Born April 20, 1937, in San Diego, CA; son of Stanley W. (a dentist) and Ila (Bark) Smith; married Gay Woodruff, August 20, 1960; children: Laralee Ellen. *Education:* University of Colorado, B.A., 1959, M.A., 1961, Ph.D., 1964. *Avocational interests:* Jogging and other sports, conservation, gardening, and politics.

ADDRESSES: Home—2911 Cedar Ave., Durango, CO 81301. *Office*—Department of History, Fort Lewis College, Durango, CO 81301.

CAREER: Fort Lewis College, Durango, CO, assistant professor, 1964-67, associate professor, 1967-72, professor of history, 1972—.

MEMBER: Society for American Baseball Research, Western History Association, Colorado Historical Society, Montana Historical Society, Mining History Association, Phi Alpha Theta.

AWARDS, HONORS: Huntington Library research grants, 1968, 1973, and 1978; Hafen Award, 1971, for outstanding magazine article; Certificate of Commendation, 1974, for *Horace Tabor: His Life and the Legend,* and Award of Merit, 1981, both from American Association for State and Local History; Westerners' Little Joe Award, 1977, for *Colorado Mining: A Photographic History;* Society for Technical Communication Award of Distinction, 1980, for *Secure the Shadow: Lachlan McLean, Colorado Mining Photographer,* and 1983, for *Song of the*

Hammer and Drill: The Colorado San Juans, 1860-1914; Colorado Humanist of the Year, 1989; Colorado Professor of the Year, 1990.

WRITINGS:

Rocky Mountain Mining Camps: The Urban Frontier, Indiana University Press (Bloomington), 1967.
(With M. Benson and C. Ubbelohde) *A Colorado History,* Pruett (Boulder, CO), 1972, revised edition, 1987.
Horace Tabor: His Life and the Legend, Colorado Associated University Press (Boulder, CO), 1973.
Silver Saga: The Story of Caribou, Colorado, Pruett, 1974.
Colorado Mining: A Photographic History, University of New Mexico Press (Albuquerque), 1977.
(With D. Weber) *Fortunes Are for the Few: Letters of a Forty-Niner,* San Diego Historical Society, 1977.
Rocky Mountain Boom Town: A History of Durango, University of New Mexico Press, 1980.
Secure the Shadow: Lachlan McLean, Colorado Mining Photographer, Colorado School of Mines (Golden), 1980.
(With D. Vandenbusche) *A Land Alone: Colorado's Western Slope,* Pruett, 1981.
Song of the Hammer and Drill: The Colorado San Juans, 1860-1914, Colorado School of Mines, 1982.
(Editor) *Natural Resources in Colorado and Wyoming,* Sunflower University Press (Manhattan, KS), 1982.
(Editor) *A Taste of the West: Essays in Honor of Robert G. Athearn,* Pruett, 1983.
When Coal Was King: A History of Crested Butte, Colorado, 1880-1952, Colorado School of Mines, 1984.
(With Fay Metcalf and Thomas Noel) *Colorado: Heritage of the Highest State* (with teacher's guide and activity tablet), Pruett, 1984.
(With Richard D. Lamm) *Pioneers and Politicians: Ten Colorado Governors in Profile,* Pruett, 1984.
Mining America: The Industry and the Environment, 1800-1980, University Press of Kansas (Lawrence), 1987.
Mesa Verde National Park, University of Kansas Press, 1987.
The Birth of Colorado: A Civil War Perspective, University of Oklahoma Press (Norman), 1989.
Rocky Mountain West, University of New Mexico Press, 1992.

WORK IN PROGRESS: The Eighth Illinois Cavalry and *Henry Teller.*

SIDELIGHTS: Duane A. Smith once told *CA:* "Probably the most important motivation for research on mining camps was the desire to uncover a more realistic and honest history as opposed to much of the literature which passes for the true history of the mining frontier.

"I believe that history is not dull, but writers and teachers of it often make it so. Therefore, my goal as a writer is to make history come alive for the reader, to 'hook' people on history."

*   *   *

SONDHEIM, Stephen (Joshua) 1930-

PERSONAL: Born March 22, 1930, in New York, NY; son of Herbert (a dress manufacturer) and Janet (a fashion designer and interior decorator; maiden name, Fox; present name, Leshin) Sondheim. *Education:* Williams College, B.A. (magna cum laude), 1950; graduate study in music composition and theory with Milton Babbitt; studied privately with Oscar Hammerstein II.

ADDRESSES: Home—New York, NY.

CAREER: Composer and lyricist, 1956—. Visiting professor of drama and musical theater and fellow at St. Catherine's College, Oxford University, 1990. Appeared in television specials, including *June Moon,* Public Broadcasting Service (PBS-TV), 1974, and *Putting It Together—The Making of the Broadway Album,* Home Box Office (HBO), 1986. Appeared in episodes of the television series *Great Performances,* including "Broadway Sings: The Music of Jule Styne," PBS-TV, 1987, and "Bernstein at 70," PBS-TV, 1989.

MEMBER: American Academy and Institute of Arts and Letters, American Society of Composers, Authors, and Publishers (ASCAP), Authors League of America, Writers Guild of America, Dramatists Guild (president, 1973-81).

AWARDS, HONORS: Hutchinson Prize, Williams College, 1950; Antoinette Perry ("Tony") Award nominations, League of American Theatres and Producers, 1958 (with composer Leonard Bernstein), for *West Side Story,* 1960 (with composer Jule Styne), for *Gypsy,* 1965 (with composer Richard Rodgers), for *Do I Hear a Waltz?,* 1976, for best score in *Pacific Overtures,* 1982, for best score in *Merrily We Roll Along,* and 1984, for best score in *Sunday in the Park with George;* Antoinette Perry ("Tony") Awards, 1963, for *A Funny Thing Happened on the Way to the Forum,* 1971, two awards for best music and best lyrics in *Company,* 1972, for best score in *Follies,* 1979, for best score in *A Little Night Music,* 1979, for *Sweeney Todd: The Demon Barber of Fleet Street,* and 1988, for best score in *Into the Woods; Evening Standard* Drama Awards for best musical, 1959, for *Gypsy,* 1973, for *A Little Night Music,* 1987, for *Follies,* and 1989, for *Into the Woods;* New York Drama Critics' polls conducted by *Va-*

riety, 1969-70, named best composer for *Company,* and 1970-71, named best composer and lyricist for *Follies;* Drama Desk Awards, 1969-70, for music and lyrics in *Company,* 1970-71, for music and lyrics in *Follies,* 1972-73, for music and lyrics in *A Little Night Music,* 1978-79, for music and lyrics in *Sweeney Todd,* 1981-82, for lyrics in *Merrily We Roll Along,* 1983-84, for lyrics in *Sunday in the Park with George,* and 1987-88, for lyrics and outstanding musical, for *Into the Woods;* New York Drama Critics' Circle Awards for best new musical, 1970, for *Company,* 1971, for *Follies,* 1973, for *A Little Night Music,* 1976, for *Pacific Overtures,* 1979, for *Sweeney Todd,* 1984, for *Sunday in the Park with George,* and 1988, for *Into the Woods.*

Grammy Awards, National Academy of Recording Arts and Sciences, 1970, for best musical cast album *Company,* 1973, for musical cast album *A Little Night Music,* 1975, for song of the year "Send in the Clowns" from the musical *A Little Night Music,* 1979, for best musical cast album *Sweeney Todd,* 1984, for best musical cast album *Sunday in the Park with George,* 1986, for best musical cast album *Follies in Concert,* and 1988, for best musical cast album *Into the Woods;* honorary doctorate, Williams College, 1971; Edgar Allan Poe Award (with Anthony Perkins), Mystery Writers of America, 1973, for best motion picture screenplay, for *The Last of Sheila;* musical salute given by the American Musical and Dramatic Academy and the National Hemophilia Foundation at Shubert Theatre, 1973; Los Angeles Drama Critics' Circle Awards, 1974-75, for music and lyrics in *A Little Night Music,* and 1989, for original musical score in *Into the Woods;* Elizabeth Hull-Kate Warriner Award, Dramatists Guild, 1979, for *Sweeney Todd;* Brandeis University Creative Arts Award in theater arts, 1982; Unique Contribution Award, Drama League of New York, 1983, "for initiating an American Young Playwrights Festival"; Common Wealth Award of Distinguished Service in dramatic arts, Bank of Delaware, 1984; Pulitzer Prize for drama, Columbia University Graduate School of Journalism, 1985, for *Sunday in the Park with George;* Laurence Olivier Award for musical of the year, Society of West End Theatre (England), 1988, for *Follies,* and 1991, for *Sunday in the Park with George;* named Lion of the Performing Arts, New York Public Library, 1989; Academy Award, Academy of Motion Picture Arts and Sciences, 1990, for best original song "Sooner or Later (I Always Get My Man)" from *Dick Tracy;* Golden Globe Award nominations, Hollywood Foreign Press Association, 1990, for original songs "Sooner or Later (I Always Get My Man)" and "What Can You Lose?" from *Dick Tracy;* National Medal of Arts Award, National Endowment for the Arts, 1992 (declined).

WRITINGS:

STAGE PRODUCTIONS

(Composer of incidental music) *The Girls of Summer,* produced at Longacre Theatre, New York City, 1956.

(Lyricist) *West Side Story* (also see below; first produced at Winter Garden Theatre, New York City, September 26, 1957, revived at New York State Theatre, New York City, June 24, 1968, revived at Minskoff Theatre, February 14, 1980), music by Leonard Bernstein, Random House (New York City), 1958, published in *Romeo and Juliet and West Side Story,* Dell (New York City), 1965.

(Lyricist) *Gypsy* (also see below; first produced at Broadway Theatre, New York City, May 21, 1959, revived at Winter Garden Theatre, September 23, 1974, revived at St. James Theatre, New York City, November 16, 1989), music by Jule Styne, Random House, 1960.

(Composer of incidental music) *Invitation to a March,* produced at Music Box Theatre, New York City, 1960.

(Composer and lyricist) *A Funny Thing Happened on the Way to the Forum* (also see below; first produced at Alvin Theatre, New York City, May 8, 1962, revived at Lunt-Fontanne Theatre, New York City, April 4, 1972), Dodd (New York City), 1963, Applause Theater (Diamond Bar, CA), 1991.

(Composer and lyricist) *Anyone Can Whistle* (also see below; first produced at Majestic Theatre, New York City, April 4, 1964), Dodd, 1965.

(Lyricist) *Do I Hear a Waltz?* (also see below; first produced at 46th Street Theatre, New York City, March 18, 1965), music by Richard Rodgers, Random House, 1966.

(Lyricist with others) *Leonard Bernstein's Theatre Songs,* produced at Theatre De Lys, New York City, 1965.

(Composer and lyricist) *Company* (also see below; first produced at Alvin Theatre, April 26, 1970), Random House, 1970.

(Composer and lyricist) *Follies* (also see below; first produced at Winter Garden Theatre, April 4, 1971), Random House, 1971.

(Composer) *The Enclave,* produced at Theatre Four, New York City, 1973.

(Composer and lyricist) *A Little Night Music* (also see below; first produced at Shubert Theatre, New York City, February 25, 1973, produced at Majestic Theatre, 1973-74), Dodd, 1974, Applause Theater, 1991.

(Coauthor of additional lyrics with John LaTouche) *Candide* (revival; also see below), original lyrics by Richard Wilbur, music by Leonard Bernstein, produced at Chelsea Theatre Center of Brooklyn, Brooklyn, NY, 1973-74, produced at Broadway Theatre, March 10,

1974, revived at New York State Theatre, October 13, 1982.

(Composer and lyricist) *The Frogs,* produced at Yale Repertory Theatre, New Haven, CT, May 20, 1974, produced at Odyssey Theatre, Los Angeles, 1983.

(Composer with John Kander and Giuseppe Verdi) *Once in a Lifetime,* produced by Public Players Inc., Central Arts Theatre, 1975.

(Lyricist with others) *By Bernstein,* produced at Chelsea Theatre Center Westside, New York City, 1975.

(Composer and lyricist) *Pacific Overtures* (also see below; first produced at Winter Garden Theatre, January 11, 1976, revived at Promenade Theatre, New York City, October 25, 1984), Dodd, 1977, Theatre Communications Group (New York City), 1991.

(Composer and lyricist) *Sweeney Todd: The Demon Barber of Fleet Street* (also see below; first produced at Uris Theatre [now Gershwin Theatre], New York City, March 1, 1979, revived as an opera at New York State Theatre, October 11, 1984), Dodd, 1979, Applause Theater, 1991.

(Composer and lyricist with others) *The Madwoman of Central Park West,* produced at 22 Steps Theatre, 1979.

(Composer and lyricist) *Merrily We Roll Along* (also see below), first produced at Alvin Theatre, November 16, 1981, revived at La Jolla Playhouse, La Jolla, CA, June 16, 1985.

(Composer and lyricist) *Sunday in the Park with George* (also see below; workshop produced at Playwrights Horizons, New York City, July 6, 1983, produced at Booth Theatre, New York City, 1984-85), Dodd, 1986, Applause Theater, 1991.

(Composer and lyricist) *Into the Woods* (also see below; produced at Old Globe Theatre, San Diego, CA, c. 1986, produced at Martin Beck Theatre, New York City, 1987-89), Theatre Communications Group, 1989.

(Composer and lyricist with others) *Jerome Robbins' Broadway,* produced at Imperial Theatre, New York City, 1989-90.

(Composer and lyricist) *Assassins* (first produced at Playwrights Horizons, 1991), Theatre Communications Group, 1991.

Composer with Mary Rodgers of song "The Boy from ..." for *The Mad Show,* produced at New Theatre, New York City, 1966. Also provided music for *Twins,* first produced at Fisher Theatre, Detroit, MI, c. 1972.

STAGE MUSICAL ANTHOLOGIES

Sondheim: A Musical Tribute (benefit production), produced at Shubert Theatre, March 11, 1973.

Side by Side by Sondheim (also see below), includes music by Leonard Bernstein, Mary Rodgers, Richard Rodgers, and Jule Styne, produced in London, 1976, produced at Music Box Theatre, April 18, 1977, revised version first performed as *A Stephen Sondheim Evening,* produced at Sotheby's, New York City, March 3, 1983.

Marry Me a Little (also see below), first produced at Production Company, October 29, 1980, produced at Actor's Playhouse, New York City, 1981.

Follies in Concert with New York Philharmonic, first produced at Lincoln Center, New York City, September 6, 1985.

Julie Wilson: From Weill to Sondheim—A Concert (one act devoted to Sondheim's work), produced at Kaufman Theatre, 1987.

You're Gonna Love Tomorrow: A Stephen Sondheim Evening, produced at New Playwrights' Theatre, Washington, DC, c. 1987.

Sondheim: A Celebration at Carnegie Hall, produced in New York City, 1992.

Putting It Together, produced by Manhattan Theatre Club, City Center Theatre, New York City, 1993.

FILM COMPOSITIONS

(Lyricist) *West Side Story* (also see below), United Artists (UA), 1961.

(Lyricist) *Gypsy* (also see below), Warner Bros., 1962.

(Composer and lyricist) *A Funny Thing Happened on the Way to the Forum* (also see below), UA, 1966.

(Composer of score) *Stavisky* (also see below), Cinemation, 1974.

(Composer and lyricist) *A Little Night Music* (also see below), New World, 1977.

(Composer of score with Dave Grusin) *Reds,* Paramount, 1981.

(Composer and lyricist with others) *Dick Tracy,* Touchstone-Buena Vista, 1990.

Also author of music and lyrics for "The Madam's Song," in *The Seven Percent Solution,* Universal, 1977.

TELEVISION PRODUCTIONS

(Composer and lyricist with Burt Shevelove) *The Fabulous 50s* (special), Columbia Broadcasting System (CBS-TV), 1960.

(Composer and lyricist) *Evening Primrose* (special), American Broadcasting Co. (ABC-TV), 1966.

(Composer and lyricist) *Annie, the Woman in the Life of a Man* (special), CBS-TV, 1970.

(Composer and lyricist) *Sweeney Todd, The Demon Barber of Fleet Street* (special; also see below), Entertainment Channel, 1982.

(Lyricist) "Candide," *Great Performances,* PBS-TV, 1986.

(Composer and lyricist) "Follies in Concert," *Great Performances,* PBS-TV, 1986.

(Composer and lyricist) "Sunday in the Park with George" (also see below), *Broadway on Showtime,* Showtime, 1986, broadcast on *American Playhouse,* PBS-TV, 1986.

(Composer and lyricist) "A Little Night Music" (also see below), *Live from Lincoln Center* (broadcast from New York State Theatre), PBS-TV, 1990.

(Composer) *Time Warner Presents the Earth Day Special,* ABC-TV, 1990.

(Composer and lyricist) "Into the Woods" (also see below), *Great Performances,* PBS-TV, 1991.

Also author of lyrics to "Somewhere," included in *Putting It Together: The Making of the Broadway Album* (special), HBO, 1986, and song "The Saga of Lenny," included in "Bernstein at 70," *Great Performances,* PBS-TV, 1989.

TELEPLAYS

(With others) *Topper* (series), National Broadcasting Co., (NBC-TV), 1953.

The Last Word (series), CBS-TV, 1957-59.

RECORDINGS

West Side Story, Columbia, 1957, released as film soundtrack, 1961.

Gypsy, Columbia, 1959.

A Funny Thing Happened on the Way to the Forum, Capitol, 1962.

Anyone Can Whistle, Columbia, 1964.

Do I Hear a Waltz?, Columbia, 1965.

Company, Columbia, 1970.

Follies, Capitol, 1971, released as *Follies in Concert,* RCA, 1985.

A Little Night Music, Columbia, 1973.

Stavisky, Polydor, 1973.

Sondheim: A Musical Tribute (anthology), Warner Bros., 1973, released as *Sondheim Evening: A Musical Tribute* (includes Sondheim singing "Anyone Can Whistle"), RCA, 1990.

Pacific Overtures, RCA, 1976.

Side by Side by Sondheim, RCA, 1977.

Sweeney Todd, The Demon Barber of Fleet Street, RCA, 1979.

Marry Me a Little, RCA, 1981.

Merrily We Roll Along, RCA, 1981.

Sunday in the Park with George, RCA, 1984.

Music of Stephen Sondheim, Book of the Month Records, 1985.

Into the Woods, RCA, 1988.

I'm Breathless (Music from and Inspired by the Film "Dick Tracy" (includes "Sooner or Later [I Always Get My Man]" and "What Can You Lose?"), Sire, 1990.

Sondheim songs are also featured in Barbra Streisand's *Broadway Album,* 1985, and *Stephen Sondheim: A Collector's Sondheim* (compilation of original cast recordings), RCA.

OTHER

(With Anthony Perkins) *The Last of Sheila,* Warner Bros., 1973.

(Author of introduction) Richard Lewine and Alfred Simon, *Songs of the American Theatre,* Dodd, 1973.

(Contributor) Otis L. Guernsey, Jr., editor, *Playwrights, Lyricists, Composers on Theatre,* Dodd, 1974.

(Author of introduction) Hugh Fordin, *Getting to Know Him,* Random House, 1977.

Stephen Sondheim's Crossword Puzzles, Harper (New York City), 1980.

(Editor) *Lyrics by Oscar Hammerstein II,* revised edition, Hal Leonard Publishing, 1985.

Also author of *The Hansen Treasury of Stephen Sondheim Songs,* 1977, *The Stephen Sondheim Songbook,* 1979, and *All Sondheim,* 1980. Contributor of crossword puzzles to *New York* magazine, 1968-69.

ADAPTATIONS: Into the Woods has been adapted as a juvenile book by Hudson Talbott, published by Crown (New York City), 1988.

SIDELIGHTS: Stephen Sondheim, according to Arthur Laurents, is "without question, the best Broadway lyricist past or present. . . . Any lyric he has written can be quoted to illustrate this contention. I think Sondheim is the only lyricist who almost always writes a lyric which could *only* be sung by the character for which it was designed, who never pads with unnecessary fillers, who never sacrifices meaning or intention for a clever rhyme and who knows that a lyric is the shortest of one-act plays, with a beginning, a middle and an end. Moreover, he knows how the words must sit on a musical phrase. I am not his agent." And Burt Shevelove remarked: "Far and away the best of the new lyric writers is Stephen Sondheim. Beside wit, ingenuity, and warmth, he brings a sense of the character to every word that is sung. He is the first and perhaps the only true *theatre* lyricist we have." Sondheim's contributions to the musical theater have been so significant that the *Dramatists Guild Literary Quarterly* designated its first ten years as the "Sondheim decade." "There can hardly have been an issue since," the editors commented, "when a work by Stephen Sondheim . . . wasn't a major attraction on the Broadway scene, and often more than one."

In nearly thirty years in the theater, Sondheim has been instrumental in revolutionizing the musical. The composer's ability to incorporate a variety of musical styles into his scores has caused T. E. Kalem of *Time* to claim after

seeing a Sondheim production that the "entire score is an incredible display of musical virtuosity." Using music, Sondheim creates an attitude for the dramatic situation so that individual songs may push the drama along. Sometimes, unlike most of his predecessors, the composer strays from the traditional rhyming structure. Too, his lyrical cynicism and satire have moved the musical comedy from the lighter and simpler shows of Rodgers and Hammerstein to what is termed "conceptual musicals."

Instead of escapism, his conceptual musicals present serious concerns and dramatic subtexts. Each of the composer's works depends on one fundamental concept to act as a framework. Though every theatrical production should have a unifying theme, "every Sondheim-Prince [renowned director Harold Prince] show," argued Jeff Sweet, a critic, composer, and librettist, "begins with a prologue in which the plot isn't entered into, saying to the audience, 'These are what your expectations should be for this show. These are our priorities, these are the ideas we're going to be concentrating on.' They are conceptual musicals, they get the concept up there in the first number." One of the creators of the new, unromantic musical production, Sondheim has helped to place the musical on a more serious level than that of the traditional Broadway show. In fact, after assessing the contemporary musical, Ray Evens decided that "many musicals today tend to the opera form, and there are marvelous counterpoints, involvements and dramatics which, when done well—as in the case of Sondheim—are a new plateau in the art."

When Sondheim composes, it is a cooperative effort. "I go about starting a song first with the collaborators," he divulged, "sometimes just with the book writer, sometimes with the director. We have long discussions and I take notes, just general notes, and then we decide what the song should be about, and I try to make a title." The composer, according to Sondheim, must stage numbers or draw "blueprints" so that the director or the choreographer may see the uses of a song.

For Sondheim, collaboration usually begins with the book and book writer from whom "you should steal." Since a good production sounds as though one writer is responsible for both the book and the score, the book writer and composer must work together if a play is to have texture. "Any book writer I work with knows what I'm going to do," explained Sondheim, "and I try to help him out wherever I can; that's the only way you make a piece, make a texture." "I keep hearing about people," he continued, "who write books and then give them to composers or composers who write scores and then get a book writer. I don't understand how that works."

Sondheim's first Broadway collaboration has an unusual history. At the age of twenty-five, the composer completed the music and lyrics for *Saturday Night,* a musical that never saw the Broadway stage owing to the death of its producer Lemuel Ayers. But *Saturday Night* still served Sondheim well. "It was my portfolio," he explained, "and as a result of it I got *West Side Story.*" Remembering the circumstances of his collaboration with Leonard Bernstein, Sondheim related: "I was at an opening night party, and I saw one familiar face, Arthur Laurents, and I went over to make small talk with him. I asked him what he was doing, and he said, 'I'm about to begin a musical of *Romeo and Juliet* with Leonard Bernstein and Jerry Robbins.' I asked, 'Who's doing the lyrics?'—just idly, because I didn't think of myself as a lyric writer, I thought of myself as a songwriter, I was composing all the time. Arthur literally smote his forehead (I think it's the only time I have ever seen anybody literally smite his forehead). He said, 'I never thought of you and I liked your lyrics very much. I didn't like your music very much, but I did like your lyrics a lot.' (Arthur is nothing if not frank.)"

The story of the ugly life on a city street, with only glimpses of beauty and love, *West Side Story* is considered one of the masterpieces of the American theater. Beginning its first run in New York in 1957, *West Side Story* ran for 734 performances on Broadway. After an extended tour of the United States, the play began a second Broadway run of 249 performances. In 1961, *West Side Story* was adapted into a motion picture that captured ten Academy Awards and became one of the greatest screen musicals in terms of commercial success.

Many critics have attributed much of *West Side Story*'s popularity to its musical score. In *The Complete Book of the American Musical Theatre,* David A. Ewen named the score as "one of the most powerful assets to this grim tragedy." Ewen cited "Maria," "I Feel Pretty," and "Somewhere" as "unforgettable lyrical episodes." Sondheim's comic songs, such as "America" and "Gee, Officer Krupke!," have also been applauded for their wittiness and their roles as satirical commentaries.

Sondheim's next production was *Gypsy,* a musical based on the autobiography of burlesque star Gypsy Rose Lee. Initially, Sondheim was contracted to write both the music and the lyrics for this show, but actress Ethel Merman felt uneasy with a little-known composer. So Jule Styne composed *Gypsy*'s music while Sondheim wrote the lyrics, a collaboration that produced, according to Harvey Schmidt, "the ideal Broadway show score." Although the play is entertaining in the tradition of Broadway musicals, its "real distinction," said Schmidt, "is in the fact that at its heart is a 'serious' musical dealing with deep human drives and needs. And it manages to avoid pitfalls that work against most attempts at 'seriousness' in musicals: sentimentality and pretentiousness. Each song is strongly rooted in character and story, yet bounces off the stage

with artful simplicity, never once violating its promise to 'Let Me Entertain You.'" One song from *Gypsy,* "Some People," is considered, at least by Jerry Herman, to be the "best single lyric ever written." "It's perfectly metered and rhymed," he proclaimed. "It's a lyric in the Larry Hart sense of a *song* lyric, and at the same time it is a piece of dramatic literature, poetry that defines the character of Madame Rose [*Gypsy*'s mother] as clearly as three scenes of dialogue. You know this woman after hearing it. It's harsh, it's bitter, it's unrelenting, it's skillful, it works on, like, three levels for me, and I admire it enormously." "In fact," he concluded, "I admire the *Gypsy* lyrics and score more than any other I can think of at this moment."

An old-fashioned burlesque, *A Funny Thing Happened on the Way to the Forum,* followed *Gypsy.* Sondheim and playwrights Burt Shevelove and Larry Gelbart adapted *Forum* from the comedies of Plautus, a classical Roman playwright. The play is bawdy, rough-and-tumble, and fun. A low comedy of lechers and courtesans done in a combination of ancient Roman and American vaudeville techniques, *Forum* is paced with ambiguous meanings, risque connotations, and not-so-subtle innuendos. For instance, a slave carrying a piece of statuary is told by a matron: "Carry my bust with pride." Typically Sondheim, the score is saturated with humor. Some critics have cited "Everybody Ought to Have a Maid" as particularly amusing while "Lovely" has been suspected, at least by one critic, of being Sondheim's satire of his own song "Tonight." For *Forum,* unlike most of his previous plays, Sondheim wrote both the lyrics and the music. "With *Forum,*" a *Time* reviewer noted, "Sondheim finally proved that he, like Noel Coward, could indeed go it alone." *Forum* received a Tony Award as the season's best musical and, in 1966, it was released by United Artists as a motion picture starring Zero Mostel, Jack Gilford, Phil Silvers, and Buster Keaton.

In 1973, when Charles Michener worried that the Broadway musical had degenerated to an embarrassing state of high camp and rock music, Sondheim's *A Little Night Music* appeared on Broadway and restored some of the reviewer's faith in musical theater. "Sondheim," he wrote, "is virtually alone in trying to preserve the great tradition of dramatic songwriting that Jerome Kern and Oscar Hammerstein II began more than 40 years ago with 'Showboat.'" Critics recognized *Night Music* to be as spectacular as the great musicals that had gone before it but, as Michener noted, the play was serious, too, "pertinent as well as diverting."

Sondheim composed all the songs for *Night Music* in three-quarter time or multiples of that meter; this served as the play's concept and tied it together. Three-quarter time was the foundation to which the composer added a Greek chorus, conons, and fuguetos. Subtexts were injected into almost every song—most notably in "Every Day a Little Death," which allows a countess to express her feelings of loneliness as a philanderer's wife. In addition, Sondheim devoted himself to the "inner monologue song," which is a song, a *Time* critic explained, "in which characters sing of their deepest thoughts, but almost never to each other."

Though *Night Music* addresses the standard musical-comedy subject—love—it "is a masquelike affair, tailor-made to fit Sondheim's flair for depicting confused people experiencing ambivalent thoughts and feelings," the *Time* reviewer assessed. Many of his songs illustrate ambivalence because Sondheim likes neurotic people. He revealed: "I like troubled people. Not that I don't like squared-away people, but I *prefer* neurotic people. I like to hear rumblings beneath the surface." The show's cast of confused characters includes the giddy child bride whose middle-aged husband takes up with his ex-mistress while his adolescent son has a crush on his new step-mother. Of course, the above-mentioned countess laments the sadness of her marriage to a straying husband, and a lusty chambermaid salutes carnal love through the play.

Critically, *Night Music* was a triumph. "This is a jewelled music box of a show," asserted Kalem, "lovely to look at, delightful to listen to, perhaps too exquisite, fragile and muted to ever be quite humanly affecting." "It is a victory of technique over texture," the reviewer asserted, "and one leaves it in the odd mental state of unbridled admiration and untouched feelings." Many reviewers agreed that the strongest element in the play was Sondheim's score. "It is a beauty," Kalem raved, "his best yet in an exceedingly distinguished career." *Night Music,* another critic insisted, "is Sondheim's most brilliant accomplishment to date." "Literate, ironic, playful, enviably clever, altogether professional," praised Kalem, "Sondheim is a quicksilver wordsmith in the great tradition of Cole Porter, Noel Coward and Lorenz Hart."

The overall effect of Sondheim's *Side by Side by Sondheim,* said Jack Kroll of *Newsweek,* "is to turn Sondheim into a kind of American Noel Coward." An anthology of the composer's work, *Side by Side* is a British tribute to the composer, and most critics were quick to add their homage. Brendan Gill of the *New Yorker* wrote that "the apotheosis of Stephen Sondheim proceeds apace, and I am eager to do my bit. At forty-seven, Mr. Sondheim may feel that he is a trifle young to be hoisted up onto a plinth as the Good Gray Tunesmith of Turtle Bay, but the body of his work is already impressively large, and his admirers are as numerous as they are importunate; besides, it is an ineradicable defect of homage that it must be accepted when it is offered, and not when it is convenient." *New York*'s Alan Rich added: "These Britishers have jour-

neyed to our midst to remind us of what we all should be aware of: That Sondheim is one of our treasures."

Sondheim once again made his presence known on Broadway with *Sweeney Todd: The Demon Barber of Fleet Street.* Sondheim became interested in the play in 1973, related Mel Gussow of the *New York Times,* "when he saw a production of the melodrama at the Stratford East Theatre in England. He was captivated by it, although, as he said, 'I found it much more passionate and serious than the audience did.'" Composed as if it were an opera, *Sweeney Todd* is the story of a murderous barber who sends his victims downstairs to a pie shop where they become the secret ingredients in Mrs. Lovett's meat pies. By Sondheim's own admission, the play "has a creepy atmosphere." The main character, Todd, is out for revenge. Judge Turpin, who desired Todd's wife and daughter, shipped the barber off to Australia as punishment for a crime that he did not commit. Todd escapes and returns seeking vengeance. His attempt to kill the judge fails, causing his revenge to snowball into mass murder. In the end, Todd kills Turpin, but by then the barber, too, is doomed.

Sweeney Todd is about revenge. Harold Prince's production, however, mirrors the industrial age, its influences, and its effects. "We are invited to see Sweeney Todd not as a man obsessed with an insane desire for revenge," Gill observed, "but as the sorry victim of the workings of a vicious society—that nineteenth century England which was reaping the rich fruit of the Industrial Revolution by dint of ignoring the cost in human suffering." The real purpose of *Sweeney Todd* is, as Gill pointed out, "to give us all a good old-fashioned scare," which it does. For as Gill said after seeing the play, "I am steering clear these days of trapdoors, straight razors, and the more complexly bestrewn pizzas."

Sweeney Todd received numerous Drama Desk Awards and Tony Awards in 1979, including best score of a musical. In the opinion of director Harold Prince, the play's music is "the most melodic and romantic score that Steve has ever written. The music is soaring." Nearly eighty percent of the show is music, and musical motifs recur throughout the score to maintain the audience's emotional level. Sondheim even incorporated a musical clue, a theme associated with a character, into the score.

In 1984, Sondheim teamed up with artist-turned-dramatist James Lapine (winner of an Obie award in 1978 for his play *Photograph*) to create the musical *Sunday in the Park with George.* For Lapine and Sondheim, their first collaboration was a remarkable success, garnering the 1985 Pulitzer Prize for drama. Their feat was made even more unusual by the fact that *Sunday in the Park with George* is centered around an idea Clive Barnes deemed "audaciously ambitious" in the *New York Post.* "It is to show us the creation of a work of art, the formulation of an artistic style based on scientific principles, and to reveal, in passing, the struggles of an artist for recognition," Barnes explained.

"I write generally experimental, unexpected work," Sondheim told Samuel G. Freedman for a *New York Times* article; he has made that truth perhaps nowhere more evident than in *Sunday in the Park with George.* Conceptual rather than plot-driven, the play structures itself around two vignettes that are performed as two separate acts. The first follows French pointillist Georges Seurat in the evolution of his renowned painting "A Sunday Afternoon on the Island of La Grande Jatte." The second is centered upon the artistic struggles of the American greatgrandson of the artist, the "George" of the play's title, who pays homage to his ancestor's work through modern laser artistry.

According to Rich, the reaction of the audience to the unusual musical was typical of the sharply divided response he's come to expect from Sondheim productions. "I never saw a performance of *Sunday in the Park with George* . . . at which some members of the audience didn't walk out early—often not even waiting until intermission to do so—while others, sobbing in their seats, refused to budge until well after the house lights were up," he wrote. The critical response to *Sunday in the Park with George* was nearly as divided. Many felt that the play confirmed the belief that the creative process is inherently undramatic. David Sterritt's review for the *Christian Science Monitor* pointed to a conflict between the desire to depict art and the desire to depict an artist as the source for the play's failure. *Sunday in the Park with George,* he wrote, "hovers between the formal elegance of *La Grande Jatte* and the living, breathing, potentially fascinating life of Seurat himself—but partakes fully of neither."

Other critics took exception to what they saw as the autobiographical note sounded by the play's theme: in the depiction of Seurat's rejection by art critics of his time, many felt, was Sondheim's venting of his frustration at his own critical reception. "It is easy to see why Stephen Sondheim should have been attracted to the idea of creating a musical about Georges Seurat, whose career is a way of discussing some of the dilemmas that confront the contemporary artist," Howard Kissel observed in a review for *Women's Wear Daily.* Kissel went on to object to what he felt was the "defensive" stance Sondheim reveals in songs like "Lesson # 8," and to dismiss the notion that the play is avant garde. Instead, the critic expressed the opinion that *Sunday in the Park with George* is merely contrived.

Yet many critics were compelled by the play's premise and convinced of its status as a breakthrough for theater. "To say that this show breaks new ground is not enough; it also breaks new sky, new water, new flesh and new spirit,"

Jack Kroll proclaimed in *Newsweek.* Kroll not only approved of the material, but he celebrated the pairing of Lapine and Sondheim, declaring that over the course of the musical, its creators "take us full circle, implying that there's still hope for vision in a high-tech world and that art and love may be two forms of the same energy . . . , in this show of beauty, wit, nobility and ardor, [that idea] makes this Sondheim's best work since . . . his classic collaborations with Harold Prince."

Not surprisingly, Lapine and Sondheim revived their partnership, collaborating on the 1986 musical *Into the Woods.* Again, their collaboration was richly rewarding. Winner of Tony Awards for lyrics and outstanding musical, the play was a greater commercial success than *Sunday in the Park with George* had been. Essentially about the loss of innocence, the play explores the "grim" in the Brothers Grimm and in other tellers of children's tales. Turning fairytales like Cinderella and Little Red Riding Hood on their heads, the two acts of *Into the Woods* move from the happily to the unhappily ever after. Yet the musical ends on the surprisingly upbeat notes of the song "No One Is Alone," prompting some critics to complain that Sondheim had sold out to public demand for lighter material. Others, however, found the musical wholly appealing. "It is that joyous rarity," wrote Elizabeth L. Bland and William A. Henry III in a *Time* review, "a work of sophisticated artistic ambition and deep political purpose that affords nonstop pleasure."

In 1990, Sondheim earned his first Academy Award for the song "Sooner or Later (I Always Get My Man)," composed for the movie *Dick Tracy* and sung by Madonna. From there, Sondheim went on to create a uniquely American show, *Assassins,* which showcases the assassins and would-be assassins of presidents of the United States. With characters such as John Wilkes Booth and Lynette "Squeaky" Fromme, the musical quickly earned the reputation of being Sondheim's darkest work to date. Undaunted, theater-goers lined up in droves for its sold-out run in 1991 at Playwrights Horizons. Frank Rich commented on Sondheim's artistic principles. "Sondheim has real guts," he wrote. "He isn't ashamed to identify with his assassins to the extreme point where he will wave a gun in a crowded theater, artistically speaking, if that's what is needed to hit the target of American complacency."

With the deepening and darkening of the themes of his work in the 1980s and 1990s, comparisons of Sondheim to the lighter Noel Coward have all but ceased. There is little doubt that this change is one Sondheim would approve. As he once told *CA:* "It was my mother who wanted me to be the American Noel Coward, not I. If I wanted to be like anybody (which I don't), it wouldn't be Noel Coward."

BIOGRAPHICAL/CRITICAL SOURCES:

BOOKS

Authors and Artists for Young Adults, Volume 11, Gale (Detroit), 1993.

Contemporary Literary Criticism, Gale, Volume 30, 1984, Volume 39, 1986.

Ewen, David A., *The Complete Book of the American Musical Theatre,* Holt (New York City), 1970.

Hughes, Catharine, editor, *American Theatre Annual 1978-1979,* Gale, 1980.

Hughes, editor, *American Theatre Annual 1979-1980,* Gale, 1981.

Hughes, editor, *New York Theatre Annual,* Gale, Volume 1, 1978, Volume 2, 1978.

Guernsey, Otis L., Jr., editor, *Playwrights, Lyricists, Composers on Theatre,* Dodd, 1974.

Lewine, Richard, and Alfred Simon, *Songs of the American Theatre,* Dodd, 1973.

Zadan, Craig, *Sondheim and Company,* Avon, 1976.

PERIODICALS

America, December 12, 1987, p. 485.
American Spectator, March, 1988, pp. 28-29.
Atlantic Monthly, December, 1984, p. 121.
Chicago Tribune, June 5, 1979; October 14, 1983; May 3, 1984; April 29, 1985; December 7, 1986; December 14, 1986; November 6, 1987; June 12, 1988.
Chicago Tribune Book World, April 15, 1984.
Christian Science Monitor, May 3, 1984, p. 27.
Commonweal, January 15, 1988.
Daily Mirror, September 27, 1957.
Daily News, September 27, 1957; April 6, 1964; April 27, 1970; February 26, 1973; March 2, 1979; February 15, 1980; May 3, 1984.
Globe and Mail (Toronto), November 7, 1987.
Harper's, April, 1979, pp. 71-74, 76, 78.
High Fidelity, August, 1979, pp. 80-81.
Insight, August 28, 1989, p. 59.
Journal American, September 27, 1957.
Journal of Popular Culture, winter, 1978, pp. 513-25.
Los Angeles Times, March 18, 1983; May 20, 1984, p. 3; November 26, 1984, pp. 1, 5; November 6, 1987; January 8, 1989, pp. 4-5, 75.
Maclean's, December 24, 1984, p. 41.
Musical Quarterly, April, 1980, pp. 309-14.
Nation, December 12, 1987, pp. 725-27.
New Leader, December 28, 1987, pp. 18-19.
New Republic, June 18, 1984, pp. 25-26; December 21, 1987, pp. 28-30; April 3, 1989, pp. 28-29; January 1, 1990, pp. 27-28.
New Statesman, August 7, 1987, pp. 23-24.
Newsweek, April 23, 1973, pp. 54-56, 61, 64; January 26, 1976, p. 59; May 2, 1977; March 12, 1979, pp. 101,

103; March 19, 1979; May 14, 1984, pp. 83-84; November 16, 1987, pp. 106-07; February 4, 1991, p. 72; June 22, 1992, p. 52.
New York, May 2, 1977; March 3, 1979; March 19, 1979; March 3, 1980; November 16, 1987, p. 109; October 2, 1989, p. 82; August 20, 1990, pp. 120, 124; February 4, 1991, p. 38.
New Yorker, August 11, 1975, pp. 74-76; May 2, 1977; March 12, 1979; November 16, 1987, pp. 147-48; February 11, 1991, pp. 68-69.
New York Post, March 19, 1965; January 12, 1976; April 19, 1977; March 2, 1979; February 15, 1980; May 3, 1984.
New York Times, January 12, 1976, p. 39; April 19, 1977; February 1, 1979; February 25, 1979; March 2, 1979, p. C3; June 2, 1979; February 14, 1980; March 14, 1981; November 17, 1981; December 13, 1981, pp. D3, D6; March 6, 1983; July 24, 1983; April 1, 1984; April 4, 1984; May 3, 1984, p. C21; May 13, 1984, pp. 7, 31; October 13, 1984; October 21, 1984; October 26, 1984; May 24, 1985; September 9, 1985; July 23, 1987; October 9, 1987; November 1, 1987; November 6, 1987; November 29, 1987; May 10, 1988; November 27, 1989, pp. C13, C15; January 22, 1990; September 30, 1990; November 7, 1990; February 3, 1991.
Opera News, November, 1985, pp. 18, 20, 22.
People, September 23, 1985, p. 78.
Saturday Review, May 1, 1971, pp. 16, 65.
Stereo Review, July, 1971, pp. 110-11; July, 1973, pp. 94-95.
Time, April 12, 1971, p. 78; May 3, 1971; March 12, 1973; March 19, 1973; February 25, 1980; June 16, 1986, p. 90; November 16, 1987, pp. 96-97; December 7, 1987, pp. 80-82; September 25, 1989, p. 76; February 4, 1991, p. 62.
Times (London), May 5, 1984; July 11, 1987; July 23, 1987; August 2, 1989; January 28, 1991, p. 16.
U.S. News and World Report, February 1, 1988, pp. 52-54.
Variety, April 8, 1964, p. 80; November 19, 1975, pp. 64-65; April 20, 1977; February 20, 1980; November 22, 1989; February 4, 1991, p. 95.
Vogue, April, 1984, p. 85.
Washington Post, November 18, 1981; November 6, 1987.
Women's Wear Daily, April 27, 1970; April 5, 1971; February 26, 1973; March 2, 1979; May 3, 1984.*

*   *   *

SOUTHALL, Ivan (Francis) 1921-

PERSONAL: Born June 8, 1921, in Canterbury, Victoria, Australia; son of Francis Gordon (in insurance) and Rachel Elizabeth (Voutier) Southall; married Joyce Blackburn, September 8, 1945 (divorced); married Susan Stanton, 1976; children: (first marriage) Andrew John, Roberta Joy, Elizabeth Rose, Melissa Frances. *Education:* Attended Melbourne Technical College, 1937-41. *Politics:* Independent. *Religion:* Methodist.

ADDRESSES: P.O. Box 25, Healesville, Victoria 3777, Australia.

CAREER: Herald and Weekly Times, Melbourne, Victoria, Australia, process engraver, 1936-41 and 1947; freelance writer, 1948—. Library of Congress, Whittall Lecturer, 1973; American Library Association, Arbuthnot Honor Lecturer, 1974. MacQuarie University, writer-in-residence, 1978. Community Youth Organization, past president; Knoxbrooke Training Centre for the Intellectually Handicapped, foundation president. *Military service:* Australian Army, 1941; Royal Australian Air Force, 1942-46, pilot, 1942-44, war historian, 1945-46; became flight lieutenant; received Distinguished Flying Cross.

MEMBER: Australian Society of Authors.

AWARDS, HONORS: Australian Children's Book of the Year Award, 1966, for *Ash Road,* 1968, for *To the Wild Sky,* 1971, for *Bread and Honey,* and 1976, for *Fly West;* Australian Picture Book of the Year Award, 1969, for *Sly Old Wardrobe;* Japanese Government's Children's Welfare and Culture Encouragement Award, 1969, for *Ash Road;* Carnegie Medal, Library Association (England), 1972, for *Josh;* Zilver Griffel (Netherlands), 1972, for *To the Wild Sky;* named member of Order of Australia, 1981; National Children's Book Award (Australia), 1986, for *The Long Night Watch.*

WRITINGS:

FICTION

Out of the Dawn: Three Short Stories, privately printed, 1942.
Third Pilot, Horwitz, 1959.
Flight to Gibraltar, Horwitz, 1959.
Mediterranean Black, Horwitz, 1959.
Sortie in Cyrenaica, Horwitz, 1959.
Mission to Greece, Horwitz, 1960.
Atlantic Pursuit, Horwitz, 1960.

NONFICTION

The Weaver from Meltham (biography), illustrated by George Colville, Whitcombe & Tombs (Christchurch), 1950.
The Story of The Hermitage: The First Fifty Years of the Geelong Church of England Girls' Grammar School, F. W. Cheshire (Harlow, Essex), 1956.
They Shall Not Pass Unseen, Angus & Robertson (London), 1956.
A Tale of Box Hill: Day of the Forest, Box Hill City Council, 1957.

Bluey Truscott: Squadron Leader Keith William Truscott, R.A.A.F., D.F.C. and Bar, Angus & Robertson, 1958.
Softly Tread the Brave: A Triumph over Terror, Devilry, and Death by Mine Disposal Officers John Stuart Mould and Hugh Randall Syme, Angus & Robertson, 1960.
Parson on the Track: Bush Brothers in the Australian Outback, Lansdowne (London), 1962.

"SIMON BLACK" SERIES FOR CHILDREN

Meet Simon Black, illustrated by Frank Norton, Angus & Robertson, 1950.
Simon Black in Peril, Angus & Robertson, 1951.
Simon Black in Space, Angus & Robertson, 1952, Anglobooks, 1953.
Simon Black in Coastal Command, Anglobooks, 1953.
Simon Black in China, Angus & Robertson, 1954.
Simon Black and the Spacemen, Angus & Robertson, 1955.
Simon Black in the Antarctic, Angus & Robertson, 1956.
Simon Black Takes Over: The Strange Tale of Operation Greenleaf, Angus & Robertson, 1959.
Simon Black at Sea: The Fateful Maiden Voyage of A.P.M.I. Arion, Angus & Robertson, 1961.

NONFICTION FOR CHILDREN

Journey into Mystery: A Story of the Explorers Burke and Willis, illustrated by Robin Goodall, Lansdowne, 1961.
Lawrence Hargrave (biography), Oxford University Press (Oxford), 1964.
Rockets in the Desert: The Story of Woomera, Angus & Robertson, 1964.
Indonesian Journey (travel), Lansdowne, 1965, Ginn (Aylebury, England), 1966.
Bushfire!, illustrated by Julie Mattox, Angus & Robertson, 1968.
Seventeen Seconds (children's adaptation of *Softly Tread the Brave;* also see below), Macmillan (Basingstoke), 1973.
Fly West, Angus & Robertson, 1974, Macmillan (New York City), 1975.

FICTION FOR CHILDREN

Hills End, illustrated by Jim Phillips, Angus & Robertson, 1962, St. Martin's (New York City), 1963.
Ash Road, illustrated by Clem Seale, Angus & Robertson, 1965, St. Martin's, 1966.
To the Wild Sky, illustrated by Jennifer Tuckwell, St. Martin's, 1967.
The Fox Hole (also see below), illustrated by Ian Ribbons, St. Martin's, 1967.
Let the Balloon Go (also see below), illustrated by Ribbons, St. Martin's, 1968.

Sly Old Wardrobe (picture book), illustrated by Ted Greenwood, F. W. Cheshire, 1968, St. Martin's, 1970.

Finn's Folly, St. Martin's, 1969.

Chinaman's Reef Is Ours, St. Martin's, 1970.

Bread and Honey, Angus & Robertson, 1970, published as *Walk a Mile and Get Nowhere*, Bradbury (Scarsdale, NY), 1970.

Josh, Angus & Robertson, 1971, Macmillan, 1972.

Over the Top (also see below), illustrated by Ribbons, Methuen (London), 1972, published as *Benson Boy*, illustrated by Ingrid Fetz, Macmillan, 1972.

Head in the Clouds, illustrated by Richard Kennedy, Angus & Robertson, 1972, Macmillan, 1973.

Matt and Jo, Macmillan, 1973.

Three Novels (contains *The Fox Hole, Let the Balloon Go*, and *Over the Top*), Methuen, 1975.

What about Tomorrow?, Macmillan, 1977.

King of the Sticks, Greenwillow (New York City), 1979.

The Golden Goose, Greenwillow, 1981.

The Long Night Watch, Methuen, 1983, Farrar, Straus (New York City), 1984.

A City out of Sight, Angus & Robertson, 1984.

Christmas in the Tree, Hodder & Stoughton (London), 1985.

Rachel, Farrar, Straus, 1986.

Blackbird, Farrar, Straus, 1988.

The Mysterious World of Marcus Leadbeater, Farrar, Straus, 1990.

OTHER

Woomera, Angus & Robertson, 1962.

Indonesia Face to Face (travel), Lansdowne, 1964.

(Editor) *The Challenge: Is the Church Obsolete?—An Australian Response to the Challenge of Modern Society* (essays), Lansdowne, 1966.

The Sword of Esau: Bible Stories Retold, illustrated by Joan Kiddell-Monroe, Angus & Robertson, 1967, St. Martin's, 1968.

The Curse of Cain: Bible Stories Retold, illustrated by Kiddell-Monroe, St. Martin's, 1968.

A Journey of Discovery: On Writing for Children (lectures), Kestrel (London), 1975, Macmillan, 1976.

Also author, with others, of a screenplay titled *Let the Balloon Go*, 1976.

SIDELIGHTS: Ivan Southall is an award-winning Australian author who is best known for his fictional works for children and young adults. Southall offers realistic portrayals of ordinary children coping with dramatic situations, usually without the guidance of adults. Although his characters are in "severely demanding circumstances . . . learning, growth and change take place," states Geoffrey Fox in an article for *Children's Literature in Education.* Southall has been criticized by some who claim that his subjects are too mature—and potentially frightening—for his readership. Other critics have suggested that the challenging vocabulary and various sophisticated literary devices evident in the author's works—such as stream-of-consciousness writing, flashbacks, and a roving point of view—are geared to an adult rather than a juvenile audience. However Southall continues to employ these techniques because he believes in treating his readers as intellectual equals, regardless of their age.

Through his fiction, Southall attempts to identify with the experiences young people have during their lives. In an essay for *Something about the Author Autobiography Series* (*SAAS*) the author remarked: "Life is everyone's undiscovered land coming little by little into view. The excitement of it all is why I've spent the last twenty-five years putting words around it. I've seen this kind of writing as a worthy pursuit and an accomplishment worth the striving. It's why I've gone on largely resisting the urge to write of wider adult experiences. One of my objectives as a writer primarily for the young has been to 'protect' the great moments of life, not to spoil them or 'give them away.' It's why so many of my endings are open and why I've brought the reader to bridges over which imagination has to cross."

Through his writing career, Southall has consistently produced works that proved popular and received critical acclaim. Four times, he won Australian Children's Book of the Year Award. *Ash Road*, received the honor in 1966. In this novel, a fire burns out of control in the dry and windy Australian foothills and is rapidly approaching a house full of children. Southall offers an hour-by-hour account that increases in tension as the focus shifts from the boy who started the fire to the children in its path and also to their worried parents. A sudden storm stops the fire before it reaches the house.

Southall again received Australia's children's book of the year award in 1968 for *To the Wild Sky*. In this work, six children are flying across Australia in a private plane in order to attend a birthday party. Midway through the flight, the pilot of the aircraft collapses and although one of the children who has some knowledge of planes is able to safely land, the group is stranded on a deserted island. Southall provides hints that the children can survive, but he ends the novel without revealing the fate of the isolated group. However, seventeen years after *To the Wild Sky* was written, Southall provided the answers about what happened to the characters in the sequel *A City out of Sight*.

In 1972 Southall won England's Carnegie Medal—annually given in recognition of an outstanding book for children—for *Josh*. The story concerns a fourteen-year-old boy who visits his aunt who lives in a country town.

Josh is a sensitive boy who writes poetry. During his five-day stay, Josh tries to get along with his somewhat strange aunt and the young people of Ryan Creek whose attitudes and behavior are foreign to him. The town kids bully him and throw him into the water even though he can't swim. Although he is rescued, Josh realizes that he will never adapt to life in this environment and consequently returns home. In his *SAAS* essay, the author remarked, "The half-jesting, half-despairing inner dialogue of *Josh* comes directly out of my own teens."

Southall has continued his success with his more recent books. *Rachel,* published in 1986, is based on the childhood of the author's mother and is set in a gold mining town in the late 1800s. A reviewer for *Horn Book* remarked that "emotional intensity, irony, and a fine sense of comedy are brilliantly intermingled" in *Rachel.* Alan Brownjohn, writing in the *Times Literary Supplement,* states that with *Rachel* Southall "has produced an unusual, oddly memorable tale."

Southall is known for his storytelling ability, his sympathy for his young characters, and his habit of leaving the conclusions of his works ambiguous so the reader must imagine an ending. His label as one of Australia's most popular children's writers indicates that Southall was able to realize his dreams of becoming a famous author even though others thought he would be limited by his lack of education. Summing up the author's positive contribution to children's literature, Fox maintains that "Ivan Southall's ability is evident not merely in his technique, but also in the directness and sensitivity with which he handles areas children want to read about, and even 'should' read about."

BIOGRAPHICAL/CRITICAL SOURCES:

BOOKS

Children's Literature Review, Volume 2, Gale, 1976, pp. 145-158.
Something about the Author Autobiography Series, Volume 3, Gale, 1987, pp. 268-277.

PERIODICALS

Children's Book Review, December, 1971.
Children's Literature in Education, November, 1971, pp. 50, 52.
Horn Book, January/February, 1987, p. 62.
Times Literary Supplement, May 25, 1967; October 3, 1968; February 24, 1984; December 12, 1986, p. 1410.
Voice of Youth Advocates, April, 1987.

SPEAR, Hilda D(oris) 1926-

PERSONAL: Born August 27, 1926, in Pinner, England; daughter of Joseph Charles (in Royal Navy) and Blanche Elizabeth (a nurse; maiden name, Collins) King; married Walter E. Spear (a university professor), 1952; children: Gillian Spear Dolan, Kathryn. *Education:* Birkbeck College, London, B.A. (with honors), 1951, M.A., 1953; University of Leicester, Ph.D., 1972.

ADDRESSES: Office—Department of English, University of Dundee, Dundee DD1 4HN, Scotland.

CAREER: Teacher of English at secondary schools in London, England, 1946-48, and Leicester, England, 1952-56; Purdue University, West Lafayette, IN, lecturer in English, 1957-58; lecturer in English and education at colleges of education in Leicester, 1958-60; University of Leicester, Leicester, lecturer in English and education, 1965-68; University of Dundee, Dundee, Scotland, lecturer, 1969-87, senior lecturer in English, 1987—, senior adviser of studies, 1978-87. Guest lecturer at schools and universities in Great Britain, the United States, Japan, China, and India. Member of Bursaries Panel, Scottish Arts Council, 1981-86.

MEMBER: International Biographical Association (fellow), English Association, Dundee Literary Society.

AWARDS, HONORS: Prizes from Scottish Arts Council, 1978, for *The Poems and Selected Letters of C. H. Sorley,* and 1980, for *Remembering, We Forget;* awards from British Academy and Carnegie Trust, 1979, for *Remembering, We Forget.*

WRITINGS:

(Editor) *The English Poems of Charles Stuart Calverley,* Leicester University Press (Leicester), 1974.
(Editor) *The Poems and Selected Letters of C. H. Sorley,* Blackness Press, 1978.
Remembering, We Forget, Davis-Poynter, 1979.
Emily Bronte: Wuthering Heights (study outline), Macmillan (Basingstoke), 1985.
Forster: A Passage to India (study outline), Macmillan, 1986.
(With Abdel Moneim Aly) *Forster in Egypt,* Woolf (London), 1987.
(With Aly) *The Uncollected Egyptian Essays of E. M. Forster,* Blackness Press, 1988.
(Editor with B. Pandrich) *Sword and Pen: Poems of 1915 from Dundee and Tayside,* Aberdeen University Press (Aberdeen), 1989.
(With O. Yamada and D. Robb) *The Contribution to Literature of Orcadian Writer George Mackay Brown,* Edwin Mellen Press, 1991.
Iris Murdoch, Macmillan, in press.

Also author of a series of study notes to classic literary works for Longman, 1980-90.

OTHER

Contributor to books, including *Pelican Guide to English Literature,* edited by Boris Ford, Volume V, Penguin, 1957, 2nd edition, 1982; *Great Writers of the English Language,* edited by James Vinson and D. L. Kirkpatrick, Macmillan, 1980; *A Guide for Readers,* edited by Ford, Penguin, 1984; *British Literary Magazines,* edited by Alvin Sullivan, Greenwood Press, 1986; *Images of Egypt in Twentieth Century Literature,* edited by Hoda Gindi, Cairo University Press, 1991; *English Language Teaching: Theory and Practice,* edited by M. Tarinayya, T.R. Publications, 1992; *The Literature of Place,* edited by N. Page and P. Preston, Macmillan, 1993; *Reference Guide to Short Fiction,* edited by Noel Watson, St. James Press, 1994; and *Writing: Region and Nation,* edited by J. Davies and G. Pursglove, University of Wales Press, 1994.

Also author of *Your Bright Promise: An Evocation of the Life of Charles Sorley,* a dramatic narration first performed in 1986. Contributor to language and literature journals, including *Use of English, English, Four Decades of Poetry, English Literature in Transition, Durham University Journal, Scottish Review,* and *Lines Review.*

SIDELIGHTS: Hilda D. Spear told *CA:* "I find writing and research both absorbing and enjoyable. I also enjoy teaching, particularly passing on to students my own enthusiasms in reading and research. Literature should always give the reader pleasure of some kind.

"I suppose that, like many writers and academics, I am a dissident liberal, I don't know the answers and wish I did; but I am aware of the problems! It is this which makes a study of war literature so especially fascinating.

"However, I believe that concentrated work on any area of literature brings its rewards; I very rarely find that I am unable to receive intellectual pleasure from poems, novels or plays that I happen to be working on. My dramatic narration *Your Bright Promise* was the result of a public performance to accompany an exhibition on the life and work of Sorley. It was one of the results of a sabbatical year; the other results were mainly academic but the year off has made me realise how important it is to be able, occasionally, to stand back and have leisure to think and to brood. I shouldn't like it all the time; I suspect that I am a bit of a workaholic; at least I enjoy working!"

*   *   *

SPYKER, John Howland
See ELMAN, Richard

STACEY, Thomas Charles Gerard 1930-
(Tom Stacey)

PERSONAL: Born January 11, 1930, in Bletchingly, England; son of David Henry and Gwen (Part) Stacey; married Caroline Clay, January 5, 1952; children: Emma, Mathilda, Isabella, Samuel, Tomasina. *Education:* Attended Eton College, Oxford. *Politics:* "Lapsed Conservative." *Religion:* Anglican.

ADDRESSES: Home—128 Kensington Church St., London W8, England. *Agent*—Jacintha Alexander Associates, 47 Emperor's Gate, London SW7 4HJ, England.

CAREER: Picture Post, London, England, writer and foreign correspondent, 1952-54; *Daily Express,* London, foreign and diplomatic correspondent, 1954, 1956-60; *Montreal Star,* Montreal, Quebec, correspondent, 1955-56; *Sunday Times,* London, chief roving correspondent, 1960-65; *Evening Standard,* London, columnist, 1965-67; Correspondents World Wide, London, managing director, 1967-71; Stacey International (formerly Tom Stacey Ltd.), London, managing director, 1969—. Occasional columnist for *Daily Telegraph.* Conservative party parliamentary candidate, North Hammersmith, 1960-64, and Dover, 1965-67; public lecturer on foreign affairs. Governor, Christopher Wren School, 1960-68, Wandsworth School, 1971-79, St. David's and St. Katharine's School, 1992—. *Military service:* Scots Guards, 1949-50, served in Malaya; became second lieutenant.

MEMBER: Royal Society of Literature (fellow), Royal Geographical Society (fellow), White's Club, Beefsteak Club, Pratts Club.

AWARDS, HONORS: John Llewellyn Rhys Memorial Prize, 1954, for *The Hostile Sun: A Malayan Journey;* Granada Award for journalism, 1961.

WRITINGS:

NOVELS UNDER NAME TOM STACEY

The Brothers M., Secker & Warburg (London), 1960, Pantheon (New York City), 1961.
The Living and the Dying, Macmillan (London), 1976.
The Pandemonium, W. H. Allen (London), 1980.
The Twelfth Night of Ramadan, Vanguard, 1983.
The Worm in the Rose, Stein & Day (Briarcliff Manor, NY), 1985.
Deadline, St. Martin's (New York City), 1988.
Decline, Heinemann (London), 1991.

NONFICTION UNDER NAME TOM STACEY

The Hostile Sun: A Malayan Journey, Duckworth (London), 1953.
Summons to Ruwenzori, Secker & Warburg, 1965.

Immigration and Enoch Powell, Tom Stacey Ltd. (London), 1970.

EDITOR UNDER NAME TOM STACEY

Today's World: A Map Notebook for World Affairs, Collins (London), 1968.
(With Caroline Hayman) *Correspondents World Wide,* Correspondents World Wide, 1968.
(With Rowland St. Oswald) *Here Come the Tories,* Tom Stacey Ltd., 1970.

Editor-in-chief, *Chambers's Encyclopaedia Yearbook,* 1969-72; editorial director, *Peoples of the World,* twenty volumes, Grolier, 1971-73.

OTHER

Deadline (screenplay), British Broadcasting Corp. Television, 1988.
Bodies and Souls (short stories), Heinemann, 1989.

Contributor to books, including *Called Up,* edited by Peter Chambers and Amy Landreth, Wingate, 1955; *Africa: A Handbook to the Continent,* edited by Colin Legum, Praeger, 1961; *Encore,* M. Joseph, 1962; *Race, Class, and Power,* edited by R. W. Mack, American Book Co., 1963; and *Bradshawe's Guide: The Best of Magazine Writing,* Frewin, 1968.

WORK IN PROGRESS: Blackness and Darkness, a book on the future of Africa.

SIDELIGHTS: During his career as a foreign correspondent, Tom Stacey traveled more than one million miles and visited over one hundred countries. He made an overland crossing of Africa in the mid-1950s, during which he conducted an anthropological study of the Bakonjo tribe. When this tribe, living in the Ruwenzori Mountains of Uganda, staged a rebellion in 1963, Stacey was called in by the government to settle the conflict. His account of the rebellion and how it was resolved is related in *Summons to Ruwenzori.* The novel *The Brothers M.* is set in Africa and draws upon Stacey's experiences there.

BIOGRAPHICAL/CRITICAL SOURCES:

PERIODICALS

Atlantic, July, 1961.
Booklist, June 1, 1961.
Christian Science Monitor, April 13, 1961.
Guardian, October 14, 1960.
Listener, February 12, 1976.
New Statesman, October 22, 1960; April 9, 1965; February 6, 1976.
New York Times Book Review, April 30, 1961.
Observer (London), February 22, 1976; February 10, 1980.
Observer Magazine, March 17, 1991.
Saturday Review, June 10, 1961.

Spectator, October 14, 1960.
Sunday Telegraph, January 27, 1980.
Time, May 12, 1961.
Time and Tide, September, 1972.
Times (London), February 19, 1976.
Times Literary Supplement, October 21, 1960; April 22, 1965; February 12, 1971; February 6, 1976; February 8, 1980.
Washington Times Magazine, March 24, 1986.

*   *   *

STACEY, Tom
See STACEY, Thomas Charles Gerard

*   *   *

STARK, Freya (Madeline)   1893-1993

PERSONAL: Born January 31, 1893, in Paris, France; died May 9, 1993, in Asolo, Italy; daughter of Robert (a sculptor) and Flora Stark (a painter and pianist); married Stewart Perowne, 1947 (separated, 1952). *Education:* Attended University of London and the School of Oriental and African Studies. *Avocational interests:* Travel, mountaineering, embroidery.

CAREER: "As for a career, I cannot tell you very much as I have only been a regular paid worker during the war when I was taken on in Aden and Egypt by our Ministry of Information, and in Iraq (Bagdad) as attache to the British Embassy. I then was sent on a mission to the United States—described in *Dust in the Lion's Paw* and Volume V of *Letters*—and for the last six months of the war to India as a personal worker for Lady Wavell, who was then the Vicereine. That is as much as I have done in an official way, and the rest of my 'working life' has been spent traveling in Persia, Turkey, or the Arab lands. All of this has been recorded in one book or another."

MEMBER: Sister of the Order of St. John of Jerusalem, 1949.

AWARDS, HONORS: Triennial Burton Memorial Medal, Royal Asiatic Society, 1934; Mungo Park Medal, Royal Scottish Geographical Society, 1936; Founders Medal, Royal Geographical Society, 1942; Percy Sykes Memorial Medal, Royal Central Asiatic Society, 1951; L.L.D., University of Glasgow, 1951; Cross of British Empire, 1953; D.Litt., University of Durham, 1971; Dame of British Empire, 1972.

WRITINGS:

The Valleys of the Assassins and Other Persian Travels, J. Murray, 1934, revised edition, Transatlantic (Albuquerque, NM), 1972.

The Southern Gates of Arabia: A Journey in the Hadhramaut, Dutton, 1936, reprinted, J. P. Tarcher (Los Angeles, CA), 1983.

Baghdad Sketches, J. Murray, 1937, Dutton (New York City), 1938.

Seen in the Hadhramaut, J. Murray, 1938, Dutton, 1939.

A Winter in Arabia, Dutton, 1940, new edition, J. Murray, 1972, reprinted, Overlook Press (New York City), 1987.

Letters from Syria, J. Murray, 1942.

The Arab Island: The Middle East, 1939-1943, Knopf (New York City), 1945.

East Is West, Knopf, 1945.

Perseus in the Wind, J. Murray, 1948, Beacon Press (Boston, MA), 1956.

Traveller's Prelude (also see below), J. Murray, 1950.

Beyond Euphrates: Autobiography, 1928-1933 (also see below), J. Murray, 1951.

The Coast of Incense: Autobiography, 1933-1939 (also see below), J. Murray, 1953.

The Freya Stark Story (condensation in one volume of *Traveller's Prelude, Beyond Euphrates,* and *The Coast of Incense*), Coward, 1953.

Ionia: A Quest, Harcourt (New York City), 1954.

The Lycian Shore, Harcourt, 1956.

(Contributor) Roloff Beny, *The Thrones of Earth and Heaven,* Abrams (New York City), 1958, 2nd edition, 1959.

Alexander's Path: From Caria to Cilicia, Harcourt, 1958, reprinted, Transatlantic, 1975, reissued, Overlook Press, 1988.

Riding to the Tigris, J. Murray, 1959, Harcourt, 1960.

Dust in the Lion's Paw: Autobiography, 1939-1946, J. Murray, 1961, Harcourt, 1962.

The Journey's Echo, J. Murray, 1963, reprinted, Ecco Press (New York City), 1988.

Rome on the Euphrates: The Story of a Frontier, J. Murray, 1966, Harcourt, 1967.

The Zodiac Arch, J. Murray, 1968, Harcourt, 1969.

The Minaret of Djam: An Excursion in Afghanistan, J. Murray, 1970, Transatlantic, 1972.

Gateways and Caravans: A Portrait of Turkey, Macmillan (New York City), 1971 (published in England as *Turkey: A Sketch of Turkish History,* Thames & Hudson (London), 1971).

Letters, edited by L. Moorehead, Volume I: *The Furnace and the Cup, 1914-30,* Compton Russell, 1974, Volume II: *The Open Door, 1930-35,* Compton Russell, 1975, Volume III: *The Growth of Danger, 1935-39,* Compton Russell, 1976, Volume IV, *Bridge of the Levant, 1940-43,* Michael Russell, 1977, Volume V: *New Worlds for Old, 1943-46,* Michael Russell, 1978.

A Peak in Darien, J. Murray, 1976, Transatlantic, 1977.

Rivers of Time, W. Blackwood, 1982.

Over the Rim of the World (selected letters), edited by Caroline Moorehead, J. Murray, 1988.

Also author of *Space, Time and Movement in Landscape,* 1969; *Letters,* Vol. VI: *The Broken Road, 1947-52,* 1981; Vol. VII: *Some Talk of Alexander, 1952-59,* 1982; Vol. VIII: *The Traveller's Epilogue, 1960-80,* 1982.

SIDELIGHTS: "To anyone familiar with the chronicles of travel in the primitive regions of the Middle East, the name of Freya Stark is an illustrious one," declared a *Canadian Forum* writer. As the author of more than two dozen autobiographical travel books which, a *Times Literary Supplement* critic stated, rank "among the best of their kind in our generation," Stark exhibited "a remarkable rapport with the people of exotic lands" as well as "a luminous style," according to the *New Yorker.* Robert Payne of the *New York Times Book Review* noted that "she writes angelically in the great tradition of Charles Doughty and T. E. Lawrence. The pulse quickens as you read, because she can bring the sights and sounds of incredible countries before you in the twinkling of an eye."

The typical Freya Stark book combines traditional travel writing with practical hints and a tough-minded personal philosophy some have called "old-fashioned" because it emphasizes the lessons man can learn from history (particularly Roman history). The finished product, stated a *Christian Science Monitor* reviewer, has "a charming but uncloying flavor, a saltiness which is not bitter, and an argumentativeness which never puffs itself up." The *Spectator's* David Stone praised Stark's ability to make her books "both entertainment and literature," while J. G. Harrison of the *Christian Science Monitor* noted: "Of very few writers, today's or the past's, can it be said that they find it almost impossible to be dull, to be in poor taste or to be less than highly literate. It can of Miss Stark. Indeed, it is hard to think of any writer alive today who so unfailingly achieves this high standard as does she."

Another *Times Literary Supplement* critic agreed with these assessments of Stark's work. He wrote: "Unlike many travellers soaked in the literature and archaeology of past civilizations, Miss Stark is constantly alive to her immediate surroundings: indeed, what gives her work its extraordinary depth and power is just this ability to focus past and present as it were stereoscopically, in a single image. . . . Yet all this would be of little avail if she did not also possess a superb prose style in which to express her vision: rich yet never rococo, each simile and metaphor sharply original, the apparent simplicity of description concealing a rare talent for picking the mot juste."

Concluded still another *Times Literary Supplement* critic: "Miss Stark unites in one mind the traveller, the historian, the philosopher and the poet: she sees life clearly, yet with passion and depth as well as wholeness. . . . [She sheds] fresh light on our own experiences and assumptions by holding up the past to us."

BIOGRAPHICAL/CRITICAL SOURCES:

PERIODICALS

Atlantic, April, 1960.
Books, December 30, 1934; October 4, 1936; February 12, 1939.
Canadian Forum, July, 1968.
Chicago Sunday Tribune, April 19, 1959; January 28, 1962.
Christian Century, December 5, 1956.
Christian Science Monitor, July 11, 1934; July 8, 1936; December 4, 1937; August 17, 1940; June 13, 1949; December 3, 1953; December 9, 1954; June 2, 1955; March 19, 1959; March 21, 1960; January 25, 1962; March 21, 1967; March 6, 1969.
Commonweal, August 12, 1955; September 7, 1956; July 8, 1960.
Economist, October 1, 1966.
Forum, November, 1936; February, 1938.
Manchester Guardian, June 23, 1936; May 22, 1956; November 14, 1958; December 4, 1959.
New Republic, November 11, 1936.
New Statesman, December 6, 1958; December 12, 1959; November 24, 1961; January 20, 1967; December 11, 1970.
New Statesman and Nation, June 2, 1934; May 30, 1936; December 4, 1937; December 17, 1938; January 1, 1949; October 9, 1954; June 16, 1956.
New Yorker, April 16, 1960; January 27, 1962; April 25, 1964; March 22, 1969.
New York Herald Tribune Book Review, November 15, 1953; June 5, 1955; August 12, 1956; March 15, 1959; April 3, 1960.
New York Times, October 11, 1936; January 9, 1938; January 29, 1939; November 10, 1940; November 18, 1945; May 1, 1949; November 1, 1953; June 12, 1955; August 12, 1956; March 15, 1959.
New York Times Book Review, March 27, 1960; January 28, 1962; April 5, 1964.
San Francisco Chronicle, May 26, 1955; August 12, 1956; March 17, 1959.
Saturday Review, June 9, 1934; August 6, 1955; May 12, 1962.
Saturday Review of Literature, October 20, 1934; November 7, 1936; February 19, 1938; March 30, 1946.
Spectator, June 15, 1934; July 10, 1936; November 19, 1937; June 28, 1940; November 26, 1948; November 12, 1954; July 6, 1956; October 17, 1958.
Times Literary Supplement, May 30, 1936; October 30, 1937; December 24, 1938; June 29, 1940; December 4, 1948; October 15, 1954; May 4, 1956; October 24, 1958; December 4, 1959; November 3, 1961; Novem-

ber 24, 1966; July 25, 1968; December 4, 1970; July 25, 1968.
Weekly Book Review, November 18, 1945.
Yale Review, spring, 1946.

OBITUARIES:

PERIODICALS

Los Angeles Times, May 11, 1993, p. A20.
New York Times, May 11, 1993, p. B7.
Times (London), May 11, 1993, p. 17.*

*   *   *

STEFFANSON, Con
   See CASSIDAY, Bruce (Bingham)

*   *   *

STEVENSON, James   1929-

PERSONAL: Born in 1929, in New York, NY; son of Harvey (an architect) and Winifred (Worcester) Stevenson; married Jane Walker, 1953; children: five sons, four daughters. *Education:* Yale University, B.A., 1951.

ADDRESSES: Home—Connecticut.

CAREER: Life, New York City, reporter, 1954-56; *New Yorker,* New York City, cartoonist and writer for "Talk of the Town," 1956-1963; creator of "Capitol Games" (syndicated political comic strip); writer and illustrator, 1962—. *Military service:* U.S. Marine Corps, 1951-53.

AWARDS, HONORS: New York Times Outstanding Children's Book of the Year and *School Library Journal* Best Books for Spring honor, both 1977, for *"Could Be Worse!";* American Library Association (ALA) Notable Book designation, 1978, for *The Sea View Hotel,* 1979, for *Fast Friends: Two Stories,* 1980, for *That Terrible Halloween Night; School Library Journal* Best Books for Spring honor, 1979, for *Monty;* Children's Choice Award, International Reading Association, 1979, for *The Worst Person in the World,* 1980, for *That Terrible Halloween Night,* 1982, for *The Night after Christmas,* 1989, for *The Supreme Souvenir Factory,* and 1990, for *Oh No, It's Waylon's Birthday!;* Best Illustrated Book and Outstanding Book honors, both *New York Times,* 1980, for *Howard; School Library Journal* Best Books of 1981 honor, for *The Wish Card Ran Out!; Boston Globe/Horn Book* honor list, 1981, for *The Night after Christmas;* Christopher Award, 1982, for *We Can't Sleep;* Parents Choice Award, 1982, for *Oliver, Clarence, and Violet; Boston Globe/Horn Book* honor list, ALA Notable Book designation, *School Library Journal* Best Books of 1983 honor, all 1983, for

What's under My Bed?; Garden State Children's Book Award, New Jersey Library Association, 1983, for *Clams Can't Sing;* ALA Notable Book designation, 1986, for *When I Was Nine; Redbook* award, 1987, for *Higher on the Door.*

WRITINGS:

Do Yourself a Favor, Kid (novel), Macmillan (New York City), 1962.

The Summer Houses, Macmillan, 1963.

Sorry, Lady, This Beach Is Private! (cartoons), Macmillan, 1963.

Sometimes, But Not Always (novel), Little, Brown (Boston), 1967.

Something Marvelous Is About to Happen (humor), Harper (New York City), 1971.

Cool Jack and the Beanstalk, Penguin (New York City), 1976.

Let's Boogie! (cartoons), Dodd (New York City), 1978.

Uptown Local, Downtown Express, Viking (New York City), 1983.

SELF-ILLUSTRATED BOOKS FOR CHILDREN

Walker, the Witch, and the Striped Flying Saucer, Little, Brown, 1969.

The Bear Who Had No Place to Go, Harper, 1972.

Here Comes Herb's Hurricane!, Harper, 1973.

"Could be Worse!," Greenwillow (New York City), 1977.

Wilfred the Rat, Greenwillow, 1977.

(With daughter, Edwina Stevenson) *"Help!" Yelled Maxwell,* Greenwillow, 1978.

The Sea View Hotel, Greenwillow, 1978.

Winston, Newton, Elton, and Ed, Greenwillow, 1978.

The Worst Person in the World, Greenwillow, 1978.

Fast Friends: Two Stories, Greenwillow, 1979.

Monty, Greenwillow, 1979.

Howard, Greenwillow, 1980.

That Terrible Halloween Night, Greenwillow, 1980.

Clams Can't Sing, Greenwillow, 1980.

The Night after Christmas, Greenwillow, 1981.

The Wish Card Ran Out!, Greenwillow, 1981.

The Whale Tale, Random House (New York City), 1981.

Oliver, Clarence, and Violet, Greenwillow, 1982.

We Can't Sleep, Greenwillow, 1982.

What's under My Bed?, Greenwillow, 1983.

The Great Big Especially Beautiful Easter Egg, Greenwillow, 1983.

Barbara's Birthday, Greenwillow, 1983.

Grandpa's Great City Tour: An Alphabet Book, Greenwillow, 1983.

Worse Than Willy!, Greenwillow, 1984.

Yuck!, Greenwillow, 1984.

Emma, Greenwillow, 1985.

Are We Almost There?, Greenwillow, 1985.

That Dreadful Day, Greenwillow, 1985.

Fried Feathers for Thanksgiving, Greenwillow, 1986.

No Friends, Greenwillow, 1986.

There's Nothing To Do!, Greenwillow, 1986.

When I Was Nine, Greenwillow, 1986.

Happy Valentine's Day, Emma!, Greenwillow, 1987.

Higher on the Door (sequel to *When I Was Nine*), Greenwillow, 1987.

No Need for Monty, Greenwillow, 1987.

Will You Please Feed Our Cat?, Greenwillow, 1987.

The Supreme Souvenir Factory, Greenwillow, 1988.

We Hate Rain!, Greenwillow, 1988.

The Worst Person in the World at Crab Beach, Greenwillow, 1988.

Grandpa's Too-Good Garden, Greenwillow, 1989.

Oh No, It's Waylon's Birthday!, Greenwillow, 1989.

Un-Happy New Year, Emma!, Greenwillow, 1989.

Emma at the Beach, Greenwillow, 1990.

Mr. Hacker, illustrated by Frank Modell, Greenwillow, 1990.

July, Greenwillow, 1990.

National Worm Day, Greenwillow, 1990.

Quick! Turn the Page!, Greenwillow, 1990.

The Stowaway, Greenwillow, 1990.

Which One Is Whitney?, Greenwillow, 1990.

Brrr!, Greenwillow, 1991.

That's Exactly the Way It Wasn't, Greenwillow, 1991.

The Worst Person's Christmas, Greenwillow, 1991.

Rolling Rose, Greenwillow, 1991.

Don't You Know There's a War On?, Greenwillow, 1992.

And Then What?, Greenwillow, 1992.

The Flying Acorns, Greenwillow, 1993.

The Pattaconk Brook, Greenwillow, 1993.

Fun—No Fun, Greenwillow, 1994.

The Mud Flat Olympics, Greenwillow, 1994.

Worst Than the Worst, Greenwillow, 1994.

OTHER

Also author of plays and television sketches. Illustrator of numerous books, including William K. Zinsser's *Weekend Guests: From "We're So Glad You Could Come" to "We're So Sorry You Have to Go,"* and *Vice-Versa,* Harper, 1963; John Donovan's *Good Old James,* Harper, 1975; Franz Brandenberg's *Otto Is Different,* Greenwillow, 1985; Jack Prelutsky's *Something Big Has Been Here,* Greenwillow, 1980; and Helen V. Griffith's *Grandaddy and Janetta,* Greenwillow, 1993. Contributor of articles to *New Yorker.*

ADAPTATIONS: Many of Stevenson's books have been adapted for filmstrip or audio cassette, including *Fast Friends,* Educational Enrichment Materials, 1981; *"Could Be Worse!"* and *That Terrible Halloween Night,* both Educational Enrichment Materials, 1982; *What's under My Bed?,* Weston Woods, 1984; *We Can't Sleep,* Random House, 1984, re-released on videocassette, 1988; *Howard* was adapted for film as *New Friends,* Made-to-Order Library Products; *"Could Be Worse!"* and *What's under My Bed?* were highlighted on *Reading Rainbow,* PBS-TV.

SIDELIGHTS: A noted humorist and children's author, James Stevenson began primarily as a suburban satirist, expanding his subjects to include social criticism, nostalgia, and children's problems. Stevenson's early novels and cartoons explored suburban lifestyles. For example, one cartoon published in the 1960s pictured an elderly commuter in a business suit sitting on a railroad bench in his living room. The commuter's wife explains: "He retired last January, but he's been tapering off gradually." After considering this cartoon and similar works, one *Newsweek* writer indicated that Stevenson's "understated and gentle humor exploited incongruity and anachronisms to penetrate facades and assumptions" of suburbia.

Likewise, other critics found that Stevenson's autobiographical novel *Sometimes, But Not Always* shows the ludicrousness of contemporary life through suburbanite Joe Roberts, a laboring gag writer plagued by financial stress. Roberts works several jobs to attain financial security for his harried wife and many children, but he nevertheless suffers with a recurring nightmare that a banker forecloses on his home and family. Roberts eventually becomes the idea man for *So What Else Is New?,* a television series affectionately known as "SWEIN." In this role he persuades Rosco Ritz, a has-been vaudevillian, to appear on a show in which the song-and-dance man is cruelly humiliated. When Ritz dies, Roberts is beset by guilt. He flees to the town dump where he decides amid the junk that everyone is "obsolete" and disposable. Reviewing *Sometimes, But Not Always,* a *Time* reviewer commented that "author Stevenson has combined a sardonic view of showbiz with verbal cartooning that veers into wild hallucination."

By the late 1960s Stevenson moved from covering suburbanites to lampooning national problems, and a *Newsweek* reporter observed that "his political art, like his suburban drawings, remains humorous and even playful." One of Stevenson's first social commentaries was a six-page *New Yorker* cartoon spread that satirized the U.S. military. Titled "The ABCs of Your ABM: A Public Service Pamphlet from Your Defense Department," the feature advocated disarmament and parodied Pentagonese. Similarly, part of Stevenson's 1971 book *Something Marvelous Is About to Happen* satirized government investigative panels by scrutinizing the credentials of a Professor Lamberti, a cult hero and xylophonist. The outcome of the inquiry is of course vague, for as S. K. Oberbeck explained in *Newsweek,* "That's Stevenson's world." "In one flourish," Oberbeck continued, "he captures the frustration and befuddlement of modern man awash in government's and media's programmed inconclusiveness." However delighted Oberbeck was with Stevenson's political satire, the

reviewer still maintained that the humorist's "forays into nostalgia are really his forte." For example, in *Something Marvelous Is About to Happen* Stevenson doodles a portrait of his early life, including a disclosure that his brother's hidden diary was boring.

In addition to recalling his childhood, Stevenson explores the predicaments of most children in his many juvenile books, particularly those featuring Mary Ann, Louie, and their grandfather. For example, *Worse Than Willy!* confronts the problem of sibling rivalry. Mary Ann and Louie quickly become jealous of their parents' doting on their new brother Willy. They complain to Grandpa, who tells them of his similar dilemma years ago when his brother Wainwright was born. Grandpa felt ignored while Wainwright was hugged and kissed. So he threw blocks at his brother, ruined the baby's toys and books, and always received full blame, for his parents never found fault with Wainwright. Mary Ann and Louie finally concede that Wainwright was "worse than Willy," so Grandpa tells them an elaborate tale of adventure in which young Wainwright saves his life.

Elizabeth Crow, for one, praised *Worse Than Willy* in the *New York Times Book Review* for putting a child's problem into perspective. "This is a terrific book for little children," she remarked, "good-humored, hysterically funny and true about sibling rivalry. . . . Mr. Stevenson understands that this too shall pass, and that it'll pass a lot quicker if you make up a funny story about it."

An earlier Mary Ann and Louie story, *That Terrible Halloween Night,* has the children attempting to frighten Grandpa because he is apparently unimpressed by the holiday. They disguise themselves and the dog, but Grandpa remains collected; rather than being scared, he frightens them with a spooky story of his adventures as a youth in a "strange" house. According to a *Washington Post Book World* reviewer, in *That Terrible Halloween Night* "Stevenson, as always, manages to convey an entire world—its style, its atmosphere, and the emotions of its inhabitants—through a few strokes of his pen."

Stevenson has expanded his cast of characters throughout his career as a children's author. Several books, including *Emma* and *Un-Happy New Year, Emma!,* are about a good-natured young witch/apprentice named Emma who triumphs over the efforts of two older sorceresses, Dolores and Lavinia, to undermine her attempts at magic. Then there are the "worst" books. The "worst," an old curmudgeon, disguises his need for companionship by grumbling and complaining where the most people will hear him. In *The Worst Person's Christmas,* the protagonist relishes the spirit of the holiday season: "That night the worst put a chair by his front window so that, when the carol singers came, he could tell them to get off his property and go away." As in Stevenson's other "worst" books, *The Worst Person in the World* and *The Worst Person in the World at Crab Beach,* a series of mishaps occur that don't exactly make the worst any nicer, but by story's end he is no longer the worst person in the whole world.

Stevenson began writing and drawing as a boy and was encouraged by his father who was a watercolorist. He says he was influenced by movies and comics rather than any of the children's books he read as a child. "I think that my experience and creative mind have been formed much more by movies and comic books," he once told *CA.* "I like the idea of a storyboard and I like the idea of a movie and all the different angles from which things can be viewed."

Stevenson's books are often illustrated in comic-book or cartoon style. The intermix of story line with dialogue "balloons" and graffiti adds energy and dimension to his humorously-drawn tales. The use of pencil as an artistic medium in drawing his appealing, scruffy characters brings an air of informality and spontaneity to his stories. Stevenson adds a wash of soft color to his drawings, avoiding the vivid contrasts of the traditional comic book in favor of a more subtle effect.

"I have no ideas until I sit here with the paper in front of me," Stevenson told Kimberly Olson Fakih in *Publishers Weekly.* "I never think of cartoon ideas until I'm here. For children's books, it's a different desk. One of the problems of working is that you try to stay fresh. You can't do it unless you just stop and do something else." To his young audience, Stevenson has continued to provide a fresh, lively view of things. As Karla Kuskin wrote in the *New York Times Book Review,* "Whether writing or drawing, Mr. Stevenson understands perfectly the strength of a simple understated line and a quiet laugh."

BIOGRAPHICAL/CRITICAL SOURCES:

BOOKS

Children's Literature Review, Volume 17, Gale, 1989, pp. 148-168.
Kingman, Lee, and others, compilers, *Illustrators of Children's Books: 1967-1976,* Horn Book, 1978.
Stevenson, James, *Sometimes, But Not Always,* Little, Brown, 1967.
Stevenson, James, *The Worst Person's Christmas,* Greenwillow, 1991.
Twentieth Century Children's Writers, 3rd edition, St. James Press, 1989, pp. 919-920.

PERIODICALS

Atlantic, July, 1963.
Best Sellers, August 15, 1967.
Books for Your Children, autumn-winter, 1985, p. 25.

Chicago Tribune Book World, October 5, 1980; April 10, 1983.
Christian Science Monitor, November 6, 1969; November 10, 1980.
Commonweal, November 11, 1977.
Horn Book, August, 1977, pp. 432-433; September-October, 1985, p. 605.
Junior Bookshelf, December, 1971, p. 367.
Los Angeles Times Book Review, August 14, 1983.
National Observer, July 24, 1967.
Newsweek, April 8, 1963; July 14, 1969; December 29, 1971; December 11, 1978; December 18, 1978; December 7, 1981.
New Yorker, July 20, 1963; August 5, 1967; December 11, 1971; December 2, 1972; December 6, 1982.
New York Times, August 4, 1972.
New York Times Book Review, July 23, 1967; August 7, 1977; November 13, 1977; April 30, 1978; June 17, 1979; October 7, 1979; April 27, 1980; October 26, 1980; April 26, 1981; November 15, 1981, p. 57; April 25, 1982; November 14, 1982; March 27, 1983; April 24, 1983; May 20, 1984.
Publishers Weekly, February 27, 1987, pp. 148-149.
Saturday Review/World, December 4, 1973.
Spectator, November 13, 1971.
Time, April 12, 1963; August 4, 1967; December 4, 1978.
Times Educational Supplement, October 21, 1977; December 14, 1979; January 18, 1980; March 27, 1981; February 18, 1983, p. 30.
Village Voice, December 11, 1978.
Washington Post Book World, October 26, 1969; April 13, 1980; October 12, 1980; December 13, 1981; May 13, 1984.

*   *   *

STEWART, J(ohn) I(nnes) M(ackintosh) 1906-1994
(Michael Innes)

PERSONAL: Born September 30, 1906, in Edinburgh, Scotland; died November 12, 1994, in Surrey, England; son of John (in education) and Eliza Jane (Clark) Stewart; married Margaret Hardwick (a physician), 1932, (died 1979); children: three sons, two daughters. *Education:* Oriel College, Oxford, M.A., 1928.

ADDRESSES: Home—Lower Park House, Occupation Road, Lindley, Huddersfield HD3 3EE, England.

CAREER: Writer. University of Leeds, Yorkshire, England, lecturer in English, 1930-35; University of Adelaide, Adelaide, South Australia, jury professor of English, 1935-45; Queen's University, Belfast, Northern Ireland, lecturer, 1946-48; Oxford University, Oxford,

England, reader in English literature, 1969-73. Student of Christ Church, Oxford, 1949-73, became emeritus; Walker Ames Professor at University of Washington, 1961.

AWARDS, HONORS: Matthew Arnold Memorial Prize, 1929; D.Litt., University of New Brunswick, 1962, University of Leicester, 1979, St. Andrews University, 1980; Honorary Fellow of the Royal Society, Edinburgh, 1990.

WRITINGS:

NOVELS

Mark Lambert's Supper, Gollancz (London), 1954.
The Guardians, Gollancz, 1955, Norton (New York City), 1957.
A Use of Riches, Norton, 1957.
The Man Who Won the Pools, Norton, 1961.
The Last Tresilians, Norton, 1963.
An Acre of Grass, Norton, 1965.
The Aylwins, Norton, 1966.
Vanderlyn's Kingdom, Norton, 1967.
Avery's Mission, Norton, 1971.
A Palace of Art, Norton, 1972.
Mungo's Dream, Norton, 1973.
The Gaudy (first book in "A Staircase in Surrey" quintet), Gollancz, 1974, Norton, 1975.
Young Pattullo (second book in "A Staircase in Surrey" quintet), Gollancz, 1975, Norton, 1976.
A Memorial Service (third book in "A Staircase in Surrey" quintet), Norton, 1976.
The Madonna of the Astrolabe (fourth book in "A Staircase in Surrey" quintet), Norton, 1977.
Full Term (fifth book in "A Staircase in Surrey" quintet), Norton, 1978.
Andrew and Tobias, Norton, 1980.
A Villa in France, Norton, 1982.
An Open Prison, Norton, 1984.
The Naylors, Norton, 1985.

NOVELS; UNDER PSEUDONYM MICHAEL INNES

Death at the President's Lodging, Gollancz, 1936, also published as *Seven Suspects,* Dodd (New York City), 1937.
Hamlet, Revenge!, Dodd, 1937.
Lament for a Maker, Dodd, 1938.
The Spider Strikes Back, Dodd, 1939, published in England as *Stop Press,* Gollancz, 1939.
A Comedy of Terrors (also see below), Dodd, 1940, published in England as *There Came Both Mist and Snow,* Gollancz, 1940.
Appleby on Ararat, Dodd, 1941.
The Daffodil Affair, Dodd, 1942.

The Weight of the Evidence, Gollancz, 1943, Dodd, 1944.
What Happened at Hazelwood, Gollancz, 1944, Dodd, 1947.
Appleby's End, Dodd, 1945.
Unsuspected Chasm, Dodd, 1945, published in England as *From London Far,* Gollancz, 1946.
Night of Errors, Gollancz, 1947, Dodd, 1948.
The Case of the Journeying Boy, Dodd, 1949, published in England as *The Journeying Boy,* Gollancz, 1949.
Paper Thunderbolt, Dodd, 1951, published in England as *Operation Pax,* Gollancz, 1951.
One Man Show (also see below), Dodd, 1952, published in England as *A Private View,* Gollancz, 1952.
Christmas at Candleshoe, Dodd, 1953.
The Man from the Sea, Dodd, 1955.
A Question of Queens, Dodd, 1956, published in England as *Old Hall, New Hall,* Gollancz, 1956.
Death on a Quiet Day, Dodd, 1957, published in England as *Appleby Plays Chicken,* Gollancz, 1957.
The Long Farewell, Dodd, 1958.
Hare Sitting Up, Dodd, 1959.
The Case of Sonia Wayward, Dodd, 1960, published in England as *The New Sonia Wayward,* Gollancz, 1960.
Silence Observed, Dodd, 1961.
The Crabtree Affair, Dodd, 1962, published in England as *A Connoisseur's Case,* Gollancz, 1962.
Money from Holme, Gollancz, 1964, Dodd, 1965.
The Bloody Wood, Dodd, 1966.
A Change of Heir, Dodd, 1966.
Death by Water, Dodd, 1968.
Appleby at Allington, Dodd, 1968.
Picture of Guilt, Dodd, 1969, published in England as *A Family Affair,* Gollancz, 1969.
Death at the Chase, Dodd, 1970.
An Awkward Lie, Dodd, 1971.
The Open House, Dodd, 1972.
Appleby's Answer, Dodd, 1973.
Appleby's Other Story, Gollancz, 1973, Dodd, 1974.
The Mysterious Commission, Gollancz, 1974, Dodd, 1975.
The Gay Phoenix, Gollancz, 1976, Dodd, 1977.
Honeybath's Haven, Gollancz, 1977, Dodd, 1978.
The Ampersand Papers, Dodd, 1978.
Going It Alone, Dodd, 1980.
Lord Mullion's Secret, Dodd, 1981.
Sheiks and Adders, Dodd, 1982.
Appleby and Honeybath, Dodd, 1983.
Carson's Conspiracy, Dodd, 1984.
Appleby and the Ospreys, Dodd, 1986.

OTHER

(Editor) Michel Eyquen de Montaigne, *Montaigne's Essays: John Florio's Translation,* Random House (New York City), 1931.
Educating the Emotions, [Adelaide, Australia], 1944.

(Contributor) Raynor Heppenstall, editor, *Imaginary Conversations: Eight Radio Scripts,* Secker & Warburg (London), 1948.

Characters and Motive in Shakespeare: Some Recent Appraisals Examined, Longman, 1949.

(Under pseudonym Michael Innes; with Heppenstall) *Three Tales of Hamlet,* Gollancz, 1950.

(Under pseudonym Michael Innes) *Dead Man's Shoes,* Dodd, 1954, published in England as *Appleby Talking: Twenty-Three Detective Stories,* Gollancz, 1954.

(Under pseudonym Michael Innes) *Appleby Talks Again: Eighteen Detective Stories,* Gollancz, 1956, Dodd, 1957.

The Man Who Wrote Detective Stories and Other Stories, Norton, 1959.

Eight Modern Writers, Oxford University Press, 1963, published as *Writers of the Early Twentieth Century: Hardy to Lawrence,* 1990.

(Under pseudonym) *Appleby Intervenes: Three Tales from Scotland Yard* (contains *One Man Show, A Comedy of Terrors,* and *The Secret Vanguard*), Dodd, 1965.

Rudyard Kipling, Dodd, 1966.

(Author of introduction) J. B. Priestley, *Thomas Love Peacock,* Penguin, 1966.

(Editor) Wilkie Collins, *Moonstone,* Penguin, 1966.

(Editor and author of introduction) William Makepeace Thackeray, *Vanity Fair,* Penguin, 1968.

Joseph Conrad, Dodd, 1968.

Cucumber Sandwiches and Other Stories, Norton, 1969.

Thomas Hardy: A Critical Biography, Dodd, 1971.

Shakespeare's Lofty Scene, Oxford University Press for the British Academy, 1971.

(Under pseudonym Michael Innes) *The Appleby File: Detective Stories,* Gollancz, 1975, Dodd, 1976.

Our England Is a Garden (short stories), Norton, 1979.

The Bridge at Arta and Other Stories (short stories), Norton, 1981.

My Aunt Christina and Other Stories, Norton, 1983.

(Under pseudonym Michael Innes) *Parlour 4 and Other Stories,* Gollancz, 1986.

Myself and Michael Innes: A Memoir, Gollancz, 1987, Norton, 1988.

SIDELIGHTS: J. I. M. Stewart distinguished himself both as a novelist and as a literary scholar. Best known for his mysteries, written under the pseudonym Michael Innes, Stewart was praised by critics for the mannered sophistication and erudition of his prose, which has drawn frequent comparisons with the nineteenth-century American novelist Henry James. Stewart also received acclaim as a literary biographer and historian, particularly for his biography of the early twentieth-century English poet and novelist Thomas Hardy and for his *Eight Modern Writers,* the fifteenth volume in the "Oxford History of English Literature" series.

Many of Stewart's novels are set in the privileged and eccentric milieu of the University of Oxford, where he himself spent a number of years as a professor of literature. In *The Gaudy,* the first of five volumes that make up the "Staircase in Surrey" quintet, Duncan Pattullo accepts a teaching fellowship at the University of Oxford after a stint as a dramatist. The subsequent volumes in the series—*Young Pattullo, A Memorial Service, The Madonna of the Astrolabe,* and *Full Term*—describe the humorous eccentricities and amorous misadventures of Pattullo and his colleagues. Stewart stated in his *Contemporary Authors Autobiography Series* (*CAAS*) entry that "in some regards these pages are closely autobiographical. . . . Duncan Pattullo . . . devotes several pages to describing his school-days at what is plainly the [Edinburgh] Academy," which Stewart himself attended for a little over eleven years.

Many critics enjoyed *The Gaudy* and its companion volumes. According to Reid Beddow in the *Washington Post Book World,* the series as a whole is "equal in entertainment to . . . Anthony Powell's *A Dance to the Music of Time* and within the genre of Oxford novels the funniest since Evelyn Waugh's *Brideshead Revisited.*" Melody Hardy, writing for *Best Sellers,* asserted that Stewart "captures the romance of an Oxford education and its impact on the men who experience it." A reviewer for the *Times Literary Supplement* was less impressed. "The present reviewer," it was noted, "hopes to be spared the next four installments." The writer added, "One feels that Mr. Stewart would have written better if he had known Christ Church, Oxford, less well." Susan Kennedy, reviewing *A Memorial Service* in the *Times Literary Supplement,* cited problems with Stewart's use of serial conventions. "One of the drawbacks of the serial novel is the need to remind the reader . . . of people and events introduced in earlier volumes," wrote Kennedy. "Mr. Stewart's way of handling this is to take up old threads in after-dinner conversations or on leisurely, companionable walks."

In spite of this mixed reception, many reviewers agreed that Stewart's autobiographical quintet presents a vivid and authentic portrait of life at Oxford. "Part of the fun in all this," wrote Beddow, "is in deciphering the true identity of some of the characters." Beddow sees many famous Oxford scholars, including J. R. R. Tolkien, Max Beerbohm, and Iris Murdoch, presented in various guises in Stewart's work. "When I look back on those years now," Stewart recollected in his *CAAS* entry, "they come to my [mind] as having been filled with frivolities—frivolities innocent enough for the most part, but compatible with our duty as students only because we found ourselves, for the time, within a highly privileged section of society. Everything of a workaday sort was done for us; we didn't even have to visit our tailor, since he came knocking at our door, smoothly anxious to know if he could be of service to us. We seemed to be—although we were not—young lords of unlimited leisure." The quintet itself, Beddow declared, presents "the graceful thanks of a man who knows he has been privileged to spend half a century in the most ivory of towers."

In addition to his scholarly works and novels, Stewart also penned several collections of short stories, including *Cucumber Sandwiches and Other Stories, Our England Is a Garden, The Bridge at Arta and Other Stories,* and *My Aunt Christina and Other Stories.* The tales in *Cucumber Sandwiches* were deemed "perfect" by a reviewer for the *New York Times Book Review,* and Stewart's short stories often remind critics of Henry James's shorter works— probably by design, for as Stewart himself stated in his *CAAS* entry, many of his early works "were made . . . distinctly under the pilotage of Henry James. I had spent the better part of a year in reading through almost everything that James wrote." Neil Millar noted in the *Christian Science Monitor* that *Cucumber Sandwiches* "exhales the drama of every battle between flesh and spirit. Its flesh never undresses in public, and nearly always dresses for dinner. Its spirit rarely raises—and never lowers—its kindly, cultured, understanding voice." The writer for the *New York Times Book Review* also noted that Stewart "shapes and polishes each sentence with respectful craftsmanship." The same writer added, "Little enough is left us these days. Let us give deep thanks to J. I. M. Stewart for his intellect, his respect for undecayed English, and his preservative humor."

In addition to his high standing as a novelist, Stewart is well-regarded as a literary biographer. Orville Prescott, in his review of *Rudyard Kipling* in the *Saturday Review,* commented that "Mr. Stewart's most important achievement in this lucid and penetrating little book is to analyze the elements that make so many of Kipling's stories immortal. . . ." He added that "Mr. Stewart is adept in performing one of the critic's most useful tasks—pointing out the less obvious merits, the nuances, and the true significances which hasty readers easily overlook." Stewart's *Joseph Conrad* received mixed reviews, while his *Thomas Hardy: A Critical Biography* was more unanimously praised. Keith Cushman, writing in *Library Journal,* declared: "Students and teachers of Hardy will find [*Thomas Hardy*] to be one of the most useful and sensible studies available," and a reviewer for the *Virginia Quarterly Review* asserted that "[Stewart's] approach [in *Thomas Hardy*] is biographical, but biographical in an intelligent and flexible way that avoids the dogma implicit in the sets of consistent philosophy or structural criticism."

Stewart also wrote numerous mysteries under the pseudonym of Michael Innes. With his first mystery, *Death at the President's Lodging,* the author exhibited some of the characteristics that made him a popular success for more than fifty years. The novel "didn't go for length, or a large cast, or extended thoughts on man, nature, and society," Stewart commented. "But it did, although all-tentatively, try for a certain lightness of air and liveliness of talk side by side with the mysteriousness. This disposition, uncanonical from the 'classical' point of view, has remained with me, and turned me into one of the Farceurs (Julian Symons's excellent word for it) of the mystery story. . . . It has also delayed the point at which the aged jester will consent (Bernard Shaw's phrase, but directed elsewhere) to be led into the wings."

Many of the crime novels feature Inspector Sir John Appleby, a resourceful crime-solver who rises in rank to become chief police commissioner of London before retiring and who is probably the most popular of all of Stewart's characters. He "came into being," Stewart revealed in Otto Penzler's *The Great Detectives,* "during a sea voyage from Liverpool to Adelaide." By the time he arrived in Australia, Stewart "had completed a novel called *Death at the President's Lodging* . . . in which a youngish inspector from Scotland Yard solves the mystery of the murder of Dr. Umpleby, the president of one of the constituent colleges of Oxford University." Although the stories themselves exist in a timeless, literary realm, Stewart declared, "Appleby himself ages, and in some respects perhaps even matures. He ages along with his creator, and like his creator ends up as a retired man who still a little meddles with the concerns of his green unknowing youth."

Stewart commented further on Appleby's longevity in *The Great Detectives.* "Appleby," he stated, "is as much concerned to provide miscellaneous and unassuming 'civilized' entertainment as he is to hunt down baddies wherever they may lurk." In the many years of the character's existence, Stewart concluded, "I have never quite got tired of John Appleby as a pivot round which farce and mild comedy and parody and freakish fantasy revolve." Even in retirement, Appleby was present in Stewart's more recent mysteries, including *The Gay Phoenix* and *Appleby and the Ospreys.* Stewart also paired Appleby with another of his recurrent mystery solvers, the Royal Academy portrait painter Charles Honeybath, in *Appleby and Honeybath.*

The Appleby adventures and Stewart's other crime novels were praised for their unassuming humor and erudition. Julian Symons, writing in *Mortal Consequences: A History—From the Detective Story to the Crime Novel,* stated, "There is no greater quotation spotter or capper in crime literature than Inspector (later Sir John) Appleby." However, Symons continued, "Appleby shows off, not out of sheer pretentiousness like [Dorothy L. Sayers' Lord Peter] Wimsey or [Harriet] Vane, but from genuine high spirits."

Washington Post Book World contributor George L. Scheper, in a review of *Myself and Michael Innes: A Memoir,* called the Appleby mysteries "highly literate, witty and, as they say, 'donnish.' " Scheper also stated that the best of the mystery novels "give us the privileged sense of having been invited to a common-room tea or Oxford High Table to hear an exceptionally witty and entertaining raconteur." And in a tribute to Stewart's continuous popularity, he declared, "Other literate mystery writers since Dorothy L. Sayers have put their oar in, and have come and gone, but Innes has stayed the course for fifty years."

BIOGRAPHICAL/CRITICAL SOURCES:

BOOKS

Contemporary Authors Autobiography Series, Volume 3, Gale, 1986, pp. 343-60.
Contemporary Literary Criticism, Gale, Volume 7, 1977, Volume 14, 1980, Volume 32, 1985.
Penzler, Otto, *The Great Detectives,* Little, Brown (Boston), 1978.
Symons, Julian, *Mortal Consequences: A History—From the Detective Story to the Crime Novel,* Harper (New York City), 1972.

PERIODICALS

Armchair Detective, fall, 1991, p. 457; spring, 1992, p. 234.
Best Sellers, June, 1975.
Books and Bookmen, June, 1983.
Book World, November 28, 1971.
British Book News, May, 1982.
Chicago Tribune Book World, June 8, 1980, p. 15; March 28, 1982, p. 4; June 22, 1986, p. 33.
Christian Science Monitor, June 13, 1970.
Economist, January 15, 1972.
Library Journal, March 1, 1972.
Listener, July 29, 1982.
London Review of Books, December 30, 1982.
Los Angeles Times Book Review, April 3, 1983, p. 9.
National Review, April 9, 1968.
New Leader, September 9, 1968.
New Statesman, December 20, 1968; September 24, 1971; February 9, 1973; June 13, 1975; April 30, 1976; July 7, 1978; August 10, 1979; November 12, 1982; May 20, 1983.
New York Times, December 11, 1982; December 2, 1983; June 19, 1987.
New York Times Book Review, April 7, 1968; June 19, 1970; May 29, 1977; June 11, 1978; April 29, 1979; February 14, 1982, p. 22; February 13, 1983, p. 31; January 1, 1984, p. 26; July 29, 1984, p. 20; September 15, 1985, p. 30; August 10, 1986, p. 19.
Observer, August 19, 1979.
Saturday Review, October 22, 1966, p. 58.

Southwest Review, autumn, 1977.
Spectator, September 22, 1967; October 31, 1981.
Times (London), April 18, 1987.
Times Literary Supplement, January 19, 1967; September 21, 1967; December 25, 1969; February 2, 1973; October 25, 1974; June 6, 1975; May 7, 1976; July 7, 1978, p. 757; January 16, 1981, p. 50; June 19, 1981, p. 690; July 2, 1982, p. 725; November 26, 1982, p. 1318; January 25, 1985, p. 86; January 31, 1986, p. 113; September 25, 1987, p. 1045.
Virginia Quarterly Review, winter, 1972.
Washington Post Book World, November 9, 1979; July 18, 1982, p. 16; October 30, 1988, p. 14.

OBITUARIES:

PERIODICALS

New York Times, November 16, 1994, p. D25.

*   *   *

STRASSER, Todd 1950-
(Morton Rhue)

PERSONAL: Born May 5, 1950, in New York, NY; son of Chester S. (a manufacturer of dresses) and Sheila (a copy editor; maiden name, Reisner) Strasser; married Pamela Older (a businesswoman), July 2, 1981; children: Lia, Geoff. *Education:* Beloit College, B.A., 1974. *Avocational interests:* Fishing, skiing, and tennis.

ADDRESSES: Agent—Ellen Levine, 432 Park Ave. S., New York, NY 10016.

CAREER: Free-lance writer, 1975—. Beloit College, Beloit, WI, worked in public relations, 1973-74; *Times Herald Record,* Middletown, NY, reporter, 1974-76; Compton Advertising, New York City, copywriter, 1976-77; *Esquire,* New York City, researcher, 1977-78; Toggle, Inc. (fortune cookie company), New York City, owner, 1978-89. Speaker at teachers' and librarians' conferences, middle schools, and at junior and senior high schools. Lectures and conducts writing workshops for adults and teenagers.

MEMBER: International Reading Association, Writers Guild of America, Authors Guild, Freedom to Read Foundation, PEN.

AWARDS, HONORS: American Library Association's Best Books for Young Adults citations, 1981, for *Friends till the End: A Novel,* and 1982, for *Rock 'n' Roll Nights: A Novel;* New York Public Library's Books for the Teen Age citations, 1981, for *Angel Dust Blues,* 1982, for *The Wave* and *Friends till the End: A Novel,* 1983, for *Rock 'n' Roll Nights: A Novel,* and 1984, for *Workin' for Peanuts;*

Friends till the End: A Novel was chosen a Notable Children's Trade Book in the Field of Social Studies by the National Council for Social Studies and the Children's Book Council, 1982; *Rock 'n' Roll Nights: A Novel* was chosen for the Acton Public Library's CRABbery Award List, 1983; Young Reader Medal nomination from the California Reading Association, 1983, for *Friends till the End: A Novel;* Book Award from the Federation of Children's Books (Great Britain), 1983, for *The Wave,* and 1984, for *Turn It Up!;* Outstanding Book Award from the Iowa Books for Young Adult Program, 1985, for *Turn It Up!;* Colorado Blue Spruce Award nomination, 1987, for *Angel Dust Blues;* Edgar Award nomination from Mystery Writers of America, for *The Accident.*

WRITINGS:

YOUNG ADULT FICTION

Angel Dust Blues, Coward, 1979.

Friends till the End: A Novel, Delacorte (New York City), 1981.

(Under pseudonym Morton Rhue) *The Wave* (novelization based on the television drama of the same title by Johnny Dawkins), Delacorte, 1981.

Rock 'n' Roll Nights: A Novel, Delacorte, 1982.

Workin' for Peanuts, Delacorte, 1983.

Turn It Up! (sequel to *Rock 'n' Roll Nights: A Novel*), Delacorte, 1984.

A Very Touchy Subject, Delacorte, 1985.

Ferris Bueller's Day Off (novelization based on film of the same title by John Hughes), New American Library (New York City), 1986.

Wildlife (sequel to *Turn It Up!*), Delacorte, 1987.

Rock It to the Top, Delacorte, 1987.

The Accident (also see below), Delacorte, 1988.

Cookie (novelization based on film of the same title by Nora Ephron), New American Library, 1989.

Moving Target, Fawcett (New York City), 1989.

Beyond the Reef, illustrations by Debbie Heller, Delacorte, 1989.

Home Alone (novelization based on film of the same title), Scholastic (New York City), 1991.

The Diving Bell, illustrations by Heller, Scholastic, 1992.

OTHER

The Complete Computer Popularity Program, Delacorte, 1984.

The Mall from Outer Space, Scholastic, 1987.

The Family Man (novel for adults), St. Martin's (New York City), 1988.

Over the Limit (teleplay based on Strasser's *The Accident*), *ABC Afterschool Special,* American Broadcasting Company, Inc., 1990.

Also contributor to periodicals, including *New Yorker, Esquire, New York Times,* and *Village Voice.*

ADAPTATIONS: Workin' for Peanuts was adapted for cable television as a Home Box Office "Family Showcase" presentation, 1985; *A Very Touchy Subject* was adapted for television as an "ABC Afterschool Special" titled *Can a Guy Say No?,* 1986.

WORK IN PROGRESS: Young adult novels about the importance of the play *Anne Frank: Diary of a Young Girl,* and about a New York teenager's adventure in Alaska; novelizations of screenplays *Honey I Blew Up the Baby* and *Home Alone II.*

SIDELIGHTS: Todd Strasser writes critically recognized realistic fiction for preteens and teenagers. In works ranging from *Friends till the End: A Novel,* the story of a young man stricken with leukemia, to *Wildlife,* a study of the breakup of a successful rock group, Strasser mixes humor and romance with timely subjects to address concerns of teens: drugs, sex, illness, and music. His understanding of the feelings of youth and adolescents has made his works popular with young people.

Angel Dust Blues appeared in 1979 and won Strasser critical acclaim. The story itself is about, Strasser tells Nina Piwoz in *Media and Methods,* "a group of fairly well-to-do, suburban teenagers who get into trouble with drugs." It was based on actual events Strasser had witnessed when he was growing up. Two years later, he published another young-adult novel, again based on his own experiences. "My second book, *Friends till the End,* is about a healthy teenager who has a friend who becomes extremely ill with leukemia," he explains to Piwoz. "When I moved to New York, I had a roommate . . . an old friend of mine. Within a few weeks, he became very ill. I spent a year visiting him in the hospital, not knowing whether he was going to live or die."

Rock 'n' Roll Nights, Strasser's third novel under his own name, was a change of pace from the serious themes of his first two works. "It's about a teenage rock and roll band—something with which I had absolutely no direct experience," he tells Piwoz. "However, I grew up in the 1960s when rock and roll was really our 'national anthem.' I relate much better to rock stars than to politicians. I always wanted to be in a rock band, as did just about everybody I knew." "I think the kind of music teens listen to may change, or what they wear may change," Strasser continues, "but dealing with being popular, friends or the opposite sex, or questions of morality and decency . . . [I don't think] those things really ever change. I hate to say this, but I think authors tell the same stories—just in today's language and in today's settings." Strasser continued the story of the band "Coming Attractions" in two sequels, *Turn It Up!* and *Wildlife.*

In his more recent works, Strasser continues to write hard-hitting, realistic stories about teenagers and their problems. Strasser once told *CA:* "Since I've written [many] books about teenagers, people often ask me how I know what today's teens are like. It's true that almost twenty years have passed since I qualified for that age group, so I suppose the question has some merit. I think the single most important thing I do to keep up with teens is accept invitations to speak at junior high and high schools all over the country. This year, for instance, I visited schools in Alaska, Iowa, Massachusetts, Pennsylvania, Ohio, and Colorado. Thus I'm not only able to keep up with teens, but with teens from all over the country.

"Another question I'm often asked is why I concentrate solely on books for teens. Well, actually, I don't. In the next few months I will publish a juvenile as well as an adult novel. I guess I originally wrote a lot of books for teens because that was where I had my first success and felt the most confident. But as I grow older, I find my interests widening not only towards writing books for older people, but for younger ones as well. I'd like to think that the day will come when I will write books for people of all ages, from three to eighty-three.

"The other day, someone who didn't know me well said that because I was a writer I must be a 'free spirit' and lead a wonderful life. At first I wanted to tell him he was completely wrong, but then I thought about it and decided he was only half wrong. In a way I am a free spirit, in that I am free to pick any idea or topic and write about it. That, indeed, is a wonderful freedom and I am grateful to have it. Along with that freedom, however, comes an awful lot of hard work. Unless you are fortunate enough to be one of the handful of perpetual best-selling writers in this world, you really can not make a living writing a book every two or three years. My work is about as close to 'nine-to-five' as my schedule allows. Being a writer is great, but I can't say it's easy."

BIOGRAPHICAL/CRITICAL SOURCES:

BOOKS

Children's Literature Review, Volume 11, Gale (Detroit), 1986.
Holtze, Sally Holmes, *Sixth Book of Junior Authors and Illustrators,* H. W. Wilson (Bronx), 1989.
Nilsen, Alleen Pace, and Kenneth L. Donelson, *Literature for Today's Young Adults,* second edition, Scott, Foresman (Glenview, IL), 1985.
Roginski, Jim, *Behind the Covers: Interviews with Authors and Illustrators of Books for Children and Young Adults,* Libraries Unlimited (Littleton, CO), 1985.

PERIODICALS

Best Sellers, May, 1983, p. 75; June, 1984, p. 118.

Bulletin of the Center for Children's Books, February, 1980, p. 120.
English Journal, September, 1982, p. 87; January, 1985; December, 1985; December, 1986; November, 1987, p. 93; March, 1988, p. 85.
Horn Book, April, 1980, p. 178; April, 1983, p. 175; May-June, 1985, p. 321; March/April, 1986; January, 1990, p. 90.
Journal of Youth Services in Libraries, fall, 1988, pp. 64-70.
Library Journal, January, 1988, p. 100.
Media and Methods, February, 1983.
New York Times, October 2, 1983; June 19, 1985.
New Yorker, January 24, 1977, p. 28.
Publishers Weekly, November 27, 1981, p. 88; April 24, 1987, p. 73; December 4, 1987, p. 63.
School Library Journal, January, 1980, p. 81; March, 1982, p. 160; August, 1983, p. 80; August, 1984, p. 87; April, 1985, p. 100; February, 1988, p. 75; June/July, 1988, p. 59; September, 1989, p. 278.
Variety, March 22, 1990, p. 14.
Voice of Youth Advocates, June, 1981, p. 32; December, 1982, p. 36; October, 1983, p. 209; June, 1984, p. 98; June, 1985, p. 136; December, 1986; December, 1988, p. 242; October, 1989, p. 217.
Wilson Library Bulletin, May, 1981, p. 691; April, 1983, p. 692; March, 1985, p. 485.
Writer's Digest, December, 1979.

*　　*　　*

STRATFORD, Michael
See CASSIDAY, Bruce (Bingham)

*　　*　　*

SWARTHOUT, Glendon (Fred) 1918-1992

PERSONAL: Born April 8, 1918, in Pinckney, MI; died from complications from emphysema, September 23, 1992, in Scottsdale, AZ; son of Fred H. and Lila (Chubb) Swarthout; married Kathryn Vaughn, 1940; children: Miles. *Education:* University of Michigan, A.B., 1939, A.M., 1946; Michigan State University, Ph.D., 1955.

ADDRESSES: Agent—William Morris Agency, 1350 Avenue of the Americas, New York, NY 10019.

CAREER: Writer, 1963-92. University of Michigan, Ann Arbor, teaching fellow, 1946-48; University of Maryland, College Park, instructor, 1948-51; Michigan State University, East Lansing, associate professor of English, 1951-59; Arizona State University, Tempe, lecturer in English,

1959-63. *Military service:* U.S. Army, Infantry, 1943-45; became sergeant; awarded two battle stars.

AWARDS, HONORS: Theatre Guild Playwriting Award, 1947; Hopwood Award in Fiction, 1948; O. Henry Prize Short Story, 1960; National Society of Arts and Letters gold medal, 1972; Spur Award from Western Writers of America for best novel, 1975; Owen Wister Award from Western Writers of America for his work, 1991.

WRITINGS:

Willow Run, Crowell, 1943, reprinted, AMS Press, 1982.
They Came to Cordura, Random House, 1958.
Where the Boys Are, Random House, 1960.
Welcome to Thebes, Random House, 1962.
(With wife, Kathryn Swarthout) *The Ghost and the Magic Saber,* Random House, 1963.
The Cadillac Cowboys, Random House, 1964.
(With K. Swarthout) *Whichaway,* Random House, 1966.
The Eagle and the Iron Cross, New American Library, 1966.
Loveland, Doubleday, 1968.
(With K. Swarthout) *The Button Boat,* Doubleday, 1969.
Bless the Beasts and Children, Doubleday, 1970.
The Tin Lizzie Troop, Doubleday, 1972.
(With K. Swarthout) *T. V. Thompson,* Doubleday, 1972.
Luck and Pluck, Doubleday, 1973.
The Shootist, Doubleday, 1975.
(With K. Swarthout) *Whales to See The,* Doubleday, 1975.
The Melodeon, Doubleday, 1977.
Skeletons, Doubleday, 1979.
Cadbury's Coffin, Doubleday, 1982.
The Old Colts, Thorndike Press, 1985.
The Homesman, Thorndike Press, 1988.
Pinch Me, I Must Be Dreaming, St. Martin's Press, 1994.

Contributor of stories to *Cosmopolitan, Collier's, New World Writing, Esquire,* and *Saturday Evening Post.*

ADAPTATIONS: They Came to Cordura was filmed by Columbia in 1959, *Where the Boys Are* was filmed by Metro-Goldwyn-Mayer in 1960, *Bless the Beasts and Children* was filmed by Columbia in 1971, and *The Shootist* was filmed by Paramount in 1976 and starred John Wayne and Lauren Bacall.

SIDELIGHTS: "Glendon Swarthout," wrote Richard Schickel in *Harper's,* "had the misfortune of selling a couple of his early books to the movies and since his sensibility seems to lead him naturally toward the linear adventure story, no one takes him very seriously. But he is a good, entertaining writer—exuberant, optimistic, maybe a little childlike (in a nice way) in his love of archetypal characters and situations, but always intelligent and alive." Peter Corodimas in *Best Sellers* appreciated Swarthout's opti-

mism. "At a time when many novelists are preoccupied with themes of absurdity and alienation," he explained, "it is enjoyable, not to say helpful to one's sanity, to read a novel about life which sees life the way novelists used to see it: at least as partly intelligible—which may in itself be a wrong view, but comforting nonetheless." A prolific writer in several genres, Swarthout wrote mysteries, westerns, comedies and books for children. His most popular book, *Bless the Beasts and Children,* has sold over two million copies worldwide.

Bless the Beasts and Children tells the story of six misfit teenagers sent to a summer camp for disturbed boys. When the camp fails to deliver on its promise to make them into responsible men, the teenagers take to the road, intent on doing it for themselves. Brian Garfield, writing in the *Saturday Review,* called the novel "a compassionate book, a true book, a book of the heart; it is also a compelling drama that grabs you with a grip that can't be pried loose." Schickel described Swarthout as "a stylist who also entertains and instructs and I say good for him. It is not as easy as it sounds." Writing in the *English Journal,* John W. Conner found *Bless the Beasts and Children* to be "an exciting adventure yarn using adolescents as major characters. It is an escellent example of literature *about* adolescents rather than literature *for* adolescents."

Another successful Swarthout effort is *The Shootist,* the story of the last Western gunfighter in 1901. J. B. Books, dying of cancer, wants to go out fighting. In the town of El Paso, Books gets his wish when three local troublemakers want to make a name for themselves by confronting him in a shootout. Although S. K. Oberbeck in *Newsweek* called the novel "a gritty but sentimental literary tintype," Victoria Glendenning in *New Statesman* found that *The Shootist* "combines the mock-heroic Hollywood myth of the West with an ideal of true heroism—which is always a private and painful matter. Mr. Swarthout is equally fascinated by both, and he has written an original book."

BIOGRAPHICAL/CRITICAL SOURCES:

BOOKS

Contemporary Literary Criticism, Volume 35, Gale, 1985.

PERIODICALS

Best Sellers, October 1, 1968, pp. 262-264; March, 1978, p. 325.
Chicago Sunday Tribune, January 17, 1960.
Commonweal, June 18, 1943.
English Journal, January, 1972, p. 139.
Harper's, April, 1970, p. 107.
Listener, January 10, 1980, pp. 62-63.
New Statesman, May 9, 1975, pp. 633-634.
Newsweek, February 3, 1975, pp. 64, 66.
New York Herald Tribune Book Review, February 9, 1958.

New York Herald Tribune Books, July 1, 1962.

New York Times, February 9, 1958, pp. 4, 28.

New York Times Book Review, May 30, 1943, p. 18; February 7, 1960, p. 34; June 17, 1962, p. 24; October 5, 1969.

Saturday Review, February 6, 1958, p. 30; January 23, 1960, p. 19; May 2, 1970, pp. 41-42.

Spectator, December 24, 1977, pp. 29-30.

Time, January 18, 1960.

Wall Street Journal, June 9, 1972, p. 8.

Washington Post Book World, July 2, 1972, p. 9.

OBITUARIES:

PERIODICALS

Chicago Tribune, September 26, 1992.

New York Times, September 26, 1992.*

*   *   *

SWIFT, Robert
See KELLY, Tim

T

TALL, Deborah 1951-

PERSONAL: Born March 16, 1951, in Washington, DC; daughter of Max M. (an engineer) and Selma (Donnerstein) Tall; married David Weiss (a writer), September 9, 1979; children: Zoe, Clea. *Education:* University of Michigan, B.A., 1972; Goddard College, M.F.A., 1979.

ADDRESSES: Office—Department of English, Hobart and William Smith Colleges, Geneva, NY 14456. *Agent*—Sterling Lord Literistic, 1 Madison Ave., New York, NY 10010.

CAREER: Freelance writer in Ireland, 1972-77; CK Studios, New York City, typographical designer, 1978-80; University of Baltimore, Baltimore, MD, assistant professor of English, 1980-82; Hobart and William Smith Colleges, associate professor of English, 1982—. Judge, New York Foundation for the Arts poetry fellowship, 1988.

MEMBER: Associated Writing Programs, Academy of American Poets, National Writers Union, Poetry Society of America.

AWARDS, HONORS: Jules and Avery Hopwood Award for poetry and Michael R. Gutterman Award for poetry, both from University of Michigan, both 1972; Yaddo fellowships, 1982, 1984, and 1991; faculty research grant, Hobart and William Smith Colleges, 1983, 1986, and 1989; Ingram Merrill Foundation grant, 1987.

WRITINGS:

Eight Colors Wide (poems), London Magazine Editions (London), 1974.
Ninth Life (poems), Ithaca House (Ithaca, NY), 1982.
The Island of the White Cow: Memories of an Irish Island (nonfiction), Atheneum (New York City), 1986.
Come Wind, Come Weather (poems), State Street Press, 1988.

(Coeditor) *Taking Note: From Poets' Notebooks,* Hobart and William Smith Colleges Press (Geneva, NY), 1991.
From Where We Stand: Recovering a Sense of Place (nonfiction), Knopf (New York City), 1993.

Contributor of poems, essays and reviews to periodicals, including *Poetry, Nation, Iowa Review, Yale Review, Ploughshares, Ironwood, Antaeus, London Magazine, Chelsea, Poet and Critic, Listener, Indiana Review, Antioch Review, Georgia Review,* and *Partisan Review.* Editor, *Seneca Review,* 1982—.

WORK IN PROGRESS: An anthology of excerpts from poets' notebooks to be published by Norton; a memoir.

BIOGRAPHICAL/CRITICAL SOURCES:

PERIODICALS

New York Times Book Review, March 16, 1986.

* * *

TAYLOR, C(ecil) P(hilip) 1929-1981

PERSONAL: Born November 6, 1929, in Glasgow, Scotland; died December 9, 1981; son of Max George (a watchmaker) and Fay (Leventhal) Taylor; married Irene Diamond, 1955; married second wife, Elizabeth Screen, 1967; children: Avram, Clair, David, Catherine. *Education:* Attended Queen's Park Secondary School.

ADDRESSES: Agent—Clive Goodwin, 79 Cromwell Rd., London, S.W.7, England.

CAREER: Playwright. Worked as an electrical engineer, radio engineer, television engineer, charity worker, record company employee, and held a "succession of non-jobs." Literary advisor, Northumberland Youth Theatre Association, Shiremoor, Northumberland, England, beginning 1968, Tyneside Theatre Trust, Liverpool, England, beginning 1971, and Everyman Theatre, Liverpool, beginning 1971; director, Writer's Workshop, Northumberland, beginning 1969.

AWARDS, HONORS: World Jewish Congress Playwriting Prize; Arts Council playwright's bursary, 1965; Scottish Television Theatre Award, 1969.

WRITINGS:

PLAYS

Aa Went te Blaydon Races (fold musical), produced at Newcastle Playhouse, 1962.

Happy Days Are Here Again (produced in London at Arts Theatre, 1964, produced Off-Off Broadway at Manhattan Theatre Club, 1972), published in *New English Dramatists,* number 12, Penguin (New York City), 1968.

Of Hope and Glory, produced in Edinburgh at Traverse Theatre Club, 1965.

Fable (produced in Glasgow at Close Theatre Club, 1965), Edinburgh University Drama Society, 1967.

Allergy (one-act; produced at Traverse Theatre Club, 1966), published in *Traverse Plays,* Penguin, 1966.

Bread and Butter (produced in London at Cochrane Theatre, 1966, produced in Washington, DC, 1969), published in *New English Dramatists,* number 10, Penguin, 1967, and *Their Very Own Golden City,* edited by Arnold Wesker, Penguin , 1967.

Who's Pinkus? Where's Chelm? (Jewish fold musical; music by Monty Norman), produced in Edinburgh, 1966, produced at Cochrane Theatre, 1967.

The Ballachulish Beat: A Play with Songs, Rapp & Carroll, 1967.

Mister David, produced in Warsaw at Jewish State Theatre, 1967.

What Can a Man Do, produced at Newcastle Theatre, 1968.

Thank You Very Much (for youth theatres; produced at Northumberland Experimental Youth Theatre, 1969), Methuen (New York City), 1970.

Lies about Vietnam/Truth about Sarajevo, produced at Traverse Theatre Club, 1969, published as *The Truth about Sarajevo: A Play for the Traverse Theatre,* Scottish Theatre Editions, 1970.

Brave (for youth), produced at Northumberland Experimental Youth Theatre, 1969.

The Cleverness of Us, produced in Liverpool at Everyman Theatre, 1971.

Bloch's Play (produced in Edinburgh at Gateway Theatre, 1971), Scottish Theatre Editions, 1971.

The Grace Darling Show, produced in Newcastle at University Theatre, 1971.

Passion Play, produced at Traverse Theatre Club, 1971.

Em'n Ben, produced in Shiremoor at Newcastle Youth Theatre, 1971.

Me, produced in Glasgow at Citizens Theatre, 1971.

Ginger Golly and the Fable Men (for youth), produced at University Theatre, 1972.

The Black and White Minstrels, produced at Traverse Theatre Club, 1972.

Happy Anniversary, produced in Edinburgh at Pool Theatre Club, 1972.

You Are My Heart's Delight, produced in London at Soho Polo Theatre, 1973.

The Grand Adultery Convention, produced in London at Almost Free Theatre, 1973.

New Year in Tel-Aviv, produced at Traverse Theatre Club, 1973.

The 5p Opera, produced in Newcastle at Gulbenkian Studio, 1973.

Oil and Water, produced on tour in Scotland by Perth Theatre Tour, 1973.

Apples (produced at Gulbenkian Studio, 1973), Hutchinson, 1973.

Columba (musical; music by Bob Stukey and Peter Brewis), produced at Traverse Theatre Club, 1973.

Carol O.K., produced at Gulbenkian Studio, 1974.

So Far, So Bad, produced at Tyneside Theatre Trust, 1974.

The Spital Tongues Plays, produced in schools in Newcastle, 1974.

Pilgrim, produced at Gulbenkian Studio, 1975.

The Killingworth Play, produced in Northumberland by Northern Counties College Drama Group, 1975.

Plumber's Progress, produced at Prince of Wales Theatre, West End, London, 1975.

And a Nightingale Sang . . . , Eyre Methuen, 1979.

Bandits!, Iron Press (Franklin, MI), 1979.

Happy Lies (for youth), produced at Albany Empire, London, 1981.

Good (produced in London at the Warehouse Theatre, 1981, produced on Broadway, 1982, produced in Los Angeles at South Coast Repertory, 1984, produced in New York City at Bouwerie Lane Theatre, 1989), revised edition, Methuen, 1983.

Live Theatre, Methuen, 1983.

PLAYS; ADAPTOR

Sophocles, *Antigone,* produced at University Theatre, 1972.

Bertolt Brecht, *The Three Penny Opera* (music by Kurt Weill), produced at University Theatre, 1972.

Brecht, *Drums in the Night,* produced at Traverse Theatre Club, 1973.

Clifford Odets, *Waiting for Lefty,* produced at University Theatre, 1973.

Carl Sternheim, *Schippel* (based on *Burger Schippel*), produced at Traverse Theatre Club, 1974.
(With Traverse Theatre Co.) Henrik Ibsen, *Gynt!* (based on *Peer Gynt;* music by Adrian Secchi), produced at Traverse Theatre Club, 1975.

TELEVISION PLAYS

Revolution (trilogy; includes *Charles and Cromwell* (also see below), *Lenin,* and *Castro*), British Broadcasting Corporation Television (BBC-TV), 1970.
Bloch's Play, STV, 1971.
Words (BBC-TV, 1972), published in *Second Playbill 2,* edited by Alan Durband, Hutchinson, 1973.
Adam Smith (series), BBC-TV, 1972.
Izzy, BBC-TV, 1975.
For Services to Myself, BBC-TV, 1976.

OTHER

Making a Television Play: A Complete Guide from Conception to BBC Production, Based on the Making of the Play "Charles and Cromwell" for BBC "Thirty Minute Theatre" (includes script of *Charles and Cromwell*), Oriel Press, 1970.

Also author of play *Bring Me Sunshine, Bring Me Smiles,* produced in 1982; also author of other television plays, including *Lone Rider,* 1966, *Myopia,* 1966, *Oil and Water,* 1967, *Friends,* 1967, *Happy Anniversary,* 1968, *Thank You for the Family Circle,* 1968, *In Case,* 1969, and *Street Fighter,* 1969; also author of a radio play, *Love Story,* 1966. Contributor to anthologies. Script editor, *Burns* series of television plays; writer for BBC Educational Television, beginning 1966.

A manuscript collection of Taylor's work is housed in the National Library, Edinburgh, Scotland.

SIDELIGHTS: Described in a London *Times* obituary as a "regional writer with an international viewpoint," the prolific C. P. Taylor eschewed London's West End and its commercial lures for practicing his craft—both playwriting and directing—mainly in his native Scotland. By working with theater groups in Scotland, particularly early in his career, he helped strengthen Scottish theater. According to the *Times* obituary, "Taylor's long attachment to the Edinburgh Traverse Theatre and later to the Tyneside Theatre, may have isolated him from the London scene but at least protected him from its careerist pressures." Writing in the *New Stateman,* Benedict Nightingale characterized Taylor as "always a committed socialist, but one who increasingly came to annoy the ideologically straight and narrow, because he couldn't help seeing the flaws in the human material from which socialism would have to be built." Taylor's characters, Nightingale suggested, "like to think of themselves as enlightened, progressive, or simply good. The drama, and

usually the comedy, comes from their attempts to deflect, suppress or ignore whatever tends to contradict their illusions and undermine their self-esteem."

Among his last plays, *Good* garnered widespread recognition. Its protagonist is a German literature professor, John Halder, turned Nazi SS officer; the drama centers on both his attempts to find philosophical justification for the existence of the SS and its actions, and the question of how a "good," average citizen could join a cause so antithetical to all the principles he previously held. In addition, the play explores relationships and their evolutions, including that of Halder and his good friend Maurice, a Jew. *Good* has enjoyed numerous stagings, including productions in London, Los Angeles, on Broadway, and a revival in New York City.

Reviewer Ned Chaillet wrote in the London *Times* that *Good* "shimmers with ideas as it sets out to show how a 'good' liberal German professor becomes a good servant of the Nazis." Frank Rich of the *New York Times* observed that the play, which has a stream-of-consciousness format, "is an undeniably provocative work, . . . written . . . with an intelligent, light touch in a most imaginative form." Yet, Rich added that the play "doesn't add anything to the generalities of the past." Dan Sullivan of the *Los Angeles Times* remarked, "If the purpose of Taylor's play is to say that Germany created Hitler as the masochist creates the sadist, it does so. What it doesn't prove is that it could happen here, among level-headed people . . . ." In another *Los Angeles Times* article, Sullivan argued, "Better men and women than [Halder] were corrupted by Hitler, and *Good* would come closer to home as a cautionary fable if it dealt with one of them. It would also generate more tension as a play." *New York Times* reviewer Wilborn Hampton found several problems with the play, but concludes, "Yet for all the play's weaknesses, *Good* is frightening and mesmerizing."

Cecil Philip Taylor once told *CA:* "[My] main themes [are] the conflict between man's ideals and his limitations. . . . [I am] obsessed with the danger presented by general rules, general diagnosis. Every play is about particular people, particular periods, particular incidents. The universal comes from a close and accurate study of the particular."

BIOGRAPHICAL/CRITICAL SOURCES:

BOOKS

Contemporary Literary Criticism, Volume 27, Gale (Detroit), 1984.
Taylor, John Russell, *Anger and After,* Methuen, 1962.
Taylor, John Russell, *The Second Wave: British Drama for the Seventies,* Hill & Wang (New York City), 1971.

PERIODICALS

Christian Science Monitor, May 24, 1969.
Los Angeles Times, October 14, 1982; February 25, 1984;
    March 31, 1986.
New Republic, November 15, 1982, pp. 23-25.
New Statesman, April 23, 1982, p. 30.
New York, October 25, 1982, pp. 77-78.
New Yorker, October 25, 1982, pp. 160-161.
New York Times, October 14, 1982; November 28, 1983;
    February 25, 1989.
Scottish Theatre, Volume 3, number 4, 1971.
Stage, April 22, 1971.
Stage and Television Today, December 3, 1970.
Times (London), September 22, 1965, p. 14; January 4,
    1967, p. 6; January 6, 1982; April 26, 1982.
Variety, May 21, 1969.
Washington Post, October 9, 1985.

OBITUARIES:

PERIODICALS

Drama, Autumn, 1982, pp. 16-17.
New Statesman, January 8, 1982, p. 23.
Times (London), December 15, 1981.*

*   *   *

THALER, M. N.
See KERNER, Fred

*   *   *

THOMAS, Cullen
See KIMES, Beverly Rae

*   *   *

TIERNEY, Tom 1928-

PERSONAL: Born October 8, 1928, in Beaumont, TX;
son of John Taylor (an accountant) and Mary Lou
(Gripon) Tierney. *Education:* University of Texas, B.F.A.,
1949; attended Pratt Institute, 1953, Art Students League,
1955, Cartoonists and Illustrators School (now School of
Visual Arts, NY), 1955. *Politics:* "Not committed." *Religion:* "Not committed." *Avocational interests:* Ballet, singing.

ADDRESSES: Drawer D, Hopewell Jct., NY 12533.

CAREER: Freelance illustrator. *Military service:* U.S.
Army, 1951-52; served as a recruiting illustrator; became
sergeant.

MEMBER: "None (I am a rabid nonjoiner!)"

AWARDS, HONORS: Purchase Award, Texas General
Exhibition, 1952, for watercolor; First Prize, Beaumont
Art Museum, 1953, for oil painting.

WRITINGS:

*SELF-ILLUSTRATED PAPER DOLL BOOKS; PUBLISHED BY
DOVER UNLESS OTHERWISE NOTED*

Thirty from the Thirties, Prentice-Hall, 1974.
Glamorous Movie Stars of the Thirties, 1978.
Attitude: An Adult Paper Doll Book, St. Martin's, 1979.
Rudolph Valentino, 1979.
Marilyn Monroe, 1979.
John Wayne, 1981.
Vivien Leigh, 1981.
Pavlova and Nijinsky, 1981.
*Cut and Assemble a Toy Theater: The Nutcracker Ballet:
    A Complete Production in Full Color,* 1981.
Judy Garland, c. 1982.
Carmen Miranda, 1982.
Great Empresses and Queens, 1982.
American Family of the Colonial Era, 1983.
Isadora Duncan, Martha Graham and Other Stars of Modern Dance, 1983.
Great Fashion Designs of the Twenties, 1983.
Cat Snips, Tribeca, 1983.
Joan Crawford, 1983.
Santa Claus, 1983.
Great Fashion Designs of the Belle Epoque, 1983.
Fashion Designers of the Twenties, 1983.
Famous Modern Dancers, 1983.
Nancy Reagan, 1984.
Pope John Paul II, 1984.
Ronald Reagan, 1984.
Great Black Entertainers, 1984.
(More) Erte Fashions, 1984.
Cupie, 1984.
Cut and Assemble a Toy Theater: Peter Pan, 1984.
Fashion Designers of the Thirties, 1984.
Opera Stars of the Golden Age, 1984.
Greta Garbo, 1985.
Great Fashion Designs of the Fifties, 1985.
Princess Diana and Prince Charles, 1985.
Legendary Baseball Stars, 1985.
Gibson Girl Fashions, 1985.
Paul Poiret's Fashions, 1985.
Fashion Designers of the Fifties, 1985.
American Family of the Civil War Era, 1985.
Ziegfield Follies, 1985.
Clarke Gable, 1986.
Grace Kelly, 1986.
Supergirl, Putnam, 1986.
Chanel Fashion Review, 1986.
American Family of the Victorian Era, 1986.
Little Cupie Paper Dolls, 1986.

Three Little Kittens, 1986.
Diaghilev's Ballets Russes, 1986.
American Family of the Puritan Era, 1987.
Duke and Duchess of Windsor, 1987.
American Family of the Early Republic, 1987.
American Family of the 1890s, 1987.
American Family of the Pilgrim Period, 1987.
Famous American Women, 1987.
Great Fashion Designs of the Forties, 1987.
Great Fashion Designs of the Victorian Era, 1987.
Schiaparelli Fashion Review, 1987.
Fun with Teddy Bear Paper Dolls, 1987.
Two Little Ducks, 1987.
American Family of the 1920s, 1988.
Abraham Lincoln and His Family, 1989.
Fashions of the Old South, 1989.
George Washington and His Family, 1989.
Notable American Women, 1989.
Theodore Roosevelt and His Family, 1989.
George Bush and His Family, 1990.
John F. Kennedy and His Family, 1990.
American Family of the 1930s, 1991.
American Family of 1900-1920, 1991.
Annie Oakley and Buffalo Bill, 1991.
Ballet Stars of the Romantic Era, 1991.
Bride and Groom Fashion, 1991.
Franklin D. Roosevelt and His Family, 1991.
Great Fashion Designs of the Sixties, 1991.
Harry S. Truman and His Family, 1991.
Woodrow Wilson and His Family, 1991.
Christopher Columbus, 1992.
Jeanette MacDonald and Nelson Eddie, 1992.
Little Indian Girl, 1992.
Little Irish Girl, 1992.
Little Italian Girl, 1992.
Little Mexican Girl, 1992.
Thomas Jefferson and His Family, 1992.

Also author of other paper doll books, including *Alice in Wonderland, American Family of the 1940s, Dorothy of Oz, Fashion Model, Jimmy Carter and His Family, Little Chinese Girl, Little Scottish Girl, Martin Luther King and His Family, Richard M. Nixon and His Family, Roaring Twenties, Southern Belles,* and *Wedding Fashion.*

ILLUSTRATOR

Clip Art: Children's Illustrations, Dover, 1982.
Clip Art: Men's Head Illustrations, Dover, 1982.
Clip Art: Women's Head Illustrations, Dover, 1982.
Clip Art: Hand Illustrations, Dover, 1983.
Day-to-Night Barbie Paper Doll Book, Western, 1985.
Jennie Abbott, *Dance Club Magic,* Golden, 1986.
Barbie and the Rockers: The Fan, Golden, 1986.
Barbie and the Rockers: The Hottest Group in Town, Golden, 1986.

Barbie and the Rockers Stamp Book, Paninni, 1986.
Clip Art: Wedding Illustrations, Dover, 1986.
Rusty Hallock, *Night of a Thousand Earrings,* Golden, 1986.
Sara Hughes, *Surprise at Starlight Mansion,* Golden, 1986.
Deborah Kovacs, *Battle of the Bands,* Golden, 1986.
Mary Packard, *Video Mischief,* Golden, 1986.
A Sleep Over Visit, Golden, 1986.
T. P. Turner, *Secret Star,* Golden, 1986.
Larry Weinberg, *Spoils of Success,* Golden, 1986.
Ready-to-Use Medical and Health Services Illustrations, Dover, 1987.
Ready-to-Use Nautical and Seashore Illustrations, Dover, 1987.
Ready-to-Use School and Education Illustrations, Dover, 1987.
Ready-to-Use Travel and Tourist Illustrations, Dover, 1987.
Ready-to-Use Office and Business Illustrations, Dover, 1988.
Ready-to-Use Wining and Dining Illustrations, Dover, 1989.
Ready-to-Use Trades and Services Silhouettes, Dover, 1990.

OTHER

Contributor of illustrations to magazines, including *Harper's Bazaar, Sports Illustrated,* and *Show.*

WORK IN PROGRESS: More paper doll books for Dover.

SIDELIGHTS: Tom Tierney once told *CA:* "My training has been as a visual artist—painting, sculpture, etc.—so most of my interests have been in these areas. I have always been a film enthusiast. This, coupled with my fashion art career, led to *Thirty from the Thirties.*" Tierney created the book of paper dolls as a gift for his mother, who still owned paper dolls she had collected during her childhood. His mother enthusiastically showed the dolls to several friends, including a literary agent. Soon after, *Thirty from the Thirties* was published, and in 1978 Dover persuaded the successful fashion illustrator to make more books of paper dolls. Tierney, whose clients in the retail fashion industry include Lane Bryant and Macy's, explained, "These paper doll books are unique in that they are designed for the serious collector of nostalgia. They include biographical data and notes, while the costumes are researched and rendered for maximum accuracy. The series seems assured of success."

TILLY, Louise A(udino) 1930-

PERSONAL: Born December 13, 1930, in Orange, NJ; daughter of Hector (an engineer) and Piera (an artist; maiden name, Roffino) Audino; married Charles Tilly (a sociologist), August 15, 1953; children: Christopher, Kathryn, Laura, Sarah. *Education:* Rutgers University, A.B., 1952; Boston University, M.A., 1955; University of Toronto, Ph.D., 1974.

ADDRESSES: Home—61 Irving Pl., No. 6C, New York, NY 10003. *Office*—Committee on Historical Studies, Graduate Faculty, New School for Social Research, 64 University Place, New York, NY 10003.

CAREER: University of Michigan, Flint, lecturer in history, 1971-72; Michigan State University, East Lansing, instructor, 1972-74, assistant professor of history, 1974-75; University of Michigan, Ann Arbor, assistant professor, 1975-77, associate professor, 1977-82, professor of history, 1982-84, director of women's studies program, 1975-77, 1980, 1983, 1984; New School for Social Research, New York City, professor of history and sociology, 1984-94, chair of Committee on Historical Studies, 1984—, Michael E. Gellert Professor of History, 1994—. Shelby Cullom Davis Center for Historical Studies, Princeton University, fellow, 1978; Ecole des Hautes Etudes en Sciences Sociales, Paris, directeur d'Etudes Associe, 1979, 1980, 1988, 1991; Social Science Research Council, board member, 1983-86; Institute for Advanced Study, Princeton University, visiting member, 1987-88; Center for Advanced Study in the Behavioral Sciences, 1991-92; member of National Research Council's Committee on Women's Employment, 1981-86, chair of Technological Change and Women's Employment panel, 1984-86; served as grant evaluator for numerous foundations, including the National Science Foundation and the National Endowment for the Humanities.

MEMBER: American Historical Association (Higby Prize Committee chair, 1980; member of council, 1985-87; president, 1993), Social Science History Association (president, 1981-82), Coordinating Committee of Women in the Historical Profession, Berkshire Conference of Women Historians, Council for European Studies, Italian Historical Studies society.

AWARDS, HONORS: Award for best article by a woman from Berkshire Conference of Women Historians, 1976, for "Women's Work and the Family in Nineteenth-Century Europe"; Rockefeller grant, 1974-76; American Philosophical Society grant, 1977-78, 1985-86; travel grants from Council for International Educational Exchange, 1979, American Council of Learned Societies, 1980, 1990; Einaudi Foundation grant, 1982; Russell Sage Foundation grant, 1985-86; Sloan Foundation grant,

1989; Council for European Studies grant, 1991; Guggenheim fellow, 1991-92.

WRITINGS:

(With Charles Tilly and Richard Tilly) *The Rebellious Century,* Harvard University Press (Cambridge), 1975.

(With Joan Scott) *Women, Work, and Family,* Holt, 1978, 2nd edition, Methuen (New York City), 1987.

(Editor and contributor with C. Tilly) *Class Conflict and Collective Action,* Sage Publications (Beverly Hills), 1981.

(Editor with Vivian Patraka) *Feminist Re-Visions: What Has Been and What Might Be,* Women's Studies Program, University of Michigan (Ann Arbor), 1983.

(Editor and translator with Kathryn L. Tilly, and author of introduction) Serge Grafteaux, *Meme Santerre: A French Woman of the People,* Schocken (New York City), 1985.

(With Heidi Hartmann and Robert Kraut) *Computer Chips and Paper Clips: Technology and Women's Employment,* National Academy Press (Washington, DC), 1986.

(Editor with Patricia Gurin) *Women, Politics, and Change,* Russell Sage (New York City), 1990.

Politics and Class in Milan, 1881-1901, Oxford University Press (New York City), 1992.

(Editor with John Gillis and David Levine) *The European Experience of Fertility Decline: The Quiet Revolution,* Blackwell, 1992.

Contributor to *Modern European Social History,* edited by Robert Bezucha, Heath (Lexington, MA), 1972; and *The Family in History,* edited by Charles Rosenberg, University of Pennsylvania Press (Philadelphia), 1975. Contributor to history journals, including the *American Historical Review.* Member of editorial boards, *Gender and History, International Labor and Working Class History, Journal of Historical Sociology, Journal of Family History, Passato e Presente, Theory and Society,* and *Women and Work.*

WORK IN PROGRESS: Industrialization and Gender Inequality in Global Perspective.

SIDELIGHTS: Louise A. Tilly told *CA:* "My translation of *Meme Santerre* was the result of my use of that autobiographical account in my own research on families and class in French cities. My Paris bookseller told me about the book, and I was thrilled and fascinated by it because it gives both a moving firsthand account of a poor woman's life (she was born in 1891) and provides an exceptionally rich description of work in the hand-weaving of linen and commercial agriculture, producing sugar beets and wheat. The family of Meme Santerre migrated between these two worlds of work on a seasonal basis."

TODD, John M(urray) 1918-1993
(John Fox)

PERSONAL: Born May 27, 1918, in Liverpool, England; died June 9, 1993, in Somerset, England; son of Murray and Elizabeth (Brancker) Todd; married Patricia Calnan (a chiropodist), May 3, 1953; children: Zia, Fabian, Stephany. *Education:* Attended Wellington College, Berkshire, England; Corpus Christi College, Cambridge, B.A. (honors), 1939, certificate of education, 1940. *Religion:* Roman Catholic.

ADDRESSES: Agent—A.M. Heath & Co. Ltd., 35 Dover St., London W.1, England.

CAREER: Free-lance journalist, 1940-56; Longmans, Green & Co. Ltd., London, England, editor of Roman Catholic books, 1956-59; Darton, Longman & Todd Ltd., London, director, 1959-83; Search Press, London, director, beginning 1970; Boston College, Boston, MA, teacher, 1972; King's College, London, teacher, 1983-86; director, Tablet Publishing, beginning 1988. Member, Shepton Mallet Rural District Council, 1952-67. *Wartime service:* Conscientious objector working on farm during World War II.

WRITINGS:

We Are Men: A Book for the Catholic Layman, Sheed, 1955.

Catholicism and the Ecumenical Movement, Longmans, Green, 1956.

John Wesley and the Catholic Church, Macmillan, 1958.

African Mission: A Historical Study of the Society of African Missions Whose Priests Have Worked on the Coast of West Africa and Inland, in Liberia, the Ivory Coast, Ghana, Togoland, Dahomey and Nigeria, and in Egypt, Since 1856, Macmillan, 1962.

Martin Luther: A Biographical Study, Newman, 1964.

(Contributor) M. de la Bedoyere, *Objections to Roman Catholicism,* Constable, 1964, Lippincott, 1965.

The Laity: The People of God, Darton, Longman & Todd, 1965, Paulist Press, 1967.

(Contributor) M. de la Bedoyere, *The Future of Catholic Christianity,* Lippincott, 1966.

Reformation, Doubleday, 1971.

Luther: A Life, Crossroad, 1982.

EDITOR

(Under pseudonym John Fox) *Christian Letters on Sex and Marriage,* Longmans, Green, 1955.

The Springs of Morality: A Catholic Symposium, Macmillan (New York), 1956.

The Arts, Artists, and Thinkers, an Inquiry into the Place of the Arts in Human Life: A Symposium, Longmans, Green (New York), 1958.

Work: Christian Thought and Practice: A Symposium, Helicon, 1960.

Problems of Authority, Helicon, 1962.

OTHER

Contributor to religious journals. Consultant editor, *Search.*

OBITUARIES:

PERIODICALS

New York Times, July 1, 1993, p. D19.*

*　　　*　　　*

TREVELYAN, (Walter) Raleigh 1923-

PERSONAL: Surname is pronounced "Trevillian"; born July 6, 1923, in Port Blair, Andaman Islands, India; son of Walter Raleigh Fetherstonhaugh Trevelyan (a colonel in the Indian Army) and Olive Beatrice (Frost) Trevelyan. *Education:* Attended Winchester College, Winchester, England, 1937-42. *Religion:* Church of England. *Avocational interests:* Travel, gardening, collecting, theater.

ADDRESSES: Home—St. Cadix, St. Veep, Lostwithiel, Cornwall PL22 0NG, England; 18 Hertford St., London W1Y 7DB, England. *Agent*—A. M. Heath & Co. Ltd., 79 St. Martin's Lane, London WC2N 4AA, England; Brandt & Brandt Literary Agents, 1501 Broadway, New York, NY 10036.

CAREER: Samuel Montagu (merchant bankers), London, England, trainee, 1947-48; William Collins Sons & Co. Ltd. (publishers), London, editor, 1948-58; Hutchinson & Co. Ltd. (publishers), London, editor and director of Arrow Books Ltd. and New Authors Ltd., 1958-61; Penguin Books Ltd. (publishers), Harmondsworth, Middlesex, England, editor, 1961-62; Michael Joseph Ltd. (publishers), London, editorial director, 1962-73; Hamish Hamilton Ltd. (publishers), London, director, 1973-80; Jonathan Cape Ltd. (publishers), London, literary adviser, 1980-86; Bloomsbury (publishers), literary adviser, 1986-88. Member of United Kingdom Goodwill Mission to Virginia for the Jamestown Festival, 1957. *Military service:* British Army, Rifle Brigade, Infantry, 1942-46; served with Military Mission to Italian Army in Rome, 1944-46; became captain; mentioned in dispatches.

MEMBER: International PEN (vice-chair of English Center), Anglo-Italian Society for the Protection of Animals (chair), Royal Society of Literature (fellow), Royal Geographical Society (fellow), British-Italian Society.

AWARDS, HONORS: John Florio Prize, Translators Association, for *The Outlaws.*

WRITINGS:

The Fortress: A Diary of Anzio and After (Book Society recommendation), Collins (London), 1956, St. Martin's (New York City), 1957.

A Hermit Disclosed (Book Society choice), Longmans, Green (London), 1960, St. Martin's, 1961.

(Translator) Giuliano Palladino, *Peace at Alamein,* Hodder & Stoughton (London), 1962.

(Editor) *Italian Short Stories/Racconti italiani,* Penguin (Baltimore, MD), 1965.

The Big Tomato, Longmans, Green, 1966.

(Editor) *Italian Writing Today,* Penguin, 1967.

(Translator from the Italian) Luigi Meneghello, *The Outlaws,* Morrow (New York City), 1967.

Princes under the Volcano, Morrow, 1972.

The Shadow of Vesuvius, M. Joseph (London), 1976.

A Pre-Raphaelite Circle, Chatto & Windus (London), 1978.

Rome '44: The Battle for the Eternal City, Secker & Warburg (London), 1981, Viking (New York City), 1982.

Shades of the Alhambra, Secker & Warburg, 1985.

The Golden Oriole: Childhood, Family and Friends in India, Viking, 1987.

Grand Dukes and Diamonds, Secker & Warburg, 1991.

(Editor) *A Clear Premonition: The Letters of Lieutenant Timothy Lloyd, 1943-44,* Leo Cooper (London), 1994.

Contributor of book reviews to periodicals, including *New York Times Book Review,* London *Sunday Times, Observer, Listener, Guardian,* and *Times Literary Supplement;* contributor of articles on art to *Apollo* and *Connoisseur;* contributor to National Trust publications.

WORK IN PROGRESS: Companion Guide to Sicily, for Everyman (tentative), 1995; *Sir Walter Raleigh and El Dorado,* for Secker & Warburg (tentative), c. 1996.

SIDELIGHTS: Raleigh Trevelyan's military histories *The Fortress: A Diary of Anzio and After* and *Rome '44: The Battle for the Eternal City* have both been praised by reviewers. Trevelyan was a twenty-year-old Rifle Brigade subaltern when he took part in the Allied landings at Anzio, Italy, in 1944, and *The Fortress* is the journal that he wrote at that time. A *Times Literary Supplement* contributor called it "a concentrated and brilliantly observed account of the dangers and confusion of infantry warfare" and noted that "the restless immediacy native to the diary form escapes the confines of journalism through the author's self-awareness." In conclusion, the reviewer stated: "The unsentimental humanity of his dealings with his men . . . and the piled-up excitements of the close-quarters action make this one of the most notable memoirs to have emerged from the Second World War." Of *Rome '44,* Norman Lewis wrote in the *New York Times Book Review:* "Raleigh Trevelyan's book is a distinguished addition to

the chronicles of war. His writing is of sensitive literary quality."

Trevelyan similarly aroused admiration with *The Golden Oriole: Childhood, Family and Friends in India,* a wide-ranging look at India under British rule during the 1800s and 1900s, unified by the author's focus on his own family's experiences. Writing in the *New York Times Book Review,* Jan Morris judged it one of the best Anglo-Indian memoirs and "one of the very few that will survive not just as a period piece but as literature." Among Trevelyan's ancestors were a number of administrators, soldiers, and writers who lived and worked in India; using his own memories and details of their lives, writings, and experiences the author "is able to evoke the whole course of the British relationship with India," Morris asserted. The critic hailed Trevelyan's writing skill and unsentimental and often humorous approach, summing up *The Golden Oriole* as a "historical memoir of the profoundest kind."

BIOGRAPHICAL/CRITICAL SOURCES:

PERIODICALS

New York Times Book Review, February 21, 1982; November 22, 1987, pp. 3, 51.
Times Literary Supplement, January 31, 1986.

*   *   *

TRIPP, Karen 1923-1993
(Karen Gershon)

PERSONAL: Born August 29, 1923, in Bielefeld, Germany; died March 24, 1993, in London, England; daughter of Paul (an architect) and Selma (Schoenfeld) Loewenthal; married Val Tripp (an art teacher), March 6, 1948; children: Christopher, Anthony, Stella, Naomi.

CAREER: Writer.

MEMBER: Society of Authors (England), Hebrew Writers' Association (Israel).

AWARDS, HONORS: British Arts Council award for poetry, 1967; *Jewish Chronicle* book prize, 1967; Haim Greenberg Literary Award, 1968.

WRITINGS:

UNDER PSEUDONYM KAREN GERSHON

(With C. Levenson and Ian Crichton Smith) *The Relentless Year: New Poets, 1959,* Eyre & Spottiswoode, 1960.

Selected Poems, Harcourt, 1966.

(Editor) *We Came as Children: A Collective Autobiography* (prose), Harcourt, 1966.

(Editor) *Postscript: A Collective Account of the Lives of Jews in West Germany since the Second World War,* Gollancz, 1969.

Legacies and Encounters: Poems, 1966-1971, Gollancz, 1972.

My Daughters, My Sisters (poems), Gollancz, 1975.

Coming Back from Babylon, Gollancz, 1979.

Burn Helen, Gollancz, 1980.

Bread of Exile, Gollancz, 1985.

The Fifth Generation, Gollancz, 1986.

Collected Poems, Gollancz, 1990.

A Lesser Child, P. Owens, 1994.

Contributor to periodicals, including *Critical Quarterly, London Magazine, Encounter, Jewish Chronicle, Midstream,* and *Jerusalem Post* (Israel).

OBITUARIES:

PERIODICALS

Times (London), April 15, 1993, p. 23A.*

*   *   *

TROGDON, William (Lewis) 1939-
(William Least Heat-Moon)

PERSONAL: Born August 27, 1939, in Kansas City, MO; son of Ralph G. (a lawyer) and Maurine (a homemaker; maiden name, Davis) Trogdon; married, 1967, wife's name, Lezlie (divorced, 1978); married Linda Keown (a teacher). *Education:* University of Missouri at Columbia, B.A. in literature, 1961, M.A., 1962, Ph.D., 1973, B.A. in photojournalism, 1978.

ADDRESSES: Office—222 Berkeley St., Boston, MA 02116. *Agent*—Lois Wallace, 177 East 70th St., New York, NY 10021.

CAREER: Stephens College, Columbia, MO, teacher of English, 1965-68, 1972, 1978; writer. Lecturer at University of Missouri School of Journalism, 1984-1987. *Military service:* U.S. Navy, served on USS *Lake Champlain,* 1964-65; became personnelman third class.

AWARDS, HONORS: Blue Highways: A Journey into America was named a notable book of 1983 by the *New York Times* and one of the five best nonfiction books of 1983 by *Time;* Christopher Award, 1984, and Books-Across-the-Sea Award, 1984, both for *Blue Highways: A Journey into America; PrairyErth (a deep map)* was selected as the best work of nonfiction by the American Library Association, was named one of the year's four best books about the West by Mountains and Plains Booksellers Association, 1991, and was named a notable book of 1991 by the *New York Times.*

WRITINGS:

UNDER PSEUDONYM WILLIAM LEAST HEAT-MOON

(And photographer) *Blue Highways: A Journey into America,* Little, Brown (Boston), 1982.

(Contributor and author of introduction) *The Red Couch: A Portrait of America,* photography by Kevin Clarke and Horst Wackerbarth, Alfred Van der Marck, 1984.

(And creator of maps and petroglyphs) *PrairyErth (a deep map),* Houghton (Boston), 1991.

Also contributor to magazines and periodicals, including *Atlantic Monthly, Esquire, Time,* and *New York Times Book Review.*

WORK IN PROGRESS: A book on American rivers.

SIDELIGHTS: William Trogdon, who writes under the name William Least Heat-Moon, has garnered more critical attention with his first two books than many writers have with twenty. These books, *Blue Highways: A Journey into America* and *PrairyErth (a deep map),* have earned him comparisons to the greatest writers about America: Alexis de Tocqueville, Mark Twain, Jack Kerouac, Herman Melville, John Steinbeck and, most frequently, Henry David Thoreau. Like these writers, Heat-Moon strives to say something important and elemental about the American psyche, speaking in a language common to all Americans. But his two books could not be more different: in *Blue Highways,* Heat-Moon skims across the surface of the entire continent, chronicling the lives of the hundreds of people he meets on the way; in *PrairyErth (a deep map)* he delves into the natural and human history of Chase County, Kansas, exploring every niche of the 774 square miles of rolling Kansas grassland. In both works he provides a moving portrait of the people and the land that make up America.

On a damp March morning in 1978, Heat-Moon left his rented apartment in Columbia, Missouri, climbed into his 1975 van and embarked on a tour that would take him from his point of departure to the Atlantic coast, then clockwise around the perimeter of the United States. As he wrote in *Blue Highways,* his travelogue of that journey, he described that he felt "a nearly desperate sense of isolation and a growing suspicion that I lived in an alien land" and was weary of "carnival midway strips of plastic-roof franchises" and his students' preoccupation with material goods.

Seeking, in his words, "places where change did not mean ruin and where time and men and deeds connected," Heat-Moon kept off of the highways and traveled the old two-lane roads delineated in blue on old maps. He received some of the inspiration for traveling such back roads from John Steinbeck's *Travels with Charley,* which recounted the author's travels around the country in a truck. Heat-Moon's journey lasted three months and covered thirteen thousand miles; the process of editing the journals and tapes into the final manuscript took four years.

Jonathan Yardley, writing in the *Washington Post Book World,* claimed that "more than anything else [Heat-Moon] is passionately, somewhat blindly in love with small-town America and with places where 'things live on . . . in the only way the past ever lives—by not dying." The towns Heat-Moon seemed to love most were those with the oddest names, for he often picked roads that would lead him to towns such as Nameless, Tennessee, and Dime Box, Texas. Heat-Moon sought in particular those residents described by *New York Times* reviewer Anatole Broyard as the "philosopher-historians" found in almost every small town—"keepers of the flame," who, according to Broyard, "wait for someone to whom [they] can explain the soul of the place and pick the colors out," and whose stories reveal, said Yardley, "a *real* past, not something Disneyfied and sentimentalized."

Reviewers commented on Heat-Moon's talent for observing people and places. Richard A. Blake in *America* explained that the author "notes wild flowers and weeds, jack rabbits and oyster beds, and even the texture of clouds and colors of fog. . . . Most of all, he observes people. He delights in the gentle and garrulous, and enjoys the unusual." "All [Heat-Moon's] energy goes into making the moments live," remarked Michael Parfit in the *Los Angeles Times Book Review,* deeming the author's view of America "more intimate and perceptive than most solitary wanderers' books." Although Craig Mellow, writing in the *New Leader,* claimed that Heat-Moon's "affection for the old . . . sometimes results in a sophomoric condemnation of the new," and added that "there is a limit to the appeal of homespun philosophy and simple good news," Peter Ross in the *Detroit News* described *Blue Highways* as "an intense, compelling travelogue of a new sort, a saga that probes the American land and character with brilliance, wit, style, and soulfulness."

Heat-Moon's next work, *PrairyErth (a deep map),* focuses on the history and people of Chase County, Kansas, which in a broader sense serves to provide an understanding of America. It took the author eight years to research; he spent six years walking the county, digging in libraries and the Chase courthouse, sleeping on the ground, and talking to people. The work examines how towns are born, why people gather in the places they do, how people receive their names, how they die, and how the environment is affected by the encroachment of man. "I'm in quest of the land and what informs it," Heat-Moon says in the first chapter of the book, "and I'm here because of shadows in me, loomings about threats to America that are alive here

too, but things I hope will show more clearly in the spareness of this county."

PrairyErth's unique narrative structure provides interesting challenges to the reader. There are no central characters other than the narrator, whom the reader knows little about, and no plot that unfolds over the course of the book. Though some characters reappear, for the most part Heat-Moon describes one aspect of the county and then moves on, making few explicit connections between the images with which he works. "Part of the idea," Heat-Moon told *Heartland Journal* interviewer Peter Gilmour, "is built upon a notion of the way that Native Americans often tell stories. There will be a kernel of the story that the narrator wants to work around. But the tale is likely to proceed by what appears to be ramblings about other things. . . . So what happens is that the listener must then assume a certain responsibility for constructing the tale."

Readers searching for help to make sense of *PrairyErth* might look to the "Commonplace Books," collections of quotations from various sources that precede each of the twelve sections of the book. Heat-Moon quotes from a wide variety of sources in these sections, from famous authors to politicians to historians to environmentalists to unnamed settlers keeping a journal as they cross the prairie. The quotations are brief, usually no more than a sentence or two, but taken together they indicate the direction of the chapters to follow and, Heat-Moon informed Gilmour, "they carry the theme and guide the motif [of *PrairyErth*]." The quotations also provide some sense of Heat-Moon's reaction to what he will describe; while he usually lets people speak for themselves within the chapters, in the commonplace book he provides, through his selections, his own perspective. "Readers either hate or love the Commonplace Book quotations," the author told Gilmour. "I thought that would probably happen. They are some of my favorite parts of the book, and, in fact, probably the only part of the book that I can sit down and read happily now. I go through and read those things. I love them."

Paul Theroux in the *New York Times Book Review* remarked of *PrairyErth,* "It is a good-hearted book about the heart of the country. Mr. Heat-Moon does not make much of the xenophobia he encounters, nor does he explore the racism—the anti-black and anti-Hispanic sentiments he hears. He takes people as he finds them and they put up with his note-taking." In conclusion, Theroux found, "Mr. Heat-Moon has succeeded in recapturing a sense of the American grain that will give the book a permanent place in the literature of our country."

In each of his books, Heat-Moon has been heading toward an earth-centered conservationist ethic: in *Blue Highways* he consistently points out the damages that a growth-oriented country has wrought on its land and its people and celebrates those people who have removed themselves from the madding crowd; in *PrairyErth* he chronicles a county that time has passed by, again demonstrating the benefits of living close to the earth, of conserving the land. In both books Heat-Moon lets the story tell itself, and it does so in a circular, roundabout fashion. In this manner Heat-Moon's Native American background again asserts itself. It is typically the white man's way to get straight to the point, to tell a linear tale. Heat-Moon's stories travel the land, taking the truths that are there without trying to force an interpretation.

BIOGRAPHICAL/CRITICAL SOURCES:

BOOKS

Contemporary Literary Criticism, Volume 29, Gale (Detroit), 1984, pp. 222-26.
Heat-Moon, William Least, *Blue Highways: A Journey into America,* Little, Brown, 1982.
Heat-Moon, *PrairyErth (a deep map),* Houghton, 1991.

PERIODICALS

America, April 9, 1983.
Chicago Tribune, February 24, 1983.
Christian Science Monitor, February 11, 1983; March 2, 1984.
Commonweal, May 20, 1983.
Detroit Free Press, February 19, 1984.
Detroit News, February 20, 1983.
Globe and Mail (Toronto), April 14, 1984.
Heartland Journal, March-April, 1992, pp. 9-11.
Hudson Review, summer, 1983, pp. 420-24.
Hungry Mind Review, spring, 1992, p. 47.
Kirkus Reviews, November 1, 1982; December 15, 1982.
London Review of Books, August 4-17, 1983.
Los Angeles Times Book Review, January 30, 1983; October 16, 1983; December 8, 1985.
Maclean's, February 7, 1983.
National Review, May 13, 1983, p. 580.
New Leader, March 21, 1983, pp. 16-17.
Newsweek, February 7, 1983, p. 63.
New Yorker, May 2, 1983, pp. 121-26.
New York Times, January 13, 1983.
New York Times Book Review, February 6, 1983, pp. 1, 22; October 27, 1991, pp. 1, 25-26.
Observer (London), July 3, 1983.
People, February 28, 1983; April 18, 1983, pp. 72-74.
Publishers Weekly, August 16, 1991, p. 40.
Time, January 24, 1983, p. 84.
Times (London), June 9, 1983.
Times Literary Supplement, August 26, 1983, p. 902.
U.S. News and World Report, November 11, 1991, pp. 58-59.

Village Voice, May 24, 1983.
Washington Post Book World, December 26, 1982, pp. 3, 7.

* * *

TUOHY, Frank
See TUOHY, John Francis

* * *

TUOHY, John Francis   1925-
(Frank Tuohy)

PERSONAL: Born May 2, 1925, in Uckfield, England; son of Patrick Gerald (a physician) and Dorothy (Annandale) Tuohy. *Education:* King's College, Cambridge, B.A. (first-class honors), 1946.

ADDRESSES: Home—Shatwell Cottage, Yarlington, near Wincanton, Somerset BA9 8DL, England. *Agent*—A. D. Peters & Co., Ltd., 10 Buckingham St., London WC2N 6BU, England.

CAREER: University of Turku, Turku, Finland, lecturer, 1947-48; University of Sao Paulo, Sao Paulo, Brazil, professor of English language and literature, 1950-56; Jagiellonian University, Krakow, Poland, contract professor, 1958-60; Waseda University, Tokyo, Japan, visiting professor, 1964-67; Purdue University, Lafayette, IN, writer-in-residence, 1970-71, 1976, and 1980; Rikkyo University, Tokyo, Japan, visiting professor, 1983—. Also taught at Texas A & M University, College Station, TX.

MEMBER: PEN, Royal Society of Literature (London; fellow), Society of Authors.

AWARDS, HONORS: Katherine Mansfield Prize, 1960, for the short story "The Admiral and the Nuns"; Society of Authors traveling fellowship, 1963, for the book *The Admiral and the Nuns;* Geoffrey Faber Memorial Prize, 1963-64, and James Tait Black Memorial Prize, 1964, both for *The Ice Saints;* E. M. Forster Memorial Award, 1971; William Heinemann Award, 1979, for *Live Bait.*

WRITINGS:

UNDER NAME FRANK TUOHY

The Animal Game (novel), Scribner (New York City), 1957.
The Warm Nights of January (novel), Macmillan (New York City), 1960.
The Admiral and the Nuns (stories), Scribner, 1962.
The Ice Saints (novel), Scribner, 1964.
Portugal (travelogue), Thames & Hudson (London), 1969, Viking (New York City), 1970.

Fingers in the Door (stories), Scribner, 1970.
Yeats: An Illustrated Biography, Macmillan, 1972.
Live Bait and Other Stories, Holt (New York City), 1979.
The Collected Stories, Holt, 1984.

Also author of television play, *The Japanese Student,* 1973. Contributor of stories to *Winter's Tales,* Macmillan, 1971, 1972, 1974, and to *Encounter.*

SIDELIGHTS: In a style that the *Observer*'s Paul Bailey termed "economical and telling," Frank Tuohy's writing explores the ways in which social, sexual, and cultural distinctions serve to alienate human beings from one another. In a critique of *Live Bait and Other Stories* for the *New York Times Book Review,* Julia O'Faolain commented, "Hierarchical social systems—Japanese, Communist, British—interest [Tuohy], and he enjoys moving characters conditioned by one code into areas in which another prevails. Signals are then misread, susceptibilities offended. . . . The codes, held against one another like transparencies, reveal not only their own limitations but those of the human condition." Kingsley Shorter of the *New Leader* offered similar remarks concerning *Fingers in the Door.* Shorter noted that Tuohy evokes "the deadly art of social classification" and added, "Tuohy knows that class, like race or creed, is only one of the grosser and more visible ways we 'classify in order to deal with one another,' he recognizes that classification is a never-ending process pursued at every level of consciousness down to the very minutiae of existence. . . . In the mute agony of his characters, Tuohy reveals the *reducto ad absurdum* of the class system: The dreadful discovery that one is all alone, the solitary member of a class of one."

Tuohy, a distant relative of James Joyce on his father's side, was born with a heart defect that was not cured until 1960, when he underwent surgery. This defect kept him out of military service during World War II, giving him an opportunity to study philosophy and English at Cambridge, where he took a degree with first-class honors. He began writing stories during his college years and soon after graduation went to Finland for the first of several teaching stints abroad.

As many critics have observed, the many countries in which Tuohy has lived and taught often provide the settings for his books and give them their unique flavor. His first two novels, *The Animal Game* and *The Warm Nights of January,* are set in South America, where Tuohy taught English language and literature for six years, and *The Animal Game,* which *Saturday Review*'s Ben Ray Redman called "one of the most entertaining books that have come my way in a long time," involves the actions and interactions of a number of expatriates in a country that appears to be Brazil. "Mr. Tuohy's writing," observed Richard Horchler in the *New York Times Book Review,* "is unob-

trusively excellent, his control of his material remarkably firm, his imagination both strong and subtle." Assessing Tuohy's second novel, *The Warm Nights of January,* Tucker credited him for being "especially skillful at capturing the struggle of the expatriate consciousness to achieve an equilibrium between the pull of European sensibilities and the lure of . . . primitive energies . . . with an economy of style that is impressive." And "as in all his work," Tucker pointed out, "the land serves as the real antagonist."

Tuohy's third book, a collection of short stories entitled *The Admiral and the Nuns,* brought its writer a Society of Authors traveling fellowship, and the title story won a 1960 Katherine Mansfield Prize. Though Michele Murray, writing for *Commonweal,* found the stories "enjoyable to read," she felt that the author left them emotionally incomplete—"an exercise in cliff-hanging." Hers represented only a small segment of reviewer opinion, however. More typical was the kind Hoke Norris provided in *Saturday Review,* comparing Tuohy's manner to that of Chekhov: "Quiet, deceptively matter-of-fact, without compromise or illusion or any desire to prettify the ugly—yet he finds beauty where others might find only moral or physical squalor."

The Ice Saints, Tuohy's third novel, grew out of his stay in Poland from 1958 to 1960. The central character of the novel, Rose Nicolson, travels to Poland to visit her sister and to attempt to bring her fourteen-year-old nephew to England. Through the account of her doomed and disastrous efforts and the harshness of the physical and political Polish landscapes, Tuohy illuminates the wide gulf between the Eastern and Western cultures of the time. Aileen Pippett, writing for the *New York Times Book Review,* hailed *The Ice Saints* as "a remarkable achievement, a tribute to [Tuohy's] skill as an artist and his honesty as a thinker." In *London Magazine,* Frank McGuiness called the book "a refreshingly unblinkered survey of contemporary Poland" and lamented Tuohy's limited fame, which he attributed to a current taste among readers for the "vulgar, the superficially tough and the flamboyant whereas Tuohy can only provide the subtle, the searchingly sympathetic and the reflective."

The general critical response to *Fingers in the Door,* a 1970 collection of stories set mostly in England, was favorable. Tuohy was called "a discerning social commentator" by *Saturday Review*'s Robert Moss, though the reviewer admitted that "the author's command of mood and his handling of character and situation are frequently faulty." He went on to cite the "glazed, mannered surfaces" of the story "Thunderbolt" as an example, and concluded by deeming the collection "a work of competence and occasional excellence, but no more." Tucker, however, described the stories in *Fingers in the Door* as "noteworthy for their small, epiphanic moments in the lives of suburban professional people." Tucker further confirmed C. P. Snow's assessment of Tuohy as "a master of the short story, one of the best now writing in English."

After a travelogue on Portugal, Tuohy took on the job of writing a biography of William Butler Yeats. Though he was influenced in this direction partly by his publisher, Macmillan, who owned the British and United States rights to Yeats' work, Tuohy had long been interested in the Irish writer (he had done a paper on Yeats while at Cambridge, and viewed him as a vehicle for exploring some of his own heritage). Though Tuohy pursued his work without the authority of Yeats's son, the book that emerged was lauded by critics. Denis Donoghue of the *New York Review of Books* hailed it as "sensible, well-written, and beautifully illustrated," while John Mole commented in the *Listener* that, rather than confirming "the popular prejudice against Yeats," Tuohy "accepts it as inevitable, making the most of everything which seems most extraordinary, as an enticement to further understanding."

Tuohy's next work, the collection *Live Bait and Other Stories,* returns to one of his favorite character types—the exile. Some of the stories are set in Japan, others in Poland and France. In this collection, John Mellors noted in *London Magazine,* Tuohy again excels in showing "the oddness of the English character by contrasting it with the quirks in the make-up of people of other nationalities." Mellors offered as an example the story "Evening in Connecticut," in which a young Englishman is painfully aware of his own reserve at the dinner party of an American academic and blunders embarrassingly because he misunderstands another guest's use of a word. "Michael in Connecticut didn't always interpret the [cultural] signals correctly," Mellors wrote in closing, "but Tuohy is the interpreter who never misses a nuance." William Boyd asserted in *New Statesman* that "Tuohy's strength lies in the way he captures the unusual mood and viewpoint of the expatriate, the exile and the temporary alien."

The Collected Stories, a compilation of all the works from *The Admiral and the Nuns, Fingers in the Door,* and *Live Bait,* elicited several long, thoughtful reviews. Looking at the body of stories, D. J. Enright in the *Times Literary Supplement* described Tuohy's favorite subjects as "people, commonly inhabitants of the Home Countries, who for one reason or another have failed to learn from experience; or else people, often Eastern Europeans, who have learnt rather too much and sometimes need to un-

learn. . . . We have good reason to feel grateful for Frank Tuohy's rare visitations." *Spectator*'s Christopher Hawtree pronounced that Tuohy had "unobtrusively but with the sharpest of eyes for all that is absurd, pretentious and unpleasant in human behavior, conveyed his liverish view of the world with a rare elegance and wit."

In his review of *The Collected Stories, Newsweek*'s Peter Prescott echoed C. P. Snow's earlier opinion by pronouncing Tuohy "one of the best living English practitioners of the short story," placing him in a trinity with V. S. Pritchett and William Trevor. "None [of the three] has any use for experimentation with form or language," Prescott continued. "Each writes deeply traditional stories about human vulnerability, psychological exploitation and the festering injuries imposed by class and cultural distinctions." The pain Tuohy's characters experience is real, Prescott said; "it is not going to go away. . . . The best his people can hope for is a temporary truce, a postponement of misery sure to come, or a quick flick of stylish revenge."

BIOGRAPHICAL/CRITICAL SOURCES:

BOOKS

Contemporary Literary Criticism, Volume 37, Gale (Detroit), 1986.
Dictionary of Literary Biography, Volume 14: *British Novelists since 1960,* Gale, 1983.

PERIODICALS

Commonweal, March 8, 1963, pp. 626-27.
Listener, October 28, 1976, p. 544.
London Magazine, December, 1964, pp. 93-96; February, 1979, pp. 59-63.
Los Angeles Times Book Review, February 18, 1979; June 30, 1985, p. 1.
New Leader, October 5, 1970.
New Statesman, October 27, 1978, pp. 554-55.
Newsweek, February 4, 1985, p. 78.
New York Review of Books, May 26, 1977, pp. 3-4, 6, 8.
New York Times, January 6, 1979.
New York Times Book Review, October 13, 1957, p. 48; September 20, 1964, p. 4; February 25, 1979; January 6, 1985, p. 20.
Observer, May 17, 1970.
Saturday Review, September 28, 1957, p. 35; March 23, 1963, pp. 45-46; November 7, 1970, pp. 45-46.
Spectator, January 12, 1985, pp. 23-24.
Times Literary Supplement, December 21, 1984, p. 1465.
Washington Post Book World, February 11, 1979.

—Sidelights by Jean W. Ross

U

UCHIDA, Yoshiko 1921-1992

PERSONAL: Surname is pronounced "Oo-*chee*-dah"; born November 24, 1921, in Alameda, CA; died after a stroke, June 21, 1992, in Berkeley, CA; daughter of Dwight Takashi (a businessman) and Iku (Umegaki) Uchida. *Education:* University of California, Berkeley, A.B. (cum laude), 1942; Smith College, M.Ed., 1944. *Politics:* Democrat. *Religion:* Protestant. *Avocational interests:* Fine arts, folk crafts.

CAREER: Elementary school teacher in Japanese relocation center in Utah, 1942-43; Frankford Friends' School, Philadelphia, PA, teacher, 1944-45; membership secretary, Institute of Pacific Relations, 1946-47; secretary, United Student Christian Council, 1947-52; full-time writer, 1952-57; University of California, Berkeley, secretary, 1957-62; full-time writer, 1962-92.

AWARDS, HONORS: Ford Foundation research fellow in Japan, 1952; Children's Spring Book Festival honor award, *New York Herald Tribune,* 1955, for *The Magic Listening Cap;* Notable Book citation, American Library Association, 1972, for *Journey to Topaz;* medal for best juvenile book by a California author, Commonwealth Club of California, 1972, for *Samurai of Gold Hill;* Award of Merit, California Association of Teachers of English, 1973; citation, Contra Costa chapter of Japanese American Citizens League, 1976, for outstanding contribution to the cultural development of society; Morris S. Rosenblatt Award, Utah State Historical Society, 1981, for article, "Topaz, City of Dust"; Distinguished Service Award, University of Oregon, 1981; Commonwealth Club of California medal, 1982, for *A Jar of Dreams;* award from Berkeley Chapter of Japanese American Citizens League, 1983; School Library Journal, Best Book of the Year citation, 1983, for *The Best Bad Thing;* New York Public Library, Best Book of the Year citation, 1983, for *The Best Bad Thing;* Best Book of 1985 citation, Bay Area Book Reviewers, 1985, for *The Happiest Ending;* Child Study Association of America, Children's Book of the Year citation, 1985, for *The Happiest Ending;* San Mateo and San Francisco Reading Associations, Young Authors' Hall of Fame award, 1985, for *The Happiest Ending;* Friends of Children and Literature award, 1987, for *A Jar of Dreams;* Japanese American of the Biennium award, Japanese American Citizens Leagues, 1988, for outstanding achievement.

WRITINGS:

JUVENILES

The Dancing Kettle and Other Japanese Folk Tales, illustrations by Richard C. Jones, Harcourt, 1949, reprinted, Creative Arts Book Co., 1986.

New Friends for Susan, illustrations by Henry Sugimoto, Scribner, 1951.

(Self-illustrated) *The Magic Listening Cap—More Folk Tales from Japan,* Harcourt, 1955, reprinted, Creative Arts Book Co., 1987.

(Self-illustrated) *The Full Circle* (junior high school study book), Friendship, 1957.

Takao and Grandfather's Sword, illustrations by William M. Hutchinson, Harcourt, 1958.

The Promised Year, illustrations by Hutchinson, Harcourt, 1959.

Mik and the Prowler, illustrations by Hutchinson, Harcourt, 1960.

Rokubei and the Thousand Rice Bowls, illustrations by Kazue Mizumura, Scribner, 1962.

The Forever Christmas Tree, illustrations by Mizumura, Scribner, 1963.

Sumi's Prize, illustrations by Mizumura, Scribner, 1964.

The Sea of Gold, and Other Tales from Japan, illustrations by Marianne Yamaguchi, Scribner, 1965.

Sumi's Special Happening, illustrations by Mizumura, Scribner, 1966.

In-Between Miya, illustrations by Susan Bennett, Scribner, 1967.

Hisako's Mysteries, illustrations by Bennett, Scribner, 1969.

Sumi and the Goat and the Tokyo Express, illustrations by Mizumura, Scribner, 1969.

Makoto, the Smallest Boy: A Story of Japan, illustrations by Akihito Shirawaka, Crowell, 1970.

Journey to Topaz: A Story of the Japanese-American Evacuation, illustrations by Donald Carrick, Scribner, 1971.

Samurai of Gold Hill, illustrations by Ati Forberg, Scribner, 1972.

The Old Man with the Bump (cassette based on story from *The Dancing Kettle*), Houghton, 1973.

The Birthday Visitor, illustrations by Charles Robinson, Scribner, 1975.

The Rooster Who Understood Japanese, illustrations by Robinson, Scribner, 1976.

The Two Foolish Cats (filmstrip with cassette based on a story from *The Sea of Gold*), Encyclopaedia Britannica Educational, 1977.

Journey Home (sequel to *Journey to Topaz*), illustrations by Robinson, McElderry Books, 1978.

The Fox and the Bear (cassette based on a story from *The Magic Listening Cap*), Science Research Associates, 1979.

A Jar of Dreams, McElderry Books, 1981.

The Best Bad Thing (sequel to *A Jar of Dreams*), McElderry Books, 1983.

Tabi: Journey through Time, Stories of the Japanese in America, United Methodist Publishing House, 1984.

The Happiest Ending (sequel to *The Best Bad Thing*), McElderry Books, 1985.

The Two Foolish Cats, illustrations by Margot Zemach, McElderry Books, 1987.

The Terrible Leak, Creative Education, 1990.

The Magic Purse, illustrations by Keiko Narahashi, McElderry Books, 1993.

The Bracelet, illustrations by Joanna Yardley, Philomel, 1993.

The Wise Old Woman, illustrations by Martin Springett, McElderry Books, 1994.

FOR ADULTS

We Do Not Work Alone: The Thoughts of Kanjiro Kawai, Folk Art Society (Japan), 1953.

(Translator of English portions) Soetsu Yanagi, editor, *Shoji Hamada,* Asahi Shimbun Publishing, 1961.

The History of Sycamore Church, Sycamore Congregational Church, 1974.

Desert Exile: The Uprooting of a Japanese-American Family, University of Washington Press, 1982.

Picture Bride (novel), Northland Press, 1987.

The Invisible Thread (an autobiography for young adults), J. Messner, 1991.

OTHER

Contributor to many books, including *Flight Near and Far,* Holt, 1970; *Scribner Anthology for Young People,* Scribner, 1976; *Literature and Life,* Scott, Foresman, 1979; *Fairy Tales of the Sea,* Harper, 1981; *Anthology of Children's Literature,* Scott, Foresman, 1984; and *Explorations,* Houghton, 1986. Author of regular column, "Letter from San Francisco," in *Craft Horizons,* 1958-61. Contributor to exhibit catalogue of Oakland Museum, 1976. Contributor of adult stories and articles to newspapers and periodicals, including *Woman's Day, Gourmet, Utah Historical Quarterly, Far East,* and *California Monthly.* The Kerlan Collection holds Uchida's manuscripts for *In-Between Miya* and *Mik and the Prowler.* Other manuscript collections are at the University of Oregon Library, Eugene, and the Bancroft Library, University of California, Berkeley.

SIDELIGHTS: Yoshiko Uchida's appreciation for her Japanese heritage inspired her to become the author of many books on Japanese culture for readers of all ages. "In fiction, the graceful and lively books of Yoshiko Uchida have drawn upon the author's own childhood to document the Japanese-American experience for middle-grade readers," Patty Campbell commented in the *New York Times Book Review.* And among her non-fiction works for adults are studies of Japanese folk artists such as *We Do Not Work Alone: The Thoughts of Kanjiro Kawai,* as well as a memoir of wartime imprisonment, *Desert Exile: The Uprooting of a Japanese-American Family.*

After the bombing of Pearl Harbor, Americans of Japanese descent were incarcerated by order of the government. Uchida was a senior at the University of California, Berkeley, when her family was sent to Tanforan Racetrack, where thousands of Japanese-Americans lived in stables and barracks. After five months at Tanforan, they were moved to Topaz, a guarded camp in the Utah desert. Uchida taught in the elementary schools there until the spring of 1943, when she was released to accept a fellowship for graduate study at Smith College. Her parents were also released that year.

Uchida earned a Master's Degree in education; but because teaching limited her time for writing, she found a secretarial job that allowed her to write in the evenings. As she explained in her contribution to *Something about the Author Autobiography Series,* "I was writing short stories at the time, sending them to the *New Yorker, Atlantic Monthly* and *Harper's*—and routinely receiving printed rejection slips. After a time, however, the slips contained encouraging penciled notes and a *New Yorker* editor even met with me to suggest that I write about my concentration camp experiences. . . . And many of the short stories I wrote during those days were published eventually in literature anthologies for young people."

By the time *Woman's Day* accepted one of her stories, Uchida found that writing for children promised more success. Her first book, *The Dancing Kettle and Other Japanese Folk Tales,* was well-received, and when a Ford Foundation grant enabled Uchida to visit Japan, she collected more traditional tales. In addition, she became fascinated with Japanese arts and crafts, and learned more about them from Soetsu Yanagi, the philosopher, and other founders of the Folk Art Movement in Japan. But her most important gain from the visit, she wrote, was the awareness "of a new dimension of myself as a Japanese-American and [a] deepened . . . respect and admiration for the culture that had made my parents what they were."

The death of the author's mother in 1966 prompted Uchida to write a book for her parents "and the other first-generation Japanese (the Issei), who had endured so much." The result was the book *Journey to Topaz: A Story of the Japanese-American Evacuation.* Based on her own experiences in the camps during the war, it marked a shift in emphasis from Japanese culture to the Japanese-American experience in the United States. Every book Uchida wrote after *Journey to Topaz* responded to the growing need for identity among third generation Japanese-Americans. Uchida once explained to *CA:* "Through my books I hope to give young Asian-Americans a sense of their past and to reinforce their self-esteem and self-knowledge. At the same time, I want to dispel the stereotypic image still held by many non-Asians about the Japanese and write about them as real people. I hope to convey the strength of spirit and the sense of hope and purpose I have observed in many first-generation Japanese. Beyond that, I write to celebrate our common humanity, for the basic elements of humanity are present in all our strivings."

BIOGRAPHICAL/CRITICAL SOURCES:

BOOKS

Children's Literature Review, Volume 6, Gale, 1984.
Something about the Author Autobiography Series, Volume 1, Gale, 1986.
Twentieth-Century Children's Writers, 3rd edition, St. James Press, 1989.

PERIODICALS

Children's Book World, November 5, 1967.
New York Times Book Review, February 9, 1986.
Young Readers' Review, January, 1967.

OBITUARIES:

PERIODICALS

Chicago Tribune, June 28, 1992, section 2, p. 6.
Los Angeles Times, June 27, 1992, p. A26.
New York Times, June 24, 1992, p. A18.
School Library Journal, August, 1992, p. 23.*

*   *   *

UNCLE SHELBY
  See SILVERSTEIN, Shel(by)

*   *   *

URI, Pierre (Emmanuel) 1911-1992

PERSONAL: Born November 20, 1911, in Paris, France; died July 21, 1992, in Paris, France; son of Isaac and Helene (Kahn) Uri; married Monique Blanchetiere, 1939; children: Jean-Michel, Marie-Helene Piccot, Noelle, Didier. *Education:* Attended Ecole Normale Superieure, 1929-33, and Princeton University, 1934-35.

CAREER: Teacher of philosophy in Lyons, France, 1935-36, Beauvais, France, 1936-37, Laon, France, 1937-38, and Reims, France, 1938-39; research economist for Institut de Sciences Economiques Appliquees, 1944-47; professor at National School for Public Administration, 1947-51; director of economics for European Coal and Steel Community, 1952-59; European Economic Community chairperson for Experts' Group on Long Term Development, 1960-64, and for Experts' Group on Competitive Capacity, 1968-70; University of Paris IX, Paris, France, professor, 1969-76. Economic and financial adviser to Common Market, 1958-59; European representative for Lehman Brothers, 1959-61; consultant to Atlantic Institute, 1962-67; vice chairperson of United Nations Group on Multi-national Corporations, 1973-74; member of French Economic and Social Council, 1974-79. *Military service:* French Army, 1939-40; received Croix de Guerre.

AWARDS, HONORS: Created Chevalier of French Legion of Honor, 1969; received the Grand Croix of the National Order of Merit, 1991.

WRITINGS:

La Reforme de l'enseignement, Reider, 1937.
Dialogue des continents, Plon, 1963, translation published as *Partnership for Progress,* Harper, 1963.
Une Politique monetaire pour l'Amerique Latine, Plon, 1965, translation published as *A Monetary Policy for Latin America,* Praeger, 1965.
La Grande-Bretagne rejoint l'European, Plon, 1968, translation published as *Pour gouverner,* Robert Laffont, 1967.

From Commonwealth to Common Market, Penguin, 1968.

Trade Investment Policies for the Seventies, Praeger, 1971.

Un Avenir pour l'Europe agricole, Cahiers Atlantiques, 1971, translation published as *A Future for European Agriculture,* Atlantic Papers, 1971. (Editor) *Israel and the Common Market,* International Publications Services, 1971.

Plan quinquennal pour une revolution, Fayard, 1973.

L'Europe se gaspille, Hachette, 1973.

Developpement sans dependance, Calmann-Levy, 1974, translation published as *Development without Dependence,* Praeger, 1976.

(With Renaud Fabre) *Aider le Tiers-Monde a se nourrir lui-meme,* Economica, 1981.

Changer l'impot (pour changer la France), Ramsay, 1981.

Penser pour l'action; un fondateur de l'Europe, O. Jacob, 1991.

Also author of *Le Fonds monetaire international,* 1945, and *Reduire les inegalites,* 1983.

SIDELIGHTS: Pierre Uri once told *CA:* "My constant effort has been bent on linking theory and action and reconciling efficiency and equity. The Third World, for example, ceases to be an economic unit as gaps are increasing between the industrializing countries (which produce oil and raw materials) and the poorest countries. The Third World remains a political unit due to our former mismanagement of relations through colonial or imperialistic exploitation.

"The European Community could have been one of the great revolutions of the century, but it falls short of the expectations of its founders for lack of the policies which would have made it a more shock-proof, internationally effective, regionally balanced, and equalitarian society."

Among Uri's many lifetime accomplishments, the *New York Times* cites his work on the drafting of "two crucial treaties that laid the cornerstone for European economic and political integration": the Treaty of Paris of 1951 and the Treaty of Rome of 1957. Jacques Delors, president of the European Commission, summarized Uri's contributions to the European Community, describing him in a London *Times* obituary as "one of the main architects of the construction of Europe."

OBITUARIES:

PERIODICALS

Chicago Tribune, July 24, 1992, p. 10.
New York Times, July 24, 1992, p. D17.
Times (London), July 24, 1992, p. 15.*

V

VANDENBERG, Philipp 1941-
(Klaus Dieter Hartel)

PERSONAL: Original name Klaus Dieter Hartel; name legally changed in 1972; born September 20, 1941, in Breslau, Germany (now Wroclaw, Poland). *Education:* Attended University of Munich, 1963-64. *Politics:* None. *Religion:* None. *Avocational interests:* Travel.

ADDRESSES: Home—D 83623 Baiernrain, Villa Vandenberg, Germany.

CAREER: Passauer Neue Presse (newspaper), Passau, Bavaria, local editor, 1964-67; *Abendzeitung,* Munich, Germany, news editor, 1967-69; *Quick* (magazine), Munich, editor and writer, 1969-74; *Playboy*—Germany, Munich, nonfiction editor, 1974-76; full-time writer, 1976—.

WRITINGS:

IN ENGLISH TRANSLATION

Der Fluch der Pharaonen, Scherz (Munich), 1973, translation by Thomas Weyr published as *The Curse of the Pharaohs,* Lippincott (Philadelphia, PA), 1975.

Nofretete: eine archaeologische Biographie, Scherz, 1975, translation by Ruth Hein published as *Nefertiti: An Archaeological Biography,* Lippincott, 1978.

Der vergessene Pharao: Unternehmen Tut-ench-Amun, das groesste Abenteuer der Archaeologie, Bertelsmann (Munich), 1978, translation published as *The Forgotten Pharaoh,* Macmillan, 1980.

IN GERMAN

Nofretete, Echnaton und ihre Zeit: Die glanzvollste Epoche Aegyptens in Bildern, Berichten und Dokumenten, Scherz, 1976.

Auf den Spuren unserer Vergangenheit, Goldmann (Munich), 1977.

Ramses der Grosse: Eine archaeologische Biographie, Scherz, 1977.

Das Geheimnis der Orakel: Archaeologen entschluesseln das bestgehuetete Mysterium der Antike (first part of title means "The Secret of the Oracles"), Bertelsmann, 1979.

Nero: Kaiser und Gott, Kuenstler und Narr, Bertelsmann, 1981.

Der Gladiator (fiction), Heyne (Munich), 1982.

Das Tal: Auf den Spuren der Pharaonen, Bertelsmann, 1983.

Die Hetaere (fiction), Heyne, 1984.

Die Pharaonin (fiction), Heyne, 1984.

Das versunkene Hellas: Die Wiederentdeckung des antiken Griechenland, Bertelsmann, 1984.

Caesar und Kleopatra, Bertelsmann, 1986.

Der Pompejaner (fiction), Luebbe (Bergisch Gladbach, Germany), 1986.

Das Tal der Pharaonen, Heyne, 1986.

Klatscht beifall, wenn das Stueck gut war, Bertelsmann, 1988.

Sixtinische Verschwoerung, Luebbe, 1988.

Das Pharao-komplott, Luebbe, 1990.

Die heimlichen Herrscher, Bertelsmann, 1991.

Das fuenfte Evangelium, Luebbe, 1993.

Der gruene Skarabaeus, Luebbe, 1994.

Vandenberg's books have been published in twenty-seven languages, including Japanese, Turkish, Spanish, Finnish, Swedish, Polish, Rumanian, Italian, and French.

*   *   *

VERCORS
See BRULLER, Jean (Marcel)

VERCORS, J. Bruller
See BRULLER, Jean (Marcel)

*   *   *

VIERECK, Peter (Robert Edwin) 1916-

PERSONAL: Born August 5, 1916, in New York, NY; son of George Sylvester (a poet) and Margaret (Hein) Viereck; married Anya de Markov, June, 1945 (divorced, May, 1970); married Betty Martin Falkenberg, August 30, 1972; children: (first marriage) John-Alexis, Valerie Edwina (Mrs. John Gibbs) *Education:* Harvard University, B.S. (summa cum laude), 1937, M.A., 1939, Ph.D., 1942; Henry fellow, Christ Church, Oxford, graduate study, 1937-38.

ADDRESSES: Home—12 Silver St., South Hadley, MA 01075-1616. *Office*—History Department, Mount Holyoke College, South Hadley, MA 01075.

CAREER: Harvard University, Cambridge, MA, instructor in German literature, tutor in history and literature departments, 1946-47; Smith College, Northampton, MA, assistant professor of history, 1947-48, visiting lecturer in Russian history, 1948-49; Mount Holyoke College, South Hadley, MA, associate professor, 1948-55, professor of modern European and Russian history, 1955-65, Mount Holyoke Alumnae Foundation Chair of Interpretive Studies, 1965-79, William R. Kenan Chair of History, Mount Holyoke College, 1979—. Whittal Lecturer in Poetry, Library of Congress, 1954, 1963; Fulbright professor in American poetry and civilization, University of Florence, 1955; Elliston Chair, poetry lecturer, University of Cincinnati, 1956; visiting lecturer, University of California, Berkeley, 1957, 1964, and City College of the City University of New York, 1964; director of poetry workshop, New York Writers Conference, 1965-67. Speaker at numerous universities. Participated in cultural exchange mission to Russia for U.S. State Department, 1961; visiting research scholar in Russia for Twentieth Century Fund, 1962-63. *Military service:* U.S. Army, Psychological Warfare, 1943-45; awarded two battle stars; taught history at U.S. Army University, Florence, Italy, 1945.

MEMBER: American Committee for Cultural Freedom (member of executive committee), PEN, Committee for Basic Education (charter member), American Historical Association, Oxford Society, Poetry Society of America, Phi Beta Kappa, Harvard Club (New York City), Harvard Club of London, Bryce Club (Oxford, England).

AWARDS, HONORS: Tietjens Prize for poetry, 1948; Pulitzer Prize for poetry, 1949, for *Terror and Decorum: Poems 1940-1948;* Guggenheim fellowship, Rome, 1949-50; Rockefeller Foundation researcher in history,

Germany, summer, 1958; most distinguished alumnus award, Horace Mann School for Boys, 1958; honorary L.H.D. from Olivet College, 1959; National Endowment for the Humanities senior research fellow, 1969; Poetry award of the Massachusetts Artists Foundation, 1978; Sadin prize, *New York Quarterly,* 1980, for lyrical poetry; Golden Rose Award of the New England Poetry Club, 1981; Varoujan Poetry Prize of the New England Poetry Club, 1983; Ingram Merrill Foundation Fellow in poetry 1985; Poetry Translation award of the Translation Center at Columbia University for translating German and Russian poets in a book called *Transplantings.*

WRITINGS:

HISTORY

Metapolitics: From the Romantics to Hitler, Scribner (New York City), 1941; revised edition published as *Metapolitics: The Roots of the Nazi Mind,* Capricorn Books (Toms River, NJ), 1961, 2nd revised edition, 1965, updated, new edition by Louisiana State University Press (Baton Rouge), 1982.

Conservatism Revisited: The Revolt against Revolt, 1815-1949, Scribner, 1949, 2nd edition published as *Conservatism Revisited and the New Conservatism: What Went Wrong?,* 1962, 3rd edition, 1972, reprinted by Greenwood Press (Westport, CT), 1978.

Shame and Glory of the Intellectuals: Babbitt, Jr. Versus the Rediscovery of Values, Beacon Press (Boston, MA), 1953, reprinted, Greenwood Press, 1978.

The Unadjusted Man: A New Hero for Americans: Reflections on the Distinction between Conserving and Conforming, Beacon Press, 1956, reprinted, Greenwood Press, 1973.

Conservatism: From John Adams to Churchill, Van Nostrand (New York City), 1956, revised edition, 1962, reprinted, Greenwood Press, 1978.

Inner Liberty: The Stubborn Grit in the Machine, Pendle Hill (Wallingford, PA), 1957.

Conservatism from Burke and John Adams till 1982: A History and an Anthology, Louisiana State University Press, 1982.

POETRY

Terror and Decorum: Poems 1940-1948, Scribner, 1948, reprinted, Greenwood Press, 1972.

Strike through the Mask: New Lyrical Poems, Scribner, 1950, reprinted, Greenwood Press, 1972.

The First Morning: New Poems, Scribner, 1952, reprinted, Greenwood Press, 1972.

Dream and Responsibility: The Tension between Poetry and Society, University Press of Washington, DC, 1953, reprinted, 1972.

The Persimmon Tree (poems), Scribner, 1956.

The Tree Witch: A Poem and a Play (First of All a Poem) (produced at Harvard University's Loeb Theater), Scribner, 1961, reprinted, Greenwood Press, 1973.

New and Selected Poems, 1932-1967, Bobbs-Merrill (Indianapolis, IN), 1967, reprinted, University Microfilms (Ann Arbor, MI), 1980.

Archer in the Marrow: The Applewood Cycles of 1967-1987 (epic poem), Norton (New York City), 1987.

Also author of *Tide and Continuities: Last and First Poems,* 1993.

OTHER

Also author of *Opcomp: A Modern Medieval Miracle Play,* 1993.

Contributor to various publications, including *Mid-Century American Poets,* Twayne, 1950; *Arts in Renewal,* University of Pennsylvania Press, 1951; *The New American Right,* Criterion, 1955; *Education in a Free Society,* University of Pittsburgh Press, 1958; *The Radical Right,* Doubleday, 1963; *Soviet Policy Making,* edited by P. H. Juviler and H. W. Morton, Burns & McEachern, 1967; *Outside Looking In,* edited by D. B. James, Harper, 1972; *A Question of Quality,* edited by Louis Filler, Bowling Green University Popular Press, 1976. Contributor of monographs, essays, reviews, and poems to popular magazines and professional journals. Author of essay on "Conservatism" in *Encyclopaedia Britannica,* 15th Edition.

WORK IN PROGRESS: An update of his books on conservatism with new chapters extremely critical of plutocracy, McCarthyism and the Reagan presidency.

SIDELIGHTS: Heralded by critics for his "comic sense" and "lyrical element," Peter Viereck has received numerous awards for his works of poetry and historical nonfiction. Endorsing a philosophy which seeks to join humankind with what he describes as the rhythmic heritage of the universe, Viereck seeks to synthesize extremes in much of his poetry. In a *Dictionary of Literary Biography* essay, Idris McElveen explained: "The lyrical element is present in finely crafted lines of sounds and rhythms. When Viereck is at his best, he can have both intelligence and lyricism in the same poem. . . . As a result of this risk-taking, his range in tone and in subject matter is exceptional. Also as a result, he often fails disastrously and conspicuously." Not surprisingly, Viereck has received similarly mixed reviews throughout his long and successful career. McElveen concluded that Viereck's risk-filled poetry can either display an "energetic control of language for purposes of wit and variety in tone and subject matter" or can occasionally "disintegrate into contrivances and verbal clowning."

Upon its publication in 1941, Viereck's first book made a strong impression on reviewers. *Books'* John Barnes called

Metapolitics: From the Romantics to Hitler "a corrosive analysis of some of the ideas of National Socialism. . . . It does as much as any book since the [Second World War] began to define the specifically German elements of what Mr. Viereck calls the 'theology of nightmare.'" A reviewer for *Christian Science Monitor* found the work "an extremely important book, notable because it makes it possible for the normal western mind to understand at least partially the disease which has warped the thinking of the German people. This is no easy task because no German has ever been able to explain it intelligently." Crane Brinton wrote in the *Saturday Review of Literature:* "This is the best account of the intellectual origins of Nazism available to the general reader. It is a controversial book, packed with points worth disputing."

Catholic World's Erik von Kuehnelt-Leddihn expressed a similar opinion of Viereck's later nonfiction book, *Shame and Glory of the Intellectuals: Babbitt, Jr. Versus the Rediscovery of Values.* He commented: "In this . . . internally cohesive and brilliant statement of a young conservative spokesman, the reader will be intellectually stimulated by a scintillating wealth of ideas. He will also be introduced to the indignation of a true American idealist and forced to shake with laughter at the salty humor of a highly amusing author." *Saturday Review's* Elmer Davis added, "[Viereck] has a good many things of importance to say and we had better listen to him."

While reviewers have been generally favorable toward Viereck's nonfiction work, some critics have commented on the time it has taken him to "mature" as a poet. Although Chad Walsh's 1956 review of *The Persimmon Tree* described Viereck as a "lyricist who is now coming into his own," this maturation process took time, as reviews of *Terror and Decorum: Poems 1940-1948* reflect. In *Nation,* Rolfe Humphries pointed out that "Mr. Viereck has. . . . A good deal to learn," and David Daiches noted in a review for the *New York Herald Tribune Weekly Book Review* that while there was great promise evident in Viereck's earlier work, "much in [*Terror and Decorum*] is still promise." Though *Saturday Review of Literature's* Selden Rodman acknowledged that "his book as a whole is so rich in experimental vigor, so full of new poetic attitudes toward civilization and its discontents, so fresh and earthy in its reanimation of the American spirit, that it seems to offer endless possibilities of development—both for Viereck himself, and for other young poets," he also wrote that Viereck's "style is much less finished."

Other reviewers of the Pulitzer Prize-winning book faulted more than Viereck's supposed lack of maturity. Robert Fitzgerald noted that "the poems are lively and a few of them sustain a neat, coarse clarity and a satiric turn of fancy that is not disagreeable. However, he has a warm, breezy, familiar way of being acutely embarrassing." Fitzgerald continued: "The favorable reception of this patter may be significant, but I judge it to be momentary, for Viereck has as yet written very little to which one could wish to return often or with serious interest." Paul Goodman agreed in a *Poetry* review, complaining "it is hard to read these verses seriously because, though Viereck has many lively talents, he seems to have no personal language."

James Reaney echoed Goodman's opinion in *Canadian Forum:* "Peter Viereck's poems, for the most part . . . are the results of forced fancy, of imagination overdriven by a sort of imagery-engine. . . . At their best these poems describe a horrifying, harsh world not even our own but always five centuries ahead. . . . His poems . . . are a perfect illustration of the proverb: One may be a visionary and a visionary with all the correct myths, symbols and assorted gobbets of erudition on their right places and still not be a poet."

At the time of its publication in 1950, the collection *Strike through the Mask* generated comments as to Viereck's classification as a lyric poet. While *New York Times* reviewer W. C. Williams argued that "Viereck's talent is . . . in the purest sense lyrical, sensitive, [and] distinguished in feeling," Rodman, writing in the *New York Herald Tribune Book Review,* contested the real trouble with *Strike through the Mask* is that Viereck is not a lyric poet at all. . . . His great gifts are in the realm of the didactic, the meditative and perhaps the pastoral. And if he exercises them in these fields with restraint, he can well become the universal catalyst he aspires to be." But Anne Freemantle's review of *The First Morning* in *Commonweal* echoes the early complaints of Viereck's maturity as a poet: "Dr. Viereck is staying young too long. His 'new poems' are still full of promise; but by now, in his thirties, he should have backed them up with performance."

Upon the publication of *The Persimmon Tree* in 1956, critics apparently sensed a difference in Viereck's tone. The book was lauded by L. B. Drake, who noted in the *Atlantic,* "Gone is that vague unease, that preoccupation with nightmare and fugue that haunted his earlier work," while *Poetry*'s Hayden Carruth found "the new poems offer a gentler flow, an easier tone of voice." Walsh wrote that "underneath the technical fireworks and plain vitality was a quieter, more tranquil Viereck, the lyricist gravely recording the eternal flow of life and experience."

A decade later, Viereck's publication of *New and Selected Poems 1932-1967* prompted Andrew Glaze to write: "It is hard to imagine a poet more out of style at this moment than Peter Viereck," and yet, "he goes on in his baroque way, turning out complicated, interesting and old-fashioned pieces in the midst of triumphant, new alien styles. . . . He has always been unpredictable and difficult. He has never made points with moderation and

safety. . . . No one has created more wonderful poems out of near-doggerel rhythms and unlikely rhymes, as though from the pure pleasure of barely skirting disaster. . . . Even when his poems fail, they are rarely as dull as the poetry we have had to grow accustomed to."

In addition, Ernest Kroll noted that "it isn't easy . . . to mistake a poem by Peter Viereck. Impulse in the saddle, with unbounded energy raring to take on any subject, is the outstanding impression one gets from his work. . . . He frequently takes his reader for a wild ride from which he alone, the poet, returns. . . . There is fortunately, however, another Viereck, the memorable one, who can and does rein his mount in tightly after the wilder rides." According to *Shenandoah*'s Lisel Mueller, Viereck "believes that poetry must communicate and that it must celebrate the emotional life, the life of meaning rather than gesture. . . . He writes for the intelligent common reader, in the traditional forms he is intent on preserving. He writes with wit, spirit, conviction and a great understanding of history and modern western culture."

Often willing to take chances and stretch his form to the limit, Viereck followed through on the dramatic intermingling of play and poem he presented in his 1961 work *The Tree Witch: A Poem and A Play (First of All a Poem)*. The ambitious and intriguing collection of twenty years' work, *Archer in the Marrow: The Applewood Cycles of 1967-1987* is highly complex, structured in eighteen lyrical cycles. *Los Angeles Times Book Review*'s George Butterick summarized *Archer in the Marrow* as "a philosophical epic starring the classic Christ-Dionysus-Osiris configuration, representing the tragicomic spirit of the human imagination." Although he found value and excitement in *Archer in the Marrow*'s lyrical lines, Butterick ultimately concluded that Viereck's poetry falls short. "Viereck's poetry can be praised for its vitality, satiric intent, rhythmic variety within its chosen confines, and occasional boldness of rhyme—but never consistently." Although willing to acknowledge Viereck's inconsistency, *Dictionary of Literary Biography* essayist McElveen contended that "in spite of these lapses in language and in spite of his persistent desire to make his ideas about morality and society clear and persuasive, Viereck has already established himself as a poet with a unique talent for merging the separate disciplines of poetry and social philosophy in a language that is at once lyrical and humane, witty and risk-taking."

BIOGRAPHICAL/CRITICAL SOURCES:

BOOKS

Contemporary Literary Criticism, Volume 4, Gale, 1975.
Dictionary of Literary Biography, Volume 5: *American Poets since World War II,* Gale, 1980.
Engle, Paul, and Joseph Langland, editors, *Poet's Choice,* Dial Press, 1962.

Henault, Marie, *Peter Viereck, Poet and Historian,* Twayne, 1966.

Nemerov, Howard, *Poetry and Fiction,* Rutgers University Press, 1963.

PERIODICALS

Atlantic, June, 1957.

Books, October 5, 1941.

Canadian Forum, April, 1949.

Catholic World, July, 1953.

Christian Science Monitor, November 7, 1941; December 24, 1953; October 11, 1956; May 27, 1987.

Commonweal, August 5, 1949; October 24, 1952.

Hudson Review, winter, 1988.

Kirkus Reviews, January 15, 1961.

Library Journal, April 1, 1961; February 15, 1987.

Los Angeles Times Book Review, June 14, 1987.

Michigan Quarterly Review, summer, 1969.

Nation, October 11, 1941; November 13, 1948.

National Review, February 5, 1988.

New Leader, April 8, 1969; August 10, 1987.

New Republic, August 8, 1949; April 24, 1950; March 16, 1953.

New Yorker, January 31, 1953; March 21, 1953; March 24, 1962.

New York Herald Tribune Book Review, March 26, 1950; March 22, 1953.

New York Herald Tribune Weekly Book Review, November 21, 1948; October 9, 1949.

New York Times, November 21, 1948; March 12, 1950; March 15, 1953; October 28, 1956.

New York Times Book Review, August 6, 1967.

Poetry, February, 1949; February, 1957.

Saturday Review, February 28, 1953; July 22, 1961; October 14, 1967.

Saturday Review of Literature, October 4, 1941; October 9, 1948.

Shenandoah, spring, 1968.*

*   *   *

**von HELLER, Marcus
See ZACHARY, Hugh**

W

WALCOTT, Derek (Alton) 1930-

PERSONAL: Born January 23, 1930, in Castries, St. Lucia; son of Warwick (a civil servant) and Alix (a teacher) Walcott; married Fay Moston, 1954 (divorced, 1959); married Margaret Ruth Maillard, 1962 (divorced); married Norline Metivier (an actress and dancer); children: one son (first marriage), two daughters (second marriage). *Education:* Attended St. Mary's College (St. Lucia); University of the West Indies (Kingston, Jamaica), B.A. 1953.

ADDRESSES: Home—(summer) 165 Duke of Edinburgh Ave., Diego Martin, Trinidad and Tobago; (winter) 71 St. Mary's, Brookline, MA 02146. *Office*—Creative Writing Department, Boston University, 236 Bay State Rd., Boston, MA 02215. *Agent*—Bridget Aschenberg, International Famous Agency, 1301 Avenue of the Americas, New York, NY 10019.

CAREER: Poet and playwright. Teacher at St. Mary's College, St. Lucia, Boys' Secondary School, Grenada, and at Kingston College, Jamaica. Founding director of Trinidad Theatre Workshop, 1959—. Visiting professor at Columbia University, 1981, and Harvard University, 1982; visiting professor in Creative Writing Department of Boston University, 1985—. Also lecturer at Rutgers University and Yale University.

AWARDS, HONORS: Rockefeller fellowship, 1957; Jamaica Drama Festival prize, 1958, for *Drums and Colours: An Epic Drama;* Guinness Award, 1961, for "A Sea-Chantey"; Borestone Mountain poetry awards, 1963, for "Tarpon," and 1976, for "Midsummer, England"; named fellow of the Royal Society of Literature, 1966; Heinemann Award, Royal Society of Literature, 1966, for *The Castaway,* and 1983, for *The Fortunate Traveller;* Cholmondeley Award, 1969, for *The Gulf;* Eugene O'Neill Foundation-Wesleyan University fellowship, 1969; Order of the Humming Bird, Trinidad and Tobago, 1969 (one source says 1979); Obie Award, 1971, for *Dream on Monkey Mountain;* honorary doctorate of letters, University of the West Indies, 1972; Officer of British Empire, 1972; Jock Campbell/*New Statesman* Prize, 1974, for *Another Life;* Guggenheim fellowship, 1977; named honorary member of the American Academy and Institute of Arts and Letters, 1979; *American Poetry Review* Award, 1979; National Writer's Prize, Welsh Arts Council, 1979; John D. and Catherine T. MacArthur Foundation grant, 1981; *Los Angeles Times Book Review* Prize in poetry, 1986, for *Collected Poems, 1948-1984;* Queen Elizabeth II Gold Medal for Poetry, 1988; Nobel Prize for literature, 1992; St. Lucia Cross, 1993.

WRITINGS:

POETRY

Twenty-Five Poems, Guardian Commercial Printery, 1948.

Epitaph for the Young: A Poem in XII Cantos, Advocate (Bridgetown, Barbados), 1949.

Poems, Kingston City Printery (Jamaica), 1953.

In a Green Night: Poems, 1948-1960, J. Cape (London), 1962.

Selected Poems (includes poems from *In a Green Night: Poems, 1948-1960*), Farrar, Straus (New York City), 1964.

The Castaway and Other Poems, J. Cape, 1965.

The Gulf and Other Poems, J. Cape, 1969, published with selections from *The Castaway and Other Poems* as *The Gulf: Poems,* Farrar, Straus, 1970.

Another Life (long poem), Farrar, Straus, 1973, second edition published with introduction, chronology and selected bibliography by Robert D. Hammer, Three Continents (Washington, DC), 1982.

Sea Grapes, J. Cape, 1976, slightly revised edition, Farrar, Straus, 1976.

Selected Verse, Heinemann (London), 1976.

The Star-Apple Kingdom, Farrar, Straus, 1979.

The Fortunate Traveller, Farrar, Straus, 1981.

Selected Poetry, selected, annotated, and introduced by Wayne Brown, Heinemann, 1981, revised edition, 1993.

The Caribbean Poetry of Derek Walcott, and the Art of Romare Beardon, Limited Editions Club (New York City), 1983.

Midsummer, Farrar, Straus, 1984.

Collected Poems, 1948-1984, Farrar, Straus, 1986.

The Arkansas Testament, Farrar, Straus, 1987.

Omeros, Farrar, Straus, 1989.

Contributor of poems to numerous periodicals, including *New Statesman, London Magazine, Encounter,* and *Bim.*

PLAYS

Henri Christophe: A Chronicle in Seven Scenes (first produced in Castries, St. Lucia, 1950, produced in London, England, 1951), Advocate, 1950.

Harry Dernier: A Play for Radio Production, Advocate, 1951.

Wine of the Country, University College of the West Indies (Mona, Jamaica), 1953.

The Sea at Dauphin: A Play in One Act (first produced in Mona, Jamaica, 1953, produced in London, 1960), Extra-Mural Department, University College of the West Indies, 1954.

Ione: A Play with Music (first produced in Port of Spain, Trinidad, 1957), Extra-Mural Department, University College of the West Indies, 1957.

Drums and Colours: An Epic Drama (first produced in Kingston, Trinidad, 1958), published in *Caribbean Quarterly,* March-June, 1961.

Ti-Jean and His Brothers, first produced in Port of Spain, Trinidad, 1958, produced Off-Broadway at Delacorte Theatre, 1972.

Malcochon; or, Six in the Rain (one-act; first produced as *Malcochon* in Castries, St. Lucia, 1959, produced in London under title *Six in the Rain,* 1960, produced Off-Broadway at St. Mark's Playhouse, 1969), Extra-Mural Department, University of West Indies, 1966.

Dream on Monkey Mountain, first produced in Toronto, 1967, produced Off-Broadway at St. Mark's Playhouse, 1971.

Dream on Monkey Mountain and Other Plays (contains *Dream on Monkey Mountain, Sea at Dauphin, Malcochon; or, Six in the Rain, Ti-Jean and His Brothers,* and the essay "What the Twilight Says: An Overture"), Farrar, Straus, 1970.

In a Fine Castle, first produced in Jamaica, 1970, produced in Los Angeles, CA, 1972.

The Joker of Seville (musical), first produced in Port of Spain, Trinidad, 1974.

The Charlatan, first produced in Los Angeles, 1974.

O Babylon!, first produced in Port of Spain, Trinidad, 1976.

Remembrance (three-act), first produced in St. Croix, Virgin Islands, December, 1977, produced Off-Broadway at The Other Stage, 1979.

Pantomime, Port of Spain, Trinidad, 1978, produced Off-Broadway at the Hudson Guild Theater, 1986.

The Joker of Seville and O Babylon!: Two Plays, Farrar, Straus, 1978.

Remembrance & Pantomime: Two Plays, Farrar, Straus, 1980.

The Isle Is Full of Noises, first produced at the John W. Huntington Theater, Hartford, CT, 1982.

Three Plays (contains *The Last Carnival, Beef, No Chicken,* and *A Branch of the Blue Nile),* Farrar, Straus, 1986.

Steel, first produced at the American Repertory Theatre, Cambridge, MA, 1991.

Odyssey: A Stage Version, Farrar, Straus, 1993.

Also author of *Franklin, a Tale of the Islands, Jourmard,* and *To Die for Grenada.*

CONTRIBUTOR

John Figueroa, editor, *Caribbean Voices,* Evans, 1966.

Barbara Howes, editor, *From the Green Antilles,* Macmillan (New York City), 1966.

Howard Sergeant, editor, *Commonwealth Poems of Today,* Murray (London), 1967.

O. R. Dathorne, editor, *Caribbean Verse,* Heinemann, 1968.

Anne Walmsley, compiler, *The Sun's Eye: West Indian Writing for Young Readers,* Longmans, Green (London) 1968.

Orde Coombs, editor, *Is Massa Day Dead?,* Doubleday (New York City), 1974.

D. J. Enright, editor, *Oxford Book of Contemporary Verse, 1945-1980,* Oxford University Press, 1980.

Errol Hill, editor, *Plays for Today,* Longman, 1985.

Also contributor to *Caribbean Literature,* edited by George Robert Coulthard; *New Voices of the Commonwealth,* edited by Sergeant; and *Young Commonwealth Poetry,* edited by Peter Ludwig Brent.

OTHER

The Poet in the Theatre, Poetry Book Society (London), 1990.

Antilles: Fragments of Epic Memory, Farrar, Straus, 1993.

Art and literature critic for *Trinidad Guardian;* feature writer for *Public Opinion* (Jamaica).

SIDELIGHTS: Although born of mixed racial and ethnic heritage on St. Lucia, a West Indian island where a French/English patois is spoken, poet and playwright Derek Walcott was educated as a British subject. Taught to speak English as a second language, he grew to be skilled in his adopted tongue. His use of the language has drawn praise from critics, including British poet and novelist Robert Graves who, according to *Times Literary Supplement* contributor Vicki Feaver, "has gone as far to state that [Walcott] handles English with a closer understanding of its inner magic than most (if not all) of his English-born contemporaries." In their statement upon awarding Walcott the Nobel Prize for Literature in 1992, the Swedish Academy, as quoted in the *Detroit Free Press,* declared: "In him, West Indian culture has found its great poet." Walcott is the first native Caribbean writer to win the prize. In its citation, the Academy noted that "in his literary works, Walcott has laid a course for his own cultural environment, but through them he speaks to each and every one of us."

The major theme of Walcott's writing is the dichotomy between black and white, subject and ruler, and the elements of both Caribbean and Western civilization present in his culture and ancestry. In "What the Twilight Says," the introduction to *Dream on Monkey Mountain and Other Plays,* Walcott refers to his "schizophrenic boyhood," in which he led "two lives: the interior life of poetry [and] the outward life of action and dialect." In his study *Derek Walcott,* Robert D. Hamner notes that this "schizophrenia" is common among West Indians and comments further that "since [Walcott] is descended from a white grandfather and a black grandmother on both paternal and maternal sides, he is living example of the divided loyalties and hatreds that keep his society suspended between two worlds."

"As a West Indian . . . writing in English, with Africa and England in his blood," Alan Shapiro writes in the *Chicago Tribune Book World,* "Walcott is inescapably the victim and beneficiary of the colonial society in which he was reared. He is a kind of a Caribbean Orestes . . . unable to satisfy his allegiance to one side of his nature without at the same time betraying the other." Caryl Phillips describes Walcott's work in much the same way in a *Los Angeles Times Book Review* essay. The critic notes that Walcott's poetry is "steeped in an ambivalence toward the outside world and its relationship to his own native land of St. Lucia."

One often-quoted poem, "A Far Cry from Africa," from *In a Green Night: Poems, 1948-1960,* deals directly with Walcott's sense of cultural confusion. "Where shall I turn, divided to the vein? / I who have cursed / The drunken officer of British rule, how choose / Between this Africa and the English tongue I love? / Betray them both, or give

back what they give?" In another poem, "The Schooner Flight," from his collection, *The Star-Apple Kingdom,* the poet uses a Trinidadian sailor named Shabine to appraise his own place as a person of mixed blood in a world divided into whites and blacks. According to the mariner: "The first chain my hands and apologize, 'History'; / the next said I wasn't black enough for their pride." Not white enough for whites, not black enough for blacks, Shabine sums up the complexity of his situation near the beginning of the poem, saying: "I had a sound colonial education, / I have Dutch, nigger and English in me, / and either I'm nobody or I'm a nation."

It is Walcott, of course, who is speaking, and *New York Review of Books* contributor Thomas R. Edwards notes how the poet suffers the same fate as his poetic alter-ego, Shabine. Edwards writes, "Walcott is a cultivated cosmopolitan poet who is black, and as such he risks irrelevant praise as well as blame, whites finding it clever of him to be able to sound so much like other sophisticated poets, blacks feeling that he's sold his soul by practicing white arts."

Although pained by the contrasts in his background, Walcott has chosen to embrace both his island and his colonial heritage. His love of both sides of his psyche is apparent in his work. As Hamner notes: "Nurtured on oral tales of gods, devils, and cunning tricksters passed down by generations of slaves, Walcott should retell folk stories; and he does. On the other hand, since he has an affinity for and is educated in Western classics, he should retell the traditional themes of European experience; and he does. As inheritor of two vitally rich cultures, he utilizes one, then the other, and finally creates out of the two his own personalized style."

Walcott seems closest to his island roots in his plays. For the most part, he has reserved his native language—patois or creole—to them. They also feature Caribbean settings and themes. According to *Literary Review* contributor David Mason, through his plays Walcott hopes to create a "catalytic theater responsible for social change or at least social identity."

Although a volume of poems was his first published work, Walcott originally concentrated his efforts on the theater. In the fifties, he wrote a series of plays in verse, including *Henri Christophe: A Chronicle in Seven Scenes, The Sea at Dauphin: A Play in One Act,* and *Ione: A Play with Music.* The first play deals with an episode in Caribbean history: ex-slave Henri Christophe's rise to kingship of Haiti in the early 1800s. The second marks Walcott's first use of the mixed French/English language of his native island in a play. Dennis Jones notes in *Dictionary of Literary Biography Yearbook: 1981* that while Walcott uses the folk idiom of the islands in the play, the speech of the characters is not strictly imitative. It is instead "made eloquent, as the common folk represented in the work are made noble, by the magic of the artist."

In "What the Twilight Says" Walcott describes his use of language in his plays. In particular, he expresses a desire to mold "a language that went beyond mimicry, . . . one which finally settled on its own mode of inflection, and which begins to create an oral culture, of chants, jokes, folk-songs, and fables." The presence of "chants, jokes, and fables" in Walcott's plays causes critics such as Jones and the *Los Angeles Times*'s Juana Duty Kennedy to use the term "folk dramas" to describe the playwright's best pieces for theater. In *Books and Bookmen* Romilly Cavan observes the numerous folk elements in Walcott's plays: "The laments of superstitious fishermen, charcoal-burners and prisoners are quickly counter-pointed by talking crickets, frogs, and birds. Demons are raised, dreams take actual shape, [and] supernatural voices mingle with the natural lilting elliptical speech rhythms of downtrodden natives." Animals who speak and a folk-representation of the devil, for example, are characters in the play *Ti-Jean and His Brothers*.

Walcott's most highly praised play, *Dream on Monkey Mountain,* is also a folk drama. It was awarded a 1971 Obie Award and deemed "a poem in dramatic form" by Edith Oliver in the *New Yorker*. The play's title is itself enough to immediately transport the viewer into the superstitious, legend-filled world of the Caribbean back country. In the play, Walcott draws a parallel between the hallucinations of an old charcoal vendor and the colonial reality of the Caribbean. Islanders subjected to the imposition of a colonial culture on their own eventually question the validity of both cultures. Ultimately, they may determine that their island culture—because it has no official status other than as an enticement for tourists—is nothing but a sterile hallucination. Conversely, as Jones notes, they may reach the conclusion at which Walcott wishes his audience to arrive: the charcoal vendor's "dreams connect to the past, and that it is in that past kept alive in the dreams of the folk that an element of freedom is maintained in the colonized world."

Perhaps because of critics' unfamiliarity with the Caribbean reality which Walcott describes in his plays, the author's work for theater has received only mixed reviews in this country. For example, while Walter Goodman writes in the *New York Times* that Walcott's *Pantomime* "stays with you as a fresh and funny work filled with thoughtful insights and illuminated by bright performances," Frank Rich's comments on the play in the same newspaper are not as favorable. "Walcott's best writing has always been as a poet . . . ," Rich observes, "and that judgment remains unaltered by *Pantomime.* For some reason, [Walcott] refuses to bring the same esthetic rigor to

his playwriting that he does to his powerfully dense verse."

In James Atlas's *New York Times Magazine* essay on Walcott, the critic confronts Rich's remarks head on, asserting that the poet would respond to Rich by commenting "that he doesn't conceive of his plays as finished works but as provisional effects to address his own people. 'The great challenge to me,' he says, 'was to write as powerfully as I could without writing down to the audience, so that the large emotions could be taken in by a fisherman or a guy on the street, even if he didn't understand every line.' "

If Walcott's plays reveal what is most Caribbean about him, his poetry reveals what is most English. If he hopes to reach the common person in his plays, the same cannot be said of his poetry. His poems are based on the traditional forms of English poetry, filled with classical allusions, elaborate metaphors, complex rhyme schemes, and other sophisticated poetic devices. In the *New York Times Book Review,* Selden Rodman calls Walcott's poems "almost Elizabethan in their richness." The *New York Times*'s Michiko Kakutani also recognizes British influences in Walcott's poetry, noting that "from England, [Walcott] appropriated an old-fashioned love of eloquence, an Elizabethan richness of words and a penchant for complicated, formal rhymes. In fact, in a day when more and more poets have adopted a grudging, minimalist style, [his] verse remains dense and elaborate, filled with dazzling complexities of style."

Some critics object that Walcott's attention to style sometimes detracts from his poetry, either by being unsuitable for his Caribbean themes or by becoming more important than the poems' content. Denis Donoghue, for example, remarks in the *New York Times Book Review,* "It is my impression that his standard English style [is] dangerously high for nearly every purpose except that of Jacobean tragedy." In Steve Ratiner's *Christian Science Monitor* review of *Midsummer,* the critic observes that "after a time, we are so awash in sparkling language and intricate metaphor, the subject of the poem is all but obscured." Helen Vendler, in the *New York Review of Books,* finds an "unhappy disjunction between [Walcott's] explosive subject . . . and his harmonious pentameters, his lyrical allusions, his stately rhymes, [and] his Yeatsian meditations."

More criticism comes from those who maintain that the influence of other poets on Walcott's work has drowned out his authentic voice. While Vendler, for instance, describes Walcott as a "man of great sensibility and talent," she dismisses much of his poetry as "ventriloquism" and maintains that in Walcott's collection *The Fortunate Traveller* he seems "at the mercy of influence, this time the influence of Robert Lowell." Poet J. D. McClatchy also notices Lowell's influence in *The Fortunate Traveller* as well as two other Walcott poetry collections: *The Star-Apple Kingdom* and *Midsummer*. In his *New Republic* review, McClatchy not only finds similarities in the two men's styles but also a similar pattern of development in their poetry. "Like Lowell," the critic notes, "Walcott's mode has . . . shifted from the mythological to the historical, from fictions to facts, and his voice has gotten more clipped and severe. There are times when the influence is almost too direct, as in 'Old New England,' [a poem from *The Fortunate Traveller*] where he paces off Lowell's own territory."

Both major criticisms of Walcott's poetry are answered in Sven Birkerts's *New Republic* essay. Birkerts observes: "Walcott writes a strongly accented, densely packed line that seldom slackens and yet never loses conversational intimacy. He works in form, but he is not formal. His agitated phonetic surfaces can at times recall Lowell's, but the two are quite different. In Lowell, one feels the torque of mind; in Walcott, the senses predominate. And Walcott's lines ring with a spontaneity that Lowell's often lack."

Other critics defend the integrity of Walcott's poems. Poet James Dickey notes in the *New York Times Book Review*, "Fortunately, for him and for us, . . . Walcott has the energy and the exuberant strength to break through his literary influences into a highly colored, pulsating realm of his own." In his *Poetry* review of *Midsummer* Paul Breslin writes: "For the most part, . . . Walcott's voice remains as distinctive as ever, and the occasional echoes of Lowell register as homage rather than unwitting imitation."

Hamner maintains that when dealing with Walcott's poetry the term assimilation rather than imitation should be used. The critic observes, "Walcott passed through his youthful apprenticeship phase wherein he consciously traced the models of established masters. He was humble enough to learn from example and honest enough to disclose his intention to appropriate whatever stores he found useful in the canon of world literature. . . . But Walcott does not stop with imitation. Assimilation means to ingest into the mind and thoroughly comprehend; it also means to merge into or become one with a cultural tradition."

In *Omeros*, whose title is the contemporary Greek word for Homer, Walcott pays homage to the ancient poet in an epic poem that replaces the Homeric Cyclades with the Antilles. Two of the main characters, the West Indian fishermen Achille and Philoctete, set out on a journey to the land of their ancestors on the West African coast. The characters are concerned not with the events of the Trojan War, but rather with the array of civilization, from African antiquity to frontier America and present-day Boston and London. Half-way through the book, the poet himself enters the narrative. Nick Owchar remarks in the *Los An-*geles *Times Book Review* that "the message of *Omeros* grows with the poet's entrance." He notes that "Walcott's philosophical intentions never come closer to being realized than when he turns . . . criticism on himself. Divestiture, as an artist, is Walcott's forte. He considers his own dangerous use of metaphors: 'When would I not hear the Trojan War / in two fishermen cursing?' he asks near the end. The poet's danger, like every person's, is to distance himself from human suffering by reinterpreting it."

Michael Heyward observes in the *Washington Post Book World:* "*Omeros* is not a translation or even a recreation of either of Homer's great epics. . . . The ancient work it resembles most . . . is Ovid's *Metamorphoses,* with its panoply of characters, its seamless episodic structure, and its panoramic treatment of a mythic world both actual and legendary." He concludes, "We are used to encountering the dynamic exploration of politics and history and folk legend in the contemporary novel, the domain—thanks to Rushdie, Marquez, Gaddis, and others—of modern epic. . . . *Omeros* is not a novel and it does not approximate the form of a novel, but it does rival the novel's mastery of a mythic, multi-dimensional narrative. Strenuous and thrilling, it swims against the tide."

The uniqueness of Walcott's work stems from his ability to interweave British and island influences, to express what McClatchy calls "his mixed state" and do so "without indulging in either ethnic chic or imperial drag." His plays offer pictures of the common Caribbean folk and comment on the ills bred by colonialism. His poetry combines native patois and English rhetorical devices in a constant struggle to force an allegiance between the two halves of his split heritage. According to *Los Angeles Times Book Review* contributor Arthur Vogelsang, "These continuing polarities shoot an electricity to each other which is questioning and beautiful and which helps form a vision all together Caribbean and international, personal (him to you, you to him), independent, and essential for readers of contemporary literature on all the continents."

BIOGRAPHICAL/CRITICAL SOURCES:

BOOKS

Brown, Stewart, editor, *The Art of Derek Walcott,* Dufour (Chester Springs, PA), 1991.
Contemporary Literary Criticism, Gale (Detroit), Volume 2, 1974, Volume 4, 1975, Volume 9, 1978, Volume 14, 1980, Volume 25, 1983, Volume 42, 1987, Volume 67, 1992, Volume 76, 1993.
Dictionary of Literary Biography, Volume 117, Gale, 1992.
Dictionary of Literary Biography Yearbook, Gale, *1981,* 1982, and *1992,* 1993.

Goldstraw, Irma, *Derek Walcott: An Annotated Bibliography of His Works,* Garland Publishing (New York City), 1984.

Hamner, Robert D., *Derek Walcott,* Twayne (Boston), 1981.

Terada, Rei, *Derek Walcott's Poetry: American Mimicry,* Northeastern University Press (Boston), 1992.

Walcott, Derek, *Collected Poems, 1948-1984,* Farrar, Straus, 1986.

Walcott, Derek, *Dream on Monkey Mountain and Other Plays,* Farrar, Straus, 1970.

Walcott, Derek, *In a Green Night: Poems, 1948-1960,* J. Cape, 1962.

Walcott, Derek, *The Star-Apple Kingdom,* Farrar, Straus, 1979.

PERIODICALS

Books and Bookmen, April, 1972.
Book World, December 13, 1970.
Chicago Tribune Book World, May 2, 1982; September 9, 1984; March 9, 1986.
Christian Science Monitor, March 19, 1982; April 6, 1984.
Detroit Free Press, October 9, 1992.
Georgia Review, summer, 1984.
Hudson Review, summer, 1984.
Literary Review, spring, 1986.
London Magazine, December, 1973-January, 1974; February-March, 1977.
Los Angeles Times, November 12, 1986.
Los Angeles Times Book Review, April 4, 1982; May 21, 1985; April 6, 1986; October 26, 1986; September 6, 1987; January 20, 1991.
Nation, February 12, 1977; May 19, 1979; February 27, 1982.
National Review, November 3, 1970; June 20, 1986.
New Republic, November 20, 1976; March 17, 1982; January 23, 1984; March 24, 1986.
New Statesman, March 19, 1982.
New Yorker, March 27, 1971; June 26, 1971.
New York Magazine, August 14, 1972.
New York Review of Books, December 31, 1964; May 6, 1971; June 13, 1974; October 14, 1976; May 31, 1979; March 4, 1982.
New York Times, March 21, 1979; August 21, 1979; May 30, 1981; May 2, 1982; January 15, 1986; December 17, 1986.
New York Times Book Review, September 13, 1964; October 11, 1970; May 6, 1973; October 31, 1976; May 13, 1979; January 3, 1982; April 8, 1984; February 2, 1986; December 20, 1987.
New York Times Magazine, May 23, 1982.
Poetry, February, 1972; December, 1973; July, 1977; December, 1984; June, 1986.
Review, winter, 1974.

Spectator, May 10, 1980.
Time, March 15, 1982; October 19, 1992.
Times Literary Supplement, December 25, 1969; August 3, 1973; July 23, 1976; August 8, 1980; September 8, 1980; September 24, 1982; November 9, 1984; October 24, 1986.
Tribune Books (Chicago), November 8, 1987.
TriQuarterly, winter, 1986.
Village Voice, April 11, 1974.
Virginia Quarterly Review, winter, 1974; summer, 1984.
Washington Post Book World, February 21, 1982; April 13, 1986; November 11, 1990.
Western Humanities Review, spring, 1977.
World Literature Today, spring, 1977; summer, 1979; summer, 1981; winter, 1985; summer, 1986; winter, 1987.
Yale Review, October, 1973.*

* * *

WALLEY, Byron
See CARD, Orson Scott

* * *

WARDE, William F.
See NOVACK, George (Edward)

* * *

WARREN, Robert Penn 1905-1989

PERSONAL: Born April 24, 1905, in Guthrie, KY; died of cancer, September 15, 1989, in Stratton, VT; son of Robert Franklin (a businessman) and Anna Ruth (Penn) Warren; married Emma Brescia, September 12, 1930 (divorced, 1950); married Eleanor Clark (a writer), December 7, 1952; children: (second marriage) Rosanna Phelps, Gabriel Penn. *Education:* Vanderbilt University, B.A. (summa cum laude), 1925; University of California, Berkeley, M.A., 1927; Yale University, graduate study, 1927-28; Oxford University, B.Litt., 1930. *Politics:* Democrat.

CAREER: Southwestern Presbyterian University (now Southwestern College at Memphis), Memphis, TN, assistant professor of English, 1930-31; Vanderbilt University, Nashville, TN, acting assistant professor, 1931-34; Louisiana State University, Baton Rouge, assistant professor, 1934-36, associate professor, 1936-42; University of Minnesota, Minneapolis, professor of English, 1942-50; Yale University, New Haven, CT, professor of playwrighting in School of Drama, 1950-56, professor of English, 1961-73, professor emeritus, 1973-89. Visiting lecturer, State University of Iowa, 1941; Jefferson Lecturer, National Endowment for the Humanities, 1974. Staff member of writers conferences, University of Colorado, 1936, 1937, and 1940, and Olivet College, 1940. Consultant in poetry, Library of Congress, 1944-45.

MEMBER: American Academy of Arts and Letters (member of board), Academy of American Poets (chancellor), American Academy of Arts and Sciences, American Philosophical Society, Modern Language Association (honorary fellow), Century Club (New York).

AWARDS, HONORS: Rhodes Scholarship, Oxford University, 1928-30; Caroline Sinkler Prize, Poetry Society of South Carolina, 1936, 1937, and 1938; Levinson Prize, *Poetry* magazine, 1936; Houghton Mifflin literary fellowship, 1936; Guggenheim fellowship, 1939-40 and 1947-48; Shelley Memorial Prize, 1942, for *Eleven Poems on the Same Theme;* Pulitzer Prize for fiction, 1947, for *All the King's Men;* Southern Prize, 1947; Robert Meltzer Award, Screenwriters Guild, 1949; Union League Civic and Arts Foundation Prize, *Poetry* magazine, 1953; Sidney Hillman Award, 1957; Edna St. Vincent Millay Memorial Award, American Poetry Society, 1958, National Book Award, 1958, and Pulitzer Prize for poetry, 1958, all for *Promises: Poems, 1954-56;* Irita Van Doren Award, *New York Herald Tribune,* 1965, for *Who Speaks for the Negro?;* Bollingen Prize in poetry, Yale University, 1967, for *Selected Poems: New and Old, 1923-1966;* National Endowment for the Arts grant, 1968.

Van Wyck Brooks Award for poetry, National Medal for Literature, and Henry A. Bellaman Prize, all 1970, all for *Audubon: A Vision;* award for literature, University of Southern California, 1973; Golden Rose Trophy, New England Poetry Club, 1975; Emerson-Thoreau Medal, American Academy of Arts and Sciences, 1975; Copernicus Prize, American Academy of Poets, 1976; Wilma and Robert Messing Award, 1977; Pulitzer Prize for poetry, 1979, for *Now and Then: Poems, 1976-1978;* Harriet Monroe Award for poetry, 1979, for *Selected Poems, 1923-1975;* MacArthur Foundation fellowship, 1980; Common Wealth Award for Literature, 1980; Hubbell Memorial Award, Modern Language Association, 1980; Connecticut Arts Council award, 1980; Presidential Medal of Freedom, 1980; National Book Critics Circle poetry award nomination, 1980, and American Book Award nomination, 1981, both for *Being Here: Poetry, 1977-1980; Los Angeles Times* poetry prize nomination, 1982, for *Rumor Verified: Poems, 1979-1980;* Brandeis University Creative Arts Award, 1984; gold medal for poetry, American Academy and Institute of Arts and Letters, 1985; National Medal of the Arts, 1987; Poet Laureate of the United States, 1986-87.

Recipient of honorary degrees from University of Louisville, 1949, Kenyon College, 1952, University of Kentucky, 1955, Colby College, 1956, Swarthmore College, 1958, Yale University, 1959, Bridgeport University, 1965, Fairfield University, 1969, Wesleyan University, 1970, Harvard University, 1973, Southwestern College at Memphis, 1974, University of the South, 1974, University of New Haven, 1974, Johns Hopkins University, 1975, Monmouth College, 1979, New York University, 1983, and Oxford University, 1983; also received honorary degrees from Arizona State University and Dartmouth College.

WRITINGS:

POETRY

Thirty-Six Poems, Alcestis Press, 1935.

Eleven Poems on the Same Theme, New Directions, 1942.

Selected Poems: 1923-43, Harcourt, 1944.

Brother to Dragons: A Tale in Verse and Voices, Random House, 1953, revised edition published as *Brother to Dragons: A Tale in Verse and Voices—A New Version,* 1979.

Promises: Poems, 1954-56, Random House, 1957.

You, Emperors and Others: Poems, 1957-60, Random House, 1960.

Selected Poems: New and Old, 1923-1966, Random House, 1966.

Incarnations: Poems, 1966-68, Random House, 1968.

Audubon: A Vision, Random House, 1969.

Or Else, Poem: Poems, 1968-1974, Random House, 1974.

Selected Poems, 1923-1975, Random House, 1976.

Now and Then: Poems, 1976-1978, Random House, 1978.

Being Here: Poetry, 1977-1980, Random House, 1980.

Rumor Verified: Poems, 1979-1980, Random House, 1981.

Chief Joseph of the Nez Perce, Random House, 1983.

New and Selected Poems, 1923-1985, Random House, 1985.

FICTION

Night Rider, Houghton, 1939, abridged edition, edited and introduced by George Mayberry, New American Library, 1950.

At Heaven's Gate, Harcourt, 1943, abridged edition, edited and introduced by Mayberry, New American Library, 1949.

All the King's Men (also see below), Harcourt, 1946.

Blackberry Winter (novelette), Cummington Press, 1946.

The Circus in the Attic, and Other Stories (short stories), Harcourt, 1947.

World Enough and Time: A Romantic Novel, Random House, 1950.

Band of Angels, Random House, 1955.

The Cave, Random House, 1959.

The Gods of Mount Olympus (adaptations of Greek myths for young readers), Random House, 1959.

Wilderness: A Tale of the Civil War, Random House, 1961.

Flood: A Romance of Our Time, Random House, 1964.

Meet Me in the Green Glen, Random House, 1971.

A Place To Come To, Random House, 1977.

NONFICTION

John Brown: The Making of a Martyr, Payson & Clarke, 1929.

(With others) *I'll Take My Stand: The South and the Agrarian Tradition,* Harper, 1930.

(Contributor) Herbert Agar and Allen Tate, editors, *Who Owns America?: A New Declaration of Independence,* Houghton, 1936.

(Author of critical essay) Samuel Taylor Coleridge, *The Rime of the Ancient Mariner,* illustrated by Alexander Calder, Reynal & Hitchcock, 1946.

Segregation: The Inner Conflict in the South, Random House, 1956.

Remember the Alamo!, Random House, 1958.

Selected Essays, Random House, 1958.

How Texas Won Her Freedom: The Story of Sam Houston and the Battle of San Jacinto (booklet), San Jacinto Museum of History, 1959.

The Legacy of the Civil War: Meditations on the Centennial, Random House, 1961.

Who Speaks for the Negro?, Random House, 1965.

A Plea in Mitigation: Modern Poetry and the End of an Era (lecture), Wesleyan College, 1966.

Homage to Theodore Dreiser: August 27, 1871-December 28, 1945, on the Centennial of His Birth, Random House, 1971.

Democracy and Poetry, Harvard University Press, 1975.

(Contributor) *A Time to Hear and Answer: Essays for the Bicentennial Season,* University of Alabama Press, 1977.

Jefferson Davis Gets His Citizenship Back (essay), University of Kentucky Press, 1980.

Portrait of a Father, University of Kentucky Press, 1988.

New and Selected Essays, Random House, 1989.

WITH CLEANTH BROOKS

(Editors with John T. Purser) *An Approach to Literature,* Louisiana State University Press, 1936, 5th edition, Prentice-Hall, 1975.

(Editors) *Understanding Poetry: An Anthology for College Students,* Holt, 1938, 4th edition, 1976.

(Editors) *Understanding Fiction,* Crofts, 1943, 2nd edition, Appleton-Century-Crofts, 1959, shortened version of 2nd edition published as *Scope of Fiction,* 1960, 3rd edition published under original title, Prentice-Hall, 1979.

Modern Rhetoric, Harcourt, 1949, published as *Fundamentals of Good Writing: A Handbook of Modern Rhetoric,* 1950, 2nd edition published under original title, 1958, 4th edition, 1979.

(Editors) *An Anthology of Stories from the Southern Review,* Louisiana State University Press, 1953.

(Editors with R. W. B. Lewis) *American Literature: The Makers and the Making,* two volumes, St. Martin's, 1974.

PLAYS

Proud Flesh (in verse), produced in Minneapolis, MN, 1947, revised prose version produced in New York City, 1948.

(With Erwin Piscator) *Blut auf dem Mond: Ein Schauspiel in drei Akten* (based on Warren's novel *All the King's Men;* produced in 1947, produced in Dallas, TX, as *Willie Stark: His Rise and Fall,* 1958, produced on Broadway, 1959), Lechte, 1956.

All the King's Men (based on Warren's novel of same title; produced Off-Broadway at East 74th St. Theatre), Random House, 1960.

Ballad of a Sweet Dream of Piece: An Easter Charade (produced in New York City), music by Alexei Haieff, Pressworks, 1981.

EDITOR

A Southern Harvest: Short Stories by Southern Writers, Houghton, 1937, reprinted, N. S. Berg, 1972.

(With Albert Erskine) *Short Story Masterpieces,* Dell, 1954, 2nd edition, 1958.

(With Erskine) *Six Centuries of Great Poetry: From Chaucer to Yeats,* Dell, 1955.

(With Erskine) *A New Southern Harvest,* Bantam, 1957.

(With Allen Tate) Denis Devlin, *Selected Poems,* Holt, 1963.

Faulkner: A Collection of Critical Essays, Prentice-Hall, 1966.

Randall Jarrell, 1914-1965, Farrar, Straus, 1967.

John Greenleaf Whittier's Poetry: An Appraisal and a Selection, University of Minnesota Press, 1971.

Selected Poems of Herman Melville, Random House, 1971.

Katherine Anne Porter: A Collection of Critical Essays, Prentice-Hall, 1979.

OTHER

Contributor to numerous publications, including *American Scholar, American Review, Botteghe Oscure, Fugitive, Harvard Advocate, Holiday, Mademoiselle, Nation, New Republic, New York Times Book Review, Poetry, Saturday Review, Sewanee Review, Southern Review, Virginia Quarterly Review,* and *Yale Review.* Warren recorded his work on *Robert Penn Warren Reads from His Own Works,*

CMS, 1975, and *Robert Penn Warren Reads Selected Poems,* Caedmon, 1980. Cofounding editor, *Fugitive,* 1922-25; founder and editor, with Cleanth Brooks, *Southern Review,* 1935-42; advisory editor, *Kenyon Review,* 1938-61.

ADAPTATIONS: Two of Warren's books have been made into films: *All the King's Men,* Columbia Pictures, 1949, and *Band of Angels,* Warner Bros., 1957. *All the King's Men* has also served as the basis for an opera written by Carlisle Floyd entitled *Willie Stark,* which was broadcast on television.

SIDELIGHTS: Robert Penn Warren, one of the most famous members of the Fugitives, a major literary movement that emerged in the American South shortly after World War I, was designated the first Poet Laureate of the United States in 1986 by the Library of Congress. A distinguished poet, novelist, critic, and teacher, he won virtually every major award given to writers in the United States, and was the only person to receive a Pulitzer Prize in both fiction (once) and poetry (twice). He also achieved a measure of commercial success in his lifetime that eludes many other serious artists. In short, observed Hilton Kramer in the *New York Times Book Review,* "Few other writers in our history have labored with such consistent distinction and such unflagging energy in so many separate branches of the literary profession. He is a man of letters on the old-fashioned, outsize scale, and everything he writes is stamped with the passion and the embattled intelligence of a man for whom the art of literature is inseparable from the most fundamental imperatives of life."

Literature did not always play a central role in Warren's life. As he recalled in an interview with John Baker published in *Conversations with Writers:* "I didn't expect to become a writer. My ambition was to be a naval officer and I got an appointment to Annapolis. . . . Then I had an accident. I couldn't go—an accident to my eyes—and then I went to [Vanderbilt University] instead, and I started out in life there as a chemical engineer. That didn't last but three weeks or so, because I found the English courses so much more interesting. History courses were also interesting, but the chemistry was taught without imagination."

The freshman English teacher that Warren found so fascinating was fellow Southerner John Crowe Ransom, "a real, live poet, in pants and vest, who had published a book and also fought in the war. . . . As a man, he made no effort to charm his students, but everything he said was interesting." Ransom, recognizing that Warren was no ordinary English student, encouraged the young man to enroll in one of his more advanced courses. He also invited Warren to join the Fugitives, a group of Vanderbilt teachers and students as well as several local businessmen who had been meeting informally since around 1915 to discuss

trends in American life and literature. By 1922, the year Warren joined, many of the Fugitives' discussions focused on poetry and critical theory, Warren's favorite subjects at the time. "In a very important way," said Warren in retrospect, "that group was my education."

The Fugitives drifted apart in the mid-1920s, about the same time Warren graduated from Vanderbilt and headed west to continue his education at the University of California at Berkeley. After receiving his M.A. there in 1927, Warren attended Yale University and then England's Oxford University, where, as he described it, he "stumbled on" writing fiction. Homesick and weary of spending his days and nights working on his dissertation, Warren, at the request of one of the editors of the literary annual *American Caravan,* agreed to compose a novelette based on the folk tales he had heard as a boy in Kentucky. As he later remarked to Baker, his contribution to the annual received "some pleasant notices in the press," and soon publishers were asking him to write novels.

Although Warren wrote several novels during the next decade (only one of which, *Night Rider,* was published), most of his time was spent trying to earn a living. Returning to Tennessee in 1930, after completing his studies at Oxford, he briefly served on the faculty of Southwestern Presbyterian University (now Southwestern at Memphis) before obtaining a teaching position at Vanderbilt. From there Warren went to Louisiana State University in 1934, teaming up with friend and fellow faculty member Cleanth Brooks to edit a series of immensely successful and influential textbooks, including *An Approach to Literature* and *Understanding Poetry: An Anthology for College Students.* Based on the editors' class notes and conversations, these books have been largely responsible for disseminating the theories of New Criticism to several generations of college students and teachers. According to Helen McNeil in the *Times Literary Supplement,* Warren and Brooks helped to establish the New Criticism as "an orthodoxy so powerful that contemporary American fiction and poetry are most easily defined by their rebellion against it."

The New Criticism—a method of analyzing a work of art that focuses attention on the work's intrinsic value as an object in and of itself, more or less independent of outside influences (such as the circumstances of its composition, the reality it creates, the effect it has on readers, and the author's intentions)—grew out of discussions Warren had participated in first as a member of the Fugitives, then as an Agrarian. (The Agrarians were former Fugitives who banded together again in the late 1920s to extol the virtues of the rural South and to promote an agrarian as opposed to an industrial economy.) Despite his close association with the Agrarians and his key role in publicizing their theories, Warren did not consider himself to be a professional critic. As he explained to Baker: "A real critic, like Cleanth Brooks or I. A. Richards, has a system. . . . He's concerned with that, primarily. I'm not. I'm interested in trying to understand this poem or that poem, but I'm not interested in trying to create a system. . . . I'm interested in my enjoyment, put it that way, more than anything else. I've certainly written some criticism, but I usually take it from my class notes. I'm just not a professional critic. . . . But writing fiction, poetry, that's serious—that's for keeps."

Poetry and fiction were thus Warren's main concerns throughout his long career. He saw nothing unusual in the fact that he had made notable contributions to both, re-marking to Baker that "a poem for me and a novel are not so different. They start much the same way, on the same emotional journey, and can go either way. . . . The inter-esting topics, the basic ideas in the poems and the basic ideas in the novels are the same."

For the most part, these "basic ideas" in Warren's poetry and fiction have sprung from his Southern agrarian heri-tage. Observed Marshall Walker in *London Magazine:* "Warren began as an enlightened conservative South-erner. Like his close associates, John Crowe Ransom, Donald Davidson, Allen Tate, Andrew Lytle, he was acutely aware of the gulf widening between an America that moved further into slavery to material progress and a minority of artists and intellectuals, self-appointed cus-todians of traditional values. . . . Agrarians, with Ran-som in the lead, were determined to re-endow nature with an element of horror and inscrutability and to bring back a God who permitted evil as well as good—in short, to give God back his thunder."

In Warren's work, especially his novels, there is a strong emphasis on what Walker referred to as "the vitality of Southern history." Continued the critic: "[Warren dis-plays] a sense of . . . history as a continuum in which he was himself involved. . . . [He] has long since left Guth-rie, Kentucky and the South, to live in the North. He has, nonetheless, remained a Southerner, and the eternal re-turn has been as much a part of his own life as it is of the lives of his characters." Warren's subject matter is mark-edly regional; he drew much of his inspiration from per-sonal reminiscences as well as from narratives, ballads, and folk legends he heard as a child in Kentucky and Ten-nessee.

Despite the fact that he relied on history for material, Warren balked at being labeled a "historical novelist." "I just happened to encounter stories that had the right germ of an idea for a novel," he once stated in a *Saturday Review* article. "I should hope that the historical novel would be a way of saying something about the present." To this end, he often changed the actual historical focus of a story to

concentrate on peripheral characters whose behavior re-vealed more about the ethical or dramatic issues *behind* the facts. Knowledge rather than history was Warren's main obsession, maintained Everett Wilkie and Josephine Helterman in the *Dictionary of Literary Biography.* Ex-plained the two critics: "His works reflect the many forms in which he himself has found knowledge. . . . [His] wis-dom is the wisdom of interpretation; his main question, 'How is one to look at life?' From an elaboration of the complex forces which shape both our lives and our percep-tions, he shows us history as a living force which can yet tell us something about ourselves."

Although Warren lived most of his adult life in Connecti-cut and Vermont, the historical events behind most of his work originate in the American South. For instance, War-ren's first novel, *Night Rider,* set in Kentucky at the begin-ning of the twentieth century, tells the story of an attorney who joins forces with a secret group of tobacco farmers. These farmers use unsavory tactics to threaten other farm-ers that refuse to join their association, which is concerned with obtaining higher prices from the large tobacco com-panies. A later novel, *World Enough and Time: A Roman-tic Novel,* recreates a 19th-century murder case in Ken-tucky, and *Band of Angels,* the story of a mulatto woman who upon her father's death recognizes that she is legally a slave and will be sold as property, takes place against the backdrop of the American Civil War and the Reconstruc-tion era. *Wilderness: A Tale of the Civil War* shares a simi-lar historical context; it is the story of a Bavarian Jew who idealistically travels to America in order to fight for free-dom in the Civil War only to realize that the Yankee sol-diers are not dedicated to the cause of racial freedom.

Warren's most famous novel, *All the King's Men,* traces the political rise and fall of demagogue Willie Stark, the fictional equivalent of populist politician Huey "Kingfish" Long of Louisiana who was assassinated in 1939. The story is told through the eyes of Stark's hard-boiled jour-nalist/historian sidekick, Jack Burden. Stark, who begins his life as an idealistic young lawyer, learns that the way to the heart of the electorate is through manipulating broad passions rather than presenting a coherent political plan. The novel sold three million copies and has been translated into twenty languages. Wrote Robin Toner in the *New York Times:* "For many people, *All the King's Men* is still the definitive novel about American politics, about the ideas and the trade-offs and the emotions that still resonate out on the hustings." Elizabeth Kastor, writ-ing in the *Washington Post,* said, "If the game of naming the Great American Novel is still being played anywhere, Warren's *All the King's Men* would easily make the final rounds."

The type of *real politik* practiced by Stark poses an ethical dilemma for several characters in the novel, including the upstanding Dr. Adam Stanton, who chooses to accept Stark's money to build a great hospital and in so doing collaborates with the politician's corrupt regime. Ultimately, Burden is also forced to confront his own role in larger events and to recognize that he is not exempt from responsibility, as he once believed. Truth itself is shown to be a dangerous proposition if it is used for the wrong ends. When Stark asks Burden to find a guilty secret to use against an honorable man, Stark says, "Man is conceived in sin and born in corruption and he passeth from the stink of the didie to the stench of the shroud. There's always something." Thus, Burden's digging up dirt on Stark's enemies becomes a modern enactment of original sin and the Fall.

"*All the King's Men,*" wrote Robert Gorham Davis in the *New York Times Book Review,* "is brilliantly done, with magnificent brief set-pieces in which Robert Penn Warren writes prose equivalent to his poems in sound and rhythm and imagery; lyric passages full of wisdom and acute observation about a boy's falling in love; about men growing old; about being a failure." However, Davis contended that the novel depicts Huey Long's career from his education to the impeachment proceedings and assassination so accurately that it should be judged on its political as well as its literary merits. The total effect, Davis said, "is to justify Long and the intellectuals who played ball with him; to romanticize him; to have a kind of love affair with him through the three women who adore him." Ultimately, Davis found that Warren never fully confronts the threat that demagogues like Stark pose to democracy.

Diana Trilling reached a similar conclusion about *All the King's Men* in the *Nation.* "For sheer virtuosity," she wrote, "for the sustained drive of its prose, for the speed and evenness of its pacing, for its precision of language, its genius of colloquialism, I doubt indeed whether it can be matched in American fiction." She, however, also questioned the political conclusions that the reader reaches through Burden's perspective: "It is in fact difficult *not* to infer . . . that a Willie Stark's absolute power is justified by such public benefactions as the fine hospital he builds, or that we are to welcome the Willie Stark type of political unpleasantness as a step in political progress."

Warren denied the existence of a direct correlation between the fictional Stark and the late Huey Long. Although he acknowledged that if he hadn't lived in Louisiana and if Long hadn't existed, the novel would not have been written, Warren pointed out in an essay in the *Yale Review:* "But this is far from saying that my 'state' in *All the King's Men* is Louisiana (or any of the other forty-nine stars in our flag), or that my Willie Stark is the late Senator. What Louisiana and Senator Long gave me was a line of thinking and feeling that did eventuate in the novel." Other critics note that Jack Burden is the central charac-

ter of the novel, and is supposed to mediate between the utilitarian politics of Stark and the saintliness of Adam Stanton. The novel does not glorify Stark or Long, they contend, so much as it examines the choices and conflicts that this type of politician faces. R. Gray, writing in *Journal of American Studies,* commented, "Stark's story is also a tragic one; as tragic and as poignant as, say, that of Brecht's *Mother Courage.* For Willie Stark and Mother Courage are both placed in situations which demand the worst of them, if they are to survive, even though they may recognize and sometimes wish for the best."

Despite its Pulitzer Prize, several critics have criticized the intricately-plotted *All the King's Men,* calling its story line melodramatic and Warren's writing overblown. In the *New Republic,* Saul Maloff called *All the King's Men* an "extraordinarily bad novel." The plot, he said, "combines elements of grand guignol and Southern Gothic with those of sentimental romance, all of it closely stage-managed." Maloff is most critical of Jack Burden, whom he described as garrulous and posturing. "Burden," wrote Maloff, "vaporizes relentlessly about History, Time, Truth, God, Fate, Chance, the Meaning Of It All; nothing can begin to happen but that it releases torrents of overblown, ornamental creative writing, whether the object—or victim—of his meditations be grand or trivial."

For Warren, individuals must undergo a process of self-discovery that is painful, yet the opposite state—ignorance—is brutish. In his book *The Poetic Vision of Robert Penn Warren,* Victor H. Strandberg declared that the contemplation of this passage from innocence to maturity is "the crucial center" of Warren's creative achievement. With this theme in mind, wrote Strandberg, Warren typically divided his characters into two groups: "those who refuse passage into a polluted and compromised adult environment" (whom Strandberg refers to as the "Clean" people) and "those who accept passage into the world's stew" (the "Dirty" people). The Clean people prefer to think of themselves as being separate from the filth and corruption of the world, while the Dirty people are willing to face life as it is in order "to proceed to the subsequent stages of spiritual development." In Warren's view, the Clean people can either be relatively harmless, reclusive fundamentalist types, or they can be almost psychopathic in their determination to purify the world and punish sinners (i.e., the Dirty people). In all Warren's writing, the "most negative characters are those who reject the osmosis of being, while his spiritual guides are those who accept it," Strandberg observed.

The "action" in most of Warren's work thus consists primarily of an idealistic narrator's search for his or her identity in an atmosphere of confusion or corruption. This search eventually leads to recognition of the world's fallen state and, consequently, of the self's "innate depravity," to use Strandberg's phrase. In an attempt to overcome the sense of alienation caused by these "warring parts of the psyche," a typical Warren character undergoes a period of intense self-examination that ideally results in a near-religious experience of conversion, rebirth, and a mystical feeling of oneness with God. This in turn opens the door to further knowledge, not only about the self but about the world as well. Though the search for identity may not always end in success, noted Strandberg, "the craving to recreate that original felicity [that existed before the Fall] is one of mankind's deepest obsessions, in Warren's judgment."

According to Wilkie's interpretation, Warren's goal is "to provide an overview of the human condition and to explicate, or mirror, the perplexities of existence in a world in which belief in God has faded. . . . Despite whatever difficulties man may face in his existence, Warren does not counsel despair or state that life is not worth living. . . . It is essential, [he] asserts, to learn whatever answers one can. . . . Though being alive may not always be easy and fun, Warren believes it is well worth the effort."

In a review of Warren's *New and Selected Poems, 1923-1985,* the *New York Times*' Michiko Kakutani summed up Warren's literary preoccupations as "man's exile from Edenic innocence; his groping search for knowledge and love; and his attempts, as a creature caught in history and the particular excesses of this 'maniacal century,' to connect time present with time past." To emphasize that this major concern carries over to his fiction, Kakutani quoted the famous final passage from *All the King's Men:* "We shall come back, no doubt, to walk down the Row and watch young people on the tennis courts by the clump of mimosas and walk down the beach by the bay. But that will be a long time from now, and soon now we shall go out of the house and go into the convulsion of the world, out of history into history and the awful responsibility of Time."

Many observers find Warren's language, style, and tone to be perfectly suited to his subject matter. His word choice, for example, is a lyrical mixture of earthiness and elegance, of the folk speech of Kentucky and Tennessee and what James Dickey referred to in the *Saturday Review* as a "rather quaintly old-fangled scholastic vocabulary." Richard Jackson offered a similar description in the *Michigan Quarterly Review;* he remarked: "[Warren's] idiom . . . is at once conversational and lyric, contemporary and historic, profane and sacred. It is, a language in which he can slip easily from necessary precept to casual observation, cosmic vision to particular sighting." In the opinion of Calvin Bedient, who wrote an article on this subject for the *Sewanee Review,* Warren's poetry is written "in a genuinely expansive, passionate style. Look at its prose ease and rapidity oddly qualified by log-rolling compounds, al-

literation, successive stresses, and an occasional inversion—something rough and serviceable as a horse-blanket yet fancy too—and you wonder how he ever came up with it. It is excitingly massive and moulded and full of momentum. Echoes of Yeats and Auden still persist, but it is wonderfully peculiar, homemade."

Charles H. Bohner was equally impressed by Warren's forceful and exuberant style. "There is about his art the prodigality of the writer who exercises his verbal gifts for the sheer magic of the effects he can produce," noted the critic in his book-length study of Warren. "About all of Warren's work there is a gusto and masculine force, a willingness to risk bathos and absurdity, reminiscent of a writer who, Warren has said, has had the greatest influence on his own work—Shakespeare. . . . He has always seemed driven to explore the boundaries of his art, to push the possibilities of his form to its outer limits."

Although Warren drew extensively from his own past for the language, settings, and themes that appear in both his fiction and poetry, he approached all of this familiar material somewhat objectively and analytically, as if he were contemplating it from a distance, either far from home or, more frequently, at a much later time. Warren's preoccupation with time and how the passage of years affects memory reveals itself in his extensive use of flashbacks to illustrate the often ironic nature of the relationship between the past and the present. Critics also find the abundance of background detail in his work to be evidence of his near obsession with time. According to James H. Justus in the *Sewanee Review,* for instance, one of the hallmarks of Warren's prose is his practice of including "periods of closely observed details strung out in an evocative rhetoric which invites nostalgia for a specific time and place or which invokes awe for a mythic history that seems to explain national and even human urges."

In his book *Robert Penn Warren,* Paul West asserted, "[No] writer has worked harder than Warren to substantiate narrative through close, doting observation of the physical, emotional world. He sees it, makes the page tremble with it. . . . His 'texture of relations'—to his past, to his work, to familiars and strangers—is something he fingers endlessly; and in the long run it is the feel, not the feel's meaning, that he communicates." This aspect of his poetry may be determined by the way Warren wrote his poetry; he once told *CA* that he often began writing a poem many years before that poem came to fruition: "I save all kinds of scraps of unfinished poems and poems that don't pan out; keep them for years. I go back now and then and read the old stuff, the discards. Several times I've found some germ for a poem or some old line that starts a whole new poem. It's a kind of mine, something you have to mine later. Because a poem may be awful, but it may have one good line in it."

Despite the fact that Warren is best known as the author of *All the King's Men,* he regarded himself primarily as a poet. He once commented in the *Sewanee Review:* "If I had to choose between my novels and my *Selected Poems,* I would keep the *Selected Poems* as representing me more fully, my vision and my self." After emerging from a ten-year-long period of "poet's block" in 1954, Warren devoted most of his creative energies to writing verse. Unlike his early (pre-1944) poetry, which sprang from either the contemplation of complex metaphysical concepts or the ballads and narratives native to his region, Warren's later poetry was inspired by a mood, a natural event, or a memory that often took shape as "a moralized anecdote," to use Warren's own phrase. It was a highly personal and often autobiographical (but by no means confessional) form of poetry. In fact, maintained Kramer, "[Warren's] poetry is so unlike that of most other poets claiming our attention. . . . [His] is a poetry haunted by the lusts and loves of the flesh, filled with dramatic incident, vivid landscapes and philosophical reflection—a poetry of passion recollected in the tragic mode. It teems with experience, and with the lessons and losses of experience."

As several critics have made clear, the natural world plays a prominent role in Warren's poetry, providing him with much of his inspiration and imagery. But according to Wilkie in his *Dictionary of Literary Biography* essay, the poet's fascination with nature did not mean he believed man could turn to nature for answers to age-old questions about life and death. "Warren argues repeatedly that the natural world is not a sympathetic or reliable guide to interpreting human life and that man's affairs are a matter of indifference to the rest of creation," asserted the critic. "Only man's pride or ignorance allows him to impute to the natural world any concern with his comings and goings."

Warren's later poetry was noted for its rambling conversational rhythm, due in part to what Edward L. Stewart referred to in the *Washington Post Book World* as its "wide range of conventional but loose-limbed, free but masterfully controlled verse patterns." Warren favored very long and very short lines, the use of which created an irregular meter and sentences that seemed to wind down the page, "run[ning] forward, as it were, into experience," said Bedient in *Parnassus: Poetry in Review.* The overall tone was one of reflection and meditation, though not in a passive sense, wrote Alan Williamson, a *Washington Post Book World* critic. "In the whiplash of [Warren's] long line, the most ordinary syntax becomes tense, muscular, searching," commented Williamson. "His ear is formidable, though given to strong effects rather than graceful ones." The *Times Literary Supplement*'s Jay Parini also found that "power is the word that comes to mind" when

reading Warren's work—power that is expressed in the "raw-boned, jagged quality" of his verse.

According to John Rees Moore of the *Sewanee Review,* these are the same features that made Warren's poetry stand out "in sharp contrast to the jittery rhythms and fragmented images—the reaching out for a style—that are characteristic of much recent poetry. Not that wit, boldness, and even a certain nervous energy are missing but that Warren's poetic quest for identity has reached a stage where he is freer to disregard whatever is not of central interest to him and mull over with increased concentration whatever is." In short, noted Peter Clothier in the *Los Angeles Times Book Review,* "in an age when the quick gratification of surface glitter often replaces slower pleasures of craft and care, Robert Penn Warren's poetry reminds us that the work of a master craftsman is literally irreplaceable. . . . [His] is work of absolute formal and intellectual integrity."

Not all reviewers agree that Warren's work deserves such unqualified praise. The focus of most negative reaction is on the author's attitude toward his material; though some critics acknowledge that Warren tackled unquestionably important themes, they believe his treatment of those themes bordered on the pompous. As Leslie Fiedler explained in *The Collected Essays of Leslie Fiedler,* a Warren poem can be "bombastic in the technical sense of the word: [there is] a straining of language and tone toward a scream which can no longer be heard, the absolute cry of bafflement and pain. Such a tone becomes in Warren . . . ridiculous on occasion, ridiculous whenever we lapse from total conviction."

In his book *Contemporaries,* Alfred Kazin pointed out that "all [of Warren's] work seems to deal with the Fall of Man. And if in reading [him] I have come to be more wary of his handling of this theme, it is because of the nostalgia it conveys, the strident impatient language with which it is expressed, the abstract use to which it is put. . . . Warren tends to make rhetoric of his philosophy." Bedient expressed a similar thought in the *Sewanee Review,* commenting that Warren "seems bitten by the Enormity of it all. He *will* have mystery." As a result, concluded Bedient, his philosophical musings are "sometimes truly awkward and sometimes pseudo-profound."

A few reviewers attributed Warren's occasional awkwardness to the very quality that has made him such a noteworthy figure in American literature: his versatility. Eric Bentley, for one, speculated that Warren's dual role as both artist and critic hindered his ability to "submerge himself in the artist." Continued Bentley in a *Kenyon Review* article: "I cannot help pointing to a duality in Warren that may well constitute his major problem: it is his combination of critical and creative power. I am far from suggesting that the critical and the creative are of their nature antithetic and I am fully ready to grant that what makes Warren remarkable among American writers is his double endowment. The problem lies precisely in his being so two-sidedly gifted; he evidently finds it endlessly difficult to combine his two sorts of awareness."

Noting in the *Virginia Quarterly Review* that "Warren has dedicated his career to proving the indivisibility of the critical and the creative imaginations," David M. Wyatt went on to state: "Such a habit of mind stations Warren on the border between . . . the artist who works from experience and the critic who works toward meaning. . . . His characters are placed out of themselves, the bemused or obsessive spectators of their own wayward acts. . . . [Warren] thus joins that central American tradition of speakers—Emerson, Thoreau, Henry Adams, Norman Mailer—who are not only the builders but the interpreters of their own designs."

Parnassus: Poetry in Review reviewer Rachel Hadas maintained that Warren's difficulties stem from "nothing as simple as a lack of talent." Explained Hadas: "[Warren exhibits an] inability or unwillingness to recognize and settle for the nature of his particular genius. . . . [He] has an imagination of generous proportions. It embraces history, human drama, perhaps above all the beauty of the natural world; it is capable at times of both beauty of form *and* splendor of color. . . . But Warren cannot do everything well. He is *not* an original thinker or a visionary poet; in his handling of condensed lyric, as well as of abstraction, he can be embarrassingly inept." Bedient, also writing in *Parnassus: Poetry in Review,* declared that in effect, "[Warren] has failed to be ruthless toward himself, and his weaknesses loom oppressively in the reflected brilliance of his accomplishments."

Many critics, of course, disagree with these evaluations of Warren's poetry. Monroe K. Spears reported in the *Sewanee Review* that Warren's failings "are hard for me to specify; I find his attitudes and themes—moral, psychological, and religious—so congenial that it is difficult for me to regard the poetry with proper detachment." He continued, "Warren's later poetry seems to me to embody most of the special virtues of 'open' poetry—accessibility, immediate emotional involvement, wide appeal—and to resist the temptations to formlessness and to moral exhibitionism, self-absorption, and sentimentality that are the chief liabilities of that school."

Even Bentley judged that Warren, despite his faults, "is worth a dozen petty perfectionists." And as poet and critic James Dickey observed in his book *Babel to Byzantium:* "When he is good, and often even when he is bad, you had as soon read Warren as live. He gives you the sense of poetry as a thing of final importance to life: as a way or *form*

of life. . . . Warren's verse is so deeply and compellingly linked to man's ageless, age-old drive toward self-discovery, self-determination, that it makes all discussion of line endings, metrical variants, and the rest of poetry's paraphernalia appear hopelessly beside the point."

One point critics agree upon, however, is the extraordinary nature of Warren's contribution to literature. In his critical study of the author, Bohner declared that "no other American literary figure of the twentieth century has exhibited greater versatility than Robert Penn Warren. . . . While arguments about his preeminence in any one field would be ultimately inconclusive, his total accomplishment . . . surpasses that of any other living writer." Marshall Walker praised Warren in the *London Magazine,* calling him "America's most distinguished man of letters in the European sense of a writer involved with books and human kind and at ease in a variety of genres. . . . The range of his achievement testifies to the scope and commitment of Warren's human sympathies. Each intellectual act, whether formally poem, novel, or one of the interviews with black leaders in *Who Speaks for the Negro?* is one of the nature of a poem, according to his own definition of the poem as 'a way of getting your reality shaped a little better.' "

Writing in the *Saturday Review,* Dickey suggested that it is Warren's depth rather than his range that should be celebrated. "[Warren] is direct, scathingly honest, and totally serious about what he feels," Dickey began. "He plunges as though compulsively into the largest of subjects: those that seem to cry out for capitalization and afflatus and, more often than not in the work of many poets, achieve only the former. . . . He is a poet of enormous courage, with a highly individual intelligence." But above all, concluded Dickey, Warren is "a man who looks, and refuses to look away. . . . [He] wounds deeply; he strikes in at blood-level and gut-level, with all the force and authority of time, darkness, and distance themselves, and of the Nothingness beyond nothingness, which may even be God."

In an introduction to a reading given by Warren, later published in *Poetry Pilot,* Stanley Kunitz summed up Warren's central achievement by saying, "No writer of our time has been so multi-faceted or myriad-minded. . . . Now, when we contemplate the accumulation of his verse—the many pages of his progress—we can begin to see this achievement in true perspective, as a work truly rare in our time, for its combination of intellect and passion, for its marriage of fierceness and grandeur."

BIOGRAPHICAL/CRITICAL SOURCES:

BOOKS

Authors in the News, Volume 1, Gale, 1976.

Baumbach, Jonathan, *The Landscape of Nightmare: Studies in the Contemporary Novel,* New York University Press, 1965.

Berger, Walter, editor, *A Southern Renascence Man: Views of Robert Penn Warren,* Louisiana State University Press, 1984.

Bohner, Charles H., *Robert Penn Warren,* Twayne, 1964, revised edition, 1981.

Bradbury, John M., *The Fugitives: A Critical Account,* University of North Carolina Press, 1958.

Brooks, Cleanth, *The Hidden God,* Yale University Press, 1963.

Burt, John, *Robert Penn Warren and American Idealism,* Yale University Press, 1988.

Casper, Leonard, *Robert Penn Warren: The Dark and Bloody Ground,* University of Washington Press, 1960.

Chambers, Robert H., *Twentieth Century Interpretations of 'All The King's Men': A Collection of Critical Essays,* Prentice-Hall, 1977.

Clark, William Bedford, editor, *Critical Essays on Robert Penn Warren,* Twayne, 1981.

Contemporary Literary Criticism, Gale, Volume 1, 1973, Volume 4, 1975, Volume 6, 1976, Volume 8, 1981, Volume 39, 1986, Volume 53, 1989, Volume 59, 1990.

Conversations with Writers, Gale, 1977.

Cowan, Louise, *The Fugitive Group,* Louisiana State University Press, 1959.

Cowley, Malcolm, editor, *Writers at Work: The Paris Review Interviews,* Viking, 1959.

Dickey, James, *Babel to Byzantium,* Farrar, Straus, 1968.

Dictionary of Literary Biography, Gale, Volume 2: *American Novelists since World War II,* 1978, *Yearbook: 1980,* 1981, Volume 48: *American Poets, 1880-1945,* 1986.

Fiedler, Leslie, *The Collected Essays of Leslie Fiedler,* Volume I, Stein & Day, 1971.

Gray, Richard, *The Literature of Memory: Modern Writers of the American South,* Johns Hopkins University Press, 1977.

Gray, editor, *Robert Penn Warren: A Collection of Critical Essays,* Prentice-Hall, 1980.

Graziano, Frank, editor, *Homage to Robert Penn Warren,* Logbridge Rhodes, 1982.

Grimshaw, James A., Jr., *Robert Penn Warren: A Descriptive Bibliography, 1922-1979,* University Press of Virginia, 1981.

Grimshaw, editor, *Robert Penn Warren's Brother to Dragons: A Discussion,* Louisiana State University Press, 1983.

Guttenberg, Barnett, *The Novels of Robert Penn Warren,* Vanderbilt University Press, 1975.

Hall, James, *The Lunatic Giant in the Drawing Room: The British and American Novel since 1930,* Indiana University Press, 1968.

Justus, James H., *The Achievement of Robert Penn Warren,* Louisiana State University Press, 1981.

Kazin, Alfred, *Contemporaries,* Atlantic-Little Brown, 1962.

Litz, A. Walton, editor, *Modern American Fiction: Essays in Criticism,* Oxford University Press, 1963.

Longley, John L., Jr., editor, *Robert Penn Warren: A Collection of Critical Essays,* New York University Press, 1965.

Nakadate, Neil, *Robert Penn Warren: Critical Perspectives,* University Press of Kentucky, 1981.

Newquist, Roy, editor, *Conversations,* Rand McNally, 1967.

Poenicke, Klaus, *Robert Penn Warren,* Heidelberg, 1959.

Rubin, Louis D., Jr., *Writers of the Modern South: The Faraway Country,* University of Washington Press, 1963.

Snipes, Katherine, *Robert Penn Warren,* Ungar, 1983.

Stewart, John Lincoln, *The Burden of Time,* Princeton University Press, 1965.

Strandberg, Victor H., *The Poetic Vision of Robert Penn Warren,* University Press of Kentucky, 1977.

Van O'Connor, William, editor, *Forms of Modern Fiction,* Indiana University Press, 1959.

Walker, Marshall, *Robert Penn Warren: A Vision Earned,* Barnes & Noble, 1979.

Watkins, Floyd C. and John T. Hiers, editors, *Robert Penn Warren Talking: Interviews, 1950-78,* Random House, 1980.

Watkins, Hiers, and Mary Louise Weaks, editors, *Talking with Robert Penn Warren,* University of Georgia Press, 1990.

Watkins, *Then & Now: The Personal Past in the Poetry of Robert Penn Warren,* University Press of Kentucky, 1982.

Weeks, Dennis L, compiler, *"To Love So Well the World": A Festschrift in Honor of Robert Penn Warren,* Peter Lang, 1992.

West, Paul, *Robert Penn Warren,* University of Minnesota Press, 1964.

PERIODICALS

Chicago Tribune, September 10, 1978; April 7, 1985; June 1, 1987.

Chicago Tribune Book World, October 14, 1979; September 7, 1980; February 28, 1982; July 7, 1985.

Christian Science Monitor, September 4, 1946.

Commonweal, October 4, 1946.

Detroit News, February 15, 1981.

Hudson Review, summer, 1977.

Journal of American Studies, December, 1972.

Kenyon Review, summer, 1948.

London Magazine, December, 1975/January, 1976.

Los Angeles Times, March 19, 1981; February 28, 1986.

Los Angeles Times Book Review, September 7, 1980; October 19, 1980; January 17, 1982; July 10, 1983, p. 6.

Michigan Quarterly Review, fall, 1978.

Nation, August 24, 1946.

New Leader, January 31, 1977.

New Republic, September 2, 1946; March 3, 1973, pp. 28-30.

New Statesman & Nation, June 5, 1948.

Newsweek, August 25, 1980; March 10, 1986.

New Yorker, August 24, 1946; December 29, 1980.

New York Times, August 18, 1946; December 16, 1969; March 2, 1977; June 2, 1981; March 27, 1983; April 24, 1985; February 27, 1986; June 13, 1986; October 6, 1986; April 20, 1987.

New York Times Book Review, August 18, 1946, p. 3; June 25, 1950; January 9, 1977; November 2, 1980; April 7, 1985, p. 24; May 12, 1985, p. 8; May 28, 1989, p. 19.

Parnassus: Poetry in Review, fall/winter, 1975; summer, 1977; spring/summer, 1979.

Poetry Pilot, November, 1989.

San Francisco Chronicle, August 18, 1946.

Saturday Review, June 24, 1950; August 20, 1955; August, 1980.

Saturday Review of Literature, August 17, 1946.

Sewanee Review, spring, 1970; spring, 1974; spring, 1975; summer, 1977; spring, 1979; summer, 1980.

Southern Review, spring, 1976; winter, 1990.

Spectator, January 26, 1974.

Time, August 18, 1975.

Times Literary Supplement, May 8, 1948; November 28, 1980; January 29, 1982; February 17, 1989.

Virginia Quarterly Review, summer, 1977; summer, 1991.

Washington Post, May 2, 1980; March 31, 1987; September 23, 1989.

Washington Post Book World, March 6, 1977; October 22, 1978; September 30, 1979; August 31, 1980; October 4, 1981; June 26, 1983; April 13, 1986; April 30, 1989, p. 5; February 3, 1991.

Yale Review, autumn, 1946; December, 1963.

OBITUARIES:

PERIODICALS

Chicago Tribune, September 16, 1989; September 17, 1989.

Globe and Mail (Toronto), September 16, 1989.

Los Angeles Times, September 16, 1989.

Newsweek, September 25, 1989.

New York Times, September 16, 1989.

Southern Review, winter, 1990.

Washington Post, September 16, 1989.*

WEATHERBY, W(illiam) J(ohn)   1930(?)-1992

PERSONAL: Born c. 1930 in Heaton Moor, England; died of cancer, August 5, 1992, in Poughkeepsie, NY; son of William (an artist) and Kathleen (Glancy) Weatherby. *Politics:* "democrat (with a small 'd')." *Religion:* "Christian of no color."

CAREER: Journalist in England and the United States, and editor for Farrar, Straus & Giroux, New York City, and Penguin Books, Inc., New York City; Simon & Schuster, Inc., New York City, editor, beginning 1972.

AWARDS, HONORS: Edgar Allan Poe Award, Mystery Writers of America, for *Death of an Informer.*

WRITINGS:

Breaking the Silence: The Negro Struggle in the U.S.A. (also see below), Penguin, 1965, published as *Love in the Shadows,* Stein & Day, 1966.

Out of Hiding (fiction), Hart-Davis, 1966, Doubleday, 1967.

(Editor with Roi Ottley) *The Negro in New York: An Informal Social History,* New York Public Library and Oceana, 1967.

One of Our Priests Is Missing (novel), Doubleday, 1968.

Breaking the Silence (play based on his nonfiction work of the same title), produced at Liverpool Playhouse, winter, 1969.

Conversations with Marilyn, Mason/Charter, 1976.

Squaring Off: Mailer versus Baldwin, Mason/Charter, 1977.

Death of an Informer, Robson Books, 1977.

Murder at the UN, Robson Books, 1977.

James Baldwin: Artist on Fire, Donald I. Fine, 1989.

Salman Rushdie: Sentenced to Death, Carroll & Graf, 1990.

Blindsight: The Secret Life of James Thurber, Donald I. Fine, 1992.

Jackie Gleason: An Intimate Portrait of the Great One, Pharos Books, 1992.

Also author of the novels *Coronation, The Moondancers,* and *Goliath.* Contributor to *Newsweek, People, New York Times, New York Post, Illustrated London News, New Society, London Evening News, Manchester Guardian, Times Literary Supplement* and *Sunday Times.*

BIOGRAPHICAL/CRITICAL SOURCES:

PERIODICALS

Best Sellers, March 15, 1967.

New York Times Book Review, March 5, 1967.

OBITUARIES:

PERIODICALS

New York Times, August 8, 1992, p. 10.*

*   *   *

WEBB, Richard   1915-1993

PERSONAL: Born in 1915 in Bloomington, IL; committed suicide, June 10, 1993, in Van Nuys, CA; son of John R. and Laura Gail (Gunnett) Webb; married Elizabeth Regina Sterns, 1942; married second wife, Florence Pauline Morse, January, 1949; children: (first marriage) Richelle Regina, Patricia Gail. *Education:* Attended John Brown University, 1930-33.

ADDRESSES: Agent—Reece Halsey, 8733 Sunset Blvd., Hollywood, CA 90069.

CAREER: Actor, producer, and author; starred in *Captain Midnight* television series, 1954-58, and in *U.S. Border Patrol* television series, 1959-61; appeared in more than sixty motion pictures, including *I Wanted Wings, Sullivan's Travels, Out of the Past, The Big Clock, Sands of Iwo Jima, I Was a Communist for the FBI, Carson City, This Woman Is Dangerous, Beware of the Blob,* and *Washington behind Closed Doors,* and in more than 260 television shows, including *Studio One, Lights Out, Mod Squad, The Time Travelers, Maverick, Death Valley Days, Name of the Game,* and *Lassie.* Writer and producer of television films. Lecturer on psychic phenomena. *Military service:* U.S. Army, First Coast Artillery, 1936-38; served in Panama Canal Zone, U.S. Army, 1941-45; became lieutenant colonel in U.S. Army Reserve.

MEMBER: Screen Actors Guild, American Federation of Television and Radio Artists, Actors Equity, Reserve Officers Association, Authors League, Writers Guild, Southern California Society for Psychical Research.

WRITINGS:

(And producer) *The Legend of Eli and Lottie Johl* (television script), American Broadcasting Co. (ABC), 1966.
Great Ghosts of the West, Nash Publishing, 1971.
Stigmata, Psychic Magazine, 1973.
These Came Back, Hawthorn, 1974.
(With Teet Carle) *The Laughs on Hollywood,* Roundtable Publishing, 1984.

Also author of *Voices from Another World* and *Flight without Wings.*

SIDELIGHTS: Richard Webb was a television and movie actor who made famous the television hero Captain Midnight, leader of the Secret Squadron. Every week from September, 1954, to May, 1956, Captain Midnight and his assistant Ichabod Mudd used advanced scientific weapons to fight evildoers. The program's many young fans could become members of the Secret Squadron by sending in a coupon from a jar of Ovaltine. In 1977, the U.S. Army and the U.S. Army Reserve made a recruiting film entitled *Captain Midnight Makes General,* based on the character Webb made famous. In 1986, the Smithsonian Institute's National Air and Space Museum held a Captain Midnight exhibit featuring items from the original program. Webb donated his character's uniform, decoder pin and, as the *Los Angeles Times* quoted him explaining, "everything but the undershorts" to the exhibit.

Discussing Captain Midnight, Webb once remarked to *CA:* "There has been such a renaissance of interest in 'the old heroes,' that I have developed a whole new television series project, with Captain Midnight now in a flying saucer. No, I won't play the character, I'll play his father, Colonel Midnight. He'll probably need some guidance from the Old Man. Hopefully, the new, younger Captain Midnight will be so popular that he too will draw 15,000 fans to a stadium on a personal appearance (when the Captain Midnight program was at the height of its popularity, six million children joined Captain Midnight's 'Secret Squadron' and his personal appearances at a stadium often drew 15,000 children and parents). Fan mail from members of the 'Secret Squadron' has continued to come in over the years."

The author of several books on ghosts and psychic phenomena, Webb once told *CA:* "My writing career began in 1970 when film work had slowed down and I was looking for something to do. It worked! Never having 'taken writing,' it has been interesting to watch the change, the progress in my work. It is still my conviction that unless a person can write, all the writing courses in the country won't accomplish that for the individual. My interest has been writing on a subject which has distinct appeal for me (I can see the beginning, middle, and end in my mind before striking keys on paper) and which I can see as a possible film project. My talent doesn't as yet include being assigned a writing project from someone else and then doing it in a satisfactory manner. Because of my lifelong training I understand screenplays and can do a credible job; with books I can only feel 'Thank God for editors!'"

Webb committed suicide in 1993 after a long bout with a debilitating respiratory illness.

OBITUARIES:

PERIODICALS

Los Angeles Times, June 12, 1993, p. A29.
Washington Post, June 14, 1993, p. B7.*

WEBSTER, Noah
See KNOX, William

*   *   *

WIDGERY, David   1947-1992

PERSONAL: Born April 27, 1947, in London, England; died in an accident at home, October 26, 1992, in London, England; son of John Howard (a designer) and Margaret (a teacher; maiden name, Finch) Widgery; married Juliet Ash; children: one daughter (deceased). *Education:* Royal Free Hospital School of Medicine, M.B.B.S., 1972. *Politics:* "International Socialist."

CAREER: House physician and surgeon at Bettnal Green Hospital, London, England; senior house officer, St. Marys, Paddington, England, 1973-74, and St. Leonards, Shoredilch, 1974-76; general medical practitioner in East London, England, beginning 1976.

WRITINGS:

The Left in Britain, 1956-1968, Penguin, 1976.
Health in Danger: The Crisis in the National Health Service, Archon Books, 1979.
Beating Time: Riot 'n' Race 'n' Rock 'n' Roll, Chatto & Windus, 1986.
The National Health: A Radical Perspective, Hogarth Press, 1988.
(Editor with Michael Rosen) *The Chatto Book of Dissent,* Chatto & Windus, 1991.

Also author of *Preserving Disorder: Selected Essays, 1966-88,* 1989, and *Some Lives!: A GP's East End,* 1991. Contributor to magazines, including *Socialist Worker, Socialist Review, New Statesman, New Society, International Socialism, Spare Rib, British Medical Journal,* and *Heathworker.* Reviews editor for *Socialist Worker,* 1974-75. Editor of *Oz, Time Out* and *City Limits.*

SIDELIGHTS: David Widgery once told *CA* that he was active in rank and file trade union politics. His interests were "British and American labour history and sexual radicalism."

OBITUARIES:

PERIODICALS

Times (London), November 4, 1992, p. 19.*

*   *   *

WIENER, Leigh Auston   1929-1993

PERSONAL: Born August 28, 1929, in New York, NY; died of complications from Sweet's syndrome, a blood dis-

ease, May 11, 1993, in Los Angeles, CA; son of Willard Lowen and Grace Louise (Katz) Wiener; married Carolyn Hadfield, December 11, 1969 (divorced); children: Devik Hunt. *Education:* Attended University of California, Los Angeles, 1948-52.

CAREER: Los Angeles Times, Los Angeles, CA, staff photographer, 1952-57; member of faculty of University of California, Los Angeles, beginning 1981. Co-host of *Talk about Pictures,* a television series; producer, photographer, and co-author of *Slice of Sunday,* a special program broadcast by Columbia Broadcasting System, Inc. (CBS-TV). Member of steering committee of State of California Earthquake Preparedness Committee. *Military service:* U.S. Army, photographer for *Stars and Stripes,* 1952-54; served in Europe.

AWARDS, HONORS: A Slice of Sunday was named one of the two most innovative documentaries of the previous 25 years by the Film Editors' Guild, 1979.

WRITINGS:

Here Comes Me, Odyssey, 1966.
Not Subject to Change, International Business Machines Corp., 1969.
How Do You Photograph People?, Viking, 1982.
(With William Everson) *The High Embrace,* Dawson's Book Shop (Los Angeles), 1986.
Marilyn: A Hollywood Farewell; The Death and Funeral of Marilyn Monroe, Seven Four One, 1990.

Also author of *Leigh Wiener: Portraits* and *1989's Tijuana Sunday.* Author of a column in *Westways,* 1980-81, and a column in the *Los Angeles Times,* beginning 1981. Contributor of photographs to *Life, Time, Look, Colliers, Fortune,* and other magazines.

OBITUARIES:

PERIODICALS

Los Angeles Times, May 14, 1993, p. A26.
New York Times, May 14, 1993, p. B7.*

*   *   *

WILDER, Amos Niven   1895-1993

PERSONAL: Born September 18, 1895, in Madison, WI; died of cancer, May 1, 1993, in Cambridge, MA; son of Amos Parker and Isabella (Niven) Wilder; married Catharine Kerlin, June 26, 1935; children: Catharine Wilder Guiles, Amos Tappan. *Education:* Yale University, B.A., 1920, B.D. (cum laude), 1924, Ph.D., 1933; graduate study at Mansfield College, Oxford, 1921-23, and Harvard University, 1929-30.

CAREER: Ordained Congregationalist minister, 1926; pastor of Congregational church in North Conway, NH, 1925-28; Hamilton College, Clinton, NY, associate professor of ethics and Christian evidences, 1930-33; Andover Newton Theological School, Newton Centre, MA, professor of New Testament interpretation, 1933-43; Chicago Theological Seminary, Chicago, IL, professor of New Testament, 1943-54; Harvard University, Cambridge, MA, professor of New Testament, 1954-56, Hollis Professor of Divinity, 1956-63, professor emeritus, beginning 1963. Visiting professor at University of Frankfurt, 1951, 1952. *Military service:* American Ambulance Field Service, 1916-17; served in France; received Croix de Guerre. U.S. Army, Field Artillery, 1918-19.

MEMBER: American Academy of Arts and Sciences, Society for the Arts, Literature, and Contemporary Culture, Massachusetts Historical Society, Alpha Delta Phi, Elizabethan Club, Winthrop Club.

AWARDS, HONORS: Belgian-American Foundation fellow at University of Brussels, 1920-21; National Council for Religion in Higher Education fellow, 1928; D.D. from Hamilton College, 1933, Oberlin College, 1952, Yale University, 1956, and Fairfield University, 1969; Bross Decennial Award from Lake Forest College, 1951, for *Modern Poetry and the Christian Tradition;* L.H.D. from University of Chicago, 1955; Guggenheim fellow, 1958-59; Th.D. from University of Basel, 1960.

WRITINGS:

Battle-Retrospect and Other Poems, Yale University Press, 1923, reprinted, AMS Press, 1971.

Arachne (poems), Yale University Press, 1928.

Eschatology and Ethics in the Teaching of Jesus, Harper, 1939, revised edition, 1950.

Spiritual Aspects of the New Poetry, Harper, 1940, reprinted, Books for Libraries, 1968.

The Healing of the Waters (poems), Harper, 1943.

Modern Poetry and the Christian Tradition: A Study In the Relation of Christianity to Culture, Scribner, 1952.

Otherworldliness and the New Testament, Harper, 1954.

New Testament Faith for Today, Harper, 1955.

Theology and Modern Literature, Harvard University Press, 1958.

The Language of the Gospel: Early Christian Rhetoric, Harper, 1964, reprinted as *Early Christian Rhetoric,* Harvard University Press, 1971.

Kerygma, Eschatology and Social Ethics, Fortress Press, 1966.

The New Voice: Religion, Literature, Hermeneutics, Herder, 1969.

(Editor) *Grace Confounding* (poems), Fortress Press, 1972.

Theopoetic: Theology and the Religious Imagination, Fortress Press, 1976.

Thornton Wilder and His Public, Fortress Press, 1980.

(Editor) *Jesus' Parables and the War of Myths: Essays on Imagination in the Scripture,* Fortress Press, 1982.

The Bible and the Literary Critic, Fortress Press, 1991.

Armageddon Revisited: A World War I Journal, Yale University Press, 1994.

SIDELIGHTS: Amos Niven Wilder once told *CA:* "My main field of scholarly study and teaching has been the New Testament and early Christian origins. But my literary interests have led me to the literary study of the Bible, and to teaching and writing on modern literature. In the Society for the Arts, Literature, and Contemporary Culture, I have long been interested in modern cultural assessment, in association with many gifted artists and qualified critics and social scientists."

OBITUARIES:

PERIODICALS

New York Times, May 4, 1993, p. B13.*

* * *

WILKINSON, Sylvia   1940-

PERSONAL: Born April 3, 1940, in Durham, NC; daughter of Thomas Noell (a building contractor) and Peggy (George) Wilkinson. *Education:* University of North Carolina at Greensboro, B.A., 1962; Hollins College, M.S., 1963; graduate study at Stanford University, 1965-66. *Avocational interests:* Sports car racing, tennis (was eastern North Carolina women's tennis champion in 1959 and Durham champion for two years), horses, painting (has had several one-artist shows), acting, dancing, hiking, skiing, motorcycle riding.

ADDRESSES: Home—109 Garden St., Chapel Hill, NC 27514; also 514 Arena St., El Segundo, CA 90245. *Agent*—Liz Darhansoff, L. D. Literary Agency, 70 E. 91st St., New York, NY 10028.

CAREER: Novelist and writer of juvenile fiction and nonfiction. Asheville-Biltmore College (now University of North Carolina at Asheville), instructor in English, art, and drama, 1963-65; College of William and Mary, Williamsburg, VA, instructor in English, 1966-67; University of North Carolina at Chapel Hill, lecturer in creative writing, 1967-70. Visiting writer, Creative Writing Learning Institute of North Carolina, 1968-69, Washington College, 1974-75 and 1984, and University of Wisconsin—Milwaukee, 1985. Writer-in-residence at Hollins College, 1969 and 1975, Richmond Humanities Center, 1972-80, Sweet Briar College, 1973-75, 1977. Participant in Poetry in the Schools program, 1972, and in various writers' workshops. National Humanities Faculty, 1975—. Has also worked in stock-car and sprintcar racing crews and as a timer and scorer of auto races.

MEMBER: Authors League of America, Authors Guild, PEN, International Motor Sports Association, Sports Car Club of America, Sierra Club, Animal Protection Society.

AWARDS, HONORS: Creative writing fellowship, Hollins College, 1963; Eugene Saxton Memorial Trust Grant, 1964, for *Moss on the North Side;* Wallace Stegner Creative Writing fellowship, Stanford University, 1965-66; Merit Award for literature, *Mademoiselle,* 1966; Sir Walter Raleigh Awards for North Carolina fiction, 1968, for *A Killing Frost,* and 1977, for *Shadow of the Mountain;* Feature Story Award, *Sports Car* magazine, 1972, for article "Chimney Rock Hillclimb"; creative writing fellowship, National Endowment for the Arts, 1973-74; Guggenheim fellowship, 1977-78; service award, University of North Carolina at Greensboro, 1978; honorable mention, Kafka Award, American Women Fiction Writers, 1978, for *Shadow of the Mountain.*

WRITINGS:

NOVELS

Moss on the North Side, Houghton (Boston), 1966.
A Killing Frost, Houghton, 1967.
Cale, Houghton, 1970, revised edition, with a foreword by Louis D. Rubin, Jr., Algonquin, 1986.
Shadow of the Mountain, Houghton, 1977.
Bone of My Bones, Putnam (New York City), 1982.

NONFICTION

(Editor) *Change: A Handbook for the Teaching of English and Social Studies in the Secondary Schools,* LINC Press (Durham, NC), 1971.
The Stainless Steel Carrot: An Auto Racing Odyssey, Houghton, 1973.
Automobiles (juvenile), Children's Press (Chicago), 1982.
Dirt Tracks to Glory: The Early Days of Stock Car Racing as Told by the Participants, Algonquin, 1983.
(With Robert Hillerich) *I Can Be a Race Car Driver* (juvenile), Children's Press, 1986.

THE "WORLD OF RACING" SERIES; FOR YOUNG ADULTS

Can-Am, Children's Press, 1981.
Endurance Racing, Children's Press, 1981.
Stock Cars, Children's Press, 1981.
Super Vee, Children's Press, 1981.
Formula One, Children's Press, 1981.
Formula Atlantic, Children's Press, 1981.
Sprint Cars, Children's Press, 1981.
Champ Cars, Children's Press, 1982.
Trans-Am, Children's Press, 1983.

Kart Racing, Children's Press, 1985.

OTHER

Also author, pseudonymously, of a children's mystery-adventure series on auto racing.

Contributor of articles and reviews to various periodicals, including *Writer, Ingenue, Sports Car, Sports Illustrated, Mademoiselle, Auto Week, Stock Car Racing, Southern Living,* and *American Scholar.*

WORK IN PROGRESS: Two novels: *Lying Dog,* for Algonquin Books, and *Sewer Lily.*

SIDELIGHTS: Sylvia Wilkinson once told *CA:* "As I entered junior high, I experienced two crises that would determine my future as a writer. 'Starrie' was my other self when I was a child. At age twelve I started putting down her stories in my Blue Horse notebook. I showed some of my writings to my seventh-grade teacher, who told me: 'You write what I tell you to write.' I held on to my manuscript then, secretly working at night in my attic room. Years later, I showed my work to Randall Jarrell, my creative writing teacher at the University of North Carolina at Greensboro. He read it and said, 'Miss Wilkinson, you have a gift.' That was the happiest day of my life. I finished the book in 1965 when I was twenty-five years old; I published it as *Moss on the North Side.*

"The other crisis that happened to me when I was twelve was a decision I made," Wilkinson continued. "Daddy told me I could have a horse or continue my dancing lessons; we couldn't afford both. I took the horse. It was on horseback that I planned all my fictional adventures, partly because I was alone (except for my dog and horse) and partly because it gave me the feeling of being in another place and another time—like a cowboy. . . . I missed the dancing lessons, but the decision was the right one.

"A big part of my motivation to be a writer came from my mother's mother, Mama George. She was a farm woman with a third-grade education from Sunday school who listened to soap operas and read newspapers and comic books. But she was a storyteller with a natural sense of form and drama. She never repeated a story and never told a dull one. I became a writer out of an oral tradition, knowing I could never equal her standards. She would start rocking in her iron porch chair and start talking. Eudora Welty once said the reason the South has so many writers is because it has so many porches."

All of Wilkinson's novels except *Cale* have young female protagonists, prompting *Washington Post Book World* reviewer Jonathan Yardley to speculate about the author's "strong autobiographical impulse." In *Moss on the North Side,* young Cary, who is half Native American, suffers the aftermath of her father's death, and then becomes aware of her sexuality through her emerging love for Johnny Strawbright, an albino African-American youth. A *Time* reviewer pronounced *Moss on the North Side* to be among "the season's most flagrantly gifted first novels."

Ramie Hopkins, the heroine of Wilkinson's second novel, *A Killing Frost,* is a thirteen-year-old emerging artist. The focus of the novel is Ramie's difficult relationship with Mama Liz, her grandmother, with whom she lives. Narrated by Ramie, the novel shows the young character's growing awareness of the complexities of human beings—both those around her and those, such as her dead parents, who have shaped her past.

Wilkinson's third novel, *Cale,* follows the growth of a boy—the eponymous Cale—from birth through high school. Like Wilkinson's first two novels, *Cale* is a coming-of-age story. Using shifting points of view, Wilkinson tells the tale through the eyes of characters of different ages, races, and genders; for the 1986 revised edition, however, Wilkinson trimmed several sections (including monologues by Cale's mother, Falissa), giving Cale a more central position in his own story.

In 1977's *Shadow of the Mountain,* Wilkinson returned to a female protagonist, this time a young woman named Jean Fitzgerald who has been trained in survival skills and gets a job for the governmental Appalachian Corps in the poverty-stricken mountains of North Carolina. Jean becomes "progressively more isolated," as Katherine Kearns writes in the *Dictionary of Literary Biography Yearbook, 1986,* and as the novel closes, she is in danger of being murdered in her cabin.

Bone of My Bones, set in rural North Carolina, is the story of Ella Ruth Higgins, a nine-year-old girl who grows to age eighteen during the course of the novel. As she grows up Ella must survive both the death of her mother and her own gang-rape by a group of male acquaintances. David Quammen, in the *New York Times Book Review,* called Ella Ruth "a vivid and sympathetic character" describing her narrative voice as "effective . . . graced at points with humor, richly raucous language and illuminations on the travail of female adolescence." Nevertheless, Quammen lamented the book's lack of shape and selectivity, claiming that Wilkinson calculated wrongly in assuming that Ella Ruth's likability would carry the novel. Yardley called *Bone of My Bones* "a modest and appealing story, told with obvious feeling." He also expressed serious reservations about the novel's construction, stating that the narrative line was too weak and that the crucial rape scene was handled perfunctorily. Yardley suggested that Wil-

kinson may have explored the coming-of-age motif sufficiently and might benefit from finding a new subject. However, the critic went on to say, "because Sylvia Wilkinson is herself an uncommonly talented writer, and because she knows her territory so well, her work always commands a serious and respectful hearing."

Though storytelling comes naturally to Wilkinson, it is by no means a simple process. "Writing is not a pleasant task for me," she once told *CA.* "I find myself seeking for a thousand escapes from the hard chair in front of my typewriter—partly because it requires so much mental effort and no physical activity, tying me into a nervous knot like a ten-year-old in church." Wilkinson conceded, however, that storytelling is a compulsion for her, "and I could not stop writing if I tried."

BIOGRAPHICAL/CRITICAL SOURCES:

BOOKS

Authors in the News, Volume 1, Gale (Detroit), 1976.
Dictionary of Literary Biography Yearbook, 1986, Gale, 1987.
Frank N. Magill, editor, *Critical Survey of Long Fiction,* Salem Press (Englewood Cliffs, NJ), 1983.

PERIODICALS

Kentucky Review, Number 2, 1981, pp. 75-88.
New York Times Book Review, February 21, 1982, p. 13.
Southern Literary Journal, fall, 1982, pp. 22-36.
Washington College Review, January, 1975.
Washington Post Book World, February 10, 1982, pp. C1, C9.*

*   *   *

WILLIAMS, William P(roctor) 1939-

PERSONAL: Born September 1, 1939, in Glade, KS; son of Joseph Earl (a farmer) and Berneice (Richardson) Williams; married Karen McKinley, August 19, 1962 (marriage dissolved, 1984); married Antonia Forster (an author); children: (first marriage) Elizabeth, William II. *Education:* Kansas State University, B.A., 1961, M.A., 1964, Ph.D., 1968; Oxford University, Certificate, 1962. *Religion:* Episcopalian.

ADDRESSES: Home—606 Grove St., DeKalb, IL 60115. *Office*—Department of English, Northern Illinois University, DeKalb, IL 60115.

CAREER: Kansas State University, Manhattan, instructor in English, 1966-67; Northern Illinois University, DeKalb, assistant professor, 1967-70, associate professor, 1970-78, professor of English, 1978—, director of graduate studies in English, 1978-81. Northern Illinois University summer session at University College, Oxford University, assistant director, 1970, 1976, and director, 1971, 1977; director and senior tutor, Northern Illinois University fall semester at Oxford University, 1979; director, Northern Illinois University summer session at St. Catherine's College, Cambridge, 1990. Reader, General Ordination Examination (national examination for admission to Holy Orders in the Episcopal Church), 1974-77. President, Friends of the Northern Illinois University Libraries, 1992-93; member of Central Renaissance Conference. Gives talks at colleges and universities and on radio programs, and presents papers at conferences, symposia, and meetings of professional organizations.

MEMBER: Modern Language Association of America, Renaissance Society of America, Bibliographical Society, Shakespeare Association of America, American Society for Eighteenth-Century Studies, Medieval and Renaissance Drama Society, Society for Textual Scholarship, Oxford Bibliographical Society, Malone Society, Midwest Modern Language Association (member of executive committee, 1987-90), Bibliographical Society of Northern Illinois (cofounder).

AWARDS, HONORS: Northern Illinois University research grants, 1968, 1969, 1971, 1972, 1975, 1980, 1981, 1983, 1985, 1987, and 1988; Folger Shakespeare Library summer fellow, 1972; American Philosophical Society fellow, 1972-73, research grant, 1987; Newberry Library fellow, 1974, travel grant, 1984; National Endowment for the Humanities research grant, 1978; American Council of Learned Societies grant-in-aid, 1975, 1979; Fulbright senior research award, United Kingdom, 1983; Bibliographical Society of America fellow, 1985.

WRITINGS:

(Compiler) *A Descriptive Catalogue of Seventeenth-Century English Religious Literature in the Kansas State University Library,* Kansas State University Libraries (Manhattan), 1966.

(Compiler with Charles A. Pennel) *Elizabethan Bibliographies,* Volume 4: *George Chapman and John Marston,* Volume 8: *Francis Beaumont, John Fletcher, Philip Massinger, John Ford, and James Shirley,* Nether Press (London), 1968.

(Compiler with Robert Gathorne-Hardy) *A Bibliography of the Writings of Jeremy Taylor to 1700,* Northern Illinois University Press (DeKalb), 1971.

(Editor and compiler) *A Bibliography of Jeremy Taylor, 1700-1980,* Garland Publishing (New York City), 1979.

(Compiler) *An Index to the Stationers' Register, 1640-1708,* Laurence McGilvery (La Jolla, CA), 1980.

(With Craig S. Abbott) *An Introduction to Bibliographical and Textual Studies,* Modern Language Association of America (New York City), 1985, 2nd edition, 1989.

(Compiler with Fred H. Higginson) *A Bibliography of the Writings of Robert Graves,* 2nd edition, University Press of Virginia (Charlottesville), 1987.

Also author or compiler of catalogues and monographs. Contributor to books, including *Studies in English and American Literature,* edited by John L. Cutler and Lawrence S. Thompson, Whitston (Troy, NY), 1978; *Essays in Paper Analysis,* edited by Stephen Spector, Folger Shakespeare Library (Washington, DC), 1987; and *Professing Shakespeare Now,* edited by Robert P. Merrix and Nicholas Ranson, Edwin Mellen (Lewiston, NY), 1992. Contributor to dictionaries and to *Papers of the Bibliographical Society of America.* Contributor to periodicals, including *Modern Language Review, Journal of English and Germanic Philology, Anglican Theological Review, Studies in Bibliography, Notes and Queries, Shakespeare Newsletter,* and *Times Literary Supplement.* Editor, *Reavis Newsletter,* 1969-71, 1973-75, and *Analytical and Enumerative Bibliography,* 1976—; associate editor, *English Literature in Transition,* 1969-71.

WORK IN PROGRESS: A new edition of *Titus Andronicus,* with Judith Rogers and William Long, for Modern Language Association of America; a critical edition of the dramatic works of Cosmo Manuche.

*   *   *

WILSON, J(ohn) Tuzo   1908-1993

PERSONAL: Born October 24, 1908, in Ottawa, Ontario, Canada; died April 15, 1993, in Toronto, Ontario, Canada; son of John Armitstead (an engineer employed as a civil servant) and Henrietta Loetitia (Tuzo) Wilson; married Isabel Jean Dickson, October 29, 1938; children: Patricia Isabel (Mrs. Michael C. Proctor), Susan Loetitia Clark. *Education:* University of Toronto, B.A. (first class honors), 1930; Cambridge University, M.A., 1932, Sc.D., 1958; Princeton University, Ph.D., 1936. *Religion:* Anglican.

CAREER: Geological Survey of Canada, Ottawa, Ontario, assistant geologist, 1936-39; University of Toronto, Ontario, professor of geophysics, beginning 1946, fellow of Massey College, beginning 1962, principal of Erindale College in Mississauga, 1967-74; Ontario Science Centre, director general, 1947-85; York University, Toronto, chancellor, 1983-86. Member of National Research Council of Canada, 1958-64, and Defence Research Board of Canada, 1960-66; visiting professor at Australian National University, 1950, 1965, Ohio State University,

1968, and California Institute of Technology, 1972; Canadian delegation to UNESCO, delegate member, 1962, 1964, 1966; lecturer at more than 170 universities throughout the world; National Museums of Canada, trustee, 1967-74. *Military service:* Canadian Army, 1939-46; served in England, North Africa, and Sicily; became colonel; received Order of the British Empire and Legion of Merit (United States).

MEMBER: International Union of Geodesy and Geophysics (president, 1957-60), Trinity College, University of Toronto (honorary fellow), Royal Society of Canada (fellow; president, 1972-73), Royal Canadian Geographic Society (former vice president), Order of Canada (officer), Royal Society of London (fellow), National Academy of Sciences (foreign associate), American Academy of Arts and Sciences (foreign honorary member), American Philosophical Society (honorary member), Arctic Institute of North America (chairperson, 1947-48), St. John's College, Cambridge University (honorary fellow), Royal Swedish Academy of Sciences (foreign honorary member), Associe Academie Royale de Belgium (foreign honorary member).

AWARDS, HONORS: Massey fellowship, Cambridge University, 1930-32; D.Sc. from University of Western Ontario and LL.D. from Carleton University, both 1958, and other honorary degrees from Acadia University, 1968, Memorial University of Newfoundland, 1968, Franklin and Marshall College, 1969, University of Calgary, 1972, and McGill University, 1973; overseas fellowship, Churchill College, 1965; Blaylock Medal from Canadian Institute of Mineralogy and Metallurgy; Miller Medal from Royal Society of Canada; Bancroft Award of Royal Society of Canada; Bucher Medal of American Geophysical Union; Penrose Medal of Geological Society of America; Logan Medal of Geological Association of Canada; Vetlesen Prize, Columbia University, 1978; Britannica Award, 1986.

WRITINGS:

One Chinese Moon, Longmans (Canada), 1959.
(With J. A. Jacobs and R. D. Russell) *Physics and Geology,* McGraw, 1959, 2nd edition, 1974.
IGY: The Year of the New Moons, Knopf, 1961.
(Editor) *Continents Adrift,* W. H. Freeman, 1972.
Unglazed China, Macmillan (Canada), 1973.

Contributor to encyclopedias. Contributor of more than 100 articles to scientific journals. Also editor of *Continents Aground,* 1976.

SIDELIGHTS: In his lifetime, J. Tuzo Wilson traveled to over 100 countries and made the first solo ascent of Mount Hague in Montana. He also conceived and conducted a 3,400-mile military expedition by snowmobile through Arctic Canada and in 1946 traveled as an observer on the first U. S. Air Force flight over the North Pole. As a geophysicist, he became an exponent of the theory of continental drift, which he dramatized at Canada's centennial exhibit at Expo 67, in May, 1967.

OBITUARIES:

PERIODICALS

Times (London), May 3, 1993, p. 17.*

*   *   *

WINTERS, Jon
    See CROSS, Gilbert B.

*   *   *

WRAGG, E(dward) C(onrad)   1938-

PERSONAL: Born June 26, 1938, in Sheffield, England; son of George William (a florist) and Maria (Brandstetter) Wragg; married Judith King, December 29, 1960; children: Josephine, Caroline, Christopher. *Education:* University of Durham, B.A. (with first class honors), 1959, diploma in education, 1960, University of Leicester, M.Ed., 1967; University of Exeter, Ph.D., 1972. *Avocational interests:* Sport, reading, travel, media.

ADDRESSES: Office—School of Education, University of Exeter, Exeter EX1 2LU, England.

CAREER: Teacher in grammar school in Wakefield, England, 1960-63; teacher of German and head of department in boys' school in Leicester, England, 1964-66; University of Exeter, Exeter, England, lecturer in education, 1966-73; University of Nottingham, Nottingham, England, professor of education, 1973-78; University of Exeter, professor of education, 1978—, director of School of Education, 1978—. Chairperson, British Broadcasting Corporation (BBC) School Broadcasting Council; specialist adviser, Parliamentary Select Committee on Education; director, Teacher Education Project, Department of Education and Science, 1976-81; member, Council for National Academic Awards; director, Leverehulme Primary Project, 1988-92, Appraisal Project, 1992-94, and Primary Improvement Project, 1994—.

MEMBER: British Educational Research Association (president), Universities Council for the Education of Teachers.

AWARDS, HONORS: D. Univ., Open University, 1993.

WRITINGS:

(Adaptor) Wolfgang Ecke, *Krimis,* Longmans, Green, 1967.

Life in Germany, Longmans, Green, 1968.
Teaching Teaching, David & Charles, 1974.
Classroom Interaction, Open University, 1976.
Teaching Mixed Ability Groups, David & Charles, 1976.
A Handbook for School Governors, Methuen, 1980.
Class Management and Control, Macmillan, 1981.
A Review of Research in Teacher Education, National Foundation for Educational Research, 1982.
Swineshead Revisited, Trentham, 1982.
Classroom Teaching Skills, Croom Helm, 1984.
More Pearls from Swineshire, Trentham, 1984.
The Domesday Project, BBC Publications, 1985.
Education: An Action Guide for Parents, BBC Publications, 1986.
Teacher Appraisal, Macmillan, 1987.
Riches from Wragg, Trentham, 1990.
Class Management, Routledge, 1993.
(With George Brown) *Explaining,* Routledge, 1993.
An Introduction to Classroom Observation, Routledge, 1993.
Primary Teaching Skills, Routledge, 1993.
(With Brown) *Questioning,* Routledge, 1993.

Author of *Education in the Market Place,* 1988, *The Wragged Edge,* 1988, *Schools and Parents,* 1989, *Mad Curriculum Disease,* 1991, *The Parents' File,* 1993, *No, Minister!,* 1993, *Effective Teaching,* 1994, and *Flying Boot,* 1994. Editor of a teaching series for David & Charles, the *Teaching Matters* series for Cassell, and *Research Papers in Education* for Routledge. Regular columnist for *Times Educational Supplement.* Contributor to language and education journals.

WORK IN PROGRESS: Research on teacher education, classroom interaction, and curriculum development.

SIDELIGHTS: E. C. Wragg told CA: "Writing a regular column for a national newspaper in which I try to bring out the humorous side of education has made me realise how hilarious human behavior is. I think of all those wasted years I took it seriously."

*   *   *

WYKES, Alan 1914-1993

PERSONAL: Born May 21, 1914, in Beddington, Surrey, England; died June 11, 1993, in Reading, Berkshire, England; son of Alan Edwin Hill and Louise Ethel (Morant) Wykes; married Muriel Edith Gillham, 1939. *Education:* Attended grammar school in England. *Avocational interests:* Music, theatre, literature, cats.

ADDRESSES: Agent—A. D. Peters, 10 Buckingham St., London WC2N 6BU, England; Harold Matson Co., Inc., 22 East 40th St., New York, NY 10016.

CAREER: Author. Fiction editor, *Housewife* (magazine), 1952-61. *Military service:* British Army, 1940-46.

MEMBER: Savage Club (London; honorary secretary).

WRITINGS:

Pursuit till Morning, Random House, 1947.
The Music Sleeping, Duckworth, 1948.
The Pen Friend, Duckworth, 1950.
Happyland, Duckworth, 1952.
A Concise Survey of American Literature, Library Publishers, 1955.
(With Lord Brabazon) *The Brabazon Story,* Heinemann, 1956.
(With J. A. Hunter) *Hunter's Tracks,* Hamish Hamilton, 1957.
(With W. H. Scott-Shawe) *Mariner's Tale,* Hamish Hamilton, 1958.
(Editor) *A Sex by Themselves,* Arthur Barker, 1958.
Snake Man, Hamish Hamilton, 1960, Simon & Schuster, 1961.
Nimrod Smith, Hamish Hamilton, 1961.
Party Games, Collins, 1963.
Gambling, Aldus Books, 1964, published as *The Complete Illustrated Guide to Gambling,* Doubleday, 1964.
The Doctor and His Enemy, M. Joseph, 1965, Dutton, 1966.
The Pan Book of Amateur Dramatics, Pan Books, 1965, published as *The Handbook of Amateur Dramatics,* A. Barker, 1966.
An Eye on the Thames, Jarrolds, 1966.
The Great Yacht Race, Davies, 1966.
Air Atlantic: A History of Civil and Military Transatlantic Flying, Hamish Hamilton, 1967, D. White, 1968.
The Siege of Leningrad, Ballantine, 1968.
The Royal Hampshire Regiment, Hamish Hamilton, 1968.
Doctor Cardano, Muller, 1969.
The Nuremberg Rallies, Ballantine, 1970.
Reading: Biography of a Town, Macmillan (London), 1970.
Lucrezia Borgia, Heron, 1970.
Hitler, Ballantine, 1970.
Goebbels, Ballantine, 1971.
Himmler, Ballantine, 1972.
Heydrich, Ballantine, 1972.
1942: The Turning Point, Macdonald & Co., 1972.
(Compiler) *Abroad: A Miscellany of English Travel Writing,* Macdonald & Co., 1973.
S. S. Leibstandarte, Ballantine, 1974.
Not So Savage, Jupiter, 1975.
Eccentric Doctors, Mowbrays, 1975.
Saucy Seaside Postcards, Jupiter, 1976.
Circus, Jupiter, 1977.
H. G. Wells in the Cinema, Jupiter, 1978.
Ale and Hearty, Jupiter, 1979.

Also author of *Eisenhower,* 1983, and, with Noel Barber, *Woman of Cairo,* 1983, and *Daughters of the Prince,* 1989. Contributor of short stories to *Collier's, Mademoiselle,* and other magazines.

OBITUARIES:

PERIODICALS

Times (London), July 13, 1993, p. 19.*

Y

YARDE, Jeanne Betty Frances 1925-
(Joan Hunter, Jeanne Montague)

PERSONAL: Born October 17, 1925, in Bath, England; daughter of Louis (a musician) and Winifred (a musician; maiden name, Smaggasgale) Field; married Graham Herbert Treasure, August 14, 1943 (divorced July, 1976); married Michael Andrew "Hank" Yarde, December 23, 1981; children: (first marriage) Anthony, Vanessa, Louise Frances, Bruce. *Education:* Attended Bath College of Art. *Politics:* "Was Conservative, not sure any more. Possibly Liberal." *Religion:* "Christened Church of England, but don't go to church. Study alternative religions, reincarnation, etc. Not an atheist, believing in a creative force and higher power."

ADDRESSES: Home and office—23 Vicarage St., Warminster, Wiltshire BA12 8JG, England. *Agent*—c/o Jane Conway Gordon, 1 Old Compton St., Soho, London W1V 5PH, England.

CAREER: Associated with Citizen House (theatrical costumers), Bath, England, 1941-42 and 1945-47; writer, 1970—.

AWARDS, HONORS: The Castle of the Winds was nominated for "Best Historical Gothic of the Year," *Romantic Times,* 1987-88; "Best Saga of the Year" award, *Romantic Times,* 1989-90, for *Diamond Heart.*

WRITINGS:

UNDER PSEUDONYM JOAN HUNTER; HISTORICAL ROMANCES

Courtney's Wench, R. Hale (London), 1973, published as *Roxanna,* Pocket Books (New York City), 1975.
The Falcon and the Dove, R. Hale, 1974, published as *Under the Raging Moon,* Pocket Books, 1975.

Rupert the Devil, R. Hale, 1976, published as *Cavalier's Woman* (bound with *Cavalier*), Pocket Books, 1977, published separately under pseudonym Jeanne Montague, Wordsworth, 1995.
Cavalier, R. Hale, 1977, published under pseudonym Jeanne Montague, Wordsworth, 1995.
The Lord of Kestle Mount, R. Hale, 1978, published as *Lord of Kestle Mount,* Pocket Books, 1979.

UNDER PSEUDONYM JEANNE MONTAGUE; HISTORICAL ROMANCES

Flower of My Heart, Macdonald Futura (London), 1981.
Touch Me with Fire, Macdonald Futura, 1981, published as *Passion Flame,* Ace Books (New York City), 1983.
Wild Bride, Zebra Books (New York City), 1994.

UNDER PSEUDONYM JEANNE MONTAGUE; GOTHIC ROMANCES

The Clock Tower, Century Publishing (London), 1983, St. Martin's (New York City), 1984.
Midnight Moon, Century Publishing, 1984, St. Martin's, 1985.
The Castle of the Winds, Century Hutchinson, 1986, St. Martin's, 1987.
Tigers of Wrath, Century Hutchinson, 1987.

UNDER PSEUDONYM JEANNE MONATAGUE; "DAWN OF LOVE" SERIES

Brave Wild Heart, Dragon Books, 1987.
The Power of Love, Dragon Books, 1987.
Sword of Honour, Dragon Books, 1987.
Vengeance Is Mine, Dragon Books, 1987.

UNDER PSEUDONYM JEANNE MONTAGUE; TEENAGE HISTORICAL SERIES

Lady Cavalier, Blackie & Son (London), 1989.
Lady Cavalier Rides Out, Blackie & Son, 1989.
The Phantom of Monksilver Abbey, Blackie & Son, 1990.

UNDER PSEUDONYM JEANNE MONTAGUE; FAMILY SAGAS

Diamond Heart, Pocket Books, 1990.
Sisters and Lovers, Piatkus Books (London), 1992.
Family Passions, Piatkus Books, 1993.
Daughters of Fury, Piatkus Books, 1994.
Creole Moon, Piatkus Books, 1995.

SIDELIGHTS: Jeanne Betty Frances Yarde wrote to *CA:* "I write all the time to make a living, and have been known to do stints of fifteen hours a day, seven days a week if the pressure is on. It is hard work, not very remunerative, alas, as it is a struggle to make much money by writing. There have been times when we've been down to bread and margarine, wondering which bill to pay first, but I am addicted to dreaming up stories, and there is a lot of satisfaction to be had from it.

"Though I may toy with different ideas when I have time, I only work on novels that have been commissioned by publishers. As these have period settings, I do a great deal of research, fussy about detail, atmosphere and accuracy, and will tackle almost any genre that my agent or editors suggests. My ambition would be to write in-depth and literary horror books, like those of Clive Barker or Anne Rice, two of my favourite authors.

"I have recently been working on a non-fiction book about the life and operas of Giacomo Puccini. I have a burning passion for opera, particularly the works of Puccini, Richard Wagner and Richard Strauss. I listen to it when not actually engaged on my word-processor, usually whilst cooking or sewing. I can't have any music on when I'm writing as this distracts me too much. When I read for relaxation I enjoy vampire books, particularly those of Anne Rice, and the family sagas of Susan Howatch and Sara Harrison but here, as with music, my taste is eclectic.

"While I lounge in the garden, I plan the next chapter of the book I happen to be working on, and have had some of my best ideas when doing something entirely different to actually sitting in front of the computer screen. I always keep paper handy to jot these down. Like all authors I sometimes suffer the dreaded 'writers' block', but find the best way to deal with this is to carry on working, no matter what rubbish comes out. One can always edit it later. I thank heavens for my computer. It has made my life so much easier, and I can sometimes work on two completely different books with the aid of my wonderful little robot."

*   *   *

YOUNT, John (Alonzo) 1935-

PERSONAL: Born July 3, 1935, in Boone, NC; son of John Luther (an electrician) and Vera (Sherwood) Yount; married Susan Childs, September 7, 1957; children: Jennifer Sherwood, Sarah Childs. *Education:* Attended Wake Forest University, 1956-57; Vanderbilt University, B.A., 1960; University of Iowa, M.F.A., 1962. *Politics:* Democrat. *Religion:* Lutheran.

ADDRESSES: Home—29 Woodridge Rd., Durham, NH 03824. *Office*—Department of English, University of New Hampshire, Durham, NH 03824. *Agent*—Robert Rosen, 7 West 51st St., New York, NY 10016.

CAREER: University of New Hampshire, Durham, instructor of English, 1962-64; Clemson University, Clemson, SC, assistant professor of English, 1964-65; University of New Hampshire, assistant professor, 1965-67, associate professor, 1967-73, professor of English, 1973—. Visiting professor at University of Arkansas, spring, 1973. *Military service:* U.S. Army, Medical Corps, 1954-56.

AWARDS, HONORS: Rockefeller Foundation grant for literature, 1967-68; Guggenheim fellow, 1974; National Endowment for the Arts grant for fiction, 1976.

WRITINGS:

NOVELS

Wolf at the Door, Random House (New York City), 1967.
The Trapper's Last Shot, Random House, 1973.
Hardcastle, Richard Marek, 1980.
Toots in Solitude, Marek-Martin, 1983.
Thief of Dreams, Viking (New York City), 1991.

Contributor to *Esquire.*

WORK IN PROGRESS: A novel.

SIDELIGHTS: Novelist John Yount is noted for his finely wrought characterizations and his ability to evoke the atmosphere of a place, especially the rural South. Although his first novel, *Wolf at the Door,* drew mixed reviews, his four later novels have been enthusiastically acclaimed.

Wolf at the Door concerns Tom Rapidan, a young, recently married undergraduate at a southern university, who "is in a state of near collapse, relying almost entirely on booze for peace, and indifferent to his wife," Herbert Mitchell reports in the *New York Times Book Review.* While Rapidan realizes that he is in trouble, he does not know what to do about it. A *Best Sellers* critic finds the novel "technically competent," but remarks: "Just what is wrong with [the character's] life we do not know; Tom's childhood recollections provide no clear answer." Robert Granat voices a similar opinion in the *Washington Post Book World.* Granat notes that "there are some fine individual scenes and characterizations and the emotional interplay is subtle and convincing," but he criticizes Yount for presenting "the anatomy of a desperate situation without making much effort to penetrate into its causes or significance." And *Punch*'s B. A. Young suggests that "Mr. Yount's hero would make a useful minor character in a more ambitious story, but as a case-history on his own he hardly rates this much attention."

Reviews of Yount's second novel, *The Trapper's Last Shot,* were far more favorable. Set in Sharaw, Georgia, during the mid-1960s, the novel details the lives of two brothers, Dan and Beau Jim Early. Dan, the eldest, is a farmer. Mel Watkins of the *New York Times Book Review* describes him as "stoic, illiterate, [and] completely baffled by anything beyond the immediate world of his daily chores." Beau Jim, who has just returned from six years in the Army, plans to enroll in a local community college and is "eager to recapture his carefree youth," according to *Newsweek*'s S. K. Oberbeck. The author recounts the brothers' ambitions and fates against the backdrop of the growing civil-rights movement. *Nation*'s Alan Cheuse calls the novel "compelling," and Watkins finds that it provides "a quietly effective portrait of rural Southerners wrestling with their personal ambitions and frustrations and the threat posed to their way of life by the civil-rights movement." Oberbeck voices similar praise, stating that *The Trapper's Last Shot* is a "precision-tooled novel with [a] tight regional focus that brilliantly describes the churning violence in a hardscrabble . . . Georgia township."

What Oberbeck and Watkins seem to admire most about Yount's novel is its characterizations. Brother Dan, they contend, is particularly noteworthy; Watkins calls him "one of the most memorable fictional characters I've run across in some time." Dan "is both vile and sensitive, evil and touching," the critic adds; "most important, Yount is able to make one feel empathy for him." Oberbeck agrees and extends his praise to all the characterizations as well as to Yount's ability to transform "a cruel clarity of vision into warm sympathy."

Hardcastle, Yount's third novel, garnered even more attention and acclaim. Jim Marks of the *Washington Post* terms *Hardcastle* a "well-crafted, absorbing and sometimes wonderfully humorous novel." Elaine Kendall, writing in the *Los Angeles Times Book Review,* finds that the novel is "direct and deceptively simple on the surface, with ramifications both wider and deeper than the plot can suggest."

Like the author's earlier works, *Hardcastle* is set in the rural South, this time during the depression. The plot revolves around Bill Music, who, as the novel opens, has given up his dream of finding work in Chicago and is returning to his parents' farm in Virginia. He is sidetracked in Kentucky, however, where he meets and becomes friends with Regus Bone, a guard for the Hardcastle Mining Company. With Bone's help, Music secures himself a

job as mine guard. But Music finds the position both dangerous and troubling, for the mineworkers are being pressured by union organizers. "Guards are armed and under orders to shoot anyone who looks like an outside agitator," Kendall explains. "Music is torn between his desperate need for money and his certain knowledge that the miners' only hope of improving their wretched lot is to unionize." Music grows more and more disillusioned with his role as "company goon" and decides to quit. He persuades Bone to join him and the two take up farming. But Music and Bone, despite their efforts otherwise, become increasingly involved in and sympathetic to the miners' plight and find it difficult to avoid the bitter conflict between labor and management. Kendall asserts that "*Hardcastle* is a story of trust, of conscience and eventually of love." And Raymond Carver comments in the *Chicago Tribune Book World:* "In a time when so much fiction is being written and published that doesn't seem to count for much, it should be said at once that this is a book about something—and something that matters. It has to do with the nature and meaning of friendship, love, obligation, responsibility, and behavior."

Critics were equally impressed by the book's concise yet evocative prose. "Yount's prose style is so economical and highly concentrated that it has the emotional impact of poetry," Kendall states. "Few contemporary novels have conveyed a sense of place so thoroughly and effectively." The *New York Times*'s Christopher Lehmann-Haupt praises Yount's "charming but not overwritten Kentucky mountain dialogue and [his] moody descriptions of the countryside." And Marks finds that with its "narrative drive, humor, finely honed language and rounded, compassionately observed characters," *Hardcastle* provides "just about everything I like in a novel."

Because of its themes, narrative style, and attention to such details as setting and dialogue, Yount's novel has been compared to John Steinbeck's *The Grapes of Wrath* and Thomas Wolfe's *You Can't Go Home Again.* Kendall maintains that until the publication of *Hardcastle,* "the Great Depression seemed to belong almost exclusively to John Steinbeck. [However, there are now] two classics of the period—*The Grapes of Wrath* and *Hardcastle.*" Marks contends that Yount "is especially close to . . . Thomas Wolfe in his use of the theme, 'You can't go home again. . . .' And his prose can rise to a lyrical, poetic lilt. But he's a good deal more disciplined than Wolfe, and he particularly lacks Wolfe's adolescent sprawl."

Finally, Carver remarks that, when he finished reading *Hardcastle,* he was reminded of Lionel Trilling's statement: "A great book reads us." "Somewhere in my 20s," Carver writes, "I read this and pondered its meaning. What exactly was the man saying? When I finished reading *Hardcastle,* this remarkably generous but unsparing novel, I [recalled] Trilling's words; and I thought, So this is what he was talking about. This is what he meant." Kendall concludes that *Hardcastle* "is an extraordinary novel, filled with deep affection for a small corner of America, illuminated by total understanding of the qualities that make a time, a place and its people truly memorable."

Yount's fourth novel, *Toots in Solitude,* returns to the contemporary South for a comedy with serious themes. Macon (Toots) Henslee, the title character, is a one-eyed veteran of the Korean War who has become a successful auto salesperson. Married but chafing against the constraints of middle-class domesticity, he quits his job, leaves his wife, and sets himself up as a hermit in a treehouse on a river. His solitude is interrupted by the arrival of Sally Ann Shaw, a country and western singer on the run from an abusive drug-dealing boyfriend whom she robbed and badly injured. Toots helps Sally Ann evade the clutches of the drug dealer's hired thugs, but after the danger has passed, the problems of modern love set in again, and Toots recognizes that his solitude has not ended. "Mr. Yount is grumpy about the prospects of boys and girls in a state of civilization," notes Christopher Lehmann-Haupt in the *New York Times,* calling *Toots in Solitude* a "charming novel." Bette Pesetsky, writing in the *New York Times Book Review,* finds the characters and the turns of plot somewhat predictable, but hails Yount as "a compelling storyteller" and his book "a tale written with zest and read with pleasure." *Newsweek*'s Gene Lyons enthusiastically dubs the novel "rueful, funny and beautifully written" and Yount "an American original with a voice distinctively his own." Peter Ross, writing in the *Detroit News,* pinpoints one of the book's distinctive strengths: "Part of John Yount's stunning success in this effortless, quietly explosive novel is making a preference for solitude comprehensible."

Thief of Dreams is "a worthy follow-up to his well-received *Toots in Solitude,*" in the opinion of Chicago *Tribune Books*'s Douglas Seibold—an opinion shared by many other reviewers. A study of male adolescence set in 1948, the book follows 13-year-old James Tally as he deals with his parents' troubled marriage and his sufferings at the hands of a school bully. James's parents lead separate lives, as illustrated in interspersed chapters: father Edward is working construction in Pittsburgh, while mother Madeline has returned to her native hills of North Carolina with James. Upset by his experiences, young James runs away to the backwoods to test his manhood; mean-

while, his father, having realized the importance of family ties, has come back from Pittsburgh to try to mend his marriage. Seibold commends Yount's originality in dealing with the issue of marital problems in the form of a period piece: "Yount takes a very contemporary sort of situation and puts a distinctive spin on it by setting it in the conservative South of 40 years ago." Rosellen Brown of the *New York Times Book Review* writes: "*Thief of Dreams* does a fine job of bringing us into all three of its main characters' thoughts. And what we see there is the unbridgeable distance between the man, the boy and the woman who is both wife and mother. It's an old scenario and a classic American one." Brown notes, however, that the estrangement of Edward and Madeline is "too persuasive a breach" to warrant the novel's optimistic ending. Katharine A. Powers, in the *Washington Post Book World,* feels differently about the ending, calling it "perfectly satisfying, even if it suggests something of the fairy tale, for in that way it captures an element of a boy's vision of the world." She ultimately describes the novel as "both exciting and moving." Similarly, John Schulian of the *Los Angeles Times Book Review* terms the novel "a triumph for John Yount." Schulian uses his review of *Thief of Dreams* as an occasion to re-appraise, in strongly favorable terms, Yount's earlier works, calling the novelist "as gifted as anyone working at the writer's trade." In *Thief of Dreams,* Schulian asserts, Yount has written "a story that is so internal, so understated that one can't help applauding its integrity."

BIOGRAPHICAL/CRITICAL SOURCES:

PERIODICALS

Best Sellers, July 1, 1967.
Chicago Tribune Book World, May 18, 1980.
Detroit News, March 18, 1984.
Los Angeles Times Book Review, June 1, 1980; April 7, 1991, p. 10.
Nation, June 15, 1974.
Newsweek, October 8, 1973; February 20, 1984.
New York Times, May 23, 1980; January 24, 1984.
New York Times Book Review, July 2, 1967; February 17, 1974; January 29, 1984; March 17, 1991, p. 13.
Punch, May 15, 1968.
Tribune Books (Chicago), April 7, 1991.
Washington Post, June 27, 1980.
Washington Post Book World, September 10, 1967; May 5, 1991.

Z

ZACHARY, Hugh 1928-
(John Dexter, Ginny Gorman, Elizabeth Hughes, Zach Hughes, Zachary Hughes, Pablo Kane, Peter Kanto, Marcus von Heller)

PERSONAL: Born January 12, 1928, in Holdenville, OK; son of John F. (a construction worker) Zachary and Ida Louise Francis (Duckworth) Boydstow; married Elizabeth Wiggs (a writer and artist), January 10, 1948; children: Whitney Leigh, Leslie Beth. *Education:* University of North Carolina, B.A., 1951. *Politics:* Republican. *Religion:* Catholic. *Avocational interests:* Stamp collecting, hunting treasure, boats, fishing, and music.

ADDRESSES: Home—7 Pebble Beach Dr., Yaupon Beach, NC 28461.

CAREER: Writer. Announcer-newsperson for numerous radio and television stations throughout the United States, including Oklahoma, Tennesee, North Carolina, and Florida, 1948-63. Member of Yaupon Beach City Council. *Military service:* U.S. Army, 1946-48.

MEMBER: Science Fiction Writers of America, American Crime Writer's League.

AWARDS, HONORS: Southern Book Award, 1972, for *The Beachcomber's Handbook of Seafood Cookery;* first runner-up in Porgy Awards, *West Coast Review of Books,* 1981, for *Of Love and Battle;* Nebula Award nomination, Science Fiction Writers of America, for *World Where Sex Was Born.*

WRITINGS:

NOVELS

One Day in Hell, Novel Books, 1961.
A Feast of Fat Things, Harris-Wolfe, 1968.
Gwen, in Green, Gold Medal (New York City), 1974.
Second Chance, Major (Canoga Park, CA), 1976.
To Guard the Right, Raven House, 1980.
Bloodrush, Leisure Publications, 1981.
Murder in White, Leisure Publications, 1981.
Top Level Death, Raven House, 1981.
(With wife, Elizabeth Zachary) *Of Love and Battle,* Ballantine (New York City), 1981.
The Lost and the Fallen, Ballantine, 1983.
Desert Battle, Dell (New York City), 1983.
Bitter Victory, Dell, 1983.
The Venus Venture, Vanguard, 1986.
The Revenant, New American Library (New York City), 1988.
Dos Caballos, M. Evans (New York City), 1989.

"SIERRA LEONE" SERIES

Flight to Freedom, Dell, 1982.
Freedom's Passion, Dell, 1982.
Treasure of Hope, Dell, 1982.
Freedom's Victory, Dell, 1982.

UNDER PSEUDONYM JOHN DEXTER

Bedroom Touchdown, Playtime, 1966.

UNDER PSEUDONYM GINNY GORMAN

Flames of Joy, Neva, 1967.

UNDER PSEUDONYM ELIZABETH HUGHES

The Competition for Alan, Lancer Books, 1971.
The Legend of the Deadly Doll, Award Books, 1973.

UNDER PSEUDONYM ZACH HUGHES

The Book of Rack the Healer, Award Books, 1973.
Legend of Miaree, Ballantine, 1974.
Seed of the Gods, Berkley Publishing (New York City), 1974.
Tide (also see below), Putnam (New York City), 1974.
The Stork Factor, Berkley Publishing, 1975.

The St. Francis Effect, Berkley Publishing, 1976.
Tiger in the Stars, Laser Books, 1976.
Il Campo Degli UFO, Urania, 1976.
For Texas and Zed, Popular Library, 1976.
Killbird, New American Library, 1980.
Pressure Man, New American Library, 1980.
Thunderworld, New American Library, 1983.
Gold Star, New American Library, 1983.
Closed System, New American Library, 1987.
Sundrinker, DAW (New York City), 1987.
The Dark Side, New American Library, 1987.
Lifeforce, DAW, 1988.
Mother Lode, DAW, 1991.
Deep Freeze, DAW, 1992.

UNDER PSEUDONYM ZACHARY HUGHES; "HOTEL DESTINY" SERIES

The Adlon Link, Jove (New York City), 1981.
Fortress London, Jove, 1981.
The Fires of Paris, Jove, 1981.
Tower of Treason, Jove, 1982.

UNDER PSEUDONYM PABLO KANE

A Dick for All Seasons, Olympia, 1970.

UNDER PSEUDONYM PETER KANTO

Lolila, Novel Books, 1964.
The Bashful Lesbian, Brandon House (Bronx, NY), 1965.
Lust Addict, Playtime, 1965.
Battalion Broads, Playtime, 1965.
A Man Called Sex, Brandon House, 1965.
Call Me Gay, Brandon House, 1965.
Two Way Beach, Brandon House, 1965.
Too Young to Wait, Brandon House, 1966.
Beach Wife, Brandon House, 1966.
One Lonely Summer, Brandon House, 1966.
License to Prowl, Brandon House, 1966.
Gold in Her Eyes, Brandon House, 1966.
Color Her Willing, Brandon House, 1967.
The Love Standard, Brandon House, 1967.
Matinee in Three Scenes, Brandon House, 1967.
The Bedroom Beat, Brandon House, 1967.
Playboy's Lament, Corinth, 1967.
The Girl with the Action, Brandon House, 1967.
Tomcat, Brandon House, 1967.
May Johnson's Girls, Brandon House, 1967.
The Love Boat, Brandon House, 1967.
Wallings Wantons, Corinth, 1967.
Neighborly Love, Brandon House, 1967.
Black and White, Playtime, 1967.
The Girls Upstairs, Playtime, 1968.
Suddenly, Wonderfully Gay, Brandon House, 1968.
Moonlighting Wives, Brandon House, 1968.
The Sullied Virgin, Man's Magazine, 1968.
Two Beds for Liz, Brandon House, 1968.

A Small Slice of War, Caravelle, 1968.
The Snake Room, United Graphics, 1968.
Angel Baby, United Graphics, 1968.
Taste of Evil, Beeline (Albany, NY), 1969.
First Experiences, Beeline, 1969.
World Where Sex Was Born, Olympia, 1969.
Back Way In, Oracle, 1969.
Unnatural Urges, Olympia, 1969.
Rosy Cheeks, Beeline, 1969.
Twenty Nights in Eros, Pendulum, 1969.
The Coupling Game, Olympia, 1969.
Naked Joy, Olympia, 1970.
Green Thumb and Silver Tongue, Olympia, 1970.
Sexpo, Danish Style, Olympia, 1970.
Rake's Junction, Lancer, 1970.
On Campus, Midwood, 1970.
Das Grofse Spiel, Olympia, 1970.
Der Sexplanet, Olympia, 1971.
Her Husband's Best Friend, Greenleaf Classics, 1971.
The Sex Experiment at Diddle U., Beeline, 1971.
Super Sex Stars, Beeline, 1971.
Doing It with Daughter, Beeline, 1972.
Lustful Nights, Beeline, 1972.
Girl in Revolt, Greenleaf Classics, 1972.
Lay-A-Day, Beeline, 1972.
Try Me!, Beeline, 1973.

UNDER PSEUDONYM MARCUS VON HELLER

Das Drachennest, Olympia, 1960.
A Nest of Vixens, Olympia, 1969.

NONFICTION

The Beachcomber's Handbook of Seafood Cookery, Blair, 1970.
How to Win at Wild-Card Poker, Stephen Greene (Brattleboro, VT), 1975.

OTHER

Also author of screenplay, *Tide,* based on his novel of the same name, for American Broadcasting Companies. Former feature writer and book reviewer for *Raleigh News and Observer* and *Star News* (Wilmington, NC). Contributor, sometimes under pseudonyms, of short stories and articles to periodicals. Hugh's works have been translated into several foreign languages, including German and Italian.

ADAPTATIONS: Movie option for *Gwen, in Green* has been sold to Bernard Bassey.

SIDELIGHTS: When Hugh Zachary left his position as an announcer and newsperson for radio and television in 1963 to write books, he initially subsidized his income by investing in an old boat and fishing commercially. "Fortunately," he once commented to *CA,* "nothing is ever wasted for a writer. Experience on the sea led to several books, including *Tide*." In addition to books based on his sea experience, Zachary's writing ouevre includes historical fiction, science fiction, and even a prize-winning cookbook. Zachary has also written books with his wife, Elizabeth. Commending Elizabeth's writing skills, Zachary elaborated that her "knowledge of people and their interactions is always a valuable part of any Zachary book."

Zachary also commented: "In addition to writing historical series, one of which is now at book number twenty-five, I venture into my favorite field of writing, science fiction, at least once a year for my own pleasure and for variety. In addition, I have written in most fields other than women's romance, a genre I leave to my wife and daughter.

"Although there are millions of copies of my books in print, my best work exists only on disc or under my desk. For example, I did a tour of duty as mate aboard an anchor handling tug in Great Britain's North Sea oil fields which represents an engineering feat comparable to the building of the Suez and Panama canals or a space mission to Mars, and wrote one damned good sea story about two Americans, a Scot engineer and fourteen Spanish seamen in one of the roughest bodies of water in the world for thirty days at a time (six months at a time for the Spanish seamen). One editor said she'd buy the book if I made the captain a woman."*